MW01681619

SPECIAL INDIAN EDITION

ORGANIZATIONAL BEHAVIOR

5th Edition

Emerging Knowledge and
Practice for the Real World

SPECIAL INDIAN EDITION

ORGANIZATIONAL BEHAVIOR

5th Edition

Steven L. McShane
The University of Western Australia

Mary Ann Von Glinow
Florida International University

Radha R. Sharma
Management Development Institute, Gurgaon, India

Tata McGraw Hill Education Private Limited
NEW DELHI

McGraw-Hill Offices
New Delhi New York St Louis San Francisco Auckland Bogotá Caracas
Kuala Lumpur Lisbon London Madrid Mexico City Milan Montreal
San Juan Santiago Singapore Sydney Tokyo Toronto

Tata McGraw-Hill

Organizational Behavior, 5/e (SIE)

Indian Adaptation done by arrangement with the McGraw-Hill Companies, Inc., New York

Sales Territories: India, Pakistan, Nepal, Bangladesh, Sri Lanka and Bhutan

Tata McGraw-Hill Edition 2011

ISBN-13: 978-0-07-107798-9
ISBN-10: 0-07-107798-7

Vice President and Managing Director—McGraw-Hill Education: Asia Pacific Region: *Ajay Shukla*
Head—Higher Education Publishing and Marketing: *Vibha Mahajan*
Publishing Manager—B&E/HSSL: *Tapas K Maji*
Deputy Manager (Sponsoring): *Surabhi Khare*
Development Editor: *Anirudh Sharan*
Executive (Editorial Services): *Yogesh Kumar*
Senior Production Manager: *Manohar Lal*
Senior Production Executive: *Atul Gupta*
Marketing Manager—Higher Education: *Vijay S Jagannathan*
Assistant Product Manager: *Daisy Sachdeva*
Senior Product Specialist: *Anusha Sharma*
General Manager—Production: *Rajender P Ghansela*
Assistant General Manager—Production: *B L Dogra*

Published by the Tata McGraw Hill Education Private Limited, 7 West Patel Nagar, New Delhi 110 008,
Typeset at The Composers, 260, C.A. Apt., Paschim Vihar, New Delhi 110 063 and printed at
AVON PRINTERS, Plot No, 16, Main Loni Road, Jawahar Nagar, Industrial Area, Shahdara, Delhi - 110 094.

Cover Design: Meenu Raghav, Graphic Designer, TMH

Cover Printer: SDR Printers

RYCCRRAGDDAXC

The McGraw·Hill Companies

About the Authors

Steven L. McShane

Steven L. McShane is Professor of Management in the Business School at the University of Western Australia (UWA), where he receives high teaching ratings from students in Perth, Singapore, Manila, and other cities where UWA offers its programs. He is also an Honorary Professor at Universiti Tunku Abdul Rahman (UTAR) in Malaysia and previously taught in the business faculties at Simon Fraser University and Queen's University in Canada. Steve has conducted executive programs with Nokia, TÜV-SÜD, Wesfarmers Group, Main Roads WA, McGraw-Hill, ALCOA World Alumina Australia, and many other organizations. He is also a popular visiting speaker, having given presentations to faculty and students in almost a dozen countries over the past four years.

Steve earned his Ph.D. from Michigan State University in organizational behavior, human resource management, and labor relations. He also holds a Master of Industrial Relations from the University of Toronto, and an undergraduate degree from Queen's University in Canada. Steve has served as President of the Administrative Sciences Association of Canada (the Canadian equivalent of the Academy of Management) and Director of Graduate Programs in the business faculty at Simon Fraser University.

Along with coauthoring *Organizational Behavior,* Fifth Edition, Steve coauthors with Mary Ann Von Glinow on *Organizational Behavior: Essentials,* Second Edition (2009). He is also the coauthor with Sandra Steen (University of Regina) of *Canadian Organizational Behaviour,* Seventh Edition (2009), with Tony Travaglione (Curtin University) of *Organisational Behaviour on the Pacific Rim,* Second Edition (2007), and with Charles Hill (University of Washington) of *Principles of Management,* First Edition (2008). Steve is also coauthor of Indian, Chinese, and Taiwanese editions or translations of his OB book. Steve has published several dozen articles and conference papers on workplace values, training transfer, organizational learning, exit-voice-loyalty, employee socialization, wrongful dismissal, media bias in business magazines, and other diverse topics.

Steve enjoys spending his leisure time swimming, body board surfing, canoeing, skiing, and traveling with his wife and two daughters.

Mary Ann Von Glinow

Dr. Von Glinow is Director of the Center for International Business Education and Research (CIBER) and is Research Professor of Management and International Business at Florida International University. She also is the 2006 Vice President of the Academy of International Business (AIB) and an editor of JIBS. Previously on the Marshall School faculty of the University of Southern California, she has an MBA and Ph.D. in Management Science from The Ohio State University. Dr. Von Glinow was the 1994–95 President of the Academy of Management, the world's largest association of academicians in management, and is a Fellow of the Academy and the Pan-Pacific Business Association. She sits on eleven editorial review boards and numerous international panels. She teaches in executive programs in Latin America, Central America, the Caribbean region, Asia, and the U.S.

Dr. Von Glinow has authored over 100 journal articles and 11 books. Her most recent books include *Managing Multinational Teams* (Elsevier, 2005) and *Organizational Learning Capability* (Oxford University Press, 1999; in Chinese and Spanish translation), which won a Gold Book Award from the Ministry of Economic Affairs in Taiwan in 2002. She has also coauthored the popular *Organizational Behavior,* Fifth Edition textbook and *Organizational Behavior: Essentials,* Second Edition (McGraw-Hill/Irwin, 2009). She heads an international consortium of researchers delving into "Best International Human Resource Management Practices," and her research in this arena won an award from the American Society for Competitiveness' Board of Trustees. She also received an NSF grant to study globally distributed work. Dr. Von Glinow is the 2005 Academy of Management recipient of the Distinguished Service Award, one of the Academy's three highest honors bestowed.

Mary Ann consults to a number of domestic and multinational enterprises, and serves as a mayoral appointee to the Shanghai Institute of Human Resources in China. Since 1989, she has been a consultant in General Electric's "Work-out" and "Change Acceleration Program" including "Coaching to Management." Her clients have included Asia Development Bank, American Express, Diageo, Knight-Ridder, Burger King, Pillsbury, Westinghouse, Southern California Edison, The Aetna, State of Florida, Kaiser Permanente, TRW, Rockwell Int'l, Motorola, N.Y. Life, Amoco, Lucent, and Joe's Stone Crabs, to name a few. She is on the Board of Friends of WLRN, Fielding University, Friends of Bay Oaks, Pan-Pacific Business Association, and Animal Alliance in Los Angeles. She is actively involved in several animal welfare organizations and received the 1996 Humanitarian Award of the Year from Miami's Adopt-a-Pet.

Radha R. Sharma

Radha R. Sharma is Senior Professor, Organizational Behavior and Human Resource Development at Management Development Institute, Gurgaon, India, and has three decades of experience in teaching, research and executive development. She is Ambassador for India for HR Division, and Member, International Members Committee of OB Division of Academy of Management, USA, which has representatives from over 100 countries. She is an alumnus of Harvard Business School from where she qualified for GCPCL. She is a member of International Consortium for Research on Emotional Intelligence in Organizations (USA) and a founder member of the Forum for Emotional Intelligence and Learning (FEIL), India. She has been a Visiting Professor to International University: European Business School, Germany, and has taught courses on ESCP-Europe International MBA programs. She teaches leadership, emotional intelligence, intercultural skills, psychometric testing and measurement and change management courses at MBA, executive MBA and Ph.D. levels.

Dr. Sharma has successfully completed a number of research projects supported by World Health Organization (WHO); UNESCO; IDRC, Canada; McClelland Centre for Research and Innovation, USA; Polish Academy of Sciences, Poland; University of Otego, New Zealand; and Government of India. She has received Outstanding Management Researcher Award, AIMS International, 2008; Outstanding Cutting Edge Research Paper Award, 2006, from Academy of Human Resource Development, USA; Best Faculty Award: Excellence in Research, 2007 and 2006 at Management Development Institute, Gurgaon, India; Best Paper Award 2003, *Indian Journal of Training & Development* during 33rd IFTDO World Conference and First Runners-Up Research Paper Award 2008 (co-author), World SME Conference and Outstanding Editor Award, 2007, from *AIMS International Journal of Management.*

Her publications include nine books, popular among them being *Change Management* (McGraw-Hill Companies, 2007, 2011); *360 Degree Feedback, Competency Mapping & Assessment Centers* (Tata McGraw-Hill, 2004); *Organizational Behavior* (co-authored with Steven McShane and Mary Ann Von Glinow, McGraw-Hill-Companies, 2006 and 2008); *Organizational Behaviour: An Online Book,* 2003, *Enhancing Academic Achievement: Role of Personality Factors* (Concept, 1985). She has published a number of research papers in national/international peer-reviewed journals/conference proceedings. She is also a member of the Editorial Board of *AIMS International Journal of Management;* XIMB, *Journal of Case Research,* and has been the Co-Editor, *Indian Journal of Training and Development;* Assistant Editor, Educational Planning and Administration Bulletin and member, Editorial Board of Survey. She has also been the Guest Editor for special issues of Vision–Journal of Business Perspective on Emotional Intelligence and Managerial Competencies.

Dr. Sharma is also on the board of Human Relations & IR Committee of PHD Chamber of Commerce & Industry and Academic Council of Indian Institute of Health Management and Research, has been on the Academic Council of Advance Diploma in Training and Development; National Diploma Board of Indian Society of Training and Development; Human Capital Development Committee of Federation of Indian Chapter of Commerce and Industry and Expert Committee of All India Council for Technical Education and is also an elected member of the Executive Board of Delhi Management Association. She has been the Founder Secretary, Indian Society of Hospital Administrators (West Bengal chapter). She has also been on various panels of judges for the Best Research Paper Award for various national and international journals; HRD Emerging Thinkers' Award; National Award for Innovative Training Practices and Award for Excellence in HR Practices.

She has undertaken training and consulting in transformational leadership development; emotional intelligence mapping and development of psychometric testing; competency mapping; organizational change through HR interventions; personality and potential testing; management of stress and burnout; culture building; 360-degree feedback; assessment centers; team building for reputed organizations in central and state governments, public and private sectors. Some of these assignments were sponsored by UNICEF and the World Bank.

A recipient of four gold medals for academic excellence, Dr. Sharma has obtained master's and Ph.D. in Psychology from Banaras Hindu University and Advanced Professional Certification in MBTI from Association of Personality Type. She also has to her credit certificate courses in Corporate Social Responsibility from British Council and New Academy of Business, UK, and the World Bank Institute.

Dedicated with love and devotion to
Donna, and to our wonderful daughters, Bryton and Madison

—S.L.M.

Dedicated to Zack, Emma, and Googun!

—M.A.V.G.

Dedicated to my inspiring parents and Chandresh and affectionate children
Anubhuti-Vishwa, Swati, and Abhinav

—R.R.S.

PREFACE

Welcome to the emerging knowledge and practice of organizational behavior! Social networks and virtual teams are replacing committee meetings. Knowledge is replacing infrastructure. Values and self-leadership are replacing command-and-control management. Companies are looking for employees with emotional intelligence and team competencies, not just technical smarts. Diversity and globalization have become challenges as well as competitive opportunities for organizations. Co-workers aren't down the hall; they're at the other end of an Internet connection located somewhere else on the planet.

Organizational Behavior, Fifth Edition, is written in the context of these emerging workplace realities. This edition explains how emotions guide employee motivation, attitudes, and decisions; how self-concept influences employee motivation and behavior, team cohesion, and leadership; how social networks are gaining importance as a source of personal power and organizational effectiveness; and how appreciative inquiry has become an important strategy for changing organizations. This book also presents the new reality that organizational behavior is not just for managers; it is relevant and useful to anyone who works in and around organizations.

LINKING THEORY WITH REALITY

Every chapter of *Organizational Behavior,* Fifth Edition, is filled with examples that make OB knowledge more meaningful and reflect the relevance and excitement of this field. These stories about real people and organizations translate academic theories into relevant knowledge. For example, you will read how Whole Foods Market and La-Z-Boy have discovered the advantages of teamwork; how Sony Europe has improved employee motivation through the positive organizational behavior practice of strengths-based feedback; how Raytheon and other companies have mapped out informal social networks throughout the organization; and how Ernst & Young, Procter & Gamble, and several other firms are sending employees to overseas social responsibility assignments to improve their global mindset and other perceptual capabilities.

These real-life stories appear in many forms. Every chapter of *Organizational Behavior,* Fifth Edition, offers several detailed photo captions and many more in-text anecdotes. Lengthier stories are distinguished in a feature we call *Connections,* because it "connects" OB concepts with real organizational incidents. Case studies in each chapter connect OB concepts to the emerging workplace realities. These stories provide representation across the United States and around the planet. They also cover a wide range of industries–from software to government, and from small businesses to the Fortune 500.

GLOBAL ORIENTATION

One of the first things you might notice about this book is its strong global orientation. This goes beyond the traditional practice of describing how U.S. companies operate in other parts of the world.

Organizational Behavior, Fifth Edition, takes a truly global approach by illustrating how organizational behavior concepts and practices are relevant to companies in every part of the world. For example, you will read how Mina Ishiwatari faced resistance to change as she transformed sleepy Tokyo-based Hoppy Beverage Co. into a high-profile brand; how Volkswagen and Porsche executives are wrapped up in high-stakes conflict over how Volkswagen should be run; how Air New Zealand CEO Rob Fyfe relies on a hands-on approach to improve his and others' perceptions; how Sweden's Svenska Handelsbanken relies on employee empowerment and organizational rewards rather than centralized budgets to manage the business; and how Mott MacDonald's oil and gas team improves emotions and camaraderie through desert safari treks in Abu Dhabi.

This global orientation is also apparent in our discussion of many organizational behavior topics. The first chapter of *Organizational Behavior,* Fifth Edition, introduces the concept of globalization. Global issues are then highlighted throughout the book, such as cross-cultural values and ethics, development of a global mindset, job satisfaction and display of emotions in different societies, cross-cultural issues in the success of self-directed work teams, problems with cross-cultural communication, cultural values and expectations as a factor in preferred influence tactics, the handling of conflict differently across cultures, and preferred leadership styles across cultures.

Contemporary Theory Foundation

Vivid real-world examples and practices are only valuable if they are connected to good theory. *Organizational Behavior* has developed a reputation for its solid foundation of contemporary and classic research and writing. You can see this in the references. Each chapter is based on dozens of articles, books, and other sources. The most recent literature receives thorough coverage, resulting in what we believe is the most up-to-date organizational behavior textbook available. These references also reveal that we reach out to marketing, information management, human resource management, and other disciplines for new ideas. At the same time, this textbook is written for students, not the scholars whose work is cited. So, although this book provides new knowledge and its practical implications, it rarely names researchers and their university affiliations. It focuses on organizational behavior knowledge rather than "who's who" in the field.

One of the driving forces for writing *Organizational Behavior* was to provide a conduit whereby emerging OB knowledge more quickly reaches students, practitioners, and fellow scholars. This objective is so important that we state it in the subtitle of this book. To its credit, *Organizational Behavior* was the first textbook to discuss workplace emotions, social identity theory, four-drive theory, appreciative inquiry, affective events theory (but without the jargon), somatic marker theory (also without the jargon), virtual teams, future-search events, Schwartz's value model, resilience, employee engagement, learning orientation, workaholism, and several other groundbreaking topics. This edition introduces additional emerging OB concepts and practices, including social networking communication, the competencies of effective team members, exceptions to media richness theory, the importance of self-concept in organizational behavior, the globally integrated enterprise, the global mindset, and strengths-based feedback.

Organizational Behavior Knowledge for Everyone

Another distinctive feature of *Organizational Behavior,* Fifth Edition, is that it is written for everyone in organizations, not just managers. The philosophy of this book is that everyone who works in and around organizations needs to understand and make use of organizational behavior knowledge. The contemporary reality is that people throughout the organization–systems analysts, production employees, accounting professionals–are assuning more responsibilities as companies remove layers of management and give the rest of us more autonomy over our work. This book helps everyone to make sense of organizational behavior and provides the conceptual tools needed to work more effectively in the workplace.

Active Learning and Critical Thinking Support

We teach organizational behavior, so we understand how important it is to use a textbook that offers deep support for active learning and critical thinking. The fact that business school accreditation associations also emphasize the importance of the learning experience further reinforces our attention to classroom activities. *Organizational Behavior,* Fifth Edition, includes more than two dozen case studies in various forms and levels of complexity. It offers three dozen self-assessments, most of which have received construct validation. This book is also a rich resource for in-class activities, some of which are not available in other organizational behavior textbooks, such as "Test Your Knowledge of Personality," "Where in the World Are We?" and "Cross-Cultural Communication Game."

Changes to the Fifth Edition

Organizational Behavior, Fifth Edition, has benefited from reviews by several dozen organizational behavior teachers and researchers in several countries over the past two years. The most significant structural change is that we have reduced the book to 15 chapters so that it more closely parallels the number of weeks in a typical OB course. This edition also continues to update current knowledge in every chapter and provides fresh examples to illustrate theories and concepts. The most notable improvements to this edition are described as follows:

Chapter 1: Organizational Behavior—Introduction, Trends and Challenges. This chapter has been substantially revised and updated. It introduces four perspectives of organizational effectiveness (the ultimate dependent variable in OB), so students now have an excellent macro-OB foundation for topics throughout this book. The organizational effectiveness section also provides better organization for open systems, organizational learning, high performance work practices, and values and ethics. The five types of individual behavior are also described in this chapter as a natural micro-OB flow from the organizational effectiveness discussion. The topic of workforce diversity now distinguishes surface from deep-level diversity. Discussion of the systematic research anchor now describes evidence-based management. We also look into OB challenges in the context of mergers and acquisitions, global economic meltdown, green management, cluster concept, inclusive growth, and focus on innovation for competitiveness, work-life balance focusing on different time zone and rapid growth organizations. The changing nature of work is also explained as is the updation on CSR in India/CSR awards 2010 and international status of CSR in management schools. The Indian perspective of OB, namely, replication, disenchantment and integration as well as the *vedantic* perspective (*adhyatmic* to *atmic*) has been explained for better understanding.

Chapter 2: Individual Behavior, Personality, and Values. This edition provides important new knowledge about self-concept, including its main components (self-enhancement, self-verification, self-evaluation, and social identity) and their relevance for organizational behavior. This edition also has a rewritten and expanded discussion of personality in line with the topic's increasing importance in OB. The Indian perspective on moral self, dimensions of the self, culture construction of self, Indian mindset, changing perspective of values in Indian youth have been added. The impact of global meltdown as well as ethical values and behavior in its context on employees has been explained. The addition of Jungian personality theory of personality in organizations lends solidarity to the concept of the individual. The MARS model now includes a fuller conceptual background.

Chapter 3: Perception and Learning in Organizations. This edition updates the section on selective attention, organization, and interpretation based on the rapidly developing research on this topic. It also introduces the increasingly popular concept of global mindset in the context of perception and learning. The chapter adds discussion about false-consensus effect as well as the implicit association test. It also re-organizes into one section the discussion about practices that minimize perceptual problems. The concept of glass ceiling and the awareness of perceptual biases along with emotional display across cultures and an update on emotional intelligence provide a detailed explanation. Positive organizational behavior, which was introduced in previous editions, is described in this chapter and mentioned again in subsequent chapters of this book.

Chapter 4: Workplace Emotions, Attitudes, and Stress. This chapter now incorporates the topic of stress, which is closely related to workplace emotions. The impact of stress on the physical, mental well-being of the employees as well as predisposition to stress is also discussed. It continues to present a clearer explanation of the dual (cognitive and emotional) processes of attitudes and provides a fuller understanding about the dimensions of emotional intelligence. Wellness programs for employees have also been explored. This chapter also discusses "shock events" in job satisfaction.

Chapter 5: Foundations of Employee Motivation. The previous edition was apparently the first OB book to discuss employee engagement. This edition moves the topic to this chapter, so employee engagement is more closely connected to employee motivation as well as the MARS model. How managers design motivating jobs and how companies use Physical Environment as a motivator for their employees is also explained here. Balanced scorecard has also been moved to this chapter, because of its emphasis on goal setting rather than rewards. The chapter also distinguishes drives from needs and explains how drives and emotions are the prime movers of human motivation. It formulates the Indian approaches to motivation–*nishkam karma, daan karma*, self-actualization, passion to learn, innovation-*jugad* (need to achieve with less or alternate resources). It describes Maslow's contribution to the field of human motivation. *Organizational Behavior* was the first OB textbook to introduce four-drive theory, and this edition further refines the description of that model and its practical implications. The need for autonomy–Entrepreneurship/Intrapreneurship and Social Entrepreneurship and Networking has also been analyzed. Finally, this chapter introduces the positive organizational behavior concept and practice called strengths-based feedback.

Chapter 6: Applied Performance Practices. This edition adds emerging information about the situational and personal influences on self-leadership as well as self-leadership contingencies. It also updates information about the meaning of money and reward practices.

Chapter 7: Decision Making and Creativity. This edition introduces three of the decision heuristic biases discovered and popularized by Kahneman and Tversky. The chapter also revises and updates the discussion of problems with problem identification, the section on the influence of emotions on making choices, and the section on characteristics of creative people. It also has a more dedicated overview of the rational choice concept of subjective expected utility, implementation of decisions, and role of technology in decision-making and creativity and innovation.

Chapter 8: Team Dynamics. This edition combines the two chapters on teams found in previous editions. It summarizes types of teams and more fully discusses the potential benefits and problems with teams. Issues arising in multi-cultural teams have also been discussed. Furthermore, this edition introduces new information on the competencies of effective team members, revises the writing on self-directed teams and virtual teams, and provides emerging knowledge about two key processes in team development: team identity and team competence.

Chapter 9: Communicating in Teams and Organizations. The previous edition was apparently the first OB textbook to discuss the role of blogs and wikis in organizations. This edition continues this leadership with new information about social networking communication. Other new knowledge in this chapter include the topic of multi-communicating, social acceptance as a contingency in the selection of communication channels, conditions that offset the effects of media richness, social acceptance, social media and its impact and four factors that influence the effectiveness of the communication process. (i.e. encoding and decoding)

Chapter 10: Power and Influence in the Workplace. This chapter further develops the section on social networking as a source of power. It also adds a separate section on the consequences of power, issues and challenges and a cultural perspective.

Chapter 11: Conflict and Negotiation in the Workplace. This edition offers a more detailed look at the contingencies of conflict handling. It also revises and updates the development of thinking about whether conflict is good or bad. This description includes emerging model of constructive versus relationship conflict and the ways to allow the former while suppressing the latter. The discussion of negotiation now includes more specific advice regarding making concessions as well as the emerging views of constructive and relationship conflict.

Chapter 12: Leadership in Organizational Settings. In this edition, the competency perspective of leadership has been rewritten to incorporate new information about personality, self-concept, practical intelligence, and other specific competencies. The topic of implicit leadership has also been revised to incorporate the distinction between leadership prototypes and the romance of leadership. The topic of shared leadership has been expanded and the concept of open leadership and leadership in the context of global meltdown has been introduced.

Chapter 13: Organizational Structure. This edition describes the globally integrated enterprise in the section on forms of departmentalization. The liability of newness is now discussed in the section on organic structures. The chapter also revises writing on span of control and tall/flat structures and introduces concurrent engineering practices in the context of informal coordinating mechanisms. The (dis)advantages of tall versus flat structures also receive a more precise discussion.

Chapter 14: Organizational Culture. This edition more specifically (than in past editions) critiques the "integration" perspective of organizational culture by referring to the alternative differentiation and fragmentation views of this topic. It discusses the Indian Cultural Perspective in terms of Indian cultural traditions, composite Indian mindset and Situational Behavior of Indians. It also describes attraction-selection-attrition theory as well as the Organizational Culture Profile model.

The sections on organizational culture and performance as well as the section on changing/ strengthening organizational culture have been substantially rewritten with added inputs on aligning artifacts and attracting, selecting and socializing with employees. Addition of socialization as a learning and adjustment process under Organization Socialization strengthens the concept while the concept of culture in MNCs entering India and vice-versa as well as importance of cultural skills have also been discussed.

Chapter 15: Organizational Change. In this edition, the topic of resistance to change is further updated regarding the three functions of resistance. We added a new section on large-group interventions as a distinct fourth approach to organizational change. The topics of urgency for change and future search conferences also received minor updates. A new approach to organizational change has been added in the form of large-group intervention.

Acknowledgements

Have you ever worked on a high-performance team where everything just seems to "click"? We have–on this fifth edition of *Organizational Behavior!* Sure, we spent plenty of time alone writing and researching for this book, and of course there were challenges along the way. But it is always amazing how teamwork *really does* make a difference. Several people provided valued expertise to smooth out the rough spots of writing, search out the most challenging photos, create a fantastic design, develop the various forms of student and instructor support, and pull together these many pieces into a comprehensive textbook. This teamwork is even more amazing when you consider that most of the team members live throughout the United States and one of the authors (Steve) spends most of his time on the other side of the world.

Executive editor John Weimeister led the way with unwavering enthusiasm and foresight. Senior developmental editor Christine (Chipper) Scheid demonstrated superhuman skills at coordinating the volumes of e-mails and files that produced this edition. Sue Gottfried was an amazing copy editor, catching the most subtle errors and improving the authors' writing. Christine Vaughan, our lead project manager, was another true professional as she guided the book through its production schedule. Jennifer Blankenship, our photo researcher, continued to raise the bar at finding the best photos, including obscure images that we thought no one could possibly track down. Pam Kontopoulos created a design that represents the philosophy and style of this book. The eye-catching cover particularly captures the "dynamic flow" of well-performing contemporary organizations. Finally, marketing manager Natalie Zook created information packages and marketing materials to help McGraw-Hill/Irwin's superb sales team. These professionals help instructors to discover that this book really does deliver the content and support needed for an excellent learning experience. Thanks to you all. This has been an exceptional team effort!

As was mentioned earlier, several dozen instructors around the world reviewed parts or all of *Organizational Behavior,* Fifth Edition, or related editions in Canada, the Pacific Rim, and elsewhere over the past two years. Their compliments were energizing, and their suggestions significantly improved the final product. The following people from U.S. colleges and universities provided the most recent feedback for improvements specifically for *Organizational Behavior,* Fifth Edition:

Forrest Aven
University of Houston–Downtown

Prasad Balkundi
State University of New York–Buffalo

Kathleen Bates
California State University–San Marcos

Lehman Benson
University of Arizona

Sandra Deacon-Carr
Boston University

Diane Galbraith
Slippery Rock University of Pennsylvania

Nathan Goates
Shippensburg University of Pennsylvania

Kanata Jackson
Hampton University

Gary Kohut
University of North Carolina–Charlotte

Jerry Kopf
Radford University

Karthik Namasivayam
Pennsylvania State University–University Park

Howard Rudd
College of Charleston

Susmita Mukhopadhyay
Vinod Gupta School of Management–IIT Kharagpur

Manodip Ray Chaudhuri
Future Business School

Harold Andrew Patrick
Christ University

Debaprasad Chattopadhyay
Globsyn Business School

We also extend our sincere thanks to Floyd Ormsbee, Clarkson University, for his exceptional work on revision of the Test Bank. We also extend our gratitude to the many instructors in the United States and abroad who contributed cases and exercises to this edition of *Organizational Behavior.*

Steve would also like to extend special thanks to his students in Perth, Manila, and Singapore for sharing their learning experiences and assisting with the development of the three organizational behavior textbooks in the United States, Canada, and the Pacific Rim. Along with working with Mary Ann, Steve is honored to work with coauthors on other editions and translations of this book, including Professor Mara Olekalns at the University of Melbourne and Professor Tony Travaglione at Curtin University for the Pacific Rim edition, Sandra Steen at the University of Regina for the Canadian edition, Professor Radha Sharma at MDI for the Indian edition, Professor Runtian Jing at UESTC for the Chinese edition, and Professor Charles Benabou at UQAM for the Quebec French edition. Steve is also very grateful to his colleagues at the University of Western Australia for their support during changing times. But more than anything else, Steve is forever indebted to his wife Donna McClement and to their wonderful daughters, Bryton and Madison. Their love and support give special meaning to Steve's life.

Mary Ann would also like to acknowledge the many professionals at McGraw-Hill/Irwin who have worked to make the Fifth Edition a reality. In addition, she would like to thank the many, many students who have used and hopefully enjoyed this book. Student appreciation of this book is apparent by the number of times Mary Ann has been stopped on various campuses all over the world by students who say that they recognize her picture and want to thank her! There are a few who have actually asked for Mary Ann's autograph, and that did not happen when she was president of the Academy of Management! Thus, it is to the students that Mary Ann says thank you, particularly for making this learning venture fun and exciting. She would also like to thank the faculty and staff at Florida International University, as well as her CIBER staff: Sonia, Juan, and Kranthi. By far and away, Mary Ann thanks coauthor Steve McShane for his tireless efforts. Finally, Mary Ann would like to thank her family, starting with the immediate ones–Emma, Zack, and Googun–but also John, Rhoda, Lauren, Lindsay, and Christy. She also wants to acknowledge the critical role that some very special people play in her life: Janet, Peter, Bill, Karen, Alan, Danny, Debra, Mary, and Linda. I thank you all!

Radha Sharma would like to acknowledge her MBA students for their feedback during her teaching of 'Human Behavior in Organizations' paper at Management Development Institute, Gurgaon, India. According to their feedback, the book required concepts and practices adopted not only in the Western context but also those prevalent in the East, particularly pertaining to the Indian subcontinent. The success of previous editions provided a clue that readers look out for new ideas and concepts; and this has been the driving force to incorporate a large number of emerging and exiting phenomena prevalent in this subcontinent in this volume.

Radha Sharma sincerely thank Steven McShane, a brilliant scholar who invited her a couple of years ago to co-author the book to cater to the needs of a large section of students in this subcontinent.

His passion for writing with global context has made his several books bestsellers in the US, Canada and the Pacific Rim. This book is an outcome of truly global teamwork–Steve in Australia, Mary Ann in the US and Radha Sharma in India, linking the three continents through this book. It has been a privilege to work with both Steve and Mary; they have been superb personally and professionally and Radha Sharma cherishes this teamwork.

Radha Sharma would also like to thank her family–Chandresh, Anubhuti-Vishwa, Swati and Abhinav, who provided immense support by accepting her long hours not only at work but over the weekends as well. She also extends her sincere thanks to the team at Tata McGraw-Hill, especially Tapas Maji for his professional commitment and sincerity of purpose, Surabhi Khare for her understanding and timely support, and Anirudh Sharan for the hard work in going through the manuscript and publication process as well.

Steven L. McShane
Mary Ann Von Glinow
Radha R. Sharma

Supporting the Learning Process

The changes described previously refer only to the text material. *Organizational Behavior,* Fifth Edition, also has improved technology supplements, cases, team exercises, and self-assessments.

Several organizational behavior practices have helped Pixar Animation Studios become the world's most successful animation studio.

One of Robert Iger's first tasks as Walt Disney Co.'s new CEO was to acquire Pixar Animation Studios and put its leaders—John Lasseter (shown in this photo) and Ed Catmull—in charge of Disney's own animation unit, Walt Disney Animation Studios. The studio that brought us *Mickey Mouse* and *The Lion King* had become moribund over the past decade, eclipsed by Pixar's award-winning productions. Disney already had lucrative distribution rights to Pixar's first five films, including any sequels, but Iger wanted something much more valuable. He wanted the organizational behavior practices that have made Pixar a powerhouse filmmaker, from *Toy Story* to *Wall-E.*

Pixar's success is founded on the notion that companies depend on the quality of their employees and how well they collaborate with each other. "From the very beginning, we recognized we had to get the best people, technically, from the computer science world, and from the artistic filmmaking animation world, and get them working together," explains John Lasseter, who is now chief creative officer of both Pixar and Disney Animation Studios. "That, right there, is probably the secret to Pixar."

Pixar enables people to work together in several ways. First, the company relies on long-term employment relationships rather than short-term project contracts. These long-term relationships improve team development and social networks. "The problem with the Hollywood model is that it's generally the day you wrap production ...u've finally figured out how to work together," says Randy Nelson, head of Pixar University. ...eap from an idea-centered business to a people-centered business." Pixar's campus in ...ia, is another reason why employees work well together. The buildings were designed to ... teams yet also to encourage chance encounters with people from other projects. "When ...h other and make eye contact, innovative things happen," says Pixar director Brad Bird. ...an, no-nonsense, perfectionist culture is a third reason why the animation studio's staff ...ffectively. The company gives power to its production teams rather than to senior ...se teams are also ruthless at writing and rendering scenes several times until they look ...es—from entry-level newcomers to the CEO—are encouraged to be creative and offer ...bout work in progress. Production teams have regular "sweatbox" sessions at which ...ussed openly. Even the most successful films receive a "postmortem" to discover how ...een improved. "Our job is to address problems even when we're successful," explains ...ation president Ed Catmull, whose leadership is identified as the foundation of Pixar's

Yasmeen Youssef's self-confidence was a bit shaky when she and her husband moved from Egypt to Canada a few years ago. "I was worried no one would take a chance on me, would believe in me," she recalls. But any self-doubts slowly disappeared after taking an entry-level job with Fairmont Hotels & Resorts corporate offices in Toronto. "Everything changed when I started working at Fairmont," says Youssef, who is now on Fairmont's human resource team and recently trained new staff in Cairo. "I can't believe the amount of value, care, respect everyone has extended to me."

Fairmont Hotels has excelled as North America's largest luxury hotel operator by hiring people such as Yasmeen Youssef (shown here) with the right values and personality and then nurturing their self-concept and cross-cultural competencies.

As North America's largest luxury hotel operator, Fairmont discovered long ago that one of the secret ingredients for employee performance and well-being is supporting the individual's self-concept. "People want to feel valued and they stay where they feel valued," says Carolyn Clark, Fairmont's senior vice president of human resources. Clark also points out that Fairmont is able to nurture this talent by selecting the best, which means hiring people with the right values and personality for superb customer service. "We believed that we could train the technical skills—that's the easy part," Clark explained a few years ago. "What we can't train is the service orientation. We just can't put people in the training program and say they are going to come out smiling if that is not inherent in them."

Along with hiring people with the right values and personality and nurturing their self-concept, Fairmont is developing staff to work effectively in a multicultural world. Sean Billing is a case in point. The economics graduate had been working as Fairmont's director of rooms in Chicago when he casually asked his boss whether the hotel chain could use his skills and knowledge elsewhere. Soon after, Billing was offered a position in Kenya, bringing Fairmont's new properties in the African country up to world-class standards through training and technology without losing the distinctive Kenyan character. Billing jumped at the opportunity, but he also recognizes the challenge of inculcating Fairmont's deep values of customer service, environmentalism, and empowerment into another culture. "It's a little bit of hotel culture shock . . . things are quite different here," he says.[1]

Opening Vignette

Each chapter begins with an engaging **opening vignette** that sets the stage for the chapter. These brief but interesting case studies introduce students to critical issues, challenge their preconceptions, and highlight some of today's hottest companies.

1

ORGANIZATIONAL BEHAVIOR—INTRODUCTION, TRENDS AND CHALLENGES

Learning Objectives

After reading this chapter, you should be able to:

1. Define *organizational behavior* and *organizations* and discuss the importance of this field of inquiry and evolution of OB in India.
2. Diagram an organization from an open-systems perspective.
3. Define *intellectual capital* and describe the organizational learning perspective of organizational effectiveness.
4. Diagnose the extent to which an organization or one of its work units applies high-performance work practices.
5. Explain how the stakeholder perspective emphasizes the importance of values, ethics, and corporate social responsibility. Discover the broad contours of CSR as applied in organizations and as ingrained as a value in MBA education.
6. Summarize the five types of individual behavior in organizations.
7. Explore the current OB trends including employer branding, inclusive workforce and green intellectual capital management.
8. Debate the organizational opportunities and challenges of globalization, the changing workplace dynamics, and virtual work.
9. Discuss the anchors on which organizational behavior knowledge is based.

LEARNING OBJECTIVES

A topical guide for the student, a list of Learning Objectives not only can be found at the beginning of each chapter, but correspondingly throughout the chapter.

Learning Objectives

After reading the next two sections, you should be able to:

2. Diagram an organization from an open-systems perspective.
3. Define *intellectual capital* and describe the organizational learning perspective of organizational effectiveness.
4. Diagnose the extent to which an organization or one of its work units applies high-performance work practices.
5. Explain how the stakeholder perspective emphasizes the importance of values, ethics, and corporate social responsibility. Discover the broad contours of CSR as applied in organizations and as ingrained as a value in MBA education.
6. Summarize the five types of individual behavior in organizations.
7. Explore the current OB trends, including employer branding, inclusive workforce and green intellectual capital management.

CAPTIONS BEYOND CURSORY

Going beyond the simple caption, richly detailed photos are accompanied by more in-depth narrative.

Google Attracts and Keeps Talent through "Cool" Campuses Google is ranked by college students in many countries as one of the top 10 places to work. One reason why the Internet technology company is able to attract so many applicants is that its workplaces look like every student's dream of a college campus and dorm. Google's headquarters (called Googleplex) in Mountain View, California, is outfitted with lava lamps, exercise balls, casual sofas, foosball, pool tables, workout rooms, video games, slides, and a restaurant with free gourmet meals. Google's new EMEA engineering hub in Zurich, Switzerland, also boasts a fun, campuslike environment. These photos show a few areas of Google's offices in Zurich, including private temporary workspaces in beehives and ski gondolas. Google's offices are so comfortable that executives occasionally remind staff of building code regulations against making Google's offices their permanent home.[115]

1.1 **GLOBAL CONNECTIONS**

Hospitals Take the Lean Journey to Efficiency

Building Nissan automobiles seems unrelated to serving surgical patients, but staff at Sunderland Royal Hospital can see the similarities. The hospital in northern England recently borrowed several lean management ideas from the nearby Nissan factory, one of the most efficient car plants in Europe, to improve its day surgery unit. "We took [Sunderland hospital staff] on a tour of our plant, showing them a variety of lean processes in action, and let them decide which ones could be applied back at the hospital," says a training manager at Nissan's factory in Sunderland.

Sunderland's day surgery staff members were actively involved in applying lean management to their work unit. After attending Nissan's two-day workshop on lean thinking, they mapped out the work processes, questioned assumptions about the value or relevance of some activities, and discovered ways to reduce the lengthy patient wait times (which were up to three hours). There was some initial resistance and skepticism, but the hospital's day surgery soon realized significant improvements in efficiency and service quality.

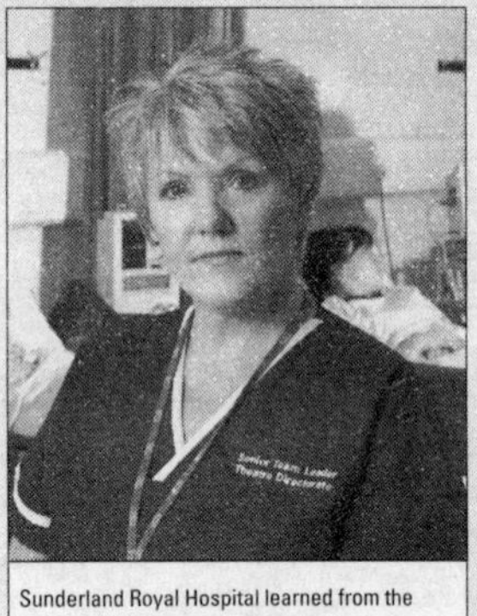

Sunderland Royal Hospital learned from the nearby Nissan factory how to implement lean management in its new day surgery unit.

"By working with Nissan's staff, we have streamlined the patient pathway from 29 to 11 discrete stages," says Anne Fleming (shown in photo), who oversees Sunderland's 32-bed day-case unit and its 54 employees. "We have done this by reducing duplication, halving the time that patients spend in the unit to three hours by giving them individual appointment times, and introducing the just-in-time approach to the patient pathway." Fleming also reports that Sunderland's operating rooms are now much more efficient.

Sunderland Royal Hospital is one of many health care centers around the world that are improving efficiency through lean thinking. After receiving training in Japan on lean practices, several teams of doctors, nurses, and other staff from Virginia Mason Medical Center in Seattle, Washington, redesigned workflows to cut out 34 miles of unnecessary walking each day. Park Nicollet Health Services in Minneapolis, Minnesota, improved efficiency at its ambulatory clinic to such an extent that the unit does not require a patient waiting area. One Park Nicollet team worked with orthopedic surgeons to reduce by 60 percent the variety of instruments and supplies they ordered for hip and knee surgery. The trauma team at Bolton Hospitals NHS Trust in the United Kingdom reduced average wait times for patients with fractured hips by 38 percent (from 2.4 to 1.7 days), which also resulted in a lower mortality rate for these patients. By smoothing out the inflow of work orders and rearranging the work process, Bolton's pathology department cut the time required to process samples, previously 24 to 30 hours, to just 2 to 3 hours and reduced the space used by 50 percent.

"We know that our case for extra funding will fall on deaf ears unless we cut out waste in the system," explains Dr. Gill Morgan, chief executive of the U.K.'s NHS Confederation. "Lean works because it is based on doctors, nurses, and other staff leading the process and telling us what adds value and what doesn't. They are the ones who know."[59]

CONNECTIONS

Connections boxes connect OB concepts with real organizational incidents. Periodically, these boxes highlight organizational behavior issues around the world and are entitled **Global Connections.**

End-of-Chapter Material Geared Toward Application

TEAM EXERCISES AND SELF-ASSESSMENTS

Experiential exercises and self-assessments represent an important part of the active learning process. *Organizational Behavior*, Fifth Edition, supports that learning process by offering team and class exercises in every chapter. Many of these learning activities are not available in other organizational behavior textbooks—for example, "Test Your Knowledge of Personality" (Chapter 2), "Cross-Cultural Communication Game" (Chapter 9), and "Contingencies of Conflict Handling" (Chapter 11). This edition also has three dozen self-assessments in the book or at the Online Learning Center. Self-assessments personalize the meaning of several organizational behavior concepts, such as extroversion/introversion, self-leadership, empathy, stress, creative disposition, and tolerance of change.

SELF-ASSESSMENT 2.7

ARE YOU INTROVERTED OR EXTROVERTED?

Purpose This self-assessment is designed to help you estimate the extent to which you are introverted or extroverted.

Instructions The statements in the scale below refer to personal characteristics that might or might not be characteristic of you. Mark the box indicating the extent to which the statement accurately or inaccurately describes you. Then use the scoring key in Appendix B at the end of this book to calculate your results. This exercise should be completed alone so that you can assess yourself honestly

IPIP Introversion-Extroversion Scale

How accurately does each of the statements listed below describe you?	Very accurate description of me	Moderately accurate	Neither accurate nor inaccurate	Moderately inaccurate	Very inaccurate description of me
1. I feel comfortable around people.	☐	☐	☐	☐	☐
2. I make friends easily.	☐	☐	☐	☐	☐
3. I keep in the background	☐	☐	☐	☐	☐
4. I don't talk a lot.	☐	☐	☐	☐	☐
5. I would describe my experiences as somewhat dull.	☐	☐	☐	☐	☐

n, M. C. Ashton, C. R. Cloninger, and H. C.
search in Personality 40 (2006), pp. 84–96.

e meaning and implications of

TEAM EXERCISE 2.6

ETHICS DILEMMA VIGNETTES

Purpose This exercise is designed to make you aware of the ethical dilemmas people face in various business situations, as well as the competing principles and values that operate in these situations.

Instructions (Small Class) The instructor will form teams of four or five students. Team members will read each case below and discuss the extent to which the company's action in each case was ethical. Teams should be prepared to justify their evaluation using ethics principles and the perceived moral intensity of each incident.

Instructions (Large Class) Working alone, read each case below and determine the extent to which the company's action in each case was ethical. The instructor will use a show of hands to determine the extent to which students believe the case represents an ethical dilemma (high or low moral intensity) and the extent to which the main people or company in each incident acted ethically.

Case One An employee who worked for a major food retailer wrote a Weblog (blog) and, in one of his writings, complained that his boss wouldn't let him go home when he felt sick and that his district manager refused to promote him because of his dreadlocks. His blog named the employer, but the employee didn't use his real name. Although all blogs are on the Internet, the employee claims that his was low-profile and that it didn't show up in a Google search of his name or the company. Still, the
vered the blog, figured out the employee's real name, and fired him for
ny in a public domain."

rinter manufacturers usually sell printers at a low margin over cost and gen-
from subsequent sales of the high-margin ink cartridges required for each
r manufacturer now designs its printers so that they work only with ink car-
region. Ink cartridges purchased in the United States will not work with the
n Europe, for example. This "region coding" of ink cartridges does not im-
er, it prevents consumers and gray marketers from buying the product at a
ion. The company says this policy allows it to maintain stable prices within
nually changing prices due to currency fluctuations.

few years, the design department of a small (40-employee) company has been
program, but the three employees who use the software have been complaining
e software is out of date and is slowing down their performance. The department
peting software program, costing several thousand dollars. However, the next
r six months and buying the current version will not allow much discount on the
has put in advance orders for the next version. Meanwhile, one employee was
urrent version of the software from a friend in the industry. The company has
es to use this current version of the software even though they did not pay for it.

s a popular talk-show radio personality and opinionated commentator on the
a popular radio station in a large U.S. city. Price is married to John Tremble,
ntly elected mayor of the city even though he had no previous experience in

Critical Thinking Questions

1. An insurance company has high levels of absenteeism among the office staff. The head of office administration argues that employees are misusing the company's sick leave benefits. However, some of the mostly female staff members have explained that family responsibilities interfere with work. Using the MARS model, as well as your knowledge of absenteeism behavior, discuss some of the possible reasons for absenteeism here and how it might be reduced.
2. As the district manager responsible for six stores in a large electronics retail chain, you have had difficulty with the performance of some sales employees. Although they are initially motivated and generally have good interpersonal skills, many have difficulty with the complex knowledge of the wide variety of store products, ranging from computers to high-fidelity sound systems. Describe three strategies you might apply to improve the match between the competencies of new sales employees and the job requirements.
3. Studies report that heredity has a strong influence on an individual's personality. What are the implications of this in organizational settings?
4. Suppose that you give all candidates applying for a management trainee position a personality test that measures the five dimensions in the five-factor model. Which personality traits would you consider to be the most important for this type of job? Explain your answer.
5. An important aspect of self-concept is the idea that almost everyone engages in self-enhancement. What problems tend to occur in organizations as a result of the self-enhancement phenomenon? What can organizational leaders do to make use of a person's inherent drive for self-enhancement?
6. This chapter discussed value congruence mostly in the context of an employee's personal values versus the organization's values. But value congruence also relates to the juxtaposition of other pairs of value systems. Explain how value congruence is relevant with respect to organizational versus professional values (i.e., values of a professional occupation, such as physician, accountant, pharmacist).
7. People in a particular South American country have high power distance and high collectivism. What does this mean, and what are the implications of this information when you (a senior executive) visit employees working for your company in that country?
8. "All decisions are ethical decisions." Comment on this statement, particularly by referring to the concepts of moral intensity and ethical sensitivity.

BUSINESSWEEK CASE STUDIES

Found at the end of each chapter, ***BusinessWeek* case studies** introduce the online full-text article and provide critical thinking questions for class discussion or assignments. These cases encourage students to understand and diagnose real-world issues using organizational behavior knowledge. For example, one case study challenges students to identify and evaluate the strategies that Merck CEO Richard Clark has applied to transform the culture of the pharmaceutical company. Another case study asks students to explain design thinking at Procter & Gamble and to relate design thinking to the decision-making process in organizations.

CASE STUDY 2.3

THE TROUBLE WITH BUSINESS ETHICS

BusinessWeek

Business ethics may have risen to the top of most executive agendas, but Wal-Mart Stores has learned that practicing ethics can also present ethical dilemmas. A few months after going through a new employee training session with a heavy emphasis on ethics, Chalace Epley Lowry acted on the guidance to report any activity that seemed the least bit suspicious. Lowry told the company's ethics office about possible insider trading by one of her supervisors. Wal-Mart's investigation concluded that the supervisor had done nothing wrong, but Lowry soon discovered that her identity as the whistle-blower had been revealed to the supervisor she accused of wrongdoing. Now Lowry is looking for another job, but there's no guarantee she'll get transferred at Wal-Mart.

This *BusinessWeek* case study examines the challenges of supporting ethics hotlines and whistle-blowing, and it discusses the reasons why employees are reluctant to communicate ethical wrongdoing. Read the full text of this *BusinessWeek* article at www.mhhe.com/mcshane5e, and prepare for the discussion questions below.

Discussion Questions

1. In an organization's efforts to maintain ethical standards, how important is it to encourage and support employees who report possible incidents of ethical wrongdoing (i.e., engage in whistle-blowing)? Why? What can companies do to support whistle-blowers?
2. What actions are described in this case study that companies have taken to improve ethical standards in their organizations? Are these actions substantive changes or mostly symbolic? Why?

Source: P. Gogoi, "The Trouble with Business Ethics," *BusinessWeek Online,* 22 June 2007.

CHAPTER CASES AND ADDITIONAL END-OF-TEXT CASES

Every chapter includes at least one short **case study** that challenges students to diagnose issues and apply ideas from that chapter. More than one dozen additional cases appear at the end of the book. Several cases are new to this book and are written by instructors from different countries.

CASE STUDY 3.1

HY DAIRIES, INC.

Syd Gilman read the latest sales figures with a great deal of satisfaction. The vice president of marketing at Hy Dairies, Inc., a large midwestern milk products manufacturer, was pleased to see that the marketing campaign to improve sagging sales of Hy's gourmet ice cream brand was working. Sales volume and market share of the product had increased significantly over the past two quarters compared with the previous year.

The improved sales of Hy's gourmet ice cream could be credited to Rochelle Beauport, who was assigned to the gourmet ice cream brand last year. Beauport had joined Hy less than two years ago as an assistant brand manager after leaving a similar job at a food products firm. She was one of the few women of color in marketing management at Hy Dairies and had a promising career with the company. Gilman was pleased with Beauport's work and tried to let her know this in the annual performance … vacated posi… modest sala… experience i… were aware … at Hy several …

Rochelle … expecting G… mentioning … marketing r… management … the company … "backroom" … the route to …

After a l… bewildered … Also, she di…

Gilman re… hearing of th… his temporar… be good for …

Beauport … events that e… Dairies and f…

Chapter Summary

Perception involves selecting, organizing, and interpreting information to make sense of the world around us. Perceptual organization engages categorical thinking—the mostly nonconscious process of organizing people and objects into preconceived categories that are stored in our long-term memory. Mental models—internal representations of the external world—also help us to make sense of incoming stimuli.

Social identity theory explains how we perceive people through categorization, homogenization, and differentiation. Stereotyping is a derivative of social identity theory, in which people assign traits to others based on their membership in a social category. Stereotyping economizes mental effort, fills in missing information, and enhances our self-perception and social identity. However, it also lays the foundation for prejudice and systemic discrimination.

The attribution process involves deciding whether an observed behavior or event is caused mainly by the person (internal factors) or the environment (external factors). Attributions are decided by perceptions of the consistency, distinctiveness, and consensus of the behavior. This process helps us to link together the various pieces of our world in cause-effect relationships, but it is also subject to attribution errors, including fundamental attribution error and self-serving bias.

Self-fulfilling prophecy occurs when our expectations about another person cause that person to act in a way that is consistent with those expectations. Essentially, our expectations affect our behavior toward the target person, which then affects that employee's opportunities and attitudes, which then influences his or her behavior. Self-fulfilling prophecies tend to be stronger when the relationship begins (such as when employees first join the department), when several people hold the expectations toward the employee, and when the employee has a history of low achievement.

Four other perceptual errors commonly noted in organizations are the halo effect, primacy effect, recency effect, and false-consensus effect. We can minimize these and other perceptual problems through aw… meaningful interaction.

Learning is a relatively permanent change in behavior (or behavior tendency) that … the environment. Much of what we learn is tacit knowledge, which is embedded in ou…

The behavior modification perspective of learning states that behavior change occu… Antecedents are environmental stimuli that provoke (not necessarily cause) behavio… that influence its future occurrence. Consequences include positive reinforcement, pun… The schedules of reinforcement also influence behavior.

Social learning theory states that much learning occurs by observing others and th… favorable outcomes and avoiding behaviors that lead to punishing consequences. …

Key Terms

attribution process	halo effect	recency effect
behavior modification	Johari Window	selective attention
categorical thinking	learning	self-fulfilling prophecy
contact hypothesis	learning orientation	self-reinforcement
empathy	mental models	self-serving bias
false-consensus effect	perception	social learning theory
fundamental attribution error	positive organizational behavior	stereotyping
global mindset	primacy effect	tacit knowledge

BRIEF CONTENTS

CONTENTS

PART 4 ORGANIZATIONAL PROCESSES

1 PART

Introduction

One of Robert Iger's first tasks as Walt Disney Co.'s new CEO was to acquire Pixar Animation Studios and put its leaders—John Lasseter (shown in this photo) and Ed Catmull—in charge of Disney's own animation unit, Walt Disney Animation Studios. The studio that brought us *Mickey Mouse* and *The Lion King* had become moribund over the past decade, eclipsed by Pixar's award-winning productions. Disney already had lucrative distribution rights to Pixar's first five films, including any sequels, but Iger wanted something much more valuable. He wanted the organizational behavior practices that have made Pixar a powerhouse filmmaker, from *Toy Story* to *Wall-E.*

Several organizational behavior practices have helped Pixar Animation Studios become the world's most successful animation studio.

Pixar's success is founded on the notion that companies depend on the quality of their employees and how well they collaborate with each other. "From the very beginning, we recognized we had to get the best people, technically, from the computer science world, and from the artistic filmmaking animation world, and get them working together," explains John Lasseter, who is now chief creative officer of both Pixar and Disney Animation Studios. "That, right there, is probably the secret to Pixar."

Pixar enables people to work together in several ways. First, the company relies on long-term employment relationships rather than short-term project contracts. These long-term relationships improve team development and social networks. "The problem with the Hollywood model is that it's generally the day you wrap production that you realize you've finally figured out how to work together," says Randy Nelson, head of Pixar University. "We've made the leap from an idea-centered business to a people-centered business." Pixar's campus in Emeryville, California, is another reason why employees work well together. The buildings were designed to cluster people into teams yet also to encourage chance encounters with people from other projects. "When people run into each other and make eye contact, innovative things happen," says Pixar director Brad Bird.

Pixar's egalitarian, no-nonsense, perfectionist culture is a third reason why the animation studio's staff members work effectively. The company gives power to its production teams rather than to senior executives, but these teams are also ruthless at writing and rendering scenes several times until they look right. All employees—from entry-level newcomers to the CEO—are encouraged to be creative and offer candid feedback about work in progress. Production teams have regular "sweatbox" sessions at which problems are discussed openly. Even the most successful films receive a "postmortem" to discover how they could have been improved. "Our job is to address problems even when we're successful," explains Pixar/Disney Animation president Ed Catmull, whose leadership is identified as the foundation of Pixar's unique culture.[1]

1

ORGANIZATIONAL BEHAVIOR—INTRODUCTION, TRENDS AND CHALLENGES

Learning Objectives

After reading this chapter, you should be able to:

1. Define *organizational behavior* and *organizations* and discuss the importance of this field of inquiry and evolution of OB in India.
2. Diagram an organization from an open-systems perspective.
3. Define *intellectual capital* and describe the organizational learning perspective of organizational effectiveness.
4. Diagnose the extent to which an organization or one of its work units applies high-performance work practices.
5. Explain how the stakeholder perspective emphasizes the importance of values, ethics, and corporate social responsibility. Discover the broad contours of CSR as applied in organizations and as ingrained as a value in MBA education.
6. Summarize the five types of individual behavior in organizations.
7. Explore the current OB trends including employer branding, inclusive workforce and green intellectual capital management.
8. Debate the organizational opportunities and challenges of globalization, the changing workplace dynamics, and virtual work.
9. Discuss the anchors on which organizational behavior knowledge is based.

Collaboration, motivation, communication, creativity, empowerment, organizational learning, leadership–these are some of the organizational behavior concepts behind the success of Pixar Animation Studios and other companies. They are also some of the topics featured in this book. Our main objective is to help you understand behavior in organizations and to work more effectively in organizational settings. We begin in this chapter by introducing the field of organizational behavior and explaining why knowledge of this field is important to organizations as well as to your career. Next, the chapter describes the four main perspectives of organizational effectiveness, which is considered the "ultimate dependent variable" in organizational behavior. This is followed by an overview of the five main types of individual behavior in organizations. The Indian perspective on organizational behavior is also discussed. This chapter also describes challenges facing organizations—globalization, increasing workforce diversity, emerging employment relationships—and highlights the anchors that guide organizational behavior knowledge development, global meltdown, inclusive growth, managing different time zones, etc.

Learning Objectives

After reading this section, you should be able to:

1. Define *organizational behavior* and *organizations* and discuss the importance of this field of inquiry and evolution of OB in India.

THE FIELD OF ORGANIZATIONAL BEHAVIOR

organizational behavior (OB)
The study of what people think, feel, and do in and around organizations.

Organizational behavior (OB) is the study of what people think, feel, and do in and around organizations. Its focus is on employee behavior, decisions, perceptions, and emotional responses. It looks at how individuals and teams in organizations relate to each other and to their counterparts in other organizations. OB also encompasses the study of how organizations interact with their external environments, particularly in the context of employee behavior and decisions. OB researchers systematically study these topics at multiple levels of analysis, namely, the individual, team (including interpersonal), and organization.[2]

Organizational Behavior's Foundations

Organizational behavior emerged as a distinct field around the 1940s, but organizations have been studied by experts in other fields for many centuries.[3] For example, the Greek philosopher Plato wrote about the essence of leadership. Around the same time, the Chinese philosopher Confucius extolled the virtues of ethics and leadership. In 1776, Adam Smith advocated a new form of organizational structure based on the division of labor. One hundred years later, German sociologist Max Weber wrote about rational organizations, the work ethic, and charismatic leadership. Soon after, industrial engineer Frederick Winslow Taylor proposed new ways to organize employees and motivate them through goal setting and rewards. In the 1920s, Elton Mayo and his colleagues reported on how formal and informal group dynamics operate in the workplace. During that same time, Mary Parker Follett pioneered new ways of thinking about several OB topics, including constructive conflict, team dynamics, organizational democracy, power, and leadership. A decade later, Chester Barnard wrote insightful views regarding individual behavior, motivation, communication, leadership and authority, and team dynamics in organizational settings. This brief historical tour indicates that OB has been around for a long time; it just wasn't organized into a unified discipline until after World War II.

Emergence of OB as a Discipline

Mary Parker Follett and Chester Barnard were pioneers of contemporary organizational behavior thinking a decade or two before OB became a distinct field of inquiry. Follett was a Boston social worker and political science scholar who suggested that conflict can be "constructive" when the parties gain a better understanding of each other. She was also a strong advocate of employee involvement and organizational democracy. Chester Barnard was a career executive (including president of New Jersey Bell Telephone Company and, later, head of two foundations), who wrote several influential books on management and organizations. He emphasized that organizations depend on effective communication and that a manager's formal authority depends on the employee's willingness to accept that power. He also discussed norms of informal groups as well as a rational perspective of employee motivation. Both Barnard and Follett described organizations as holistic cooperative organisms. This was a refreshing contrast to the machinelike metaphor of organizations that dominated management theory and practice in those days.[4]

OB is an interdisciplinary field and its emergence can be traced back to Human Relations Movement stimulated by Hawthorne experiments during 1920s. The idea of scientific management, propounded by Frederick Winslow Taylor, had come up with fundamental principles of the subject based on Motion and Time Studies, which were introduced in industry in the United States on a large scale. The major contributions of the scientific management have been (i) standardization of work; (ii) equality in payment of wages, and (iii) precision in training. However, following the support of business leaders, academicians, plus shortage of World War II led to the surge of interest in the Human Relations Movement and legalization of union-management relations in 1930s. During this period, extensive experiments were being conducted by behaviour scientists in industry, highlighting the importance of 'human' factor or the man behind the machine. There has been a shift from 'mechanization' of management to 'humanization' of management. Human relations management laid emphasis on the mutuality of interest between employers and employees, respect for individual differences in motivation, productivity and dignity. This led to better human relations and better working conditions.

Hawthorne Studies Hawthorne studies were conducted at Hawthorne Works of Western Electric Company near Chicago. The first study aimed at experimentally testing the effects of varying degrees of illumination on worker-productivity. The study was conducted on two groups of female workers in control and experimental group design. While the experimental group was subjected to different degrees of illumination ranging from very high to very low; the control group worked under constant conditions. When the productivity of the groups was compared, the researchers were baffled to find that at the end of the experiment the productivity showed an increase in both the control and experimental groups. The productivity increase was expected from the group which worked under constant lighting but not in the other group which worked under different conditions. After their analysis, they concluded that it was the complex human variable which caused the increase in the productivity of the experimental group.

The Next Phase: Relay-room Experiments The relay-room experiments commenced in 1927 and lasted for five years. These were led by Elton Mayo and involved his colleagues from Harvard and representatives of the company. The study tested the effect of thirteen variables like the effect of place of work, method of payment, rest pauses, length of work day, and length of work week, on productivity.

The same control and experimental design was used and the researchers found the results to be practically identical to the illumination experiment. Every test period resulted in higher productivity. This implied the presence of another variable (other than independent and dependent) which accounted for increase in the output.

The Bank-Wiring-Room Study The bank-wiring-room studies commenced in 1931 and lasted till May 1932. The methodology used in this study was different; it was based on the observational analysis of the informal work groups. There were no experimental changes introduced in the bank-wiring study. Also, supervisors of the department acted as observers and their role was to ensure that there was order and control. Unlike the previous studies, the result of the bank-wiring study revealed no continual increases in productivity. The results were essentially opposite of the relay-room experiments. Here, the output was restricted by the bank wirers. The logic of restricted output was that there was fear among the wirers of raising the standard by the contractor. Also, fear of unemployment, protection of slow workers and satisfaction on the part of management were the explanations for workers' low output. Dynamics among the members, group pressure, ridicule and sarcastic remarks were used by the group to prevent high performers give high output.

Contribution of Hawthorne studies to OB This led to understanding of human behavior, despite the conceptual and methodological limitations of research of that time as compared to the present.[5] When the workers were asked the reason for higher productivity in Hawthorne experiments (except the bank-wiring room), they gave a number of reasons like the size of the group, personal attention during the experiment, novel experience, and desire to participate in it.[6] The role of human factors was labeled as 'Hawthorne Effect' which laid the foundation of future studies in human behavior.

WHAT ARE ORGANIZATIONS?

organizations
Groups of people who work interdependently toward some purpose.

The definition of organizational behavior begs the question: What are organizations? **Organizations** are groups of people who work interdependently toward some purpose.[7] Notice that organizations are not buildings or government-registered entities. In fact, many organizations exist without either physical walls or government documentation to confer their legal status. Organizations have existed for as long as people have worked together.[8] Massive temples dating back to 3500 BC were constructed through the organized actions of multitudes of people. Craftspeople and merchants in ancient Rome formed guilds, complete with elected managers. More than 1,000 years ago, Chinese factories were producing 1,25,000 tons of iron each year. Throughout history, organizations have consisted of people who communicate, coordinate, and collaborate with each other to achieve common objectives.

One key feature of organizations is that they are collective entities. They consist of human beings (typically, but not necessarily, employees), and these people interact with each other in an *organized* way. This organized relationship requires some minimal level of communication, coordination, and collaboration to achieve organizational objectives. As such, all organizational members have degrees of interdependence with each other; they accomplish goals by sharing materials, information, or expertise with co-workers.

A second key feature of organizations is that their members have a collective sense of purpose. There is some debate among OB experts about whether all organizations really have a collective sense of purpose. The collective purpose isn't always well defined or agreed on. Furthermore, although most companies have vision and mission statements, these documents are sometimes out of date or don't describe what employees and leaders try to achieve in reality. These points may be true, but imagine an organization without goals: It would consist of a mass of people wandering around aimlessly without any sense of direction. So, whether they are producing animated feature films at Pixar Animation Studios or designing and building automobiles at General Motors, organizational members do have some sense of collective purpose. "A company is one of humanity's most amazing inventions," says Steve Jobs, CEO of Apple, Inc. (and former CEO of Pixar Animation Studios). "It's totally abstract. Sure, you have to build something with bricks and mortar to put the people in, but basically a company is this abstract construct we've invented, and it's incredibly powerful."[9]

Why Study Organizational Behavior?

Organizational behavior instructors face a challenge: On the one hand, students just beginning their careers tend to value courses related to specific jobs, such as accounting and marketing.[10] However, OB doesn't have a specific career path–there is no "VP of OB"–so these students sometimes have difficulty recognizing the value that OB knowledge can offer to their future. On the other hand, students with several years of work experience place OB near the top of their list of important courses. Why? Because they have directly observed that OB *does make a difference* to their career success. To begin with, they have learned that OB theories help us to make sense of the workplace. These theories also give us the opportunity to question and rebuild our personal mental models that have developed through observation and experience. Thus, OB is important because it helps to fulfill our need to understand and predict the world in which we live.[11]

But the main reason why people with work experience value OB knowledge is that they have discovered how it helps them to get things done in organizations. This practical side of organizational behavior

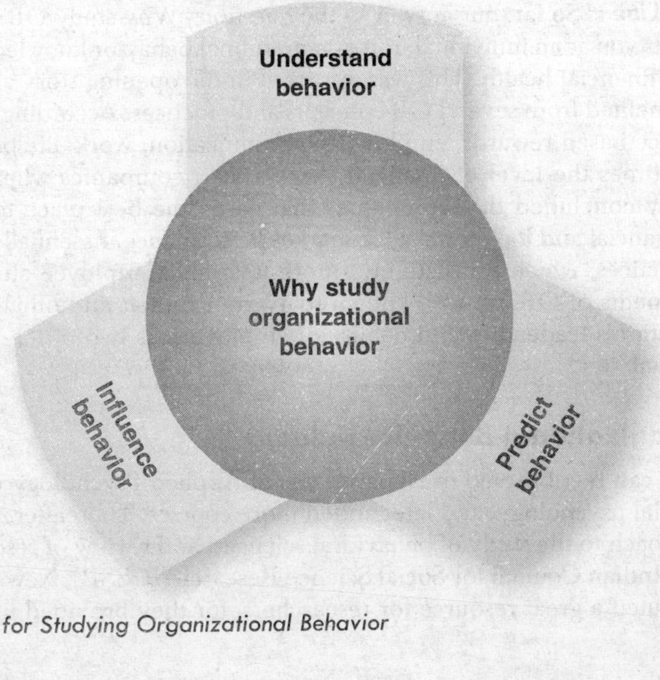

Exhibit 1.1 *Reasons for Studying Organizational Behavior*

is, according to some experts, a critical feature of the best OB theories.[12] Everyone in the organization needs to work with other people, and OB provides the knowledge and tools for working with and through others. Building a high-performance team, motivating co-workers, handling workplace conflicts, influencing your boss, and changing employee behavior are just a few of the areas of knowledge and skills offered in organizational behavior. No matter what career path you choose, you'll find that OB concepts play an important role in performing your job and working more effectively within organizations.

Understanding, Predicting, and Influencing Each of us has an inherent need to understand and predict the world in which we live. Because much of our time is spent working in or around organizations, OB theories are particularly helpful in satisfying this innate drive to make sense of the workplace. OB theories also give you the opportunity to question and rebuild your personal mental models that have developed through observation and experience.

Understanding and predicting are important, but most of us also need to influence the organization in various ways. Whether you are trying to introduce a new marketing strategy, encourage staff to adopt new information technology, or negotiate more flexible work arrangements with your boss, you'll find that OB concepts play an important role in performing your job and working more effectively within organizations. This practical side of organizational behavior is, according to some experts, a critical feature of the best OB theories.

Organizational Behavior is for Everyone Our explanation of why organizational behavior is important for your career success does not assume that you are, or intend to be, a manager. In fact, this book pioneered the notion that OB knowledge is for everyone. Whether you are a geologist, financial analyst, customer service representative, or chief executive officer, you need to understand and apply the many organizational behavior topics that are discussed in this book. Yes, organizations will continue to have managers, but their roles have changed and the rest of us are increasingly expected to manage ourselves in the workplace. In the words of one forward-thinking OB writer many years ago: Everyone is a manager.[13]

OB and the Bottom Line So far, our answer to the question "Why study OB?" has focused on how OB knowledge benefits you as an individual. But organizational behavior knowledge is just as important for the organization's financial health. This was apparent in the opening story about Pixar Animation Studios, which has benefited from several OB concepts and practices. According to one estimate, firms that apply performance-based rewards, employee communication, work–life balance, and other OB practices have three times the level of financial success than companies where these practices are absent. Another study concluded that companies that earn "the best place to work" awards have significantly higher financial and long-term stock market performance. Essentially, these firms leverage the power of OB practices, which translate into more favorable employee attitudes, decisions, and performance. The benefits of OB are well known to Warren Buffett and other financial gurus; they consider the organization's leadership and quality of employees as two of the best predictors of the firm's financial potential.[14]

Evolution of Organizational Behavior in India

The beginning of OB can be observed in Departments of Applied Psychology which offered courses in clinical and industrial psychology, and later added more courses. Thereafter, there has emerged an interdisciplinary approach to the study of behavioral sciences, and review of researches in psychology have been funded by Indian Council for Social Science Research (ICSSR), New Delhi, and published. These surveys constituted a great resource for researchers, for they provided literature for review as the internet technology had not developed by then. In 1962, the Behavioral Science Centre was established at New Delhi, which published directories of research in behavioral sciences and Indian Behavioural Science Abstracts (ABS). Another development, observed in early 1960s, was adoption of the process methodology of training for dealing with interpersonal and group issues by Rolf Lynton and Udai Pareek in the form of Learning groups (L-groups) and Training groups (T-groups). Thereafter, some social scientists received training at the National Training Laboratory Institute (NTL), and came together to create a professional body, called the Indian Society for Applied Social Sciences (ISABS) in 1971, which has since been running basic and advanced courses, and also theme based courses, using process methodology. ISABS also introduced a system of accreditation and thereby developed a group of professionals, who are carrying its mission forward. Later, courses on organizational behavior were introduced in the psychology departments of universities, and in management institutes.[15]

The literature of organizational behavior in the Indian context classifies evolution as follows:

1. Imitating the Western theories and concepts
2. Disenchantment
3. Integration of Western and Indian theories and concepts

Imitating the Western theories and concepts In the first stage of evolution of organizational behavior in India, many Western theories were imitated based on their universal validity. However, the replications failed due to incorrect translation of the research instruments, lack of rigor in the research design or faulty sampling. Initially, the Indian scholars did not have organizational-behavior theories or conceptual framework to give a more realistic viewpoint; neither had they challenged the Western theories and concepts. To cover up the inconsistencies in research findings, Indian cultural angle was used by both Indian and Western scholars. However, there were differences in viewpoint regarding Indian culture between Indian and Western scholars.

Disenchantment Early researches by few Indian scholars revealed that the Indians were authoritarian and had clear demarcation of dos and don'ts, strong orientation towards hierarchy. They were conscious about status, high need for power, but there was no conclusive evidence on whether they possessed the fundamental psychodynamics [free floating anxiety, ego-alien sexuality][16]. Participative leaders were perceived to be weak as they relinquished responsibility of decision making. Indians preferred and worked effectively under nurturing supervisors[17].

In the Indian organizations, Maslow's need hierarchy theory was not found to hold true. Money, security and status remained the most important needs across all levels and industries[18]. In India, the two-factor theory was shown to be artifact of the methodology implemented by Herzberg and the T-group methodology, which was individual-based was found to be ineffective in India's collectivist culture; system-wide interventions were found to be more effective[19]. Rice introduced the concept of socio-technology system which was experimented in textile looms sheds of Ahmedabad[20] later experimented by De[21] in a number of public-sector organizations. However, it revealed that underlying values like egalitarianism and participatory orientation were lacking in the Indian culture. Indians dodged work through various means in order to get rest or to meet social obligations[22]. This non-work orientation was partly due to traditional Indian culture making inroads into organizational settings[23].

Integration In this approach, scholars attempted to integrate Western and Indian aspects of organizational behavior which resulted into five approaches: Ancient Indian approach to management, Ancient Indian concepts examined by Western methods, finding relevance of Western concepts in India,

Assimilative synthesis of Western and Indian concepts, and Indigenous conceptualization with universally applicable processes.

- *Ancient Indian Approach to Management (Vedantic path):* There were many Indian organizations which followed the Vedantic approach, i.e. spiritual route to organizational development. Organizations like State Bank of India, Indian Oil, Infosys, etc.[24] followed values and practices drawn primarily on vedantic thoughts[25] and Sharma[26]. In studies by Garg and Parikh[27], the managers who inculcated Western values were found to experience identity crisis because they alienated themselves from their inner self.
- *Ancient Indian Concepts examined by Western Methods:* Experimental method was employed to study the impact of yogic exercises and meditation on behavior[28]. Empirical studies on *nishkam karm* (working sincerely without any preoccupation with the results) have shown results that decreased work-related stress[29], executive burnout symptoms[30] and increase satisfaction[31].
- *Relevance of Western Concepts in the Indian Context:* The Machiavellian tendency (ingratiation and manipulation process) was investigated by Pandey[32] and Tripathi[33] who found that it was pervasive and risk-free in India than in the West. Indians, in order to gain favors, indulged in name-dropping; self demeaning behavior, and changed views according to situation. The psychological consequence of crowding is not always negative in India unlike in the West[34]. Aspects like the need for achievement[35], distributive justice[36] and morality[37] which existed in western frameworks, were studied in Indian context and had unique Indian cultural components and dynamics.
- *Assimilative Synthesis of Western and Indian Concepts:* Through research it was found, there was need to assimilate western values like openness, collaboration, trust, authenticity, autonomy and confrontation to resolve problems, along with Indian's concern for others, efforts to synthesize difference of views and respect for knowledge and expertise, so as to build an effective organization[38]. Another research indicated that Indian managers working in MNCs behaved with expatriates in the same manner as expatriates conducted with them but had typical Indian behavior when dealing with another Indian colleague[39].
- *Indigenous Conceptualization with Universally Applicable Processes:* This school of thought suggested that universally applicable processes can be adapted in a way suitable for the Indian organizations and its people based on Goal Theory of Motivation[40]. In localizing the process of the Goal Theory of Motivation, it was suggested, that setting the appropriate goals, module of the training program and the appraisal format needed to be determined taking into consideration the Indian culture. Similarly, taking into consideration the Indian cultural preference for a nurturing superior and compliant subordinate, the reinforcement theory was put into use in a contingency framework to postulate a model of leadership suitable for Indian organizations.[41]

Traditional Indian Organizational Behavior Concepts

Organizational behavior from the Indian perspective has been discussed in various Indian ancient scriptures and literature. Some of these concepts have been discussed here briefly.

Loksangraha/Collective Interest *Loksangraha* means that actions of an individual or organization should be in collective interest. The concept of *loksangraha* has been discussed in the *Bhagvad Gita*, the holy book for Hindus. Actions, behavior, etc. should be undertaken for the welfare and interest of the society[42]. Inclusive growth, which has become the pivotal point across organizations and economies in recent years, has ideologies similar to that of *loksangraha* found in the ancient Indian literature.

Parasparam Bhavayantaha/Affinity and Interdependence An individual or an organization, both cannot sustain on their own in a society. According to the *Gita*, affinity and interdependence is essential to live and thrive in a society which paves the way for cooperation, despite differences. Focus is on harmonization in the context of an organization[43]. Inclusion of diversity has similarities with *Parasparam Bhavayantaha*, which is gaining importance and challenging organizations and individuals to accept and thrive along with individuals from diverse cultures, with difference in values, beliefs, etc. A workplace with diversity inclusion can be one of the enablers for organizations to strive in the midst of globalized economies and uncertainties.

Swadharma/Performing One's Duty *Bhagvad Gita's* articulation of *swadharma* means, an individual should perform duties and responsibilities assigned to them. The duties should be performed with positive inclination and effectiveness. An individual should take care that they do not overstep into others roles and responsibilities, otherwise it would lead to conflict in the organization.[44]

Cultural Perspective to Understand Organizational Behavior in Indian Organizations

India is a multi-cultural country. The multi-dimensional culture of India has been pruned and churned over centuries through influence of foreign cultures which descended on the Indian soil. Research reveals that there are three important features of Indian culture which can be seen and experienced in the behavior of individuals, group/s and organization/s: (a) Pluralistic World View, (b) Synthesizing Mindset, and (c) High Context Sensitivity[45].

(a) **Pluralistic World View:** Indians are open to new ideas, influences and adopt values, norms, beliefs and practices of other cultures.
(b) **Synthesizing Mindset:** Indians integrate influences from diverse cultures which they come across. However, those influences which are not acceptable for integration are also allowed to co-exist. Due to this mindset, there is consistency, inconsistency as well as opposite elements in the Indian culture.
(c) **High Context Sensitivity:** Indians' behavior/response differs according to the different organizational context and the person or group with whom they come in contact.

Influencers on Indian Culture

Indian culture has mixed influence of ancient Hindu mythologies, indigenous mindset, colonial experiences and global exposure[46].

Ancient Hindu View It is based on Hindu mythologies comprising cosmic collectivism, hierarchical order and spiritual orientation. Cosmic collectivism is based on the assumption that the Universe consists of diverse forms and elements which are compatible and also conflicting, but are related. Hierarchical order signifies that all things within the Universe are arranged in order of being superior or inferior to the other. Spirituality was conceived to enable human beings to rise above their physical and material well-being, i.e. well-being of the soul.

Indigenous Mindset Under indigenous mindset, ancient Hindu culture is retained, but at the same time, it has assimilated some aspects of the Mughal and the Muslim culture which were acceptable. The Indians also allowed early immigrants and invaders to retain their religions and cultures despite differences.

Influences of Colonial Rule The colonial experience was totally different. In order to gain and retain power, the colonial rule adopted a bureaucratic style which led to the divide-and-rule policy. The adverse effects of colonial rule of bureaucracy were syndrome of 'amoral familism', i.e. concern for own family members at the cost of organizational goals, unwillingness to make any small sacrifice for the benefit of society at large, and lack of respect for law and the society[47].

Influences from Global Exposure In the pre-independence era, few Indians got exposure to and experience in English language, literature, education systems of the West, modern sciences and medicine, legal and administrative system of the British. The *Westernized* exposure increased in the post-independence era due to international connections and business exchanges, and mass media. Organizations adopted modernization practices, management principles, organizational structure, etc. from the West. Values like achievement, advancement, individualism, confidence, ambition, etc. had begun to influence and over a period of time, these values have been nurtured by Indians. The Indian economy was liberalized in 1991, which led to the evolution of global Indians. Globalized features of the Indians include enterprising people, being knowledge of modern science and technology, possession of in-depth knowledge and exposure to international markets (e.g. Tata Tetley, Mahindra & Mahindra, Infosys, Maruti Suzuki, Bajaj Auto Ltd.), have expertise as well as recognition as management gurus (e.g., C.K. Prahlad, Gita Piramal, Sumantra Ghoshal, Ram Charan, Vijay Govindrajan, Rakesh Khurana). Global Indians are balancing between Indian and Western values for the larger canvass of life, and social responsibility is important to them.

The Indian Mindset: Coexistence of the Opposites

'There is much more of an ability [of Indians] to live with inconsistency and dissonance than what it tends to be characteristics of most Westerners'[48]. The Indian mind has co-existence of the opposites, characteristics like collective-individual approach, personal-contract based relationship, hierarchical orientation, evading and tolerance for uncertainty, gender-based complexity (the Indian culture has male dominance), harmony-conflict, spirituality-materialism, emotional-rational attitude, perfectionism-least care for perfectionism or *chalta hai* attitude (poor quality is also acceptable), dependence-independence (spirit of entrepreneurship). The Indian mindset is the existences of opposites, which acts or interprets taking into consideration the respective individual, group, place (organization) and time.

Learning Objectives

After reading the next two sections, you should be able to:

2. Diagram an organization from an open-systems perspective.
3. Define *intellectual capital* and describe the organizational learning perspective of organizational effectiveness.
4. Diagnose the extent to which an organization or one of its work units applies high-performance work practices.
5. Explain how the stakeholder perspective emphasizes the importance of values, ethics, and corporate social responsibility. Discover the broad contours of CSR as applied in organizations and as ingrained as a value in MBA education.
6. Summarize the five types of individual behavior in organizations.
7. Explore the current OB trends, including employer branding, inclusive workforce and green intellectual capital management.

Perspectives of Organizational Effectiveness

Almost all organizational behavior theories have the implicit or explicit objective of making organizations more effective.[49] Indeed, organizational effectiveness is considered the "ultimate dependent variable" in organizational behavior.[50] The first challenge, however, is to define

organizational effectiveness
A broad concept represented by several perspectives, including the organization's fit with the external environment, internal-subsystems configuration for high performance, emphasis on organizational learning, and ability to satisfy the needs of key stakeholders.

organizational effectiveness. Experts agree that this topic is burdened with too many labels–organizational performance, success, goodness, health, competitiveness, excellence, and so on–with no consensus on the meaning of each label.

Long ago, organizational effectiveness was defined as the extent to which an organization achieved its stated goals.[51] According to this view, Pixar is effective because it achieves its stated objective of producing animation features on time, on budget, and on target regarding box office sales. The goal attainment view is no longer accepted, however, because a company can be considered effective simply by establishing easily achievable goals. Also, some goals–such as social responsibility to the community–are so abstract that it is difficult to know how well the organization has achieved them. A third flaw with the goal attainment definition is that a company's stated objectives might threaten its long-term survival. For example, some corporate leaders receive incentives (such as stock options) to maximize short-term profits. Some accomplish this objective by slashing expenditures, including funds for marketing and product development. The result is often a lack of new products and deterioration in the company's brand value in the long run. In extreme cases, the company achieves its short-term profitability targets but eventually goes out of business.

How is organizational effectiveness defined today? The answer is that there are several perspectives of effectiveness, so this concept is defined in terms of *all of these perspectives.*[52] Organizations are considered effective when they have a good fit with their external environment, when their internal subsystems are configured for a high-performance workplace, when they are learning organizations, and when they satisfy the needs of key stakeholders. Over the next few pages, we will discuss each of these four perspectives of organizational effectiveness in some detail.

Open-Systems Perspective

open systems
A perspective which holds that organizations depend on the external environment for resources, affect that environment through their output, and consist of internal subsystems that transform inputs to outputs.

The **open-systems** perspective of organizational effectiveness is one of the earliest and deeply entrenched ways of thinking about organizations. In fact, the other major organizational effectiveness perspectives might be considered detailed extensions of the open-systems model.[53] As depicted in Exhibit 1.2, the open-systems perspective views organizations as complex organisms that "live" within an external environment. The word *open* describes this permeable relationship, whereas *closed* systems can exist without dependence on an external environment.

As open systems, organizations depend on the external environment for resources, including raw materials, employees, financial resources, information, and equipment. Pixar, Disney, and other companies could not survive without employees, raw materials, knowledge, and so forth. The open-systems perspective also describes numerous subsystems within the organization, such as processes (communication and reward systems), work units (production, marketing), and social dynamics (informal networks, power relationships). With the aid of technology (such as equipment, work methods, and information), these subsystems transform inputs into various outputs. Some outputs (e.g., products and services) may be valued by the external environment, whereas other outputs (e.g., employee layoffs, pollution) have adverse effects. The organization receives feedback from the external environment regarding the value of its outputs and the availability of future inputs.

According to the open-systems perspective, successful organizations monitor their environments and are able to maintain a close fit with changing conditions.[54] One way they do this is by finding new

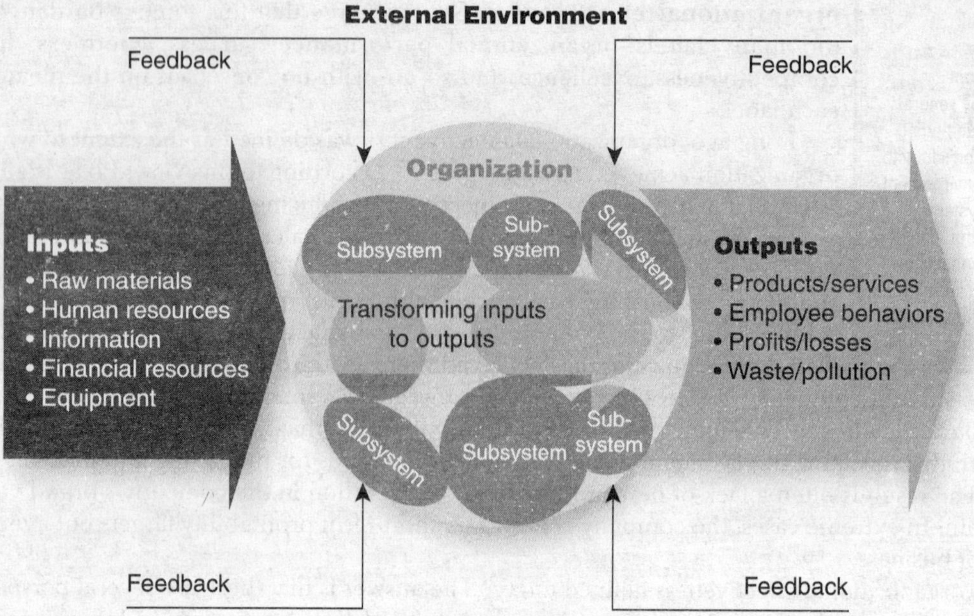

Exhibit 1.2 *Open-Systems Perspective of Organizations*

opportunities to secure essential inputs. For instance, many fast-food restaurants struggle to find enough employees. To ensure that it has enough qualified staff, McDonald's restaurants were among the first to recruit retirees. More recently, McDonald's UK introduced the "family contract," an employment arrangement that allows members of the employee's family (spouses, grandparents, and children over the age of 16) to swap shifts without notifying management.[55] Successful organizations also redesign outputs so that they remain compatible with demands from the external environment. Food manufacturers have changed their ingredients to satisfy more health-conscious consumers. Automobile manufacturers have redesigned cars to satisfy demands for more fuel efficiency and safety, while also continually adapting to customer preferences in models and styling.

Internal-Subsystems Effectiveness The open-systems perspective considers more than an organization's fit with the external environment. It also examines how well the organization operates internally, that is, how well it transforms inputs into outputs. The most common indicator of this internal transformation process is **organizational efficiency** (also called *productivity*), which is the amount of outputs relative to inputs.[56] Companies that produce more goods or services with less labor, materials, and energy are more efficient.

organizational efficiency The amount of outputs relative to inputs in the organization's transformation process.

lean management A cluster of practices to improve organizational efficiency by continuously reducing waste, unevenness, and overburden in the production process.

A popular strategy for improving efficiency in the transformation process is **lean management.**[57] Based on practices developed by Toyota Motor Company, lean management involves continuously reducing waste, unevenness, and overburden in the production process. Waste (called *muda*) takes many forms, such as excess travel of the product or service through the production process, too much time during which the work is sitting idle (waiting for the next step in production), too much inventory, too much employee physical movement, and too much finished product without a buyer. Lean management also involves minimizing situations in which people and equipment are overloaded (too much demand per unit time) and smoothing out the production process (e.g., reducing bottlenecks). The "lean" movement originated in manufacturing, but it is now being adopted by hospitals, government, accounting firms, and other service providers.[58] Global Connections 1.1 describes how British and American hospitals have improved efficiency and effectiveness through various lean practices.

1.1 Global Connections

Hospitals Take the Lean Journey to Efficiency

Building Nissan automobiles seems unrelated to serving surgical patients, but staff at Sunderland Royal Hospital can see the similarities. The hospital in northern England recently borrowed several lean management ideas from the nearby Nissan factory, one of the most efficient car plants in Europe, to improve its day surgery unit. "We took [Sunderland hospital staff] on a tour of our plant, showing them a variety of lean processes in action, and let them decide which ones could be applied back at the hospital," says a training manager at Nissan's factory in Sunderland.

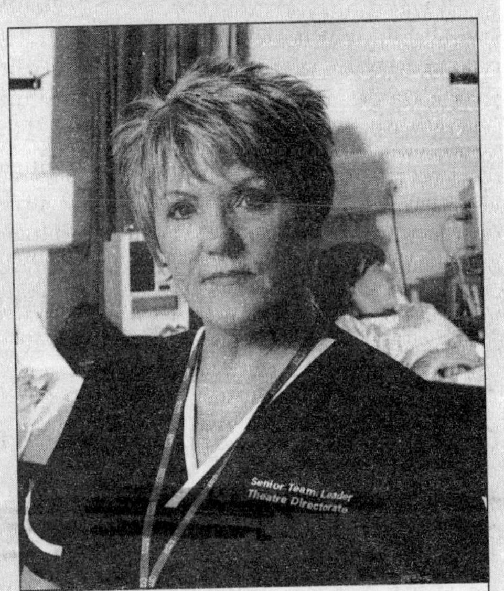

Sunderland Royal Hospital learned from the nearby Nissan factory how to implement lean management in its new day surgery unit.

Sunderland's day surgery staff members were actively involved in applying lean management to their work unit. After attending Nissan's two-day workshop on lean thinking, they mapped out the work processes, questioned assumptions about the value or relevance of some activities, and discovered ways to reduce the lengthy patient wait times (which were up to three hours). There was some initial resistance and skepticism, but the hospital's day surgery soon realized significant improvements in efficiency and service quality.

"By working with Nissan's staff, we have streamlined the patient pathway from 29 to 11 discrete stages," says Anne Fleming (shown in photo), who oversees Sunderland's 32-bed day-case unit and its 54 employees. "We have done this by reducing duplication, halving the time that patients spend in the unit to three hours by giving them individual appointment times, and introducing the just-in-time approach to the patient pathway." Fleming also reports that Sunderland's operating rooms are now much more efficient.

Sunderland Royal Hospital is one of many health care centers around the world that are improving efficiency through lean thinking. After receiving training in Japan on lean practices, several teams of doctors, nurses, and other staff from Virginia Mason Medical Center in Seattle, Washington, redesigned workflows to cut out 34 miles of unnecessary walking each day. Park Nicollet Health Services in Minneapolis, Minnesota, improved efficiency at its ambulatory clinic to such an extent that the unit does not require a patient waiting area. One Park Nicollet team worked with orthopedic surgeons to reduce by 60 percent the variety of instruments and supplies they ordered for hip and knee surgery. The trauma team at Bolton Hospitals NHS Trust in the United Kingdom reduced average wait times for patients with fractured hips by 38 percent (from 2.4 to 1.7 days), which also resulted in a lower mortality rate for these patients. By smoothing out the inflow of work orders and rearranging the work process, Bolton's pathology department cut the time required to process samples, previously 24 to 30 hours, to just 2 to 3 hours and reduced the space used by 50 percent.

"We know that our case for extra funding will fall on deaf ears unless we cut out waste in the system," explains Dr. Gill Morgan, chief executive of the U.K.'s NHS Confederation. "Lean works because it is based on doctors, nurses, and other staff leading the process and telling us what adds value and what doesn't. They are the ones who know."[59]

Keep in mind that efficiency does not necessarily translate into effectiveness. Efficiency is about *doing things right,* whereas effectiveness is about *doing the right things.* A company might be highly efficient at making a product or providing a service, but it will be ineffective if no one wants that product or service, for example. Also, efficiency often requires standardization, whereas companies operating in rapidly changing environments need to remain nimble and responsive. Organizations often need more *adaptive* and *innovative* transformation processes, not just more efficient ones. For example, German engineering conglomerate Siemens AG has an effective transformation process because its subsystems are innovative and responsive, not necessarily the most efficient. "Whether I have additional costs or not doesn't matter as much as the speed to market and the quality of the design," says a Siemens executive. "We're not talking about a pure cost game."[60]

Another important issue in the transformation process is how well the organization's subsystems coordinate with each other. The more each subsystem depends on other subsystems, the higher the risk of problems that undermine the transformation process.[61] Information gets lost, ideas are not shared, materials are hoarded, communication messages are misinterpreted, resources and rewards are distributed unfairly, and so forth. These coordination challenges are amplified as organizations grow, such as when employees are clustered into several departments and when departments are clustered into several organizational divisions. That's why even the best-laid plans are paved with unintended consequences. A slight change in work practices in one subsystem may ripple through the organization and affect other subsystems in adverse ways. For example, an adjustment in accounting procedures might have the unintended effect of motivating sales staff to sell more products with lower profit margin or discouraging administrative staff from accurately completing documents that are vital for executive decisions.

Organizational Learning Perspective

organizational learning
A perspective which holds that organizational effectiveness depends on the organization's capacity to acquire, share, use, and store valuable knowledge.

The open-systems perspective has traditionally focused on physical resources that enter the organization and are processed into physical goods (outputs). This was representative of the industrial economy but not the "new economy," where the most valued input is knowledge. Knowledge is the driver of competitive advantage, however, in the **organizational learning** perspective (also called *knowledge management*). Through this lens, organizational effectiveness depends on the organization's capacity to acquire, share, use, and store valuable knowledge.[62]

Knowledge acquisition occurs when information is brought into the organization from the external environment. This can include hiring people, acquiring companies, and scanning the environment for the latest trends. It also includes the process of creative insight–experimenting and discovering new ideas.[63] *Knowledge sharing* refers to the distribution of knowledge throughout the organization. For example, Pixar Animation Studios deliberately centralized its cafeteria, mailroom, and restroom facilities so that employees would "bump into" and coincidentally share knowledge with people from other areas of the organization rather than just their own team members. Knowledge sharing also occurs through electronic whiteboards, wikis, blogs, and other computer-mediated technology. *Knowledge use* is the application of knowledge to organizational processes in ways that improve the organization's effectiveness. Essentially, new work activities involve knowledge use because they require the application of new knowledge to break out of past routines and practices. *Storage* refers to ways that companies retain valuable knowledge. They retain employees, document best practices, record experiments (including those that didn't work out), and keep samples of past products.

To understand knowledge acquisition, sharing, use, and storage, consider how Google engages in organizational learning. The company that brought us the ubiquitous Internet search engine acquires knowledge by hiring the best talent, buying entire companies (such as Keyhole, Inc., whose knowledge created Google Earth), and encouraging employees to try out new ideas. Employees are expected to devote 20 percent of their time to discovering new knowledge of their choosing. Google encourages knowledge sharing in many ways. It has a team-oriented project culture that encourages staff to share information as part of their job. Its campuslike environment (called the Googleplex) increases the chance that employees from different parts of the organization will mingle and casually share information, whether dining at the company's subsidized gourmet restaurant or playing a game of volleyball in the sports area. Google also relies on sophisticated information technologies–wikis, blogs, and intranet repositories–to support knowledge sharing. Along with promoting knowledge acquisition and sharing, Google encourages knowledge use by giving employees the freedom to apply their newfound knowledge and encouraging them to experiment with that knowledge. "Google is truly a learning organization," says Google's chief financial officer, George Reyes.[64]

absorptive capacity
The ability to recognize the value of new information, assimilate it, and use it for value-added activities.

An interesting dilemma in organizational learning is that the ability to acquire, share, and use new knowledge is limited by the company's existing store of knowledge. To recognize the value of new information, assimilate it, and use it for value-added activities, organizations require sufficient **absorptive capacity.**[65] For example, many companies were slow to develop online marketing practices because no one in the organization had enough knowledge about the Internet to fathom its potential or apply that knowledge to the company's business. In some cases, companies had to acquire entire teams of people with the requisite knowledge to realize the potential of this marketing channel. Entire countries also suffer from a lack of absorptive capacity. Without sufficient knowledge, a society is slow or completely unable to adopt new information that may improve social and economic conditions.[66]

intellectual capital
A company's stock of knowledge, including human capital, structural capital, and relationship capital.

human capital
The stock of knowledge, skills, and abilities among employees that provides economic value to the organization.

Intellectual Capital: The Stock of Organizational Knowledge Knowledge acquisition, sharing, and use represent the flow of knowledge. The organizational learning perspective also considers the company's stock of knowledge, called its **intellectual capital.**[67] The most obvious form of intellectual capital is **human capital**–the knowledge, skills, and abilities that employees carry around in their heads. This is an important part of a company's stock of knowledge, and it is a huge risk in companies where knowledge is the main competitive advantage. When key people leave, they take with them some of the knowledge that makes the company effective.

Even if every employee left the organization, intellectual capital would still remain in the form of *structural capital.* This includes the knowledge captured and retained in an organization's systems and structures, such as the documentation of work procedures and the physical layout of the production line. Structural capital also includes the organization's finished products because knowledge can be extracted by taking them apart to discover how they work and are constructed (i.e., reverse engineering). Finally, intellectual capital includes *relationship capital,* which is the value derived from an organization's relationships with customers, suppliers, and others who provide added mutual value for the organization.

organizational memory
The storage and preservation of intellectual capital.

Organizational Memory and Unlearning Corporate leaders need to recognize that they are the keepers of an **organizational memory.**[68] This unusual metaphor refers to the storage and preservation of intellectual capital. It includes knowledge that employees possess as well as knowledge embedded in the organization's systems and structures. It includes documents, objects, and anything else that provides meaningful information about how the organization should operate.

How do organizations retain intellectual capital? One way is by keeping good employees. Progressive companies achieve this by adapting their employment practices to become more compatible with emerging workforce expectations, including work–life balance, an egalitarian hierarchy, and a workspace that generates more fun. A second organizational memory strategy is to systematically transfer knowledge to other employees. This occurs when newcomers apprentice with skilled employees, thereby acquiring knowledge that is not documented. A third strategy is to transfer knowledge into structural capital. This includes bringing out hidden knowledge, organizing it, and putting it in a form that can be available to others (such as written instructions or a video clip showing the task being performed).

The organizational learning perspective states not only that effective organizations learn but also that they unlearn routines and patterns of behavior that are no longer appropriate.[69] Unlearning removes knowledge that no longer adds value and, in fact, may undermine the organization's effectiveness. Some forms of unlearning involve replacing dysfunctional policies, procedures, and routines. Other forms of unlearning erase attitudes, beliefs, and assumptions. For instance, employees rethink the "best way" to perform a task and how to serve clients.

High-Performance Work Practices Perspective

Although the open-systems perspective states that successful companies are good at transforming inputs into outputs, it does not identify the most important subsystem characteristics of effective organizations. Consequently, an entire field of research has blossomed around the objective of determining specific "bundles" of organizational practices that offer competitive advantage. This research has had various labels over the years, but it is now most widely called **high-performance work practices (HPWP).**[70]

high-performance work practices (HPWP)
A perspective which holds that effective organizations incorporate several workplace practices that leverage the potential of human capital.

The HPWP perspective begins with the idea that *human capital*–the knowledge, skills, and abilities that employees possess–is an important source of competitive advantage for organizations.[71] Human capital helps the organization realize opportunities or minimize threats in the external environment. Furthermore, human capital is neither widely available nor easily duplicated. For instance, a newly formed company cannot instantly develop a workforce identical to a workforce at an established company. Nor can technology replace the capabilities that employees bring to the workplace. In short, human capital is valuable, rare, difficult to imitate, and nonsubstitutable.[72] Therefore, organizations excel by introducing a bundle of systems and structures that leverage the potential of their workforce.

Many high-performance work practices have been studied over the years.[73] Four practices with strong research support are employee involvement, job autonomy, employee competence, and performance- and/or skill-based rewards. As you will learn later in this book, employee involvement and job autonomy tend to strengthen employee motivation as well as improve decision-making, organizational responsiveness, and commitment to change. In high-performance workplaces, employee involvement and job autonomy often take the form of self-directed teams, which are discussed in Chapter 8.

Another key variable in the HPWP model is employee competence. Specifically, organizations are more effective when they recruit and select people with relevant skills, knowledge, values, and other personal characteristics. Furthermore, successful companies invest in their employees by supporting further competency development (see Chapter 2). A fourth characteristic of high-performance organizations is that they link performance and skill development to various forms of financial and nonfinancial rewards valued by employees. We discuss reward systems in Chapter 6 as one of several practices to improve employee performance.

The HPWP perspective is currently popular among OB experts and practitioners, but it also has its share of critics. One concern is that many studies try to find out which practices predict organizational performance without understanding *why* those practices should have this effect.[74] In other words, some of the practices identified as HPWPs lack theoretical foundation; the causal connection between work practices and organizational effectiveness is missing. Without this explanation, it is difficult to be confident that the practice will be valuable in the future and in other situations. A second concern with the HPWP perspective is that it may satisfy shareholder and customer needs at the expense of employee well-being.[75] Some experts point out that HPWPs increase work stress and that management is reluctant to delegate power or share the financial benefits of productivity improvements. If high-performance work practices improve organizational performance at a cost to employee well-being, then this perspective (along with the open-systems and organizational learning perspectives) offers an incomplete picture of organizational effectiveness. The remaining gaps are mostly filled by the stakeholder perspective of organizational effectiveness.

Stakeholder Perspective

The three organizational effectiveness perspectives described so far mainly consider processes and resources, yet they only minimally recognize the importance of relations with **stakeholders.** Stakeholders include individuals, organizations, and other entities that affect, or are affected by, the organization's objectives and actions. They include anyone with a stake in the company–employees, shareholders, suppliers, labor unions, government, communities, consumer and environmental interest groups, and so on. The essence of the stakeholder perspective is that companies must take into account how their actions affect others, and this requires that they understand, manage, and satisfy the interests of their stakeholders.[76] The stakeholder perspective personalizes the open-systems perspective; it identifies specific people and social entities in the external and internal environment. It also recognizes that stakeholder relations are dynamic; they can be negotiated and managed, not just taken as a fixed condition.[77]

stakeholders
Individuals, organizations, and other entities that affect, or are affected by, the organization's objectives and actions.

Consider the troubles that Wal-Mart has faced in recent years.[78] For decades, the world's largest retailer concentrated on customers by providing the lowest possible prices and on shareholders by generating healthy financial returns. Yet emphasizing these two stakeholders exposed the company to increasing hostility from other groups in society. Some interest groups accused Wal-Mart of destroying America's manufacturing base and tacitly allowing unethical business practices (such as child labor) in countries where it purchased goods. Other groups pointed out that Wal-Mart had a poor record of environmental and social responsibility. Still other groups lobbied to keep Wal-Mart out of their communities because the giant retailer typically builds in outlying suburbs where land is cheap, thereby fading the vibrancy of the community's downtown area. These stakeholder pressure points existed for some time, but Wal-Mart mostly ignored them until they became serious threats. In fact, Wal-Mart recently created the position "senior director of stakeholder engagement" to ensure that it pays more attention to most stakeholders and to proactively manage stakeholder relationships.

Understanding, managing, and satisfying the interests of stakeholders is more challenging than it sounds because stakeholders have conflicting interests and organizations don't have the resources to satisfy every stakeholder to the fullest. Therefore, organizational leaders need to decide how much priority to give to each group. One commonly cited factor is to favor stakeholders with the most power.[79] This makes sense when one considers that the most powerful stakeholders hold the greatest threat and opportunity to the company's survival. Yet stakeholder power should not be the only criterion for determining organizational strategy and resource allocation. Ignoring less powerful stakeholders might motivate them to become more powerful by forming coalitions or seeking government support. It might also irritate more powerful stakeholders if ignoring weaker interests violates the norms and standards of society.

Values, Ethics, and Corporate Social Responsibility This brings us to one of the key strengths of the stakeholder perspective, namely, that it incorporates values, ethics, and corporate social responsibility into the organizational effectiveness equation.[80] The stakeholder perspective states that to manage the interests of diverse stakeholders, leaders ultimately need to rely on their personal and organizational values for guidance. **Values** are relatively stable, evaluative beliefs that guide our preferences for outcomes or courses of action in a variety of situations.[81] Values help us to know what is right or wrong, or good or bad, in the world. Chapter 2 explains how values are an important part of our self-concept and, as such, motivate our actions. Although values exist within individuals, groups of people often hold similar values, so we tend to ascribe these *shared values* to the team, department, organization, profession, or entire society. For example, Chapter 14 discusses the importance and dynamics of organizational culture, which includes shared values across the company or within subsystems.

values
Relatively stable, evaluative beliefs that guide a person's preferences for outcomes or courses of action in a variety of situations.

Values have become a popular topic in corporate boardrooms because leaders are discovering that the values-driven organizational approach to guiding employee behavior is potentially more effective, as well as more popular, than the old command-and-control approach (i.e., top-down decisions with close supervision of employees). Bank of Montreal (BMO) is a case in point. A few years ago, in a series of meetings, BMO's top executives reflected on the financial institution's history and had deep conversations to identify the values on which the Canadian financial institution was built. Out of this dialogue emerged four value statements that were distributed to employees and built into a revised reward system. Why did BMO go to such trouble to identify and communicate its shared values? "[BMO's values] provide a stable base for guiding employee decisions and actions in an otherwise rapidly changing workplace," explains a BMO executive who attended the meetings. "Simply put, *values matter* and employees care that the organizations they work for and represent are ethical and walk the talk of their values."[82]

Values-Based Leadership at Dubai's Department of Economic Development The senior management team at the Department of Economic Development (DED) in the Emirate of Dubai recently devoted several months to identifying the agency's core values: accountability, teamwork, and continuous improvement. Each of these three values is anchored with specific behavior descriptions to ensure that employees and other stakeholders understand their meaning. DED also organized a series of workshops (shown in photo) in which employees participated in a "Values Mystery" exercise to help them recognize values-consistent behaviors. To develop a values-based organization, DED will also use these three values to evaluate employee performance, assess employee competencies, and identify management potential.[83]

By incorporating values into organizational effectiveness, the stakeholder perspective also provides the strongest case for ethics and corporate social responsibility. In fact, the stakeholder perspective emerged out of earlier writing on ethics and corporate

ethics
The study of moral principles or values that determine whether actions are right or wrong and outcomes are good or bad.

corporate social responsibility (CSR)
Organizational activities intended to benefit society and the environment beyond the firm's immediate financial interests or legal obligations.

social responsibility. **Ethics** refers to the study of moral principles or values that determine whether actions are right or wrong and outcomes are good or bad. We rely on our ethical values to determine "the right thing to do." Ethical behavior is driven by the moral principles we use to make decisions. These moral principles represent fundamental values. Chapter 2 provides more detail about ethical principles and related influences on moral reasoning.

Corporate social responsibility (CSR) consists of organizational activities intended to benefit society and the environment beyond the firm's immediate financial interests or legal obligations.[84] It is the view that companies have a contract with society, in which they must serve stakeholders beyond shareholders and customers. In some situations, the interests of the firm's shareholders should be secondary to those of other stakeholders.[85] As part of CSR, many companies have adopted the triple bottom line philosophy: They try to support or "earn positive returns" in the economic, social, and environmental spheres of sustainability. Firms that adopt the triple bottom line aim to survive and be profitable in the marketplace (economic), but they also intend to maintain or improve conditions for society (social) as well as the physical environment.[86]

Not everyone agrees with the idea that organizations are more effective when they cater to a wide variety of stakeholders. More than 30 years ago, economist Milton Friedman pronounced that "there is one and only one social responsibility of business–to use its resources and engage in activities designed to increase its profits." Although few writers take this extreme view today, some point out that companies can benefit other stakeholders only if those with financial interests in the company receive first priority. Yet four out of five Americans say that a company's commitment to a social issue is an important factor in deciding whether to work for the company and whether to buy its products or services. In another survey, more than two-thirds of North American students said they would not apply for a job if the company is considered irresponsible. Most American and European MBA students also claim they would accept lower financial rewards to work for an organization with a better ethical/CSR reputation. However, another recent survey indicated that while most American MBA students believe socially responsible companies have a better reputation, less than half of these respondents believe CSR improves revenue, employee loyalty, customer satisfaction, community well-being, or the company's long-term viability.[87]

Focus on Stakeholders Makes Lockheed Martin "Ideal" When choosing a future employer, college graduates look beyond salary and career opportunities. These factors are important, but recent surveys indicate that the company's ethical standards, values, and corporate social responsibility (CSR) are also top considerations. Based on its reputation for ethics, diversity, and CSR, Lockheed Martin Corporation is ranked by American undergraduate engineering students as one of the top companies for an ideal career and is among the top 60 companies identified by all undergraduate students. "Students have always been impressed with Lockheed Martin's commitment to diversity and social responsibility," says the CEO of Universum Communications, the company that surveys more than 37,000 students annually. "The company is well known for its charitable contributions and strong values." For example, this photo shows a team of Lockheed Martin employees assisting cleanup of New Orleans following Hurricane Katrina.[88]

Capgemini recently discovered the importance of corporate social responsibility when the Netherlands-based information technology (IT) consulting firm tried to fill 800 IT and management consulting positions in that country. Rather than offering a T-shirt for completing the 30-minute online survey on recruitment issues, Capgemini advised respondents (IT and management consultants) that for each completed survey it would provide funding for a street kid in Kolkata, India, to have one week of schooling and accommodation. The survey included an option for respondents to find out more about employment with the consulting firm. Far beyond its expectations, Capgemini received more than 10,000 completed surveys and 2,000 job inquiries from qualified respondents. The company filled its 800 jobs and developed a waiting list of future prospects. Furthermore, media attention about this initiative raised Capgemini's brand reputation for corporate social responsibility. The consulting firm supported 10,400 weeks of housing and education for children in Kolkata.[89]

Corporate Social Responsibility in India

The concept of CSR is not new to Indian industry as a number of business houses in the public and private sectors have been doing their bit for the community. The pioneering efforts in India were made in the nineteenth century by the Tata Group, which was founded in 1868. It built the first steel mill in India in 1911. Later, Mahatma Gandhi, the Father of the Nation, influenced various companies to play an active role in nation building and promoting socio-economic development. As a result, social responsibility was discharged through corporate philanthropy–by offering donations in cash or kind and provision of services like hospitals, schools, etc. The Statist approach emerged after India's independence in 1947, when a number of labor laws and management principles were introduced. The state sponsored corporate philanthropy still operates in public sector organizations in India. However, there is a trend to move towards stakeholders' approach by some progressive private organizations.

The Indian constitution provides for social justice and equity for all sections of the society in every work organization. There is reservation in government jobs for socially disadvantaged groups-labeled as scheduled castes and scheduled tribes and physically challenged persons. There exist various labor legislations, e.g. payment of wages, minimum wages, etc. Of late, there have been strict legislations against environmental pollution.

Ministry of Corporate Affairs, Government of India has developed Corporate Social Responsibility Voluntary Guidelines (2009). These guidelines facilitate business houses to contribute in the interest of stakeholders and society and towards sustainable business development. The essence of these guidelines comprises the fundamental principles, core elements and implementation guidance. The fundamental principles address the importance of CSR for business entities and its need to be an integral part of all its strategic initiatives and policies. Business entities should have a CSR policy and a framework aligned with its business goals. The core elements covered are as follows:[90]

- To care for all the stakeholders
- Functioning should be ethical, transparent and accountable
- To respect workers' rights and welfare
- To respect human rights
- To respect the environment
- Social and inclusive development activities

Triple Bottom Line (TBL) has become an important and integral part of many business entities in India. It gauges business performance on three parameters: Economic, Environmental and Social factors. Another important development in India Incorporation includes practice of sustainability reporting through GRI (Global Reporting Institute) guidelines by few business entities.[91]

Initiatives to Promote CSR

Tata Energy Research Institute, UNDP, UN Volunteers, and New Academy of Business, UK, organized a national workshop on Corporate Citizenship in India in collaboration with the British Council, India, at New Delhi, during 2002.[92] There were also India Partnership Forum and Consultative Meeting with CEOs. UNDP and CII jointly organized a half-day roundtable consultation on introducing 'Value Based Management Education in Business Schools' with selected Business/Management Institutes in 2002, in New Delhi. Based on the discussions, the following action points were identified and implemented.

The meeting was organized to assess industry interest for demand of CSR education in Management/Business Schools. More specifically, it proposed to focus on:

- Developing knowledge base and case studies that greatly impact at operational and strategic levels
- Sharing knowledge, experience, and practices in value-based education
- Initiating a larger consultative process on role of business in society
- Gauging business demand on CSR education

The CEO's Meeting on CSR Education in 2002 held at New Delhi made the following recommendations:

- CSR education/course should be a part of mainstream/general theme in management/business schools, and not as an elective. Such mainstream course would give students value underpinning in business/sensitize on ethical approach to business
- Management institutes are best placed to impart value underpinnings, ethical approaches to business to students
- Industry would like to see future managers with the strong basic value underpinnings of value-based ethical approach to business
- Set up educational labs with the help of corporate to develop need based curriculum for tomorrow
- Business schools would like the top management in corporate sector to help in putting together such types of case studies–open discussions on the viewpoint of contending stakeholders (be it environmental, trade unions, labor movement, etc.)–bring this kind of dialogue and debate into classrooms, for ethical reasoning with students, rather than preaching such issues.
- Viewpoint of the company, viewpoint of societal stakeholders–to let the students look at the reasoning behind each of these stakeholders and actually look at what the main protagonist (CEO here) has actually recommended and strategised–"this would be a form of case study"
- Top corporate management could help management institutes put together such case studies (they should be allowed to express their views), build a dialogue/ethical reasoning in classrooms (case studies that contain various groups' views on 'a' product and also promote the business stakeholders' dialogue with a set of contending societal stakeholders in the classroom. The CEO can be invited to interact on 'ethical reasoning' or action points.
- Generate/develop case studies on CSR–corporate governance industry will cooperate and make available the data. CII members could help identify specific case studies on CSR/corporate governance.
- Specific examples from industry: Captains of industry to interact with management students and deliver talks to the students
- Broaden and support the dialogue on role of business in society – changing role of business and CSR
- Management institutes to develop course material – design one extension course – develop a few cases – run these courses – have workshop with CEOs

Business and Social Responsibility: A Collaborative Initiative among British Council, Management Development Institute, Gurgaon, and New Academy of Business, UK, in 2002-03 The collaborative initiative aimed at influencing business leaders and academics on issues of CSR and impact of business in building a society based on equality and justice. Thus, in order to promote links between management educators and corporates through curriculum development and practitioner experience, British Council, India, in collaboration with Management Development Institute (MDI), Gurgaon, India, and New Academy of Business, UK, launched an initiative in a phased manner.

The launch of the initiative was done with a videoconference between UK and India. Mr. Chris Marsden, Chair, Amnesty International, UK Business Group, experts from New Academy of Business, UK, and professionals from academia and industry representing four regions of India participated in the VC at the four Indian regional centers of the British Council.

This was followed by an online course on Business and Social Responsibility between UK and India. After the completion of the course the participants underwent an intensive workshop at Management Development Institute, Gurgaon, India, during December 2002, coordinated by Prof. Radha R. Sharma of MDI. As a follow-up of the workshop, projects were undertaken by the participants for applying their learnings and sharing the results with their peers and UK faculty through a videoconference in 2003 between UK and India.

TERI-BCSD India (TERI-Business Council for Sustainable Development) is an independent platform which encourages Indian corporate diaspora to develop sustainable business, helps in translating a company's vision into management action, and making it sustainable for competitive advantage. TERI-BCSD addressed the aspects of TBL. It is a partner of the World Business Council for Sustainable Development, Geneva (TERI-BSCD)[92].

CSR and Business Ethics in Management Education: International Status

A survey was conducted by QS (Quacquarelli Symonds) among Global Top 200 Business Schools for 2010-2011, in the category of specializations, with focus on Corporate Social Responsibility (CSR) and Business Ethics [QS Top MBA, 2010]. The corporate debacles which have troubled the economies of the world during the past few years, have changed the notion of CSR and business ethics dramatically, which is also reflected in the way business schools are adapting and integrating these issues in their respective MBA programs. It has also been noted that there is a rise in the number of courses offered in CSR and business ethics who integrate these aspects in every class. The top 10 B-Schools selected were Stanford University, Harvard Business School, Tuck School of Business, INSEAD, Wharton Business School, Columbian Business School, University of Michigan: Ross School of Business, Northwestern University: Kellogg School of Management, IESE Business School, and Yale School of Management.

Stanford The B-School at Stanford offers *Ethics in Management* and *Strategic Leadership* in the first year which cover issues of ethics and CSR in business. Another course titled *Real-Life Ethics* has been developed in collaboration with practitioners to examine complex and nuanced ethical situations.

Harvard Business School (HBS) Ethics is an integral part of HBS curriculum since its inception. There are stand-alone or integrated courses in Human Resource Management and Corporate Finance, etc. Leadership and Corporate Accountability is an interdisciplinary course that prepares students for leadership challenges in the changing global society. Under Community Values Programme, outreach events, special initiatives, informal conversations and the like are organized for members to keep value-based decision-making on top of their mind. There is a Leadership and Ethics Forum of students which "challenges the HBS community to confront, consider and debate leadership and ethical issues."[93]

Tuck School of Business Tuck has made mandatory credits for students in topics of CSR and business ethics. The elective courses offered are Ethics in Action, Business Strategies for Sustainability, Entrepreneurship in the Social Sector, and Corporate Responsibility. There is an Allwin Initiative for Corporate Citizenship which facilitates expansion of career horizons for students, collaborates with non-profit organizations across the world, and also brings issues on the nexus between business and society to the classroom.

INSEAD Amongst the European schools, INSEAD is ahead in giving importance to CSR and ethics. The five areas of their interest include CSR, Business and Marketing Ethics from normative perspective, Ethical Consumerism, Ethics of Defaults and the Opening of Firm Boundaries. There is INSEAD Social Innovation Centre which focuses on business models and market-based mechanisms which deliver sustainable economic, environmental and social prosperity.

Wharton Wharton provides a doctoral program titled 'Ethics and Legal Studies' which is the only one and unique in the world. This program focuses on ethical and legal norms relevant to both business and individuals in decision making. In a recent revision of its MBA program, there is explicit stress on integrated focus on ethical and legal responsibility in business.

Columbia Business School The Columbia Business School has a curriculum titled 'Individual, Business and Society (IBS)'. Through this curriculum, issues like leadership, personal integrity, CSR and Corporate Governance are addressed. The modules include core courses, special sessions and also new-student orientation sessions.[94]

Ross School of Business Ross offers elective courses focused on Environmentally Sustainable Business, Ethics of Corporate Management, and Business Strategies for the Base of the Pyramid in its full-time MBA program.[95]

Kellogg School of Management It offers a course on Values and Crisis Decision-Making in the second year of the full-time MBA program. This is a compulsory course and has half-credit.[96]

IESE Business School It offers a compulsory course on 'Leading Organizations: Systems, Values and Ethics' in the first year of the full-time MBA program. In the second year, there is a course on Business Ethics.[97]

Yale School of Management Yale offers an elective course 'Business Ethics Meets Behavioral Economics' in the second year of the MBA program. In another MBA program for executives: Leadership in Healthcare, a course titled 'Ethics in Healthcare Management' is offered in the second year.[98]

CSR in Management Education in India

Management schools produce managers for tomorrow, therefore, inclusion of CSR in the management education curriculum will not only provide required knowledge but also develop the right kind of attitude among future managers to manage the organizations they would join.

A group of CEOs in India had recommended introduction of value based education in management schools in the CEOs' meeting held in August 2002. A sample survey of perception of management students by Sharma[99] had revealed that all the students were in favor of introduction of CSR in management/business school curriculum. 32% of them wanted it to be introduced as a core course whereas another 32% as an elective. The remaining 36% students were in favor of CSR being made an integral component of a paper on Corporate Strategy/Corporate Ethics. Also, 77% of them wanted that CSR be given weightage in campus placement or recruitment by companies. As the sample consisted of students with work experience, 91% mentioned that CSR policies of a company could give it competitive edge. The remaining 9% believed that CSR policies give a boost to a company's image.

Recent Developments at Indian Business Schools Management Development Institute (MDI India) has a Centre for Corporate Governance. It not only offers courses on corporate social responsibility at MBA and PhD levels, but also undertakes research and case development in this field. It had undertaken a project under the aegis of UNDP-CII-AICTE-MDI for preparing cases from various industries focusing on the process and decision-making content implicit in the introduction, implementation, and evaluation of various facets of CSR during 2004. The outcome has been a book containing 18 illustrative cases and 6 conceptual papers edited by Professors CV Baxi and Ajit Prasad. CSR conferences/seminars/workshops were organized in various business schools across the country. MBA students at MDI organize blood donation camps, arrange books, and impart education to poor children during off time. They also organize marketing events for handicrafts produced by non-government organizations (NGOs) to raise funds for their social work.

Indian Insitute of Mannagement (IIM), Bangalore, has also established a Centre for Corporate Governance and Citizenship which is engaged in teaching, training, research, and case development in this field. It organized a case competition during 2007, sponsored by Tata Steel Ltd. It undertook a Indo-UK project on 'Curriculum Design, Teaching and Research on CSR.'. During January 3-4, 2008, it organized a curriculum-roll-out workshop', participation largely by faculty from business schools, to encourage them to adopt and adapt the curriculum for their use. It has also launched a website dedicated to teaching of CSR which provides basic teaching aids and links to online resources on the subject. The Management Center for Human Values at IIM, Calcutta provides training to its students in business ethics and CSR. CSR is receiving considerable attention from students of other IIMs as well. In 2008, 22 students from four IIMs at Ahmedabad, Bangalore, Kolkata, and Lucknow business schools of Indian Institute of Technology, Bombay have taken up their summer internship with The National Kidney Foundation (NKF) in Singapore[100]. Besides, in S P Jain Business School at Mumbai all the students are required to undertake a 6-week project with a non-government organization or a CSR division of a corporate organization. All the above efforts are geared to making a socially responsible corporate manager.

Many management schools in India offer a general course on Business Ethics. A number of schools, including the Indian Institute of Management, Bangalore, have organized conferences and workshops on CSR. But there is need for concerted effort to promote teaching and research on CSR in a big way as there are about 1500 management/business schools in India.

CSR in Industry

CEOs of progressive corporates support CSR as is revealed by the Consultative Committee Meeting of CEOs and the CEOs Meeting on CSR Education. Large corporate houses have CSR policies and/or programs existing in various forms. Organizations like Tatas have a long tradition of discharging social responsibility through institutionalized mechanisms. The survey of management students by Sharma[101] revealed that TISCO and TELCO were among the most respected corporates in India. Other respected Indian corporates/companies, besides Tata organizations, are Hero Honda, Infosys, Birla Group, and Lijjat Papad (a women cooperative in India) which are transparent and ethical

Public sector organizations in India have a well-defined policy for pursuing CSR. 38% of the companies surveyed (in the CSR Survey 2002–India) earmarked resources for CSR a priori. An analysis of Indian companies that follow CSR would reveal the following reasons:

(i) to build a good corporate image
(ii) to improve relations with local community
(iii) to pursue their founder's values and vision
(iv) to pursue long-term business interests
(v) to promote shareholder value
(vi) to improve relations with internal customers
(vii) to build corporate brand globally
(viii) to adhere to legal compliance/to avail of tax/duty exemption
(ix) to penetrate global market
(x) to fulfil requirement of their business partners
(xi) to have competitive edge
(xii) to follow the industrial trend

A survey called 'Altered Images' was conducted by Tata Energy Research Institute (TERI) (2001), India, which collected feedback from various stakeholders, viz., executives and workers from the firms and the public. The survey revealed many concerns internal to the company and related to the environment; to name a few—discrimination of employees, product quality, environment pollution, social issues, and role of NGOs. There is now greater awareness among people about ethics, values, integrity, and responsibility, and there is data to support the link between good ethics and good business. We have examples of this in various IT firms viz., TCS, Infosys, and Wipro, etc. which allocate a considerable amount of their profits for the social cause. Also, other companies, like Tata Consultancy Services (TCS), NIIT, Infoway, and Cognizant Technology Solutions have set aside sizeable sums for CSR. However, a large number of small and medium private enterprises are unable to link business with CSR. In such organizations, CSR is discharged either though legislative compliance or through occasional corporate philanthropy.

India Corporate Week (ICW) was started by the Ministry of Corporate Affairs in 2009, in order to join hands with industry associations at both national and state level to promote importance of being "Corporate" and its responsibility in fulfilling societal obligation and inclusive growth. This initiative was started off after some scandals had hit a few Indian Corporates. This event is held every year in the second week of December. In 2009, the theme was 'Corporate Sector and Inclusive Growth'; in 2010 focus was on 'Sustainable Business'.[102]

CSR Awards

Various awards have been introduced over the years in India, to recognize the efforts of business entities in their contribution towards CSR. These include Golden Peacock Award for CSR, Golden Peacock Environment Management Award, Businessworld-FICCI-SEDF, CII-ITC Sustainability Award, TERI Corporate Environment Award, TERI CSR award, and The Asian CSR award.

An award for Corporate Social Responsibility in India was instituted in 1999 by Business World-Federation of Indian Chamber of Commerce & Industry (FICCI)-SEDF to recognize the efforts of Indian corporates in social responsibility.[103] A number of companies in India take time off from their core business activities and undertake projects with a social cause. The sponsor of the award developed a three-stage rigorous selection process. After inviting the entries Stage I involved assessment of these companies on pre-defined parameters, including Institutionalization of CSR, Community as a stakeholder, Community Development, and various CSR practices – including HR practices, Environmental Practices, etc. Stage II involved an onsite assessment by a recognized Non-Government Organization and Business and Community Foundation (BCF) who visited the shortlisted companies and their project sites for qualitative assessment and evaluation of their work. Stage III was the stage for final selection by a four-member jury drawn from corporate and social spheres. The shortlisted companies made a presentation before the honourable jury, and the top three companies, based on their scores in the three stage process, were awarded the top three prizes.

(a) Businessworld-FICCI-SEDF CSR Award In 2009–10, the winner in Large Enterprise Corporate Citizen was Tata Steel Ltd., and Jury Special Commendation was given to Bharti Airtel Ltd., in Small and Medium Enterprises Corporate Citizen winner was Smaat Aqua Technologies Pvt Ltd., and Jury Commendation was given away to Elin Appliances Private Ltd. Exemplary Innovation Promoting CSR Corporate Citizen award was given to Multi Commodity Exchange of India Ltd[104].

(b) Golden Peacock Award This award is administered by the Golden Peacock Global Awards Secretariat, a London-based organization. It was instituted in India in 1991 and has become popular across industries. It has a framework based on IOD Business Excellence Model. Public Sector Units, Private Sector Organizations, Government/Municipality Organizations, Undertakings and Public Utility Services, and NGOs are invited. Applications are invited from both Indian and MNCs based in the country. The assessment is done by both the business unit themselves and by external evaluators. The information based on which an organization is assessed includes Business Overview and General Information (5% weightage), Marketplace (10% weightage), Corporate Governance Policies (15% weightage), Social Community Initiatives (20% weightage), CSR Management Practices (20% weightage), and Social Project (30%). The jury shortlists the finalists which go for a closer review by another committee. The finalist organizations are invited to make presentations before the winners are announced. After evaluation process is over, a feedback report is written by evaluators and forwarded to organizations for improvements[105].

(c) CII-ITC Sustainability Award The Confederation of Indian Industries (CII)-Indian Tobacco Company (ITC) Sustainability award has been instituted in 2006. The overall process includes invitation of application, assessment by individual assessors, consensus on assessment results, providing the marks, thereafter short listing, visiting and assessing the business unit sites, reviewing scores and assessment, and the findings are presented to the jury which finalizes the winners, and those which are not shortlisted are provided with a feedback report. The Sustainability Excellence Model is based on European Foundation for Quality Management. Equal weightage is given to both enablers and the results. Enablers include leadership, internal and external stakeholders, key resources, and process. Results include learning and innovation, results for internal and external stakeholders, and key performance results (KRA). Along with these aspects, economic, social and environmental dimensions are also given equal weightage. In 2010, Sustainability Prize was given to Babrala Plant of Tata Chemicals Ltd., in the independent unit category[106].

(d) The Energy and Resource Institute (TERI) CSR Award It was instituted in 2001-02. This award distinguishes best practices and innovations of Indian corporate houses which fulfill their duty towards the stakeholders in the society. The objectives of this award include: (a) CSR concerns integrated with corporate functioning, (b) receptiveness to the needs of different stakeholders, and (c) fostering innovative partnership models to fulfill social responsibilities. They have three categories classified on the basis of turnover. In 2008-09, Tata Refractories Limited (first prize in 2nd category), GMR Infrastructure Limited (first prize in 3rd category) and Vikram Cement & Aditya Cement, a unit of Grasim Industries Ltd. (second prize in 3rd category)[107].

(e) Asian CSR Award It is presented by the Asian Institute of Management and Ramon V. del Rosario, Sr. Centre for Corporate Responsibility. The awards are given in the following categories: Environmental Excellence, Support and Improvement of Education, Poverty Alleviation, Best Workplace Practices, and Concern for Health[108].

CSR survey of 2002–India, on a sample of 102 Indian companies, has revealed that the most important driver within Indian Industry is the desire to become a good corporate citizen. As this is being linked to brand reputation and improved ties with communities, the companies would benefit from engaging in/providing funds for promotion of CSR.

In the context of WTO, CSR and business links are being established across the globe. It is now becoming imperative for a company to follow the CSR. There is need for a multi-pronged strategy for development and promotion of CSR education in India in which industry could play an active role. Mainstreaming CSR in teaching and research in management schools will go a long way in integrating education, business, and society.

TYPES OF INDIVIDUAL BEHAVIOR

The four perspectives described over the past few pages–open systems, organizational learning, high-performance work practices, and stakeholder–provide a multidimensional view of what makes companies effective. Within these models, however, are individual behaviors that enable companies to interact with their environments; acquire, share, and use knowledge to the best advantage; process inputs to outputs efficiently and responsively; and meet the needs of various stakeholders. While organizational effectiveness is the ultimate dependent variable, these employee behaviors are the individual-level dependent variables found in most OB research. Exhibit 1.3 highlights the five types of behavior

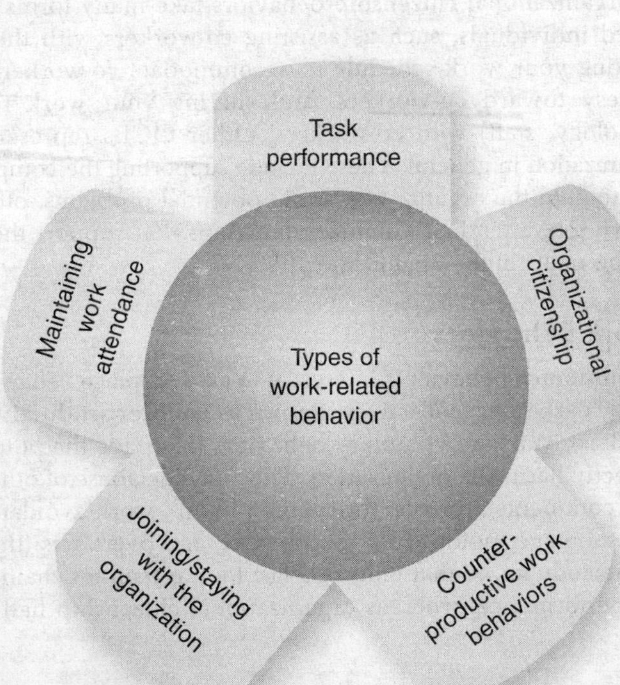

Exhibit 1.3 *Types of Work-Related Behavior*

discussed most often in the organizational behavior literature: task performance, organizational citizenship, counterproductive work behaviors, joining and staying with the organization, and work attendance.

Task Performance

Task performance refers to goal-directed behaviors under the individual's control that support organizational objectives. Task performance behaviors transform raw materials into goods and services or support and maintain technical activities.[109] For example, foreign exchange traders at Wachovia make decisions and take actions to exchange currencies. Employees in most jobs have more than one performance dimension. Foreign exchange traders must be able to identify profitable trades, work cooperatively with clients and co-workers in a stressful environment, assist in training new staff, and work on special telecommunications equipment without error. Some of these performance dimensions are more important than others, but only by considering all of them can we fully evaluate an employee's contribution to the organization.

Organizational Citizenship

Companies could not effectively compete, transform resources, or serve the needs of their stakeholders if employees performed only their formal job duties. Employees also need to engage in **organizational citizenship behaviors (OCBs)**–various forms of cooperation and helpfulness to others that support the organization's social and psychological context.[110] In other words, companies require contextual performance (i.e., OCBs) along with task performance.

organizational citizenship behaviors (OCBs) Various forms of cooperation and helpfulness to others that support the organization's social and psychological context.

Organizational citizenship behaviors take many forms. Some are directed toward individuals, such as assisting co-workers with their work problems, adjusting your work schedule to accommodate co-workers, showing genuine courtesy toward co-workers, and sharing your work resources (supplies, technology, staff) with co-workers. Other OCBs represent cooperation and helpfulness toward the organization in general. These include supporting the company's public image, taking discretionary action to help the organization avoid potential problems, offering ideas beyond those required for your own job, attending voluntary functions that support the organization, and keeping up with new developments in the organization.[111]

Counterproductive Work Behaviors

counterproductive work behaviors (CWBs) Voluntary behaviors that have the potential to directly or indirectly harm the organization.

Organizational behavior is interested in all workplace behaviors, including those on the "dark side," collectively known as **counterproductive work behaviors (CWBs).** CWBs are voluntary behaviors that have the potential to directly or indirectly harm the organization. They include abuse of others (e.g., insults and nasty comments), threats (threatening harm), work avoidance (e.g., tardiness), work sabotage (doing work incorrectly), and overt acts (theft). CWBs are not minor concerns. One recent study found that units of a fast-food restaurant chain with higher CWBs had a significantly worse performance, whereas organizational citizenship had a relatively minor benefit.[112]

Joining and Staying with the Organization

Task performance, organizational citizenship, and the lack of counterproductive work behaviors are obviously important, but if qualified people don't join and stay with the organization, none of these performance-related behaviors will occur. Attracting and retaining talented people is particularly important as worries about skill shortages heat up. For instance, a shortage of qualified truck drivers is the main factor restricting growth at Contract Freighters in Joplin, Missouri. "We have plenty of freight; we have plenty of trucks," says company president Herb Schmidt, but the "severe shortage" of qualified drivers is making it impossible to satisfy the growing customer base. Hotels in many parts of the United States are also struggling to find enough staff to keep up with demand. "We're woefully understaffed," says the owner of a St. Petersburg, Florida, resort that employs 265 people and still has 40 unfilled vacancies. "It's horrible.[113]"

Companies survive and thrive not just by hiring people with talent or potential; they also need to ensure that these employees stay with the company. Organizations with high turnover suffer because of the high cost of replacing people who leave. More important, as mentioned earlier in this chapter, much of an organization's intellectual capital is the knowledge carried around in employees' heads. When people leave, some of this vital knowledge is lost, often resulting in inefficiencies, poorer customer service, and so forth. This threat is not trivial: Between one-third and one-half of employees say they would change companies if offered a comparable job.[114]

Maintaining Work Attendance

Along with attracting and retaining employees, organizations need everyone to show up for work at scheduled times. Situational factors–such as severe weather or car breakdown–explain some work absences. Motivation is another factor. Employees who experience job dissatisfaction or work-related stress are more likely to be absent or late for work because taking time off is a way to temporarily

Google Attracts and Keeps Talent through "Cool" Campuses Google is ranked by college students in many countries as one of the top 10 places to work. One reason why the Internet technology company is able to attract so many applicants is that its workplaces look like every student's dream of a college campus and dorm. Google's headquarters (called Googleplex) in Mountain View, California, is outfitted with lava lamps, exercise balls, casual sofas, foosball, pool tables, workout rooms, video games, slides, and a restaurant with free gourmet meals. Google's new EMEA engineering hub in Zurich, Switzerland, also boasts a fun, campuslike environment. These photos show a few areas of Google's offices in Zurich, including private temporary workspaces in beehives and ski gondolas. Google's offices are so comfortable that executives occasionally remind staff of building code regulations against making Google's offices their permanent home.[115]

withdraw from stressful or dissatisfying conditions. Absenteeism is also higher in organizations with generous sick leave because this benefit limits the negative financial impact of taking time away from work. Studies have found that absenteeism is also higher in teams with strong absence norms, meaning that team members tolerate and even expect co-workers to take time off.[116]

Organization Behavior Trends—Impacting Emerging Economies

There has never been a better time to learn about organization behavior. The pace of change is accelerating, and most of the transformation is occuring in the workplace. Let's take a brief tour through the various trends.

Outsourcing

In the present globally competitive environment, outsourcing of business processes through which in-house operations/processes are contracted to an outside party is adopted. It is one of the management tools adopted by companies which are either faced with personnel shortage or have increased customer demands or have launched new products or services. It is also a method to reduce operational costs and gain access to superior technologies or more efficient personnel at reduced cost. By outsourcing noncore activities, the companies are able to concentrate on their core competencies, thereby increasing productivity and enhancing job satisfaction of the employees. Industry trends show that companies that have been asking the question 'why outsource' have become vocal advocates of the offshore model. There are several other reasons for a company to outsource, to name a few, cost restructuring, improving quality, availability of expert knowledge and operational expertise, people problems, introducing change, access to new market, capacity management, and taking advantage of the different time zones to make the services seamlessly available 24 x 7. Opposite of outsourcing is 'insourcing', where the provider of services 'embeds' specialists at the client's location to perform specific tasks.

Offshoring

Despite outsourcing generating a lot of controversies in recent times, it is predicted that outsourcing as a business practice is on a growth mode. More and more companies are drawing up plans to outsource work to offshore locations. Offshoring is generally in two forms-production offshoring and services offshoring. China has emerged as a prominent destination for production offshoring after its accession to the WTO in 2001. With technical advancements in telecommunications, India has become a leading country in this domain, and now many parts of the world are emerging as offshore destinations.

The terms *outsourcing and offshoring* are often used interchangeably but there is a technical difference. Outsourcing involves using a third party for certain processes which may or may not involve some degree of offshoring. Offshoring, however, is shifting of a part of an organizational function to another country, regardless of whether the work is outsourced or stays within the same corporation. This is done due to lower tax, low labour cost, or subsidised services. The various operating models of outsourcing across the globe have resulted in new terms such as *nearshoring, noshoring,* and *rightshoring* that reflect the changing mix of locations. In nearshore outsourcing, the outsourcing partner is located geographically closer than the outsourcing partner in offshore outsourcing and has similar time zone, similar culture, and language. This leads to better coordination, communication, and greater efficiency. This economises frequent visits to the outsourcing partner. This is seen in the opening of offices and operations centers by Indian companies in the US and UK.[117]

Multisourcing

One of the main drivers behind the multisourcing approach is the perception that it better leverages competitive pressures. It refers to large (predominantly IT) outsourcing agreements.[118] In this arrangement, there is disciplined provisioning and blending of business and IT services[119] provided by an optimum mix of internal and external providers to achieve business goals. In other words, multisourcing enables different parts of the client business to be sourced from different suppliers. This requires a governance model that communicates strategy, clearly defines responsibility, and has end-to-end integration.Multisourcing facilitates 'mix-and-match' approach to procurement, improved service quality by offering 'best of the class' solutions to customers through allocation of different tasks to suppliers, and avoids being 'locked in' to a broad, long-term relationship with a single supplier which makes it difficult to award new projects to other suppliers.

Opensourcing

As the name indicates, there is free sharing of new knowledge and information under an open source or free software license. Some academics/scholars or self managed groups create a network and pool the knowledge/information free of cost which is available to all. One such example is Wikipedia, the other is Linux operating system. In 1984, Richard Stallman, a MIT researcher, spearheaded the 'free software movement' in an effort to develop a free operating system known as GNU, the source codes of which would not only be available to all but would also be always modifiable. With this in view, he established a Free Software Foundation called *General Public License (GPL)* which allowed its users to freely use the source code in any manner they liked, or improve upon it with the condition that all the changes would be made available under the same license as the original code, and would be freely available to all. In 1991, Linus Torvalds improved upon it and developed Linux operating system as a rival software to Microsoft Windows operating system. This GNU/Linux operating system continues to be free, and firms using this software are required to respect its copyright. There is a large body of knowledge available on the web as opensourcing.

Business Process Outsourcing (BPO) in India

Business Process Outsourcing (BPO) is the transfer of one or more IT-intensive business processes to an external provider who administers and manages the agreed upon processes in measurable performance criteria. This industry in India has boomed at 70% a year and is now worth $1.6 billion, employing 100,000 people. According to a report by McKinsey, it is expected to grow only 27% till 2008 to deliver $17 billion in revenue and employment of a million people.[120] The services provided by it include a wide range-like telemarketing services, employee IT help-desk services, customer support services, technical support services, insurance processing, new business/promotion, policy maintenance/management, data processing services, data conversion services, e-book conversion, etc., scanning, book keeping and accounting services, and form processing services (insurance claim form, medical bills, etc.).

Google's recent announcement about setting up an R&D center in Bangalore reflects this new mindset. The company's move is motivated by the vast engineering talent pool in India, and is not a cost cutting move.[121]

The IT enabled services (ITES)-BPO segment contributes 30% of the total ITES exports from India. Some of the people centric exports are described below.

Call Centers Call centers are capital intensive Business Process Outsourcing (BPO), but at the same time, these are one of the most critical marketing and sales elements for an accomplished business.

These have dedicated or shared staffs who are engaged in customer relationship management, acquisition of new customers, interactive voice response, data collection, lead generation, and customer analysis. These centers have gained considerable importance as a marketing and customer retention platform for a company. India is an important destination for telemarketing outsourcing, having the largest English speaking population. Offshore call centers, which offer telemarketing services, convert potential clients into customers, and the existing customers into long-term customers. The telemarketing agents are trained professionals who have good communication, sales, and presentation skills. The challenge before the manager of a call center is meeting customer expectations from across the world, through staff who, along with communication skills, are expected to be proficient in managing expectations of customers from countries they have not visited. High attrition is reported in call centers in India.

During 1970s, outsourcing in the US comprised of payroll processing, and it extended to billing, accounting services, and word processing. However, during the past couple of years, outsourcing has extended from low end operations to high end knowledge work. Whereas BPO is more about volume and report, knowledge process outsourcing is driven by knowledge, skills, and experience.

Knowledge Process Outsourcing (KPO) The success of business process outsourcing has encouraged companies to outsource their high end knowledge work. It involves highly value added processes which are dependent on advanced knowledge, technical skills, and relevant experience. It involves software solutions, E-business integration, IT enabled services, web solutions, Customer Relationship Management, ERP and data warehousing, financial services, biotechnology research, computer aided simulations and engineering design, and services–such as business research and legal services. KPO has become an industry in itself. India is one of the important destinations, apart from Philippines, China, and Eastern Europe, in offshored outsourcing. "India and China are already the leading destinations for offshoring", said Daniel Franklin, Editorial Director of the Economist Intelligence Unit."

Since outsourcing is done from countries which have world class systems and quality, and are talent rich and low cost destinations; it helps the companies in these countries to reduce the cost of infrastructure and of hiring employees, and focus on optimum use of competitive resources available across the globe. The disadvantage of outsourcing is that the employees of the outsourcer company may feel insecure. But, so far as the company is concerned, it gets the benefit of flexibility, technological agility, and cost and competitive advantage.

Challenges and Implications for Organizational Behavior The BPO industry attracts a large number of young people as it employs people with a wide range of educational and skill levels, offers them good work environment, flexibility of time, attractive lifestyle, and a number of perks. Despite these privileges, there is high attrition in this industry. The reasons for attrition are lack of growth opportunities, lack of promotion, physical strain, monotony, uneasy relationship with peers or managers, higher salary offered by another employer or pursuing higher education.

Thus, the major problems faced by BPOs and KPOs are high attrition, ongoing recruitment, and continuous need for training and development of employees. It being an emerging field, there are hardly any published studies, but media reports and web postings indicate that it is due to young and ambitious people who take up these jobs to get global market exposure but do not see career growth in the organization. They, thus, develop dissatisfaction due to expectation mismatch. However, media also reports that call center professionals in India are well taken care of, get good salaries, promotions shift changes, and provided with other incentives. The delegation from the US which visited call centers and firms in cities like Chennai, Mumbai, Bangalore, and Hyderabad in 2005 remarked, "We are very much impressed by the welfare measures for the workers here."[122] Considering the momentum and growth in this industry, it is expected that there would be both vertical and lateral career opportunities at supervisory and middle levels of management. In the high end KPO industry, poaching and talent management are serious issues, and firms offer very attractive incentive schemes and developmental opportunities to attract and retain talent.

BPO work is still considered to be of low value, thus making it difficult to attract the best talent. Further, demands on parameters–such as quality, turn-around timeliness, information security, business continuity, and disaster recovery are very high. Employees are required to work in different time zones in tight time schedules which is stressful. For low end operations, no standard curriculum can be designed and followed, and therefore, no standard pre-job training is possible. There is also a lack of benchmarks for HR policies on compensation, benefits, and performance and most companies evolve these, based on their experience or market trends.

A recent trend is that many Indian IT firms are expanding their operations abroad for 'nearshoring', or are acquiring software firms there. In these acquisitions, cultural integration is one of the major OB challenges. Also, company HR policies need to be tailored to the specific labor laws and compensation packages prevalent in these countries.

Employer Branding

Employer branding is defined as "a targeted, long-term strategy to manage the awareness and perceptions of employees, potential employees, and related stakeholders with regard to a particular firm"[123]. Companies are interested in building and sustaining their 'employer brand' as it is an enabler in building competitive advantage, helps employees internalize values of the company, and for employee retention. Employer branding is important for a company's various stakeholders. However, it is crucial for internal employees as well to attract potential employees.

Research yields that for success of 'Employer Branding', certain characteristics are essential. These include (a) to be noticeable, (b) to be seen as relevant and resonant, and (c) to have differentiation from direct competitors. These characteristics should be consistent with a company's consumer and corporate branding. Other additional characteristics include (a) to fulfill the psychological contract, and (b) unintended appropriation of brand values[124].

Why Employer Branding? Employer branding is crucial in order to communicate the values and culture of the company to various stakeholders, especially potential employees as their values should match with that of the company. Moreover, the potential candidate would be able to evaluate in the context of 'desirability for the workplace' within the industry. Employer branding can play a crucial role in attracting and growing the high quality workforce and has a positive impact on organizational performance. Moreover, it gives an insight into the work culture and the way human resource is managed and contingency measures taken for the workforce in times of uncertainty.

Role of Employer Branding in Corporate Branding There are similar characteristics between corporate branding and employer branding. These are: the brand needs to be visible, should have significance for its stakeholders, and be resonant and exclusive[125]. The success of employer branding depends on its propositions developed on rational and emotional basis in sync with the expectations of existing and potential employees[126]. The promises made through employer branding, if delivered appropriately to existing and newly recruited employees, have positive and direct impact on their and also on the organization's performance. To ensure effectiveness and success of corporate branding, an organization needs to align corporate branding and employer branding appropriately. Employees are one of the interfaces of corporate brand. Their behavior, approach with customers and other stakeholders leads to either positive or negative perceptions. Employees' approach and behavior also reflect an organization's culture, values and attractiveness as a workplace to external stakeholders. Appropriate integration of employer branding and corporate branding is crucial in providing an organization a competitive advantage; otherwise it could lead to negative repercussions.

Great Places to Work Survey, 2010: India[127]

Great Places to Work Survey is conducted by the Great Places to Work Institute Incorporation, based in the U.S., which has its affiliate offices across the world. The study is undertaken in 45 countries across the world with participation from 5,500 organizations and 2 million employees every year. In India, the survey is conducted by the Great Places to Work Institute, India. In the year 2010, it captured the workplace experience of 53,000 employees in India. The study is conducted based on a model which comprises Trust Index (which is from employee perspective) and Culture Audit (which is from management perspective). Trust Index covers the following variables: Credibility, Respect, Fairness, Pride, and Camaraderie. Culture Audit covers the following variables: Hiring, Inspiring, Speaking, Listening, Thanking, Developing, Caring, Celebrating and Sharing.

Name of the Company	Unique Features
Google India Pvt Ltd	Work culture
Make My Trip (India) Pvt Ltd	Empowerment, trust, practical processes
Intel Technology India Pvt Ltd	Leadership development, work life balance, gender diversity, work life effectiveness and corporate social responsibility
Marriot Hotels India Pvt Ltd	Culture audit practices which includes spirit to serve
NetApp India Pvt Ltd	Flexibility and attention towards employees involved in decision-making, buddy mentor approach for new employees, 360 degree appraisal with emphasis on trust and transparency, work culture values – creativity, innovation, teamwork, leadership and productivity
American Express, India	Care for people, valued team work, collaboration, equal opportunity employer
NTPC Ltd	Empowerment attributes, transparent culture, encouragements for innovation
PayPal India Pvt Ltd	Indianized work culture, empowerment to technologist, women empowerment, pro-employee policies
Ajuba Solutions India Pvt Ltd	Integrity, pursuit for excellence, employees as valuable assets
SAS Institute (India) Pvt Ltd	Team work, integrity & loyalty, competency building of employees

Source: Great Place to Work Institute (2010), India's Best Companies to Work For. http://www.greatplacetowork.com/what_we_do/lists-in-in-2010.htm, accessed on 26/2/2011

Exhibit 1.4 *Ranking of Best Places to Work—2010*

Cross-Culture Perspective Corporates which operate in the international markets are dependent on a talent pool which comprises individuals of different nationalities and have differences in their cultural and individual value system. The issue of attracting potential applicants is highly challenging because of competition for talented people in the market. For potential applicants, the key drivers are job characteristics, remuneration, growth potential, and reputation of the company in the respective industry. However, these drivers are influenced by an applicant's culture as well as individual perceptions and needs. In countries with a collectivist culture, corporates at the time of recruitment should focus on creating congruence between personal, cultural and organizational values as well as maintaining its global competitiveness. In countries with an individualist culture, the need for power and achievement are related to employer reputation. So, MNCs need to design their existing job offers and career paths which match with individual and cultural values of the target group of applicants in the respective country in order to attract and retain the talented workforce. When undertaking employer branding, MNCs need to consider the cultural matters of the country in which they are operating.

Inclusive Workplace

An organization can be an *inclusive workplace* when it adopts broader and open vision of inclusion which includes the organization as well as stakeholders from the adjoining community, national and international levels[128]. He defines an inclusive workplace wherein inclusion occurs at four levels, the first two are at micro level and latter two at macro level:

- Level 1: Inclusion through diversified workforce
- Level 2: Inclusion through organizational collaborations
- Level 3: Inclusion through national collaborations
- Level 4: Inclusion through international collaborations

Level 1: Inclusion through Diversified Workforce *Inclusive workplace* focuses on developing a diversified culture and leverages and utilizes these differences for competitive advantage, and for attracting and retaining talented workforce. Diversity exists in terms of gender, religion, race, nationality, ability, sexual orientation and thought differences, etc. A conducive climate can be created through nurturing positive interdependent work, symbolic interactions, positive organizational change through development of feelings of inclusion among employees, and by developing relationship irrespective of the differences. An inclusive workplace ensures employee safety, encourages innovation, and provides for equal opportunity and values contribution of employees. Such workplaces have positive impact on the organization, the employees, communities and other stakeholders. There is psychological and physical well-being which facilitates transfer of knowledge and cooperative action and economic strength.

Coca-Cola SABCO planned an innovative distribution channel which has become core of its business operations in Ethiopia. This innovation has facilitated access to those markets which it was unable due to logistic problem. It has provided employment to uneducated or less educated from the surrounding community. It was unable to reach small bars, kiosks and shops located in congested and thickly populated localities. There was potential market for non-alcoholic beverages in such locations. The large delivery vans were unable to reach these localities as the lanes were narrow and congested. In 1999, with funding from International Finance Corporation (IFC), it devised the use of small handcarts in its distribution channel to reach the target consumers residing in such localities. This was a win-win situation for both the company and the surrounding community. The local people were roped in and signed as distributors for the company who delivered the products on time and reliably each week. There are approximately 650 privately operating distribution businesses in Ethiopia, mainly operated by the first-time entrepreneurs. This innovative distribution facilitated the poor to gain entrepreneurial skills, cheap credit, income generation and move out of hassles of an informal sector.

Source: International Finance Corporation (2010), "Ethiopia–Distribution: Reaching Hidden Markets", In Telling Our Story: Base of the Pyramid Investments–Inclusive Business, http://www.ifc.org/ifcext/media.nsf/AttachmentsByTitle/TOS_BOP_Apr10/$FILE/TOS_BOP_Apr10.pdf, accessed on 1/2/2011.

Tata Consultancy Services (TCS) has started an initiative named TCS–*Maitree* to open employment opportunities for the visually impaired, in 2008. It started with Advanced Computer Training Centre which offers courses according to the industry requirements that enables differently abled people with life-affirming employment opportunities. It helps to overcome their disability through technology, able guidance, recognition and conducive environment. To enhance employability, the focus is on training in IT infrastructure and service management, developing competencies for BPO and soft skills. These individuals after the completion of the course are provided employment within TCS or any of the Tata group companies or other organizations in the industry.

Source: Tata Consultancy Service (2009). *Rising to their Right Potential.* TCS Maitree is Opening the Door of Opportunity for the Visually Impaired through Training and Skills Development. http://www.tata.com/media/articles/inside.aspx?artid=yhfbFqV3Dlc=, accessed on 1/2/2011.

Level 2: Inclusion through Organizational Collaboration An organization needs to pursue inclusiveness with its outside stakeholders to make it an *inclusive workplace.* Organizations can consider inclusion through financial, social, education and training, physical infrastructure, economic, and equal opportunities. These enter into collaboration with institutions or Non-Governmental Organizations (NGOs) which have better access and knowledge of communities. Employees are also encouraged to contribute in this process of inclusion through sharing of knowledge, skills and to consider the well-being of the communities and society in their routine professional-level decision-making activities.

PepsiCo India and Punjab Agriculture University have co-developed an innovative tractor-driven machine which enables Direct Seeding of Rice (DSR). It is an eco-friendly technique that reduces water usage in rice paddies by 30% and reduction in carbon emission by 70%. This is beneficial for farmers as they face issues of water scarcity. This initiative has been successful and in order to reach its benefits to farmers across India, the company has collaborated with Indian Agriculture Research Institute (IARI). The company also has partnerships with state governments, NGOs and local communities which enable it to implement inclusive business models that are scaleable and sustainable.

Source: Radjou Navi, Prabhu Jaideep, Kaipa Prasad, and Ahuja Simone (2011), *Indian Tales of Inclusive Business Models*, http://blogs.hbr.org/cs/2011/01/indian_tales_of_inclusive_busi.html, accessed on 1/2/2011.

Level 3: Inclusion through State/National Collaborations Inclusion at state/national level enables an organization to reach the disadvantaged groups on a large scale. An organization collaborates with government-affiliated organizations/institutions in their programs or initiatives at state and/or national level. These collaborations can be undertaken through various modes such as Public Private Partnership (PPP) model and SPV (Special Purpose Vehicle). The organization can contribute by providing vocational training, financial inclusive services, education, training on entrepreneurship to women, other minority groups or disadvantaged groups, generate or provide job opportunities either at the place of the respective community's residence or within the organization.

DuPont's Indian unit has entered into an innovative PPP model with various state governments in India through which they strive to improve upon productivity and profitability of agriculture for farmers and also aim to improve food availability through accessibility to resilient seeds at reasonable prices.

Source: Radjou Navi, Prabhu Jaideep, Kaipa Prasad, and Ahuja Simone (2011), "Indian Tales of Inclusive Business Models", http://blogs.hbr.org/cs/2011/01/indian_tales_of_inclusive_busi.html, accessed on 1/2/2011.

Level 4: Inclusion through International Collaborations Organizations operating on international or global level can ensure that inclusion is practiced by all its subsidiaries/units/branches wherever these are located. Organizations can enter into collaboration with individuals/groups/organizations cutting across national and cultural boundaries.

Hindustan Unilever's Livelihood Initiative Hindustan Unilever Ltd., a subsidiary of Unilever Global, undertakes initiatives and actions with the aim of sustainability. The company's focus areas are Water Conservation, Livelihoods and Community Initiatives. The Indian subsidiary has partnered with Aide et Action, to set up vocational training centers for the youths from communities surrounding their Silvasa Plant, the capital of Dadar and Nagar Haveli (union territory) in India. These vocational training centers, called iLEAD, provide courses in tailoring, basic knowledge of computers, electrical wiring, and so on. The courses offered are according to demands and needs of the industries located in the city. Till 2010, 60% of the youths trained in these centers have been employed at various organizations in the city. The youth intending to set up their own enterprise are provided with necessary space and useful advice. The alumni of iLEAD facilitate in job placement of the new trainees outside the city.

Source: Hindustan Unilever (2011), "Project in Partnership with Aide et Action", http://www.hul.co.in/sustainability/society/livelihoods/?WT.LHNAV=Livelihoods, accessed on 11/2/2011.

Green Management with Focus on Environment

The deteriorating environment is causing a concern to all the stakeholders of the society. Various initiatives, regulations and laws have been formulated over the years both at the international and national levels. At the international level, Montreal Convention (1987), Declaration of Rio Earth Summit (1992), Kyoto Protocol (1997), Sustainable Development Announcements of Johannesburg World Summit (2002), Restrictions to the Use of Certain Hazardous Substances in EEE (Electronic Electric Equipment), etc. have brought in tremendous pressures on industries across the globe. Additionally, there are pressures from pro-environmental organizations and consumers.

Corporate Environment Management Companies are no longer left with a choice, but are required to integrate environment-protection activities which comply with international and national regulatory frameworks. The companies which are proactive make use of environment-friendly innovative methods and technologies. Consumers too are keen to buy environment-friendly products and are ready to pay a higher price. The companies aggressively pursuing environment management have a competitive edge. Environment management also gives cushion to corporate bodies against unwanted protests and penalties and helps in enhancing its image and competitive advantage.

Green Intellectual Capital Green Intellectual Capital concept was proposed by Chen[129]. Green Intellectual Capital is classified as green human capital, green structural capital and green relational capital based on Ulrich's concept of human capital.[130] Green human capital means employees possess knowledge, potential, experience, attitude, wisdom, level of creativity, commitment, etc. on environment protection and environment-friendly actions which can enable a company to gain competitiveness. Green structural capital comprises an organization's capabilities, commitments, knowledge-management systems, information-technology systems, databases, managerial institutions, operational processes, managerial philosophies, organizational culture, images of the company, patents, trademarks, copyrights, etc. for environment-friendly practices and environment protection. Green relational capital includes a company's cumulative interactive relationships with customers, suppliers and partners regarding corporate environmental management for a competitive benefit. It was found from the study that green human capital, green structural capital and green relational capital had positive correlation with competitive advantage for the firms. Investment in green human capital, green structural capital and green relational capital is beneficial for business growth.

Sustainability Strategy in the midst of Green Passion Environment/green standards are a hotly debated subject at various platforms across the globe. Unruh and Ettenson[131] have developed four strategies which companies can adopt to sustain in the midst of green passion:

1. Adopt the existing standards of the concerned industry
2. Choose and modify the standards to suit the organization's capabilities and processes
3. First mover–define standards for the concerned industry
4. Define and set your own standards

This trend could lead to changes in organizational behavior of an entity. Organizations would have to relook at various aspects of organizational behavior from the perspective of environment and endorse the same.

Innovation for Organizational Competitiveness[132]

Innovativeness is, "the degree to which an individual or other unit of adoption is relatively earlier in adopting new ideas than other members of a system"[133].

Necessity breeds opportunity which sows the seeds of innovation for an organization to compete under constraints and gain competitive advantage. Organizations, in order to gain competitive advantage need to boost both efficiency and sensitivity to consumers' needs. Organizations face challenges for carrying out trade-off between the two, under constraints from both inside and outside environment. Competitive advantage through innovation depends on competencies/knowledge advantage, management and strategy of innovation and culture.

Competencies Competencies which are enablers for the innovativeness depend on secret skills, distinctive technologies, processes, updated knowledge, integration of resources and capabilities across the organization, which are superior to those of its competitors. Knowledge of an organization has a direct relation with innovation. An organization can innovate based on its existing knowledge or its attempt to develop or obtain knowledge. In other words, the innovativeness of an organization reflects its knowledge level. An organization needs to pursue its distinctiveness on a continuous basis for its sustainability. The challenge remains for competencies in organizations to be dynamic in all aspects that need to be renovated, developed and cultivated constantly under changing and unpredictable environment.

Ambuja Cement, to gain competitive advantage, undertook a two-pronged strategy, i.e. to reduce transportation cost and improve responsiveness to customers. Transportation cost forms a major chunk in any cement manufacturer's operating expenses. Cement factories are located near limestone mines, but such mines are far away from the markets causing major expenditures. The company found an innovative way to overcome these constraints through 'Split Plants'. Through Split Plants, the initial processing of the product is completed at plants located near the mines and reduces weight of the materials. These lightweight materials are easier to transport to plants located near the markets, which undertake grinding and packaging. This served two purposes for the company, i.e. reduction in transportation cost and efficiency improvement and improved responsiveness to customers. In India, 90% of the cement is transported either by rail or road. The company thought of a different approach to speed up transportation, i.e. the sea route. It is India's first company to introduce bulk movement of cement through the sea route, which enabled it to overcome the bottlenecks in road transportation and also opened opportunity to access coastal markets that were previously untapped.

Source: Chaudari, Atanu; Giffi, Craig; Kumar, Kandaswami and Singh Shalab Kumar (2009), "Necessity Breeds Opportunity: Constraints, Innovation and Competitive Advantage", http://www.deloitte.com/assets/Dcom-SouthAfrica/Local%20Assets/Documents/Necessity%20Breed%20Opportunity.pdf, accessed on 5/2/2011.

Management and Strategy for Innovation Innovation can occur in a variety of areas, i.e. products/services, technology, prices, operational execution and to improve the understanding of customers and markets. An organization's position on innovation is reflected through their level of focus on developing external and internal innovations. External innovations concentrate on product/service used or experienced by customers, while internal innovations concentrate on processes and procedures. Another aspect revealed is the extent of innovation–whether it is incremental enhancements or radical changes and its degree of innovativeness or newness for the market. Sie, Chu and Chen[134] have classified management innovation into three categories: Organizational Innovation, Informational Innovation and Technological Innovation.

Indian Tobacco Company (ITC) Ltd. introduced an innovative channel to source raw materials from farmers at low cost for its agri-business. Traditionally, the Indian agriculture market was run by middlemen who provided credit and raw materials of agriculture to the farmers, and thereafter at the time of harvesting bought their output to be sold in the market. In this system, middlemen kept large surpluses for themselves; this pushed up procurement costs. ITC developed an innovative channel for sourcing raw materials by unbundling information (information on price) and transaction (weight and delivery)—the two aspects of supply chain. E-Choupals, i.e. the Information and Communication Technology (ICT) kiosks, were set up in villages to give farmers information on crop price, grading standards, and lowest cost of the raw material. This innovation was a win-win situation for both the farmers and the company. Farmers were relieved from the clutches of middlemen and received better return on investment. Warehousing hubs were also set up by the company, being managed by people who were middlemen previously. The resultant benefits were reduction in transaction cost, screening of products for quality and creation of efficient logistics that was traceable. The company improved upon its responsiveness to the customers through these kiosks. Quality of inputs was ensured by the company, which reflected in the output and also was able to customize products according to local needs. E-Choupal has also opened new opportunities for the company to use it as retail channel to reach out to the underserved rural markets.

Source: Chaudhari, Atanu; Giffi, Craig; Kumar, Kandaswami and Singh, Shalab Kumar (2009), "Necessity Breeds Opportunity: Constraints, Innovation and Competitive Advantage", http://www.deloitte.com/assets/Dcom-SouthAfrica/Local%20Assets/Documents/Necessity%20Breed%20Opportunity.pdf, accessed on 5/2/2011.

Culture of an Organization Culture of an organization is also crucial for innovation. An organization needs to foster a culture with values of commitment to innovation, to be a leader for providing innovative products/services; dynamic entrepreneurial workplace, which highlights teamwork. Leadership commitment is essential to develop such a culture, along with the need to understand innovative process and commitment to policies. Organizations also need to balance cost and efficiency and risks and profits. A culture that fosters innovation also paves the way for competition among individuals and between departments[135].

Mahindra and Mahindra Group launched an intranet-based innovation pad in May, 2009. This platform cuts across all its 104 group companies and approximately 1 lakh employees. About 39,000 employees have used this innovation pad from across the group companies and have helped in generating 400 ideas which are related to products, process and new ways of doing things. The idea behind this initiative was to generate and pool knowledge by bringing together the employees and also to share the knowledge. This would enable the company to innovate faster, bridge the digital divide and cross-breed ideas. The older generation in the organization too is open to such initiatives, which is a boost to develop and sustain innovative culture.

Source: Live Mint (2009), "Mahindra Employees Play with Ideas", http://www.livemint.com/2009/07/27224908/Mahindra-employeesplay-with-i.html?h=B, accessed on 5/2/2011.

Innovation can enable organizations to gain competitive edge, if there is a strategy that aligns between product/service/market, knowledge/competencies level of the organization with the stage of innovation.

Cluster Concept[136]

According to UNIDO report, cluster is defined as "a local agglomeration of enterprises (mainly SMEs, but often also including some large enterprises), which produce and sell a range of related and complementary products and services"[137]. According to Michael E. Porter, clusters are "geographic concentrations of interconnected companies, specialized suppliers, service providers and associated institutions in a particular field that are present in a nation or region".[138]

Increase in competition arising out of globalization and increasing importance to knowledge intensity has changed the role of clusters in competition. Clusters influence market competition by raising the productivity of constituent firms or industries, improving capability to innovate and stimulate growth. Clusters can impact market competition, if there is networking and communication within the cluster among individuals and institutions.

Role of Clusters There is growing importance of clusters, as these are pivotal to develop modern industrial innovation policy, attract foreign direct investment (FDI), promote excellence in various industries, give impetus to employment generation and other complementary developments. Clusters are used as a competitive strategy.

Boosters for Clusters Boosting the development of clusters and sustaining them require appropriate business environment, suitable government policies for development and sustainability of clusters, technological support, government incentives, encouragement of grassroot or local innovations, training and development for skill enhancement or acquiring new skills.

In India, development of industrial clusters has led to employment generation, development of entrepreneurship and has contributed to industrial growth and exports. Other benefits generated through clusters include (a) rise in the levels of skilled labor and inputs in the market, (b) paving the way for infrastructure development and (c) innovation generated through informal exchanges. These clusters have been successful in promotion and development of small, micro and medium enterprises. Each firm in a cluster provides employment to people from range of 5 to 500 persons depending on production facilities and capacity. A cluster's success depends on building networks to establish cooperation, capacity building and specialization.

Challenges The challenges faced include global economic crisis, competition from competing clusters, global competition, disruptive changes, traditional clusters reeling under pressures of modernization, pressures to remain competitive and innovative for sustenance, etc.

Corporate Entrepreneurship Culture in Organizations

Entrepreneurship is not new for organizations. Entrepreneurial thinking within organizations was recognized by Peter Drucker in 1985 in his pioneering book *Innovation and Entrepreneurship*. Covin and Miles[139] define corporate entrepreneurship as

> "the presence of innovation with the objective of rejuvenating or redefining organizations, markets or industries in order to create or sustain competitive superiority."

Morris and Kuratko[140] defined corporate entrepreneurship as "a term used to describe entrepreneurial behavior inside established mid-sized and large organizations". It is also known as *intrapreneurship.*

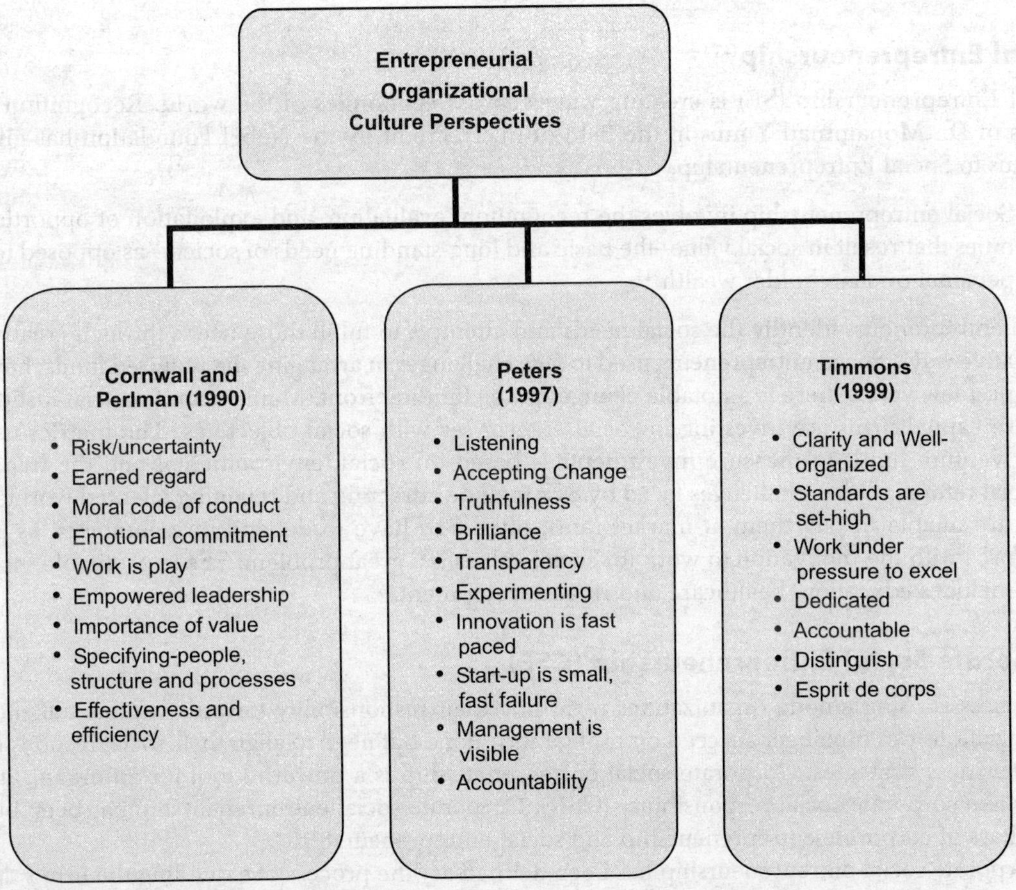

Source: Adapted from Morris, M.H.; Kuratko, D.F.; Covin, J.G.: "Corporate Entrepreneurship and Innovation", Thomson South-Western; Second Edition, 2008, p. 259.

Exhibit 1.5 *Characteristics of Intrapreneurship*

Factors that Drive Corporate Entrepreneurship The factors which are crucial to initiate and drive corporate entrepreneurship include top-down approach, vision, alignment between organizational structure and vision, flexibility of the organization to internal and external environments, new technologies, and value proposition of the company that helps to align different work groups. Besides, managing team conflicts is crucial; compensation should have a good mix of variety which is decided at the top; recognition, encouragement for entrepreneurial activities, and enhanced status drive corporate entrepreneurship.

Entrepreneurial Organizational Culture According to Kuratko et al.[141], the intensity and level of entrepreneurial activities in an organization can be measured on the parameters of innovativeness, risk-taking and proactivity. Morris et al.[142] gave an overview of the characteristics of an entrepreneurial organizational culture based on studies of Cornwall and Perlman, Peters and Timmons.

An organizational culture which possesses the characteristics essential for entrepreneurship can open opportunities for employees who have entrepreneurial flair and give competitive advantage to the organization to sustain in a globally competitive and uncertain environment.

Social Entrepreneurship[143]

Social Entrepreneurship (SE) is creating waves across economies of the world. Recognition to the works of Dr. Mohammad Yunus in the field of micro-credit by the Nobel Foundation has given an impetus to Social Entrepreneurship.

> Social entrepreneurship involves the recognition, evaluation, and exploitation of opportunities that result in social value–the basic and long-standing needs of society–as opposed to personal or shareholder wealth[144].

Social entrepreneurs identify the social needs and attempts to fulfill those needs through creative and innovative ways. Social entrepreneurs used to face challenges in arranging the required funds, however, since past few years, there is a notable change on the funding front. Mainstream financial institutions, venture capital firms are investing in social enterprises with social objectives. The metrics used by social venture funds to measure investments is based on social, environmental and the traditional financial returns. Other challenges faced by SEs include attracting and retaining talented workforce as these are unable to pay them at market rates, often SEs have to depend on volunteers, as getting workforce with the motivation to work for social values is a great problem. SEs in profitable sectors in India includes education, healthcare and rural development.

Corporate Social Entrepreneurship (CSE)

Awareness is rising among organizations regarding their responsibility towards various stakeholders. Organizations can no longer succeed on profitability alone but need to align their social responsibilities with business strategies. Corporate social entrepreneurship is a powerful tool for an organization to undertake corporate social responsibility (CSR). Corporate social entrepreneurship has been built on the pillars of corporate entrepreneurship and social entrepreneurship.

Corporate social entrepreneurship has been defined as "the process of extending the firm's domain of competence and corresponding opportunity set through innovative leveraging of resources, both within and outside its direct control, aimed at the simultaneous creation of economic and social value"[145].

Motivational Factors for CSE The motivation for organizations to invest in social actions is varied–some do it for altruistic reasons, whereas others would have utilitarian motives[146]. However, the intensity of these motivational factors is crucial to arouse commitment, generate required amount of resources to make it sustainable and which has transformative impact. The outcomes of these social investments need to be holistic i.e. both social and economic gains.

Enablers for Corporate Social Entrepreneurship According to Austin and Reficco[147], the enablers to develop corporate social entrepreneurship include encouraging environment, corporate social intrapreneur (role of both entrepreneur and manager), value proposition of the organization, value creation (optimizing returns to stakeholders) and creating value collaboratively.

Encouraging Environment Change is needed in the mindset of top leadership and top management to be open to developing and nurturing entrepreneurial culture and environment, value-based culture within the organization and bringing in transformation. To bring in sustainable transformation, change is needed in vision, strategy, structures and processes. During the process of transformation, the leadership needs to ensure alignment between social needs and business strategy. Silos need to be broken; all the stakeholders need to be brought together to work upon various issues, focussing on the social value and out-of-the-box thinking.

Corporate Social Intrapreneur An organization can succeed in corporate social entrepreneurship when it has people with the following characteristics[148]: advocates/champions rigorously advocating business and social integration, clear articulators/communicators about the importance of corporate social entrepreneurship, creators of innovative products and services, catalysts for change, coordinating and mobilizing resources, contributors, and cost conscious.

Value Proposition of the Organization An organization's value proposition should be based on social outcomes and to fulfill an organization's responsibility toward the society. These values need to be translated into actions through ethical behaviors, and innovative products/services. Strategies should be chalked out considering the value propositions. Over a period of time, it should build trust amongst all stakeholders.

Value Creation – Optimizing Returns to Stakeholders Taking this into consideration the needs of all the stakeholders. This enables sustainability of organizations.

Creating Value Collaboratively An organization collaborates or forms alliance with governments, or business organization/s or NGOs or civil society. These collaborations help in leveraging competencies and resources of both the organization and outside stakeholders, which creates new capabilities, opportunities and innovations.

Challenges to adopt corporate social entrepreneurship include managing disruptive change, change in business models, persuading employees to adopt corporate social entrepreneurship approach, resistance as the change takes place at the core, and to create and maintain synergies.

Learning Objectives

After reading the next two sections, you should be able to:

8. Debate the organizational opportunities and challenges of globalization, the changing workplace dynamics, and virtual work.
9. Discuss the anchors on which organizational behavior knowledge is based.

CONTEMPORARY CHALLENGES FOR ORGANIZATIONS

Throughout the earlier discussion on organizational effectiveness was an underlying theme that organizations are deeply affected by the external environment. These need to maintain a good fit with their external environment by continuously monitoring and adjusting to changes in that environment. This external environment is continuously changing, but some changes, over the past decade and in the decade to come, are more profound than others. These changes require that corporate leaders and all other employees adjust to new realities. In this section, we highlight three of the major challenges facing organizations: globalization, increasing workforce diversity, and emerging employment relationships.

Globalization

The term 'globalization' implies integration of economies and societies through cross border flow of goods, services, finance, capital, ideas, information, technologies, and people. This integration across countries may involve several aspects—social, political, economic, and cultural which may impact the native culture. In the present scenario, economic integration is taking place in the form of (a) trade in goods and services, (b) movement of capital, and (c) flow of finance, besides movement of people. Globalization offers both opportunities and challenges in the form of conflicts on tariff and other trade matters. If development is viewed as the major objective, as proclaimed by Doha declaration, the countries can try and work out a trading arrangement beneficial to all countries.[149]

You might not have heard of Fonterra, but chances are that you have purchased or eaten one of its products recently. The New Zealand–based company is the world's largest dairy exporting business and the world's lowest-cost dairy ingredient producer. It operates in 140 countries, employs 20,000 people, and represents 40 percent of the global dairy trade. In many countries, it forms joint partnerships, such as those with the Dairy Farmers of America, SanCor in Argentina, and Aria in Europe. Fonterra's current position on the world stage is quite different from the situation a decade ago, when three New Zealand dairy companies joined forces. They realized that globalization was shaking up the industry and that forming a global enterprise was essential to their survival. The merged company was so globally focused from the outset that it was temporarily called GlobalCo until the name Fonterra was chosen. Fonterra's adjustment to a global operation was not easy. Executives were replaced as the company needed to adopt a different mindset. "A lot of people in the [pre-merger companies] were very New Zealand–centric and culturally did not understand the global challenges of the teams offshore and the different operating companies," acknowledges a Fonterra executive.[150]

globalization
Economic, social, and cultural connectivity with people in other parts of the world.

Fonterra is a rich example of the globalization of business over the past few decades. **Globalization** refers to economic, social, and cultural connectivity with people in other parts of the world. Fonterra and other organizations globalize when they actively participate in other countries and cultures. Although businesses have traded goods across borders for centuries, the degree of globalization today is unprecedented because information technology and transportation systems allow a much more intense level of connectivity and interdependence across the planet.[151]

Globalization offers numerous benefits to organizations in terms of larger markets, lower costs, and greater access to knowledge and innovation. At the same time, there is considerable debate about whether globalization benefits developing nations and whether it is primarily responsible for increasing work intensification, as well as reducing job security and work–life balance in developed countries.[152] Globalization is now well entrenched, so the real issue in organizational behavior is how corporate leaders and employees alike can lead and work effectively in this emerging reality.[153] OB researchers are turning their attention to this topic. In Project GLOBE, for example, dozens of experts are studying leadership and organizational practices worldwide.[154]

Globalization and its Impact on India India opened up its economy in 1991 and went through various economic reforms. Domestic and external sector policy measures were partly prompted by the immediate needs and partly by the demands of the multilateral organizations. The reforms included reduction in import duty, abolition of restrictions on imports, removal of permission for starting new enterprises or expanding the existing ones, disinvestment and privatization of some public sector firms. India, as a developing country, has some strengths as well as some limitations. Its one billion population, with about 250 million middle class with buying power, offers tremendous marketing opportunities to many global firms. A large number of multinational firms have moved to India after liberalization; some of these are Honda, Suzuki, General Motors, Ford, Hyundai in the auto sector; Coke, Pepsi, McDonalds, Pizza Hut, KFC, Barista in the food and beverage sector; Nike, Adidas in sports wear and goods; Levi's, Reid & Taylor in the apparels and garment sector; LG, Samsung and GE in white goods; Star, National Geograhic, Sony and Discovery in the entertainment sector; Revelon, Oriflame and Maybellene in the cosmetic sector; HP, IBM, Dell, Compaq in the computer sector; to name a few, and many others in pharmaceuticals and other sectors. The Government of India has also promoted foreign direct investment (FDI).

The economy showed steady upward trend post liberalization. India has highly skilled manpower which has led to India's rise to the top in the world IT industry, but there is shortage of talent and high employee attrition. The Government has taken a decision to establish many institutions of higher learning and excellence in the next five years (the 11th plan period). Considering the pace of growth and demands due to globalization, there is shortage of power and a variety of infrastructure problems which are being addressed. Some labor reforms have been introduced; India has the cost advantage with labor, and has low energy costs as well, which makes it an attractive outsourcing destination for auto components and IT enabled services. Some negative effects of globalization have been restructuring, downsizing, and voluntary retirement schemes (VRS) implemented by organizations, shift in employment from large to small and medium enterprises, and availability of qualified people for lower level jobs.

The positive impacts of globalization can be summarized as easy access to international brands and consumer durables, global connectivity through technological advancements, flow of investments, air travel at competitive rates, greater efficiency in public sector and professionalisation of family owned firms, exponential growth of BPO and ITes services, global acquisitions and expansion of business (Ranbaxy, Tata Motors, Aditya Birla Group, Cipla, Tata Steel, Mahindra & Mahindra, Dr. Reddy's, and Asian Paints etc.), strong R&D by MNCs and innovative marketing strategies, and use of innovative HR practices. The revolution in telecommunications and IT is simultaneously creating a huge market economy. The key to India's growth lies in improving productivity and efficiency and promoting entrepreneurship. India needs to consolidate its position and delineate the path for different industries to achieve productivity and efficiency levels comparable to the world class organizations.

Source: Rangarajan, C. 2006. Responding To Globalization: India's Answer http://eac.gov.in/aboutus/chspe/55GLOBALIZATION%20AND%20CHALLENGES%20BEFORE%20INDIA-Gen%20(single%20space).doc; Balakrishnan, Chandrasekaran. 2004. Impact of Globalisation on Developing Countries and India. http://economics.about.com/od/globalizationtrade/l/aaglobalization.htm; Mehrotra, Rajen. 2005. Globalisation and its Impact on Indian Industry. ILO, Jan. 4, New Delhi. http://www.gmupolicy.net/india/GlobalCompetitiveBusinessNov04.ppt#8.

Global Meltdown[155]

The global financial meltdown which erupted due to the speculative bubble of the housing market (sub-prime crisis) in the US in 2008 had shaken up both the developed and the developing countries.

The US economy was straining under the housing bubble since 2006 due to the rising default rate on sub-prime and Adjustable Rate Mortgages (ARM). The banks had encouraged potential home owners to buy high loans with the belief that they would be able to pay-back quickly, but neglected the interest rates. From mid-2007, interest rates had begun to rise and housing prices witnessed downward trend. During the housing boom, Mortgage Backed Securities (MBS) and Collateralized Debt Obligations (CDO) were used whose value were derived from mortgage payments and housing prices. However, the decline in housing prices spelled the trouble for major global financial institutions which had borrowed and heavily invested in sub-prime MBS which reported huge losses. Defaults and losses on other types of loans also increased. These financial maladies had eroded the financial capacity of the banking system and caused huge drain of wealth from the consumers.

Global meltdown of such an enormous size erupted not only due to the weakness of the systems and regulations of global economy, but also due to crisis in leadership. Leaders who were unable to gauge such crisis were blinded by greed, avoided uncertainties, and lacked vision. Self-interest caused harm to all the stakeholders.

Major and well-established financial institutions like Lehman Brothers, Freddie and Fannie, Citigroup, Merill Lynch, etc. in the USA collapsed, and financial institutions around the world were shaken. This global economic crisis was considered to be the worse compared to the 1980's economic crisis. The negative aspect of globalization is that the world economy is integrated; any downturn or tumult in any nation would have its repercussions on all the nations. According to Nobel Laureate Joseph Stiglitz (2009), this global meltdown affected all the countries directly through shakeout of the financial markets, i.e. financial inflow into the market decreased leading to problem in accessing finance in developing countries, fall in exports, decline in remittances, and impact on labor force/employment (both native and immigrant). Countries across the world are, even after three years, striving to recover from the aftereffects of this global meltdown.

Impact on Organizations Organizations were caught off the guard due to this uncertain event. Factors like a volatile financial market, extreme volatility of the world economy, and collapsed world trade affected developing countries adversely despite having disciplined systems and regulations in place. Late 2008 and the almost the whole year of 2009 was gloomy. Indian organizations were affected due to economic stagnation, adverse impact on exports, cut on consumers' spending power, and financial pressures. These factors propelled corporates, financial institutions, SMEs (Small and Medium Enterprises), etc. to take drastic measures like putting on hold investments in new projects, cutting down on production capacity, laying off employees, cutting down on perks and incentives to employees, etc. in order to survive through the recessionary period. Global meltdown caused corporates to undergo financial, emotional and security turmoil. Retrenchment/lay-off has further aggravated the problem of unemployment in India and in other countries across the globe.

Impact on People Employees were the most panicked across industries. Many organizations took drastic steps, like retrenchment, lay-offs, remuneration cut; put on hold incentives, etc. which caused panic, psychological break-downs, and employees were in the dark about the future. Those employees, whose jobs were not secured, constantly underwent fears of losing their job. Along with panic and insecurities related to the job, they were worried about responses from their family and the society.

Impact on Society Impact on society due to the global meltdown has been dreadful. The issues which have worsened in post-global meltdown are inequality, jealousy, attitude of hoarding for oneself and family, security threats, emotional and psychological insecurity, cutting down or stoppage on semi-luxurious and luxurious expenses, saving or investing in financial or non-financial resources, for securing the future.

Implications for Organizational Behavior From the global economic crisis what emerges is that, organizations need to have value-based and responsible leadership who takes care of not only of their positions in the organization but also of other stakeholders, i.e. customers, employees and the society at large. It has indeed caused large-scale unemployment, financial loss, loss of status and self-esteem and personal hardships causing anxiety, frustration and depression.

Increasing Workforce Diversity

Walk into the offices of Verizon Communications and you can quickly see that the communications service giant reflects the communities it serves. Minorities make up 35 percent of Verizon's 230,000 employees and 29 percent of management positions. Women represent 42 percent of its workforce and 38 percent of management positions. Verizon's inclusive culture has won awards from numerous organizations and publications representing Hispanics, African-Americans, gays and lesbians, people with disabilities, and other groups. "A commitment to diversity is as much about good business as it is about doing the right thing," says Magda Yrizarry, vice president of workplace culture, diversity and compliance for Verizon. "As a company, we serve some of the most diverse markets; so from our leadership to our frontline employees, we understand and value diversity."[156]

Verizon Communications is a model employer and a reflection of the increasing diversity of people living in the United States and in many other countries. The description of Verizon's diversity refers to **surface-level diversity**–the observable demographic and other overt differences in people, such as their race, ethnicity, gender, age, and physical capabilities. Surface-level diversity has changed considerably in the United States over the past few decades. People with nonwhite or Hispanic origin represent one-third of the American population, and the percentage is projected to increase substantially over the next few decades. Within the next 50 years, one in four Americans will be Hispanic, 14 percent will be African American, and 8 percent will be of Asian descent. By 2060, people with European non-Hispanic ethnicity will be a minority.[157] Many other countries are also experiencing increasing levels of racial and ethnic diversification.

surface-level diversity The observable demographic or physiological differences in people, such as their race, ethnicity, gender, age, and physical disabilities.

Diversity also includes differences in the psychological characteristics of employees, including personalities, beliefs, values, and attitudes.[158] We can't directly see this **deep-level diversity,** but it is evident in a person's decisions, statements, and actions. One illustration of deep-level diversity is the different attitudes and expectations held by employees across generational cohorts.[159] *Baby boomers*–people born between 1946 and 1964–seem to expect and desire more job security and are more intent on improving their economic and social status. In contrast, *Generation-X* employees–those born between 1965 and 1979–expect less job security and are motivated more by workplace flexibility, the opportunity to learn (particularly new technology), and egalitarian and "fun" organizations. Meanwhile, some observers suggest that *Generation-Y* employees (those born after 1979) are noticeably self-confident, optimistic, multitasking, and more independent than even Gen-X co-workers. These statements certainly don't apply to everyone in each cohort, but they do reflect the dynamics of deep-level diversity and shifting values and expectations across generations.

deep-level diversity Differences in the psychological characteristics of employees, including personalities, beliefs, values, and attitudes.

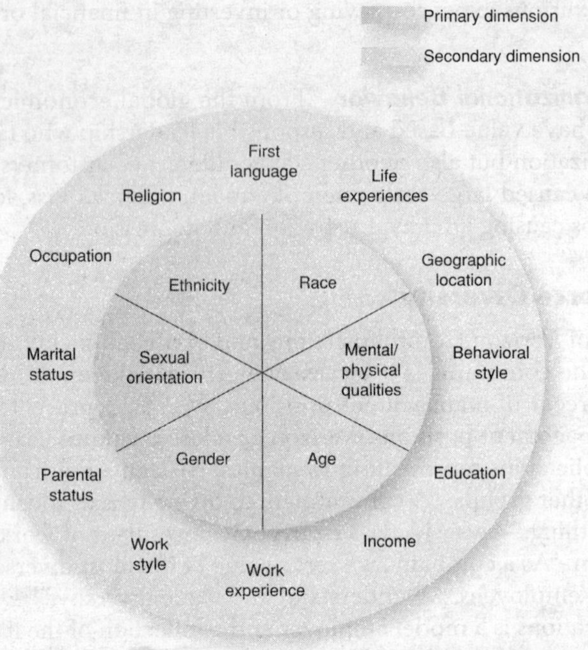

Sources: Adapted from M. Loden, *Implementing Diversity* (Chicago: Irwin, 1996); S. Bradford, "Fourteen Dimensions of Diversity: Understanding and Appreciating Differences in the Workplace," in J. W. Pfeiffer (Ed.), *1996 Annual: Volume 2 Consulting* (San Diego: Pfeiffer and Associates, 1996), pp. 9–17.

Exhibit 1.6 *Primary and Secondary Dimensions of Workforce Diversity*

Consequences of Diversity Diversity presents both opportunities and challenges in organizations.[160] In some circumstances and to some degree, diversity can become a competitive advantage by improving decision-making and team performance on complex tasks. Studies suggest that teams with some forms of diversity (particularly occupational diversity) make better decisions on complex problems than do teams whose members have similar backgrounds. A few studies also report that companies that win diversity awards have higher financial returns, at least in the short run.[161] This is consistent with anecdotal evidence from many corporate leaders, namely, that having a diverse workforce improves customer service and creativity. For instance, PepsiCo estimates that one-eighth of its revenue growth is directly attributable to new products inspired by diversity efforts.[162]

Based on this evidence, the popular refrain is that workforce diversity is a sound business proposition. Unfortunately, it's not that simple. There is growing evidence that most forms of diversity offer both advantages and disadvantages.[163] Teams with diverse employees usually take longer to perform effectively. Diversity brings numerous communication problems as well as "faultlines" in informal group dynamics. Diversity is also a source of conflict, which can lead to lack of information sharing and, in extreme cases, morale problems and higher turnover.

Whether or not workforce diversity is a business advantage, companies need to make it a priority because surface-level diversity is a moral and legal imperative. Ethically, companies that offer an inclusive workplace are, in essence, making fair and just decisions regarding employment, promotions, rewards, and so on. Fairness is a well-established influence on employee loyalty and satisfaction.

"Diversity is about fairness; we use the term inclusive meritocracy," says Ann M. Limberg, president of Bank of America New Jersey. "What it does for our workforce is build trust and assures that individual differences are valued."[164] Our main point here is that workforce diversity is the new reality and that organizations need to adjust to this reality both to survive and to experience its potential benefits for organizational success.

Workforce Diversity in India

Walk into the offices of Verizon Communications around the United States and you can quickly see that the communications service giant reflects the communities it serves. Minorities make up 30 percent of Verizon's workforce of 200,000 and 18 percent of top management positions. Women represent 43 percent of its workforce and 32 percent of top management. Verizon's inclusive culture has won awards from numerous organizations representing Hispanics, African Americans, gays and lesbians, people with disabilities, and other groups. You can also see this diversity at Google. Its California headquarters employs people from most countries, which creates a challenge for the company's restaurant staff. "It's a global community here, and you can't just go with one kind of cuisine," says Charlie Ayers, the chef who created Google's kitchens. Even Google's smaller European operations in Dublin, Ireland, employ people from more than 40 nationalities.[165]

surface-level diversity Observable demographic or physiological differences in people, such as their race, ethnicity, gender, age, and physical disabilities.

Verizon Communications and Google are model employers that reflect the increasing diversity of people living in the United States and in many other countries. Workforce diversity takes many forms. The primary categories in Exhibit 1.6 represent **surface-level diversity,** which include observable demographic or physiological differences in people, such as their race, ethnicity, gender, age, and physical disabilities. This most obvious form of diversity has changed considerably in the United States over the past few decades.

People with nonwhite or Hispanic origin represent one-third of the American population, and this fraction is projected to increase substantially over the next few decades. The Hispanic population recently replaced African Americans as the second largest ethnic group. Within the next 50 years one in four Americans will be Hispanic, 14 percent will be African American, and 8 percent will be of Asian descent. By 2060 non-Hispanic whites will be a minority[166]. Many other countries are also experiencing increasing levels of racial and ethnic diversification. Meanwhile women now account for nearly half of the paid workforce in the United States–more than double the participation rate a few decades ago. Gender-based shifts continue to occur within many occupations. For example, women represent 59 percent of accountants in the United States, compared to just 17 percent in 1960. Similarly, the percentage of women enrolled in medical schools has jumped from 9 percent in 1970 to almost 50 percent today[167].

Deep-Level Diversity Surface-level diversity is the most obvious and easiest-to-measure form of diversity. In contrast, **deep-level diversity** represents differences in the psychological characteristics of employees, including personalities, beliefs, values, and attitudes. We can't directly see deep-level diversity, but it is evident in a person's decisions, statements, and actions. The secondary dimensions of diversity shown in Exhibit 1.6 don't represent psychological differences, but they and the primary dimensions influence deep-level diversity. Religion and geographic location, for example, influence a person's personal values. Education and work experience shape a person's beliefs and attitudes on a variety of issues. An individual's personal wealth (income), parental status, and other factors influence personal needs and preferences.

Emerging Employment Relationships

Globalization and increasing workforce diversity have produced two contrasting changes in relationships between employers and employees: (1) aligning the workplace with emerging workforce expectations and (2) increasing workforce flexibility to increase organizational competitiveness.

work–life balance Minimizing conflict between work and nonwork demands.

Aligning the Workplace with Emerging Workforce Expectations Work–life **balance**–minimizing conflict between work and nonwork demands–was seldom mentioned a couple of decades ago. Most employees assumed that they would put in long hours to rise up through the corporate ladder. Asking the boss to accommodate nonwork responsibilities and interests was almost a sign of betrayal[168]. But as Connections 1.1 describes, work–life balance has become one of the most important factors in the employment relationship. Probably the main reason is that technology has turned many former 9-to-5 jobs into 24/7 employment, so people are pushing back with demands for more work–life balance. A second reason is that two-income families put more demands on both partners to provide time for household duties. Gen-X/Gen-Y expectations represent a third factor. Young people today are less willing to completely wrap themselves in their jobs, possibly because they witnessed the problems with this workaholic style in their baby boomer parents.

Along with providing more work–life balance, companies are adjusting to emerging workforce expectations of a more egalitarian workplace by reducing hierarchy and replacing command-and-control management with facilitating and teaching-oriented leaders. Gen-X/Gen-Y employees also want to work in companies that make a difference, which may explain why employers are paying more attention to serving the community rather than just shareholders–a trend we'll discuss in more detail later in this chapter.

Younger employees tend to view the workplace as a community where they spend a large part of their lives (even with work–life balance), so many expect opportunities for more social fulfillment and fun. Again, several companies are making this shift in the employment relationship. Google is a sparkling example. The company's Googleplex (headquarters) in Mountain View, California, "resembles a glimmering playground for 20-somethings," says one observer. The building is outfitted with lava lamps, exercise balls, casual sofas, foosballs, pool tables, workout rooms, video games, a restaurant with free gourmet meals, and a small pool where swimmers exercise against an artificial current. Beach volleyball matches are held in the courtyard, and roller hockey games are in the parking lot. Google executives had to remind some employees that making the Googleplex their permanent residence was against building code regulations[169].

Increasing Workforce Flexibility As some companies are aligning employment practices with emerging workforce expectations, they are also demanding more flexibility from employees to remain responsive to globalization and other sources of turbulence. This increased flexibility occurs partly through **employability,** in which employees are expected to manage their own careers by anticipating future organizational needs and developing new competencies that match those needs[170]. From this

employability
An employment relationship in which people perform a variety of work activities rather than hold specific jobs, and are expected to continuously learn skills that will keep them employed.

perspective, organizations are customers, and employees keep their jobs by continuously developing new competencies for the future and performing a variety of work activities over time. Furthermore, employability shifts the burden of this adaptability to employees rather than employers, although the latter are expected to offer the resources and opportunities to assist in the process. "I think people are starting to understand the concept of lifetime employability rather than lifetime employment," says Rich Hartnett, global staffing director at aerospace manufacturer Boeing. "It's a good idea to stay current with what's out there and take personal responsibility for our own employability.[171]"

contingent work
Any job in which the individual does not have an explicit or implicit contract for long-term employment, or one in which the minimum hours of work can vary in a nonsystematic way.

Contingent Work Along with employability, companies are making more use of **contingent work** to increase workforce flexibility. Contingent work includes any job in which the individual does not have an explicit or implicit contract for long-term employment, or one in which the minimum hours of work can vary in a nonsystematic way. This employment relationship includes anyone with temporary or seasonal employment, freelance contractors (sometimes called "free agents"), and temporary staffing agency workers. By some estimates more than 15 percent of the U.S. workforce is employed in some sort of contingent work arrangement. Some experts predict that this trend will continue.

Why has contingent work increased? One reason is that it allows companies to reduce costs by more closely matching employment levels and competencies with product or service demands. This is particularly apparent in service industries, where casual work is most common. It is also the preferred employment relationship for "free agents" with high-demand skills who enjoy a variety of interesting assignments. At the same time, research suggests that contingent workers potentially have higher accident rates as well as lower performance and loyalty. However, these outcomes depend on the type of contingent workers (for example, "free agent" contractors versus new hires on temporary status) as well as whether contingent workers are separated from, or interact regularly with, permanent staff. Another concern is that permanent employees may feel injustice against their employers if contingent workers are treated as second-class citizens[172].

Virtual Work

Rush hour isn't much of a rush for Tan Swee Hoong. She enjoys breakfast with her three children, heads them off to school, then walks from the kitchen to her study. There the relocation manager at Hewlett-Packard's offices in Singapore checks e-mail and uses the telephone to connect with teammates on her work projects[173]. Tan Swee Hoong's daily routine is an example of **virtual work,** whereby employees use information technology to perform their jobs away from the traditional physical workplace. Tan's variation of virtual work, called *telecommuting* or *teleworking,* involves working at home rather than commuting to the office. Virtual work also includes employees connected to the office while on the road or at clients' offices.

virtual work
Work practices whereby employees use information technology to perform their jobs away from the traditional physical workplace.

Telecommuting is still rare in most Asian countries, making Tan Swee Hoong more of a pioneer than a typical employee in that region. It is somewhat more common in Japan, where 6 percent of employees telecommute. To ease traffic congestion and air pollution, the Japanese government wants to increase that figure to 20 percent by 2010. Various surveys estimate that around 20 percent of Americans work at home at least one day each month. In some firms telecommuting and other forms of virtual work are the norm rather than the exception. For instance, nearly 50 percent of employees at Sun Microsystems complete some of their work from home, cafés, drop-in centers, or clients' offices. More than two-thirds of the employees at Agilent Technologies engage in virtual work some or all of the time[174].

Some research suggests that virtual work, particularly telecommuting, potentially reduces employee stress by offering better work–life balance and dramatically reducing time lost through commuting to the office. AT&T estimates that by avoiding daily travel, telecommuters reduce pollution and are about 10 percent more productive than before they started working from home. Nortel Networks reports that 71 percent of its U.K. staff feels more empowered through virtual work arrangements. Others point out that virtual work reduces the cost of office space and reduces traffic congestion[175].

Against these potential benefits, virtual workers face a number of real or potential challenges[176]. Although telecommuting is usually introduced to improve work–life balance, family relations may suffer rather than improve if employees lack sufficient space and resources for a home office. Some virtual workers complain of lack of recognition, although virtual work does not seem to undermine career progression or performance ratings. Social isolation is another common complaint, particularly among virtual workers who rarely visit the office. Virtual work is clearly better suited to people who are self-motivated, organized, can work effectively with broadband and other technology, and have sufficient fulfillment of social needs elsewhere in their life. Virtual work also functions better in organizations that evaluate employees by their performance outcomes rather than by "face time."

virtual teams
Teams whose members operate across space, time, and organizational boundaries, and who are linked through information technologies to achieve organizational goals.

Virtual Teams Another variation of virtual work occurs in **virtual teams:** cross-functional groups that operate across space, time, and organizational boundaries with members who communicate mainly through information technology[177]. Virtual teams exist when some members telecommute, but also when team members are located on company premises at different sites around the country or world. Teams have varying degrees of virtualness, depending on how often and how many team members interact face-to-face or at a distance. Currently a flurry of research activity is studying the types of work best suited to virtual teams and the conditions that facilitate and hinder their effectiveness. As with telecommuting, some people are also better suited than others to virtual team dynamics. Chapter 10 will examine these virtual team issues in detail.

Organization's Growth with Inclusiveness[178]

Inclusive growth has become a buzzword in recent years across economies of the world and amongst various stakeholders. Research and Development, debates, consultations, initiatives, etc. are being aggressively undertaken in the area of inclusive development/inclusive growth by federal institutions/organizations, industries, corporate bodies, MSMEs (Micro, Small and Medium Enterprises) regulatory bodies and international organizations.

> According to the World Bank's report, inclusive growth is all about, "lifting the pace of growth and to enlarge the size of the economy, while providing level playing field for investment and to increase productive opportunities"[179].

Inclusive growth/development is possible only through cooperation amongst the stakeholders of an economy. Effective inclusive growth is possible when there is inclusion at social, financial, economic and developmental level for all communities. Corporate bodies are one of the stakeholders who have crucial role in inclusive growth of an economy. These corporate bodies need to be inclusive organizations, to be enablers of inclusive growth.

In India, there are organizations like the Tatas and Birlas, which have been practicing inclusive growth/development since decades, even before it became a buzzword amongst the corporate bodies. No longer can an organization sustain on the goal of profitability only. It needs to consider the growth of other stakeholders too. Organizations need to awaken their hearts and souls, and connect it with their minds for sustainable growth and development. The core of an organization to contribute in inclusive growth lies in the fact that how inclusive an organization is.

Leadership, Value and Cultural Aspects

An organization which pursues or intends to pursue inclusive growth depends on leadership, values framework, and inclusive culture.

Leadership Leader of an organization is the role model for all employees and they look upto him/her. The leadership of an organization pursuing or intending to pursue need to propagate, endorse and practice inclusive growth, e.g. Ratan Tata, Chairman of Tata Group, Kumaramangalam Birla, Chairman of Aditya Birla Group, Azim Premji, Chairman, Wipro, etc.

Values It should have pluralistic value framework that gives due respect to a variety of cultural values which exist in the organization due to diversified workforce and strives to modify its values and norms to continuously pursue inclusiveness.

Inclusive Culture According to Pless and Maak[180], the principles of building an inclusive culture are: principle of recognition (emotional, solidarity, legal and political recognitions), reciprocal understanding, standpoint plurality and mutual enabling, trust, and integrity. Principle of recognition is to recognize differences but also includes looking for the common bond in emotional solidarity, political, and legal aspects. Reciprocal understanding means to be familiar with each other, and to be open and able to communicate. Standpoint plurality and mutual enabling means in multi-cultural and diversified organization, there should be openness to hear all voices—both of majority and minority—and through deliberations find common approach on the concerned issue or topic. Trust can be built over a period of time through continuous nurturing and it is crucial in building an inclusive culture. Integrity can be developed through moral reliability, consistency and quality of moral self-governance.

However, there are challenges in building and sustaining inclusive culture. These include challenging existing value systems, mindsets, habits and to bring change to embedded ways in thinking and behavioral aspects, to question the dominating thinking styles, to challenge hierarchical leadership thoughts, and openly reveal teamwork barriers.

Transformational Phases towards Inclusive Organization

An organization intending to build an inclusive culture undergoes the following transformation phases: Phase 1: To raise awareness and create understanding on inclusive culture and open for reflection; Phase 2: To develop a vision focused on inclusion; Phase 3: To rethink on concepts and principles of management; and Phase 4: Acclimatize the HR systems and processes to inclusive culture. Exhibit 1.7 gives a diagrammatic representation of the stages of transformation.

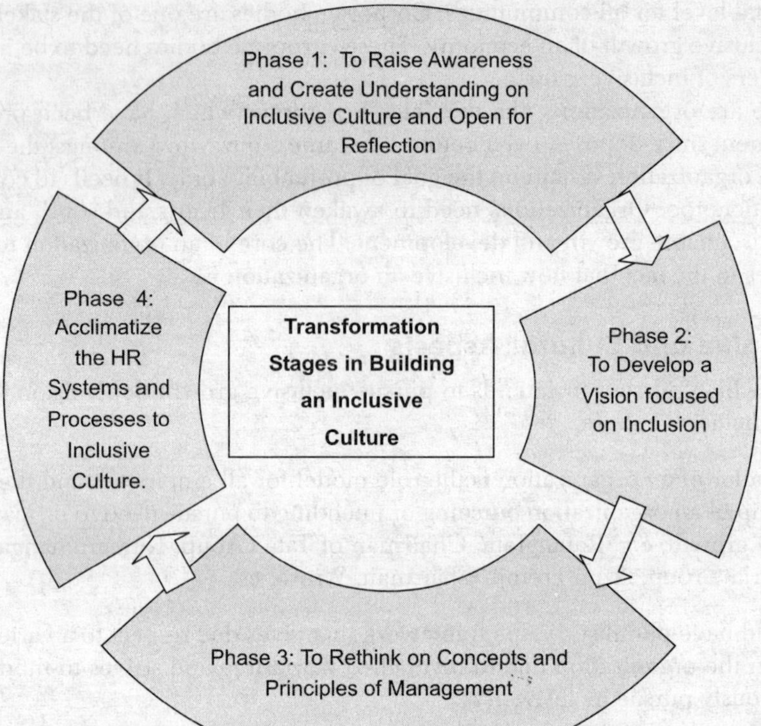

Exhibit 1.7 *Stages of Transformation*

Source: Adapted from Pless and Maak (2004), *Building an Inclusive Diversity Culture: Principles, Process and Practice, Journal of Business Ethics*, 54: 129–147, 2004.

Affinity Groups as Enablers Affinity groups are those which are formed based on commonalities among members of an organization and these include communities of people who share ethnicity, gender, sexual orientation or other aspects. The members of an affinity group face similar issues and challenges and come together for mutual support. Affinity groups can be crucial for organizations in their efforts towards an inclusive-culture organization, to better understand the diversified workforce, accessibility to each group/community for equal opportunities, giving ear to each of the diversified voices, access to information, productive links with co-workers and management, opportunity to contribute and innovate, and opportunity to advance in professional arena. Formation of an affinity group undergoes: Awareness creation for both the organization and the respective group/community, followed by affiliation, i.e. community building and connecting, access, i.e. through networking and advancement which can be provided through training and education. Affinity groups play the role of advocates, connectors, and communicators and enable organization to competitively leverage on diverse strengths of its members towards inclusiveness and sustainable growth.

Organizations intending to bring in a culture of inclusion need to identify and leverage on environmental and internal pressures. The initial drivers can be legal, moral and economic aspects to give an impetus to diversity along with inclusiveness. The managers and change agents need to put across competitive edge that can be gained by including diversity and inclusion. The impact of such a change on groups, inter-group relations, individual reaction and communication within the organization

Stakeholders / Actions	Organizations	Individuals	Diversity and Inclusion Practitioners
Actions to enable Gender Inclusion	Discuss, educate and create awareness on flexibility and flexi careers Identify jobs/careers which are flexible Advocate through men and women practicing flexi work arrangements.	Need to communicate about flexi-work arrangements, Understand implications career opportunities and progression.	Identify jobs/careers which can be flexible considering the industry and environment in which the organization operates, Create enablers, Create training programs and message to educate leaders, executives and people, Creates measures to understand the effectiveness of flexi work, Work with regulators to understand statutory guidelines.
Actions to enable Differently Able	To create policies, practices, and procedures, Organizational readiness at infrastructure and emotional level, Identifying jobs suitable for them and the career paths, learning opportunities, Engage external organization for better understanding, Sensitizing across all levels, Focus on incremental change.	Develop and polish skills, Abled employees need to work with differently abled themselves.	Role of conscience keeper of the organization, Work upon getting leadership and financial support, Diversity and inclusion training, Start on pilot basis Choose the appropriate manager
Actions to enable LGBT (Lesbian Gay, Bisexual and Transgender)	Commitment from the top leadership, Training to all employees to overcome prejudice and stereotypes, sensitizing and create positive workplace.		

Source: Adapted from Accenture (2010), 'Key Actions' in Future Forward: Inclusion and Diversity for a High Performance Nation', http://microsite.accenture.com/vaahini/Documents/pdf/Inclusion-and-diversity-Brochure.pdf, accessed on 1/2/2010.

Exhibit 1.8 *Measures to Integrate Inclusion and Diversity*

needs to be understood both, the adverse effects and to capitalize upon the positives. An initiative of diversity change should include demographic, cultural and political elements for sustainable diversity change.

Changing Nature of Work[181]

Penetration of information technology (IT) in the workplace has changed the dynamics of work, and has led to continuous change. The world is becoming closer with the help of technology, which has opened up opportunities and also brought challenges for both the organization and its human resource. Competition is on the increase; an organization faces it from within the industry as well as from unexpected quarters. Post global meltdown of 2008, organizations have become cautious. In the past, organizations grew in stable environment, but over the years uncertainty has made the environment unpredictable and sometimes turbulent. The organization, to some extent, can sustain through adaptability.

> "Work will become less routine, characterized by increased volatility, hyper-connectedness, 'swarming' and more," said Tom Austin, Vice President and Gartner fellow.[182]

Change in the nature of work has been fuelled by changes at the workplace. The factors include globalization, economic and social uncertainties, unpredictable business environment, workforce diversity, constant technological upgradation, competition, etc. Due to globalization, organizations have been expanding their operations across countries. Therefore, employees are required to understand the new cultures, government regulations, markets and business scenario and the people. There is an increasing concern regarding change in demographics, i.e. GenX and GenY form the largest proportion of employees. While working population is aging in most countries in Europe and the US, in India over 65% of the population is below the age of 35 which is often referred to as its demographic dividend[183]. The number of women employees have increased at workplaces, thus enabling them to manage their dual roles at work and at home effectively. Organizations have introduced flexi hours and provision of support systems like crèche, personal services like bill and school fess deposit, etc. Intercultural skills are gaining importance as globalization has increased movement of people across countries, and many expatriates are part of the workforce. Updating or honing new skills has become crucial. These skills include self-development skills, cross-cultural communication and etiquettes, new marketing techniques, and cross-cultural adaptation skills. Employees are becoming techno-nomads and are required to use technology extensively—i-phone, i-pads, internet, video-conferencing, webinars, con calls, etc. to make optimum utilization of resources, leveraging technologies to produce the best output.

Features of Changing Nature of Work According to a study by Gartner, the changes expected in nature of work over the next few years include de-routinization of work, work swarms, weak links, working with the collective, work sketch-ups, spontaneous work, simulation and experimentation, pattern sensitivity, hyperconnected and individual workspace.

De-routinization of work means each individual would have their own uniqueness in analytical or interactive contribution which would result in discovery, innovation, team work, leadership, selling and learning. This uniqueness cannot be automated which each individual would bring to the work place. Importance would be given to collective or team work.

Within team work, there is an emergence of *swarming trend* wherein individuals known or unknown, or from within or outside the organization come together to attack a problem or opportunity and quickly disperse. This is an agile response in unplanned action requirements and has displaced structured or bureaucratic conditions. Networking across professional, personal and social spaces has become crucial for individuals to survive in the workplace.

The organization also needs to *work collectively with informal groups* outside the organization who can have an impact on its performance. The managers need to identify such external collective and key people through whom market intelligence can be collected and also who would be enablers in various business strategies. The nonroutine process would be highly informal. Emphasis would be on *sketch-ups.* Though now organizations attempt to capture the criteria followed in decision-making, over the years standard patterns won't be followed. This means structured way of decision-making or the pattern to follow frameworks would be replaced with simple sketch-ups.

Spontaneity would increase, i.e. being proactive at work and seeking out for new opportunities, new models and designs.

Encouraging *simulation and experimentation* at workplace would be on rise, considering the ever changing and increasing usage of technologies. This would lead to development of a large number of dimensional virtual representations from a variety of data. People would interact and juggle with the data, manipulate it on various parameters and reshape the virtual world according to their visualization.

Pattern sensitivity becomes important, especially in the context of volatile business environment where the focus is on disruptive change. Groups would be created to identify, understand and evaluate divergent emerging patterns and suggest ways to exploit the opportunities emerging from it or to protect the organization.

Hyper networking/connectedness is increasing across organizations through various channels and an organization is unable to control these. Through this connectivity, there would be rush for more work from both informal and formal relationships and it would impact the way people work, and role of IT in supporting this work would be important.

Employees would be on the move *24 × 7* as they would be connected with people who they may or may not know across countries in different time zones. People won't need large physical space either at the workplace or at home. They would be equipped with gadgets easy to handle, carry and operate and work from the comforts of home. The lines between personal, professional and family life would slowly disappear and demands from each of the sphere would overlap. Individuals would need to manage this complexity to maintain work-life balance. Individuals would be faced with stress due to information overload and constant movement at work, which may also impact their performance if not appropriately managed.

Other Aspects of Changing Work[184] At present individuals have the option to work either as *consultant or employee or agent or part-time employee.* This trend will increase depending on the talent of the individual, need of the company and opportunity and growth for future.

Face-to-Screen interactions would increase, saving time, money and also contributing towards betterment of environment and saving upon resources.

No more superannuation, i.e. employees would continue to work till it is suitable for them.

Socially oriented approaches would be crucial in every aspect of the workplace.

Greater Transparency is increasingly required in organizations regarding employees, decision-making and business transactions.

Cultural Adjustment is becoming crucial, with increase in workforce diversity and employees taking up foreign postings/assignments. It is vital for organizations operating at international levels to train their employees in cross-cultural skills and to adopt appropriate strategies to survive and thrive in the global context.

Change in role of HR – The role of HR professionals is no longer limited to HR function, but now they are supposed to be strategic business partners. They have knowledge about the business of the organization, and take up pivotal tasks relating to management of culture, change management, need-based training and development along with the traditional role they used to perform.

Ethics and social responsibility of an organization are gaining importance among employees and other stakeholders. These aspects would be given significant weightage for monetary and other incentives and benefits given to employees.

Challenge of employee retention is keeping organizations on tenterhooks due to increasing competition. Current and future employees would no longer be loyal to one organization for lifetime. HR needs to constantly explore creative ways to attract and retain skilled and talented workforce.

Issues of Different Timezone Work Culture

Globalization and liberalization has raised many opportunities along with the challenges for organizations. Organizations have spread their wings across various countries which lie in different time zones. According to research studies[185], the following challenges and issues have emerged in the context of different timezones:

Readiness to Collaborate Readiness of individuals spread across a country or countries to collaborate and participate with other individuals from different cultures and nations. Aspects to be considered include whether each of the individual possesses skills to collaborate and whether the organizational culture encourages collaboration. Alignment between goals of collaborating and incentive schemes is crucial for the success of collaboration/s.

Promptness to adopt Technologies Technology savvy level of both the individual and organization is vital, especially in the context of geographically distributed work. There are a variety of technologies available and new technologies are being rolled out to assist geographically distributed work. However, if there is limitation on the part of an employee or the organization, it would obstruct the efficiency of work. Organizations need to be equipped with support systems to train individuals in handling new technologies efficiently.

Commonality Working with multi-cultural, multi-disciplinary and dispersed workforce requires a basis of commonality in terms of knowledge and vocabulary. This is most challenging when it comes to collaborative work, spread across a distance. So, training in language, culture, communication etiquettes, work etiquettes, etc. is not only essential, but also stressful for employees. Along with work responsibilities, they have to learn, understand and practice additional matters which are integral to the job. This leads to stress and takes toll on psychological, physical and emotional facets of an individual.

Characteristics of Work Characteristics of work needs to be assessed to know its feasibility in long-distance and different timezone work environment. This would require rich communication.

Management of the Organization and Decision-Making Process Culture, leadership and management style of an organization has an impact on distributed work environment. Leadership would send clear messages, and decision-making would need to be transparent, fair and clear.

Coordinating Different Timezones Coordination is a challenge when individuals in a collaboration are dispersed and located in different time zones. Employees would be in different points in their diurnal rhythms.

Cultural Issues Cultural issues would be at three levels: organizational cultural differences, cultural differences within a country and cross-national cultural differences. Juggling culture issues at these different levels is mindboggling for an organization and it is highly sensitive which can have long-term impact on its performance and growth.

Building and Maintaining Trust Building and maintaining trust in multi-cultured and multi-disciplinary collaboration, spread geographically is an ongoing and consistent process. Organizations need to have a support system to handle aspects of trust building.

Impact of Mergers and Acquisitions

Mergers and Acquisitions (M&As) have been worldwide phenomena during the last few decades. Some M&As have been fruitful while others have met with fallout. The initial concerns for many organizations have been strategic, financial or operational side of mergers. However, the human side involved in M&As is gaining importance in the recent years. The human side of M&As needs to be understood from psychological, social and cultural perspectives. The psychological perspective looks into impact of M&A on an individual's stress level, coping mechanism and commitment level.[186] The social perception includes group dynamics, group membership, social comparison and status[187]. The cultural perspective considers the whole organization and cultural clashes which erupt during M&A processes.

Psychological Perspective The employees of an organization whether from the one which is to be acquired or from the one which is the acquirer assess an M&A scenario based on the information and context provided to them. They would assess cultural similarity, their own position in the deal structure, impact on their job, etc. to make sense of the M&A deal. Whenever an M&A deal is proposed, employees of the organization undergo anxiety regarding their job, career path and they experience uncertainty and conflicts regarding their roles. If these aspects are not dealt with appropriately, these result in low productivity, job dissatisfaction, self-centered behavior, mental and physical illness and lack of motivation. Organizations can touch upon psychological perspective of its human resources through top-down communication, two way communication, social support, encourage participation in decision making, train managers to empathize with employees, constant and consistent communication, clarification regarding roles and responsibilities, golden parachutes, and thereby speed up the M&A process[188].

Social Perspective An individual is concerned about impact of M&A on his/her identity within the organization at professional level and among work groups as well as at social level, i.e. within the society. M&A deal can have either positive or negative impact on group dynamics, group membership, social comparison and status. If the social perspective is not handled properly, it would lead to loss of identity of an individual, give rise to grief and anger, resistance to change, inter-group bias, conflicts and non-compliant behaviors/actions. The social perspective can be handled by organizations through disengagement efforts, to assess the strengths of existing identities and to frame attractive new identities, foster cross-organizational arrangements and activities[189].

An employee's position in a deal structure has a strong influence on his/her perceptions regarding in-group power. Employees on the buying side perceive significantly higher levels of power. However, higher perceived power does not reduce perceived uncertainty, but has direct impact on an employee's satisfaction level with the merger and his/her intention to leave the organization. Perception regarding uncertainty in an M&A has significant impact on the employees' reaction.

Higher levels of uncertainty have direct relation with higher anticipated conflict. Intention to leave, willingness to collaborate and satisfaction levels are low, and vice-versa. Organizations when plan to undertake an M&A, they need to have tailor-made communication for each group of employees in accordance with the context of the deal and their position in the deal structure. The classification of groups can be on dimensions like functional, hierarchical, unitwise and acquired-acquirer perspective. The communication should clearly address the condition of the respective group in order to reduce uncertainty. Moreover, improvement of power position of certain group of employees may reduce their intention to leave. However, equal importance need to given to in-group power of groups as each of the group may be equally important. Perceived power has positive relationship with the employees' satisfaction with M&A. So, organizations need to monitor and enhance employee satisfaction and this would have positive impact on organizational citizenship behaviors.

Cultural perspective Culture is crucial for any M&A deal. An individual's perception about cultural match between two organizations enables him/her make sense of the deal. Cultural clash potential affects employees' perception regarding cultural similarity. There is an inverse relationship between *cultural clash potential* and *cultural similarity.* Aspects of cultural adjustment need to be considered; otherwise it would lead to acculturative stress and resistance, inter-organizational conflicts and tension and cultural clash. This can be taken care of through cultural due-diligence, developing multiculturalism, encouraging inter-cultural learning, and by creating awareness about behaviors and thoughts which fuels clashes. In the context of international M&A deals, national cultures also need to be taken care of. Through various researches, it has been found that there is no relation between national cultural differences and employee resistance to M&A[190]. This could be because organizations easily adjust to national cultures, e.g. by making operations methods adaptable to local environment. Organizational cultural differences increase post-acquisition conflicts due to in-group and out-group categorization[191]. Conflicts increase post-acquisition because acquisition partners are likely to be less accepting and more attentive to cultural differences and have low inclination towards building a new shared culture. There are acculturation factors which need to be considered, i.e. partner's attractiveness, organization culture preservation and multiculturalism. When two organizations in a M&A deal have mutual attraction towards each other it would have positive impact on post-acquisition, preservation of new shared organization culture. Managing diversified workforce plays key role in managing cultural aspects. In order to reduce potential cultural clash during communication to different group of employees, importance should be given to communicate cultural similarities. Communicating cultural similarities may significantly reduce uncertainty and negative attitudes associated with M&A.

Employees' perception on uncertainty, power position in the deal and cultural similarity result into collaboration (satisfaction) or intention to leave (conflict). Assumption should not be made that employees' who are in a better position in the deal structure, (i.e. acquirer's side) would experience lower uncertainty because announcement of the merger may still create a great deal of uncertainty for them. Organizations along with strategic and financial aspects should also concurrently take care of the human resource which is crucial to make an M&A deal successful. Uncertainty is more painful than bad news and poor communication creates uncertainty[192]. So, engaging and reassuring employees through effective and consistent communication is essential. Level of organizational virtues, i.e. empathy and warmth towards employees has direct relation to employees who perceive job insecurity, especially in times of uncertainty. Empathy and warmth given by the organization ensures emotional attachment and loyalty of key employees in turbulent times.

Downsizing

> "Employee downsizing is a planned set of organizational policies and practices aimed at workforce reduction with the goal of improving firm's performance."[193]

Downsizing, as a management tool, is not new. Organizations have been using it, whenever the need arose, in order to remain competitive. However, its magnitude has crippled and shaken up industries, employees, and various stakeholders, especially in the context of global meltdown in 2008. Massive lay-offs were witnessed in the United States and significant employee reduction were experienced in Ireland, Japan, China, Hong Kong, Taiwan, India, etc. Downsizing has a far-reaching impact and implications both economically and socially. In recent years, various terms like redundancies, headcount reductions, hyperboles, smart sizing, canning are used which actually means downsizing[194]. A research by Guthrie and Dattta (2008), which studied 122 firms that had been engaged in downsizing, has revealed that though firms consider downsizing to be a quick fix to improve performance, these efforts have failed to achieve the desired economic goals.

Reasons Leading to Downsizing

Macro Economic Factors Macro economic factors include environmental and institutional pressures, i.e. regulatory, cognitive and normative, which influence restructuring. Environmental factors include industry deregulation, economic peaks, industry adopting downsizing, industry culture, privatization, reduction in state subsidies, deregulated wages, declining industry conditions, changes in industry employment, etc.[195]

Industry factors Industry factors include the type of industry in which the company operates, demand scenario, technological and capital intensity and competition[196].

Organizational factors Organizational factors include the organization's performance, its market position, business strategy, nature and status of merger and acquisition, HR policies, competencies of the employees, diversification, characteristics of Board of Directors, ownership structure and leadership. Highly leveraged firms which experienced short-term distress exhibited greater tendency to adopt employee downsizing. Research studies have found mutual trust between top management team and employees have negative association with employee downsizing. Current ration and inventory levels have positive association with announcement of lay-off. Decrease in market share, shareholder value and ownership status were positively associated with downsizing. Changes in an organization's strategy, adoption of new technologies, decline in productivity, decline in profits, hostile M&As, etc. lead to employee downsizing[197].

Consequences of Downsizing

Financial Consequences Through various research studies it has been found that majority of the firms have not been able to gain desired levels of efficiency, effectiveness, productivity and profitability[198].

Organizational Consequences Employees form a major chunk of an organization's operating costs, so it seems rational and natural response to downsize and aim to increase shareholder value. Few have been able to gain positive outcomes. However, majority of the downsized firms fell short of their goals[199].

Human Consequences In downsizing three types of people are affected—the executioner, employees who are downsized and employees who survive. The most prominent symptom is survivor syndrome. Brockner[200] asserts downsizing causes variety of psychological problems like guilt, positive inequity, anger, relief, and job insecurity. These psychological attributes have the potential to impact surviving employees' work behaviors and attitudes.

Modern Downsizing Practices Two widely adopted downsizing practices include Stealth downsizing and Non-selective downsizing.

Stealth Downsizing It is an approach under which managers are not permitted to discuss about downsizing openly, that is through meetings, memos or emails, due to the fear of negative publicity. This is to avoid negative press at all costs, but cerates an atmosphere of distrust and unease among employees. Organizations lay off their employees quietly[201].

Nonselective Downsizing Through empirical research evidence, it has been found that nonselective downsizing is practiced by large firms in particular. Nonselective downsizing means announcement of large scale lay-offs, and closure of plants. Lehman Brothers closed its Indian operations in 2008, after it filed for bankruptcy.

Research yields that the factors important to make downsizing successful are flexibility, innovativeness and creativity of the organization, improved communication with stakeholders who have doubts about downsizing. Trust and empowerment play a crucial role in such gripping situations.

ANCHORS OF ORGANIZATIONAL BEHAVIOR KNOWLEDGE

Globalization, increasing workforce diversity, and emerging employment relationships are just a few of the trends that challenge organizations and make OB knowledge more relevant than ever before. To understand these and other topics, the field of organizational behavior relies on a set of basic beliefs or knowledge structures (see Exhibit 1.9). These conceptual anchors represent the principles on which OB knowledge is developed and refined.

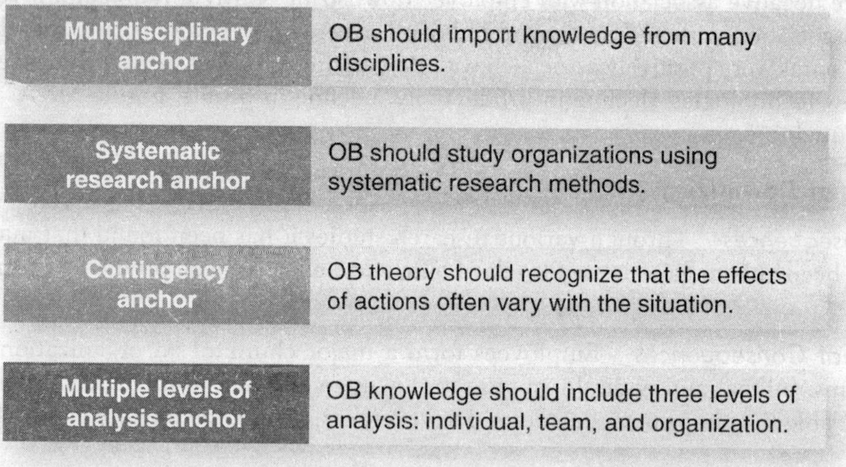

Exhibit 1.9 *Anchors of Organizational Behavior Knowledge*

The Multidisciplinary Anchor

Organizational behavior is anchored around the idea that the field should develop from knowledge in other disciplines, not just from its own isolated research base. For instance, psychological research has aided our understanding of individual and interpersonal behavior. Sociologists have contributed to our knowledge of team dynamics, organizational socialization, organizational power, and other aspects of the social system. OB knowledge has also benefited from knowledge in emerging fields such as communications, marketing, and information systems. Some OB experts have recently argued that the field suffers from a "trade deficit"–importing far more knowledge from other disciplines than is exported to other disciplines. Although this may be a concern, organizational behavior has thrived through its diversity of knowledge from other fields of study.[202]

The Systematic Research Anchor

A critical feature of OB knowledge is that it should be based on *systematic research,* which typically involves forming research questions, systematically collecting data, and testing hypotheses against those data. Appendix A at the end of this book details some of the features of the systematic research process, including hypotheses, sampling, research design, and qualitative methods research. When research is founded on theory and conducted systematically, we can be more confident that the results are meaningful and useful for practice. This is known as **evidence-based management**–making decisions and taking actions based on research evidence.

evidence-based management
The practice of making decisions and taking actions based on research evidence.

Evidence-based management makes sense, yet OB experts are often amazed at how frequently corporate leaders embrace fads, consulting models and their own pet beliefs without bothering to find out if they actually work![203] There are many reasons that people have difficulty applying evidence-based management. One explanation is that corporate decision-makers are bombarded with so many ideas from newspapers, books, consultant reports, and other sources that they have difficulty figuring out which ones are based on good evidence. Another reason why people ignore evidence and embrace fads is that good OB research is necessarily generic; it is rarely described in the context of a specific problem in a specific organization. Managers therefore have the difficult task of figuring out which theories are relevant to their unique situation. A third reason is that many consultants and popular book writers are rewarded for marketing their concepts and theories, not for testing to see if they actually work. Indeed, some management concepts have become popular (and are even found in some OB textbooks!) because of heavy marketing, not because of any evidence that they are valid. Finally, as you will learn in Chapter 3, people form perceptions and beliefs quickly and tend to ignore evidence that their beliefs are inaccurate.

The Contingency Anchor

People and their work environments are complex, and the field of organizational behavior recognizes this by stating that a particular action may have different consequences in different situations. In other words, no single solution is best in all circumstances.[204] Of course, it would be so much simpler if we could rely on "one best way" theories, in which a particular concept or practice has the same results in every situation. OB experts do search for simpler theories, but they also remain skeptical about "surefire" recommendations; an exception is somewhere around the corner. Thus, when faced with a particular problem or opportunity, we need to understand and diagnose the situation and select the strategy most appropriate *under those conditions.*[205]

The Multiple Levels of Analysis Anchor

This textbook divides organizational behavior topics into three levels of analysis: individual, team, and organization. The *individual level* includes the characteristics and behaviors of employees as well as the thought processes that are attributed to them, such as motivation, perceptions, personalities, attitudes, and values. The *team level* of analysis looks at the way people interact. This includes team dynamics, communication, power, organizational politics, conflict, and leadership. At the *organizational level,* we focus on how people structure their working relationships and on how organizations interact with their environments.

Although an OB topic is typically pegged into one level of analysis, it usually relates to multiple levels.[206] For instance, communication is located in this book as a team (interpersonal) process, but we also recognize that it includes individual and organizational processes. Therefore, you should try to think about each OB topic at the individual, team, and organizational levels, not just at one of these levels.

Chapter Summary

Organizational behavior is the study of what people think, feel, and do in and around organizations. Organizations are groups of people who work interdependently toward some purpose. Although OB doesn't have a specific career path, it offers knowledge and skills that are vitally important to anyone who works in organizations. OB knowledge also has a significant effect on the success of organizations. This book takes the view that OB is for everyone, not just managers.

An important aspect of OB is that it is a subject which is applied in the real-world. This book looks at the entire globe for context, and lays a special emphasis on India and Asian countries.

Organizational effectiveness is a multidimensional concept represented by four perspectives: open systems, organizational learning, high-performance work practices, and stakeholder. The open-systems perspective says that organizations need to adapt to their external environment and configure their internal subsystems to maximize efficiency and responsiveness. For the most part, the other perspectives of organizational effectiveness are detailed extensions of the open-systems model. The organizational learning perspective states that organizational effectiveness depends on the organization's capacity to acquire, share, use, and store valuable knowledge. Intellectual capital is knowledge that resides in an organization, including its human capital, structural capital, and relationship capital. Effective organizations also "unlearn," meaning that they remove knowledge that no longer adds value.

The high-performance work practices (HPWP) perspective states that effective organizations leverage the human capital potential of their employees. Specific HPWPs have been identified, and experts in this field suggest that they need to be bundled together for maximum benefit. The stakeholder perspective states that effective organizations take into account how their actions affect others, and this requires them to understand, manage, and satisfy the interests of their stakeholders. This perspective incorporates values, ethics, and corporate social responsibility into the organizational effectiveness equation.

To be sustainable, businesses have to inculcate values like being responsible to the society, to the natural environment, and also drive-in key enablers like social entrepreneurship, employer branding and so on.

The five main types of workplace behavior are task performance, organizational citizenship, counterproductive work behaviors, joining and staying with the organization, and work attendance. These represent the individual-level dependent variables found in most OB research.

Three environmental shifts that are challenging organizations include globalization, increasing workforce diversity, and emerging employment relationships. Globalization refers to economic, social, and cultural connectivity with people in other parts of the world. Workforce diversity includes both surface-level and deep-level diversity. Three emerging employment relationship changes are demands for work–life balance, virtual work and culture.

Several conceptual anchors represent the principles on which OB knowledge is developed and refined. These anchors include beliefs that OB knowledge should be multidisciplinary and based on systematic research, that organizational events usually have contingencies, and that organizational behavior can be viewed from three levels of analysis (individual, team, and organization).

Key Terms

absorptive capacity
corporate social responsibility (CSR)
counterproductive work behaviors (CWBs)
deep-level diversity
ethics
evidence-based management
globalization
high-performance work practices (HPWPs)
human capital
intellectual capital
lean management
open systems
organizational behavior (OB)
organizational citizenship behaviors (OCBs)
organizational effectiveness
organizational efficiency
organizational learning
organizational memory
organizations
stakeholders
surface-level diversity
values
virtual work
work–life balance

Critical Thinking Questions

1. A friend suggests that organizational behavior courses are useful only to people who will enter management careers. Discuss the accuracy of your friend's statement.
2. A number of years ago, employees in a city water distribution department were put into teams and encouraged to find ways to improve efficiency. The teams boldly crossed departmental boundaries and areas of management discretion in search of problems. Employees working in other parts of the city began to complain about these intrusions. Moreover, when some team ideas were implemented, the city managers discovered that a dollar saved in the water distribution unit may have cost the organization two dollars in higher costs elsewhere. Use the open-systems perspective to explain what happened here.
3. After hearing a seminar on organizational learning, a mining company executive argues that this perspective ignores the fact that mining companies cannot rely on knowledge alone to stay in business. They also need physical capital (such as digging and ore-processing equipment) and land (where the minerals are located). In fact, these two may be more important than what employees carry around in their heads. Evaluate the mining executive's comments.
4. A common refrain among executives is "People are our most important asset." Relate this statement to any two of the four perspectives of organizational effectiveness presented in this chapter. Does this statement apply better to some perspectives than to others? Why or why not?
5. Corporate social responsibility is one of the hottest issues in corporate boardrooms these days, partly because it is becoming increasingly important to employees and other stakeholders. In your opinion, why have stakeholders given CSR more attention recently? Does abiding by CSR standards potentially cause companies to have conflicting objectives with some stakeholders in some situations?
6. Look through the list of chapters in this textbook, and discuss how globalization could influence each organizational behavior topic.
7. "Organizational theories should follow the contingency approach." Comment on the accuracy of this statement.
8. What does *evidence-based management* mean? Describe situations you have heard about in which companies have practiced evidence-based management, as well as situations in which companies have relied on fads that lacked sufficient evidence of their worth.

CASE STUDY 1.1

JERSEY DAIRIES, INC.

Jersey Dairies, Inc. faced increasing competition that threatened its dominant market share in the Pacific Northwest. Senior management at the 300-employee dairy food processing company decided that the best way to maintain or increase market share was to take the plunge into a quality management (QM) program. Jersey hired consultants to educate management and employees about the QM process, and sent several managers to QM seminars. A steering team of managers and a few employees visited other QM companies throughout North America.

To strengthen the company's QM focus, Jersey president Tina Stavros created a new position called vice-president of quality, and hired James Alder into that position. Alder, who previously worked as a QM consultant at a major consulting firm, was enthusiastic about implementing a complete QM program. One of Alder's first accomplishments was convincing management to give every employee in the organization several days of training in quality measurement (e.g., Pareto diagrams), structured problem solving, and related QM practices. Jersey's largely unskilled workforce had difficulty learning this material, so the training took longer than expected and another round was required one year later.

Alder worked with production managers to form continuous improvement (CI) teams–groups of employees who looked for ways to cut costs, time, and space throughout the work process. Although Alder was enthusiastic about CI teams, most supervisors and employees were reluctant to get involved. Supervisors complained that the CI teams were "asking too many questions" about activities in their department. Less than one-quarter of the production areas formed CI teams because employees thought QM was a fancy way for management to speed up the work. This view was reinforced by some of management's subsequent actions, such as setting higher production targets and requiring employees to complete the tasks of those who were absent from work.

To gain more support for QM, Jersey president Tina Stavros spoke regularly to employees and supervisors about how QM was their answer to beating the competition and saving jobs. Although these talks took her away from other duties, she wanted every employee to know that their primary objective was to improve customer service and production efficiency in the company. To encourage more involvement in the CI teams, Stavros and Alder warned employees that they must support the QM program to save their jobs. To further emphasize this message, the company placed large signs throughout the company's production facilities that said, "Our Jobs Depend on Satisfied Customers" and "Quality Management: Our Competitive Advantage."

Alder and Stavros agreed that Jersey's suppliers must have a strong commitment toward the QM philosophy, so Jersey's purchasing manager was told to get suppliers "on board" or find alternative sources. Unfortunately, the purchasing manager preferred a more collegial and passive involvement with suppliers, so he was replaced a few months later. The new purchasing manager informed suppliers that they should begin a QM program immediately because Jersey would negotiate for lower prices in the next contracts and would evaluate their bids partly based on their QM programs.

Twenty months after Jersey Dairies began its QM journey, Tina Stavros accepted a lucrative job offer from a large food products company in the Midwest. Jersey Dairies promoted its vice-president of finance, Thomas Cheun, to the president's job. The board of directors was concerned about Jersey's falling profits over the previous couple of years and wanted Cheun to strengthen the bottom line. Although some CI teams did find cost savings, these were mostly offset by higher expenses. The company had nearly tripled its training budget and had significantly higher paid-time-off costs as employees took these courses. A considerable sum was spent on customer surveys and focus groups. Employee turnover was higher, mainly due to dissatisfaction with the QM program. Just before Stavros left the company, she received word that several employees had contacted the Commercial Food Workers Union about organizing Jersey's nonunion production workforce.

A group of suppliers asked for a confidential meeting in which they told Cheun to reconsider the QM demands on them. They complained that their long-term relationships with Jersey were being damaged and that other dairies were being more realistic about price, quality, and delivery requirements. Two major suppliers bluntly stated that they might decide to end their contracts with Jersey rather than agree to Jersey's demands.

Almost two years after Jersey Dairies began QM, Thomas Cheun announced that James Alder was leaving Jersey Dairies, that the position of vice-president of quality would no longer exist, and that the company would end several QM initiatives begun over the previous two years. Instead, Jersey Dairies, Inc. would use better marketing strategies and introduce new technologies to improve its competitive position in the marketplace.

Discussion Questions

1. What perspective of organizational effectiveness did Tina Stavros and James Alder attempt to apply in this case? Describe how specific elements of that perspective related to their interventions.

2. Explain what went wrong in this case, using one or more of the other perspectives of organizational effectiveness.

Source: Steven L. McShane, © 1995.

CASE STUDY 1.2

WORKING FROM HOME—IT'S IN THE DETAILS

BusinessWeek

Roads leading to Microsoft's headquarters in Redmond, Washington, simply weren't designed to handle the 35,000 commuters who report for work there each day. The daily gridlock has become so acute that it nearly caused Washington State's governor to miss his own speech at the software maker on a recent morning. Microsoft has figured out how to tackle the commuter crisis: it has introduced a program to get more staff telecommuting, either working from home or other off-site locales.

About 14% of the U.S. workforce gets its job done at a home office more than two days per week. That's up from 11% in 2004, and will be around 17% in another year or two. But the growth of telecommuting has also awakened many companies to the reality that not everyone is ready for virtual work. Companies also need to make adjustments to the way they operate in order for telecommuting to have lasting benefits.

This *BusinessWeek* case study discusses the issues that companies are facing with the rising tide of telecommuting, as well as the strategies these organizations are applying to overcome these obstacles. Read the full text of this *BusinessWeek* article at www.mhhe.com/mcshane5e, and prepare for the discussion questions below.

Discussion Questions

1. Identify and discuss the main problems or concerns mentioned in this case study regarding telecommuting. In your opinion, do most of these problems originate with the company or the employee?
2. Describe the characteristics of people who adjust more easily to telecommuting. How can companies identify these employees or develop others to be better prepared for telecommuting?

Source: R. King, "Working from Home: It's in the Details," *BusinessWeek,* 12 February 2007, p. 9.

TEAM EXERCISE 1.3

HUMAN CHECKERS

PURPOSE This exercise is designed to help students understand the importance and application of organizational behavior concepts.

MATERIALS None, but the instructor has more information about the team's task.

INSTRUCTIONS

1. Form teams with eight students. If possible, each team should have a private location where team members can plan and practice the required task without being observed or heard by other teams.

2. All teams receive special instructions in class about their assigned task. All teams have the same task and have the same amount of time to plan and practice the task. At the end of this planning and practice, each team will be timed while completing the task in class. The team that completes the task in the least time wins.
3. No special materials are required or allowed (see rules below) for this exercise. Although the task is not described here, students should learn the following rules for planning and implementing the task:
   a. You cannot use any written form of communication or any props to assist in the planning or implementation of this task.
   b. You may speak to other students on your team at any time during the planning and implementation of this task.
   c. When performing the task, you can move only forward, not backward. (You are not allowed to turn around.)
   d. When performing the task, you can move forward to the next space, but only if it is vacant. In Exhibit 1, the individual (dark circle) can move directly into an empty space (light circle).
   e. When performing the task, you can move forward two spaces if that space is vacant. In other words, you can move around a person who is one space in front of you to the next space if that space is vacant. (In Exhibit 2, two people occupy the dark circle, and the light circle is an empty space. A person can move around the person in front to the empty space.)
4. When all teams have completed their task, the class will discuss the implications of this exercise for organizational behavior.

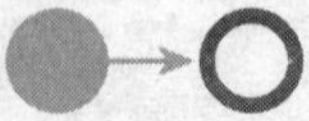

Exhibit 1

Exhibit 2

Discussion Questions

1. Identify organizational behavior concepts that the team applied to complete this task.
2. What personal theories of people and work teams were applied to complete this task?
3. What organizational behavior problems occurred, and what actions were (or should have been) taken to solve them?

CLASS EXERCISE 1.4

DIAGNOSING ORGANIZATIONAL STAKEHOLDERS

PURPOSE This exercise is designed to help you understand how stakeholders influence organizations as part of the open-systems anchor.

MATERIALS Students need to select a company and, prior to class, retrieve and analyze publicly available information over the past year or two about that company. This may include annual reports, which are usually found on the websites of publicly traded companies. Where possible, students should also scan full-text newspaper and magazine databases for articles published over the previous year about the company.

INSTRUCTIONS The instructor may have students work alone or in groups for this activity. Students will select a company and investigate the relevance and influence of various stakeholder groups on the organization. Stakeholders can be identified from annual reports, newspaper articles, website statements, and other available sources. Stakeholders should be rank-ordered in terms of their perceived importance to the organization.

Students should be prepared to present or discuss their rank ordering of the organization's stakeholders, including evidence for this ordering.

Discussion Questions

1. What are the main reasons why certain stakeholders are more important than others for this organization?
2. On the basis of your knowledge of the organization's environmental situation, is this rank order of stakeholders in the organization's best interest, or should specific other stakeholders be given higher priority?
3. What societal groups, if any, are not mentioned as stakeholders by the organization? Does this lack of reference to these unmentioned groups make sense?

SELF-ASSESSMENT 1.5

IT ALL MAKES SENSE?

PURPOSE This exercise is designed to help you comprehend how organizational behavior knowledge can help you to understand life in organizations.

INSTRUCTIONS (*Note:* This activity may be done as a self-assessment or as a team activity.) Read each of the statements below and circle whether each statement is true or false, in your opinion. The class will consider the answers to each question and discuss the implications for studying organizational behavior.

Due to the nature of this activity, the instructor will provide the answers to these questions. There is no scoring key in Appendix B.

1.	True	False	A happy worker is a productive worker.
2.	True	False	Decision-makers tend to continue supporting a course of action even though information suggests that the decision is ineffective.
3.	True	False	Organizations are more effective when they prevent conflict among employees.
4.	True	False	It is better to negotiate alone than as a team.
5.	True	False	Companies are more successful when they have strong corporate cultures.
6.	True	False	Employees perform better without stress.
7.	True	False	The best way to change people and organizations is by pinpointing the source of their current problems.
8.	True	False	Female leaders involve employees in decisions to a greater degree than do male leaders.
9.	True	False	The best decisions are made without emotion.
10.	True	False	If employees feel they are paid unfairly, nothing other than changing their pay will reduce their feelings of injustice.

SELF-ASSESSMENT 1.6

IS TELECOMMUTING FOR YOU?

Some employees adapt better than others to telecommuting (also called *teleworking*) and other forms of virtual work. This self-assessment measures personal characteristics that seem to relate to telecommuting, and therefore it provides a rough indication of how well you would adapt to telework. The instrument asks you to indicate how much you agree or disagree with each of the statements provided. You need to be honest with yourself to get a reasonable estimate of your telework disposition. Please keep in mind that this scale considers only your personal characteristics. Other factors, such as organizational, family, and technological systems support, must also be taken into account.

2

PART

Individual Behavior and Processes

Yasmeen Youssef's self-confidence was a bit shaky when she and her husband moved from Egypt to Canada a few years ago. "I was worried no one would take a chance on me, would believe in me," she recalls. But any self-doubts slowly disappeared after taking an entry-level job with Fairmont Hotels & Resorts corporate offices in Toronto. "Everything changed when I started working at Fairmont," says Youssef, who is now on Fairmont's human resource team and recently trained new staff in Cairo. "I can't believe the amount of value, care, respect everyone has extended to me."

Fairmont Hotels has excelled as North America's largest luxury hotel operator by hiring people such as Yasmeen Youssef (shown here) with the right values and personality and then nurturing their self-concept and cross-cultural competencies.

As North America's largest luxury hotel operator, Fairmont discovered long ago that one of the secret ingredients for employee performance and well-being is supporting the individual's self-concept. "People want to feel valued and they stay where they feel valued," says Carolyn Clark, Fairmont's senior vice president of human resources. Clark also points out that Fairmont is able to nurture this talent by selecting the best, which means hiring people with the right values and personality for superb customer service. "We believed that we could train the technical skills—that's the easy part," Clark explained a few years ago. "What we can't train is the service orientation. We just can't put people in the training program and say they are going to come out smiling if that is not inherent in them."

Along with hiring people with the right values and personality and nurturing their self-concept, Fairmont is developing staff to work effectively in a multicultural world. Sean Billing is a case in point. The economics graduate had been working as Fairmont's director of rooms in Chicago when he casually asked his boss whether the hotel chain could use his skills and knowledge elsewhere. Soon after, Billing was offered a position in Kenya, bringing Fairmont's new properties in the African country up to world-class standards through training and technology without losing the distinctive Kenyan character. Billing jumped at the opportunity, but he also recognizes the challenge of inculcating Fairmont's deep values of customer service, environmentalism, and empowerment into another culture. "It's a little bit of hotel culture shock . . . things are quite different here," he says.[1]

2

Individual Behavior, Personality, and Values

Learning Objectives

After reading this chapter, you should be able to:

1. Describe the four factors that directly influence voluntary individual behavior and performance.
2. Summarize the "Big Five" personality traits in the five-factor model and discuss their influence on organizational behavior and its bearing on attrition and retention of employees.
3. Define *personality* and discuss what determines an individual's personality characteristics.
4. Describe self-concept in terms of self-enhancement, self-verification, and self-evaluation. Compare and contrast the Indian and Western perspectives of self.
5. Explain how social identity theory relates to a person's self-concept.
6. Distinguish personal, shared, espoused, and enacted values and explain why value congruence is important.
7. Summarize five values commonly studied across cultures. Explore the Indian values at the workplace.
8. Explain how moral intensity, ethical sensitivity, and the situation influence ethical behavior.

What makes Fairmont Hotels & Resorts a successful company? There is no single explanation, but this opening vignette reveals that North America's largest luxury hotel company applies many of the theories and practices discussed in this chapter. It hires people with the right personality traits and values, trains them well, and nurtures their self-concept. As a global enterprise, Fairmont also ensures that its staff members develop cross-cultural competencies.

This chapter concentrates our attention on the role of the individual in organizations. We begin by presenting the MARS model, which outlines the four direct drivers of individual behavior and results. Next, we introduce the most stable aspect of individuals–personality–including personality development, personality traits, and how personality relates to organizational behavior. We then look at the individual's self-concept, including self-enhancement, self-verification, self-evaluation, and social identity. The latter part of this chapter examines another relatively stable characteristic of individuals: their personal values. We look at types of values, issues of value congruence in organizations, cross-cultural values, and ethical values and practices.

Learning Objectives

After reading this section, you should be able to:

1. Describe the four factors that directly influence voluntary individual behavior and performance.

MARS Model of Individual Behavior and Performance

For most of the past century, experts in psychology, sociology, and, more recently, organizational behavior have investigated the direct predictors of individual behavior and performance.[2] One of the earliest formulas was *performance* = *person* × *situation,* where *person* includes individual characteristics and *situation* represents external influences on the individual's behavior. Another frequently mentioned formula is *performance* = *ability* × *motivation*. Sometimes known as the "skill-and-will" model, this formula elaborates two specific characteristics within the person that influence individual performance. Ability, motivation, and situation are by far the most commonly mentioned direct predictors of individual behavior and performance, but in the 1960s researchers identified a fourth key factor: role perceptions (the individual's expected role obligations).[3]

Exhibit 2.1 illustrates these four variables–motivation, ability, role perceptions, and situational factors–which are represented by the acronym *MARS*.[4] All four factors are critical influences on an individual's voluntary behavior and performance; if any one of them is low in a given situation, the employee would perform the task poorly. For example, motivated salespeople with clear role perceptions and sufficient resources (situational factors) will not perform their jobs as well if they lack sales skills and related knowledge (ability). Let's look at each of these four factors in more detail.

Employee Motivation

motivation
The forces within a person that affect his or her direction, intensity, and persistence of voluntary behavior.

Motivation represents the forces within a person that affect his or her direction, intensity, and persistence of voluntary behavior.[5] *Direction* refers to the path along which people engage their effort. People have choices about where they put their effort; they have a sense of what they are trying to achieve and at what level of quality, quantity, and so forth. In other words, motivation is goal-directed, not random. People are motivated to arrive at work on time, finish a project a few hours early, or aim for many other targets. The second element of

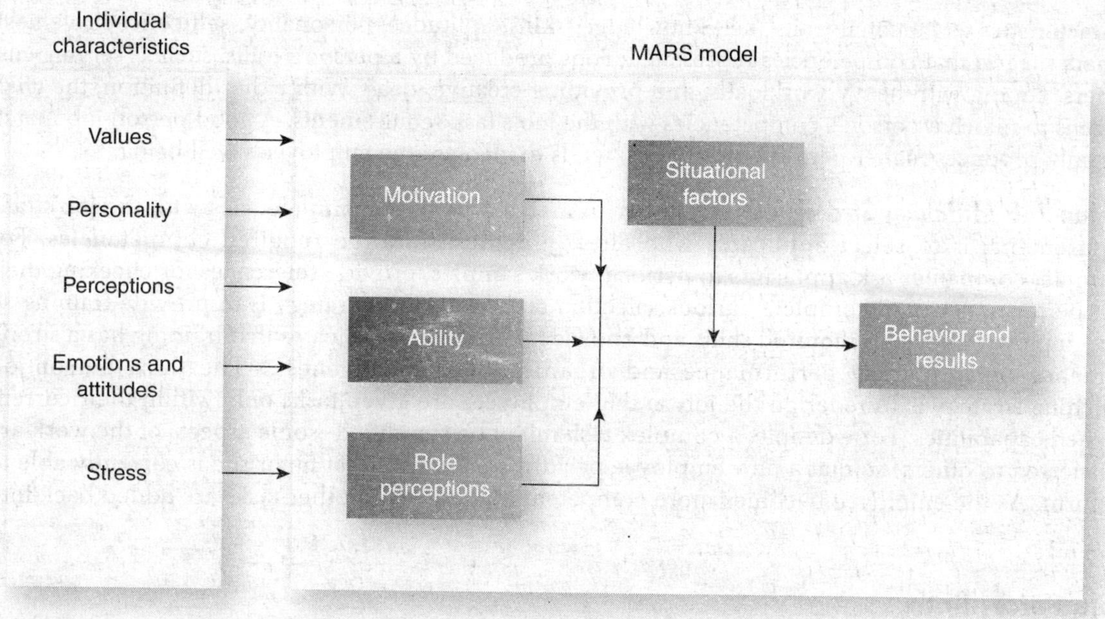

Exhibit 2.1 *MARS Model of Individual Behavior and Results*

motivation, called *intensity,* is the amount of effort allocated to the goal. Intensity is all about how much people push themselves to complete a task. For example, two employees might be motivated to finish their project a few hours early (direction), but only one of them puts forth enough effort (intensity) to achieve this goal.

Finally, motivation involves varying levels of *persistence,* that is, continuing the effort for a certain amount of time. Employees sustain their effort until they reach their goal or give up beforehand. Remember that motivation exists within individuals; it is not their actual behavior. Thus, direction, intensity, and persistence are cognitive (thoughts) and emotional conditions that directly cause us to move.

Ability

ability
The natural aptitudes and learned capabilities required to successfully complete a task.

Employee abilities also make a difference in behavior and task performance. **Ability** includes both the natural aptitudes and the learned capabilities required to successfully complete a task. *Aptitudes* are the natural talents that help employees learn specific tasks more quickly and perform them better. There are many physical and mental aptitudes, and our ability to acquire skills is affected by these aptitudes. For example, finger dexterity is an aptitude by which individuals learn more quickly and potentially achieve higher performance at picking up and handling small objects with their fingers. Employees with high finger dexterity are not necessarily better than others at first; rather, their learning tends to be faster and performance potential tends to be higher. *Learned capabilities* are the skills and knowledge that you currently possess. These capabilities include the physical and mental skills and knowledge you have acquired. Learned capabilities tend to wane over time when not in use.

competencies
Skills, knowledge, aptitudes, and other personal characteristics that lead to superior performance.

Aptitudes and learned capabilities are closely related to *competencies,* which has become a frequently used term in business. **Competencies** are characteristics of a person that result in superior performance.[6] Many experts describe these characteristics as personal traits (i.e., knowledge, skills, aptitudes, personality, self-concept, values). Others suggest that competencies represent actions produced by a person's traits, such as serving customers, coping with heavy workloads, and providing creative ideas. With either definition, the challenge is to match a person's competencies with the job's task requirements. A good person-job match not only produces higher performance; it also tends to increase the employee's well-being.

Person-Job Matching Strategies One way to match a person's competencies with the job's task requirements is to select applicants who already demonstrate the required competencies. For example, companies ask applicants to perform work samples, provide references for checking their past performance, and complete various selection tests. A second strategy is to provide training so that employees develop required skills and knowledge. Research indicates that training has a strong influence on individual performance and organizational effectiveness.[7] The third person-job matching strategy is to redesign the job so that employees are given tasks only within their current learned capabilities. For example, a complex task might be simplified–some aspects of the work are transferred to others–so that a new employee performs only tasks that he or she is currently able to perform. As the employee becomes more competent at these tasks, other tasks are added back into the job.

Role Perceptions

role perceptions
The extent to which people understand the job duties (roles) assigned to or expected of them.

Motivation and ability are important influences on individual behavior and performance, but employees also require accurate **role perceptions** to perform their jobs well. Role perceptions are the extent to which people understand the job duties (roles) assigned to them or expected of them. These perceptions are critical because they guide the employee's direction of effort and improve coordination with co-workers, suppliers, and other stakeholders. Unfortunately, many employees do not have clear role perceptions. According to one large-scale survey, most employees understand their organization's business goals, but only 39 percent know what to do in their own jobs to achieve those goals.[8]

The role perceptions concept has three components. First, employees have accurate role perceptions when they understand the specific tasks assigned to them, that is, when they know the specific duties or consequences for which they are accountable. This may seem obvious, but employees have been (unjustly) fired for failing to perform tasks that they didn't even know were part of their job duties. Second, people have accurate role perceptions when they understand the priority of their various tasks and performance expectations. This includes the quantity versus quality dilemma, such as how many customers to serve in an hour (quantity) versus how well the employee should serve each customer (quality). It also refers to properly allocating time and resources to various tasks, such as how much time a manager should spend coaching employees in a typical week. The third component of role perceptions is understanding the preferred behaviors or procedures for accomplishing the assigned tasks. This refers to situations in which more than one method could be followed to perform the work. Employees with clear role perceptions know which of these methods is preferred by the organization.

Situational Factors

Employees' behavior and performance also depend on how much the situation supports or interferes with their task goals. Situational factors include conditions beyond the employee's immediate control that constrain or facilitate behavior and performance.[9] Some situational characteristics–such as consumer preferences and economic conditions–originate from the external environment and,

Best Buy Sorts Out Role Perceptions for Black Friday It's 5 a.m. on Black Friday, and hundreds of eager shoppers are pouring through the doors of the Best Buy retail outlet in Columbia, Maryland, to grab up the advertised bargains. Fortunately, Best Buy's 225 employees in Columbia know what is expected of them on this extremely busy day after Thanksgiving. A huge floor plan in the back office has color-coded stickers marking where every staff member will be located; six green dots indicate where employees will stand outside to monitor and support customers who have lined up for hours. Many Best Buy stores held special rehearsals—complete with acting customers—during the week before Black Friday to help employees understand their roles and hone their customer service skills. For example, this photo shows customer assistance supervisor Aaron Sanford orchestrating a Black Friday practice run at a Best Buy store in Denver. "If you do it right, you're very profitable," advises Kevin McGrath, Best Buy's store manager in Columbia. McGrath explains that clear role perceptions are just as important for a retail outlet as for a winning sports team. "The [Baltimore] Ravens are successful because [the players] know what is expected of them," he says.[10]

consequently, are beyond the employee's and organization's control. However, other situational factors–such as time, people, budget, and physical work facilities–are controlled by people within the organization. Therefore, corporate leaders need to carefully arrange these conditions so that employees can achieve their performance potential.

The four elements of the MARS model–motivation, ability, role perceptions, and situational factors–affect all voluntary workplace behaviors and their performance outcomes. These elements are themselves influenced by other individual differences. In the remainder of this chapter, we introduce three of the most stable individual characteristics: personality, self-concept, and values.

Learning Objectives

After reading the next two sections, you should be able to:

2. Summarize the "Big Five" personality traits in the five-factor model and discuss their influence on organizational behavior and its bearing on attrition and retention of employees.
3. Define *personality* and discuss what determines an individual's personality characteristics.
4. Describe self-concept in terms of self-enhancement, self-verification, and self-evaluation. Compare and contrast the Indian and Western perspectives of self.
5. Explain how social identity theory relates to a person's self-concept.

TYPES OF INDIVIDUAL BEHAVIOR IN ORGANIZATIONS

People engage in many different types of behavior in organizational settings. Exhibit 2.2 highlights the five types of behavior discussed most often in organizational behavior literature: task performance, organizational citizenship, counterproductive work behaviors, joining and staying with the organization, and work attendance.

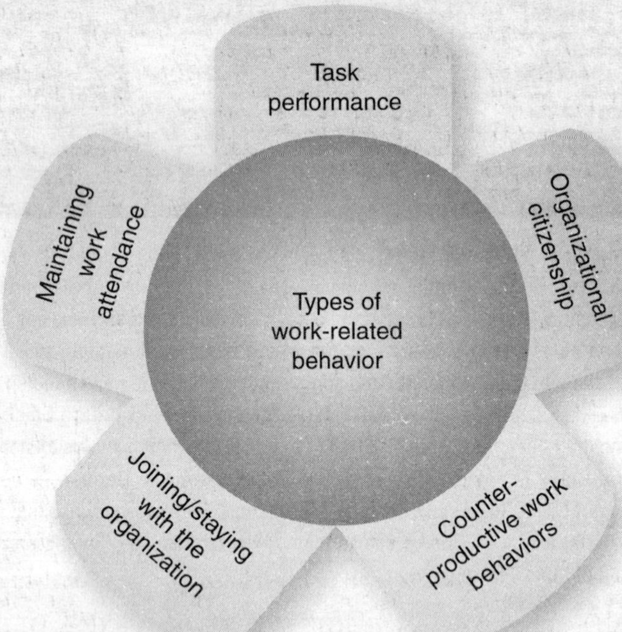

Exhibit 2.2 *Types of Work-Related Behavior*

Task Performance

Task performance refers to goal-directed behaviors under the individual's control that support organizational objectives. Task performance behaviors transform raw materials into goods and services or support and maintain technical activities.[11] For example, foreign exchange traders at Wachovia make decisions and take actions to exchange currencies. Employees in most jobs have more than one performance dimension. Foreign exchange traders must be able to identify profitable trades, work cooperatively with clients and co-workers in a stressful environment, assist in training new staff, and work on special telecommunications equipment without error. Some of these performance dimensions are more important than others, but only by considering all of them can we fully evaluate an employee's contribution to the organization.

Exhibiting Organizational Citizenship

One of the defining characteristics of engaged employees is that they perform beyond task-performance standards or expectations. "When employees become engaged, they develop a stronger conscientiousness about what they can do," explains Bill Erikson, vice chairman of consulting firm Kenexa. "They will go the extra step, or maybe even the extra mile, to support the interest of the organization." In short, engaged employees practice **organizational citizenship**. They help others without selfish intent, are actively involved in organizational activities, avoid unnecessary conflicts, perform tasks beyond normal role requirements, and gracefully tolerate impositions. Several factors described throughout this book explain why some employees are good organizational citizens and others are not. Later in this chapter, for example, we learn that people with a conscientiousness personality trait have higher organizational citizenship.[12]

organizational citizenship
Behaviors that extend beyond the employee's normal job duties.

Counterproductive Work Behaviors

Although organizations benefit from task performance and organizational citizenship, we also need to recognize that employees sometimes succumb to **counterproductive work behaviors (CWBs)**—voluntary behaviors that have the potential to directly or indirectly harm the organization. Organizational behavior experts have organized CWBs into five categories: abuse of others (insults and nasty comments), threats (threatening harm), work avoidance (tardiness), work sabotage (doing work incorrectly), and overt acts (theft). CWBs are not minor concerns. One recent study found that units of a fast-food restaurant chain with higher CWBs had a significantly worse performance, whereas organizational citizenship had a relatively minor benefit. Throughout this book we'll identify several ways to minimize counterproductive work behaviors, including better organizational justice (Chapter 5) and less workplace stress (Chapter 7), as well as the propensity of people with a political personality trait known as Machiavellianism to engage in CWBs (Chapter 12).[13]

counterproductive work behaviors (CWBs)
Voluntary behaviors that are potentially harmful to the organization's effectiveness.

Joining and Staying with the Organization

Task performance, organizational citizenship, and the lack of counterproductive work behaviors are obviously important; but if qualified people don't join and stay with the organization, none of these performance-related behaviors will occur. Attracting and retaining talented people is particularly important as worries about skills shortages heat up. For instance, a shortage of qualified truck drivers is the main factor restricting growth at Contract Freighters in Joplin, Missouri. "We have plenty of freight; we have plenty of trucks," says company president Herb Schmidt, but the "severe shortage" of qualified drivers is making it impossible to satisfy the growing customer base. Hotels in many parts of the United States are also struggling to find enough staff to keep up with demand. "We're woefully understaffed," says the owner of a St. Petersburg, Florida, resort that employs 265 people and still has 40 unfilled vacancies. "It's horrible."[14] Even Google, which is one of the most widely recognized employer "brands," is feeling the challenge in the war for talent. However, as Connections 2.1 describes, the California-based Internet search engine company has reduced some of its skills shortage through various guerilla recruiting tactics.

A reputable employer brand may attract qualified applicants, but the war for talent also includes ensuring that they stay with the company. Chapter 1 described how much of an organization's intellectual capital is the knowledge carried around in employees' heads. Organizations may try to document information about work processes, corporate values, and customer needs; but much of it remains in employees' heads. Consequently, retaining valued employees is a critical knowledge management strategy. The problem is that many employees don't plan on staying with their current employer very long. A few surveys report that between one-third and one-half of employees say they would change companies if offered a comparable job.[15]

job satisfaction
A person's evaluation of his or her job and work context.

Why do people quit their jobs? Traditionally, OB experts have identified low job satisfaction as the main cause of turnover. **Job satisfaction** is a person's evaluation of his or her job and work context (see Chapter 4). Employees become dissatisfied with their employment relationship, which motivates them to search for and join another organization with better conditions. Although job dissatisfaction builds over time and eventually affects turnover, the most recent opinion is that specific "shock events" need to be considered.[16] These shock events, such as a boss's unfair decision or a conflict episode with a co-worker, create strong emotions that trigger employees to think about and search for alternative employment.

Attrition and Employee-retention Strategies in India

Attrition does not always have a negative connotation. A healthy attrition rate in any industry is necessary for new ideas and innovation to flow in, as well as to facilitate the overall growth of the industry in terms of knowledge sharing. But, after a particular level, the same boon becomes a bane. There is another perspective regarding attrition specific to the BPO industry in India. It has had low cost, high quality labor advantage for lower-end business processes compared to other competitors, such as Philippines, South Africa, and Ireland. For companies to remain competitive, the cost has to be kept low. Therefore, if the tasks performed by an agent are standard and do not require added skills, there is no benefit in retaining a highly experienced employee. At the floor level operation, after minimal training, a non-experienced candidate can work with the same efficiency as a 2-3 years experienced employee. Hence, the industry players consider the present attrition as positive attrition because it is serving the industry by keeping the cost low. The primary reason for people leaving the low-end BPO is that the industry is viewed as a gap-filler occupation. The industry has been mainly dependent on youngsters who take out time to work, make money in the process, and also explore career options. Hence, for this group, BPO is never a long-term career but only a part-time job. The easy availability of BPO jobs is a source of easy money until there is another source of funding. Also, the unfriendly working conditions, late-night work shifts, and stressful nature of the job act as a deterrent for people to stick to this industry for long. In addition, the BPO jobs are not being taken with a positive spirit by the society at large. Surveys indicate that nearly 50 per cent leave the industry. Regarding the attrition between firms, the chief cause is the high demand for skilled resource as compared to the supply. Presently, there is no certified institute providing BPO specific training and education. The scarce resource in the market has lead to a widescale poaching and head hunting amongst the competitors for the common pool. Due to the immaturity prevalent in the industry, the industry lacks

2.1 CONNECTIONS

Google Goes Guerrilla in the War for Talent

To keep up with its blistering growth, Google needs to hire thousands of people in the United States each year. The California-based company that created the world's most popular Internet search engine is also expanding rapidly in India and many other countries. The problem is that Google can't find enough talent to keep up with its growth plans. "Can we hire the quality and quantity of people we want to? No," cofounder Sergey Brin admitted to several hundred investment analysts. "We're underinvesting in our business because of the limitations of hiring."

Google relies on guerrilla recruiting, including this innovative ad, to win the war for talent.

Fortunately Google has also become a master of guerrilla recruiting. Rather than passively waiting for applicants to reply to recruitment ads, Google actively and creatively seeks out talent. One successful tactic has been to host competitions such as "Code Jam," in which contestants around the world are challenged to write code to solve specific problems, then find ways to "break" the code that others have written. Winners in the final round of 100 contestants (out of thousands in the first round) receive up to $10,000, a trip to the Googleplex (Google headquarters), and a job offer.

A related form of guerrilla recruiting is to host internships. Google recently funded a "Summer of Code" event in which 410 college-level students (out of thousands who submitted proposals) received mentoring support from several partner organizations while writing open-source software code. Google paid a small stipend to mentors at the other organizations and $4,500 to students who completed their projects. Summer of Code gave Google (and the other mentoring firms) an inside track on high-quality applicants. "It was a way to start a dialogue with people around the world who might not necessarily be looking for a job—but might become a future employee," says Judy Gilbert, Google's staffing program director.

Even Google's recruitment ads take on a creative guerrilla twist. One example is the billboard (shown in the accompanying photo) and subway banners Google has created, luring curious commuters to follow a series of Web sites with math problems. Only those with top-notch math skills could decipher each puzzle, which eventually led to Google's website with an invitation to submit a résumé. "One thing we learned while building Google is that it's easier to find what you're looking for if it comes looking for you," said the Google Web page. "What we're looking for are the best engineers in the world. And here you are!"

Sources: "Google Entices Job Searchers with Math Puzzle," *NPR*, 14 September 2004; S. Olsen, "Google Recruits Eggheads with Mystery Billboard," *CNET News.com*, 9 July 2004; "Google Expansion Is Being Held Back by Hiring Process," *The Wall Street Journal*, 10 February 2005, p. B5; C. Hymowitz, "Busy Executives Fail to Give Recruiting Attention It Deserves," *The Wall Street Journal*, 21 November 2005, p. B1; V. Kopytoff, "How Google Woos the Best and Brightest," *San Francisco Chronicle*, 18 December 2005, p. A1; J. Puliyenthuruthel, "How Google Searches—for Talent," *BusinessWeek*, 11 April 2005; P.-W. Tam and K.J. Delaney, "Talent Search: Google's Growth Helps Ignite Silicon Valley Hiring Frenzy," *The Wall Street Journal*, 23 November 2005, p. A1; "Google Code Jam 2005" (Mountain View, California, 2005), http://www.google.com/codejam/ (accessed 1 March 2006).

mature HR processes such as human resource planning. Thus, to meet their unplanned needs, the firms resort to poaching employees working on similar projects in other firms. Attrition impacts business performance in more ways than is usually perceived, based on the HR perspective. It is an issue which affects organizational climate, morale, and motivation of employees, and impacts tangible aspects, such as shareholder return and value. In service industries, like the BPO and the IT/ITES, which are thriving, the workforce is young and dynamic. However, very high levels of job expectations, intense competition, and pressure to deliver has caused attrition. The psychological contracts that develop between the employees and the organization are, at best, transactional. There is no organizational commitment. Attrition, as a problem, is also seen as the origin of further dialogues about *talent management* and sourcing.[17]

Recent Trends in Attrition

Employee turnover is at an all-time high in Asia, according to a study by Hewitt Associates, a global human-resources services company. Organizations throughout the region experienced a 16% attrition rate in 2005, up from 14% in 2004 and 10% in 2003. According to a study,[18] the banking and finance sector saw the largest employee turnover at 25%, which is likely to have been brought on by stable economies, growing markets, and increased retail investor confidence. At 23%, attrition was also high in the outsourcing industry, which has experienced unprecedented levels of growth in the recent years. The lowest turnover was recorded in the manufacturing sector at 11%.

Across all industries, more than a third of the participating companies (36%) agreed that sales is their most vulnerable function with respect to employee turnover. As companies compete for new business and customers, organizations increasingly attempt to attract salespeople with strong incentive schemes.

From an employee perspective, turnover was highest at the professional/supervisor/technical level at 39% of total attrition and lowest among senior/top management at just 0.1% of the total attrition. Interestingly, attrition among employees identified as high performers was considerably lower than other employees, indicating that most organizations are successfully retaining their top performers. To what extent an employer is able to retain his colleagues is dependent on how well an organization integrates its people practices to its business objectives.

Attrition in BPOs in India

Attrition rates and retention have become a major threat and the biggest challenge for the human resource professionals of the BPO sector in India, which is one of the most rapidly growing sectors. The BPO industry, both voice based and nonvoice based, is grappling with the issues of high attrition rates and skill shortages. According to NASSCOM, the attrition rate for call centers (voice-based BPO's) is around 55-60%, whereas for other BPOs, it is around 15-20%. The reasons for attrition cited are repetitive and monotonous work, long working hours with little personal time, stress and physical strain, lack of professional growth opportunities, lack of conducive environment and interpersonal problems, offer of higher salary, and pursuing higher education. This not only adversely affects organizational productivity but also causes tremendous loss. According to an estimate, attrition cost is approximately 76% of the annual salary cost of low-end BPOs. As regards voice-based BPOs, it has been estimated to be 27% of the total operating costs.

One reason for attrition is 'poaching', which is weaning away experienced professionals by competitors by offering attractive perks and wages. Another reason is night shifts which is not appreciated socially in India. Moreover, the call-center jobs are treated as time-gap arrangements by most employees.

Thus, HR professionals need to come up with appropriate HR policies for the Indian BPO industry to attract and retain talent and create synergy between work and life. A lot is being done by the BPO industry by way of creating sophisticated work environment, and providing fun and entertainment, besides transport and other facilities to make the employees comfortable.

Employee Retention

Employee retention is a proactive action by organizations to retain their employees. It has been observed that employee loss results in loss of productivity, customer dissatisfaction, sagging morale of remaining employees, and increased cost of replacement. If one analyzes the question why employees leave, one would find that an organization spends a lot for keeping external customers happy, but does little to treat its internal customers, i.e. employees happy. Happy employees deliver better service, offer better customer care, and record lower absenteeism and turnover rates. It has been observed that high-performing companies have employees who enjoy their work and get support and recognition from the organization.

A sample survey of a high-performing manufacturing organization in India by Sharma[19] revealed that responsibility and growth received the highest rating followed by the job itself, recognition, salary, work environment and interpersonal relations, and company policies and administration. The company offered performance-based incentives.

Strategies adopted by Indian firms vary from company to company, particularly in the private sector. Employee stock option scheme (ESOP) is one of the strategies for employee retention. Companies chart out well-defined career path, provide empowerment,[20] flexi-time, and job enrichment, in addition to paid holidays and allowances like housing, car allowance, medical allowance, etc. Companies also celebrate birthdays of employees and provide dating allowance to young and unmarried ones; dating is a recent phenomenon among young Indians. Prominent Indian BPOs, like Essar Group's Aegis BPO, WNS and Capgemini, are designing in-house curricula to meet the industry's requirements. However, firms like Wipro and HCL Technologies are partnering some key universities for certified courses.[21] The companies look after personal aspiration of employees and provide coaching and mentoring, professional development opportunities, and monthly awards. Work environment and work-life balance play an important role in employee retention.

Maintaining Work Attendance

Along with attracting and retaining employees, organizations need everyone to show up for work at scheduled times. Absenteeism occurs for a variety of reasons. One factor is conditions largely beyond employees' control, such as a major storm, car breakdowns, or sick kids with no one else to care for them. Motivation is another factor. Employees who experience job dissatisfaction or work-related stress are more likely to be absent or late for work because taking time off is a way to temporarily withdraw from stressful or dissatisfying conditions. Absenteeism is also higher in organizations with generous sick leave because this benefit limits the negative financial impact of taking time away from work. Yet another factor is team norm. Studies have found that absenteeism is higher in teams with strong absence norms, meaning that team members tolerate and even expect co-workers to take time off.

The MARS model and the five types of individual behavior and results provide a foundation for the ideas presented over the next few chapters. For the remainder of this chapter, we will look at two of the most stable individual differences: personality and values.

Personality in Organizations

Personality is an important individual characteristic, which explains why Empower MediaMarketing and many other companies are increasingly testing the personality traits of job applicants and employees. **Personality** is the relatively enduring pattern of thoughts, emotions, and behaviors that characterize a person, along with the psychological processes behind those characteristics.[22] It is, in essence, the bundle of characteristics that make us similar to or different from other people. We estimate an individual's personality by what he or she says and does, and we infer the person's internal states–including thoughts and emotions–from these observable behaviors. A basic premise of personality theory is that people have inherent characteristics or traits that can be identified by the consistency or stability of their behavior across time and situations.[23] For example, you probably have some friends who are more talkative than others. You might know some people who like to take risks and others who are risk-averse. This consistency is an essential requirement for personality theory because it attributes a person's behavior to something within him or her–the individual's personality–rather than to purely environmental influences.

personality
The relatively enduring pattern of thoughts, emotions, and behaviors that characterize a person, along with the psychological processes behind those characteristics.

Of course, people do not act the same way in all situations; in fact, such consistency would be considered abnormal because it indicates a person's insensitivity to social norms, reward systems, and other external conditions.[24] People vary their behavior to suit the situation, even if the behavior is at odds with their personality. For example, talkative people remain relatively quiet in a library where "no talking" rules are explicit and strictly enforced. People typically exhibit a wide range of behaviors, yet within that variety are discernible patterns that we refer to as *personality traits.* Traits are broad concepts that allow us to label and understand individual differences. Furthermore, traits predict an individual's behavior far into the future. For example, studies report that an individual's personality in childhood predicts various behaviors and outcomes in adulthood, including educational attainment, employment success, marital relationships, illegal activities, and health-risk behaviors.[25]

Personality Determinants: Nature versus Nurture

What determines an individual's personality? Most experts now agree that personality is shaped by both nature and nurture, although the relative importance of each continues to be debated and studied. *Nature* refers to our genetic or hereditary origins–the genes that we inherit from our parents. Studies of identical twins, particularly those separated at birth, reveal that heredity has a very large effect on personality; up to 50 percent of variation in behavior and 30 percent of temperament preferences can be attributed to a person's genetic characteristics.[26] In other words, genetic code not only determines our eye color, skin tone, and physical shape but also has a significant effect on our attitudes, decisions, and behavior.

Some similarities of identical twins raised apart are surreal. Consider Jim Springer and Jim Lewis, twins who were separated when only four weeks old and didn't meet each other until age 39. In spite of being raised in different families and communities in Ohio, the "Jim twins" held similar jobs, smoked the same type of cigarettes, drove the same make and color of car, spent their vacations on the same Florida beach, had the same woodworking hobby, gave their first sons almost identical names, and had been married twice. Both their first and second wives also had the same first names![27]

Although personality is heavily influenced by heredity, it is also affected to some degree by *nurture*–the person's socialization, life experiences, and other forms of interaction with the environment. Studies have found that the stability of an individual's personality increases up to at least age 30 and possibly to age 50, indicating that some personality development and change occurs when people are young.[28] The main explanation of why personality becomes more stable over time is that people form clearer and more rigid self-concepts as they get older. The executive function–the part of the brain that manages goal-directed behavior–tries to keep our behavior consistent with our self-concept.[29] As self-concept becomes clearer and more stable with age, behavior and personality therefore also become more stable and consistent. We discuss self-concept in more detail later in this chapter. The main point here is that personality is not completely determined by heredity; life experiences, particularly early in life, also shape each individual's personality traits.

Personality and Organizational Behavior

Brigitte Catellier's final hurdle to become vice president of legal affairs at Astral Media Inc. wasn't quite what she might have anticipated. For seven hours Catellier sat through eight aptitude, preferences, and personality tests, some of which asked unusual questions such as whether she would prefer to be an astronaut or an acrobat. "I was told very directly there are two candidates and you are both doing the same tests," says Catellier, who was later offered the job at the Montreal-based media giant. Astral decided a few years ago to include psychological tests in the hiring process, including instruments that measure personality traits such as dominance and tolerance. "This helps us to avoid mistakes, and we have made mistakes from time to time in the past," says Astral's vice president of human resources, referring to people hired in the past whose personality didn't fit the company or job requirements.[30]

Astral Media is among the growing number of firms around North America that have introduced psychological testing in the hiring process. Although aptitude tests have been used regularly for decades, personality tests have had a rocky experience in choosing job applicants. At one time scholars commonly explained employee behavior in terms of personality traits, and companies regularly administered personality tests to job applicants. This changed in the 1960s when researchers reported that the relationship between personality and job performance is very weak.[31] They cited problems with measuring personality traits and explained that the connection between personality and performance exists only under narrowly defined conditions. Companies stopped using personality tests due to concerns that these tests might unfairly discriminate against visible minorities and other identifiable groups.

Over the past decade, personality has regained some of its credibility in organizational settings.[32] Recent studies have reported that specific personality traits predict specific work-related behaviors, stress reactions, and emotions fairly well under specific conditions. Research indicates that effective leaders have identifiable traits and that personality explains some of a person's positive attitudes and life happiness. Personality traits also seem to help people find the jobs that best suit their needs. Personality is a remote concept, so it isn't the best predictor of most jobs; but it is increasingly clear that some personality traits are relevant. Some of the most relevant personality traits for job performance and well-being are found in the Big Five personality dimensions.

five-factor model (FFM) The five abstract dimensions representing most personality traits: conscientiousness, emotional stability, openness to experience, agreeableness, and extroversion.

Five-Factor Model of Personality

One of the most important elements of personality theory is that people possess specific personality traits. Traits such as sociable, depressed, cautious, and talkative represent clusters of thoughts, feelings, and behaviors that allow us to identify, differentiate, and understand people.[33] The most widely respected model of personality traits is the **five-factor model (FFM).** Several decades ago, personality experts identified more than 17,000 words in Roget's thesaurus and Webster's dictionary that describe an individual's personality. These words were aggregated into 171 clusters and then further reduced to five abstract personality dimensions. Using more sophisticated techniques, recent investigations identified the same five personality dimensions. Analyses of trait words in several other languages have produced strikingly similar results, although they also lend support for the notion of six or possibly seven dimensions of personality. Generally, though, the five-factor model is fairly robust across cultures.[34] These "Big Five" dimensions, represented by the handy acronym *CANOE,* are outlined in Exhibit 2.3 and described below:

conscientiousness
A personality dimension describing people who are careful, dependable, and self-disciplined.

neuroticism
A personality dimension describing people with high levels of anxiety, hostility, depression, and self-consciousness.

- *Conscientiousness.* **Conscientiousness** characterizes people who are careful, dependable, and self-disciplined. Some scholars argue that this dimension also includes the will to achieve. People with low conscientiousness tend to be careless, less thorough, more disorganized, and irresponsible.
- *Agreeableness.* This dimension includes the traits of being courteous, good-natured, empathic, and caring. Some scholars prefer the label "friendly compliance" for this dimension, with its opposite being "hostile noncompliance." People with low agreeableness tend to be uncooperative, short-tempered, and irritable.
- *Neuroticism.* **Neuroticism** characterizes people with high levels of anxiety, hostility, depression, and self-consciousness. In contrast, people with low neuroticism (high emotional stability) are poised, secure, and calm.
- *Openness to experience.* This dimension is the most complex and has the least agreement among scholars. It generally refers to the extent to which people are imaginative, creative, curious, and aesthetically sensitive. Those who score low on this dimension tend to be more resistant to change, less open to new ideas, and more conventional and fixed in their ways.

Personality dimension	People with a high score on this dimension tend to be more:
Conscientiousness	Careful, dependable, self-disciplined
Agreeableness	Courteous, good-natured, empathic, caring
Neuroticism	Anxious, hostile, depressed
Openness to experience	Imaginative, creative, curious, sensitive
Extroversion	Outgoing, talkative, sociable, assertive

Exhibit 2.3 *Five-Factor Model's Big Five Personality Dimensions*

extroversion
A personality dimension describing people who are outgoing, talkative, sociable, and assertive.

- *Extroversion.* **Extroversion** characterizes people who are outgoing, talkative, sociable, and assertive. The opposite is *introversion,* which characterizes those who are quiet, shy, and cautious. Extroverts get their energy from the outer world (people and things around them), whereas introverts get their energy from the internal world, such as personal reflection on concepts and ideas. Introverts do not necessarily lack social skills. Rather, they are more inclined to direct their interests to ideas than to social events. Introverts feel quite comfortable being alone, whereas extroverts do not.

These five personality dimensions are not independent of each other. Some experts suggest that conscientiousness, agreeableness, and low neuroticism (high emotional stability) represent a common underlying characteristic broadly described as "getting along"; people with these traits are aware of and more likely to abide by rules and norms of society. The other two dimensions share the common underlying factor called "getting ahead"; people with high scores on extroversion and openness to experience exhibit more behaviors aimed at achieving goals, managing their environment, and advancing themselves in teams.[35]

Studies report fairly strong associations between personality and several workplace behaviors and outcomes, even when employee ability and other factors are taken into account. Conscientiousness and emotional stability (low neuroticism) stand out as the personality traits that best predict individual performance in almost every job group.[36] Both are motivational components of personality because they energize a willingness to fulfill work obligations within established rules (conscientiousness) and to allocate resources to accomplish those tasks (emotional stability). Various studies have reported that conscientious employees set higher personal goals for themselves, are more motivated, and have higher performance expectations than do employees with low levels of conscientiousness. They also tend to have higher levels of organizational citizenship and work better in organizations that give employees more freedom than is found in traditional command-and-control workplaces.[37]

The other three personality dimensions predict more specific types of employee behavior and performance. Extroversion is associated with performance in sales and management jobs, where employees must interact with and influence people. Agreeableness is associated with performance in jobs where employees are expected to be cooperative and helpful, such as working in teams, customer relations, and other conflict-handling situations. People high on the openness-to-experience personality dimension tend to be more creative and adaptable to change. Finally, personality influences employee well-being in various ways. Studies report that personality influences a person's general emotional reactions to her or his job, how well the person copes with stress, and what type of career paths make that person happiest.[38]

Myers-Briggs Type Indicator

Myers-Briggs Type Indicator (MBTI)
A personality inventory designed to identify individuals' basic preferences for perceiving and processing information.

More than half a century ago the mother-and-daughter team of Katherine Briggs and Isabel Briggs-Myers developed the **Myers-Briggs Type Indicator (MBTI),** a personality inventory designed to identify individuals' basic preferences for perceiving and processing information. The MBTI builds on the personality theory proposed in the 1920s by Swiss psychiatrist Carl Jung that identifies the way people prefer to perceive their environment as well as obtain and process information. Jung suggested that everyone is either extroverted or introverted in orientation and has particular preferences for perceiving (sensing or intuition) and judging or deciding on action (thinking or feeling). The MBTI is designed to measure these as well as a fourth dimension relating to how people orient themselves to the outer world (judging versus perceiving)[39]. Extroversion and introversion were discussed earlier, so let's examine the other dimensions:

- *Sensing/intuition.* Some people like collecting information through their five senses. Sensing types use an organized structure to acquire factual and preferably quantitative details. In contrast, intuitive people collect information nonsystematically. They rely more on subjective evidence as well as their intuition and sheer inspiration. Sensers are capable of synthesizing large amounts of seemingly random information to form quick conclusions.
- *Thinking/feeling.* Thinking types rely on rational cause–effect logic and systematic data collection to make decisions. They weigh the evidence objectively and unemotionally. Feeling types, on the other hand, consider how their choices affect others. They weigh the options against their personal values more than rational logic.
- *Judging/perceiving*–Some people prefer order and structure in their relationship with the outer world. These judging types enjoy the control of decision making and want to resolve problems quickly. In contrast, perceiving types are more flexible. They like to spontaneously adapt to events as they unfold and want to keep their options open.

The MBTI questionnaire combines the four pairs of traits into 16 distinct types. For example, ESTJ is one of the most common types for managers, meaning that they are extroverted, sensing, thinking, and judging types. Each of the 16 types has its strengths and weaknesses. ENTJs are considered natural leaders, ISFJs have a high sense of duty, and so on. These types indicate people's preferences, not the way they necessarily behave all of the time.

Eastern Concept of Personality

According to Indian scriptures, there are three types of personalities which include: *Tamasik, Rajasik* and *Satvik.*

- *Tamasik* personality type–violent and dark, such personality sends negative vibes or energy.
- *Rajasik*–vibrant and colorful, individuals with such personality have positive vibes.
- *Satvik*–illuminated and purity, such individuals are silent and have synergy.

According to Sharma (2007)[40], an ideal personality for leadership would be a combination of *rajasik* and *satvik* personality qualities. The combination of these two personalities leads to *rajarshi* which has been articulated in ancient Indian scriptures.

Other Personality Traits

The Big Five personality dimensions represent a broad categorization of personality traits, but organizational behavior also considers traits that are more specific or fall outside the five clusters. Two other personality traits that help to explain individual behavior in the workplace are locus of control and self-monitoring.

locus of control
A personality trait referring to the extent to which people believe events are within their control.

Locus of Control **Locus of control** refers to a generalized belief about the amount of control people have over their own lives. Individuals who feel that they are very much in charge of their own destiny have an internal locus of control; those who think that events in their life are due mainly to fate, luck, or powerful others have an external locus of control. Locus of control is a generalized belief, so people with an external locus can feel in control in familiar situations (such as opening a door or serving a customer). However, their underlying locus of control would be apparent in new situations in which control over events is uncertain. Compared to people with an external locus of control, people with a moderately strong internal locus of control tend to perform better in most employment situations, are more successful in their careers, earn more money, and are better suited for leadership positions. Internals are also more satisfied with their jobs, cope better in stressful situations, and are more motivated by performance-based reward systems.[41]

self-monitoring
A personality trait referring to an individual's level of sensitivity to the expressive behavior of others and the ability to adapt appropriately to these situational cues.

Self-Monitoring **Self-monitoring** refers to an individual's level of sensitivity to the expressive behavior of others and the ability to adapt appropriately to these situational cues. High self-monitors can adjust their behavior quite easily, whereas low self-monitors are more likely to reveal their emotions, so predicting their behavior from one situation to the next is relatively easy.[42] The self-monitoring personality trait has been identified as a significant factor in many organizational activities. Employees who are high self-monitors tend to be better at social networking, interpersonal conversations, and leading people. They are also more likely than low self-monitors to be promoted within the organization and to receive better jobs elsewhere.[43]

Personality and Vocational Choice

Self-monitoring, locus of control, conscientiousness, and the many other personality traits help to explain individual behavior in organizations. One fairly successful application of personality is in the area of vocational choice. Vocational choice is not just about matching your skills with job requirements. It is a complex alignment of personality, values, and competencies with the requirements of work and characteristics of the work environment.[44] You might be very talented at a particular job, but your personality and values must also be aligned with what the job offers.

John Holland, a career development scholar, was an early proponent of this notion that career success depends on the degree of congruence between the person and his or her work environment. Holland argued that people can be classified into different types relating to their personality and that they seek out and are more satisfied in work environments that are congruent with their particular profiles. Thus, *congruence* refers to the extent that someone has the same or similar personality type as the environment in which he or she is working. Some research has found that high congruence leads to better performance, satisfaction, and length of time in that career; but other studies are less supportive of the model.[45]

Holland's Six Types Holland's theory classifies both individual personalities and work environments into six categories: realistic, investigative, artistic, social, enterprising, and conventional. Exhibit 2.4 defines these types of people and work environments and suggests sample occupations representing those environments. Few people fall squarely into only one of Holland's classifications. Instead Holland refers to a person's degree of *differentiation*–that is, the extent to which the individual fits into one or several types. A highly differentiated person is aligned with a single category, whereas most people fit into two or more categories.

Because most individuals fit into more than one personality type, Holland developed a model shaped like a hexagon with each personality type around the points of the model. Consistency refers to the extent that a person is aligned with similar types, which are next to each other in the hexagon, whereas dissimilar types are opposite. For instance, the enterprising and social types are next to each other in Holland's model, so individuals with both enterprising and social personalities have high consistency.

Holland type	Personality traits	Work environment characteristics	Sample occupations
Realistic	Practical, shy, materialistic, stable.	Work with hands, machines, or tools; focus on tangible results.	Assembly worker; dry cleaner, mechanical engineer.
Investigative	Analytic, introverted, reserved, curious, precise, independent.	Work involves discovering, collecting, and analyzing; solving problems.	Biologist, dentist, systems analyst.
Artistic	Creative, impulsive, idealistic, intuitive, emotional.	Work involves creation of new products or ideas, typically in an unstructured setting.	Journalist, architect, advertising executive.
Social	Sociable, outgoing, conscientious, need for affiliation.	Work involves serving or helping others; working in teams.	Social worker, nurse, teacher, counselor.
Enterprising	Confident, assertive, energetic, need for power.	Work involves leading others; achieving goals through others in a results-oriented setting.	Salesperson, stockbroker, politician.
Conventional	Dependable, disciplined, orderly, practical, efficient.	Work involves systematic manipulation of data or information.	Accountant, banker, administrator.

Sources: Based on information in D.H. Montross, Z.B. Leibowitz, and C.J. Shinkman, *Real People, Real Jobs* (Palo Alto, CA: Davies-Black, 1995); and J.H. Greenhaus, *Career Management* (Chicago: Dryden, 1987).

Exhibit 2.4 *Holland's Six Types of Personalities and Work Environments*

Practical Implications of Holland's Theory Holland's vocational fit model is the basis of much career counseling today. Still, some aspects of the model don't seem to work. Holland's personality types represent only some of the Big Five personality dimensions, even though other dimensions should be relevant to vocational fit.[46] Also, research has found that some "opposing" categories in Holland's hexagon are not really opposite to each other. There are also doubts about whether Holland's model can be generalized to other cultures. Aside from these concerns, Holland's model seems to explain individual attitudes and behavior to some extent, and it is the dominant model of career testing today.[47]

Personality and values lay some of the foundation for our understanding of individual behavior in organizations. However, people are, of course, also influenced by the environments in which they live and work. These environments are perceived and learned, the two topics presented in the next chapter.

SELF-CONCEPT: THE "I" IN ORGANIZATIONAL BEHAVIOR

self-concept
An individual's self-beliefs and self-evaluations.

To more fully understand individual behavior in organizations, we need to realize that people develop, nurture, and act in ways that maintain and enhance their self-concept. **Self-concept** refers to an individual's self-beliefs and self-evaluations. It is the "Who am I?" and "How do I feel about myself?" that people ask themselves and that guide their decisions and actions. Self-concept has not received much attention in organizational behavior research, but scholars in psychology, social psychology, and other disciplines have discovered that it is a critically important concept for understanding individual perceptions, attitudes, decisions, and behavior. Indeed, as the opening vignette to this chapter illustrated, managers at Fairmont Hotels & Resorts have known for years that nurturing an employee's self-concept can be a powerful way to strengthen his or her motivation and well-being.

People do not have a single unitary self-concept.[48] Rather, they think of themselves in several ways in various situations. For example, you might think of yourself as a creative employee, a health-conscious vegetarian, and an aggressive skier. A person's self-concept has higher *complexity* when it consists of many categories. Along with varying in complexity, self-concept varies in the degree of its *consistency.* People have high consistency when similar personality traits and values are required across all aspects of self-concept. Low consistency occurs when some aspects of self require personal characteristics that conflict with the characteristics required for other aspects of self. A third structural feature of self-concept is *clarity,* that is, the degree to which a person's self-conceptions are clearly and confidently described, internally consistent, and stable across time. A clear self-concept necessarily requires a consistent self-concept. Generally, people develop a clearer self-concept as they get older.

These three structural dimensions of self-concept–complexity, consistency, and clarity–influence an individual's adaptability and well-being. People function better when their self-concept has many elements (high complexity) that are compatible with each other (high consistency) and are relatively clear. In contrast, people are more rigid and inflexible, and therefore less adaptable, when their self-view consists of only a few similar characteristics (low complexity). People also have poorer psychological adjustment when their self-concept is less clear and includes conflicting elements.

Self-Enhancement

A key ingredient in self-concept is the desire to feel valued. People are inherently motivated to promote and protect a self-view of being competent, attractive, lucky, ethical, and important.[49] This *self-enhancement* is observed in many ways. Individuals tend to rate themselves above average, selectively recall positive feedback while forgetting negative feedback, attribute their successes to personal motivation or ability while blaming the situation for their mistakes, and believe that they have a better than average probability of success. People don't see themselves as above average in all circumstances, but this bias is apparent for conditions that are common rather than rare and that are important to them.[50]

Self-enhancement has both positive and negative consequences in organizational settings.[51] On the positive side, research has found that individuals have better personal adjustment and experience better mental and physical health when they view their self-concept in a positive light. On the negative side, self-enhancement can result in bad decisions. For example, studies report that self-enhancement causes managers to overestimate the probability of success in investment decisions.[52] Generally, though, successful companies, such as Fairmont Hotels & Resorts, strive to help employees feel they are valued and integral members of the organization. Global Connections 2.1 describes how Johnson & Johnson, Inc.'s businesses worldwide also support employees' self-concept by making them feel valued and by aligning their career plans with their self-view.

Self-Verification

Along with being motivated by self-enhancement, people are motivated to verify and maintain their existing self-concept.[53] *Self-verification* stabilizes an individual's self-concept, which, in turn, provides an important anchor that guides his or her thoughts and actions. Self-verification differs from self-enhancement because people usually prefer feedback that is consistent with their self-concept even when that feedback is unflattering. Self-verification has several implications for organizational behavior.[54] First, it affects the perceptual process because employees are more likely to remember information that is consistent with their self-concept. Second, the more confident employees are in their self-concept, the less they will accept feedback–positive or negative–that is at odds with their self-concept. Third, employees are motivated to interact with others who affirm their self-concept, and this affects how well they get along with their boss and with co-workers in teams.

Self-Evaluation

Almost everyone strives to have a positive self-concept, but some people have a more positive evaluation of themselves than do others. This self-evaluation is mostly defined by three concepts: self-esteem, self-efficacy, and locus of control.[55]

Self-Esteem *Self-esteem*–the extent to which people like, respect, and are satisfied with themselves–represents a global self-evaluation. People with high self-esteem are less influenced by others, tend to

2.2 GLOBAL CONNECTIONS

Feeling Valued Adds Value at Johnson & Johnson

Johnson & Johnson is one of the world's most respected employers because it recognizes the value of supporting each employee's self-concept. "We make them feel the company belongs to them," says Narendra Ambwani (shown here), the company's managing director in India.

Every Saturday, Vikas Shirodkar takes his daughter to dance lessons and pops into his office at Johnson & Johnson's Indian headquarters in Mumbai, which is located next door to the dance class. Doing work at the office saves Shirodkar the trouble of driving home and back again to pick up his daughter after class. After three weeks, Shirodkar received a call from J&J's managing director, Narendra Ambwani, asking if he was overburdened and needed additional staff. Shirodkar was surprised by the question, until Ambwani explained that he noticed the executive's name on the register every Saturday and was concerned about his workload.

The managing director's call was a defining moment for Shirodkar because it reflected J&J's value system, in which every employee "must be considered as an individual" and the company "must respect [employees'] dignity and recognize their merit." The credo recognizes employees, customers, communities, and the environment, as well as shareholders. In India, where job-hopping has become the norm, the average J&J employee has more than 15 years of service. Asked about J&J's success at attracting and retaining talented workers, India managing director Narendra Ambwani answers: "We make them feel the company belongs to them."

J&J also supports each employee's self-concept through day-to-day coaching. For example, J&J's Pharmaceutical Research & Development division in the United States discovered that a key ingredient of employee motivation and well-being is to have managers ensure that employees feel valued as contributors to the company's success. The European operations of J&J's Global Pharmaceutical Supply Group also introduced a new career program that takes into account employees' self-concept by matching their personal values with corresponding job preferences.[56]

persist in spite of failure, and think more rationally. Self-esteem regarding specific aspects of self (e.g., a good student, a good driver, a good parent) predicts specific thoughts and behaviors, whereas a person's overall self-esteem predicts only large bundles of thoughts and behaviors.[57]

self-efficacy
A person's belief that he or she has the ability, motivation, correct role perceptions, and favorable situation to complete a task successfully.

Self-Efficacy **Self-efficacy** refers to a person's belief that he or she can successfully complete a task.[58] Those with high self-efficacy have a "can do" attitude. They believe they possess the energy (motivation), resources (situational factors), understanding of the correct course of action (role perceptions), and competencies (ability) to perform the task. In other words, self-efficacy is an individual's perception regarding the MARS model in a specific situation. Although originally defined in terms of specific tasks, self-efficacy is also a general trait related to self-concept.[59] General self-efficacy is a perception of one's competence to perform across a variety of situations. The higher the person's general self-efficacy, the higher is his or her overall self-evaluation.

locus of control
A person's general belief about the amount of control he or she has over personal life events.

Locus of Control **Locus of control,** the third concept related to self-evaluation, is defined as a person's general belief about the amount of control he or she has over personal life events. Individuals with more of an internal locus of control believe that their personal characteristics (i.e., motivation and competencies) mainly influence life's outcomes. Those with more of an external locus of control believe that events in their life are due mainly to fate, luck, or conditions in the external environment. Locus of control is a generalized belief, so people with an external locus can feel in control in familiar situations (such as performing common tasks). However, their underlying locus of control would be apparent in new situations in which control over events is uncertain. People with a more internal locus of control have a more positive self-evaluation. They also tend to perform better in most employment situations, are more successful in their careers, earn more money, and are better suited for leadership positions. Internals are also more satisfied with their jobs, cope better in stressful situations, and are more motivated by performance-based reward systems.[60]

The Social Self

A person's self-concept can be organized into two fairly distinct categories: personal identity characteristics and social identity characteristics.[61] *Personal identity* consists of characteristics that make us unique and distinct from people in the social groups to which we have a connection. For instance, an unusual achievement that distinguishes you from other people typically becomes a personal identity characteristic. Personal identity refers to something about you as an individual without reference to a larger group. At the same time, human beings are social animals; they have an inherent drive to be associated with others and to be recognized as part of social communities. This drive to belong is reflected in self-concept by the fact that all individuals define themselves to some degree by their association with others.[62]

social identity theory
A theory that explains self-concept in terms of the person's unique characteristics (personal identity) and membership in various social groups (social identity).

This social element of self-concept is described by **social identity theory.** According to social identity theory, people define themselves by the groups to which they belong or have an emotional attachment. For instance, someone might have a social identity as an American, a graduate of the University of Massachusetts, and an employee at IBM (see Exhibit 2.5). Social identity is a complex combination of many memberships arranged in a hierarchy of

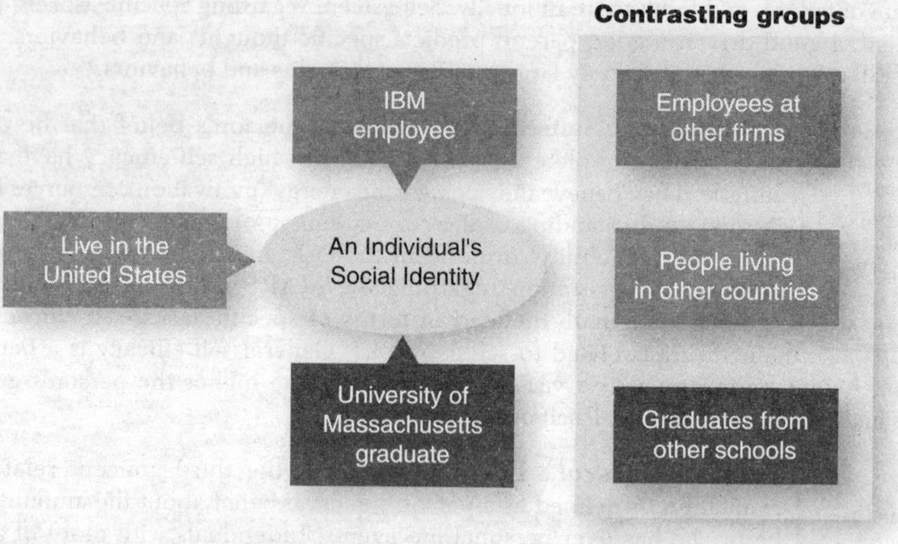

Exhibit 2.5 *Social Identity Theory Example*

importance. One factor determining importance is how easily we are identified as a member of the reference group, such as by our gender, age, and ethnicity. It is difficult to ignore your gender in a class where most other students are the opposite gender, for example. In that context, gender tends to become a stronger defining feature of your social identity than it is in social settings where there are many people of the same gender.

Along with our demographic characteristics, a group's status is typically an important influence on whether we include the group in our social identity. We identify with groups that have high status or respect because this aids the self-enhancement of our self-concept. Medical doctors usually define themselves by their profession because of its high status, whereas people in low-status jobs tend to define themselves by nonjob groups. Some people define themselves in terms of where they work because their employer has a positive reputation in the community. In contrast, other people never mention where they work because their employer is noted for poor relations with employees and has a poor reputation in the community.[63]

SELF-CONCEPT: INDIAN AND WESTERN PERSPECTIVES

Dimensions of Self

The construct of self can be viewed from various perspectives according to the purpose of understanding and utilization of this construct[64]. The various perspectives are discussed below:

Hindu view of Self According to *Taittiriya Upanishad,* there are five layers of self in an individual which are connected to each other. These layers are physical, vital breath, sensory, cognitive, and joyous. Among all these layers of self, joyous is the true self. Joyous is known as *atman*, which is the centre of a living being[65]. Joyous is the psychic organizing principle of mind which is independent and observes and directs the functioning of other layers of the self. Realization of *atman* or Joyous is crucial for the holistic well-being of an individual.

Another perspective of self is *turiya avastha* which is one of the normative aspects of self and is popular in Indian literature. Paranjpe based on *Upanishad's* assertion regarding self, defines turiya avastha as a state of self in which "the distinction between the subject and the object, knower and known, which is characteristic of the ordinary state of consciousness disappears. It is a trans-cognitive state, and as such cannot be adequately accounted for in terms of concepts and words". This state of mind can be attained through consistent practice of yogic exercises.

Hierarchical Structure *Viewing from Outer to Inner Layer of Individual:* Outer layer is the body and the body language of an individual which is visible to any perceiver. In body, physical health, strength, attractiveness, attire, hairstyle, etc. form the first layer of an individual's personality which creates an impression. This impression is further influenced by body language, i.e., speech, gestures, postures and other non-verbal signals. An individual may or may not be aware of these body languages, but sends messages to other individuals which reinforces the earlier impression based on physical aspects or modifies the impressions. Perceptions like friendly or unfriendly, expressive or reserved, etc. However, these perceptions based on outer layer can be either right or wrong. For example, Tulsidas wrote in his epic *Ramayana* that a handsome person with a mean mind is just like a pot of gold that is full of venom. Inner layer is crucial to understand an individual, as it comprises feelings, thoughts, and action orientations which enable a person to relate with other individuals.

Moral Self According to scholars, human beings have in-built bio-genetic features which drive them to strive for biological needs and in-built moral dispositions to fulfill one's own aspirations. *According to* Vivekanand (1953)[66], a conscious mind is like, "a monkey, restless by nature, drunk with wine, smarting under the scorpion bite, and possessed as if, by a demon". Though these are the qualities of a conscious mind, it strives to transform itself into a moral and spiritual form. Kanungo and Mendonca[67], stated that moral laws are universal because they incorporate fundamental values, i.e. truth, goodness, beauty, courage and justice. These values are found in all cultures, although cultures may differ with regard to the application of these values'.

Cultural Construct of Self Culture affects the process of social perception and provides a model for culturally-shared self. According to Markus and Kitayama (1991)[68], the western culture has individualistic perspective while non-western have collectivistic cultures. According to Roland[69], the American self is individualized, characterized by self is developed on 'I', individualistic narcissistic structures, ego-ideal, super-ego, communications are direct, and rational orientation. However, in the context of Indian self states it has two strands familial and spiritual. The familial strand comprises the following features *symbiosis-reciprocity*, *self-esteem* derived from strong identification with family reputation and honour, socially contextual ego ideal, super-ego based on demands of hierarchical family or group. The mode of communication is both explicit and implicit, and modes of functioning are highly contextual. The *spiritual* strand comprises identification with gods and goddesses and religious rites, rituals and *gurus.*

Western Perspective

Levels of Consciousness Freud[70] classified three levels of the mind as *conscious, subconscious* and *unconscious.* The conscious mind comprises of perceptions, emotions, memories, thoughts, needs, impulses, habits, attitudes, etc. which an individual is aware of. The unconscious level of mind consists of bio-genetically generated animal impulses, desires, and strivings which are not allowed in the conscious mind. The subconscious level is a grey area between the other two levels of the mind. So, human behavior is the resultant of these three levels of mind. In an organization, individuals behave as per the relative strength of these three levels of their minds.

Another classification of the three levels of the mind in an individual is parent ego-state, adult-ego state and child-ego state which is called *Transactional Analysis*[71]. Transactional analysis is widely used tool for management in organizations. Child form denotes spontaneity in desires, joyfulness, and playfulness, which stimulates an individual to defy organizational norms of thinking within the limits. Parent form in an individual enables to be restrictive and moralizing, and the adult form guides the individual to be focused on work, to adopt a problem-solving approach, and to regulate the self to perform one's own tasks.

Self-Concept and Organizational Behavior

We began this section by stating that self-concept is an important topic for understanding individual perceptions, attitudes, decisions, and behavior. In fact, self-concept may eventually be recognized as one of the more useful ways to understand and improve an employee's performance and well-being. Some aspects of self-concept, such as self-efficacy and locus of control, already are known influences on job performance. Self-concept also affects how people select and interpret information, as well as their biases in judgments (such as probability of success). Furthermore, as you will learn in future chapters, the social identity component of self-concept influences team dynamics, organizational commitment, and other OB concepts.

Learning Objectives

After reading the next three sections, you should be able to:

6. Distinguish personal, shared, espoused, and enacted values and explain why value congruence is important.
7. Summarize five values commonly studied across cultures. Explore the Indian values at the workplace.
8. Explain how moral intensity, ethical sensitivity, and the situation influence ethical behavior.

VALUES IN THE WORKPLACE

A person's self-concept is connected to his or her personal values.[72] *Values* are stable, evaluative beliefs that guide our preferences for outcomes or courses of action in a variety of situations. They are perceptions about what is good or bad, right or wrong. Values tell us what we "ought" to do. They serve as a moral compass that directs our motivation and, potentially, our decisions and actions. Values are related to self-concept because they partly define who we are as individuals and as members of groups with similar values.

People arrange values into a hierarchy of preferences, called a *value system*. Some individuals value new challenges more than they value conformity. Others value generosity more than frugality. Each person's unique value system is developed and reinforced through socialization from parents, religious institutions, friends, personal experiences, and the society in which he or she lives. As such, a person's hierarchy of values is stable and long-lasting. For example, one study found that value systems of a sample of adolescents were remarkably similar 20 years later when they were adults.[73]

Notice that our description of values has focused on individuals, whereas executives often describe values as though they belong to the organization. In reality, values exist only within individuals–we call them *personal values*. However, groups of people might hold the same or similar values, so we tend to ascribe these *shared values* to the team, department, organization, profession, or entire society. The values shared by people throughout an organization *(organizational values)* receive fuller discussion in Chapter 14 because they are a key part of corporate culture. The values shared across a society *(cultural values)* receive attention later in this chapter.

Before discussing workplace values in more detail, we need to distinguish between espoused and enacted values.[74] *Espoused values* represent the values that we say we use and, in many cases, think we use. Corporate leaders might say they value environmentalism, creativity, and politeness, whether or not they really do value these things in practice. Values are socially desirable, so people create a positive public image by claiming to believe in values that others expect them to embrace. Also, corporate values are usually considered espoused values because, although leaders might abide by them, we don't know whether lower-level employees share this commitment. *Enacted values,* on the other hand, represent the values we actually rely on to guide our decisions and actions. These values-in-use are apparent by watching people in action. Just as we judge an individual's personality by behavioral tendencies, so too do we judge enacted values by behavioral tendencies.

Types of Values

Values come in many forms, and experts on this topic have devoted considerable attention to organizing them into clusters. Several decades ago, social psychologist Milton Rokeach developed two lists of values, distinguishing means (instrumental values) from end goals (terminal values). Although Rokeach's lists are still mentioned in some organizational behavior sources, they are no longer considered acceptable representations of personal values. The instrumental-terminal values distinction was neither accurate nor useful, and experts have identified values that were excluded from Rokeach's lists.

Today, by far the most respected and widely studied set of values is the model developed and tested by social psychologist Shalom Schwartz and his colleagues.[75] Schwartz's list of 57 values builds on Rokeach's earlier work but does not distinguish instrumental from terminal values. Instead, through painstaking empirical research, Schwartz reported that human values are organized into the circular model (circumplex) shown in Exhibit 2.6.[76] The model organizes values into 10 broad categories, each representing several specific values. For example, conformity consists of four values: politeness, honoring parents, self-discipline, and obedience.

These 10 categories of values are further reduced to two bipolar dimensions. One dimension has the opposing value domains of openness to change and conservation. *Openness to change* refers to the extent to which a person is motivated to pursue innovative ways. It includes the value domains of self-direction (creativity, independent thought) and stimulation (excitement and challenge). *Conservation* is the extent to which a person is motivated to preserve the status quo. This dimension includes the value clusters of conformity (adherence to social norms and expectations), security (safety and stability), and tradition (moderation and preservation of the status quo).

The other bipolar dimension in Schwartz's model has the opposing value domains of self-enhancement and self-transcendence. *Self-enhancement*–how much a person is motivated by self-interest–includes the value categories of achievement (pursuit of personal success) and power (dominance over others). The opposite of self-enhancement is *self-transcendence,* which refers to motivation to promote the welfare of others and nature. Self-transcendence includes the values of benevolence (concern for others in one's life) and universalism (concern for the welfare of all people and nature).

Values and Individual Behavior

Personal values guide our decisions and actions to some extent, but this connection isn't always as strong as some would like to believe. Habitual behavior tends to be consistent with our values, but our everyday conscious decisions and actions apply our values much less consistently. The main reason for

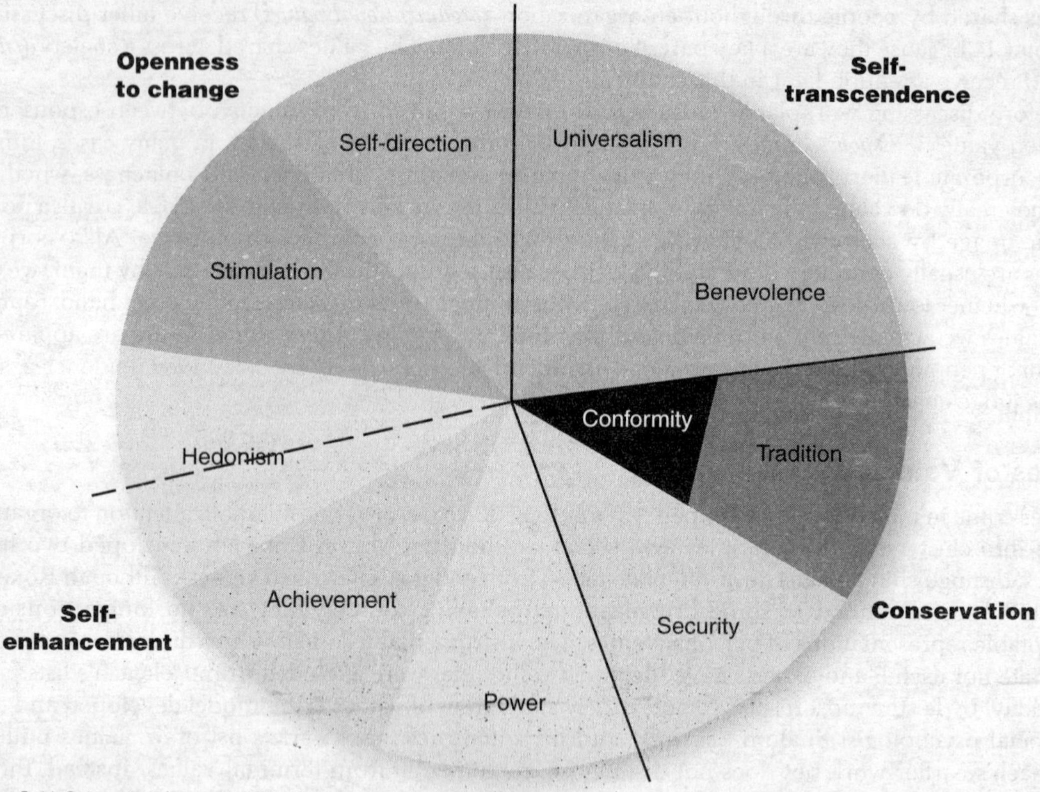

Sources: S. H. Schwartz, "Universals in the Content and Structure of Values: Theoretical Advances and Empirical Tests in 20 Countries," *Advances in Experimental Social Psychology,* 25 (1992), pp. 1–65; S. H. Schwartz and G. Sagie, "Value Consensus and Importance: A Cross-National Study," *Journal of Cross-Cultural Psychology,* 31 (July 2000), pp. 465–497.

Exhibit 2.6 *Schwartz's Values Circumplex*

the "disconnect" between personal values and individual behavior is that values are abstract concepts that sound good in theory but are less easily followed in practice.

Three conditions strengthen the linkage between personal values and behavior.[77] First, we are more likely to apply values when we are reminded of them. For example, co-workers tend to treat each other with much more respect and consideration immediately after a senior executive gives a speech on the virtues of benevolence in the workplace. Second, we tend to apply our values only when we can think of specific reasons for doing so. In other words, we need logical reasons for applying a specific value in a specific situation. Third, we tend to apply our values in situations that facilitate doing so. Work environments shape our behavior, at least in the short term, so they necessarily encourage or discourage value-consistent behavior.

Value Congruence

Personal values not only define the person's self-concept; they also affect how comfortable that person is with being associated with the organization and working with specific people. The key concept here is *value congruence,* which refers to how similar a person's value hierarchy is to the value hierarchy of the organization, a co-worker, or another source of comparison. *Person-organization value congruence* occurs when the employee's and organization's dominant values are similar. Values are guideposts, so employees whose values are similar to the dominant organizational values are more likely to make decisions compatible with the organization's value-based mission and objectives. Person-organization value congruence also leads to higher job satisfaction, loyalty, and organizational citizenship as well as lower stress and turnover. "The most difficult but rewarding accomplishment in any career is 'living true' to your values and finding companies where you can contribute at the highest level while being your authentic self," says Cynthia Schwalm, president of the U.S. commercial division of biopharmaceutical company Eisai Co. Ltd. "There is nothing more important in my estimation."[78]

Do the most successful organizations have the highest possible levels of person-organization value congruence? Not at all! While a comfortable degree of value congruence is necessary for the reasons just noted, organizations also benefit from some level of value incongruence. Employees with diverse values offer different perspectives, which potentially lead to better decision-making. Also, too much congruence can create a "corporate cult" that potentially undermines creativity, organizational flexibility, and business ethics.

A second type of value congruence involves how consistent the values apparent in our actions (enacted values) are with what we say we believe in (espoused values). This *espoused-enacted value congruence* is especially important for people in leadership positions because any obvious gap between espoused and enacted values undermines their perceived integrity, a critical feature of effective leaders. One global survey reported recently that 55 percent of employees believe senior management behaves consistently with the company's core values.[79] Meyners & Co., the Albuquerque, New Mexico, accounting firm, tries to maintain high levels of espoused-enacted value congruence by surveying subordinates and peers about whether managers' decisions and actions are consistent with the company's espoused values.[80]

A third type of value congruence involves the compatibility of an organization's dominant values with the prevailing values of the community or society in which it conducts business.[81] For example, an organization headquartered in one country that tries to impose its value system on employees and other stakeholders located in another culture may experience higher employee turnover and have more difficult relations with the communities in which the company operates. Thus, globalization calls for a delicate balancing act: Companies depend on shared values to maintain consistent standards and behaviors, yet they need to operate within the values of different cultures around the world. Let's look more closely at how values vary across cultures.

VALUES ACROSS CULTURES

Fairmont Hotels & Resorts operates world-class hotels in several countries and is rapidly expanding its operations into the Middle East, Africa, and other regions. As the opening story in this chapter described, Fairmont actively develops cross-cultural competencies in its staff through work experience and formal training. Sean Billing and other Fairmont staff soon realize that they need to be sensitive to the fact that cultural differences exist and, although often subtle, can influence decisions, behavior, and interpersonal relations.

Individualism and Collectivism

individualism
A cross-cultural value describing the degree to which people in a culture emphasize independence and personal uniqueness.

Many values have been studied in the context of cross-cultural differences, but the two most commonly mentioned are individualism and collectivism. **Individualism** is the extent to which we value independence and personal uniqueness. Highly individualist people value personal freedom, self-sufficiency, control over their own lives, and appreciation of the unique qualities that distinguish them from others. As shown in Exhibit 2.7, Americans and Italians

Country	Individualism	Collectivism	Power distance	Uncertainty avoidance	Achievement orientation
United States	High	Low	Medium low	Medium low	Medium high
Denmark	Medium	Medium low	Low	Low	Low
India	Medium high	Medium	High	Medium low	Medium high
Italy	High	High	Medium	High	High
Japan	Medium high	Low	Medium	High	High
Taiwan	Low	High	Medium	High	Medium

Sources: Individualism and collectivism results are from the meta-analysis reported in D. Oyserman, H. M. Coon, and M. Kemmelmeier, "Rethinking Individualism and Collectivism: Evaluation of Theoretical Assumptions and Meta-Analyses," *Psychological Bulletin,* 128 (2002), pp. 3–72. The other results are from G. Hofstede, *Culture's Consequences,* 2nd ed (Thousand Oaks, CA: Sage, 2001).

Exhibit 2.7 *Five Cross-Cultural Values in Selected Countries*

collectivism
A cross-cultural value describing the degree to which people in a culture emphasize duty to groups to which people belong and to group harmony.

generally exhibit high individualism, whereas Taiwanese tend to have low individualism. **Collectivism** is the extent to which we value our duty to groups to which we belong and to group harmony. Highly collectivist people define themselves by their group memberships and value harmonious relationships within those groups.[82] Americans generally have low collectivism, whereas Italians and Taiwanese have relatively high collectivism.

Contrary to popular belief, individualism is not the opposite of collectivism. In fact, an analysis of previous studies reports that the two concepts are unrelated.[83] Some cultures that highly value duty to one's group do not necessarily give a low priority to personal freedom and self-sufficiency. The distinction between individualism and collectivism makes sense when we realize that people across all cultures define themselves in terms of both their uniqueness (personal identity) and their relationship to others (social identity). Some cultures clearly reflect one more than the other, but both have a place in a person's values and self-concept.

Power Distance

power distance
A cross-cultural value describing the degree to which people in a culture accept unequal distribution of power in a society.

A third frequently mentioned cross-cultural value is **power distance**–the extent to which people accept unequal distribution of power in a society.[84] Those with high power distance accept and value unequal power. They value obedience to authority and are comfortable receiving commands from their superiors without consultation or debate, and they prefer to resolve differences indirectly through formal procedures rather than directly. In contrast, people with low power distance expect relatively equal power sharing. They view the relationship with their boss as one of interdependence, not dependence; that is, they believe their boss is also dependent on them, so they expect power sharing and consultation before decisions affecting them are made. People in India tend to have high power distance, whereas people in Denmark generally have low power distance.

uncertainty avoidance
A cross-cultural value describing the degree to which people in a culture tolerate ambiguity (low uncertainty avoidance) or feel threatened by ambiguity and uncertainty (high uncertainty avoidance).

Uncertainty Avoidance

Uncertainty avoidance is the degree to which people tolerate ambiguity (low uncertainty avoidance) or feel threatened by ambiguity and uncertainty (high uncertainty avoidance). Employees with high uncertainty avoidance value structured situations in which rules of conduct and decision making are clearly documented. They usually prefer direct rather than indirect or ambiguous communications. Uncertainty avoidance tends to be high in Italy and Taiwan and very high in Japan. It is generally low in Denmark.

The financial meltdown which hit the U.S. economy in 2008 led to major global meltdown. The root causes for such mayhem were high degree of low uncertainty avoidance, loopholes in governance, encouragement to risk-taking behavior, ambiguity in information and assessment, etc.

Individuals and organizations were pre-occupied with the future and always aimed to adopt new technologies, and grab new opportunities, but overlooked the associated risks. To tackle the uncertainty, individuals or organization put in all possible resources to mitigate its impact. Tendency gets formed to avoid uncertainty and control risks and develop mechanisms to manipulate risks and develop safety measures. However, when there is evidence of reduced risks, it tends to change behavior and the individual becomes less responsible. Organizations attempt to provide secured and controlled environment for all its stakeholders, which is difficult in an environment of uncertainty. As the scope of risk and uncertainty increased for organizations, the need for new governance structures and procedures arose and led to the development of global practices and audit regimes. New designations like Risk Managers, Chief Risk Officers, Risk Management Boards in organizations emerged which indicate obsession with risk factor.[85]

Despite all the tactics and measures to mitigate risks, it paved the way for new risks in a competitive environment. This high degree of low uncertainty-avoidance behavior occurred because organizations and individuals anticipated reduced risks, and it led to reckless behavior. Organizations began to bundle risk as a commodity which was packaged and traded. Risk was attractively wrapped with accountable governance structures and appropriate legislation under the eagle eyes of the regulatory bodies and governments. Uncertainties had increased due to global competition. There was rise in complexities and situations, and high stakes for all stakeholders were overlooked.

The learning has been that organizations cannot fully eliminate risk and uncertainties. People need to balance i.e. control risks and also evolve and survive in an uncertain environment. In other words, organizations need to be resilient as advancements and progress bring along with them an advanced level of uncertainties and risks.

Lehman Brothers' Impact on India A job in Lehman Brothers was once considered to be posh in the financial and banking industry. However, this major financial institution with its corporate office in America turned up a surprise when it filed for bankruptcy in the year 2008. This dream job for those in America as well in other countries including India turned into a nightmare. The Indian operations in Mumbai was the largest in Asia which comprised of 2500 employees. The grave signs of lay-off emerged when employees were asked to continue work as usual with no clarity on their roles, but all connections of contact were suspended. Frequent meetings were held and in one such meeting, employees were asked to update their CVs and to look up for job. In the words of a former employee "The fear of a job loss is now real. The most difficult part will be to explain things to family and friends. A job loss in this country is a social disgrace – nobody cares, if it is because of a global meltdown". The RBI had given strict instructions to Lehman Brothers that it needs to take clearance from the central bank for any operations it undertook and ordered to stop trading in government securities. Lehman Brothers' Indian office had tried to rope in counselors in order to soften the big blow. Another former employee from their investment-banking division had quoted, "With the markets down and brokerages scaling back operations, retrenchment could not have come at a worse time for the Lehman staff". The employees of this organization, mostly graduates of elite business schools and drawing huge salaries were doubtful about getting a similar job.

Sources:

1. Goswami Samyabrata Ray (17 Sept., 2008), *Lehman Crisis: India Impact*. http://www.businessworld.in/index.php/Economy-and-Banking/Layoff-Fears-Wash-Ashore.html, accessed on 13/12/2010.
2. Silicon India (17 Sept, 2008), *Lehman Brothers issues 24 Hour Notice to Indian Employees*, http://www.siliconindia.com/shownews/Lehman_Brothers_issues_24hour_short_notice_to_Indian_employees_-nid-46640.html, accessed on 16/12/2010.

Achievement-Nurturing Orientation

achievement-nurturing orientation
A cross-cultural value describing the degree to which people in a culture emphasize competitive versus cooperative relations with other people.

Achievement-nurturing orientation reflects a competitive versus cooperative view of relations with other people.[86] People with a high achievement orientation value assertiveness, competitiveness, and materialism. They appreciate people who are tough, and they favor the acquisition of money and material goods. In contrast, people in nurturing-oriented cultures emphasize relationships and the well-being of others. They focus on human interaction and caring rather than competition and personal success. People in Sweden, Norway, and Denmark score very low on achievement orientation (i.e., they have a high nurturing orientation). In contrast, very high achievement orientation scores have been reported in Japan and Hungary, with fairly high scores in the United States and Italy.

Before leaving this topic, we need to point out two concerns about cross-cultural values.[87] One concern is that country scores on power distance, uncertainty avoidance, and achievement-nurturing orientation are based on a survey of IBM staff worldwide more than a quarter century ago. More than 100,000 IBM employees in dozens of countries completed that survey, but IBM employees might not represent the general population. There is also evidence that values have since changed considerably in some countries. A second concern is the assumption that everyone in a society has similar cultural values. This may be true in a few countries, but *multiculturalism*–in which several microcultures coexist in the same country–is becoming the more common trend. By attributing specific values to an entire society, we are engaging in a form of stereotyping that limits our ability to understand the more complex reality of that society.

Indian Values and Workplace Behavior

India is a diverse and demographically complex country, therefore, what would qualify as Indian values would be based to what the majority of people of India attach significance, and what reflects in their belief or behavior pattern. Thus, dominant Indian values are affinity to family, humility, non competitiveness, spiritual harmony, respect for wisdom and age, patience, cosmic harmony, or harmony with nature, cooperation, generosity, and cultural pluralism. The famous Indian scripture, *Bhagavad Gita*[88] focuses on '*karma*', or work, and considers it to be the sacred duty of every person. Work is considered as an offering to the 'supreme', therefore, all work is sacred and should be done with utmost dedication, for spiritual growth and not for material gains. The work, as a duty, is to be performed regularly with non-attachment. As we are the sum total of the impressions produced by our thoughts and deeds; if we have good thoughts and perform good deeds, it would leave a good impression. These tendencies make up our character. Both pleasure and pain leave an impression on our mind in such a way that we become strong and enlightened. We have tremendous power in us to produce great results, since it is our own *karma* which determines everything. Thus, *Bhagawad Gita* summarizes that the work done with the ideals of truth and selfishness and love, and not for personal gains of money, power, and fame, equips us with great power. However, times have changed and so have people.

The traditional Indian values are being influenced by native and other cultures, with education and exposure through satellite-based communications, which allow people to be exposed to global cultures, values, styles, and behavior. Unlike the past, people are becoming more individualistic, and keep self interest above the interest of the community or society and, in some cases, above the interest of their joint family. However, there are still people who focus on their *karma* (work), are conscientious and sincere, and contribute to organizational and country's productivity, but there are others who lack accountability and fall short of their duties and responsibilities, not due to lack of ability but due to their attitude and a lax performance-management system in the organization. It may be said that an organization is a subsystem of the society, therefore societal values are reflected in the organizational behavior. But each organization has its own values, and wherever these values are institutionalized, we find that the organization is able to achieve its goals effectively. Companies like Infosys have spelt out their values, and they carry out management of the organization on the basis of these values.

Facets of Indian Mindset A research study based on the views of 47 social scientists, spread across 17 locations in India, found the following four facets of personality which are typical to an Indian personality:

Dependence proneness An Indian who does not have surety about himself/herself, suffers from inferiority complex, is obedient and submissive to authority, and impassive about quality, standards and norms.

Collectivist approach Indians with a collectivist's personality are those who are bonded in relationship-based roles and submissive to authority. They are weak on individualistic orientations. They have tendency to change according to situation and possess analytical skills.

Materialistic These are Indians who are selfish and aggressive to attain power, money, prestige, and control. They make very calculative moves, are enterprising in nature, and make adjustments in order to fulfill their selfish needs. A person with materialistic approach possesses highly individualistic personality characteristics.

Holistic These Indians are balanced in emotional, rational and spiritual spheres. They think rationally, give equal importance to personal relationships, and their spiritual awareness enables them to not get fascinated by materialistic gains and they constantly strive for excellence.

From an organizational-behavior perspective, an individual with collectivistic personality would suit a workplace who values relationships more than performance, while the dependence-prone people would have a negative impact. Materialistic individuals are highly suitable for organizations which are task oriented, highly competitive, globalized and focus on profit making. Holistic individuals would suit organizations that have concern for people, society and its own business.

There are organizations in India which have practiced holistic approach for decades, like the Tatas, Birlas, and others. Among the emergent organizations, Infosys, Wipro, etc. practice this approach. However, organizations and individuals have realized or realizing that they can no longer succeed and sustain on narrow approaches. Progress of oneself along with progress of others is crucial for success and sustenance. Corporate Social Responsibility, Triple Bottom Line, Sustainability Index, GRI (Global Reporting Initiatives), United Nations Global Compact, etc. are initiatives being undertaken to encourage holistic approach and behavior in individuals, leaders and organizations.

Sources:

Sinha, J.B.P. and A. Pandey (2007), "Indians' Mindsets and the Conditions that Evoke Them", *Psychological Studies*, 52: 1–13.

Sihna, J.B.P. (2008), Self and Personality, in *Culture and Organizational Behaviour*, New Delhi: Sage Publications, pp. 81–109.

Institutionalization of Values at Infosys Infosys, an Indian software company, was founded in 1981 by Narayana Murthy along with his six friends, with a modest sum of money saved by Sudha Murthy, wife of Narayana Murthy. "His vision has been to make Infosys a globally respected software corporation delivering the best of solutions and employing the best in class professionals."[89] The company grew rapidly in domestic and international markets. In 1999, Infosys became the first Indian company to be listed on the NASDAQ. It has grown exponentially, and is one of the highly respected companies in India, delivering high quality services in the globally competitive environment. Mr. Narayana Murthy, the chief mentor of Infosys drew inspiration from his teachers, and imbibed the values of 'public good before private good' and 'truthfulness' of his parents. He stands by his principles, leads by example, and the company treats all its stakeholders with fairness, honesty, and transparency. Infosys is a value driven organization the values that drive Infosys are:

- *Customer Delight:* A commitment to surpassing our customer expectations.
- *Leadership by Example:* A commitment to set standards in our business and transactions, and be an exemplar for the industry and our own teams.
- *Integrity and Transparency:* A commitment to be ethical, sincere, and open in our dealings.
- *Fairness:* A commitment to be objective and transaction-oriented, thereby earning trust and respect.
- *Pursuit of Excellence:* A commitment to strive relentlessly, to constantly improve ourselves, our teams, our services and products so as to become the best.[90]

The unique feature of the company is that despite its exponential growth and global success, the company is transaction driven, and is not driven by personality. It has a long-term vision it focuses on the world-class operational model and its intellectual capital. The employees of the company have a lot of empowerment and also have a stock option plan. They have inculcated the value of treating corporate resources as personal resources. The company expects people to make value added contributions towards a company. Thus, Infosys is a company driven by knowledge and values, and attracts the best talent in the industry.

Ethical Values and Behavior

When employees are asked to list the most important characteristic they look for in a leader, the top factor isn't intelligence, courage, or even being inspirational. Although these characteristics are important, the most important factor in most surveys is honesty/ethics.[91] *Ethics* refers to the study of moral principles or values that determine whether actions are right or wrong and outcomes are good or bad. People rely on their ethical values to determine "the right thing to do."

Unfortunately, incidents involving corporate wrongdoing continue to raise serious questions about the ethical values of many corporate leaders. Scandals at Enron, WorldCom, Tyco, and other companies led to the Sarbanes-Oxley Act in 2002, which put more controls on U.S. companies and auditing firms to minimize conflict of interest and disclose the company's financial picture more fully. This legislation might reduce some unethical conduct, but wrongdoing is unlikely to disappear completely.

Three Ethical Principles

To better understand business ethics, we need to consider three distinct types of ethical principles: utilitarianism, individual rights, and distributive justice.[92] While you might prefer one principle more than the others on the basis of your personal values, all three should be actively considered to put important ethical issues to the test.

- *Utilitarianism.* This principle advises us to seek the greatest good for the greatest number of people. In other words, we should choose the option that provides the highest degree of satisfaction to those affected. This is sometimes known as a *consequential principle* because it focuses on the consequences of our actions, not on how we achieve those consequences. One problem with utilitarianism is that it is almost impossible to evaluate the benefits or costs of many decisions, particularly when many stakeholders have wide-ranging needs and values. Another problem is that even if the objective of our behavior is ethical according to utilitarianism, the means to achieving that objective is sometimes considered unethical.

- *Individual rights.* This principle reflects the belief that everyone has entitlements that let her or him act in a certain way. Some of the most widely cited rights are freedom of movement, physical security, freedom of speech, fair trial, and freedom from torture. The individual-rights principle includes more than legal rights; it also includes human rights that everyone is granted as a moral norm of society. One problem with individual rights is that certain individual rights may conflict with others. The shareholders' right to be informed about corporate activities may ultimately conflict with an executive's right to privacy, for example.
- *Distributive justice.* This principle suggests that people who are similar to each other should receive similar benefits and burdens; those who are dissimilar should receive different benefits and burdens in proportion to their dissimilarity. For example, we expect that two employees who contribute equally in their work should receive similar rewards, whereas those who make a lesser contribution should receive less. A variation of the distributive justice principle says that inequalities are acceptable when they benefit the least well off in society. Thus, employees in risky jobs should be paid more if their work benefits others who are less well off. One problem with the distributive justice principle is that it is difficult to agree on who is "similar" and what factors are "relevant."

Moral Intensity, Ethical Sensitivity, and Situational Influences

moral intensity
The degree to which an issue demands the application of ethical principles.

Along with ethical principles and their underlying values, three other factors influence ethical conduct in the workplace: the moral intensity of the issue, the individual's ethical sensitivity, and situational factors. **Moral intensity** is the degree to which an issue demands the application of ethical principles. Decisions with high moral intensity are more important, so the decision-maker needs to more carefully apply ethical principles to resolve it. Several factors influence the moral intensity of an issue, including those listed in Exhibit 2.8. Keep in mind that this list represents the factors people tend to think about; some of them might not be considered morally acceptable when people are formally making ethical decisions.[93]

ethical sensitivity
A personal characteristic that enables people to recognize the presence of an ethical issue and determine its relative importance.

Even if an issue has high moral intensity, some employees might not recognize its ethical importance because they have low **ethical sensitivity.** Ethical sensitivity is a personal characteristic that enables people to recognize the presence of an ethical issue and determine its relative importance.[94] Ethically sensitive people are not necessarily more ethical. Rather, they are more likely to recognize whether an issue requires ethical consideration; that is, they can more accurately estimate the moral intensity of the issue. Ethically sensitive people tend to have higher empathy. They also have more information about the specific situation. For example, accountants would be more ethically sensitive regarding the appropriateness of specific accounting procedures than would someone who has not received training in this profession.

The third important factor explaining why good people engage in unethical decisions and behavior is the situation in which the conduct occurs. Employees say they regularly experience pressure from top management that motivates them to lie to customers, breach regulations, or otherwise act unethically.[95] Situational factors do not justify unethical conduct. Rather, we need to recognize these factors so that organizations can reduce their influence in the future.

Moral intensity factor	Moral intensity question	Moral intensity is higher when:
Magnitude of consequences	How much harm or benefit will occur to others as a result of this action?	The harm or benefit is larger.
Social consensus	How many other people agree that this action is ethically good or bad?	Many people agree.
Probability of effect	(a) What is the chance that this action will actually occur? (b) What is the chance that this action will actually cause good or bad consequences?	The probability is higher.
Temporal immediacy	How long after the action will the consequences occur?	The consequences are immediate rather than delayed.
Proximity	How socially, culturally, psychologically, and/or physically close to me are the people affected by this decision?	Those affected are close rather than distant.
Concentration of effect	(a) How many people are affected by this action? (b) Are the people affected by this action easily identifiable as a group?	Many people are affected. Those affected are easily identifiable as a group.

Source: Based on information in T. J. Jones, "Ethical Decision Making by Individuals in Organizations: An Issue Contingent Model," *Academy of Management Review* 16 (1991), pp. 366–395.

Exhibit 2.8 *Factors Influencing Perceived Moral Intensity**

Supporting Ethical Behavior

Most large and medium-size organizations in the United States, United Kingdom, and several other countries apply one or more strategies to improve ethical conduct. Creating ethical codes of conduct is the most common. Almost all Fortune 500 companies in the United States and the majority of the 500 largest U.K. companies now have codes of ethics. These statements communicate the organization's ethical standards and signal to employees that the company takes ethical conduct seriously. However, critics point out that ethics codes alone do little to reduce unethical conduct. After all, Enron had a well-developed code of ethics, but that document didn't prevent senior executives from engaging in wholesale accounting fraud, resulting in the energy company's bankruptcy.[96]

Jet Airways Retrenchment—Uproar and Lurking Fear Jet Airways, like many other Indian organizations, was impacted adversely due to the global meltdown. It had taken measures like suspending operations on routes which were not viable, retrenchment of the staff, tied-up alliance with Kingfisher Airlines, etc. in order to survive global meltdown. The company had suspended initially around 800 flight attendants who were recruited for the planned expansion on 15th October, 2008. The Jet Airways management also had planned to lay-off personnel under probation and those whose jobs were unconfirmed. 800 flight attendants who received the news of their employment termination were shocked as the termination letters did not provide any reason. Quotes from some of the Jet Airways employees who were sacked give an insight into the panic and trauma they underwent. a staff quoted "I can't believe that I am unemployed now. Everything changed in hours". Another employee had quoted "My father was very happy when I got the job with the airlines in March this year. I had completed my training and was based at Delhi airport. Now our future is in dark. My father is shocked to hear about all this."

*These are factors people tend to ask themselves about when determining the moral intensity of an issue. Whether some of these questions should be relevant is itself an ethical question.

However, the sacked employees revolted back, by holding protests and also brought in political pressures in order to get back their jobs. Immediately within a day or two, Mr. Naresh Goyal, Chairman, Jet Airways announced reinstatement of all the sacked employees. Goyal had said in a press meet in the context of employees reinstatement: "All the employees are like family members to me and I am the head of that family. The decision to retrench was taken by the management considering economic realities. But, as the head of the family my conscience does not allow me to be dictated by only economics and money. So, the employees will start working from tomorrow as usual." However, the repercussions of global meltdown are always threatening both for the organization and the employees. In February 2009, it had to terminate the services of 27 expatriate pilots due to fleet reduction.

Sources:

1. India Today (16 Oct, 2008), *Jet Airways Employees Protest Retrenchment Drive.* http://indiatoday.intoday.in/site/Story/17753/Jet+Airways+employees+protest+retrenchment+drive.html, accessed on 13/12/2010.
2. BBC News (15 Oct, 2008), *Jet Airways Lays off 800 Staff.* http://news.bbc.co.uk/2/hi/7670874.stm, accessed on 16/12/2010.
3. Business Standard (17 Oct, 2008), *Jet Caves in Under Pressure, to Take Back Sacked Staff'.* http://www.business-standard.com/india/news/jet-caves-in-under-pressure-to-take-back-sacked-staff/337648/, accessed on 16/12/2010.
4. Sharma Rajeshwarei (2 Feb, 2008),*Layoffs Needn't be the First Option.* http://www.livemint.com/2009/02/02205740/Layoffs-needn8217t-be-the-f.html, Live Mint, accessed on 16/12/2010.

To supplement ethics codes, many firms provide ethics training. At Texas Instruments, employees learn to ask the following questions as their moral compass: "Is the action legal? Does it comply with our values? If you do it, will you feel bad? How would it look in the newspaper? If you know it's wrong, don't do it! If you're not sure, ask. Keep asking until you get an answer." Molson Coors developed an award-winning online training program set up as an expedition: Employees must resolve ethics violations at each "camp" as they ascend a mountain. The first few camps present real scenarios with fairly clear ethical violations of the company's ethics code; later camps present much fuzzier dilemmas requiring more careful thought about the company's underlying values.[97]

Some companies have also introduced procedures whereby employees can communicate possible ethical violations in confidence. Food manufacturer H. J. Heinz Co. has an ethics hotline that operates around the clock and in 150 languages for its global workforce. Heinz's director of ethics says

Protecting E&Y's Brand with Value-Based Ethics Training As a leading accounting and professional services firm, Ernst & Young (E&Y) has a lot at stake in maintaining its reputation for ethical conduct. "We can't ever be in a position to have our ethics challenged," says Michael Hamilton, E&Y's chief learning and development officer for the Americas. Although the financial world has become very rule-based, the rules still leave gaps where ethical missteps can occur. To minimize this risk, E&Y invests heavily in values-based ethics training. "Ethics training and value training are about providing all of our people with a clear message and some guiding principles about what to do when the rules don't address a situation or area," Hamilton explains. All E&Y staff members are required to complete a two-hour Web-based ethics course called "Living Our Core Values" in which they learn about the company's values and ethical principles, followed by analysis of several specific case situations. Ethical topics are also being integrated throughout E&Y's professional development courses. "We're trying to bake ethics training into all of our curriculum," says Jeffrey Hoops, ethics and compliance officer for the Americas and chief privacy officer. "It's about continually reminding people that doing the right thing and speaking up when you see the wrong thing is not just accepted—it is the expected way we do things at Ernst & Young."[98]

that the hotline "has provided an early warning signal of problems we were not aware of." Rogers Cable Communications Inc. also has an anonymous "star hotline" as well as a Web link that employees can use to raise ethical issues or concerns about ethical conduct. Rogers employees can even call back to find out what actions have been taken to resolve an ethical issue.[99]

These additional measures support ethical conduct to some extent, but the most powerful foundation is a set of shared values that reinforce ethical conduct. "If you don't have a culture of ethical decision-making to begin with, all the controls and compliance regulations you care to deploy won't necessarily prevent ethical misconduct," warns a senior executive at British communications giant Vodafone. This culture is supported by the ethical conduct and vigilance of corporate leaders. By acting with the highest standards of moral conduct, leaders not only gain support and trust from followers; they role-model the ethical standards that employees are more likely to follow.[100]

Karma/Action Theory—Indian Concept[101]

The old adage goes, "As you sow, so you reap". In India, there is emphasis on *karma/actions.* This theory is about action-result linkage, which means if positive actions are sowed, it will reap positively, and vice versa. An organization and individual, both should keep their actions and results in perspective. The theory focuses on ethical actions of an organization. *Gunas/*personality of an individual has an impact on one's actions. In an organizational context, an entity's culture, leadership, and organizational behavior gets reflected in the actions undertaken and in its outcome, i.e. goodwill in the market, customer satisfaction, market share, sustainability, etc. Despites uncertainties, and rush for staying ahead in the competitive environment, organizations and individuals need to practice self-regulation. An organization uses the right strategies, means and fundamentals to earn the right profit. As corporate social responsibility is becoming crucial, organizations can leverage the *karma* theory to strengthen ethical foundation and practices in organizations that can result into competitive advantage.

Ethical Lapses Causing Toxic Behavior in the Context of Global Meltdown

Ethical lapse is one of the causes which caused the meltdown of 2008 and impacted not only the US economy, but also economies across the globe. Breakdown of ethics had led to breakdown or closure of organizations; employees lost their jobs overnight and were left in the dark along with their families; people who had trust in the organization and had invested their hard earned money, lost it in the subprime crisis and stock-exchange meltdown.

Ethical Lapses

Values of an individual form their attitude and give shape to behaviors. These values can be either ethical or non-ethical, consequences of which are according to the seeds sowed. Some of the noted ethical lapses which are being considered as the cause behind this global meltdown in various research studies are as follows:

Greed Greed is caused by various factors like desire for gain, disregard for risk, a psychological motivation to grab and leverage opportunities, and desire for excess. The disastrous financial meltdown happened because of the greed in individuals, institutions, investors, and federal organizations. In the spree to gain more wealth, risk, regulations and impact on the economy were overlooked. According to Paul Krugman, the Princeton Nobel Laureate economist, "Greed is bad….a system that lavishly rewards executives for success attempts those executives who control much of the information to outsiders, to fabricate the appearance of success–aggressive accounting, fictitious transactions, that inflates sales, whatever it takes"[102]. For example, people burn their fingers in stock markets or get swayed in stock scams when they chase fast moving or over priced stocks[103].

Overconfidence Over-optimism about future which occurs when risks and associated losses are overlooked. Over-optimism causes overconfidence which affects decision making. Individuals rely highly on their own skills; they get overconfident based on their past success and totally ignore good fortunes which too has a key role. Overconfident individuals start to believe on their own that they are competent ahead of others, they are honest and fair in their practices.

Abuse of Power Individuals misuse the power and authority which comes along with their position for individual or collective benefit. They abuse power by involving in corporate wrong doing, management fraud, and illegal corporate behavior[104].

Selfish Motives There is rise in selfish motives among individuals and organizations. They would contribute and get involved only if they foresee benefits in materialistic terms.

Low Levels of Uncertainty Avoidance Individuals and organizations are so much addicted to achieve their goals that they overlook risks and do not want to loose at any cost. This risk aversion behavior is the result of emotional attachment to what they own.

Toxic Behaviors Resultant of Ethical Lapses

Employee bad behavior has been defined as "voluntary behavior that violates significant organizational norms and in doing so threatens the well-being of the organization, its members, or both"[105].

Narcissist Behavior Individuals with narcissist behavior have high ego, they think and feel that they have the right to entitlements. They are arrogant in nature. They think in visionary terms, are very demanding and ruthless to achieve their goals. Narcissists can be productive or unproductive for organizations.

Materialism In the past, individuals worked under fixed timing and were content with their fixed salaries. However, the Gen X and Y are competitive, they would struggle and strive to achieve and succeed in work life and also in their lifestyle. They work for late hours, strive to compete and go ahead of other colleagues, in order to receive higher salaries, perk and better positions and reputation. They earn lumpsum salaries which is spent in buying rich and lavish lifestyle, to provide higher levels of comforts and materialistic needs for their family and children. Self-interest, freedom, high level of optimism, and endeavor has fueled materialism. Compulsive drive for more which is unending causes materialism.

Job Insecurity Organizations no longer guarantee job security in an ever-rising competitive and uncertainties ridden environment. Employees spend long hours at the workplace as the organization expects performance excellence from them. Moreover, employees cannot deny working for long hours on professional terms, and also have fear of losing their job. In the process of keeping their jobs safe, they tend to practice unethical methods and ways for shortcut to success.

Rat Race Workplaces have become increasingly competitive, so each individual strives to be in the good books of their managers. This means they work for long hours, take up additional responsibilities, etc. leading to rat race. These factors cause stress, pressures, imbalance, desire to get benefits both in kind and praise increases at uncontrollable levels. The Gen X and Y are quickly climbing the corporate ladder. There is increase in proportion of young generation occupying senior positions in organizations.

Chapter Summary

Individual behavior is influenced by motivation, ability, role perceptions, and situational factors (MARS). Motivation consists of internal forces that affect the direction, intensity, and persistence of a person's voluntary choice of behavior. Ability includes both the natural aptitudes and the learned capabilities required to successfully complete a task. Role perceptions are a person's beliefs about what behaviors are appropriate or necessary in a particular situation. Situational factors are environmental conditions that constrain or facilitate employee behavior and performance.

Personality is the relatively enduring pattern of thoughts, emotions, and behaviors that characterize a person, along with the psychological processes behind those characteristics. Most experts now agree that personality is shaped by both nature and nurture. Most personality traits are represented within the five-factor model, which includes conscientiousness, agreeableness, neuroticism, openness to experience, and extroversion. Another set of traiis, measured by the Myers-Briggs Type Indicator, represents how people prefer to perceive and judge information. Conscientiousness and emotional stability (low neuroticism) stand out as the personality traits that best predict individual performance in almost every job group. The other three personality dimensions predict more specific types of employee behavior and performance.

Self-concept includes an individual's self-beliefs and self-evaluations. It has three structural dimensions: complexity, consistency, and clarity. People are inherently motivated to promote and protect their self-concept; this is self-enhancement. At the same time, people are motivated to verify and maintain their existing self-concept; this is self-verification.

Self-evaluation, an important aspect of self-concept, consists of self-esteem, self-efficacy, and locus of control. Self-esteem is the extent to which people like, respect, and are satisfied with themselves. Self-efficacy is a person's belief that he or she has the ability, motivation, correct role perceptions, and favorable situation to complete a task successfully; general self-efficacy is a perception of one's competence to perform across a variety of situations. Locus of control is defined as a person's general belief about the amount of control he or she has over personal life events. Self-concept consists of both personality identity and social identity. Social identity theory explains how people define themselves in terms of the groups to which they belong or have an emotional attachment.

Values are stable, evaluative beliefs that guide our preferences for outcomes or courses of action in a variety of situations. People arrange values into a hierarchy of preferences, called a *value system*. Espoused values—what we say and think we use as values—are different from enacted values, which are values evident from our actions. Values have been organized into a circle with 10 clusters. Value congruence is the similarity of value systems between two entities.

Five values that differ across cultures are individualism, collectivism, power distance, uncertainty avoidance, and achievement-nurturing orientation. Three values that guide ethical conduct are utilitarianism, individual rights, and distributive justice. Three factors that influence ethical conduct are the extent to which an issue demands ethical principles (moral intensity), the person's ethical sensitivity to the presence and importance of an ethical dilemma, and situational factors that cause people to deviate from their moral values. Companies improve ethical conduct through a code of ethics, ethics training, ethics hotlines, and the conduct of corporate leaders.

Key Terms

ability
achievement-nurturing orientation
collectivism
competencies
conscientiousness
ethical sensitivity
extroversion
five-factor model (FFM)
individualism
locus of control
moral intensity
motivation
Myers-Briggs Type Indicator (MBTI)
neuroticism
personality
power distance
role perceptions
self-concept
self-efficacy
social identity theory
uncertainty avoidance

Critical Thinking Questions

1. An insurance company has high levels of absenteeism among the office staff. The head of office administration argues that employees are misusing the company's sick leave benefits. However, some of the mostly female staff members have explained that family responsibilities interfere with work. Using the MARS model, as well as your knowledge of absenteeism behavior, discuss some of the possible reasons for absenteeism here and how it might be reduced.
2. As the district manager responsible for six stores in a large electronics retail chain, you have had difficulty with the performance of some sales employees. Although they are initially motivated and generally have good interpersonal skills, many have difficulty with the complex knowledge of the wide variety of store products, ranging from computers to high-fidelity sound systems. Describe three strategies you might apply to improve the match between the competencies of new sales employees and the job requirements.
3. Studies report that heredity has a strong influence on an individual's personality. What are the implications of this in organizational settings?
4. Suppose that you give all candidates applying for a management trainee position a personality test that measures the five dimensions in the five-factor model. Which personality traits would you consider to be the most important for this type of job? Explain your answer.
5. An important aspect of self-concept is the idea that almost everyone engages in self-enhancement. What problems tend to occur in organizations as a result of the self-enhancement phenomenon? What can organizational leaders do to make use of a person's inherent drive for self-enhancement?
6. This chapter discussed value congruence mostly in the context of an employee's personal values versus the organization's values. But value congruence also relates to the juxtaposition of other pairs of value systems. Explain how value congruence is relevant with respect to organizational versus professional values (i.e., values of a professional occupation, such as physician, accountant, pharmacist).
7. People in a particular South American country have high power distance and high collectivism. What does this mean, and what are the implications of this information when you (a senior executive) visit employees working for your company in that country?
8. "All decisions are ethical decisions." Comment on this statement, particularly by referring to the concepts of moral intensity and ethical sensitivity.

CASE STUDY 2.1

SK TELECOM GOES EGALITARIAN IN A HIERARCHICAL SOCIETY

Until recently, Hur Jae-hoon could end debate with junior staff members just by declaring that the discussion was over. Employed at the fourth tier in SK Telecom Co.'s five-tier management/professional hierarchy, the 33-year-old strategist held the corresponding title of "Hur Daeri" and received plenty of respect from people in lower positions. No one below Hur was allowed to question his decisions, and Hur was expected to silently comply with requests from above. South Korea's culture of deferring to people in higher positions was deeply ingrained in the telecommunications company. In some South Korean companies, such as Samsung, junior staff members aren't even allowed to initiate conversations with anyone above their boss.

Now, in spite of South Korea's strong hierarchical culture, SK Telecom wants to support more egalitarian values. It has already removed its five management ranks and their differentiated titles and status. The English word *Manager* is now used to address anyone employed throughout the five former ranks. (Hur Jae-hoon's title has changed from Hur Daeri to "Hur Manager"). Only vice presidents and above retain their previous status titles. People in charge of projects or people are also called "Team Leader." Furthermore, the company is assigning project leadership responsibilities to employees in their twenties, whereas these roles were previously held only by older staff with much more seniority. As an added change, the company is allowing a more casual dress code at work.

Through this dramatic shift in values and practices, SK Telecom's senior executives hope that junior staff will speak up more freely, thereby improving creativity and decision-making. They particularly want to avoid incidents such as one that occurred several years ago in which an excellent idea from younger employees was initially shot down by their bosses. The junior staff suggested that allowing customers to change their cell phone ringtones to music chosen by the friend they've phoned would generate revenue through music licensing. Fortunately, the idea was introduced several months later, after a few persistent employees proposed the idea again.

SK Telecom's initiative is not completely new to South Korea. Small high-tech companies already embrace egalitarian values and flatter corporate structures. But SK Telecom is among the first large firms in the country to attempt this culture shift, and it has met with resistance along the way. SK Telecom executives were initially divided over how quickly and to what extent the company should distance itself from South Korea's traditional hierarchical culture. "There were ideas for gradual versus all-out reforms," recalls chief executive Kim Shin-bae. "But the word 'gradually' means 'not now' to some people. So we decided to go all-out."

According to a company survey, 80 percent of employees support the changes. However, even with the changes in titles, many still look for subtle evidence of who has higher status and, therefore, should receive more deference. Some also rely on what positions managers held under the old five-tier hierarchy. "I know what the old titles were," says an LG Electronics Co. manager who supplies cell phones to SK Telecom. "So unconsciously, I keep that in mind."

Hur Jae-hoon admits there are times when he prefers a more hierarchical culture, but he believes that SK Telecom's more egalitarian values and practices are already showing favorable results. In one recent meeting, a younger colleague sparred with Hur over the better way to complete a strategy project. "For a moment, I wished it was back in the old days when I could have shut that guy down," Hur recalls. "But I had to admit his opinion was better than mine, and I adjusted. So the system worked."

Discussion Questions

1. SK Telecom is attempting to distance itself from which South Korean cultural value? What indicators of this value are identified in this case study? What other artifacts of this cultural value would you notice while visiting a South Korean company that upheld this national culture?
2. In your opinion, why is this hierarchical value so strong in South Korea? What are the advantages and disadvantages of this value in societies?
3. Do you think SK Telecom will be successful in integrating a more egalitarian culture, even though it contrasts with South Korea's culture? What are some of the issues that may complicate or support this transition?

Source: Based on E. Ramstad, "Pulling Rank Gets Harder at One Korean Company," *Wall Street Journal,* 20 August 2007, p. B1.

CASE STUDY 2.2

PUSHING PAPER CAN BE FUN

A large city government was putting on a number of seminars for managers of various departments throughout the city. At one of these sessions, the topic discussed was motivation–how we can get public servants motivated to do a good job. The plight of a police captain became the central focus of the discussion:

I've got a real problem with my officers. They come on the force as young, inexperienced rookies, and we send them out on the street, either in cars or on a beat. They seem to like the contact they have with the public, the action involved in crime prevention, and the apprehension of criminals. They also like helping people out at fires, accidents, and other emergencies.

The problem occurs when they get back to the station. They hate to do the paperwork, and because they dislike it, the job is frequently put off or done inadequately. This lack of attention hurts us later on when we get to court. We need clear, factual reports. They must be highly detailed and unambiguous. As soon as one part of a report is shown to be inadequate or incorrect, the rest of the report is suspect. Poor reporting probably causes us to lose more cases than any other factor.

I just don't know how to motivate them to do a better job. We're in a budget crunch and I have absolutely no financial rewards at my disposal. In fact, we'll probably have to lay some people off in the near future. It's hard for me to make the job interesting and challenging because it isn't–it's boring, routine paperwork, and there isn't much you can do about it.

Finally, I can't say to them that their promotions will hinge on the excellence of their paperwork. First of all, they know it's not true. If their performance is adequate, most are more likely to get promoted just by staying on the force a certain number of years than for some specific outstanding act. Second, they were trained to do the job they do out in the streets, not to fill out forms. All through their career it is the arrests and interventions that get noticed.

Some people have suggested a number of things, like using conviction records as a performance criterion. However, we know that's not fair–too many other things are involved. Bad paperwork increases the chance that you lose in court, but good paperwork doesn't necessarily mean you'll win. We tried setting up team competitions based upon the excellence of the reports, but the officers caught on to that pretty quickly. No one was getting any type of reward for winning the competition, and they figured why should they bust a gut when there was no payoff.

I just don't know what to do.

Discussion Questions

1. What performance problems is the captain trying to correct?
2. Use the MARS model of individual behavior and performance to diagnose the possible causes of the unacceptable behavior.
3. Has the captain considered all possible solutions to the problem? If not, what else might be done?

Source: T. R. Mitchell and J. R. Larson, Jr., *People in Organizations,* 3rd ed. (New York: McGraw-Hill, 1987), p. 184. Reproduced with permission from The McGraw-Hill Companies.

CASE STUDY 2.3

THE TROUBLE WITH BUSINESS ETHICS

BusinessWeek

Business ethics may have risen to the top of most executive agendas, but Wal-Mart Stores has learned that practicing ethics can also present ethical dilemmas.

A few months after going through a new employee training session with a heavy emphasis on ethics, Chalace Epley Lowry acted on the guidance to report any activity that seemed the least bit suspicious. Lowry told the company's ethics office about possible insider trading by one of her supervisors. Wal-Mart's investigation concluded that the supervisor had done nothing wrong, but Lowry soon discovered that her identity as the whistle-blower had been revealed to the supervisor she accused of wrongdoing. Now Lowry is looking for another job, but there's no guarantee she'll get transferred at Wal-Mart.

This *BusinessWeek* case study examines the challenges of supporting ethics hotlines and whistle-blowing, and it discusses the reasons why employees are reluctant to communicate ethical wrongdoing. Read the full text of this *BusinessWeek* article at www.mhhe.com/mcshane5e, and prepare for the discussion questions below.

Discussion Questions

1. In an organization's efforts to maintain ethical standards, how important is it to encourage and support employees who report possible incidents of ethical wrongdoing (i.e., engage in whistle-blowing)? Why? What can companies do to support whistle-blowers?
2. What actions are described in this case study that companies have taken to improve ethical standards in their organizations? Are these actions substantive changes or mostly symbolic? Why?

Source: P. Gogoi, "The Trouble with Business Ethics," *BusinessWeek Online*, 22 June 2007.

CLASS EXERCISE 2.4

TEST YOUR KNOWLEDGE OF PERSONALITY

PURPOSE This exercise is designed to help you think about and understand the effects of the Big Five personality dimensions on individual preferences and outcomes.

INSTRUCTIONS (LARGE CLASS) Below are several questions relating to the Big Five personality dimensions and various preferences or outcomes. Answer each of these questions relying on your personal experience or best guess. Later, the instructor will show you the answers based on scholarly results. You will *not* be graded on this exercise, but it may help you to better understand the effect of personality on human behavior and preferences.

INSTRUCTIONS (SMALL CLASS)

1. The instructor will organize students into teams. Members of each team work together to answer each of the questions below relating to the Big Five personality dimensions and various preferences or outcomes.
2. The instructor will reveal the answers based on scholarly results. (*Note:* The instructor might create a competition to see which team has the most answers correct.)

PERSONALITY AND PREFERENCES QUESTIONS

1. Which two Big Five personality dimensions are positively associated with enjoyment of workplace humor?

   ____________________ ____________________

2. Listed below are several jobs. Please check no more than two personality dimensions that you believe are positively associated with preferences for each occupation.
3. Rank order (1 = highest, 5 = lowest) the Big Five personality dimensions in terms of how much you think they predict a person's degree of life satisfaction. (*Note:* Personality dimensions are ranked by their absolute effect, so ignore the negative or positive direction of association.)

Job	Personality Dimension				
	Extroversion	Conscientiousness	Agreeableness	Neuroticism	Openness to experience
Budget analyst	☐	☐	☐	☐	☐
Corporate executive	☐	☐	☐	☐	☐
Engineer	☐	☐	☐	☐	☐
Journalist	☐	☐	☐	☐	☐
Life insurance agent	☐	☐	☐	☐	☐
Nurse	☐	☐	☐	☐	☐
Physician	☐	☐	☐	☐	☐
Production supervisor	☐	☐	☐	☐	☐
Public relations director	☐	☐	☐	☐	☐
Research analyst	☐	☐	☐	☐	☐
School teacher	☐	☐	☐	☐	☐
Sculptor	☐	☐	☐	☐	☐

___ Conscientiousness
___ Agreeableness
___ Neuroticism
___ Openness to experience
___ Extroversion

TEAM EXERCISE 2.5

COMPARING CULTURAL VALUES

PURPOSE This exercise is designed to help you determine the extent to which students hold similar assumptions about the values that dominate in other countries.

INSTRUCTIONS (SMALL CLASS) The terms in the left column represent labels that a major consulting project identified with businesspeople in a particular country, based on its national culture and values. These terms appear in alphabetical order. In the right column are the names of countries, also in alphabetical order, corresponding to the labels in the left column.

1. Working alone, connect the labels with the countries by relying on your perceptions of these countries. Each label is associated with only one country, so each label should be connected to only

one country, and vice versa. Draw a line to connect the pairs, or put the label number beside the country name.

2. The instructor will form teams of four or five members. Members of each team will compare their results and try to reach consensus on a common set of connecting pairs.
3. Teams or the instructor will post the results so that all can see the extent to which students hold common opinions about businesspeople in other cultures. Class discussion can then consider the reasons why the results are so similar or different, as well as the implications of these results for working in a global work environment.

Value Labels and Country Names

Value label (alphabetical)	Country name (alphabetical)
1. Affable humanists	Australia
2. Ancient modernizers	Brazil
3. Commercial catalysts	Canada
4. Conceptual strategists	China
5. Efficient manufacturers	France
6. Ethical statesmen	Germany
7. Informal egalitarians	India
8. Modernizing traditionalists	Netherlands
9. Optimistic entrepreneurs	New Zealand
10. Quality perfectionists	Singapore
11. Rugged individualists	Taiwan
12. Serving merchants	United Kingdom
13. Tolerant traders	United States

Source: Based on R. Rosen, P. Digh, M. Singer, and C. Phillips, *Global Literacies* (New York: Simon & Schuster, 2000).

INSTRUCTIONS (LARGE CLASS)

1. Working alone, connect the labels with the countries by relying on your perceptions of these countries. Each label is associated with only one country, so each label should be connected to only one country, and vice versa. Draw a line to connect the pairs, or put the label number beside the country name.
2. Asking for a show of hands, the instructor will find out which country is identified by most students with each label. The instructor will then post the correct answers.

TEAM EXERCISE 2.6

ETHICS DILEMMA VIGNETTES

PURPOSE This exercise is designed to make you aware of the ethical dilemmas people face in various business situations, as well as the competing principles and values that operate in these situations.

INSTRUCTIONS (SMALL CLASS) The instructor will form teams of four or five students. Team members will read each case below and discuss the extent to which the company's action in each case was ethical. Teams should be prepared to justify their evaluation using ethics principles and the perceived moral intensity of each incident.

INSTRUCTIONS (LARGE CLASS) Working alone, read each case below and determine the extent to which the company's action in each case was ethical. The instructor will use a show of hands to determine the extent to which students believe the case represents an ethical dilemma (high or low moral intensity) and the extent to which the main people or company in each incident acted ethically.

CASE ONE An employee who worked for a major food retailer wrote a Weblog (blog) and, in one of his writings, complained that his boss wouldn't let him go home when he felt sick and that his district manager refused to promote him because of his dreadlocks. His blog named the employer, but the employee didn't use his real name. Although all blogs are on the Internet, the employee claims that his was low-profile and that it didn't show up in a Google search of his name or the company. Still, the employer somehow discovered the blog, figured out the employee's real name, and fired him for "speaking ill of the company in a public domain."

CASE TWO Computer printer manufacturers usually sell printers at a low margin over cost and generate much more income from subsequent sales of the high-margin ink cartridges required for each printer. One global printer manufacturer now designs its printers so that they work only with ink cartridges made in the same region. Ink cartridges purchased in the United States will not work with the same printer model sold in Europe, for example. This "region coding" of ink cartridges does not improve performance. Rather, it prevents consumers and gray marketers from buying the product at a lower price in another region. The company says this policy allows it to maintain stable prices within a region rather than continually changing prices due to currency fluctuations.

CASE THREE For the past few years, the design department of a small (40-employee) company has been using a particular software program, but the three employees who use the software have been complaining for more than a year that the software is out of date and is slowing down their performance. The department agreed to switch to a competing software program, costing several thousand dollars. However, the next version won't be released for six months and buying the current version will not allow much discount on the next version. The company has put in advance orders for the next version. Meanwhile, one employee was able to get a copy of the current version of the software from a friend in the industry. The company has allowed the three employees to use this current version of the software even though they did not pay for it.

CASE FOUR Judy Price is a popular talk-show radio personality and opinionated commentator on the morning phone-in show of a popular radio station in a large U.S. city. Price is married to John Tremble, an attorney who was recently elected mayor of the city even though he had no previous experience in public office. The radio station's board of directors is very concerned that the station's perceived objectivity will be compromised if Price remains on air as a commentator and talk-show host while her husband holds such a public position. For example, the radio station manager believes that Price gave minimal attention to an incident in which environmental groups criticized the city for its slow progress on recycling. Price denied that her views are biased and stated that the incident didn't merit as much attention as other issues that particular week. To ease the board's concerns, the station manager transferred Price from her talk-show host and commentator position to the hourly news reporting position, where most of the script is written by others. Although the reporting job is technically a lower position, Price's total salary package remains the same. Price is now seeking professional advice to determine whether the radio station's action represents a form of discrimination on the basis of marital status.

SELF-ASSESSMENT 2.7

ARE YOU INTROVERTED OR EXTROVERTED?

PURPOSE This self-assessment is designed to help you estimate the extent to which you are introverted or extroverted.

INSTRUCTIONS The statements in the scale below refer to personal characteristics that might or might not be characteristic of you. Mark the box indicating the extent to which the statement accurately or inaccurately describes you. Then use the scoring key in Appendix B at the end of this book to calculate your results. This exercise should be completed alone so that you can assess yourself honestly

IPIP Introversion-Extroversion Scale

How accurately does each of the statements listed below describe you?	Very accurate description of me	Moderately accurate	Neither accurate nor inaccurate	Moderately inaccurate	Very inaccurate description of me
1. I feel comfortable around people.	☐	☐	☐	☐	☐
2. I make friends easily.	☐	☐	☐	☐	☐
3. I keep in the background.	☐	☐	☐	☐	☐
4. I don't talk a lot.	☐	☐	☐	☐	☐
5. I would describe my experiences as somewhat dull.	☐	☐	☐	☐	☐
6. I know how to captivate people.	☐	☐	☐	☐	☐
7. I don't like to draw attention to myself.	☐	☐	☐	☐	☐
8. I am the life of the party.	☐	☐	☐	☐	☐
9. I am skilled in handling social situations.	☐	☐	☐	☐	☐
10. I have little to say.	☐	☐	☐	☐	☐

Source: Adapted from instruments described and/or presented in L. R. Goldberg, J. A. Johnson, H. W. Eber, R. Hogan, M. C. Ashton, C. R. Cloninger, and H. C. Gough, "The International Personality Item Pool and the Future of Public-Domain Personality Measures," *Journal of Research in Personality* 40 (2006), pp. 84–96.

without concerns of social comparison. Class discussion will focus on the meaning and implications of extroversion and introversion in organizations.

SELF-ASSESSMENT 2.8

WHAT ARE YOUR DOMINANT VALUES?

Values have taken center stage in organizational behavior. Increasingly, OB experts are realizing that our personal values influence our motivation, decisions, and attitudes. This self-assessment is designed to help you estimate your personal values and value system. The instrument consists of several words and phrases, and you are asked to indicate whether each word or phrase is highly opposite or highly similar to your personal values or is at some point between these two extremes. As with all self-assessments, you need to be honest with yourself when completing this activity in order to get the most accurate results.

SELF-ASSESSMENT 2.9

INDIVIDUALISM-COLLECTIVISM SCALE

Two of the most important concepts in cross-cultural organizational behavior are individualism and collectivism. This self-assessment measures your levels of individualism and collectivism with one of the most widely adopted measures. This scale consists of several statements, and you are asked to indicate how well each statement describes you. You need to be honest with yourself to receive a reasonable estimate of your level of individualism and collectivism.

SELF-ASSESSMENT 2.10

ESTIMATING YOUR LOCUS OF CONTROL

This self-assessment is designed to help you estimate the extent to which you have an internal or external locus-of-control personality. The instrument asks you to indicate the degree to which you agree or disagree with each of the statements provided. As with all self-assessments, you need to be honest with yourself when completing this activity to get the most accurate results. The results show your relative position on the internal-external locus continuum and the general meaning of this score.

SELF-ASSESSMENT 2.11

IDENTIFYING YOUR GENERAL SELF-EFFICACY

Self-efficacy refers to a person's belief that he or she has the ability, motivation, and resources to complete a task successfully. Self-efficacy is usually conceptualized as a situation-specific belief. You may believe that you can perform a certain task in one situation but may be less confident with that task in another situation. However, there is evidence that people develop a more general self-efficacy. This exercise helps you estimate your general self-efficacy. Read each of the statements in this self-assessment and select the response that best fits your personal belief. This self-assessment should be completed alone so that you rate yourself honestly without concerns of social comparison. Class discussion will focus on the meaning and importance of self-efficacy in the workplace.

In his regular job, John Leiter helps American companies carry out internal investigations into financial wrongdoing. But the Boston-based Ernst & Young senior manager found himself in a completely different environment as a participant in the accounting firm's corporate social responsibility fellows program. For three months, Leiter was transplanted to Montevideo, Uruguay, assisting Infocorp, a young information technology company, with its first real five-year strategic plan. Leiter was performing different work in a different country with a different culture and language. "I worked out of my comfort zone the entire time," he recalls.

John Leiter (second from left) and other employees at Ernst & Young are developing more cosmopolitan perceptions of the world by assisting entrepreneurs in other cultures, such as this information technology company in Uruguay.

Leiter particularly noticed that he had to adjust his fast-paced American business style to the more personal approach in Uruguay, which included traditional quarter-hour chitchats before meetings. The experience gave him a different perspective of the world and his approach to working with clients. "Often times, we have such a myopic focus, and it doesn't allow us to take a large view of the issue," says Leiter, who now spends more time learning about the client's needs before launching into the work.

International corporate volunteering is more than an important form of corporate social responsibility; it is also a valuable tool to help employees at Ernst & Young and other companies develop more cosmopolitan perceptions of the world. "We need people with a global mindset, and what better way to develop a global mindset, and what more realistic way, than for somebody to have an immersion experience with just enough safety net," says Deborah K. Holmes, Ernst & Young Americas director of corporate responsibility.

Ernst & Young has sent John Leiter and two dozen other high-performing employees to work with entrepreneurs in South America. At Pfizer, the world's largest pharmaceutical company, between 25 and 45 employees work up to six months in Africa and elsewhere each year to combat HIV-AIDS and other illnesses. Through its Project Ulysses program, PricewaterhouseCoopers sends 25 partners each year to developing countries, where they spend eight weeks working with nongovernmental organizations (NGOs) on community projects.

IBM has also made international corporate volunteering part of its global leadership development curriculum through its recently launched Corporate Service Corps program. IBM CEO Sam Palmisano explains that these corporate social responsibility initiatives will develop its global leaders because participants "work in these other kinds of environments, so they can get a perspective and learn . . . how to think about problems from another perspective, from another point of view."[1]

3

Perception and Learning in Organizations

Learning Objectives

After reading this chapter, you should be able to:

1. Outline the perceptual process.
2. Explain how social identity and stereotyping influence the perceptual process, and how one can minimize stereotyping bias.
3. Describe the attribution process and two attribution errors.
4. Summarize the self-fulfilling-prophecy process.
5. Explain how halo, primacy, recency, and false-consensus effects bias our perceptions.
6. Discuss three ways to improve social perception, with specific application to organizational situations.
7. Describe the A-B-C model of behavior modification and the four contingencies of reinforcement.
8. Describe the three features of social learning theory.
9. Outline the elements of organizational learning and ways to improve each element.

global mindset
The capacity for complex perceiving and thinking characterized by superior awareness of and openness to different ways that others perceive their environment.

International corporate volunteering programs have become a key component of global leadership development because they nurture a **global mindset.**[2] They help employees develop a superior awareness of and openness to different "spheres of meaning and action," that is, the various ways that others perceive their environment. Global mindset is gaining interest among organizational behavior experts. It is also a fitting topic to begin this chapter because it encompasses the dynamics of perceptions and learning. From a perceptual view, global mindset begins with self-awareness–understanding our own beliefs, values, and attitudes. Through self-awareness, we are more open-minded and nonjudgmental when receiving and processing complex information for decision making. Having a global mindset also relates to learning because employees working in a global environment need to quickly absorb large volumes of information about the diverse environments in which they work. Furthermore, people with a global mindset have a strong learning orientation. They welcome new situations as learning opportunities rather than view them as threats, and they continually question rather than quickly confirm what they know.

This chapter describes these two related topics of perceptions and learning in organizations. We begin by describing the perceptual process, that is, the dynamics of selecting, organizing, and interpreting external stimuli. Next, we examine the perceptual processes of social identity and stereotyping, attribution, and self-fulfilling prophecy, including biases created within these processes. Four other perceptual biases–halo, primacy, recency, and false consensus–are also briefly introduced. We then identify potentially effective ways to improve perceptions, including practices similar to corporate volunteering. The latter part of this chapter looks at three perspectives of learning: behavior modification, social learning theory, and experiential learning, followed by the key elements in organizational learning.

Learning Objectives

After reading the next two sections, you should be able to:

1. Outline the perceptual process.
2. Explain how social identity and stereotyping influence the perceptual process, and how one can minimize stereotyping bias.

THE PERCEPTUAL PROCESS

perception
The process of receiving information about and making sense of the world around us.

selective attention
The process of attending to some information received by our senses and ignoring other information.

Perception is the process of receiving information about and making sense of the world around us. It entails determining which information to notice, how to categorize this information, and how to interpret it within the framework of our existing knowledge. This perceptual process is far from perfect, as you will learn in this chapter, but it generally follows the steps shown in Exhibit 3.1. Perception begins when environmental stimuli are received through our senses. Most stimuli that bombard our senses are screened out; the rest are organized and interpreted. The process of attending to some information received by our senses and ignoring other information is called **selective attention.** Selective attention is influenced by characteristics of the person or object being perceived, particularly size, intensity, motion, repetition, and novelty. For example, a small, flashing red light on a nurse station console is immediately noticed because it is bright (intensity),

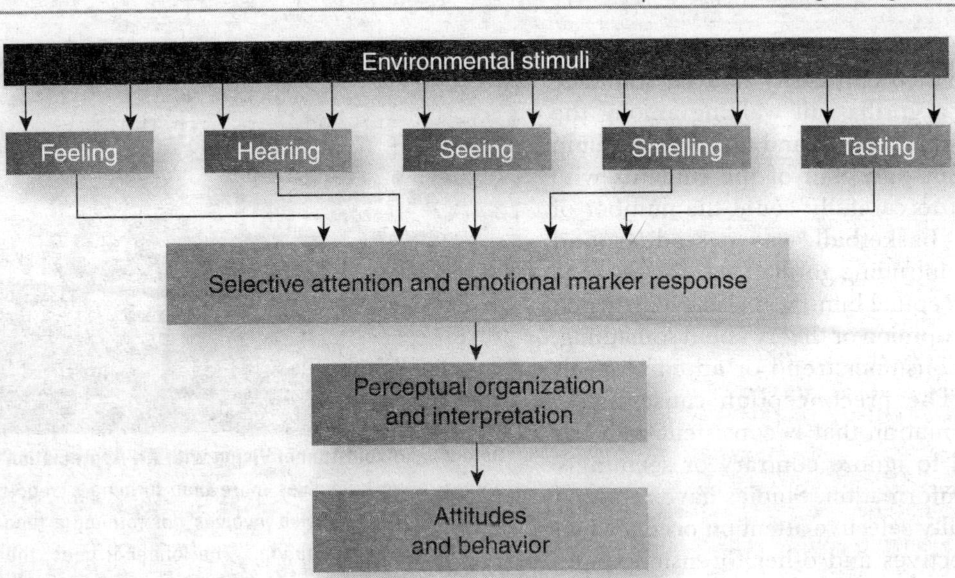

Exhibit 3.1 *Model of the Perceptual Process*

flashing (motion), a rare event (novelty), and has symbolic meaning that a patient's vital signs are failing. Notice that selective attention is also influenced by the context in which the target is perceived. The selective attention process is triggered by things or people who might be out of context, such as hearing someone with a foreign accent in a setting where most people have American accents.

Characteristics of the perceiver play an important role in selective attention, much of it without the perceiver's awareness.[3] When information is received through the senses, our brain quickly and nonconsciously assesses whether it is relevant or irrelevant to us and then attaches emotional markers (worry, happiness, boredom) to that information. The emotional markers help us to store information in memory; they also reproduce the same emotions when we are subsequently thinking about this information.[4]

The selective attention process is far from perfect. As mentioned in Chapter 2, we have a natural and usually nonconscious tendency to seek out information that supports our self-concept or puts us in a favorable light and to ignore or undervalue information that is contrary to our self-concept. This *confirmation bias* also screens out information that is contrary to our values and assumptions.[5] Several studies have found that people fail to perceive (or soon forget) statements and events that undermine political parties that they support. One recent study examined how people perceived and accepted stories during the first weeks of the Iraq War that were subsequently retracted (acknowledged by the media as false stories). The study found that most of the Germans and Australians surveyed dismissed the retracted events, whereas a significantly large percentage of Americans continued to believe these false stories, even though many of them recalled that the stories had been retracted by the media. In essence, people in the American sample were reluctant to reject and forget about information that supported their beliefs about the Iraq War.[6]

Finally, selective attention is influenced by our assumptions and conscious anticipation of future events. You are more likely to notice a co-worker's e-mail among the daily bombardment of messages when you expect to receive that e-mail (particularly when it is important to you). Unfortunately, expectations and assumptions also cause us to screen out potentially important information. In one study, students were asked to watch a 30-second video clip in which several people passed around two basketballs. Students who were asked just to watch the video clip easily noticed someone dressed in a gorilla suit walking among the players for nine seconds and stopping to thump its chest. But only half of the students who were asked to carefully count the number of times one basketball was passed around noticed the intruding gorilla.[7]

This perceptual blindness also occurs when we form an opinion or theory about something, such as a consumer trend or an employee's potential. The preconception causes us to select information that is consistent with the theory and to ignore contrary or seemingly irrelevant information. Studies have reported that this faulty selective attention occurs when police detectives and other forensic experts quickly form theories about what happened.[8] These experts are now increasingly aware of the need to avoid selective attention traps by keeping an open mind, absorbing as much information as possible, and avoiding theories too early in the investigation.

Detectives Avoid Tunnel Vision with Art Appreciation Good detective work involves more than forming a good theory about the crime. It also involves *not* forming a theory too early in the investigation. "The longer it goes, the more theories there are," warns FBI special agent Mark MacKizer when describing a six-year-old investigation in which a family was murdered in Henry County, Virginia. "We're very careful to let the evidence drive the investigation, not theories. All the investigators on this case are cognizant of not having tunnel vision." Keith Findley, codirector of the Wisconsin Innocence Project, advises that becoming preoccupied with a single theory "leads investigators, prosecutors, judges, and defense lawyers alike to focus on a particular conclusion and then filter all evidence in a case through the lens provided by that conclusion." To minimize this selective attention problem, officers in the New York Police Department are attending art classes, where they learn to be more mindful and take multiple perspectives of all information. "[The class] reminded me to stop and take in the whole scene and not just have tunnel vision," says NYPD captain David Grossi, adding that the class helped him to discover evidence outside the area he normally would have investigated.[9]

Perceptual Organization and Interpretation

categorical thinking
Organizing people and objects into preconceived categories that are stored in our long-term memory.

People make sense of information even before they become aware of it. This sense making partly includes **categorical thinking**—the mostly nonconscious process of organizing people and objects into preconceived categories that are stored in our long-term memory.[10] Categorical thinking relies on a variety of automatic perceptual grouping principles. Things are often grouped together on the basis of their similarity or proximity to others. If you notice that a group of similar-looking people includes several professors, for instance, you will likely assume that the others in that group are also professors. Another form of perceptual grouping is based on the need for cognitive closure, such as filling in missing information about what happened at a meeting that you didn't attend (e.g., who was there, where it was held). A third form of grouping occurs when we think we see trends in otherwise ambiguous information. Several studies have found that people have a natural tendency to see patterns that really are random events, such as presumed winning streaks among sports stars or in gambling.[11]

The process of "making sense" of the world around us also involves interpreting incoming information. This happens quickly as selecting and organizing because the previously mentioned emotional markers are tagged to incoming stimuli, which are essentially quick judgments about whether that information is good or bad for us. To give you an idea of how quickly and systematically this nonconscious perceptual interpretation process occurs, consider the following study:[12] After viewing video clips of university instructors teaching an undergraduate class, eight observers rated the instructors on several personal characteristics (optimistic, likable, anxious, active, etc.). The observers, who had never seen the instructors before, were similar to each other on how they rated the instructors, even though they completed their ratings alone. Equally important, these ratings were very similar to the ratings completed by students who attended the actual class.

These results may be interesting, but they become extraordinary when you realize that the observers formed their perceptions from as little as *six seconds* of video–three segments of two seconds each selected randomly from the one-hour class! Furthermore, the video didn't have any sound. In other words, people form similar perceptions and judgments on the basis of very thin slices of information. Other studies have reported similar findings for observations of high school teachers, courtroom judges, and physicians. Collectively, these "thin slice" studies reveal that selective attention, as well as perceptual organization and interpretation, operates very quickly and to a large extent without our awareness.

mental models
Visual or relational images in our mind that represent the external world.

Mental Models To achieve our goals with some degree of predictability and sanity, we need road maps of the environments in which we live. These road maps, called **mental models,** are internal representations of the external world.[13] They consist of visual or relational images in our mind, such as what the classroom looks like or, conceptually, what happens when we submit an assignment late. We rely on mental models to make sense of our environment through perceptual grouping; the models fill in the missing pieces, including the causal connection among events. For example, you have a mental model about attending a class lecture or seminar, including assumptions or expectations about where the instructor and students arrange themselves in the room, how they ask and answer questions, and so forth. We can create a mental image of a class in progress.

Mental models play an important role in sense making, yet they also make it difficult to see the world. For example, accounting professionals tend to see corporate problems in terms of accounting solutions, whereas marketing professionals see the same problems from a marketing perspective. Mental models also block our recognition of new opportunities. How do we change mental models? That's a tough challenge. After all, we developed models from several years of experience and reinforcement. The most important way to minimize the perceptual problems with mental models is to constantly question them. We need to ask ourselves about the assumptions we make. Working with people from diverse backgrounds is another way to break out of existing mental models. Colleagues from different cultures and areas of expertise tend to have different mental models, so working with them makes our own assumptions more obvious.

Social Identity and Stereotyping

In the previous chapter, you learned that social identity is an important component of a person's self-concept. We define ourselves to a large extent by the groups to which we belong or have an emotional attachment. Along with shaping our self-concept, social identity theory explains the dynamics of *social perception*–how we perceive others.[14] Social perception is influenced by three activities in the process of forming and maintaining our social identity: categorization, homogenization, and differentiation.

- *Categorization.* Social identity is a comparative process, and the comparison begins by categorizing people into distinct groups. By viewing someone (including yourself) as a Texan, for example, you remove that person's individuality and, instead, see him or her as a prototypical representative of the group "Texans." This categorization then allows you to distinguish Texans from people who live in, say, California or New Hampshire.
- *Homogenization.* To simplify the comparison process, we tend to think that people within each group are very similar to each other. For instance, we think Texans collectively have similar attitudes and characteristics, whereas Californians collectively have their own set of characteristics. Of course, every individual is unique, but we tend to lose sight of this fact when thinking about our social identity and how we compare to people in other social groups.
- *Differentiation.* Social identity fulfills our inherent need to have a distinct and positive self-concept. To achieve this, we do more than categorize people and homogenize them; we also differentiate groups by assigning more favorable characteristics to people in our groups than to people in other groups. This differentiation is often subtle, but it can escalate into a "good-guy–bad-guy" contrast when groups are in conflict with each other.[15]

Stereotyping in Organizations

stereotyping
The process of assigning traits to people on the basis of their membership in a social category.

Stereotyping is an extension of social identity theory and a product of our natural process of organizing information through categorical thinking.[16] Stereotyping has three elements. First, we develop social categories and assign traits that are difficult to observe. For instance, students might form the stereotype that professors are both intelligent and absentminded. Personal experiences shape stereotypes to some extent, but stereotypes are mainly provided to us through cultural upbringing and media images (e.g., movie characters). Second, we assign people to one or more social categories on the basis of easily observable information about them, such as their gender, appearance, or physical location. Third, people who seem to belong to the stereotyped group are assigned nonobservable traits associated with the group. For example, if we learn that someone is a professor, we implicitly tend to assume the person is also intelligent and absentminded.

Why Stereotyping Occurs?

One reason why people engage in stereotyping is that, as a form of categorical thinking, it is a natural and mostly nonconscious "energy-saving" process that simplifies our understanding of the world. It is easier to remember features of a stereotype than the constellation of characteristics unique to everyone we meet.[17] A second reason is that we have an innate need to understand and anticipate how others will behave. We don't have much information when first meeting someone, so we rely heavily on stereotypes to fill in the missing pieces. People with a strong need for cognitive closure have a higher tendency to rely on stereotypes. A third reason is that stereotyping enhances our self-concept. As mentioned earlier, the social identity process includes differentiation–we have more favorable views of members of our own groups than we do of people in other groups. When out-group members threaten our self-concept, we are particularly motivated (often without our awareness) to assign negative stereotypes to them.[18]

Problems with Stereotyping Stereotypes are not completely fictional, but neither do they accurately describe every person in a social category. For instance, the widespread "bean counter" stereotype of accountants views people in this profession as "single-mindedly preoccupied with

Glass Ceiling in Organizations Globalization has enabled the rise in proportion of women workforce across the world. However, women (now) continue to face new challenges in progress and development of their professional life. Glass Ceiling "is a metaphor intended to describe invisible barriers to women's achievement of the highest corporate levels".[19] According to *Morrison and Von Glinow,*[20] Glass Ceiling "is a barrier so subtle that it is transparent yet so strong that it prevents women and minorities from moving up in the management hierarchy". This barrier is invisible from the bottom, but it grows visible and stronger when they move-up the career ladder.

Variants of Glass Ceiling

Glass Border This denotes the barriers that women face in their international assignments.[21] It is also known as Expatriate Glass Ceiling.[22] ***Concrete Ceiling*** This denotes density of barriers faced by ethnic and minority women groups.[23] ***Double Pane Glass*** This denotes obstacles that women face in workplace.[24] ***Greenhouse*** This denotes constraints faced in horizontal and vertical careers.

Effect of Glass Ceiling The effects of glass ceiling include: obstacles in advancement of career and moving up the career ladder, discrimination in pay and perks, inequalities in benchmarking and assessment of performance, differences while assigning international assignments, etc.

Challenges to Reach Top Management Organizations have explored and continued to strive to break this glass ceiling, but there are challenges hindering progress of women to top level of organization. Eagly (2007)[25] names these challenges as 'Labyrinth of Leadership'. These are remnants of prejudice, confrontation to women's leadership, matters of leadership style, demands of family life, and underinvestment in social capital.

Interventions required from management of organizations include dispelling prejudices and perceptions regarding female leaders, shift focus from long-hour norms, bring objectivity in performance evaluation, use open recruitment tools, increase intake of women in executive positions, avoid forming teams with only single female member, encourage social networking among women, prepare female candidates in line management with proper tasks, encourage HR practices which support family life, provide considerable time to those employees who have considerable family responsibilities to prove their entitlement for promotion, give chance to women who have taken break from careers, and encourage male employees too to take benefit of family friendly HR policies.

precision and form, methodical and conservative, and a boring joyless character."[26] Although this may be true of some accountants, it is certainly not characteristic of all–or even most–people in this profession. Even so, once we categorize someone as an accountant, the features of accountants in general rather than the features of the specific person get recalled, even when the person does not possess many of the stereotypic traits.

Another problem with stereotyping is that it lays the foundation for discriminatory attitudes and behavior. Most of this perceptual bias occurs as *unintentional (systemic) discrimination,* whereby decision-makers rely on stereotypes to establish notions of the "ideal" person in specific roles. A person who doesn't fit the ideal tends to receive a less favorable evaluation. This subtle discrimination often shows up in age discrimination claims, such as the case in which Ryanair's recruitment advertising said it was looking for "young dynamic" employees. Recruiters at the Irish discount airline probably didn't intentionally discriminate against older people, but the tribunal concluded that systemic discrimination did occur because none of the job applicants were over 40 years old.[27]

The more serious form of stereotype bias is *intentional discrimination* or *prejudice,* in which people hold unfounded negative attitudes toward people belonging to a particular stereotyped group.[28] Overt prejudice seems to be less common today than a few decades ago, but it still exists. Over each of the past four years, for instance, more than one-quarter of Americans say they overhead racial slurs in the workplace.[29] In one recent case, three female advisers in California successfully sued their employer, Smith Barney, on the grounds that their male co-workers were deliberately assigned more lucrative clients (and therefore received higher pay) and more administrative support. These complaints were raised less than a decade after Smith Barney was ordered to correct discriminatory practices in its New York offices, where female employees complained of sexist and discriminatory behavior. A tribunal in Quebec was shocked to discover that one of Canada's largest vegetable farms prevented black employees from eating in the regular cafeteria. Instead, they were relegated to a "blacks only" eating area that lacked heat, running water, proper toilets, and refrigeration.[30] As Global Connections 3.1 describes, France is also coming to terms with both intentional and unintentional discrimination against non-Caucasian job applicants.

If stereotyping is such a problem, shouldn't we try to avoid this process altogether? Unfortunately, it's not that simple. Most experts agree that categorical thinking (including stereotyping) is an automatic and nonconscious process. Intensive training can minimize stereotype activation to some extent, but for the most part the process is hardwired in our brain cells.[31] Also remember that stereotyping helps us in several valuable (although fallible) ways described earlier: minimizing mental effort, filling in missing information, and supporting our social identity. The good news is that while it is very difficult to prevent the *activation* of stereotypes, we can minimize the *application* of stereotypic information. Later in this chapter, we identify ways to minimize stereotyping and other perceptual biases.

Minimizing Stereotyping Bias

If stereotyping is such a problem, shouldn't we try to avoid this process altogether? Unfortunately, it's not that simple. Most experts agree that categorical thinking (including stereotyping) is an automatic and unconscious process. Intensive training can minimize stereotype activation to some extent, but for the most part the process is hardwired in our brain cells.[32] Also remember that stereotyping helps us in several valuable (although fallible) ways described earlier: minimizing mental effort, filling in missing information, and supporting our social identity. The good news is that although it is very difficult to prevent the *activation* of stereotypes, we can minimize the *application* of stereotypical information. In other words, we can avoid using our stereotypes in our decisions and actions toward other people. Three strategies for minimizing the application of stereotyping are diversity awareness training, meaningful interaction, and decision-making accountability.

Diversity Awareness Training and Assessment Diversity awareness training tries to minimize discrimination by dispelling myths about people from various cultural and demographic groups and by identifying the organizational benefits of diversity and the problems with stereotyping. Some sessions rely on role-playing and other exercises to help employees discover the subtle yet pervasive effects of stereotyping in their decision making and behavior. Another approach is to complete self-assessments, such as the Implicit Association Test (IAT), which detect subtle race, age, and gender bias in people.[33]

Diversity training and assessment do not correct deep-rooted prejudice; they probably don't even change stereotypes in tolerant people. What they can potentially do, however, is to increase our sensitivity to equality and motivate us to block inaccurate perceptions arising from ingrained stereotypes. Consider Jennifer Smith-Holladay, who recently completed the IAT. Smith-Holladay was surprised to learn that she is biased in favor of white people, a group to which she belongs, and in favor of heterosexuals, a group to which she does not belong. "I discovered that I not only have some ingroup favoritism lurking in my subconscious, but also possess some internalized oppression in terms of my sexuality." Smith-Holladay suggests that this revelation will make her more aware of personal biases and help her minimize their application in decision making. "In the case of my own subconscious ingroup favoritism for white people, for example, my charge is to be color-conscious, not color-blind, and to always explicitly consider how race may affect behaviors and decisions," she says.[34]

3.1 Global Connections

"Your Name Says Everything in France"

Hamid Senni was born and raised in France but eventually moved to the United Kingdom because race discrimination in his home country limited job opportunities.

Hamid Senni wears a shirt and tie whenever he strolls along the Champs Elysées in Paris. The reason for this formality? "If I'm in jeans, people think I'm a shoplifter," he says. What makes this misperception even worse is that Senni, the son of Moroccan immigrants, was born and raised in France. And in spite of his education (three degrees in economics) and fluent language skills, Senni was told more than once that he would never find a job in France. A well-intentioned high school teacher once told him that he should replace Hamid with a more traditional French name. Incensed by the daily discrimination he experienced in his own country, Senni moved to Sweden and now lives in London, where he advises companies on ethnic diversity and has written a book on his experience. "Going abroad was like an exorcism," he says bluntly. "In the U.K., diversity is seen as an opportunity. In France it's still seen as a problem."

Senni's perception of racial and ethnic discrimination in France is supported by a recent study conducted jointly by the French government and the International Labour Organization (ILO). Researchers submitted two nearly identical job applications to 2,440 help-wanted ads. The main difference was that the candidate in one application had a French-sounding name whereas the individual in the other application had a North African or sub-Saharan African name. Almost 80 percent of employers preferred the applicant with the French-sounding name. Furthermore, when applicants personally visited human resource staff, those who had foreign names seldom received job interviews; instead, they were often told that the job had been filled or that the company would not be hiring after all. The report concluded that "almost 90 percent of overall discrimination occurred before the employer had even bothered to interview both test candidates."

One young black resident near Paris who calls himself Billy Fabrice knows about the undercurrents of racial discrimination. "Your name says everything in France," says Fabrice. "If you are called Diallo or Amir, that's all they want to know. If you are called Jean-Pierre, you show up for a job and they take you." Some employers specifically ask hiring agencies for applicants who are "BBR." This acronym for the colors of the French flag (bleu, blanc, rouge) is apparently a well-known employment code to hire only white French people. In one recent court case, prosecutors claimed that Garnier, a division of L'Oréal, tried to hire mostly white staff for in-store promotions. Garnier sent its temporary recruitment agency a fax specifying that those hired should be within a specific age range (18 to 22), have a certain clothing size, and be "BBR." Initially, 38 percent of candidates sent by the recruitment agency were non-Caucasian. After the fax was sent, this dropped to less than 5 percent.

While many French employers, including Garnier, deny prejudice or even systemic discrimination against non-Caucasian applicants, others are taking steps to make the hiring process more color-blind. Axa SA, the giant French insurance company, introduced anonymous résumés, in which job applicants provide their qualifications but not their names, addresses, gender, or age. Serge Simon, a 20-something French resident with Haitian origins, is hopeful. "I think that with an anonymous résumé, a person will be hired for what they are—for their qualifications and not for the color of their skin," he believes.[35]

Meaningful Interaction The more meaningful interaction we have with someone, the less we rely on stereotypes to understand that person.[36] This statement, which describes the **contact hypothesis,** sounds simple enough; but in reality it works only under specific conditions. Participants must have close and frequent interaction working toward a shared goal where they need to rely on each other (that is, cooperate rather than compete with each other). Everyone should have equal status in that context and should be engaged in a meaningful task. An hour-long social gathering between executives and frontline employees does not satisfy these conditions. On the other hand, having executives work in frontline jobs, which we described at the beginning of this chapter, does seem to represent meaningful interaction. By working in frontline jobs these executives reduce their status differences with other staff, cooperate toward a common goal, and have close and frequent interaction with frontline employees.

contact hypothesis
A theory stating that the more we interact with someone, the less we rely on stereotypes to understand that person.

Decision-Making Accountability A third way to minimize the biasing effects of stereotyping is to hold employees accountable for their decisions.[37] This accountability encourages more active information processing and, consequently, motivates decision makers to suppress stereotypical perceptions in favor of more precise and logical information. In contrast, less concern about accountability allows decision makers to engage in more passive information processing, which includes more reliance on discriminatory stereotypes.

Overall, social-identity theory and stereotyping are central activities in the perceptual process, most of which occurs automatically and unconsciously. Without our awareness, our brain identifies and organizes the incoming information around preconceived categories and assigns emotional markers representing an initial reaction to whether the information is good, bad, or irrelevant. It may be difficult to prevent this categorization and activation of stereotypes, but we can consciously control the application of stereotypes in decision making and behavior. Now let's look at another perceptual activity: attribution.

Learning Objectives

After reading the next three sections, you should be able to:

3. Describe the attribution process and two attribution errors.
4. Summarize the self-fulfilling-prophecy process.
5. Explain how halo, primacy, recency, and false-consensus effects bias our perceptions.

Attribution Theory

The **attribution process** involves deciding whether an observed behavior or event is caused mainly by the person (internal factors) or by the environment (external factors).[38] Internal factors include the person's ability or motivation, whereas external factors include lack of resources, other people, or just luck. If a co-worker doesn't show up for an important meeting, for instance, we infer either internal attributions (the co-worker is forgetful, lacks motivation, etc.) or external attributions (traffic, a family emergency, or other circumstances prevented the co-worker from attending).

attribution process
The perceptual process of deciding whether an observed behavior or event is caused largely by internal or external factors.

People rely on the three attribution rules shown in Exhibit 3.2 to determine whether someone's behavior mainly has an internal or external attribution. Internal attributions are made when the observed individual behaved this way in the past (high consistency), he or she behaves like this toward other people or in different situations (low distinctiveness), and other people do not behave this way in similar situations (low consensus). On the other hand, an external attribution is made when there is low consistency, high distinctiveness, and high consensus.

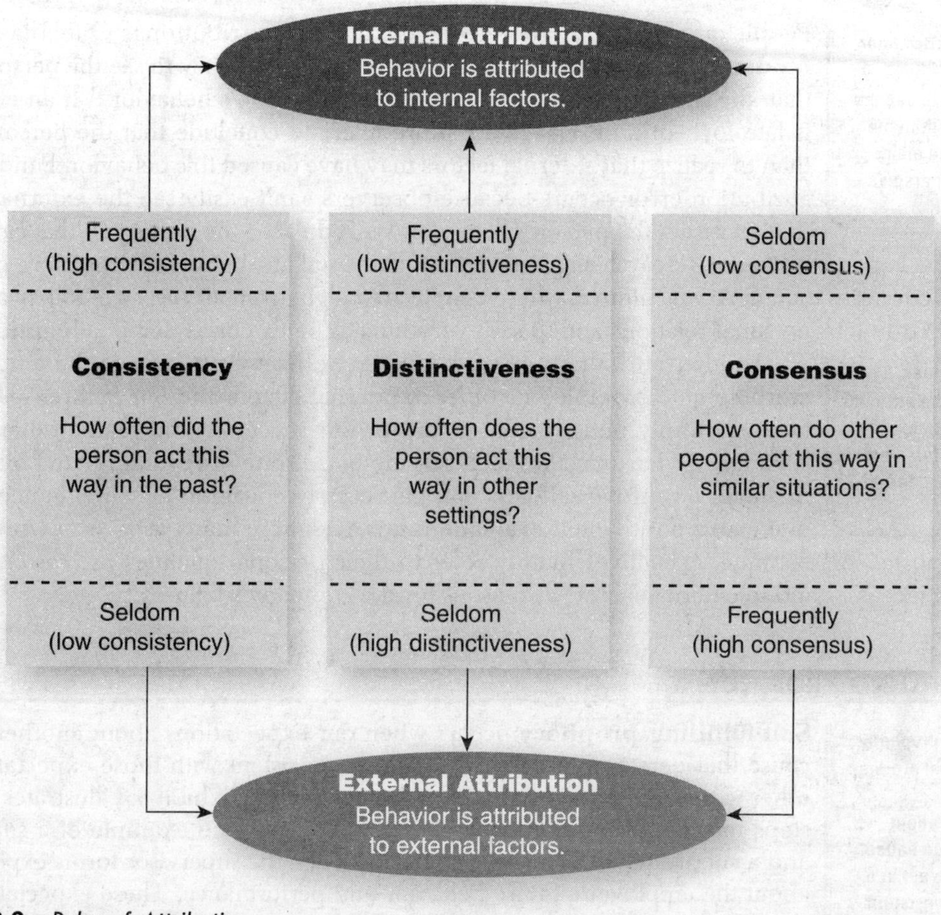

Exhibit 3.2 *Rules of Attribution*

To illustrate how these three attribution rules operate, suppose that an employee is making poor-quality products one day on a particular machine. We would probably conclude that there is something wrong with the machine (an external attribution) if the employee has made good-quality products on this machine in the past (low consistency), the employee makes good-quality products on other machines (high distinctiveness), and other employees have recently had quality problems on this machine (high consensus). We would make an internal attribution, on the other hand, if the employee usually makes poor-quality products on this machine (high consistency), other employees produce good-quality products on this machine (low consensus), and the employee also makes poor-quality products on other machines (low distinctiveness).[39]

Attribution is an essential perceptual process because it forms cause-effect relationships, which, in turn, affect how we respond to others' behavior and how we act in the future. How we react to a co-worker's poor performance depends on our internal or external attribution of that performance. Students who make internal attributions about their poor performance are more likely to drop out of their programs, for instance.[40]

Attribution Errors

fundamental attribution error
The tendency to see the person rather than the situation as the main cause of that person's behavior.

People are far from perfect when making attributions. One bias, called **fundamental attribution error,** refers to our tendency to see the person rather than the situation as the main cause of that person's behavior.[41] If an employee is late for work, observers are more likely to conclude that the person is lazy than to realize that external factors may have caused this behavior. Fundamental attribution error occurs because observers can't easily see the external factors that constrain the person's behavior. We didn't see the traffic jam that caused the person to be late, for instance. Research suggests that fundamental attribution error is more common in Western countries than in Asian cultures, where people are taught from an early age to pay attention to the context in interpersonal relations and to see everything as being connected in a holistic way.[42]

self-serving bias
The tendency to attribute our favorable outcomes to internal factors and our failures to external factors.

Another attribution error, known as **self-serving bias,** is the tendency to attribute our favorable outcomes to internal factors and our failures to external factors. Simply put, we take credit for our successes and blame others or the situation for our mistakes. Self-serving bias is one of several related biases that maintain a positive self-concept, particularly engaging in self-enhancement to maintain a positive self-evaluation. It is evident in many aspects of work life. In annual reports, for example, executives mainly refer to their personal qualities as reasons for the company's successes and to external factors as reasons for the company's failures.[43]

Self-Fulfilling Prophecy

self-fulfilling prophecy
The perceptual process in which our expectations about another person cause that person to act in a way that is consistent with those expectations.

Self-fulfilling prophecy occurs when our expectations about another person cause that person to act in a way that is consistent with those expectations. In other words, our perceptions can influence reality. Exhibit 3.3 illustrates the four steps in the self-fulfilling prophecy process using the example of a supervisor and a subordinate.[44] The process begins when the supervisor forms expectations about the employee's future behavior and performance. These expectations are sometimes inaccurate, because first impressions are usually formed from limited information. The supervisor's expectations influence his or her treatment of employees. Specifically, high-expectancy employees (those expected to do well) receive more emotional support through nonverbal cues (e.g., more smiling and eye contact), more frequent and valuable feedback and reinforcement, more challenging goals, better training, and more opportunities to demonstrate good performance.

The third step in self-fulfilling prophecy includes two effects of the supervisor's behavior on the employee. First, through better training and more practice opportunities, a high-expectancy employee learns more skills and knowledge than a low-expectancy employee. Second, the employee becomes more self-confident, which results in higher motivation and willingness to set more challenging goals.[45]

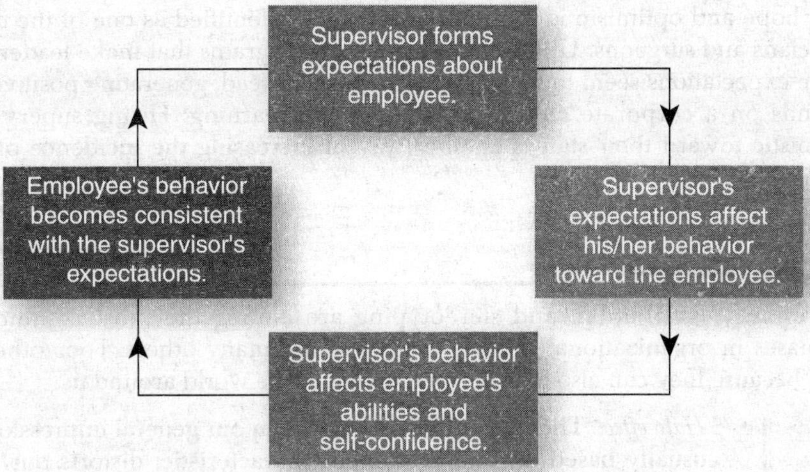

Exhibit 3.3 *The Self-Fulfilling Prophecy Cycle*

In the final step, high-expectancy employees have higher motivation and better skills, resulting in better performance, while the opposite is true of low-expectancy employees.

There are plenty of examples of self-fulfilling prophecies in work and school settings.[46] Research has found that women perform less well on math tests after being informed that men tend to perform better on them. Women perform better on these tests when they are not exposed to this negative self-fulfilling prophecy. Similarly, people over 65 receive lower results on memory tests after hearing that mental ability declines with age. Another study reported that the performance of Israeli Defense Force trainees was influenced by their instructor's expectations regarding the trainee's potential in the program. Self-fulfilling prophecy was at work here because the instructor's expectations were based on a list provided by researchers showing which recruits had high and low potential, even though the researchers had actually listed these trainees randomly.

Contingencies of Self-Fulfilling Prophecy

Self-fulfilling prophecies are more powerful under some conditions than others. The self-fulfilling prophecy effect is stronger at the beginning of a relationship, such as when employees are first hired. It is also stronger when several people (rather than just one person) hold the same expectations of the individual. In other words, we might be able to ignore one person's doubts about our potential but not the collective doubts of several people. The self-fulfilling prophecy effect is also stronger among people with a history of low achievement. High achievers can draw on their past successes to offset low expectations, whereas low achievers do not have past successes to support their self-confidence. Fortunately, the opposite is also true: Low achievers respond more favorably than high achievers to positive self-fulfilling prophecy. Low achievers don't receive this positive encouragement very often, so it probably has a stronger effect on their motivation to excel.[47]

positive organizational behavior
A perspective of organizational behavior that focuses on building positive qualities and traits within individuals or institutions as opposed to focusing on what is wrong with them.

The main lesson from the self-fulfilling prophecy literature is that leaders need to develop and maintain a positive, yet realistic, expectation toward all employees. This recommendation is consistent with the emerging philosophy of **positive organizational behavior,** which suggests that focusing on the positive rather than negative aspects of life will improve organizational success and individual well-being. Communicating hope and optimism is so important that it is identified as one of the critical success factors for physicians and surgeons. Unfortunately, training programs that make leaders aware of the power of positive expectations seem to have minimal effect. Instead, generating positive expectations and hope depends on a corporate culture of support and learning. Hiring supervisors who are inherently optimistic toward their staff is another way of increasing the incidence of positive self-fulfilling prophecies.

Other Perceptual Errors

Self-fulfilling prophecy, attribution, and stereotyping are among the most common perceptual processes and biases in organizational settings, but there are many others. Four others are briefly described below because they can also bias our perception of the world around us.

halo effect
A perceptual error whereby our general impression of a person, usually based on one prominent characteristic, colors our perception of other characteristics of that person.

- *Halo effect*. The **halo effect** occurs when our general impression of a person, usually based on one prominent characteristic, distorts our perception of other characteristics of that person.[48] If a supervisor who values punctuality notices that an employee is sometimes late for work, the supervisor might form a negative image of the employee and evaluate that person's other traits unfavorably as well. The halo effect is most likely to occur when concrete information about the perceived target is missing or we are not sufficiently motivated to search for it. Instead, we use our general impression of the person to fill in the missing information.

primacy effect
A perceptual error in which we quickly form an opinion of people on the basis of the first information we receive about them.

- *Primacy effect*. The **primacy effect** is our tendency to quickly form an opinion of people on the basis of the first information we receive about them.[49] This rapid perceptual organization and interpretation occurs because we need to make sense of the world around us. The problem is that first impressions–particularly negative first impressions–are difficult to change. After categorizing someone, we tend to select subsequent information that supports our first impression and screen out information that opposes that impression.

recency effect
A perceptual error in which the most recent information dominates our perception of others.

- *Recency effect*. The **recency effect** occurs when the most recent information dominates our perceptions.[50] This perceptual bias is most common when people (especially those with limited experience) are making an evaluation involving complex information. For instance, auditors must digest large volumes of information in their judgments about financial documents, and

the most recent information received prior to the decision tends to get weighed more heavily than information received at the beginning of the audit. Similarly, when supervisors evaluate the performance of employees over the previous year, the most recent performance information dominates the evaluation because it is the most easily recalled.

false-consensus effect
A perceptual error in which we overestimate the extent to which others have beliefs and characteristics similar to our own.

- *False-consensus effect.* Sometimes called the *similar-to-me effect,* the **false-consensus effect** is a widely observed bias in which we overestimate the extent to which others have beliefs and characteristics similar to our own.[51] Employees who are thinking of quitting their jobs believe that a large percentage of their co-workers are also thinking about quitting. This bias occurs to some extent because we associate with others who are similar to us, and we selectively remember information that is consistent with our own views. We also believe "everyone does it" to reinforce our self-concept regarding behaviors that do not have a positive image (quitting, parking illegally, etc.).

Learning Objectives

After reading this section, you should be able to:

6. Discuss three ways to improve social perception, with specific application to organizational situations.

IMPROVING PERCEPTIONS

We can't bypass the perceptual process, but we should make every attempt to minimize perceptual biases and distortions. Three potentially effective ways to improve perceptions include awareness of perceptual biases, self-awareness, and meaningful interaction.

Awareness of Perceptual Biases

One of the most obvious and widely practiced ways to reduce perceptual biases is by knowing that they exist. For example, diversity awareness training tries to minimize discrimination by making people aware of systemic discrimination as well as prejudices that occur through stereotyping. This training also attempts to dispel myths about people from various cultural and demographic groups. Awareness of perceptual biases can reduce these biases to some extent by making people more mindful of their thoughts and actions. However, awareness has only a limited effect.[52] For example, trying to correct misinformation about demographic groups has limited effect on people with deeply held prejudices against those groups. Also, self-fulfilling prophecy training informs managers about this perceptual bias and encourages them to engage in more positive rather than negative self-fulfilling prophecies, yet research has found that managers continue to engage in negative self-fulfilling prophecies after they complete the training program.

Improving Self-Awareness

A more powerful way to minimize perceptual biases is to help people become more aware of biases in their own decisions and behavior. As mentioned at the beginning of this chapter, self-awareness is a critical foundation for developing a global mindset. We need to understand our beliefs, values, and attitudes to be more open-minded and nonjudgmental toward others. Self-awareness is equally important in other ways. The emerging concept of authentic leadership, for instance, emphasizes self-awareness as the first step in a person's ability to effectively lead others (see Chapter 12).[53]

But how do we become more self-aware? One formal procedure, called the Implicit Association Test (IAT), detects subtle race, age, and gender bias by associating positive and negative words with specific demographic groups.[54] Many people are much more cautious about their stereotypes and prejudices after discovering that their test results show a personal bias against older people or individuals from different ethnic backgrounds. For example, Jennifer Smith-Holladay was surprised to learn after taking the IAT that she is biased in favor of white people, a group to which she belongs, and in favor of heterosexuals, a group to which she does not belong. "I discovered that I not only have some in-group favoritism lurking in my subconscious, but also possess some internalized oppression in terms of my sexuality," says Smith-Holladay. She adds that the IAT results will make her more aware of personal biases and help her to minimize their application in decision making. "In the case of my own subconscious in-group favoritism for white people, for example, my charge is to be color-conscious, not color-blind, and to always explicitly consider how race may affect behaviors and decisions."[55]

Johari Window
A model of mutual understanding that encourages disclosure and feedback to increase our own open area and reduce the blind, hidden, and unknown areas.

More generally, people tend to reduce their perceptual biases by "knowing themselves"–increasing awareness of their own values, beliefs, and prejudices.[56] The **Johari Window** is a popular model for understanding how co-workers can increase their mutual understanding.[57] Developed by Joseph Luft and Harry Ingram (hence the name "Johari"), this model divides information about you into four "windows"–open, blind, hidden, and unknown–based on whether your own values, beliefs, and experiences are known to you and to others (see Exhibit 3.4). The *open area* includes information about you that is known both to you and to others. The *blind area* refers to information that is known to others but not to you. For example, your colleagues might notice that you are self-conscious and awkward when meeting the company chief executive, but you are unaware of this fact. Information known to you but unknown to others is found in the *hidden area*. Finally, the *unknown area* includes your values, beliefs, and experiences that aren't known to you or others.

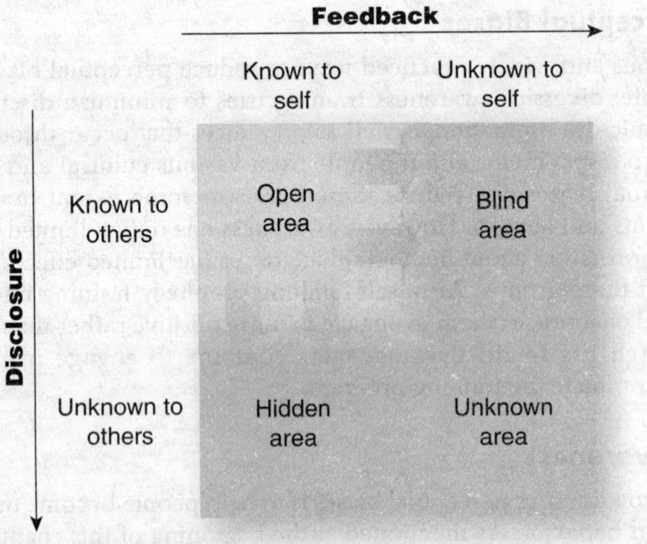

Source: Based on J. Luft, *Group Processes* (Palo Alto, CA: Mayfield, 1984).

Exhibit 3.4 *The Johari Window Model of Self-Awareness and Mutual Understanding*

The main objective of the Johari Window is to increase the size of the open area so that both you and colleagues are aware of your perceptual limitations. This is partly accomplished by reducing the hidden area through *disclosure*–informing others of your beliefs, feelings, and experiences that may influence the work relationship.[58] The open area also increases through *feedback* from others about your behavior. This information helps you to reduce your blind area, because co-workers often see things in you that you do not see. Finally, the combination of disclosure and feedback occasionally produces revelations about information in the unknown area.

Air New Zealand Executives Get Meaningful Interaction If the meal service seems a bit slower than usual on your next Air New Zealand flight, it might be that CEO Rob Fyfe is doing the serving while chatting with passengers. Every month, Fyfe and his top executive team fill the roster as flight attendants, check-in counter staff, or baggage handlers. (The executives had to pass tests to work as cabin crew.) The frontline jobs give the Air New Zealand executives a regular reality check while working alongside employees. It also gives employees an opportunity to see that the airline's leaders are human beings who care about staff and customers. The process is also somewhat reversed; every month one staff member spends a day with the CEO. "That will include sitting in on an executive briefing and possibly even a lunch with a politician," Fyfe explains. "They go everywhere with me for the entire day." That program has been extended to other senior executives. The result of this meaningful interaction and many other initiatives to support employees is that morale and customer service at Air New Zealand have soared in recent years.[60]

Meaningful Interaction

While the Johari Window relies on dialogue, self-awareness and mutual understanding can also improve through *meaningful interaction.*[59] This statement is based on the **contact hypothesis,** which states that, under certain conditions, people who interact with each other will be less prejudiced or perceptually biased against each other. Simply spending time with members of other groups can improve your understanding and opinion of those persons to some extent. However, the contact hypothesis effect is much stronger when people have close and frequent interaction working toward a shared goal and need to rely on each other (i.e., cooperate rather than compete with each other). Everyone should have equal status in that context and should be engaged in a meaningful task.

contact hypothesis
A theory stating that the more we interact with someone, the less prejudiced or perceptually biased we will be against that person.

An hour-long social gathering between executives and frontline employees would not satisfy the contact hypothesis conditions. On the other hand, meaningful interaction might occur in many of the international volunteering activities described in the opening vignette to this chapter. In these programs, professionals from developed countries work alongside people from developing countries. Although the volunteers have expertise (and therefore status), they often perform work outside that expertise and in unfamiliar environments requiring the expertise of people in the local community. Another potential application of the contact hypothesis occurs when senior executives and other staff from headquarters work in frontline jobs frequently or for an extended time. Everyone at Domino's head office in Ann Arbor, Michigan, attends Pizza Prep School, where they learn how to make pizzas and run a pizza store. Every new hire at 1-800-GOT-JUNK? (North America's largest rubbish removal company) spends an entire week on a junk removal truck to better understand how the business works. "How can you possibly empathize with someone out in the field unless you've been on the truck yourself?" asks CEO and founder Brian Scudamore.[61]

empathy
A person's understanding of and sensitivity to the feelings, thoughts, and situations of others.

Meaningful interaction does more than reduce our reliance on stereotypes. It also potentially improves **empathy** toward others, that is, the extent to which we understand and are sensitive to the feelings, thoughts, and situations of others.[62] You have empathy when actively visualizing the other person's situation and feeling that person's emotions in that situation. Empathizing with others improves our sensitivity to the external causes of another person's performance and behavior, thereby reducing fundamental attribution error. A supervisor who imagines what it's like to be a single mother, for example, would become more sensitive to the external causes of lateness and other events among such employees.

The perceptual process represents the filter through which information passes from the external environment to our memory. As such, it is really the beginning of the learning process, which we discuss next.

Learning Objectives

After reading the next two sections, you should be able to:

7. Describe the A-B-C model of behavior modification and the four contingencies of reinforcement.
8. Describe the three features of social learning theory.
9. Outline the elements of organizational learning and ways to improve each element.

LEARNING IN ORGANIZATIONS

learning
A relatively permanent change in behavior (or behavioral tendency) that occurs as a result of a person's interaction with the environment.

Learning is a relatively permanent change in behavior (or behavioral tendency) that occurs as a result of a person's interaction with the environment. Learning occurs when the learner behaves differently. For example, you have "learned" computer skills when you operate the keyboard and software more quickly than before. Learning occurs when interaction with the environment leads to behavior change. This means that we learn through our senses, such as through study, observation, and experience.

tacit knowledge
Knowledge that is embedded in our actions and ways of thinking and is transmitted only through observation and experience.

Some of what we learn is *explicit knowledge,* such as reading information in this book. However, explicit knowledge is really only the tip of the knowledge iceberg. Most of what we know is **tacit knowledge.**[63] Tacit knowledge is not documented; rather, it is acquired through observation and direct experience. For example, airline pilots learn to operate commercial jets more by watching experts and practicing on flight simulators than by attending lectures. They acquire tacit knowledge by directly experiencing the complex interaction of behavior with the machine's response.

Three perspectives of learning tacit and explicit knowledge are reinforcement, social learning, and direct experience. Each perspective offers a different angle for understanding the dynamics of learning.

behavior modification
A theory that explains learning in terms of the antecedents and consequences of behavior.

Behavior Modification: Learning through Reinforcement

One of the oldest perspectives on learning, called **behavior modification** (also known as *operant conditioning* and *reinforcement theory*), takes the rather extreme view that learning is completely dependent on the environment. Behavior modification does not question the notion that thinking is part of the learning process, but it views human thoughts as unimportant intermediate stages between behavior and the environment. The environment teaches us to alter our behaviors so that we maximize positive consequences and minimize adverse consequences.[64]

A-B-Cs of Behavior Modification The central objective of behavior modification is to change behavior (B) by managing its antecedents (A) and consequences (C). This process is nicely illustrated in the A-B-C model of behavior modification, shown in Exhibit 3.5.[65]

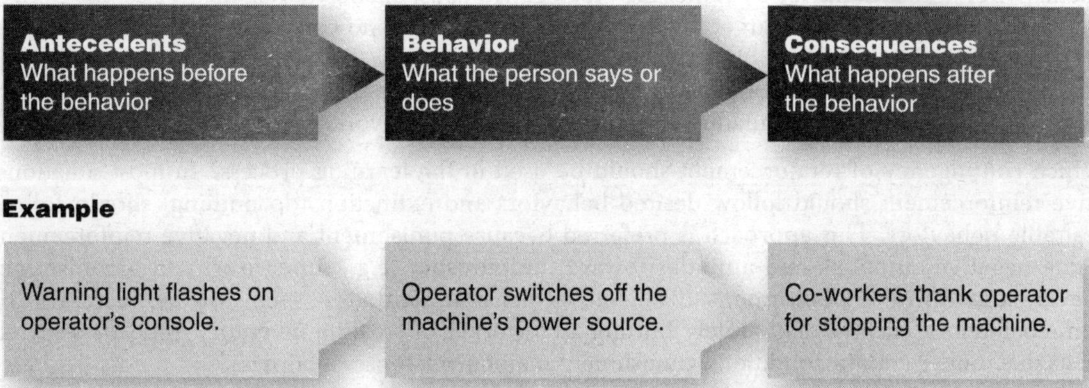

Sources: Adapted from T. K. Connellan, *How to Improve Human Performance* (New York: Harper & Row, 1978), p. 50; F. Luthans and R. Kreitner, *Organizational Behavior Modification and Beyond* (Glenview, IL: Scott, Foresman, 1985), pp. 85–88.

Exhibit 3.5 *A-B-Cs of Behavior Modification*

Antecedents are events preceding the behavior, informing employees that certain behaviors will have particular consequences. An antecedent may be a sound from your computer signaling that an e-mail has arrived or a request from your supervisor asking you to complete a specific task by tomorrow. Such antecedents let employees know that a particular action will produce specific consequences. Notice that antecedents do not cause behaviors. The computer sound doesn't cause us to open our e-mail. Rather, the sound is a cue telling us that certain consequences are likely to occur if we engage in certain behaviors. In behavior modification, *consequences* are events following a particular behavior that influence its future occurrence. Generally speaking, people tend to repeat behaviors that are followed by pleasant consequences and are less likely to repeat behaviors that are followed by unpleasant consequences or no consequences at all.

Contingencies of Reinforcement Behavior modification identifies four types of consequences, called the *contingencies of reinforcement,* that increase, maintain, or reduce the probability that behavior will be repeated.[66]

- *Positive reinforcement* occurs when the *introduction* of a consequence *increases or maintains* the frequency or future probability of a specific behavior. Receiving a bonus after successfully completing an important project is considered positive reinforcement because it typically increases the probability that you will use that behavior in the future.
- *Punishment* occurs when a consequence decreases the frequency or future probability of a behavior. This consequence typically involves introducing something that employees try to avoid. For

instance, most of us would consider being demoted or being ostracized by our co-workers as forms of punishment.[67]

- *Negative reinforcement* occurs when the removal or avoidance of a consequence increases or maintains the frequency or future probability of a specific behavior. Supervisors apply negative reinforcement when they stop criticizing employees whose substandard performance has improved. When the criticism is withheld, employees are more likely to repeat behaviors that improved their performance. Notice that negative reinforcement is not punishment. Whereas punishment extinguishes behavior by introducing a negative consequence, negative reinforcement actually reinforces behavior by removing the negative consequence.
- *Extinction* occurs when the target behavior decreases because no consequence follows it. In this respect, extinction is a do-nothing strategy. Generally, behavior that is no longer reinforced tends to disappear; it becomes extinct. For instance, research suggests that performance tends to decline when managers stop congratulating employees for their good work.[68]

Which contingency of reinforcement should be used in the learning process? In most situations, positive reinforcement should follow desired behaviors and extinction (do nothing) should follow undesirable behaviors. This approach is preferred because punishment and negative reinforcement generate negative emotions and attitudes toward the punisher (e.g., supervisor) and organization. However, some form of punishment (dismissal, suspension, demotion, etc.) may be necessary for extreme behaviors, such as deliberately hurting a co-worker or stealing inventory. Indeed, research suggests that, under certain conditions, punishment maintains a sense of fairness.[69]

Schedules of Reinforcement Along with the types of reinforcement, the frequency and timing of the reinforcers also influence employee behaviors.[70] These reinforcement schedules can be continuous or intermittent. The most effective reinforcement schedule for learning new tasks is *continuous reinforcement*–providing positive reinforcement after every occurrence of the desired behavior. Employees learn desired behaviors quickly, and when the reinforcer is removed, extinction also occurs very quickly.

The best schedule for reinforcing learned behavior is a *variable ratio schedule* in which employee behavior is reinforced after a variable number of times. Salespeople experience variable ratio reinforcement because they make a successful sale (the reinforcer) after a varying number of client calls. They might make four unsuccessful calls before receiving an order on the fifth one, then make 10 more calls before receiving the next order, and so on. The variable ratio schedule makes behavior highly resistant to extinction because the reinforcer is never expected at a particular time or after a fixed number of accomplishments.

Behavior Modification in Practice Everyone practices behavior modification in one form or another. We thank people for a job well done, are silent when displeased, and sometimes try to punish those who go against our wishes. Behavior modification also occurs in various formal programs to reduce absenteeism, improve task performance, encourage safe work behaviors, and have a healthier lifestyle.[71] In Arkansas, for example, the North Little Rock School Board introduced an absenteeism reduction plan in which teachers can earn $300 after every six months with perfect attendance. Those with no more than one day of absence receive $100. ExxonMobil's Fawley refinery in the United Kingdom introduced a "Behave Safely Challenge" program in which supervisors rewarded employees and contractors on the spot when they exhibited good safety behavior or intervened to improve the safe behavior of co-workers. These rewards were a form of positive reinforcement using a variable ratio schedule (safe work behaviors were reinforced after a variable number of times that they occurred).[72]

Reinforcing the Long (and Healthy) Walk For many of Horton Group's 350 employees, the best parking spots aren't closest to the building; they are deep in the outfield. The Chicago-based insurance broker reinforces the healthy lifestyle of walking by rewarding staff who take at least 7,000 steps each day—more than twice the normal daily average. Humana, Inc., has introduced a similar program. Employees at the Kentucky-based health insurance company use a pedometer to count the number of steps, and the results are uploaded from the pedometer to a Website. The more steps taken, the higher the rewards in the form of cash cards that can be used at popular retail stores. "This program has changed the culture within Humana," says Phil Smeltzer, Humana's wellness strategy leader. "People have started paying attention to how many steps they are taking. When it gets late in the day and they haven't walked enough, they take the long way to their car."[73]

Although a natural part of human interaction, behavior modification has a number of limitations when applied strategically in organizational settings. One limitation is "reward inflation," in which the reinforcer is eventually considered an entitlement. For this reason, most behavior modification programs must run infrequently and for a short duration. Another concern is that the variable ratio schedule of reinforcement tends to create a lottery-style reward system, which is unpopular with people who dislike gambling. Probably the most significant problem is behavior modification's radical view that behavior is learned only through personal interaction with the environment.[74] This view is no longer accepted; instead, learning experts recognize that people also learn by observing others and thinking logically about possible consequences. This learning-through-observation process is explained by social learning theory.

Social Learning Theory: Learning by Observing

social learning theory
A theory stating that much learning occurs by observing others and then modeling the behaviors that lead to favorable outcomes and avoiding behaviors that lead to punishing consequences.

Social learning theory states that much learning occurs by observing others and then modeling the behaviors that lead to favorable outcomes and avoiding behaviors that lead to punishing consequences.[75] This form of learning occurs in three ways: behavior modeling, learning behavior consequences, and self-reinforcement.

- *Behavior modeling*. People learn by observing the behaviors of a role model on a critical task, remembering the important elements of the observed behaviors, and then practicing those behaviors.[76] This is a valuable form of learning because tacit knowledge and skills are mainly acquired through observation and practice. As an example, it is difficult to document or explain in a conversation all the steps necessary to bake professional-quality bread. Student chefs also need to observe the master baker's subtle behaviors. Behavioral modeling also increases self-efficacy because people gain more self-confidence after seeing someone else perform the task. This is particularly true when observers identify with the model, such as someone who is similar in age, experience, gender, and related features.

- *Learning behavior consequences.* People learn the consequences of behavior through logic and observation, not just through direct experience. They logically anticipate consequences after completing a task well or poorly. They also learn behavioral consequences by observing the experiences of other people. Consider the employee who observes a co-worker receiving a stern warning for working in an unsafe manner. This event would reduce the observer's likelihood of engaging in unsafe behaviors because he or she has learned to anticipate a similar reprimand following those behaviors.[77]

self-reinforcement
Reinforcement that occurs when an employee has control over a reinforcer but doesn't "take" it until completing a self-set goal.

- *Self-reinforcement.* **Self-reinforcement** occurs whenever an employee has control over a reinforcer but doesn't "take" it until completing a self-set goal.[78] For example, you might be thinking about having a snack after you finish reading the rest of this chapter. Raiding the refrigerator is a form of self-induced positive reinforcement for completing this reading assignment. Self-reinforcement takes many forms, such as taking a short walk, watching a movie, or simply congratulating yourself for completing a task.

Learning through Experience

Along with behavior modification and social learning, another way that employees learn is through direct experience. In fact, most tacit knowledge and skills are acquired through experience as well as observation. Generally, experiential learning begins when we engage with the environment; then we reflect on that experience and form theories about how the world around us works. This is followed by experimentation, in which we find out how well the newly formed theories work.[79] Experiential learning requires all these steps, although people tend to prefer one step more than the others.

learning orientation
An individual attitude and organizational culture in which people welcome new learning opportunities, actively experiment with new ideas and practices, view reasonable mistakes as a natural part of the learning process, and continuously question past practices.

One of the most important ingredients for learning through experience is that the organization and its employees should possess a strong **learning orientation.**[80] As mentioned at the beginning of this chapter, people with a global mindset have a strong learning orientation, meaning that they welcome new learning opportunities, actively experiment with new ideas and practices, view reasonable mistakes as a natural part of the learning process, and continuously question past practices. This individual orientation becomes part of the organization's culture when it is held by many people throughout the organization.

Organizations develop and maintain a learning orientation culture by supporting experimentation, acknowledging reasonable mistakes without penalty, and supporting the mindset that employees should engage in continuous learning. They encourage employees to question long-held assumptions or mental models and to actively "unlearn" practices that are no longer ideal. Without a learning orientation, mistakes are hidden and problems are more likely to escalate or reemerge later. It's not surprising, then, that one of the most frequently mentioned lessons from the best-performing manufacturers is to expect mistakes. "At CIMB we have learnt to admit our mistakes openly," says Datuk Nazir Razak, chief executive of CIMB Group, Malaysia's second-largest financial services company. "Some of these mistakes cost us a lot of money," he adds, but "each mistake is a learning opportunity."[81]

Concrete experience involves sensory and emotional engagement in some activity. It is followed by *reflective observation,* which involves listening, watching, recording, and elaborating on the experience. The next stage in the learning cycle is *abstract conceptualization.* This is the stage in which we develop concepts and integrate our observations into logically sound theories. The fourth stage, *active experimentation,* occurs when we test our previous experience, reflection, and conceptualization in a particular context. People tend to prefer and operate better in some stages than in others due to their unique competencies and personality. Still, experiential learning requires all four stages in proper balance.

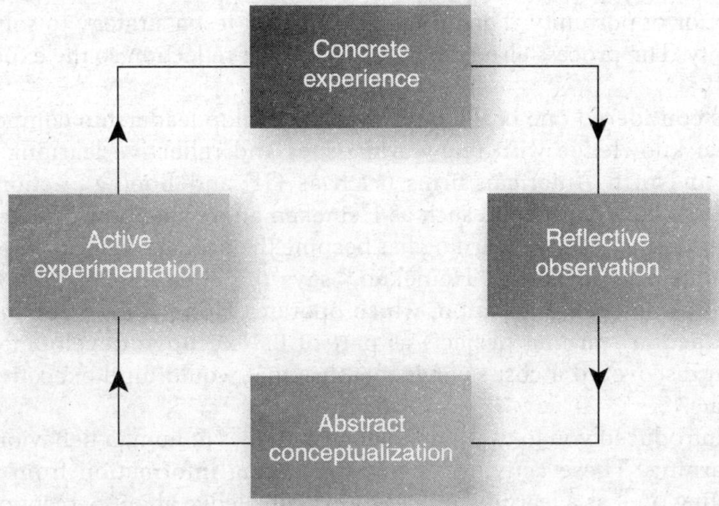

Exhibit 3.6 *Kolb's Experiential Learning Model*

Experiential Learning in Practice

learning orientation
The extent that an organization or individual supports knowledge management, particularly opportunities to acquire knowledge through experience and experimentation.

Learning through experience works best in organizations with a strong **learning orientation**–they value learning opportunities and, in particular, the generation of new knowledge while employees perform their jobs. If an employee initially fails to perform a task, then the experience might still be a valuable learning opportunity. In other words, such organizations encourage employees to appreciate the process of individual and team learning, not just the performance results.

Organizations achieve a learning orientation culture by rewarding experimentation and recognizing mistakes as a natural part of the learning process. They encourage employees to take reasonable risks to ultimately discover new and better ways of doing things. Without a learning orientation, mistakes are hidden and problems are more likely to escalate or reemerge later. It's not surprising, then, that one of the most frequently mentioned lessons from the best-performing manufacturers is to expect mistakes. "[Mistakes] are a source of learning and will improve operations in the long run," explains an executive at Lockheed Martin in

Bethesda, Maryland. "[They] foster the concept that no question is dumb, no idea is too wild, and no task or activity is irrelevant."[82]

action learning
A variety of experiential learning activities in which employees are involved in a "real, complex, and stressful problem," usually in teams, with immediate relevance to the company.

Action Learning One application of workplace experiential learning that has received considerable interest, particularly in Europe, is **action learning.** Action learning occurs when employees, usually in teams, investigate and apply solutions to a situation that is both real and complex, with immediate relevance to the company.[83] In other words, the task becomes the source of learning. Kolb's experiential learning model presented earlier is usually identified as the main template for action learning. Action learning requires concrete experience with a real organizational problem or opportunity, followed by "learning meetings" in which participants reflect on their observations about that problem or opportunity. Then they develop and test a strategy to solve the problem or realize the opportunity. The process also encourages plenty of reflection so the experience becomes a learning process.

Action learning is considered one of the best ways to develop leadership competencies because it combines conceptual knowledge with real-world issues and reflective learning. Although slowly gaining popularity in North American firms (such as GE and Boeing), action learning is well established in Europe, where companies such as Heineken appreciate how this learning process can add value to the organization. "Action learning has become the primary vehicle for generating creative ideas and building business success at Heineken," says the chairman of the executive board at Europe's largest brewer. MTR Corporation, which operates Hong Kong's commuter train system, recently introduced action learning projects as part of its executive development program. One action-learning team discovered a cost savings measure that would fund executive development at MTR for several years.[84]

This chapter has introduced you to two fundamental activities in human behavior in the workplace: perceptions and learning. These activities involve receiving information from the environment, organizing it, and acting on it as a learning process. Our knowledge about perceptions and learning in the workplace lays the foundation for the next chapter, which looks at workplace emotions, attitudes and stress.

FROM INDIVIDUAL TO ORGANIZATIONAL LEARNING

One of the most popular contemporary perspectives of organizational effectiveness is *organizational learning,* which was defined in Chapter 1 as any structured activity that improves an organization's capacity to acquire, share, and use knowledge in ways that improve its survival and success. Organizational learning is heavily dependent on individual learning, but the "capacity" to acquire, share, and use knowledge means that companies establish systems, structures, and organizational values that support the knowledge management process.[85]

- *Knowledge acquisition.* This includes extracting information and ideas from the external environment as well as through insight. One of the fastest and most powerful ways to acquire knowledge is by hiring individuals or acquiring entire companies. Knowledge also enters the organization when employees learn from external sources, such as by discovering new resources from suppliers or becoming aware of new trends from clients. A third knowledge acquisition strategy is experimentation. Companies receive knowledge through insight as a result of research and other creative processes.

- *Knowledge sharing.* This aspect of organizational learning involves distributing knowledge to others across the organization. Although typically associated with computer intranets and digital repositories of knowledge, knowledge sharing also occurs through informal online or face-to-face communication.[71] Most social learning (such as behavioral modeling) and experiential learning are forms of knowledge sharing because the learning is transferred from one employee to another.
- *Knowledge use.* The competitive advantage of knowledge comes from applying it in ways that add value to the organization and its stakeholders. To do this, employees must realize that the knowledge is available and that they have enough freedom to apply it. This requires a culture that supports the learning process.

This chapter has introduced two fundamental activities in human behavior in the workplace: perceptions and learning. These activities involve receiving information from the environment, organizing it, and acting on it as a learning process. Our knowledge about perceptions and learning in the workplace lays the foundation for the next chapter, which looks at workplace emotions and attitudes.

Chapter Summary

Perception involves selecting, organizing, and interpreting information to make sense of the world around us. Perceptual organization engages categorical thinking—the mostly nonconscious process of organizing people and objects into preconceived categories that are stored in our long-term memory. Mental models—internal representations of the external world—also help us to make sense of incoming stimuli.

Social identity theory explains how we perceive people through categorization, homogenization, and differentiation. Stereotyping is a derivative of social identity theory, in which people assign traits to others based on their membership in a social category. Stereotyping economizes mental effort, fills in missing information, and enhances our self-perception and social identity. However, it also lays the foundation for prejudice and systemic discrimination.

The attribution process involves deciding whether an observed behavior or event is caused mainly by the person (internal factors) or the environment (external factors). Attributions are decided by perceptions of the consistency, distinctiveness, and consensus of the behavior. This process helps us to link together the various pieces of our world in cause-effect relationships, but it is also subject to attribution errors, including fundamental attribution error and self-serving bias.

Self-fulfilling prophecy occurs when our expectations about another person cause that person to act in a way that is consistent with those expectations. Essentially, our expectations affect our behavior toward the target person, which then affects that employee's opportunities and attitudes, which then influences his or her behavior. Self-fulfilling prophecies tend to be stronger when the relationship begins (such as when employees first join the department), when several people hold the expectations toward the employee, and when the employee has a history of low achievement.

Four other perceptual errors commonly noted in organizations are the halo effect, primacy effect, recency effect, and false-consensus effect. We can minimize these and other perceptual problems through awareness of perceptual bias, self-awareness, and meaningful interaction.

Learning is a relatively permanent change in behavior (or behavior tendency) that occurs as a result of a person's interaction with the environment. Much of what we learn is tacit knowledge, which is embedded in our actions without conscious awareness.

The behavior modification perspective of learning states that behavior change occurs by altering its antecedents and consequences. Antecedents are environmental stimuli that provoke (not necessarily cause) behavior. Consequences are events following behavior that influence its future occurrence. Consequences include positive reinforcement, punishment, negative reinforcement, and extinction. The schedules of reinforcement also influence behavior.

Social learning theory states that much learning occurs by observing others and then modeling the behaviors that seem to lead to favorable outcomes and avoiding behaviors that lead to punishing consequences. It also recognizes that we often engage in self-reinforcement. Behavior modeling is effective because it transfers tacit knowledge and enhances the observer's confidence in performing the task.

Many companies now use experiential learning because employees do not acquire tacit knowledge through formal classroom instruction. Experiential learning begins with concrete experience, followed by reflection on that experience, formation of a theory from that experience, and then testing of that theory in the environment.

Organizational learning is any structured activity that improves an organization's capacity to acquire, share, and use knowledge in ways that improve its survival and success. Organizations acquire knowledge through individual learning and experimentation. Knowledge sharing occurs mainly through various forms of communication and training. Knowledge use occurs when employees realize that the knowledge is available and that they have enough freedom to apply it.

Key Terms

attribution process
behavior modification
categorical thinking
contact hypothesis
empathy
false-consensus effect
fundamental attribution error
global mindset
halo effect
Johari Window
learning
learning orientation
mental models
perception
positive organizational behavior
primacy effect
recency effect
selective attention
self-fulfilling prophecy
self-reinforcement
self-serving bias
social learning theory
stereotyping
tacit knowledge

Critical Thinking Questions

1. Several years ago, senior executives at energy company CanOil wanted to acquire an exploration company (HBOG) that was owned by another energy company, AmOil. Rather than face a hostile takeover and unfavorable tax implications, CanOil's two top executives met with the CEO of AmOil to discuss a friendly exchange of stock to carry out the transaction. AmOil's chief executive was previously unaware of CanOil's plans, and as the meeting began, the AmOil executive warned that he was there merely to listen. The CanOil executives were confident that AmOil wanted to sell HBOG because energy legislation at the time made HBOG a poor investment for AmOil. AmOil's CEO remained silent for most of the meeting, which CanOil executives interpreted as an implied agreement to proceed to buy AmOil stock on the market. But when CanOil launched the stock purchase a month later, AmOil's CEO was both surprised and outraged. He thought he had given the CanOil executives the cold shoulder, remaining silent to show his disinterest in the deal. The misunderstanding nearly bankrupted CanOil because AmOil reacted by protecting its stock. What perceptual problem(s) likely occurred that led to this misunderstanding?
2. What mental models do you have about attending a college or university lecture? Are these mental models helpful? Could any of these mental models hold you back from achieving the full benefit of the lecture?
3. Do you define yourself in terms of the university or college you attend? Why or why not? What are the implications of your answer for your university or college?
4. During a diversity management session, a manager suggests that stereotypes are a necessary part of working with others. "I have to make assumptions about what's in the other person's head, and stereotypes help me do that," she explains. "It's better to rely on stereotypes than to enter a working relationship with someone from another culture without any idea of what they believe in!" Discuss the merits of and problems with the manager's statement.
5. Describe how a manager or coach could use the process of self-fulfilling prophecy to enhance an individual's performance.
6. Describe a situation in which you used behavior modification to influence someone's behavior. What specifically did you do? What was the result?

7. Why are organizations moving toward the use of experiential approaches to learning? What conditions are required for success?
8. BusNews Corp. is the leading stock market and business news service. Over the past two years, BusNews has experienced increased competition from other news providers. These competitors have brought in Internet and other emerging computer technologies to link customers with information more quickly. There is little knowledge within BusNews about how to use these computer technologies. On the basis of the knowledge acquisition processes for knowledge management, explain how BusNews might gain the intellectual capital necessary to become more competitive in this respect.

CASE STUDY 3.1

HY DAIRIES, INC.

Syd Gilman read the latest sales figures with a great deal of satisfaction. The vice president of marketing at Hy Dairies, Inc., a large midwestern milk products manufacturer, was pleased to see that the marketing campaign to improve sagging sales of Hy's gourmet ice cream brand was working. Sales volume and market share of the product had increased significantly over the past two quarters compared with the previous year.

The improved sales of Hy's gourmet ice cream could be credited to Rochelle Beauport, who was assigned to the gourmet ice cream brand last year. Beauport had joined Hy less than two years ago as an assistant brand manager after leaving a similar job at a food products firm. She was one of the few women of color in marketing management at Hy Dairies and had a promising career with the company. Gilman was pleased with Beauport's work and tried to let her know this in the annual performance reviews. He now had an excellent opportunity to reward her by offering her the recently vacated position of market research coordinator. Although technically only a lateral transfer with a modest salary increase, the marketing research coordinator job would give Beauport broader experience in some high-profile work, which would enhance her career with Hy Dairies. Few people were aware that Gilman's own career had been boosted by working as marketing research coordinator at Hy several years earlier.

Rochelle Beauport had also seen the latest sales figures on Hy's gourmet ice cream and was expecting Gilman's call to meet with her that morning. Gilman began the conversation by briefly mentioning the favorable sales figures and then explained that he wanted Beauport to take the marketing research coordinator job. Beauport was shocked by the news. She enjoyed brand management and particularly the challenge involved with controlling a product that directly affected the company's profitability. Marketing research coordinator was a technical support position–a "backroom" job–far removed from the company's bottom-line activities. Marketing research was not the route to top management in most organizations, Beauport thought. She had been sidelined.

After a long silence, Beauport managed a weak "Thank you, Mr. Gilman." She was too bewildered to protest. She wanted to collect her thoughts and reflect on what she had done wrong. Also, she did not know her boss well enough to be openly critical.

Gilman recognized Beauport's surprise, which he naturally assumed was her positive response to hearing of this wonderful career opportunity. He, too, had been delighted several years earlier about his temporary transfer to marketing research to round out his marketing experience. "This move will be good for both you and Hy Dairies," said Gilman as he escorted Beauport from his office.

Beauport was preoccupied with several tasks that afternoon, but she was able to consider the day's events that evening. She was one of the top women and few minorities in brand management at Hy Dairies and feared that she was being sidelined because the company didn't want women or people of color in top management. Her previous employer had made it quite clear that women "couldn't take the heat" in marketing management and tended to place women in technical support positions after a brief term in lower brand management jobs. Obviously Syd Gilman and Hy Dairies were following the same game plan. Gilman's comment that the coordinator job would be good for her was just a nice way of saying that Beauport couldn't go any further in brand management at Hy Dairies.

Beauport now faced the difficult decision of whether to confront Gilman and try to change Hy Dairies' sexist and possibly racist practices or to leave the company.

Discussion Questions

1. Apply your knowledge of stereotyping and social identity theory to explain what went wrong here.
2. What other perceptual error is apparent in this case study?
3. What can organizations do to minimize misperceptions in these types of situations?

CASE STUDY 3.2

HOW FAILURE BREEDS SUCCESS

BusinessWeek

Coca-Cola chairman and former CEO E. Neville Isdell knows that the best companies embrace their mistakes and learn from them. That's why Isdell doesn't mind rhyming off the list of Coke's failures over the years. In fact, he is keen to convince employees and shareholders that he will tolerate the failures that will inevitably result from the bigger risks that he wants Coke to take. At the same time, say analysts, balancing a learning culture with a performance culture is a perennial challenge. Intuit, the tax software company, thinks it has a solution. When one of its marketing strategies recently flopped, the company celebrated the failure and spent a lot of time dissecting it.

This *BusinessWeek* case study describes several ways that companies learn from their mistakes while still maintaining a strong focus on performance and the bottom line. Read the full text of this *BusinessWeek* article at www.mhhe.com/mcshane5e, and prepare for the discussion questions below.

Discussion Questions

1. Describe the experiential learning process that companies mentioned in this case study apply to learn from their mistakes and failures.
2. What perceptual problems do managers need to overcome with failures? How can these perceptual problems be minimized?

Source: J. McGregor, "How Failure Breeds Success," *BusinessWeek,* 10 July 2006, p. 42.

CLASS EXERCISE 3.3

THE LEARNING EXERCISE

PURPOSE This exercise is designed to help you understand how the contingencies of reinforcement in behavior modification affect learning.

MATERIALS Any objects normally available in a classroom will be acceptable for this activity.

INSTRUCTIONS (LARGE OR SMALL CLASS) The instructor will ask for three volunteers, who are then briefed outside the classroom. The instructor will spend a few minutes briefing the remaining students in the class about their duties. Then, one of the three volunteers will enter the room to participate in the exercise. When completed, the second volunteer enters the room and participates in the exercise. When completed, the third volunteer enters the class and participates in the exercise.

For students to gain the full benefit of this exercise, no other information will be provided here. However, the instructor will have more details at the beginning of this fun activity.

CLASS EXERCISE 3.4

STEREOTYPING IN CORPORATE ANNUAL REPORTS

PURPOSE This exercise is designed to help you diagnose evidence of stereotyping and identify corporate role models that minimize stereotyping in corporate annual reports.

MATERIALS Students need to complete their research for this activity prior to class, including selecting a publicly traded company and downloading the past four or more years of its fully illustrated annual reports.

INSTRUCTIONS The instructor may have students work alone or in groups for this activity. Students will select a company that is publicly traded and posts its annual reports on the company website. Ideally, annual reports for at least the past four years should be available, and these reports should be presented in the final illustrated format (typically PDF replicas of the original hard-copy report).

Students will closely examine images in the selected company's recent annual reports in terms of how women, visible minorities, and older employees and clients are presented. Specifically, students should be prepared to discuss and provide details in class regarding:

1. The percentage of images showing (i.e., visual representation of) women, visible minorities, and older workers and clients. Students should also be sensitive to the size and placement of these images on the page and throughout the annual report.
2. The roles in which women, visible minorities, and older workers and clients are depicted. For example, are women shown more in traditional or nontraditional occupations and nonwork roles in these annual reports?

If several years of annual reports are available, students should pick one that is a decade or more old and compare its visual representation of and role depiction of women, visible minorities, and older employees and clients.

If possible, students should pick one of the most blatantly stereotypic illustrations they can find in these annual reports to show in class, either as a hard-copy printout or as a computer projection.

SELF-ASSESSMENT 3.5

HOW MUCH PERCEPTUAL STRUCTURE DO YOU NEED?

PURPOSE This self-assessment is designed to help you estimate your personal need for perceptual structure.

Instructions Read each of the statements below and decide how much you agree with each according to your attitudes, beliefs, and experiences. Then use the scoring key in Appendix B at the end of this book to calculate your results. It is important for you to realize that there are no right or wrong answers to these questions. This self-assessment should be completed alone so that you can rate yourself honestly without concerns of social comparison. Class discussion will focus on the meaning of need for structure in terms of how we engage differently in the perceptual process at work and in other settings.

Personal Need for Structure Scale

To what extent do you agree or disagree with each of these statements about yourself?	Strongly agree	Moderately agree	Slightly agree	Slightly disagree	Moderately disagree	Strongly disagree
1. It upsets me to go into a situation without knowing what I can expect from it.	☐	☐	☐	☐	☐	☐
2. I'm not bothered by things that interrupt my daily routine.	☐	☐	☐	☐	☐	☐
3. I enjoy being spontaneous.	☐	☐	☐	☐	☐	☐
4. I find that a well-ordered life with regular hours makes my life tedious.	☐	☐	☐	☐	☐	☐
5. I find that a consistent routine enables me to enjoy life more.	☐	☐	☐	☐	☐	☐
6. I enjoy having a clear and structured mode of life.	☐	☐	☐	☐	☐	☐
7. I like to have a place for everything and everything in its place.	☐	☐	☐	☐	☐	☐
8. I don't like situations that are uncertain.	☐	☐	☐	☐	☐	☐
9. I hate to change my plans at the last minute.	☐	☐	☐	☐	☐	☐
10. I hate to be with people who are unpredictable.	☐	☐	☐	☐	☐	☐
11. I enjoy the exhilaration of being in unpredictable situations.	☐	☐	☐	☐	☐	☐
12. I become uncomfortable when the rules in a situation are not clear.	☐	☐	☐	☐	☐	☐

Source: M. M. Thompson, M. E. Naccarato, and K. E. Parker, "Assessing Cognitive Need: The Development of the Personal Need for Structure and the Personal Fear of Invalidity Scales," paper presented at the annual meeting of the Canadian Psychological Association, Halifax, Nova Scotia, 1989. Reprinted with permission.

SELF-ASSESSMENT 3.6

ASSESSING YOUR PERSPECTIVE TAKING (COGNITIVE EMPATHY)

Empathy is an important perceptual ability in social relations, but the degree to which people empathize varies considerably. This self-assessment provides an estimate of one form of empathy, known as *cognitive empathy* or *perspective taking*. That is, it measures the level of your cognitive awareness of another person's situational and individual circumstances. To complete this scale, indicate the degree to which each of the statements presented does or does not describe you very well. You need to be honest with yourself for a reasonable estimate of your level of perspective taking. The results show your relative position along the perspective-taking continuum and the general meaning of this score.

SELF-ASSESSMENT 3.7

ASSESSING YOUR EMOTIONAL EMPATHY

Empathy is an important perceptual ability in social relations, but the degree to which people empathize varies considerably. This self-assessment provides an estimate of one form of empathy, known as *emotional empathy*–the extent that you are able to experience the emotions or feelings of another person. To complete this scale, indicate the degree to which each of the statements presented does or does not describe you very well. You need to be honest with yourself for a reasonable estimate of your level of emotional empathy. The results show your relative position along the emotional empathy continuum and the general meaning of this score.

You know the fun is about to begin at Suntech Optics when employees spot the pineapple wearing sunglasses. The bespectacled fruit is the mascot for the eyewear supplier's Have Fun Team, which is responsible for creating various forms of workplace levity. Employees at the company's headquarters in Vancouver, Canada, might discover a puzzle on their desk, with a prize awarded to the person who solves it first. Dozens of stuffed bears are brought to work on Bring Your Teddy Bear to Work Day. Halloween is a special treat as staff dress up for the occasion and show off their pumpkin-carving skills. "We try to infuse having fun into our whole corporate culture," says Suntech manager Deborah Peck. "It's one of our core strategies. It's part of our life."

Having fun is part of the culture at Mott MacDonald. This photo shows a Mott employee during the Abu Dhabi oil and gas team's annual desert safari for staff and families.

Fun at work? It sounds like an oxymoron. But to attract and keep talented employees, companies are finding creative ways to generate positive emotions in the workplace. Don't be surprised if you see staff at John Laing Homes, a construction firm in California, walking around in slippers on one of their crazy-dress days. AstraZeneca's "Fun Department" set up a mock doctor's office where employees with "terminal seriousness" receive "prescriptions to play." The pharmaceutical company is also known for fun pranks, such as surprising an employee on his birthday with a cubicle filled to the brim with colorful peanut-shaped packing material. Employees at Mott MacDonald, a global management, engineering, and development consulting firm, also have plenty of fun. For example, the Abu Dhabi oil and gas team has an annual desert safari, complete with camel rides (shown in photo).

Another fun-focused company is Dixon Schwabl, a 75-employee marketing and public relations firm in Rochester, New York. "Fun is not just a word here, it is a way of life!" wrote one employee in a recent survey. Employees enjoy bocce tournaments, softball leagues, golf chipping contests, water balloon toss events, Halloween pumpkin-decorating contests, a padded primal scream room to release tension, and a spiral slide for those who want to descend more quickly to the main floor. "At the end of the day, everyone's going to be happier and the product will be far better than if they're not happy," says Dixon Schwabl CEO Lauren Dixon.[1]

4

WORKPLACE EMOTIONS, ATTITUDES, AND STRESS

Learning Objectives

After reading this chapter, you should be able to:

1. Explain how emotions and cognition (conscious reasoning) influence attitudes and behavior.
2. Identify the conditions that require, and the problems associated with, emotional labor.
3. Describe the four dimensions of emotional intelligence.
4. Summarize the consequences of job dissatisfaction in terms of the exit-voice-loyalty-neglect model.
5. Discuss the effects of job satisfaction on job performance and customer service.
6. Distinguish affective and continuance commitment and discuss their influence on employee behavior.
7. Describe five strategies for increasing organizational (affective) commitment.
8. Understand the dynamics of psychological contracts.
9. Define *stress* and describe the stress experience including job burnout.
10. Explain why a stressor might produce different stress levels in two people.
11. Identify five ways to manage workplace stress.

Dixon Schwabl, Mott MacDonald, AstraZeneca, John Laing Homes, Suntech Optics, and many other companies around the world are discovering that emotions and attitudes make a difference in individual behavior and well-being, as well as in the organization's performance and customer service. Over the past decade, the field of organizational behavior has experienced a sea change in thinking about workplace emotions, so this chapter begins by introducing the concept and explaining why researchers are so eager to discover how emotions influence attitudes and behavior. Next, we consider the dynamics of emotional labor, followed by the popular topic of emotional intelligence. The specific work attitudes of job satisfaction and organizational commitment are then discussed, including their association with various employee behaviors and work performance. The latter part of this chapter examines work-related stress, beginning with an overview of the stress experience and the consequences of distress. Three major work-related stressors are then described, followed by coverage of five ways to manage stress in the workplace.

Learning Objectives

After reading this section, you should be able to:

1. Explain how emotions and cognition (conscious reasoning) influence attitudes and behavior.

EMOTIONS IN THE WORKPLACE

Emotions have a profound effect on almost everything we do in the workplace. This is a strong statement, and one that you would rarely find a decade ago in organizational behavior research or textbooks. Until recently, OB experts assumed that a person's thoughts and actions are governed primarily by conscious reasoning (called *cognition*). Yet groundbreaking neuroscience discoveries have revealed that our perceptions, attitudes, decisions, and behavior are influenced by both cognition and emotion.[2] In fact, emotions may have a greater influence because emotional processes often occur before conscious cognitive processes and, consequently, influence the latter. By ignoring emotionality, many theories have overlooked a large piece of the puzzle about human behavior in the workplace.

emotions
Physiological, behavioral, and psychological episodes experienced toward an object, person, or event that create a state of readiness.

Emotions are physiological, behavioral, and psychological episodes experienced toward an object, person, or event that create a state of readiness.[3] These "episodes" are very brief events that typically subside or occur in waves lasting from milliseconds to a few minutes. Emotions are directed toward someone or something. For example, we experience joy, fear, anger, and other emotional episodes toward tasks, customers, or a software program we are using. This differs from *moods,* which are less intense and longer-term emotional states that are not directed toward anything in particular.[4]

Emotions are experiences. They represent changes in our physiological state (e.g., blood pressure, heart rate), psychological state (e.g., ability to think clearly), and behavior (e.g., facial expression). Most of these emotional reactions are subtle and occur without our awareness. This is a particularly important point because people often think about "getting emotional" when the subject of emotions is mentioned. In reality, you experience emotions every minute but aren't even aware of most of them. Finally, emotions put us in a state of readiness. When we get worried, for example, our heart rate and blood pressure increase to make our body better prepared to engage in fight or flight. Strong emotions also trigger our conscious awareness of a threat or opportunity in the external environment.[5]

Types of Emotions

People experience many emotions as well as various combinations of emotions, but all of them have two common features. First, emotions generate a global evaluation (called *core affect*) that something is good or bad, helpful or harmful, to be approached or to be avoided. Second, all emotions produce some level of activation. However, they vary considerably in this activation, that is, in how much they demand our attention and motivate us to act. These two dimensions of emotions are the foundation of the circumplex model shown in Exhibit 4.1.[6] Distressed is a negative emotion that generates a high level of activation, whereas relaxed is a pleasant emotion that has fairly low activation.

"Biosensors. The whole company knows instantly when I'm displeased."

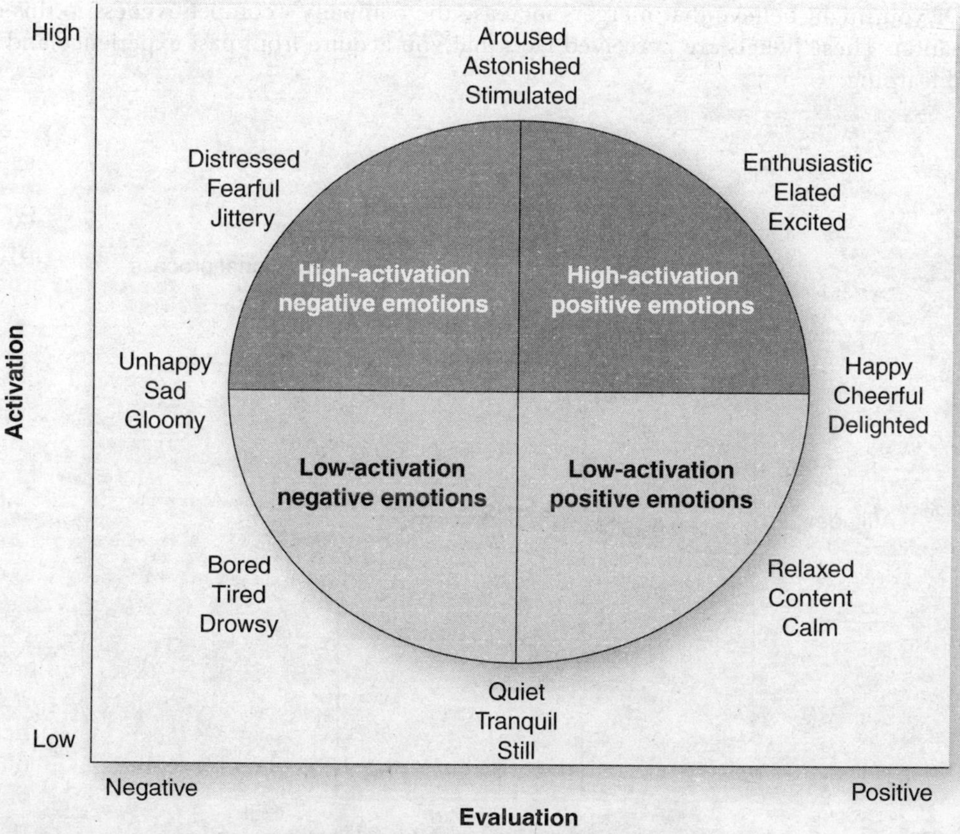

Source: Adapted from R. J. Larsen, E. Diener, and R. E. Lucas, "Emotion: Models, Measures, and Individual Differences," in *Emotions in the Workplace*, ed. R. G. Lord, R. J. Klimoski, and R. Kanfer (San Francisco: Jossey-Bass, 2002), pp. 64–113; J. A. Russell, "Core Affect and the Psychological Construction of Emotion," *Psychological Review* 110, no. 1 (2003), pp. 145–172.

Exhibit 4.1 *Circumplex Model of Emotions*

Emotions, Attitudes, and Behavior

attitudes
The cluster of beliefs, assessed feelings, and behavioral intentions toward a person, object, or event (called an *attitude object*).

To understand how emotions influence our thoughts and behavior in the workplace, we first need to know about attitudes. **Attitudes** represent the cluster of beliefs, assessed feelings, and behavioral intentions toward a person, object, or event (called an *attitude object*).[7] Attitudes are *judgments,* whereas emotions are *experiences.* In other words, attitudes involve conscious logical reasoning, whereas emotions operate as events, usually without our awareness. We also experience most emotions briefly, whereas our attitude toward someone or something is more stable over time.

Until recently, experts described attitudes in terms of the three cognitive components illustrated on the left side of Exhibit 4.2: beliefs, feelings, and behavioral intentions. Now we have good evidence that a parallel emotional process is also at work, shown on the right side of the exhibit.[8] Using attitude toward mergers as an example, let's look more closely at this model, beginning with the traditional cognitive perspective of attitudes.

- *Beliefs.* These are your established perceptions about the attitude object–what you believe to be true. For example, you might believe that mergers reduce job security for employees in the merged firms. Or you might believe that mergers increase the company's competitiveness in this era of globalization. These beliefs are perceived facts that you acquire from past experience and other forms of learning.

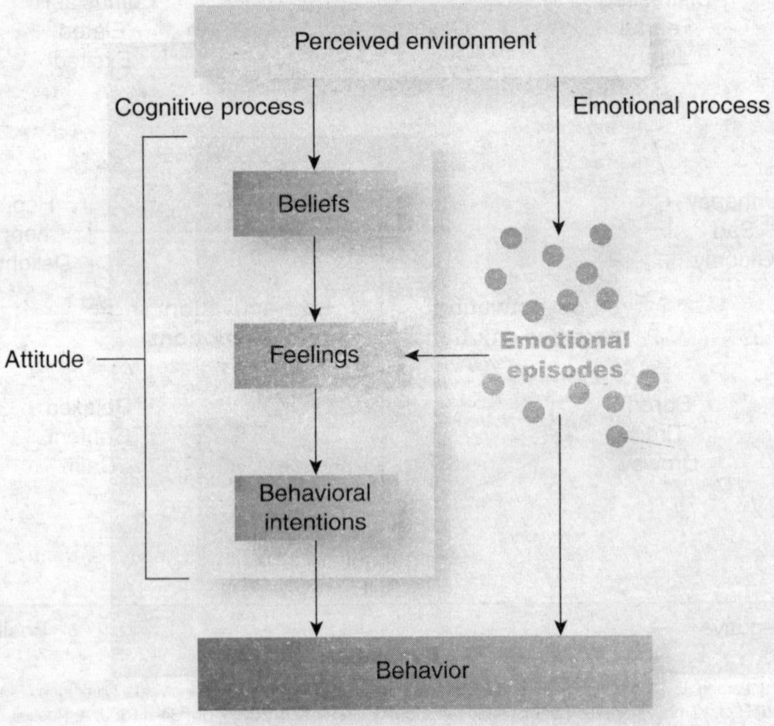

Exhibit 4.2 *Model of Emotions, Attitudes, and Behavior*

- *Feelings.* Feelings represent your positive or negative evaluations of the attitude object. Some people think mergers are good; others think they are bad. Your like or dislike of mergers represents your assessed feelings. According to the traditional cognitive perspective of attitudes (left side of the model), feelings are calculated from your beliefs about mergers. If you believe that mergers typically have negative consequences such as layoffs and organizational politics, you will form negative feelings toward mergers in general or about a specific planned merger in your organization.
- *Behavioral intentions.* Intentions represent your motivation to engage in a particular behavior regarding the attitude object.[9] Upon hearing that the company will merge with another organization, you might become motivated to look for a job elsewhere or possibly to complain to management about the merger decision. Your feelings toward mergers motivate your behavioral intentions, and which actions you choose depends on your past experience, self-concept (values, personality), and social norms of appropriate behavior.

Exhibit 4.2 also illustrates that behavioral intentions directly predict behavior. However, whether your intentions translate into behavior depends on all four elements of the MARS model, such as opportunity and ability to act. Attitudes are also more likely to influence behavior when they are strong, meaning that they are anchored by strong emotions.

How Emotions Influence Attitudes and Behavior As we mentioned, emotions play a central role in forming and changing employee attitudes.[10] The right side of Exhibit 4.2 illustrates this process, which (like the cognitive process) also begins with perceptions of the world around us. The emotional centers of our brain quickly and imprecisely tag emotional markers to incoming sensory information on the basis of whether that information supports or threatens our innate drives. These markers are not calculated feelings; they are automatic and nonconscious emotional responses based on very thin slices of sensory information.[11]

Returning to the example of your attitude toward mergers, you might experience excitement, worry, nervousness, or happiness upon learning that your company intends to merge with a competitor. The large dots on the right side of Exhibit 4.2 illustrate the numerous emotional episodes you experience upon hearing the merger announcement, subsequently thinking about the merger, discussing the merger with co-workers, and so on. These emotions are transmitted to the logical reasoning process, where they are logically analyzed along with other information about the attitude object.[12] Thus, while you are consciously evaluating whether the merger is good or bad, your emotions have already formed an opinion, which then sways your conscious evaluation. In fact, we often deliberately "listen in" on our emotions to help us consciously decide whether to support or oppose something.[13] If you experience mainly positive emotions whenever you think about or discuss the merger, these positive emotional episodes will lean your logical reasoning toward positive feelings regarding the merger.

The dual cognitive-emotional attitude process helps us to understand why Dixon Schwabl and many other companies want their employees to experience plenty of positive emotional episodes each day. Work attitudes are shaped by the almost continuous bombardment of emotional experiences people have at work. Those who experience more positive emotions tend to have more favorable attitudes toward their jobs and organizations, even when they aren't consciously aware of many of these emotional experiences. And when they do think about how they feel about their jobs, they listen in on the emotions regenerated from past positive or negative events in the workplace.

The influence of both cognitive reasoning and emotions on attitudes is most apparent when they disagree with each other. People occasionally experience this mental tug-of-war, sensing that something isn't right even though they can't think of any logical reason to be concerned. This conflicting experience indicates that the person's logical analysis of the situation (left side of Exhibit 4.2) can't identify reasons to support the automatic emotional reaction (right side of Exhibit 4.2).[14] Should we pay attention to our emotional response or our logical analysis? This question is not easy to answer, but some studies indicate that while executives tend to make quick decisions based on their gut feelings (emotional response), the best decisions tend to occur when executives spend time logically evaluating the situation.[15] Thus, we should pay attention to both the cognitive and emotional sides of the attitude model, and hope they agree with each other most of the time!

One last comment about Exhibit 4.2: Notice the arrow from the emotional episodes to behavior. It indicates that emotions directly (without conscious thinking) influence a person's behavior. This occurs when we jump suddenly if someone sneaks up on us. It also occurs in everyday situations because even low-intensity emotions automatically change our facial expressions. These actions are not carefully thought out. They are automatic emotional responses that are learned or hardwired by heredity for particular situations.[16]

When Cognitions and Emotions Conflict The influence of both logical reasoning and emotions on attitudes is most apparent when they disagree with each other. Everyone occasionally experiences this mental tug-of-war, sensing that something isn't right even though they can't think of any logical reason to be concerned. This conflicting experience indicates that our logical analysis of the situation (left side of Exhibit 4.2) can't identify reasons to support the automatic emotional reaction (right side of Exhibit 4.2). Should we pay attention to our emotional response or our logical analysis? This question is not easy to answer because, as we just learned, the emotional and rational processes interact with each other so closely. However, some studies indicate that while executives tend to make quick decisions based on their gut feelings (emotional response), the best decisions tend to occur when executives spend time, logically evaluating the situation[17]. Thus, we should pay attention to both the cognitive and emotional sides of the attitude model, and hope they agree with each other most of the time!

One last observation about the attitude model in Exhibit 4.2 relates to the arrow directly from the emotional episodes to behavior. This indicates that people have direct behavioral reactions to their emotions. Even low-intensity emotions automatically change your facial expressions. High-intensity emotions can have a more powerful effect, which is apparent when an upset employee bangs a fist on a desk or an overjoyed colleague embraces someone nearby. These actions are not carefully thought out. They are fairly automatic emotional responses that serve as coping mechanisms in that situation.[18]

cognitive dissonance Condition that occurs when we perceive an inconsistency between our beliefs, feelings, and behavior.

Cognitive Dissonance Emotions and attitudes usually lead to behavior, but the opposite sometimes occurs through the process of **cognitive dissonance.**[19] Cognitive dissonance occurs when we perceive an inconsistency between our beliefs, feelings, and behavior. When this inconsistency violates our self-concept, it generates emotions that motivate us to change one or more of these elements. For example, let's say that you agreed to accept a foreign posting, even though it didn't interest you, because you believed it might be necessary for promotion into senior management. However, you later learn that many people become senior managers in the firm without spending any time on foreign assignment. In this situation, you will likely experience cognitive dissonance because of the inconsistency between your beliefs and feelings (dislike foreign assignments) and behavior (accepted a foreign posting).

Behavior is usually more difficult to change than beliefs and feelings. This is particularly true when the dissonant behavior has been observed by others, was done voluntarily, and can't be undone. In the foreign assignment example, you experience cognitive dissonance because others know that you accepted the assignment, it was accepted voluntarily (e.g., you weren't threatened with dismissal if you refused the assignment), and working overseas can't be undone (although you might be able to change your mind beforehand). Thus, people usually change their beliefs and feelings to reduce the inconsistency. For example, you might convince yourself that the foreign posting is not so bad after all because it will develop your management skills. Alternatively, you might downplay the features that previously made the foreign posting less desirable. Over time, a somewhat negative attitude toward foreign assignments becomes a more favorable one.

Emotions and Personality Our coverage of the dynamics of workplace emotions wouldn't be complete unless we mentioned that emotions are also partly determined by a person's personality, not just workplace experiences.[20] Some people experience positive emotions as a natural trait. These people are generally extroverted–outgoing, talkative, sociable, and assertive (see Chapter 2). In contrast, other people have a personality with a tendency to experience more negative emotions. Positive and negative emotional traits affect a person's attendance, turnover, and long-term work attitudes. For example, several studies report that people with a negative emotional trait have lower levels of job satisfaction and higher levels of job burnout.[21] While positive and negative personality traits have some effect, other research concludes that the actual situation in which people work has a noticeably stronger influence on their attitudes and behavior.[22]

Learning Objectives

After reading this section, you should be able to:

2. Identify the conditions that require, and the problems associated with, emotional labor.
3. Describe the four dimensions of emotional intelligence.

MANAGING EMOTIONS AT WORK

The Elbow Room Café is packed and noisy on this Saturday morning. A customer at the Vancouver restaurant half shouts across the room for more coffee. A passing waiter scoffs: "You want more coffee, get it yourself!" The customer only laughs. Another diner complains loudly that he and his party are running late and need their food. This time, restaurant manager Patrick Savoie speaks up: "If you're in a hurry, you should have gone to McDonald's." The diner and his companions chuckle. To the uninitiated, the Elbow Room Café is an emotional basket case, where staff turn rudeness into a fine art. But it's all a performance–a place where guests can enjoy good food and play out their emotions about dreadful customer service. "It's almost like coming to a theatre," says Savoie, who spends much of his time inventing new ways to insult the clientele.[23]

emotional labor
The effort, planning, and control needed to express organizationally desired emotions during interpersonal transactions.

Whether giving the most insulting service at Elbow Room Café in Vancouver or the friendliest service at Dixon Schwabl in Rochester, New York, people are expected to manage their emotions in the workplace. They must conceal their frustration when serving an irritating customer, display compassion to an ill patient, and hide their boredom in a long meeting with senior management. These are all forms of **emotional labor**–the effort, planning, and control needed to express organizationally desired emotions during interpersonal transactions.[24] Almost everyone is expected to abide by *display rules*–norms requiring us to display specific emotions and to hide other emotions.

Emotional labor is higher in jobs requiring a variety of emotions (e.g., anger as well as joy) and more intense emotions (e.g., showing delight rather than smiling weakly), as well as in jobs where interaction with clients is frequent and has a longer duration. Emotional labor also increases when employees must precisely rather than casually abide by the display rules.[25] This particularly occurs in the service industries, where employees have frequent face-to-face interaction with clients. For instance, the Ritz-Carlton Hotel Co.'s motto is "Smile–we are on stage." To ensure that this standard is maintained at the dozens of properties it manages around the world, the Ritz developed a detailed training program that teaches staff how to look pleasant in front of guests. Its orientation manual even includes two pages on phrases to use and to avoid saying, such as "My pleasure" rather than "OK, sure."[26]

Emotional Display Norms across Cultures

How much we are expected to hide or reveal our true emotions in public depends to some extent on the culture in which we live. Cultural values in some countries–particularly Ethiopia, Korea, Japan,

All Smiles in Berlin Five months before the World Cup soccer finals arrived in Germany, the country's national tourist board launched a campaign encouraging Berliners to smile more often for the million visitors attending the wildly popular tournament. The customer service campaign covered a dozen German cities where the games were played, but the tourist board particularly targeted Berlin, a city known for somewhat abrupt and gruff service. "Smiles create more smiles, and in this city we need a bit more smiling," said Klaus Böger, Berlin's senator for education and sport. Berlin's advertising program, called "The Most Beautiful Smile for Our Guests" *(Das schönste Lächeln für unsere Gäste),* displayed one of a dozen smiling citizens, four of whom are shown in this photo, on hundreds of billboards around the city. "We won't get this opportunity again for another 50 years, so it's worth at least smiling for a few weeks," said German World Cup organizing committee president (and German soccer legend) Franz Beckenbauer, with apparent sympathy for those uncomfortable with displaying friendly emotions to strangers.[27]

and Austria–expect people to subdue their emotional expression and minimize physical contact with others. Even voice intonation tends to be monotonic. In other countries–notably Kuwait, Egypt, Spain, and Russia–cultural values allow or encourage open display of one's true emotions. People are expected to be transparent in revealing their thoughts and feelings, dramatic in their conversational tones, and animated in their use of nonverbal behaviors to get their message across. These cultural variations in emotional display can be quite noticeable. One survey reported that 83 percent of Japanese believe it is inappropriate to get emotional in a business context, compared with 40 percent of Americans, 34 percent of French, and only 29 percent of Italians. In other words, Italians are more likely to accept or tolerate people who display their true emotions at work, whereas emotional behavior would be considered rude or embarrassing in Japan.[28]

Emotional Dissonance

Emotional labor can be challenging for most of us because it is difficult to conceal true emotions and to display the emotions required by the job. Joy, sadness, worry, and other emotions automatically activate a complex set of facial muscles that are difficult to prevent and equally difficult to fake. Pretending to be cheerful or concerned requires adjustment and coordination of several specific facial muscles and body positions. Meanwhile, our true emotions tend to reveal themselves as subtle gestures, usually without our awareness. More often than not, observers see when we are faking and sense that we feel a different emotion.[29]

emotional dissonance
The conflict between required and true emotions.

Emotional labor also creates conflict between required and true emotions, which is called **emotional dissonance.** The larger the gap between the required and true emotions, the more employees tend to experience stress, job burnout, and psychological separation from self.[30] Hiring people with a natural tendency to display the emotions required for the job can minimize emotional dissonance. For example, The Container Store expects employees to display positive emotions on the job, so its unofficial motto is "Grouchy People Need Not Apply." St. Wilfred's Hospice in Chichester, England, takes a similar view. "We have standards of behavior," says chief executive Alison Moorey. "We expect anyone who comes into the hospice to be treated with smiles and courtesy."[31]

Emotional dissonance is also minimized through deep acting rather than surface acting.[32] People engage in *surface acting* when they try to modify their behavior to be consistent with required emotions but continue to hold different internal feelings. For instance, we force a smile while greeting a customer whom we consider rude. *Deep acting* involves changing true emotions to match the required emotions. Rather than feeling irritated by a rude customer, you might view your next interaction with that person as an opportunity to test your sales skills. This change in perspective can potentially generate more positive emotions next time you meet that difficult customer, thereby producing friendlier displays of emotion. However, deep acting also requires considerable emotional intelligence, which we discuss next.

Emotional Intelligence

Exactech, Inc., is growing quickly, so the Gainesville, Florida, orthopedic device manufacturer introduced a program to develop future leaders. Two dozen high-potential employees were identified among the staff of 260 and then given intensive yearlong training. This program didn't focus completely on technical skill development. Rather, participants learned how to improve their self-awareness and interaction with other staff members. "Especially as people rise to higher levels in organizations, their ability to do their job effectively depends on emotional intelligence qualities more than technical qualities," explains Exactech cofounder Bill Petty.[33]

emotional intelligence (EI)
A set of abilities to perceive and express emotion, assimilate emotion in thought, understand and reason with emotion, and regulate emotion in oneself and others.

Exactech is one of many organizations discovering that **emotional intelligence (EI)** can significantly improve individual, team, and organizational effectiveness. Emotional intelligence includes a set of *abilities* to perceive and express emotion, assimilate emotion in thought, understand and reason with emotion, and regulate emotion in oneself and others.[34] One popular model, shown in Exhibit 4.3, organizes EI into four dimensions representing the recognition of emotions in ourselves and in others, as well as the regulation of emotions in ourselves and in others.[35] These four dimensions are also found in other models of EI, but experts disagree on the definitive list of abilities representing EI. For example, the authors of the model shown here include a list of "abilities" for each cell, but others warn that the list includes personality traits and personal values (e.g., achievement, optimism) as well as task outcomes (e.g., teamwork, inspirational leadership).[36]

	Self (personal competence)	Other (social competence)
Recognition of emotions	**Self-Awareness** • Emotional self-awareness • Accurate self-assessment • Self-confidence	**Social Awareness** • Empathy • Organizational awareness • Service
Regulation of emotions	**Self-Management** • Emotional self-control • Transparency • Adaptability • Achievement • Initiative • Optimism	**Relationship Management** • Inspirational leadership • Influence • Developing others • Change catalyst • Conflict management • Building bonds • Teamwork and collaboration

Sources: D. Goleman, R. Boyatzis, and A. McKee, *Primal Leadership* (Boston: Harvard Business School Press, 2002), Chapter 3; D. Goleman, "An EI-Based Theory of Performance," in *The Emotionally Intelligent Workplace, ed.* C. Cherniss and D. Goleman (San Francisco: Jossey-Bass, 2001), p. 28.

Exhibit 4.3 *Dimensions of Emotional Intelligence*

- *Self-awareness.* Self-awareness is the ability to perceive and understand the meaning of your own emotions. You are more sensitive to subtle emotional responses to events and understand their message. Self-aware people are better able to eavesdrop on their emotional responses to specific situations and to use this awareness as conscious information.[37]
- *Self-management.* Self-management is the ability to manage your own emotions, something that we all do to some extent. We keep disruptive impulses in check. We try not to feel angry or frustrated when events go against us. We try to feel and express joy and happiness toward others when the occasion calls for these emotional displays. We try to create a second wind of motivation later in the workday. Notice that self-management goes beyond displaying behaviors that represent desired emotions in a particular situation. It includes generating or suppressing emotions. In other words, the deep acting described earlier requires high levels of the self-management component of emotional intelligence.
- *Social awareness.* Social awareness is the ability to perceive and understand the emotions of other people. To a large extent, this ability is represented by *empathy*–having an understanding of and sensitivity to the feelings, thoughts, and situations of others (see Chapter 3). This includes

understanding another person's situation, experiencing the other person's emotions, and knowing his or her needs even though unstated. Social awareness extends beyond empathy to include being organizationally aware, such as sensing office politics and understanding social networks.

- *Relationship management.* This dimension of EI involves managing other people's emotions. This includes consoling people who feel sad, emotionally inspiring your team members to complete a class project on time, getting strangers to feel comfortable working with you, and managing dysfunctional emotions among staff who experience conflict with customers or other employees. Some emotional intelligence experts link this component of EI to a wide variety of interpersonal activities, but we must remember that relationship management is restricted to managing other people's emotions, whereas working effectively with other people extends to other competencies.

These four dimensions of emotional intelligence form a hierarchy.[38] Self-awareness is the lowest level of EI because it is a prerequisite for the other three dimensions but does not require the other dimensions. Self-management and social awareness are necessarily above self-awareness in the EI hierarchy. You can't manage your own emotions (self-management) if you aren't good at knowing your own emotions (self-awareness). Relationship management is the highest level of EI because it

4.1 GLOBAL CONNECTIONS

GM Holden Revs Up Emotional Intelligence

General Motors carefully selected staff for its new GM Holden production facility at Port Melbourne, Australia, but it wasn't long before the project unraveled due to infighting and interpersonal tensions. Consultants called in to analyze the problems offered the following solution: Employees need to improve their emotional intelligence. With this advice, the 30 plant design team members and more than 300 other employees completed a detailed assessment of their emotional intelligence. The automaker then introduced a variety of training modules targeting different aspects of emotional intelligence, such as effective self-expression, understanding others, and controlling emotions.

Emotional intelligence training helped employees at GM Holden, the Australian division of General Motors, to get along better.

Some staff were skeptical about these touchy-feely seminars, so GM Holden evaluated the program to see whether employee scores improved and behavior changed. The company discovered that employee scores on the emotional intelligence test improved by almost 50 percent and that employees became much more cooperative and diplomatic in their behavior. "It has greatly improved communication within the team and with other teams outside the plant," says GM Holden quality systems engineer Vesselka Vassileva. Some employees also note that it has improved their interpersonal behavior outside the workplace. "I'm not so aggressive or assertive," says manufacturing engineer Alf Moore. "I feel better and it's helped me at home."[39]

requires all three other dimensions. In other words, we require a high degree of emotional intelligence to master relationship management because this set of competencies requires sufficiently high levels of self-awareness, self-management, and social awareness.

Most jobs involve social interaction with co-workers or external stakeholders, so employees need emotional intelligence to work effectively. Research indicates that people with high EI are better at interpersonal relations, perform better in jobs requiring emotional labor, are superior leaders, make better decisions involving social exchanges, and are more successful in many aspects of job interviews. Teams whose members have high emotional intelligence initially perform better than teams with low EI.[40] However, emotional intelligence does not improve some forms of performance, such as tasks that require minimal social interaction.[41]

Improving Emotional Intelligence

Emotional intelligence is associated with some personality traits, as well as with the emotional intelligence of one's parents. For this reason, some companies have attempted to test the levels of EI in applicants. For example, all new pilots at Air Canada receive EI testing. Pilots are team leaders of the on-board crew and need to work effectively with staff on the ground, so they must have the ability to understand and manage their own emotions as well as the emotions of others. "If you have to interact well with other people, these [emotional intelligence tests] are instruments that we can use during the selection process to identify people that have these enhanced skills," says Captain Dave Legge, vice president of Air Canada flight operations. "At the end of the day, we want to have a better idea of who we're hiring."[42]

Emotional intelligence is not completely innate, however. It can also be learned, which is why Exactech invests in developing EI skills in its future leaders.[43] Sony Europe also incorporates EI training in its executive development program, including an exercise in which leaders keep a journal of their emotional experiences throughout a week of work. One study reported that business students scored higher on emotional intelligence after taking an undergraduate interpersonal skills course.[44] As Global Connections 4.1 describes, employees at GM Holden in Australia also improved their interpersonal relations after completing an emotional intelligence training program. Personal coaching, plenty of practice, and frequent feedback are particularly effective at developing EI. Emotional intelligence also increases with age; it is part of the process called maturity. Overall, emotional intelligence offers considerable potential, but we also have a lot to learn about its measurement and effects on people in the workplace.

So far, this chapter has introduced the model of emotions and attitudes, as well as emotional intelligence as the means by which we manage emotions in the workplace. The next two sections of this chapter introduce the concepts of job satisfaction and organizational commitment. These two attitudes are so important in our understanding of workplace behavior that some experts suggest that together they should be called "overall job attitude."[45]

Learning Objectives

After reading this section, you should be able to:

4. Summarize the consequences of job dissatisfaction in terms of the exit-voice-loyalty-neglect model.
5. Discuss the effects of job satisfaction on job performance and customer service.
6. Distinguish affective and continuance commitment and discuss their influence on employee behavior.
7. Describe five strategies for increasing organizational (affective) commitment.
8. Understand the dynamics of psychological contracts.

Job Satisfaction

job satisfaction
A person's evaluation of his or her job and work context.

Job satisfaction, a person's evaluation of his or her job and work context, is probably the most studied attitude in organizational behavior.[46] It is an *appraisal* of the perceived job characteristics, work environment, and emotional experiences at work. Satisfied employees have a favorable evaluation of their jobs, based on their observations and emotional experiences. Job satisfaction is best viewed as a collection of attitudes about different aspects of the job and work context. You might like your co-workers but be less satisfied with your workload, for instance.

How satisfied are employees at work? The answer depends, of course, on the person, the workplace, and the country. Global surveys indicate with some consistency that job satisfaction tends to be highest in the Nordic countries (Denmark, Sweden, Norway, and Finland) as well as in India and the United States. The lowest levels of overall job satisfaction are usually recorded in Hungary and several Asian countries (e.g., China [including Hong Kong] and South Korea).[47] Exhibit 4.4 reveals that more than 85 percent of Americans are moderately or very satisfied with their jobs, a level that has been consistent for the past three decades.[48]

Can we conclude from these results that Americans are happy at work? Possibly, but not as much as these statistics suggest. The problem is that surveys often use a single direct question, such as "How satisfied are you with your job?" Many dissatisfied employees are reluctant to reveal their feelings in a direct question because this is tantamount to admitting that they made a poor job choice and are not

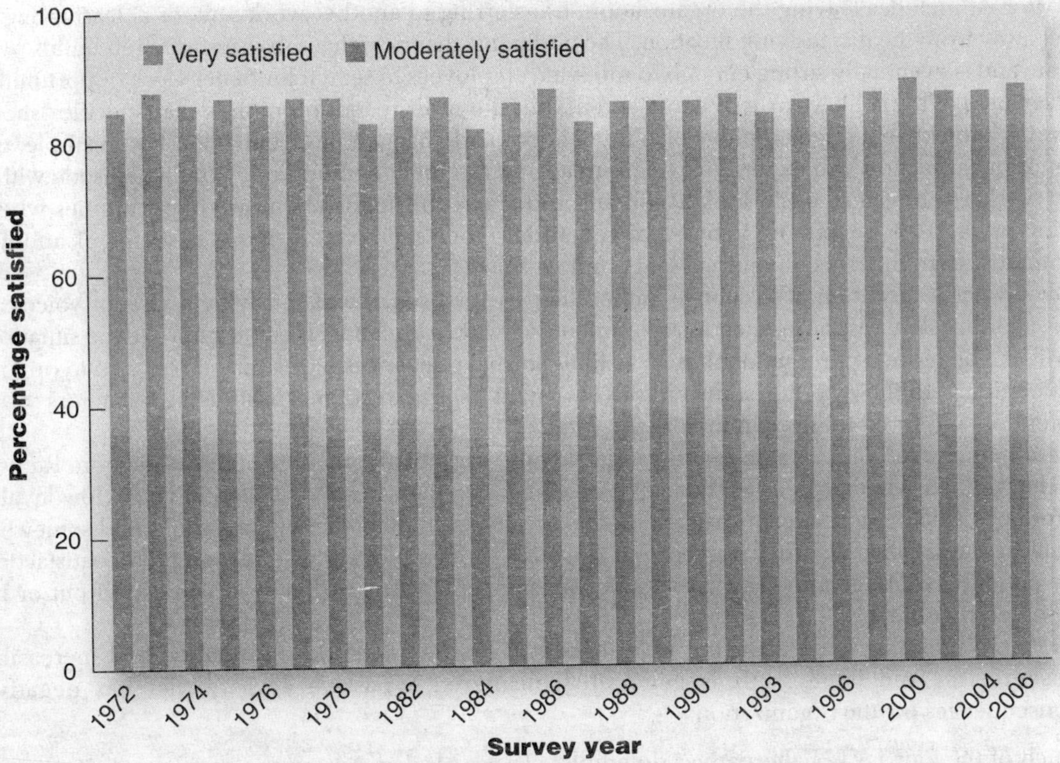

Exhibit 4.4 *Stability of Job Satisfaction in America*

enjoying life. For instance, surveys in the United States, Canada, and Malaysia found that although most employees in those countries say they are satisfied with their jobs and work environment, more than half would abandon their employer if offered a comparable job elsewhere.[49] Another indication is that employees rate almost all aspects of the job lower than their overall satisfaction.

Job Satisfaction and Work Behavior

Brad Bird pays a lot of attention to job satisfaction. "In my experience, the thing that has the most significant impact on a budget–but never shows up in a budget–is morale," advises Bird, who directed *Ratatouille* and other award-winning films at Pixar Animation Studios. "If you have low morale, for every dollar you spend, you get 25 cents of value. If you have high morale, for every dollar you spend, you get about $3 of value."[50]

Brad Bird's opinion about the importance of job satisfaction is consistently reflected in the actions of leaders in many companies. Along with their increasing competition to win best-workplace awards, many companies carefully monitor job satisfaction and related employee attitudes. In some firms, executive bonuses depend partly on employee satisfaction ratings. The reason for this attention is simple: Job satisfaction affects many of the individual behaviors introduced in Chapter 1. A useful template for organizing and understanding the consequences of job dissatisfaction is the **exit-voice-loyalty-neglect (EVLN) model.** As the name suggests, the EVLN model identifies four ways that employees respond to dissatisfaction:[51]

exit-voice-loyalty-neglect (EVLN) model
The four ways, as indicated in the name, that employees respond to job dissatisfaction.

- *Exit.* Exit includes leaving the organization, transferring to another work unit, or at least trying to get away from the dissatisfying situation. The traditional theory is that job dissatisfaction builds over time and is eventually strong enough to motivate employees to search for better work opportunities elsewhere. This is likely true to some extent, but the most recent opinion is that specific "shock events" quickly energize employees to think about and engage in exit behavior. For example, the emotional reaction you experience to an unfair management decision or a conflict episode with a co-worker motivates you to look at job ads and speak to friends about job opportunities where they work. This begins the process of redefining your self-concept more in terms of another company than in terms of your current employer.[52]
- *Voice.* Voice is any attempt to change, rather than escape from, the dissatisfying situation. Voice can be a constructive response, such as recommending ways for management to improve the situation, or it can be more confrontational, such as filing formal grievances or forming a coalition to oppose a decision.[53] In the extreme, some employees might engage in counterproductive behaviors to get attention and force changes in the organization.
- *Loyalty.* In the original version of this model, loyalty was not an outcome of dissatisfaction. Rather, it determined whether people chose exit or voice (i.e., high loyalty resulted in voice; low loyalty produced exit).[54] More recent writers describe loyalty as an outcome, but in various and somewhat unclear ways. Generally, they suggest that "loyalists" are employees who respond to dissatisfaction by patiently waiting–some say they "suffer in silence"–for the problem to work itself out or be resolved by others.[55]
- *Neglect.* Neglect includes reducing work effort, paying less attention to quality, and increasing absenteeism and lateness. It is generally considered a passive activity that has negative consequences for the organization.

Which of the four EVLN alternatives do employees use? It depends on the person and situation.[56] One determining factor is the person's self-concept. Some people avoid the self-image of being a complainer, whereas others view themselves very much as taking action when they dislike a work situation. Self-concept relates to personal and cultural values as well as personality. For example, people with a high-conscientiousness personality are less likely to engage in neglect and more likely to engage in voice. Past experience also influences which EVLN action is applied. Employees who were unsuccessful with voice in the past are more likely to engage in exit or neglect when experiencing job dissatisfaction in the future. Another factor is loyalty, as it was originally intended. Specifically, employees are more likely to quit when they have low loyalty to the company, and they are more likely to engage in voice when they have high loyalty. Finally, the response to dissatisfaction depends on the situation. Employees are less likely to use the exit option when there are few alternative job prospects, for example.

Job Satisfaction and Performance For almost a century, OB researchers have challenged the popular belief that "a happy worker is a productive worker." For most of that time, they concluded that job satisfaction had a minimal effect on job performance. Now the evidence suggests that the popular saying may be correct after all: There is a *moderate* relationship between job satisfaction and job performance. In other words, happy workers really are more productive workers *to some extent*.[57] Even with a moderate association between job satisfaction and performance, there are a few underlying reasons why the relationship isn't stronger. One argument is that general attitudes (such as job satisfaction) don't predict specific behaviors very well. As we learned with the EVLN model, job dissatisfaction can lead to a variety of outcomes other than lower job performance (neglect). Some employees continue to work productively while they complain (voice), look for another job (exit), or patiently wait for the problem to be fixed (loyalty).

A second explanation is that job performance leads to job satisfaction (rather than vice versa), but only when performance is linked to valued rewards. Higher performers receive more rewards and, consequently, are more satisfied than low-performing employees who receive fewer rewards. The connection between job satisfaction and performance isn't stronger because many organizations do not reward good performance. The third explanation is that job satisfaction influences employee motivation but doesn't affect performance in jobs where employees have little control over their job output (such as assembly-line work).

Job Satisfaction and Customer Satisfaction Another popular belief is that happy customers are the result of happy employees. This belief is strongly held at Dixon Schwabl, the Rochester, New York, advertising, marketing, and public relations agency described at the beginning of this chapter. "You might think our clients are No. 1, but really it's our employees," says Dixon Schwabl CEO Lauren Dixon. "If we make our employees No. 1, they'll make our clients No. 1." Ralph Norris, the CEO of Commonwealth Bank of Australia and previously CEO of Air New Zealand, agrees. "I'm not primarily interested in shareholder returns," says Norris. "If we look after and inspire the staff, they will look after the customers and that will take care of shareholder returns."[58]

These executives are referring to the *service profit chain model,* which proposes that increasing employee satisfaction and loyalty results in higher customer perceptions of value, thereby improving the company's profitability. In other words, job satisfaction has a positive effect on customer service.[59] There are two main reasons for this relationship. First, employees are usually in a more positive mood when they feel satisfied with their jobs and working conditions. Employees in a good mood display friendliness and positive emotions more naturally and frequently, and this causes customers to experience positive emotions. Second, satisfied employees are less likely to quit their jobs, so they have better knowledge and skills to serve clients. Lower turnover also enables customers to have the same employees serve them, so there is more consistent service. Some evidence indicates that

Employee First Customer Second—HCL Technologies[60] HCL Technologies is one of the IT services providing company in India. It adopted a new strategy, i.e. '*Employees First Customer Second*' in 2005. Through this strategy company intended to put employees' needs before its customers' needs which is radical and totally opposite to the service industry's mantra 'serve the customer first'. Through this strategy, the objective has been to provide unique environment to the employees, wherein they are considered as partners, responsible for transformation, and think of ways to provide value to customers.

This initiative has helped to empower employees, improve value for its customers, and management and supporting functions are accountable to frontline managers.

The enablers for this management philosophy included virtual assistants, sabbaticals for employees' talent transformation, guidance from experts, to explore and develop inner peace and freedom of empowerment. The benefits reaped are reflected in its financial statement, its revenues have grown three folds in the past four years.

customers build their loyalty to specific employees, not to the organization, so keeping employee turnover low tends to build customer loyalty.[61]

The Ethics of Job Satisfaction

Before leaving the topic of job satisfaction, we should mention that job satisfaction does more than improve work behaviors and customer satisfaction. Job satisfaction is also an ethical issue that influences the organization's reputation in the community. People spend a large portion of their time working in organizations, and many societies now expect companies to provide work environments that are safe and enjoyable. Indeed, employees in several countries closely monitor ratings of the best companies to work for, an indication that employee satisfaction is a virtue worth considerable goodwill to employers. This virtue is apparent when an organization has low job satisfaction. The company tries to hide this fact, and when morale problems become public, corporate leaders are usually quick to improve the situation.

ORGANIZATIONAL COMMITMENT

organizational (affective) commitment
The employee's emotional attachment to, identification with, and involvement in a particular organization.

continuance commitment
An employee's calculative attachment to the organization, whereby the employee is motivated to stay only because leaving would be costly.

Along with studying job satisfaction, OB researchers have been very interested in an attitude called organizational commitment. **Organizational (affective) commitment** is the employee's emotional attachment to, identification with, and involvement in a particular organization.[62] This definition pertains specifically to *affective commitment* because it is an emotional attachment–our feelings of loyalty–to the organization. Organizational (affective) commitment differs from **continuance commitment,** which is a calculative attachment.[63] Employees have high continuance commitment when they do not particularly identify with the organization where they work but feel bound to remain there because it would be too costly to quit. In other words, they choose to stay because the calculated (typically financial) value of staying is higher than the value of working somewhere else. You can tell an employee has high calculative commitment when he or she says: "I hate this place but can't afford to quit!" This reluctance to quit may exist because the employee might lose a large bonus by leaving early or is well established in the community where he or she works.[64]

Consequences of Organizational Commitment

Organizational (affective) commitment can be a significant competitive advantage.[65] Loyal employees are less likely to quit their jobs and be absent from work. They also have higher work motivation and organizational citizenship, as well as somewhat higher job performance. Organizational commitment also improves customer satisfaction because long-tenure employees have better knowledge of work practices and because clients like to do business with the same employees. One warning is that employees with very high loyalty tend to have high conformity, which results in lower creativity. There are also cases of dedicated employees who violated laws to defend the organization. However, most companies suffer from too little rather than too much employee loyalty.

Affective commitment is usually beneficial, whereas continuance commitment tends to be dysfunctional. In fact, employees with high levels of continuance commitment tend to have *lower* performance ratings and are *less* likely to engage in organizational citizenship behaviors. Furthermore, unionized employees with high continuance commitment are more likely to use formal grievances, whereas employees with high affective commitment engage in more constructive problem solving when employee-employer relations sour.[66] Although some level of financial connection may be necessary, employers should not confuse continuance commitment with employee loyalty. Employers still need to win employees' hearts (affective commitment) beyond tying them financially to the organization (continuance commitment).

Building Organizational Commitment

There are almost as many ways to build organizational loyalty as there are topics in this textbook, but the following list is most prominent in the literature:

- *Justice and support.* Affective commitment is higher in organizations that fulfill their obligations to employees and abide by humanitarian values, such as fairness, courtesy, forgiveness, and moral integrity. These values relate to the concept of organizational justice, which we discuss in the next chapter. Similarly, organizations that support employee well-being tend to cultivate higher levels of loyalty in return.[67]
- *Shared values.* The definition of affective commitment refers to a person's identification with the organization, and that identification is highest when employees believe their values are congruent with the organization's dominant values. Also, employees experience more comfort and predictability when they agree with the values underlying corporate decisions. This comfort increases their motivation to stay with the organization.[68]
- *Trust.* **Trust** refers to positive expectations one person has toward another person in situations involving risk.[69] Trust means putting faith in the other person or group. It is also a reciprocal activity: To receive trust, you must demonstrate trust. Employees identify with and feel obliged to work for an organization only when they trust its leaders. This explains why layoffs are one of the greatest blows to employee loyalty–by reducing job security, companies reduce the trust employees have in their employer and the employment relationship.[70]

trust
Positive expectations one person has toward another person in situations involving risk.

- *Organizational comprehension.* Organizational comprehension refers to how well employees understand the organization, including its strategic direction, social dynamics, and physical layout. This awareness is a necessary prerequisite to affective commitment because it is difficult to identify with something that you don't know very well. The practical implication here is to ensure that employees are able to develop a reasonably clear and complete mental picture of the organization. This occurs by giving staff information and opportunities to keep up to date about organizational events, interact with co-workers, discover what goes on in different parts of the organization, and learn about the organization's history and future plans.[71]

- *Employee involvement.* Employee involvement increases affective commitment by strengthening the employee's social identity with the organization. Employees feel that they are part of the organization when they participate in decisions that guide the organization's future. Employee involvement also builds loyalty because giving this power is a demonstration of the company's trust in its employees.

Organizational commitment and job satisfaction represent two of the most often studied and discussed attitudes in the workplace. Each is linked to emotional episodes and cognitive judgments about the workplace and relationship with the company. Emotions also play an important role in another concept that is on everyone's mind these days: stress. The final section of this chapter provides an overview of work-related stress and how it can be managed.

PSYCHOLOGICAL CONTRACTS

When Katherine Certain joined an ad agency not long ago, her expectations included a wide range of job duties, such as calling potential clients and evaluating marketing plans. The recent college graduate did get those responsibilities, along with a few that weren't on her list–such as watering the plants and walking the owner's dogs each day. After the initial shock that she had been given these tasks, Certain began to feel degraded and confused. Less than a year later Certain jumped to a larger ad agency, where so far she hasn't experienced any surprises.[72]

Katherine Certain experienced the shock of having her psychological contract violated. This isn't unusual. According to one university study, 24 per cent of employees are "chronically" angry at work, mostly because they feel their employer violated their basic promises and they didn't fulfill the psychological contract.[73] The **psychological contract** refers to the individual's beliefs about the terms and conditions of a reciprocal exchange agreement between that person and another party. This is inherently perceptual, so one person's understanding of the psychological contract may differ from the other party's understanding. In employment relationships, psychological contracts consist of beliefs about what the employee is entitled to receive and is obliged to offer the employer in return[74]. For example, Katherine Certain believed that her employer would give her responsibilities related to her career interests. Being assigned the duties of watering plants and walking the boss's dogs clearly violated her expectations.

psychological contract
The individual's beliefs about the terms and conditions of a reciprocal exchange agreement between that person and another party.

Types of Psychological Contracts

Psychological contracts vary in many ways.[75] One of the most fundamental differences is the extent to which they are transactional or relational. As Exhibit 4.5 indicates, *transactional contracts* are primarily short-term economic exchanges. Responsibilities are well defined around a fairly narrow set of obligations that do not change over the life of the contract. People hired in temporary positions and as consultants tend to have transactional contracts. To some extent, new employees also form transactional contracts until they develop a sense of continuity with the organization.

Relational contracts, on the other hand, are rather like marriages; they are long-term attachments that encompass a broad array of subjective mutual obligations. Employees with a relational psychological contract are more willing to contribute their time and effort without expecting the organization to pay back this debt in the short term. Relational contracts are also dynamic, meaning that the parties are more flexible regarding when they expect a payback for their contributions to the relationship. Not surprisingly, organizational citizenship behaviors are more likely to prevail under relational than transactional contracts. Permanent employees are more likely to believe they have a relational contract.

Contract Characteristics	Transactional	Balanced	Relational
Focus	Economic		Economic and socioemotional
Time frame	Closed-ended and short-term		Open-ended and indefinite
Stability	Static		Dynamic
Scope	Narrow		Pervasive
Tangibility	Well-defined		More subjective

Source: Based on information in D.M. Rousseau and J.M. Parks, "The Contracts of Individuals and Organizations," *Research in Organizational Behavior* 15 (1993), pp. 1–43; D.M. Rousseau, *Psychological Contracts in Organizations* (Thousand Oaks, CA: Sage, 1995).

Exhibit 4.5 *Types of Psychological Contracts in Employment*

Psychological Contracts across Cultures and Generations

Psychological contracts are influenced by the social contexts in which the contracting process occurs[76]. In other words, they vary across cultures and groups of employees based on their unique cultures and cohort experiences. For instance, employees in the United States, United Kingdom, and several other countries expect some involvement in company decisions (that is, they have low power distance), whereas employees in Taiwan and Mexico are more willing to accept arbitrary orders from their supervisors (they have high power distance).

In Japan, employees traditionally expected lifetime employment in return for loyalty and hard work. However, this relational psychological contract shifted as a result of the country's extended recession in the 1990s. The emerging psychological contract among many young Japanese is a startling contrast to their parents. Specifically, Japan is experiencing a rising tide of "freeters" – young people

Japan's Freeters Turn the Psychological Contract Upside Down More than 2 million young Japanese have become "freeters": casual workers with an equally casual psychological contract that emphasizes personal freedom over loyalty. Generally they want employment that is short-term, transactional, and flexible—just the opposite of what their parents expected in an employment relationship. "Living as a freeter, I get more freedom and I like that," says Mika Onodera, a 28-year-old bakery employee in Tokyo (shown in this photo). Japan's struggling economy partially explains why an increasing number of young people are willing to accept temporary work; but recent surveys also suggest that freeters simply don't worry at all about long-term careers, and they think job-hopping is a badge of honor. The Japanese government is so concerned about the freeter trend that it provides financial aid to companies who hire freeters so they can "test-drive" a permanent job. It has also introduced a program in high schools to teach students the value of holding a full-time job.[77]

who hop from one job to the next, usually with a distinctly transactional psychological contract. The psychological contract expectations of freeters has motivated the Japanese government to introduce various schemes intended to change their views on the employment relationship.

Psychological contracts also seem to vary across generations of employees. Older employees grew up with "organization man" expectations in which dedicated employees worked in secure jobs with steady promotions through the hierarchy. They often devoted their entire lives to the same company, put in regular hours, and rarely thought about changing employers.[78] The implicit contract was that if you are loyal to the company and perform your job reasonably well, the company will be loyal to you by providing job security and managing your career development. When the "new deal" of employability arrived, these older employees felt betrayed–their psychological contracts had been violated.

However, some scholars suggest that job security has less value to Generation-X and Generation-Y employees than to baby boomers. Workforce newcomers have mainly experienced a psychological contract based on employability and are comfortable with weaker job security. "Employees are developing the view that their only job security in the future must be based on their ability and their competence," says Gary L. Howard, a Motorola vice president, "and not on keeping a job at some particular company."[79]

Psychological contracts are changing, as is the entire field of organizational behavior as it embraces new knowledge about emotions in the workplace. Emotional brain centers, emotional labor, emotional intelligence, and other topics in this chapter were unheard of 10 or 15 years ago. Now they are essential reading to improve our grasp of the complex dynamics of employee attitudes and behavior. You will see several references to emotions-related concepts throughout this book, including the next chapter about employee motivation.

Learning Objectives

After reading this section, you should be able to:

9. Define *stress* and describe the stress experience including job burnout.
10. Explain why a stressor might produce different stress levels in two people.
11. Identify five ways to manage workplace stress.

WORK-RELATED STRESS AND ITS MANAGEMENT

Josh Holmes has fond memories of working at Electronic Arts (EA) but admits that the long hours at the electronic-game company were stressful. "From the minute I joined [EA], I put every waking hour of my day into my work. . . . It definitely took its toll," says Holmes. After 10 years at EA, Holmes was burned out, so he quit. "We had done a lot of really long grueling hours. I know I was thinking that there's got to be a way to do things a little differently." So, in their quest for a less stressful electronic-game company, Holmes and three other senior EA staff members formed Propaganda Games (now a creative center within Disney's video game division), with the unique values of creativity, risk taking, and work–life balance. "We want you to come into the studio, do great work, then get out and live your life," says Propaganda's Web site. "We foster a start-up attitude without the start-up stress."[80]

stress
An adaptive response to a situation that is perceived as challenging or threatening to a person's well-being.

Experts have trouble defining **stress,** but it is most often described as an adaptive response to a situation that is perceived as challenging or threatening to the person's well-being.[81] Stress is a physiological and psychological condition that prepares us to adapt to hostile or noxious environmental conditions. Our heart rate increases, muscles tighten, breathing speeds up, and perspiration increases. Our body also moves more blood to the brain, releases adrenaline and other hormones, fuels the system by releasing more glucose and fatty acids, activates systems that sharpen our senses, and conserves resources by shutting down our immune system. One school of thought suggests that stress is a negative evaluation of the external environment. However, critics of this cognitive appraisal perspective point out that the stress experience is an emotional experience, which may occur before or after a conscious evaluation of the situation.[82]

Whether stress is a complex emotion or a cognitive evaluation of the environment, it has become a pervasive experience in the daily lives of most people. Three out of four Americans (and a similar percentage of people in Germany, Canada, Australia, and the United Kingdom) say they frequently or sometimes feel stress in their daily lives. Approximately one in every four employees in the United Kingdom feels "very or extremely stressed," and this condition has become the top cause of absenteeism there. More than one-quarter of Canadians say they experience high levels of stress each day. A survey of 4,700 people across Asia reported that one-third were feeling more stress than they had in the recent past. The percentage of people reporting stress was highest in Taiwan and lowest in Thailand. The Japanese government, which tracks work-related stress every five years, has found that the percentage of Japanese employees who feel "strong worry, anxiety or stress at work or in daily working life" has increased from 51 percent in 1982 to almost two-thirds of the population today.[83]

As these surveys imply, stress is typically described as a negative experience. This is known as *distress*–the degree of physiological, psychological, and behavioral deviation from healthy functioning. However, some level of stress–called *eustress*–is a necessary part of life because it activates and motivates people to achieve goals, change their environments, and succeed in life's challenges.[84] Our focus is on the causes and management of distress, because it has become a chronic problem in many societies.

General Adaptation Syndrome

general adaptation syndrome
A model of the stress experience, consisting of three stages: alarm reaction, resistance, and exhaustion.

More than 500 years ago, people began using the word *stress* to describe the human response to harsh environmental conditions. However, it wasn't until the 1930s that Hans Selye (often described as the father of stress research) first documented the stress experience, called the **general adaptation syndrome.** Selye determined (initially by studying rats) that people have a fairly consistent and automatic physiological response to stressful situations, which helps them to cope with environmental demands.

The general adaptation syndrome consists of the three stages shown in Exhibit 4.6.[85] The *alarm reaction* stage occurs when a threat or challenge activates the physiological stress responses that were noted above. The individual's energy level and coping effectiveness decrease in response to the initial shock. The second stage, *resistance,* activates various biochemical, psychological, and behavioral mechanisms that give the individual more energy and engage coping mechanisms to overcome or remove the source of stress. To focus energy on the source of the stress, the body reduces resources to the immune system during this stage. This explains why people are more likely to catch a cold or some other illness when they experience prolonged stress. People have a limited resistance capacity, and if the source of stress persists, the individual will eventually move into the third stage, *exhaustion.* Most of us are able to remove the source of stress or remove ourselves from that source before becoming too exhausted. However, people who frequently reach exhaustion have increased risk of long-term physiological and psychological damage.[86]

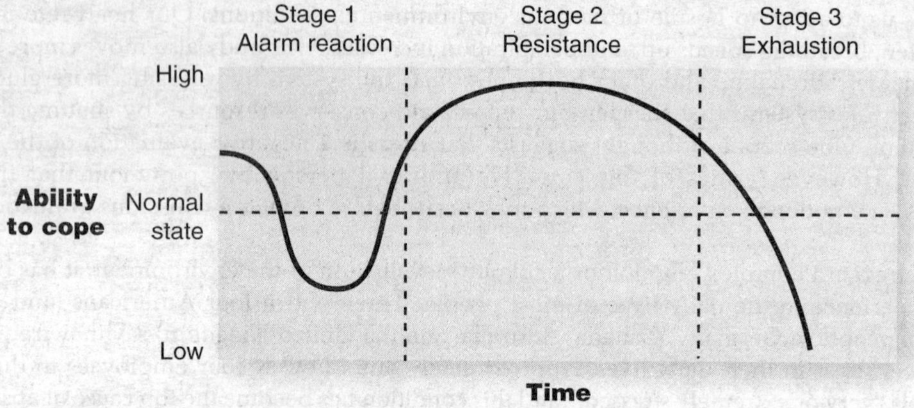

Source: Adapted from H. Selye, *The Stress of Life* (New York: McGraw-Hill, 1956).

Exhibit 4.6 *General Adaptation Syndrome*

Consequences of Distress

Stress takes its toll on the human body.[87] Many people experience tension headaches, muscle pain, and related problems mainly due to muscle contractions from the stress response. Studies have found that high stress levels also contribute to cardiovascular disease, including heart attacks and strokes, and may be associated with some forms of cancer. Stress also produces various psychological consequences, such as job dissatisfaction, moodiness, depression, and lower organizational commitment. Furthermore, various behavioral outcomes have been linked to high or persistent stress, including lower job performance, poor decision making, and increased workplace accidents and aggressive behavior. Most people react to stress through "fight or flight," so increased absenteeism is another outcome because it is a form of flight.[88]

Physiological Consequences

Stress takes its toll on the human body.[89] The stress response shuts down the immune system, which makes us more vulnerable to viral and bacterial infection. Many people experience tension headaches due to stress. Others get muscle pain and related back problems. These physiological ailments are attributed to muscle contractions that occur when people are exposed to stressors.

Cardiovascular disease is one of the most disturbing effects of stress in modern society. Strokes and heart attacks were rare a century ago but are now among the leading causes of death among adults in the United States and other countries. Stress also influences hypertension (high blood pressure). In spite of better lifestyle and medical treatment, recent evidence suggests that hypertension continues to increase, particularly among older people and non-Hispanic blacks in the United States. Along with these health problems, a recent study of 60,000 people in Norway found that those with high scores on an anxiety test were 25 per cent more likely to have premalignant tumors seven years later.

Psychological Consequences

Stress produces various psychological consequences, including job dissatisfaction, moodiness, depression, and lower organizational commitment.[90] Emotional fatigue is another psychological consequence of stress and is related to job burnout.

job burnout
The process of emotional exhaustion, cynicism, and reduced efficacy (lower feelings of personal accomplishment) resulting from prolonged exposure to stress.

Job Burnout **Job burnout** refers to the process of emotional exhaustion, cynicism, and reduced feelings of personal accomplishment resulting from prolonged exposure to stress.[91] It is a complex process that includes the dynamics of stress, coping strategies, and stress consequences. Burnout is caused by excessive demands made on people who serve or frequently interact with others. In other words, burnout is due mainly to interpersonal and role-related stressors, and is most common in helping occupations (nurses, teachers, police officers).

Exhibit 4.7 diagrams the relationship among the three components of job burnout. *Emotional exhaustion*, the first stage, is characterized by a lack of energy, tiredness, and a feeling that one's emotional resources are depleted. Emotional exhaustion is sometimes called *compassion fatigue* because the employee no longer feels able to give as much support and care to clients.

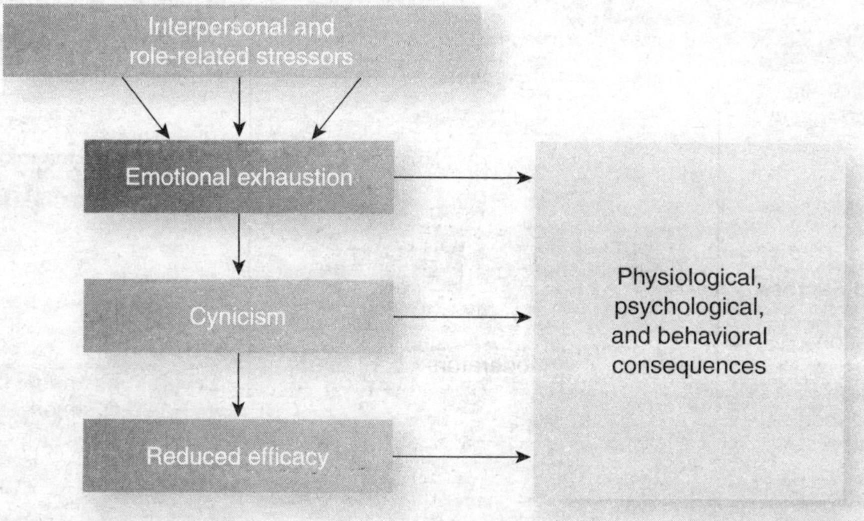

Exhibit 4.7 *The Job Burnout Process*

Cynicism (also called *depersonalization*) follows emotional exhaustion. It is identified by an indifferent attitude toward work and the treatment of others as objects rather than people. At this stage employees become emotionally detached from clients and cynical about the organization. This detachment is to the point of callousness–far beyond the normal level in helping occupations. Cynicism is also apparent when employees strictly follow rules and regulations rather than trying to understand the client's needs and searching for a mutually acceptable solution.

Reduced professional efficacy (also called *reduced personal accomplishment*), the final component of job burnout, refers to feelings of diminished confidence in one's ability to perform the job well. In these situations employees develop a sense of learned helplessness as they no longer believe that their efforts make a difference.

Indian Perspective on Job Burnout

The Indian model of Executive Burnout was developed by Sharma[92] which differs from the western model in construct, causes, and consequences. Studies carried out by Sharma yielded that burnout is not confined to helping occupations but is prevalent among executives as well. The Western construct of burnout, using Maslach Burnout Inventory (MBI), has largely been based on people occupations (like nurses and teachers) and later extended to non-service occupations. When tested by the author[93] on Indian sample of executives, she found that there was difference in the dimension of diminished personal accomplishment which was not valid for the Indian sample. Those suffering from burnout did not have low personal accomplishment; on the contrary, high achieving executives were mostly found to suffer from burnout. Some dimensions, viz., ambiguity, dissatisfaction and powerlessness, inadequacy, and physical exhaustion, which were empirically found vital for executives in the Indian context, were not covered by MBI. She evolved the construct of Executive Burnout, not only in the industrial context but also in the Indian context, and standardized an instrument for diagnosis of executive burnout. She has also identified determinants of burnout among executives. The Indian model of executive burnout is presented in Exhibit 4.8.

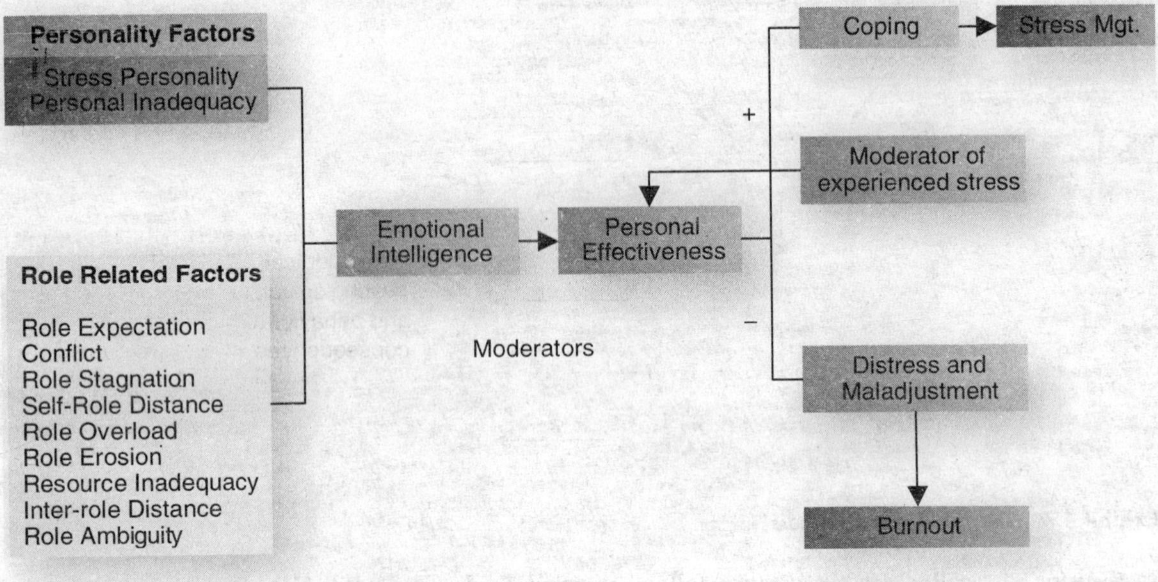

Exhibit 4.8 *Indian Model of Executive Burnout*

The adverse effects of burnout are seen not only on the employees but also on the organization as a whole. The behavior patterns observed among staff are absenteeism, non-compliance, interpersonal and group conflict, lack of team work, low productivity, and alcoholism. Burnout is being observed in other spheres as well. There are media reports on burnout among players. As a number of matches are arranged in quick succession, players do not get sufficient time to recover from the fatigue of test cricket. Consequently, their workload and inability to cope with it is causing burnout among players in many countries. One of the world-class cricket players, Sachin Tendulkar, shares this view.

Behavioral Consequences

Moderate levels of stress focus our attention and concentrate resources where they are most needed. But when stress becomes distress, job performance falls, memory becomes impaired, workplace accidents are more frequent, and decisions are less effective.[94] You have probably experienced this in an exam or emergency work situation. You forget important information, make mistakes, and otherwise "draw a blank" under intense pressure.

Overstressed employees also tend to have higher levels of absenteeism. One reason is that stress makes people susceptible to viral and bacterial infections. The other reason is that absenteeism is a coping mechanism. At a basic level, we react to stress through "fight or flight." Absenteeism is a form of flight–temporarily withdrawing from the stressful situation so that we can reenergize. Companies may try to minimize absenteeism, but it sometimes helps employees avoid the exhaustion stage of the stress experience.[95]

Workplace Aggression Workplace aggression is more than the serious interpersonal stressor described earlier. It is also an increasingly worrisome behavioral consequence of stress. Aggression represents the fight (instead of flight) reaction to stress. In its mildest form, employees engage in verbal harassment. They "fly off the handle" and are less likely to empathize with co-workers. Like most forms of workplace behavior, co-worker aggression is caused by both the person and the situation. Although certain individuals are more likely to be aggressive, their behavior is also usually a consequence of extreme stress to some extent.[96] In particular, employees are more likely to engage in aggressive behavior if they believe they have been treated unfairly, experience other forms of frustration beyond their personal control, and work in physical environments that are stressful (such as being hot or noisy).

Stressors: The Causes of Stress

stressors
Any environmental conditions that place a physical or emotional demand on a person.

Before identifying ways to manage work-related stress, we must first understand its causes, known as stressors. **Stressors** include any environmental conditions that place a physical or emotional demand on a person.[97] There are numerous stressors in the workplace and in life in general. In this section, we'll highlight three of the most common stressors: harassment and incivility, workload, and lack of task control.

Interpersonal Stressors

Among the four types of stressors, interpersonal stressors seem to be the most pervasive in the workplace. The trend toward teamwork generates interpersonal stressors because employees must interact more with co-workers. Organizational politics, which we'll discuss in Chapter 12, are another interpersonal stressor. Bad bosses can also be quite stressful. For instance, one study discovered that female health care assistants experienced much higher blood pressure when working with an ineffective rather than an effective supervisor. Over a sustained period this higher blood pressure would increase the risk of stroke by 38 percent![98] Two other interpersonal stressors are workplace violence and harassment, which are discussed next.

Workplace Violence Workplace violence is a serious interpersonal stressor. In the United States more than 600 employees are murdered on the job each year, and 2 million others experience lesser forms of physical violence. An International Labor Organization study reported that more than 60 percent of health care staff in Bulgaria, Australia, South Africa, and Portugal experienced at least one incident of physical or psychological violence in the previous year. A recent survey reported that more than a quarter of the 3,000 British nurses questioned had been physically attacked at work, half of those within the previous 12 months.[99]

Victims of workplace violence experience severe stress symptoms. Those who observe the violence also tend to experience stress. After a serious workplace incident, counselors assist many employees, not just the direct victims. Even employees who have not directly experienced or observed violence may show signs of stress if they work in jobs that expose them to a higher incidence of violence.

Five-Star Bullying in Posh London Hotels Working at a London five-star hotel has not been pleasant for Ahmet (not his real name). For the past six long months the Moroccan migrant worker has experienced racial harassment, as well as shouting and screaming from managers and customers who pointed their fingers at his head. At one point the harassment became so severe that Ahmet burst into tears, had to go on medication, and received counseling. Another five-star hotel, which welcomes migrant workers in its induction as a "home away from home," is apparently just as abusive. Workers there complain about the daily verbal attacks from managers, who hurl profanities and ridicule one ethnic group against another. "These are the top luxury hotels. Just imagine the rest of them," says Julio Haro, race equality officer of Britain's General Union, adding that these incidents are the norm, not the exception, in the hotel industry.[100]

psychological harassment
Repeated and hostile or unwanted conduct, verbal comments, actions, or gestures that affect an employee's dignity or psychological or physical integrity and that result in a harmful work environment for the employee.

Harassment and Incivility One of the fastest-growing sources of workplace stress is **psychological harassment**. Psychological harassment includes repeated and hostile or unwanted conduct, verbal comments, actions, and gestures that affect an employee's dignity or psychological or physical integrity and that result in a harmful work environment for the employee. This covers a broad landscape of behaviors, from threats and bullying to subtle yet persistent forms of incivility.[101] Two-thirds of Americans think people are less civil today than 20 years ago; 10 percent say they witness incivility daily in their workplaces and are targets of that abuse at least once each week. More than half of U.K. human resource managers and Australian lawyers say they have been bullied or intimidated.[102]

sexual harassment
Unwelcome conduct of a sexual nature that detrimentally affects the work environment or leads to adverse job-related consequences for its victims.

Sexual harassment is a type of harassment in which a person's employment or job performance is conditional and depends on unwanted sexual relations (called *quid pro quo* harassment) and/or the person experiences sexual conduct from others (such as posting pornographic material) that unreasonably interferes with work performance or creates an intimidating, hostile, or offensive working environment (called *hostile work environment* harassment). The number of charges alleging sexual harassment in the United States has declined steadily from 16,000 in 2000 to less than 13,000 today. Approximately 15 percent of sexual harassment claims are filed by men.[103] The Equal Employment Opportunity Commission attributes the improvement to better supervisor training and concerted management action to address harassment issues before they reach litigation.

Role-Related Stressors

role conflict
Incongruity or incompatibility of expectations associated with a person's role.

Role-related stressors include conditions in which employees have difficulty understanding, reconciling, or performing the various roles in their lives. Three types of role-related stressors are role conflict, role ambiguity, and work overload. **Role conflict** refers to the degree of incongruity or incompatibility of expectations associated with a person's role. Some people experience stress when they have two roles that conflict with each other. For example, various studies have recently reported this inter-role conflict among human service workers and healthcare providers, where workloads and bureaucratic procedures interfered with their ability to serve clients or patients.[104] Role conflict also occurs when an employee's personal values are incompatible with organizational values.

role ambiguity
A lack of clarity and predictability of the outcomes of a person's behavior.

Role ambiguity refers to the lack of clarity and predictability of the outcomes of a person's behavior. Role ambiguity produces unclear role perceptions, which directly affect job performance. It is also a source of stress in a variety of situations, such as joining an organization or working in a new joint venture, because people are uncertain about task and social expectations.[105]

Work Overload Half a century ago, social scientists predicted that technology would allow employees to enjoy a 15-hour workweek at full pay by 2030.[106] So far, it hasn't turned out that way. As the opening vignette to this section on workplace stress described, employees at Electronic Arts and many other companies in the video game industry are experiencing stress due to *work overload*–working more hours, and more intensely during those hours, than they can reasonably manage. Surveys by the Families and Work Institute report that 44 percent of Americans say they are overworked, up from 28 percent who felt this way three years earlier. Almost 25 percent of Canadian employees work more than 50 hours per week, compared with only 10 percent a decade ago. Work overload is an important

BlackBerry Addiction Nick Salaysay (shown in photo) admits that his work routinely gets mixed in with his personal time. "I have a BlackBerry, so I check my e-mail a lot when I'm supposed to be on vacation," says the lawyer in Calgary, Canada. Salaysay also acknowledges that having work spill over into his time off "really annoys my girlfriend." Amy Schulman is another dedicated BlackBerry user. The New York City lawyer recalls that "the BlackBerry was at first a significant intrusion on family life," but she can't resist how the device helps her to process several hundred e-mails each day. As a consolation, Schulman says she usually avoids looking at her e-mail while dining with her family, "and I try not to look at it in movie theaters." Although Nick Salaysay and Amy Schulman are comfortable using their BlackBerries during family time, research indicates that the increased workload and work preoccupation caused by these devices can result in the additional stress of relationship and marital problems. One law report recently warned that employers who issue BlackBerries could also incur liability for stress-related illnesses as the devices keep employees on an "electronic leash."[107]

predictor of job burnout. It is also a major cause of work–family conflicts, because overworked employees have insufficient time to satisfy their nonwork roles of being a parent, a spouse, and so forth.[108]

Why do employees work such long hours? One explanation is the combined effect of technology and globalization. "Everyone in this industry is working harder now because of e-mail, wireless access, and globalization," says Christopher Lochhead, chief marketing officer of Mercury Interactive, a California-based consulting firm. "You can't even get a rest on the weekend." A second cause, according to a recent study, is that many people are caught up in consumerism; they want to buy more goods and services, and doing so requires more income through longer work hours. A third reason, called the "ideal worker norm," is that professionals expect themselves and others to work longer work hours. For many, toiling away far beyond the normal workweek is a badge of honor, a symbol of their superhuman capacity to perform above others.[109] This badge of honor is particularly serious in several (but not all) Asian countries, to the point where "death from overwork" is now part of the common language (*karoshi* in Japanese and *guolaosi* in Chinese). For example, two young faculty members at China's top engineering school died suddenly, apparently from exhaustion and overwork.[110]

Low Task Control An increasingly popular model of job burnout suggests that emotional exhaustion depends on both job demands and job resources.[111] *Job demands* are aspects of work that require sustained physical or psychological effort. High workload is one of the more significant job demands in the contemporary workplace. At the same time, the effect of job demands on burnout (or stress in general) depends on the individual's job resources. *Job resources* represent aspects of the job that help employees to achieve work goals, reduce job demands, and/or stimulate personal growth and development.

An important job resource is autonomy or control over the pace of work. Low task control increases employee exposure to the risk of burnout because they face high workloads without the ability to adjust the pace of the load to their own energy, attention span, and other resources. Furthermore, the degree to which low task control is a stressor increases with the burden of responsibility the employee must carry.[112] Assembly-line workers have low task control, but their stress can be fairly low if their level of responsibility is also low. In contrast, sports coaches are under immense pressure to win games (high responsibility), yet they have little control over what happens on the playing field (low task control).

Organizational and Physical Environment Stressors

Organizational and physical environment stressors come in many forms. Downsizing is stressful for those who lose their jobs. Even those who keep their jobs (called layoff survivors) experience stress because of the reduced job security, chaos of change, additional workloads, and guilt of having a job as others lose theirs. For example, one study reported that long-term sick leave doubled among surviving government employees in Finland after a major downsizing.[113] Physical work environment stressors include excessive noise and poor lighting. People working in dangerous environments also tend to experience higher stress levels.

Work–Nonwork Stressors

There are three types of work–nonwork stressors: time-based, strain-based, and role-based conflict.

Time-Based Conflict *Time-based conflict* refers to the challenge of balancing the time demanded by work with family and other nonwork activities. Time-based conflict relates back to the work overload stressor described earlier. The problem of longer work hours that we discussed earlier (as well as more intensely during those hours) is compounded by the fact that employees have little time or energy left for themselves and their family. Inflexible work schedules, business travel, and rotating shift schedules also take a heavy toll because they reduce the ability to effectively juggle work and nonwork.[114] Time-based conflict is usually more acute for women than for men because housework and child care continue to fall more on their shoulders as a "second shift" in most dual-career families.

Strain-Based Conflict *Strain-based conflict* occurs when stress from one domain spills over to the other. Relationship problems, financial difficulties, and loss of a loved one usually top the list of nonwork stressors. New responsibilities, such as marriage, birth of a child, and a mortgage, are also stressful to most of us. Stress at work spills over to an employee's personal life and often becomes the foundation of stressful relations with family and friends. Strain-based conflict may be increasing as technology allows work and nonwork activities to spread from one domain to the other. For instance, many professionals now routinely use their cell phones, pagers, and BlackBerry wireless devices for work-related tasks while at home and even on vacation. Similarly, many employees use technology at work to complete household obligations, such as online banking or purchases.[115]

Role Behavior Conflict A third work–nonwork stressor, called *role behavior conflict,* occurs when people are expected to act quite differently at work than in nonwork roles. For instance, people who act logically and impersonally at work have difficulty switching to a more compassionate behavioral style in their personal lives. Thus stress occurs in this adjustment from one role to the other.[116]

Stress and Occupations

Several studies have attempted to identify which jobs have more stressors than others.[117] These lists are not in complete agreement, but Exhibit 4.9 identifies a representative sample of jobs and their relative level of stressors. We need to view this information with some caution, however. One problem with rating occupations in terms of their stress levels is that a particular occupation may have considerably different tasks and job environments across organizations and societies. A nurse's job may be less stressful in a small-town medical clinic, for instance, than in the emergency room of a large city hospital.

Another important point to remember when looking at Exhibit 4.9 is that a major stressor to one person may be less significant to another. Thus not everyone in so-called high-stress occupations

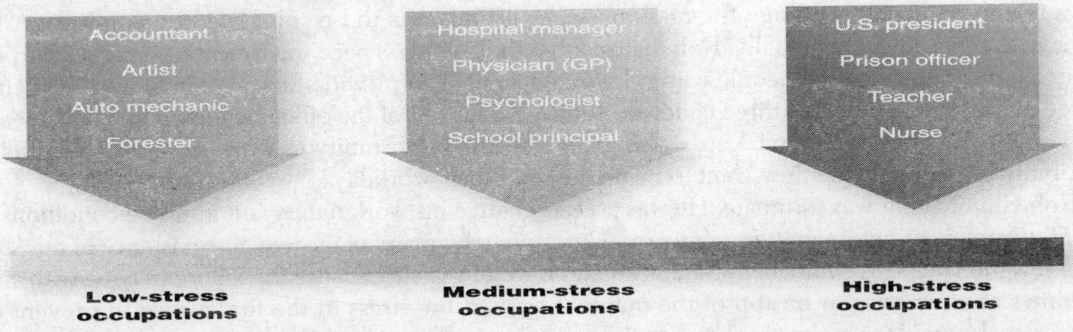

Exhibit 4.9 *Stressors in Occupations*

actually experiences more stress than people in other occupations. High-stress jobs have more stressors, but people don't experience more stress if they are carefully selected and trained for this type of work. The next section discusses individual differences in stress.

Individual Differences in Stress

Because of unique personal characteristics, people have different stress experiences when exposed to the same stressor. One reason for this is that people have different threshold levels of resistance to the stressor. Those who exercise and have healthy lifestyles have a larger store of energy to cope with high stress levels. A second reason for different stress responses is that people use different coping strategies, some of which are more effective than others. Research suggests that employees who try to ignore or deny the existence of a stressor suffer more in the long run than those who try to find ways to weaken the stressor and seek social support.[118]

resilience
The capability of individuals to cope successfully in the face of significant change, adversity, or risk.

A third reason why some people experience less stress than others is that some have higher resilience.[119] **Resilience** is the capability of individuals to cope successfully in the face of significant change, adversity, or risk. Those with high resilience are able to withstand adversity as well as recover more quickly from it. Resilient people possess personality traits (such as high extroversion and low neuroticism) that generate more optimism, confidence, and positive emotions. Resilience also involves specific competencies and behaviors for responding and adapting more effectively to stressors. Research indicates that resilient people have higher emotional intelligence and good problem-solving skills. They also apply productive coping strategies, such as analyzing the sources of stress and finding ways to neutralize these problems.[120]

workaholic
A person who is highly involved in work, feels compelled to work, and has a low enjoyment of work.

While resilience helps people to withstand stress, another personal characteristic–workaholism–attracts more stressors and weakens the capacity to cope with them. The classic **workaholic** (also called *work addict*) is highly involved in work, feels compelled or driven to work because of inner pressures, and has a low enjoyment of work. Workaholics are compulsive and preoccupied with work, often to the exclusion and detriment of personal health, intimate relationships, and family.[121] Classic workaholics are more prone to job stress and have significantly higher scores on depression, anxiety, and anger.[122]

Managing Work-Related Stress

A few years ago, Koh Ching Hong would dutifully arrive at work around 7:30 in the morning and stay until 10 at night. The managing director of Fuji Xerox in Singapore would continue working at home for a few more hours, sending off e-mail messages listing tasks to be completed by employees "first thing in the morning." Eventually, Koh realized that the relentless pace was defeating a higher purpose. "It came to a point that the people whom I worked so hard to provide for, my family, weren't getting to see me," says the father of three children. Today, Koh is out of the office by 6:30 p.m. and shoos his staff out at the same time. Fuji Xerox also gives staff the opportunity to work from home as well as flexibility regarding when they want to begin and end their workday.[123]

Koh Ching Hong was fortunate. He was able to change his work habits and improve conditions for his 500 employees before matters got worse. Unfortunately, many of us deny the existence of our stress until it is too late. This avoidance strategy creates a vicious cycle because the failure to cope with stress becomes another stressor on top of the one that created the stress in the first place. To prevent this vicious cycle, employers and employees need to apply one or more of the stress management strategies described below: remove the stressor, withdraw from the stressor, change stress perceptions, control stress consequences, and receive social support.[124]

Exhibit 4.10 *Stress Management Strategies*

Remove the Stressor Removing the stressor usually begins by identifying areas of high stress and determining the main causes of the stress. By identifying the specific stressors that adversely affect specific areas of the organization, such "stress audits" recognize that a one-size-fits-all approach to stress management is ineffective. Ericsson conducts this diagnosis in its North American operations through an annual survey that includes a stress index. Executives at the telecommunications company use the index to identify departments where stress problems may be developing. "We look at those scores and if there appears to be a problem in a particular group, we put in action plans to try and remedy and improve the work situation that may be causing the stress," explains an Ericsson executive.[125]

There are many ways to remove the stressor, but some of the more common actions involve assigning employees to jobs that match their skills and preferences, reducing excessive workplace noise, having a complaint system and taking corrective action against harassment, and giving employees more control over the work process. Another important way that companies can remove stressors is by facilitating better work–life balance. Work–life balance initiatives minimize conflict between the employee's work and nonwork demands. Five of the most common work–life balance initiatives are flexible and limited work time, job sharing, telecommuting, personal leave, and child care support.[126]

- *Flexible and limited work time.* An important way to improve work–life balance is limiting the number of hours that employees are expected to work and giving them flexibility in scheduling those hours. Propaganda Games, which was described earlier in this chapter, stands out in an overworked industry because it keeps work hours within reasonable limits. Best Buy has become a role model in work–life balance by giving employees very flexible work hours.

- *Job sharing.* Job sharing splits a career position between two people so that they experience less time-based stress between work and family. They typically work different parts of the week, with some overlapping work time in the weekly schedule to coordinate activities. This strategy gives employees the ability to work part-time in jobs that are naturally designed for full-time responsibilities.
- *Telecommuting.* Telecommuting, which was described in Chapter 1, reduces the time and stress of commuting to work and makes it easier to fulfill family obligations, such as temporarily leaving the home office to pick the kids up from school. Research suggests that telecommuters tend to experience better work–life balance.[127] However, telecommuting may increase stress for those who crave social interaction and who lack the space and privacy necessary to work at home.
- *Personal leave.* Employers with strong work–life values offer extended maternity, paternity, and personal leave for employees to care for a new family or take advantage of a personal experience. The U.S. Family and Medical Leave Act gives expecting mothers and anyone considered to have an illness 12 weeks of unpaid, job-protected leave. However, most countries provide 12 to16 weeks of paid leave, with some offering one year or more of fully or partially paid maternity leave.[128]
- *Child care support.* According to one estimate, almost one-quarter of large American companies provide on-site or subsidized child care facilities. Child care support reduces stress because employees are less rushed to drop off children and less worried during the day about how well their children are doing.[129]

Withdraw from the Stressor Removing the stressor may be the ideal solution, but it is often not feasible. An alternative strategy is to permanently or temporarily remove employees from the stressor. Permanent withdrawal occurs when employees are transferred to jobs that better fit their competencies and values. Temporarily withdrawing from stressors is the most frequent way that employees manage stress. Vacations and holidays are important opportunities for employees to recover from stress and reenergize for future challenges. Approximately 5 percent of U.S. companies offer paid sabbaticals to some of their employees. McDonald's Corp. has had paid sabbaticals for the past 40 years, offering employees eight weeks of paid time off after every 10 years of service.[130]

Some companies have innovative ways to help employees withdraw from stressful work throughout the day. SAS Institute employees in Cary, North Carolina, enjoy live piano recitals at lunch. Consulting firms Segal Co. in New York and Vielife in London have nap rooms where staff can recover with a few winks of sleep. The opening vignette to this chapter mentioned that Dixon Schwabl, the Rochester-based marketing and public relations firm, has a scream room where employees can verbalize their daily frustrations. Liggett-Stashower, Inc., the Cleveland-based creative agency, has three theme rooms, including a karaoke room where employees can sing away their stress. "The higher the stress level, the more singing there is going on," says the company's art director.[131]

Change Stress Perceptions Earlier, we learned that employees experience different stress levels because they have different levels of resilience, including self-confidence and optimism. Consequently, another way to manage stress is to help employees improve their self-concept so that job challenges are not perceived as threatening. One study reported that personal goal setting and self-reinforcement can also reduce the stress that people experience when they enter new work settings. Other research suggests that some (but not all) forms of humor can improve optimism and create positive emotions by taking some psychological weight off the situation.[132]

Control Stress Consequences Coping with workplace stress also involves controlling its consequences. For this reason, many companies have fitness centers or subsidize the cost of membership at

ROWEing to Better Work–Life Balance Mark Wells's work space has an odd assortment of objects: a huge bowl holding 5 pounds of peanuts, an audio turntable, and a trophy with the inscription "Worst Attendance Record." Wells (shown in photo) works full time as an e-learning specialist, yet he was away from the office 42 days last year attending concerts (including four in Europe), festivals, and other fun events. His employer, Best Buy, didn't mind because Wells's productivity increased markedly. Wells and 3,000 other head-office employees are evaluated by their results, not their face time, through the Minneapolis-based retailer's results-only work environment (ROWE) initiative. For example, Steve Hance is in the office only a few days each month. Most of the time, the Best Buy employee relations manager works 285 miles away from his home in Cedar Rapids, Iowa. Thanks to ROWE, Best Buy promotion manager Dawn Paulson was able to work from home during a complicated pregnancy, an arrangement that she says "benefited the company . . . and helped keep me from going stir-crazy." Best Buy strengths coach Christy Runningen also appreciates ROWE's benefits. "ROWE has helped me to find the right balance in my work and home life, and now I actually have a life," says Runningen. "I know my family would tell you that I am a lot less stressed out overall than I used to be."[133]

off-site centers. Research indicates that physical exercise reduces the physiological consequences of stress by helping employees moderate their breathing and heart rate, muscle tension, and stomach acidity.[134] A few firms, such as AstraZeneca, encourage employees to practice relaxation and meditation techniques during the workday. Research has found that various forms of meditation reduce anxiety, reduce blood pressure and muscle tension, and moderate breathing and heart rate.[135]

Along with fitness and relaxation/meditation, wellness programs can also help control the consequences of stress. In the United States, 81 percent of employers with at least 50 employees have wellness programs. Through education and support, these programs help employees to develop better nutrition and fitness, regular sleep, and other good health habits. For example, employees at Pitney Bowes receive up to $200 for completing online wellness surveys three times each year. More than 80 percent of the Minitab, Inc., employees in State College, Pennsylvania, participate in the software developer's wellness program, which includes annual on-site checkups and meditation classes.[136] Many large employers offer *employee assistance programs (EAPs)*–counseling services that help employees resolve marital, financial, or work-related troubles. EAPs also target specific stressors in the industry (e.g., bank robberies).

Receive Social Support Social support occurs when co-workers, supervisors, family members, friends, and others provide emotional and/or informational support to buffer an individual's stress experience. It potentially improves the person's resilience (particularly her or his optimism and self-confidence) because support makes people feel valued and worthy. Social support also provides information to help the person interpret, comprehend, and possibly remove the stressor. For instance, to reduce a new employee's stress, co-workers could describe ways to handle difficult customers. Seeking social support is called a "tend and befriend" response to stress, and research suggests that women often follow this route rather than the "fight-or-flight" response mentioned earlier.[137]

Employee emotions, attitudes, and stress influence employee behavior mainly through motivation. Recall, for instance, that behavioral intentions are judgments or expectations about the motivation to engage in a particular behavior. The next chapter introduces the prominent theories of employee motivation.

Wellness Programs for Employees

Wellness of employees is crucial and a matter of concern for organizations. Changes in lifestyle and work styles, along with stresses caused due to pressures of competition and sustainability, have severely impacted overall wellness of employees. Various studies have revealed that organizations, which do not have effective wellness programs, have low employee turnover. Rise in lifestyle diseases is impacting organizations. According to Berry et. al. (2010), Wellness program, "is an organized employer sponsored program that is designed to support employees (sometimes their families) as they adopt and sustain behaviors that reduce health risks, improve quality of life, enhance personal effectiveness, and benefit the organization's bottom-line".[138]

Wellness Programs have also been defined "as those designed to improve the health and well-being of employees (and their families), in order to enhance organizational performance and reduce costs"[139].

Foundation of Valuable Wellness Program Wellness program to be beneficial for both the employer and the employees will depend on the foundation of Leadership across levels, alignment with organization's culture, scope, significance and quality, cost aspect, collaborations, effective communications and Rewards (University of Michigan's Health Management Research Centre).

Components of Wellness Program The components of a wellness program include health risk assessments, biometric screenings, health coaching, lifestyle change programs, health fairs, seminars, creating awareness through communication campaigns and usage of latest technologies.

Global Wellness Survey (2009) According to a study conducted by Buck Consultants, there is a rise in number of organizations which have implemented wellness strategy. Out of the 1,103 companies from across the globe 64% (2009) had wellness strategy in place, which is the highest in comparison to 60% (2008) and 49% (2007) despite the global recession.

The studies found that the most common objective of implementing wellness strategy was 'to improve productivity and to reduce presenteeism'. Presenteeism means employees are physically present, but not fully productive. This objective was common in companies located in Africa, Australia, Canada, Europe, and Latin America. In Asia it was *to improve workforce morale/engagement* and in the U.S. *to reduce healthcare/insurance costs.* The global financial meltdown hit the U.S. economy severely and employers wanted to reduce their financial burdens. The other popular objectives which drove wellness programs in Asia included *to improve productivity/presenteeism, and reduce employee absenteeism.*

The health risks which drove the wellness strategy include stress matter of concern across most of the continents and lack of physical activity/exercise (Latin America and the U.S.). The global economic meltdown which left its impact across nations intensified 'stress' and the U.S. and Latin America reflected the risks of obesity prevalent in the region. In Asia, other health risks which were of major concern included physical exercise, nutrition/healthy eating habits.

The popular components of a wellness program included immunizations/flu shots (U.S., Canada and Latin America), Biometric health screening (Asia and Africa) and Fitness (Europe). In Asia, other popular components include on-site health classes, company-sponsored sports teams, executive screening program and health-risk appraisal.

The popular health element in a wellness program in 2009 included cycle to work (Asia, U.S. and Latin America), caregiver support (Africa), personal health/ lifestyle coaching (Canada), and Vending machine highlight on healthy food options (Europe).

Through various studies it has been found that there is growing importance of employee wellness programs as it has direct impact on employees' wellness (productivity and health) and organizational performance. According to Berry et al. (2010), organizations can develop metrics to measure the effectiveness of employee wellness programs. The metrics would broadly comprise of *healthcare, safety, productivity and organizational culture.* Healthcare includes cost of medial care and medicines, utilization of claims, disability costs, and worker's compensation cost. Safety metric includes safety incident rate (classification by types), lost and modified workdays in safety incidents, productivity i.e. absenteeism/ presenteeism. Organizational culture metric includes trust in leadership/management, recommendation of the firm as employer and employee turnover.

Chapter Summary

Emotions are physiological, behavioral, and psychological episodes experienced toward an object, person, or event that create a state of readiness. Emotions differ from attitudes, which represent a cluster of beliefs, feelings, and behavioral intentions toward a person, object, or event. Beliefs are a person's established perceptions about the attitude object. Feelings are positive or negative evaluations of the attitude object. Behavioral intentions represent a motivation to engage in a particular behavior with respect to the target.

Attitudes have traditionally been described as a purely rational process in which beliefs predict feelings, which predict behavioral intentions, which predict behavior. We now know that emotions have an influence on behavior that is equal to or greater than that of cognitions. This dual process is apparent when we internally experience a conflict between what logically seems good or bad and what we emotionally feel is good or bad in a situation. Emotions also affect behavior directly. Behavior sometimes influences our subsequent attitudes through cognitive dissonance.

Emotional labor consists of the effort, planning, and control needed to express organizationally desired emotions during interpersonal transactions. It is more common in jobs requiring a variety of emotions and more intense emotions, as well as in jobs where interaction with clients is frequent and has a long duration. Cultures also differ on the norms of displaying or concealing a person's true emotions. Emotional dissonance occurs when required and true emotions are incompatible with each other. Deep acting can minimize this dissonance, as can the practice of hiring people with a natural tendency to display desired emotions.

Emotional intelligence is the ability to perceive and express emotion, assimilate emotion in thought, understand and reason with emotion, and regulate emotion in oneself and others. This concept includes four components arranged in a hierarchy: self-awareness, self-management, social awareness, and relationship management. Emotional intelligence can be learned to some extent, particularly through personal coaching.

Job satisfaction represents a person's evaluation of his or her job and work context. The exit-voice-loyalty-neglect model outlines four possible consequences of job dissatisfaction. Job satisfaction has a moderate relationship with job performance and with customer satisfaction. Affective organizational commitment (loyalty) is the employee's emotional attachment to, identification with, and involvement in a particular organization. This contrasts with continuance commitment, which is a calculative bond with the organization. Companies build loyalty through justice and support, shared values, trust, organizational comprehension, and employee involvement.

Stress is an adaptive response to a situation that is perceived as challenging or threatening to a person's well-being. The stress experience, called the general adaptation syndrome, involves moving through three stages: alarm, resistance, and exhaustion. Stressors are the causes of stress and include any environmental conditions that place a physical or emotional demand on a person. Three stressors that have received considerable attention are harassment and incivility, work overload, and low task control.

Two people exposed to the same stressor may experience different stress levels. Many interventions are available to manage work-related stress, including removing the stressor, withdrawing from the stressor, changing stress perceptions, controlling stress consequences, and receiving social support.

Key Terms

attitudes
cognitive dissonance
continuance commitment
emotional dissonance
emotional intelligence (EI)
emotional labor
emotions
exit-voice-loyalty-neglect (EVLN) model
general adaptation syndrome
job burnout
job satisfaction
organizational (affective) commitment
psychological harassment
resilience
sexual harassment
stress
stressors
trust
workaholic

Critical Thinking Questions

1. A recent study reported that instructors at colleges and universities are frequently required to engage in emotional labor. Identify the situations in which emotional labor is required for this job. In your opinion, is emotional labor more troublesome for college instructors or for telephone operators working at an emergency service?
2. "Emotional intelligence is more important than cognitive intelligence in influencing an individual's success." Do you agree or disagree with this statement? Support your perspective.
3. Describe a time when you effectively managed someone's emotions. What happened? What was the result?
4. "Happy employees create happy customers." Explain why this statement might be true, and identify conditions in which it might not be true.
5. What factors influence an employee's organizational loyalty?
6. Is being a full-time college or university student a stressful role? Why or why not? Contrast your response with other students' perspectives.

7. Two recent college graduates join the same major newspaper as journalists. Both work long hours and have tight deadlines for completing their stories. They are under constant pressure to scout out new leads and be the first to report new controversies. One journalist is increasingly fatigued and despondent and has taken several days of sick leave. The other is getting the work done and seems to enjoy the challenges. Use your knowledge of stress to explain why these two journalists are reacting differently to their jobs.
8. A senior official of a labor union stated: "All stress management does is help people cope with poor management. [Employers] should really be into stress reduction." Discuss the accuracy of this statement.

CASE STUDY 4.1

RIDING THE EMOTIONAL ROLLER COASTER

Louise Damiani's work is an emotional roller coaster most days. The oncology nurse at CentraState Healthcare System in Freehold Township, New Jersey, soars with joy as patients beat their cancer into remission. Then there are the low points when one of her patients is given grim news about his or her cancer. She also battles with the frustration of office politics.

But even after a long shift, Damiani doesn't let her negative emotions surface until she gets into her car and heads home. "You have to learn how to pick and choose and not bring that emotion up," Damiani advises. "You say, 'OK, I can deal with this. I can focus on the priority, and the priority is the patient.'"

As well as managing her own emotions, Damiani has mastered the skill of creating positive emotions in others. She recently received an award in recognition of her extraordinary sensitivity toward patients' needs and concerns. For example, one of Damiani's patients wanted to return to her native Mexico but, with an advanced stage of cancer, such a journey wasn't possible. Instead, Damiani brought "Mexico" to the hospital by transforming a visitors' lounge into a fiesta-type setting and inviting the patient's family, friends, and hospital staff to attend the special event.

Lisa Salvatore, a charge nurse at the recently built Leon S. Peters Burn Center in Fresno, California, also recognizes that her job involves supporting patients' emotional needs, not just their physical problems. "With burns, you don't just treat something on the outside," she says. "You treat something on the inside that you can't see." Salvatore also experiences the full range of emotions, including the urgency of getting burn patients out of emergency within an hour to improve their prospects of recovery. "I like high stress. I like trauma," she says. Still, she acknowledges the emotional challenges of treating children with burns. "I deal with it and then I cry all the way home. I just sob on my way driving home."

Anil Shandil, a medic from the 328th Combat Support Hospital in Fort Douglas, Utah, has witnessed more severe burns and injuries than most medical professionals. For two years at the Landstuhl Army Regional Medical Center in Germany, he aided soldiers who had been wounded in Iraq or Afghanistan. The tour of duty was extremely emotionally taxing. "You get a lot of severed limbs, a lot of traumatic brain injuries, a lot of death and dying," says Shandil. "So the compassion fatigue is rather high." People who work closely with victims of trauma often suffer compassion fatigue, also known as secondary traumatic stress disorder. The main symptom is a decreasing ability to feel compassion for others.

In spite of the risk of compassion fatigue, Shandil has volunteered for an even more challenging assignment. He and 85 other soldiers in the 328th are now in Iraq providing medical care for Iraqi detainees being held there by the U.S. military. So, along with managing emotions from constant exposure to trauma cases, these medics must also show respectful compassion to those who fought against American comrades. Shandil knows it will be hard. "Yes, these are people who were not kind to us. But as a medic, it's our job to care for them, no matter if that is your friend or your enemy."

Discussion Questions

1. To what extent do the three people featured in this case study manage their own emotions on the job? How do they accomplish this? To what extent do you think they effectively manage emotions under these circumstances?
2. This case study states that nurses and other medical staff need to manage the emotions of their patients. Why is emotions management important in this job? In what ways do medical staff alter the emotions of their patients?
3. Stress is mentioned throughout this case study. How does this stress occur? What stress outcomes occur for people in these types of jobs? How can these people try to minimize high levels of stress?

Sources: "Providing Emotional Comfort," *Journeys* (CentraState Medical Center Magazine), 4 (Winter 2008), p. 1; M. L. Diamond, "When Job Stress Bubbles Up, Keep a Lid on Your Emotions," *Seattle Times,* 4 May 2008, p. H2; B. Anderson, "First Stop on a Long Road," *Fresno Bee,* 25 May 2008, p. A1; M. D. LaPlante, "Medics' Compassion to Be Tested," *Salt Lake Tribune,* 17 Sep-tember 2008.

CASE STUDY 4.2

DISPATCHES FROM THE WAR ON STRESS

BusinessWeek

Mark Ostermann had been working in the Chicago office of Boston Consulting Group for less than a year when he attracted the attention of the Red Zone police. Ostermann's infraction: working too hard. He had been putting in 60-plus-hour weeks for a month and a half straight, and his colleagues were worried he was burning out. Now his bosses were stepping in to get Ostermann the help he needed.

This *BusinessWeek* case study discusses the ongoing battle against workplace stress, including some of its causes and consequences, as well as corporate strategies to minimize it. Read the full text of this *BusinessWeek* article at www.mhhe.com/mcshane5e, and prepare for the discussion questions below.

Discussion Questions

1. This case study describes various ways that companies try to manage workplace stress. In terms of the types of stress management strategies described in this chapter, which approaches are applied most and least often?
2. What stress outcomes are mentioned in this case study? What stressors are noted in association with these stress outcomes?
3. Some of the stress problems described in this chapter relate to winning or losing in performance management. Why would the risk of failing to achieve performance goals result in such serious stress outcomes?

Source: J. Goudreau, "Dispatches from the War on Stress," *BusinessWeek,* 6 August 2007, p. 74.

CLASS EXERCISE 4.3

STRENGTH-BASED COACHING

PURPOSE To help students practice a form of interpersonal development built on the dynamics of positive emotions.

MATERIALS None.

BACKGROUND Several chapters in this book introduce and apply the emerging philosophy of *positive organizational behavior*, which suggests that focusing on the positive rather than negative aspects of life will improve organizational success and individual well-being. An application of positive OB is strength-based or appreciative coaching, in which the coach focuses on the person's strengths rather than weaknesses and helps to realize the person's potential. As part of any coaching process, the coach listens to the employee's story and uses questions and suggestions to help that person redefine her or his self-concept and perceptions of the environment. Two important skills in effective coaching are active listening and probing for information (rather than telling the person a solution or direction). The instructions below identify specific information and issues that the coach and coachee will discuss.

INSTRUCTIONS (SMALL CLASS)

1. Form teams of four people. One team can have six people if the class does not have multiples of four. For odd-numbered class sizes, one person may be an observer. Divide into pairs in which one person is coach and the other coachee. Ideally for this exercise, the coach and coachee should have *little* knowledge of each other.
2. Coachees will describe something about themselves in which they excel and for which they like to be recognized. This competency might be work-related, but not necessarily. It would be a personal achievement or ability that is close to their self-concept (how they define themselves). The coach mostly listens, but also prompts more details from the coachee using "probe" questions ("Tell me more about that." "What did you do next?" "Could you explain that further, please?" "What else can you remember about that event?"). As the coachee's story develops, the coach will guide the coachee to identify ways to leverage this strength. For example, the pair would explore situational barriers to practicing the coachee's strength as well as aspects of this strength that require further development. The strength may also be discussed as a foundation for the coachee to develop strengths in other, related ways. The session should end with some discussion of the coachee's goals and action plans. The first coaching session can be any length of time specified by the instructor, but 15 to 25 minutes is typical for each coaching session.
3. After completing the first coaching session, regroup so that each pair consists of different partners than those in the first pair (i.e., if pairs were A-B and C-D in session 1, pairs are A-C and B-D in session 2). The coaches become coachees to their new partners in session 2.
4. The class will debrief regarding the emotional experience of discussing personal strengths, the role of self-concept in emotions and attitudes, the role of managers and co-workers in building positive emotions in people, and the value and limitations of strength-based coaching.

Note: For further information about strength-based coaching, see Sara L. Orem, Jacqueline Binkert, and Ann L. Clancy, *Appreciative Coaching* (San Francisco: Jossey-Bass, 2007); Marcus Buckingham and C. Coffman, *First, Break All the Rules* (New York: Simon & Schuster, 1999).

TEAM EXERCISE 4.4

RANKING JOBS ON THEIR EMOTIONAL LABOR

PURPOSE This exercise is designed to help you understand the jobs in which people tend to experience higher or lower degrees of emotional labor.

INSTRUCTIONS

1. Individually rank-order the extent to which the jobs listed below require emotional labor. In other words, assign a "1" to the job you believe requires the most effort, planning, and control to express organizationally desired emotions during interpersonal transactions. Assign a "10" to the job you believe requires the least amount of emotional labor. Mark your rankings in column 1.
2. The instructor will form teams of four or five members, and each team will rank-order the items on the basis of consensus (not simply averaging the individual rankings). These results are placed in column 2.
3. The instructor will provide expert ranking information. This information should be written in column 3. Then students calculate the differences in columns 4 and 5.
4. The class will compare the results and discuss the features of jobs with high emotional labor.

Occupational Emotional Labor Scoring Sheet

Occupation	(1) Individual ranking	(2) Team ranking	(3) Expert ranking	(4) Absolute difference of 1 and 3	(5) Absolute difference of 2 and 3
Bartender					
Cashier					
Dental hygienist					
Insurance adjuster					
Lawyer					
Librarian					
Postal clerk					
Registered nurse					
Social worker					
Television announcer					
			TOTAL		
(The lower the score, the better.)				Your score	Team score

TEAM EXERCISE 4.5

STAGE FRIGHT!

PURPOSE This exercise is designed to help you diagnose a common stressful situation and determine how stress management practices apply to this situation.

BACKGROUND Stage fright–including the fear of public speaking–is one of the most stressful experiences many people have in everyday life. According to some estimates, nearly three-quarters of us frequently get stage fright, even when speaking or acting in front of a small audience. Stage fright is an excellent topic for this team activity on stress management because the psychological and physiological symptoms of stage fright are really symptoms of stress. In other words, stage fright is the stress experience in a specific context involving a public audience. On the basis of the personal experiences of team members, your team will be asked to identify the symptoms of stage fright and to determine specific stress management activities that effectively combat stage fright.

INSTRUCTIONS

1. Students are organized into teams, typically four to six students per team. Ideally, each team should have one or more people who acknowledge that they have experienced stage fright.
2. Each team's first task is to identify the symptoms of stage fright. The best way to organize these symptoms is to look at the three categories of stress outcomes described in this chapter: physiological, psychological, and behavioral. The specific stage fright symptoms may be different from the stress outcomes described in the chapter, but the three broad categories are relevant. Teams should be prepared to identify several symptoms and to present one or two specific examples of stage fright symptoms based on personal experiences of team members. (Please remember that individual students are not required to describe their experiences to the entire class.)
3. Each team's second task is to identify specific strategies people could or have applied to minimize stage fright. The five categories of stress management presented in the chapter will likely provide a useful template for organizing the specific stage fright management activities. Each team should document several strategies for minimizing stage fright and be able to present one or two specific examples to illustrate some of these strategies.
4. The class will congregate to hear each team's analysis of symptoms of and solutions to stage fright. This information will then be compared to the stress experience and stress management practices, respectively.

SELF-ASSESSMENT 4.6

SCHOOL COMMITMENT SCALE

PURPOSE This self-assessment is designed to help you understand the concept of organizational commitment and to assess your commitment to the college or university you are currently attending.

OVERVIEW The concept of commitment is as relevant to students enrolled in college or university courses as it is to employees working in various organizations. This self-assessment adapts a popular organizational commitment instrument so that it refers to your commitment as a student to the school you are attending.

INSTRUCTIONS Read each of the statements below and circle the response that best fits your personal belief. Then use the scoring key in Appendix B at the end of this book to calculate your results. This self-assessment should be completed alone so that you can rate yourself honestly without concerns of social comparison. However, class discussion will focus on the meaning of the different types of organizational commitment and how well this scale applies to the commitment of students toward the college or university they are attending.

School Commitment Scale

To what extent do you agree or disagree with each of these statements?	Strongly agree	Moderately agree	Slightly agree	Neutral	Slightly disagree	Moderately disagree	Strongly disagree
1. I would be very happy to complete the rest of my education at this school.	☐	☐	☐	☐	☐	☐	☐
2. One of the difficulties of leaving this school is that there are few alternatives.	☐	☐	☐	☐	☐	☐	☐
3. I really feel as if this school's problems are my own.	☐	☐	☐	☐	☐	☐	☐
4. Right now, staying enrolled at this school is a matter of necessity as much as desire.	☐	☐	☐	☐	☐	☐	☐
5. I do not feel a strong sense of belonging to this school.	☐	☐	☐	☐	☐	☐	☐
6. It would be very hard for me to leave this school right now even if I wanted to.	☐	☐	☐	☐	☐	☐	☐
7. I do not feel emotionally attached to this school.	☐	☐	☐	☐	☐	☐	☐
8. Too much of my life would be disrupted if I decided to move to a different school now.	☐	☐	☐	☐	☐	☐	☐
9. I do not feel like part of the "family" at this school.	☐	☐	☐	☐	☐	☐	☐
10. I feel that I have too few options to consider leaving this school.	☐	☐	☐	☐	☐	☐	☐
11. This school has a great deal of personal meaning for me.	☐	☐	☐	☐	☐	☐	☐
12. If I had not already put so much of myself into this school, I might consider completing my education elsewhere.	☐	☐	☐	☐	☐	☐	☐

Source: Adapted from J. P. Meyer, N. J. Allen, and C. A. Smith, "Commitment to Organizations and Occupations: Extension and Test of a Three-Component Model," *Journal of Applied Psychology* 78 (1993), pp. 548–551.

SELF-ASSESSMENT 4.7

DISPOSITIONAL MOOD SCALE

This self-assessment is designed to help you understand mood states or personality traits of emotions and to assess your own mood or emotional personality. This self-assessment consists of several words representing various emotions that you might have experienced. For each word presented, indicate the extent to which you have felt this way generally across all situations *over the past six months*. You need to be honest with yourself to receive a reasonable estimate of your mood state or personality trait on these scales. The results provide an estimate of your level on two emotional personality scales. This instrument is widely used in research, but it is only an estimate. You should not assume that the results are accurate without a more complete assessment by a trained professional.

SELF-ASSESSMENT 4.8

WORK ADDICTION RISK TEST

This self-assessment is designed to help you identify the extent to which you are a workaholic. This instrument presents several statements and asks you to indicate the extent to which each statement is true of your work habits. You need to be honest with yourself for a reasonable estimate of your level of workaholism.

SELF-ASSESSMENT 4.9

PERCEIVED STRESS SCALE

This self-assessment is designed to help you estimate your perceived general level of stress. The items in this scale ask you about your feelings and thoughts during the last month. In each case, please indicate how often you felt or thought a certain way. You need to be honest with yourself for a reasonable estimate of your general level of stress.

SELF-ASSESSMENT 4.10

STRESS COPING PREFERENCE SCALE

This self-assessment is designed to help you identify the type of coping strategy you prefer to use in stressful situations. This scale lists a variety of things you might do when faced with a stressful situation. You are asked how often you tend to react in these ways. You need to be honest with yourself for a reasonable estimate of your preferred coping strategy.

Founded only a decade ago in San Antonio, Texas, Rackspace Hosting, Inc., already employs more than 2,000 employees and has become one of the best-known brands in enterprise-level Web hosting and the information technology services industry. This success demands highly motivated employees who will deliver fast, reliable service. "To enable us to meet our high service levels, we have to have a very high level of employee engagement, so our staff are extremely important to us," says Fabio Torlini, Rackspace's marketing director in the United Kingdom. Rackspace scores in the top 14 percent on employee engagement among 100,000 workplaces worldwide.

Rackspace Hosting motivates its employees through recognition and appreciation of what it takes to make employee engagement central to business operations.

Rackspace generates this high level of engagement through rewards and fulfillment of personal needs. Rackspace employees—called "Rackers"—receive quarterly bonuses based on meeting companywide goals. Those who receive great customer feedback or perform beyond the call of duty are awarded free restaurant dinners for the entire family, a weekend vacation in the river residence guest house of cofounder Graham Weston, or the key for a week to one of Weston's BMWs (called the "Rackmobile"). "If you gave somebody a $200 bonus, it wouldn't mean very much," observes Weston. "When someone gets to drive my car for a week, they never forget it." The top-performing Rackers each month receive special treatment; they are tied up in a straitjacket and have a photograph of them in the outfit hung on the Wall of Fanatics.

To fulfill their social needs and minimize dysfunctional internal competition, Rackspace organizes employees into teams and has a healthy social budget that funds monthly outings such as dinners, theatrical events, boating trips, and scavenger hunts. In addition, due to plentiful training and career development opportunities, 85 percent of Rackers say that work fulfills their need for personal growth.

Rackspace also motivates staff through the power of strength-based coaching. In some offices, every employee's photograph is posted on a board with a list of his or her five key strengths. "Each Racker is an individual and has unique strengths," the company's three founders and CEO recently wrote in an annual letter to investors. "We help them develop their strengths rather than ask them to change who they are. We encourage Rackers to talk about their strengths and to find positions in the company that leverage their inherent talents. This approach creates happier, more engaged Rackers who look forward to coming to work."[1]

5

Foundations of Employee Motivation

Learning Objectives

After reading this chapter, you should be able to:

1. Diagram and discuss the relationship between human drives, needs, and behavior.
2. Summarize Maslow's needs hierarchy and discuss Maslow's contribution to the field of motivation.
3. Give an overview of Herzberg's theory in the field of motivation.
4. Summarize McClelland's learned needs theory, including the three needs he studied.
5. Describe four-drive theory and discuss its implications for motivating employees.
6. Diagram the expectancy theory model and discuss its practical implications for motivating employees.
7. Describe the characteristics of effective goal setting and feedback.
8. Summarize equity theory and describe how to improve procedural justice.
9. Identify the factors that influence procedural justice, as well as the consequences of procedural justice.

motivation
The forces within a person that affect the direction, intensity, and persistence of voluntary behavior.

Rewards, social events, strength-based feedback, and various celebrations for good performance are designed to maintain and improve employee motivation at Rackspace Hosting. This motivation has catapulted the company's performance in a highly competitive market. Rackspace is also recognized as one of the best places to work. Recall from Chapter 2 that **motivation** refers to the forces within a person that affect the direction, intensity, and persistence of voluntary behavior.[2] Motivated employees are willing to exert a particular level of effort (intensity), for a certain amount of time (persistence), toward a particular goal (direction). Motivation is one of the four essential drivers of individual behavior and performance.

This chapter introduces the core theories of employee motivation. We begin by introducing employee engagement, an increasingly popular concept associated with motivation. Next, we distinguish between drives and needs and explain how needs are shaped through the individual's self-concept and other personal factors. Three theories that focus on drives and needs–Maslow's needs hierarchy, McClelland's learned needs theory, and four-drive theory–are introduced and evaluated. Next, we turn our attention to the popular rational decision model of employee motivation: expectancy theory. This is followed by a discussion of the key elements of goal setting and feedback. In the final section, we look at organizational justice, including the dimensions and dynamics of equity theory and procedural justice.

EMPLOYEE ENGAGEMENT

employee engagement
The employee's emotional and cognitive motivation, self-efficacy to perform the job, perceived clarity of the organization's vision and his or her specific role in that vision, and belief that he or she has the resources to get the job done.

When Rackspace Hosting executives discuss employee motivation, they are just as likely to use the phrase *employee engagement*. This concept, which is closely connected to employee motivation, has become so popular in everyday language that we introduce it here. Employee engagement's popularity far exceeds its conceptual development; its definition varies across studies, and its distinction from job satisfaction, organizational commitment, and other variables is unclear.[3] Even so, there are enough threads of similarity that we can cautiously define **employee engagement** as the employee's emotional and cognitive motivation, self-efficacy to perform the job, perceived clarity of the organization's vision and his or her specific role in that vision, and belief that he or she has the resources to get the job done.[4] This definition relates to the four cornerstones of individual behavior and performance identified in the MARS model (see Chapter 2): motivation, ability, role perceptions, and situational factors. Employee engagement encompasses the employee's beliefs about and emotional responses to these conditions. Additionally, some writers suggest that employee engagement includes a high level of absorption in the work–the experience of "getting carried away" while working.

Employee engagement is a hot topic among executives and consultants. One report estimates that one in every four large organizations has a formal employee engagement program, and three out of five intend to develop plans to improve employee engagement.[5] Some companies even have employee engagement departments or managers. The popularity of employee engagement is partly due to preliminary evidence that it improves organizational effectiveness. Royal Bank of Scotland calculated that when its employee engagement scores increase, productivity rises and staff turnover falls. British retailer Marks & Spencer claims that a 1 percent improvement in the engagement levels of its workforce produces a 2.9 percent increase in sales per square foot. JCPenney has calculated that stores with higher employee engagement produce higher sales. Other research indicates that employee engagement is associated with higher organizational citizenship and lower turnover intentions.[6]

Getting Engaged at JCPenney In the hypercompetitive retail industry, the number-one ingredient for winning the hearts and pocketbooks of customers is the quality, style, and price of the merchandise. What's the second most important ingredient? It's employee engagement, according to executives at JCPenney. "We feel strongly there's a correlation between engaged associates and store profitability," says Myron "Mike" Ullman, CEO of the Plano, Texas, retailer. In fact, the company's internal research revealed that stores with the top-quartile engagement scores generate about 10 percent more in sales per square foot and 36 percent greater operating income than similar-size stores in the lowest quartile. A few years ago, about two-thirds of JCPenney associates were "engaged." Thanks to improved training, career development, and other management practices, more than three-quarters of employees now are engaged. Per-share earnings have more than doubled since JCPenney management focused on improving employee engagement. "We see a 200 basis-point [increase in] profit when we engage the associates," Ullman claims. "This isn't just warm, fuzzy stuff. It's solid business logic."[7]

The challenge facing organizational leaders is that most employees aren't very engaged. Several consulting reports estimate that only about one-quarter of American employees are highly engaged, which is slightly above the global average. Less than 60 percent are somewhat engaged, and approximately one-fifth have low engagement or are actively disengaged. Actively disengaged employees tend to be disruptive at work, not just disconnected from work. Globally, employees in Mexico and Brazil seem to have the highest levels of engagement, whereas several Asian countries (notably Japan, China, and South Korea) and a few European countries (notably Italy, Netherlands, and France) have the lowest levels.[8] Some writers suggest that globalization, information technology, corporate restructuring, and other changes have potentially undermined the levels of trust and commitment necessary to motivate employees beyond minimum standards.[9] Others point out that companies have not adjusted to the changing needs and expectations of new workforce entrants.[10] Overall, these reports of low employee engagement imply that many employees are not very motivated to perform their jobs. To create a more motivated workforce, we first need to understand employee drives and needs and how these concepts relate to individual goals and behavior.

Learning Objectives

After reading this section, you should be able to:

1. Diagram and discuss the relationship between human drives, needs, and behavior.
2. Summarize Maslow's needs hierarchy and discuss Maslow's contribution to the field of motivation.
3. Give an overview of Herzberg's theory in the field of motivation.
4. Summarize McClelland's learned needs theory, including the three needs he studied.
5. Describe four-drive theory and discuss its implications for motivating employees.

Employee Drives and Needs

To figure out how to create a more engaged and motivated workforce, we first need to understand the motivational "forces" within people. Unfortunately, many writers conveniently avoid this topic, and

drives
Hardwired characteristics of the brain that correct deficiencies or maintain an internal equilibrium by producing emotions to energize individuals.

the result is a stream of confusing phrases such as *innate drives, learned needs, motivations, instincts, secondary drives,* and *primary needs.*[11] We define **drives** (also called *primary needs* or *innate motives*) as hardwired characteristics of the brain that correct deficiencies or maintain an internal equilibrium by producing emotions to energize individuals.[12] Drives are the "prime movers" of behavior because they generate emotions, which put people in a state of readiness to act on their environment (see Chapter 4). Although typically overlooked in organizational behavior, emotions play a central role in motivation.[13] In fact, both words *(emotion* and *motivation)* are derivations of the same Latin word, *movere,* which means "to move." Although there is no clear list of human drives, several are consistently identified in research, such as the drives for social interaction, understanding of the environment, competence or status, and defense of oneself against physiological and psychological harm.[14]

needs
Goal-directed forces that people experience.

We define **needs** as goal-directed forces that people experience. Needs are the motivational forces of emotions channeled toward particular goals to correct deficiencies or imbalances. So drives produce emotions, and needs are essentially the emotional experience channeled toward goals believed to address the source of emotion. Consider the following example: Everyone has a drive to bond–an inherent need to be associated with other people to some degree. The drive to bond generates negative emotions when we are rejected by others or lack social interaction over time. These negative emotions are experienced as unfulfilled needs; they motivate us to do something that will increase our connectedness to and acceptance by other people.

Individual Differences in Needs

Even though all people have the same drives, they don't have the same emotional responses (such as loneliness, curiosity, or anger) or needs in the same situation. Exhibit 5.1 explains why this difference occurs. The left side of the model shows that the individual's self-concept (including personality and values), social norms, and past experience amplify or suppress drive-based emotions, thereby resulting in stronger or weaker needs.[15] People who define themselves as very sociable typically experience a strong need for social interaction if alone for a while, whereas people who view themselves as less sociable would experience a less intense need to socialize over that time. These individual differences also explain, as you shall discover later in this chapter, why needs can be "learned" to some extent. Socialization and reinforcement may cause people to alter their self-concept somewhat, resulting in a stronger or weaker need for social interaction, achievement, and so on.

Self-concept, social norms, and past experience do more than adjust the emotions generated by our built-in drives. The right side of Exhibit 5.1 shows that these individual characteristics also regulate a person's motivated goals and behavior. Even if you have a strong desire for social interaction, you probably wouldn't walk up to strangers and start talking to them; this action is contrary to social norms of behavior in most (but not all) cultures. Similarly, suppose that you dislike your boss's decision to assign you to a particular project. Openly confronting the boss about this assignment is common in some companies and cultures and much less common in other contexts. People regulate their goals and behavior on the basis of these social and cultural norms, as well as their self-concept and reinforcement (or observation of others) in previous situations. Employees are more likely to direct their emotional energy toward speaking up if they view themselves as being forthright, live in a low power distance culture, and work in a company that encourages constructive debate.

We have presented this detail about needs and drives for a few reasons.[16] First, as mentioned, motivation theories use the terms *needs, drives,* and *motivations* so loosely that they make it difficult to

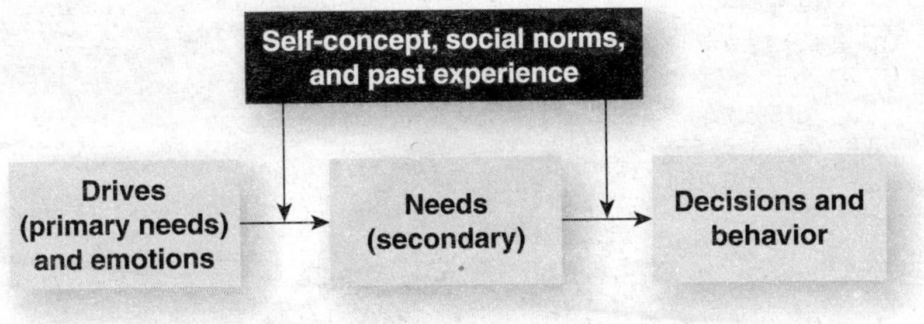

Exhibit 5.1 *Drives, Needs, and Behavior*

compare theories, so it is important to settle this confusion at the outset. Second, the field of organizational behavior has been woefully slow to acknowledge the central role of emotions in employee motivation, as will be apparent when we review most motivation theories in this chapter. Third, Exhibit 5.1 provides a useful template for understanding various motivation theories. In fact, you will see pieces of this theory when we discuss four-drive theory, expectancy theory, goal setting, and other concepts in this chapter. The remainder of this section describes theories that try to explain the dynamics of drives and needs. Later theories in this chapter explain how experiences–such as expectancies, feedback, and work experiences–influence the motivation process.

Maslow's Needs Hierarchy Theory

Maslow's needs hierarchy theory
A motivation theory of needs arranged in a hierarchy, whereby people are motivated to fulfill a higher need as a lower one becomes gratified.

By far, the most widely known theory of human motivation is **Maslow's needs hierarchy theory** (see Exhibit 5.2). Developed by psychologist Abraham Maslow in the 1940s, the model condenses and integrates the long list of needs that had been studied previously into a hierarchy of five basic categories (from lowest to highest):[17]

Physiological. The need for food, air, water, shelter, and the like.

Safety. The need for a secure and stable environment and the absence of pain, threat, or illness.

Belongingness/love. The need for love, affection, and interaction with other people.

Esteem. The need for self-esteem through personal achievement as well as social esteem through recognition and respect from others.

Self-actualization. The need for self-fulfillment, realization of one's potential.

Along with developing these five categories, Maslow identified the desire to know and the desire for aesthetic beauty as two innate drives that do not fit within the hierarchy.

Maslow's list represents drives (primary needs) because they are described as innate and universal. According to Maslow, we are motivated simultaneously by several needs but the strongest source is the lowest unsatisfied need at the time. As the person satisfies a lower-level need, the next higher need in the hierarchy becomes the primary motivator and remains so even if never satisfied. Physiological needs are initially the most important, and people are motivated to satisfy them first. As they become gratified, the desire for safety emerges as the strongest motivator. As safety needs are satisfied, belongingness needs become most important, and so forth. The exception to this need fulfillment process is self-actualization; as people experience self-actualization, they desire more rather than less of this need. Thus, while the bottom four groups are *deficiency needs* because they become activated

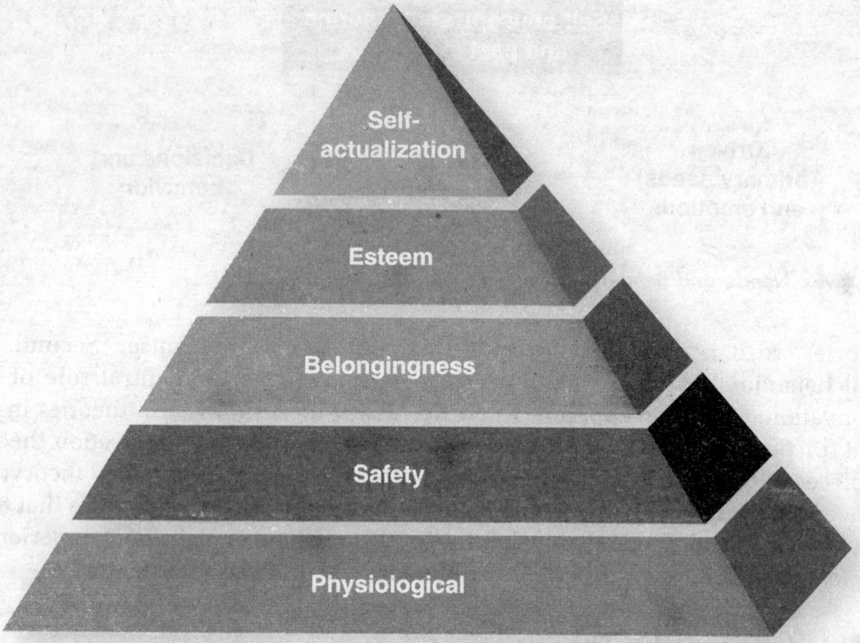

Source: Based on information in A. H. Maslow, "A Theory of Human Motivation," *Psychological Review* 50 (1943), pp. 370–396.

Exhibit 5.2 *Maslow's Needs Hierarchy*

when unfulfilled, self-actualization is known as a *growth need* because it continues to develop even when fulfilled.

Limitations and Contributions of Maslow's Work In spite of its popularity, Maslow's needs hierarchy theory has been dismissed by most motivation experts.[18] Maslow developed the theory from only his professional observations, and he was later surprised that it was so widely accepted before anyone tested it. Empirical studies have concluded that people do not progress through the hierarchy as the theory predicts. For example, some people strive more for self-esteem before their belongingness needs have been satisfied. The theory also assumes that needs priorities shift over a long time, whereas in reality needs priorities rise and fall far more frequently with the situation. A person's needs for status, food, social interaction, and so forth, change daily or weekly, not every few years. As Global Connections 5.1 describes, companies around the world routinely motivate all staff through recognition. These examples illustrate that people regularly need–and are motivated to receive–respect and belongingness in the workplace.

Although needs hierarchy theory has failed the reality test, Maslow deserves credit for bringing a more holistic, humanistic, and positive approach to the study of human motivation.[19] First, Maslow brought a more holistic perspective by explaining that needs and drives should be studied together because human behavior is typically initiated by more than one of them at the same time. Previously, motivation experts had splintered needs or drives into dozens of categories, each studied in isolation.[20]

Second, Maslow brought a more humanistic perspective to the study of motivation. In particular, he suggested that higher-order needs are influenced by personal and social influences, not just instincts. In other words, he was among the first to recognize that human thoughts (including self-concept, social

5.1 Global Connections

Shining the Spotlight on Employee Recognition

David Gachuru lives by a motto that motivates employees with much more than money: "If an employee's work calls for a thumbs-up, I will appreciate him or her as many times as possible." Translating this advice into practice is a daily event for the general manager of Sarova Panafric Hotel in Nairobi, Kenya. In addition to thanking staff personally and through e-mails, Gachuru holds bimonthly meetings at which top-performing employees are congratulated and receive paid holidays with their family. Employee achievements are also celebrated in the hotel's newsletter, which is distributed to guests as well as to employees.

David Gachuru (left in photo) motivates staff at Sarova Panafric Hotel in Nairobi, Kenya, through plenty of praise and recognition.

Sarova Panafric Hotel and other firms are returning to good old-fashioned praise and recognition to regularly motivate staff. Good thing, because recent surveys in several countries identify lack of praise, recognition, or appreciation as a major reason why employees are demotivated and disengaged and decide to find work elsewhere. For instance, on the basis of 1,000 exit interviews, Ireland's Small Firms Association (SMA) recently reported that lack of recognition was a top reason why employees in that country quit their jobs. "Increasingly people need to feel that their contribution is valued," suggests SMA director Patricia Callan. "If people do not feel important, they are not motivated to stay."

The challenge of recognition is to "catch" employees doing extraordinary work or showing organizational citizenship. Peer recognition, in which co-workers identify exemplary performers, is an increasingly popular way for companies to identify employees deserving special recognition and reward. At the Ritz-Carlton Hotel in Kuala Lumpur, Malaysia, co-workers write words of appreciation to each other using First Class Cards. "This serves as a motivational aspect of the work environment," says an executive at Ritz-Carlton Kuala Lumpur, which is rated as one of the best places to work in Asia.

Amgen, the California-based biotechnology company, recently introduced globally a more intricate peer recognition program called Bravo! Tier I recognition is an e-mail–based thank-you sent by co-workers through a special Bravo Web site. Tier II peer recognitions are accompanied by an electronic gift certificate. At Tier III, employees nominate individuals or teams, and an "award wizard" determines the amount of the reward (ranging from $100 to $500). A Tier IV recognition is accompanied by a larger financial reward for those who significantly improved the company's operations. The Tier V award, which is reviewed by the executive team, is received by employees who have made the highest material impact on company performance.[21]

norms, and past experience) play a role in motivation. Previous motivation experts had focused almost entirely on human instincts without considering that motivation could be shaped by human thought.

Third, Maslow brought a more positive perspective of employee motivation by focusing on need gratification rather than only on need deprivation. In particular, he popularized the previously developed concept of *self-actualization,* suggesting that people are naturally motivated to reach their potential and that organizations and societies need to be structured to help people continue and develop this motivation.[22] Due to his writing on self-actualization and the power of need gratification, Maslow is a pioneer in *positive organizational behavior.* Recall from Chapter 3 that positive OB says that focusing on the positive rather than negative aspects of life will improve organizational success and individual well-being. In other words, this approach advocates building positive qualities and traits within individuals or institutions as opposed to focusing on trying to fix what might be wrong with them.[23]

What's Wrong with Needs Hierarchy Models?

ERG theory
A needs hierarchy theory consisting of three fundamental needs—existence, relatedness, and growth.

Maslow's theory is not the only attempt to map employee needs onto a single hierarchy. Another hierarchy model, called **ERG theory,** reorganizes Maslow's five groups into three–existence, relatedness, and growth.[24] Unlike Maslow's theory, which only explained how people progress up the hierarchy, ERG theory also describes how people regress down the hierarchy when they fail to fulfill higher needs. ERG theory seems to explain human motivation somewhat better than Maslow's needs hierarchy, but that's mainly because it is easier to cluster human needs around ERG's three categories than Maslow's five categories. Otherwise, research studies have found that ERG theory only marginally improves our understanding of human needs.[25]

Why have Maslow's needs hierarchy theory, ERG theory, and other needs hierarchies largely failed to explain the dynamics of employee needs? The most glaring explanation is that people don't fit into a single needs hierarchy. Some people place social status at the top of their personal hierarchy; others consider personal development and growth an ongoing priority over social relations or status. There is increasing evidence that needs hierarchies are unique to each person, not universal, because needs are strongly influenced by each individual's self-concept, including personal values and social identity. If your most important values lean toward stimulation and self-direction, you probably pay more attention to self-actualization needs. If power and achievement are at the top of your value system, status needs will likely be at the top of your needs hierarchy. This connection between values and needs suggests that a needs hierarchy is unique to each person and can possibly change over time, just as values change over a lifetime.[26]

Herzberg's Motivation-Hygiene Theory

Frederick Herzberg (1957)[27] conducted his study on accounts and engineers to determine the factors in an employee's work environment which caused satisfaction or dissatisfaction. He developed the two-factor model called the *Motivation-Hygiene Theory.* The research involved interviewing employees where they were asked what satisfied or dissatisfied them about their work. Herzberg found that the factors causing job satisfaction (and presumably motivation) were different from those causing job dissatisfaction. He labeled the satisfiers as motivators and the dissatisfiers as *hygiene factors,* (the term 'hygiene' was used to indicate maintenance factors that are necessary to avoid dissatisfaction, but they by themselves, do not provide satisfaction).

The following table presents the factors causing dissatisfaction and satisfaction, listed in the order of higher to lower importance.

Hygiene factors	**Motivators**
Company policy	Achievement
Supervision	Recognition
Relationship w/Boss	Work itself
Work conditions	Responsibility
Salary	Advancement
Relationship w/Peers	Growth

Herzberg reasoned that the opposite of satisfaction is not dissatisfaction, but rather, it is no satisfaction. His argument was that the factors causing satisfaction are different from those causing dissatisfaction, the two feelings cannot simply be treated as opposites of each other. From the above one observes that the factors that determine dissatisfaction or no dissatisfaction are not part of the work itself, but rather, they are external to work. Thus, Hygiene factors are environment-centric, that is, they are concerned with avoiding unpleasantness at work. If these factors are considered inadequate by the employees, then this can result in dissatisfaction with work.

Motivator factors are based on an individual's need for personal growth and satisfaction-like promotion and advancement-and are intrinsic to job. If these are effective then they can motivate an individual to achieve above average performance and effort.

There is some similarity between Herzberg's and Maslow's (1954) models.[28] Both suggest that needs have to be satisfied for an employee to be motivated. However, Herzberg argues that only the higher order needs of the Maslow's Hierarchy (e.g. self-actualization, esteem needs) act as motivators. The remaining needs if not addressed can only cause dissatisfaction. Many management researchers (Guest, 1992)[29] do not subscribe to motivation- hygiene model but, in India, these models are still relevant.

Learned Needs Theory

Earlier in this chapter we said that drives (primary needs) are innate whereas needs are shaped, amplified, or suppressed through self-concept, social norms, and past experience. Maslow noted that individual characteristics influence the strength of higher-order needs, such as the need to belong. Psychologist David McClelland further investigated the idea that need strength can be altered through social influences. In particular, he recognized that a person's needs can be strengthened through reinforcement, learning, and social conditions. McClelland examined three "learned" needs: achievement, power, and affiliation.[30]

need for achievement (nAch)
A need in which people want to accomplish reasonably challenging goals and desire unambiguous feedback and recognition for their success.

Need for Achievement People with a strong **need for achievement (nAch)** want to accomplish reasonably challenging goals through their own effort. They prefer working alone rather than in teams, and they choose tasks with a moderate degree of risk (i.e., neither too easy nor impossible to complete). High-nAch people also desire unambiguous feedback and recognition for their success. Money is a weak motivator, except when it provides feedback and recognition.[31] In contrast, employees with a low nAch perform their work better when money is used as an incentive. Successful entrepreneurs tend to have a high nAch, possibly because they establish challenging goals for themselves and thrive on competition.[32]

need for affiliation (nAff)
A need in which people seek approval from others, conform to their wishes and expectations, and avoid conflict and confrontation.

Need for Affiliation **Need for affiliation (nAff)** refers to a desire to seek approval from others, conform to their wishes and expectations, and avoid conflict and confrontation. People with a strong nAff try to project a favorable image of themselves. They tend to actively support others and try to smooth out workplace conflicts. HighnAff employees generally work well in coordinating roles to mediate conflicts and in sales positions where the main task is cultivating long-term relations. However, they tend to be less effective at allocating scarce resources and making other decisions that potentially generate conflict. People in decision-making positions must have a relatively low need for affiliation so that their choices and actions are not biased by a personal need for approval.[33]

need for power (nPow)
A need in which people want to control their environment, including people and material resources, to benefit either themselves (personalized power) or others (socialized power).

Need for Power People with a high **need for power (nPow)** want to exercise control over others and are concerned about maintaining their leadership position. They frequently rely on persuasive communication, make more suggestions in meetings, and publicly evaluate situations more often. McClelland pointed out that there are two types of nPow. Individuals who enjoy their power for its own sake, use it to advance personal interests, and wear their power as a status symbol have *personalized power*. Others mainly have a high need for *socialized power* because they desire power as a means to help others.[34] McClelland argues that effective leaders should have a high need for socialized rather than personalized power. They must have a high degree of altruism and social responsibility and be concerned about the consequences of their own actions on others.

Learning Needs McClelland's research supported his theory that needs can be learned (more accurately, strengthened or weakened), so he developed training programs for this purpose. In his achievement motivation program, trainees write achievement-oriented stories and practice achievement-oriented behaviors in business games. They also complete a detailed achievement plan for the next two years and form a reference group with other trainees to maintain their newfound achievement motivation style.[35] These programs seem to work. Participants attending a need-for-achievement course in India subsequently started more new businesses, had greater community involvement, invested more in expanding their businesses, and employed twice as many people as nonparticipants did. Research on similar achievement motivation courses for American small-business owners reported dramatic increases in the profitability of the participants' businesses. In essence, these programs attempt to alter the individual's self-concept or experiences such that they amplify or suppress related drive-generated emotions.

Practical Implications of Needs/Drive-Based Theories

Needs- and drive-based theories, and particularly four-drive theory, offer some practical advice for motivating employees. The main recommendation that Lawrence and Nohria provide from four-drive theory is to ensure that individual jobs and workplaces provide balanced opportunities to fulfill the drives to acquire, bond, learn, and defend.[36] There are really two key recommendations here. The first one is that everyone in the workplace needs to regularly fulfill all four drives. This contrasts sharply with the ill-fated needs hierarchy theories, which suggested that employees are motivated mainly by one need at a time. The four-drive theory says that each of us continuously seeks fulfillment of our innate drives. Thus, the best workplaces for motivation and morale provide sufficient rewards, learning opportunities, social interaction, and so forth for all employees.

The second recommendation from the four-drive theory is that these four drives must be kept in "balance"; that is, organizations should avoid too much or too little opportunity to fulfill each drive. The reason for this advice is that the four drives counterbalance each other. Companies that help employees fulfill one drive but not the others will face long-term problems. An organization that energizes the drive to acquire without the drive to bond may eventually suffer from organizational politics and dysfunctional conflict. Change and novelty in the workplace will aid the drive to learn, but too much of it will trigger the drive to defend so that employees become territorial and resistant to change. Creating a workplace that supports the drive to bond can, at extreme levels, undermine the diversity and constructive debate required for effective decision making.

Another recommendation from the needs/drives-based theories is to offer employees a choice of rewards rather than giving everyone the same specific reward. Although we possess the same drives and require their ongoing fulfillment, people differ in their needs at any given time. Due to their unique value systems and experiences, some employees generally have a strong need to achieve, whereas others are motivated more by social factors. A narrow application of this recommendation is to let employees choose their own rewards. Farm Fresh Supermarkets accomplishes this by awarding points to employees for good customer service. These points are later redeemed for reward gifts from a catalog. "There are several hundred items in [the catalog], and they can get everything from a T-shirt to a toaster oven, coffee maker, and a vacuum cleaner," explains Ron Dennis, president of the Virginia Beach, Virginia–based grocery chain.[37] At a broader level, employees need to have career choices and diverse opportunities to discover and experience their potential. One of the enduring recommendations from Maslow's work on self-actualization is that employees must have sufficient freedom to discover their potential. It cannot be assumed or dictated by management.

Four-Drive Theory

One of the central messages of this chapter is that emotions play a significant role in employee motivation. This view is supported by a groundswell of research in neuroscience, but it is almost completely absent from contemporary motivation theories in organizational behavior. Also, social scientists in several fields (psychology, anthropology, etc.) increasingly agree that human beings have several hardwired drives, including social interaction, learning, and dominance. One of the few theories to apply this emerging knowledge is **four-drive theory.**[38] Developed by Harvard Business School professors Paul Lawrence and Nitin Nohria, four-drive theory states that everyone has the drive to acquire, bond, learn, and defend:

four-drive theory
A motivation theory that is based on the innate drives to acquire, bond, learn, and defend and that incorporates both emotions and rationality.

- *Drive to acquire.* This is the drive to seek, take, control, and retain objects and personal experiences. The drive to acquire extends beyond basic food and water; it includes enhancing one's self-concept through relative status and recognition in society.[39] Thus, it is the foundation of competition and the basis of our need for esteem. Four-drive theory states that the drive to acquire is insatiable because the purpose of human motivation is to achieve a higher position than others, not just to fulfill one's physiological needs.
- *Drive to bond.* This is the drive to form social relationships and develop mutual caring commitments with others. It explains why people form social identities by aligning their self-concept with various social groups (see Chapter 2). It may also explain why people who lack social contact are more prone to serious health problems.[40] The drive to bond motivates people to cooperate and, consequently, is a fundamental ingredient in the success of organizations and the development of societies.
- *Drive to learn.* This is the drive to satisfy our curiosity, to know and understand ourselves and the environment around us.[41] When observing something that is inconsistent with or beyond our current knowledge, we experience a tension that motivates us to close that information gap. In fact, studies have revealed that people who are removed from any novel information will crave even boring information; the drive to learn generated such strong emotions that the study participants eventually craved month-old stock reports![42] The drive to learn is related to the higher-order needs of growth and self-actualization described earlier.
- *Drive to defend.* This is the drive to protect ourselves physically and socially. Probably the first drive to develop, it creates a "fight-or-flight" response in the face of personal danger. The drive to

defend goes beyond protecting our physical self. It includes defending our relationships, our acquisitions, and our belief systems.

These four drives are innate and universal, meaning that they are hardwired in our brains and are found in all human beings. They are also independent of each other. There is no hierarchy of drives, so one drive is neither dependent on nor inherently inferior or superior to another drive. Four-drive theory also states that these four drives are a complete set–there are no fundamental drives excluded from the model. Another key feature is that three of the four drives are proactive–we regularly try to fulfill them. Only the drive to defend is reactive–it is triggered by threat. Thus, any notion of fulfilling drives is temporary, at best.

How Drives Influence Employee Motivation Four-drive theory draws from current neuroscience knowledge to explain how drives translate into goal-directed effort. To begin with, recall from previous chapters that the information we receive is quickly and nonconsciously tagged with emotional markers that subsequently shape our logical analysis of a situation.[43] According to four-drive theory, the four drives determine which emotions are tagged to incoming stimuli. If you arrive at work one day to see a stranger sitting in your office chair, you might quickly experience worry, curiosity, or both. These emotions are automatically created by one or more of the four drives. In this example, the emotions produced are likely strong enough to demand your attention and motivate you to act on this observation.

Most of the time, we aren't aware of our emotional experiences because they are subtle and fleeting. However, emotions do become conscious experiences when they are sufficiently strong or when we experience conflicting emotions. Under these circumstances, our mental skill set relies on social norms, past experience, and personal values to direct the motivational force of our emotions to useful and acceptable goals that address the source of those emotions (see Exhibit 5.3). In other words, the emotions generated by the four drives motivate us to act, and our mental skill set chooses courses of action that are acceptable to society and our own moral compass.[44] This is the process described at the

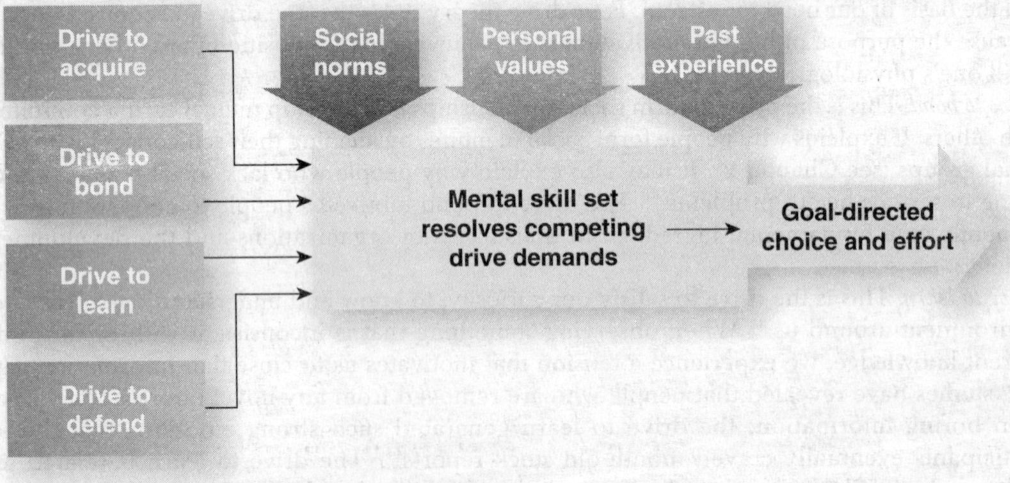

Source: Based on information in P. R. Lawrence and N. Nohria, *Driven: How Human Nature Shapes Our Choices* (San Francisco: Jossey-Bass, 2002).

Exhibit 5.3 *Four-Drive Theory of Motivation*

beginning of this chapter, namely, that drives produce emotions; our self-concept, social norms, and past experience translate these emotions into goal-directed needs, and these individual characteristics also translate needs into decisions and behavior.

Evaluating Four-Drive Theory Although four-drive theory was introduced very recently, it is based on a deep foundation of research that dates back more than three decades. The drives have been identified from psychological and anthropological studies. The translation of drives into goal-directed behavior originates from considerable research on emotions and neural processes. The theory avoids the assumption that everyone has the same needs hierarchy, and it explains why needs vary from one person to the next. Notice, too, that four-drive theory is both holistic (it relates to all drives, not just one or two) and humanistic (it acknowledges the role of human thought and social influences, not just instinct). Maslow had identified these two principles as important features of an effective motivation theory. Four-drive theory also provides a much clearer understanding of the role of emotional intelligence in employee motivation and behavior. Employees with high emotional intelligence are more sensitive to competing demands from the four drives, are better able to avoid impulsive behavior from those drives, and can judge the best way to act to fulfill those drive demands in a social context.

Even with its well-researched foundations, four-drive theory is far from complete. First, most experts would argue that one or two other drives exist that should be included. Second, social norms, personal values, and past experience probably don't represent the full set of individual characteristics that translate emotions into goal-directed effort. For example, other elements of self-concept beyond personal values, such as personality and social identity, likely play a significant role in translating drives into needs and needs into decisions and behavior.

Practical Implications of Four-Drive Theory The main recommendation from four-drive theory is to ensure that individual jobs and workplaces provide a balanced opportunity to fulfill the drives to acquire, bond, learn, and defend.[45] There are really two recommendations here. The first is that the best workplaces for employee motivation and well-being offer conditions that help employees fulfill all four drives. Employees continually seek fulfillment of their innate drives, so successful companies provide sufficient rewards, learning opportunities, social interaction, and so forth, for all employees.

The second recommendation is that fulfillment of the four drives must be kept in balance; that is, organizations should avoid too much or too little opportunity to fulfill each drive. The reason for this advice is that the four drives counterbalance each other. The drive to bond counterbalances the drive to acquire; the drive to defend counterbalances the drive to learn. An organization that energizes the drive to acquire without the drive to bond may eventually suffer from organizational politics and dysfunctional conflict. Change and novelty in the workplace will aid the drive to learn, but too much of it will trigger the drive to defend to such an extent that employees become territorial and resistant to change. Thus, the workplace should offer enough opportunity to keep all four drives in balance.

These recommendations help explain why Rackspace Hosting, described at the beginning of this chapter, has a motivated workforce and is rated as one of the best places to work in America and the United Kingdom. Rackspace has internal competitions that fulfill the drive to acquire, yet it balances the competitive conditions with generously funded social events where employees maintain a supportive social environment. The opening vignette also noted that the Web hosting and IT services company encourages staff to learn through training and career-enhancing assignments. At the same time, these are balanced by a nurturing environment that emphasizes employee strengths rather than faults. The company likely also minimizes the drive to defend because it is in a growth phase with little probability of layoffs or other risks to personal well-being.

Motivation and Commitment among Indian Managers

A number of researches on motivation, using a variety of methods, have been undertaken and reported which probe the question, 'what motivates a manager or a worker in an Indian organization'. Among managers, promotion has been found to be the most important incentive and dissatisfier and recognition as the most important job factor in satisfaction and dissatisfaction.[46] In a study of Indian executives, Kalyansundram and Arason[47] found executives to be extensively dominated by dependency and control motives. Sharma and Kaur[48], in their study of 163 executives from a public sector organization reported 44.9% variation in job satisfaction due to job-related factors.

Organizational commitment is an intense positive orientation towards an organization, one's identification with it, viewing organization's goals as one's own, and overstretching oneself to achieve the same. Motivation, a driving force for goal-directed activity and OC, exerts considerable influence on various aspects of work performance and withdrawal behavior. Sharma and Sharma[49] studied determinants of organizational commitment and motivation from among Indian managers involving 11 organizational variables. Based on a sample of 254 middle-level managers from a high-performing organization, the study revealed the determinants of motivation among Indian managers shown in Exhibit 5.4.

Determinants of Motivation	Job Satisfaction	Organizational Commitment	Social Satisfaction
Job Content	62%	35%	33%
Scope for Advancement	18%	22%	18%
Objectivity & Rationality	15%	17%	14%
Monetary Benefits	10%	12%	
Safety and Security		15%	17%
Grievance Handling			24%

Exhibit 5.4 *Determinants of Motivation: Standardised Beta Co-efficients*[49]

Of all the three determinants identified by this study, job content has emerged as the most critical determinant of managerial motivation as it predicts variance in all the three dimensions of motivation. The net contribution of this variable is the highest. The next highest predictors of variance in all the three forms of motivation are scope for advancement and monetary benefits, respectively. Other significant determinants of motivation which predict variance in two out of three forms of motivation are safety and security, and objectivity and rationality. Grievance handling has been able to account for only 24% variance in social satisfaction.

Learning Objectives

After reading the next three sections, you should be able to:

6. Diagram the expectancy theory model and discuss its practical implications for motivating employees.
7. Describe the characteristics of effective goal setting and feedback.
8. Summarize equity theory and describe how to improve procedural justice.
9. Identify the factors that influence procedural justice, as well as the consequences of procedural justice.

Expectancy Theory of Motivation

expectancy theory
A motivation theory based on the idea that work effort is directed toward behaviors that people believe will lead to desired outcomes.

The theories described so far mainly explain the internal origins of employee motivation. But how do these drives and needs translate into specific effort and behavior? Four-drive theory recognizes that social norms, personal values, and past experience direct our effort, but it doesn't offer any more detail. **Expectancy theory,** on the other hand, offers an elegant model based on rational logic to predict the chosen direction, level, and persistence of motivation. Essentially, the theory states that work effort is directed toward behaviors that people believe will lead to desired outcomes. In other words, we are motivated to achieve the goals with the highest expected payoff.[50] As illustrated in Exhibit 5.5, an individual's effort level depends on three factors: effort-to-performance (E-to-P) expectancy, performance-to-outcome (P-to-O) expectancy, and outcome valences. Employee motivation is influenced by all three components of the expectancy theory model. If any component weakens, motivation weakens.

- *E-to-P expectancy.* This is the individual's perception that his or her effort will result in a particular level of performance. In some situations, employees may believe that they can unquestionably accomplish the task (a probability of 1.0). In other situations, they expect that even their highest level of effort will not result in the desired performance level (a probability of 0.0). In most cases, the E-to-P expectancy falls somewhere between these two extremes.
- *P-to-O expectancy.* This is the perceived probability that a specific behavior or performance level will lead to a particular outcome. In extreme cases, employees may believe that accomplishing a particular task (performance) will definitely result in a particular outcome (a probability of 1.0), or they may believe that successful performance will have no effect on this outcome (a probability of 0.0). More often, the P-to-O expectancy falls somewhere between these two extremes.
- *Outcome valences.* A *valence* is the anticipated satisfaction or dissatisfaction that an individual feels toward an outcome. It ranges from negative to positive. (The actual range doesn't matter; it may be from −1 to +1 or from −100 to +100.) An outcome valence represents a person's anticipated

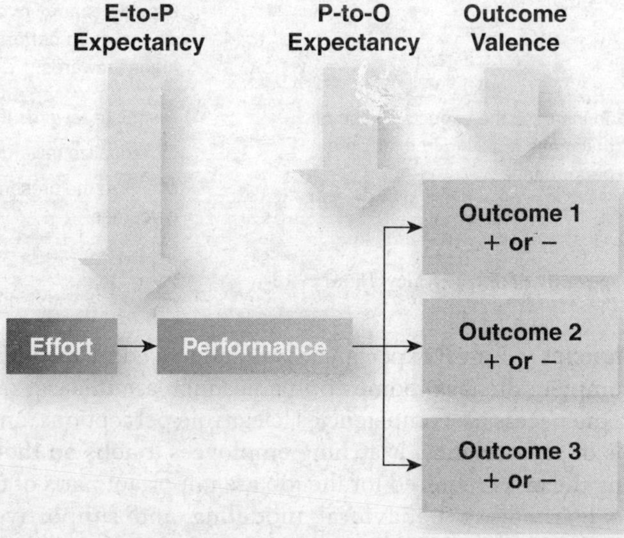

Exhibit 5.5 *Expectancy Theory of Motivation*

satisfaction with the outcome.[51] Outcomes have a positive valence when they are consistent with our values and satisfy our needs; they have a negative valence when they oppose our values and inhibit need fulfillment.

Expectancy Theory in Practice

One of the appealing characteristics of expectancy theory is that it provides clear guidelines for increasing employee motivation.[52] Several practical applications of expectancy theory are listed in Exhibit 5.6 and described below.

Expectancy theory component	Objective	Applications
E→P expectancies	To increase the belief that employees are capable of performing the job successfully.	• Select people with the required skills and knowledge. • Provide required training and clarify job requirements. • Provide sufficient time and resources. • Assign simpler or fewer tasks until employees can master them. • Provide examples of similar employees who have successfully performed the task. • Provide coaching to employees who lack self-confidence.
P→O expectancies	To increase the belief that good performance will result in certain (valued) outcomes.	• Measure job performance accurately. • Clearly explain the outcomes that will result from successful performance. • Describe how the employee's rewards were based on past performance. • Provide examples of other employees whose good performance has resulted in higher rewards.
Outcome valences	To increase the expected value of outcomes resulting from desired performance.	• Distribute rewards that employees value. • Individualize rewards. • Minimize the presence of countervalent outcomes.

Exhibit 5.6 *Practical Applications of Expectancy Theory*

Increasing E-to-P Expectancies E-to-P expectancies are influenced by the individual's belief that he or she can successfully complete the task. Some companies increase this can-do attitude by assuring employees that they have the necessary competencies, clear role perceptions, and necessary resources to reach the desired levels of performance. Matching employees to jobs on the basis of their abilities and clearly communicating the tasks required for the job are important parts of this process. Similarly, E-to-P expectancies are learned, so behavioral modeling and supportive feedback (positive reinforcement) typically strengthen the individual's belief that he or she is able to perform the task.

Increasing P-to-O Expectancies The most obvious ways to improve P-to-O expectancies are to measure employee performance accurately and distribute more valued rewards to those with higher job performance. P-to-O expectancies are perceptions, so employees need to know that higher performance will result in higher rewards, and they need to know how that connection occurs. Companies meet these needs by explaining how specific rewards are connected to specific past performance and by using examples, anecdotes, and public ceremonies to illustrate when behavior has been rewarded.

Many companies claim they provide higher rewards to people with higher performance, yet surveys repeatedly find that the performance-to-outcome linkage is foggy to most staff. Less than half of the 6,000 American employees surveyed in one study said they know how to increase their base pay or cash bonuses. Another poll reported that only 32 percent of employees believe that people at their company are paid more for doing a better job. Less than half of employees in a large-scale Malaysian survey said they believe their company rewards high performance or deals appropriately with poor performers. Only one-quarter of 10,000 Canadian employees recently surveyed said they regularly receive rewards for a job well done. This is consistent with another survey which reported that only 27 percent of Canadian employees say there is a clear link between their job performance and pay.[53]

Increasing Outcome Valences Everyone has unique values and experiences, which translate into different needs at different times. Consequently, individualizing rather than standardizing rewards and other performance outcomes is an important ingredient in employee motivation. At the same time, leaders need to watch for countervalent outcomes–consequences with negative valences that reduce rather than enhance employee motivation. For example, peer pressure may cause some employees to perform their jobs at the minimum standard even though formal rewards and the job itself would otherwise motivate them to perform at higher levels.

Overall, expectancy theory is a useful model that explains how people rationally figure out the best direction, intensity, and persistence of effort. It has been tested in a variety of situations and predicts employee motivation in different cultures.[54] However, critics have a number of concerns with how the theory has been tested. Another concern is that expectancy theory ignores the central role of emotion in employee effort and behavior. The valence element of expectancy theory captures some of this emotional process, but only peripherally.[55]

Does Expectancy Theory Fit Reality?

The expectancy theory remains one of the better theories for predicting work effort and motivation. In particular, it plays a valuable role by detailing a person's thinking process when translating the competing demands of the four drives into specific effort. The expectancy theory has been applied to a wide variety of studies, such as predicting student motivation to participate in teaching evaluations, using a decision support system, leaving the organization, and engaging in organizational citizenship behaviors.[56] Research also indicates that the expectancy theory predicts employee motivation in different cultures.[57]

One limitation is that the expectancy theory seems to ignore the central role of emotion in employee effort and behavior. As we learned earlier in this and previous chapters, emotions serve an adaptive function that demands our attention and energizes us to take action. The valence element of expectancy theory captures some of this emotional process, but only peripherally. Thus theorists probably need to redesign the expectancy theory model in light of new information about the importance of emotions in motivation and behavior.

Indian Approaches to Motivation for Well-being of Employees

The Indian approaches to motivation are radically opposite to western approaches, the focus being on motivation that should drive from within an individual as a process towards self-realization. The two Indian approaches to motivation are *Nishkam Karm* and *Daan Karm.*

Nishkam Karm *Nishkam Karm* is an approach of motivation to work diligently without getting concerned for the results. Here, an individual works with right and pure motive, whose results are expected to be wholesome. The goal needs to be imagined as a series of collective and interconnected small goals and to concentrate one at a time, this enables a person to give best performance. The process orientation of this approach causes less stress, which is manageable.[58]

Daan Karm This motivation approach is based on the concept of '*giving*'. Chakraborty[59] quoted from Taittirya Upanishad regarding *daan karma.* 'The offering (daan) should be with honour, should be plenty, with modesty, with awe, and with sympathy'. The offering should be given to those who are worthy and one must not expect anything in return. This motivates both the donor and the receiver, and helps to create social capital.

Innovating with Less—The Indian Scenario[60]

Innovation is not just an idea. It is converting that idea into growing revenues, improving margins and winning customers

—Ram Charan

Corporate Dossier – The Economic Times, 17 December, 2010.

The global financial meltdown has changed the approach and parameters for organizations toward innovation. Prior to the major recession, innovations were based on assumptions of affluence and abundance. There is a growing population of middle class and lower middle class from both developed and developing countries who demand affordable, durable and environmental friendly goods and services. So, the driving forces for innovation in the existing context are affordability and sustainability. Thus, strategies for innovation need to focus on creation of more products with meager resources, with low cost manufacturing, new sources of knowledge, variation in supply chain, cross-border interdependence and to selling at affordable prices. These complexities have created new opportunities of serving those markets which were previously not considered as potent.

Developing countries are the pioneers in innovating with fewer resources. Some of the well-known innovation with meager resources in India include Tata Nano– the ₹ 1lac car, Arvind Eye Care – which provides cataract surgery at reasonable cost $30, Tata Swatch (₹ 1000) – the cost effective water filter, etc. The reasons for fuelling such innovations include constraints of resources, shortage of technology and talent, to cater the growing middle class and the poor population, and the spirit of entrepreneurship and ambition. In India, this phenomena is called '*Jugaad*', i.e. to find or develop alternatives, make improvisations, and to be creative in overcoming resource constraints and to solve problems. But, there is one negative notion with regard to *Jugaad*, i.e. compromising on quality.

Prahlad and Mashelkar have unveiled a framework to capture this innovation trend in India based on Gandhian philosophy, the tenets of which include: "I would prize every invention of science made for the benefit of all" and "Earth provides enough to satisfy every man's need, but not every man's greed". There are three types of Gandhian innovations:

To Disrupt Existing Business Models In this type of innovation, organizations have used western technologies, but have created business models which impacted the industry economics, for example, the 'Outsourcing' concept by IT companies. Well-known IT companies used off-the-shelf hardware, but employ new talent-based business models for competitive advantage. IT companies like Infosys and Wipro and others were offering cost-effective and quality processes. Now the focus is on providing end-to-end business solutions to organizations.

Bring Alterations in Organizational Capabilities An organization which has created new technologies which have led to alternation in organizational capabilities, e.g. Computational Research Laboratories (CRL) developed world's fourth fastest and Asia's first supercomputer era. This computer was developed in a cost-effective way using whole new design with standard components by its engineers. This led to an opportunity for CRL. It is the first company to offer supercomputing services. Its services are availed of by 40 companies including Boeing and Tata Motors.

Construct New Competencies New capabilities are developed by either developing or acquiring new technologies or through collaborations. Tata Motors created Tata Nano through this approach. It collaborated with several companies within India and abroad to develop various components according to its specifications, e.g. Bosch (Germany) for new engine management system, I.D.E.A. Institute and Trilix (Italy) for its exterior design and styling, Sona Koya (India) for lightweight steering shaft, Johnson Controls (USA) for seating system, Toyo (Japan) for engine cooling module, Behr (Germany) for heating, ventilation and air-conditioning system and Madras Rubber Factor [MRF] (India) for tough—than normal rear tires.

Based on the above types of innovation, there are three distinct innovation categories which include Innovations that bring Changes in Business Dynamics; Innovation that blend different Technologies; and Innovation that produce New Technologies.

Innovations that bring Changes in Business Dynamics For example, Bharati Airtel, used to charge high price from its customers like its competitors when it entered mobile services market in 1995. However, by 2002, it faced challenges from new entrants and was facing financial crunch. These challenges led the top management to recognize that instead of focusing on Average Revenue Per User (ARPU) [the standard industry metric of few thousand customers], it needed to provide services at lower rates and attract millions of customers. The focus was changed from gross revenue and profit, ratio of operating expenses to gross revenue, and ratio of revenue to capital expenditure. This new innovative approach led it to expand its presence across India.

Innovation that blends different technologies The Emergency Management and Research Institute (India) has synthesized latest telecommunication, computing, medical, and transportation technology to provide free emergency services in tribal, rural, and urban areas.

Innovation that Produce New Technologies Lupin Pharmaceutical reversed its normal drug development process. It gathered clinical data before it undertook lab tests in order to create an affordable treatment for psoriasis. Lupin came up with effective formulation with fraction of money.

Guiding Principles for Gandhian Innovation The guiding principles for organizations include: goal for inclusive growth, vision needs to be unambiguous, stretch targets, innovate under constraints, and to consider consumers as people, suppliers as people, and employees as innovators.

Metrics for these Innovations These include profits and losses, balance sheets, return of capital, cash flow, capital intensity, access and influence, innovation efficiency, volume, costs, concentrate on creating new markets.

Source: Adapted from Prahlad C.K, and R.A. Mashelkar (2010), *Innovation's Holy Grail*, Harvard Business Review, July–August.

Goal Setting and Feedback

Walk into almost any customer contact center (i.e., call center)–whether it's Sitel's offices in Albuquerque, New Mexico, or Dell's contact center in Quezon City in the Philippines–and you will notice that work activities are dominated by goal setting and plenty of feedback.[61] Contact-center performance is judged on several *key performance indicators (KPIs),* such as average time to answer the call, length of time per call, and abandon rates (customers who hang up before the call is handled by a customer service representative). Some contact centers have large electronic boards showing how many customers are waiting, the average time they have been waiting, and the average time before someone talks to them. A few even have "emotion detection" software, which translates words and voice intonation into a measure of the customer's level of happiness or anger during the telephone conversation.[62]

goal setting
The process of motivating employees and clarifying their role perceptions by establishing performance objectives.

Goal setting is the process of motivating employees and clarifying their role perceptions by establishing performance objectives. It potentially improves employee performance in two ways: (1) by amplifying the intensity and persistence of effort and (2) by giving employees clearer role perceptions so that their effort is channeled toward behaviors that will improve work performance. Goal setting is more complex than simply telling someone to "do your best." It requires several specific characteristics. Some consultants refer to these as "SMART goals," but the acronym doesn't quite capture all of the key ingredients identified by goal-setting research. The six key characteristics are specific goals, relevant goals, challenging goals, goal commitment, participation in goal formation (sometimes), and goal feedback.[63]

- *Specific goals*. Employees put more effort into a task when they work toward specific goals rather than "do your best" targets. Specific goals have measurable levels of change over a specific and relatively short time frame. For example, New York City mayor Michael Bloomberg has set the goal of replacing 300 gas-guzzling yellow cabs with fuel-efficient models every month. Specific goals communicate more precise performance expectations, so employees can direct their effort more efficiently and reliably.
- *Relevant goals*. Goals must also be relevant to the individual's job and be within his or her control. For example, a goal to reduce waste materials would have little value if employees don't have much control over waste in the production process.
- *Challenging goals*. Challenging goals (rather than easy ones) cause people to raise the intensity and persistence of their work effort and to think through information more actively. They also fulfill a person's achievement or growth needs when the goal is achieved. General Electric, Goldman Sachs, and many other organizations emphasize *stretch goals*. These goals don't just stretch a person's abilities and motivation; they are goals that people don't even know how to reach, so they need to be creative to achieve them.

Goal Setting Makes Every Day Count in NYC When New York City mayor Michael R. Bloomberg gives a speech or writes a memo, he lets it be known that the time remaining in his second mayoral term is quickly passing by. The successful entrepreneur-turned-politician has announced challenging goals to accomplish, and he doesn't want any of his remaining tenure wasted. To be sure that New York City employees also experience this deadline urgency, Bloomberg had special clocks installed in a dozen city government offices that count down how many days remain in his mayoral term. Above many of these countdown clocks is the catchphrase: "Make every day count." Bloomberg's penchant for specific, challenging, measurable goals is most apparent in PlaNYC, which includes 127 environmental initiatives captured in 10 overarching goals. Bloomberg aims to reduce greenhouse gas emissions citywide by 30 percent by 2030. He recently announced plans to have 300 new hybrid taxis on the road each month until the city's entire fleet of 13,000 taxis is fuel-efficient by 2012. (Bloomberg is shown here in front of one of the new "green" hybrid taxis.) Another goal is to plant 1 million trees over the next decade, including at least 10,000 street trees per year.[64]

- *Goal commitment.* Ideally, goals should be challenging without being so difficult that employees lose their motivation to achieve them.[65] This is the same as the E-to-P expectancy that you learned about in the section on expectancy theory. The lower the E-to-P expectancy that the goal can been accomplished, the less committed (motivated) the employee is to the goal.
- *Goal participation* (sometimes). Goal setting is usually (but not always) more effective when employees participate in setting the goals.[66] Participation potentially creates a higher level of goal commitment than is found when goals are set alone by the supervisor. Participation may also improve goal quality, because employees have valuable information and knowledge that may not be known to those who initially formed the goal.
- *Goal feedback.* Feedback is another necessary condition for effective goal setting.[67] Feedback is any information that lets us know whether we have achieved the goal or are properly directing our effort toward it. Feedback redirects our effort, but it potentially also fulfills our growth needs.

Balanced Scorecard

balanced scorecard (BSC)
A goal-setting and reward system that translates the organization's vision and mission into specific, measurable performance goals related to financial, customer, internal, and learning/growth (i.e., human capital) processes.

A popular form of organizational-level goal setting is the **balanced scorecard (BSC).** The balanced scorecard translates the organization's vision and mission into specific, measurable performance goals related to financial, customer, internal, and learning/growth (i.e., human capital) processes. The objective of BSC is to ensure that the full range of organizational performance is captured in the goal-setting process. Each dimension includes several goals related to specific operations within the organization, thereby connecting each work unit to the overall corporate objectives. For example, an airline might include on-time performance as one of its customer process goals and number of hours of safety training per employee as a learning and growth process goal. These specific goals are often weighted and scored to create a composite measure of achievement across the organization each year.

The Richmond, Virginia, school board implemented a BSC to help it achieve six goals, including improving student achievement, promoting a safe and nurturing environment, and providing strong leadership for effective and efficient operations. Each goal has several outcome measures. For instance, the goal of improving student achievement includes a dozen measures, such as percentage of students who meet a state-sanctioned completion rate, percentage of special education students moving to a higher reading level, and percentage of students enrolling in specific math and science courses. "Our BSC lays out a challenging set of process measures and targets for us, and it holds us accountable for reaching our goals," explains Yvonne Brandon, superintendent of Richmond Public Schools.[68]

Characteristics of Effective Feedback

Whirlpool Corp. employees complained that they weren't getting enough feedback from their bosses, so the appliance manufacturer asked managers to meet with their immediate subordinates quarterly rather than the previous schedule's every six months. Jeffrey Davidoff, head of marketing for Whirlpool's North American consumer brands, has taken the feedback frequency even further; he meets with his eight direct reports for up to 45 minutes every two weeks. "I'm noticing much better results," Mr. Davidoff says.[69]

Whirlpool managers are discovering that feedback is an important practice in employee motivation and performance. Along with clarifying role perceptions and improving employee skills and knowledge, feedback motivates when it is constructive and when employees have strong self-efficacy.[70]

As with goal setting, feedback should be *specific* and *relevant.* In other words, the feedback should refer to specific metrics (e.g., sales increased by 5 percent last month) and to the individual's behavior or outcomes within his or her control. Feedback should also be *timely;* the information should be available soon after the behavior or results occur so that employees see a clear association between their actions and the consequences.

Effective feedback is also *sufficiently frequent.* How frequent is "sufficiently"? The answer depends on at least two things. One consideration is the employee's knowledge and experience with the task. Feedback is a form of reinforcement, so employees working on new tasks should receive more frequent corrective feedback because they require more behavior guidance and reinforcement (see Chapter 3). Employees who perform repetitive or familiar tasks can receive less frequent feedback. The second factor is how long it takes to complete the task. Feedback is necessarily less frequent in jobs with a long cycle time (e.g., executives and scientists) than in jobs with a short cycle time (e.g., grocery store cashiers). The final characteristic of effective feedback is that it should be *credible.* Employees are more likely to accept feedback (particularly corrective feedback) from trustworthy and credible sources.

Feedback through Strength-Based Coaching Forty years ago, Peter Drucker recognized that leaders are more effective when they focus on strengths rather than weaknesses. "The effective executive builds on strengths–their own strengths, the strengths of superiors, colleagues, subordinates; and on the strength of the situation," wrote the late management guru.[71] Rackspace Hosting, Inc., which was described at the beginning of this chapter, has adopted this positive OB approach. It gives employees opportunities to develop their strengths rather than requiring them to focus on areas where they have limited interest or talent. This is the essence of **strength-based coaching** (also known as *appreciative coaching*)–maximizing the person's potential by focusing on her or his strengths rather than weaknesses.[72] In strength-based coaching, the employee describes areas of work where he or she excels. The coach guides this discussion by asking exploratory questions and by helping the employee to discover ways of leveraging his or her strength. For example, the pair would explore situational barriers to practicing the coachee's strength as well as aspects of this strength that require further development.

strength-based coaching
A positive organizational behavior approach to coaching and feedback that focuses on building and leveraging the employee's strengths rather than trying to correct his or her weaknesses.

Strength-based coaching is logical because people inherently seek feedback about their strengths, not their flaws. Recall from Chapter 2 that people engage in self-enhancement, at least for those domains of self which are most important. Strength-based coaching also makes sense because personality becomes quite stable before a person reaches midcareer, and this stability limits the flexibility of the person's interests, preferences, and competencies.[73] In spite of these research observations, most companies focus goal setting and feedback on tasks that employees are performing poorly. After the initial polite compliments, many coaching or performance feedback sessions analyze the employee's weaknesses, including determining what went wrong and what the employee needs to do to improve. These inquisitions sometimes produce so much negative feedback that employees become defensive; they can also undermine self-efficacy, thereby making the employee's performance worse rather than better. By focusing on weaknesses, companies fail to realize the full potential of the employee's strengths. One survey reports that only 20 percent of employees in large organizations say that they have an opportunity to perform tasks that they do best.[74]

Sources of Feedback

Feedback can originate from nonsocial or social sources. Nonsocial sources provide feedback without someone communicating that information. Employees at contact centers view electronic displays

Sony Europe Builds on Strengths When competition from Korea and China threatened Sony Europe's market position, the electronics and music company decided that its competitive advantage would be to leverage the power of strengths rather than battle against weaknesses. Employees were asked to identify activities in which they excel, enjoy the work, and feel at ease. On the basis of this information, Sony Europe designed jobs around these strengths, instead of molding people to fit into existing, rigid job structures. For example, the performance of a Sony Europe employee dropped after he moved to another sales position. Rather than pushing the employee to deliver higher performance in the new job, Sony compared the individual's strengths against the job requirements. The company learned that the employee's strength was in face-to-face communication, whereas his new job required very little social interaction. Sony created a new role for the employee that leveraged his strengths. Within a year, the employee's team had delivered record sales and increased profits at a lower cost. Strength-based coaching "ensures that everybody in Sony is focusing on what they do best," says Ray White, Sony Europe's vice president of human resources. "They're aligning their 'A' talents to make their best contribution to the business and their best contributions are outstanding."[75]

showing how many callers are waiting and the average time they have been waiting. Nova Chemicals operators receive feedback from a computer screen that monitors in real time the plant's operational capacity, depicted as a gently flowing green line, and actual production output, shown as a red squiggly line. Soon after Nova installed the feedback system, employees engaged in friendly bouts of rivalry to determine who could keep the actual production output as close as possible to the plant's maximum capacity.[76]

Corporate intranets allow many executives to receive feedback instantaneously on their computer, usually in the form of graphic output on an executive dashboard. Almost half of Microsoft's employees use a dashboard to monitor project deadlines, sales, and other metrics. Microsoft CEO Steve Ballmer regularly reviews dashboard results in one-on-one meetings with his division leaders. "Every time I go to see Ballmer, it's an expectation that I bring my dashboard with me," says the head of the Microsoft Office division.[77]

Multisource (360-Degree) Feedback Erik Djukastein knew that he needed feedback on his leadership skills, but asking his boss for performance feedback wasn't possible because Djukastein owns the company, Contech Electronics. Instead, he asked all 20 employees and managers at the company to anonymously complete a written report about his strengths and weaknesses. "It was illuminating and scary looking at the results–when your staff say you don't follow through on your commitments, that hurts," Djukastein admits. "But the good news is that it enabled me to open my eyes to things that were instrumental in changing my mental attitude."[78]

multisource (360-degree) feedback
Information about an employee's performance collected from a full circle of people, including subordinates, peers, supervisors, and customers.

Erik Djukastein relied on **multisource (360-degree) feedback** to provide him with meaningful feedback. As the name implies, multisource feedback is information about an employee's performance collected from a full circle of people, including subordinates, peers, supervisors, and customers. Almost all the Fortune 500 companies use multisource feedback, typically for managers rather than nonmanagement employees.[79] Multisource feedback tends to provide more complete and accurate information than feedback from a supervisor alone. It is particularly useful when the supervisor is unable to observe the employee's behavior or performance throughout the year. Lower-level employees also feel a greater sense of fairness and open communication when they are able to provide upward feedback about their boss's performance.[80]

However, multisource feedback also creates challenges. Having several people review so many other people can be expensive and time-consuming. With multiple opinions, the 360-degree process can also produce ambiguous and conflicting feedback, so employees may require guidance to interpret the results. A third concern is that peers may provide inflated rather than accurate feedback to avoid conflicts during the forthcoming year. A final concern is that employees experience a stronger emotional reaction when they receive critical feedback from many people rather than from just one person (such as the boss). "Initially you do take it personally," admits a manager at software maker Autodesk. "[360-degree feedback] is meant to be constructive, but you have to internally battle that."[81]

Choosing Feedback Sources With so many sources of feedback–multisource feedback, executive dashboards, customer surveys, equipment gauges, nonverbal communication from your boss–which one works best under which conditions? The preferred feedback source depends on the purpose of the information. To learn about their progress toward goal accomplishment, employees usually prefer nonsocial feedback sources, such as computer printouts or feedback directly from the job. This is because information from nonsocial sources is considered more accurate than information from social sources. Corrective feedback from nonsocial sources is also less damaging to self-esteem. In contrast, social sources tend to delay negative information, leave some of it out, and distort the bad news in a positive way.[82] When employees want to improve their self-image, they seek out positive feedback from social sources. It feels better to have co-workers say that you are performing the job well than to discover this from a computer screen.

Evaluating Goal Setting and Feedback

Goal setting represents one of the "tried-and-true" theories in organizational behavior, so much so that scholars consider it to be one of the top OB theories in terms of validity and usefulness.[83] In partnership with goal setting, feedback also has an excellent reputation for improving employee motivation and performance. At the same time, putting goal setting into practice can create problems.[84] One concern is that goal setting tends to focus employees on a narrow subset of measurable performance indicators while ignoring aspects of job performance that are difficult to measure. The saying, "What gets measured, gets done" applies here. A second problem is that when goal achievement is tied to financial rewards, many employees are motivated to set easy goals (while making the boss think they are difficult) so that they have a higher probability of the bonus or pay increase. As a former CEO at Ford Motor Company once quipped: "At Ford, we hire very smart people. They quickly learn how to make relatively easy goals look difficult!"[85] A third problem is that setting performance goals is effective in established jobs but seems to interfere with the learning process in new, complex jobs. Thus, we need to be careful not to apply goal setting where an intense learning process is occurring.

Organizational Justice

The government of Tasmania, Australia's island state, recently bought the unfinished Bell Bay power station when the original owners experienced financial problems. United Group, the construction company hired to finish building the electricity generation station, brought in crews from other states to work alongside the Tasmanian workers at the site. It wasn't long before the Tassie workers discovered a huge gap in pay rates. The new interstate workers were being paid $31.50 per hour, whereas the Tasmanian workers were paid $22 for doing the same job at the same work site. "The situation is basically unfair and the Tasmanian workers are very angry," says the local labor union leader.[86]

Most organizational leaders know that treating employees fairly is both morally correct and good for employee motivation, loyalty, and well-being. Yet the feelings of injustice that the Tasmanian workers at the Bell Bay power station site recently experienced are regular occurrences in the workplace. To minimize these incidents, we need to first understand that there are two forms of organizational justice: distributive justice and procedural justice.[87] **Distributive justice** refers to perceived fairness in the outcomes we receive compared to our contributions and the outcomes and contributions of others. **Procedural justice,** on the other hand, refers to fairness of the procedures used to decide the distribution of resources. The Tasmanian workers experienced distributive injustice because co-workers from other parts of Australia earned much bigger paychecks for doing the same work. Depending on how this pay gap was determined and how the employer, United Group, addresses these grievances, the workers might also experience procedural injustice.

distributive justice
Perceived fairness in the individual's ratio of outcomes to contributions compared with a comparison other's ratio of outcomes to contributions.

procedural justice
Perceived fairness of the procedures used to decide the distribution of resources.

Equity Theory

The first thing we usually think about and experience in situations of injustice is distributive injustice–the belief (and its emotional response) that the pay and other outcomes we receive in the exchange relationship are unfair. What is considered "fair" varies with each person and situation. We apply an *equality principle* when we believe that everyone in the group should receive the same outcomes (such as when everyone at Rackspace gets free dinners with teammates). The *need principle* is applied when we believe that those with the greatest need should receive more outcomes than others with less need. The *equity principle* infers that people should be paid in proportion to their contribution. The equity principle is the most common distributive justice rule in organizational settings, so let's look at it in more detail.

To explain how the equity principle operates, OB scholars developed **equity theory,** which says that employees determine feelings of equity by comparing

equity theory
A theory explaining how people develop perceptions of fairness in the distribution and exchange of resources.

their own outcome/input ratio to the outcome/input ratio of some other person.[88] The *outcome/input ratio* is the value of the outcomes you receive divided by the value of the inputs you provide in the exchange relationship. Inputs include such things as skill, effort, reputation, performance, experience, and hours worked. Outcomes are what employees receive from the organization in exchange for the inputs, such as pay, promotions, recognition, preferential treatment, or preferred jobs in the future. In our example, the Tasmanian workers likely believed that collectively they and the interstate workers provided the same skills, effort, and hours of work, but the interstate workers received much more favorable outcomes–bigger paychecks.

Equity theory states that we compare our outcome/input ratio with that of a comparison other.[89] In our example, the Tasmanian workers compared themselves to other employees in the same job, namely, the interstate workers at the same work site. In other situations, the comparison other might be another person or group of people in other jobs (e.g., comparing your pay against how much the CEO is paid) or another organization. Some research suggests that employees frequently collect information on several referents to form a "generalized" comparison other.[90] For the most part, however, the comparison other varies from one person to the next and is not easily identifiable.

People develop feelings of equity or inequity by comparing their own outcome/input ratio with the comparison other's ratio. Exhibit 5.7 diagrams the three equity evaluations. In the underreward inequity situation–which the Tasmanian workers experienced–people believe their outcome/input ratio is lower than the comparison other's ratio. In the equity condition, people believe that their outcome/input ratio is similar to the ratio of the comparison other. In the overreward inequity condition, people believe their ratio of outcomes/inputs is higher than the comparison other's ratio. However, overreward inequity isn't as common as underreward inequity because people often change their perceptions to justify the favorable outcomes.

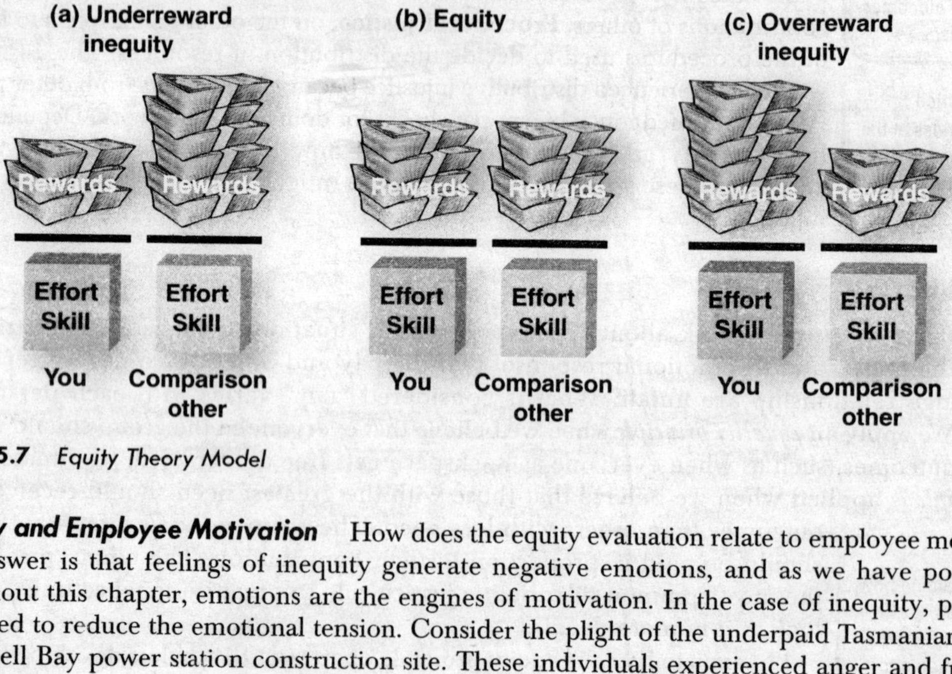

Exhibit 5.7 *Equity Theory Model*

Inequity and Employee Motivation How does the equity evaluation relate to employee motivation? The answer is that feelings of inequity generate negative emotions, and as we have pointed out throughout this chapter, emotions are the engines of motivation. In the case of inequity, people are motivated to reduce the emotional tension. Consider the plight of the underpaid Tasmanian workers at the Bell Bay power station construction site. These individuals experienced anger and frustration when they discovered how much less they earned than co-workers who came in from other places in

Australia. These emotions motivated the workers to contact their labor union to correct the problem. There are many other ways that people respond to feelings of underreward inequity. The most common responses (some of which are unethical) include:[91]

- *Reduce our inputs.* Perform the work more slowly, give fewer helpful suggestions, engage in less organizational citizenship behavior.
- *Increase our outcomes.* Ask for a pay increase directly or through a labor union, make unauthorized use of company resources.
- *Increase the comparison other's inputs.* Subtly ask the better-off co-worker to do a larger share of the work to justify his or her higher pay or other outcomes.
- *Reduce the comparison other's outcomes.* Ask the company to reduce the co-worker's pay.
- *Change our perceptions.* Believe that the co-worker really is doing more (e.g., working longer hours) or that the higher outcomes (e.g., better office) he or she receives really aren't so much better than what you get.
- *Change the comparison other.* Compare yourself to someone else closer to your situation (job duties, pay scale).
- *Leave the field.* Avoid thinking about the inequity by keeping away from the work site where the overpaid co-worker is located, take more sick leave, move to another department, or quit your job.

Although the seven responses to inequity remain the same, people who feel overreward inequity would, of course, act differently. Some overrewarded employees reduce their feelings of inequity by working harder. "What helps motivate me is that I look around the office and I see people who are working as hard or harder than I am. You feel guilty if you're not pulling your weight," says a New Jersey accountant. However, many overrewarded employees don't work harder. Some might encourage the underrewarded co-worker to work at a more leisurely pace. A common reaction, however, is that the overrewarded employee changes his or her perceptions to justify the more favorable outcomes. As author Pierre Berton once said: "I was underpaid for the first half of my life. I don't mind being overpaid for the second half."[92]

"O.K., if you can't see your way to giving me a pay raise, how about giving Parkerson a pay cut?"

Individual Differences: Equity Sensitivity Thus far, we have described equity theory as though everyone has the same feelings of inequity in a particular situation. The reality, however, is that people vary in their **equity sensitivity,** that is, their outcome/input preferences and reaction to various outcome/input ratios.[93] At one end of the equity sensitivity continuum are the "benevolents"–people who are tolerant of situations where they are underrewarded. They might still prefer equal outcome/input ratios, but they don't mind if others receive more than they do for the same inputs. In the middle are people who fit the standard equity theory model. These "equity sensitives" want their outcome/input ratio to be equal to the outcome/input ratio of the comparison other. Equity sensitives feel increasing inequity as the ratios become different. At the other end are the "entitleds." These people feel more comfortable in situations where they receive proportionately more than others. They might accept having the same outcome/input ratio as others, but they would prefer receiving more than others performing the same work.

equity sensitivity
An individual's outcome/input preferences and reaction to various outcome/input ratios.

Evaluating Equity Theory Equity theory is widely studied and quite successful at predicting various situations involving feelings of workplace injustice.[94] However, equity theory isn't so easy to put into practice because it doesn't identify the comparison other and doesn't indicate which inputs or outcomes are most valuable to each employee. The best solution here is for leaders to know their employees well enough to minimize the risk of inequity feelings. Open communication is also a key, enabling employees to let decision makers know when they feel decisions are unfair. A second problem is that equity theory accounts for only some of our feelings of fairness or justice in the workplace. Experts now say that procedural justice is at least as important as distributive justice.

Costco Wholesale CEO Keeps Executive Pay Equitable John Pierpont Morgan, who in the 1800s founded the financial giant now called J.P. Morgan Chase, warned that no CEO should earn more than 20 times an average worker's pay. That advice didn't stop James L. Dimon from earning an average of $40 million in total compensation for each of his first two years as the current CEO of J.P. Morgan Chase. Dimon took home more than 1,200 times the pay of the average employee in the United States. Costco Wholesale chief executive Jim Sinegal (shown in photo) thinks such a large wage gap is blatantly unfair and can lead to long-term employee motivation problems. "Having an individual who is making 100 or 200 or 300 times more than the average person working on the floor is wrong," says Sinegal, who cofounded the Issaquah, Washington, company. Even though Costco is one of the world's largest retailers, Sinegal's annual salary and bonus usually amount to less than $600,000. Stock options raised his latest total compensation to $3.2 million, which was much less than Costco's board wanted to pay him. Sinegal explained that receiving higher pay would not affect his motivation and performance. At the same time, Costco employees enjoy some of the highest pay rates in the retail industry (averaging $17 per hour).[95]

Procedural Justice

Recall that *procedural justice* refers to fairness of the procedures used to decide the distribution of resources. How do companies improve procedural justice?[96] A good way to start is by giving employees "voice" in the process; encourage them to present their facts and perspectives on the issue. Voice also provides a "value-expressive" function; employees tend to feel better after having an opportunity to speak their mind. Procedural justice is also higher when the decision maker is perceived as unbiased, relies on complete and accurate information, applies existing policies consistently, and has listened to all sides of the dispute. If employees still feel unfairness in the allocation of resources, their feelings tend to weaken if the company allows the employee to appeal the decision to a higher authority.

Finally, people usually feel less inequity when they are given a full explanation of the decision and their concerns are treated with respect. If employees believe a decision is unfair, refusing to explain how the decision was made could fuel their feelings of inequity. For instance, one study found that nonwhite nurses who experienced racism tended to file grievances only after experiencing disrespectful treatment in their attempt to resolve the racist situation. Another study reported that employees with repetitive strain injuries were more likely to file workers' compensation claims after experiencing disrespectful behavior from management. A third recent study noted that employees have stronger feelings of injustice when the manager has a reputation of treating people unfairly most of the time.[97]

Consequences of Procedural Injustice Procedural justice has a strong influence on a person's emotions and motivation. Employees tend to experience anger toward the source of the injustice, which generates various response behaviors that scholars categorize as either withdrawal or aggression.[98] Notice how these response behaviors are similar to the fight-or-flight responses described earlier in the chapter regarding situations that activate our drive to defend. Research suggests that being treated unfairly threatens our self-concept and social status, particularly when others see that we have been unjustly treated. Employees retaliate to restore their self-concept and reinstate their status and power in the relationship with the perpetrator of the injustice. Employees also engage in these counterproductive behaviors to educate the decision maker, thereby trying to minimize the likelihood of future injustices.[99]

Organizational Justice in Practice

One of the clearest lessons from equity theory is that we need to continually treat people fairly in the distribution of organizational rewards. Unfortunately, this is perhaps one of life's greatest challenges because most of us seem to have unique opinions about the value of inputs and outcomes. Decision makers need to carefully understand these dynamics along with the distribution rules–equity, equality, or need–that the organization wants to apply. From the procedural justice literature, we can see that justice also depends on whether employees believe the decision-making process follows a fair set of rules and whether they are personally treated fairly in that process.

In spite of the many challenges of creating justice in the workplace, managers can improve their procedural fairness through training programs. In one study, supervisors participated in role-play exercises to develop several procedural justice practices in the disciplinary process, such as maintaining the employee's privacy, giving employees some control over the process, avoiding arbitrariness, and exhibiting a supportive demeanor. Judges subsequently rated supervisors who received the procedural justice training as behaving more fairly than supervisors who did not receive the training. In another study, managers received procedural justice training through lectures, case studies, role-playing, and discussion. Three months later, subordinates of the trained managers had significantly higher organizational citizenship behaviors than the subordinates of managers who did not receive procedural justice training.[100] Overall it seems that justice can be improved in the workplace.

Chapter Summary

Motivation consists of the forces within a person that affect his or her direction, intensity, and persistence of voluntary behavior in the workplace. Drives (also called primary needs) are neural states that energize individuals to correct deficiencies or maintain an internal equilibrium. They are the "prime movers" of behavior, activating emotions that put us in a state of readiness to act. Needs—goal-directed forces that people experience—are shaped by the individual's self-concept (including personality and values), social norms, and past experience.

Maslow's needs hierarchy groups needs into a hierarchy of five levels and states that the lowest needs are initially most important but higher needs become more important as the lower ones are satisfied. Although very popular, the theory lacks research support, as does ERG theory, which attempted to overcome some of the limitations in Maslow's needs hierarchy. Both models assume that everyone has the same hierarchy, whereas the emerging evidence suggests that needs hierarchies vary from one person to the next according to their personal values.

McClelland's learned needs theory argues that needs can be strengthened through learning. The three needs studied in this respect have been need for achievement, need for power, and need for affiliation. Four-drive theory states that everyone has four innate drives—the drives to acquire, bond, learn, and defend. These drives activate emotions that we regulate through a skill set that considers social norms, past experience, and personal values. The main recommendation from four-drive theory is to ensure that individual jobs and workplaces provide a balanced opportunity to fulfill the four drives.

Expectancy theory states that work effort is determined by the perception that effort will result in a particular level of performance (E-to-P expectancy), the perception that a specific behavior or performance level will lead to specific outcomes (P-to-O expectancy), and the valences that the person feels for those outcomes. The E-to-P expectancy increases by improving the employee's ability and confidence to perform the job. The P-to-O expectancy increases by measuring performance accurately, distributing higher rewards to better performers, and showing employees that rewards are performance-based. Outcome valences increase by finding out what employees want and using these resources as rewards.

Goal setting is the process of motivating employees and clarifying their role perceptions by establishing performance objectives. Goals are more effective when they are specific, relevant, and challenging; have employee commitment; and are accompanied by meaningful feedback. Participative goal setting is important in some situations. Effective feedback is specific, relevant, timely, credible, and sufficiently frequent.

Organizational justice consists of distributive justice (perceived fairness in the outcomes we receive relative to our contributions and the outcomes and contributions of others) and procedural justice (fairness of the procedures used to decide the distribution of resources). Equity theory has four elements: outcome/input ratio, comparison other, equity evaluation, and consequences of inequity. The theory also explains what people are motivated to do when they feel inequitably treated. Companies need to consider not only equity of the distribution of resources but also fairness in the process of making resource allocation decisions.

Key Terms

balanced scorecard (BSC)
distributive justice
drives
employee engagement
equity sensitivity
equity theory
ERG theory
expectancy theory
four-drive theory
goal setting
Maslow's needs hierarchy theory
motivation
multisource (360-degree) feedback
need for achievement (nAch)
need for affiliation (nAff)
need for power (nPow)
needs
procedural justice
strength-based coaching

Critical Thinking Questions

1. Four-drive theory is conceptually different from Maslow's needs hierarchy (as well as ERG theory) in several ways. Describe these differences. At the same time, needs are based on drives, so the four drives should parallel the seven needs that Maslow identified (five in the hierarchy and two additional needs). Map Maslow's needs onto the four drives in four-drive theory.
2. Learned needs theory states that needs can be strengthened or weakened. How might a company strengthen the achievement needs of its management team?
3. Exhibit 5.1 illustrates how a person's drives and needs result in decisions and behavior. Explain where the expectancy theory of motivation fits into this model.
4. Use all three components of expectancy theory to explain why some employees are motivated to show up for work during a severe storm whereas others make no effort to leave their home.
5. Two friends who have just completed an organizational behavior course at another college inform you that employees must fulfill their need for self-esteem and social esteem before they can reach their full potential through self-actualization. What theory are these friends referring to? How does their statement differ from what you learned about that theory in this chapter?
6. Using your knowledge of the characteristics of effective goals, establish two meaningful goals related to your performance in this class.
7. Several service representatives are upset that the newly hired representative with no previous experience will be paid $3,000 a year above the usual starting salary in the pay range. The department manager explained that the new hire would not accept the entry-level rate, so the company raised the offer by $3,000. All five reps currently earn salaries near the top of the scale ($15,000 higher than the new recruit), although they all started at the minimum starting salary a few years earlier. Use equity theory to explain why the five service representatives feel inequity in this situation.
8. Organizational injustice can occur in the classroom as well as in the workplace. Identify classroom situations in which you experienced feelings of injustice. What can instructors do to maintain an environment that fosters both distributive and procedural justice?

CASE STUDY 5.1

VÊTEMENTS LTÉE

Vêtements Ltée is a chain of men's retail clothing stores located throughout the province of Quebec, Canada. Two years ago, the company introduced new incentive systems for both store managers and sales employees. Store managers in each store receive a salary with annual merit increases based on sales above targeted goals, store appearance, store inventory management, customer complaints, and several other performance measures. Some of this information (e.g., store appearance) is gathered during visits by senior management, while other information is based on company records (e.g., sales volume).

Sales employees are paid a fixed salary plus a commission based on the percentage of sales credited to that employee over the pay period. The commission represents about 30 percent of a typical paycheck and is intended to encourage employees to actively serve customers and to increase sales volume. Because returned merchandise is discounted from commissions, sales employees are discouraged from selling products that customers do not really want.

Soon after the new incentive systems were introduced, senior management began to receive complaints from store managers regarding the performance of their sales staff. They observed that sales employees tended to stand near the store entrance waiting to "tag" customers as their own. Occasionally, sales staff would argue over "ownership" of the customer. Managers were concerned that this aggressive behavior intimidated some customers. It also tended to leave some parts of the store unattended by staff.

Many managers were also concerned about inventory duties. Previously, sales staff would share responsibility for restocking inventory and completing inventory reorder forms. Under the new compensation system, however, few employees were willing to do these essential tasks. On several occasions, stores have faced stock shortages because merchandise was not stocked or reorder forms were not completed in a timely manner. Potential sales have suffered from empty shelves when plenty of merchandise was available in the back storeroom or at the warehouse. The company's new automatic inventory system could reduce some of these problems, but employees must still stock shelves and assist in other aspects of inventory management.

Store managers have tried to correct the inventory problem by assigning employees to inventory duty, but this has created resentment among the employees selected. Other managers have threatened sales staff with dismissal if they do not do their share of inventory management. This strategy has been somewhat effective when the manager is in the store, but staff members sneak back onto the floor when the manager is away. It has also hurt staff morale, particularly relations with the store manager.

To reduce the tendency of sales staff to hoard customers at the store entrance, some managers have assigned employees to specific areas of the store. This has also created some resentment among employees stationed in areas with less traffic or lower-priced merchandise. Some staff have openly complained of lower paychecks because they have been placed in a slow area of the store or have been given more than their share of inventory duties.

Discussion Questions

1. What symptom(s) in this case suggest that something has gone wrong?
2. What are the main causes of these symptoms?
3. What actions should Vêtements executives take to correct these problems?

CASE STUDY 5.2

MOTIVATING STAFF WHEN THE MONEY IS TIGHT

BusinessWeek

College grads aren't exactly beating a path to the hotel industry to get rich quick. New staff would be lucky to earn $40,000 in their first year. Yet when Marriott International visited the University of Delaware, it was able to attract recruits with something else that motivates–the chance to help run a hotel. In industries where the money is tight, companies are using other incentives to motivate people to join and stay with them. Many offer the lure of interesting work; others point out the work–life balance or "cool" workplace perks. A growing number of employers are also trying the carrot-and-stick approach by restructuring their 401(k) matches and vesting schedules to entice new employees to stay until the richer benefits kick in.

This *BusinessWeek* case study describes how companies with limited payroll budgets try to win the war for talent. Read the full text of this *BusinessWeek* article at www.mhhe.com/mcshane5e, and prepare for the discussion questions below.

Discussion Questions

1. This case study describes several different strategies for attracting and retaining new employees. On the basis of the four drives described in four-drive theory and the needs listed in Maslow's

needs hierarchy, identify the drives and needs associated with each of these initiatives. Which needs or drives seem to dominate in this article?

2. If Claire Pignataro and some other recruits earn less pay than people in other industries, to what extent would the attraction and retention initiatives described in this case study reduce feelings of inequity?

Source: L. Gerdes, "The Best Places to Launch a Career," *BusinessWeek*, 15 September 2008, p. 36.

CLASS EXERCISE 5.3

NEEDS PRIORITY EXERCISE

PURPOSE This class exercise is designed to help you understand the characteristics and contingencies of employee needs in the workplace.

INSTRUCTIONS (LARGE CLASS)

1. The table below lists in alphabetical order 14 characteristics of the job or work environment. Working alone, use the far-left column to rank-order these characteristics in terms of how important they are to you personally. Write in "1" beside the most important characteristic, "2" for the second most important, and so on through to "14" for the least important characteristic on this list.

Importance to *you*	What HR managers believe are important to employees	
______	______	Autonomy and independence
______	______	Benefits (health care, dental, etc.)
______	______	Career development opportunities
______	______	Communication between employees and senior management
______	______	Compensation/pay
______	______	Feeling safe in the work environment
______	______	Flexibility to balance work–life issues
______	______	Job security
______	______	Job-specific training
______	______	Management recognition of employee job performance
______	______	Opportunities to use skills and abilities
______	______	Organization's commitment to professional development
______	______	Relationship with immediate supervisor
______	______	The work itself

2. In the second column, rank-order these characteristics in the order that you think human resource managers believe they are important for their employees.
3. The instructor will ask students, by a show of hands (or use of classroom technology), to identify the top-ranked options.
4. The instructor will provide results of a recent large-scale survey of employees. When these results are presented, identify the reasons for any noticeable differences. Relate the differences to your understanding of the emerging view of employee needs and drives in work settings.

INSTRUCTIONS (SMALL CLASS)

Same as above for steps 1 to 4.

5. Students are assigned to teams, where they compare their rank-order results and explain their ranking. Rationales for different rankings should be noted and discussed with the entire class. Students should pay close attention to different needs, self-concepts, and various forms of diversity (culture, profession, age, etc.) to identify possible explanations for any variation of results across students.

TEAM EXERCISE 5.4

A QUESTION OF FEEDBACK

PURPOSE This exercise is designed to help you understand the importance of feedback, including problems that occur with imperfect communication in the feedback process.

MATERIALS The instructor will distribute a few pages of exhibits to one person on each team. The other students will require a pencil with eraser and blank paper. Movable chairs and tables in a large area are helpful.

INSTRUCTIONS (SMALL CLASS)

1. The class is divided into pairs of students. Each pair is ideally located in a private area, where they are away from other students and one person can write. One student is given the pages of exhibits from the instructor. The other student in each pair is not allowed to see these exhibits.
2. The student holding the materials will describe each of the exhibits and the other student's task is to accurately replicate each exhibit. The pair of students can compare the replication with the original at the end of each drawing. They may also switch roles for each exhibit, if they wish. If roles are switched, the instructor must distribute exhibits separately to each student so that they are not seen by the other person. Each exhibit has a different set of limitations, as described below:

- *Exhibit 1.* The student describing the exhibit cannot look at the other student or his or her diagram. The student drawing the exhibit cannot speak or otherwise communicate with the person describing the exhibit.
- *Exhibit 2.* The student describing the exhibit may look at the other student's diagram. However, he or she may say only "yes" or "no," when the student drawing the diagram asks a specific question. In other words, the person presenting the information can use only these words for feedback and can use them only when asked a question by the student doing the drawing.
- *Exhibit 3*: (optional, if time permits). The student describing the exhibit may look at the other student's diagram and may provide any feedback at any time to the person replicating the exhibit.

3. The class will gather to analyze this exercise. This may include discussion on the importance of feedback and the characteristics of effective feedback for individual motivation and learning.

INSTRUCTIONS (LARGE CLASS)

Some parts of this exercise are possible in large classes. Here is one variation:

1. Students are asked to prepare for the exercise by having a pencil and paper ready.
2. One student volunteers to provide instructions from the front of the class regarding Exhibit 1. The volunteer receives the first exhibit and describes it to the class, while other students try to replicate the exhibit. When finished, the exhibit is shown to the class on a transparency or computer projection.
3. For Exhibit 2, one student volunteers to provide instructions and a few other students serve as feedback helpers. The helpers have a copy of Exhibit 2, which they may view, but it cannot be shown to students doing the drawing. The helpers are dispersed to various parts of the room to provide feedback to a group of students under their care (if the class has 100 students, the exercise might have 5 helpers, each responsible for feedback to 20 students). Helpers can say only "yes" or "no," but they may point to specific locations of the student's drawing when uttering these words (because these helpers provide feedback to many students). Throughout this activity, the student describing the exhibit must *not* stop his or her description. After the speaker has finished and the drawings are completed, the helpers might be asked to select the most accurate drawing among those within their domain. The students who drew the accurate depictions might be asked to discuss their experience with feedback.

SELF-ASSESSMENT 5.5

NEED-STRENGTH QUESTIONNAIRE

Although everyone has the same innate drives, our secondary or learned needs vary on the basis of our self-concept. This self-assessment provides an estimate of your need strength on selected secondary needs. Read each of the statements on next page and check the response that you believe best reflects your position regarding each statement. Then use the scoring key in Appendix B at the end of the book to calculate your results. To receive a meaningful estimate of your need strength, you need to answer each item honestly and with reflection on your personal experiences. Class discussion will focus on the meaning of the needs measured in this self-assessment as well as their relevance in the workplace.

SELF-ASSESSMENT 5.6

MEASURING YOUR GROWTH-NEED STRENGTH

Abraham Maslow's need hierarchy theory distinguished between deficiency needs and growth needs. Deficiency needs become activated when unfulfilled, such as the need for food or belongingness. Growth needs, on the other hand, continue to develop even when temporarily fulfilled. Maslow identified self-actualization as the only category of growth needs. Research has found that Maslow's needs hierarchy theory overall doesn't fit reality but that specific elements, such as the

Personal Needs Questionnaire

How accurately do each of the following statements describe you?	Very accurate description of me	Moderately accurate	Neither accurate nor inaccurate	Moderately inaccurate	Very inaccurate description of me
1. I would rather be myself than be well thought of.	☐	☐	☐	☐	☐
2. I'm the type of person who never gives up.	☐	☐	☐	☐	☐
3. When the opportunity occurs, I want to be in charge.	☐	☐	☐	☐	☐
4. I try not to say things that others don't like to hear.	☐	☐	☐	☐	☐
5. I find it difficult to talk about my ideas if they are contrary to group opinion.	☐	☐	☐	☐	☐
6. I tend to take control of things.	☐	☐	☐	☐	☐
7. I am not highly motivated to succeed.	☐	☐	☐	☐	☐
8. I usually disagree with others only if I know my friends will back me up.	☐	☐	☐	☐	☐
9. I try to be the very best at what I do.	☐	☐	☐	☐	☐
10. I seldom make excuses or apologize for my behavior.	☐	☐	☐	☐	☐
11. If anyone criticizes me, I can take it.	☐	☐	☐	☐	☐
12. I try to outdo others.	☐	☐	☐	☐	☐
13. I seldom change my opinion when people disagree with me.	☐	☐	☐	☐	☐
14. I try to achieve more than what others have accomplished.	☐	☐	☐	☐	☐
15. To get along and be liked, I tend to be what people expect me to be.	☐	☐	☐	☐	☐

Sources: Adapted from instruments described and/or presented in L. R. Goldberg, J. A. Johnson, H. W. Eber, R. Hogan, M. C. Ashton, C. R. Cloninger, and H. C. Gough, "The International Personality Item Pool and the Future of Public-Domain Personality Measures," *Journal of Research in Personality* 40 (2006), pp. 84–96; H. J. Martin, "A Revised Measure of Approval Motivation and Its Relationship to Social Desirability," *Journal of Personality Assessment* 48 (1984), pp. 508–519.

concept of growth needs, remain valid concepts. This self-assessment is designed to estimate your level of growth-need strength. This instrument asks you to consider what it is about a job that is most important to you. Please indicate which of the two jobs you personally would prefer if you had to make a choice between them. In answering each question, assume that everything else about the jobs is the same. Pay attention only to the characteristics actually listed.

SELF-ASSESSMENT 5.7

YOUR EQUITY SENSITIVITY

Some people experience stronger or weaker feelings of unfairness in specific situations. This self-assessment estimates your level of equity sensitivity. Read each of the statements in this questionnaire, and indicate the response that you believe best reflects your position regarding each statement. This exercise should be completed alone so that you assess yourself honestly, without concerns of social comparison. Class discussion will focus on equity theory and the effect of equity sensitivity on perceptions of fairness in the workplace.

Strange as this may seem, one of Europe's most successful banks doesn't believe in budgets or centralized financial targets. Executives at Svenska Handelsbanken AB learned decades ago that these costly controls from the head office motivate dysfunctional behavior rather than customer-focused performance. Therefore, the Swedish bank gives local managers and their staff autonomy to run their local branches as their own. "Nobody knows the local market or the customers better than our branch managers and their staff," explains Handelsbanken CEO Pär Boman.

Svenska Handelsbanken is one of the most successful banks in Europe, in part because it engages employees through financial rewards, motivating jobs, and empowerment.

Even with 10,000 employees across more than 450 branches in 21 countries (mostly Nordic countries and the United Kingdom), Handelsbanken leaves most decisions to branch managers and staff. "We decide which of the bank's products to offer and at what price," says a Handelsbanken branch manager. "My staff are fully involved in the preparation of the work program (the branch's action plan)." Branch managers also decide how to advertise products, how many people to employ and at what salary, and how much to pay for property leases. Only mutual fund management, high-level risk decisions, office equipment, and the bank's computer systems are centralized.

Handelsbanken further motivates staff by distributing a monthly report card on each branch's cost-to-income ratio, profit per employee, and total profit. Branch performance is also compared to that of competing banks in the area. "[We] find that our people are driven by their urge to show a better result than their competitors—to be above average," says Jan Wallander, the former Handelsbanken CEO who transformed the 140-year-old bank in the 1970s.

This competitive culture apparently does not undermine cooperation because employees are rewarded through a unique form of profit sharing and employee stock ownership, not individual or branch performance. In years when Handelsbanken is more profitable than the average of competing banks, it transfers one-third of the excess profits to an employee fund (called the Octogonen Foundation). Everyone receives the same number of shares in the fund for each year of service, which can be cashed out at 60 years of age. About 75 percent of the fund is invested in Handelsbanken. It currently holds 10 percent of the bank's stock, making employees the bank's largest shareholder.[1]

6

APPLIED PERFORMANCE PRACTICES

Learning Objectives

After reading this chapter, you should be able to:

1. Discuss the advantages and disadvantages of the four reward objectives.
2. Identify several team- and organizational-level performance-based rewards.
3. Describe five ways to improve reward effectiveness.
4. Discuss the advantages and disadvantages of job specialization.
5. Diagram the job characteristics model of job design.
6. Identify three strategies for improving employee motivation through job design.
7. Define *empowerment* and identify strategies that support empowerment.
8. Describe the five elements of self-leadership.
9. Identify specific personal and work environment influences on self-leadership.

Handelsbanken's success is a testament to the organizational behavior benefits of rewards, job design, empowerment, and self-leadership. The company relies on prudent reward systems, offers jobs with high motivating potential, expects staff members to manage themselves, and delegates power to branches, resulting in high levels of employee empowerment. This chapter looks at each of these applied performance practices. The chapter begins by examining the meaning of money. This is followed by an overview of financial reward practices, including the different types of rewards and how to implement rewards effectively. Next, we look at the dynamics of job design, including specific job design strategies for motivating employees. We then consider the elements of empowerment, as well as conditions that support empowerment. The final part of the chapter explains how employees manage their own performance through self-leadership.

Learning Objectives

After reading this section, you should be able to:

1. Discuss the advantages and disadvantages of the four reward objectives.
2. Identify several team- and organizational-level performance-based rewards.
3. Describe five ways to improve reward effectiveness.

The Meaning of Money in the Workplace

Rewarding people with money is one of the oldest and certainly the most widespread applied performance practices. At the most basic level, money and other financial rewards represent a form of exchange; employees provide their labor, skill, and knowledge in return for money and benefits from the organization. From this perspective, money and related rewards align employee goals with organizational goals. This concept of economic exchange can be found across cultures. The word for *pay* in Malaysian and Slovak means "to replace a loss"; in Hebrew and Swedish it means "making equal."[2]

However, money is much more than an object of compensation for an employee's contribution to organizational objectives. Money relates to our needs, our emotions, and our self-concept. It is a symbol of achievement and status, a reinforcer and motivator, and a source of enhanced or reduced anxiety.[3] According to one source, "Money is probably the most emotionally meaningful object in contemporary life: only food and sex are its close competitors as common carriers of such strong and diverse feelings, significance, and strivings."[4]

The meaning of money varies considerably from one person to the next.[5] Studies report that money may be viewed as a symbol of status and prestige, as a source of security, as a source of evil, or as a source of anxiety or feelings of inadequacy. It is considered a "taboo" topic in many social settings. It has been described both as a "tool" (i.e., money is valued because it is an instrument for acquiring other things of value) and as a "drug" (i.e., money is an object of addictive value in itself). One large-scale study revealed that money generates a variety of emotions, most of which are negative, such as anxiety, depression, anger, and helplessness.[6] A widely studied model of money attitudes suggests that people have a strong "money ethic" when they believe that money is not evil; that it is a symbol of achievement, respect, and power; and that it should be budgeted carefully. These attitudes toward money influence an individual's ethical conduct, organizational citizenship, and many other behaviors and attitudes.[7]

The meaning of money seems to differ between men and women. One large-scale survey revealed that in almost all 43 countries studied men attach more importance or value to money than do women. Men particularly tend to view money as a symbol of power and status.[8] Personal and cultural values influence the meaning of money. People in countries with high power distance (such as China and Japan) tend to have a high respect and priority for money, whereas people in countries with a strong egalitarian culture (such as Denmark, Austria, and Israel) are discouraged from openly talking about money or displaying their personal wealth. One study suggests that Swiss culture values saving money whereas Italian culture places more value on spending it.[9]

Many experts now believe that money is a much more important motivator than was previously believed, more because of its inherent or symbolic value than because of what it can buy.[10] Philosopher John Stuart Mill made this observation 150 years ago when he wrote: "The love of money is not only one of the strongest moving forces of human life, but money is, in many cases, desired in and for itself."[11] One recent study found that people who are more highly paid have higher job performance because the higher paycheck makes them feel more valued in the organization (i.e., they have a more positive self-concept). Others have pointed out that the symbolic value of money and other rewards is particularly motivational when a few people receive more than others. This is because the higher reward gives beneficiaries a degree of social distinction, which is consistent with the drive to acquire, introduced in Chapter 5.

Overall, current organizational behavior knowledge indicates that money is much more than a means of exchange between employer and employee. It fulfills a variety of needs, influences emotions, and shapes or represents a person's self-concept. This is important to remember when the employer is distributing financial rewards in the workplace. Over the next few pages, we look at various reward practices and how to improve the implementation of performance-based rewards.

FINANCIAL REWARD PRACTICES

Financial rewards come in many forms, which can be organized into the four specific objectives identified in Exhibit 6.1: membership and seniority, job status, competencies, and performance.

Membership- and Seniority-Based Rewards

Membership-based and seniority-based rewards (sometimes called "pay for pulse") represent the largest part of most paychecks. Some employee benefits, such as free or discounted meals in the company cafeteria, remain the same for everyone, whereas others increase with seniority. For example, legislative staff in Nevada with eight years or more service receive an additional $150 annually. This jumps to $2,350 for those with 30 years or more service. Many Asian companies distribute a "13th month" bonus, which every employee expects to receive each year no matter how well the company performed over the previous year. Although many Japanese firms have shifted to performance-based pay, others have retained or returned to wage scales based on the employee's age. "Even during that period [when the employee's performance is below expectations], we raise salaries according to their age," says the president of Tokai Rubber Industries Ltd., which returned to age-based salaries after discarding a short-lived performance-based pay plan.[12]

These membership- and seniority-based rewards potentially attract job applicants (particularly those who desire predictable income) and reduce turnover. However, they do not directly motivate job performance; on the contrary, they discourage poor performers from seeking work better suited to their abilities. Instead, the good performers are lured to better-paying jobs. Some of these rewards are also "golden handcuffs"– they discourage employees from quitting because of deferred bonuses or generous benefits that are not available elsewhere. However golden handcuffs potentially weaken job performance because they generate continuance rather than affective commitment (see Chapter 4).

Reward objective	Sample rewards	Advantages	Disadvantages
Membership/seniority	• Fixed pay • Most employee benefits • Paid time off	• May attract applicants • Minimizes stress of insecurity • Reduces turnover	• Doesn't directly motivate performance • May discourage poor performers from leaving • Golden handcuffs may undermine performance
Job status	• Promotion-based pay increase • Status-based benefits	• Tries to maintain internal equity • Minimizes pay discrimination • Motivates employees to compete for promotions	• Encourages hierarchy, which may increase costs and reduce responsiveness • Reinforces status differences • Motivates job competition and exaggerated job worth
Competencies	• Pay increase based on competency • Skill-based pay	• Improves workforce flexibility • Tends to improve quality • Is consistent with employability	• Subjective measurement of competencies • Skill-based pay plans are expensive
Task performance	• Commissions • Merit pay • Gainsharing • Profit sharing • Stock options	• Motivates task performance • Attracts performance-oriented applicants • Organizational rewards create an ownership culture • Pay variability may avoid layoffs during downturns	• May weaken job content motivation • May distance reward giver from receiver • May discourage creativity • Tends to address symptoms, not underlying causes, of behavior

Exhibit 6.1 *Reward Objectives, Advantages, and Disadvantages*

Job Status-Based Rewards

job evaluation
Systematically rating the worth of jobs within an organization by measuring their required skill, effort, responsibility, and working conditions.

Almost every organization rewards employees to some extent on the basis of the status or worth of the jobs they occupy. **Job evaluation** is widely used to assess the worth or status of each job. Most job evaluation methods give higher value to jobs that require more skill and effort, have more responsibility, and have more difficult working conditions.[13] Aside from receiving higher pay, employees with more valued jobs sometimes receive larger offices, company-paid vehicles, and other perks.

Job status–based rewards try to improve feelings of fairness by assigning higher pay to people working in jobs with higher value to the organization. These rewards also motivate employees to compete for promotions. However, at a time when companies are trying to be more cost-efficient and responsive to the external environment, job status–based rewards potentially do the opposite by encouraging a bureaucratic hierarchy. These rewards also reinforce a status mentality, whereas Generation-X and Generation-Y employees expect a more egalitarian workplace. Furthermore, status-based pay potentially motivates employees to compete with each other for higher-status jobs and to raise the value of their own jobs by exaggerating job duties and hoarding resources.[14]

Competency-Based Rewards

Over the past two decades, many companies have shifted reward priorities from job status to skills, knowledge, and other competencies that lead to superior performance. The most common competency-based reward practices identify a set of competencies (adaptability, team orientation, technical expertise, leadership, etc.) relevant to all jobs within a broad pay group and give employees within each group higher pay rates as they improve those competencies.[15] In other words, rather than paying people for the specific job that they perform, competency-based plans pay people on the basis of their assessed skills and knowledge, whether or not they actually use those competencies in their current job duties. Job status–based pay has not been completely abandoned, because the broad pay groups reflect job status (e.g., the technical staff pay range is lower than the senior executive pay range). Within those pay groups, however, employees are rewarded for skills, knowledge, and other competencies. This reward system is sometimes known as *broadbanding* because several jobs with narrow pay ranges are grouped together into a much broader pay range.

Skill-based pay plans are a more specific variation of competency-based rewards in which people receive higher pay based on their mastery of measurable skills. For example, technicians at the City of Flagstaff, Arizona, are paid for the number of skill blocks they have mastered. New hires must complete the first skill block during probation, and they can eventually progress through the five other skill blocks to earn almost twice the base (single skill block) salary. Technicians demonstrate proficiency in a skill block through in-house or formal certification assessments.[16]

Competency-based rewards motivate employees to learn new skills.[17] This tends to improve organizational effectiveness by creating a more flexible workforce; more employees are multiskilled for performing a variety of jobs, and they are more adaptive to embracing new practices in a dynamic environment. Product or service quality also tends to improve because employees with multiple skills are more likely to understand the work process and know how to improve it. However, competency-based pay plans have not always worked out as well as promised by their advocates. They are often overdesigned, making it difficult to communicate these plans to employees. Competency definitions are often vague, which raises questions about fairness when employers are relying on these definitions to award pay increases. Skill-based pay systems measure specific skills, so they are usually more objective. However, they are expensive because employees spend more time learning new tasks.[18]

Performance-Based Rewards

Performance-based rewards have existed since Babylonian days 4,000 years ago, but their popularity has increased dramatically over the past couple of decades.[19] Here is an overview of some of the most popular individual, team, and organizational performance-based rewards.

Individual Rewards Many employees receive individual bonuses or awards for accomplishing a specific task or exceeding annual performance goals. Real estate agents and other salespeople typically earn *commissions,* in which their pay increases with sales volume. Piece-rate systems reward employees according to the number of units produced. For example, lawn care staff at The Lawn Mowgul in Dallas, Texas, earn a form of piece rate (called "piecemeal") that is based on the number of yards cut;

housekeeping staff in some British hotels earn a piece rate for each room they clean (about $3 per room). Hong Kong communications company PCCW rewards employees with up to one month's pay if they exceed their performance goals.[20]

Team Rewards Over the past two decades, many organizations have shifted their focus from individuals to teams. Consequently, employees in these companies are finding that a larger part of their total paycheck is determined by team performance. At Forrest General Hospital in Hattiesburg, Mississippi, for example, all employees in patient accounts and registration receive a bonus if the team meets its time-of-service and self-pay collections targets. "[The team incentive] is set up so that either everyone gets the incentive, or no one gets it," explains Forrest General Hospital's director of revenue cycle.[21] One of the most successful companies to apply team (as well as organizational) rewards is Nucor, Inc. As Connections 6.1 describes, America's largest steelmaker rewards teams for higher output and applies financial penalties if their output falls below satisfactory quality.

gainsharing plan
A team-based reward that calculates bonuses from the work unit's cost savings and productivity improvement.

Gainsharing plans are a form of team-based compensation that calculates bonuses from the work unit's cost savings and productivity improvement. Whole Foods Market uses this form of team incentive. Each department within a store is run by a team with a monthly payroll budget. If payroll money is unspent at the end of the month, the surplus is divided among members of that Whole Foods Market team.[22] American hospitals have cautiously introduced a form of gainsharing whereby physicians and medical staff in a medical unit (cardiology, orthopedics, etc.) are collectively rewarded for cost reductions in surgery and patient care. The cost reductions occur in two ways: (1) by standardizing purchasing decisions so that hospitals can negotiate larger supplier discounts on devices and medicines and (2) by reducing discretionary use of products. One recent study found that introduction of gainsharing in six hospital cardiology units reduced costs per patient by more than 7 percent. Almost all of this cost reduction occurred through lower prices (likely due to standardized purchasing) rather than reduced use of supplies.[23] More generally, gainsharing plans tend to improve team dynamics, knowledge sharing, and pay satisfaction. They also create a reasonably strong link between effort and performance because much of the cost reduction and labor efficiency is within the team's control.[24]

Organizational Rewards Along with using individual and team-based rewards, many firms rely on organizational-level rewards to motivate employees. Some firms reward all staff members for achieving challenging sales goals or other indicators of organizational performance. These rewards are usually financial bonuses, but a few firms reward employees with travel. At Staffing Alternatives, all 25 employees and their spouses or partners were treated to a three-day vacation at Walt Disney World. "We wanted it to reward everybody for their hard work during the year and make it something that they would remember," says Christopher Moyes, CEO of the staffing services business in North Brunswick, New Jersey. Staffing Alternatives employees also receive quarterly bonuses based on both organizational and individual performance.[25]

employee stock ownership plan (ESOP)
A reward system that encourages employees to buy company stock.

Employee stock ownership plans (ESOPs) encourage employees to buy company stock, usually at a discounted price or through a no-interest loan. The financial incentive occurs as dividends and market appreciation of the stock. Due to tax concessions in the United States and a few other countries, most ESOPs are designed as retirement plans. Sears Roebuck and UPS were two of the earliest companies to introduce ESOPs. Today, more than 20 percent of Americans working in the private sector hold stock in their companies.[26] Handelsbanken, the Swedish bank described at the beginning of this chapter, has a unique ESOP in which employees own company

6.1 CONNECTIONS

Nucor Rewards the Team

Two decades ago, Nucor was an upstart in an industry dominated by Bethlehem Steel, National Steel, and other mega-firms. Today, battered by global competition, two-thirds of American steel companies have disappeared or are under bankruptcy protection. Nucor, on the other hand, has become the largest steel company in America and the tenth largest in the world. Although it now employs more than 12,000 people (most in the United States), Nucor remains nimble, highly competitive, and profitable.

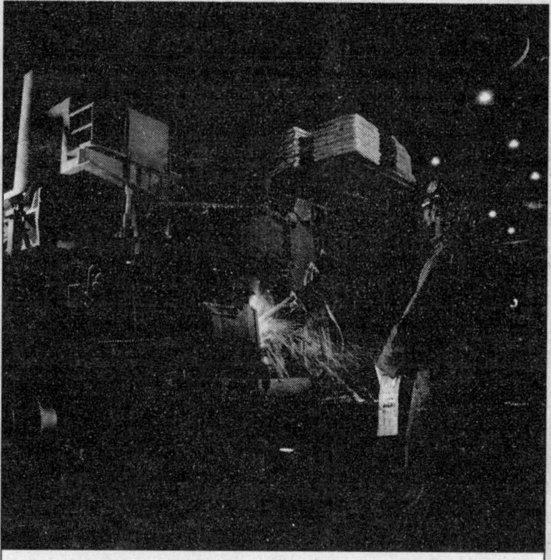

Nucor's high-performance culture is fueled by team and organizational rewards representing up to two-thirds of annual pay.

What's Nucor's secret to success? One of the most important factors is its performance-based reward system. In recent years, the average Nucor steelworker has annually earned more than $80,000, but most of that pay is variable—it depends on team and organization performance. "We pay a real low base wage, but high bonuses on a weekly basis," explains a Nucor executive. "The bonuses are based on the quality and tons produced and shipped through a team. The average base pay is about $9 to $10 an hour, but they could get an additional $15 to $20 an hour for bonuses." These bonuses are paid to everyone on the team, which ranges from 12 to 20 people. Nucor does not limit the amount of bonus a team can receive, but it is usually equal or double the base pay.

Nucor's team bonus system relies on quality of output, not just quantity. If employees catch a bad batch of steel before it leaves their work area, that tonnage of product is subtracted from the team's weekly bonus calculation. If the bad batch makes its way to the next internal customer or shipping department within the minimill, two times the tonnage of bad product is subtracted from the team's bonus. And if the bad product makes its way to the customer, the team loses a bonus amount equal to three times that amount of product.

Production employees have the highest variable pay, but Nucor's professional and administrative employees also earn bonuses representing about one-third of their salary that are based on their division's performance. In addition to these team and division rewards, Nucor employees receive an annual profit-sharing bonus representing 10 percent of the company's operating profit. This has been as much as $18,000 per employee in some recent years.[27]

stock through an independent retirement fund. Phelps County Bank in Rolla, Missouri, operates another form of ESOP. Each year, the employee-owned bank contributes stock equal to 15 percent of each employee's salary into her or his ESOP account. The stock is vested (legally transferred) to the employee after seven years of service. "Stock ownership was the vehicle that really made us focus on what it meant to be an owner," says Phelps County Bank CEO Bill Marshall.[28]

stock option
A reward system that gives employees the right to purchase company stock at a future date at a predetermined price.

While ESOPs involve purchasing company shares, **stock options** give employees the right to purchase shares from the company at a future date at a predetermined price up to a fixed expiration date. For example, an employer might offer employees the right to purchase 100 shares at $50 at any time between two and six years from now. If the stock price is, say, $60 two years later, employees could earn $10 per share from these options, or they could wait up to six years for the stock price to rise further. If the stock never rises above $50 during that time, they are "out of the money" and employees would just let the options expire. The intention of stock options is to motivate employees to make the company more profitable, thereby raising the company's stock price and enabling them to reap the value above the exercise price of the stock options.

profit-sharing plan
A reward system that pays bonuses to employees on the basis of the previous year's level of corporate profits.

Profit-sharing plans, a fourth organizational-level reward, calculate bonuses from the previous year's level of corporate profits. As mentioned in Connections 6.1, Nucor employees earn a profit-sharing bonus on top of their fixed pay and team bonuses. Each year, the steelmaker distributes 10 percent of its earnings before taxes to employees, a percentage that recently amounted to more than $18,000 per employee. Handelsbanken also has a profit-sharing plan, in which a share of profits above the average profitability of other banks is deposited into the employees' retirement plan.

Evaluating Organizational-Level Rewards How effective are organizational-level rewards? Research indicates that ESOPs and stock options tend to create an "ownership culture" in which employees feel aligned with the organization's success.[29] Profit sharing tends to create less ownership culture, but it has the advantage of automatically adjusting employee compensation with the firm's prosperity, thereby reducing the need for layoffs or negotiated pay reductions during recessions.

The main problem with ESOPs, stock options, and profit sharing is that employees often perceive a weak connection between individual effort and corporate profits or the value of company shares. Even in small firms, the company's stock price or profitability is influenced by economic conditions, competition, and other factors beyond the employee's immediate control. This low individual performance-to-outcome expectancy weakens employee motivation. Another concern is that some companies use ESOPs as a replacement for employee pension plans. This is a risky strategy because the pension funds lack diversification. If the company goes bankrupt, employees lose both their jobs and a large portion of their retirement nest egg.[30]

Improving Reward Effectiveness

Performance-based rewards have come under attack over the years for discouraging creativity, distancing management from employees, distracting employees from the meaningfulness of the work itself, and being quick fixes that ignore the true causes of poor performance. While these issues have kernels of truth under specific circumstances, they do not necessarily mean that we should abandon performance-based pay. On the contrary, as the high-performance work practices perspective of organizational effectiveness advises (see Chapter 1), top-performing companies are more likely to have performance-based rewards.[31] Reward systems do motivate most employees, but only under the right conditions. Here are some of the more important strategies for improving reward effectiveness.

Link Rewards to Performance Behavior modification theory (Chapter 3) and expectancy theory (Chapter 5) both recommend that employees with better performance should be rewarded more than those with poorer performance. Unfortunately, as was noted in Chapter 5, this simple principle seems to be unusually difficult to apply. Few employees see a relationship between job performance and the amount of pay they and co-workers receive. A Gallup survey at an American telecommunications company revealed an equally devastating observation: Management's evaluation of 5,000 customer service employees was uncorrelated with the performance ratings that customers gave those employees. "Whatever behaviors the managers were evaluating were irrelevant to the customers," concluded Gallup executives. "The managers might as well have been rating the employees' shoe sizes, for all the customers cared."[32]

How can companies improve the pay–performance linkage? Inconsistencies and bias can be minimized by introducing gainsharing, ESOPs, and other plans that use objective performance measures. Where subjective measures of performance are necessary, companies should rely on multiple sources of information. Companies also need to apply rewards soon after the performance occurs, and in a large-enough dose (such as a bonus rather than a pay increase), so that employees experience positive emotions when they receive the reward.[33]

Ensure That Rewards Are Relevant Companies need to align rewards with performance within the employee's control. The more employees see a "line of sight" between their daily actions and the reward, the more they are motivated to improve performance. Wal-Mart applies this principle by awarding bonuses to top executives on the basis of the company's overall performance, whereas frontline employees earn bonuses based on the sales volume of the store where they work. Reward systems also need to correct for situational factors. Salespeople in one region may have higher sales because the economy is stronger there than elsewhere, so sales bonuses need to be adjusted for such economic factors.

Use Team Rewards for Interdependent Jobs Team rewards should be used rather than individual rewards when employees work in highly interdependent jobs because it is difficult to measure individual performance in these situations. Nucor relies on team-based bonuses for this reason; steelmaking is a team effort, so employees earn bonuses based on team performance. Team rewards also encourage cooperation, which is more important when work is highly interdependent. A third benefit of team rewards is that they tend to support employee preferences for team-based work. One concern, however, is that employees (particularly the most productive employees) in the United States and many other low-collectivism cultures prefer rewards based on their individual performance rather than team performance.[34]

Ensure That Rewards Are Valued It seems obvious that rewards work best when they are valued. Yet companies sometimes make false assumptions about what employees want, with unfortunate consequences. The solution, of course, is to ask employees what they value. Campbell Soup did this a few years ago at its distribution centers in Canada. Executives thought the employees would ask for more money in a special team reward program. Instead, distribution staff said the most valued reward was a leather jacket with the Campbell Soup logo on the back. The leather jackets cost much less yet were worth much more than the financial bonus the company had intended to distribute.[35]

Watch Out for Unintended Consequences Performance-based reward systems sometimes have an unexpected–and undesirable–effect on employee behaviors. Consider the pizza company that decided to reward its drivers for on-time delivery. The plan got more hot pizzas to customers on time, but it also increased the accident rates of the company's drivers because the incentive motivated them to drive recklessly.[36] Global Connections 6.2 describes a few other examples in which reward systems had unintended consequences. The solution here is to carefully think through the consequences of rewards and, where possible, test incentives in a pilot project before applying them across the organization.

Financial rewards come in many forms and, as mentioned at the outset of this section, influence employees in complex ways. But money isn't the only thing that motivates people to join an

6.2 GLOBAL CONNECTIONS

When Rewards Go Wrong

There is an old saying that "what gets rewarded gets done." But what companies reward isn't always what they had intended their employees to do. Here are a few dramatic examples of how performance-based rewards produce unintended consequences:

UBS suffered a $37 *billion* loss in one year because its bonus system rewarded staff for short-term revenue without imposing any penalties for buying high-risk securities to generate that revenue.

- UBS AG recently lost more than $37 billion (yes, *billion*) in one year because of its exposure to high-risk mortgage securities. The massive loss forced Switzerland's largest bank to lay off staff, close down a hedge fund business, borrow from foreign governments, and suffer an exodus of clients. Many financial institutions suffered horrendous losses (and a few went bankrupt) during this subprime mortgage crisis, but UBS openly acknowledged that a faulty reward system was partly responsible. Specifically, its bonus plan motivated its traders to generate short-term revenue without penalizing them for exposing the bank to high-risk investments. "Essentially, bonuses were measured against gross revenue with no formal account taken of the quality or sustainability of those earnings," says a UBS report submitted to the Swiss banking regulator.[37]
- Stock options are supposed to motivate executives to improve corporate performance. Instead, they seem to motivate some leaders to use dodgy accounting practices to distort or misrepresent the company's performance. One recent study found that financial misrepresentation was associated with executive stock options but not with bonuses or other forms of executive compensation. Another report estimated that for every 25 percent increase in stock options awarded to executives, the risk of fraud rises by 68 percent. Companies with the largest corporate frauds in recent years have, on average, eight times as many options as similar companies that did not experience fraud.[38]
- Donnelly Mirrors (now part of Magna International) introduced a gainsharing plan that motivated employees to reduce labor but not material costs. Employees at the automobile parts manufacturer knew they worked faster with sharp grinding wheels, so they replaced the expensive diamond wheels more often. This action reduced labor costs, thereby giving employees the gainsharing bonus. However, the labor savings were more than offset by much higher costs for diamond grinding wheels.[39]
- Integrated steel companies often rewarded managers for increased labor efficiency. The lower the labor-hours required to produce a ton of steel, the larger the manager's bonus. Unfortunately, steel firms usually didn't count the work of outside contractors in the formula, so the reward system motivated managers to hire expensive contractors in the production process. By employing more contractors, the true cost of production increased, not decreased.[40]
- Toyota rewards its dealerships on the basis of customer satisfaction surveys, not just car sales. What Toyota discovered, however, is that this motivates dealers to increase satisfaction scores, not customer satisfaction. One Toyota dealership received high ratings because it offered free detailing to every customer who returned a "Very Satisfied" survey. The dealership even had a special copy of the survey showing clients which boxes to check off. This increased customer ratings, but not customer satisfaction.[41]

organization and perform effectively. "High performers don't go for the money," warns an executive at Imation Corp. "Good people want to be in challenging jobs and see a future where they can get even more responsibilities and challenges." The director of Xerox's research center agrees with this assessment. "Our top stars say they want to make an impact–that's the most important thing," he says. "Feeling they are contributing and making a difference is highly motivational for them."[42] In other words, companies motivate employees mainly by designing interesting and challenging jobs, the topic we discuss next.

Learning Objectives

After reading this section, you should be able to:

4. Discuss the advantages and disadvantages of job specialization.
5. Diagram the job characteristics model of job design.
6. Identify three strategies for improving employee motivation through job design.

JOB DESIGN PRACTICES

How do you build a better job? That question has challenged organizational behavior experts as well as psychologists, engineers, and economists for a few centuries. Some jobs have very few tasks and usually require very little skill. Other jobs are immensely complex and require years of experience and learning to master them. From one extreme to the other, jobs have different effects on work efficiency and employee motivation. The challenge, at least from the organization's perspective, is to find the right combination so that work is performed efficiently but employees are motivated and engaged.[43] This challenge requires careful **job design**–the process of assigning tasks to a job, including the interdependency of those tasks with other jobs. A *job* is a set of tasks performed by one person. To understand this issue more fully, let's begin by describing early job design efforts aimed at increasing work efficiency through job specialization.

job design
The process of assigning tasks to a job, including the interdependency of those tasks with other jobs.

Job Design and Work Efficiency

Chrysler Corp. outsources European manufacturing of its minivan to Magna Steyr, a subsidiary of Magna International. On average, employees assigned to Magna Steyr's Chrysler minivan assembly line in Graz, Austria, take three minutes to attach their assigned pieces to the chassis before repeating their work on the next vehicle. Meanwhile, employees assembling the same vehicle at Chrysler's own assembly plants in North America have an average job cycle time of 64.5 seconds.[44] The difference isn't that Austrian employees are slower. Rather, Chrysler's North American employees are assigned fewer tasks. They have a higher degree of **job specialization.**

job specialization
The result of division of labor in which work is subdivided into separate jobs assigned to different people.

Job specialization occurs when the work required to build an automobile–or any other product or service–is subdivided into separate jobs assigned to different people. Each resulting job includes a narrow subset of tasks, usually completed in a short cycle time. *Cycle time* is the time required to complete the task before starting over with a new work unit. Employees at Chrysler's minivan assembly operations in North America have an average cycle time of 64.5 seconds, which means they repeat the same set of tasks about 58 times each hour and probably about 230 times before they take a meal break.

Why would companies divide work into such tiny bits? The simple answer is that job specialization improves work efficiency. Efficiency is higher because employees have fewer tasks to juggle and therefore spend less time changing activities. They also require fewer physical and mental skills to accomplish the assigned work, so less time and fewer resources are needed for training. A third reason is that employees practice their tasks more frequently with shorter work cycles, so jobs are mastered quickly. A fourth reason why work efficiency increases is that employees with specific aptitudes or skills can be matched more precisely to the jobs for which they are best suited.[45]

The efficiency of job specialization was noted more than 2,300 years ago by the Chinese philosopher Mencius and Greek philosopher Plato. In the 1400s and 1500s, the Arsenal of Venice employed up to 4,000 people in specialized jobs (caulkers, paymasters, division managers, carpenters, iron workers, warehouse supervisors, etc.) to build ships and many accessories such as cannons, ropes, oars, and armor. The state-owned organization became so efficient that in 1570 it built 100 ships in two months. After construction, the galleons traveled along a waterway where workers apportioned food, ammunition, cordage, and other supplies from specially designed warehouses. This assembly line could outfit 10 galleons in just six hours.[46] The benefits of job specialization were also recorded by Adam Smith 250 years ago. The Scottish economist described a small factory where 10 pin makers collectively produced as many as 48,000 pins per day because they performed specialized tasks, such as straightening, cutting, sharpening, grinding, and whitening the pins. In contrast, Smith explained that if these 10 people worked alone producing complete pins, they would collectively manufacture no more than 200 pins per day.[47]

Scientific Management One of the strongest advocates of job specialization was Frederick Winslow Taylor, an American industrial engineer who introduced the principles of **scientific management** in the early 1900s.[48] Scientific management consists of a toolkit of activities. Some of these interventions–training, goal setting, and work incentives–are common today but were rare until Taylor popularized them. However, scientific management is mainly associated with high levels of job specialization and standardization of tasks to achieve maximum efficiency.

scientific management The practice of systematically partitioning work into its smallest elements and standardizing tasks to achieve maximum efficiency.

According to Taylor, the most effective companies have detailed procedures and work practices developed by engineers, enforced by supervisors, and executed by employees. Even the supervisor's tasks should be divided: One person manages operational efficiency, another manages inspection, and another is the disciplinarian. Taylor and other industrial engineers demonstrated that scientific management significantly improves work efficiency. No doubt, some of the increased productivity can be credited to the training, goal setting, and work incentives, but job specialization quickly became popular in its own right.

Problems with Job Specialization Frederick Taylor and his contemporaries focused on how job specialization reduces labor "waste" by improving the mechanical efficiency of work (i.e., matching skills, faster learning, less switchover time). Yet they didn't seem to notice how this extreme job specialization adversely affects employee attitudes and motivation. Some jobs–such as assembling Chrysler minivans–are so specialized that they may soon become tedious, trivial, and socially isolating. Employee turnover and absenteeism tend to be higher in specialized jobs with very short cycle times. Companies sometimes have to pay higher wages to attract job applicants to this dissatisfying, narrowly defined work.[49]

Job specialization often reduces work quality because employees see only a small part of the process. As one observer of an automobile assembly line reports: "Often [employees] did not know how their jobs related to the total picture. Not knowing, there was no incentive to strive for quality–what did quality even mean as it related to a bracket whose function you did not understand?"[50]

Equally important, job specialization can undermine the motivational potential of jobs. As work becomes specialized, it tends to become easier to perform but less interesting. As jobs become more complex, work motivation increases but the ability to master the job decreases. Maximum job performance occurs somewhere between these two extremes, where most people can eventually perform the job tasks efficiently yet the work is interesting.

Job Design and Work Motivation

motivator-hygiene theory
Herzberg's theory stating that employees are primarily motivated by growth and esteem needs, not by lower-level needs.

Industrial engineers may have overlooked the motivational effect of job characteristics, but it is now the central focus of many job design changes. Organizational behavior scholar Frederick Herzberg is credited with shifting the spotlight when he introduced **motivator-hygiene theory** in the 1950s.[51] Motivator-hygiene theory proposes that employees experience job satisfaction when they fulfill growth and esteem needs (called *motivators*) and they experience dissatisfaction when they have poor working conditions, job security, and other factors categorized as lower-order needs (called *hygienes*). Herzberg argued that only characteristics of the job itself motivate employees, whereas the hygiene factors merely prevent dissatisfaction. It might seem obvious to us today that the job itself is a source of motivation, but the concept was radical when Herzberg proposed the idea.

job characteristics model
A job design model that relates the motivational properties of jobs to specific personal and organizational consequences of those properties.

Motivator-hygiene theory has been soundly rejected due to lack of research support, but Herzberg's ideas generated new thinking about the motivational potential of the job itself.[52] Out of subsequent research emerged the **job characteristics model,** shown in Exhibit 6.2. The job characteristics model identifies five core job dimensions that produce three psychological states. Employees who experience these psychological states tend to have higher levels of internal work motivation (motivation from the work itself), job satisfaction (particularly satisfaction with the work itself), and work effectiveness.[53]

skill variety
The extent to which employees must use different skills and talents to perform tasks within their jobs.

Core Job Characteristics The job characteristics model identifies five core job characteristics. Under the right conditions, employees are more motivated and satisfied when jobs have higher levels of these characteristics:

- *Skill variety.* **Skill variety** refers to the use of different skills and talents to complete a variety of work activities. For example, sales clerks who normally only serve customers might be assigned the additional duties of stocking inventory and changing storefront displays.

task identity
The degree to which a job requires completion of a whole or an identifiable piece of work.

- *Task identity.* **Task identity** is the degree to which a job requires completion of a whole or identifiable piece of work, such as assembling an entire broadband modem rather than just soldering in the circuitry.
- *Task significance.* **Task significance** is the degree to which the job affects the organization and/or larger society. For instance, many employees at Medtronic, the Minneapolis-based maker of pacemakers and other medical equipment, have high job specialization, yet 86 percent say their work has special meaning and 94 percent feel pride in what they accomplish. The reason for their high task significance is that they attend seminars that show how the products they manufacture save lives. "We have patients who come in who would be dead if it wasn't for us," says a Medtronic production supervisor.[54]

task significance
The degree to which a job has a substantial impact on the organization and/or larger society.

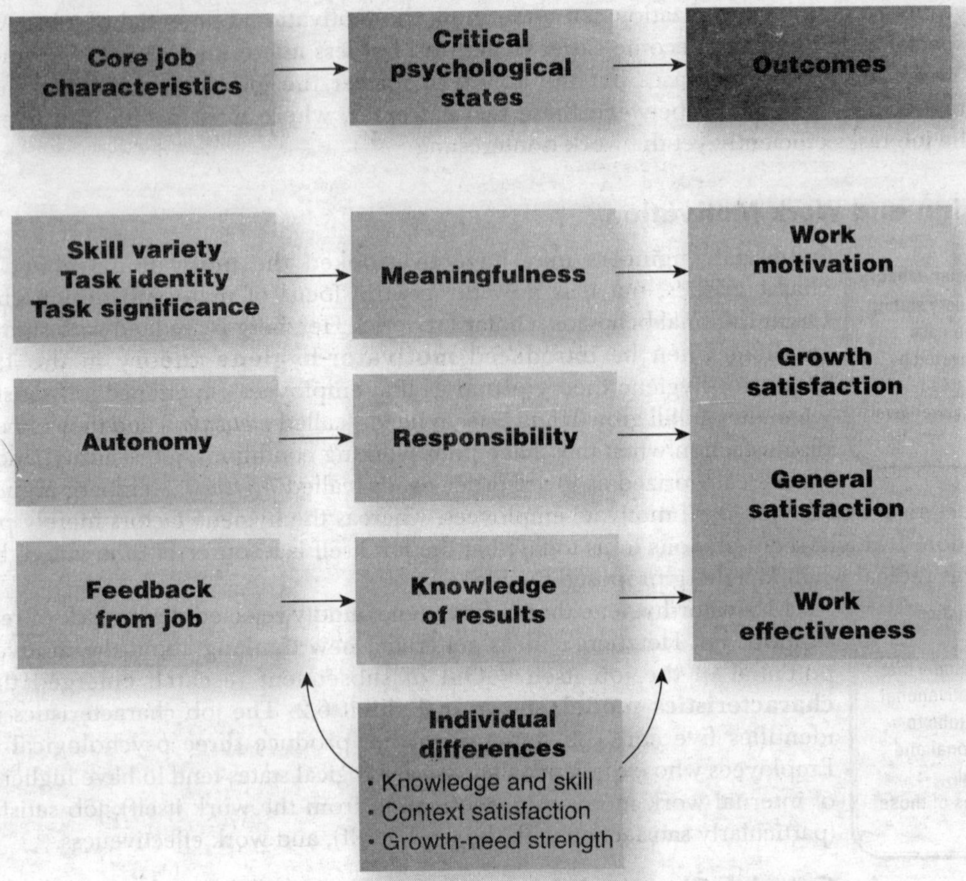

Source: J. Richard Hackman and Greg R. Oldham, *Work Redesign* (Prentice Hall Organizational Development Series), 1st Edition, Copyright © 1980. Reproduced by permission of Pearson Education, Inc., Upper Saddle River, New Jersey.

Exhibit 6.2 *The Job Characteristics Model*

autonomy
The degree to which a job gives employees the freedom, independence, and discretion to schedule their work and determine the procedures used in completing it.

- *Autonomy.* Jobs with high levels of **autonomy** provide freedom, independence, and discretion in scheduling the work and determining the procedures to be used to complete the work. In autonomous jobs, employees make their own decisions rather than relying on detailed instructions from supervisors or procedure manuals.
- *Job feedback.* Job feedback is the degree to which employees can tell how well they are doing on the basis of direct sensory information from the job itself. Airline pilots can tell how well they land their aircraft, and road crews can see how well they have prepared the roadbed and laid the asphalt.

Critical Psychological States The five core job characteristics affect employee motivation and satisfaction through three critical psychological states, shown in Exhibit 6.2. One of these psychological states is *experienced meaningfulness*–the belief that one's work is worthwhile or important. Skill variety, task identity, and task significance directly contribute to the job's meaningfulness. If the job has high

Customer Talks Raise Task Significance and Identity Repairing aircraft engines is a complex business involving the specialized work of dozens of people. However, employees working in specialized jobs tend to have lower task identity and task significance. "We work on airplane engines, but individual employees work on different parts, and don't necessarily know what the customer uses it for," says Maurice Carter, a bearing technician lead hand at the Rolls Royce Engine Services facility in Oakland, California. For this reason, Rolls Royce introduced "Voice of the Customer," an initiative in which customer representatives visit the facility and talk to production staff about why the quality of these engines is important to them. "[A customer's visit] allows you to know that your quality is key to the rescue of someone who may be stranded in a remote area, who relies on your ability to make sure that engine starts and continues to run in any adverse circumstance," says Carter. "Voice of the Customer isn't just a nicety," explains a Rolls Royce Engine Services executive. "It gives employees with relatively repetitive jobs the sense that they're not just working on a part but rather are key in keeping people safe."[55]

levels of all three characteristics, employees are likely to feel that their jobs are highly meaningful. The meaningfulness of a job drops as one or more of these characteristics declines.

Work motivation and performance increase when employees feel personally accountable for the outcomes of their efforts. Autonomy directly contributes to this feeling of *experienced responsibility*. Employees must be assigned control of their work environment to feel responsible for their successes and failures. The third critical psychological state is *knowledge of results*. Employees want information about the consequences of their work effort. Knowledge of results can originate from co-workers, supervisors, or clients. However, job design focuses on knowledge of results from the work itself.

Individual Differences Job design doesn't increase work motivation for everyone in every situation. Employees must have the required skills and knowledge to master the more challenging work. Otherwise, job design tends to increase stress and reduce job performance. The original model also suggests that increasing the motivational potential of jobs will not motivate employees who are dissatisfied with their work context (e.g., working conditions, job security) or who have a low growth-need strength. However, research findings have been mixed, suggesting that employees might be motivated by job design no matter how they feel about their job context or how high or low they score on growth needs.[56]

Job Design Practices That Motivate

Three main strategies can increase the motivational potential of jobs: job rotation, job enlargement, and job enrichment. This section also identifies several ways to implement job enrichment.

Job Rotation At the beginning of this section on job design, we mentioned that assembly-line employees at Chrysler have a high degree of specialization. Chrysler executives are aware of the motivational and physiological problems that this repetitive work can create, so they have introduced a policy whereby employees work in teams and rotate to a different workstation within that team every few hours. **Job rotation** is the practice of moving employees from one job to another. "The whole idea of job rotation makes a big difference," says Chrysler's vice president of manufacturing. "The job naturally gets better, quality improves, throughput improves." Chrysler reported significant improvements in productivity and morale within the first year of its job rotation program. Job rotation offers "important ergonomic benefits to workers, improvements in product quality, and higher employee satisfaction," says a senior manager at Chrysler's plant in Toledo, Ohio.[57]

job rotation
The practice of moving employees from one job to another.

From the experience at Chrysler and many other companies, we can identify three potential benefits of job rotation. First, it minimizes health risks from repetitive strain and heavy lifting because employees use different muscles and physical positions in the various jobs. Second, it supports multiskilling (employees learn several jobs), which increases workforce flexibility in staffing the production process and in finding replacements for employees on vacation. A third benefit of job rotation is that it potentially reduces the boredom of highly repetitive jobs. However, organizational behavior experts continue to debate whether job rotation really is a form of job redesign because the jobs remain the same; they are still highly specialized. Critics argue that job redesign requires changes within the job, such as job enlargement.

Job Enlargement **Job enlargement** adds tasks to an existing job. This might involve combining two or more complete jobs into one or just adding one or two more tasks to an existing job. Either way, skill variety increases because there are more tasks to perform. Video journalists represent a clear example of an enlarged job. As Exhibit 6.3 illustrates, a traditional news team consists of a camera operator, a sound and lighting specialist, and the journalist who writes and presents or narrates the story. One video journalist performs all of these tasks.

job enlargement
The practice of adding more tasks to an existing job.

Job enlargement significantly improves work efficiency and flexibility. However, research suggests that simply giving employees more tasks won't affect motivation, performance, or job satisfaction. These benefits result only when skill variety is combined with more autonomy and job knowledge.[58] In other words, employees are motivated when they perform a variety of tasks *and* have the freedom and knowledge to structure their work to achieve the highest satisfaction and performance. These job characteristics are at the heart of job enrichment.

Job Enrichment **Job enrichment** occurs when employees are given more responsibility for scheduling, coordinating, and planning their own work.[59] Generally, people in enriched jobs experience higher job satisfaction and work motivation, along with lower absenteeism and turnover. Productivity is also

job enrichment
The practice of giving employees more responsibility for scheduling, coordinating, and planning their own work.

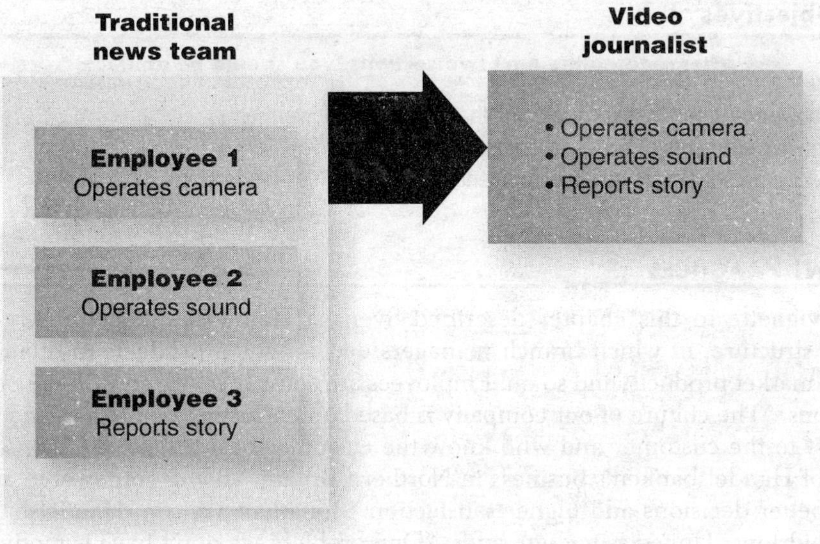

Exhibit 6.3 *Job Enlargement of Video Journalists*

higher when task identity and job feedback are improved. Product and service quality tend to improve because job enrichment increases the jobholder's felt responsibility and sense of ownership over the product or service.[60]

One way to increase job enrichment is by combining highly interdependent tasks into one job. This *natural grouping* approach is reflected in the video journalist job. Video journalist was earlier described as an enlarged job, but it is also an example of job enrichment because it naturally groups tasks together to complete an entire product (i.e., a news clip). By forming natural work units, jobholders have stronger feelings of responsibility for an identifiable body of work. They feel a sense of ownership and, therefore, tend to increase job quality. Forming natural work units increases task identity and task significance because employees perform a complete product or service and can more readily see how their work affects others.

A second job enrichment strategy, called *establishing client relationships,* involves putting employees in direct contact with their clients rather than using the supervisor as a go-between. By being directly responsible for specific clients, employees have more information and can make decisions affecting those clients.[61] Establishing client relationships also increases task significance because employees see a line-of-sight connection between their work and consequences for customers. This was apparent among medical secretaries at a large regional hospital in Sweden after the hospital reduced its workforce by 10 percent and gave the secretaries expanded job duties. Although these employees experienced more stress from the higher workloads, some of them also felt more motivated and satisfied because they now had direct interaction with patients. "Before, I never saw a patient; now they have a face," says one medical secretary. "I feel satisfied and pleased with myself; you feel someone needs you."[62]

Forming natural task groups and establishing client relationships are common ways to enrich jobs, but the heart of the job enrichment philosophy is to give employees more autonomy over their work. This basic idea is at the core of one of the most widely mentioned–and often misunderstood–practices, known as empowerment.

Learning Objectives

After reading the next two sections, you should be able to:

7. Define *empowerment* and identify strategies that support empowerment.
8. Describe the five elements of self-leadership.
9. Identify specific personal and work environment influences on self-leadership.

EMPOWERMENT PRACTICES

The opening vignette to this chapter described Svenska Handelsbanken's highly decentralized organizational structure, in which branch managers decide which products to offer, what price to charge, how to market products, and so on. Employees are actively involved with the branch manager in these decisions. "The culture of our company is based on entrusting employees and allowing those who are closest to the customer and who know the customer best to take decisions," says Anders Bouvin, head of Handelsbanken's business in Northern Britain. "Being empowered and having this trust leads to better decisions and higher satisfaction." Jonathan Watson, Handelsbanken's branch manager in Maidstone, United Kingdom, adds: "One problem we don't have is motivating our staff. Thanks to the decentralized way Handelsbanken operates and empowers staff with the responsibility to do their jobs to the best of their ability, motivation is easy and morale remains high."[63]

empowerment
A psychological concept in which people experience more self-determination, meaning, competence, and impact regarding their role in the organization.

The word **empowerment** is often mentioned in writing and conversations about Handelsbanken because, unlike too many financial institutions, the Swedish bank's employees really do experience the feeling of being empowered. Empowerment is a psychological concept represented by four dimensions: self-determination, meaning, competence, and impact of the individual's role in the organization. If any dimension weakens, the employee's sense of empowerment will weaken.[64]

- *Self-determination.* Empowered employees feel that they have freedom, independence, and discretion over their work activities.
- *Meaning.* Employees who feel empowered care about their work and believe that what they do is important.
- *Competence.* Empowered people are confident about their ability to perform the work well and have a capacity to grow with new challenges.
- *Impact.* Empowered employees view themselves as active participants in the organization; that is, their decisions and actions have an influence on the company's success.

Supporting Empowerment

Chances are that you have heard leaders say they are "empowering" the workforce. Yet empowerment is a state of mind, so what these executives really mean is that they are changing the work environment to support the feeling of empowerment.[65] Numerous individual, job design, and organizational or work-context factors support empowerment. At the individual level, employees must possess the necessary competencies to be able to perform the work as well as handle the additional decision-making requirements.[66] Job characteristics clearly influence the degree to which people feel empowered.[67] Employees are much more likely to experience self-determination when working in jobs with a high degree of autonomy and minimal bureaucratic control. They experience more meaningfulness when working in jobs with high levels of task identity and task significance. They experience more

Semco's Radical Empowerment Most executives like to say they empower their workforce, but few come close to the freedom that employees experience at Semco Corporation, SA. "Can an organization let people do what they want, when they want, and how they want?" asks Ricardo Semler, who took over his father's marine pump business in Sao Paulo, Brazil, 20 years ago. The answer appears to be yes. Today, the industrial manufacturing and services company has 3,000 employees who work in teams of 6 to 10 people. Employees choose their objectives, hire co-workers, calculate budgets, set their own salaries, decide when to come to work, and elect their own bosses. The only policy manual is a comic book that introduces newcomers to Semco's democratic culture. Semler, shown here with some head office staff resting in hammocks, complains that too few companies have tried to liberate employees. "Treating employees like two-year-olds is a comfortable norm for too many businesses. Perpetuating this behavior will deal the killing blow to any organization," Semler warns. "Treating employees like intelligent adults and allowing them to manage themselves is a business model that worked at Semco."[68]

self-confidence when working in jobs that allow them to receive feedback about their performance and accomplishments.

Several organizational and work-context factors also influence empowerment. Employees experience more empowerment in organizations where information and other resources are easily accessible. Empowerment also requires a learning orientation culture. In other words, empowerment flourishes in organizations that appreciate the value of employee learning and that accept reasonable mistakes as a natural part of the learning process. Furthermore, as mentioned above in describing Handelsbanken, empowerment requires corporate leaders who trust employees and are willing to take the risks that empowerment creates."[69]

With the right individuals, job characteristics, and organizational environment, empowerment can substantially improve motivation and performance. For instance, a study of bank employees concluded that empowerment improved customer service and tended to reduce conflict between employees and their supervisors. A study of nurses reported that empowerment is associated with higher trust in management, which ultimately influences job satisfaction, belief and acceptance of organizational goals and values, and effective organizational commitment. Empowerment also tends to increase personal initiative because employees identify with and assume more psychological ownership of their work.[70]

Self-Leadership Practices

What is the most important characteristic that companies look for in their employees? Leadership potential, ability to work in a team, and good communication skills are important, but a survey of 800 British employers concludes that they don't top the list. Instead, the most important employee characteristic is self-motivation. Jack Harding can identify with these survey results. The founder of eSilicon Corp., which designs and manufactures custom chips for electronics companies, believes that the best-performing businesses prosper when employees manage their own motivation and performance. "You look for character and experience" when hiring new employees, Harding suggests. "They need to be smart, team players, and self-motivated--and you can't instill that."[71]

Bayer CropScience Searches for Self-Leaders With production increasing at its facility in Research Triangle Park, North Carolina, Bayer CropScience wants to hire two dozen more chemical process operators. The task won't be easy, though. Bayer CropScience, a division of Germany-based conglomerate Bayer AG, is looking for job applicants with special characteristics. "It's difficult to fill [these jobs]," says site leader Nick Crosby. "We're not in the game these days of just getting people who can read, write and shovel stuff around." Instead, Bayer CropScience wants employees who practice self-leadership. "We need self-motivated people who work well with empowered teams—people who can think for themselves, do basic diagnosis, and keep the plants operating at an optimum," he says.[72]

Most of the concepts introduced in this chapter and in Chapter 5 have assumed that leaders do things to motivate employees. Certainly, these theories and practices are valuable, but they overlook the fact that the most successful employees ultimately motivate and manage themselves. In other words, they engage in self-leadership.

self-leadership
The process of influencing oneself to establish the self-direction and self-motivation needed to perform a task.

Self-leadership refers to the process of influencing oneself to establish the self-direction and self-motivation needed to perform a task.[73] This concept includes a toolkit of behavioral activities borrowed from social learning theory and goal setting. It also includes constructive thought processes that have been extensively studied in sports psychology. Overall, self-leadership takes the view that individuals mostly regulate their own actions through these behavioral and cognitive (thought) activities.

Self-Leadership Strategies

Although self-leadership consists of several processes, the five main activities are identified in Exhibit 6.4. These elements, which generally follow each other in a sequence, are personal goal setting, constructive thought patterns, designing natural rewards, self-monitoring, and self-reinforcement.[74]

Exhibit 6.4 *Elements of Self-Leadership*

Personal Goal Setting The first step in self-leadership is to set goals for your own work effort. This applies the ideas learned in Chapter 5 on goal setting, such as identifying goals that are specific, relevant, and challenging. The main difference is that self-leadership involves setting goals alone, rather than having them assigned by or jointly decided with a supervisor. Research suggests that employees are more focused and perform better when they set their own goals, particularly in combination with other self-leadership practices.[75] Personal goal setting also requires a high degree of self-awareness, because people need to understand their current behavior and performance before establishing meaningful goals for personal development.

Constructive Thought Patterns Before beginning a task and while performing it, employees should engage in positive (constructive) thoughts about that work and its accomplishment. In particular, employees are more motivated and better prepared to accomplish a task after they have engaged in positive self-talk and mental imagery.

self-talk
The process of talking to ourselves about our own thoughts or actions.

Positive Self-Talk Do you ever talk to yourself? Most of us do, according to a major study of university students.[76] **Self-talk** refers to any situation in which we talk to ourselves about our own thoughts or actions. Some of this internal communication assists the decision-making process, such as weighing the advantages of a particular choice. Self-leadership is mostly interested in evaluative self-talk, in which you evaluate your capabilities and accomplishments.

The problem is that most evaluative self-talk is negative; we criticize much more than encourage or congratulate ourselves. Negative self-talk undermines our confidence and potential to perform a particular task. In contrast, positive self-talk creates a "can-do" belief and thereby increases motivation by raising our effort-to-performance expectancy. We often hear that professional athletes "psych" themselves up before an important event. They tell themselves that they can achieve their goal and that they have practiced enough to reach that goal. They are motivating themselves through positive self-talk.

mental imagery
The process of mentally practicing a task and visualizing its successful completion.

Mental Imagery You've probably heard the phrase "I'll cross that bridge when I come to it!" Self-leadership takes the opposite view. It suggests that we need to mentally practice a task and imagine successfully performing it beforehand. This process, known as **mental imagery,** has two parts. One part involves mentally practicing the task, anticipating obstacles to goal accomplishment, and working out solutions to those obstacles before they occur. By mentally walking through the activities required to accomplish the task, we begin to see problems that may occur. We can then imagine what responses would be best for each contingency.[77]

While one part of mental imagery helps us to anticipate things that could go wrong, the other part involves visualizing successful completion of the task. You might imagine the experience of completing the task and the positive results that follow, such as being promoted, receiving a prestigious award, or taking time off work. This visualization increases goal commitment and motivates people to complete the task effectively. This is the strategy that Tony Wang applies to motivate himself. "Since I am in sales, I think about the reward I get for closing new business–the commission check–and the things it will allow me to do that I really enjoy," explains Wang. "Or I think about the feeling I get when I am successful at something and how it makes me feel good, and use that to get me going."[78]

Designing Natural Rewards Self-leadership recognizes that employees actively craft their jobs. To varying degrees, they can alter tasks and work relationships to make the work more motivating.[79] One way to build natural rewards into the job is to alter the way a task is accomplished. People often have enough discretion in their jobs to make slight changes to suit their needs and preferences. For instance, you might try out a new software program to design an idea, rather than sketch the image with a pencil. By using the new software, you are making more challenging and appealing a task that may have otherwise been mundane.

Self-Monitoring Self-monitoring is the process of keeping track at regular intervals of one's progress toward a goal by using naturally occurring feedback. Some people can receive feedback from the job itself, such as members of a lawn maintenance crew who can see how they are improving the appearance of their client's property. But many of us are unable to observe our work output so readily. Instead, many people need to design feedback systems. Salespeople might arrange to receive monthly reports on sales levels in their territory. Production staff might have gauges or computer feedback systems installed so that they can see how many errors are made on the production line. Research suggests that people who have control over the timing of performance feedback perform their tasks better than do those with feedback assigned by others.[80]

Self-Reinforcement Self-leadership includes the social learning theory concept of self-reinforcement (see Chapter 3). Self-reinforcement occurs whenever an employee has control over a reinforcer but doesn't "take" the reinforcer until completing a self-set goal.[81] A common example is taking a break after reaching a predetermined stage of your work. The work break is a self-induced form of positive reinforcement. Self-reinforcement also occurs when you decide to do a more enjoyable task after completing a task that you dislike. For example, after slogging through a difficult report, you might decide to spend time doing a more pleasant task, such as catching up on industry news by scanning Web sites.

Effectiveness of Self-Leadership

Self-leadership is shaping up to be a valuable applied performance practice in organizational settings. A respectable body of research shows consistent support for most elements of self-leadership. Self-set goals and self-monitoring increased the frequency of wearing safety equipment among employees in a mining operation. Airline employees who received constructive thought training experienced better mental performance, enthusiasm, and job satisfaction than co-workers who did not receive this training. Mental imagery helped supervisors and process engineers in a pulp-and-paper mill to transfer what they learned in an interpersonal communication skills class back to the job.[82] Studies also indicate that constructive thought processes improve individual performance in cycling, hockey goaltending, ice skating, soccer, and other sports. Indeed, studies show that almost all Olympic athletes rely on mental rehearsal and positive self-talk to achieve their performance goals.[83]

Self-Leadership Contingencies

As with most other organizational behavior theories, self-leadership is more or less likely to occur depending on the person and the situation. With respect to individual differences, preliminary research suggests that self-leadership behaviors are more frequently found in people with higher levels of conscientiousness and extroversion. Some writers also suggest that people with a positive self-concept evaluation (i.e., self-esteem, self-efficacy, and internal locus of control) are more likely to apply self-leadership strategies.[84]

Although the research is still very sparse, the work environment also seems to influence the extent to which employees engage in self-leadership strategies. In particular, employees require sufficient autonomy to engage in some or most aspects of self-leadership. They probably also feel more confident with self-leadership when their boss is empowering rather than controlling and where there is a high degree of trust between them. Employees are also more likely to engage in self-monitoring in companies that emphasize continuous measurement of performance.[85] Overall, self-leadership promises to be an important concept and practice for improving employee motivation and performance.

Chapter Summary

Money and other financial rewards are a fundamental part of the employment relationship, but their value and meaning vary from one person to the next. Organizations reward employees for their membership and seniority, job status, competencies, and performance. Membership-based rewards may attract job applicants, and seniority-based rewards reduce turnover, but these reward objectives tend to discourage turnover among those with the lowest performance. Rewards based on job status try to maintain internal equity and motivate employees to compete for promotions. However, they tend to encourage a bureaucratic hierarchy, support status differences, and motivate employees to compete and hoard resources. Competency-based rewards are becoming increasingly popular because they improve workforce flexibility and are consistent with the emerging idea of employability. However, they tend to be subjectively measured and can result in higher costs as employees spend more time learning new skills.

Awards and bonuses, commissions, and other individual performance-based rewards have existed for centuries and are widely used. Many companies are shifting to team-based rewards such as gainsharing plans and to organizational rewards such as employee stock ownership plans (ESOPs), stock options, and profit sharing. ESOPs and stock options create an ownership culture, but employees often perceive a weak connection between individual performance and the organizational reward.

Financial rewards have a number of limitations, but reward effectiveness can be improved in several ways. Organizational leaders should ensure that rewards are linked to work performance, rewards are aligned with performance within the employee's control, team rewards are used where jobs are interdependent, rewards are valued by employees, and rewards have no unintended consequences.

Job design is the process of assigning tasks to a job, including the interdependency of those tasks with other jobs. Job specialization subdivides work into separate jobs for different people. This increases work efficiency because employees master the tasks quickly, spend less time changing tasks, require less training, and can be matched more closely with the jobs best suited to their skills. However, job specialization may reduce work motivation, create mental health problems, lower product or service quality, and increase costs through discontentment, absenteeism, and turnover.

Contemporary job design strategies reverse job specialization through job rotation, job enlargement, and job enrichment. The job characteristics model is a template for job redesign that specifies core job dimensions, psychological states, and individual differences. Organizations introduce job rotation to reduce job boredom, develop a more flexible workforce, and reduce the incidence of repetitive strain injuries. Two ways to enrich jobs are clustering tasks into natural groups and establishing client relationships.

Empowerment is a psychological concept represented by four dimensions: self-determination, meaning, competence, and impact regarding the individual's role in the organization. Individual characteristics seem to have a minor influence on empowerment. Job design is a major influence, particularly autonomy, task identity, task significance, and job feedback. Empowerment is also supported at the organizational level through a learning orientation culture, sufficient information and resources, and corporate leaders who trust employees.

Self-leadership is the process of influencing oneself to establish the self-direction and self-motivation needed to perform a task. This includes personal goal setting, constructive thought patterns, designing natural rewards, self-monitoring, and self-reinforcement. Constructive thought patterns include self-talk and mental imagery. Self-talk occurs in any situation in which a person talks to himself or herself about his or her own thoughts or actions. Mental imagery involves mentally practicing a task and imagining successfully performing it beforehand.

Key Terms

autonomy
employee stock ownership plans (ESOPs)
empowerment
gainsharing plans
job characteristics model
job design
job enlargement
job enrichment
job evaluation
job rotation
job specialization
mental imagery
motivator-hygiene theory
profit-sharing plans
scientific management
self-leadership
self-talk
skill variety
stock options
task identity
task significance

Critical Thinking Questions

1. As a consultant, you have been asked to recommend either a gainsharing plan or a profit-sharing plan for employees who work in the four regional distribution and warehousing facilities of a large retail organization. Which reward system would you recommend? Explain your answer.
2. You are a member of a team responsible for developing a reward system for your college or university faculty unit. Assume that the faculty is nonprofit, so profit sharing is not an option. What other team or organization-level rewards might work in this situation? Describe specific measures that could be used to calculate the amount of bonus.
3. Alaska Tire Corporation redesigned its production facilities around a team-based system. However, the company president believes that employees will not be motivated unless they receive incentives based on their individual performance. Give three explanations of why Alaska Tire should introduce team-based rather than individual rewards in this setting.
4. What can organizations do to increase the effectiveness of financial rewards?
5. Most of us have watched pizzas being made while waiting in a pizzeria. What level of job specialization do you usually notice in these operations? Why does this high or low level of specialization exist? If some pizzerias have different levels of specialization than others, identify the contingencies that might explain these differences.
6. Can a manager or supervisor "empower" an employee? Discuss fully.
7. Describe a time when you practiced self-leadership to successfully perform a task. With reference to each step in the self-leadership process, describe what you did to achieve this success.
8. Can self-leadership replace formal leadership in an organizational setting?

CASE STUDY 6.1

THE REGENCY GRAND HOTEL

Elizabeth Ho, Prada Singapore under the supervision of Steven L. McShane

The Regency Grand Hotel is a five-star hotel in Bangkok, Thailand. The hotel was established 15 years ago by a local consortium of investors and has been operated by a Thai general manager throughout this time. The hotel is one of Bangkok's most prestigious hotels, and its 700 employees enjoyed the prestige of being associated with the hotel. The hotel provided good welfare benefits, above-market-rate salary, and job security. In addition, a good year-end bonus amounting to four months' salary was rewarded to employees regardless of the hotel's overall performance during the year.

Recently, the Regency was sold to a large American hotel chain that was very keen to expand its operations into Thailand. When the acquisition was announced, the general manager decided to take early retirement when the hotel changed ownership. The American hotel chain kept all of the Regency employees, although a few were transferred to other positions. John Becker, an American with 10 years of management experience with the hotel chain, was appointed as the new general manager of the Regency Palace Hotel. Becker was selected as the new general manager because of his previous successes in integrating newly acquired hotels in the United States. In most of the previous acquisitions, Becker took over operations with poor profitability and low morale.

Becker is a strong believer in empowerment. He expects employees to go beyond guidelines and standards to consider guest needs on a case-by-case basis. That is, employees must be guest-oriented at all times to provide excellent customer service. From his U.S. experience, Becker has found that empowerment increases employee motivation, performance, and job satisfaction, all of which contribute to the hotel's profitability and customer service ratings. Soon after becoming general manager of Regency Palace, Becker introduced the practice of empowerment to replicate the successes that he had achieved back home.

The Regency Grand Hotel has been very profitable since it opened 15 years ago. The employees have always worked according to management's instructions. Their responsibility was to ensure that the instructions from their managers were carried out diligently and conscientiously. Innovation and creativity were discouraged under the previous management. Indeed, employees were punished for their mistakes and discouraged from trying out ideas that had not been approved by management. As a result, employees were afraid to be innovative and to take risks.

Becker met with Regency's managers and department heads to explain that empowerment would be introduced in the hotel. He told them that employees must be empowered with decision-making authority so that they can use their initiative, creativity, and judgment to satisfy guest needs and handle problems effectively and efficiently. However, he stressed that the more complex issues and decisions were to be referred to superiors, who were to coach and assist rather than provide direct orders. Furthermore, Becker stressed that mistakes were allowed but that making the same mistakes more than twice would not be tolerated. He advised his managers and department heads not to discuss with him minor issues or problems and not to consult with him about minor decisions. Nevertheless, he told them that they were to discuss important, major issues and decisions with him. He concluded the meeting by asking for feedback. Several managers and department heads told him that they liked the idea and would support it, while others simply nodded their heads. Becker was pleased with the response and was eager to have his plan implemented.

In the past, the Regency had emphasized administrative control, resulting in many bureaucratic procedures throughout the organization. For example, the front-counter employees needed to seek approval from their manager before they could upgrade guests to another category of room. The front-counter manager would then have to write and submit a report to the general manager justifying the upgrade. Soon after his meeting with the managers, Becker reduced the number of bureaucratic rules at the Regency and allocated more decision-making authority to frontline employees. This action upset those who previously had decision-making power over these issues. As a result, several of these employees left the hotel.

Becker also began spending a large portion of his time observing and interacting with the employees at the front desk, lobby, restaurants, and various departments. This direct interaction with Becker helped many employees to understand what he wanted and expected of them. However, the employees had much difficulty trying to distinguish between a major and a minor issue or decision. More often than not, supervisors would reverse employee decisions by stating that they were major issues requiring management approval. Employees who displayed initiative and made good decisions in satisfying the needs of the guests rarely received any positive feedback from their supervisors. Eventually, most of these employees lost confidence in making decisions and reverted back to relying on their superiors for decision making.

Not long after the implementation of the practice of empowerment, Becker realized that his subordinates were consulting him more frequently than before. Most of them came to him with minor issues and consulted with him about minor decisions. He had to spend most of his time attending to his subordinates. Soon he began to feel highly frustrated and exhausted, and very often he would tell his secretary that "unless the hotel is on fire, don't let anyone disturb me."

Becker thought that the practice of empowerment would benefit the overall performance of the hotel. However, contrary to his expectation, the business and overall performance of the hotel began to deteriorate. There was an increasing number of guest complaints. In the past, the hotel had minimal guest complaints. Now there was a significant number of formal written complaints every month. Many other guests voiced their dissatisfaction verbally to hotel employees. The number of mistakes made by employees was on the increase. Becker was very upset when he realized that two of the local newspapers and an overseas newspaper had published negative feedback on the hotel in terms of service standards. He was most distressed when an international travel magazine voted the hotel "one of Asia's nightmare hotels."

The stress levels of the employees were continuously mounting since the introduction of the practice of empowerment. Absenteeism due to illness was increasing at an alarming rate. In addition, the employee turnover rate reached an all-time high. The good working relationships that were established under the old management had been severely strained. The employees were no longer united and supportive of each other. They were quick to "point fingers" at or to "backstab" one another when mistakes were made and when problems occurred.

Discussion Questions

1. Identify the symptoms indicating that problems exist in this case.
2. Diagnose the problems in this case using organizational behavior concepts.
3. Recommend solutions that overcome or minimize the problems and symptoms in this case.

Note: This case is based on true events, but the industry and names have been changed. Reprinted with permission.

CASE STUDY 6.2

HOW TO MAKE A MICROSERF SMILE

BusinessWeek

Microsoft CEO Steve Balmer had an epic morale problem; the company suffered from software delays, Google envy, and a stock price that had been drifting sideways for too long. To help the world's largest software company out of this morass, Balmer asked veteran product manager Lisa Brummel to become the next human resources chief. Brummel couldn't do much about the company's stock price, but she did transform many of Microsoft's performance and reward practices.

This *BusinessWeek* case study describes how Microsoft is revamping its reward practices and, indirectly, helping employees to feel more empowered. Read the full text of this *BusinessWeek* article at www.mhhe.com/mcshane5e, and prepare for the discussion questions below.

Discussion Questions

1. What changes did Lisa Brummel make to Microsoft's performance and reward practices? Why did Microsoft have these performance and reward practices in place?
2. In your opinion, are these performance and reward management changes beneficial, or will any of them cause long-term problems?
3. In your opinion, which actions, if any, introduced by Lisa Brummel have improved feelings of empowerment at Microsoft?

Source: M. Conlin and J. Greene, "How to Make a Microserf Smile," *BusinessWeek,* 10 September 2007, pp. 56–59.

TEAM EXERCISE 6.3

IS STUDENT WORK ENRICHED?

PURPOSE This exercise is designed to help you learn how to measure the motivational potential of jobs and evaluate the extent that jobs should be further enriched.

INSTRUCTIONS (SMALL CLASS) Being a student is like a job in several ways. You have tasks to perform, and someone (such as your instructor) oversees your work. Although few people want to be students most of their lives (the pay rate is too low!), it may be interesting to determine how enriched your job is as a student.

1. Students are placed into teams (preferably four or five people).
2. Working alone, each student completes both sets of measures in this exercise. Then, using the guidelines on page 193, they individually calculate the score for the five core job characteristics as well as the overall motivating-potential score for the job.
3. Members of each team compare their individual results. The group should identify differences of opinion for each core job characteristic. They should also note which core job characteristics have the lowest scores and recommend how these scores could be increased.
4. The entire class will then meet to discuss the results of the exercise. The instructor may ask some teams to present their comparisons and recommendations for a particular core job characteristic.

INSTRUCTIONS (LARGE CLASS)

1. Working alone, each student completes both sets of measures in this exercise. Then, using the guidelines on page 193, each student individually calculates the score for the five core job characteristics as well as the overall motivating-potential score for the job.
2. Using a show of hands or classroom technology, students indicate their results for each core job characteristic. The instructor will ask for results for several bands across the range of the scales. Alternatively, students can complete this activity prior to class and submit their results through online classroom technology. Later, the instructor will provide feedback to the class showing the collective results (i.e., distribution of results across the range of scores).
3. Where possible, the instructor might ask students with very high or very low results to discuss their views with the class.

Job Diagnostic Survey

Circle the number on the right that best describes student work.	Very little ▼			Moderately ▼			Very much ▼
1. To what extent does student work permit you to decide on your own how to go about doing the work?	1	2	3	4	5	6	7
2. To what extent does student work involve doing a whole or identifiable piece of work, rather than a small portion of the overall work process?	1	2	3	4	5	6	7
3. To what extent does student work require you to do many different things, using a variety of your skills and talents?	1	2	3	4	5	6	7
4. To what extent are the results of your work as a student likely to significantly affect the lives and well-being of other people (e.g., within your school, your family, or society)?	1	2	3	4	5	6	7
5. To what extent does working on student activities provide information about your performance?	1	2	3	4	5	6	7

(Contd.)

Circle the number on the right that best describes student work.	Very inaccurate ▼			Uncertain ▼			Very accurate ▼
6. Being a student requires me to use a number of complex and high-level skills.	1	2	3	4	5	6	7
7. Student work is arranged so that I do *not* have the chance to do an entire piece of work from beginning to end.	7	6	5	4	3	2	1
8. Doing the work required of students provides many chances for me to figure out how well I am doing.	1	2	3	4	5	6	7
9. The work students must do is quite simple and repetitive.	7	6	5	4	3	2	1
10. The work of a student is one where a lot of other people can be affected by how well the work gets done.	1	2	3	4	5	6	7
11. Student work denies me any chance to use my personal initiative or judgment in carrying out the work.	7	6	5	4	3	2	1
12. Student work provides me the chance to completely finish the pieces of work I begin.	1	2	3	4	5	6	7
13. Doing student work by itself provides few clues about whether I am performing well.	7	6	5	4	3	2	1
14. As a student, I have considerable opportunity for independence and freedom in how I do the work.	1	2	3	4	5	6	7
15. The work I perform as a student is *not* very significant or important in the broader scheme of things.	7	6	5	4	3	2	1

Source: Adapted from the Job Diagnostic Survey, developed by J. R. Hackman and G. R. Oldham. The authors have released any copyright ownership of this scale [see J. R. Hackman and G. Oldham, ***Work Redesign*** (Reading, MA: Addison-Wesley, 1980), p. 275].

Calculating The Motivating-Potential Score

Scoring Core Job Characteristics: Use the following set of calculations to estimate the motivating-potential score for the job of being a student. Use your answers from the Job Diagnostic Survey that you completed on page 192.

Skill variety (SV) $\frac{\text{Questions } 3 + 6 + 9}{3} = \_\_\_\_$

Task identity (TI) $\frac{\text{Questions } 2 + 7 + 12}{3} = \_\_\_\_$

Task significance (TS) $\frac{\text{Questions } 4 + 10 + 15}{3} = \_\_\_\_$

Autonomy $\frac{\text{Questions } 1 + 11 + 14}{3} = \_\_\_\_$

Job feedback $\frac{\text{Questions } 5 + 8 + 13}{3} = \_\_\_\_$

Calculating Motivating-Potential Score (MPS):.Use the following formula and the results to the left to calculate the motivating-potential score. Notice that skill variety, task identity, and task significance are averaged before being multiplied by the score for autonomy and job feedback.

$$\left(\frac{SV + TI + TS}{3}\right) \times \text{Autonomy} \times \text{Job feedback}$$

$$\left(\frac{\_\_ + \_\_ + \_\_}{3}\right) + \_\_\_\_ + \_\_\_\_ = \_\_\_\_$$

SELF-ASSESSMENT 6.4

WHAT IS YOUR ATTITUDE TOWARD MONEY?

PURPOSE This exercise is designed to help you understand the types of attitudes toward money and assess your attitude toward money.

INSTRUCTIONS Read each of the statements on page 194 and circle the response that you believe best reflects your position regarding each statement. Then use the scoring key in Appendix B at the end of the book to calculate your results. This exercise should be completed alone so that you can assess yourself honestly without concerns of social comparison. Class discussion will focus on the meaning of money, including the dimensions measured here and other aspects of money that may have an influence on behavior in the workplace.

Money Attitude Scale

To what extent do you agree or disagree that . . .	Strongly agree ▼	Agree ▼	Neutral ▼	Disagree ▼	Strongly disagree ▼
1. I sometimes purchase things because I know they will impress other people.	5	4	3	2	1
2. I regularly put money aside for the future.	5	4	3	2	1
3. I tend to get worried about decisions involving money.	5	4	3	2	1
4. I believe that financial wealth is one of the most important signs of a person's success.	5	4	3	2	1
5. I keep a close watch on how much money I have.	5	4	3	2	1
6. I feel nervous when I don't have enough money.	5	4	3	2	1
7. I tend to show more respect to people who are wealthier than I am.	5	4	3	2	1
8. I follow a careful financial budget.	5	4	3	2	1
9. I worry about being financially secure.	5	4	3	2	1
10. I sometimes boast about my financial wealth or how much money I make.	5	4	3	2	1
11. I keep track of my investments and financial wealth.	5	4	3	2	1
12. I usually say "I can't afford it," even when I can afford something.	5	4	3	2	1

Sources: Adapted from J. A. Roberts and C. J. Sepulveda, "Demographics and Money Attitudes: A Test of Yamauchi and Templer's (1982) Money Attitude Scale in Mexico," *Personality and Individual Differences,* 27 (July 1999), pp. 19–35; K. Yamauchi and D. Templer, "The Development of a Money Attitude Scale," *Journal of Personality Assessment,* 46 (1982), pp. 522–528.

SELF-ASSESSMENT 6.5

ASSESSING YOUR SELF-LEADERSHIP

This exercise is designed to help you understand self-leadership concepts and assess your self-leadership tendencies. Self-leadership is the process of influencing oneself to establish the self-direction and self-motivation needed to perform a task. Please indicate the extent to which each statement in this instrument describes you very well or does not describe you at all. Complete each item honestly to get the best estimate of your score on each self-leadership dimension.

SELF-ASSESSMENT 6.6

STUDENT EMPOWERMENT SCALE

Empowerment is a concept that applies to people in a variety of situations. This instrument is specifically adapted to your position as a student at this college or university. Indicate the extent to which you agree or disagree with each statement in this instrument; then request the results, which provide an overall score as well as scores on each of the four dimensions of empowerment. Complete each item honestly to get the best estimate of your level of empowerment.

Google is a hotbed of creativity and innovation in an industry already famed for churning out new ideas. Among the many conditions that support Google's creative culture is its policy of giving engineers 20 percent of their time to develop projects of their choosing. "Almost everything that is interesting which Google does started out as a 20 percent time idea," says Google CEO Eric Schmidt. Google News and the photos linked to Google Maps were two projects developed from the 20 percent time rule. When an idea gets developed far enough, Google assigns more people to work on it.

Google is a hotbed of creativity and innovation by giving staff 20 percent of their time to work on pet projects, using evidence-based experiments to test ideas, and involving employees in organizational decisions.

Although Google employees are passionate about their creative projects, the company also relies on razor-sharp analytic decision making. "Employees know that decisions about the business are data-driven," says Laszlo Bock, Google's top human resource executive. Bock's human resource team carefully analyzes two dozen performance variables of current staff to make better decisions about choosing job applicants. Google's business product management team has experimented with the placement, color, and size of ads on Google results pages to decide which characteristics yield the most clicks and the best revenue.

When a problem or opportunity lacks information, Google tries to fill in some of the missing pieces through "prediction markets" in which employees use play money (called Goobles) to cast their bets on strategic and operational questions. Google has conducted hundreds of these markets on issues ranging from whether a particular project will be completed on time to how many people will use Gmail (Google's e-mail system) by the end of the quarter. "Google uses these bets for its own planning. It helps them make decisions," says an economist studying Google's prediction markets.[1]

7

DECISION MAKING AND CREATIVITY

Learning Objectives

After reading this chapter, you should be able to:

1. Describe the six stages in the rational choice decision process.
2. Explain why people have difficulty identifying problems and opportunities.
3. Explain why people do not follow the rational choice model when evaluating alternative choices.
4. Describe three ways in which emotions influence the selection of alternatives.
5. Outline how intuition operates.
6. Describe four causes of escalation of commitment.
7. Describe four benefits of employee involvement in decision making.
8. Identify four contingencies that affect the optimal level of employee involvement.
9. Outline the four steps in the creative process.
10. Describe the characteristics of employees and the workplace that support creativity.

Many Google watchers claim that the company's success is largely driven by its superb execution of decision making and creativity. One recent article even "reverse-engineered" Google's innovation process as a guide for others to follow. At the same time, critics point to signs that Google's rapid growth (it now employs almost 20,000 people) is creating a bureaucracy that undermines its creativity and that Google's obsession with hiring elite engineers has constrained its diversity.[2] **Decision making** is the conscious process of making choices among alternatives with the intention of moving toward some desired state of affairs.[3] This chapter begins by outlining the rational choice paradigm of decision making. Then we examine this perspective more critically by recognizing how people identify problems and opportunities, choose among alternatives, and evaluate the success of their decisions differently from the rational model. Bounded rationality, escalation of commitment, and intuition are three of the more prominent topics in this section. Next, we explore the role of employee involvement in decision making, including the benefits of involvement and the factors that determine the optimal level of involvement. The final section of this chapter examines the factors that support creativity in decision making, including characteristics of creative people, work environments that support creativity, and creativity activities.

decision making
The conscious process of making choices among alternatives with the intention of moving toward some desired state of affairs.

Learning Objectives

After reading the next two sections, you should be able to:

1. Describe the six stages in the rational choice decision process.
2. Explain why people have difficulty identifying problems and opportunities.

RATIONAL CHOICE PARADIGM OF DECISION MAKING

How should people make decisions in organizations? Most business leaders would likely answer this question by saying that effective decision making involves identifying, selecting, and applying the best possible alternative. In other words, the best decisions use pure logic and all available information to choose the alternative with the highest value–such as highest expected profitability, customer satisfaction, employee well-being, or some combination of these outcomes. For example, Google relics on careful analysis to choose the best job applicants, the best way to present its advertisements on the Web page, the best companies to acquire, the best projects to fund, and so on. These decisions sometimes involve complex calculations of data to produce a formula that points to the best choice.

In its extreme form, this calculative view of decision making represents the **rational choice paradigm,** which has dominated the philosophy and scholarship of decision making in Western societies for most of written history. It was established 2,500 years ago when Plato and his contemporaries in ancient Greece raised logical debate and reasoning to a fine art. A few centuries later, Greek and Roman Stoics insisted that one should always "follow where reason leads" rather than fall victim to passion and emotions. About 400 years ago, Descartes and other European philosophers emphasized that the ability to make logical decisions is one of the most important accomplishments of human beings. In the 1700s, Scottish philosophers proposed that the best choice is the one that offers the "greatest good for the greatest number." This eventually evolved into the ethical principle of utilitarianism (described in Chapter 2), as well as maximization, which is at the heart of contemporary economics. By the 1900s, social scientists and mathematicians had developed elegant rational choice

rational choice paradigm
The view in decision making that people should—and typically do—use logic and all available information to choose the alternative with the highest value.

models and formulas that are now embedded in operations research, economics, and other decision sciences.[4]

subjective expected utility
The probability (expectation) of satisfaction (utility) resulting from choosing a specific alternative in a decision.

The ultimate principle of the rational choice paradigm is to choose the alternative with the highest **subjective expected utility.**[5] Subjective expected utility is the probability (expectation) of satisfaction (utility) for each alternative. Rational choice assumes that decision makers should (and do) select the alternative that offers the greatest level of happiness (i.e., maximization), such as highest returns for stockholders and highest satisfaction for customers, employees, government, and other stakeholders. Subjective expected utility involves calculating (1) the probability that each alternative will cause any of the possible outcomes to occur and (2) the value (or happiness) of those possible outcomes. Consider Google's hiring process, which involves screening several hundred thousand applications each year to select a few thousand of those applicants. The company wants to hire the best people–those who will provide the greatest value to Google. In other words, it wants to choose applicants with the highest subjective expected utility. Google estimates the potential of each applicant using a selection formula and selects those with the highest scores.

Along with its principle of making decisions around subjective expected utility, the rational choice paradigm assumes that decision makers follow the systematic process illustrated in Exhibit 7.1.[6] The first step is to identify the problem or recognize an opportunity. A *problem* is a deviation between the current and the desired situation–the gap between "what is" and "what ought to be." This deviation is a symptom of more fundamental root causes that need to be corrected.[7] An *opportunity* is a deviation between current expectations and a potentially better situation that was not previously expected. In other words, decision makers realize that some decisions may produce results beyond current goals or expectations.

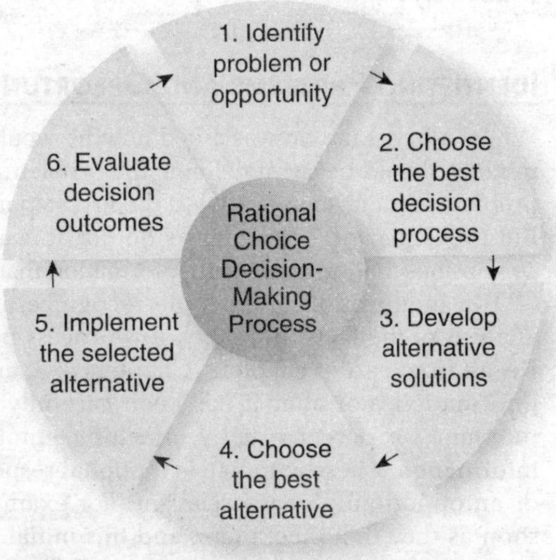

Exhibit 7.1 *Rational Choice Decision-Making Process*

The second step involves deciding how to process the decision.[8] One issue is whether the decision maker has enough information or needs to involve others in the process. Later in this chapter, we'll examine the contingencies of employee involvement in the decision. Another issue is whether the decision is programmed or nonprogrammed. *Programmed decisions* follow standard operating procedures; they have been resolved in the past, so the optimal solution has already been identified and documented. In contrast, *nonprogrammed decisions* require all steps in the decision model because the problems are new, complex, or ill-defined. The third step is to identify and develop a list of possible solutions. This usually begins by searching for ready-made solutions, such as practices that have worked well on similar problems. If an acceptable solution cannot be found, then decision makers need to design a custom-made solution or modify an existing one.

The fourth step in the rational choice decision process is to choose the alternative with the highest subjective expected utility. This calls for all possible information about all possible alternatives and their outcomes, but the rational choice paradigm assumes this can be accomplished with ease. The fifth step in the rational choice decision process is to implement the selected alternative. Rational choice experts have little to say about this step because they assume implementation occurs without any problems. This is followed by the sixth step, evaluating whether the gap has narrowed between "what is" and "what ought to be." Ideally, this information should come from systematic benchmarks so that relevant feedback is objective and easily observed.

Problems with the Rational Choice Paradigm

The rational choice paradigm seems so logical, yet it is impossible to apply in reality. One reason is that the model assumes people are efficient and logical information processing machines. But as we will discuss over the next few pages, people have difficulty recognizing problems; they cannot (or will not) simultaneously process the huge volume of information needed to identify the best solution; and they have difficulty recognizing when their choices have failed. The second reason why the rational model doesn't fit reality is that it focuses on logical thinking and completely ignores the fact that emotions also influence–perhaps even dominate–the decision-making process. As we shall discover in this chapter, emotions both support and interfere with our quest to make better decisions.[9] With these points in mind, let's look again at each step in the rational choice decision-making process, but with more detail about what really happens.

Identifying Problems and Opportunities

When Albert Einstein was asked how he would save the world in one hour, he replied that the first 55 minutes should be spent defining the problem and the last 5 minutes solving it.[10] Einstein's point is that problem identification is not just the first step in decision making; it is arguably the most important step. But problems and opportunities do not appear on our desks as well-labeled objects. Instead, they are conclusions that we form from information that something is wrong or that a higher standard is possible.

You might think that people recognize problems and opportunities on the basis of systematic analysis of the facts. In reality, this process begins much earlier and without conscious deliberation. Recall from earlier chapters (Chapters 3, 4, and 5) that preferences are formed as soon as we receive information, not after it has been carefully analyzed.[11] Specifically, we evaluate information the moment we perceive it by attaching emotional markers (anger, caution, delight, etc.) to that information. These automatic emotional responses shape our perception that something is a problem or an opportunity or is irrelevant. For example, employees form an opinion of new co-workers as soon as they first meet them, and this initial impression influences how quickly new employees are viewed as successes (opportunities) or failures (problems). If the new employee is viewed negatively, any instances of failure are quickly labeled as problems. But if co-workers form a positive initial impression of a new employee, that newcomer's failures are less likely to be viewed as problems–they are ignored or dismissed as temporary setbacks.

Problems with Problem Identification

The problem identification stage is, itself, filled with problems. Below are five of the most widely recognized concerns.[12]

Stakeholder Framing Employees, clients, and other stakeholders with vested interests try to "frame" the situation by persuading decision makers that the available information points to a problem or an opportunity or does not have any importance at all. This framing of facts tends to short-circuit the decision maker's full assessment of the situation.

Perceptual Defense People sometimes block out bad news as a coping mechanism. Their brain refuses to see information that threatens their self-concept. This phenomenon is not true for everyone. Some people inherently avoid negative information, whereas others are more sensitive to it. Recent studies also report that people are more likely to disregard danger signals when they have limited control over the situation.[13] For example, an investigation of the space shuttle *Columbia* disaster revealed that NASA managers rejected suggestions and evidence that the shuttle and its seven crew members were in trouble (see photo below).

Mental Models *Mental models* are visual or relational images in our mind of the external world (see Chapter 3); they fill in information that we don't immediately see, which helps us understand and navigate in our surrounding environment. Many mental images are also prototypes–they represent models of how things should be. Unfortunately, these mental models also blind us from seeing unique problems or opportunities because they produce a negative evaluation of things that are dissimilar to the mental model. If an idea doesn't fit the existing mental model of how things should work, the idea is dismissed as unworkable or undesirable.

Restrictive mental models explain why many excellent products and creative ideas are initially rejected by industry veterans. For example, Apple, Inc.'s "1984" television commercial, which launched the Apple Macintosh during the 1984 Super Bowl, is considered the best television commercial in history (as rated by *Advertising Age*), yet it almost didn't see the light of day. Unlike traditional commercials, which name the product throughout and illustrate its features, the 60-second "1984" ad shows a female athlete hurling a sledgehammer at a giant TV screen of an Orwellian Big Brother, liberating thousands of subjugated followers. The Macintosh computer isn't shown at all, and its name is revealed only during the last eight seconds. Apple's external board members loathed the ad because

No Problem, Houston? In February 2003, the NASA space shuttle *Columbia* disintegrated during reentry, killing all seven crew members. The disintegration was technically caused by a hole in the left wing, created when a large piece of foam debris struck the wing during liftoff. However, a special accident investigation board concluded that NASA's middle management continually resisted attempts to recognize that the *Columbia* was in trouble and therefore made no attempt to prevent loss of life. For example, photos from military satellites would have determined whether the foam caused serious wing damage. But when a team of engineers requested these photos, NASA management shot back an e-mail just 26 minutes later rejecting the request without explanation. Managers also questioned tests suggesting that a chunk of foam debris could cause wing damage, yet they were quick to accept a faulty test showing that the foam could not damage the wing. In addition, the accident board reported that NASA managers criticized those who believed that a problem existed. One engineer was called "alarmist"; NASA's lead flight director said that the "rationale was lousy" in a report submitted by an engineering team concerned about the wing damage. In one meeting, *Columbia's* lead flight director candidly admitted: "I don't think there is much we can do, so you know it's not really a factor during the flight because there isn't much we can do about it."[14]

it was so contrary to their mental prototype of what a good ad should look like. Some claimed it was the worst commercial in history; others proposed firing Apple's ad agency. On the basis of this reaction, Apple CEO John Sculley asked Jay Chiat (the head of Apple's ad agency, Chiat-Day) to sell the company's only two Super Bowl time slots. Instead, Chiat sold the short 30-second space but claimed that he could not find a buyer for the 60-second slot. The single 60-second ad shown during the Super Bowl had such a huge effect that it was featured on evening news broadcasts over the next several days. A month later, Apple's board members applauded the Macintosh team for a successful launch and apologized for their misjudgment of the "1984" commercial.[15]

Decisive Leadership Studies report that employees rate leaders as more effective when they are more decisive.[16] Being decisive includes quickly forming an opinion of whether an event signals a problem or opportunity. Consequently, eager to look effective, many leaders quickly announce problems or opportunities before having a chance to logically assess the situation. The result, according to research, is more often a poorer decision than would result if more time had been devoted to identifying the problem and evaluating the alternatives.

Solution-Focused Problems Decision makers have a tendency to define problems as veiled solutions.[17] For instance, someone might say: "The problem is that we need more control over our suppliers." This statement doesn't describe the problem; it is really a slightly rephrased presentation of a solution to an ill-defined problem. Decision makers engage in solution-focused problem identification because it provides comforting closure to the otherwise ambiguous and uncertain nature of problems. People with a strong need for cognitive closure (those who feel uncomfortable with ambiguity) are particularly prone to solution-focused problems. Some decision makers take this solution focus a step further by seeing all problems as solutions that have worked well for them in the past, even though they were applied under different circumstances. Again, the familiarity of past solutions makes the current problem less ambiguous or uncertain.

Identifying Problems and Opportunities More Effectively

Recognizing problems and opportunities will always be a challenge, but one way to improve the process is by becoming aware of the five problem identification biases described above. For example, by recognizing that mental models restrict a person's perspective of the world, decision makers are more motivated to consider other perspectives of reality. Along with increasing their awareness of problem identification flaws, leaders require considerable willpower to resist the temptation of looking decisive when a more thoughtful examination of the situation should occur. A third way to improve problem identification is for leaders to create a norm of "divine discontent." They are never satisfied with the status quo, and this aversion to complacency creates a mindset that more actively searches for problems and opportunities.[18]

Finally, employees can minimize problem identification blunders by discussing the situation with colleagues. The logic here is that blind spots in problem identification are more easily identified by hearing how others perceive certain information and diagnose problems. Opportunities also become

"My team has created a very innovative solution, but we're still looking for a problem to go with it."

apparent when outsiders explore this information from their different mental models. Google, described at the beginning of this chapter, actively applies this practice. The company deliberately puts employees into teams so that they bounce ideas off each other. In addition, the company has an online "suggestion box" where employees post their ideas (including perspectives of a problem or opportunity) so that other Google employees can comment on and rate them.[19]

Learning Objectives

After reading the next two sections, you should be able to:

3. Explain why people do not follow the rational choice model when evaluating alternative choices.
4. Describe three ways in which emotions influence the selection of alternatives.
5. Outline how intuition operates.
6. Describe four causes of escalation of commitment.

EVALUATING AND CHOOSING ALTERNATIVES

According to the rational choice paradigm of decision making, people rely on logic to evaluate and choose alternatives. This paradigm assumes that decision makers have well-articulated and agreed-on organizational goals, that they efficiently and simultaneously process facts about all alternatives and the consequences of those alternatives, and that they choose the alternative with the highest payoff.

bounded rationality
The view that people are bounded in their decision-making capabilities, including access to limited information, limited information processing, and tendency toward satisficing rather than maximizing when making choices.

Nobel Prize–winning organizational scholar Herbert Simon questioned these assumptions a half century ago. He argued that people engage in **bounded rationality** because they process limited and imperfect information and rarely select the best choice.[20] Simon and other OB experts report that the rational choice paradigm differs in several ways from how people actually evaluate and choose alternatives. These differences, as shown in Exhibit 7.2, are so significant that even economists have shifted from rational choice to bounded rationality assumptions in their theories. Let's look at these differences in terms of goals, information processing, and maximization.

Problems with Goals

The rational choice paradigm assumes that organizational goals are clear and agreed-on. In fact, these conditions are necessary to identify "what ought to be" and, therefore, provide a standard against which each alternative is evaluated. Unfortunately, organizational goals are often ambiguous or in conflict with each other. One survey reported that 25 percent of managers and employees felt decisions are delayed because of difficulty agreeing on what they want the decision to achieve.[21]

Problems with Information Processing

The rational choice paradigm also makes several assumptions about the human capacity to process information. It assumes that decision makers can process information about all alternatives and their consequences, whereas this is not possible in reality. Instead, people evaluate only a few alternatives and only some of the main outcomes of those alternatives.[22] For example, there may be dozens of computer brands to choose from and dozens of features to consider, yet people typically evaluate only a few brands and a few features.

Rational Choice Paradigm Assumptions	Observations from Organizational Behavior
Goals are clear, compatible, and agreed-on.	Goals are ambiguous, in conflict, and lack full support.
Decision makers can calculate all alternatives and their outcomes.	Decision makers have limited information processing abilities.
Decision makers evaluate all alternatives simultaneously.	Decision makers evaluate alternatives sequentially.
Decision makers use absolute standards to evaluate alternatives.	Decision makers evaluate alternatives against an implicit favorite.
Decision makers use factual information to choose alternatives.	Decision makers process perceptually distorted information.
Decision makers choose the alternative with the highest payoff.	Decision makers choose the alternative that is good enough (satisficing).

Exhibit 7.2 *Rational Choice Assumptions versus Organizational Behavior Findings about Choosing Alternatives*

implicit favorite
A preferred alternative that the decision maker uses repeatedly as a comparison with other choices.

A related problem is that decision makers typically evaluate alternatives sequentially rather than all at the same time. As a new alternative comes along, it is immediately compared to an **implicit favorite**–an alternative that the decision maker prefers and that is used as a comparison with other choices. When choosing a new computer system, for example, people typically have an implicit favorite brand or model in their heads that they use to compare with the others. This sequential process of comparing alternatives with an implicit favorite occurs even when decision makers aren't consciously aware that they are doing this.[23]

Although the implicit-favorite comparison process seems to be hardwired in human decision making (i.e., we naturally compare things), it often undermines effective decision making because people distort information to favor their implicit favorite over the alternative choices. They tend to ignore problems with the implicit favorite and advantages of the alternative. Decision makers also overweight factors on which the implicit favorite is better and underweight areas in which the alternative is superior.[24]

Biased Decision Heuristics According to the rational choice paradigm, the best choices have the highest subjective expected utility. However, psychologists Amos Tversky and Daniel Kahneman discovered that human beings have built-in *decision heuristics*–unstructured and often nonconscious modes of reasoning or rules of thumb–that bias an individual's perceived probabilities that specific outcomes will occur. Probabilities represent the expectancies in rational choice thinking, so biased probabilities result in less rational decision making. Three of the most widely studied heuristic biases are the anchoring and adjustment heuristic, availability heuristic, and representativeness heuristic:[25]

anchoring and adjustment heuristic
A natural tendency for people to be influenced by an initial anchor point such that they do not sufficiently move away from that point as new information is provided.

availability heuristic
A natural tendency to assign higher probabilities to objects or events that are easier to recall from memory, even though ease of recall is also affected by nonprobability factors (e.g., emotional response, recent events).

representativeness heuristic
A natural tendency to evaluate probabilities of events or objects by the degree to which they resemble (are representative of) other events or objects rather than on objective probability information.

- **Anchoring and adjustment heuristic.** This heuristic states that we are influenced by an initial anchor point and do not sufficiently move away from that point as new information is provided.[26] The result is that the initial anchor point biases our estimate above or below the true value of what we are trying to estimate. The anchoring and adjustment heuristic is used to advantage when negotiators start with a high initial offer. The other party in the negotiation may initially experience sticker shock but eventually feels more comfortable accepting a high price than he or she would if the initial offer had been lower. Some experts suggest that the anchoring and adjustment heuristic also partially explains the primacy effect–people do not adjust their perceptions and attitudes toward someone after they have formed an initial impression of the person.
- **Availability heuristic.** Objects or events are assigned higher probabilities of occurring if they are easier to recall from memory. This makes sense to some extent, because we generally do have an easier time recalling frequent events. However, the ease of recalling something is also affected by other factors, which distort our probability estimates.[27] One biasing influence is that recent events are easier to recall than are events further in the past. Our estimate of the percentage of executives who are greedy is higher soon after hearing news about high executive salaries than at a time when there is no recent news about executive salaries. This ease of recall increases our perception that executives are highly paid and greedy. Another influence on our recall is the emotional strength of the event. Shark attacks are an example. These attacks on human beings receive considerable media attention and generate gory images in our minds, so they are easy to recall. Because of this ease of recollection, we think the probability of being bitten by sharks is much higher than is true.
- **Representativeness heuristic.** People tend to evaluate probabilities of events or objects by the degree to which they resemble (are representative of) other events or objects rather than on objective probability information.[28] Stereotyping is one form of this bias. Suppose you are asked to identify a student's college major on the basis of only the person's personality profile and the fact that the person is in a population of 25 engineers and 75 social science students. If the personality fits your stereotype of engineers, you would likely identify the student as an engineer even though he or she is three times as likely to be a social science major. Another form of the representativeness heuristic, known as the *clustering illusion,* is the tendency to see patterns on the basis of a small sample of events that, in fact, are random. For example, most players and coaches believe that players are more likely to have a successful shot on the net when their previous two or three shots have been successful. The representativeness heuristic is at work here because players and coaches believe these sequences are causally connected (representative) when, in reality, they are random events.

Problems with Maximization

satisficing
Selecting an alternative that is satisfactory or "good enough," rather than the alternative with the highest value (maximization).

One of the main assumptions of the rational choice paradigm is that people want to (and are able to) choose the alternative with the highest payoff (i.e., the highest subjective expected utility). Yet rather than aiming for maximization, people engage in **satisficing**–they choose an alternative that is satisfactory or "good enough."[29] In effect, they evaluate alternatives sequentially and select the first one perceived to be above a standard of acceptance for their needs and preferences. One reason why satisficing occurs is that, as mentioned earlier, decision makers have a natural tendency to evaluate alternatives sequentially, not all at the same time. They evaluate each alternative against the implicit favorite and eventually select an option that scores above a subjective minimum point considered to be good enough.

The other reason why people engage in satisficing rather than maximization is that choosing the best alternative demands more information processing capacity than people possess or are willing to apply. Studies have found that people like to have choices, but when exposed to many alternatives, they become cognitive misers by engaging in less optimal decision making.[30] Such decision-making efficiencies include discarding alternatives that fail a threshold level on one or two factors (such as color or size), comparing among only a few alternatives rather than all choices, and choosing the first alternative above a preset standard (i.e., satisficing). One study found that, compared to people given few alternatives, those given a large number of alternatives subsequently experienced less physical stamina, had more difficulty performing arithmetic calculations, were less resilient in the face of failure, and engaged in more procrastination. In other words, making the best choice among many alternatives can be cognitively and emotionally draining.

One other observation suggests that people lack information processing capacity to select the best alternative. Research has found that when people are given more alternatives, they are less likely to make any choice at all. This problem was highlighted in a study of consumer responses to two jam-tasting booths in a grocery store, one displaying 6 types of jam and the other displaying 24 flavors. Thirty percent of shoppers who stopped at the 6-jam display bought some jam; only 3 percent of shoppers who stopped by the 24-jam display bought jam. The larger number of choices discouraged customers from making any purchase decision. These results are similar to those in other studies where people made decisions about chocolates, term essays, and pension plan investment options.[31] Four decades ago, futurist Alvin Toffler warned about the increasing risk of choice overload: "People of the future may suffer not from an absence of choice, but from a paralyzing surfeit of it. They may turn out to be victims of that peculiarly super-industrial dilemma: overchoice."[32]

Evaluating Opportunities

Opportunities are just as important as problems, but what happens when an opportunity is "discovered" is quite different from when a problem is discovered. According to a recent study of decision failures, decision makers do not evaluate several alternatives when they find an opportunity; after all, the opportunity *is* the solution, so why look for others! An opportunity is usually experienced as an exciting and rare revelation, so decision makers tend to have an emotional attachment to the opportunity. Unfortunately, this emotional preference motivates decision makers to apply the opportunity and short-circuit any detailed evaluation of it.[33]

Short-Circuited by Choice Overload Companies in many countries typically offer defined-contribution pension plans [typically 401(k) plans in the United States]. The employee contributes a fixed amount of pretax earnings into the plan each year (often with matching employer contributions), and retirement income depends on the investment performance of those funds. Increasingly, companies are giving employees the responsibility of deciding how their pension assets should be invested. In some cases, employees are presented with a list of up to 100 investment alternatives (money market, balanced funds, property funds, ethical funds, growth funds, etc.). However, studies have found that when presented with a large number of investment alternatives, employees choose the least cognitively challenging choice—they don't make any decision at all. They avoid signing up for the pension plan, even though participation in the plan offers short-term tax advantages and long-term retirement financial security. Fortunately, some companies have found a way to increase pension plan participation rates—they give staff only a few investment alternatives. In one extreme example, employees receive a card on which they tick one choice—a small pretax deduction invested in a combination of money market and balanced mutual funds. Companies that have introduced this very simple decision form report a 25 percent increase in employee participation rates in the company's pension plan.[34]

Emotions and Making Choices

Herbert Simon and many other experts have presented plenty of evidence that people do not evaluate alternatives nearly as well as is assumed by the rational choice paradigm. However, they neglected to mention another glaring weakness with rational choice: It completely ignores the effect of emotions in human decision making. Just as both the rational and emotional brain centers alert us to problems, they also influence our choice of alternatives.[35] Emotions affect the evaluation of alternatives in three ways.

Emotions Form Early Preferences The emotional marker process described earlier in this chapter as well as in previous chapters (Chapters 3 through 5) determines our preferences for each alternative. Our brain very quickly attaches specific emotions to information about each alternative, and our preferred alternative is strongly influenced by those initial emotional markers. Of course, logical analysis also influences which alternative we choose, but it requires strong logical evidence to change our initial preferences (initial emotional markers). Yet even logical analysis depends on emotions to sway our decision. Specifically, neuroscientific evidence says that information produced from logical analysis is tagged with emotional markers that then motivate us to choose or avoid a particular alternative. Ultimately, emotions, not rational logic, energize us to make the preferred choice. In fact, people with damaged emotional brain centers have difficulty making choices.

Emotions Change the Decision Evaluation Process A considerable body of literature indicates that moods and specific emotions influence the *process* of evaluating alternatives.[36] For instance, we pay more attention to details when in a negative mood, possibly because a negative mood signals that there is something wrong that requires attention. When in a positive mood, on the other hand, we pay less attention to details and rely on a more programmed decision routine. Research also suggests that decision makers rely on stereotypes and other shortcuts to speed up the choice process when they experience anger. Anger also makes them more optimistic about the success of risky alternatives, whereas the emotion of fear tends to make them less optimistic. Overall, emotions shape *how* we evaluate information, not just which choice we select.

Emotions Serve as Information When We Evaluate Alternatives The third way that emotions influence the evaluation of alternatives is through a process called "emotions as information." Marketing experts have found that we listen in on our emotions to help identify the preferred option.[37] You might think of this as a temporary improvement in emotional intelligence. Most emotional experiences remain below the level of conscious awareness, but people actively try to be more sensitive to these subtle emotions when making a decision.

When buying a new car, for example, you not only logically evaluate each vehicle's features; you also try to gauge your emotions when visualizing what it would be like to own each of the alternative cars on your list of choices. Even if you have solid information about the quality of each vehicle on key features (purchase price, fuel efficiency, maintenance costs, resale value, etc.), you are swayed by your emotional reaction to each vehicle and actively try to sense that emotional response when thinking about it. Some people pay more attention to these gut feelings, and personality tests such as the Myers-Briggs Type Indicator (see Chapter 2) identify individuals who listen in on their emotions more than others.[38] But all of us use our emotions as information to some degree. This phenomenon ties directly into our next topic, intuition.

Intuition and Making Choices

Greg McDonald felt uneasy about a suspicious-looking crack in the rock face, so the veteran miner warned a co-worker to stay away from the area. "There was no indication there was anything wrong–just a little crack," McDonald recalled. A few minutes later, the ceiling in the mine shaft 3,000 feet underground caved in. Fortunately, the co-worker had heeded McDonald's advice. "If he had been there, he would be dead," McDonald said in an interview following a near-sleepless night after the incident.[39]

The gut instinct that helped Greg McDonald save his co-worker's life is known as **intuition**–the ability to know when a problem or opportunity exists and to select the best course of action without conscious reasoning.[40] Intuition is both an emotional experience and a rapid nonconscious analytic process. As mentioned in the previous section, the gut feelings we experience are emotional signals that have enough intensity to make us consciously aware of them. These signals warn us of impending danger, such as a dangerous mine wall, or motivate us to take advantage of an opportunity. Some intuition also directs us to preferred choices relative to other alternatives in the situation.

intuition
The ability to know when a problem or opportunity exists and to select the best course of action without conscious reasoning.

All gut feelings are emotional signals, but not all emotional signals are intuition. The key distinction is that intuition involves rapidly comparing our observations with deeply held patterns learned through experience.[41] These templates represent tacit knowledge that has been implicitly acquired over time. They are mental models that help us to understand whether the current situation is good or bad, depending on how well that situation fits our mental model. When a template fits or doesn't fit the current situation, emotions are produced that motivate us to act. Greg McDonald's years of experience produced mental templates of unsafe rock faces that matched what he saw on that fateful day. Studies have also found that chess masters receive emotional signals when they sense an opportunity through quick observation of a chessboard. When given the opportunity to think about the situation, chess masters can explain why they see a favorable move on the chessboard. However, their intuition signals the opportunity long before this rational analysis takes place.

As mentioned, some emotional signals are not intuition. As a result, some experts warn that we should not trust our gut feelings. The problem is that emotional responses are not always based on well-grounded mental models. Instead, they occur when we compare the current situation to more remote templates, which may or may not be relevant. A new employee might feel confident about relations with a supplier, whereas an experienced employee senses potential problems. The difference is that the new employee relies on templates from other experiences or industries that might not work well in this situation. Thus, whether the emotions we experience in a situation represent intuition or not depends largely on our level of experience in that situation.

So far, we have described intuition as an emotional experience (gut feeling) and a process in which we compare the current situation with well-established templates of the mind. Intuition also relies on *action scripts*–programmed decision routines that speed up our response to pattern matches or mismatches.[42] Action scripts effectively shorten the decision-making process by jumping from problem identification to selection of a solution. In other words, action scripting is a form of programmed decision making. Action scripts are generic, so we need to consciously adapt them to the specific situation.

Making Choices More Effectively

It is very difficult to get around the human limitations of making choices, but a few strategies help to minimize these concerns. One important discovery is that decisions tend to have a higher failure rate when leaders are decisive rather than contemplative about the available options. Of course, decisions can also be ineffective when leaders take too long to make a choice, but research indicates that a lack of logical evaluation of alternatives is a greater concern. By systematically assessing alternatives against relevant factors, decision makers minimize the implicit-favorite and satisficing problems that occur when they rely on general subjective judgments. This recommendation does not suggest that we ignore intuition; rather, it suggests that we use it in combination with careful analysis of relevant information.[43]

A second piece of advice is that we need to remember that decisions are influenced by both rational and emotional processes. With this awareness, some decision makers deliberately revisit important issues so they look at the information in different moods and have allowed their initial emotions to subside. For example, if you sense that your team is feeling somewhat too self-confident when making an important competitive decision, you might decide to have the team members revisit the decision a few days later when they are thinking more critically. Another strategy is **scenario planning,** which is a disciplined method for imagining possible futures. It typically involves thinking about what would happen if a significant environmental condition changed and what the organization should do to anticipate and react to such an outcome.[44] Scenario planning is a useful vehicle for choosing the best solutions under possible scenarios long before they occur, because alternative courses of action are evaluated without the pressure and emotions that occur during real emergencies.

scenario planning
A systematic process of thinking about alternative futures and what the organization should do to anticipate and react to those environments.

IMPLEMENTING DECISIONS

Implementing decisions is often skipped over in most writing about the decision-making process. Yet leading business writers emphasize that execution–translating decisions into action–is one of the most important and challenging tasks of leaders. A survey of 3,600 managers identified the "drive for results" as one of the five most important competencies of effective managers. This evidence is backed up by Larry Bossidy's experience leading thousands of managers. "When assessing candidates, the first thing I looked for was energy and enthusiasm for execution," says the former CEO of Honeywell and Allied Signal. The art and science of implementing decisions will be covered more fully in later chapters, particularly those on leadership and organizational change.[45]

EVALUATING DECISION OUTCOMES

postdecisional justification
The tendency to support the selected alternative in a decision by forgetting or downplaying the negative features of that alternative, emphasizing its positive features, and doing the opposite for alternatives not selected.

Contrary to the rational choice paradigm, decision makers aren't completely honest with themselves when evaluating the effectiveness of their decisions. One concern is that after making a choice, decision makers tend to support their choice by forgetting or downplaying the negative features of the selected alternative and emphasizing its positive features. This perceptual distortion, known as **postdecisional justification,** results from the need to maintain a positive self-concept.[46] Postdecisional justification gives people an excessively optimistic evaluation of their decisions, but only until they receive very clear and undeniable information to the contrary. Unfortunately, it also inflates the decision maker's initial evaluation of the decision, so reality often comes as a painful shock when objective feedback is finally received.

Escalation of Commitment

escalation of commitment
The tendency to repeat an apparently bad decision or allocate more resources to a failing course of action.

In addition to postdecisional justification, people poorly evaluate their decision outcomes due to **escalation of commitment**–the tendency to repeat an apparently bad decision or allocate more resources to a failing course of action.[47] Scotland's new parliament building is one example of escalation of commitment. Originally estimated at £50 million (US$80 million), the Holyrood building eventually cost £400 million and took twice as long to construct. Another example is the construction of Denver International Airport, which was delayed because of a badly flawed state-of-the-art automated baggage-handling system. The airport opened 16 months late and between $1 and $2 billion overbudget, using mainly an older baggage system; the new baggage system was put to some use but was abandoned a decade later due to high costs. A third example is the Darlington nuclear power plant in Ontario, Canada, which had an estimated cost of $2 billion (some claim the estimate was $5 billion) and was eventually completed at a cost of more than $14 billion. This huge debacle prompted the Ontario government to deregulate the electricity industry and split Ontario Hydro (now called Hydro One) into two operating companies. Ironically, a former CEO of Ontario Hydro warned that Darlington and other megaprojects invite escalating commitment because "once you commit to them, there's very little you can do to reverse that commitment."[48]

Causes of Escalating Commitment The four main reasons why people are led deeper and deeper into failing projects are self-justification, prospect theory effect, perceptual blinders, and closing costs.

- *Self-justification.* Individuals are motivated to maintain their course of action when they have a high need to justify their decision. This self-justification is particularly evident when decision makers are personally identified with the project and have staked their reputations to some extent on the project's success.[49] The Irish government's PPARS project (see photo) likely experienced escalation

Irish Health under re-PPARS In the mid-1990s, executives at five health boards across Ireland decided to develop a common payroll system, called PPARS (payroll, payment, and related systems). Using well-established SAP software, the project would be done in three years at a total estimated cost of US$12 million. Health department officials were enthusiastic about PPARS' many benefits, but four years later the system was still far from completion even though costs had more than doubled to $25 million. Asked in 2002 to evaluate the project, Hay Associates concluded that PPARS was worth continuing, even if only to recoup the funds spent so far. The catch, however, was that the government needed to fork over another $120 million, which it agreed to do. By 2005, Ireland's finance department was sounding alarm bells that PPARS costs had spiraled out of control and the operational parts of the system were error-prone. The most embarrassing example was a health department employee who received a $1.5 million paycheck one week. The Irish government halted the rollout of PPARS, yet senior health officials remained confident in its success, ordering staff as late as May 2007 to "realize the benefits" of the system. PPARS was officially axed in July 2007. The estimated cost of the failed project: somewhere between $250 and $350 million.[50]

to some degree for this reason. The reputations of government politicians and health board officials depended on the success of PPARS, and pouring more money into the project symbolized their continued support and evidence that the decision was a wise one.

prospect theory
A natural tendency to feel more dissatisfaction from losing a particular amount than satisfaction from gaining an equal amount.

- *Prospect theory effect.* You would think that people dislike losing $50 just as much as they like receiving $50, but that isn't true for most of us. The negative emotions we experience when losing a particular amount are stronger than the positive emotions we experience when gaining the same amount. Consequently, we have a tendency to take more risks to avoid losses. This effect, called **prospect theory,** is a second explanation for escalation of commitment. Stopping a project is a certain loss, which is more painful to most people than the uncertainty of success associated with continuing to fund the project. Given the choice, decision makers choose the less painful option.[51]

- *Perceptual blinders.* Escalation of commitment sometimes occurs because decision makers do not see the problems soon enough.[52] They nonconsciously screen out or explain away negative information to protect self-esteem. Serious problems initially look like random errors along the trend line to success. Even when decision makers see that something is wrong, the information is sufficiently ambiguous that it can be misinterpreted or justified.
- *Closing costs.* Even when a project's success is in doubt, decision makers will persist because the costs of ending the project are high or unknown. Terminating a major project may involve large financial penalties, a bad public image, or personal political costs.

These four conditions make escalation of commitment look irrational. Usually it is, but there are exceptions. Studies suggest that throwing more money into a failing project is sometimes a logical attempt to further understand an ambiguous situation. This strategy is essentially a variation of testing unknown waters. By adding more resources, the decision maker gains new information about the effectiveness of these funds, which provides more feedback about the project's future success. This strategy is particularly common where the project has high closing costs.[53]

Evaluating Decision Outcomes More Effectively

One of the most effective ways to minimize escalation of commitment and postdecisional justification is to ensure that the people who made the original decision are not the same people who later evaluate that decision. This separation of roles minimizes the self-justification effect because the person responsible for evaluating the decision is not connected to the original decision. A second strategy is to publicly establish a preset level at which the decision is abandoned or reevaluated. This is similar to a stop-loss order in the stock market, whereby the stock is sold if it falls below a certain price. The problem with this solution is that conditions are often so complex that it is difficult to identify an appropriate point to abandon a project.[54]

A third strategy is to find a source of systematic and clear feedback.[55] For example, the phenomenally large cost overruns at Scotland's new parliament building might have been smaller if the Scottish government had received less ambiguous or less distorted information from civil servants about the true costs of the project during the first few years. (In fact, civil servants hid some of these costs from elected officials.)[56] A fourth strategy to improve the decision evaluation process is to involve several people in the evaluation. Co-workers continuously monitor each other and might notice problems sooner than someone working alone on the project. Employee involvement offers these and other benefits to the decision-making process, as we discuss next.

Learning Objectives

After reading the next two sections, you should be able to:

7. Describe four benefits of employee involvement in decision making.
8. Identify four contingencies that affect the optimal level of employee involvement.
9. Outline the four steps in the creative process.
10. Describe the characteristics of employees and the workplace that support creativity.

Employee Involvement in Decision Making

In this world of rapid change and increasing complexity, leaders rarely have enough information to make the best decision alone. Consequently, they need to rely on the knowledge and multiple perspectives of employees to more effectively solve problems or realize opportunities. "The Information Age has brought us into a democratic age, an age of participation and influence," says Traci Fenton, founder and CEO of WorldBlu, a consulting firm that specializes in employee involvement and organizational democracy.[57]

Employee involvement (also called *participative management*) refers to the degree to which employees influence how their work is organized and carried out.[58] Every organization has some form and various levels of employee involvement. At the lowest level, participation involves asking employees for information. They do not make recommendations and might not even know what the problem is about. At a moderate level of involvement, employees are told about the problem and provide recommendations to the decision maker. At the highest level of involvement, the entire decision-making process is handed over to employees. They identify the problem, choose the best alternative, and implement their choice.

employee involvement
The degree to which employees influence how their work is organized and carried out.

Benefits of Employee Involvement

For the past half century, organizational behavior scholars have advised that employee involvement potentially improves decision-making quality and commitment.[59] Involved employees can help improve decision quality by recognizing problems more quickly and defining them more accurately. Employees are, in many respects, the sensors of the organization's environment. When the organization's activities misalign with customer expectations, employees are usually the first to know. Employee involvement ensures that everyone in the organization is quickly alerted to such problems.[60] Employee involvement can also potentially improve the number and quality of solutions generated. In a well-managed meeting, team members create synergy by pooling their knowledge to form new alternatives. In other words, several people working together can potentially generate more and better solutions than the same people working alone.

Employee Involvement Keeps Thai Carbon Black in the Black Thai Carbon Black, which makes the black coloring agent in tires, inks, and many other products, views all of its employees as problem solvers. "The 'can do' attitude of every employee is important," says the president of the Thai-Indian joint venture. Each year, the staff submits over 600 productivity improvement suggestions, placing their ideas in one of the little red boxes located around the site. Participatory management meetings are held every month, at which employees are encouraged to come up with new ideas on ways to improve day-to-day operations. For instance, the company cut its transport costs by more than 10 percent after employees developed a special shipping bag allowing packers to stuff more product into the same volume. Thanks in part to its emphasis on employee involvement, Thai Carbon Black is one of the few companies outside Japan to receive the Deming Prize for total quality management. It has also received the Thailand Quality Class award, *Forbes* magazine's recognition as one of the best-managed companies, and Hewitt Associates' ranking as one of the best employers in Asia and Thailand.[61]

A third benefit of employee involvement is that, under specific conditions, it improves the evaluation of alternatives. Numerous studies on participative decision making, constructive conflict, and team dynamics have found that involvement brings out more diverse perspectives, tests ideas, and provides more valuable knowledge, all of which help the decision maker to select the best alternative.[62] A mathematical theorem introduced in 1785 by the Marquis de Condorcet also supports the view that many people outshine individuals alone when choosing among two alternatives.[63] To explain this idea (called *Condorcet's jury theorem*), let's suppose that you need to choose one of two firms for your company's accounting services. Furthermore, you and members of your team have, on average, a better than random chance of picking the firm that will provide superior service. Condorcet's theory states that the alternative selected by the team's majority is more likely to be correct than is the alternative selected by you or any other individual team member. Furthermore, the majority's accuracy will increase as you involve more people in the vote. Google applied Condorcet's theory in its prediction markets, which were described in the opening vignette to this chapter. By encouraging a large number of employees to vote on various alternatives, Google executives get better choices or estimates about future events.

Along with improving decision quality, employee involvement tends to strengthen employee commitment to the decision. Rather than viewing themselves as agents of someone else's decision, staff members feel personally responsible for its success. Involvement also has positive effects on employee motivation, satisfaction, and turnover. A recent study reported that employee involvement also increases skill variety, feelings of autonomy, and task identity, all of which increase job enrichment and potentially employee motivation. Participation is also a critical practice in organizational change because employees are more motivated to implement the decision and less likely to resist changes resulting from the decision.[64]

Contingencies of Employee Involvement

If employee involvement is so wonderful, why don't leaders leave all decisions to employees? The answer is that the optimal level of employee involvement depends on the situation. The employee involvement model shown in Exhibit 7.3 lists four contingencies: decision structure, source of decision knowledge, decision commitment, and risk of conflict in the decision process.

- *Decision structure.* At the beginning of this chapter, we described how some decisions are programmed, whereas others are nonprogrammed. Programmed decisions are less likely to need employee involvement because the solutions are already worked out from past incidents. In other words, the benefits of employee involvement increase with the novelty and complexity of the problem or opportunity.
- *Source of decision knowledge.* Subordinates should be involved in some level of decision making when the leader lacks sufficient knowledge and subordinates have additional information to improve decision quality. In many cases, employees are closer to customers and production activities, so they often know where the company can save money, improve product or service quality, and realize opportunities. This is particularly true for complex decisions where employees are more likely to possess relevant information.
- *Decision commitment.* Participation tends to improve employee commitment to the decision. If employees are unlikely to accept a decision made without their involvement, some level of participation is usually necessary.
- *Risk of conflict.* Two types of conflict undermine the benefits of employee involvement. First, if employee goals and norms conflict with the organization's goals, only a low level of employee involvement is advisable. Second, the degree of involvement depends on whether employees will

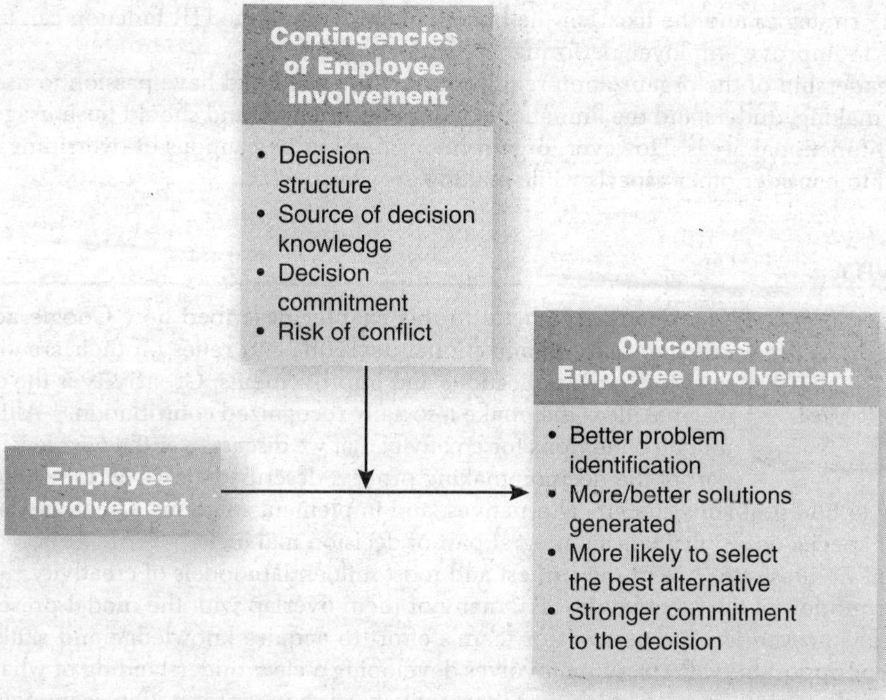

Exhibit 7.3 *Model of Employee Involvement in Decision Making*

reach agreement on the preferred solution. If conflict is likely, high involvement (i.e., employees make the decision alone) would be difficult to achieve.

Employee involvement is an important component of the decision-making process. To make the best decisions, we need to involve people who have the most valuable information and who will increase commitment to implement the decision. Another important component of decision making is creativity, which we discuss next.

Role of Technology in Decision Making[65]

Information and Communication Technology (ICT) has a key role in decision making across levels and functional areas within an organization. The leadership and organizational culture that are open to new technologies and technological changes make rigorous use of these in various decision making processes.

ICT has transformed itself from just being a supporting technology to a strategic tool. Organizations deploying technology for decision-making processes have implemented various analytical applications, data capturing tools, forecasting techniques and the like, which are operated and analyzed by specialists. Employees are also trained in new techniques and technologies which facilitate optimization of operation and meeting of customer expectations. ICT enables gathering of data on buying trends of consumers, their demands, cues which trigger buying behavior, data on cost of production, sales turnover, compensation costs, information on criteria for performance evaluation, etc. This large volume of data is useful for various functional divisions and for overall decision making.

Based on the analysis and forecasting of the data, the organization takes decisions regarding production target, sales target, alteration or improvements in supply chain, devising pricing and marketing strategies and the like. For the benefit of employees, the HR function can take decision on strategies to improve employee performance, perks/benefits, etc.

The leadership of the organization requires to see the need and have passion to use technology in decision making, understand the limitations of these techniques, and should push usage of technology across all functional areas. However, organizations need to be cautious of overriding on technology, and need to consider other aspects while making decisions.

CREATIVITY

creativity
The development of original ideas that make a socially recognized contribution.

The opening vignette to this chapter described how Google actively engages employees in organizational decisions and relies on their creativity to identify new software applications and improvements. **Creativity** is the development of original ideas that make a socially recognized contribution.[66] Although there are unique conditions for creativity that we discuss over the next few pages, it is really part of the decision-making process described earlier in the chapter. We rely on creativity to find problems, identify alternatives, and implement solutions. Creativity is not something saved for special occasions. It is an integral part of decision making.

Exhibit 7.4 illustrates one of the earliest and most influential models of creativity.[67] Although there are other models of the creative process, many of them overlap with the model presented here. The first stage is *preparation*–the person's or team's effort to acquire knowledge and skills regarding the problem or opportunity. Preparation involves developing a clear understanding of what you are trying to achieve through a novel solution and then actively studying information seemingly related to the topic.

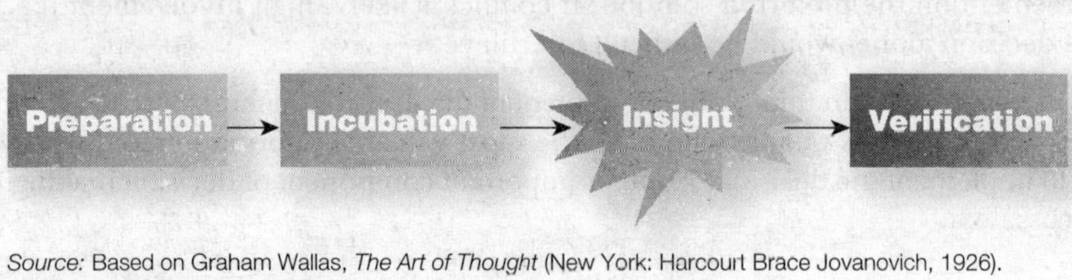

Source: Based on Graham Wallas, *The Art of Thought* (New York: Harcourt Brace Jovanovich, 1926).

Exhibit 7.4 *The Creative Process Model*

The second stage, called *incubation,* is the period of reflective thought. We put the problem aside, but our mind is still working on it in the background.[68] The important condition here is to maintain a low-level awareness by frequently revisiting the problem. Incubation does not mean that you forget about the problem or issue. Incubation assists **divergent thinking**–reframing the problem in a unique way and generating different approaches to the issue. This contrasts with *convergent thinking*–calculating the conventionally accepted "right answer" to a logical problem. Divergent thinking breaks us away from existing mental models so that we can apply concepts or processes from completely different areas of life. Consider the following classic example: Years ago, the experimental lightbulbs in Thomas Edison's lab kept falling off their fixtures until a technician wondered whether the threaded caps that screwed down tightly on kerosene bottles would work on lightbulbs. They did, and the design remains to this day.[69]

divergent thinking
Reframing a problem in a unique way and generating different approaches to the issue.

Insight, the third stage of creativity, refers to the experience of suddenly becoming aware of a unique idea.[70] Insight is often visually depicted as a lightbulb, but a better image would be a brief flash of light or perhaps a briefly flickering candle, because these bits of inspiration are fleeting and can be quickly lost if not documented. For this reason, many creative people keep a journal or notebook nearby at all times so that they can jot down their ideas before they disappear. Also, flickering ideas don't keep a particular schedule; they might come to you at any time of day or night.

Insights are merely rough ideas. Their usefulness still requires verification through detailed logical evaluation, experimentation, and further creative insight. Thus, although *verification* is labeled the final stage of creativity, it is really the beginning of a long process of creative decision making toward development of an innovative product or service. This ongoing process, as well as the conditions and practices that support creativity, are apparent at Nottingham-Spirk Design Associates, Inc. As Connections 7.1 describes, the successful Cleveland-based industrial-design firm relies on divergent and convergent meetings, prototyping, focus groups, and an inspiring work environment to produce dozens of marketable new ideas every year.

Creativity—The Foundation for Innovation

Creativity is one of the foundation pillars for innovation. Culture and traditions have an influence on creative interests, levels of creativity and nature and style of its outcome. The expressions of creativity can be in the form of art, culture, music, products, services to sustain in deprived or harsh conditions, to make optimum utilization of scarce resources, etc. The combination of creativity and commercialization leads to innovation where knowledge too has key role to play. According to Fienstein[71], "Creativity is making a connection between or combining two elements, which were not previously connected or combined."

Three conditions are essential to foster creativity among individuals in a society and provide competitive advantage to organizations and a country's economy[72].

a) The culture of the society needs to give high value to learning and encourage talent by providing conducive family environment from early childhood.
b) Equal importance is required to be given to nutrition and health from early childhood as it has implications for later stages of life.
c) Specialized knowledge is required among growing number of students and researchers to sustain in the competitive-knowledge environment.

Features of Creativity According to Stamm[73], following are the features of creativity:

- Creativity is an inherent quality in an individual, but to transform it into an idea and innovation requires team effort.
- Creativity does not come out of the blue, but it is based on the body of knowledge acquired by an individual and also undergoes the process of refinement over the years.
- The trait of creativity exists in all the individuals, but only the level differs.

Environmental Factors required to Promote Creativity in Organizations In order to promote and support creativity in an organization, the following aspects deserve attention as creativity, to a large extent, depends on these[74]:

1. Support for Creativity: This requires an environment of openness, transparency, open flow of information and support for new ideas.

7.1 CONNECTIONS

Going for *Wow* at Nottingham-Spirk

You might say that creativity is a religious experience at Nottingham-Spirk Design Associates, Inc. A few years ago, the industrial-design company moved into an old church in Cleveland's university park area. Perched atop an escarpment on 5 acres of property, the 1920s octagon-shaped limestone building looks like a Roman temple. Inside, employees work in a large rotunda below a domed ceiling supported by 20 columns. Symbols of the original church remain, including a choir loft and soaring pipe organ. "You can't help but walk in here and say, 'I want to create something new,'" says John Nottingham, who cofounded Nottingham-Spirk with John Spirk three decades ago.

Team members at Nottingham-Spirk Design Associates, Inc., give co-worker Craig Saunders (standing) a "WOW" rating for one of the firm's creative products, the Swiffer SweeperVac.

Along with having an inspiring church building, Nottingham-Spirk supports creativity through its risk-tolerant learning orientation culture. "We stick our necks out," says Nottingham. "If we fail, we go down the wrong path, we dust ourselves off and go the other way. We understand that's innovation." The cofounders and their 70 employees also discover ideas by looking around store shelves. "We're trying to figure out what consumers will want two years down the road," explains Spirk. "We look and see what's not there," Nottingham adds. "We literally visualize an innovation sitting on the shelf next to the competition at a price point."

These activities produce sparks of insight, but they are only the starting point in the creative process. "Anyone can have a good idea," says Nottingham. "The difficult thing is to get it to market. You've got to make the idea work and prove its feasibility as a product." To transform ideas to profitable products, Nottingham-Spirk forms teams of up to 10 employees who hold two types of meetings. In the first meeting, called a *diverging session,* team members brainstorm ideas. "We start with a creative session, people from our team that can complement each other, and we come up with as many ideas as you can," says Nottingham. These ideas are documented as scribbles and sketches on slips of paper; up to 100 of them plaster the walls by the end of the session.

In the second round of meetings, called *converging sessions,* each idea is systematically evaluated by the team. "I pass around note cards, each with a word or phrase on it that says, *who cares, nice,* or *wow,*" Nottingham explains. The person who introduced an idea can explain it further, and then each team member judges the idea by selecting one of the three cards. "If everyone holds up a *wow* card, you know you've got something," says Nottingham. The *who cares* ideas get tossed out. Some of the *nice* ideas are developed further by an idea champion. For example, the SwivelStraight one-minute Christmas tree stand received mainly *nice* ratings when it was first proposed, but co-workers gave it *wow* ratings after Nottingham-Spirk designer Craig Saunders refined it further. Almost 1 million SwivelStraight stands were sold in the product's first five years on the market.

Diverging and converging sessions are complemented by focus group meetings and client feedback to improve prototypes. Nottingham-Spirk's redesign of the round metal paint can, which has changed little over the past century, is a case in point. Employees knew from experience the frustration of working with traditional paint cans. "We couldn't think of another consumer product that you need a screwdriver to open and a hammer to close," says designer Craig Saunders. So Saunders and his co-workers created a paint can with a twist top and built-in no-drip pour spout. When shown an early prototype, potential users claimed the container wouldn't stack well in warehouses and stores, so the revised prototype was made wider and more stackable. Next, users were concerned that the plastic container would break if it was dropped. "So we took a bunch of them up on ladders and dropped them," says Nottingham. "They bounced." This feedback made the Twist and Pour paint can an instant success; Sherwin-Williams tripled sales of its Dutch Boy paint in the first six months.

Thanks to its creative work environment and innovation process, Nottingham-Spirk has registered close to 500 patents and helped clients achieve more than $30 billion sales over the past three decades. Its most visible innovations include the Crest SpinBrush, Invacare Corp. wheelchairs, Swiffer SweeperVac, wide oval-shaped antiperspirant containers, MRI scanner design, and the Twist and Pour paint can.[75]

2. Autonomy: This needs to be provided in daily conduct of work and enables to create a sense of ownership and control over work.
3. Resources: Organization should provide all necessary resources in the form of information, facilities, and materials which support and sustain creative environment.
4. Challenging Environment: The environment should provide negative and positive incentives to challenge the employees and stimulate their creative senses.
5. Organizational Limitations: Conservatism and internal conflicts need to be considered as they obstruct creativity in an organization.

In order to survive in an environment of uncertainties and growing pressures of globalization, creativity would lead to development of innovative products/services/processes and thereby provide competitive advantage to organizations.

Characteristics of Creative People

Everyone is creative, but some people have a higher potential for creativity. Four of the main characteristics that give individuals more creative potential are intelligence, persistence, knowledge and experience, and a cluster of personality traits and values representing independent imagination. First, creative people have above-average intelligence to synthesize information, analyze ideas, and apply their ideas.[76] Like the fictional sleuth Sherlock Holmes, creative people recognize the significance of small bits of information and are able to connect them in ways that no one else could imagine. Then they have the capacity to evaluate the potential usefulness of their ideas.

Although intelligence helps people to discover new ideas, an equally (or more) important characteristic is the person's persistence to seek out these ideas through trial and error in the face of resistance. In other words, creative potential includes the persistence of trying out more ideas, whereas less creative people give up sooner. Creative people have persistence because of a higher need for achievement, a strong motivation from the task itself, and a moderate or high degree of self-esteem. In support of this, a recent study reported that inventors have higher levels of confidence and optimism than do people in the general population, and these traits motivate inventors to continue working on and investing in a project after receiving diagnostic advice to quit.[77] Inventor Thomas Edison highlighted the importance of persistence when he famously said that genius is 1 percent inspiration and 99 percent perspiration. Edison and his staff discovered hundreds of ways *not* to build a lightbulb before they got it right!

A third feature of creative people is that they possess sufficient knowledge and experience on the subject.[78] Creativity experts explain that discovering new ideas requires knowledge of the fundamentals. For example, the 1960s rock group The Beatles produced most of their songs only after they had played together for several years. They developed extensive experience singing and adapting the music of other people before their creative talents soared.

Although knowledge and experience may be important in one sense, they can also undermine creativity because people develop mental models that lead to "mindless behavior," whereby they stop questioning their assumptions.[79] This relates to the discussion earlier in this chapter on mental models, namely, that they sometimes restrict the decision maker's ability to see different perspectives. To overcome this limitation, some corporate leaders like to hire people from other industries and areas of expertise. For instance, Geoffrey Ballard, founder of Ballard Power Systems, hired a chemist to develop a better battery. When the chemist protested that he didn't know anything about batteries, Ballard replied: "That's fine. I don't want someone who knows batteries. They know what won't work."[80] Ballard explained that he wanted to hire people who would question and investigate avenues that experts had long ago closed their minds to. The point here is that knowledge and experience is a double-edged sword. It is an important prerequisite for creativity, but too much routinization of knowledge and experience can cause people to be less investigative.

The fourth characteristic of creative people is a cluster of personality traits and values that support an independent imagination: high openness to experience, moderately low need for affiliation, and strong values around self-direction and stimulation. Several studies report that these personal characteristics improve the individual's creative potential under some circumstances.[81] Let's examine each of them:

- *High openness to experience.* This Big Five personality dimension represents the extent to which a person is imaginative, curious, sensitive, open-minded, and original (see Chapter 2).
- *Moderately low need for affiliation.* People are more creative when they have less need for social approval and have a somewhat high (but not necessarily very high) degree of nonconformity. Because of these characteristics, creative people are less embarrassed when they make mistakes, and they remain motivated to explore ideas even when others criticize them for their persistence.
- *High self-direction and stimulation values.* Self-direction includes the values of creativity and independent thought; stimulation includes the values of excitement and challenge. Together, these values form openness to change–representing the motivation to pursue innovative ways (see Chapter 2).

Organizational Conditions Supporting Creativity

Intelligence, persistence, knowledge and experience, and independent imagination represent a person's creative potential, but the extent to which the person has more creative output depends on a work environment that supports the creative process.[82] Before describing the contextual influences on creativity, we need to point out that different combinations of situations can equally support creativity; there isn't one best work environment.[83] With this caveat in mind, let's consider some of the conditions that seem to unleash creative potential.

One of the most important conditions that supports creative practice is that the organization has a learning orientation; that is, leaders recognize that employees make reasonable mistakes as part of the creative process. "Creativity comes from failure," Samsung Electronics CEO and vice chairman Yun Jong-yong recently advised employees. "We should reform our corporate culture to forgive failure if workers did their best."[84] Motivation from the job itself is another important condition for creativity.[85] Employees tend to be more creative when they believe their work benefits the organization and/or larger society (i.e., task significance) and when they have the freedom to pursue novel ideas without bureaucratic delays (i.e., autonomy). Creativity is about changing things, and change is possible only when employees have the authority to experiment. More generally, jobs encourage creativity when they are challenging and aligned with the employee's competencies.

Along with supporting a learning orientation and intrinsically motivating jobs, companies foster creativity through open communication and sufficient resources. They also provide a reasonable level of job security, which explains why creativity suffers during times of downsizing and corporate restructuring.[86] Some companies support the reflection stage of creativity by designing nontraditional workspaces.[87] Google is one example. The Internet innovator has funky offices in several countries that include hammocks, gondola- and hive-shaped privacy spaces, slides, and brightly painted walls.

To some degree, creativity also improves with support from leaders and co-workers. One study reported that effective product champions provide enthusiastic support for new ideas. Other studies suggest that co-worker support can improve creativity in some situations whereas competition among co-workers improves creativity in other situations.[88] Similarly, it isn't clear how much pressure should be exerted on employees to produce creative ideas. Extreme time pressure is a well-known creativity inhibitor, but lack of pressure doesn't seem to produce the highest creativity, either.

Activities That Encourage Creativity

Hiring people with strong creative potential and providing a work environment that supports creativity are two cornerstones of a creative workplace. The third cornerstone consists of various activities that help employees think more creatively. One set of activities involves redefining the problem. Employees might be encouraged to revisit old projects that have been set aside. After a few months of neglect, these projects might be seen in new ways.[89] Another strategy involves asking people unfamiliar with the issue (preferably with different expertise) to explore the problem with you. You would state the objectives and give some facts and then let the other person ask questions to further understand the situation. By verbalizing the problem, listening to questions, and hearing what others think, you are more likely to form new perspectives on the issue.[90]

A second set of creativity activities, known as *associative play,* ranges from art classes to impromptu storytelling and acting. For example, British media giant OMD sends employees to two-day retreats in the countryside, where they play grapefruit croquet, chant like medieval monks, and pretend to be dog collars. "Being creative is a bit like an emotion; we need to be stimulated," explains Harriet Frost, one of OMD's specialists in building creativity. "The same is true for our imagination and its ability to come up with new ideas. You can't just sit in a room and devise hundreds of ideas."[91]

Another associative play activity, called *morphological analysis,* involves listing different dimensions of a system and the elements of each dimension and then looking at each combination. This encourages people to carefully examine combinations that initially seem nonsensical. Tyson Foods, the world's largest poultry producer, applied this activity to identify new ways to serve chicken for lunch. The marketing and research team assigned to this task focused on three categories: occasion, packaging, and taste. Next, the team worked through numerous combinations of items in the three categories. This created unusual ideas, such as cheese chicken pasta (taste) in pizza boxes (packaging) for concessions at baseball games (occasion). Later, the team looked more closely at the feasibility of these combinations and sent them to customer focus groups for further testing.[92]

A third set of activities that promote creative thinking falls under the category of *cross-pollination.*[93] Cross-pollination occurs when people from different areas of the organization exchange ideas. "Creativity comes out of people bumping into each other and not knowing where to go," claims Laszlo Bock, Google's top human resource executive. IDEO, the California-based product design company, engages in cross-pollination by mixing together employees from different past projects so that they share new knowledge with each other.

Cross-pollination highlights the fact that creativity rarely occurs alone. Some creative people may be individualistic, but most creative ideas are generated through teams and informal social interaction.

Mother's Creative Cross-Pollination Mother is an unusual creative agency with an equally unusual name, located in a converted warehouse in an artsy district of London. All of this quirkiness fuels creativity, but the ad agency's most creative practice is its workspace arrangement. The company's 100 or so employees perform their daily work around one monster-size table—an 8-foot-wide reinforced-concrete slab that extends 300 feet like a skateboard ramp around the entire floor. If that image isn't sufficiently unusual, consider this: Every three weeks, employees are asked to relocate their laptop, portable telephone, and trolley to another area around the table. "At the end of every three weeks we have a tidy Friday, which helps keep the mess down, and then we move the following Monday," explains Stef Calcraft, one of Mother's founding partners. "One week, you may be sitting next to a finance person and opposite a creative. The next, you'll be sitting between one of the partners and someone from production." Why the musical-chairs exercise? "It encourages cross-pollination of ideas," Calcraft answers. "You have people working on the same problem from different perspectives. It makes problem-solving much more organic."[94]

This probably explains why Jonathan Ive, the award-winning designer of Apple computer products, always refers to his team's creativity rather than his own. "The only time you'll hear [Jonathan Ive] use the word 'I' is when he's naming some of the products he helped make famous: iMac, iBook, iPod," says one writer.[95] The next chapter turns our attention to the main concepts in team effectiveness, as well as ways to improve team decision making and creativity.

Chapter Summary

Decision making is a conscious process of making choices among one or more alternatives with the intention of moving toward some desired state of affairs. The rational choice paradigm of decision making includes identifying problems and opportunities, choosing the best decision style, developing alternative solutions, choosing the best solution, implementing the selected alternative, and evaluating decision outcomes.

Stakeholder framing, perceptual defense, mental models, decisive leadership, and solution-oriented focus affect our ability to identify problems and opportunities. We can minimize these challenges by being aware of the human limitations and discussing the situation with colleagues.

Evaluating and choosing alternatives is often challenging because organizational goals are ambiguous or in conflict, human information processing is incomplete and subjective, and people tend to satisfice rather than maximize. Decision makers also short-circuit the evaluation process when faced with an opportunity rather than a problem. Emotions shape our preferences for alternatives and the process we follow to evaluate alternatives. We also listen to our emotions for guidance when making decisions. This activity relates to intuition—the ability to know when a problem or opportunity exists and to select the best course of action without conscious reasoning. Intuition is both an emotional experience and a rapid nonconscious analytic process that involves both pattern matching and action scripts.

People generally make better choices by systematically evaluating alternatives. Scenario planning can help to make future decisions without the pressure and emotions that occur during real emergencies.

Postdecisional justification and escalation of commitment make it difficult to accurately evaluate decision outcomes. Escalation is mainly caused by self-justification, the prospect theory effect, perceptual blinders, and closing costs. These problems are minimized by separating decision choosers from decision evaluators, establishing a preset level at which the decision is abandoned or reevaluated, relying on more systematic and clear feedback about the project's success, and involving several people in decision making.

Employee involvement (or participation) is the degree to which employees influence how their work is organized and carried out. The level of participation may range from low (an employee providing specific information to management without knowing the problem or issue) to high (complete involvement in all phases of the decision process). Employee involvement may lead to higher decision quality and commitment, but several contingencies need to be considered, including the decision structure, source of decision knowledge, decision commitment, and risk of conflict.

Creativity is the development of original ideas that make a socially recognized contribution. The four creativity stages are preparation, incubation, insight, and verification. Incubation assists divergent thinking, which involves reframing the problem in a unique way and generating different approaches to the issue.

Four of the main features of creative people are intelligence, persistence, knowledge and experience, and independent imagination personality traits and values. Creativity is also strengthened for everyone when the work environment supports a learning orientation, the job has high intrinsic motivation, the organization provides a reasonable level of job security, and project leaders provide appropriate goals, time pressure, and resources. Three types of activities that encourage creativity are redefining the problem, associative play, and cross-pollination.

Key Terms

anchoring and adjustment heuristic
availability heuristic
bounded rationality
creativity
decision making
divergent thinking
employee involvement
escalation of commitment
implicit favorite
intuition
postdecisional justification
prospect theory
rational choice paradigm
representativeness heuristic
satisficing
scenario planning
subjective expected utility

Critical Thinking Questions

1. A management consultant is hired by a manufacturing firm to determine the best site for its next production facility. The consultant has had several meetings with the company's senior executives regarding the factors to consider when making the recommendation. Discuss the decision-making problems that might prevent the consultant from choosing the best site location.

2. You have been asked to personally recommend a new travel agency to handle all airfare, accommodation, and related travel needs for your organization of 500 employees. One of your colleagues, who is responsible for the company's economic planning, suggests that the best travel agent could be selected mathematically by inputting the relevant factors for each agency and the weight (importance) of each factor. What decision-making approach is your colleague recommending? Is this recommendation a good idea in this situation? Why or why not?
3. Intuition is both an emotional experience and an nonconscious analytic process. One problem, however, is that not all emotions signaling that there is a problem or opportunity represent intuition. Explain how we would know if our "gut feelings" are intuition or not, and if they are not intuition, suggest what might be causing them.
4. A developer received financial backing for a new business financial center along a derelict section of the waterfront, a few miles from the current downtown area of a large European city. The idea was to build several high-rise structures, attract to those sites prestigious tenants requiring large leases, and have the city extend transportation systems out to the new center. Over the next decade, the developer believed that others would build in the area, thereby attracting the regional or national offices of many financial institutions. Interest from potential tenants was much lower than initially predicted, and the city did not build transportation systems as quickly as expected. Still, the builder proceeded with the original plans. Only after financial support was curtailed did the developer reconsider the project. Using your knowledge of escalation of commitment, discuss three possible reasons why the developer was motivated to continue with the project.
5. Ancient Book Company has a problem with new book projects. Even when others are aware that a book is far behind schedule and may engender little public interest, sponsoring editors are reluctant to terminate contracts with authors whom they have signed. The result is that editors invest more time with these projects than on more fruitful projects. Describe two methods that Ancient Book Company can use to minimize this problem, which is a form of escalation of commitment.
6. Employee involvement applies just as well to the classroom as to the office or factory floor. Explain how student involvement in classroom decisions typically made by the instructor alone might improve decision quality. What potential problems may occur in this process?
7. Think of a time when you experienced the creative process. Maybe you woke up with a brilliant (but usually sketchy and incomplete) idea or you solved a baffling problem while doing something else. Describe the incident to your class and explain how the experience followed the creative process.
8. Two characteristics of creative people are that they have relevant experience and are persistent in their quest. Does this mean that people with the most experience and the highest need for achievement are the most creative? Explain your answer.

CASE STUDY 7.1

EMPLOYEE INVOLVEMENT CASES

Case 1: The Sugar Substitute Research Decision

You are the head of research and development (R&D) for a major beer company. While working on a new beer product, one of the scientists in your unit seems to have tentatively identified a new chemical compound that has few calories but tastes closer to sugar than current sugar substitutes. The company has no foreseeable need for this product, but it could be patented and licensed to manufacturers in the food industry.

The sugar-substitute discovery is in its preliminary stages and would require considerable time and resources before it would be commercially viable. This means that it would necessarily take some resources away from other projects in the lab. The sugar-substitute project is beyond your technical expertise, but some of the R&D lab researchers are familiar with that field of chemistry. As with most forms of research, it is difficult to determine the amount of research required to further identify and perfect the sugar substitute. You do not know how much demand is expected for this product. Your department has a decision process for funding projects that are behind schedule. However, there are no rules or precedents about funding projects that would be licensed but not used by the organization.

The company's R&D budget is limited, and other scientists in your work group have recently complained that they require more resources and financial support to get their projects completed. Some of these R&D projects hold promise for future beer sales. You believe that most researchers in the R&D unit are committed to ensuring that the company's interests are achieved.

Case 2: Coast Guard Cutter Decision Problem

You are the captain of a 200-foot Coast Guard cutter, with a crew of 16, including officers. Your mission is general at-sea search and rescue. At 2:00 a.m. this morning, while en route to your home port after a routine 28-day patrol, you received word from the nearest Coast Guard station that a small plane had crashed 60 miles offshore. You obtained all the available information concerning the location of the crash, informed your crew of the mission, and set a new course at maximum speed for the scene to commence a search for survivors and wreckage.

You have now been searching for 20 hours. Your search operation has been increasingly impaired by rough seas, and there is evidence of a severe storm building. The atmospherics associated with the deteriorating weather have made communications with the Coast Guard station impossible. A decision must be made shortly about whether to abandon the search and place your vessel on a course that would ride out the storm (thereby protecting the vessel and your crew, but relegating any possible survivors to almost certain death from exposure) or to continue a potentially futile search and the risks it would entail.

Before losing communications, you received an updated weather advisory concerning the severity and duration of the storm. Although your crew members are extremely conscientious about their responsibility, you believe that they would be divided on the decision to leave or stay.

Discussion Questions (for both cases)

1. To what extent should your subordinates be involved in this decision? Select one of the following levels of involvement:
   - *No involvement.* You make the decision alone without any participation from subordinates.
   - *Low involvement.* You ask one or more subordinates for information relating to the problem, but you don't ask for their recommendations and might not mention the problem to them.
   - *Medium involvement.* You describe the problem to one or more subordinates (alone or in a meeting) and ask for any relevant information as well as their recommendations on the issue. However, you make the final decision, which might or might not reflect their advice.
   - *High involvement.* You describe the problem to subordinates. They discuss the matter, identify a solution without your involvement (unless they invite your ideas), and implement that solution. You have agreed to support their decision.
2. What factors led you to choose this level of employee involvement rather than the others?
3. What problems might occur if less or more involvement occurred in this case (where possible)?

Sources: The Sugar Substitute Research Decision: © 2002 Steven L. McShane. The Coast Guard cutter case is adapted from V. H. Vroom and A. G. Jago, *The New Leadership: Managing Participation in Organizations,* Copyright © 1988. Reproduced by permission of Pearson Education, Inc., Upper Saddle River, NJ.

CASE STUDY 7.2

P&G'S DESIGN THINKING

BusinessWeek

To transform Procter & Gamble into an innovation colossus, CEO A. G. Lafley asked vice-president for design Claudia Kotchka to "get design into the DNA of the company." Kotchka asked several prominent business and design schools: "How do we teach people what design thinking is and how to use it in a way that it could scale across a company with 130,000 employees?" After an initial stumble, P&G refined its workshops so leaders can more easily apply a different way to see problems and opportunities. "Once business leaders see they can use design thinking to reframe problems, they are transformed," says Cindy Tripp, marketing director at P&G Global Design.

This *BusinessWeek* case study describes "design thinking" and how P&G is encouraging its key decision makers to make decisions from this different perspective. Read the full text of this *BusinessWeek* article at www.mhhe.com/mcshane5e, and prepare for the discussion questions below.

Discussion Questions

1. What is design thinking? How does it differ from traditional models of decision making?
2. In your opinion, should most organizations adopt a design-thinking perspective? Why or why not?
3. Prototyping is a central element in design thinking, yet it is not explicitly mentioned in the rational choice decision-making process. How is prototyping inherent in this process, or how does it differ from rational choice decision making?

Source: J. Rae, "P&G Changes Its Game," *BusinessWeek,* 29 July 2008.

TEAM EXERCISE 7.3

WHERE IN THE WORLD ARE WE?

PURPOSE This exercise is designed to help you understand the potential advantages of involving others in decisions rather than making decisions alone.

MATERIALS Students require an unmarked copy of the map of the United States with grid marks (Exhibit 2). Students are not allowed to look at any other maps or use any other materials. The instructor will provide a list of communities located somewhere on Exhibit 2. The instructor will also provide copies of the answer sheet after students have individually and in teams estimated the locations of communities.

INSTRUCTIONS

1. Write down in Exhibit 1 the list of communities identified by your instructor. Then, working alone, estimate the location in Exhibit 2 of these communities, all of which are in the United States. For example, mark a small "1" in Exhibit 2 on the spot where you believe the first community is located. Mark a small "2" where you think the second community is located, and so on. Please be sure to number each location clearly and with numbers small enough to fit within one grid space.

2. The instructor will organize students into approximately equal-size teams (typically five or six people per team). Working with your team members, reach a consensus on the location of each community listed in Exhibit 1. The instructor might provide teams with a separate copy of the map, or each member can identify the team's numbers using a different-color pen on their individual maps. The team's decision for each location should occur by consensus, not voting or averaging.
3. The instructor will provide or display an answer sheet, showing the correct locations of the communities. Using the answer sheet, students will count the minimum number of grid squares between the location they individually marked and the true location of each community. Write the number of grid squares in the second column of Exhibit 1, and then add up the total. Next, count the minimum number of grid squares between the location the team marked and the true location of each community. Write the number of grid squares in the third column of Exhibit 1, and then add up the total.
4. The instructor will ask for information about the totals, and the class will discuss the implication of these results for employee involvement and decision making.

Number	Community	Individual distance in grid units from the true location	Team distance in grid units from the true location
1			
2			
3			
4			
5			
6			
7			
8			
		Total:	Total:

Exhibit 1 *List of Selected Communities in the United States*

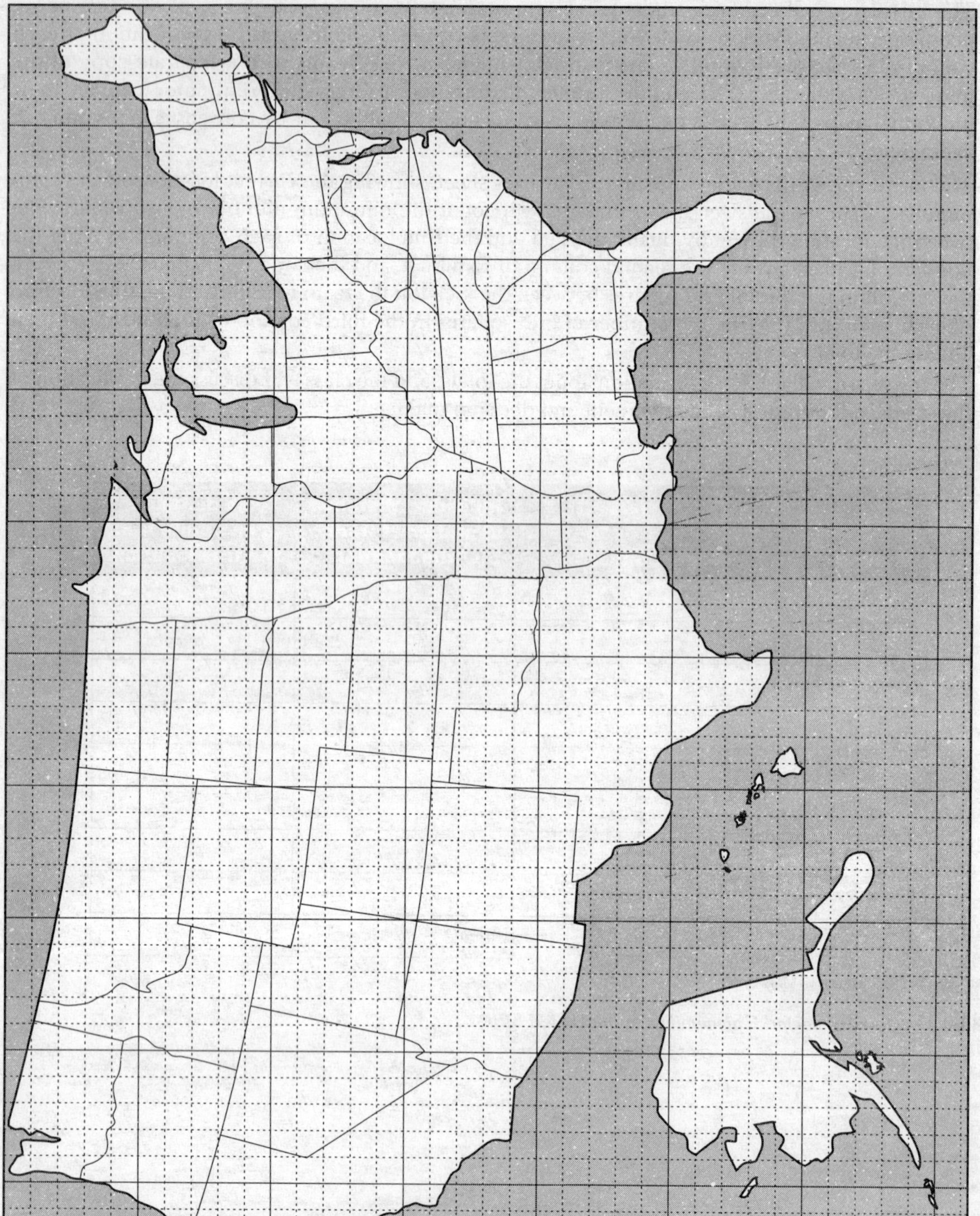

Exhibit 2 *Map of the United States*

TEAM EXERCISE 7.4

WINTER SURVIVAL EXERCISE

PURPOSE This exercise is designed to help you understand the potential advantages of involving others in decisions rather than making decisions alone.

INSTRUCTIONS

1. Read the "Situation" section in the next column. Then, working alone, rank-order the 12 items shown in the chart on page 228 according to their importance to your survival. In the "individual ranking" column, indicate the most important item with "1," going through to "12" for the least important. Keep in mind the reasons why each item is or is not important.
2. The instructor will divide the class into small teams (four to six people). Each team will rank-order the items in the second column. Team rankings should be based on consensus, not simply averaging the individual rankings.
3. When the teams have completed their rankings, the instructor will provide the expert's ranking, which can be entered in the third column.
4. Each student will compute the absolute difference (i.e., ignore minus signs) between the individual ranking and the expert's ranking, record this information in column 4, and sum the absolute values at the bottom of column 4.
5. In column 5, record the absolute difference between the team's ranking and the expert's ranking, and sum these absolute scores at the bottom. A class discussion will follow regarding the implications of these results for employee involvement and decision making.

SITUATION You have just crash-landed somewhere in the woods of southern Manitoba or possibly northern Minnesota. It is 11:32 a.m. in mid-January. The small plane in which you were traveling crashed on a small lake. The pilot and copilot were killed. Shortly after the crash, the plane sank completely into the lake with the pilot's and copilot's bodies inside. Everyone else on the flight escaped to land dry and without serious injury.

The crash came suddenly before the pilot had time to radio for help or inform anyone of your position. Since your pilot was trying to avoid the storm, you know the plane was considerably off course. The pilot announced shortly before the crash that you were 45 miles northwest of a small town that is the nearest known habitation.

You are in a wilderness area made up of thick woods broken by many lakes and rivers. The snow depth varies from above the ankles in windswept areas to more than knee-deep where it has drifted. The last weather report indicated that the temperature would reach minus 15 degrees Celsius in the daytime and minus 26 degrees at night. There are plenty of dead wood pieces and twigs in the area around the lake. You and the other surviving passengers are dressed in winter clothing appropriate for city wear–suits, pantsuits, street shoes, and overcoats. While escaping from the plane, your group salvaged the 12 items listed in the chart below. You may assume that the number of persons in the group is the same as the number in your group and that you have agreed to stay together.

Winter Survival Tally Sheet

Items	Step 1 Your individual ranking	Step 2 Your team's ranking	Step 3 Survival expert's ranking	Step 4 Difference between steps 1 and 3	Step 5 Difference between steps 2 and 3
Ball of steel wool					
Newspaper					
Compass					
Hand ax					
Cigarette lighter					
45-caliber pistol					
Section air map					
Canvas					
Shirt and pants					
Can of shortening					
Whiskey					
Chocolate bars					
			Total	Your score	Team score

(The lower the score, the better)

Source: Adapted from "Winter Survival" in D. Johnson and F. Johnson, *Joining Together,* 3d ed. (Englewood Cliffs, NJ: Prentice Hall, 1984).

CLASS EXERCISE 7.5

THE HOPPING ORANGE

PURPOSE This exercise is designed to help students understand the dynamics of creativity and team problem solving.

INSTRUCTIONS

You will be placed in teams of six students. One student serves as the official timer for the team and must have a watch, preferably with a stopwatch timer. The instructor will give each team an orange (or similar object) with a specific task involving use of the orange. The objective is easily understood and nonthreatening, and it will be described by the instructor at the beginning of the exercise. Each team will have a few opportunities to achieve the objective more efficiently. To maximize the effectiveness of this exercise, no other information is provided here.

CLASS EXERCISE 7.6

CREATIVITY BRAINBUSTERS

PURPOSE This exercise is designed to help students understand the dynamics of creativity and team problem solving.

INSTRUCTIONS

The instructor describes the problem, and students are asked to figure out the solution working alone. When enough time has passed, the instructor may then ask specific students who think they have the solution to describe (or show using overhead transparency) their answer. The instructor will review the solutions and discuss the implications of this exercise. In particular, be prepared to discuss what you needed to solve these puzzles and what may have prevented you from solving them more quickly (or at all).

1. *Double-circle problem.* Draw two circles, one inside the other, with a single line and with neither circle touching the other (as shown below). In other words, you must draw both of these circles without lifting your pen (or other writing instrument).

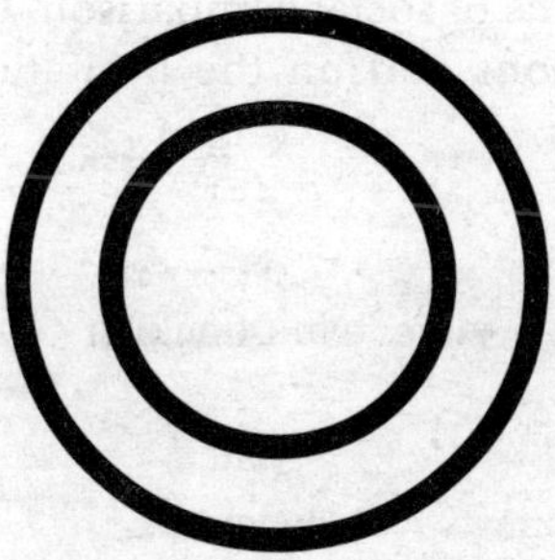

2. *Nine-dot problem.* The next column contains nine dots. Without lifting your pencil, draw no more than four straight lines that pass through all nine dots.

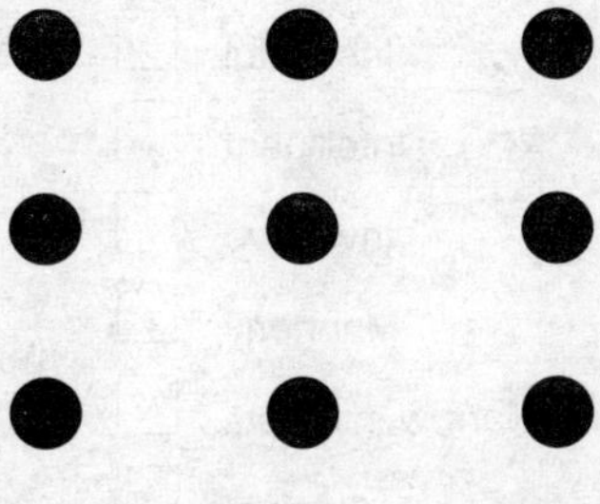

3. *Nine-dot problem revisited.* Referring to the nine-dot exhibit above, describe how, without lifting your pencil, you could pass a pencil line through all dots with three or fewer straight lines.
4. *Word search.* In the following line of letters, cross out five letters so that the remaining letters, without altering their sequence, spell a familiar English word.

CFRIVEELATETITEVRSE

5. *Burning ropes.* You have two pieces of rope of unequal lengths and a box of matches. In spite of their different lengths, each piece of rope takes one hour to burn; however, parts of each rope burn at unequal speeds. For example, the first half of one piece might burn in 10 minutes. Use these materials to accurately determine when 45 minutes has elapsed.

SELF-ASSESSMENT 7.7

MEASURING YOUR CREATIVE PERSONALITY

PURPOSE This self-assessment is designed to help you measure the extent to which you have a creative personality.

INSTRUCTIONS Presented on page 230 is an adjective checklist with 30 words that may or may not describe you. Put a mark in the box beside each word that you think accurately describes you. Please do *not* mark the boxes for words that do not describe you. When finished, you can score the test using the scoring key in Appendix B at the end of the book. This exercise should be completed alone so that you can assess yourself without concerns of social comparison. Class discussion will focus on how this scale might be applied in organizations and on the limitations of measuring creativity in work settings.

Adjective Checklist		
Affected ☐	Honest ☐	Reflective ☐
Capable ☐	Humorous ☐	Resourceful ☐
Cautious ☐	Individualistic ☐	Self-confident ☐
Clever ☐	Informal ☐	Sexy ☐
Commonplace ☐	Insightful ☐	Sincere ☐
Confident ☐	Intelligent ☐	Snobbish ☐
Conservative ☐	Inventive ☐	Submissive ☐
Conventional ☐	Mannerly ☐	Suspicious ☐
Dissatisfied ☐	Narrow interests ☐	Unconventional ☐
Egotistical ☐	Original ☐	Wide interests ☐

Source: Adapted from and based on information in H. G. Gough and A. B. Heilbrun, Jr., *The Adjective Check List Manual* (Palo Alto, CA: Consulting Psychologists Press, 1965).

SELF-ASSESSMENT 7.8

TESTING YOUR CREATIVE BENCH STRENGTH

This self-assessment takes the form of a self-scoring quiz. It consists of 12 questions that require divergent thinking to identify the correct answers. For each question, type your answer in the space provided. When finished, look at the correct answer for each question, along with the explanation for that answer.

SELF-ASSESSMENT 7.9

DECISION-MAKING STYLE INVENTORY

People have different styles of decision making that are reflected in how they identify problems or opportunities and make choices. This self-assessment estimates your decision-making style through a series of statements describing how individuals go about making important decisions. Please indicate whether you agree or disagree with each statement. Answer each item as truthfully as possible so that you get an accurate estimate of your decision-making style. This exercise should be completed alone so that you can assess yourself honestly without concerns of social comparison. Class discussion will focus on the decision-making style that people prefer in organizational settings.

3 PART

Team Processes

When Whole Foods Market opens new stores, the organic food retailer isn't just looking for staff with good customer service skills. It is looking for people who also work well in teams. Every Whole Foods Market store is divided into about 10 teams, such as the prepared-foods team, the cashier/front-end team, and the seafood team. Teams are "self-directed" because team members make the decisions about their work unit with minimal interference from management.

Whole Foods Market relies on teams to more effectively serve customers and fulfill employee needs.

"Each team is . . . responsible for managing its own business," explains Whole Foods Market cofounder John Mackey. "It gets a profit-and-loss statement, it's responsible for managing inventory, labor productivity, gross margins; and its members are responsible for many of the product-placement decisions." Whole Foods Market introduced a team-based structure when it was founded in Austin, Texas, in 1980. The idea came from the then-popular Japanese management books, which espoused the value of teamwork. Even today, with almost 200 stores employing 40,000 people in the United States, the United Kingdom, and Canada, Whole Foods Market remains true to its team-based structure.

Along with making departmental decisions, Whole Foods Market teams decide on whether new hires get to remain on the team. After a recruit is temporarily employed for 30 to 45 days, team members vote on whether the individual should become a permanent member; at least two-thirds must vote in favor for the recruit to join the team permanently. Team members take these hiring decisions seriously because their monthly bonuses are based on team performance. Every four weeks, the company calculates each team's performance against goals and cost efficiencies. When the team finds ways to work more effectively, the unused budget is divided among the team members. This team bonus can add up to hundreds of extra dollars in each paycheck.[1]

8

TEAM DYNAMICS

Learning Objectives

After reading this chapter, you should be able to:

1. Define *teams* and discuss their benefits and limitations.
2. Explain why people are motivated to join informal groups.
3. Diagram the team effectiveness model.
4. Discuss how task characteristics, team size, and team composition influence team effectiveness.
5. Summarize the team development process.
6. Discuss how team norms develop and how they may be altered.
7. List six factors that influence team cohesion.
8. Describe the three foundations of trust in teams and other interpersonal relationships.
9. Discuss the characteristics and factors required for success of self-directed teams and virtual teams.
10. Identify four constraints on team decision making.
11. Discuss the advantages and disadvantages of four structures that potentially improve team decision making.

Several factors explain why Whole Foods Market has become a retail success story and one of the best places to work in America; the company's focus on teams is clearly one of those factors. Teamwork has become an important practice in most industries and countries. A cross-functional team of employees at the City of Indianapolis conducted a "chuckhole kaizen response" to identify more efficient ways to repair potholes. The team found ways to address pothole complaints in 48 hours rather than the previous average of 19 days. Hong Kong–based Regal Printing relies on advanced technology to print up to 40,000 softcover books per day, but it also created a special team of 20 staff members to handle urgent jobs. Ford Motor Company's legal department is rated as one of the best in North America, partly because almost everything the department does is achieved through project teams. Rackspace Hosting, Inc., physically organizes most of its 1,900 employees into teams of 14 to 20 people. The San Antonio, Texas, provider of enterprise-level Web infrastructure assigns every customer to one of these dedicated teams, which provides around-the-clock service.[2]

This chapter begins by defining *teams* and examining the reasons why organizations rely on teams and why people join informal groups in organizational settings. A large segment of this chapter examines a model of team effectiveness, which includes team and organizational environment, team design, and the team processes of development, norms, cohesion, and trust. We then turn our attention to two specific types of teams: self-directed teams and virtual teams. The final section of this chapter looks at the challenges and strategies for making better decisions in teams.

Learning Objectives

After reading the next two sections, you should be able to:

1. Define *teams* and discuss their benefits and limitations.
2. Explain why people are motivated to join informal groups.

TEAMS AND INFORMAL GROUPS

teams
Groups of two or more people who interact and influence each other, are mutually accountable for achieving common goals associated with organizational objectives, and perceive themselves as a social entity within an organization.

Teams are groups of two or more people who interact and influence each other, are mutually accountable for achieving common goals associated with organizational objectives, and perceive themselves as a social entity within an organization.[3] This definition has a few important components worth repeating. First, all teams exist to fulfill some purpose, such as assembling a product, providing a service, designing a new manufacturing facility, or making an important decision. Second, team members are held together by their interdependence and need for collaboration to achieve common goals. All teams require some form of communication so that members can coordinate and share common objectives. Third, team members influence each other, although some members may be more influential than others regarding the team's goals and activities. Finally, a team exists when its members perceive themselves to be a team.

Exhibit 8.1 briefly describes various types of teams in organizations. Some teams are permanent, while others are temporary; some are responsible for making products or providing services, while others exist to make decisions or share knowledge. Each type of team has been created deliberately to serve an organizational purpose. Some teams, such as skunkworks teams, are not initially sanctioned by management, yet are called "teams" because members work toward an organizational objective.

Team type	Description
Departmental teams	Teams that consist of employees who have similar or complementary skills and are located in the same unit of a functional structure; usually minimal task interdependence because each person works with employees in other departments.
Production/service/leadership teams	Typically multiskilled (employees have diverse competencies), team members collectively produce a common product/service or make ongoing decisions; production/service teams typically have an assembly-line type of interdependence, whereas leadership teams tend to have tight interactive (reciprocal) interdependence.
Self-directed teams	Similar to production/service teams except (1) they are organized around work processes that complete an entire piece of work requiring several interdependent tasks and (2) they have substantial autonomy over the execution of those tasks (i.e., they usually control inputs, flow, and outputs with little or no supervision).
Advisory teams	Teams that provide recommendations to decision makers; include committees, advisory councils, work councils, and review panels; may be temporary, but often are permanent, some with frequent rotation of members.
Task force (project) teams	Usually multiskilled, temporary teams whose assignment is to solve a problem, realize an opportunity, or design a product or service.
Skunkworks	Multiskilled teams that are usually located away from the organization and are relatively free of its hierarchy; often initiated by an entrepreneurial team leader who borrows people and resources (*bootlegging*) to design a product or service.
Virtual teams	Teams whose members operate across space, time, and organizational boundaries and are linked through information technologies to achieve organizational tasks; may be a temporary task force or permanent service team.
Communities of practice	Teams (but often informal groups) bound together by shared expertise and passion for a particular activity or interest; main purpose is to share information; often rely on information technologies as the main source of interaction.

Exhibit 8.1 *Types of Teams in Organizations*

Informal Groups

Although most of our attention in this chapter is on formal teams, employees also belong to informal groups. All teams are groups, but many groups do not satisfy our definition of teams. Groups include people assembled together, whether or not they have any interdependence or organizationally focused objective. The friends you meet for lunch are an *informal group,* but they wouldn't be called a team because they have little or no interdependence (each person could just as easily eat lunch alone) and no organizationally mandated purpose. Instead, they exist primarily for the benefit of their members. Although the terms are used interchangeably, *teams* has largely replaced *groups* in the language of business when referring to employees who work together to complete organizational tasks.[4]

Why do informal groups exist? One reason is that human beings are social animals. Our drive to bond is hardwired through evolutionary development, creating a need to belong to informal groups.[5] This is evidenced by the fact that people invest considerable time and effort forming and maintaining social relationships without any special circumstances or ulterior motives. A second explanation is provided by social identity theory, which states that individuals define themselves by their group affiliations. Thus, we join groups–particularly those that are viewed favorably by others and that have values similar to our own–because they shape and reinforce our self-concept.[6]

A third reason why people are motivated to form informal groups is that such groups accomplish goals that cannot be achieved by individuals working alone. For example, employees will sometimes create a group to oppose organizational changes because the group collectively has more power than individuals complaining alone. A fourth explanation for informal groups is that in stressful situations we are comforted by the mere presence of other people and are therefore motivated to be near them. When in danger, people congregate near each other even though doing so serves no protective purpose. Similarly, employees tend to mingle more often after hearing rumors that the company might be acquired by a competitor. As you learned in Chapter 4, this social support minimizes stress by providing emotional and/or informational support to buffer the stress experience.[7]

Informal Groups and Organizational Outcomes Although informal groups are not created to serve organizational objectives, they have a profound influence on organizations and individual employees. Informal groups are the backbone of *social networks,* which are important sources of trust building, information sharing, power, influence, and employee well-being in the workplace.[8] As you will learn in Chapter 9, some companies have established social networking sites similar to Facebook and MySpace to encourage the formation of informal groups and associated communication. These companies recognize that informal groups build trust and mutual understanding, which transfers tacit knowledge more effectively through these informal networks than through formal reporting relationships.

social capital
The knowledge and other resources available to people from a durable network that connects them to others.

Social networks also play an important role in employee power and influence. As you will learn in Chapter 10, informal groups tend to increase an employee's **social capital**–the knowledge and other resources available to people from a durable network that connects them to others. Employees with strong informal networks tend to have more power and influence because they receive better information and preferential treatment from others and their talent is more visible to key decision makers. Finally, informal groups potentially minimize employee stress because, as mentioned above, group members provide emotional and informational social support. This stress-reducing capability of informal groups improves employee well-being, thereby improving organizational effectiveness.

Advantages and Disadvantages of Teams

When 1,760 professionals were recently asked about their work, 86 percent agreed that working in teams is more important to business success today than it was five years ago. This is certainly true in scientific research. A study of almost 20 million research publications reported that the percentage of journal articles written by teams rather than individuals has increased substantially over the past five decades. Furthermore, team-based articles had a much higher number of subsequent citations, which indicates that the quality of these publications is higher when they are written by teams rather than individuals.[9] "One of the things I think people overlook is the quality of the team," says Rose Marie Bravo, the American executive who engineered the remarkable turnaround of Burberry, the London fashion house. "It isn't one person, and it isn't two people. It is a whole group of people–a team that works cohesively towards a goal–that makes something happen or not."[10]

Why is teamwork so important? The answer to this question has a long history, dating back to research on British coal mining in the 1940s and the Japanese economic miracle of the 1970s.[11] These early studies and a huge number of investigations since then have revealed that *under the right conditions,* teams make better decisions, develop better products and services, and create a more engaged workforce than do employees working alone.[12] Similarly, team members can quickly share information and coordinate tasks, whereas these processes are slower and prone to more errors in traditional departments led by supervisors. Teams typically provide superior customer service because they offer more breadth of knowledge and expertise to customers than individual "stars" can offer.

In many situations, people are potentially more motivated when working in teams than when working alone.[13] One reason for this motivation is that, as we mentioned a few paragraphs ago, employees have a drive to bond and are motivated to fulfill the goals of groups to which they belong. This motivation is particularly strong when the team is part of the employee's social identity. Second, people are more motivated in teams because they are accountable to fellow team members, who monitor performance more closely than a traditional supervisor. This is particularly true where the team's performance depends on the worst performer, such as on an assembly line, where how fast the product is assembled depends on the speed of the slowest employee. Third, under some circumstances, performance improves when employees work near others because co-workers become benchmarks of comparison. Employees are also motivated to work harder because of apprehension that their performance will be compared to others' performance.

The Challenges of Teams

In spite of the many benefits of teams, they are not always as effective as individuals working alone.[14] Teams are usually better suited to complex work, such as designing a building or auditing a company's financial records. Under these circumstances, one person rarely has all the necessary knowledge and skills. Instead, the work is performed better by dividing its tasks into more specialized roles, with people in those specialized jobs coordinating with each other. In contrast, work is typically performed more effectively by individuals alone when they have all the necessary knowledge and skills and the work cannot be divided into specialized tasks or is not complex enough to benefit from specialization. Even where the work can and should be specialized, a team structure might not be necessary if the tasks performed by several people require minimal coordination.

process losses
Resources (including time and energy) expended toward team development and maintenance rather than the task.

The main problem with teams is that they have additional costs called **process losses**–resources (including time and energy) expended toward team development and maintenance rather than the task.[15] It is much more efficient for an individual to work out an issue alone than to resolve differences of opinion with other people. For a team to perform well, team members need to agree and have mutual understanding of their goals, the strategy for accomplishing those goals, their specific roles, and informal rules of conduct.[16] Developing and maintaining these team requirements divert time and energy away from performing the work.

Brooks's law
The principle that adding more people to a late software project only makes it later. Also called the *mythical man-month*.

The process-loss problem is particularly apparent when more staff are added or replace others on the team. Team performance suffers when a team adds members, because those employees need to learn how the team operates and how to coordinate efficiently with other team members. The software industry even has a name for this: **Brooks's law** (also called the "mythical man-month") says that adding more people to a late software project only makes it later! According to some sources, Apple Computer may have fallen into this trap in the recent development of its professional photography software program, called Aperture. When the project started to fall behind schedule, the manager in charge of the Aperture project increased the size of the team–some sources say it ballooned from 20 to almost 150 engineers and quality assurance staff within a few weeks. Unfortunately, adding so many people further bogged down the project. The result? When Aperture was finally released, it was nine months late and considered one of Apple's buggier software offerings.[17]

social loafing
The problem that occurs when people exert less effort (and usually perform at a lower level) when working in teams than when working alone.

Social Loafing Perhaps the best-known limitation of teams is the risk of productivity loss due to **social loafing.** Social loafing occurs when people exert less effort (and usually perform at a lower level) when working in teams than when working alone.[18] It is most likely to occur in large teams where individual output is difficult to identify. In particular, employees tend to put out less effort when the team produces a single output, such as solving a customer's problem. Under these conditions, employees aren't as worried that their individual performance will be noticed. There is less social loafing when each team member's contribution is more noticeable; this can be achieved by reducing the size of the team, for example, or measuring each team member's performance. Social loafing is also less likely to occur when the task is interesting, because individuals are more motivated by the work itself to perform their duties. Social loafing is also less common when the team's objective is important, possibly because individuals experience more pressure from co-workers to perform well. Finally, social loafing occurs less frequently among members who value team membership and believe in working toward the team's objectives.[19]

How to Minimize Social Loafing By understanding the causes of social loafing, we can identify ways to minimize this problem. Some of the strategies listed here reduce social loafing by making each member's performance more visible. Others increase each member's motivation to perform his or her tasks within the group[20]:

- *Form smaller teams.* Splitting a team into several smaller groups reduces social loafing because each person's performance becomes more noticeable and important for the overall team performance. A smaller group also potentially increases cohesiveness, so would-be shirkers feel a greater obligation to perform fully for their team.
- *Specialize tasks.* Each person's contribution is easier to see when each team member performs a different work activity. For example, rather than pooling their effort for all incoming customer inquiries, each customer service representative might be assigned a particular type of client.
- *Measure individual performance.* Social loafing is minimized when each member's contribution is measured. Of course, individual performance is difficult to measure in some team activities, such as problem-solving projects in which the team's performance depends on one person discovering the best answer.
- *Increase job enrichment.* Social loafing is minimized when team members are assigned more motivating jobs, such as requiring more skill variety or having direct contact with clients. More generally, social loafing is less common among employees with high job satisfaction.
- *Select motivated employees.* Social loafing can be minimized by carefully selecting job applicants who are motivated by the task and have a collectivist value orientation. Those with a collectivist value are motivated to work harder for the team because they value their membership in the group.

This chapter has laid the foundation for our understanding of team dynamics. To build an effective team requires time, the right combination of team members, and the right environment. We will apply these ingredients of environment and team processes in the next chapter, which looks at high-performance teams, including self-directed teams and virtual teams.

In summary, teams can be very powerful forces for competitive advantage, or they can be much more trouble than they are worth, so much so that job performance and morale decline when employees are placed in teams. To understand when teams are better than individuals working alone, we need to more closely examine the conditions that make teams effective or ineffective. The next few sections of this chapter discuss the model of team effectiveness.

Learning Objectives

After reading the next two sections, you should be able to:

3. Diagram the team effectiveness model.
4. Discuss how task characteristics, team size, and team composition influence team effectiveness.

A Model of Team Effectiveness

Let's begin by clarifying the meaning of team effectiveness. A team is effective when it benefits the organization, its members, and its own survival.[21] First, most teams exist to serve some organizational purpose, so effectiveness is partly measured by the achievement of those objectives. Second, a team's effectiveness relies on the satisfaction and well-being of its members. People join groups to fulfill their personal needs, so effectiveness is partly measured by this need fulfillment. Finally, team effectiveness includes the team's viability–its ability to survive. It must be able to maintain the commitment of its members, particularly during the turbulence of the team's development. Without this commitment, people leave and the team will fall apart. The team must also secure sufficient resources and find a benevolent environment in which to operate.

Why are some teams effective while others fail? This question has challenged organizational researchers for some time, and as you might expect, numerous models of team effectiveness have been proposed over the years.[22] Exhibit 8.2 presents a model that integrates the main components of team effectiveness, each of which will be examined closely over the next several pages. This model is best viewed as a template of several theories because each component (team development, team cohesion, etc.) includes its own set of theories and models to explain how that component operates.

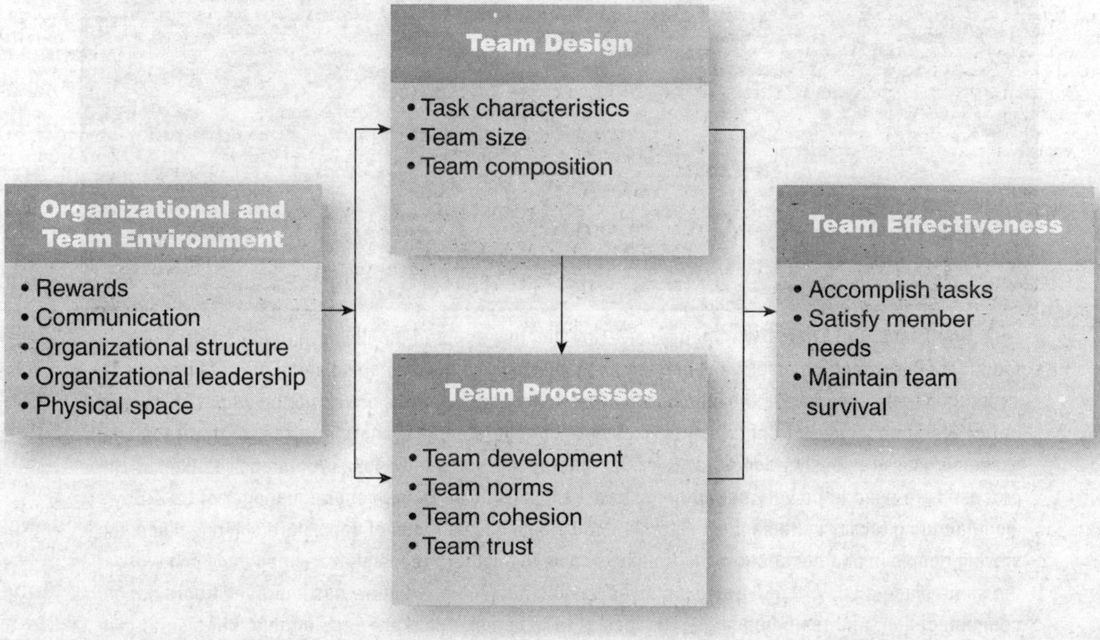

Exhibit 8.2 *Team Effectiveness Model*

Organizational and Team Environment

The organizational and team environment represents all conditions beyond the team's boundaries that influence its effectiveness. Team members tend to work together more effectively when they are at least partly rewarded for team performance.[23] For instance, part of an employee's paycheck at Whole Foods Market is determined by the team's productivity. Communication systems can influence team effectiveness, particularly in virtual teams, which are highly dependent on information technologies to coordinate work. Another environmental factor is the organizational structure; teams flourish when organized around work processes because this structure increases interaction and interdependence among team members and reduces interaction with people outside the team. High-performance teams also depend on organizational leaders who provide support and strategic direction while team members focus on operational efficiency and flexibility.[24]

The physical layout of the team's workspace can also make a difference. Medrad, Inc., reorganized its production workspace so that teams now work in U-shaped "cells" rather than along a straight assembly line. The Indianola, Pennsylvania, medical device manufacturer discovered that this cellular layout improved team performance by making it easier for team members to observe and assist each

La-Z-Boy Teams Get Their Own Space La-Z-Boy Inc. has adopted a cellular manufacturing model of production by organizing employees into teams responsible for building complete pieces of furniture. To strengthen team dynamics, the five to seven cross-functional members of each team work side by side rather than in specialized departments. This new configuration is a sharp contrast to the traditional assembly line previously adopted at the Michigan-based company's four production facilities. "The process here used to be very departmentalized," explains Jovie Dabu, general manager of La-Z-Boy's manufacturing facility in Redlands, California. "You would have a group of upholsterers in one place, the sewing people in another section, the framing people in another area, and everyone would just work in the same place all day." La-Z-Boy executives say the new team structure has improved coordination, communication, and team bonding. "The idea is to help make workers accountable, but also to give them a sense of ownership of what they do," said Greg Bachman, Redlands' production manager.[25]

other. Toyota Motor Corporation also recognizes the importance of physical layout in team effectiveness by congregating people in a large open-space room (called an *obeya*). In some projects, such as development of the Prius hybrid vehicle, department managers are brought together into the obeya to resolve issues and improve collaboration across functions. In other projects, a few dozen development staff from engineering, design, production, marketing, and other areas spend several weeks or longer working together in the obeya. Toyota claims the obeya arrangement has significantly cut product development time and costs. "The reason obeya works so well is that it's all about immediate face-to-face human contact," explains an executive at Toyota's North American headquarters.[26]

TEAM DESIGN ELEMENTS

Along with setting up a team-friendly environment, leaders need to carefully design the team itself, including task characteristics, team size, team composition, and team roles.

Task Characteristics

What type of work is best for teams? As we noted earlier, teams operate better than individuals working alone on work that is sufficiently complex, such as launching the business in a new market, developing a computer operating system, or constructing a bridge. Complex work requires skills and knowledge beyond the competencies of one person. Teams are particularly well suited when the complex work can be divided into more specialized roles and the people in the specialized roles require frequent coordination with each other. Some evidence also suggests that teams work best with well-structured tasks because it is easier to coordinate such work among several people.[27] The challenge, however, is to find tasks with the uncommon combination of being both well structured and complex.

task interdependence
The extent to which team members must share materials, information, or expertise in order to perform their jobs.

One task characteristic that is particularly important for teams is **task interdependence**–the extent to which team members must share materials, information, or expertise to perform their jobs.[28] Aside from complete independence, there are three levels of task interdependence, as illustrated in Exhibit 8.3. The lowest level of interdependence, called *pooled interdependence,* occurs when an employee or work unit shares a common resource, such as machinery, administrative support, or a budget, with other employees or work units. This would occur in a team setting where each member works alone but shares raw materials or machinery to perform her or his otherwise independent tasks. Interdependence is higher under *sequential interdependence,* in which the output of one person becomes the direct input for another person or unit. Sequential interdependence occurs where team members are organized in an assembly line.

Reciprocal interdependence, in which work output is exchanged back and forth among individuals, produces the highest degree of interdependence. People who design a new product or service would typically have reciprocal interdependence because their design decisions affect others involved in the design process. Any decision made by the design engineers would influence the work of the manufacturing engineer and purchasing specialist, and vice versa. Employees with reciprocal interdependence should be organized into teams to facilitate coordination in their interwoven relationship.

As a rule, the higher the level of task interdependence, the greater the need to organize people into teams rather than have them work alone. A team structure improves interpersonal communication and thus results in better coordination. High task interdependence also motivates most people to be part of the team. However, the rule that a team should be formed when employees have high interdependence applies when team members have the same task goals, such as serving the same

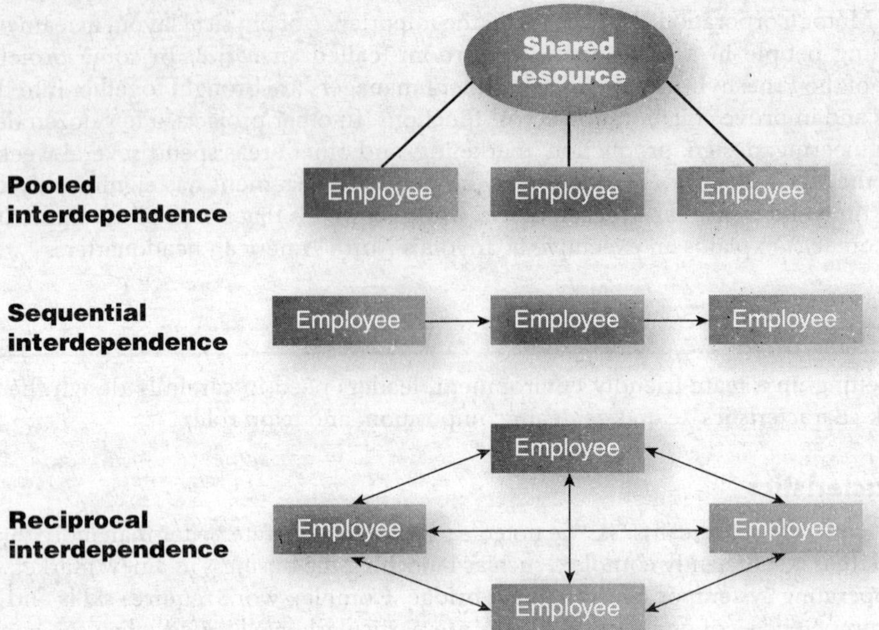

Exhibit 8.3 *Levels of Task Interdependence*

clients or collectively assembling the same product. When team members have different goals (such as serving different clients) but must depend on other team members to achieve those unique goals, teamwork might create excessive conflict. Under these circumstances, the company should try to reduce the level of interdependence or rely on supervision as a buffer or mediator among employees.

Team Size

What is the ideal size for a team? One popular (but untested) rule is that the optimal team size is between five and seven people. Yet some observers have recently argued that tasks are getting so complex that many teams need to have more than 100 members.[29] Unfortunately, the former piece of advice is overly simplistic, and the latter seems to have lost sight of the meaning and dynamics of real teams. Generally, teams should be large enough to provide the necessary competencies and perspectives to perform the work, yet small enough to maintain efficient coordination and meaningful involvement of each member.[30] As a Sun Microsystems executive explains: "You need to have a balance between having enough people to do all the things that need to be done, while keeping the team small enough so that it is cohesive and can make decisions effectively and speedily."[31] Small teams (say, less than a dozen members) operate effectively because they have less process loss. Members of smaller teams also tend to feel more engaged because they get to know their teammates (which improves trust), have more influence on the group's norms and goals, and feel more responsible for the team's successes and failures.

Should companies have 100-person teams if the task is highly complex? The answer is that a group this large probably isn't a team, even if management calls it one. A team exists when its members interact and influence each other, are mutually accountable for achieving common goals associated with organizational objectives, and perceive themselves as a social entity within an organization. It is very difficult for everyone in a 100-person work unit to influence each other and experience enough cohesion to perceive themselves as team members. Executives at Whole Foods Market were aware that real teams are much smaller than 100 people when the company opened its huge store in New York City's Columbus Circle. The store had 140 cashiers–far too many people for one cashier team–so Whole Foods Market divided the group into teams with a dozen employees each. All cashiers meet as one massive group every month to discuss production issues, but the smaller teams work effectively on a day-to-day basis.[32]

Team Composition

Choosing a new team member is too important a decision at Whole Foods Market to be left to management. Instead, as this chapter's opening vignette noted, new hires are approved for permanent employment by their teammates. Royal Dutch/Shell is also serious about selecting job applicants who have excellent team skills. As Global Connections 8.1 describes, the global energy giant hosts a special five-day exercise in Europe, North America, Asia, and the Middle East to observe how well participants work under pressure with others from diverse backgrounds.

To work effectively in a team, employees must have more than technical skills and self-leadership to perform their own work; they must also be able and willing to perform that work in a team environment. The most frequently mentioned characteristics or behaviors of effective team members are the "five C's" illustrated in Exhibit 8.4: cooperating, coordinating, communicating, comforting,

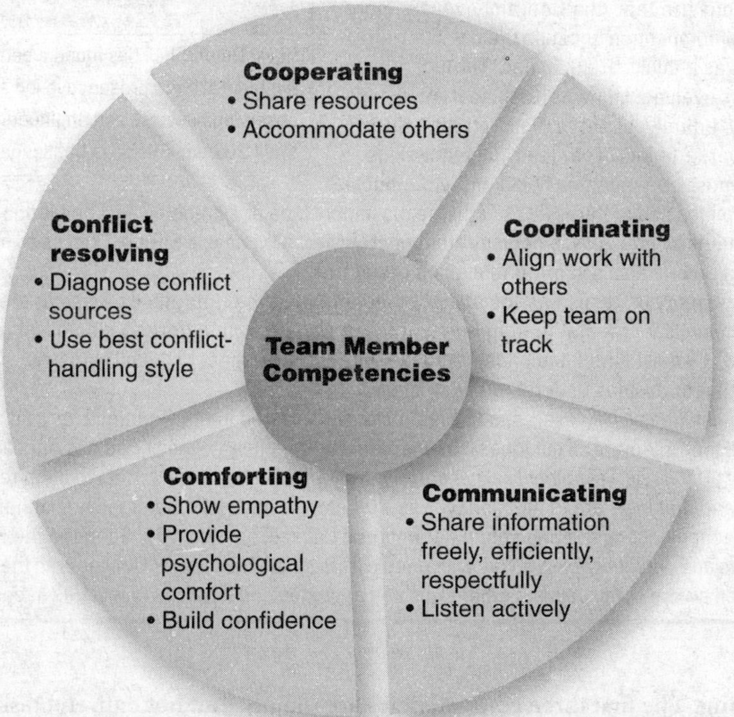

Sources: Based on information in V. Rousseau, C. Aubé, and A. Savoie, "Teamwork Behaviors: A Review and an Integration of Frameworks," *Small Group Research* 37, no. 5 (2006), pp. 540–570; M. L. Loughry, M. W. Ohland, and D. D. Moore, "Development of a Theory-Based Assessment of Team Member Effectiveness," *Educational and Psychological Measurement* 67, no. 3 (2007), pp. 505–524.

Exhibit 8.4 *Five C's of Team Member Competency*

8.1 GLOBAL CONNECTIONS

Royal Dutch Shell Finds Team Players in Gourami

Royal Dutch Shell (Shell) discovered long ago that a job interview isn't the best way to determine a job applicant's technical skills or how well he or she works in a team environment. That's why the global energy company launched the Shell Gourami Business Challenge a decade ago in Europe and very recently in the United States, Asia, and the Middle East. The five-day event involves several dozen engineering and business university students who are split into several teams representing different departments (exploration, refining, manufacturing, finance, etc.). Teams initially develop a business plan for their own department; later, they must merge the departmental plans into an organizationwide business strategy. On the final day, the multiteam's strategy is presented to Gourami's board of directors, which consists of several Shell senior executives.

Royal Dutch/Shell has found a better way to identify the team skills of prospective job applicants by observing business and engineering students in the Shell Gourami Business Challenge.

Shell leaders emphasize that the Gourami event is more like an audition than a competition because the company hires as many participants as it thinks are qualified. Throughout the event, Shell assessors evaluate students' technical knowledge and skills, but they equally observe how effectively the students work in diverse teams. The need for team skills is quickly apparent to most participants. "Working with people from all sorts of disciplines and cultures has taught me the importance of expanding my knowledge to beyond my field," acknowledges Yoganathan Periasamy, a geology student at Universiti Malaysia Sabah. "You need to be able to combine your expertise with everyone else's in order to make a project work."

Arpan Shah, a University of Texas finance student who attended the Gourami exercise in the United States, also recognized that team skills were vital to help him work with people from different specializations. "Coming from a business background, it's most difficult to understand the engineering aspect of the oil industry," says Shah. "We have to work together so that both sides understand each other."

Team cooperation isn't easy, however, due to the challenges created in the Gourami exercise. "Having to come up with the proposal, and then integrate all our ideas into one plan was definitely not easy," admits Angela Bong, a mechanical engineering student at Universiti Teknologi Malaysia. "Initially, we did have conflict. But we soon realized that everyone operates differently, and that if we are to function well as a whole, we have to understand how others work."

Claire Gould, a mechanical engineering student at Imperial College, London, who attended the European event, also noticed the challenges and potential of teamwork with people from other disciplines. "Dealing with the 'real-life' challenges of Gourami made us all aware of the value of other skills and aptitudes and the need to work as a team," says Gould.[33]

and conflict resolving. The first three competencies are mainly (but not entirely) task-related, while the last two mostly assist team maintenance:[34]

- *Cooperating*. Effective team members are willing and able to work together rather than alone. This includes sharing resources and being sufficiently adaptive or flexible to accommodate the needs and preferences of other team members, such as rescheduling use of machinery so that another team member with a tighter deadline can use it.

- *Coordinating.* Effective team members actively manage the team's work so that it is performed efficiently and harmoniously. For example, effective team members keep the team on track and help to integrate the work performed by different members. This typically requires that effective team members know the work of other team members, not just their own.
- *Communicating.* Effective team members transmit information freely (rather than hoarding), efficiently (using the best channel and language), and respectfully (minimizing arousal of negative emotions). They also listen actively to co-workers.
- *Comforting.* Effective team members help co-workers to maintain a positive and healthy psychological state. They show empathy, provide psychological comfort, and build co-worker feelings of confidence and self-worth.
- *Conflict resolving.* Conflict is inevitable in social settings, so effective team members have the skills and motivation to resolve dysfunctional disagreements among team members. This requires effective use of various conflict-handling styles as well as diagnostic skills to identify and resolve the structural sources of conflict.

These characteristics of effective team members are associated with conscientiousness and extroversion personality traits, as well as with emotional intelligence. Furthermore, the old saying "One bad apple spoils the barrel" seems to apply to teams; one team member who lacks these teamwork competencies may undermine the dynamics of the entire team.[35]

Team Diversity Another important dimension of team composition is diversity. There are two distinct and sometimes opposing issues relating to team diversity.[36] One issue is the notion that diverse teams possess better resources for tackling complex or novel problems. One reason why diverse teams are more effective under these conditions is that people from different backgrounds see a problem or opportunity from different angles. Team members have different mental models, so they are more likely to identify viable solutions to difficult problems. A second reason is that diverse teams have a broader pool of technical competencies. For example, each team at Rackspace, the San Antonio, Texas, provider of enterprise-level Web infrastructure, consists of more than a dozen people with diverse skills such as account management, systems engineering, technical support, billing expertise, and data center support. Rackspace teams require these diverse technical competencies to serve the needs of customers assigned to the team. A third reason favoring teams with diverse members is that they provide better representation of the team's constituents, such as other departments or clients from similarly diverse backgrounds. A team responsible for designing and launching a new service, for instance, should have representation from the organization's various specializations so that people in those work units will support the team's decisions.

The second issue regarding diverse teams is that diversity often creates challenges to the internal functioning of the team.[37] One problem is that diverse employees take longer to become a high-performing team. This partly occurs because team members take longer to bond with people who are different from them, particularly when others hold different perspectives and values (i.e., deep diversity). Diverse teams are susceptible to "fault lines"–hypothetical dividing lines that may split a team into subgroups along gender, ethnic, professional, or other dimensions. These fault lines reduce team effectiveness by reducing the motivation to communicate and coordinate with teammates on the other side of the hypothetical divisions. In contrast, members of teams with minimal diversity experience higher satisfaction, less conflict, and better interpersonal relations. Consequently, homogeneous teams tend to be more effective on tasks requiring a high degree of cooperation and coordination, such as emergency response teams.

Learning Objectives

After reading this section, you should be able to:

5. Summarize the team development process.
6. Discuss how team norms develop and how they may be altered.
7. List six factors that influence team cohesion.
8. Describe the three foundations of trust in teams and other interpersonal relationships.

TEAM PROCESSES

The third set of elements in the team effectiveness model, collectively known as *team processes,* includes team development, norms, cohesion, and trust. These elements represent characteristics of the team that continuously evolve.

Team Development

A few years ago, the National Transportation Safety Board (NTSB) studied the circumstances under which airplane cockpit crews were most likely to have accidents and related problems. What the NTSB discovered was startling: 73 percent of all incidents took place on the crew's first day, and 44 percent occurred on the crew's very first flight together. This isn't an isolated example. NASA studied fatigue of pilots after returning from multiple-day trips. Fatigued pilots made more errors in the NASA flight simulator, as one would expect. But the NASA researchers didn't expect the discovery that fatigued crews who had worked together made fewer errors than did rested crews who had not yet flown together.[38]

The NTSB and NASA studies reveal that team members must resolve several issues and pass through several stages of development before emerging as an effective work unit. They need to get to know and trust each other, understand and agree on their respective roles, discover appropriate and inappropriate behaviors, and learn how to coordinate with each other. The longer team members work together, the better they develop common or complementary mental models, mutual understanding, and effective performance routines to complete the work.

A popular model that captures many team development activities is shown in Exhibit 8.5.[39] The model shows teams moving systematically from one stage to the next, while the dashed lines illustrate that teams might fall back to an earlier stage of development as new members join or other conditions disrupt the team's maturity. *Forming,* the first stage of team development, is a period of testing and orientation in which members learn about each other and evaluate the benefits and costs of continued membership. People tend to be polite, will defer to authority, and try to find out what is expected of them and how they will fit into the team. The *storming* stage is marked by interpersonal conflict as members become more proactive and compete for various team roles. Members try to establish norms of appropriate behavior and performance standards.

During the *norming* stage, the team develops its first real sense of cohesion as roles are established and a consensus forms around group objectives and a common or complementary team-based mental model. By the *performing* stage, team members have learned to efficiently coordinate and resolve conflicts. In high-performance teams, members are highly cooperative, have a high level of trust in each other, are committed to group objectives, and identify with the team. Finally, the *adjourning* stage occurs when the team is about to disband. Team members shift their attention away from task orientation to a relationship focus.

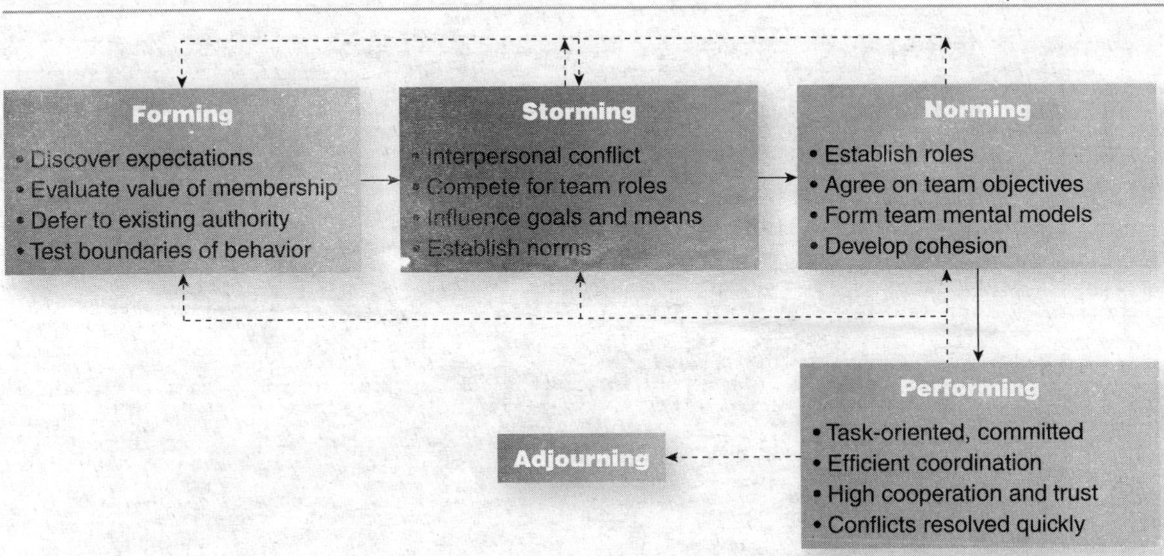

Exhibit 8.5 *Stages of Team Development*

The five-stage model is consistent with what students experience on team projects, but it is far from a perfect representation of the team development process.[40] For instance, it does not show that some teams remain in a particular stage longer than others. It also masks two distinct processes during team development: (1) developing team identity and (2) developing team competence.[41] *Developing team identity* refers to the transition that individuals make from viewing the team as something "out there" to something that is part of themselves. In other words, team development occurs when employees shift their view of the team from "them" to "us." This relates to becoming familiar with the team, making it part of their social identity, and shaping the team to better fit their prototype of an ideal team.

The other process–*developing team competence*–includes several changes related to team learning. Team members develop habitual routines that increase work efficiency. They also form shared or complementary mental models regarding team resources, goals and tasks, social interaction, and characteristics of other team members.[42] Team mental models are visual or relational mental images that are shared by team members. For example, members of a newly formed team might have different views about customer service (quality of interaction, speed of service, technical expertise provided, etc.). As the team develops, these views converge into more of a shared mental model of customer service.

role
A set of behaviors that people are expected to perform because of the positions they hold in a team and organization.

Team Roles An important part of the team development process is forming and reinforcing team roles. A **role** is a set of behaviors that people are expected to perform because they hold certain positions in a team and organization.[43] In a team setting, some roles help the team achieve its goals; other roles maintain relationships within the team. Some team roles are formally assigned to specific people. For example, team leaders are usually expected to initiate discussion, ensure that everyone has an opportunity to present his or her views, and help the team reach agreement on the issues discussed.

Team members are typically assigned specific roles as their formal job responsibilities. Yet, throughout the continuous team development process, people vary their formal roles to suit their

Sky-High Team Development Reaching the performing stage of team development isn't just a goal for the Blue Angels; it's an absolute necessity to ensure the U.S. Navy's aerial demonstration team completes its maneuvers with near-perfect timing. Although highly experienced before joining the squad, the pilots put in long hours of practice to reach the pinnacle of team development. The F/A-18A Hornets initially fly with a large space between them, but the team gradually tightens up the formation over the 10-week training program until the fighter jets are at times only 18 inches apart. Lieutenant Commander John Saccomando, who flies the No. 2 position, explains that the training improves trust and common mental models about each maneuver. "I know exactly what [the lead] jet is going to do, and when," he says. "It takes awhile to build that confidence." Team development is also sped up through candid debriefings after every practice. "We close the door, and there's no rank," says Saccomando, who is expected to offer frank feedback to commanding officer and flight leader Commander Stephen R. Foley. Foley points out that the safety and success of the Blue Angels depends on how well the team development process works. "The team concept is what makes [everything] here click," Foley emphasizes.[44]

personality and values as well as the wishes of other team members. Furthermore, many roles exist informally, such as being a cheerleader, initiator of new ideas, or an adviser who encourages the group to soberly rethink their actions. The informal roles are shared among team members, but many are eventually associated with specific team members. Again, the informal role assignment process is influenced by each team member's personal preferences (personality and values) as well as through negotiated dynamics with other team members.[45]

team building
A process that consists of formal activities intended to improve the development and functioning of a work team.

Accelerating Team Development through Team Building Team development, including sorting out team roles, takes time, so many companies try to speed up the process through team-building activities. **Team building** consists of formal activities intended to improve the development and functioning of a work team.[46] It can help new teams, but it is more commonly applied to existing teams that have regressed to earlier stages of team development due to membership turnover or loss of focus. Some team-building interventions clarify the team's performance goals, increase the team's motivation to accomplish these goals, and establish a mechanism for systematic feedback on the team's goal performance. Others try to improve the team's problem-solving skills. A third category of team building clarifies and reconstructs each member's perceptions of her or his role as well as the role expectations that member has of other team members. Role definition team building also helps the team to develop shared mental models–common internal representations of the external world, such as how to interact with clients, maintain machinery, and engage in meetings. Research studies indicate that team processes and performance depend on how well teammates share common mental models about how they should work together.[47]

A popular form of team building is aimed at improving relations among team members. This includes activities that help team members learn more about each other, build trust in each other, and develop ways to manage conflict within the team. Popular interventions such as wilderness team activities, paintball wars, and obstacle-course challenges are typically offered to build trust. "If two colleagues hold the rope for you while you're climbing 10 meters up, that is truly team-building," suggests a partner in a German communications consulting firm who participated in that team-building event.[48]

Although team-building activities are popular, their success is less certain than many claim.[49] One problem is that team-building activities are used as general solutions to general team problems. A better approach is to begin with a sound diagnosis of the team's health and then select team-building interventions that address weaknesses.[50] Another problem is that team building is applied as a one-shot medical inoculation that every team should receive when it is formed. In truth, team building is an ongoing process, not a three-day jump start.[51] Finally, we must remember that team building occurs on the job, not just on an obstacle course or in a national park. Organizations should encourage team members to reflect on their work experiences and to experiment with just-in-time learning for team development.

Team Norms

norms
The informal rules and shared expectations that groups establish to regulate the behavior of their members.

Norms are the informal rules and shared expectations that groups establish to regulate the behavior of their members. Norms apply only to behavior, not to private thoughts or feelings. Furthermore, norms exist only for behaviors that are important to the team.[52] Norms are enforced in various ways. Co-workers grimace if we are late for a meeting, or they make sarcastic comments if we don't have our part of the project completed on time. Norms are also directly reinforced through praise from high-status members, more access to valued resources, or other rewards available to the team. But team members often conform to prevailing norms without direct reinforcement or punishment because they identify with the group and want to align their behavior with the team's values. The more closely the person's social identity is connected to the group, the more the individual is motivated to avoid negative sanctions from that group.[53]

How Team Norms Develop Norms develop as soon as teams form because people need to anticipate or predict how others will act. Even subtle events during the team's formation, such as how team members initially greet each other and where they sit in the first meetings, can initiate norms that are later difficult to change. Norms also form as team members discover behaviors that help them function more effectively (such as the need to respond quickly to e-mail). In particular, a critical event in the team's history can trigger formation of a norm or sharpen a previously vague one. A third influence on team norms is the past experiences and values that members bring to the team. If members of a new team value work–life balance, norms are likely to develop that discourage long hours and work overload.[54]

Preventing and Changing Dysfunctional Team Norms Team norms often become deeply anchored, so the best way to avoid norms that undermine organizational success or employee well-being is to establish desirable norms when the team is first formed. One way to do this is to clearly state desirable norms as soon as the team is created. Another approach is to select people with appropriate values. If organizational leaders want their teams to have strong safety norms, they should hire people who already value safety and who clearly identify the importance of safety when the team is formed.

The suggestions so far refer to new teams, but how can organizational leaders maintain desirable norms in older teams? First, as one recent study affirmed, leaders often have the capacity to alter existing norms.[55] By speaking up or actively coaching the team, they can often subdue dysfunctional norms while developing useful norms. Team-based reward systems can also weaken counterproductive norms; however, studies report that employees might continue to adhere to a dysfunctional team norm (such as limiting output) even though this behavior reduces their paycheck. Finally, if dysfunctional norms are deeply ingrained and the previous solutions don't work, it may be necessary to disband the group and replace it with people having more favorable norms.

Team Cohesion

team cohesion
The degree of attraction people feel toward the team and their motivation to remain members.

Team cohesion refers to the degree of attraction people feel toward the team and their motivation to remain members. It is a characteristic of the team, including the extent to which its members are attracted to the team, are committed to the team's goals or tasks, and feel a collective sense of team pride.[56] Thus, team cohesion is an emotional experience, not just a calculation of whether to stay or leave the team. It exists when team members make the team part of their social identity. Team cohesion is therefore associated with team development because, as mentioned earlier, team members develop a team identity as part of the team development process.

Influences on Team Cohesion Several factors influence team cohesion: member similarity, team size, member interaction, difficult entry, team success, and external competition or challenges. For the most part, these factors reflect the individual's social identity with the group and beliefs about how team membership will fulfill personal needs.

- *Member similarity.* For more than 2,000 years, philosophers and researchers have observed that people with similar backgrounds and values are more comfortable with and attractive to each other. In team settings, this similarity-attraction effect means that teams have higher cohesion–or become cohesive more quickly–when members are similar to each other. Diversity tends to undermine cohesion, but this depends on the type of diversity. For example, teams consisting of people from different job groups seem to gel together just as well as teams of people from the same job.[57]
- *Team size.* Smaller teams tend to have more cohesion than larger teams because it is easier for a few people to agree on goals and coordinate work activities. However, small teams have less cohesion when they lack enough members to perform the required tasks.
- *Member interaction.* Teams tend to have more cohesion when team members interact with each other fairly regularly. This occurs when team members perform highly interdependent tasks and work in the same physical area.

- *Somewhat difficult entry.* Teams tend to have more cohesion when entry to the team is restricted. The more elite the team, the more prestige it confers on its members, and the more they tend to value their membership in the unit. At the same time, research suggests that severe initiations can weaken team cohesion because of the adverse effects of humiliation, even for those who successfully endure the initiation.[58]
- *Team success.* Cohesion is both emotional and instrumental, with the latter referring to the notion that people feel more cohesion to teams that fulfill their needs and goals. Consequently, cohesion increases with the team's level of success.[59] Furthermore, individuals are more likely to attach their social identity to successful teams than to those with a string of failures.
- *External competition and challenges.* Team cohesion tends to increase when members face external competition or a valued objective that is challenging. This might include a threat from an external competitor or friendly competition from other teams. Employees value their membership on the team because of its ability to overcome the threat or competition and as a form of social support. However, cohesion can dissipate when external threats are severe because these threats are stressful and cause teams to make less effective decisions.[60]

Consequences of Team Cohesion Every team must have some minimal level of cohesion to maintain its existence. People who belong to high-cohesion teams are motivated to maintain their membership and to help the team perform effectively. Compared to low-cohesion teams, high-cohesion team members spend more time together, share information more frequently, and are more satisfied with each other. They provide each other with better social support in stressful situations.[61]

Members of high-cohesion teams are generally more sensitive to each other's needs and develop better interpersonal relationships, thereby reducing dysfunctional conflict. When conflict does arise, members tend to resolve their differences swiftly and effectively. With better cooperation and more conformity to norms, high-cohesion teams usually perform better than low-cohesion teams.[62] However, as Exhibit 8.6 illustrates, this relationship holds true only when team norms are compatible with

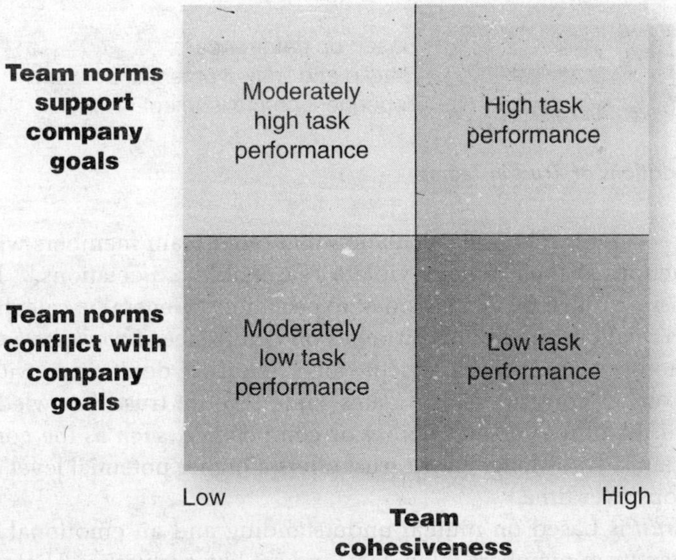

Exhibit 8.6 *Effect of Team Cohesion on Task Performance*

organizational values and objectives. Cohesion motivates employees to perform at a level more consistent with team norms, so when those norms conflict with the organization's success (such as when norms support high absenteeism or acting unethically), high cohesion will reduce team performance.[63]

Team Trust

trust
Positive expectations one person has toward another person in situations involving risk.

Any relationship–including the relationship among team members–depends on a certain degree of trust.[64] **Trust** refers to positive expectations one person has toward another person in situations involving risk. A high level of trust occurs when others affect you in situations where you are at risk but you believe they will not harm you. Trust includes both your beliefs and conscious feelings about the relationship with other team members. In other words, a person both logically evaluates the situation as trustworthy and feels that it is trustworthy.[65] Trust can also be understood in terms of the foundation of the trust. From this perspective, people trust others on the basis of three foundations: calculus, knowledge, and identification (see Exhibit 8.7).

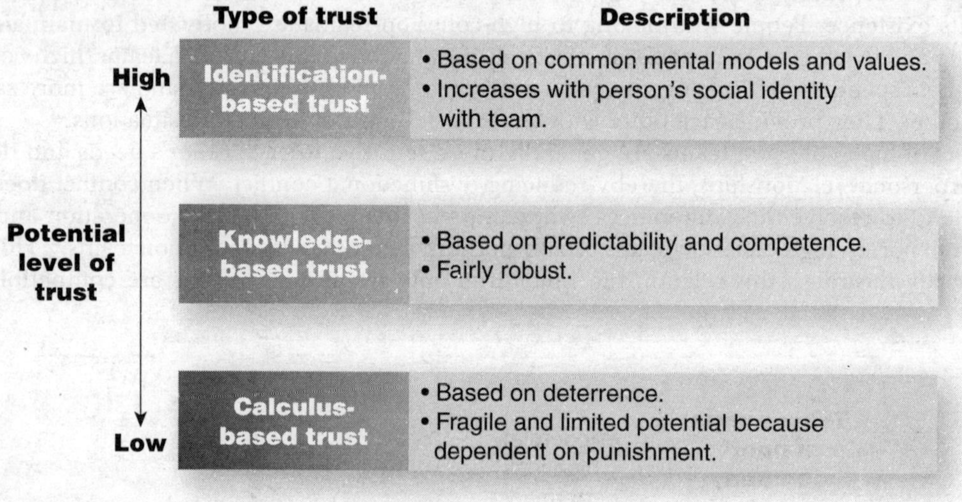

Exhibit 8.7 *Three Foundations of Trust in Teams*

Calculus-based trust represents a logical calculation that other team members will act appropriately because they face sanctions if their actions violate reasonable expectations.[66] It offers the lowest potential trust and is easily broken by a violation of expectations. Generally, calculus-based trust alone cannot sustain a team's relationship, because it relies on deterrence. *Knowledge-based trust* is based on the predictability of another team member's behavior. Even if we don't agree with a particular team member's actions, his or her consistency generates some level of trust. Knowledge-based trust also relates to confidence in the other person's ability or competence, such as the confidence that exists when we trust a physician.[67] Knowledge-based trust offers a higher potential level of trust and is more stable because it develops over time.

Identification-based trust is based on mutual understanding and an emotional bond among team members. It occurs when team members think, feel, and act like each other. High-performance teams exhibit this level of trust because they share the same values and mental models. Identification-based trust is potentially the strongest and most robust of all three types of trust. The individual's self-concept is based partly on membership in the team, and he or she believes the members' values highly overlap, so any transgressions by other team members are quickly forgiven. People are more reluctant to acknowledge a violation of this high-level trust because it strikes at the heart of their self-concept.

Dynamics of Team Trust Employees typically join a team with a moderate or high level–not a low level–of trust in their new co-workers. The main explanation for the initially high trust (called *swift trust*) in organizational settings is that people usually believe their teammates are reasonably competent (knowledge-based trust) and they tend to develop some degree of social identity with the team (identification-based trust). Even when working with strangers, most of us display some level of trust, if only because it supports our self-concept of being a nice person.[68] However, trust is fragile in new relationships because it is based on assumptions rather than well-established experience. Consequently, recent studies report that trust tends to decrease rather than increase over time. This is unfortunate because employees become less forgiving and less cooperative toward others as their level of trust decreases, and this undermines team and organizational effectiveness.[69]

The team effectiveness model is a useful template for understanding how teams work–and don't work–in organizations. With this knowledge in hand, let's briefly investigate two types of teams that have received considerable attention among OB experts and practitioners: self-directed teams and virtual teams.

Individual Differences in Trust

Along with these three foundations of trust, the level of trust depends on a person's general *propensity to trust*.[70] Some people are inherently more willing than others to trust in a given situation. When joining a new work team, you might initially have very high trust in your new teammates, whereas another new team member might only feel a moderate level of trust. This difference is due to each individual's personality, values, and socialization experiences. Our willingness to trust others also varies with the emotions experienced at the moment. In particular, we trust people more when experiencing pleasant emotions than when angry, even if those emotions aren't connected with the other person.

Learning Objectives

After reading the next three sections, you should be able to:

9. Discuss the characteristics and factors required for success of self-directed teams and virtual teams.
10. Identify four constraints on team decision making.
11. Discuss the advantages and disadvantages of four structures that potentially improve team decision making.

Self-Directed Teams

Chrysler believes that one of the key success factors for the automaker's future is "smart manufacturing," which includes applying lean manufacturing principles in plants operated by **self-directed teams (SDTs).** The automaker introduced SDTs a decade ago at its operations in Mexico. Today, employees at Chrysler's plant in Saltillo, Mexico, are organized into teams of a dozen people responsible for a specific set of integrated tasks, including maintenance, quality control, safety, and productivity in their work area. Some of Chrysler's Mexican operations already exceed the efficiency levels of Toyota, which pioneered lean manufacturing.[71]

self-directed teams (SDTs)
Cross-functional work groups that are organized around work processes, complete an entire piece of work requiring several interdependent tasks, and have substantial autonomy over the execution of those tasks.

Self-directed teams are defined by two distinctive features.[72] First, the team completes an entire piece of work requiring several interdependent tasks. This type of work arrangement clusters the team members together while minimizing interdependence and interaction with employees outside the team. The result is a close-knit group of employees who depend on each other to accomplish their individual tasks. For example, Chrysler employees responsible for assembling engines would naturally work more closely with each other than with members of other teams. La-Z-Boy also recently shifted from a traditional assembly line to self-directed teams. As described earlier in this chapter, the furniture manufacturer reorganized production employees into teams responsible for constructing an entire product. Members of each team work closely with each other and minimally with members of other teams.

The second distinctive feature of SDTs is that they have substantial autonomy over the execution of their tasks. In particular, these teams plan, organize, and control work activities with little or no direct involvement of a higher-status supervisor. The teams at Whole Foods Market, which was described at the beginning of this chapter, are considered self-directed because of their autonomy: Every team "gets a profit-and-loss statement, it's responsible for managing inventory, labor productivity, gross margins; and its members are responsible for many of the product-placement decisions," says Whole Foods Market cofounder and CEO John Mackey.[73]

Self-directed teams are found in many industries, ranging from petrochemical plants to aircraft parts manufacturing. Almost all the top-rated manufacturing firms in North America rely on SDTs.[74] The popularity of SDTs is consistent with research indicating that they potentially increase both productivity and job satisfaction. For instance, one study found that car dealership service shops that organize employees into SDTs are significantly more profitable than shops where employees work without a team structure. Another study reported that both short- and long-term measures of customer satisfaction increased after street cleaners in a German city were organized into SDTs.[75]

Sociotechnical Systems Theory and Self-directed Work Teams (SDWTs)

sociotechnical systems (STS) theory
A theory stating that effective work sites have joint optimization of their social and technological systems, and that teams should have sufficient autonomy to control key variances in the work process.

How do companies create successful self-directed work teams? To answer this question, we need to look at **sociotechnical systems (STS) theory,** which is the main source of current SDWT practices. STS theory was introduced during the 1940s at Britain's Tavistock Institute, where researchers had been studying the effects of technology on coal mining in the United Kingdom.[76]

The Tavistock researchers observed that the new coal mining technology (called the "long wall" method) led to a lower, not higher, job performance. They analyzed the causes of this problem and established the idea that organizations need "joint optimization" between the social and technical systems of the work unit. In other words, they need to introduce technology in a way that creates the best structure for semi-autonomous work teams. Furthermore, the Tavistock group concluded that teams should be sufficiently autonomous so that they can control the main "variances" in the system. This means that the team must control the factors with the greatest impact on quality, quantity, and the cost of the product or service. From this overview of STS, we can identify four main conditions for high-performance SDWTs.[77]

Responsible for an Entire Work Process STS theory suggests that self-directed teams work best when they are responsible for making an entire product, providing a service, or otherwise completing an entire work process. By making an entire product or service, the team is sufficiently independent that it can make adjustments without interfering, or having interference from, other work units. At the same time, the primary work unit ensures that employees perform interdependent subtasks within their team so they have a sense of cohesiveness by working toward a common goal.[78]

Sufficient Autonomy STS theory says that an SDWT must have sufficient autonomy to manage the work process. The team should be able to organize and coordinate work among its members to respond more quickly and effectively to its environment. This autonomy also motivates team members through feelings of empowerment.

Control Key Variances STS theory says that high-performance SDWTs have control over "key variances." These variances represent the disturbances or interruptions in the work process that affect the quality or performance of the product or service. For instance, the mixture of ingredients would be a key variance for employees in food processing because the mixture is within the team's control and influences the quality of the final product. In contrast, self-directed teams have fewer advantages when the primary causes of good or poor performance are mainly due to technology, supplies, or other factors beyond the team's control.

joint optimization
A key requirement in sociotechnical systems theory that a balance must be struck between social and technical systems to maximize an operation's effectiveness.

Operate under Joint Optimization Perhaps the most crucial feature of STS theory is **joint optimization**–the notion that the work process needs to balance the social and technical subsystems.[79] In particular, the technological system should be implemented in a way that encourages or facilitates team dynamics, job enrichment, and meaningful feedback. This idea of joint optimization was quite radical in the 1940s when many thought that technology dictated how employees should be organized. In many cases technology resulted in people working alone with little opportunity to directly coordinate their work or share knowledge and ideas. Sociotechnical systems theory, on the other hand, says that companies can and must introduce technology so that it supports a semi-autonomous, team-based structure.

Applying STS Theory and Self-Directed Work Teams

Numerous studies have found that with a few important caveats to consider, self-directed work teams make a difference. A decade ago Canon Inc. introduced self-directed teams at all 29 of its Japanese plants. The camera and copier company claims that a team of a half-dozen people can now produce as much as 30 people in the old assembly line system. One study found that car dealership service garages that organized employees into self-directed teams were significantly more profitable than service garages where employees worked without a team structure. Another reported that both short- and long-term measures of customer satisfaction increased after street cleaning employees in a German city were organized into SDWTs.[80] DaimlerChrysler improved productivity and quality at its Mexican operations by switching to SDWTs. As Connections 10.1 describes, the Chrysler group is now transforming its American plants to "smart manufacturing" with SDWTs.

STS theory provides some guidance for designing self-directed work teams, but it doesn't provide enough detail regarding the optimal alignment of the social and technical systems. Volvo's Uddevalla manufacturing plant in Sweden is an example.[81] Opened in 1988 as a model of sociotechnical design, the Uddevalla plant replaced the traditional assembly line with fixed workstations at which teams of approximately 20 employees assembled and installed components in an unfinished automobile chassis. The work structure created a strong team orientation, but productivity was among the lowest in the automobile industry. (Producing a car at Uddevalla took 50 hours versus 25 hours at a traditional Volvo plant and 13 hours at a Toyota plant.)

The Uddevalla plant was shut down in 1993 and reopened two years later. The plant still uses highly skilled teams, but they are organized around a more traditional assembly line process (similar to Toyota's production system). Some writers argue that organizational politics and poor market demand closed the Uddevalla experiment prematurely. However, Federal Signal recently had a similar experience in its truck assembly plant in the United States. It seems that both Volvo and Federal Signal failed to identify the best alignment of the social and technical subsystems.

Challenges to Self-Directed Work Teams

Along with determining the best combination of social and technical subsystems, corporate leaders need to recognize and overcome at least three potential barriers to self-directed work teams: cross-cultural issues, management resistance, and employee and labor-union resistance.

Cross-Cultural Issues SDWTs are more difficult to implement in high power—distance cultures.[82] Employees in these cultures are more comfortable when supervisors give them directions, whereas low power distance employees value their involvement in decisions. One study reported that SDWTs may be more difficult to introduce in Mexico because employees in that country (which has a high power distance culture) expect managers to make decisions affecting their work. However, as Connections 8.2 described, Chrysler was able to introduce these teams at its Mexican operations almost a decade before they were introduced in the United States. One explanation may be that Chrysler's Mexican employees and managers were more motivated to improve productivity due to competitive threats from other low-wage countries. Also, Mexico has relatively high collectivism, so employees may feel more comfortable working in teams compared to their American counterparts. Overall, cultural values might be an impediment to SDWTs, but they are unlikely to completely prevent them in most countries.

Management Resistance Poet Robert Frost once wrote, "The brain is a wonderful organ; it starts working the moment you get up in the morning and does not stop until you get into the office." Frost's humor highlights the fact that many organizations expect employees to park their brains at the door. Consistent with this view, studies report that supervisors and higher-level managers are often the main source of resistance to the transition to self-directed work teams. Their main worry is losing power when employees gain power through empowered teams. Some are concerned that their jobs will lose value, whereas others believe that they will not have any jobs at all.[83]

Self-directed teams operate best when supervisors shift from "hands-on" controllers to "hands-off" facilitators, but many supervisors have difficulty changing their style. This was one of the biggest stumbling blocks to self-directed work teams at a TRW auto parts plant. Many supervisors kept slipping back into their command-and-control supervisory style. As one TRW employee explains, "One of the toughest things for some of them was to shift from being a boss to a coach, moving from saying, 'I know what's good for you' to 'How can I help you?'" Research suggests that supervisors are less likely to resist self-directed work teams when they have personally worked in a high-involvement workplace and receive considerable training in their new facilitation role.[84]

Employee and Labor-Union-Resistance Employees sometimes oppose SDWTs because they require new skills or appear to require more work. Many feel uncomfortable as they explore their new roles, and they may be worried that they lack the skills to adapt to the new work requirements. For instance, professional surveyors at a Swedish company reported increased stress when their company

8.2 **CONNECTIONS**

Chrysler's Lean Self-Directed Work Teams

The "Big Three" automakers—General Motors, Ford, and Chrysler—are under intense pressure to improve productivity and quality. Chrysler CEO Tom La Sorda believes one of the key ingredients to the company's future is "smart manufacturing," which includes introducing lean manufacturing in plants operated by self-directed work teams (SDWTs).

SDWTs were introduced a decade ago at Chrysler's operations in Mexico, where management and employees were determined to make the team-based process successful. The plant in Saltillo, Mexico, for instance, organizes employees into teams of a dozen people responsible for a specific set of integrated tasks, including maintenance, quality control, safety, and productivity in that work area. Team members operate a workstation within their team for a few hours before rotating to another workstation. This mandatory rotation process increases skill flexibility, minimizes repetitive strain, and creates a sense of team ownership over the tasks within their mandate. Saltillo's productivity has increased by almost 30 percent since the team-based structure was introduced.

Chrysler CEO Tom La Sorda is pushing the automaker into an era of "smart manufacturing" that relies more on self-directed work teams (SDWTs). This photo shows La Sorda meeting employees at the company's plant in Saltillo, Mexico, which has already introduced SDWTs.

Now Chrysler is introducing SDWTs in its U.S. plants, including the assembly plants in Toledo, Ohio, and Belvidere, Illinois, where union members voted in favor of more flexible work arrangements. "The people within Belvidere say we should have done this a long time ago," says United Auto Workers union vice president Nate Gooden. "The boredom and everything they have (had) on the job—it's a different culture. You don't have to come to work every day and do the same job over and over again."

To assist the culture change, team leaders completed 40 hours of training to understand their new role as service leaders—serving the teams rather than vice versa. The physical workspace was also rearranged to create a more intimate team environment. Even the lockers were relocated near the teams' work area to maximize efficiency and create a sense of common team space. "Since the plant went to teams, [the assembly area] feels smaller," says Le Etta Bush, a team member at the Belvidere assembly plant.

The transformation to SDWTs has already had a noticeable effect. Scott Dahle, a supervisor on a traditional assembly line, discovered the change when he was asked to cover one day for Margo Barr, a team leader of one of Belvidere's new SDWTs. "The day he filled in for Margo, his pager never went off, his phone never rang, and no one called him on his radio. He even checked the batteries to see if they were dead," recalls Belvidere plant manager Kurt Kavajecz. "This traditional first-line supervisor, who is used to putting out fires and reacting to crises, came into the new area and was amazed because the team members and the team leaders were running the area. They were taking care of business."

Sources: M. Connelly, "Chrysler Wants to Put Team Assembly in All Plants," *Automotive News*, 30 May 2005, p. 53; J.B. White, "LaSorda's Chrysler Challenge," *The Wall Street Journal*, 15 August 2005, p. B5; J. Leute, "Union, Management Work in Lockstep at Belvidere, Ill., Plant," *Janesville Gazette* (Illinois), 18 July 2005; J. Smith, "Building Cars, Building Teams," *Plant Engineering*, 1 December 2005; M. Connelly, "Chrysler Boosts Belvidere Flexibility," *Automotive News*, 13 February 2006, p. 44.

Learning to Lead Self-Directed Teams When Standard Motor Products (SMP) introduced self-directed work teams at its Edwardsville, Kansas, plant, supervisors had a tough challenge replacing their command-and-control management style with something closer to a mentor or facilitator. "It wasn't easy for managers who were raised in the top-down authority model," recalls Darrel Ray, the nationally recognized consultant who worked with the auto parts company during the transition. "It is far easier to be a tyrant than it is to be a psychologist or a teacher," explains distribution manager Don Wakefield. Steve Domann was one of the managers who had difficulty adjusting. "I thought about quitting when the changes were announced," says Domann, who now oversees plant work teams as a team developer. "Some of the old management team couldn't conform to the team, but I'm glad I did."[85]

introduced customer-focused self-directed teams.[86] Chrysler employees in Belvidere, Illinois, initially rejected the switch to self-directed work teams, possibly fearing increased workload due to job rotation and multiskilling requirements under the proposed flexible agreement.

Labor unions supported the early experiments in sociotechnical change in Europe and India, but some unions in other parts of the world have reservations about SDWTs.[87] One concern is that teams improve productivity at the price of higher stress levels among employees, which is sometimes true. Another worry is that SDWTs require more flexibility by reversing work rules and removing job categories that unions have negotiated over the years. Labor union leaders are therefore concerned that regaining these hard-fought union member rights will be a difficult battle.

In spite of these challenges, self-directed work teams offer enormous potential for organizations when they are implemented under the right conditions, as specified by sociotechnical systems theory. Meanwhile information technologies and knowledge work have enabled virtual teams to gain popularity. The next section examines this new breed of team, including strategies to create high-performance virtual teams.

Success Factors for Self-Directed Teams

Self-directed teams probably would add value in most organizations, but several conditions must be in place to realize their benefits.[88] In addition to managing the team dynamics issues described earlier in this chapter, SDTs operate best when they are responsible for an entire work process, such as making an entire product or providing a service. Organization around a work process keeps each team sufficiently independent from other teams, yet it demands a relatively high degree of interdependence among employees within the team.[89] SDTs should also have sufficient autonomy to organize and coordinate their work. Autonomy allows them to respond more quickly and effectively to client and stakeholder demands. It also motivates team members through feelings of empowerment. Finally, SDTs are more successful when the work site and technology support coordination and communication among team members and increase job enrichment.[90] Too often, management calls a group of employees a "team," yet the work layout, assembly-line structure, and other technologies isolate the employees from each other.

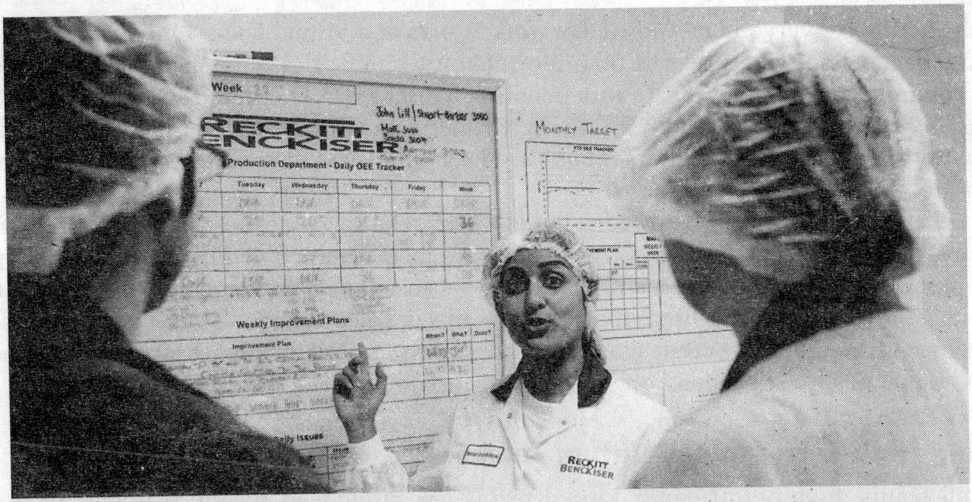

Reckitt Benckiser's Prescription for Productivity: Self-Directed Teams Through teamwork and lean manufacturing practices, Reckitt Benckiser Healthcare has become one of the most productive pharmaceutical operations in Europe. In fact, teamwork is one of the company's four core values. At its facility in Hull, United Kingdom, for example, every line is operated by a dedicated self-directed team. "The people on the lines decide how they are going to run over the next three to four weeks," says Lisa Adams, team leader of the area that packages products in sachets and tubes. Mark Smith, a crew leader of one line, proudly notes that his team has become "one of the most efficient in northern Europe" because "we were given the opportunity to take ownership of the line." The benefits of self-directed teams were apparent when the team responsible for producing Gaviscon antacid tablets tackled a problem with the delivery of tablets in the production process. The team changed the tablet-feed angle and, after a few trials, found a solution. That production line hasn't experienced any tablet-feed problems, and this has significantly reduced costs and improved efficiency due to fewer downtimes and less wasted product.[91]

Virtual Teams

PricewaterhouseCoopers (PwC) employs 190 training professionals in 70 offices across the United States. These professionals, along with many more consultants and academics who provide employee development services, routinely form virtual teams for new projects. "Virtual teaming is the norm for us," says Peter Nicolas, PwC's learning solutions manager in Florham Park, New Jersey.[92]

virtual teams
Teams whose members operate across space, time, and organizational boundaries and are linked through information technologies to achieve organizational tasks.

PwC has had plenty of experience with the growing trend toward **virtual teams.** Virtual teams are teams whose members operate across space, time, and organizational boundaries and are linked through information technologies to achieve organizational tasks.[93] Virtual teams differ from traditional teams in two ways: (1) They are not usually colocated (do not work in the same physical area), and (2) due to their lack of colocation, members of virtual teams depend primarily on information technologies rather than face-to-face interaction to communicate and coordinate their work effort.

According to one estimate, more than 60 percent of employees in professions are members of a virtual team at some point during the year. In global companies such as IBM, almost everyone in knowledge work is part of a virtual team. One reason why virtual teams have become so widespread is that information technologies have made it easier than ever before to communicate and coordinate with people at a distance.[94] The shift from production-based to knowledge-based work is a second reason why virtual teamwork is feasible. It isn't yet possible to make a physical product when team members are located apart, but most of us are now in jobs that mainly process knowledge.

Information technologies and knowledge-based work make virtual teams *possible,* but organizational learning and globalization are two reasons why they are increasingly *necessary.* Virtual teams represent a natural part of the organizational learning process because they encourage employees to share and use knowledge where geography limits more direct forms of collaboration. Globalization makes virtual teams increasingly necessary because employees are spread around the planet rather than around one city. Thus, global businesses depend on virtual teamwork to leverage their human capital.

Designing High-Performance Virtual Teams

As with all teams, high-performance virtual teams are influenced by the elements of the team effectiveness model. Exhibit 8.8 outlines the key design issues for virtual teams that we wiil discuss over the next couple of pages.

Team design element	Special virtual team requirements
Team environment	• Virtual teams need several communication channels available to offset lack of face-to-face communication.
Team tasks	• Virtual teams operate better with structured rather than complex and ambiguous tasks.
Team size and composition	• Virtual teams usually require smaller team size than conventional teams. • Virtual team members must have skills in communicating through information technology and be able to process multiple threads of conversation. • Virtual team members are more likely than conventional team members to require cross-cultural awareness and knowledge.
Team processes	• Virtual team development and cohesiveness require some face-to-face interaction, particularly when the team forms.

Exhibit 8.8 *Designing High-Performance Virtual Teams*

Virtual Team Environment Reward systems, communication systems, organizational environment, organizational structure, and leadership influence the effectiveness of all teams, including virtual teams. Communication systems are particularly important because, unlike conventional teams, virtual teams cannot rely on face-to-face meetings whenever they wish. As we will learn in the next chapter, face-to-face communication transfers the highest volume and complexity of information and offers the timeliest feedback. In contrast, e-mail, telephone, and other information technologies fall far behind in their ability to exchange information. "Having a four- to five-hour discussion is hard to do by phone, especially where you need to read body language," says an executive at accounting giant PricewaterhouseCoopers. Even videoconferencing, which seems similar to face-to-face meetings, actually communicates much less than we realize.[95]

Invensys Employees Are Virtually There Invensys PLC, the British-based process and control engineering company, relies on information technologies to make the best use of its far-reaching talent, often organizing employees into virtual teams at a moment's notice. "Our development projects operate in a virtual mode and [gather] people from multiple sites based on project needs," explains Joe Ayers, a manager at Invensys's process simulation unit in Lake Forest, California. "It is common for projects to utilize developers from three different time zones in a 'follow the sun' development mode." To assist the virtual teams that routinely develop out of this global business structure, Invensys provides a variety of communication tools, such as desktop sharing tools, voice over IP telephony, instant messaging, and video conferencing.[96]

To support high-performance virtual teams, organizations need to provide a variety of communication media so that virtual team members have the freedom to creatively combine these media to match the task demands.[97] For instance, virtual team members might rely on e-mail to coordinate routine tasks but quickly switch to videoconferences and electronic whiteboards when emergencies arise. The lack of face-to-face communication isn't all bad news for virtual teams. Working through e-mail or intranet systems can minimize status differences. Team members whose first language is not English may be overwhelmed into silence in face-to-face meetings but have time to craft persuasive messages in cyberspace.

Virtual Team Tasks Experts suggest that virtual teams operate best with structured tasks requiring only moderate levels of task interdependence.[98] Consider the task structure of client service engineers at BakBone Software. Each day BakBone engineers in San Diego pick up customer-support problems passed on from colleagues in Maryland and England. At the end of the workday, they pass some of these projects on to BakBone co-workers in Tokyo. The assignments sent on to Tokyo must be stated clearly because overseas co-workers can't ask questions in the middle of San Diego's night.

BakBone's virtual team works well with these structured tasks, whereas the lack of colocation makes it difficult for them to consult and communicate about complex and ambiguous tasks. "You don't have the time for open-ended conversation [in a virtual team],"[99] admits BakBone engineer Roger Rodriguez. "You can't informally brainstorm with someone." Generally, complex and ambiguous tasks should be assigned to colocated teams. Similarly, virtual teams should work on tasks requiring moderate levels of interdependence among team members. High levels of interdependence require more intense communication, so they are better assigned to colocated teams.

Virtual Team Size and Composition The problems of team size described in the previous chapter are amplified in virtual teams due to the limits of information technologies. In other words, virtual teams need to be smaller than comparable colocated teams to develop as quickly and coordinate as effectively. The team composition issues covered in this chapter also apply to virtual teams, with the added requirement that virtual team members need additional communication skills. They need to be sensitive to emotional reactions to e-mails and listen to more subtle nonverbal signals in teleconferences. "On a call, I use subtle listening," explains Procter & Gamble executive Karim Ladak, whose virtual team members live in six cities around the world. "I listen for a quiver or a pause. And even then I know that I can very quickly miss something."[100]

Virtual teams often span cultures, so team members must also be aware of cross-cultural issues. For example, one study reported that virtual teams of American and Belgian college students were easily confused by differing conventions in the use of commas versus decimal points in numbers (such as $2.953 million versus $2,953 million). They also experienced cultural differences in socializing. The American students were willing to engage in social communication after they completed the assignment, whereas the Belgian students were more interested in developing a relationship with their partners before beginning work on the project.[101]

Team Processes Team development and cohesiveness are particular concerns for virtual teams because they lack the face-to-face interaction that supports these processes. For example, one recent university study found that face-to-face teams communicate better than virtual teams during the early stages of a project; only after gaining experience did virtual teams share information as openly as face-to face teams. Other studies have reported that employees who work at a distance (such as through telecommuting) from other team members tend to feel less connected with their teams.[102]

Some companies try to ensure that virtual team members have good skills for communicating across distances. Others attempt to create virtual social events. For example, Grant Marshall, Australian country manager for California-based Agilent Technologies, strengthens the bonding process with his virtual team by scheduling a virtual "coffee pot chat" meeting once each month. "All the virtual team [members] call in via a conference line," explains Marshall, whose team members live throughout Asia. "There is no specific preplanned business agenda–the objective is to discuss general activities of what we have been doing." The casual meeting lasts 15 minutes to half an hour and includes such topics as "personal accomplishments, sporting activities, films, holidays, etc.–the type of discussion that you might have around the coffee station."[103]

Another solution, ironically, is to have virtual team members meet face-to-face once in a while. This is what leaders at PricewaterhouseCoopers discovered long ago. PwC virtual teams in the training and development unit meet every few months, whereas global teams in PwC's transaction services group rendezvous every 18 months.

Success Factors for Virtual Teams

Virtual teams have all the challenges of traditional teams, along with the complications of distance and time. Fortunately, OB researchers have been keenly interested in virtual teams, and their studies are now yielding ways to improve virtual-team effectiveness.[104] First, along with having the team competencies described earlier in this chapter, members of successful virtual teams must have the ability to communicate easily through technology, strong self-leadership skills to motivate and guide their behavior without peers or bosses nearby, and higher emotional intelligence so that they can decipher the feelings of teammates from e-mail and other limited communication media. Second, studies have found that leaders typically impose technology on virtual teams rather than allow them to adopt technology that suits their needs at a particular time. The best situation occurs when virtual teams have a toolkit of communication vehicles (e-mail, virtual whiteboards, videoconferencing, etc.), which gain and lose importance over different parts of the project.

The final recommendation is that virtual-team members should meet face-to-face fairly early in the team development process. This idea may seem contradictory to the entire notion of virtual teams, but so far, no technology has replaced face-to-face interaction for high-level bonding and mutual understanding. "I always try to do the kickoff meeting face-to-face," says Scott Patterson, PwC's

Leading CulturalConnect with a Virtual Connect As social media manager at Sun Microsystems, Sumaya Kazi (shown in photo) gets plenty of experience working in virtual teams, but her virtual-team skills are really put to the test in her moonlighting job as executive director and founder of CulturalConnect. CulturalConnect is an online media company Kazi created a few years ago to highlight young people of ethnic backgrounds who are making their mark in the world. CulturalConnect's five online magazines (each representing a different ethnic group) operate entirely with a virtual team of two dozen volunteer staff spread across 18 cities in eight states and two other countries. Although the dispersed workforce presents challenges, Kazi says she is proud of her ability to form a team "and energize it, even though it's virtual."[105]

e-learning manager in Atlanta. "We also try to bring the group back together for major milestones in a project." Similarly, when IBM formed a virtual team to build an electronic customer-access system for Shell, employees from both firms began with an "all hands" face-to-face gathering to assist the team development process. The two firms also made a rule that the dispersed team members should have face-to-face contact at least once every six weeks throughout the project. Without this, "after about five or six weeks we found some of that communication would start to break down," says the IBM comanager for the project.[106]

Team Decision Making

Self-directed teams, virtual teams, and practically all other groups are expected to make decisions. Under certain conditions, teams are more effective than individuals at identifying problems, choosing alternatives, and evaluating their decisions. To leverage these benefits, however, we first need to understand the constraints on effective team decision making. Then, we look at specific team structures that try to overcome these constraints.

Constraints on Team Decision Making

Anyone who has spent enough time in the workplace can reel off several ways in which teams stumble in decision making. The four most common problems are time constraints, evaluation apprehension, pressure to conform, and groupthink.

Time Constraints There's a saying that "committees keep minutes and waste hours." This reflects the fact that teams take longer than individuals to make decisions.[107] Unlike individuals, teams require extra time to organize, coordinate, and maintain relationships. The larger the group, the more time is required to make a decision. Team members need time to learn about each other and build rapport. They need to manage an imperfect communication process so that there is sufficient understanding of each other's ideas. They also need to coordinate roles and rules of order within the decision process.

production blocking
A time constraint in team decision making due to the procedural requirement that only one person may speak at a time.

Another time-related constraint found in most team structures is that only one person can speak at a time.[108] This problem, known as **production blocking,** undermines idea generation in several ways. First, team members need to listen in on the conversation to find an opportune time to speak up, and this monitoring makes it difficult for them to concentrate on their own ideas. Second, ideas are fleeting, so the longer they wait to speak up, the more likely these flickering ideas will die out. Third, team members might remember their fleeting thoughts by concentrating on them, but this causes them to pay less attention to the conversation. By ignoring what others are saying, team members miss other potentially good ideas as well as the opportunity to convey their ideas to others in the group.

evaluation apprehension
A decision-making problem that occurs when individuals are reluctant to mention ideas that seem silly because they believe (often correctly) that other team members are silently evaluating them.

Evaluation Apprehension Individuals are reluctant to mention ideas that seem silly because they believe (often correctly) that other team members are silently evaluating them.[109] This **evaluation apprehension** is based on the individual's desire to create a favorable self-presentation and need to protect self-esteem. It is most common when meetings are attended by people with different levels of status or expertise or when members formally evaluate each other's performance throughout the year (as in 360-degree feedback). Creative ideas often sound bizarre or illogical when first presented, so evaluation apprehension tends to discourage employees from mentioning them in front of co-workers.

Pressure to Conform Team cohesion leads employees to conform to the team's norms. This control keeps the group organized around common goals, but it may also cause team members to suppress their dissenting opinions, particularly when a strong team norm is related to the issue. When someone does state a point of view that violates the majority opinion, other members might punish the violator or try to persuade him or her that the opinion is incorrect. Conformity can also be subtle. To some extent, we depend on the opinions that others hold to validate our own views. If co-workers don't agree with us, we begin to question our own opinions even without overt peer pressure.

groupthink
The tendency of highly cohesive groups to value consensus at the price of decision quality.

Groupthink **Groupthink** is the tendency of highly cohesive groups to value consensus at the price of decision quality.[110] The concept includes the dysfunctional effects of conformity on team decision making, which were described above. It also includes the dysfunctionval consequences of trying to maintain harmony within the team. This desire for harmony exists as a group norm and is most apparent when team members have a strong social identity with the group. Groupthink supposedly occurs most often when the team is isolated from outsiders, the team leader is opinionated (rather than impartial), the team is under stress due to an external threat, the team has experienced recent failures or other decision-making problems, and the team lacks clear guidance from corporate policies or procedures.

The term *groupthink* is now part of everyday language, so much so that some experts worry that it commonly refers to almost any problem in team decision making. Meanwhile, scholarly studies have found that the symptoms of groupthink do not cluster together as the concept assumes; some of these characteristics actually tend to improve rather than undermine decision making in some situations. Although many cases of groupthink have been documented, a recent study found that this evidence is illusory because observers retrospectively make sense of bad decisions by incorrectly perceiving evidence of groupthink.[111]

In spite of the problems with the groupthink concept, some of its specific elements continue to be relevant because they explain specific problems with team decision making. One of these elements, conformity, was described above as a concern. Another important element is the team's overconfidence. Studies consistently report that highly confident teams have a false sense of invulnerability, which makes them less attentive in decision making than are moderately confident teams.[112]

group polarization
The tendency of teams to make more extreme decisions than individuals working alone.

Group Polarization **Group polarization** refers to the tendency of teams to make more extreme decisions than individuals working alone.[113] Suppose a group of people meets to decide the future of a new product. Individual team members might come to the meeting with various degrees of support or opposition to the product's future. Yet by the end of the meeting, chances are that the team will agree on a more extreme solution than the average person had when the meeting began.

There are three reasons why group polarization occurs (see Exhibit 8.9). First, team members become comfortable with more extreme positions when they realize that co-workers also generally support the same position. Second, persuasive arguments favoring the dominant position convince doubtful members and help form a consensus around the extreme option. Finally, individuals feel less personally responsible for the decision consequences because the decision is made by the team. Social support, persuasion, and shifting responsibility explain why teams make extreme decisions, but they also make *riskier* decisions due to the natural tendency to take higher risks when facing certain losses. This higher risk preference is caused by the prospect theory effect described in Chapter 7–people try to avoid losses because they are more painful than the equivalent gain.[114]

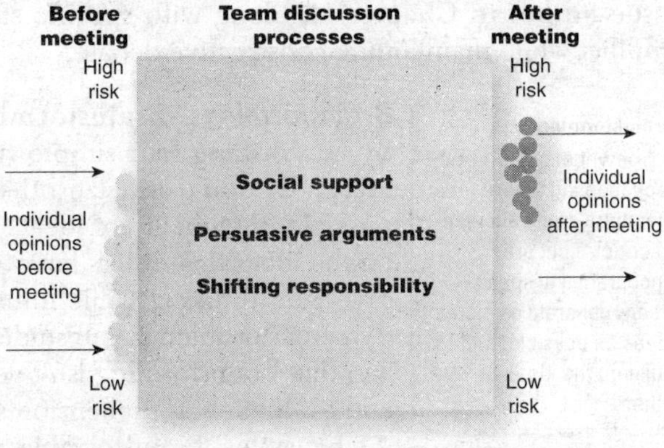

Exhibit 8.9 *The Group Polarization Process*

Team Structures to Improve Decision Making

There is plenty of research revealing problems with team decision making, but several solutions also emerge from these bad-news studies. Team members need to be confident in their decision making but not so confident that they collectively feel invulnerable. This calls for team norms that encourage critical thinking as well as team membership with sufficient diversity. Checks and balances need to be in place to prevent one or two people from dominating the discussion. The team should also be large enough to possess the collective knowledge to resolve the problem yet small enough that the team doesn't consume too much time or restrict individual input.

Team structures also help to minimize the problems described over the previous few pages. Four structures potentially improve team decision making in team settings: constructive conflict, brainstorming, electronic brainstorming, and nominal group technique.

Constructive Conflict A popular way to improve team decision making at Corning Inc. is to assign promising ideas to two-person teams, who spend up to four months analyzing the feasibility of their assigned idea. The unique feature about this process is that the team is deliberately designed so that one person is from marketing and the other has technical expertise. This oil-and-water combination sometimes ruffles feathers, but it seems to generate better ideas and evaluations. "We find great constructive conflict this way," says Deborah Mills, who leads Corning's early-stage marketing team.[115]

constructive conflict
The type of conflict that occurs when people focus their discussion on the issue while maintaining respect for people having other points of view.

Constructive conflict occurs when people focus their discussion on the issue while maintaining respect for people having other points of view. This conflict is called "constructive" because different viewpoints are encouraged so that ideas and recommendations can be clarified, redesigned, and tested for logical soundness. The main advantage of this debate is that it presents different points of view and thus encourages all participants to reexamine their assumptions and logic. The main challenge with constructive conflict is that healthy debate too often slides into personal attacks, a problem that may explain why the evidence of constructive conflict on team decision making is inconsistent.[116] We explore this issue further in Chapter 11, along with specific strategies for minimizing the emotional effects of conflict while maintaining constructive debate.

brainstorming
A freewheeling, face-to-face meeting where team members aren't allowed to criticize but are encouraged to speak freely, generate as many ideas as possible, and build on the ideas of others.

Brainstorming **Brainstorming** tries to leverage the creative potential of teams by establishing four simple rules: (1) Speak freely–describe even the craziest ideas; (2) don't criticize others or their ideas; (3) provide as many ideas as possible–the quality of ideas increases with the quantity of ideas; and (4) build on the ideas that others have presented. These rules are supposed to encourage divergent thinking while minimizing evaluation apprehension and other team dynamics problems. Lab studies using university students concluded many years ago that brainstorming isn't very effective, largely because production blocking and evaluation apprehension still interfere with team dynamics.[117]

However, brainstorming may be more beneficial than the earlier studies indicated.[118] The earlier lab studies measured the number of ideas generated, whereas recent investigations within companies using brainstorming indicate that this team structure results in more *creative* ideas, which is the main reason why companies use brainstorming. Also, evaluation apprehension is less of a problem in high-performing teams that embrace a learning orientation culture than it is for students brainstorming in lab experiments. Another overlooked advantage of brainstorming is that participants interact and participate directly, thereby increasing decision acceptance and team cohesion. Finally, brainstorming sessions often spread enthusiasm, which tends to generate more creativity. Overall, while brainstorming might not always be the best team structure, it seems to be more valuable than some of the earlier research studies indicated.

electronic brainstorming
A recent form of brainstorming that relies on networked computers for submitting and sharing creative ideas.

Electronic Brainstorming **Electronic brainstorming** is a more recent form of brainstorming that relies on networked computers for submitting and sharing creative ideas. After receiving the question or issue, participants enter their ideas using special computer software. The ideas are distributed anonymously to other participants, who are encouraged to piggyback on those ideas. Team members eventually vote electronically on the ideas presented. Face-to-face discussion usually follows. Electronic brainstorming can be quite effective at generating creative ideas with minimal production blocking, evaluation apprehension, or conformity problems.[119] Despite these numerous advantages, electronic brainstorming seems to be too structured and technology-bound for some executives. Some leaders may also feel threatened by the honesty of statements generated through this process and by their limited ability to control the discussion.

NASA's Constructive Conflict Room The ill-fated flight of the space shuttle *Columbia* in 2003 was a wake-up call for how NASA's mission management team makes decisions. The *Columbia* accident investigation team concluded that concerns raised by engineers were either deflected or watered down because the mission management team appeared to be "immersed in a culture of invincibility" and hierarchical authority discouraged constructive debate. If top decision makers had more fully considered the extent of damage during takeoff, they might have been able to save *Columbia's* seven crew members. To foster more open communications and constructive conflict, the mission management team's assigned-seating rectangular table has been replaced by a C-shaped arrangement where people sit wherever they want (shown in photo). None of the 24 members stands out above the others in the new setup. Around the walls of the room are pearls of wisdom reminding everyone of the pitfalls of team decision making. "People in groups tend to agree on courses of action which, as individuals, they know are stupid," warns one poster.[120]

nominal group technique A variation of brainstorming consisting of three stages: Participants (1) silently and independently document their ideas, (2) collectively describe these ideas to the other team members without critique, and then (3) silently and independently evaluate the ideas presented.

Nominal Group Technique **Nominal group technique** is a variation of traditional brainstorming that tries to combine the benefits of team decision making without the problems mentioned earlier.[121] The method is called "nominal" because participants form a group in name only during two of its three stages. After the problem is described, team members silently and independently write down as many solutions as they can. In the second stage, participants describe their solutions to the other team members, usually in a round-robin format. As with brainstorming, there is no criticism or debate, although members are encouraged to ask for clarification of the ideas presented. In the third stage, participants silently and independently rank-order or vote on each proposed solution. Nominal group technique tends to generate a higher number of ideas and better-quality ideas than do traditional interacting and possibly brainstorming groups.[122] Due to its high degree of structure, nominal group technique usually maintains a high task orientation and relatively low potential for conflict within the team. However, production blocking and evaluation apprehension still occur to some extent.

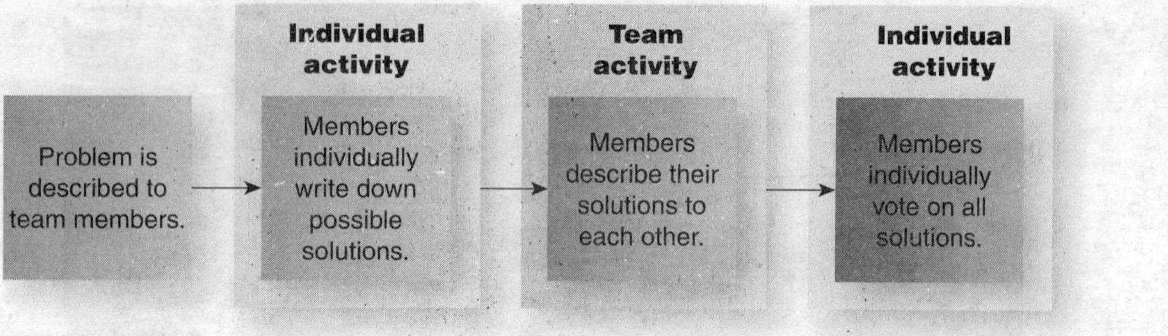

Exhibit 8.10 *Nominal Group Technique*

The nominal group technique tends to generate more and better-quality ideas compared with traditionally interacting and possibly brainstorming groups.[123] Due to its high degree of structure, the nominal group technique usually maintains a high task orientation and relatively low potential for conflict within the team. However, team cohesiveness is generally lower in nominal decisions because the structure minimizes social interaction. Production blocking and evaluation apprehension still occur to some extent.

Delphi method
A structured team decision-making process of systematically pooling the collective knowledge of experts on a particular subject to make decisions, predict the future, or identify opposing views.

Delphi Method The **Delphi method** was developed by the RAND think tank in the 1950s and has regained attention over the past decade. Delphi systematically pools the collective knowledge of experts on a particular subject to make decisions, predict the future, identify opposing views (called *dissensus*), or identify multiple causes of events.[124] One recent example is a Delphi analysis of the challenges facing agriculture in Finland. Another developed and prioritized a list of indicators that people use to evaluate ecotourism in Taiwan. A third study of 50 experts identified a range of causes of obesity in Australia, then in a second round rank ordered the importance of each cause, along with an explanation of their rankings. The results revealed a dissensus of opinion about why Australians are gaining weight.[125]

There are a few variations, but most Delphi groups have the following features. They do not meet face-to-face; in fact, participants are often located in different parts of the world and may not know each other's identity. As with electronic brainstorming, Delphi participants do not know who "owns" the ideas submitted. Typically Delphi group members submit possible solutions or comments regarding an issue to the central convener, although computer technology is turning this stage into an automatic compilation process. The compiled results are returned to the panel for a second round of comments. This process may be repeated a few more times until consensus or dissensus emerges.

Team Building

HellermanTyton's 60 senior marketing executives recently gathered in what appeared to be the middle of a South American jungle. In reality the executives at the global maker of wire and cable products were participating in a team-building exercise located in a private wildlife reserve in Naples, Florida, complete with giraffes, leopards, chimpanzees, and alligators. "You would never think we were still in Naples, but we were," says Terry Tuttle, HellermannTyton's vice president of marketing. The safari-themed program tested the managers' teamwork, communication, and leadership skills in a realistic setting. One activity even put participants up close with a live Florida alligator. "Although many were

Volunteering Builds Better Teams When E.ON UK, the United Kingdom's largest integrated energy company, recently formed a social and corporate affairs team, it didn't rely on firewalking, camping in the woods, or the other usual forms of team building. Instead team members spent time creating pathways, tree guards, and fencing in parks operated by the National Trust. "We wanted to give something back to the local community, and as we were a new team we also wanted to bond," says team member Suzanne Doxey. "When we got back to the office we were more relaxed and had better relationships with each other." Community volunteering has become the latest trend in team building. Lockheed Martin employees, including the team shown in this photo helping with the New Orleans clean up following hurricune Katrina, have logged more than 2 million hours over the past three years, volunteering their services for environmental and community improvement projects while improving interpersonal relationships back at work. PricewaterhouseCoopers is another company that sees the dual benefits of volunteering. "It's a great opportunity for people to get to know each other in an environment where they're all doing exactly the same task so there's no hierarchy," says an executive at the global accounting firm. "It really does help people to understand each other and build teams."[126]

skeptical at first, you could see the teams form and build with each exercise," says Tuttle. "By the end, everyone was pumped up. We established camaraderie as a group that is essential to getting business goals accomplished throughout the year."[127]

team building
Any formal activity intended to improve the development and functioning of a work team.

The executives at HellermannTyton rejuvenated team dynamics more quickly through **team building**–formal activities intended to improve the development and functioning of a work team.[128] Some team-building activities also reshape team norms and strengthen cohesiveness. Team building is sometimes applied to newly established teams because team members are at the earliest stages of team development. However, it is more common among existing teams, such as at HellermannTyton, where employees need to reestablish camaraderie or where the team has regressed to earlier stages of team development. Team building is therefore most appropriate when the team experiences high membership turnover or members have lost focus on their respective roles and team objectives.

Types of Team Building

There are four main types of team building: goal setting, role definition, interpersonal processes, and problem solving.[129]

- *Goal setting.* Some team-building interventions clarify the team's performance goals, increase the team's motivation to accomplish these goals, and establish a mechanism for systematic feedback on the team's goal performance. This is very similar to individual goal setting described in Chapter 5, except that the goals are applied to teams.

- *Role definition.* Clarifying role definitions is often associated with goal-setting team building. Role definition team building involves clarifying and reconstructing members' perceptions of their roles as well as the role expectations they have of other team members. Various interventions may be applied, ranging from open discussion to structured analysis of the work process. Role definition encompasses the emerging concept of *team mental models.* Recall from Chapter 3 that mental models are internal representations of the external world. Research studies indicate that team processes and performance depend on how well teammates share common mental models about how they should work together.[130] Team-building activities help team members clarify and form a more unified perspective of their team mental models.
- *Interpersonal processes.* This category of team building covers a broad territory. Conflict management fits under this heading, both as a symptom to identify the team's underlying weaknesses and as an ongoing interpersonal process that team members learn to continuously manage constructively. Early team-building interventions relied on direct confrontation sessions to give the sources of conflict an airing. This can work with professional facilitation, but experts warn that open dialogue is not always the most effective way to solve team conflicts.[131] Another interpersonal process is building (or rebuilding) trust among team members. Popular interventions such as wilderness team activities, paintball wars, and obstacle course challenges are typically offered to build trust. "If two colleagues hold the rope for you while you're climbing 10 meters up, that is truly team-building," explains Jan Antwerpes, a partner in a German communications consulting firm.
- *Problem solving.* This type of team building focuses on decision making, including the issues mentioned earlier in this chapter and the decision-making process. To improve their problem-solving skills, some teams participate in simulation games that require team decisions in hypothetical situations. PwC's adventure at Disney's EPCOT Center, which was described at the beginning of this chapter, is one such example of team building that improves problem-solving skills among team members.

Is Team Building Effective?

Are team-building interventions effective? Is the money well spent? So far the answer is an equivocal "maybe." Studies suggest that some team-building activities are successful, but just as many fail to build high-performance teams.[132] One problem is that corporate leaders assume team-building activities are general solutions to general team problems. No one bothers to diagnose the team's specific needs (such as problem solving or interpersonal processes) because the team-building intervention is assumed to be a broad-brush solution. A better approach is to begin with a sound diagnosis of the team's health, then select team-building interventions that address weaknesses.

Another problem is that corporate leaders tend to view team building as a one-shot medical inoculation that every team should receive when it is formed. In truth, team building is an ongoing process, not a three-day jump start. Some experts suggest, for example, that wilderness experiences often fail because they rarely include follow-up consultation to ensure that team learning is transferred back to the workplace.[133]

Finally, we must remember that team building occurs on the job, not just on an obstacle course or in a national park. Organizations should encourage team members to reflect on their work experiences and to experiment with just-in-time learning for team development. This dialogue requires open communication, so employees can clarify expectations, coordinate work activities, and build common mental models of working together. The next chapter looks at the dynamics of communicating in teams and organizations.

Chapter Summary

Teams are groups of two or more people who interact and influence each other, are mutually accountable for achieving common goals associated with organizational objectives, and perceive themselves as a social entity within an organization. All teams are groups, because they consist of people with a unifying relationship; not all groups are teams, because some groups do not exist to serve organizational objectives.

People join informal groups (and are motivated to be on formal teams) for four reasons: (1) People have an innate drive to bond, (2) group membership is an inherent ingredient in a person's self-concept, (3) some personal goals are accomplished better in groups, and (4) individuals are comforted in stressful situations by the mere presence of other people. Teams have become popular because they tend to make better decisions, support the organizational learning process, and provide superior customer service. People also tend to be more motivated working in teams. However, teams are not always as effective as individuals working alone. Process losses and social loafing are two particular concerns that drag down team performance.

Team effectiveness includes the team's ability to achieve its objectives, fulfill the needs of its members, and maintain its survival. The model of team effectiveness considers the team and organizational environment, team design, and team processes. Three team design elements are task characteristics, team size, and team composition. Teams tend to be better suited for situations in which the work is complex and the tasks among employees have high interdependence. Teams should be large enough to perform the work yet small enough for efficient coordination and meaningful involvement. Effective teams are composed of people with the competencies and motivation to perform tasks in a team environment. Team member diversity has advantages and disadvantages for team performance.

Teams develop through the stages of forming, storming, norming, performing, and eventually adjourning. Within these stages are two distinct team development processes: developing team identity and developing team competence. Team development can be accelerated through team building—any formal activity intended to improve the development and functioning of a work team. Teams develop norms to regulate and guide member behavior. These norms may be influenced by initial experiences, critical events, and the values and experiences that team members bring to the group.

Team cohesion—the degree of attraction people feel toward the team and their motivation to remain members—increases with member similarity, smaller team size, higher degree of interaction, somewhat difficult entry, team success, and external challenges. Cohesion increases team performance when the team's norms are congruent with organizational goals. Trust is a psychological state comprising the intention to accept vulnerability on the basis of positive expectations of the intent or behavior of another person. People trust others on the basis of three foundations: calculus, knowledge, and identification.

Self-directed teams (SDTs) complete an entire piece of work requiring several interdependent tasks, and they have substantial autonomy over the execution of their tasks. Members of virtual teams operate across space, time, and organizational boundaries and are linked through information technologies to achieve organizational tasks. Virtual teams are more effective when the team members have certain competencies, the team has the freedom to choose the preferred communication channels, and the members meet face-to-face fairly early in the team development process.

Team decisions are impeded by time constraints, evaluation apprehension, conformity to peer pressure, and groupthink (specifically overconfidence). Four structures potentially improve decision making in team settings: constructive conflict, brainstorming, electronic brainstorming, and nominal group technique.

Key Terms

brainstorming
Brooks's law
constructive conflict
electronic brainstorming
evaluation apprehension
groupthink
nominal group technique
norms
process losses
production blocking
role
self-directed teams (SDTs)
social capital
social loafing
task interdependence
team building
team cohesion
teams
trust
virtual teams

Critical Thinking Questions

1. Informal groups exist in almost every form of social organization. What types of informal groups exist in your classroom? Why are students motivated to belong to these informal groups?
2. The late management guru Peter Drucker said: "The now-fashionable team in which everybody works with everybody on everything from the beginning rapidly is becoming a disappointment." Discuss three problems associated with teams.
3. You have been put in charge of a cross-functional task force that will develop enhanced Internet banking services for retail customers. The team includes representatives from marketing, information services, customer service, and accounting, all of whom will move to the same location at headquarters for three months. Describe the behaviors you might observe during each stage of the team's development.
4. You have just been transferred from the Kansas office to the Denver office of your company, a national sales organization of electrical products for developers and contractors. In Kansas, team members regularly called customers after a sale to ask whether the products arrived on time and whether they are satisfied. But when you moved to the Denver office, no one seemed to make these follow-up calls. A recently hired co-worker explained that other co-workers discouraged her from making those calls. Later, another co-worker suggested that your follow-up calls were making everyone else look lazy. Give three possible reasons why the norms in Denver might be different from those in the Kansas office, even though the customers, products, sales commissions, and other characteristics of the workplace are almost identical.
5. You have been assigned to a class project with five other students, none of whom you have met before. To what extent would team cohesion improve your team's performance on this project? What actions would you recommend to build team cohesion among student team members in this situation?
6. Suppose that you were put in charge of a virtual team whose members are located in different cities around the country or region. What tactics could you use to build and maintain team trust, as well as minimize the decline in trust that often occurs in teams?
7. You are responsible for convening a major event in which senior officials from several state governments will try to come to an agreement on environmental issues. It is well known that some officials posture so that they appear superior, whereas others are highly motivated to solve the environmental problems that cross adjacent states. What team decision-making problems are likely to be apparent in this government forum, and what actions can you take to minimize these problems?
8. Bangalore Technologies wants to use brainstorming with its employees and customers to identify new uses for its technology. Advise Bangalore's president about the potential benefits of brainstorming, as well as its potential limitations.

CASE STUDY 8.1

THE SHIPPING INDUSTRY ACCOUNTING TEAM

For the past five years, I have been working at McKay, Sanderson, and Smith Associates, a midsize accounting firm in Boston that specializes in commercial accounting and audits. My particular specialty is accounting practices for shipping companies, ranging from small fishing fleets to a couple of the big firms with ships along the East Coast.

About 18 months ago, McKay, Sanderson, and Smith Associates became part of a large merger involving two other accounting firms. These firms have offices in Miami, Seattle, Baton Rouge, and Los Angeles. Although the other two accounting firms were much larger than McKay, all three firms agreed to avoid centralizing the business around one office in Los Angeles. Instead, the new firm–called Goldberg, Choo, and McKay Associates–would rely on teams across the country to "leverage the synergies of our collective knowledge" (an often-cited statement from the managing partner soon after the merger).

The merger first affected me a year ago when my boss (a senior partner and vice president of the merger firm) announced that I would be working more closely with three people from the other two firms to become the firm's new shipping industry accounting team. The other team members were Elias in Miami, Susan in Seattle, and Brad in Los Angeles. I had met Elias briefly at a meeting in New York City during the merger, but had never met Susan or Brad, although I knew that they were shipping accounting professionals at the other firms.

Initially, the shipping team activities involved e-mailing each other about new contracts and prospective clients. Later, we were asked to submit joint monthly reports on accounting statements and issues. Normally, I submitted my own monthly reports, which summarized activities involving my own clients. Coordinating the monthly report with three other people took much more time, particularly since different accounting documentation procedures across the three firms were still being resolved. It took numerous e-mails and a few telephone calls to work out a reasonable monthly report style.

During this aggravating process, it became apparent–to me at least–that this team business was costing me more time than it was worth. Moreover, Brad in Los Angeles didn't have a clue about how to communicate with the rest of us. He rarely replied to e-mails. Instead, he often used the telephone voice mail system, which resulted in lots of telephone tag. Brad arrives at work at 9:30 a.m. in Los Angeles (and is often late), which is early afternoon in Boston. I typically have a flexible work schedule from 7:30 a.m. to 3:30 p.m. so that I can chauffeur my kids after school to sports and music lessons. So Brad and I have a window of less than three hours to share information.

The biggest nuisance with the shipping specialist accounting team started two weeks ago when the firm asked the four of us to develop a new strategy for attracting more shipping firm business. This new strategic plan is a messy business. Somehow, we have to share our thoughts on various approaches, agree on a new plan, and write a unified submission to the managing partner. Already, the project is taking most of my time just writing and responding to e-mails and talking in conference calls (which none of us did much before the team formed).

Susan and Brad have already had two or three misunderstandings via e-mail about their different perspectives on delicate matters in the strategic plan. The worst of these disagreements required a conference call with all of us to resolve it. Except for the most basic matters, it seems that we can't understand each other, let alone agree on key issues. I have come to the conclusion that I would never want Brad to work in my Boston office (thank goodness he's on the other side of the country). While Elias and I seem to agree on most points, the overall team can't form a common vision or strategy. I don't know how Elias, Susan, or Brad feel, but I would be quite happy to work somewhere that did not require any of these long-distance team headaches.

Discussion Questions

1. What type of team was formed here? Was it necessary, in your opinion?
2. Use the team effectiveness model and related information in this chapter to identify the strengths and weaknesses of this team's environment, design, and processes.
3. Assuming that these four people must continue to work as a team, recommend ways to improve the team's effectiveness.

CASE STUDY 8.2

PHILANTHROPIC TEAM BUILDING

The top dozen executives from Adolph Coors and Molson breweries wanted to accelerate their team development to kick off the postmerger integration of the two companies. But rather than doing the usual team building in the woods or at a friendly game of golf, the Molson Coors leaders spent a full day helping to build a house for Habitat for Humanity. "We quickly got past the idea of a ropes course or golf outing," recalls Samuel D. Walker, Molson Coors' chief legal officer. "We really wanted something where we would give back to one of the communities where we do business." According to Walker, the volunteering experience exceeded everyone's expectations. "We had to unload this truck full of cement roof tiles. We actually had to figure out how to have kind of a bucket line, handing these very heavy tiles from one person to the next. That's the ultimate team-building exercise."

Molson Coors and other companies are discovering that volunteering is just as successful as a team-building event as it is as a form of corporate social responsibility. Credit Suisse held a team-building session in New Orleans that included a day working on a home damaged by Hurricane Katrina. "I think people learned a lot about each other," says Glenn W. Welling, a Credit Suisse managing director who participated in the event. "It was not uncommon seeing a managing director trying to tear down some mold-damaged wall and to watch a 25-year-old analyst come over to help him."

Kimberly Senter, director for category management at Unilever U.S., believes that volunteering events help her to know her colleagues better without the pressure of formal networking. "You're connecting on a very personal level," she suggests. "There's not a lot of talking shop. It's more, 'Pass me the hammer.'"

Timberland is a pioneer in donating employee time to community events. Since 1992, the New Hampshire–based outdoor clothing and accessories company has granted employees 40 hours of paid leave each year to work on community projects. This paid volunteering time includes Earth Day, when Timberland shuts its entire operation so that employees can participate in community projects. It doesn't take long for employees to realize that Timberland is doing more than giving back to the community; it is also developing team skills and cohesion within the company.

"It is a team-building event," says Lisa Rakaseder, a Timberland employee who participated in an Earth Day project at a YMCA camp where she and co-workers built canoe racks and raked leaves. "It gets you to interact with other people at the company." Fabienne Verschoor, who organized the YMCA project, explains further: "You have senior staff, the loading dock crew, customer service, all working together. And you won't know the difference when you see a team working. They are all putting heart and soul into it."

UPS, the package delivery company, is another organization that endorses volunteering as an activity to improve team dynamics as well as employee leadership skills. Along with supporting voluntary work throughout the year, UPS funds an annual Global Volunteer Week, which takes place in 200 countries and most recently involved 23,000 UPS employees. UPS staff in each country coordinate local projects that address issues relevant to their communities. UPS Hong Kong, for example, has worked with the Hong Kong Red Cross, the Hong Kong Society for the Protection of Children, and the Hong Kong Blind Union.

"Giving back to the community is one of the core values of UPS," says David Cheung Yu-hok, human resources manager of UPS Hong Kong. "This builds teamwork across departments because in the workplace, staff might not find the time to get along. Through these projects, they get a chance to know each other better, and sometimes they even get to meet each other's families."

Discussion Questions

1. What type of team building best describes these volunteering activities?
2. Explain how the corporate social responsibility element of volunteering contributes to team building.
3. Along with team building, in what other ways do these volunteering activities improve organizations?

Sources: M. C. White, "Doing Good on Company Time," *New York Times,* 8 May 2007; R. Notarianni, "Voluntary Work Boosts Productivity, Loyalty," *South China Morning Post,* 28 June 2008, p. 4; A. Hall, "Timberland Shows Up," *Corporate Meetings & Incentives* 27 (July) 2008, pp. 16–21.

CASE STUDY 8.3

SEAGATE'S MORALE-ATHON

BusinessWeek

Team-building activities come in many forms and are widely practiced, but few companies go as far as Seagate Technology. Each year, the giant American computer storage hardware manufacturer has been sending hundreds of employees from a dozen countries to a weeklong team-building program called Eco-Seagate. CEO Bill Watkins championed the event to break down barriers, boost confidence, and make staffers better team players. "Some of you will learn about teamwork because you have a great team," Watson advised one group of participants. "Some of you will learn because your team is a disaster."

This *BusinessWeek* case study details the team-building events that "tribes" of employees participated in throughout a recent Eco-Seagate program in New Zealand. It describes how employees reacted to these activities, including the marathon race on the final day. Read the full text of this *BusinessWeek* article at www.mhhe.com/mcshane5e, and prepare for the discussion questions below.

Discussion Questions

1. What type(s) of team building best represent the Eco-Seagate event? In your opinion, is this type of event effective for team building? Why or why not?
2. What practices in the Eco-Seagate program help team members to become more cohesive?

Source: S. Max, "Seagate's Morale-athon," *BusinessWeek,* 3 April 2006, p. 110.

TEAM EXERCISE 8.4

TEAM TOWER POWER

PURPOSE This exercise is designed to help you understand team roles, team development, and other issues in the development and maintenance of effective teams.

MATERIALS The instructor will provide enough Lego pieces or similar materials for each team to complete the assigned task. All teams should have identical (or very similar) amounts and types of pieces. The instructor will need a measuring tape and stopwatch. Students may use writing materials during the design stage (step 2, below). The instructor will distribute a "Team Objectives Sheet" and "Tower Specifications Effectiveness Sheet" to all teams.

INSTRUCTIONS

1. The instructor will divide the class into teams. Depending on class size and space availability, teams may have between four and seven members, but all should be approximately equal size.
2. Each team is given 20 minutes to design a tower that uses only the materials provided, is freestanding, and provides an optimal return on investment. Team members may wish to draw their tower on paper or a flipchart to facilitate the tower's design. Teams are free to practice building their tower during this stage. Preferably, teams are assigned to their own rooms so that the design can be created privately. During this stage, each team will complete the Team Objectives Sheet distributed by the instructor. This sheet requires the Tower Specifications Effectiveness Sheet, also distributed by the instructor.
3. Each team will show the instructor that it has completed its Team Objectives Sheet. Then, with all teams in the same room, the instructor will announce the start of the construction phase. The time allowed for construction will be closely monitored, and the instructor will occasionally call out the time elapsed (particularly if there is no clock in the room).
4. Each team will advise the instructor as soon as it has completed its tower. The team will write down the time elapsed that the instructor has determined. It may be asked to assist the instructor by counting the number of blocks used and measuring the height of the tower. This information is also written on the Team Objectives Sheet. Then the team calculates its profit.
5. After presenting the results, the class will discuss the team dynamics elements that contribute to team effectiveness. Team members will discuss their strategy, division of labor (team roles), expertise within the team, and other elements of team dynamics.

Source: Several published and online sources describe variations of this exercise, but there is no known origin to this activity.

SELF-ASSESSMENT 8.5

WHAT TEAM ROLES DO YOU PREFER?

PURPOSE This self assessment is designed to help you identify your preferred roles in meetings and similar team activities.

INSTRUCTIONS Read each of the statements on page 266 and circle the response that you believe best reflects your position regarding each statement. Then use the scoring key in Appendix B at the end of the book to calculate your results for each team role. This exercise should be completed alone so that you can assess yourself honestly without concerns of social comparison. Class discussion will focus on the roles that people assume in team settings. This scale assesses only a few team roles.

Team Roles Preferences Scale

Circle the number that best reflects your position regarding each of these statements.	Does not describe me at all ▼	Does not describe me very well ▼	Describes me somewhat ▼	Describes me well ▼	Describes me very well ▼
1. I usually take responsibility for getting the team to agree on what the meeting should accomplish.	1	2	3	4	5
2. I tend to summarize to other team members what the team has accomplished so far.	1	2	3	4	5
3. I'm usually the person who helps other team members overcome their disagreements.	1	2	3	4	5
4. I try to ensure that everyone gets heard on issues.	1	2	3	4	5
5. I'm usually the person who helps the team determine how to organize the discussion.	1	2	3	4	5
6. I praise other team members for their ideas more than do others in the meetings.	1	2	3	4	5
7. People tend to rely on me to keep track of what has been said in meetings.	1	2	3	4	5
8. The team typically counts on me to prevent debates from getting out of hand.	1	2	3	4	5
9. I tend to say things that make the group feel optimistic about its accomplishments.	1	2	3	4	5
10. Team members usually count on me to give everyone a chance to speak.	1	2	3	4	5
11. In most meetings, I am less likely than others to criticize the ideas of teammates.	1	2	3	4	5
12. I actively help teammates to resolve their differences in meetings.	1	2	3	4	5
13. I actively encourage quiet team members to describe their ideas about each issue.	1	2	3	4	5
14. People tend to rely on me to clarify the purpose of the meeting.	1	2	3	4	5
15. I like to be the person who takes notes or minutes of the meeting.	1	2	3	4	5

SELF-ASSESSMENT 8.6

ARE YOU A TEAM PLAYER?

How much do you like working in teams? Some of us avoid teams whenever possible; others tolerate teamwork; still others thrive in team environments. This exercise is designed to help you estimate the extent to which you are positively predisposed to work in teams. Read each statement in the scale and indicate the extent to which you agree or disagree with the statement. This exercise should be completed alone so that you can assess yourself honestly without concerns of social comparison. Class discussion will focus on the characteristics of individuals who are more or less compatible with working in teams.

SELF-ASSESSMENT 8.7

HOW TRUSTING ARE YOU?

Trust refers to positive expectations one person has toward another person in situations involving risk. While trust varies from one situation to the next, some people have a higher or lower propensity to trust. In other words, some people are highly trusting of others, even when first meeting them, whereas others have difficulty trusting anyone, even over a long time. This self-assessment provides an estimate of your propensity to trust. Indicate your preferred response to each statement, being honest with yourself for each item. This self-assessment should be completed alone, although class discussion will focus on the meaning of propensity to trust, why it varies from one person to the next, and how it affects teamwork.

Imagine IBM chief executive Samuel Palmisano speaking to a throng of 7,000 employees with Beijing's famous Forbidden City towering behind him. Does this scenario sound a bit too fantastic to be real? Well, Palmisano *was* in Beijing speaking face-to-face to about 2,000 staff members in an auditorium, but he also communicated part of his talk to another 5,000 IBMers globally through his avatar (graphic character representing a person) in front of a virtual version of the Forbidden City on the Second Life Web site.

Standing in front of Beijing's Forbidden City, IBM chief executive Sam Palmisano communicates through his Second Life avatar to several thousand employees worldwide.

Second Life, an online world where individuals can cruise around various islands, is becoming one of IBM's locations for sharing information. Along with participating in Palmisano's virtual town hall meeting, IBMers have held hundreds of virtual meetings at a large boardroom that IBM created on its Second Life islands. "It's just a very powerful way of meeting, interacting, and doing work with other people," says IBM executive consultant Doug McDavid. Labor unions have also discovered the communication value of Second Life. More than 1,000 people from 30 countries picketed IBM's islands in support of the company's Italian workers, who had their annual performance bonus forfeited.

Although Second Life accommodates voice and visual media, most communication around IBM's virtual islands—whether formal meetings or union protests—occurs through written text messages. Unlike instant-messaging text chats, however, each person's avatar adds a personal touch that improves the communication experience. "There's a sense that you're actually at the meeting," explains Chuck Hamilton, director of IBM's center for advanced learning. "If I stop moving my mouse, eventually my avatar will slump forward, and the other people in the room will say, 'Hey, Chuck, are you still there?' "[1]

9

Communicating in Teams and Organizations

Learning Objectives

After reading this chapter, you should be able to:

1. Explain why communication is important in organizations.
2. Diagram the communication process and identify four ways to improve this process.
3. Discuss problems with communicating through electronic mail.
4. Identify two ways in which nonverbal communication differs from verbal communication.
5. Appraise the appropriateness of a communication medium for a particular situation on the basis of social acceptance and media-richness factors.
6. Identify four common communication barriers.
7. Discuss the degree to which men and women communicate differently.
8. Outline the key strategies, including transactional analysis, for getting your message across and engaging in active listening.
9. Summarize three communication strategies in organizational hierarchies.
10. Debate the benefits and limitations of the organizational grapevine.

Information technologies have transformed how we communicate in organizations, yet we may still be at the beginning of this revolution. Wire cablegrams and telephones introduced a century ago are giving way to e-mail, instant messaging, Weblogs, podcasting, and virtual reality social networking. Each of these inventions creates fascinating changes in how people communicate with each other in the workplace, as well as new opportunities to improve organizational effectiveness and employee well-being.

communication
The process by which information is transmitted and understood between two or more people.

Communication refers to the process by which information is transmitted and *understood* between two or more people. We emphasize the word *understood* because transmitting the sender's intended meaning is the essence of good communication. This chapter begins by discussing the importance of effective communication and outlining a model of the communication process. Next, we identify types of communication channels, including computer-mediated communication, followed by factors to consider when choosing a communication medium. This chapter then identifies barriers to effective communication. This is followed by an overview of ways to communicate in organizational hierarchies and the pervasive organizational grapevine.

Learning Objectives

After reading the next two sections, you should be able to:

1. Explain why communication is important in organizations.
2. Diagram the communication process and identify four ways to improve this process.

The Importance of Communication

Effective communication is vital to all organizations, so much so that no company could exist without it. The reason? In Chapter 1 we defined organizations as groups of people who work interdependently toward some purpose. People can work interdependently only through communication. Communication is the vehicle through which people clarify their expectations and coordinate work, which allows them to achieve organizational objectives more efficiently and effectively. Chester Barnard, a telecommunications CEO and a respected pioneer in organizational behavior theory, stated this point back in 1938: "An organization is born when there are individuals who are able to communicate."[2]

Communication is also an important instrument for organizational learning and decision making. Chapter 1 explained that one perspective of organizational effectiveness is organizational learning, which is the firm's capacity to acquire, share, use, and store valuable knowledge. These processes depend on various forms of communication. Effective communication minimizes "silos of knowledge," the situation in which knowledge is cloistered or hoarded rather than distributed to others throughout the organization.[3] IBM improves organizational learning through various informal and computer-mediated communication media. For instance, when IBM employees need to find expertise for a client, they tap into the company's "Small Blue" search engine, which quickly identifies people with various forms of expertise throughout the company.[4]

Communication also aids employee well-being.[5] Information communicated from co-workers helps employees manage their work environment, telling them, for instance, how to complete work procedures correctly or handle difficult customers. Equally important, employee well-being benefits from the communication experience itself, so much so that people who experience social isolation are much more susceptible to colds, cardiovascular disease, and other physical and mental illnesses.[6]

Why? As we learned in Chapter 5, people have an inherent drive to bond, and communication is the means through which that drive is fulfilled. Communicating with others is an important means through which individuals validate their self-worth and maintain their social identity. This occurs even in the virtual world of Second Life. "In Second Life we gather and mingle before the meeting, and when it finishes, some people stop and talk again," explains Ian Hughes, an IBM employee who attends the virtual meetings as a pudgy avatar with spiky green hair. "We start to form social networks and the kinds of bonds you make in real life."[7]

A Model of Communication

The communication process model presented in Exhibit 9.1 provides a useful "conduit" metaphor for thinking about the communication process.[8] According to this model, communication flows through channels between the sender and the receiver. The sender forms a message and encodes it into words, gestures, voice intonations, and other symbols or signs. Next, the encoded message is transmitted to the intended receiver through one or more communication channels (media). The receiver senses the incoming message and decodes it into something meaningful. Ideally, the decoded meaning is what the sender had intended.

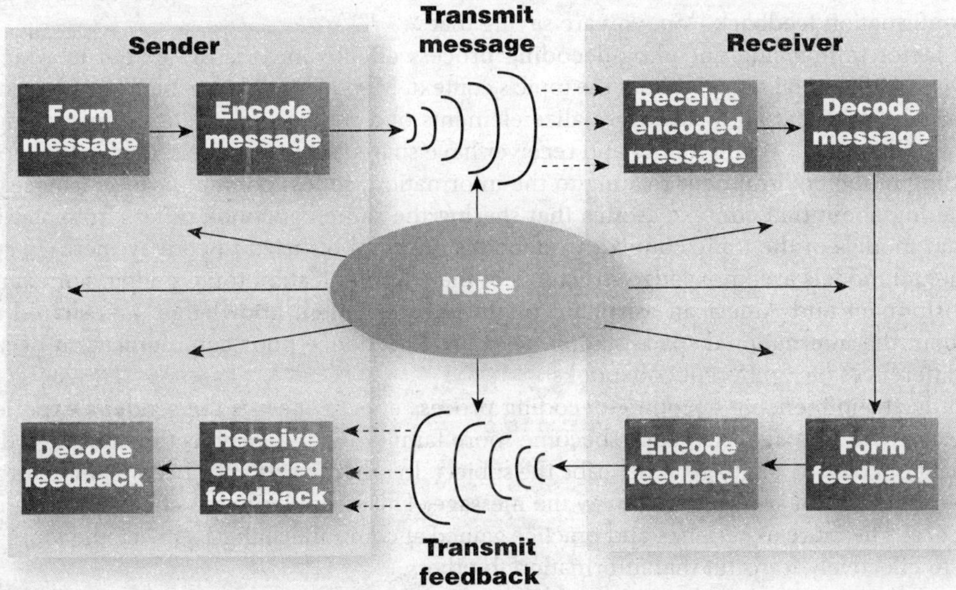

Exhibit 9.1 *The Communication Process Model*

In most situations, the sender looks for evidence that the other person received and understood the transmitted message. This feedback may be a formal acknowledgment, such as "Yes, I know what you mean," or indirect evidence from the receiver's subsequent actions. Notice that feedback repeats the communication process. Intended feedback is encoded, transmitted, received, and decoded from the receiver to the sender of the original message. This model recognizes that communication is not a free-flowing conduit. Rather, the transmission of meaning from one person to another is hampered by *noise*—the psychological, social, and structural barriers that distort and obscure the sender's intended message. If any part of the communication process is distorted or bro' :n, the sender and receiver will not have a common understanding of the message.

Influences on Effective Encoding and Decoding

The communication process model suggests that communication effectiveness depends on the ability of sender and receiver to efficiently and accurately encode and decode information. Experts have identified four factors that influence the effectiveness of the encoding-decoding process.[9] One factor is the sender's and receiver's ability and motivation to communicate through the communication channel. Some people communicate better through face-to-face conversation and prefer using this communication channel. Others are awkward in conversations, yet are quite good at communicating via BlackBerry or similar text message technologies. Generally, the encoding-decoding process is more effective when both parties are skilled at using the selected communication channel and enjoy using that channel.[10]

A second factor is the extent to which both parties have similar "codebooks"–dictionaries of symbols, language, gestures, idioms, and other tools used to convey information. With similar codebooks, the communication participants are able to encode and decode more accurately because they both have tools with the same or similar meanings. Communication efficiency also improves because there is less need for redundancy (such as saying the same thing in different ways) and less need for confirmation feedback ("So, you are saying that . . . ?").

A third factor influencing encoding-decoding process effectiveness is the extent to which both parties have shared mental models about the topic's context. Mental models are internal representations of the external world that allow us to visualize elements of a setting and relationships among those elements (see Chapter 3). When sender and receiver have shared mental models, they have a common understanding of the environment relating to the information, so less communication is necessary to clarify meaning about that context. Notice that sharing the same codebook differs from sharing the same mental models of the topic context. Codebooks are symbols used to convey message content, whereas mental models are knowledge structures of the communication topic setting. For example, a Russian cosmonaut and American astronaut might have excellent knowledge (i.e., shared mental models) about the international space station, yet they experience poor communication because of language differences (i.e., different codebooks).

A fourth factor influencing encoding-decoding process effectiveness is the sender's experience at communicating the message. As people become more familiar with the subject matter, they develop more efficient or colorful language to describe the subject. In other words, they become more proficient at using the codebook of symbols to convey the message. This is similar to the effect of job training or sports practice. The more experience and practice gained at communicating a subject, the more people learn how to effectively transmit that information to others.

Learning Objectives

After reading the next two sections, you should be able to:

3. Discuss problems with communicating through electronic mail.
4. Identify two ways in which nonverbal communication differs from verbal communication.
5. Appraise the appropriateness of a communication medium for a particular situation on the basis of social acceptance and media-richness factors.

COMMUNICATION CHANNELS

A critical part of the communication model is the channel or medium through which information is transmitted. There are two main types of channels: verbal and nonverbal. *Verbal communication* uses words and occurs through either spoken or written channels. *Nonverbal communication* is any part of communication that does not use words. Although spoken and written communication are both verbal (i.e., they both use words), you will learn in this section that they are quite different from each other and have different strengths and weaknesses in communication effectiveness. Also, written communication has traditionally been a much slower means than spoken communication for transmitting messages, but electronic mail, Weblogs, and other computer-mediated communication channels have significantly improved written communication efficiency.

Computer-Mediated Communication

Two decades ago, computer-mediated communication was a novel development. Today, it seems that many of us rely more on computer channels than on the old-fashioned options. By far, the most widely used of these is electronic mail (e-mail), which has revolutionized the way we communicate in organizational settings. E-mail has become the medium of choice in most workplaces because messages are quickly written, edited, and transmitted. Information can be appended and conveyed to many people with a simple click of a mouse. E-mail is asynchronous (messages are sent and received at different times), so there is no need to coordinate a communication session. E-mail software has also become an efficient filing cabinet.[11] Employees increasingly rely on e-mail to filter, store, sort, and search messages and attachments far more quickly than is possible with paper-based memos.

E-mail tends to be the preferred medium for coordinating work (e.g., confirming deadlines with a co-worker's schedule) and for sending well-defined information for decision making. It often increases the volume of communication and significantly alters the flow of information within groups and throughout the organization.[12] Specifically, it reduces some face-to-face and telephone communication but increases communication with people further up the hierarchy. Some social and organizational status differences still exist with e-mail,[13] but they are somewhat less apparent than is the case in face-to-face communication. By hiding age, race, and other features, e-mail reduces stereotype biases. However, it also tends to increase reliance on stereotypes when we are already aware of the other person's personal characteristics.[14]

Problems with E-mail E-mail is wonderful in many ways, but it does have limitations. In fact, as Connections 9.1 describes, some companies are trying to reduce employee dependence on e-mail. Here are the top four complaints about e-mail:

1. *Is a poor medium for communicating emotions.* People rely on facial expressions and other nonverbal cues to interpret the emotional meaning of words; e-mail lacks this parallel communication channel. Senders try to clarify the emotional tone of their messages by using expressive language ("Wonderful to hear from you!"), highlighting phrases in boldface or quotation marks, and inserting graphic faces (called *emoticons* or "smileys") representing the desired emotion. These actions help, but they do not replace the full complexity of real facial expressions, voice intonations, and hand movements.[15]
2. *Reduces politeness and respect.* E-mail messages are often less diplomatic than written letters because individuals can post e-mail messages before their emotions subside. Also, e-mail has low social presence (it's more impersonal), so people are more likely to write things that would never be spoken in face-to-face conversation. "It is much easier to have a row by email than it is face to face, and people are often ruder as a result," says Justin Beddows, a spokesperson at Welsh-based Admiral

Insurance. "Orders can be issued out and people can be quite abrupt because they feel protected by the distance the email provides."[16] These "flaming" e-mails are aggravated by misinterpretation of the emotional tone of the message. Fortunately, research has found that flaming decreases as teams move to later stages of development and when explicit norms and rules of communication are established.[17]

3. *Is a poor medium for ambiguous, complex, and novel situations.* E-mail is usually fine for well-defined situations, such as giving basic instructions or presenting a meeting agenda, but it can be cumbersome in ambiguous, complex, and novel situations. As we will describe later in this section, these circumstances require communication channels that transmit a larger volume of information with more rapid feedback. "I've stopped using email volleys where you just keep going back and forth and back and forth and nothing is going in the right direction," says a manager at an oil refinery. By talking face-to-face or by telephone in complex situations, the manager has discovered that he is "coming up with much better outcomes and a much better understanding of an issue."[18] In other words, when the issue gets messy, stop e-mailing and start talking, preferably face-to-face.
4. *Contributes to information overload.* E-mail contributes to information overload.[19] An estimated 22.3 trillion e-mails are now transmitted annually, up from just 1.1 trillion in 1998. According to one survey, professionals spend an average of two hours per day processing e-mail. The e-mail glut occurs because messages are created and copied to many people without much effort. The number of e-mail messages will probably decrease as people become more familiar with it, but to date e-mail volume continues to rise. To reduce e-mail overload and encourage more face-to-face interaction, some firms now have days when e-mail is banned (see Connections 9.1).

Social Networking Communication The opening vignette in this chapter described how IBM is experimenting with innovative forms of computer-mediated communication. In fact, while e-mail likely remains the most popular medium, IBMers have flocked to computer-mediated technologies that support *social networking*.[20] Social networking sites such as Facebook, MySpace, and LinkedIn are rapidly becoming part of popular culture. University students rate Facebook as the second most "in" thing (iPods are number one). These technologies allow people to form communities around friendships, common interests, expertise, and other themes, resulting in closer interaction in the communication experience. Indeed, many social networking technologies (from Facebook to online forums) gain value as more people participate in the technology.[21]

Yet just as corporate leaders stumbled their way through Web 1.0 (the Internet's first stage) over the past two decades, many are fighting rather than leveraging the potential of the more socially interactive second stage (called Web 2.0). A large number of companies have banned employee access to social networking sites after discovering that staff spend too much work time looking at these sites. Yet recognizing the popularity of social networking technology, a few organizational leaders are experimenting with ways to use it as a conduit for employees to communicate productively with each other, as well as with customers and other external stakeholders. Procter & Gamble employees use Facebook to keep in touch with summer intern students. Serena Software has made Facebook its new corporate intranet. The Redwood City, California, company introduced "Facebook Fridays" sessions in which teenagers are hired to teach older staff how to use Facebook. IBM developed Beehive, a corporate version of Facebook, where employees can post their profiles, photos, interests, and comments about work or other aspects of their lives.[22]

wikis
Collaborative Web spaces at which anyone in a group can write, edit, or remove material from the Web site.

IBM has also been at the forefront of another form of social networking communication, called **wikis.** Wikis are collaborative Web spaces in which anyone in a group can write, edit, or remove material from the site. Wikipedia,

9.1 **CONNECTIONS**

About-Face on Workplace E-mail

HiWired executives introduced "Home Week," a week in each month during which they must not travel. This initiative has helped them rediscover the benefits of face-to-face rather than e-mail communication.

A few years ago, Jay Ellison concluded that his employees were relying too much on e-mail and not enough on spoken communication. The vice president of operations at Chicago-based U.S. Cellular had a simple solution: Ban e-mail on Fridays. "Get out to meet your teams face to face," Ellison wrote to staff in the original announcement. "Pick up the phone and give someone a call." Ellison's Friday e-mail ban was unpopular at first, but most of Cellular's 8,000 staff members now appreciate its benefits. "While e-mail is quick and convenient it may not be the best way to communicate," Ellison suggests. "The e-mail ban has been very valuable for team-building and encouraging associates to improve their communication skills."

John Coyle, a Cellular executive, is one of the many converts. For some time, Coyle and a colleague from another department whom he had never met were e-mailing each other regarding financial reports. But when Coyle had to exchange information on an e-mail-free Friday, he picked up the phone instead. Both immediately realized from their similar phone numbers that they were located not only in the same city but in the same building. After exchanging more details, Coyle discovered that the colleague worked just a few yards away. "I literally got up, walked around the corner and there he was," says Coyle.

U.S. Cellular wasn't the first company to introduce e-mail–free days, but its success has enticed other companies. For example, Intel recently introduced "zero e-mail Fridays" for 300 engineers and other staff at its chip design operations in Austin, Texas, and Chandler, Arizona. "We're trying to address the problem that people get so addicted to e-mail that they will send an e-mail across an aisle, across a partition, and that's not a good thing," explains Brad Beavers, Intel's Austin site manager. Admiral Insurance introduced a similar initiative to wean staff from e-mail dependence. "We hold 'no email days' to encourage people to get off their backsides and visit people face to face," says Justin Beddows, a spokesperson at the Welsh insurance company.

HiWired took a different approach to increasing face-to-face communication. Executives at the Needham, Massachusetts, technology support start-up company realized that e-mail was popular because managers were traveling throughout the month. HiWired now has one "Home Week" each month, during which managers are expected to be around the office rather than on the road. Home Week includes meetings for the management team as well as social events for all 60 employees. "We embrace chat and e-mail and collaboration tools," says HiWired copresident Singu Srinivas. "Those are additives to face-to-face relationship building, but they can't be a replacement for it."[23]

the popular online encyclopedia, is a massive public example of a wiki. Wikis hold considerable promise for communicating in organizational settings because they are democratic, collaborative social networking spaces that rapidly document new knowledge. IBM introduced wiki technology a few years ago in the form of WikiCentral, which now hosts more than 20,000 wiki projects involving

100,000 employees. One of IBM's many wiki projects involved gathering from staff ideas and issues about a new patent policy within IBM. "Wikis are good for project management, for to do's, status reports, creating an issues log–you're always up to date," explains Brad Kasell, an IBM manager for emerging technologies. "There's no collating reports from everyone at the end of the week for an update." The accuracy of wikis depends on the quality of participants, but Kasell says that errors are quickly identified by IBM's online community.[24]

Nonverbal Communication

Nonverbal communication includes facial gestures, voice intonation, physical distance, and even silence. This communication channel is necessary when noise or physical distance prevents effective verbal

BlueShirt Nation Communication How can employees communicate with each other and feel connected when their company employs 150,000 people in the United States, Canada, United Kingdom, and China? For Best Buy, part of the answer is a social networking Web site called blueshirtnation.com. The site, which now boasts 22,000 members, gives staff the opportunity to create their own Facebook-like Web pages and to host forums on topics that interest them. These features have dramatically improved the rapid exchange of ideas. "Now, [employees] have the means to connect with people they've never met before," says Steve Bendt, shown in the photo with Gary Koelling, both of whom are senior managers of social technology and founders of blueshirtnation.com. The social networking site also serves as an important conduit of employee opinions to management. For example, Best Buy management canceled proposed changes to its employee discount rates after feedback from blueshirtnation.com forums revealed the depth of employee opposition to the proposal. Bendt acknowledges that this open forum for discussion requires courage from management. "It says a lot about Best Buy culture that people here are willing to take risks," says Bendt.[25]

exchanges and the need for immediate feedback precludes written communication. But even in quiet face-to-face meetings, most information is communicated nonverbally. Rather like a parallel conversation, nonverbal cues signal subtle information to both parties, such as reinforcing their interest in the verbal conversation or demonstrating their relative status in the relationship.[26]

Nonverbal communication differs from verbal (i.e., written and spoken) communication in a couple of ways. First, it is less rule-bound than verbal communication. We receive plenty of formal training on how to understand spoken words but very little on understanding the nonverbal signals that accompany those words. Consequently, nonverbal cues are generally more ambiguous and susceptible to misinterpretation. At the same time, many facial expressions (such as smiling) are hardwired and universal, thereby providing the only reliable means of communicating across cultures.

The other difference between verbal and nonverbal communication is that the former is typically conscious, whereas most nonverbal communication is automatic and nonconscious. We normally plan the words we say or write, but we rarely plan every blink, smile, or other gesture during a conversation. Indeed, as we just mentioned, many facial expressions communicate the same meaning across cultures because they are hardwired nonconscious responses to human emotions.[27] For example, pleasant emotions cause the brain center to widen the mouth, whereas negative emotions produce constricted facial expressions (squinting eyes, pursed lips, etc.).

emotional contagion
The nonconscious process of "catching" or sharing another person's emotions by mimicking that person's facial expressions and other nonverbal behavior.

Emotional Contagion One of the most fascinating effects of emotions on nonverbal communication is the phenomenon called **emotional contagion,** which is the automatic process of "catching" or sharing another person's emotions by mimicking that person's facial expressions and other nonverbal behavior. Consider what happens when you see a co-worker accidentally bang his or her head against a filing cabinet. Chances are, you wince and put your hand on your own head as if you had hit the cabinet. Similarly, while listening to someone describe a positive event, you tend to smile and exhibit other emotional displays of happiness. While some of our nonverbal communication is planned, emotional contagion represents nonconscious behavior–we automatically mimic and synchronize our nonverbal behaviors with other people.[28]

Emotional contagion serves three purposes. First, mimicry provides continuous feedback, communicating that we understand and empathize with the sender. To consider the significance of this, imagine employees remaining expressionless after watching a co-worker bang his or her head! The lack of parallel behavior conveys a lack of understanding or caring. Second, mimicking the nonverbal behaviors of other people seems to be a way of receiving emotional meaning from those people. If a co-worker is angry with a client, your tendency to frown and show anger while listening helps you share that emotion more fully. In other words, we receive meaning by expressing the sender's emotions as well as by listening to the sender's words.

The third function of emotional contagion is to fulfill the drive to bond that was described in Chapter 5. Social solidarity is built out of each member's awareness of a collective sentiment. Through nonverbal expressions of emotional contagion, people see others share the same emotions that they feel. This strengthens relations among team members, as well as between leaders and followers, by providing evidence of their similarity.[29]

Choosing the Best Communication Channel

Which communication channel is most appropriate in a particular situation? Two important elements to consider are social acceptance and media richness.

Social Acceptance

Social acceptance refers to how well the communication medium is approved and supported by the organization, teams, and individuals.[30] One factor in social acceptance is the organization's and team's norms regarding the use of specific communication channels. Norms partly explain why telephone conversations are more common among staff in some firms, whereas e-mail or instant messaging is the medium of choice in other organizations. Some companies expect employees to meet face-to-face, whereas meetings and similar conversations are rare events elsewhere. Norms also shape the use of communication media for people in specific positions. For instance, frontline employees are more likely to write an e-mail and less likely to telephone or personally visit the company's CEO.

A second social acceptance factor is individual preferences for specific communication channels.[31] You may have discovered that a co-worker prefers e-mail rather than voice mail or wants to meet in person more than you think is necessary. These preferences are due to personality traits as well as previous experience and reinforcement with particular channels. A third social acceptance factor to consider is the symbolic meaning of a channel. Some communication channels are viewed as impersonal, whereas others are more personal; some are considered professional, whereas others are casual; some are "cool," whereas others are not. To illustrate the importance of a channel's symbolic meaning, consider stories about corporate leaders who use e-mails or cell phone text messages to tell employees that they are fired or laid off. Such actions make front-page headlines because e-mail and text messages are considered inappropriate (too impersonal) for transmission of that particular information.[32]

Media Richness

media richness
A medium's data-carrying capacity, that is, the volume and variety of information that can be transmitted during a specific time.

Along with social acceptance, people select communication media on the basis of their **media richness.** Media richness is the medium's data-carrying capacity–the volume and variety of information that can be transmitted during a specific time.[33] Exhibit 9.2 illustrates various communication channels arranged in a hierarchy of richness, with face-to-face interaction at the top and lean data-only reports at the bottom. A communication channel has high richness when it is able to convey multiple cues (such as both verbal and nonverbal information), allows timely feedback from receiver to sender, allows the sender to customize the message to the receiver, and makes use of complex symbols (such as words and phrases with multiple meanings). Face-to-face communication is at the top of media richness because it allows us to communicate both verbally and nonverbally at the same time, to receive feedback almost immediately from the receiver, to quickly adjust our message and style, and to use complex language such as metaphors and idioms (e.g., "spilling the beans").

According to media-richness theory, rich media are better than lean media when the communication situation is nonroutine and ambiguous. In nonroutine situations (such as an unexpected and unusual emergency), the sender and receiver have little common experience, so they need to transmit a large volume of information with immediate feedback. Lean media work well in routine situations because the sender and receiver have common expectations through shared mental models. Ambiguous situations also require rich media because the parties must share large amounts of information with immediate feedback to resolve multiple and conflicting interpretations of their observations and experiences.[34] Choosing the wrong medium reduces communication effectiveness. When the situation is routine or clear, using a rich medium–such as holding a special meeting–would seem like a waste of time. On the other hand, if a unique and ambiguous issue is handled through e-mail or another lean medium, issues take longer to resolve and misunderstandings are more likely to occur.

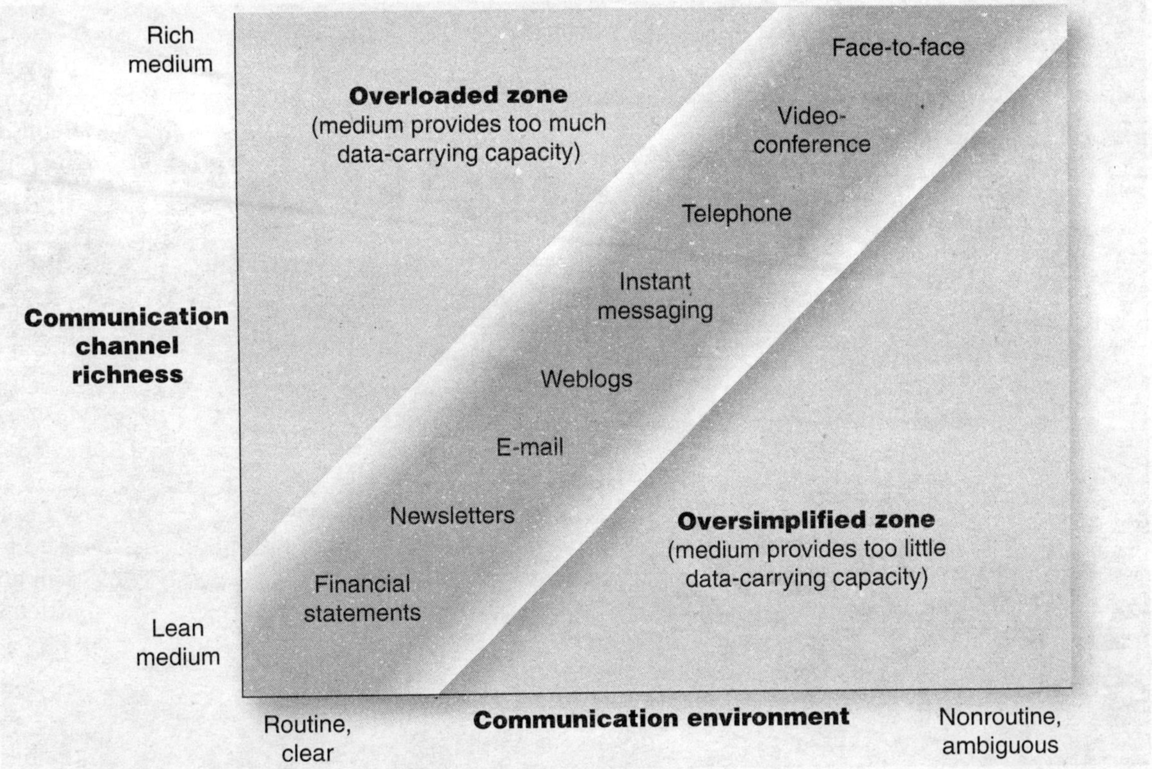

Sources: Based on R. Lengel and R. Daft, "The Selection of Communication Media as an Executive Skill," *Academy of Management Executive* 2, no. 3 (August 1988), p. 226; R. L. Daft and R. H. Lengel, "Information Richness: A New Approach to Managerial Behavior and Organization Design," *Research in Organizational Behavior,* 1984, p. 199.

Exhibit 9.2 *Media-Richness Hierarchy*

Evaluating Media-Richness Theory Research generally supports the relevance of media richness for traditional channels (face-to-face, written memos, etc.). However, the evidence is mixed when computer-mediated communication channels are studied. Three factors seem to override or blur the medium's richness:

1. *The ability to multicommunicate.* It is usually difficult (as well as rude) to communicate face-to-face with someone while simultaneously transmitting messages to someone else by using another medium. Most computer-mediated technologies, on the other hand, require less sensory demand, so employees can easily engage in two or more communication events at the same time. In other words, they can multicommunicate.[35] For example, people routinely scan Web pages while carrying on telephone conversations. Some write text messages to a client while simultaneously listening to a discussion at a large meeting. Although people do not multitask as efficiently as is often believed, some employees have become good enough at multicommunicating that they likely exchange as much information through two or more lean-media-richness channels as through one high-media-richness channel during the same time period.
2. *More varied proficiency levels.* Earlier in this chapter we explained that communication effectiveness is partially determined by the sender's competency with the communication channel. People with higher proficiency can "push" more information through the channel, thereby increasing the channel's

I Love Rewards Gets Media Rich Quick Every day at 11:15 a.m., I Love Rewards Inc. employees meet face-to-face for 10 minutes to communicate priorities and coordinate their efforts. Although each meeting at the Toronto-based incentive marketing company is brief and highly structured, verbal communication allows the team to receive immediate feedback on daily issues such as "Today's Must-Do" and "Red Flags." For two minutes of each 10-minute meeting, each employee shares a "Headline" summary of something important to her or him, ranging from the results of a client meeting to ultrasound photos of a pregnant employee's baby. Each week a new meeting facilitator is announced, giving employees the chance to enhance their communication and facilitation skills. I Love Rewards CEO Razor Suleman says these quick meetings provide a personal connection and highly interactive feedback. Suleman also values other opportunities for media-rich communication, such as coaching employees on work-related issues and hosting a book club in which staff get a chance to chat about new books.[36]

information flow. Experienced BlackBerry users, for instance, can whip through messages in a flash, whereas new users struggle to type notes and organize incoming messages. In contrast, there is less variation in the ability to communicate through casual conversation and other natural channels because most of us develop good levels of proficiency throughout life and possibly through hardwired evolutionary development.[37]

3. *Social distractions of rich channels.* Channels with high media richness tend to involve more direct social interaction. However, social presence sensitizes both parties to their relative status and self-presentation, and this diverts their attention from the message.[38] In other words, the benefits of media-richness channels such as face-to-face communication may be offset by social distractions from the message content, whereas lean media have much less social presence.

Symbolic Meaning of the Medium

"The medium is the message."[39] This famous phrase by communications guru Marshall McLuhan means that the channel of communication has social consequences as much as (or perhaps more than) the content that passes through that medium. McLuhan was referring mainly to the influence of television and other "new media" on society; but this concept applies equally well to how the symbolic meaning of a communication medium influences our interpretation of the message and the relationship between sender and receiver.

The medium-as-message principle was apparent when KPMG gave layoff notices to hundreds of its British employees via e-mail. The public swiftly criticized the consulting firm–not because of the content of the message but because of the medium through which it was transmitted. Ironically, KPMG delivered the bad news by e-mail because most employees had specifically asked for this method. Yet even the KPMG executives who sent the layoff notices were hesitant. "I was horrified about telling staff via e-mail as I knew it would make us look callous," admitted one executive.[40] The point here is that we need to be sensitive to the symbolic meaning of the communication medium to ensure that it amplifies rather than misinterprets the meaning found in the message content.

Communication Channels and Persuasion

persuasion
The use of facts, logical arguments, and emotional appeals to change another person's beliefs and attitudes, usually for the purpose of changing the person's behavior.

Media richness and social acceptance lay the foundation for understanding which communication channels are more effective for **persuasion,** that is, changing another person's beliefs and attitudes. Recent studies support the long-held view that spoken communication, particularly face-to-face interaction, is more persuasive than e-mails, Web sites, and other forms of written communication. There are three main reasons for this persuasive effect.[41] First, spoken communication is typically accompanied by nonverbal communication. People are often persuaded more when they receive both emotional and logical messages, and the combination of spoken and nonverbal communication provides this dual punch. A lengthy pause, raised voice tone, and (in face-to-face interaction) animated hand gestures can amplify the emotional tone of the message, thereby signaling the vitality of the issue.

Second, spoken communication offers the sender high-quality immediate feedback on whether the receiver understands and accepts the message (i.e., is being persuaded). This feedback allows the sender to adjust the content and emotional tone of the message more quickly than is possible with written communication. Third, people are persuaded more under conditions of high social presence than under those of low social presence. In face-to-face conversations (high social presence), people are more sensitive to how they are perceived by others in that social setting, so they pay attention to the sender's message and are more willing to actively consider that viewpoint. This is particularly true when the sender is a member of the receiver's social identity group. In contrast, when people receive persuasion attempts through a Web site, e-mail, or other source of written communication, they experience a higher degree of anonymity and psychological distance from the persuader. These conditions reduce the motivation to think about and accept the persuasive message.

Although spoken communication tends to be more persuasive, written communication can also persuade others to some extent. Written messages have the advantage of presenting more technical detail than can occur through conversation. This factual information is valuable when the issue is important to the receiver. Also, people experience a moderate degree of social presence in written communication when they are exchanging messages with close associates, so messages from friends and co-workers can be persuasive.

Learning Objectives

After reading the next two sections, you should be able to:

6. Identify four common communication barriers.
7. Discuss the degree to which men and women communicate differently.

COMMUNICATION BARRIERS (NOISE)

In spite of the best intentions of sender and receiver to communicate, several barriers (called "noise" in Exhibit 9.1) inhibit the effective exchange of information. As author George Bernard Shaw wrote, "The greatest problem with communication is the illusion that it has been accomplished." One barrier is the imperfect perceptual process of both sender and receiver. As receivers, we don't listen as well as senders assume we do, and our needs and expectations influence what signals get noticed and ignored. We aren't any better as senders, either. Some studies suggest that we have difficulty stepping out of our own perspectives and stepping into the perspectives of others, so we overestimate how well other people understand the message we are communicating.[42]

"That's my commendation for deciphering all the sales talk when we needed to upgrade the computer."

Even if the perceptual process is well tuned, messages sometimes get filtered on their way up or down the corporate hierarchy. Filtering may involve deleting or delaying negative information or using less harsh words so that the message sounds more favorable.[43] Filtering is most common in organizations that reward employees who communicate mainly positive information and among employees who have strong career mobility aspirations. Language differences represent a third source of communication noise. But even if two people speak the same language, they might have different meanings for particular words and phrases. For example, a French executive might call an event a "catastrophe" as a casual exaggeration, whereas someone in Germany usually interprets this word literally as an earth-shaking event.[44]

Jargon, which includes specialized words and phrases for specific occupations or groups, is designed to improve communication efficiency. However, it has the opposite effect when senders transmit jargon to people who do not possess the jargon codebook. Furthermore, people who use jargon to excess put themselves in an unflattering light. For example, soon after Robert Nardelli became Chrysler's new CEO, he proudly announced: "I'm blessed to have individuals with me who can take areas of responsibility and do vertical dives to really get the granularity and make sure that we're coupling horizontally across those functions so that we have a pure line of sight toward the customer." Business journalists weren't impressed, even if they did figure out what Nardelli meant.[45]

No matter how well we know a language, words and phrases have enough ambiguity to create confusion. Consider the question "Can you close the door?" You might assume the sender is asking whether shutting the door is permitted. But the question might be asking whether you are physically able to shut the door or whether the door is designed such that it can be shut. In fact, this question might not be a question at all; the person could be politely *telling* you to shut the door.[46]

The ambiguity of language isn't always dysfunctional noise.[47] Corporate leaders sometimes rely on metaphors and other vague language to describe ill-defined or complex ideas. Ambiguity is also used to avoid conveying or creating undesirable emotions. For example, one study reported that people rely on more ambiguous language when communicating with people who have different values and beliefs. In these situations, ambiguity minimizes the risk of conflict.

Information Overload

information overload
A condition in which the volume of information received exceeds the person's capacity to process it.

Start with a daily avalanche of e-mail, and then add in voice mail, cell phone text messages, PDF file downloads, Web pages, hard-copy documents, instant messages, blogs, wikis, and other sources of incoming information. Together, you have created a perfect recipe for **information overload.**[48] As Exhibit 9.3 illustrates, information overload occurs whenever the job's information load exceeds the individual's capacity to get through it. Employees have a certain *information processing capacity*–the amount of information that they are able to process in a fixed unit of time. At the same time, jobs have a varying *information load*–the amount of information to be processed per unit of time. Information overload creates noise in the communication system because information gets overlooked or misinterpreted when people can't process it fast enough. The result is poorer-quality decisions as well as higher stress.[49]

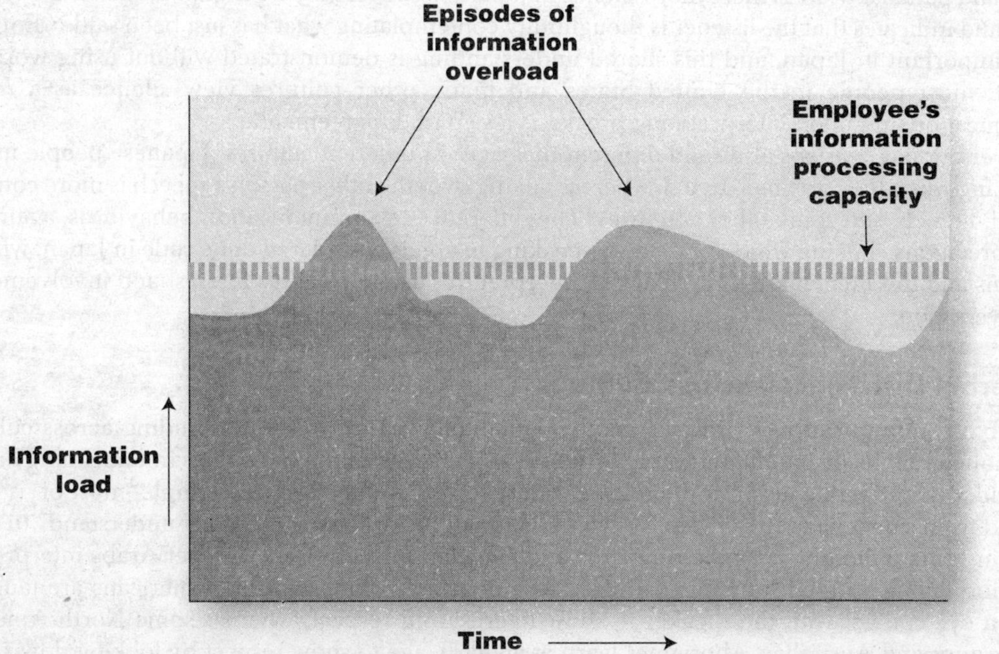

Exhibit 9.3 *Dynamics of Information Overload*

Information overload problems can be minimized by increasing our information processing capacity, reducing the job's information load, or doing a combination of both. Studies suggest that employees often increase their information processing capacity by temporarily reading faster, scanning through documents more efficiently, and removing distractions that slow information processing speed. Time management also increases information processing capacity. When information overload is temporary, information processing capacity can increase by working longer hours. Information load can be reduced by buffering, omitting, and summarizing. *Buffering* involves having incoming communication filtered, usually by an assistant. *Omitting* occurs when we decide to overlook messages, such as using software rules to redirect e-mails from distribution lists to folders that we never look at. An example of *summarizing* is reading executive summaries rather than the full reports.

CROSS-CULTURAL AND CROSS-GENDER COMMUNICATION

As globalization and cultural diversity increase, you can be sure that cross-cultural communication problems will also increase.[50] Language is the most obvious cross-cultural communication challenge. Words are easily misunderstood in verbal communication, either because the receiver has a limited vocabulary or the sender's accent distorts the usual sound of some words. Voice intonation is another cross-cultural communication barrier. How loudly, deeply, and quickly people speak varies across cultures, and these voice intonations send secondary messages that have different meanings in different cultures.

Communication includes silence, but the use and meaning of silence varies from one culture to another.[51] One study estimated that silence and pauses represented 30 percent of conversation time between Japanese doctors and patients, compared with only 8 percent of the time between American doctors and patients. Why is there more silence in Japanese conversations? In Japan, silence symbolizes respect and indicates that the listener is thoughtfully contemplating what has just been said.[52] Empathy is very important in Japan, and this shared understanding is demonstrated without using words. In contrast, most people in the United States and many other cultures view silence as a *lack* of communication and often interpret long breaks as a sign of disagreement.

Conversational overlaps also send different messages in different cultures. Japanese people usually stop talking when they are interrupted, whereas talking over the other person's speech is more common in Brazil, France, and some other countries. The difference in communication behavior is, again, due to interpretations. Talking while someone is speaking to you is considered quite rude in Japan, whereas Brazilians and the French are more likely to interpret this as the person's interest and involvement in the conversation.

Nonverbal Differences across Cultures

Nonverbal communication represents another potential area for misunderstanding across cultures. Many nonconscious or involuntary nonverbal cues (such as smiling) have the same meaning around the world, but deliberate gestures often have different interpretations. For example, most of us shake our head from side to side to say "No," but a variation of head shaking means "I understand" to many people in India. Filipinos raise their eyebrows to give an affirmative answer, yet Arabs interpret this expression (along with clicking one's tongue) as a negative response. Most Americans are taught to maintain eye contact with the speaker to show interest and respect, whereas some North American native groups and Australian Aborigines learn at an early age to show respect by looking down when an older or more senior person is talking to them.[53]

Silence and Conversational Overlaps Communication includes silence, but its use and meaning varies from one culture to another.[54] A recent study estimated that silence and pauses represented 30 percent of conversation time between Japanese doctors and patients, compared to only 8 percent of the time between American doctors and patients. Why is there more silence in Japanese conversations?

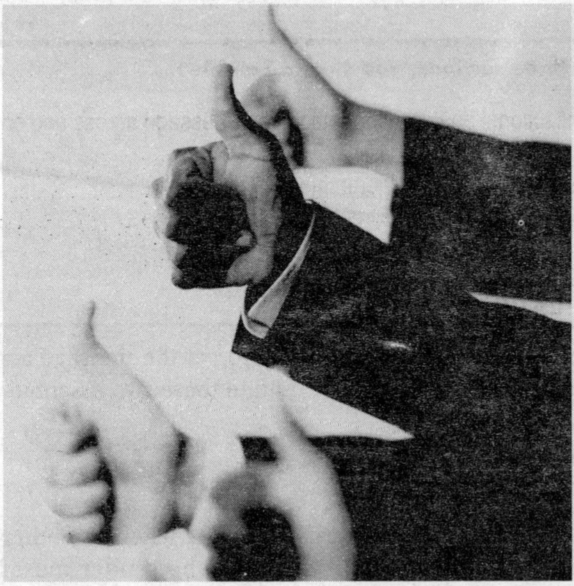

Thumbs-Up for Cross-Cultural (Mis) Communication Patricia Oliveira made several cultural adjustments when she moved from Brazil to Australia. One of the more humorous incidents occurred in the Melbourne office where she works. A co-worker would stick his thumbs up when asked about something, signaling that everything was OK. But the gesture had a totally different meaning to Oliveira and other people from Brazil. "He asked me why I was laughing and I had to explain that in Brazil, that sign means something not very nice," recalls Oliveira. "After that, everyone started doing it to the boss. It was really funny."[55]

In Japan silence symbolizes respect and indicates that the listener is thoughtfully contemplating what has just been said.[56] Empathy is also important in Japan, and this shared understanding is demonstrated without using words. In contrast, most people in the United States and many other cultures view silence as a *lack* of communication and often interpret long breaks as a sign of disagreement.

Conversational overlaps also send different messages in different cultures. Japanese people usually stop talking when they are interrupted, whereas talking over the other person's speech is more common in Brazil and some other countries. The difference in communication behavior is again due to interpretations. Talking while someone is speaking to you is considered quite rude in Japan, whereas Brazilians are more likely to interpret this as a person's interest and involvement in the conversation.

Gender Differences in Communication

Men and women have similar communication practices, but there are subtle distinctions that can occasionally lead to misunderstanding and conflict.[57] One distinction is that men are more likely than women to view conversations as negotiations of relative status and power. They assert their power by directly giving advice to others (e.g., "You should do the following") and using combative language. There is also evidence that men dominate the talk time in conversations with women, as well as interrupt more and adjust their speaking style less than do women.

Men engage in more "report talk," in which the primary function of the conversation is impersonal and efficient information exchange. Women also do report talk, particularly when conversing with men, but conversations among women have a higher incidence of relationship building through "rapport talk." Women make more use of indirect requests ("Do you think you should . . ."), apologize more often, and seek advice from others more quickly than do men. Finally, research fairly consistently indicates that women are more sensitive than men to nonverbal cues in face-to-face meetings.[58] Together, these conditions can create communication conflicts. Women who describe problems get frustrated that men offer advice rather than rapport, whereas men become frustrated because they can't understand why women don't appreciate their advice.

Learning Objectives

After reading the next three sections, you should be able to:

8. Outline the key strategies for, including transactional analysis, for getting your message across and engaging in active listening.
9. Summarize three communication strategies in organizational hierarchies.
10. Debate the benefits and limitations of the organizational grapevine.

IMPROVING INTERPERSONAL COMMUNICATION

Effective interpersonal communication depends on the sender's ability to get the message across and the receiver's performance as an active listener. In this section, we outline these two essential features of effective interpersonal communication.

Getting Your Message Across

This chapter began with the statement that effective communication occurs when the other person receives and understands the message. To accomplish this difficult task, the sender must learn to empathize with the receiver, repeat the message, choose an appropriate time for the conversation, and be descriptive rather than evaluative:

- *Empathize.* Recall from earlier chapters that empathy is a person's ability to understand and be sensitive to the feelings, thoughts, and situations of others. In conversations, this involves putting yourself in the receiver's shoes when encoding the message. For instance, be sensitive to words that may be ambiguous or trigger the wrong emotional response.
- *Repeat the message.* Rephrase the key points a couple of times. The saying "Tell them what you're going to tell them; tell them; then tell them what you've told them" reflects this need for redundancy.
- *Use timing effectively.* Your message competes with other messages and noise, so find a time when the receiver is less likely to be distracted by these other matters.
- *Be descriptive.* Focus on the problem, not the person, if you have negative information to convey. People stop listening when the information attacks their self-esteem. Also, suggest things the listener can do to improve, rather than point to him or her as a problem.

Active Listening

"Nature gave people two ears but only one tongue, which is a gentle hint that they should listen more than they talk."[59] To follow this advice, we need to recognize that listening is a process of actively sensing the sender's signals, evaluating them accurately, and responding appropriately. These three components of listening–sensing, evaluating, and responding–reflect the listener's side of the communication model described at the beginning of this chapter. Listeners receive the sender's signals, decode them as intended, and provide appropriate and timely feedback to the sender (see Exhibit 9.4). Active listeners constantly cycle through sensing, evaluating, and responding during the conversation and engage in various activities to improve these processes.[60]

Sensing Sensing is the process of receiving signals from the sender and paying attention to them. Active listeners improve sensing in three ways. First, they postpone evaluation by not forming an opinion until the speaker has finished. Second, they avoid interrupting the speaker's conversation.

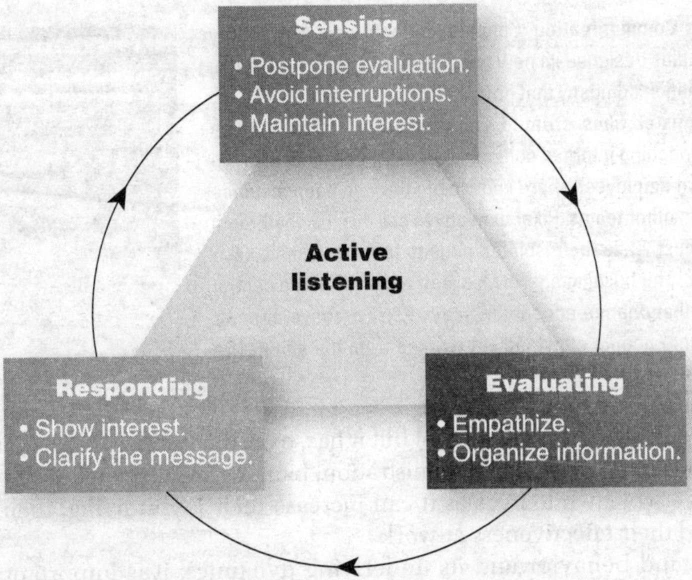

Exhibit 9.4 *Active Listening Process and Strategies*

Third, they remain motivated to listen to the speaker.

Evaluating The evaluating component of listening includes understanding the message's meaning, evaluating the message, and remembering the message. To improve their evaluation of the conversation, active listeners empathize with the speaker–they try to understand and be sensitive to the speaker's feelings, thoughts, and situation. Evaluation also improves by organizing the speaker's ideas during the communication episode.

Responding Responding, the third component of listening, is giving feedback to the sender, thereby motivating and directing the speaker's communication. Active listeners accomplish this by maintaining sufficient eye contact and sending back channel signals (e.g., "I see"), both of which show interest. They also respond by clarifying the message–rephrasing the speaker's ideas at appropriate breaks ("So you're saying that . . . ?").

IMPROVING INTERPERSONAL COMMUNICATION THROUGH TRANSACTIONAL ANALYSIS

Transactional Analysis (TA) as a method of analyzing and understanding behavior was developed by Eric Berne. Behavior Scientists view it as an outgrowth of earlier Freudian Psychology. Sigmund Freud was the first to suggest that there are three sources within the individual's personality that stimulate, monitor and control behaviors. The Freudian *id*, *ego* and *superego* are important concepts but their definitions are difficult for practitioners to comprehend or apply without extensive training in psychotherapy. Therefore, a significant contribution of TA theorists is that they have, in a sense, borrowed from Freud but have put some of his concepts into language that everyone can understand and, without being trained psychiatrists, can use for diagnostic purposes in understanding why people behave the way they do.

People in managerial positions and influencing roles affect not only organizational work but also relations with clients, employees and others. Through their interactions, they may help others become self-sufficient and capable of solving problems or may make them dependent and devoid of autonomy. TA can provide a useful tool for improving one's interpersonal skills and effectiveness on the job. TA

Pixar Building Animates Communication Communication was a top priority when Pixar Animation Studios designed its new campus in Emeryville, California, a few years ago. The animation company that brought us *The Incredibles, Finding Nemo,* and other blockbuster films created work areas that cluster team members and encourage ongoing informal communication. At the same time the campus is designed so that employees share knowledge through happenstance interactions with people on other teams. Pixar executives call this the "bathroom effect": Team members must leave their isolated pods to fetch their mail, have lunch, or visit the restroom. The building also invites staff to mingle in the central airy atrium. "It promotes that chance encounter," says Pixar creative director John Lasseter. "You run into people constantly. It worked from the minute we arrived. We just blossomed here."[61]

was originally used as a psychotherapeutic tool but it has, over the years, spread to all parts of the world and to many professions like education, administration, banking, service organizations and social work etc. It helps people live worthwhile lives as it can increase their joy in living, their harmony with the family and friends, and their effectiveness at work.

In order to understand behavior and its underlying dynamics, it is important to study the basic components of behavior or its structure.

Ego States

An ego state is a consistent and coherent pattern of thinking, feeling and behaving. The personality of a person is the collection of behavior patterns developed over time that other people begin to recognize as that person. These behavior pattens are evoked in differing degrees from the three ego states Parent, Adult and Child, where the capitalized PA and C refer to the three ego states and are usually diagrammed as shown in Exhibit 9.5.

The **Parent** ego state is borrowed from parents or those who took their place or from parental or authoritarian figures in our early life. It is a huge collection of recordings in the brain of unquestioned or imposed external events perceived by a person in his/her early years. The "tapes" are in place, stored and ready to go. Thus a person is operating from the parent Ego State when the "old tapes" from his/her childhood are mentally played back.

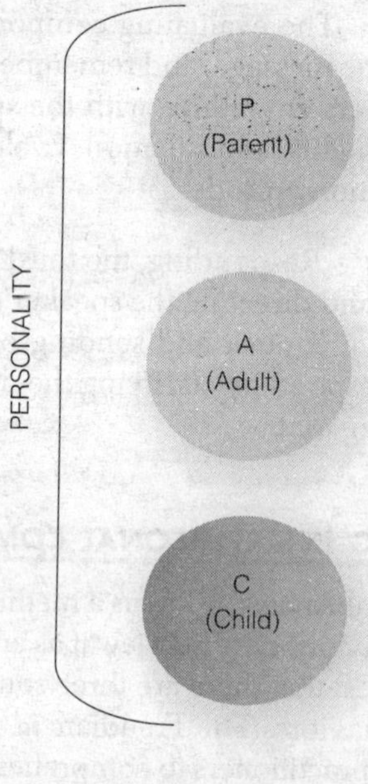

Exhibit 9.5 *The Ego States : Structural Analysis*

There are two kinds of parent ego states: (a) Nurturing Parent and (b) Critical Parent. The Nurturing Parent is that part of a person that understands, and is caring, sympathetic and protective about people. The Critical Parent is evaluative, judgmental, accusing, criticizing and controling.

The **Adult** ego state evokes a behavior that could be described simply as logical, reasonable, rational and unemotional. It functions as a human computer because it collects facts/data, processes them, makes predictions about the future and calculates probabilities. Reality testing is an important function of this ego state and it evaluates not only the current situations in an impassive manner but also the past experiences before arriving at a decision.

The **Child** ego state contains the natural impulses and attitudes learnt from the childhood experiences. Child ego state is not a synonym for childish or immature. This ego state develops further into four discernible parts. The Natural Child is that part of the child ego state that is impulsive, untrained, expressive, playful and curious. The Little Professor is intuitive, creative or imaginative and manipulative, responding to nonverbal messages and playing hunches. The Adapted Child is that part of the child ego state that is complying, withdrawing, procrastinating, fearful, obedient, guilty or ashamed. Another Child ego state, Rebellious Child rebels when there is something to rebel against, as when parents became unrealistic in their demands.

In India, the authors have come across a pattern in the ego states in employees from government and public sector organizations. As these organizations follow a system of annual confidential report, the majority of employees at the middle level of management behave from their adapted child ego state in order to be in the good books of their superiors. Therefore, the adapted child has been found to be the dominant ego state. Also, the nurturing parent has been found to be high among them. In a large number of cases, both the adapted child and the nurturing parent have almost equal scores. This is the due to the cultural factors that they act in paternalistic way with their subordinates and in adaptive way with their bosses. However, private-sector employees have mostly been found to behave from their adult ego state.

Interpersonal Transactions

Transactions are exchanges between two or more persons that consist of at least one stimulus and one response. All transactions can be classified as :

(a) Complementary transactions
(b) Crossed transactions
(c) Ulterior transactions

A ***complementary transaction*** occurs when a message sent from a specific ego state gets the predicted response from a specific ego state in the other person. Berne describes a complementary transaction as one which is "appropriate and expected and follows the natural order of healthy human relationships". A complementary transactions can occur between any two ego states.

Stimulus: "For how tong have your been a Regional Manager in Eastern India"
Response: "For the past two years"
Another Example :
Stimulus: '"Why do you come late every other day ?"
Response: "I am sorry Sir"

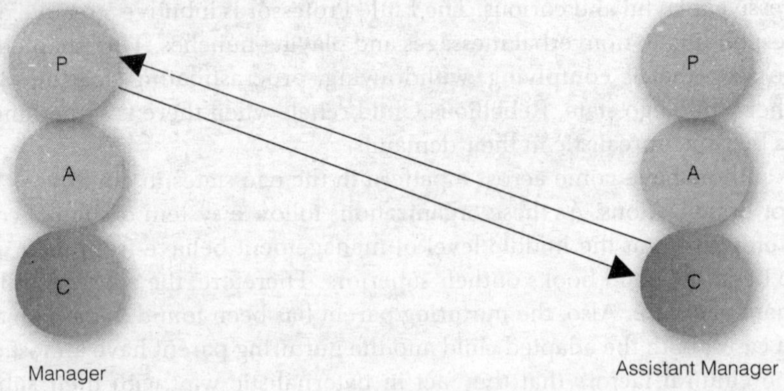

A crossed transaction occurs when an unexpected response is made to a stimulus. Thus, when the stimulus the and response cross on the PAC transactional diagram, the communication stops. At this point, people tend to withdraw, turn away from each other, or switch the conversation in another direction. If there are a number of crossed transactions, there are likely to be more interpersonal problems.

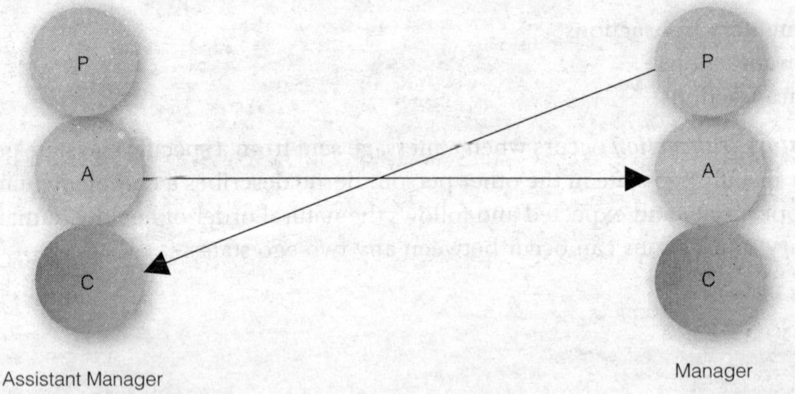

Stimulus: I have to finish a report tonight that's due tomorrow. I will have to detain two typists.
Response: Why do you always leave things till the last minute?

Ulterior Transactions are most complex. An ulterior transaction happens when someone appears to be sending one kind of message but is secretly sending another. Thus the real message is disguised under a socially acceptable transaction. The transaction originates in two or more ego states the and communication proceeds at the psychological as well as the social level.

A Healthy Personality

All persons behave from these three ego states at different times. A healthy person has a personality that maintains a balance among all the three, particularly among Nurturing Parent, Adult and Natural (Free) Child. This implies that these people are able at times, to let the Adult ego state takeover and think very rationally and engage in problem solving. At other times, these people are able to free the Child ego state and have fun and are found to be spontaneous and emotional. At still other times, healthy people are able to refer to the Parent ego state and learn from experiences. They develop values that aid in the speed and effectiveness of decision making.

While balance among the three ego states seems to be most healthy, some persons seem dominated at times by one or two ego states. This is specifically a problem when the Adult ego state is not in the 'executive position' and a person's personality is being dominated by the Critical Parent or the Rebellious (Destructive) Child. When this occurs in people, it poses problems for their managers at work.

More specifically, Child dominated people mainly coming from Rebellious Child do not engage in much rational problem solving. They try to get things done by screaming and being emotional which they learnt in their early years. It is difficult to reason with them in many situations. Instead of solving their own problems, these persons want some other persons to tell them what to do and how to do or what's wrong. Parent-dominated people who mainly come from Critical Parent also do not engage in much rational problem solving because they already know what's right and what's wrong. They seem to have an answer for everything. Even Adult dominated people can be troublesome, because they can be very boring people to work with. They are often "workaholics" and don't seem to act like other persons. Thus a balance between the three ego states makes for a healthy person.

A person uses strokes (feedback) both positive and negative while interacting with others. Thus, TA helps in developing an understanding of another person's ego state and facilitates in behaving from an appropriate ego state to improve interpersonal relations.[62]

IMPROVING COMMUNICATION THROUGHOUT THE HIERARCHY

So far, we have focused on "micro-level" issues in the communication process, namely, the dynamics of sending and receiving information between two employees or the informal exchanges of information across several people. But in this era where knowledge is a competitive advantage, corporate leaders also need to maintain an open flow of communication up, down, and across the organization. In this section, we discuss three communication strategies: workspace design, Web-based communication, and direct communication with top management.

Workspace Design

Executives at Japan Airlines decided that knocking down a few walls might reverse the airline's recent financial woes. The airline's board members and senior executive team moved out of individual offices into a single large room, where it is easier for them to spontaneously share information. The new space also includes an elliptical conference table at which they can hold meetings.[63] Japan Airlines executives have discovered that people communicate more with each other when there are no walls between them.[64] The location and design of hallways, offices, cubicles, and communal areas (cafeterias, elevators) all shape to whom we speak as well as the frequency of such communication.

Japan Airlines has applied a widely adopted workspace strategy of replacing traditional offices with an open space where all employees (including management) work together. One recent convert to open space is Continuum, the Boston-based design and innovation firm. "We do not have doors," explains a

Continuum executive. "It's structured that way to stimulate conversation and to allow people to work collaboratively. Anyone from the chief operating officer to our interns shares space and sits next to each other. You can stop in and have a conversation with anyone, anytime you want."[65] Although these open-space arrangements increase communication, they also potentially increase noise, distractions, and loss of privacy.[66] The challenge is to increase social interaction without these stressors.

Another workspace strategy is to cloister employees into team spaces but also encourage sufficient interaction with people from other teams. Pixar Animation Studios constructed its campus in Emeryville, California, with these principles in mind. The buildings encourage communication among team members. At the same time, the campus encourages happenstance interactions with people on other teams. Pixar executives call this the "bathroom effect," because team members must leave their isolated pods to fetch their mail, have lunch, or visit the restroom.[67]

Web-Based Organizational Communication

For decades, employees received official company news through hard-copy newsletters and magazines. Many firms still use these communication devices, but most have supplemented or replaced them completely with Web-based sources of information. The traditional company magazine is now typically published on Web pages or distributed in PDF format. The advantage of such *e-zines* is that company news can be prepared and distributed quickly.

However, employees are increasingly skeptical of information that has been screened and packaged by management. In response, Children's Hospital and Regional Medical Center in Seattle keeps employees up to date through staff members who volunteer to write news about their departments on the hospital's central Weblog site. "The distributed authorship of people from different departments means the content is fresher" than the hospital's previous newsletter or e-zine, says the Children's Hospital manager responsible for the Web site. IBM relies on e-zines, but employees increasingly rely on BlogCentral, an inward-facing (i.e., for IBM employees' eyes only) blog-hosting service, where several thousands employees write about their own news of the week. A search engine helps staff find important information on any of the several thousand blogs.[68]

Employee Surveys

Almost all of the "best companies to work for," as well as the majority of large firms throughout the United States and several other countries, conduct employee surveys at least once each year. In fact, leaders in two-thirds of high-performing companies claim that surveying employees is one of their most effective ways to strengthen employee engagement levels. Surveys are useful upward communication devices for a variety of purposes. Tennessee Valley Authority surveys its employees annually using a 60-item "cultural health index" that the energy producer found predicts subsequent productivity in each work unit. Bell Canada surveys its 60,000 employees each year using 84 questions about several themes, including career mobility, job challenge, information sharing, and trust in the company's leadership. Canada's largest telephone company also has quarterly "pulse surveys" that measure attitudes about specific policies, such as early retirement.[69]

Direct Communication with Top Management

"The best fertilizer in any field is that of the farmer's footsteps!" This old Chinese saying suggests that farmers will be more successful by spending more time in the fields directly observing the crop's development. Translated into an organizational context, this means that senior executives will

Kowloon Shangri-La's "State of the Hotel" Meetings Communicating with employees can be a challenge when the organization is a large hotel that operates around the clock. But these conditions haven't prevented senior management at Kowloon Shangri-La from holding "state of the hotel" meetings with all 700 staff members twice each year. Two sessions are held—one in the morning, the other in the afternoon—so that all employees at the Hong Kong hotel can attend without leaving the hotel short-staffed. "It was clear from the outset that it is a very good way of communicating with staff from top to bottom," says Kowloon Shangri-La general manager Mark Heywood. During these sessions, Heywood updates employees on the hotel's financial performance, upcoming events, and renovations. "It's a chance to communicate about the good, the bad and the ugly," he explains.[70]

management by walking around (MBWA)
A communication practice in which executives get out of their offices and learn from others in the organization through face-to-face dialogue.

understand their business better if they meet directly with employees and other stakeholders. Nearly 40 years ago, people at Hewlett-Packard coined a phrase for this communication strategy: **management by walking around (MBWA).** At 1-800-Got-Junk?, founder and CEO Brian Scudamore takes this practice further. "I don't have my own office, and I very often move around to different departments for a day at a time," says Scudamore.[71]

Along with practicing MBWA, executives communicate more directly with employees through "town hall meetings." For example, soon after becoming chief executive of McDonald's in the United Kingdom, Peter Beresford instituted a monthly online town hall event where board members answer questions from any McDonald's staff.[72] Some executives also conduct employee roundtable forums to hear opinions from a small representation of staff about various issues. At the departmental level, some companies hold daily or weekly "huddles"–brief stand-up meetings in which staff and their manager discuss goals and hear good-news stories. These direct communication strategies potentially minimize filtering because executives listen directly to employees. They also help executives acquire a deeper meaning and quicker understanding of internal organizational problems. A third benefit of direct communication is that employees might have more empathy for decisions made further up the corporate hierarchy.

Communicating through the Grapevine

grapevine
An unstructured and informal network founded on social relationships rather than organizational charts or job descriptions.

No matter how much corporate leaders try to communicate through e-zines, blogs, wikis, MBWA, and other means, employees will still rely on the oldest communication channel: the corporate **grapevine.** The grapevine is an unstructured and informal network founded on social relationships rather than organizational charts or job descriptions. What do employees think about the grapevine? Surveys of employees in two firms–one in Florida, the other in California–found that almost all employees use the grapevine but very few of them prefer this source of information. The California survey also reported that only one-third of employees believe grapevine information is credible. In other words, employees turn to the grapevine when they have few other options.[73]

Grapevine Characteristics

Research conducted several decades ago reported that the grapevine transmits information very rapidly in all directions throughout the organization. The typical pattern is a cluster chain, whereby a few people actively transmit rumors to many others. The grapevine works through informal social networks, so it is more active where employees have similar backgrounds and are able to communicate easily. Many rumors seem to have at least a kernel of truth, possibly because they are transmitted through media-rich communication channels (e.g., face-to-face) and employees are motivated to communicate effectively. Nevertheless, the grapevine distorts information by deleting fine details and exaggerating key points of the story.[74]

Some of these characteristics might still be true, but other features of the grapevine almost certainly have changed as e-mail, social networking sites, and blogs have replaced the traditional watercooler as sources of gossip. For example, several Facebook sites are themed around specific companies, allowing employees and customers to vent their complaints about the organization. Along with altering the speed and network of corporate grapevines, information technologies have expanded the networks around the globe, not just around the next cubicle.

Grapevine Benefits and Limitations

Should the grapevine be encouraged, tolerated, or quashed? The difficulty in answering this question is that the grapevine has both benefits and limitations.[75] One benefit, as mentioned earlier, is that employees rely on the grapevine when information is not available through formal channels. It is also the main conduit through which organizational stories and other symbols of the organization's culture are communicated. A third benefit of the grapevine is that this social interaction relieves anxiety. This explains why rumor mills are most active during times of uncertainty.[76] Finally, the grapevine is associated with the drive to bond. Being a recipient of gossip is a sign of inclusion, according to evolutionary psychologists. Trying to quash the grapevine is, in some respects, an attempt to undermine the natural human drive for social interaction.[77]

While the grapevine offers these benefits, it is not a preferred communication medium. Grapevine information is sometimes so distorted that it escalates rather than reduces employee anxiety. Furthermore, employees develop more negative attitudes toward the organization when management is slower than the grapevine in communicating information. What should corporate leaders do with the grapevine? The best advice seems to be to listen to the grapevine as a signal of employee anxiety and then correct the cause of this anxiety. Some companies also listen to the grapevine and step in to correct blatant errors and fabrications. Most important, corporate leaders need to view the grapevine as a competitor and meet this challenge by directly informing employees of news before it spreads throughout the grapevine.

Chapter Summary

Communication is the process by which information is transmitted and *understood* between two or more people. Communication supports work coordination, organizational learning, decision making, and employee well-being. The communication process involves forming, encoding, and transmitting the intended message to a receiver, who then decodes the message and provides feedback to the sender. Effective communication occurs when the sender's thoughts are transmitted to and understood by the intended receiver. To improve this process, both sender and receiver should have common codebooks, share common mental models, be familiar with the message topic, and be proficient with the communication channel.

The two main types of communication channels are verbal and nonverbal. Various forms of computer-mediated communication are widely used in organizations, with e-mail being the most popular. Although it is efficient and serves as a useful filing cabinet, e-mail is relatively poor at communicating emotions; it tends to reduce politeness and respect; it is an inefficient medium for communicating in ambiguous, complex, and novel situations; and it contributes to information overload. Facebook-like Web sites, wikis, virtual reality platforms, and other forms of virtual social networking are also gaining popularity as forms of communication. Nonverbal communication includes facial gestures, voice intonation, physical distance, and even silence. Unlike verbal communication, nonverbal communication is less rule-bound and is mostly automatic and nonconscious.

The most appropriate communication medium partly depends on social acceptance factors, including organization and team norms, individual preferences for specific communication channels, and the symbolic meaning of a channel. A communication medium should also be chosen for its data-carrying capacity (media richness). Nonroutine and ambiguous situations require rich media. However, we also need to recognize that lean media allow people to multicommunicate, that the capacity of computer-mediated communication is varied due to the proficiency of individual users, and that social distractions can reduce the efficient processing of information in high-media-richness channels.

Several barriers create noise in the communication process. People misinterpret messages because of perceptual biases. Some information is filtered out as it gets passed up the hierarchy. Jargon and ambiguous language are barriers when the sender and receiver have different interpretations of the words and symbols used. People also screen out or misinterpret messages due to information overload. These problems are often amplified in cross-cultural settings because of language barriers and differences in meanings of nonverbal cues. There are also some communication differences between men and women, such as the tendency for men to exert status and engage in report talk in conversations whereas women use more rapport talk and are more sensitive than are men to nonverbal cues.

To get a message across, the sender must learn to empathize with the receiver, repeat the message, choose an appropriate time for the conversation, and be descriptive rather than evaluative. Listening includes sensing, evaluating, and responding. Active listeners support these processes by postponing evaluation, avoiding interruptions, maintaining interest, empathizing, organizing information, showing interest, and clarifying the message.

Some companies try to encourage communication through workspace design, as well as through Web-based sites. Some executives also meet directly with employees, such as through management by walking around (MBWA), to facilitate communication across the organization.

In any organization, employees rely on the grapevine, particularly during times of uncertainty. The grapevine is an unstructured and informal network founded on social relationships rather than organizational charts or job descriptions. Although early research identified several unique features of the grapevine, some of these features may be changing as the Internet plays an increasing role in grapevine communication.

Key Terms

communication
emotional contagion
grapevine
information overload
management by walking around (MBWA)
media richness
persuasion
wikis

Critical Thinking Questions

1. You have been hired as a consultant to improve communication between engineering and marketing employees in a large high-technology company. Use the communication model and the four ways to improve that process to devise strategies to improve communication effectiveness among employees in these two work units.
2. A company in a country that is just entering the information age intends to introduce e-mail for office staff at its three buildings located throughout the city. Describe two benefits as well as two potential problems that employees will likely experience with this medium.
3. Senior management at a consumer goods company wants you to investigate the feasibility of using a virtual reality platform (such as Second Life) for monthly online meetings involving its three-dozen sales managers located in several cities and countries. Use the social acceptance and media-richness factors described in this chapter to identify information you need to consider when conducting this evaluation.
4. Wikis are collaborative Web sites where anyone in the group can post, edit, or delete any information. Where might this communication technology be most useful in organizations?
5. Under what conditions, if any, do you think it is appropriate to use e-mail to notify an employee that he or she has been laid off or fired? Why is e-mail usually considered an inappropriate channel to convey this information?
6. Suppose that you are part of a virtual team and must persuade other team members about an important matter (such as switching suppliers or altering the project deadline). Assuming that you cannot visit these people in person, what can you do to maximize your persuasiveness?
7. Explain why men and women are sometimes frustrated with each other's communication behaviors.
8. In your opinion, has the introduction of e-mail and other information technologies increased or decreased the amount of information flowing through the corporate grapevine? Explain your answer.

CASE STUDY 9.1

COMMUNICATING WITH THE MILLENNIALS

The Millennials (Generation Y, born between 1980 and 1995) have arrived in the workplace, and they are bringing new ways to communicate. Surveys report that this generation lives by computer and cell phone communication. Three out of four Gen Y's use instant messaging (IM); 15 percent of them are logged on to IM 24/7! Most Gen Y's either have a space on a social network site such as Facebook or frequent such sites where they have friends. These digital natives also get most of their news from the Internet rather than from TV or newspapers.

"Employers are going to find this generation communicates differently. They IM (instant message), send text messages, and can't live without a cell phone," says Dave O'Brien, regional manager of Berbee, a company that helps businesses with their information technology needs. Frank Albi, president of Inacom, a technology and business consulting firm, agrees. "The way they (Millennials) exchange information is vastly different. It's all about IMs and text messages–nice and short."

Albi also notes that Millennials are much more active in multicommunicating. "You can be on the phone with someone and easily instant message someone who you see is online to answer a question or share an idea with," Albi says. However, managers also worry that too much of this multicommunication isn't work-related. "There's a fine line about what can be allowed at work and what can't," suggests Steve Hoeft, a recruiting manager at Time Warner Cable. "Instant messaging is very popular, but if it's affecting their work, that's when there's a problem."

Corporate leaders at BT, Britain's largest telecommunications company, are also aware that Millennials (and to some extent Gen-X employees) live in different communication channels from baby boomers. "Young people in BT communicate much more informally and in real-time," says Richard Dennison, BT's intranet and channel strategy manager. "They're not intimidated by hierarchy or status; to them BT is flat." Dennison adds that Generation-Y employees want bit-size information, not long treatises.

Dennison also emphasizes that, more than previous generations, Millennials demand authentic communication, not marketing hype. "Corporate speak won't cut it anymore," Dennison warns. "First, people won't read it–if they ever did–and second, people won't believe it–if they ever did." Dennison also notices that if Gen Y's get corporate babble, they find ways to let the source know that it lacks authenticity. Remember, this is the generation that has always had a place to write comments after reading the original message.

From these observations, you might think that executive blogs are the answer to Gen-Y communication needs. Not so, argues Dennison. "Force all our senior managers to blog? My experience is that the more senior a manager is, the less likely they'll be able to blog successfully." He adds that executives have too little time to nurture a blog and that they tend to have communication experts who want to meddle (thereby undermining the blog's authenticity).

So how can the company's top dogs communicate effectively with Millennial employees? At BT, the chief executive has held 90-minute online Web chats with staff every six weeks. This medium works well for young BT employees because the communication is in real time and is authentic–the questions aren't screened and the CEO's answers aren't edited. "Thousands of people participate in these chats and it has helped to build up a significant amount of trust" in the CEO, says Dennison. These online Web chats also work well with BT executives because they represent a fixed chunk of time and provide direct contact with the concerns and issues facing employees throughout the hierarchy.

Discussion Questions

1. Take a poll of your class (at least, the Gen-X and Gen-Y members). At school or work, how many regularly (e.g., daily or every few days) send or receive information (not entertainment) using (a) e-mail, (b) instant messages (such as MSN), (c) cell phone text messages, (d) blogs, (e) social network sites (e.g., Facebook), (f) online videos (e.g., YouTube)?
2. Even within each generation, there are different preferences for communication media. After conducting the poll above, ask students who don't regularly use one or more of the listed methods why they don't like that particular communication medium. Ask those who very often use these sources to give their point of view.
3. Companies have been slow and reluctant to adopt social networking sites, online videos, and similar forms of communication. If you were a senior manager, how would you introduce these communication technologies in the workplace to share information and knowledge more effectively?

Sources: MaryBeth Matzek, "R U on 2 Gen Y?" *Marketplace,* 4 September 2007, p. 10; Richard Dennison, "Encouraging BT's Authentic Voice of Leadership," *Strategic Communication Management* 12, no. 2 (2008), p. 12.

CASE STUDY 9.2

IT'S ALL ABOUT THE FACE-TO-FACE

BusinessWeek

If there is one thing corporate globetrotters agree on, it's that there is no substitute for face time. "I don't want to sound like a whirling dervish," says Paul Calello, Credit Suisse's investment banking chief. "But in a global world you have to get in front of your employees, spend time with your clients, and show commitment when it comes to joint ventures, mergers, and alliances. The key is thoughtful travel–traveling when necessary."

Many predicted that technology and globalization would bring the end of face time. Instead, these conditions have made personal interaction all the more important. Executives increasingly feel the inhuman pull of having to be in two, three, four places around the world at the same time. Those who master this new reality are able to strategically identify their face-to-face priorities and finesse tight travel schedules to make these events happen with a reasonably sane schedule.

This *BusinessWeek* case study relates stories and advice from executives who tolerate outlandish travel schedules to meet others eyeball to eyeball rather than from a distance. Read the full text of this *BusinessWeek* article at www.mhhe.com/mcshane5e, and prepare for the discussion questions below.

Discussion Questions

1. Identify the main reasons raised in this article why executives meet employees and clients face-to-face rather than through other communication channels. Are all of these reasons logical, or are some overstated?
2. In this world of globalization and information technology, discuss the skills and knowledge that these world-traveling executives require to make face-to-face communication work effectively.

Source: T. Lowry, F. Belfour, D. Foust, J. McGregor, and M. Conlin, "It's All about the Face-to-Face," *BusinessWeek,* 28 January 2008, pp. 48–51.

TEAM EXERCISE 9.3

ANALYZING THE BLOGOSPHERE

PURPOSE This exercise is designed to help you understand the dynamics of corporate blogs as a way to communicate within organizations.

INSTRUCTIONS This activity is usually conducted in between classes as a homework assignment. The instructor will divide the class into teams (although the exercise can also be conducted individually). Each team will identify a corporate blog (written by a company or government executive and meant for customers, employees, or the wider community). The team will analyze content on the selected blog and answer the following questions for class (preferably with brief samples where applicable):

1. Who is the main intended audience of the selected blog?
2. To what extent do you think this blog attracts the interest of its intended audience? Please explain.
3. What are the main topics in recent postings about this organization? Are they mostly good or bad news? Why?

TEAM EXERCISE 9.4

ACTIVE LISTENING EXERCISE

Mary Gander, Winona State University

PURPOSE This exercise is designed to help you understand the dynamics of active listening in conversations and develop active listening skills.

INSTRUCTIONS For each of the four vignettes presented below, student teams (or students working individually) will compose three statements that demonstrate active listening. Specifically, one statement will indicate that you show empathy for the situation; the second will ask for clarification and detail in a nonjudgmental way; and the third statement will provide nonevaluative feedback to the speaker. Here are details about each of these three types of responses:

- *Showing empathy: Acknowledge feelings.* Sometimes it sounds like a speaker wants you to agree with him or her, but in reality the speaker mainly wants you to understand how he or she feels. "Acknowledging feelings" involves taking in the speaker's statements while looking at the "whole message," including body language, tone of voice, and level of arousal, and trying to determine what emotion the speaker is conveying. Then you let the speaker know that you realize what he or she is feeling by acknowledging it in a sentence.
- *Asking for clarification and detail while withholding your judgment and own opinions.* This conveys that you are trying to understand and not just trying to push your opinions onto the speaker. To formulate a relevant question in asking for more clarification, you will have to listen carefully to what the speaker says. Frame your question as someone trying to understand in more detail; often asking for a specific example is useful. This also helps the speaker evaluate his or her own opinions and perspective.
- *Providing nonevaluative feedback: Feeding back the message you heard.* This will allow the speaker to determine whether he or she conveyed the message to you and will help prevent troublesome miscommunication. It will also help the speaker become more aware of how he or she is coming across to another person (self-evaluation). Just think about what the speaker is conveying; paraphrase it in your own words, and say it back to the speaker (without judging the correctness or merit of what was said), asking him or her if that is what was meant.

After teams (or individual students) have prepared the three statements for each vignette, the instructor will ask them to present their statements and explain how these statements satisfy the active listening criteria.

VIGNETTE 1 A colleague stops by your desk and says, "I am tired of the lack of leadership around here. The boss is so wishy-washy, he can't get tough with some of the slackers around here. They just keep milking the company, living off the rest of us. Why doesn't management do something about these guys? And you are always so supportive of the boss; he's not as good as you make him out to be."

Develop three statements that respond to the speaker in this vignette by (a) showing empathy, (b) seeking clarification, and (c) providing nonevaluative feedback.

VIGNETTE 2 Your co-worker stops by your cubicle; her voice and body language show stress, frustration, and even some fear. You know she has been working hard and has a strong need to get her work done on time and done well. You are trying to concentrate on some work and have had a number of interruptions already. She abruptly interrupts you and says, "This project is turning out to be a mess. Why can't the other three people on my team quit fighting with each other?"

Develop three statements that respond to the speaker in this vignette by (a) showing empathy, (b) seeking clarification, and (c) providing nonevaluative feedback.

VIGNETTE 3 One of your subordinates is working on an important project. He is an engineer who has good technical skills and knowledge and was selected for the project team for this reason. He stops by your office and appears to be quite agitated: His voice is loud and strained, and his face has a look of bewilderment. He says, "I'm supposed to be working with four other people from four other departments on this new project, but they never listen to my ideas and seem to hardly know I'm at the meeting!"

Develop three statements that respond to the speaker in this vignette by (a) showing empathy, (b) seeking clarification, and (c) providing nonevaluative feedback.

VIGNETTE 4 Your subordinate comes into your office in a state of agitation, asking if she can talk to you. She is polite and sits down. She seems calm and does not have an angry look on her face. However, she says, "It seems like you consistently make up lousy schedules; you are unfair and unrealistic in the kinds of assignments you give certain people, me included. Everyone else is so intimidated they don't complain, but I think you need to know that this isn't right and it's got to change."

Develop three statements that respond to the speaker in this vignette by (a) showing empathy, (b) seeking clarification, and (c) providing nonevaluative feedback.

TEAM EXERCISE 9.5

CROSS-CULTURAL COMMUNICATION GAME

PURPOSE This exercise is designed to develop and test your knowledge of cross-cultural differences in communication and etiquette.

MATERIALS The instructor will provide one set of question-and-answer cards to each pair of teams.

INSTRUCTIONS

1. The class is divided into an even number of teams. Ideally, each team would have three students. (Two- or four-student teams are possible if matched with an equal-size team.) Each team is then paired with another team, and the paired teams (team "A" and team "B") are assigned a private space away from other matched teams.
2. The instructor will hand each pair of teams a stack of cards with the multiple-choice questions face down. These cards have questions and answers about cross-cultural differences in communication and etiquette. No books or other aids are allowed.
3. The exercise begins with a member of team A picking up one card from the top of the pile and asking the question on that card to the members of team B. The information given to team

B includes the question and all alternative answers listed on the card. Team B has 30 seconds after the question and alternatives have been read to give an answer. Team B earns one point if the correct answer is given. If team B's answer is incorrect, however, team A earns that point. Correct answers to each question are indicated on the card and, of course, should not be revealed until the question is correctly answered or time is up. Whether or not team B answers correctly, team B picks up the next card on the pile and reads it to members of team A. In other words, cards are read alternately to each team. This procedure is repeated until all the cards have been read or time has expired. The team receiving the most points wins.

Important note: The textbook provides very little information pertaining to the questions in this exercise. Rather, you must rely on past learning, logic, and luck to win.

SELF-ASSESSMENT 9.6

ACTIVE LISTENING SKILLS INVENTORY

PURPOSE This self-assessment is designed to help you estimate your strengths and weaknesses on various dimensions of active listening.

INSTRUCTIONS Think back to face-to-face conversations you have had with a co-worker or client in the office, hallway, factory, or other setting. Indicate the extent to which each item on next page describes your behavior during those conversations. Answer each item as truthfully as possible so that you get an accurate estimate of where your active listening skills need improvement. Then use the scoring key in Appendix B at the end of the book to calculate your results for each scale. This exercise should be completed alone so that you can assess yourself honestly without concerns of social comparison. Class discussion will focus on the important elements of active listening.

Active Listening Skills Inventory

Circle the response to the right that best indicates the extent to which each statement describes you when listening to others.	Not at all	A little	Somewhat	Very much
1. I keep an open mind about the speaker's point of view until he or she has finished talking.	☐	☐	☐	☐
2. While listening, I mentally sort out the speaker's ideas in a way that makes sense to me.	☐	☐	☐	☐
3. I stop the speaker and give my opinion when I disagree with something he or she has said.	☐	☐	☐	☐
4. People can often tell when I'm not concentrating on what they are saying.	☐	☐	☐	☐
5. I don't evaluate what a person is saying until he or she has finished talking.	☐	☐	☐	☐
6. When someone takes a long time to present a simple idea, I let my mind wander to other things.	☐	☐	☐	☐
7. I jump into conversations to present my views rather than wait and risk forgetting what I wanted to say.	☐	☐	☐	☐
8. I nod my head and make other gestures to show I'm interested in the conversation.	☐	☐	☐	☐
9. I can usually keep focused on what people are saying to me even when they don't sound interesting.	☐	☐	☐	☐
10. Rather than organizing the speaker's ideas, I usually expect the person to summarize them for me.	☐	☐	☐	☐
11. I always say things like "I see" or "uh-huh" so that people know I'm really listening to them.	☐	☐	☐	☐
12. While listening, I concentrate on what is being said and regularly organize the information.	☐	☐	☐	☐
13. While a speaker is talking, I quickly determine whether I like or dislike his or her ideas.	☐	☐	☐	☐
14. I pay close attention to what people are saying even when they are explaining something I already know.	☐	☐	☐	☐
15. I don't give my opinion until I'm sure the other person has finished talking.	☐	☐	☐	☐

Denise Revine's review was supposed to uncover more efficient uses of the human resource budget within the Royal Canadian Mounted Police (RCMP). Instead, the human resource director discovered misappropriations that would shake the foundations of the law enforcement agency: pension funds were being siphoned off for questionable and unrelated operating expenses, including excessive payments to family members. Two auditor reports later confirmed Revine's findings.

Revine informed her boss, Chief Superintendent Fraser Macaulay, who reported the preliminary evidence to the RCMP's ethics adviser. Macaulay was then asked to brief the RCMP commissioner (the organization's chief executive), Giuliano Zaccardelli, on this matter. To Macaulay's surprise, the RCMP commissioner accused Macaulay of hiding this wrongdoing and, soon after, transferred him to the Department of National Defence "so he could learn from his mistake." A Canadian government investigation into the RCMP pension affair concluded that Zaccardelli's claims against Macaulay were unfounded. Equally important, it concluded that the transfer scuttled Macaulay's career and sent "a message throughout the organization that one brings bad news to the Commissioner at one's peril."

Subversive power, influence, and politics derailed the careers of Royal Canadian Mounted Police (RCMP) human resource director Denise Revine and her boss, Chief Superintendent Fraser Macaulay (both shown here), as well as other RCMP staff who tried to discover and report wrongdoing in RCMP pension fund expenditures.

Revine submitted her final report a few months after her boss's fateful meeting with the RCMP commissioner. Soon after, Revine's position was declared surplus during a human resource department restructuring. When an HR staff member tried to find work in other departments for Revine, his boss warned: "No, don't touch her!" After 33 years with the RCMP, Revine was suddenly out of a job.

The Canadian government investigation concluded that some members of the RCMP executive were "using the restructuring process in the Human Resources Branch to try to force [Revine] out of the organization." According to the Canadian government report, at least three other RCMP officers apparently suffered career setbacks or were forced into retirement due to pressure from the RCMP's top brass.

The Canadian government's independent investigator noted, significantly, that the RCMP commissioner "enjoyed the status and privileges of his office," often "reminding people that 'I am the Commissioner.'" The investigation concluded that the RCMP suffered from this "absolute power exercised by the Commissioner" and that the best way to prevent similar problems in the future is restructuring "aimed at whittling down the power of the Commissioner."[1]

10

Power and Influence in the Workplace

Learning Objectives

After reading this chapter, you should be able to:

1. Define *power* and *countervailing power.*
2. Describe the five sources of power in organizations.
3. Explain how information relates to power in organizations.
4. Discuss the four contingencies of power.
5. Summarize the effects of power on the power holder's own performance and well-being.
6. Summarize the eight types of influence tactics.
7. Discuss three contingencies to consider when deciding which influence tactic to use.
8. Distinguish influence from organizational politics.
9. Describe the organizational conditions and personal characteristics that support organizational politics.
10. Identify ways to minimize organizational politics.

The Canadian government's independent investigation, along with separate parliamentary committee meetings, reveals the extent to which some members of the RCMP's senior executive abused their power, used assertive influence tactics, and engaged in organizational politics to suppress or subvert evidence of wrongdoing. Some RCMP executives may have taken these actions to hide their own inappropriate actions; others likely used their power and influence in a perverse attempt to protect the RCMP's public image. Although this story illustrates the dark side of power and influence, these concepts are equally relevant to ethical conduct and organizational performance. In fact, some OB experts point out that power and influence are inherent in all organizations. They exist in every business and in every decision and action.

This chapter unfolds as follows: First, we define *power* and present a basic model depicting the dynamics of power in organizational settings. The chapter then discusses the five sources of power, as well as information as a power base. Next, we look at the contingencies necessary to translate those sources into meaningful power. The latter part of this chapter examines the various types of influence in organizational settings as well as the contingencies of effective influence strategies. The final section of this chapter looks at situations in which influence becomes organizational politics, as well as ways of minimizing dysfunctional politics.

Learning Objectives

After reading the next three sections, you should be able to:

1. Define *power* and *countervailing power*.
2. Describe the five sources of power in organizations.
3. Explain how information relates to power in organizations.
4. Discuss the four contingencies of power.
5. Summarize the effects of power on the power holder's own performance and well-being.

The Meaning of Power

power
The capacity of a person, team, or organization to influence others.

countervailing power
The capacity of a person, team, or organization to keep a more powerful person or group in the exchange relationship.

Power is the capacity of a person, team, or organization to influence others.[2] Power is not the act of changing someone's attitudes or behavior; it is only the potential to do so. People frequently have power they do not use; they might not even know they have power. Also, power is not a personal feeling of power. You might feel powerful or think you have power over someone else, but this is not power unless you truly have the capacity to influence that person. The most basic prerequisite of power is that one person (or group) believes he or she is dependent on another person (or group) for a resource of value.[3] This relationship, shown in Exhibit 10.1, occurs when Person A has power over Person B by controlling something that Person B wants. You might have power over others by controlling a desired job assignment, useful information, important resources, or even the privilege of being associated with you. However, power requires the *perception* of dependence, so people might gain power by convincing others that they have something of value, whether or not they actually control that resource. Thus, power exists when others believe that you control resources they want.

Although dependence is a key element of power relationships, it is really more accurate to say that the parties are *interdependent*.[4] In Exhibit 10.1, Person A dominates in the power relationship, but Person B also has some **countervailing power**–enough power to keep Person A in the exchange relationship and ensure

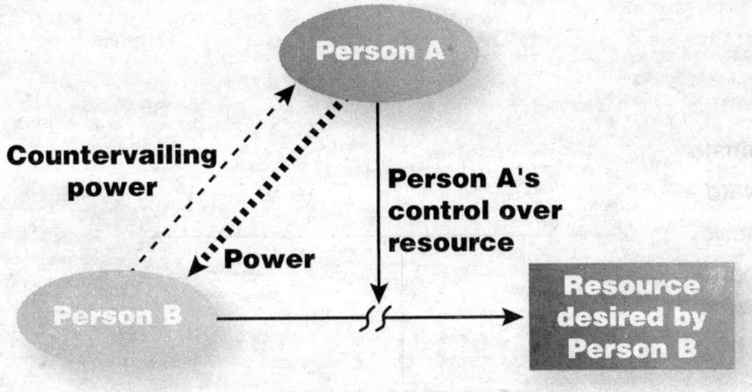

Exhibit 10.1 *Dependence in the Power Relationship*

that Person A uses her or his dominant power judiciously. For example, executives have power over subordinates by controlling their job security and promotional opportunities. At the same time, employees have countervailing power by possessing skills and knowledge that keep production humming and customers happy, something that executives can't accomplish alone. Finally, the power relationship depends on some minimum level of trust. Trust indicates a level of expectation that the more powerful party will deliver the resource. For example, you trust your employer to give you a paycheck at the end of each pay period. Even those in extremely dependent situations will usually walk away from the relationship if they lack a minimum level of trust in the more powerful party.

A Model of Power in Organizations

Power involves more than just dependence or interdependence. As Exhibit 10.2 illustrates, power is derived from five sources: legitimate, reward, coercive, expert, and referent. The model also indicates that these sources yield power only under certain conditions. The four contingencies of power include the employee's or department's substitutability, centrality, discretion, and visibility. Finally, as you will read later in this chapter, the type of power applied affects the type of influence the power holder has over the other person or work unit.

Sources of Power in Organizations

Power derives from several sources and a few contingencies that determine the potential of those power sources.[5] Three sources of power–legitimate, reward, and coercive–originate mostly from the power holder's formal position or informal role. In other words, the person is granted these sources of power formally by the organization or informally by co-workers. Two other sources of power–expert and referent–originate from the power holder's own characteristics; that is, the person brings these power bases to the organization. Sources of power are resources that help the dependent person directly or indirectly achieve his or her goals. For example, your expertise is a source of power when others need that expertise to accomplish their objectives.

legitimate power
An agreement among organizational members that people in certain roles can request certain behaviors of others.

Legitimate Power

Legitimate power is an agreement among organizational members that people in certain roles can request certain behaviors of others. This perceived right

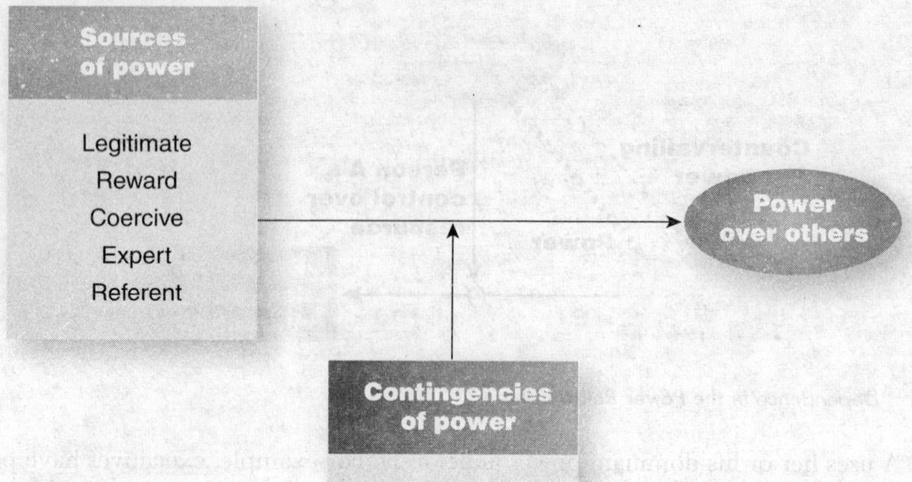

Exhibit 10.2 *A Model of Power within Organizations*

originates from formal job descriptions as well as informal rules of conduct. Legitimate power extends to employees, not just managers. For example, an organization might give employees the right to receive customer files held by the boss if this information is required for their jobs. Legitimate power depends on more than job descriptions. It also depends on mutual agreement from those expected to abide by this authority. Your boss's power to make you work overtime partly depends on your agreement to this authority. Thus, legitimate power operates within a "zone of indifference"–the range within which people are willing to accept someone else's authority.[6]

The size of this zone of indifference (and, consequently, the magnitude of legitimate power) increases with the extent to which the power holder is trusted and makes fair decisions. Some people are also more obedient than others to authority, particularly those who value conformity and tradition. People in high power distance cultures (i.e., those who accept an unequal distribution of power) also tend to have higher obedience to authority compared with people in low power distance cultures. The organization's culture represents a third factor. A 3M scientist might continue to work on a project after being told by superiors to stop working on it because the 3M culture supports an entrepreneurial spirit, which includes ignoring the boss's authority from time to time.[7]

Reward Power

Reward power is derived from the person's ability to control the allocation of rewards valued by others and to remove negative sanctions (i.e., negative reinforcement). Managers have formal authority that gives them power over the distribution of organizational rewards such as pay, promotions, time off, vacation schedules, and work assignments. Likewise, employees have reward power over their bosses through the use of 360-degree feedback systems. Employee feedback affects supervisors' promotions and other rewards, so supervisors tend to behave differently toward employees after 360-degree feedback is introduced.

Coercive Power

Coercive power is the ability to apply punishment. The opening story to this chapter described how the RCMP commissioner and likely other senior RCMP executives used coercive power to suppress and remove employees who may have spread word of the financial wrongdoing. Employees also have coercive power, ranging from sarcasm to ostracism, to ensure that co-workers conform to team norms. Many firms rely on this coercive power to control co-worker behavior in team settings. Nucor is one such example: "If you're not contributing with the team, they certainly will let you know about it," says Dan Krug, manager of HR and organizational development at the Charlotte, North Carolina, steelmaker. "The few poor players get weeded out by their peers." Similarly, when asked how AirAsia maintained attendance and productivity after the Malaysian discount airline removed its time clocks, Chief Executive Tony Fernandes replied: "Simple. Peer pressure sees to that. The fellow employees, who are putting their shoulders to the wheel, will see to that."[8]

Expert Power

For the most part, legitimate, reward, and coercive power originate from the position.[9] In contrast, expert power originates from within the person. It is an individual's or work unit's capacity to influence others by possessing knowledge or skills that others value. Employees are gaining expert power as our society moves from an industrial to a knowledge-based economy.[10] The reason is that employee knowledge becomes the means of production and is ultimately outside the control of those who own the company. And without this control over production, owners are more dependent on employees to achieve their corporate objectives.

The power of expertise is most apparent when observing how people respond to authority figures.[11] In one classic study, a researcher posing as a hospital physician telephoned on-duty nurses to prescribe a specific dosage of medicine to a hospitalized patient. None of the nurses knew the person calling, and hospital policy prohibited them from accepting treatment orders by telephone. Furthermore, the medication was unauthorized, and the prescription was twice the maximum daily dose. Yet almost all 22 nurses who received the telephone call followed the "doctor's" orders until stopped by the researchers.[12]

Referent Power

referent power
The capacity to influence others on the basis of an identification with and respect for the power holder.

People have **referent power** when others identify with them, like them, or otherwise respect them. Like expert power, referent power comes from within the person. It is largely a function of the person's interpersonal skills and tends to develop slowly. Referent power is usually associated with charismatic leadership. Experts have difficulty agreeing on the meaning of *charisma,* but it is most often described as a form of interpersonal attraction whereby followers ascribe almost magical powers to the charismatic individual.[13] Some experts describe charisma as a special "gift" or trait within the charismatic person, while others say it is mainly in the eyes of the beholder. However, all agree that charisma produces a high degree of trust, respect, and devotion toward the charismatic individual.

Information and Power

Information is power.[14] In one form, people gain information power when they control (through legitimate power) the flow of information to others. Employees are ultimately dependent on these information gatekeepers to release the information required to perform their jobs. Furthermore, by deciding what information is distributed to whom, those who control information flow also control perceptions of the situation by releasing information favoring one perspective more than another.[15] This right to control information flow is a form of legitimate power and is most common in highly bureaucratic firms. The wheel formation in Exhibit 10.3 depicts this highly centralized control over information flow. The all-channels structure, on the other hand, depicts a situation where no one has control over the flow of information. The former would occur when information must flow through your boss to you, whereas the latter occurs when information is distributed to many people, such as co-workers in a self-directed team.

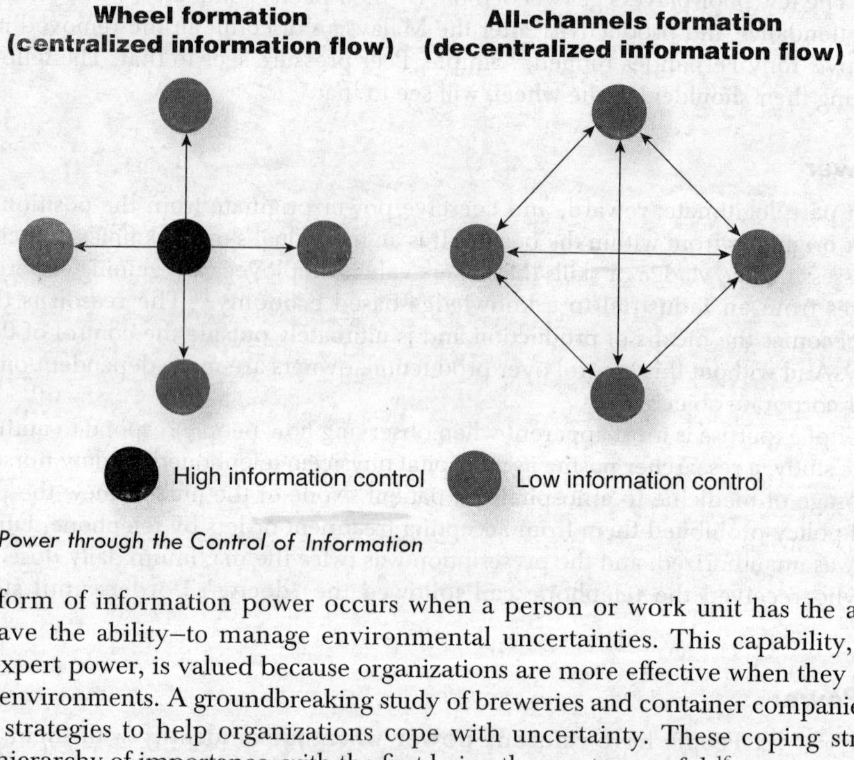

Exhibit 10.3 *Power through the Control of Information*

The other form of information power occurs when a person or work unit has the ability–or is believed to have the ability–to manage environmental uncertainties. This capability, which is a derivative of expert power, is valued because organizations are more effective when they can operate in predictable environments. A groundbreaking study of breweries and container companies identified three general strategies to help organizations cope with uncertainty. These coping strategies are arranged in a hierarchy of importance, with the first being the most powerful:[16]

- *Prevention.* The most effective strategy is to prevent environmental changes from occurring. For example, financial experts acquire power by preventing the organization from experiencing a cash shortage or defaulting on loans.
- *Forecasting.* The next best strategy is to predict environmental changes or variations. In this respect, trendspotters and other marketing specialists gain power by predicting changes in consumer preferences.
- *Absorption.* People and work units also gain power by absorbing or neutralizing the impact of environmental shifts as they occur. An example is the ability of maintenance crews to come to the rescue when machines break down and the production process stops.

DeCourcy's Trendspotting Power Colleen DeCourcy has seen the future of digital marketing . . . and we're definitely not there yet. "I think we have a long way to go before we're really using technology in marketing," says the chief digital officer at advertising agency TBWA. "We're all in this very sophomoric stage, trying to figure out a new medium." Digital media may be new, but many people in the creative business say DeCourcy is better than most people at predicting digital trends and helping clients to benefit from them. "Her knowledge of the digital landscape, grounded in creativity, makes her an invaluable addition to TBWA," says DeCourcy's boss, TBWA Worldwide CEO Tom Carroll. Ty Montague, copresident of JWT in New York and DeCourcy's former employer, agrees: "It's hard to overstate the impact she's had." For example, DeCourcy was an early adopter of marketing to the younger generation through cell phone ringtones and social network media (e.g., Facebook). Her ability to predict and manage the volatile digital marketing landscape has given her considerable power in the industry. For example, sportswear company Adidas recently picked TBWA to handle its global digital marketing work; TBWA put DeCourcy in charge of a new company in Amsterdam (called Riot) to exclusively handle this account. Also, DeCourcy was selected as president of the jury that picks the best digital advertising entries at the Cannes Lions International Advertising Festival.[17]

CONTINGENCIES OF POWER

Let's say that you have expert power because of your ability to forecast and possibly even prevent dramatic changes in the organization's environment. Does this expertise mean that you are influential? Not necessarily. As we saw earlier in Exhibit 10.2, sources of power generate power only under certain conditions. Four important contingencies of power are substitutability, centrality, discretion, and visibility.[18]

Substitutability

substitutability
A contingency of power pertaining to the availability of alternatives.

Substitutability refers to the availability of alternatives. Power is strongest when someone has a monopoly over a valued resource. Conversely, power decreases as the number of alternative sources of the critical resource increases. If you–and no one else–have expertise across the organization on an important issue, you will be more powerful than you would be if several people in your company possess this valued knowledge. Substitutability refers not only to other sources that offer the resource but also to substitutions of the resource itself. For instance, labor unions are weakened when companies introduce technologies that replace the need for their union members. Technology is potentially a substitute for production employees and, consequently, reduces union power.

Controlling access to valued resources increases nonsubstitutability. Professions and labor unions gain power by controlling the knowledge, tasks, or labor needed to perform important activities. For instance, the medical profession is powerful because it controls who can perform specific medical procedures. Labor unions that dominate an industry effectively control access to the labor needed to perform key jobs. Employees become nonsubstitutable when they possess knowledge (such as how to operate equipment or serve clients) that is not documented or readily available to others. Nonsubstitutability also occurs when people differentiate their resource from the alternatives. Some people claim that consultants use this tactic. They take skills and knowledge that many other consulting firms can provide and wrap them in a package (with the latest buzzwords, of course) so that it looks like they provide a service that no one else can offer.

Centrality

centrality
A contingency of power pertaining to the degree and nature of interdependence between the power holder and others.

Centrality refers to the degree and nature of interdependence between the power holder and others.[19] Think about your own centrality for a moment: If you decided not to show up for work or school tomorrow, how many people would be affected, and how much time would pass before they were affected? If you have high centrality, most people in the organization would be adversely affected by your absence, and they would be affected quickly.

The effect of centrality on power is apparent in well-timed labor disputes. When Boeing workers recently walked off the job in Seattle, they immediately shut down final assembly of the aerospace company's commercial jets. Analysts estimate that the resulting delivery delays cost Boeing $2.8 billion in revenue for every month that the strike continued.[20] The New York City transit strike during the busy Christmas shopping season a few years ago also displayed centrality. The illegal three-day work stoppage immediately clogged roads and prevented most city workers from showing up to work on time or at all. "[The Metropolitan Transit Authority] told us we got no power, but we got power," said one striking transit worker. "We got the power to stop the city."[21]

Discretion

The freedom to exercise judgment–to make decisions without referring to a specific rule or receiving permission from someone else–is another important contingency of power in organizations. Consider the plight of first-line supervisors. It may seem that they have legitimate, reward, and coercive power over employees, but this power is often curtailed by specific rules. The lack of discretion makes supervisors less powerful than their positions would indicate. "Middle managers are very much 'piggy-in-the-middle,'" complains a middle manager at Britain's National Health System. "They have little power, only what senior managers are allowed to give them."[22] More generally, research indicates that managerial discretion varies considerably across industries and that managers with an internal locus of control are viewed as more powerful because they act like they have plenty of discretion in their jobs.[23]

Visibility

Several years ago, as a junior copywriter at advertising agency Chiat/Day, Mimi Cook submitted an idea for a potential client to her boss, who then presented it to cofounder Jay Chiat. Chiat was thrilled with the concept, but Cook's boss "never mentioned the idea came from me," recalls Cook. Cook confronted her boss, who claimed the oversight was unintentional. But when a similar incident occurred a few months later, Cook left the agency for another firm.[24]

Mimi Cook, who has since progressed to associate creative director at another ad agency, knows that power does not flow to unknown people in the organization. Those who control valued resources or knowledge will yield power only when others are aware of these sources of power, in other words, when they are visible. One way to increase visibility is to take people-oriented jobs and work on projects that require frequent interaction with senior executives. "You can take visibility in steps," advises a pharmaceutical industry executive. "You can start by making yourself visible in a small group, such as a staff meeting. Then when you're comfortable with that, seek out larger arenas."[25]

Employees also gain visibility by being, quite literally, visible. Some people strategically locate themselves in more visible offices, such as those closest to the elevator or staff coffee room. People often use public symbols as subtle (and not-so-subtle) cues to make their power sources known to others. Many professionals display their educational diplomas and awards on office walls to remind visitors of their expertise. Medical professionals wear white coats with a stethoscope around their neck to symbolize their legitimate and expert power in hospital settings. Other people play the game of "face time"–spending more time at work and showing that they are working productively.

Social Networking and Power

social capital
The knowledge and other resources available to people or social units (teams, organizations) from a durable network that connects them to others.

"It's not what you know, but whom you know that counts!" This often-heard statement reflects the idea that employees get ahead not just by developing their competencies but by *social networking*–cultivating social relationships with others to accomplish one's goals. Networking increases a person's power in three ways. First, as we noted in Chapter 8, networks represent a critical component of **social capital**–the knowledge and other resources available to people or social units (teams, organizations) from a durable network that connects them to others. Networks consist of people who trust each other, and this increases the flow of knowledge among those within the network. The more you network, the more likely it is that you will receive valuable information that increases your expert power in the organization.[26]

Second, people tend to identify more with partners within their own networks, and this identification increases referent power among people within each network. Network-based referent power may lead to more favorable decisions by others in the network. Finally, effective networkers are better known by others in the organization, so their talents are more readily recognized. This power increases when networkers place themselves in strategic positions in the network, thereby gaining centrality.[27] For example, an individual might be regarded as the main person who distributes information in the network or who keeps the network connected through informal gatherings. Social networks are important foundations of power for individuals and, as Global Connections 10.1 describes, companies are applying social network analysis tools to discover who has this power. By identifying who is the most connected, leaders know whom to approach for information, who might be the most influential over other employees, and who would be the most costly if he or she left the company.

Social networks are natural elements of all organizations, yet a network can create a formidable barrier to those who are not actively connected to it.[28] Women are often excluded from informal management networks because they usually do not participate in golf games and other male-dominated social events. Nina Smith, who leads Sage Software's Business Management Division, has had several conversations with female executives about these power dynamics. "I'm still trying to knock down the Boys Club and I still have women at Sage coming to me and saying, 'Nina, that's the boys' network and I can't get in.'"[29] Several years ago, executives at Deloitte Touche Tohmatsu discovered that inaccessibility to powerful social networks partly explained why many junior female employees left the accounting and consulting firm before reaching partnership level. The Swiss-based firm now relies

10.1 GLOBAL CONNECTIONS

Powered by the Social Network

Engineering and environmental consulting firm MWH Global reorganized its information technology (IT) operations into a single global division and located its main service center in New Zealand. Ken Loughridge was transferred from England to manage the new service center, but he didn't know who the key players were on his New Zealand team. "By and large, the staff I'd adopted were strangers," he says. Fortunately, Loughridge was able to consult a report displaying the informal social network of relationships among his staff. MWH Global had surveyed its IT employees a few months earlier about whom they communicated with most often for information. The data produced a weblike diagram of nodes (people) connected by a maze of lines (relationships). From this picture, Loughridge could identify the "go-to" people in the work unit. "It's as if you took the top off an ant hill and could see where there's a hive of activity," he says of the map. "It really helped me understand who the players were."

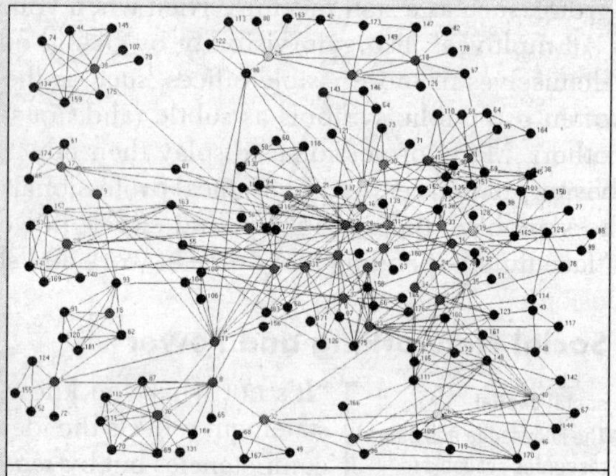

This is one of several social network analysis diagrams that helped Raytheon engineering director Karl Arunski determine who has the most social network power.

For the past half century, sociologists have mapped informal power relationships in organizations. Now, social network analysis is becoming a powerful management tool as practitioners discover that visual displays of relationships and information flows can help them to tap into employees with expertise and influence. "You look at an org chart within a company and you see the distribution of power that should be," says Eran Barak, global head of marketing strategies at Thomson Reuters. "You look at the dynamics in the social networks [to] see the distribution of power that is. It reflects where information is flowing—who is really driving things."

Karl Arunski, director of Raytheon's engineering center in Colorado, can appreciate these words. The defense and technology company's organizational chart didn't show how mission management specialists influenced people across departmental boundaries. So Arunski asked two executives to name up to 10 experts who didn't fit squarely in a particular department, and then he conducted social network analysis to see how these people collaborated with engineers throughout the organization.

The resulting maps (one of which is shown here), showed Arunski the influence and knowledge flow of various experts. It also highlighted problems where a cluster of employees is almost completely disconnected from the rest of the engineering group (such as the top left side of this diagram). One team's isolation was worrisome because its members were experts in systems architecture, an important growth area for Raytheon. To increase the team's network power, Arunski encouraged the team leader to hold meetings at which engineers could share information about systems architecture. The number of people attending eventually grew to 75, reducing the team's isolation from others. "Social Network Analysis helped Rocky Mountain Engineering understand how organizations develop architectures, and it enabled us to know how engineers become architects," says Arunski.[30]

on mentoring, formal women's network groups, and measurement of career progress to ensure that female staff members have the same career development opportunities as their male colleagues.[31]

Consequences of Power

How does power affect the power holder? We partly answered this question earlier in this book when describing empowerment–an individual's feelings of self-determination, meaning, competence, and impact in the organization. Under the right conditions, employees who receive more power feel more empowered, and this tends to increase their motivation, job satisfaction, organizational commitment, and job performance. In addition, research suggests that as people become more powerful, they are more goal-directed and tend to act on their environment rather than hide from it.

At the same time, increasing power over others can potentially undermine an individual's effectiveness and interpersonal relations. Some studies have found that people who have (or believe they have) more power over others are more likely to cling to stereotypes, have more difficulty empathizing, and generally have less accurate perceptions compared with people who have less power. They also engage in more automatic rather than mindful thinking, possibly because powerful people are less concerned about the consequences of their actions.[32] These findings may explain the widely criticized decisions and actions of the former RCMP commissioner, including his response to the pension fund abuses described at the beginning of this chapter.[33]

Learning Objectives

After reading this section, you should be able to:

6. Summarize the eight types of influence tactics.
7. Discuss three contingencies to consider when deciding which influence tactic to use.

INFLUENCING OTHERS

influence
Any behavior that attempts to alter someone's attitudes or behavior.

Up to this point, we have focused on the sources and contingencies of power. But power is only the capacity to influence others. It represents the potential to change someone's attitudes and behavior. **Influence,** on the other hand, refers to any behavior that attempts to alter someone's attitudes or behavior.[34] Influence is power in motion. It applies one or more sources of power to get people to alter their beliefs, feelings, and activities. Consequently, our interest in the remainder of this chapter is in how people use power to influence others.

Influence tactics are woven throughout the social fabric of all organizations. This is because influence is an essential process through which people coordinate their effort and act in concert to achieve organizational objectives. Indeed, influence is central to the definition of leadership. Influence operates down, across, and up the corporate hierarchy. Executives ensure that subordinates complete required tasks. Employees influence co-workers to help them with their job assignments. Subordinates engage in upward influence tactics so that corporate leaders make decisions compatible with subordinates' needs and expectations.

Types of Influence Tactics

Organizational behavior researchers have devoted considerable attention to the various types of influence tactics found in organizational settings. They do not agree on a definitive list of influence tactics, but the most commonly identified are listed in Exhibit 10.4 and described over the next few pages.[35] The first five are known as "hard" influence tactics because they force behavior change through position power (legitimate, reward, and coercion). The last three–persuasion, ingratiation and

Influence tactic	Description
Silent authority	Influencing behavior through legitimate power without explicitly referring to that power base
Assertiveness	Actively applying legitimate and coercive power by applying pressure or threats
Information control	Explicitly manipulating someone else's access to information for the purpose of changing their attitudes and/or behavior
Coalition formation	Forming a group that attempts to influence others by pooling the resources and power of its members
Upward appeal	Gaining support from one or more people with higher authority or expertise
Persuasion	Using logical arguments, factual evidence, and emotional appeals to convince people of the value of a request
Ingratiation and impression management	Attempting to increase liking by, or perceived similarity to, some targeted person
Exchange	Promising benefits or resources in exchange for the target person's compliance

Exhibit 10.4 *Types of Influence Tactics in Organizations*

impression management, and exchange–are called "soft" tactics because they rely more on personal sources of power (referent, expert) and appeal to the target person's attitudes and needs.

Silent Authority The silent application of authority occurs when someone complies with a request because of the requester's legitimate power as well as the target person's role expectations. This condition is known as *deference to authority*.[36] This deference occurs when you comply with your boss's request to complete a particular task. If the task is within your job scope and your boss has the right to make the request, then this influence strategy operates without negotiation, threats, persuasion, or other tactics. Silent authority is the most common form of influence in high power distance cultures.[37]

Assertiveness In contrast to silent authority, assertiveness might be called "vocal authority" because it involves actively applying legitimate and coercive power to influence others. Assertiveness includes persistently reminding the target of his or her obligations, frequently checking the target's work, confronting the target, and using threats of sanctions to force compliance. Assertiveness typically applies or threatens to apply punishment if the target does not comply. Explicit or implicit threats range from losing one's job to losing face by letting down the team. Extreme forms of assertiveness include blackmailing colleagues, such as by threatening to reveal the other person's previously unknown failures unless he or she complies with your request. In reference to the opening story to this chapter, evidence suggests that senior RCMP executives relied on various forms of assertiveness to suppress investigation of pension fund abuses.

Information Control Information control involves explicitly manipulating others' access to information for the purpose of changing their attitudes and/or behavior. With limited access to potentially valuable information, others are at a disadvantage. The opening story on RCMP pension fund abuses suggests that information control was used as an influence tactic. One investigator told a parliamentary committee: "I was met with inaction, delays, roadblocks, obstruction and lies." He pointed to the RCMP's top leaders as the source of this information control.[38] According to one major survey, almost half of employees believe that co-workers keep others in the dark about work issues if doing so helps their own cause. Employees also influence executive decisions by screening out (filtering) information flowing up the hierarchy. One study found that CEOs influence their board of directors by selectively feeding and withholding information.[39]

coalition
A group that attempts to influence people outside the group by pooling the resources and power of its members.

Coalition Formation When people lack sufficient power alone to influence others in the organization, they might form a **coalition** of people who support the proposed change. A coalition is influential in three ways.[40] First, it pools the power and resources of many people, so the coalition potentially has more influence than any number of people operating alone. Second, the coalition's mere existence can be a source of power by symbolizing the legitimacy of the issue. In other words, a coalition creates a sense that the issue deserves attention because it has broad support. Third, coalitions tap into the power of the social identity process introduced in Chapter 2. A coalition is essentially an informal group that advocates a new set of norms and behaviors. If the coalition has a broad-based membership (i.e., its members come from various parts of the organization), other employees are more likely to identify with that group and, consequently, accept the ideas the coalition is proposing.

Upward Appeal The opening vignette to this chapter mentions that other RCMP officers left the force because of their efforts to uncover pension fund wrongdoing. One of these people was Staff Sergeant Ron Lewis. As the RCMP staff relations representative for headquarters, Lewis had received information before most other people about suspicious activity in human resources, including nepotism and pension fund mismanagement. When RCMP top brass failed to launch an investigation, Lewis threatened to take his information to political leaders and to the public. This tactic, called **upward appeal,** involves calling on people with higher authority or expertise or symbolically relying on these sources to support the influencer's position. Lewis's threat of upward appeal influenced RCMP leaders enough to fire two human resource managers linked to the pension fund scheme, but not enough to

upward appeal
A type of influence in which someone with higher authority or expertise is called on in reality or symbolically to support the influencer's position.

Entering the Reality Distortion Field Wearing his trademark black turtleneck and faded blue jeans, Apple Computer cofounder and CEO Steve Jobs is famous for drawing crowds into his *reality distortion field.* "In his presence, reality is malleable," said Guy "Bud" Tribble (currently Apple's vice president of software technology) to newly hired Andy Hertzfeld in 1981 when Tribble was manager of the original Macintosh development team. "He [Steve Jobs] can convince anyone of practically anything. It wears off when he's not around, but it makes it hard to have realistic schedules." Tribble borrowed the phrase from the TV series *Star Trek* to describe Jobs's overwhelming persuasiveness. More recently, one journalist wrote: "[Reality distortion field] refers, of course, to Jobs's incredible ability to turn anyone—even skeptical reporters—into near-mindless fanboys. Reality distortion wears off, but not before a blizzard of uncritical media coverage of what frequently are routine announcements."[41]

investigate further. Unfortunately for Lewis, when he did take the case to political leaders (including the minister responsible for the RCMP), they apparently took no action.[42]

Along with seeking support from higher sources, another aspect of upward appeal is relying on the authority of the firm's policies or values. By reminding others that your request is consistent with the organization's overarching goals, you are implying support from senior executives without formally involving them.

persuasion
The presentation of facts, logical arguments, and emotional appeals to change another person's attitudes and behavior.

Persuasion **Persuasion** is one of the most effective influence strategies for career success. The ability to present facts, logical arguments, and emotional appeals to change another person's attitudes and behavior is not just an acceptable way to influence others; in many societies, it is a noble art and a quality of effective leaders. The effectiveness of persuasion as an influence tactic depends on characteristics of the persuader, message content, communication medium, and the audience being persuaded.[43] People are more persuasive when listeners believe they have expertise and credibility, such as when the persuader does not seem to profit from the persuasion attempt and states a few points against the position.

The message is more important than the messenger when the issue is important to the audience. Persuasive message content acknowledges several points of view so that the audience does not feel cornered by the speaker. The message should also be limited to a few strong arguments, which are repeated a few times but not too frequently. The message should use emotional appeals (such as graphically showing the unfortunate consequences of a bad decision), but only in combination with logical arguments and specific recommendations to overcome the threat. Finally, message content is more persuasive when the audience is warned about opposing arguments. This **inoculation effect** causes listeners to generate counterarguments to the anticipated persuasion attempts, which makes the opponent's subsequent persuasion attempts less effective.[44]

inoculation effect
A persuasive communication strategy of warning listeners that others will try to influence them in the future and that they should be wary about the opponent's arguments.

Two other considerations when persuading people are the medium of communication and characteristics of the audience. Generally, persuasion works best in face-to-face conversations and through other media-rich communication channels. The personal nature of face-to-face communication increases the persuader's credibility, and the richness of this channel provides faster feedback that the influence strategy is working. With respect to audience characteristics, it is more difficult to persuade people who have high self-esteem and intelligence, as well as those whose targeted attitudes are strongly connected to their self-identity.[45]

ingratiation
Any attempt to increase liking by, or perceived similarity to, some targeted person.

Ingratiation and Impression Management Silent authority, assertiveness, information control, coalitions, and upward appeals are somewhat (or very!) forceful ways to influence other people. In contrast, a very soft influence tactic is **ingratiation**–any attempt to increase liking by, or perceived similarity to, some targeted person.[46] Ingratiation comes in several flavors. Employees might flatter their boss in front of others, demonstrate that they have similar attitudes to those of their boss (e.g., agreeing with the boss's proposal), or ask their boss for advice. Ingratiation is one of the more effective influence tactics at boosting a person's career success (i.e., performance appraisal feedback, salaries, and promotions).[47] However, people who engage in high levels of ingratiation are less (not more) influential and less likely to get promoted.[48] The explanation for the contrasting evidence is that those who engage in too much ingratiation are viewed as insincere and self-serving. The terms "apple polishing" and "brown-nosing" are applied to those who ingratiate to excess or in ways that suggest selfish motives for the ingratiation.

impression management
The practice of actively shaping our public images.

Ingratiation is part of a larger influence tactic known as impression management. **Impression management** is the practice of actively shaping our public images.[49] These public images might be crafted as being important, vulnerable, threatening, or pleasant. For the most part, employees routinely engage in pleasant impression management behaviors to satisfy the basic norms of social behavior, such as the way they dress and how they behave toward colleagues and customers. Impression management is a common strategy for people trying to get ahead in the workplace. In fact, career professionals encourage people to develop a personal "brand," that is, to demonstrate and symbolize a distinctive competitive advantage.[50] Just as running shoes and soft drinks have brand images that represent an expectation, successful individuals build a personal brand in which they deliver valued knowledge or skills. Furthermore, people who are adept at personal branding rely on impression management through distinctive personal characteristics. You can more easily recall people who wear distinctive clothing or accoutrements.

Unfortunately, a few individuals carry impression management beyond ethical boundaries by exaggerating their credentials and accomplishments on their résumé. For instance, a Lucent Technologies executive lied about having a PhD from Stanford University and hid his criminal past involving forgery and embezzlement. Ironically, the executive was Lucent's director of recruiting![51] One of the most elaborate misrepresentations occurred a few years ago when a Singaporean entrepreneur sent out news releases claiming to be a renowned artificial-intelligence researcher, the author of several books, and the recipient of numerous awards from MIT and Stanford University (one of the awards was illustrated on his Web site). These falsehoods were so convincing that the entrepreneur almost received a real award, the "Internet Visionary of the Year," at the Internet World Asia Industry Awards.[52]

Exchange Exchange activities involve the promise of benefits or resources in exchange for the target person's compliance with your request. This tactic also includes reminding the target of past benefits or favors, with the expectation that the target will now make up for that debt. The norm of reciprocity is a central and explicit theme in exchange strategies. According to the norm of reciprocity, individuals are expected to help those who have helped them.[53] Negotiation is also an integral part of exchange influence activities. For instance, you might negotiate with your boss for a day off in return for working a less desirable shift at a future date. Networking is another form of exchange as an influence strategy. Active networkers build up "exchange credits" by helping colleagues in the short term for reciprocal benefits in the long term.

"Our task is to find out what management thinks we should be doing, and then to make management think we're doing it."

Networking as an influence strategy is a deeply ingrained practice in several cultures. The Chinese term *guanxi* refers to special relationships and active interpersonal connectedness. *Guanxi* is based on traditional Confucian values of helping others without expecting future repayment. However, some writers suggest that the original interpretation and practice of *guanxi* has shifted to include implicit long-term reciprocity, which can slip into cronyism. As a result, some Asian governments are discouraging *guanxi*-based decisions, preferring more arm's-length transactions in business and government decisions.[54]

Consequences and Contingencies of Influence Tactics

Now that the main influence strategies have been described, you are probably asking, Which ones are best? The best way to answer this question is to identify the three ways that people react when others try to influence them: resistance, compliance, and commitment.[55] *Resistance* occurs when people or work units oppose the behavior desired by the influencer and, consequently, refuse, argue, or delay engaging in the behavior. *Compliance* occurs when people are motivated to implement the influencer's request at a minimal level of effort and for purely instrumental reasons. Without external sources to motivate the desired behavior, it would not occur. *Commitment* is the strongest form of influence, whereby people identify with the influencer's request and are highly motivated to implement it even when extrinsic sources of motivation are no longer present.

Generally, people react more favorably to soft tactics than to hard tactics (see Exhibit 10.5). Soft influence tactics rely on personal sources of power (expert and referent power), which tend to build commitment to the influencer's request. In contrast, hard tactics rely on position power (legitimate, reward, and coercion), so they tend to produce compliance or, worse, resistance. Hard tactics also tend to undermine trust and thus can hurt future relationships.

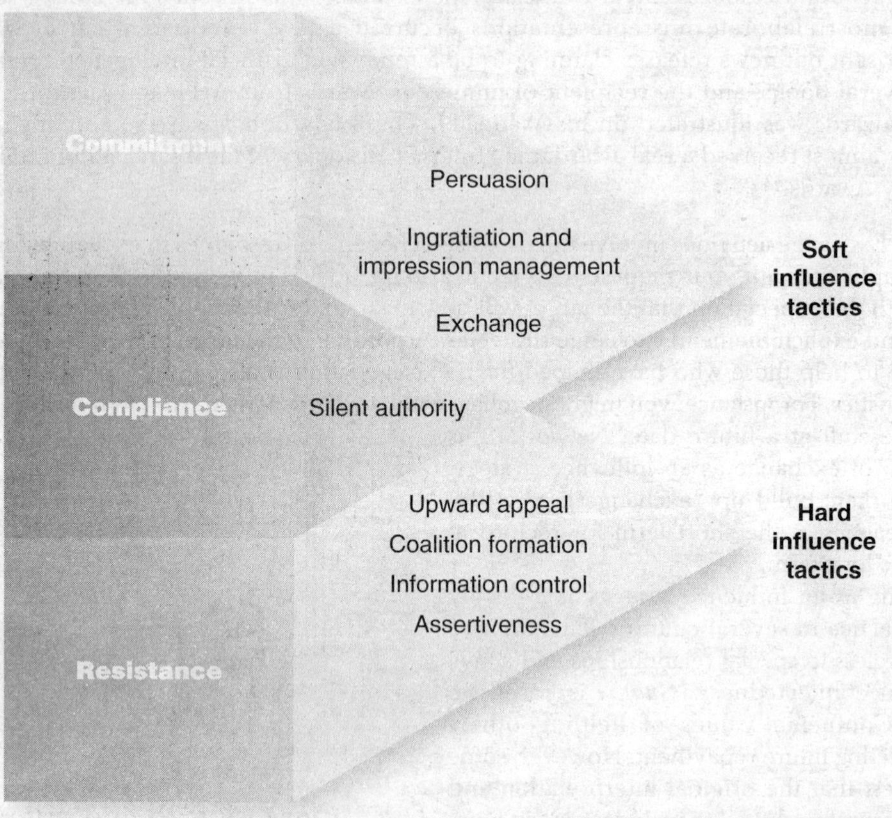

Exhibit 10.5 *Consequences of Hard and Soft Influence Tactics*

Apart from the general preference for soft rather than hard tactics, the most appropriate influence strategy depends on a few contingencies. One obvious contingency is which sources of power are strongest. People with expertise tend to have more influence using persuasion, whereas those with a strong legitimate power base are usually more successful applying silent authority.[56] A second contingency is whether, compared to the influencer, the person being influenced is higher, lower, or at the same level in the organization. As an example, employees may face adverse career consequences by being too assertive with their boss. Meanwhile, supervisors who engage in ingratiation and impression management tend to lose the respect of their staff.

Finally, the most appropriate influence tactic depends on personal, organizational, and cultural values.[57] People with a strong power orientation might feel more comfortable using assertiveness, whereas those who value conformity might feel more comfortable with upward appeals. At an organizational level, firms with a competitive culture might instigate more use of information control and coalition formation, whereas companies with a learning orientation would likely encourage more influence through persuasion. The preferred influence tactics also vary across societal cultures. Research indicates that ingratiation is much more common among managers in the United States than in Hong Kong, possibly because this tactic disrupts the more distant roles that managers and employees expect in high power distance cultures.

Learning Objectives

After reading this section, you should be able to:

8. Distinguish influence from organizational politics.
9. Describe the organizational conditions and personal characteristics that support organizational politics.
10. Identify ways to minimize organizational politics.

Influence Tactics and Organizational Politics

You might have noticed that *organizational politics* has not been mentioned yet, even though some of the practices or examples described over the past few pages are usually considered political tactics. The phrase was carefully avoided because, for the most part, organizational politics is in the eye of the beholder. You might perceive a co-worker's attempt to influence the boss as normal behavior, whereas someone else might perceive the co-worker's tactic as brazen organizational politics.

This perceptual issue explains why OB experts increasingly discuss influence tactics as behaviors and organizational politics as perceptions.[58] The influence tactics described earlier are perceived as **organizational politics** when observers view the tactics as self-serving behaviors at the expense of others and sometimes contrary to the interests of the entire organization or work unit. Of course, some tactics are so blatantly selfish that almost everyone views them as political. But, in most situations, there is no consensus that a person is engaging in organizational politics. When employees perceive many incidents of organizational politics, the result is lower job satisfaction, organizational commitment, and organizational citizenship, as well as high levels of work-related stress.[59] And because political tactics serve individuals rather than organizations, they potentially divert resources away from the organization's effective functioning and potentially threaten its survival.

organizational politics
Behaviors that others perceive as self-serving tactics for personal gain at the expense of other people and possibly the organization.

Gender Differences in Influence Tactics

Men and women seem to differ in their use of influence tactics. Some writers say that men are more likely than women to rely on direct impression management tactics. Specifically, men tend to advertise their achievements and take personal credit for successes of others reporting to them, whereas women are more reluctant to force the spotlight on themselves, preferring instead to share the credit with others. At the same time, women are more likely to apologize, personally take blame, even for problems not caused by them. Men are more likely to assign blame and less likely to assume it.[60]

Some research also suggests that women generally have difficulty in exerting some forms of influence in organizations, and this has limited their promotional opportunities. In particular, women are viewed as less (not more) influential when they try to influence others directly by exerting their authority or expertise. In job interviews, for example, direct and assertive female job applicants were less likely to be hired than were male applicants using the same influence tactics. Similarly, women who directly disagreed in conversations were less influential than women who agreed with the speaker[61]. These findings suggest that women may face problems applying "hard" influence tactics such as assertiveness. Instead, until stereotypes change, women need to rely on softer and more indirect influence strategies, such as ingratiation.

Conditions Supporting Organizational Politics

Organizational politics flourishes under the right conditions.[62] One of those conditions is scarce resources. When budgets are slashed, people rely on political tactics to safeguard their resources and maintain the status quo. Office politics also flourishes when resource allocation decisions are ambiguous or complex or lack formal rules. This is because decision makers are given more discretion over resource allocation, so potential recipients of the resources use political tactics to influence the factors that should be considered in the decision. Organizational change encourages political behaviors for this reason. Change creates uncertainty and ambiguity as the company moves from an old set of rules and practices to a new set. During such times, employees apply political strategies to protect their valued resources, position, and self-concept.[63]

Personal Characteristics

Machiavellian values
The beliefs that deceit is a natural and acceptable way to influence others and that getting more than one deserves is acceptable.

Several personal characteristics affect a person's motivation to engage in self-serving behavior.[64] One such characteristic is a strong need for personal as opposed to socialized power. People with a need for personal power seek power for its own sake and try to acquire more power. Some individuals have strong **Machiavellian values.** Machiavellianism is named after Niccolò Machiavelli, the 16th-century Italian philosopher who wrote *The Prince,* a famous treatise about political behavior. People with high Machiavellian values are comfortable with getting more than they deserve, and they believe that deceit is a natural and acceptable way to achieve this goal. They seldom trust co-workers, and they tend to use cruder influence tactics, such as bypassing one's boss or being assertive, to get their own way.[65]

Minimizing Organizational Politics and Its Consequences The conditions that fuel organizational politics also give us some clues about how to control dysfunctional political activities.[66] One strategy to keep organizational politics in check is to introduce clear rules and regulations to specify the use of scarce resources. Organizational politics can become a problem during times of organizational change, so politics can be minimized through effective organizational change practices. Leaders also need to actively manage group norms to curtail self-serving influence activities. In particular, they can support organizational values that oppose political tactics, such as altruism and customer focus. One of the most important strategies is for leaders to become role models of organizational citizenship rather than symbols of successful organizational politicians.

Along with minimizing organizational politics, companies can limit the adverse effects of political perceptions by giving employees more control over their work and keeping them informed of organizational events. Research has found that employees who are kept informed of what is going on in the organization and who are involved in organizational decisions are less likely to experience organizational politics, which results in less stress, job dissatisfaction, and absenteeism.

Chapter Summary

Power is the capacity to influence others. It exists when one party perceives that he or she is dependent on the other for something of value. However, the dependent person must also have countervailing power—some power over the dominant party—to maintain the relationship.

There are five sources of power. Legitimate power is an agreement among organizational members that people in certain roles can request certain behaviors of others. Reward power is derived from the ability to control the allocation of rewards valued by others and to remove negative sanctions. Coercive power is the ability to apply punishment. Expert power is the capacity to influence others by possessing knowledge or skills that they value. People have referent power when others identify with them, like them, or otherwise respect them. Information plays an important role in organizational power. Employees gain power by controlling the flow of information that others need and by being able to cope with uncertainties related to important organizational goals.

Four contingencies determine whether these sources of power translate into real power. Individuals and work units are more powerful when they are nonsubstitutable, that is, when there is a lack of alternatives. Employees, work units, and organizations reduce substitutability by controlling tasks, knowledge, and labor and by differentiating themselves from competitors. A second contingency is centrality. People have more power when they have high centrality, that is, when the number of people affected is large and people are quickly affected by their actions. Discretion, the third contingency of power, is the freedom to exercise judgment. Power increases when people have freedom to use their power. The fourth contingency, visibility, is the idea that power increases to the extent that a person's or work unit's competencies are known to others.

Social networking involves cultivating social relationships with others to accomplish one's goals. This activity increases an individual's social capital, thereby strengthening expert power, referent power, visibility, and possibly centrality. Power has both beneficial and adverse consequences for individuals. On the positive side, empowerment strengthens their well-being and effectiveness. On the negative side, research indicates that when people become more powerful, their perceptual and decision-making skills can suffer.

Influence is any behavior that attempts to alter someone's attitudes or behavior. The most widely studied influence tactics are silent authority, assertiveness, information control, coalition formation, upward appeal, persuasion, ingratiation and impression management, and exchange. "Soft" influence tactics such as friendly persuasion and subtle ingratiation are more acceptable than "hard" tactics such as upward appeal and assertiveness. However, the most appropriate influence tactic also depends on the influencer's power base; on whether the person being influenced, compared with the influencer, is higher, lower, or at the same level in the organization; and on personal, organizational, and cultural values regarding influence behavior.

Organizational politics consists of influence tactics that observers perceive to be self-serving behaviors at the expense of others and sometimes contrary to the interests of the entire organization or work unit. Organizational politics is more prevalent when scarce resources are allocated using complex and ambiguous decisions and when the organization tolerates or rewards political behavior. Individuals with a high need for personal power and strong Machiavellian values have a higher propensity to use political tactics.

Organizational politics can be minimized by providing clear rules for resource allocation, establishing a free flow of information, using education and involvement during organizational change, supporting team norms and a corporate culture that discourage dysfunctional politics, and having leaders who role-model organizational citizenship rather than political savvy.

Key Terms

centrality
coalition
countervailing power
impression management
influence
ingratiation
inoculation effect
legitimate power
Machiavellian values
organizational politics
persuasion
power
referent power
social capital
substitutability
upward appeal

Critical Thinking Questions

1. What role does countervailing power play in the power relationship? Give an example of your own encounter with countervailing power at school or work.
2. Several years ago, the Major League Baseball Players Association went on strike in September, just before the World Series started. The players' contract expired at the beginning of the season (May), but they held off the strike until September when they would lose only one-sixth of their salaries. In contrast, a September strike would hurt the owners financially because they earn a larger portion of their revenue during the playoffs. As one player explained: "If we strike next spring, there's nothing stopping [the club owners] from letting us go until next June or July because they don't have that much at stake." Use your knowledge of the sources and contingencies of power to explain why the baseball players association had more power in negotiations by walking out in September rather than March.
3. You have just been hired as a brand manager of toothpaste for a large consumer products company. Your job mainly involves encouraging the advertising and production groups to promote and manufacture your product more effectively. These departments aren't under your direct authority, although company procedures indicate that they must complete certain tasks requested by brand managers. Describe the sources of power you can use to ensure that the advertising and production departments will help you make and sell toothpaste more effectively.
4. How does social networking increase a person's power? What social networking strategies could you initiate now to potentially enhance your future career success?
5. List the eight influence tactics described in this chapter in terms of how they are used by students to influence their course instructors. Which influence tactic is applied most often? Which is applied least often, in your opinion? To what extent is each influence tactic considered legitimate behavior or organizational politics?
6. How do cultural differences affect the following influence factors: (a) silent authority and (b) upward appeal?
7. A few years ago, the CEO of Apple Computer invited Steve Jobs (who was not associated with the company at the time) to serve as a special adviser and raise morale among Apple employees and customers. While doing this, Jobs spent more time advising the CEO on how to cut costs, redraw the organization chart, and hire new people. Before long, most of the top people at Apple were Jobs's colleagues, who began to systematically evaluate and weed out teams of Apple employees. While publicly supporting Apple's CEO, Jobs privately criticized him and, in a show of nonconfidence, sold 1.5 million shares of Apple stock he had received. This action caught the attention of Apple's board of directors, who soon after decided to replace the CEO with Steve Jobs. The CEO claimed Jobs was a conniving backstabber who used political tactics to get his way. Others suggest that Apple would be out of business today if he hadn't taken over the company. In your opinion, were Steve Jobs's actions examples of organizational politics? Justify your answer.
8. This book frequently emphasizes that successful companies engage in organizational learning. How do political tactics interfere with organizational learning objectives?

CASE STUDY 10.1

THE RISE AND FALL OF WORLDCOM

Bernie Ebbers built WorldCom, Inc. (now part of Verizon, Inc.) into one of the world's largest telecommunications firms. Yet he and chief financial officer (CFO) Scott Sullivan have become better known for creating a massive corporate accounting fraud that led to the largest bankruptcy in U.S. history. Two investigative reports and subsequent court cases concluded that WorldCom executives were responsible for billions in fraudulent or unsupported accounting entries. How did this mammoth accounting scandal occur without anyone raising the alarm? Evidence suggests that Ebbers and Sullivan held considerable power and influence that prevented accounting staff from complaining, or even knowing, about the fraud.

Ebbers's inner circle held tight control over the flow of all financial information. The geographically dispersed accounting groups were discouraged from sharing information. Ebbers's group also restricted distribution of company-level financial reports and prevented sensitive reports from being prepared at all. Accountants didn't even have access to the computer files in which some of the largest fraudulent entries were made. As a result, employees had to rely on Ebbers's executive team to justify the accounting entries that were requested.

Another reason why employees complied with questionable accounting practices was that CFO Scott Sullivan wielded immense personal power. He was considered a "whiz kid" with impeccable integrity who had won the prestigious "CFO Excellence Award." Thus, when Sullivan's office asked staff to make questionable entries, some accountants assumed Sullivan had found an innovative–and legal–accounting loophole. If Sullivan's influence didn't work, other executives took a more coercive approach. Employees cited incidents where they were publicly berated for questioning headquarters' decisions and intimidated if they asked for more information. When one employee at a branch refused to alter an accounting entry, WorldCom's controller threatened to fly in from WorldCom's Mississippi headquarters to make the change himself. The employee changed the entry.

Ebbers had similar influence over WorldCom's board of directors. Sources indicate that his personal charisma and intolerance of dissension produced a passive board that rubber-stamped most of his recommendations. As one report concluded: "The Board of Directors appears to have embraced suggestions by Mr. Ebbers without question or dissent, even under circumstances where its members now readily acknowledge they had significant misgivings regarding his recommended course of action."

Discussion Questions

1. What power bases did Bernie Ebbers and Scott Sullivan rely on to get away with accounting fraud?
2. What influence tactics did Bernie Ebbers and Scott Sullivan use to control employees and the company's board?
3. Did Bernie Ebbers and Scott Sullivan engage in organizational politics? Explain your answer.

Sources: U.S. Bankruptcy Court, Southern District of New York, *In Re: WorldCom, Inc., et al., Debtors,* Chapter 11 Case No. 02-15533 (AJG), Jointly Administered Second Interim Report of Dick Thornburgh, Bankruptcy Court Examiner, June 9, 2003; Report of Investigation by the Special Investigative Committee of the Board of Directors of WorldCom, Inc., Dennis R. Beresford, Nicholas deB. Katzenbach, C. B. Rogers, Jr., Counsel, Wilmer, Cutler & Pickering, Accounting Advisors, PricewaterhouseCoopers LLP, March 31, 2003. Also see T. Catan et al., "Before the Fall," *Financial Times* (London), 19 December 2002, p. 17; J. O'Donnell and A. Backover, "Ebbers' High-Risk Act Came Crashing Down on Him," *USA Today,* 12 December

2002, p. B1; C. Stern, "Ebbers Dominated Board, Report Says," *Washington Post,* 5 November 2002, p. E1; D. S. Hilzenrath, "How a Distinguished Roster of Board Members Failed to Detect Company's Problems," *Washington Post,* 16 June 2003, p. E1; S. Pulliam and A. Latour, "Lost Connection," *Wall Street Journal,* 12 January 2005, p. A1; S. Rosenbush, "Five Lessons of the WorldCom Debacle," *BusinessWeek Online,* 16 March 2005.

CASE STUDY 10.2

RHONDA CLARK: TAKING CHARGE AT THE SMITH FOUNDATION

Joseph C. Santora, Essex County College and TST, Inc.

Dr. Rhonda Clark was ecstatic as she hung up the telephone. Bennett Mitchell, chairperson of KLS Executive Search firm, had just informed her that she landed the coveted position of chief executive officer (CEO) at the Smith Foundation, a nonprofit organization whose mission was to fund public awareness campaigns and research programs about eye care. Clark knew that she had just pulled off a major coup. Her appointment to this new, challenging position would indeed be *the* high point in a long, arduous climb to the executive suite. As an organizational outsider–one with no work experience within the hiring organization–she assumed that her appointment as CEO signaled a strong desire by the board to shake up the organizational status quo. However, she heard from a very reliable inside source that the very board that hired her and charged her with the responsibility of transforming the foundation was extremely fragmented. The often-rambunctious board had forced the last five CEOs to resign after very short tenures. Clark's feeling of exhilaration was rapidly being replaced by cautious optimism. As a new CEO, she pondered the rather thorny question: How could she take charge of the board of directors to ensure the mission of the organization would be accomplished?

Background

Charlie Smith, an industrialist and philanthropist, founded the Smith Foundation 40 years ago with a multimillion-dollar endowment. Despite this generous financial start-up capital and additional income derived from several financial investments and major corporate donations, in recent years the foundation's endowment has been slowly dwindling as a result of rather significant funding awards to academics, community organizations, and smaller, less well-funded foundations. Board members have held some preliminary discussions about developing new innovative strategies to strengthen the balance sheet of the organization. Currently, the foundation operates on an annual budget of slightly less than $1,500,000 (USD).

In the last five years, some foundation board members have begun to abandon many of their fiduciary responsibilities. Over the past few months, several board meetings have been canceled because the meetings lacked a quorum. In general, this 13-member board seemed to drift aimlessly in one direction or another. The board has been operating at only 70 percent capacity for the past two years with nine active board members–five men and four women.

Challenges

Dr. Rhonda Clark believed she was the one who could lead the Smith Foundation. She had great academic credentials and management experience that would help her tackle her new position as the foundation head. In the last 30 years, the 54-year old Clark, who holds a PhD in political science and policy analysis from a major U.S. West Coast university, has gained an enviable amount of managerial experience in the nonprofit and public sectors. Past professional experiences included being a graduate school professor, a director of research for a major statewide political office holder, the director of planning in a large metropolitan hospital, and the director of programs at a small foundation.

Immediately upon taking office, Clark was astounded to learn that a small, but active and influential, faction on the board had withdrawn its initial verbal promise to assist her in working closely with the corporate community. Essentially, she was informed that she was solely responsible for all external corporate relations. Clark thought to herself, "I wonder if they hired me because they thought they would get a 'do-nothing' female leader. These folks want me to either sink or swim on my own. Perhaps they set me up for failure by giving me a one-year appointment." She lamented: "I won't let this happen. I really need to learn about the key decision makers and stakeholders on the board and in the larger community, and fast."

At the last board meeting, Clark detailed the major elements of her latest proposal. Yet several board members seemed totally unfazed by it. Soon she began to encounter stiff resistance from some male board members. Jim Jackson, in particular, told Clark: "We are disappointed that you failed to win a city contract to conduct a feasibility study to determine if we can erect a facility in another section of town. We're not certain if you have the right stuff to run this foundation, and we certainly won't help you to gain financial support for the foundation by using our personal, corporate, or political contacts." Jackson thought to himself: "We've removed CEOs before, we can remove Clark, too."

After hearing Jackson's comments, Clark decided to take another tack. She began to focus her attention on making external and internal inroads which she believed could result in some modest gains for the foundation. For example, she identified and developed a close relationship with a few well-connected city agency executives, persuaded some supporters to nominate her for membership on two very influential boards, and forged a relationship with two key foundation decision makers and political power brokers. She reconfigured the internal structure of the foundation to increase maximum productivity from the staff, and she tightened budgetary controls by changing some fiscal policies and procedures.

Clark also sought the support of Susan Frost, a board member who likely had been instrumental in Clark's appointment as CEO. Clark said to herself, "If I can develop a strong symbiotic relationship with some female board members, like Sue, to support my plan, then maybe I'll get some traction." To do this, Clark held a number of late-evening meetings with Sue and another female board member. They indicated their willingness to help her, but only if she would consider implementing a few of their ideas for the foundation as well as recommending their close friend for a current staff vacancy. Clark knew they were trying to exercise their political influence, yet she believed that everyone could benefit from this *quid pro quo* relationship. She said to herself, "I guess it's a matter of you scratch my back, and I scratch yours." She eagerly agreed to move their agenda along. In a matter of a few weeks, as promised, they began working on a couple of relatively "sympathetic" board members. One day Clark got a very terse but crucial telephone call from Sue. "Several of us support you. Proceed!"

Once she heard this, Clark began to move at lightning speed. She formed a 15-member coalition of community, educational, and quasi-governmental agencies that would apply for a collaborative federal grant to create a public awareness eye campaign for children. Through the dissemination of various media, coalition members would help to inform the community-at-large about various eye diseases that afflict young, school-age children. Shortly afterward, Clark received notification from a federal agency that this multiagency project would be awarded a million-dollar grant. Clark would serve as the administrative and fiscal agent of the grant, and, as a result, she would be able to earmark a considerable amount of the administrative oversight dollars for the foundation's budget. For her efforts at coordinating this project, Clark received high marks from coalition and community members alike.

Yet, despite this important initial accomplishment, Clark had the unpleasant task of notifying the full board that, due to some unforeseen problems and their lack of support on certain key initiatives, the foundation would still experience a financial deficit. She heard several rumors that her next employment contract would not be renewed by the executive committee of the board. At this point she thought about directly confronting the obstructionists on the board by telling them that they were unreasonable and, in fact, that they were the cause of the foundation's not recovering during the past year . . . but she hesitated: She had signed on to do a job, and she was unsure if this was the wisest course of action to take at this time.

Despite this latest conflict between her and certain board members, she paused to reflect on what she believed to have been a tumultuous year as CEO.

Discussion Questions

1. Does Clark have any sources of power and any contingencies of power? If so, list and discuss them.
2. To what degree were Clark's methods of influencing board members the most effective possible under the circumstances presented in the case?
3. Do you think her methods of getting things done at the foundation were ethical? Why or why not?

Note: The names and some managerial actions in this case have been altered to preserve the integrity and anonymity of the organization. This case is intended to be used as a basis for class discussion rather than to illustrate either effective or ineffective handling of a management situation.

CASE STUDY 10.3

SHAKING UP OXFORD

BusinessWeek

John Hood may be soft-spoken, but the New Zealand–born vice-chancellor of Oxford University shows flashes of the steely determination that first convinced Oxford's search committee to hire him to give the place a top-to-bottom management overhaul. Hood's decisive actions have created few friends among the scholars, but he claims he is merely working in the university community's best interests. "I am here as the servant of the scholars," says Hood. "One has no power or authority in this job."

This *BusinessWeek* case study describes the changes that John Hood is making at Oxford and how academics at the British university are responding to those changes. The article looks at Hood's influence strategies, the methods used by Oxford's professors to resist those changes, and some of the politics of change that has occurred. Read the full text of this *BusinessWeek* article at www.mhhe.com/mcshane5e, and prepare for the discussion questions below.

Discussion Questions

1. John Hood claims that he has no power or authority in his job. Is he correct? What sources of power work for and against him during this change process?
2. What influence tactics has Hood used that are most apparent in this case study?
3. What influence tactics have professors and other stakeholders used to resist Hood's changes? Would you call any of these influence tactics "organizational politics"?

Source: S. Reed, "Shaking Up Oxford," *BusinessWeek,* 5 December 2005, p. 48.

TEAM EXERCISE 10.4

BUDGET DELIBERATIONS

Sharon Card

PURPOSE This exercise is designed to help you understand some of the power dynamics and influence tactics that occur across hierarchical levels in organizations.

MATERIALS This activity works best where one small room leads to a larger room, which leads to a larger area.

INSTRUCTIONS These exercise instructions are based on a class size of about 30 students. The instructor may adjust the size of the first two groups slightly for larger classes. The instructor will organize students as follows: A few (three or four) students are assigned the positions of executives. They are preferably located in a secluded office or corner of a large classroom. Another six to eight students are assigned positions as middle managers. These people will ideally be located in an adjoining room or space, allowing privacy for the executives. The remaining students represent the nonmanagement employees in the organization. They are located in an open area outside the executive and management rooms.

RULES Members of the executive group are free to enter the space of either the middle-management or nonmanagement groups and to communicate whatever they wish, whenever they wish. Members of the middle-management group may enter the space of the nonmanagement group whenever they wish, but they must request permission to enter the executive group's space. The executive group can refuse the middle-management group's request. Members of the nonmanagement group are not allowed to disturb the top group in any way unless specifically invited by members of the executive group. The nonmanagement group does have the right to request permission to communicate with the middle-management group. The middle-management group can refuse the lower group's request.

TASK Your organization is in the process of preparing a budget. The challenge is to balance needs with financial resources. Of course, the needs are greater than the resources. The instructor will distribute a budget sheet showing a list of budget requests and their costs. Each group has control over a portion of the budget and must decide how to spend the money over which they have control. Nonmanagement has discretion over a relatively small portion, and the executive group has discretion over the greatest portion. The exercise is finished when the organization has negotiated a satisfactory budget or when the instructor calls time-out. The class will then debrief with the following questions and others the instructor might ask.

Discussion Questions

1. What can we learn from this exercise about power in organizational hierarchies?
2. How is this exercise similar to relations in real organizations?
3. How did students in each group feel about the amount of power they held?
4. How did they exercise their power in relations with the other groups?

SELF-ASSESSMENT 10.5

GUANXI ORIENTATION SCALE

Guanxi, which is translated as "interpersonal connections," is an important element of doing business in China and some other Asian countries with strong Confucian cultural values. *Guanxi* is based on traditional Confucian values of helping others without expecting future repayment. This instrument estimates your *guanxi* orientation, that is, the extent to which you accept and apply *guanxi* values. This self-assessment should be completed alone so that you can rate yourself honestly without concerns of social comparison. Class discussion will focus on the meaning of *guanxi* and its relevance for organizational power and influence.

SELF-ASSESSMENT 10.6

MACHIAVELLIANISM SCALE

Machiavellianism is named after Niccolò Machiavelli, the 16th-century Italian philosopher who wrote *The Prince,* a famous treatise about political behavior. Out of Machiavelli's work emerged this instrument that estimates the degree to which you have a Machiavellian personality. Indicate the extent to which you agree or disagree that each statement in this instrument describes you. Complete each item honestly to get the best estimate of your level of Machiavellianism.

SELF-ASSESSMENT 10.7

PERCEPTIONS OF POLITICS SCALE (POPS)

Organizations have been called "political arenas"–environments where political tactics are common because decisions are ambiguous and resources are scarce. This instrument estimates the degree to which you believe the school where you attend classes has a politicized culture. The scale consists of several statements that might or might not describe your school. The statements refer to the administration of the school, not the classroom. Please indicate the extent to which you agree or disagree with each statement.

To reward themselves for a job well done, a team of young employees at Western Technical College like to create funny mock videos or throw a pizza party during office hours. Those events bother some older staff at the La Crosse, Wisconsin, school. This conflict comes as no surprise to Linda Gravett. "We had a sense that there was tension," says Gravett, a human resource consultant at Xavier University in Cincinnati. Gravett and colleague Robin Throckmorton identified many forms of intergenerational conflict in their recent book on that subject. "This was confirmed in our research. We found there was a lot of generational tension around the use of technology and work ethics."

Technologically savvy and ambitious, Generation-X and -Y employees' attributes and attitudes toward work have the potential to induce generational conflicts in the workplace.

Some writers claim that Generation-X and -Y employees (those born after 1964) are not that different from their baby-boomer counterparts (born between 1946 and 1964). For example, some surveys report that both younger and older generations share similar values and needs. However, differences do occur in each generation's norms and expectations, such as regarding work behavior and attire, and these differences are sometimes interpreted critically by people in the other age group. "As offices go, the editorial suites at Time Inc. are pretty laid back," claims editor Dan Kadlec. "Yet there's a limit to what passes for acceptable appearance, and I was sure a recent bunch of college interns had breached it spectacularly with their nose rings, tattoos and low-rise pants. These were bright, ambitious kids. Why the blatant show of disrespect?"

To help minimize these conflicts, Ernst & Young introduced a special program that alerts new hires to multigenerational differences. One topic, "Strategies to Connect with Baby Boomers," offers the following advice: It is probably not a good time to request time off, even for a volunteer commitment, just after your boss says that the members of his or her team of young staff are "spending too much time text-messaging each other and listening to iPods."[1]

11

Conflict and Negotiation in the Workplace

Learning Objectives

After reading this chapter, you should be able to:

1. Debate the positive and negative consequences of conflict in the workplace.
2. Distinguish constructive conflict from relationship conflict.
3. Describe three strategies for minimizing relationship conflict during constructive-conflict episodes.
4. Diagram the conflict process model.
5. Identify six structural sources of conflict in organizations.
6. Outline the five conflict-handling styles and discuss the circumstances in which each would be most appropriate.
7. Summarize six structural approaches to managing conflict.
8. Outline four situational influences on negotiations.
9. Describe four skills of effective negotiators.
10. Compare and contrast the three types of third-party dispute resolution.

One of the facts of life is that people hold different points of view. They have unique values hierarchies, develop unique perceptions of reality, and establish different norms about how to act in social settings. At the same time, organizations are living systems that demand dynamic, rather than static, relationships among employees. In other words, employees at Ernst & Young, Western Technical College, Time, and other organizations need to frequently agree on new work arrangements, revise the company's strategic direction, and renegotiate the allocation of scarce resources required to perform their jobs.

conflict
A process in which one party perceives that his or her interests are being opposed or negatively affected by another party.

Without identical viewpoints, and with the need to frequently adjust to change, conflict is bound to occur. **Conflict** is a process in which one party perceives that his or her interests are being opposed or negatively affected by another party.[2] It may occur when one party obstructs or plans to obstruct another's goals in some way. For example, a baby-boomer manager experiences conflict with Gen-X or Gen-Y employees who spend time text messaging because the manager believes that this practice interferes with her goal of completing departmental deadlines on time. Text-messaging employees experience conflict with their boss because they view this form of communication as a valuable way to network, keep informed, and (contrary to the boss's opinion) achieve departmental objectives. Conflict is ultimately based on perceptions; it exists whenever one party *believes* that another might obstruct his or her efforts, whether or not the other party actually intends to do so.

This chapter investigates the dynamics of conflict in organizational settings. We begin by considering the age-old question "Is conflict good or bad?" Next, we describe the conflict process and examine in detail the main factors that cause or amplify conflict. The five styles of handling conflict are then described, followed by a discussion of the structural approaches to conflict management. The last two sections of this chapter introduce two procedures for resolving conflict: negotiation and third-party resolution.

Learning Objectives

After reading the next two sections, you should be able to:

1. Debate the positive and negative consequences of conflict in the workplace.
2. Distinguish constructive conflict from relationship conflict.
3. Describe three strategies for minimizing relationship conflict during constructive-conflict episodes.
4. Diagram the conflict process model.

Is Conflict Good or Bad?

For at least the past century, and likely much longer, experts have been debating whether conflict is good or bad for organizational effectiveness. The *conflict-is-bad perspective* has prevailed for most of that time.[3] Exhibit 11.1(*a*) illustrates this view; the downward line shows that as the level of conflict increases, it produces more adverse outcomes. According to this perspective, even moderately low levels of disagreement tatter the fabric of workplace relations and sap energy away from productive activities. Conflict with one's supervisor not only wastes productive time but also violates the hierarchy of command and questions the efficient assignment of authority (in which managers made the decisions and employees followed them).

Although the conflict-is-bad perspective is now considered oversimplistic, numerous studies report that conflict can potentially undermine team cohesion, information sharing, decision making, and employee well-being (increased stress and lower job satisfaction). It also seems to distort perceptions and increase organizational politics.[4] Conflict distracts employees from their work and, in some cases,

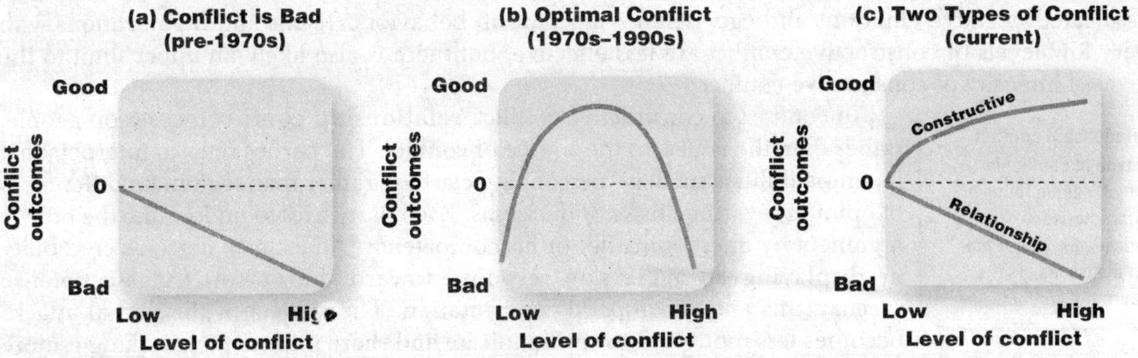

Exhibit 11.1 *Past and Present Perspectives of Conflict*

motivates them to withhold valuable knowledge and other resources. People who experience conflict are less motivated to communicate or try to understand the other party, and this further escalates conflict as each side relies increasingly on distorted perceptions and stereotypes. One survey estimates that 42 percent of a manager's time is spent dealing with workplace conflict and that conflict triggers most voluntary and involuntary employee turnover.[5]

More than 80 years ago, social worker and political science scholar Mary Parker Follett proposed the then-radical notion that conflict can be beneficial.[6] Her ideas were slow to gain support. By the 1970s, however, the conflict-is-bad perspective had been replaced by the *optimal-conflict perspective,* which holds that organizations are most effective when employees experience some level of conflict in discussions but that organizations become less effective when they have high levels of conflict. The belief that companies should have neither too little nor too much conflict, which is illustrated by the upside-down U-shaped relationship in Exhibit 11.1(*b*), remains popular today.[7]

Many studies support Follett's groundbreaking thesis that a moderate level of conflict is good. One outcome is improved decision making. Conflict energizes people to debate issues and evaluate alternatives more thoroughly. The debate tests the logic of arguments and encourages participants to reexamine their basic assumptions about the problem and its possible solution. Another apparent benefit of moderate conflict is that it prevents organizations from stagnating and becoming nonresponsive to their external environment. This reflects our earlier observation that conflict occurs in organizations because they are living systems. Moderate levels of conflict are inevitable and necessary as employees try to keep the organization responsive to the needs of customers and other stakeholders.[8] A third benefit, which we discussed in the chapter on teams, is that conflict with people outside the team potentially increases cohesion within the team. People are more motivated to work together when faced with an external threat, such as conflict with people outside the team.

The Emerging View: Constructive and Relationship Conflict

constructive conflict
A type of conflict in which people focus their discussion on the issue while maintaining respect for people having other points of view.

The upside-down U-shaped model of conflict was replaced in the 1990s by the perspective that there are two types of conflict with opposing consequences [see Exhibit 11.1(*c*)].[9] **Constructive conflict** occurs when people focus their discussion on the issue while showing respect for people with other points of view. This conflict is called "constructive" because different positions are encouraged so that ideas and recommendations can be clarified, redesigned, and tested for logical soundness. Keeping the debate focused on the issue helps participants reexamine their assumptions and beliefs without triggering the drive to defend and its associated negative emotions and ego–defense mechanism behaviors. Teams and organizations with very low levels of constructive conflict are less effective, but there is also likely an upper limit to the level of intensity of constructive conflict.[10]

relationship conflict
A type of conflict in which people focus on characteristics of other individuals, rather than on the issues, as the source of conflict.

In contrast to constructive conflict, **relationship conflict** focuses on people, rather than the issues, as the source of conflict. The parties refer to interpersonal incompatibilities such as "personality clashes" rather than legitimate differences of opinion regarding tasks or decisions. Each party tries to undermine the other's argument by questioning her or his competency. Attacking a person's credibility or displaying an aggressive response toward the person triggers defense mechanisms and a competitive orientation. The subject of the verbal attacks becomes less motivated to communicate and share information, making it more difficult for the parties to discover common ground and ultimately resolve the conflict. Instead, they increasingly rely on more distorted perceptions and stereotypes, and this, as we noted earlier, tends to further escalate the conflict. Relationship conflict is sometimes called *socioemotional* or *affective* conflict because people experience and react to strong emotional responses during such conflict episodes.

Separating Constructive Conflict from Relationship Conflict The current perspective that there are two types of conflict leads to the logical conclusion that we should encourage constructive conflict and minimize relationship conflict. This recommendation sounds good in theory, but recent evidence suggests that separating these two types of conflict isn't easy. Most of us experience some degree of relationship conflict during and after any constructive debate.[11] In other words, any attempt to engage in constructive conflict, no matter how calmly and rationally, may still sow the seeds of relationship conflict. The stronger the level of debate and the more the issue is tied to the individual's self-concept, the higher the chance that the constructive conflict will evolve into (or mix with) relationship conflict. As Connections 11.1 describes, even though Intel staff are taught the fine art of constructive debate, many of them experience relationship conflict.

Fortunately, conflict management experts have identified three strategies that potentially minimize the level of relationship conflict during constructive-conflict episodes:[12]

- *Emotional intelligence.* Relationship conflict is less likely to occur, or is less likely to escalate, when team members have high levels of emotional intelligence. Emotionally intelligent employees are better able to regulate their emotions during debate, thus reducing the risk of escalating perceptions of interpersonal hostility. People with high emotional intelligence are also more likely to view a co-worker's emotional reaction as valuable information about that person's needs and expectations, rather than as a personal attack.
- *Cohesive team.* Relationship conflict is suppressed when the conflict occurs within a highly cohesive team. The longer people work together, get to know each other, and develop mutual trust, the more latitude they give each other to show emotions without being personally offended. Strong cohesion also allows each person to know about and anticipate the behaviors and emotions of teammates. Another benefit is that cohesion produces a stronger social identity with the group, so team members are motivated to avoid escalating relationship conflict during otherwise emotionally turbulent discussions.
- *Supportive team norms.* Various team norms can hold relationship conflict at bay during constructive debate. When team norms encourage openness, for instance, team members learn to appreciate honest dialogue without personally reacting to any emotional display during the disagreements.[13] Other norms might discourage team members from displaying negative emotions toward co-workers. Team norms also encourage tactics that diffuse relationship conflict when it first appears. For instance, research has found that teams with low relationship conflict use humor to maintain positive group emotions, thereby offsetting negative feelings team members might develop toward some co-workers during debate.

11.1 CONNECTIONS

Constructive Confrontation inside Intel

Constructive conflict is part of Intel's culture, but some people say the computer-chip maker's task-focused discussion descends into relationship conflict.

Former Goldman Sachs president John Thornton has had his share of executive debates, but even he was surprised by the animated discussion that permeates Intel, the chip maker, where Thornton is a member of the board. "It can be kind of shocking at first," says Thornton, recalling his first few Intel meetings. "You realize quickly that [Intel managers] practice a form of honesty that borders on brutality." Intel cofounder and former chairman Andy Grove nurtured this culture of conflict—called constructive confrontation—many years ago when he noticed that meetings generate better ideas when staff actively debate, rather than politely defer to, ideas that others put forward. The practice is so important that new Intel employees are taught the fine art of confrontation through supervised debates and role plays.

Andy Grove emphasizes that conflict is constructive only under specific circumstances. "Constructive confrontation does not mean being loud, unpleasant or rude, and it is not designed to affix blame," warns Grove. "The essence of it is to attack a problem by speaking up in a businesslike way." If you target the other person, the benefits of constructive debate disintegrate. But some people claim that Intel's constructive confrontation never was very constructive. Instead, like John Thornton, some staff also experience a heavy dose of relationship conflict. "I can tell you unequivocally that constructive confrontation was a license for a**holes to be a**holes and express themselves," says former Intel employee Logan Shrine, who coauthored a book with Bob Coleman on Intel's changing culture. "Intel's culture is dysfunctional and anomalous to what's considered acceptable behavior in any other corporation."[14]

Learning Objectives

After reading the next three sections, you should be able to:

5. Identify six structural sources of conflict in organizations.
6. Outline the five conflict-handling styles and discuss the circumstances in which each would be most appropriate.
7. Summarize six structural approaches to managing conflict.

CONFLICT PROCESS MODEL

Now that we have outlined the history of and current knowledge about conflict and its outcomes, let's look at the model of the conflict process, shown in Exhibit 11.2.[15] This model begins with the sources of conflict, which we will describe in more detail in the next section. At some point, the sources of conflict lead one or both parties to perceive that conflict exists. One (or each) party becomes aware that the other party's statements and actions are incompatible with his or her own goals. Such perceptions usually interact with emotions experienced about the conflict.[16] Conflict perceptions and emotions manifest themselves in the decisions and behaviors of one party toward the other. These *conflict episodes* may range from subtle nonverbal behaviors to warlike aggression. Particularly when

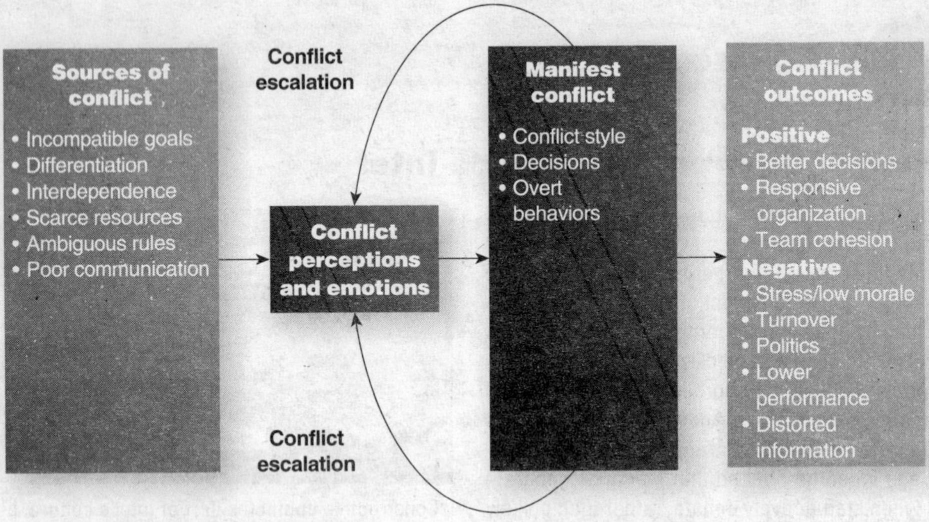

Exhibit 11.2 *Model of the Conflict Process*

people experience high levels of conflict emotions, they have difficulty finding the words and expressions that communicate effectively without further irritating the relationship.[17] Conflict is also manifested by the style each side uses to resolve the conflict. Some people tend to avoid the conflict, whereas others try to defeat those with opposing views.

Exhibit 11.2 shows arrows looping back from manifest conflict to conflict perceptions and emotions. These arrows illustrate that the conflict process is really a series of episodes that potentially cycle into conflict escalation.[18] It doesn't take much to start this conflict cycle–just an inappropriate comment, a misunderstanding, or an action that lacks diplomacy. These behaviors cause the other party to perceive that conflict exists. Even if the first party did not intend to demonstrate conflict, the second party's response may create the perception that conflict exists.

Conflict Perceptions and Emotions

At some point the sources of conflict lead one or both parties to perceive that a conflict exists. They become aware that one party's statements and actions are incompatible with their own goals. These perceptions usually interact with emotions experienced about the conflict. Infighting at Microsoft is likely stoked with emotions, such as the anger employees experience when they work late completing monthly performance reports for the management rather than spending more time meeting customers. "Instead of promoting the product to customers, I'd get stuck in the office until midnight preparing slides for my monthly product review," complains a frustrated Windows XP marketing employee.[19]

Manifest Conflict

Conflict perceptions and emotions usually manifest themselves in the decisions and overt behaviors of one party toward the other. These conflict episodes may range from subtle nonverbal behaviors to warlike aggression. Particularly when people experience high levels of conflict emotions, they have difficulty finding words and expressions that communicate effectively without further irritating the relationship.[20] Conflict is also manifested by the style each side uses to resolve the conflict. Some people tend to avoid the conflict, whereas others try to defeat those with opposing views. Conflict management styles will be described later in this chapter. At this point you should know

Constructive Confrontation Inside Intel Former Goldman Sachs president John Thornton has had his share of executive debates, but even he was surprised after joining the board of Intel Corp. regarding the "constructive confrontation" that permeates the chipmaker's culture. "It can be kind of shocking at first," says Thornton. "You realize quickly that [Intel managers] practice a form of honesty that borders on brutality." Intel cofounder and former chairman Andy Grove nurtured constructive confrontation many years ago when he noticed that meetings generate better ideas when staff actively debate rather than politely defer to ideas that others put forward. But Grove emphasizes that this conflict is constructive only under specific circumstances. "Constructive confrontation does not mean being loud, unpleasant, or rude, and it is not designed to affix blame," warns Grove. "The essence of it is to attack a problem by speaking up in a businesslike way." Intel also holds confrontation training seminars to help staff become more comfortable with the brutal honesty in its meetings.[21]

that these styles influence the other party's perceptions and actions regarding the conflict, which then either defuse or further escalate the conflict.

Conflict Escalation Cycle The conflict process in Exhibit 11.2 shows arrows looping back from manifest conflict to conflict perceptions and emotions. These loops represent the fact that the conflict process is really a series of episodes that potentially link in an escalation cycle or spiral.[22] It doesn't take much to start this conflict cycle–just an inappropriate comment, a misunderstanding, or an action that lacks diplomacy. These behaviors communicate to the other party in a way that creates a perception of conflict. If the first party did not intend to demonstrate conflict, the second party's response may create that perception.

If the conflict remains focused on perceptions, both parties can often resolve the conflict through logical analysis. However, the communication process has enough ambiguity that a wrong look or word may trigger strong emotions and set the stage for further conflict escalation. These distorted beliefs and emotions reduce each side's motivation to communicate, making it more difficult for them to discover common ground and ultimately resolve the conflict. The parties then rely more on stereotypes and emotions to reinforce their perceptions of the other party. Some structural conditions increase the likelihood of conflict escalation. Employees who are more confrontational and less diplomatic also tend to escalate conflict.[23]

Conflict Outcomes

Recent events at Microsoft illustrate some of the dysfunctional consequences of conflict: delayed product releases because one group obstructs another group's product launch; restricted flow of information across divisions; and lower morale and higher turnover of key employees. Employees are often distracted from their work by internal feuds and, in some cases, engage in dysfunctional behaviors such as withholding valuable knowledge and other resources. Ongoing conflict also increases stress and turnover while reducing organizational commitment and job satisfaction. At the intergroup level, conflict with people outside the team may cause the team to become more insular–increasing their cohesiveness while distancing themselves from outsiders who are critical of the team's past decisions.[24]

Structural Sources of Conflict in Organizations

The conflict model starts with the sources of conflict, so we need to understand these sources to effectively diagnose conflict episodes and subsequently resolve the conflict or occasionally to generate conflict where it is lacking. The six main conditions that cause conflict in organizational settings are incompatible goals, differentiation, interdependence, scarce resources, ambiguous rules, and communication problems (see Exhibit 11.3).

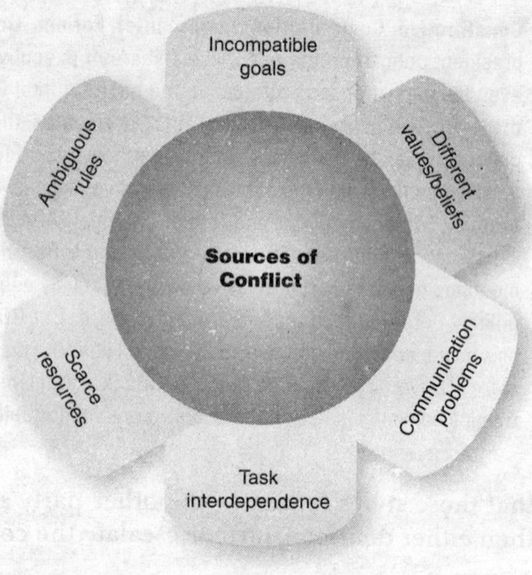

Exhibit 11.3 *Sources of Conflict in Organizations*

Incompatible Goals

Microsoft Corp. has been highly successful with its host of products and services, yet various sources conclude that the company suffers from vicious infighting across product groups. "Pretty much across the board people are saying that Microsoft is dysfunctional," concludes one industry analyst. "They are not cooperating across business groups." One of the major sources of this conflict is that some work units have goals that are incompatible with those of other units. For example, the MSN group had developed desktop search software that would compete against Google Desktop. However, Microsoft's Windows group opposed release of the MSN software because the Windows group had developed similar software for its Vista operating system. The MSN group also fought against the Office people over MSN's desire to connect their online calendar with the calendar in Office. The Office group balked because "then MSN could cannibalize Office," says an employee who recently left Microsoft. "Windows and Office would never let MSN have more budget or more control."[25]

The battles between the Microsoft MSN and Windows work units illustrate how *goal incompatibility*–in which the goals of one person or department seem to interfere with another person's or department's goals–can be a source of conflict in organizations.[26] MSN's goal of competing against Google with desktop search software threatened the Windows group's goals of launching new features in Microsoft Vista. MSN's goal of providing users with better calendar integration threatened the Microsoft Office group's product territory, which might undermine its profitability or control over the calendar feature.

Differentiation

Another source of conflict is *differentiation*–differences among people, departments, and other entities regarding their training, values, beliefs, and experiences. Differentiation can be distinguished from goal incompatibility because two people or departments may agree on a common goal but have profound differences in how to achieve that goal. Consider the classic tension between employees from two companies brought together through a merger. Employees in each organization fight over the "right way" to do things because of their unique experiences in the separate companies. This source of conflict is apparent as Porsche AG takes control of Volkswagen Group. As Global Connections 11.2 describes, VW chairman Ferdinand Piëch and his allies are battling Porsche CEO Wendelin Wiedeking and his executive team because they have substantially different views on how Europe's largest automaker should be run.

Intergenerational conflicts, which were described in the opening story to this chapter, are also mainly caused by differentiation. Younger and older employees have different needs, different expectations, and different workplace practices, and this sometimes produces conflicting preferences and actions. Recent studies suggest that intergenerational differences occur because people develop social identities around technological developments and other pivotal social events.[27] Information technology also

11.2 GLOBAL CONNECTIONS

Conflict Overdrive at VW and Porsche

Behind the smiling faces of Volkswagen Group chairman Ferdinand Piëch (left) and Porsche CEO Wendelin Wiedeking (right) is a deep conflict over how to run VW as Porsche takes control of Europe's largest carmaker.

Volkswagen Group (VW) became a den of internal conflict over the past decade as it acquired several fiefdoms—Audi, Lamborghini, Bentley, Bugatti, Skoda, SEAT—that jealously guarded their brands and continuously rebelled against sharing knowledge. One member of VW's supervisory board (the German equivalent of a board of directors) commented that managing the company is "like trying to ride a chariot with four or five horses, each of which pulls in a different direction." Now Porsche AG is entering the fray. The luxury sports car company, which relies on VW for some of its production work, began acquiring stock in VW a few years ago and recently achieved a controlling interest. Porsche CEO Wendelin Wiedeking is aware of VW's internal rivalries. "If you mix the Porsche guys with the Audi guys and the VW guys you will have trouble," says Wiedeking. "Each is proud to belong to his own company."

Yet Wiedeking is stirring up a different type of conflict as Porsche tightens its grip over VW's supervisory board. Through an unswerving drive for efficient production and astute marketing, Wiedeking and his executive team transformed Porsche into the world's most profitable and prestigious car company. Wiedeking now wants to apply those practices at VW by closing down inefficient operations and money-losing car lines. "Wiedeking is a Porsche CEO from another corporate culture," says German auto analyst Christoph Stuermer. "He's out to maximize profits by cutting costs. And he snubbed everyone, telling off VW management, interfering with their way of doing business." Ferdinand Dudenhoeffer, director of Germany's Center of Automotive Research (CAR), agrees. "Porsche is very successful in being lean and profitable. It's not going to be harmonious."

Particularly offended by Wiedeking's plans is VW chairman Ferdinand Piëch, who has a different vision for Europe's largest automaker. Piëch, whose grandfather developed the VW Beetle, places more emphasis on spectacular engineering than exceptional profits. For example, he continues to support the money-losing Bugatti brand, which VW acquired several years ago when Piëch was CEO. More recently, Piëch championed the Phaeton, VW's luxury car that broke new ground in innovation (it boasts 100 patents) but has not been a commercial success.

Wiedeking, on the other hand, believes that VW could be more profitable if it stopped producing the Phaeton and Bugatti. "Piëch sees his vision endangered by Wiedeking," says Dudenhoeffer. "Wiedeking said that there are no holy cows at VW, no more Phaetons, no more Bugattis." These ideas make Piëch's blood boil. "Anyone who says that VW should pull the Phaeton doesn't understand the world," grumbles Piëch, explaining that luxury cars represent the only segment with double-digit growth.

There is an unusual twist in the conflict involving Piëch, Wiedeking, and Porsche. Piëch is a member of the Porsche family. He is a cousin of Porsche chairman Wolfgang Porsche and owns a 10 percent share of the Porsche company. Piëch began his career at Porsche and became its chief engineer before moving to Audi and later VW. Furthermore, in what many consider a blatant conflict of interest, Piëch supported Porsche's initial investment in VW. But with Piëch and Wiedeking on a collision course, that initial friendly investment in the partnership has turned into all-out corporate war. "There was always a cease-fire between Piëch and the Porsches, but now it's war," claims auto analyst Ferdinand Dudenhoeffer. "This is like *Dallas* and *Dynasty* in Wolfsburg (VW's German headquarters). No company in the world is so self-absorbed with its problems."[28]

maintains differentiation because without face-to-face experiences, employees have more difficulty forming common mental models and norms. For instance, recent investigations indicate that virtual teams have a high incidence of conflict because technology makes it difficult for them to form common experiences and perspectives.[29]

Interdependence

Conflict tends to increase with the level of interdependence. *Interdependence* exists when team members must share common inputs to their individual tasks, need to interact in the process of executing their work, or receive outcomes (such as rewards) that are partly determined by the performance of others.[30] Higher interdependence increases the risk of conflict because there is a greater chance that each side will disrupt or interfere with the other side's goals.[31]

Other than when they have complete independence, employees tend to have the lowest risk of conflict when working with others in a pooled-interdependence relationship. *Pooled interdependence* occurs where individuals operate independently except for reliance on a common resource or authority (see Chapter 8). The potential for conflict is higher in sequential interdependence work relationships, such as on an assembly line. The highest risk of conflict tends to occur in reciprocal interdependence situations. With reciprocal interdependence, employees are highly dependent on each other and, consequently, have a higher probability of interfering with each other's work and personal goals.

Scarce Resources

Resource scarcity generates conflict because each person or unit requiring the same resource necessarily undermines others who also need that resource to fulfill their goals. Consider the lively debates among employees at Intel, described earlier in Connections 11.1. These conflict episodes occur partly because there aren't enough financial, human capital, and other resources for everyone to accomplish her or his goals, so employees need to justify why they should receive the resources. The more resources one project receives, the fewer resources another project will have available to accomplish its goals.

Ambiguous Rules

Ambiguous rules–or the complete lack of rules–breed conflict. This occurs because uncertainty increases the risk that one party intends to interfere with the other party's goals. Ambiguity also encourages political tactics, and, in some cases, employees enter a free-for-all battle to win decisions in their favor. This explains why conflict is more common during mergers and acquisitions. Employees from both companies have conflicting practices and values, and few rules have developed to minimize the maneuvering for power and resources.[32] When clear rules exist, on the other hand, employees know what to expect from each other and have agreed to abide by those rules.

Communication Problems

Conflict often occurs due to the lack of opportunity, ability, or motivation to communicate effectively. Let's look at each of these causes. First, when two parties lack the opportunity to communicate, each tends to rely more on stereotypes to understand the other party in the conflict. Unfortunately, stereotypes are sufficiently subjective that emotions can negatively distort the meaning of an opponent's actions, thereby escalating perceptions of conflict. Second, some people lack the necessary skills to communicate in a diplomatic, nonconfrontational manner. When one party communicates his or her disagreement arrogantly, opponents are more likely to heighten their perception of the conflict. This may lead the other party to reciprocate with a similar response, which further escalates the conflict.[33]

A third problem is that the perception of conflict reduces the motivation to communicate. Relationship conflict is uncomfortable, so people avoid interacting with others in a conflicting relationship. Unfortunately, less communication can further escalate the conflict because there is less opportunity to empathize with the opponent's situation and opponents are more likely to rely on distorted stereotypes of the other party. In fact, conflict tends to further distort these stereotypes through the process of social identity (see Chapter 3). We begin to see competitors less favorably so that our self-concept remains positive during these uncertain times.[34]

Interpersonal Conflict-Handling Styles

The six structural conditions described above set the stage for conflict, and these sources lead to conflict perceptions and emotions that, in turn, motivate people to take some sort of action to address the conflict. Along with pioneering the view that some conflict is beneficial, Mary Parker Follett suggested that there are different conflict-handling styles. The number of styles identified by conflict experts has varied over the years, but most common are variations of the five-category model shown in Exhibit 11.4 and described below:[35]

win-win orientation
The belief that conflicting parties will find a mutually beneficial solution to their disagreement.

- *Problem solving.* Problem solving tries to find a mutually beneficial solution to the disagreement. This is known as the **win-win orientation** because people

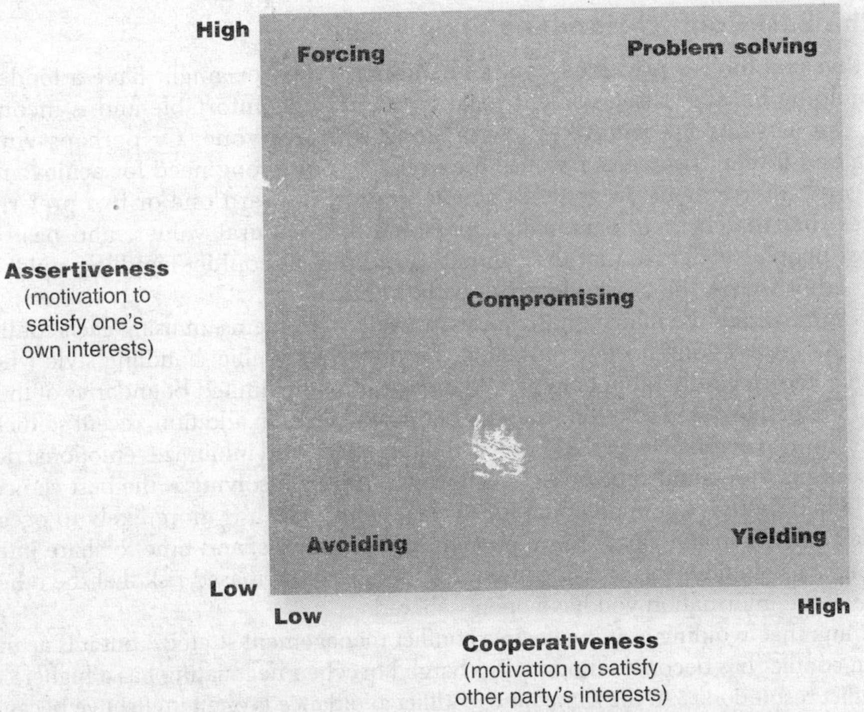

Source: C. K. W. de Dreu, A. Evers, B. Beersma, E. S. Kluwer, and A. Nauta, "A Theory-Based Measure of Conflict Management Strategies in the Workplace," *Journal of Organizational Behavior* 22 (2001), pp. 645–668. For other variations of this model, see T. L. Ruble and K. Thomas, "Support for a Two-Dimensional Model of Conflict Behavior," *Organizational Behavior and Human Performance* 16 (1976), p. 145; R. R. Blake, H. A. Shepard, and J. S. Mouton, *Managing Intergroup Conflict in Industry* (Houston: Gulf, 1964); M. A. Rahim, "Toward a Theory of Managing Organizational Conflict," *International Journal of Conflict Management* 13, no. 3 (2002), pp. 206–235.

Exhibit 11.4 *Interpersonal Conflict-Handling Styles*

win-lose orientation
The belief that conflicting parties are drawing from a fixed pie, so the more one party receives, the less the other party will receive.

using this style believe the resources at stake are expandable, rather than fixed, if the parties work together to find a creative solution. Information sharing is an important feature of this style because both parties collaborate to identify common ground and potential solutions that satisfy everyone involved.

- *Forcing*. Forcing tries to win the conflict at the other's expense. People who use this style typically have a **win-lose orientation**–they believe the parties are drawing from a fixed pie, so the more one party receives, the less the other party will receive. Consequently, this style relies on some of the "hard" influence tactics described in Chapter 10, particularly assertiveness, to get one's own way.
- *Avoiding*. Avoiding tries to smooth over or avoid conflict situations altogether. It represents a low concern for both self and the other party; in other words, avoiders try to suppress thinking about the conflict. For example, some employees will rearrange their work area or tasks to minimize interaction with certain co-workers.[36]
- *Yielding*. Yielding involves giving in completely to the other side's wishes, or at least cooperating, with little or no attention to your own interests. This style involves making unilateral concessions and unconditional promises, as well as offering help with no expectation of reciprocal help.
- *Compromising*. Compromising involves looking for a position in which you make concessions to some extent. It involves matching the other party's concessions, making conditional promises or threats, and actively searching for a middle ground between the interests of the two parties.

Choosing the Best Conflict-Handling Style

Chances are that you have a preferred conflict-handling style. You might have a tendency toward avoiding or yielding because disagreement makes you feel uncomfortable and is inconsistent with your self-concept as someone who likes to get along with everyone. Or perhaps you prefer the compromising and forcing strategies because they reflect your strong need for achievement and for control over your environment. In general, people gravitate toward one or two preferred conflict-handling styles that match their personality, personal and cultural values, and past experience. However, most people recognize that they should use different conflict-handling styles in different situations.[37] In other words, the best style varies with the situation.[38]

Exhibit 11.5 summarizes the main contingencies, as well as problems, in using each conflict-handling style. Problem solving has long been identified as the preferred conflict-handling style where possible because dialogue and clever thinking help people break out of the limited boundaries of their opposing alternatives to find an integrated solution whereby both gain value. In addition, recent studies report that problem solving improves long-term relationships, reduces stress, and minimizes emotional defensiveness and other indications of relationship conflict.[39] However, problem solving is the best choice of conflict handling only when there is some potential for mutual gains, which is more likely to occur when the issue is complex and when the parties have enough trust, openness, and time to share information. If problem solving is used under the wrong conditions, there is an increased risk that the other party will take advantage of the information you have openly shared.

You might think that avoiding is an ineffective conflict management strategy, but it is actually the best approach when conflict has become emotionally charged or when negotiating has a higher cost than the benefits of conflict resolution.[40] At the same time, conflict avoidance is often ineffective because it doesn't resolve the conflict and may increase the other party's frustration. The forcing style of conflict resolution is usually inappropriate because research indicates that it generates relationship conflict more quickly or intensely than other conflict-handling styles. However, forcing may be necessary when you know you are correct (e.g., the other party's position is unethical or based on obviously flawed logic), the dispute requires a quick solution, or the other party would take advantage of a more cooperative conflict-handling style.

Conflict-handling style	Preferred style when . . .	Problems with this style
Problem solving	• Interests are not perfectly opposing (i.e., not pure win-lose). • Parties have trust, openness, and time to share information. • Issues are complex.	• Involves sharing information that the other party might use to his or her advantage.
Avoiding	• Conflict has become too emotionally charged. • Cost of trying to resolve the conflict outweighs the benefits.	• Doesn't usually resolve the conflict. • May increase other party's frustration.
Forcing	• You have a deep conviction about your position (e.g., believe the other person's behavior is unethical). • Dispute requires a quick solution. • The other party would take advantage of more cooperative strategies.	• Has highest risk of relationship conflict. • May damage long-term relations, reducing future problem solving.
Yielding	• Other party has substantially more power. • Issue is much less important to you than to the other party. • Value and logic of your position aren't as clear.	• Increases other party's expectations in future conflict episodes.
Compromising	• Parties have equal power. • Time pressure exists for resolving the conflict. • Parties lack trust and openness for problem solving.	• Results in suboptimal solution when mutual gains are possible.

Exhibit 11.5 *Conflict-Handling-Style Contingencies and Problems*

The yielding style may be appropriate when the other party has substantially more power, the issue is not as important to you as it is to the other party, and you aren't confident that your position has the best value or logical consistency. On the other hand, yielding behaviors may give the other side unrealistically high expectations, thereby motivating her or him to seek more from you in the future. In the long run, yielding may produce more conflict rather than resolve it. The compromising style may be best when there is little hope for mutual gain through problem solving, both parties have equal power, and both are under time pressure to settle their differences. However, we rarely know for certain that mutual gains are not available, so entering a conflict with the compromising style may cause the parties to overlook better solutions.

Cultural and Gender Differences in Conflict-Handling Styles

Cultural differences are more than just a source of conflict. Cultural background also affects the preferred conflict-handling style.[41] Some research suggests that people from collectivist cultures–where

NHLPA Stick Handles the Extremes of Conflict Handling Former National Hockey League Players' Association (NHLPA) boss Bob Goodenow (left in the photo) was called the Darth Vader of hockey. He relied on a forcing style that catapulted NHL player salaries into the stratosphere, but he also soured relations with the NHL commissioner and team owners, resulting in cancellation of an entire NHL season. Goodenow stepped down after the canceled season, replaced by Ted Saskin (right), who promised a more diplomatic problem-solving approach. "I just think that in any business you need a spirit of cooperation to move forward, and I think Ted Saskin will handle that well," said NHL board of governors chairman Harley Hotchkiss when Saskin was appointed NHLPA executive director. But Saskin may have been too cozy with the NHL team owners and too mistrusting of the players he represented. Some players opposed Saskin's appointment, so the NHL commissioner's staff allegedly gave Saskin the names of players who were conspiring against him. Saskin apparently had the e-mails of these conspiring players monitored so he could anticipate their actions against him. When news of the e-mail monitoring went public, Saskin was fired. Replacing Saskin is Paul Kelly, who so far has been careful not to display too much yielding or forcing in his dealings with the NHL commissioner.[42]

people emphasize duty to groups to which they belong–are motivated to maintain harmonious relations and, consequently, are more likely than those from low collectivism cultures to manage disagreements through avoidance or problem solving. However, this view may be somewhat simplistic because people in some collectivist cultures are also more likely to publicly shame those whose actions conflict with expectations.[43]

Some writers suggest that men and women also tend to rely on different conflict-handling styles.[44] Generally, women pay more attention than do men to the relationship between the parties. Consequently, they tend to adopt a compromising or, occasionally, problem-solving style in business settings and are more willing to compromise to protect the relationship. Men tend to be more competitive and take a short-term orientation to the relationship. In low collectivism cultures, men are more likely than women to use the forcing approach to conflict handling. However, we must be cautious about these observations because gender usually has a weak influence on conflict management style.

Structural Approaches to Conflict Management

Conflict management styles pertain to how we approach the other party in a conflict situation. But conflict management also involves altering the underlying structural causes of potential conflict. The main structural approaches are emphasizing superordinate goals, reducing differentiation, improving communication and understanding, reducing task interdependence, increasing resources, and clarifying rules and procedures (see Exhibit 11.6).

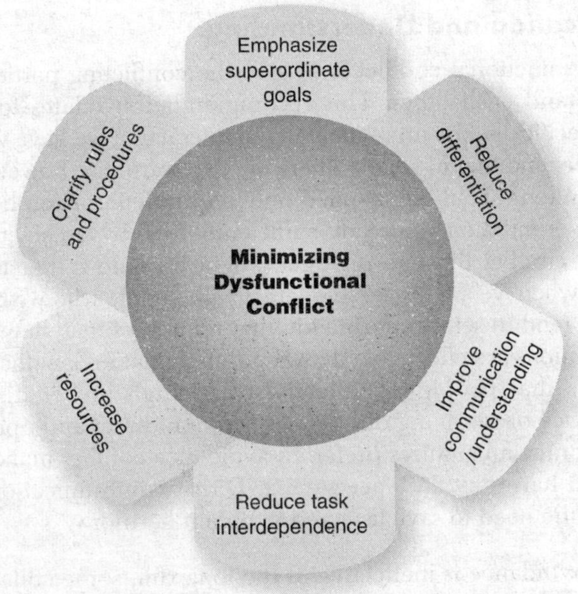

Exhibit 11.6 *Structural Approaches to Conflict Management*

Emphasizing Superordinate Goals

One of the oldest recommendations for resolving conflict is to seek and find common goals.[45] In organizational settings, this typically takes the form of a *superordinate goal*, which is any goal that both conflicting parties value and whose attainment is beyond the resources and effort of either party alone.[46] By increasing commitment to corporatewide goals, employees pay less attention to competing individual or departmental-level goals, thus reducing their perceived conflict with co-workers. They also potentially reduce the problem of differentiation by establishing a common frame of reference. For example, research indicates that the most effective executive teams frame their decisions as superordinate goals that rise above each executive's departmental or divisional goals.[47]

Reducing Differentiation

Another way to minimize dysfunctional conflict is to reduce the differences that produce the conflict in the first place. The more employees think they have common backgrounds or experiences with co-workers, the more motivated they are to coordinate their activities and resolve conflict through constructive discussion with those co-workers.[48] One way to increase this commonality is by creating common experiences. SAP, the German enterprise software company, applied this strategy when it recently acquired Business Objects, a French company with a strong U.S. presence. Conflict is common following many acquisitions because employees at each company have different cultures, experiences, and loyalties. SAP minimized this differentiation by immediately intermingling people from the two organizations. "In the first six months after the acquisition, more than 35 percent of senior managers transferred from SAP while all of the original Business Objects corporate services people are now a part of a global shared services team," says Business Objects CEO John Schwarz. "We also encourage cross-border, cross-functional teamwork on projects such as major product releases. In this way team members come to depend on each other."[49]

Improving Communication and Understanding

A third way to resolve dysfunctional conflict is to give the conflicting parties more opportunities to communicate and understand each other. This recommendation relates to the contact hypothesis described in Chapter 3. Specifically, the more meaningful interaction we have with someone, the less we rely on stereotypes to understand that person.[50] There are two warnings, however. First, communication and understanding interventions should be applied only *after* differentiation between the two sides has been reduced or when differentiation is already sufficiently low. If perceived differentiation remains high, attempts to manage conflict through dialogue might escalate rather than reduce relationship conflict. The reason is that when we are forced to interact with people who we believe are quite different and in conflict with us, we tend to select information that reinforces that view.[51] Thus, communication and understanding interventions are effective only when differentiation is sufficiently low.

The second warning is that people in collectivist and high power distance cultures are less comfortable with the practice of resolving differences through direct and open communication.[52] As noted earlier, people in Confucian cultures prefer an avoidance conflict management style because it is the most consistent with harmony and face saving. Direct communication is a high-risk strategy because it easily threatens the need to save face and maintain harmony.

Talking Circles Where avoidance is ineffective in the long run, some collectivist groups engage in structured forms of dialogue that enable communication with less risk of upsetting harmony. One such practice in Native American culture is the *talking circle*[53]. A talking circle is an ancient group process used to educate, make decisions, and repair group harmony due to conflict. Participants sit in a circle and often begin with song, prayer, shaking hands with the next person, or some other communal activity. Then they share their experiences, information, and stories relating to the issue.

A talking stick or other natural object (such as a rock or feather) is held by the speaking person, which minimizes interruptions and dysfunctional verbal reactions by others. Talking circles are not aimed at solving problems through negotiated discussion. In fact, talking circle norms usually discourage participants from responding to someone else's statements. Rather, the emphasis is on healing relationships and restoring harmony, typically through the circle's communal experience and improved understanding of each person's views. Talking circles are still rare in business organizations, but they have been applied in meetings between aboriginal people and government representatives in several countries.

Reducing Interdependence

Conflict increases with the level of interdependence, so minimizing dysfunctional conflict might involve reducing the level of interdependence between the parties. If cost-effective, this can occur by dividing the shared resource so that each party has exclusive use at different times. Sequentially or reciprocally interdependent jobs might be combined so that they form a pooled interdependence. For example, rather than having one employee serve customers and another operate the cash register, each employee could handle both customer activities alone. Buffers also help to reduce interdependence between people. Buffers include resources; for instance, more inventory could be added between people who perform sequential tasks. Organizations also use human buffers–people who serve as intermediaries between interdependent people or work units that do not get along through direct interaction.

Increasing Resources

An obvious way to reduce conflict caused by resource scarcity is to increase the amount of resources available. Corporate decision makers might quickly dismiss this solution because of the costs involved. However, they need to carefully compare these costs with the costs of dysfunctional conflict arising out of resource scarcity.

Clarifying Rules and Procedures

Conflicts that arise from ambiguous rules can be minimized by establishing rules and procedures. Armstrong World Industries, Inc., applied this strategy when consultants and information system employees clashed while working together on development of a client-server network. Information system employees at the flooring and building materials company thought they should be in charge, whereas consultants believed they had the senior role. Also, the consultants wanted to work long hours and take Friday off to fly home, whereas Armstrong employees wanted to work regular hours. The company reduced these conflicts by having both parties agree on specific responsibilities and roles. In addition, two executives were assigned responsibility for establishing more rules if future disagreements arose.[54]

Rules establish changes to the terms of interdependence, such as an employee's hours of work or a supplier's fulfillment of an order. In most cases, the parties affected by these rules are involved in the process of deciding these terms of interdependence. Thus, by redefining the terms of interdependence, the strategy of clarifying rules involves negotiation, which we discuss next.

Learning Objectives

After reading the next two sections, you should be able to:

8. Outline four situational influences on negotiations.
9. Describe four skills of effective negotiators.
10. Compare and contrast the three types of third-party dispute resolution.

Resolving Conflict through Negotiation

Think back through yesterday's events. Maybe you had to work out an agreement with other students about what tasks to complete for a team project. Chances are that you shared transportation with someone, so you had to clarify the timing of the ride. Then perhaps there was the question of who

negotiation
The process whereby two or more conflicting parties attempt to resolve their divergent goals by redefining the terms of their interdependence.

made dinner. Each of these daily events created potential conflict, and they were resolved through negotiation. **Negotiation** occurs whenever two or more conflicting parties attempt to resolve their divergent goals by redefining the terms of their interdependence. In other words, people negotiate when they think that discussion can produce a more satisfactory arrangement (at least for them) in their exchange of goods or services.

As you can see, negotiation is not an obscure practice reserved for labor and management bosses when hammering out a collective agreement. Everyone negotiates, every day. Most of the time, you don't even realize that you are in negotiations. Negotiation is particularly evident in the workplace because employees work interdependently with each other. They negotiate with their supervisors over next month's work assignments, with customers over the sale and delivery schedules of their product, and with co-workers over when to have lunch. And yes, they occasionally negotiate with each other in labor disputes and workplace agreements.

Some writers suggest that negotiations are more successful when the parties adopt a problem-solving style, whereas others caution that this conflict-handling style is sometimes costly.[55] We know that any win-lose style (forcing, yielding, etc.) is unlikely to produce the optimal solution because the parties have not shared information necessary to discover a mutually satisfactory solution. On the other hand, we must be careful about openly adopting a problem solving style until mutual trust has been established.

The concern with the problem-solving style is that information is power, so information sharing gives the other party more power to leverage a better deal if the opportunity occurs. Skilled negotiators often cautiously adopt the problem-solving style at the outset by sharing information slowly and determining whether the other side will reciprocate. In this respect, they try to establish trust with the other party.[56] They switch to one of the win-lose styles only when it becomes apparent that a win-win solution is not possible or the other party is unwilling to share information with a cooperative orientation.

Bargaining-Zone Model of Negotiations

The negotiation process moves each party along a continuum with an area of potential overlap called the *bargaining zone.*[57] Exhibit 11.7 displays one possible bargaining-zone situation. This linear diagram illustrates a purely win-lose situation–one side's gain will be the other's loss. However, the bargaining-zone model can also be applied to situations in which both sides potentially gain from the negotiations. As this model illustrates, the parties typically establish three main negotiating points. The *initial-offer point* is the team's opening offer to the other party. This may be its best expectation or a pie-in-the-sky starting point. The *target point* is the team's realistic goal or expectation for a final agreement. The *resistance point* is the point beyond which the team will make no further concessions.

The parties begin negotiations by describing their initial-offer point for each item on the agenda. In most cases, the participants know that this is only a starting point that will change as both sides offer concessions. In win-lose situations, neither the target nor the resistance point is revealed to the other party. However, people try to discover the other side's resistance point because this knowledge helps them determine how much they can gain without breaking off negotiations. When the parties have a win-win orientation, on the other hand, the objective is to find a creative solution that keeps both parties close to their initial-offer points. They hope to find an arrangement by which each side loses relatively little value on some issues and gains significantly more on other issues.

Situational Influences on Negotiations

The effectiveness of negotiating depends on both the situation and the behaviors of the negotiators. Four of the most important situational factors are location, physical setting, time, and audience.

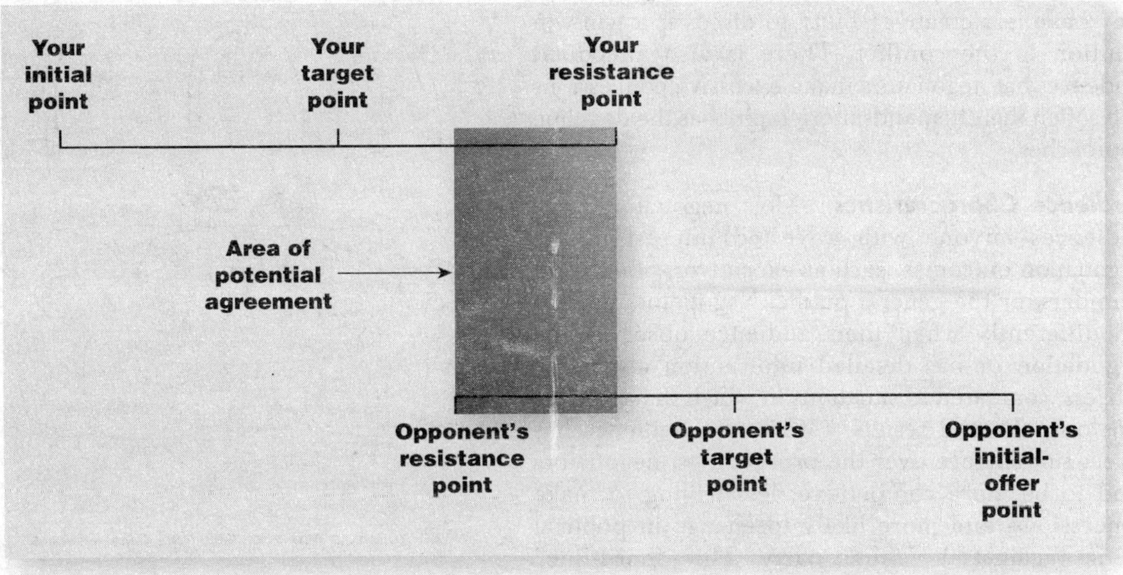

Exhibit 11.7 *Bargaining-Zone Model of Negotiations*

Location It is easier to negotiate on your own turf because you are familiar with the negotiating environment and are able to maintain comfortable routines.[58] Also, there is no need to cope with travel-related stress or depend on others for resources during the negotiation. Of course, you can't walk out of negotiations as easily when on your own turf, but this is usually a minor issue. Considering these strategic benefits of home turf, many negotiators agree to neutral territory. Phone calls, videoconferences, and other forms of information technology potentially avoid territorial issues, but skilled negotiators usually prefer the media richness of face-to-face meetings. Frank Lowy, cofounder of retail property giant Westfield Group, says that telephones are "too cold" for negotiating. "From a voice I don't get all the cues I need. I go by touch and feel and I need to see the other person."[59]

Physical Setting The physical distance between the parties and formality of the setting can influence their orientation toward each other and the disputed issues. So can the seating arrangements. People who sit face-to-face are more likely to develop a win-lose orientation toward the conflict situation. In contrast, some negotiation groups deliberately intersperse participants around the table to convey a win-win orientation. Others arrange the seating so that both parties face a whiteboard, reflecting the notion that both parties face the same problem or issue.

Time Passage and Deadlines The more time people invest in negotiations, the stronger is their commitment to reaching an agreement. This increases the motivation to resolve the conflict, but it also fuels the escalation of commitment problems, described in Chapter 7. For example, the more time put into negotiations, the stronger the tendency to make unwarranted concessions so that the negotiations do not fail.

Time deadlines may be useful when they motivate the parties to complete negotiations. However, time pressures are usually a liability in negotiations.[60] One problem is that time pressure inhibits a problem-solving conflict-handling style because the parties have less time to exchange information or present flexible offers. Negotiators under time pressure also process information less effectively, so they have less creative ability to discover a win-win solution to the conflict. There is also anecdotal evidence that negotiators make excessive concessions and soften their demands more rapidly as the deadline approaches.

"MAYBE YOU SHOULD RECONSIDER THOSE PLACE CARDS, MS. HARRIS?"

Audience Characteristics Most negotiators have audiences–anyone with a vested interest in the negotiation outcomes, such as executives, other team members, or the general public. Negotiators tend to act differently when their audience observes the negotiation or has detailed information about the process, compared to situations in which the audience sees only the end results.[61] When the audience has direct surveillance over the proceedings, negotiators tend to be more competitive, less willing to make concessions, and more likely to engage in political tactics against the other party. This "hard-line" behavior shows the audience that the negotiator is working for their interests. With the audience watching, the negotiator also has more interest in saving face.

Negotiator Skills

Negotiator skills play an important role in resolving conflict. Four of the most important skills are setting goals, gathering information, communicating effectively, and making concessions.

Preparation and Goal Setting Research consistently reports that people have more favorable negotiation results when they prepare for the negotiation and set goals.[62] In particular, negotiators should carefully think through their initial-offer, target, and resistance points. They need to consider alternative strategies in case the negotiation fails. Negotiators also need to check their underlying assumptions, as well as goals and values. Equally important is the need to research what the other party wants from the negotiation. "You have to be prepared every which way about the people, the subject, and your fallback position," advises Paul Tellier, the former president of Bombardier, Inc. "Before walking into the room for the actual negotiation, I ask my colleagues to throw some curve balls at me," he says.[63]

Gathering Information "Seek to understand before you seek to be understood." This popular philosophy from management guru Stephen Covey applies to effective negotiations. It means that we should spend more time listening closely to the other party and asking for details.[64] One way to improve the information-gathering process is to have a team of people participate in negotiations. Asian companies tend to have large negotiation teams for this purpose.[65] With more information about the opponent's interests and needs, negotiators are better able to discover low-cost concessions or proposals that will satisfy the other side.

Communicating Effectively Effective negotiators communicate in a way that maintains effective relationships between the parties. Specifically, they minimize socioemotional conflict by focusing on issues rather than people. Effective negotiators also avoid irritating statements such as "I think you'll agree that this is a generous offer." Third, effective negotiators are masters of persuasion. They structure the content of their message so that it is accepted by others, not merely understood.[66]

Making Concessions Concessions are important because they (1) enable the parties to move toward the area of potential agreement, (2) symbolize each party's motivation to bargain in good faith, and (3) tell the other party of the relative importance of the negotiating items.[67] However, concessions move the parties toward agreement only under certain conditions.[68] First, concessions need to be labeled–the other party needs to be aware that your action is a concession, that this concession is costly to you, and that it is beneficial to the other party. Second, concessions should be accompanied by an expectation that the other party should reciprocate. In fact, when there is a lack of trust, a concession should be contingent on a specific reciprocal action by the other party. Finally, concessions should be given in installments, not all at once. The rationale is that people experience more positive emotions from two smaller concessions than they would if those concessions were combined into one larger concession. For example, rather than making one concession to complete the project a month earlier than initially offered, you first offer to finish the work three weeks earlier and then later make a concession to complete it an additional week earlier.

How many concessions should you make, and when should you make them? This varies with the other party's expectations and the level of trust between you and the other party. For instance, many Chinese negotiators are wary of people who change their position during the early stages of negotiations. Similarly, some writers warn that Russian negotiators tend to view concessions as a sign of weakness, rather than a sign of trust.[69] Generally, the best strategy is to be moderately tough and give just enough concessions to communicate sincerity and motivation to resolve the conflict.[70] Being too tough can undermine relations between the parties; giving too many concessions implies weakness and encourages the other party to use power and resistance.

THIRD-PARTY CONFLICT RESOLUTION

third-party conflict resolution
Any attempt by a relatively neutral person to help conflicting parties resolve their differences.

Most of this chapter has focused on people directly involved in a conflict, yet many disputes in organizational settings are resolved with the assistance of the manager responsible for the feuding parties or of some other third party. **Third-party conflict resolution** is any attempt by a relatively neutral person to help conflicting parties resolve their differences. There are generally three types of third-party dispute resolution activities: arbitration, inquisition, and mediation. These activities can be classified by their levels of control over the process and control over the decision (see Exhibit 11.8).[71]

- *Arbitration.* Arbitrators have high control over the final decision but low control over the process. Executives engage in this strategy by following previously agreed-on rules of due process, listening to arguments from the disputing employees, and making a binding decision. Arbitration is applied as the final stage of grievances by unionized employees in many countries, but it is also becoming more common in nonunion conflicts.
- *Inquisition.* Inquisitors control all discussion about the conflict. Like arbitrators, they have high decision control because they choose the form of conflict resolution. However, they also have high process control because they choose which information to examine and how to examine it, and they generally decide how the conflict resolution process will be handled.
- *Mediation.* Mediators have high control over the intervention process. In fact, their main purpose is to manage the process and context of interaction between the disputing parties. However, the parties make the final decision about how to resolve their differences. Thus, mediators have little or no control over the conflict resolution decision.

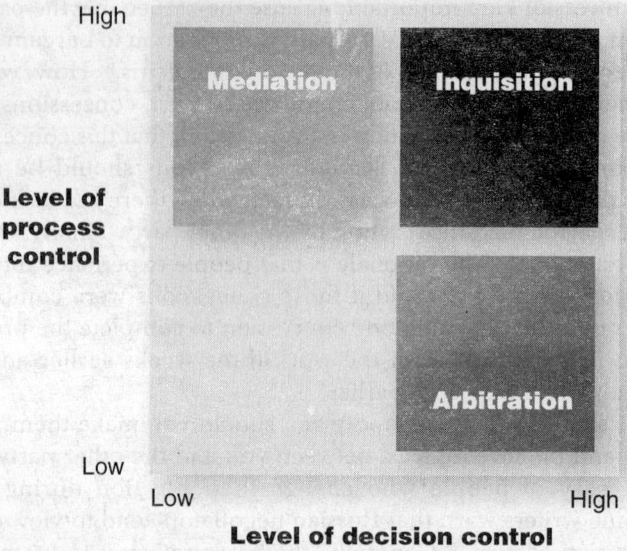

Exhibit 11.8 *Types of Third-Party Intervention*

Choosing the Best Third-Party Intervention Strategy

Team leaders, executives, and co-workers regularly intervene in disputes between employees and departments. Sometimes they adopt a mediator role; other times they serve as arbitrators. Occasionally, they begin with one approach and then switch to another. However, research suggests that people in positions of authority (e.g., managers) usually adopt an inquisitional approach, whereby they dominate the intervention process as well as make a binding decision.[72] Managers prefer the inquisition approach because it is consistent with the decision-oriented nature of managerial jobs, gives them control over the conflict process and outcome, and tends to resolve disputes efficiently.

However, the inquisitional approach to third-party conflict resolution is usually the least effective in organizational settings.[73] One problem is that leaders who take an inquisitional role tend to collect limited information about the problem, so their imposed decision may produce an ineffective solution to the conflict. Another problem is that employees often view inquisitional procedures and outcomes as unfair because they have little control over this approach. In particular, the inquisitional approach potentially violates several practices required to support procedural justice (see Chapter 5).

Which third-party intervention is most appropriate in organizations? The answer partly depends on the situation, such as the type of dispute, the relationship between the manager and employees, and cultural values such as power distance.[74] But generally speaking, for everyday disagreements between two employees, the mediation approach is usually best because it gives employees more responsibility for resolving their own disputes. The third-party representative merely establishes an appropriate context for conflict resolution. Although not as efficient as other strategies, mediation potentially offers the highest level of employee satisfaction with the conflict process and outcomes.[75] When employees cannot resolve their differences through mediation, arbitration seems to work best because the predetermined rules of evidence and other processes create a higher sense of procedural fairness.[76] Moreover, arbitration is preferred where the organization's goals should take priority over individual goals.

Alternative Dispute Resolution Rather than battle each other in court or external arbitration, the U.S. Air Force and its civilian staff have resolved most workplace conflicts quickly and with improved mutual understanding through alternative dispute resolution (ADR). "The parties, in essence, maintain control over the [ADR] process and its outcome," explains Air Mobility Command civilian programs branch chief Diana Hendrix. Some Air Force bases retain a mediator to identify issues and explore options with the parties without imposing a solution. Other bases use peer review panels, consisting of four or six union and nonunion employees who examine facts, listen to the parties, and make a final binding decision. But even with these formal third-party systems in place, Hendrix explains that supervisors are the first line of defense in resolving workplace conflict. "Ultimately, it's about Air Force employees and supervisors resolving conflicts in an efficient and effective manner so they can continue performing the Air Force mission of supporting and defending the United States of America," she says.[77]

Redress at USPS Over the past 15 years, the United States Postal Service (USPS) has applied evidence-based management practices to discover the best approach for resolving employee disputes, specifically equal employment opportunity complaints between staff members and their direct supervisors. The program began as a pilot project in the Florida Panhandle region using professional mediators, while another variation (using employees trained in mediation) was tested in upstate New York. USPS also compared the traditional *facilitation* approach, in which mediators actively move the parties toward settlement, with the *transformative* approach, in which both parties are given more power and recognition to resolve their own disputes. The emerging mediation process, called REDRESS (Resolve Employment Disputes, Reach Equitable Solutions Swiftly), adopts the transformative approach with external professional mediators. The employee may bring a representative or engage in the process alone. The USPS employment mediation program is now the world's largest and has received favorable recognition from conflict resolution experts.[78]

alternative dispute resolution (ADR)
An orderly process of third-party dispute resolution, typically including mediation followed by arbitration.

The U.S. Air Force has joined a growing list of organizations that have taken third-party resolution one step further through an **alternative dispute resolution (ADR)** process (for employees only, also called *internal dispute resolution* or *employee dispute resolution*). ADR includes third-party dispute resolution in an orderly sequence. ADR typically begins with a meeting between the employee and employer to clarify and negotiate their differences. If this fails, a mediator is brought in to help the parties reach a mutually agreeable solution. If mediation fails, the parties submit their case to an arbitrator, whose decision may be either binding or voluntarily accepted by the employer. Although most ADR systems rely on professional arbitrators, some firms, such as Eastman Kodak and some U.S. Air Force bases, prefer peer arbitration, which includes a panel of co-workers and managers who are not involved in the dispute.[79]

Whether resolving conflict through third-party dispute resolution or direct dialogue, we need to recognize that many solutions come from the sources of conflict that were identified earlier in this chapter. This may seem obvious, but in the heat of conflict, people often focus on each other rather than the underlying causes. Recognizing conflict sources is the role of effective leadership, which is discussed in the next chapter.

Chapter Summary

Conflict is the process in which one party perceives that his or her interests are being opposed or negatively affected by another party. For many years, conflict was viewed as undesirable and counterproductive. There is evidence that conflict can produce undesirable outcomes such as lower job satisfaction, team cohesion, and knowledge sharing as well as higher organizational politics and turnover. However, experts later formed the opinion that organizations suffer from too little as well as too much conflict. Research reports that moderate conflict can improve decision making, organizational responsiveness to the environment, and team cohesion (when conflict is with sources outside the team).

The current perspective involves distinguishing constructive conflict from relationship conflict. The former focuses on issues and a logical evaluation of ideas, whereas the latter pays attention to interpersonal incompatibilities and flaws. Although the ideal would be to encourage constructive conflict and minimize relationship conflict, relationship conflict tends to emerge in most constructive-conflict episodes. However, relationship conflict is less likely to dominate when the parties are emotionally intelligent, have a cohesive team, and have supportive team norms.

The conflict process model begins with the six structural sources of conflict: incompatible goals, differentiation (different values and beliefs), interdependence, scarce resources, ambiguous rules, and communication problems. These sources lead one or more parties to perceive a conflict and to experience conflict emotions. This, in turn, produces manifest conflict, such as hostile behaviors toward the other side. The conflict process often escalates through a series of episodes.

Organizational behavior experts have identified several conflict-handling styles: problem solving, forcing, avoiding, yielding, and compromising. People who use problem solving have a win-win orientation. Other styles, particularly forcing, assume a win-lose orientation. In general, people gravitate toward one or two preferred conflict-handling styles that match their personality, personal and cultural values, and past experience. However, the best style depends on various characteristics of the situation.

Structural approaches to conflict management include emphasizing superordinate goals, reducing differentiation, improving communication and understanding, reducing interdependence, increasing resources, and clarifying rules and procedures.

Negotiation occurs whenever two or more conflicting parties attempt to resolve their divergent goals by redefining the terms of their interdependence. Negotiations are influenced by several situational factors, including location, physical setting, time passage and deadlines, and audience. Important negotiator behaviors include preparation and goal setting, gathering information, communicating effectively, and making concessions.

Third-party conflict resolution is any attempt by a relatively neutral person to help the parties resolve their differences. The three main forms of third-party dispute resolution are mediation, arbitration, and inquisition. Managers tend to use an inquisition approach, although mediation and arbitration are more appropriate, depending on the situation.

Key Terms

alternative dispute resolution (ADR)
conflict
constructive conflict
negotiation
relationship conflict
third-party conflict resolution
win-lose orientation
win-win orientation

Critical Thinking Questions

1. Distinguish constructive conflict from relationship conflict, and explain how to apply the former with minimal levels of the latter.
2. The chief executive officer of Creative Toys, Inc., read about cooperation in Japanese companies and vowed to bring the same philosophy to the company. The goal is to avoid all conflict so that employees will work cooperatively and be happier at Creative Toys. Discuss the merits and limitations of the CEO's policy.
3. Conflict among managers emerged soon after a French company acquired a Swedish firm. The Swedes perceived the French management as hierarchical and arrogant, whereas the French thought the Swedes were naive and cautious and lacked an achievement orientation. Describe ways to reduce dysfunctional conflict in this situation.
4. This chapter describes three levels of interdependence that exist in interpersonal and intergroup relationships. Identify examples of each level in your work or school activities. How do these three levels affect potential conflict for you?
5. Jane has just been appointed as purchasing manager of Tacoma Technologies Corp. The previous purchasing manager, who recently retired, was known for his "winner-take-all" approach to suppliers. He continually fought for more discounts and was skeptical about any special deals that suppliers would propose. A few suppliers refused to do business with Tacoma Technologies, but senior management was confident that the former purchasing manager's approach minimized the company's costs. Jane wants to try a more collaborative approach to working with suppliers. Will her approach work? How should she adopt a more collaborative approach in future negotiations with suppliers?
6. You are a special assistant to the commander-in-chief of a peacekeeping mission to a war-torn part of the world. The unit consists of a few thousand peacekeeping troops from the United States, France, India, and four other countries. The troops will work together for approximately one year. What strategies would you recommend to improve mutual understanding and minimize conflict among these troops?
7. The chief operating officer (COO) has noticed that production employees in the company's Mexican manufacturing operations are unhappy with some of the production engineering decisions made by engineers in the company's headquarters in Chicago. At the same time, the engineers complain that production employees aren't applying their engineering specifications correctly and don't understand why those specifications were put in place. The COO believes that the best way to resolve this conflict is to have a frank and open discussion between some of the engineers and employees representing the Mexican production crew. This open-dialogue approach worked well recently among managers in the company's Chicago headquarters, so it should work equally well between the engineers and production staff. On the basis of your knowledge of communication and mutual understanding as a way to resolve conflict, discuss the COO's proposal.
8. Describe the inquisitional approach to resolving disputes between employees or work units. Discuss its appropriateness in organizational settings, including the suitability of its use with a multigenerational workforce.

CASE STUDY 11.1

TAMARACK INDUSTRIES

David J. Cherrington, Brigham Young University

Tamarack Industries manufactures motorboats primarily used for waterskiing. During the summer months, a third production line is normally created to help meet the heavy summer demand. This third line is usually created by assigning the experienced workers to all three lines and hiring college students who are home for summer vacation to complete the crews. In the past, however, experienced workers resented having to break up their teams to form a third line. They also resented having to work with a bunch of college kids and complained that the kids were slow and arrogant.

The foreman, Dan Jensen, decided to try a different strategy this summer and have all the college students work on the new line. He asked Mark Allen to supervise the new crew because Mark claimed that he knew everything about boats and could perform every job "with my eyes closed." Mark was happy to accept the new job and participated in selecting his own crew. Mark's crew was called "the Greek Team" because all the college students were members of a fraternity or sorority named with Greek letters.

Mark spent many hours in training to get his group running at full production. The college students learned quickly, and by the end of June their production rate was up to standard, with an error rate that was only slightly above normal. To simplify the learning process, Dan Jensen assigned the Greek Team long production runs that generally consisted of 30 to 40 identical units. Thus the training period was shortened and errors were reduced. Shorter production runs were assigned to the experienced teams.

By the middle of July, a substantial rivalry had been created between the Greek Team and the older workers. At first, the rivalry was good-natured. But after a few weeks, the older workers became resentful of the remarks made by the college students. The Greek Team often met its production schedules with time to spare at the end of the day for goofing around. It wasn't uncommon for someone from the Greek Team to go to another line pretending to look for materials just to make demeaning comments. The experienced workers resented having to perform all the shorter production runs and began to retaliate with sabotage. They would sneak over during breaks and hide tools, dent materials, install something crooked, and in other small ways do something that would slow production for the Greek Team.

Dan felt good about his decision to form a separate crew of college students, but when he heard reports of sabotage and rivalry, he became very concerned. Because of complaints from the experienced workers, Dan equalized the production so that all of the crews had similar production runs. The rivalry, however, did not stop. The Greek Team continued to finish early and flaunt their performance in front of the other crews.

One day the Greek Team suspected that one of their assemblies was going to be sabotaged during the lunch break by one of the experienced crews. By skillful deception, they were able to substitute an assembly from the other experienced line for theirs. By the end of the lunch period, the Greek Team was laughing wildly because of their deception, while one experienced crew was very angry with the other one.

Dan Jensen decided that the situation had to be changed and announced that the job assignments between the different crews would be shuffled. The employees were told that when they appeared for work the next morning, the names of the workers assigned to each crew would be posted on the bulletin board. The announcement was not greeted with much enthusiasm, and Mark Allen decided to stay late to try to talk Dan out of his idea. Mark didn't believe the rivalry was serious enough for this type of action, and he suspected that many of the college students would quit if their team was broken up.

Discussion Questions

1. What are the signs (symptoms) of conflict in this case?
2. Use the conflict model to (a) identify the structural causes of conflict and (b) discuss the escalation of conflict described in this case.
3. If you were Dan Jensen, what action would you take in this situation?

Sources: Reprinted with permission of David Chemington, Brigham Young University.

CASE STUDY 11.2

THE NEW HEAT AT FORD

BusinessWeek

Soon after Alan Mulally became Ford Motor Co.'s new chief executive, he and two senior engineers endured a grueling critique by *Consumer Reports* magazine's automobile testing staff of the company's current lineup of vehicles. After a couple of hours on the firing line, Ford's engineers started interrupting the testers in attempts to defend their products. Sensing the building conflict, Mulally handed the two engineers pads and pens. "You know what? Let's just listen and take notes," he said. This episode, and many others, illustrated that Ford has become a troubled organization where people are more focused on fighting each other than on learning from disagreement.

This *BusinessWeek* case study describes several conflict-related events that Mulally has experienced or created since his arrival at Ford. It also provides Ford's history of generating or avoiding conflict episodes. Read the full text of this *BusinessWeek* article at www.mhhe.com/mcshane5e, and prepare for the discussion questions below.

Discussion Questions

1. Identify the main conditions at Ford described in this case study that seem to have generated dysfunctional conflict.
2. What has Mulally done to reduce or remove these sources of conflict? In what ways has he encouraged or created more conflict?
3. The opening paragraphs of this case study describe a conflict incident involving *Consumer Reports* staff and two senior Ford engineers. Discuss this incident in terms of the conflict model. Was Mulally's intervention in this incident a good idea? Why or why not?

Source: D. Kiley, "The New Heat at Ford," *BusinessWeek,* 4 June 2007, pp. 32–38.

CLASS EXERCISE 11.3

THE CONTINGENCIES OF CONFLICT HANDLING

Gerard A. Callanan and David F. Perri, West Chester University of Pennsylvania

PURPOSE This exercise is designed to help you understand the contingencies of applying conflict-handling styles in organizational settings.

INSTRUCTIONS

1. Participants will read each of the five scenarios presented below and select the most appropriate response from among the five alternatives. Each scenario has a correct response for that situation.
2. *(Optional)* The instructor may ask each student to complete the Dutch Test for Conflict Handling self-assessment in this chapter (Self-Assessment 11.5) or a similar instrument. This instrument will provide an estimate of your preferred conflict-handling style.
3. As a class, participants give their feedback on the responses to each of the scenarios, with the instructor guiding discussion on the contextual factors embodied in each scenario. For each scenario, the class should identify the response selected by the majority. In addition, participants will discuss how they decided on the choices they made and the contextual factors they took into account in making their selections.

4. *(Optional)* Students will compare their responses to the five scenarios with their results from the conflict-handling self-assessment. Discussion will focus on the extent to which each person's preferred conflict-handling style influenced her or his alternatives in this activity and on the implications of this style preference for managing conflict in organizations.

Scenario 1

Setting: You are a manager of a division in the accounting department of a large eastern U.S. bank. Nine exempt-level analysts and six nonexempt clerical staff report to you. Recently, one of your analysts, Jane Wilson, has sought the bank's approval for tuition reimbursement for the cost of an evening MBA program specializing in organizational behavior. The bank normally encourages employees to seek advanced degrees on a part-time basis. Indeed, through your encouragement, nearly all of the members of your staff are pursuing additional schoolwork. You consult the bank's policy manual and discover that two approvals are necessary for reimbursement–yours and that of the manager of training and development, Kathy Gordon. Further, the manual states that approval for reimbursement will only be granted if the coursework is "reasonably job related." Based on your review of the matter, you decide to approve Jane's request for reimbursement. However, Kathy Gordon rejects it outright by claiming that coursework in organizational behavior is not related to an accounting analyst position. She states that the bank will only reimburse the analyst for a degree in either accounting or finance. In your opinion, however, the interpersonal skills and insights to be gained from a degree in organizational behavior are job-related and can also benefit the employee in future assignments. The analyst job requires interaction with a variety of individuals at different levels in the organization, and it is important that interpersonal and communication skills be strong.

After further discussion it becomes clear that you and Kathy Gordon have opposite views on the matter. Since both of you are at the same organization level and have equal status, it appears that you are at an impasse. Although the goal of reimbursement is important, you are faced with other pressing demands on your time. In addition, the conflict has diverted the attention of your work group away from its primary responsibilities. Because the school term is about to begin, it is essential that you and Kathy Gordon reach a timely agreement to enable Jane to pursue her coursework.

Action Alternatives for Scenario 1: Please indicate your first (1) and second (2) choices from among the following alternatives by writing the appropriate number in the space provided.

Action alternative	Ranking (1st and 2d)
1. You go along with Kathy Gordon's view and advise Jane Wilson to select either accounting or finance as a major for her MBA.	______
2. You decide to withdraw from the situation completely and tell Jane to work it out with Kathy Gordon on her own.	______
3. You decide to take the matter to those in higher management levels and argue forcefully for your point of view. You do everything in your power to ensure that a decision will be made in your favor.	______
4. You decide to meet Kathy Gordon halfway in order to reach an agreement. You advise Jane to pursue her MBA in accounting or finance, but also recommend she minor in organizational behavior by taking electives in that field.	______
5. You decide to work more closely with Kathy Gordon by attempting to get a clear as well as flexible policy written that reflects both of your views. Of course, this will require a significant amount of your time.	______

Scenario 2

Setting: You are the vice president of a relatively large division (80 employees) in a medium-sized consumer products company. Due to the recent turnover of minority staff, your division has fallen behind in meeting the company's goal for equal employment opportunity (EEO) hiring. Because of a scarcity of qualified minority candidates, it appears that you may fall further behind in achieving stated EEO goals.

Although you are aware of the problem, you believe that the low level of minority hiring is due to increased attrition in minority staff as well as the lack of viable replacement candidates. However, the EEO officer believes that your hiring criteria are too stringent, resulting in the rejection of minority candidates with the basic qualifications to do the job. You support the goals and principles of EEO; however, you are concerned that the hiring of less-qualified candidates will weaken the performance of your division. The EEO officer believes that your failure to hire minority employees is damaging to the company in the short term because corporate goals will not be met, and in the long term because it will restrict the pool of minority candidates available for upward mobility. Both of you regard your concerns as important. Further, you recognize that both of you have the company's best interests in mind and that you have a mutual interest in resolving the conflict.

Action Alternatives for Scenario 2: Please indicate your first (1) and second (2) choices from among the following alternatives by writing the appropriate number in the space provided.

Action alternative	Ranking (1st and 2d)
1. You conclude that the whole problem is too complex an issue for you to handle right now. You put it on the "back burner" and decide to reconsider the problem at a later date.	_______
2. You believe that your view outweighs the perspective of the EEO officer. You decide to argue your position more vigorously and hope that your stance will sway the EEO officer to agree with your view.	_______
3. You decide to accept the EEO officer's view. You agree to use less stringent selection criteria and thereby hire more minority employees.	_______
4. You give in to the EEO officer somewhat by agreeing to relax your standards a little bit. This would allow slightly more minority hiring (but not enough to satisfy the EEO goal) and could cause a small reduction in the overall performance of your division.	_______
5. You try to reach a consensus that addresses each of your concerns. You agree to work harder at hiring more minority applicants and request that the EEO officer agree to help find the most qualified minority candidates available.	_______

Scenario 3

Setting: You are the manager in charge of the financial reporting section of a large insurance company. It is the responsibility of your group to make periodic written and oral reports to senior management regarding the company's financial performance. The company's senior management has come to rely on your quick and accurate dissemination of financial data as a way to make vital decisions in a timely fashion. This has given you a relatively high degree of organizational influence. You rely on various operating departments to supply you with financial information according to a preestablished reporting schedule.

In two days, you must make your quarterly presentation to the company's board of directors. However, the claims department has failed to supply you with several key pieces of information that are critical to your presentation. You check the reporting schedule and realize that you should have had the information two days ago. When you call Bill Jones, the claims department manager, he informs you that he cannot possibly have the data to you within the next two days. He states that other pressing work has a higher priority. Although you explain the critical need for these data, he is unwilling to change his position. You believe that your presentation is vital to the company's welfare and explain this to Bill Jones. Although Bill has less status than you, he has been known to take advantage of individuals who are unwilling or unable to push their point of view. With your presentation less than two days away, it is critical that you receive information from the claims department within the next 24 hours.

Action Alternatives for Scenario 3: Please indicate your first (1) and second (2) choices from among the following alternatives by writing the appropriate number in the space provided.

Action alternative	Ranking (1st and 2d)
1. Accept the explanation from Bill Jones and try to get by without the figures by using your best judgment as to what they would be.	______
2. Tell Bill Jones that unless you have the data from his department on your desk by tomorrow morning, you will be forced to go over his head to compel him to give you the numbers.	______
3. Meet Bill Jones halfway by agreeing to receive part of the needed figures and using your own judgment on the others.	______
4. Try to get your presentation postponed until a later date, if possible.	______
5. Forget about the short-term need for information and try to achieve a longer-term solution, such as adjusting the reporting schedule to better accommodate your mutual needs.	______

Scenario 4

Setting: You are the production manager of a medium-sized building products company. You control a production line that runs on a three-shift basis. Recently, Ted Smith, the materials handling manager, asked you to accept a different packaging of the raw materials for the production process than what has been customary. He states that new machinery he has installed makes it much easier to provide the material in 100-pound sacks instead of the 50-pound bags that you currently receive. Ted further explains that the provision of the material in the 50-pound bags would put an immense strain on his operation, and he therefore has a critical need for you to accept the change. You know that accepting materials in the new packaging will cause some minor disruption in your production process but should not cause long-term problems for any of the three shifts. However, you are a little annoyed by the proposed change because Ted did not consult with you before he installed the new equipment. In the past, you and he have been open in your communication. You do not think that this failure to consult you represents a change in your relationship.

Because you work closely with Ted, it is essential that you maintain the harmonious and stable working relationship that you have built over the past few years. In addition, you may need some help from him in the future, since you already know that your operation will have special material requirements in about two months. You also know that Ted has influence at higher levels of the organization.

Action Alternatives for Scenario 4: Please indicate your first (1) and second (2) choices from among the following alternatives by writing the appropriate number in the space provided.

Action alternative	Ranking (1st and 2d)
1. Agree to accept the raw material in the different format.	______
2. Refuse to accept the material in the new format because it would cause a disruption in your operation.	______
3. Propose a solution where you accept material in the new format during the first shift but not during the second and third.	______
4. Tell Ted Smith that you do not wish to deal with the issue at this time but that you will consider his request and get back to him at a later date.	______
5. Tell Ted Smith of your concern regarding his failure to consult with you before installing new equipment. Inform him that you wish to find longer-term solutions to the conflict between you and him.	______

SCENARIO 5

Setting: You are employed as supervisor of the compensation and benefits section in the human resources department of a medium-sized pharmaceutical company. Your staff of three clerks is responsible for maintaining contacts with the various benefits providers and answering related questions from the company's employees. Your section shares secretarial, word processing, and copier resources with the training and development section of the department. Recently, a disagreement has arisen between you and Beth Hanson, the training and development supervisor, over when the secretarial staff should take their lunches. Beth would like the secretarial staff to take their lunches an hour later to coincide with the time most of her people go to lunch. You know that the secretaries do not want to change their lunchtimes. Further, the current time is more convenient for your staff.

At this time, you are hard-pressed to deal with the situation. You have an important meeting with the provider of dental insurance in two days. It is critical that you are well prepared for this meeting, and these other tasks are a distraction.

Action Alternatives for Scenario 5: Please indicate your first (1) and second (2) choices from among the following alternatives by writing the appropriate number in the space provided.

Action alternative	Ranking (1st and 2d)
1. Take some time over the next day and propose a solution whereby three days a week the secretaries take their lunch at the earlier time and two days at the later.	______
2. Tell Beth Hanson you will deal with the matter in a few days, after you have addressed the more pressing issues.	______
3. Let Beth Hanson have her way by agreeing to a later lunch hour for the secretarial staff.	______
4. Flat out tell Beth Hanson that you will not agree to a change in the secretaries' lunchtime.	______
5. Devote more time to the issue. Attempt to achieve a broad-based consensus with Beth Hanson that meets her needs as well as yours and those of the secretaries.	______

Source: G. A. Callanan and D. F. Perri, "Teaching Conflict Management Using a Scenario-Based Approach," *Journal of Education for Business,* 81 (January–February 2006), pp. 131–139. Reprinted with permission of the Helen Dwight Reid Educational Foundation. Published by Heldref Publications, 1319 Eighteenth St., NW, Washington, D.C. 20036-1802. Copyright © 2006.

TEAM EXERCISE 11.4

UGLI ORANGE ROLE PLAY

PURPOSE This exercise is designed to help you understand the dynamics of interpersonal and intergroup conflict as well as the effectiveness of negotiation strategies under specific conditions.

MATERIALS The instructor will distribute information on roles for Dr. Roland, Dr. Jones, and a few observers. Ideally, each negotiation should occur in a private area away from other negotiations.

INSTRUCTIONS

1. The instructor will divide the class into an even number of teams of three people each, with one participant left over for each team formed (e.g., six observers if there are six teams). One-half of the teams will take the role of Dr. Roland, and the other half will be Dr. Jones. The instructor will distribute information about the roles after these teams have been formed.
2. Members within each team are given 10 minutes (or some other time limit stated by the instructor) to learn their roles and decide on a negotiating strategy.
3. After reading their roles and discussing strategy, each Dr. Jones team is matched with a Dr. Roland team to conduct negotiations. Observers will receive observation forms from the instructor, and two observers will be assigned to watch the paired teams during prenegotiations and subsequent negotiations.
4. As soon as Roland and Jones reach agreement or at the end of the time allotted for the negotiation (whichever comes first), the Roland and Jones teams report to the instructor for further instruction.
5. At the end of the exercise, the class will congregate to discuss the negotiations. Observers, negotiators, and instructors will then discuss their observations and experiences and the implications for conflict management and negotiation.

Source: This exercise was developed by Robert J. House, Wharton Business School, University of Pennsylvania. A similar incident is also attributed to earlier writing by R. R. Blake and J. S. Mouton.

SELF-ASSESSMENT 11.5

THE DUTCH TEST FOR CONFLICT HANDLING

PURPOSE This self-assessment is designed to help you identify your preferred conflict-management style.

INSTRUCTIONS Read each of the statements below and circle the response that you believe best reflects your position regarding each statement. Then use the scoring key in Appendix B at the end of the book to calculate your results for each conflict-management style. This exercise should be completed alone so that you can assess yourself honestly without concerns of social comparison. Class discussion will focus on the different conflict-management styles and the situations in which each is most appropriate.

Dutch Test for Conflict Handling

When I have a conflict at work, I do the following:	Not at all ▼				Very much ▼
1. I give in to the wishes of the other party.	1	2	3	4	5
2. I try to realize a middle-of-the-road solution.	1	2	3	4	5
3. I push my own point of view.	1	2	3	4	5
4. I examine issues until I find a solution that really satisfies me and the other party.	1	2	3	4	5
5. I avoid confrontation about our differences.	1	2	3	4	5
6. I concur with the other party.	1	2	3	4	5
7. I emphasize that we have to find a compromise solution.	1	2	3	4	5
8. I search for gains.	1	2	3	4	5
9. I stand for my own and other's goals and interests.	1	2	3	4	5
10. I avoid differences of opinion as much as possible.	1	2	3	4	5
11. I try to accommodate the other party.	1	2	3	4	5
12. I insist that we both give in a little.	1	2	3	4	5
13. I fight for a good outcome for myself.	1	2	3	4	5
14. I examine ideas from both sides to find a mutually optimal solution.	1	2	3	4	5
15. I try to make differences seem less severe.	1	2	3	4	5
16. I adapt to the parties' goals and interests.	1	2	3	4	5
17. I strive whenever possible toward a 50-50 compromise.	1	2	3	4	5
18. I do everything to win.	1	2	3	4	5
19. I work out a solution that serves my own and the other's interests as well as possible.	1	2	3	4	5
20. I try to avoid a confrontation with the other.	1	2	3	4	5

Source: C. K. W. de Dreu, A. Evers, B. Beersma, E. S. Kluwer, and A. Nauta, "A Theory-Based Measure of Conflict Management Strategies in the Workplace," *Journal of Organizational Behavior* 22 (2001), pp. 645–668.

When Anne Sweeney took the reins of the ABC television network a few years ago, pundits said she was accepting the toughest job in the industry. The network was floundering in fourth place; only two of its programs were in the top 20; several new high-potential programs fizzled; employee morale was as low as the network's ratings. Sweeney successfully built the Disney, Nickelodeon, and FX cable networks, but many observers wondered whether anyone could lead ABC television out of its deep hole. Yet in less than four years under Sweeney, ABC was competing for the top spot with popular programs such as *Desperate Housewives, Lost,* and *Grey's Anatomy.*

Employees and experts alike say that Anne Sweeney's leadership has been a decisive factor in the remarkable turnaround of the ABC television network.

How did this remarkable turnaround occur? Sweeney credits ABC's managers and creative talent, but these people point to Sweeney's leadership as the key factor that unleashed their potential. Disney Channel Entertainment president Rich Ross suggests that Sweeney avoids micromanaging her staff but applies her analytic skill to challenge managers to think through their ideas. "[She] asks the tough questions. . . . It trains you to anticipate it," says Ross. Fred Silverman agrees: "[News Corporation founder] Rupert Murdoch was once quoted as saying she has a steel fist in a velvet glove," says the famed television producer and executive. "There's great resolve and strength there."

Others emphasize Sweeney's supportive leadership style. "She has been incredibly supportive through all the ups and downs of rebuilding a network schedule, which made it possible for us to achieve so much so fast," says ABC Entertainment president Stephen McPherson. Albert Cheng echoes this view: "Anne makes it a point to engage with everyone," says the Disney Digital Media executive vice president. "She's very concerned about the people who work for her."

Still others say that Sweeney's leadership strength is her ability to engage staff in a vision of the future. "Anne draws upon her optimism and her grace in keeping her focus firmly on the future—the future of our own organization and the future of the entire industry," says ABC News president David Westin. "In short, none of us could wish for a better leader, through whatever may come our way."[1]

12

LEADERSHIP IN ORGANIZATIONAL SETTINGS

Learning Objectives

After reading this chapter, you should be able to:

1. Define *leadership* and *shared leadership*.
2. List the main competencies of effective leaders and discuss the limitations of the competency perspective of leadership.
3. Describe the people-oriented and task-oriented leadership styles.
4. Outline the path-goal theory of leadership.
5. Summarize leadership substitutes theory.
6. Distinguish transformational leadership from transactional and charismatic leadership.
7. Describe the four elements of transformational leadership.
8. Describe the implicit leadership perspective.
9. Discuss similarities and differences in the leadership styles of women and men.
10. Understand leadership development through 360 degree feedback.
11. Explore the eight archetypes of open leadership.

Learning Objectives

After reading the next two sections, you should be able to:

1. Define *leadership* and *shared leadership.*
2. List the main competencies of effective leaders and discuss the limitations of the competency perspective of leadership.

WHAT IS LEADERSHIP?

What makes someone an effective leader? This question has challenged great thinkers for most of written history, and it is the focus of this chapter. The opening vignette, which described the leadership of Anne Sweeney, cochair of Disney Media Networks and president of Disney-ABC Television Group, offers a few clues. Sweeney's leadership is viewed from several perspectives, all of which are important. The opening vignette also reveals that leadership is no longer yesteryear's image of the command-and-control boss. Although Sweeney steps in when the situation requires, followers say her success as a leader comes, in part, from trusting them to do their jobs without micromanagement. Also notice that Sweeney's leadership is a contrast to the heroic leadership model; she routinely directs the spotlight of success toward her staff rather than herself.

leadership
Influencing, motivating, and enabling others to contribute toward the effectiveness and success of the organizations of which they are members.

A few years ago, 54 leadership experts from 38 countries reached a consensus that **leadership** is about influencing, motivating, and enabling others to contribute toward the effectiveness and success of the organizations of which they are members.[2] Leaders apply various forms of influence–particularly persuasion and related tactics that build commitment–to ensure that followers have the motivation and role clarity to achieve specified goals. Leaders also arrange the work environment–such as allocating resources and altering communication patterns–so that employees can achieve organizational objectives more easily.

Leadership in the Context of Global Meltdown

The global financial meltdown and the Satyam episode in the recent past, and Enron and WorldCom debacles in the past occurred due to failure of leadership. Leadership is one of the trusted identities of an organization. However, there are leaders who have failed to strengthen that trust and have caused misfortune to the lives of their stakeholders.

Why did Leadership fail? The leaders failed because of their short-sighted focus; drive for short-term results and rewards; self-interests (power, recognition, wealth) put ahead of organizational interests; risk-aversion attitude; sole reliability on knowledge and latest techniques and technologies; lack of self-awareness about their motives and actions; and pressures of competition leading them to strive for success and not accept mistakes or failure.

Need for Dependable and Mindful Leadership According to Bill George, in order to revive the shaken confidence and trust after global meltdown, the need is to develop dependable and mindful leadership at all levels in an organization[3]. According to him, a mindful leadership is the one which has secular ideas to sustain the effectiveness of leadership, has self-awareness and its impact on others, focused to achieve organizational goals. Mindful leaders have been found to be compassionate.

Shared Leadership

shared leadership
The view that leadership is broadly distributed, rather than assigned to one person, such that people within the team and organization lead each other.

Leadership isn't restricted to the executive suite. Anyone in the organization may be a leader in various ways and at various times.[4] This view is known as **shared leadership** or the *leaderful organization.* From this emerging view, *leadership* is plural, not singular. It doesn't operate out of one formally assigned position or role. Instead, a team or work unit may have several leaders at the same time. One team member might champion the introduction of new technology, while a co-worker keeps the work unit focused on key performance indicators. Some organizations, such as SEMCO SA and W. L. Gore & Associates, depend on shared leadership because there are no formal leaders.[5] Anyone can be a leader, if he or she has an idea or vision that other employees are eager to follow.

Shared leadership flourishes in organizations where the formal leaders are willing to delegate power and encourage employees to take initiative and risks without fear of failure (i.e., a learning orientation culture). Shared leadership also calls for a collaborative rather than internally competitive culture because employees take on shared leadership roles when co-workers support them for their initiative. Furthermore, shared leadership lacks formal authority, so it operates best when employees learn to influence others through their enthusiasm, logical analysis, and involvement of co-workers in their idea or vision.

Consider, for example, the emergence of shared leadership at Rolls-Royce Engine Services in Oakland, California. As part of its employee engagement initiative, the aircraft engine repair facility involved employees directly with clients, encouraged weekly huddles for information sharing, and accepted employee requests for less micromanagement. Employees not only experienced higher levels of engagement and empowerment; they also accepted more leadership responsibilities. "I saw people around me, all front-line employees, who were leaders," says a machine programmer at the Rolls-Royce Oakland plant. "They weren't actually leading the company, but they were people you would listen to and follow. We didn't have titles, but people had respect for what we did."[6]

Leadership is one of the most researched, and possibly the most complex, topics in organizational behavior. This has resulted in an enormous volume of leadership literature, most of which can be

Shared Leadership at W. L. Gore & Associates W. L. Gore & Associates has no formal (called *vertical*) leaders. Instead, the company's 7,000 associates work with champions of projects and other initiatives because they are willing to follow them. "There is no positional power," explains a Gore team leader. "You are only a leader if teams decide to respect and follow you." Diane Davidson discovered this extreme version of shared leadership when the newly hired apparel industry sales executive asked her "starting sponsor" to identify her boss. The sponsor replied that she had no boss and eventually advised her to "stop using the B-word." Davidson initially thought the company must have formal managers who downplayed their position, but she soon realized that Gore really is a shared leadership organization. "Your team is your boss, because you don't want to let them down," says Davidson. "Everyone's your boss, and no one's your boss." In fact, when Gore employees are asked in annual surveys "Are you a leader?" more than 50 percent of them answer "Yes."[7]

organized into five perspectives: competency, behavioral, contingency, transformational, and implicit.[8] Although some of these perspectives are currently more popular than others, each helps us to more fully understand the complex issue of leadership. This chapter explores each of these five perspectives of leadership. In the final section, we also consider cross-cultural and gender issues in organizational leadership.

Competency Perspective of Leadership

Since the beginning of recorded civilization, people have been interested in the personal characteristics that distinguish great leaders from the rest of us.[9] In the 6th century BCE, the Chinese philosopher Lao-tzu described effective leaders as selfless, honest, fair, and hardworking. The Greek philosopher Plato claimed that great leaders have wisdom and a superior capacity for logical thinking. For the past century, hundreds of leadership studies have tried to empirically identify the traits of effective leaders. However, a major review in the late 1940s concluded that no consistent list of traits could be distilled from this research. This conclusion was revised a decade later, suggesting that a few traits are associated with effective leaders.[10] These paltry findings caused many scholars to give up their search for personal characteristics that distinguish effective leaders.

Over the past two decades, leadership researchers and consultants have returned to the notion that effective leaders possess specific personal characteristics.[11] The earlier research was apparently plagued by methodological problems, lack of theoretical foundation, and inconsistent definitions of leadership. The emerging work has identified several leadership *competencies,* that is, skills, knowledge, aptitudes, and other personal characteristics that lead to superior performance (see Chapter 2). The main categories of leadership competencies are listed in Exhibit 12.1 and described below:[12]

- *Personality.* Most of the Big Five personality dimensions (see Chapter 2) are associated with effective leadership to some extent, but the strongest predictors are high levels of extroversion (outgoing, talkative, sociable, and assertive) and conscientiousness (careful, dependable, and self-disciplined). With high extroversion, effective leaders are comfortable having an influential role in social settings. With higher conscientiousness, effective leaders set higher personal goals for themselves and are more motivated to pursue those goals.
- *Self-concept.* Successful leaders have a positive self-evaluation, including high self-esteem, self-efficacy, and internal locus of control (see Chapter 2).[13] They are confident in their leadership skills and ability to achieve objectives. These leaders also have a complex, internally consistent, and clear self-concept. They know themselves and act consistently with that self-concept. These characteristics are essential for *authentic leadership,* which refers to how well leaders know themselves (have a clear self-concept) and act consistently with that self-concept (such as being consistent with their personal values).[14]
- *Drive.* Related to their high conscientiousness and positive self-concept, successful leaders have a high need for achievement (see Chapter 5). This drive represents the inner motivation that leaders possess to pursue their goals and encourage others to move forward with theirs. Drive inspires inquisitiveness, an action orientation, and boldness to take the organization or team into uncharted waters. In fact, Larry Bossidy, the former CEO of Honeywell and Allied Signal, says that drive is so important for leadership that "if you have to choose between someone with a staggering IQ . . . and someone with a lower IQ who is absolutely determined to succeed, you'll always do better with the second person."[15]
- *Integrity.* Integrity involves truthfulness and consistency of words and actions, qualities that are related to honesty and ethicality. Leaders have a high moral capacity to judge dilemmas on the

Leadership competency	Description
Personality	The leader's higher levels of extroversion (outgoing, talkative, sociable, and assertive) and conscientiousness (careful, dependable, and self-disciplined).
Self-concept	The leader's self-beliefs and positive self-evaluation about his or her own leadership skills and ability to achieve objectives.
Drive	The leader's inner motivation to pursue goals.
Integrity	The leader's truthfulness and tendency to translate words into deeds.
Leadership motivation	The leader's need for socialized power to accomplish team or organizational goals.
Knowledge of the business	The leader's tacit and explicit knowledge about the company's environment, enabling the leader to make more intuitive decisions.
Cognitive and practical intelligence	The leader's above-average cognitive ability to process information (cognitive intelligence) and ability to solve real-world problems by adapting to, shaping, or selecting appropriate environments (practical intelligence).
Emotional intelligence	The leader's ability to monitor his or her own and others' emotions, discriminate among them, and use the information to guide his or her thoughts and actions.

Exhibit 12.1 *Competencies of Effective Leaders*

basis of sound values and to act accordingly. Notice that integrity is ultimately based on the leader's values, which provide an anchor for consistency. Several large-scale studies have reported that integrity and honesty are the most important characteristics of effective leaders.[16] Unfortunately, numerous surveys report that employees don't trust their leaders and don't think they have integrity. For example, only 2 percent of Americans have a great deal of trust in the people who run big companies; 30 percent say they don't trust these leaders at all![17]

- *Leadership motivation.* Effective leaders are motivated to lead others. They have a strong need for *socialized power,* meaning that they want power as a means to accomplish organizational objectives and similar good deeds. This contrasts with a need for *personalized power,* which is the desire to have power for personal gain or for the thrill one might experience from wielding power over others (see Chapter 5).[18] Leadership motivation is also necessary because, even in collegial firms, leaders are in contests for positions further up the hierarchy. Effective leaders thrive rather than wither in the face of this competition.[19]
- *Knowledge of the business.* Effective leaders possess tacit and explicit knowledge of the business environment in which they operate.
- *Cognitive and practical intelligence.* Leaders have above-average cognitive ability to process enormous amounts of information. Leaders aren't necessarily geniuses; rather, they have a superior ability to analyze a variety of complex alternatives and opportunities. Furthermore, leaders have practical intelligence; they are able to use their knowledge of the business to solve real-world problems by adapting to, shaping, or selecting appropriate environments. Unlike cognitive intelligence, which is assessed by performance on clearly defined problems with sufficient information and usually

one best answer, practical intelligence is assessed by performance in real-world settings, where problems are poorly defined, information is missing, and more than one solution may be plausible.[20]

- *Emotional intelligence.* Effective leaders have a high level of emotional intelligence.[21] They are able to perceive and express emotion, assimilate emotion in thought, understand and reason with emotion, and regulate emotion in themselves and others (see Chapter 4).

Competency Perspective Limitations and Practical Implications

Although the competency perspective is gaining popularity (again), it has a few limitations.[22] First, it assumes that all effective leaders have the same personal characteristics that are equally important in all situations. This is probably a false assumption; leadership is far too complex to have a universal list of traits that apply to every condition. Some competencies might not be important all the time. Second, alternative combinations of competencies may be equally successful; two people with different sets of competencies might be equally good leaders. Third, the competency perspective views leadership as something within a person, yet experts emphasize that leadership is relational. People are effective leaders because of their favorable relationships with followers, so effective leaders cannot be identified without considering the quality of these relationships.[23]

As we will learn later in this chapter, several leadership researchers have also warned that some personal characteristics might influence only our perception that someone is a leader, not whether the individual really makes a difference to the organization's success. People who exhibit self-confidence, extroversion, and other traits are called leaders because they fit our prototype of an effective leader. Or we might see a successful person, call that person a leader, and then attribute unobservable traits that we consider essential for great leaders.

The competency perspective of leadership does not necessarily imply that leadership is a talent acquired at birth rather than developed throughout life. On the contrary, competencies indicate only leadership *potential,* not leadership performance. People with these characteristics become effective leaders only after they have developed and mastered the necessary leadership behaviors. People with somewhat lower leadership competencies may become very effective leaders because they have leveraged their potential more fully.

Learning Objectives

After reading the next two sections, you should be able to:

3. Describe the people-oriented and task-oriented leadership styles.
4. Outline the path-goal theory of leadership.
5. Summarize leadership substitutes theory.

Behavioral Perspective of Leadership

In the 1940s and 1950s, leadership experts at several universities launched an intensive research investigation to answer the question "What behaviors make leaders effective?" Questionnaires were administered to subordinates, asking them to rate their supervisors on a large number of behaviors. This study distilled two clusters of leadership behaviors from literally thousands of leadership behavior items.[24]

One cluster represents people-oriented behaviors. This cluster includes behaviors such as showing mutual trust and respect for subordinates, demonstrating a genuine concern for their needs, and having a desire to look out for their welfare. Leaders with a strong people-oriented style listen to employee suggestions, do personal favors for employees, support their interests when required, and treat employees as equals. The other cluster represents a task-oriented leadership style and includes behaviors that define and structure work roles. Task-oriented leaders assign employees to specific tasks, clarify their work duties and procedures, ensure that they follow company rules, and push them to reach their performance capacity. They establish stretch goals and challenge employees to push beyond those high standards.

Choosing Task- versus People-Oriented Leadership

Should leaders be task-oriented or people-oriented? This is a difficult question to answer because each style has its advantages and disadvantages. Recent evidence suggests that both styles are positively associated with leader effectiveness, but differences are often apparent only in very high or very low levels of each style. Generally, absenteeism, grievances, turnover, and job dissatisfaction are higher among employees who work with supervisors with very low levels of people-oriented leadership. Job performance is lower among employees who work for supervisors with low levels of task-oriented leadership.[25] Research suggests that university students value task-oriented instructors because they want clear objectives and well-prepared lectures that abide by the unit's objectives.[26]

One problem with the behavioral leadership perspective is that the two categories are broad generalizations that mask specific behaviors within each category. For instance, task-oriented leadership includes planning work activities, clarifying roles, and monitoring operations and performance. Each of these clusters of activities are fairly distinct and likely have different effects on employee well-being and performance. A second concern is that the behavioral approach assumes that high levels of both styles are best in all situations. In reality, the best leadership style depends on the situation.[27] On a positive note, the behavioral perspective lays the foundation for two of the main leadership styles–people-oriented and task-oriented–found in many contemporary leadership theories. These contemporary theories adopt a contingency perspective, which is described next.

Contingency Perspective of Leadership

The contingency perspective of leadership is based on the idea that the most appropriate leadership style depends on the situation. Most (although not all) contingency leadership theories assume that effective leaders must be both insightful and flexible.[28] They must be able to adapt their behaviors and styles to the immediate situation. This isn't easy to do, however. Leaders typically have a preferred style. It takes considerable effort for leaders to choose and enact different styles to match the situation. As we noted earlier, leaders must have high emotional intelligence so they can diagnose the circumstances and match their behaviors accordingly.

path-goal leadership theory
A contingency theory of leadership based on the expectancy theory of motivation that relates several leadership styles to specific employee and situational contingencies.

Path-Goal Theory of Leadership

Several contingency theories have been proposed over the years, but **path-goal leadership theory** has withstood scientific critique better than the others. Indeed, one recent study found that the path-goal theory explained more about effective leadership than did another popular perspective of leadership (transformational, which we describe later in this chapter).[29] Path-goal leadership theory has its roots in the expectancy theory of motivation (see Chapter 5).[30] Early research incorporated expectancy theory into the study of how leader behaviors influence employee perceptions of expectancies (paths) between employee effort and performance (goals). Out of this early work was born path-goal theory as a contingency leadership model.

servant leadership
The view that leaders serve followers, rather than vice versa; leaders help employees fulfill their needs and are coaches, stewards, and facilitators of employee performance.

Path-goal theory states that effective leaders ensure that employees who perform their jobs well receive more valued rewards than those who perform poorly. Effective leaders also provide the information, support, and other resources necessary to help employees complete their tasks.[31] In other words, path-goal theory advocates **servant leadership.**[32] Servant leaders do not view leadership as a position of power; rather, they are coaches, stewards, and facilitators. Leadership is an obligation to understand employee needs and to facilitate their work performance. Servant leaders ask, "How can I help you?" rather than expect employees to serve them. "The role of the leader is to create environments where others can do great work–and then to get out of the way," suggests Microsoft executive Steve Vamos. Similarly, when Financial Planning Association president Jim Barnash was recently asked about his leadership style, he replied: "I try to live a servant-leader's life, which means being more interested in your needs than my needs."[33]

Path-Goal Leadership Styles Exhibit 12.2 presents the path-goal theory of leadership. This model specifically highlights four leadership styles and several contingency factors leading to three indicators of leader effectiveness. The four leadership styles are:[34]

- *Directive.* This leadership style consists of clarifying behaviors that provide a psychological structure for subordinates. The leader clarifies performance goals, the means to reach those goals, and the standards against which performance will be judged. It also includes judicious use of rewards and disciplinary actions. Directive leadership is the same as task-oriented leadership, described earlier, and echoes our discussion in Chapter 2 on the importance of clear role perceptions in employee performance.

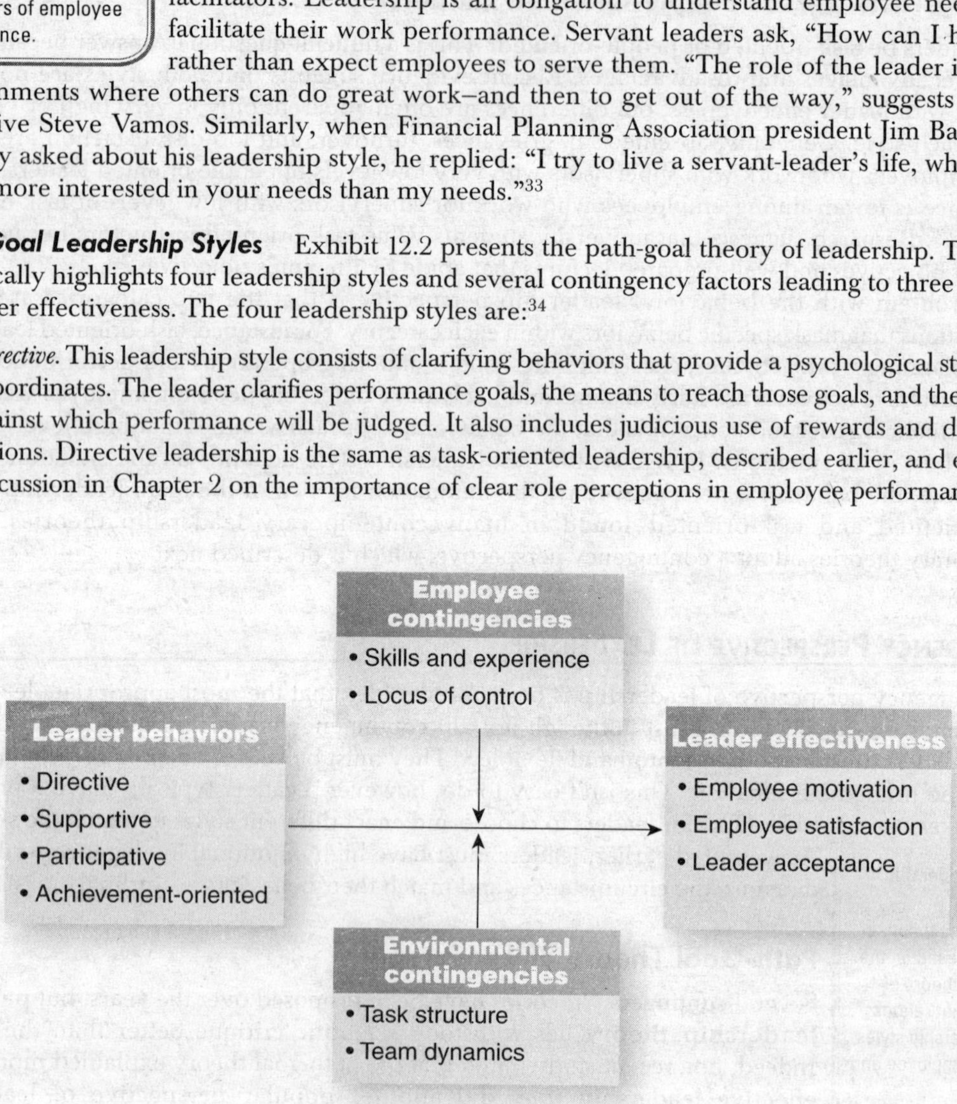

Exhibit 12.2 *Path-Goal Leadership Theory*

- *Supportive*. In this style, the leader's behaviors provide psychological support for subordinates. The leader is friendly and approachable; makes the work more pleasant; treats employees with equal respect; and shows concern for the status, needs, and well-being of employees. Supportive leadership is the same as people-oriented leadership, described earlier, and reflects the benefits of social support to help employees cope with stressful situations.
- *Participative*. Participative leadership behaviors encourage and facilitate subordinate involvement in decisions beyond their normal work activities. The leader consults with employees, asks for their suggestions, and takes these ideas into serious consideration before making a decision. Participative leadership relates to involving employees in decisions.
- *Achievement-oriented*. This leadership style emphasizes behaviors that encourage employees to reach their peak performance. The leader sets challenging goals, expects employees to perform at their highest level, continuously seeks improvement in employee performance, and shows a high degree of confidence that employees will assume responsibility and accomplish challenging goals. Achievement-oriented leadership applies goal-setting theory as well as positive expectations in self-fulfilling prophecy.

The path-goal model contends that effective leaders are capable of selecting the most appropriate behavioral style (or styles) for each situation. Leaders might simultaneously use two or more styles. In the opening vignette to this chapter, for example, Disney-ABC executive Anne Sweeney was applauded for her supportive as well as achievement-oriented leadership styles. Furthermore, she is both supportive and participative in situations where these leadership styles are most appropriate.

Contingencies of Path-Goal Theory As a contingency theory, path-goal theory states that each of the four leadership styles will be effective in some situations but not in others. The path-goal

Striving to Become the Starbucks of Sushi Douglas Foo has high expectations of himself and of his executive team at Apex-Pal International. "When we opened our first Sakae Sushi restaurant, we didn't want it to be just another restaurant, we wanted it to be a global brand," says the award-winning Singaporean entrepreneur who launched the Sakae Sushi chain of restaurants a decade ago. Foo's achievement-oriented leadership style is apparent when he says: "We want to be the Starbucks of sushi. We want to be everywhere." So far, his executive team seems to be delivering on Foo's high expectations. Sakae Sushi now boasts more than 80 outlets across seven countries in Asia, and it recently opened restaurants in New York City. "My proudest achievement to date would be my team of driven people. They are the reason why my business is accelerating and they are the biggest value in the company," says Foo. Along with his achievement-oriented leadership style, Foo is considered a supportive boss. He emphasizes family values, holds Family Days, and hands out vouchers so that staff can bring their families to the restaurant to celebrate birthdays. "He's a great boss and treats us more like his family," says Apex-Pal's marketing executive, Joyce Lee.[35]

leadership model specifies two sets of situational variables that moderate the relationship between a leader's style and effectiveness: (1) employee characteristics and (2) characteristics of the employee's work environment. Several contingencies have already been studied within the path-goal framework, and the model is open for more variables in the future.[36] However, only four contingencies are reviewed here (see Exhibit 12.3).

- *Skill and experience.* A combination of directive and supportive leadership is best for employees who are (or perceive themselves to be) inexperienced and unskilled.[37] Directive leadership gives subordinates information about how to accomplish the task, whereas supportive leadership helps them cope with the uncertainties of unfamiliar work situations. Directive leadership is detrimental when employees are skilled and experienced because it introduces too much supervisory control.
- *Locus of control.* Recall from Chapter 2 that people with an internal locus of control believe that they have control over their work environment. Consequently, these employees prefer participative and achievement-oriented leadership styles and may become frustrated with a directive style. In contrast, people with an external locus of control believe that their performance is due more to luck and fate, so they tend to be more satisfied with directive and supportive leadership.
- *Task structure.* Leaders should adopt the directive style when the task is nonroutine, because this style minimizes role ambiguity that tends to occur in complex work situations (particularly for inexperienced employees).[38] The directive style is ineffective when employees have routine and simple tasks because the manager's guidance serves no purpose and may be viewed as unnecessarily close control. Employees in highly routine and simple jobs may require supportive leadership to help them cope with the tedious nature of the work and lack of control over the pace of work. Participative leadership is preferred for employees performing nonroutine tasks because the lack of rules and procedures gives them more discretion to achieve challenging goals. The participative style is ineffective for employees in routine tasks because they lack discretion over their work.
- *Team dynamics.* Cohesive teams with performance-oriented norms act as a substitute for most leader interventions. High team cohesion substitutes for supportive leadership, whereas performance-oriented team norms substitute for directive and possibly achievement-oriented leadership. Thus, when team cohesiveness is low, leaders should use the supportive style. Leaders should apply a directive style to counteract team norms that oppose the team's formal objectives. For example, the team leader may need to use legitimate power if team members have developed a norm to "take it easy" rather than get a project completed on time.

	Directive	Supportive	Participative	Achievement-oriented
Employee contingencies				
Skill and experience	Low	Low	High	High
Locus of control	External	External	Internal	Internal
Environmental contingencies				
Task structure	Nonroutine	Routine	Nonroutine	???
Team dynamics	Negative norms	Low cohesion	Positive norms	???

Exhibit 12.3 *Selected Contingencies of Path-Goal Theory*

Path-goal theory has received more research support than other contingency leadership models, but the evidence is far from complete. A few contingencies (e.g., task structure) have limited research support. Other contingencies and leadership styles in the path-goal leadership model haven't been investigated at all (as noted by the question marks in Exhibit 12.3).[39] Another concern is that as path-goal theory expands, the model may become too complex for practical use. Few people would be able to remember all the contingencies and the appropriate leadership styles for those contingencies. In spite of these limitations, path-goal theory remains a relatively robust contingency leadership theory.

Other Contingency Theories

At the beginning of this chapter we noted that numerous leadership theories have developed over the years. Most of them are found in the contingency perspective of leadership. Some overlap with the path-goal model in terms of leadership styles, but most use simpler and more abstract contingencies. We will very briefly mention only two here because of their popularity and historical significance to the field.

situational leadership theory
A commercially popular but poorly supported leadership model stating that effective leaders vary their style (telling, selling, participating, delegating) with the "readiness" of followers.

Situational Leadership Theory One of the most popular contingency theories among practitioners is the **situational leadership theory (SLT)** also called the *life-cycle theory* of leadership, developed by Paul Hersey and Ken Blanchard.[40] SLT suggests that effective leaders vary their style with the "readiness" of followers. (An earlier version of the model called this "maturity.") *Readiness* refers to the employee's or work team's ability and willingness to accomplish a specific task. *Ability* refers to the extent to which the follower has the skills and knowledge to perform the task without the leader's guidance. *Willingness* refers to the follower's motivation and commitment to perform the assigned task. The model compresses these distinct concepts into a single situational condition.

The situational leadership model also identifies four leadership styles–telling, selling, participating, and delegating–that Hersey and Blanchard distinguish in terms of the amount of directive and supportive behavior provided. For example, "telling" has high task behavior and low supportive behavior. The situational leadership model has four quadrants, with each quadrant showing the leadership style that is most appropriate under different circumstances.

In spite of its popularity, several studies and at least three reviews have concluded that the situational leadership model lacks empirical support.[41] Only one part of the model apparently works, namely, that leaders should use "telling" (i.e., directive style) when employees lack motivation and ability. (Recall that this is also documented in path-goal theory.) The model's elegant simplicity is attractive and entertaining, but most parts don't represent reality very well.

Fiedler's contingency model
Developed by Fred Fiedler, an early contingency leadership model that suggests that leader effectiveness depends on whether the person's natural leadership style is appropriately matched to the situation.

Fiedler's Contingency Model **Fiedler's contingency model,** developed by Fred Fiedler and his associates, is the earliest contingency theory of leadership.[42] According to this model, leader effectiveness depends on whether the person's natural leadership style is appropriately matched to the situation. The theory examines two leadership styles that essentially correspond to the previously described people-oriented and task-oriented styles. Unfortunately, Fiedler's model relies on a questionnaire that does not measure either leadership style very well.

Fiedler's model suggests that the best leadership style depends on the level of *situational control,* that is, the degree of power and influence that the leader possesses in a particular situation. Situational control is affected by three factors in the following order of importance: leader-member relations, task structure, and position power.[43] *Leader-member relations* refers to how much employees trust and respect the leader and are willing to follow his or her guidance. *Task structure* refers to the clarity or ambiguity of operating procedures. *Position power* is the extent to which the leader possesses legitimate, reward, and coercive power over subordinates. These three contingencies form the eight possible combinations of *situation favorableness* from the leader's viewpoint. Good leader-member relations, high task structure, and strong position power create the most favorable situation for the leader because he or she has the most power and influence under these conditions.

Fiedler has gained considerable respect for pioneering the first contingency theory of leadership. However, his theory has fared less well. As mentioned, the leadership-style scale used by Fiedler has been widely criticized. There is also no scientific justification for placing the three situational control factors in a hierarchy. Moreover, the concept of leader-member relations is really an indicator of leader effectiveness (as in path-goal theory) rather than a situational factor. Finally, the theory considers only two leadership styles, whereas other models present a more complex and realistic array of behavior options. These concerns explain why the theory has limited empirical support.[44]

Changing the Situation to Match the Leader's Natural Style Fiedler's contingency model may have become a historical footnote, but it does make an important and lasting contribution by suggesting that leadership style is related to the individual's personality and, consequently, is relatively stable over time. Leaders might be able to alter their style temporarily, but they tend to use a preferred style in the long term. More recent scholars have also proposed that leadership styles are "hardwired" more than most contingency leadership theories assume.[45]

If leadership style is influenced by a person's personality, organizations should engineer the situation to fit the leader's dominant style, rather than expect leaders to change their style with the situation. A directive leader might be assigned inexperienced employees who need direction rather than seasoned people who work less effectively under a directive style. Alternatively, companies might transfer supervisors to workplaces where their dominant style fits best. For instance, directive leaders might be parachuted into work teams with counterproductive norms, whereas leaders who prefer a supportive style should be sent to departments in which employees face work pressures and other stressors.

Leadership Substitutes

leadership substitutes
A theory identifying contingencies that either limit a leader's ability to influence subordinates or make a particular leadership style unnecessary.

So far, we have looked at theories that recommend using different leadership styles in various situations. But one theory, called **leadership substitutes,** identifies conditions that either limit the leader's ability to influence subordinates or make a particular leadership style unnecessary. The literature identifies several conditions that possibly substitute for task-oriented or people-oriented leadership. For example, performance-based reward systems keep employees directed toward organizational goals, so they might replace or reduce the need for task-oriented leadership. Task-oriented leadership is also less important when employees are skilled and experienced. These propositions are similar to path-goal leadership theory; namely, directive leadership is unnecessary–and may be detrimental–when employees are skilled or experienced.[46]

Some research suggests that effective leaders help team members learn to lead themselves through leadership substitutes; in other words, co-workers substitute for leadership in high-involvement team structures.[47] Co-workers instruct new employees, thereby providing directive leadership. They also provide social support, which reduces stress among fellow employees. Teams with norms that support organizational goals may substitute for achievement-oriented leadership, because employees encourage (or pressure) co-workers to stretch their performance levels.[48]

Self-leadership–the process of influencing oneself to establish the self-direction and self-motivation needed to perform a task (see Chapter 6)–is another possible leadership substitute.[49] Employees with high self-leadership set their own goals, reinforce their own behavior, maintain positive thought processes, and monitor their own performance, thereby managing both personal motivation and abilities. As employees become more proficient in self-leadership, they presumably require less supervision to keep them focused and energized toward organizational objectives.

The leadership substitutes model has intuitive appeal, but the evidence so far is mixed. Some studies show that a few substitutes do replace the need for task- or people-oriented leadership, but others do not. The difficulties of statistically testing for leadership substitutes may account for some problems, but a few writers contend that the limited support is evidence that leadership plays a critical role regardless of the situation.[50] At this point, we can conclude that a few conditions such as self-directed work teams, self-leadership, and reward systems might reduce the importance of task- or people-oriented leadership but probably won't completely replace leaders in these roles.

Learning Objectives

After reading this section, you should be able to:

6. Distinguish transformational leadership from transactional and charismatic leadership.
7. Describe the four elements of transformational leadership.

TRANSFORMATIONAL PERSPECTIVE OF LEADERSHIP

transformational leadership
A leadership perspective that explains how leaders change teams or organizations by creating, communicating, and modeling a vision for the organization or work unit and inspiring employees to strive for that vision.

In the opening vignette to this chapter, ABC News president David Westin described his boss, Disney-ABC executive Anne Sweeney, as an excellent leader because she focuses on the future of the company and the industry. In fact, Sweeney is considered an entrepreneurial visionary who experiments with new channels through which the television industry delivers content. Under Sweeney's leadership, ABC was the first network to sign up shows for iTunes. It was also an innovator in online content, including delivering ad-supported free streaming programs on the Internet. In fact, Sweeney embodies the company's unofficial motto: Create what's next.

Through her vision, communication, and actions, Anne Sweeney is transforming ABC as well as the television industry. In other words, she practices **transformational leadership.** Transformational leaders such as Anne Sweeney, Herb Kelleher (Southwest Airlines), A. G. Lafley (Procter & Gamble), Carlos Ghosn (Renault/Nissan), and Richard Branson (Virgin) dot the corporate landscape. These leaders are agents of change. They create, communicate, and model a shared vision for the team or organization, and they inspire followers to strive for that vision.[51]

transactional leadership
Leadership that helps organizations achieve their current objectives more efficiently, such as by linking job performance to valued rewards and ensuring that employees have the resources needed to get the job done.

Transformational versus Transactional Leadership

Transformational leadership differs from **transactional leadership.**[52] The leadership literature offers a confusing array of definitions for transactional leadership, but we shall define it as helping organizations achieve their current objectives more efficiently, such as by linking job performance to valued rewards and ensuring that employees have the resources needed to get the job done. The contingency and behavioral theories described earlier adopt the transactional perspective because they focus on leader behaviors that improve employee performance and satisfaction. Transactional leadership is considered by some writers as "managing" or "doing things right" because leaders concentrate on improving employee performance and well-being.[53] In contrast, transformational leadership is about "leading"–changing the organization's strategies and culture so that they have a better fit with the surrounding environment. Transformational leaders are change agents who energize and direct employees to a new set of corporate values and behaviors.

Organizations require both transactional and transformational leadership.[54] Transactional leadership improves organizational efficiency, whereas transformational leadership steers companies onto a better course of action. Transformational leadership is particularly important in organizations that require significant alignment with the external environment. Unfortunately, too many leaders get trapped in the daily managerial activities that represent transactional leadership.[55] They lose touch with the transformational aspect of effective leadership. Without transformational leaders, organizations stagnate and eventually become seriously misaligned with their environments.

Transformational versus Charismatic Leadership

Another topic that has generated some confusion and controversy is the distinction between *transformational* and *charismatic* leadership.[56] Many researchers either use the words interchangeably, as if they have the same meaning, or view charismatic leadership as an essential ingredient of transformational leadership. Others take this view further by suggesting that charismatic leadership is the highest degree of transformational leadership.

However, the emerging view, which this book adopts, comes from a third group of experts who contend that charisma is distinct from transformational leadership. These academics point out that charisma is a personal trait or relational quality that provides referent power over followers, whereas transformational

Leading without Charisma *Charisma* is not a word that comes to mind when seeing Alan George Lafley in action as a leader. Various sources say that the Procter & Gamble (P&G) CEO is distinctly "unassuming," with "a humble demeanor that belies his status." Lafley is so soft-spoken that colleagues have to bend forward to hear him. One industry observer declared that "if there were 15 people sitting around the conference table, it wouldn't be obvious that he was the CEO." Lafley may lack charisma, but that hasn't stopped him from transforming the household products company where his charismatic predecessor had failed (and was ousted after just 18 months). Lafley's consistent vision, as well as symbolic and strategic actions toward a more customer-friendly and innovative organization, have provided the direction and clarity that P&G lacked. Importantly, Lafley also walks the talk; for 10 to 15 days each year, he personally interviews and observes customers using P&G products in their homes, from Germany to Venezuela. The result: P&G has become the industry's hotspot for innovation, its market share and profitability have experienced sustained growth, and its stock price has soared.[57]

leadership is a set of behaviors that people use to lead the change process.[58] Charismatic leaders might be transformational leaders; indeed, their personal power through charisma is a tool to change the behavior of followers. However, some research points out that charismatic or "heroic" leaders easily build allegiance in followers but do not necessarily change the organization. Other research suggests that charismatic leaders produce dependent followers, whereas transformational leaders have the opposite effect–they build follower empowerment, which tends to reduce dependence on the leader. For example, one study reported a negative relationship between charismatic leadership and the self-efficacy of followers.[59]

The main point here is that transformational leaders are not necessarily charismatic. Alan G. Lafley, the CEO of Procter & Gamble, is not known for being charismatic, but he has transformed the household goods company like no leader in recent memory. Similarly, IBM CEO Sam Palmisano speaks with humility yet continues to drive IBM's success. "I don't have much curb appeal," Palmisano says of his minimal charisma, adding that IBM has more than 300,000 brilliant people to drive the organization. "I just try to lead them and get them to come together around a common point of view," he explains.[60] In other words, Palmisano and Lafley lead by applying transformational leadership behaviors.

Elements of Transformational Leadership

There are several descriptions of transformational leadership, but most include the following four elements: Create a strategic vision, communicate the vision, model the vision, and build commitment toward the vision (see Exhibit 12.4).

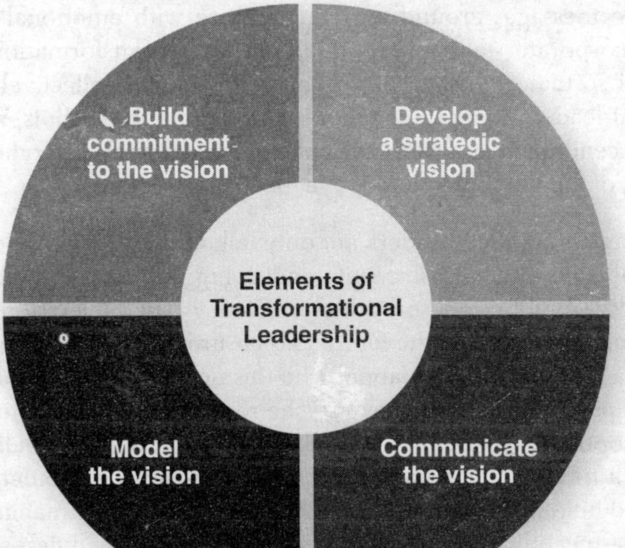

Exhibit 12.4 *Elements of Transformational Leadership*

Create a Strategic Vision Transformational leaders establish a vision of the company's future state that engages employees to achieve objectives they didn't think possible. These leaders shape a strategic vision of a realistic and attractive future that bonds employees together and focuses their energy toward a superordinate organizational goal.[61] A shared strategic vision represents the substance of transformational leadership. It reflects a future for the company or work unit that is ultimately accepted and valued by organizational members. "In essence, leadership is about dreaming the impossible and helping followers achieve the same," says Nandan Nilekani, CEO of India's information technology giant, Infosys. "Moreover, the dream has to be built on sound and context-invariant values to sustain the enthusiasm and energy of people over a long time."[62]

Strategic vision creates a "higher purpose" or superordinate goal that energizes and unifies employees.[63] A strategic vision might originate with the leader, but it is just as likely to emerge from employees, clients, suppliers, or other stakeholders. A shared strategic vision plays an important role in organizational effectiveness.[64] Visions offer the motivational benefits of goal setting, but they are compelling future states that bond employees and motivate them to strive for those objectives. Visions are typically described in a way that distinguishes them from the current situation yet makes the goal both appealing and achievable.

Communicate the Vision If vision is the substance of transformational leadership, communicating that vision is the process. CEOs say that the most important leadership quality is being able to build and share their vision for the organization. "Part of a leader's role is to set the vision for the company and to communicate that vision to staff to get their buy-in," explains Dave Anderson, president of WorkSafeBC (the Workers' Compensation Board of British Columbia, Canada).[65]

Transformational leaders communicate meaning and elevate the importance of the visionary goal to employees. They frame messages around a grand purpose with emotional appeal that captivates employees and other corporate stakeholders. Framing helps transformational leaders establish a common mental model so that the group or organization will act collectively toward the desirable goal.[66] Transformational leaders bring their visions to life through symbols, metaphors, stories, and other vehicles that transcend plain language. Metaphors borrow images of other experiences, thereby creating richer meaning of the vision that has not yet been experienced.

Model the Vision Transformational leaders not only talk about a vision; they enact it. They "walk the talk" by stepping outside the executive suite and doing things that symbolize the vision.[67] For example, when Anne Sweeney became president of Disney-ABC Television Group, she put much effort into communicating her vision of the future and ensuring that her actions were consistent with her words. "There was a lot of uncertainty about who this new team was, what they were going to be about and how the company would be managed," she recalls. "My job was to let people know what my management philosophy was and to not just talk the talk, but walk the walk."[68]

Leaders walk the talk through significant events such as visiting customers, moving their offices closer to employees, and holding ceremonies to destroy outdated policy manuals. However, they also alter mundane activities–meeting agendas, dress codes, executive schedules–so that the activities are more consistent with the vision and its underlying values. Modeling the vision is important because doing so legitimizes and demonstrates what the vision looks like in practice. "As an executive, you're always being watched by employees, and everything you say gets magnified–so you teach a lot by how you conduct yourself," advises Carl Bass, CEO of California software company Autodesk.

Modeling the vision is also important because it builds employee trust in the leader. The greater the consistency between the leader's words and actions, the more employees will believe in and be willing to follow the leader. In fact, one survey reported that leading by example is the most important characteristic of a leader. "There are lots of people who talk a good story, but very few deliver one," warns Peter Farrell, founder and chairman of San Diego–based ResMed. "You've got to mean what you say, say what you mean, and be consistent."[69]

Build Commitment toward the Vision Transforming a vision into reality requires employee commitment. Transformational leaders build this commitment in several ways. Their words, symbols, and stories build a contagious enthusiasm that energizes people to adopt the vision as their own. Leaders demonstrate a "can do" attitude by enacting their vision and staying on course. Their persistence and consistency reflect an image of honesty, trust, and integrity. Finally, leaders build commitment by involving employees in the process of shaping the organization's vision.

Evaluating the Transformational Leadership Perspective

Transformational leaders do make a difference. Subordinates are more satisfied and have higher affective organizational commitment under transformational leaders. They also perform their jobs better, engage in more organizational citizenship behaviors, and make better or more creative decisions. One study of bank branches reported that organizational commitment and financial performance seemed to increase where the branch manager completed a transformational leadership training program.[70]

Transformational leadership is currently the most popular leadership perspective, but it faces a number of challenges. One problem is that some writers engage in circular logic by defining transformational leadership by the leader's success.[71] They suggest that leaders are transformational when they *successfully* bring about change, rather than when they engage in certain behaviors we call transformational. This circular definition makes it impossible to determine whether transformational leadership is effective. Another concern is that transformational leadership is usually described as a universal rather than contingency-oriented model. Only very recently have writers begun to explore the idea that transformational leadership is more valuable in some situations than others.[72] For instance, transformational leadership is probably more appropriate when organizations need to adapt than when environmental conditions are stable. Preliminary evidence suggests that the transformational leadership perspective is relevant across cultures. However, there may be specific elements of transformational leadership, such as the way visions are formed and communicated, that are more appropriate in North America than in other cultures.

Brijmohan Lall Munjal: Leader of a World Class Organization When Hero Cycles and Honda Motor Company of Japan inked their joint venture in India in April 1984, few could have imagined that the two would go on to create history and become the subject of a case study at London Business School. But, that is the Hero Honda saga. In a little over two decades, the world's largest manufacturer of bicycles and the global leader in motorcycles has created not only the world's single largest motorcycle company but also the most endearing and successful joint venture for Honda Motor Company, worldwide. The company has sold over 15 million motorcycles and has consistently sustained the growth rate in double digits since its inception and, today, every second motorcycle sold in the country is a Hero Honda. In two decades, Hero Honda has built two world-class manufacturing facilities at Dharuhera and Gurgaon, in Haryana, India, that now churn out over 3 million bikes per year. To meet the growing demand, the company is now in the process of setting up a third plant.

"Don't dream if you can't fulfill your dreams," Brijmohan Lall Munjal is often fond of saying. The founder and patriarch of the $ 2.8 billion Hero Group is a classic first generation entrepreneur. He is a man who started small, dreamt big, and used a combination of grit and perseverance to create one of the country's largest corporate groups, and the World's No.1 Two Wheeler Company.

A visionary, Brijmohan made a rather unusual start in life. Around the time when the freedom movement in India was taking shape in the late 1920s, he walked into a newly opened *Gurukul* (Indian heritage school) near his home in Kamalia (now in Pakistan). Then he was only six years old. Thus began an extraordinary tale of courage and perseverance. Brijmohan began his business story after partition, in 1947, when he and his brothers relocated to Ludhiana. The family set up a company that provided the poor people with the basic transport (bicycles). Three decades later, as India evolved, he added a second crucial chapter—affordable and technologically superior transport to millions of middle class Indians. The rest is history.

Building Relationships

When Brijmohan and his brothers started out, there was no concept of organized dealer networks. Companies were just involved in production, and most dealers functioned like traders. Brijmohan changed the rules of the business by trusting his gut instincts—introducing business norms that were ahead of their time, and investing in strategic relationships. Brijmohan built a series of bonds and networks with hundreds of family members, vendors, dealers, and employees. Similar to the Japanese *keiretsu* system, these networks are now the glue that holds the Hero Group together.

"Thanks to the relationships that we have nurtured so passionately in the Hero family, the younger generations of some of our bicycle dealers have become dealers of Hero Honda. These relationships have survived through generations – through bad times and good times," the patriarch reminiscences.

Besides bonding with his vendors and dealers, Brijmohan has been personally responsible for kindling a spirit of entrepreneurship in his employees, and, today, 40 of his former employees are successful entrepreneurs.

Staying Ahead

Though not technically qualified in the conventional sense, few of his contemporaries have understood the dynamics of technology better than Brijmohan. He could always visualize the applicability of technology before others. For example, in the 1980s, when all two-wheeler companies in India opted for two-stroke engine technology, Brijmohan preferred a four-stoke engine – a technology that dramatically increased fuel efficiency and reduced maintenance costs. This technology was one of the biggest reasons for Hero Honda's stupendous success.

Time and again, Brijmohan managed to steal a march over his industry peers. For example, when Honda Motors of Japan was looking for a collaborator in the 1980s, the Hero Group was initially not high up the pecking order, as there were other more eligible and established suitors.Yet, it did not take long for the astute Japanese to realize that the Hero Group and Honda had much more in common than earlier perceived—there was a sharp focus on financial and raw material management, and employee turnover was low. Honda officials were also amazed that the Munjals were already practicing "just-in-time-inventory" system (JIT). It turned out that Brijmohan's aspiration to provide cheap transportation to India's poor by default ensured lean and cost-effective operations. This, in turn, increased vendor efficiency and led to near-zero inventories.

A Corporate Citizen

A frugal upbringing and a value system modeled on the famous *Gurukul* system– which stresses the sanctity of the teacher-pupil relationship—imbibed a strong sense of social commitment and responsibility in Brijmohan.

There is a special place in his heart for Ludhiana, the city where he took roots. Today, Ludhiana is a modern, bustling city, but Brijmohan has played no mean role in its evolution. Several schools and educational institutions in Ludhiana owe their existence to the Munjal family. The Ludhiana Stock Exchange owes its existence to Brijmohan's vision, as does the Ludhiana Flying Club. He has also set up the not-for-profit Dayanand Medical College and Hospital, an institute now rated as one of the best medical colleges in India—in terms of infrastructure, quality of staff, and alumni profile.

In and around Dharuhera too, near the first Hero Honda plant, Brijmohan and his family have left their stamp of philanthropy. The Raman Kant Munjal Foundation, Brijmohan's set up in memory of eldest son, runs a higher secondary school and a very modern and well-equipped 100-bed hospital there. The group has also adopted numerous villages, and provides education, vocational training, drinking water, roads, streetlights, and sewerage.

Prominent Awards and Accolades Conferred on Brijmohan Lall Munjal

2006	'Lifetime Achievement Award' for Translating Excellence in Corporate Governance into Reality by The Institute of Company Secretaries of India
2005	Indian Automotive Hall of Pride by Overdrive CNBC TV18 Commendation of Business Leadership displaying extraordinary Corporate Leadership and Entrepreneurial Spirit Padma Bhushan by the Government of India Doctor of Letters (Honoris Causa) by Hemwati Nandan Bahuguna Garhwal University, Srinagar, Garhwal Lifetime Achievement Award' by ET Awards, for Corporate Excellence
2004	Life Time Achievement Award for Management by All India Management Association D. Litt. (Honoris Causa) by Banaras Hindu University Lifetime Achievement Award by Amity Business School Lifetime Achievement Award by HT Power Jobs
2002	Entrepreneur of the Year Award by Business Standard Giants International Award to the Chairman in the field of Business & Industry Business Leadership Award by Madras Management Association
2001	Entrepreneur of the Year Award by Ernst & Young
2000	Sir Jehangir Ghandy Medal for Industrial Peace by XLRI, Jamshedpur
1998	Business Leader of the Year by Business Baron
1997	Distinguished Entrepreneurship Award by PHD Chambers of Commerce & Industry
1995	National Award for outstanding contribution to the Development of Indian Small Scale Industry (NSIC Award – Presented by President of India)
1994	Businessman of the Year by Business India Group of Publications
1992	Honorary Membership, Indian Institution of Industrial Engineering Award

Source: Hero Honda Ltd.

Learning Objectives

After reading the next two sections, you should be able to:

8. Describe the implicit leadership perspective.
9. Discuss similarities and differences in the leadership styles of women and men.
10. Understand leadership development through 360-degree feedback.
11. Explore the eight archetypes of open leadership.

implicit leadership theory
A theory stating that people evaluate a leader's effectiveness in terms of how well that person fits preconceived beliefs about the features and behaviors of effective leaders (leadership prototypes) and that people tend to inflate the influence of leaders on organizational events.

Implicit Leadership Perspective

The competency, behavior, contingency, and transformational leadership perspectives make the basic assumption that leaders "make a difference." Certainly, there is evidence that senior executives do influence organizational performance. However, leadership also involves followers' perceptions about the characteristics and influence of people they call leaders. This perceptual perspective of leadership is collectively called **implicit leadership theory.**[73]

Prototypes of Effective Leaders

Implicit leadership theory consists of two related concepts. The main part of this theory states that everyone has *leadership prototypes*–preconceived beliefs about the features and behaviors of effective leaders. These prototypes, which develop through socialization within the family and society,[74] shape our expectations and acceptance of others as leaders, and this in turn affects our willingness to serve as followers. In other words, we are more willing to allow someone to influence us as a leader if that person looks and acts like our prototype of a leader. For example, one recent study established that inherited personality characteristics significantly influence the perception that someone is a leader in a leaderless situation.[75] Such leadership prototypes not only support a person's role as leader; they also form or influence our perception of the leader's effectiveness. If the leader looks like and acts consistently with our prototype, we are more likely to believe that the leader is effective.[76] This prototype comparison process occurs because people have an inherent need to quickly evaluate individuals as leaders, yet leadership effectiveness is often ambiguous and might not be apparent for a long time.

Attributing Leadership

Implicit leadership is also influenced by attribution errors. Research has found that (at least in Western cultures) people tend to attribute organizational events to the leader, even when those events are largely caused by factors beyond the leader's control. This attribution is partly caused by fundamental attribution error (see Chapter 3) in which leaders are given credit or blame for the company's success or failure because employees do not readily see the external forces that also influence these events. Leaders reinforce this belief by taking credit for organizational successes.[77]

Need for Situational Control

A third perceptual distortion of leadership suggests that people want to believe leaders make a difference. There are two basic reasons for this belief.[78] First, leadership is a useful way for us to simplify life events. It is easier to explain organizational successes and failures in terms of the leader's ability than by analyzing a complex array of other forces. For example, there are usually many reasons why a company fails to change quickly enough in the marketplace, yet we tend to simplify this explanation down to the notion that the company president or some other corporate leader was ineffective.

Second, there is a strong tendency in the United States and other Western cultures to believe that life events are generated more from people than from uncontrollable natural forces.[79] This illusion of control is satisfied by believing that events result from the rational actions of leaders. In short, employees feel better believing that leaders make a difference, so they actively look for evidence that this is so.

The implicit leadership perspective not only questions the importance of leadership, but it also provides valuable advice to improve leadership acceptance. This approach highlights the fact that leadership is a perception of followers as much as the actual behaviors and characteristics of people calling themselves leaders. Potential leaders must be sensitive to this fact, understand what followers expect, and act accordingly. Individuals who do not make an effort to fit leadership prototypes will have more difficulty bringing about necessary organizational change.

The Romance of Leadership

Along with relying on implicit prototypes of effective leaders, followers tend to distort their perception of the influence that leaders have on the environment. This "romance of leadership" effect exists because in most cultures people want to believe that leaders make a difference. Consider the experience of Ricardo Semler, the charismatic CEO of Brazilian conglomerate SEMCO SA:

> At the company, no matter what you do, people will naturally create and nurture a charismatic figure," Semler suggests. "The charismatic figure, on the other hand, feeds this; it doesn't just happen, and it is very difficult to check your ego at the door. The people at SEMCO don't look and act like me. They are not yes-men by any means. What is left, however, is a certain feeling that has to do with the cult of personality. They credit me with successes that are not my own, and they don't debit me my mistakes. They give undue importance to what I say, and I think that doesn't go away.[80]

There are two basic reasons why people inflate their perceptions of the leader's influence over the environment.[81] First, leadership is a useful way for us to simplify life events. It is easier to explain organizational successes and failures in terms of the leader's ability than by analyzing a complex array of other forces. Second, there is a strong tendency in the United States and other Western cultures to believe that life events are generated more from people than from uncontrollable natural forces.[82] This illusion of control is satisfied by believing that events result from the rational actions of leaders. In other words, employees feel better believing that leaders make a difference, so they actively look for evidence that this is so.

One way that followers support their perceptions that leaders make a difference is through fundamental attribution error (see Chapter 3). Research has found that (at least in Western cultures) leaders are given credit or blame for the company's success or failure because employees do not readily see the external forces that also influence these events. Leaders reinforce this belief by taking credit for organizational successes.[83]

The implicit leadership perspective provides valuable advice to improve leadership acceptance. It highlights the fact that leadership is a perception of followers as much as the actual behaviors and formal roles of people calling themselves leaders. Potential leaders must be sensitive to this fact, understand what followers expect, and act accordingly. Individuals who do not make an effort to fit leadership prototypes will have more difficulty bringing about necessary organizational change.

Leadership Development Through 360 Degree Feedback: Case of Companies in India

The 360 degree method is a contrived method of providing feedback to an employee, and is referred to as the multi-rater, multi-source, or full-circle feedback, where upward, downward, and lateral feedback is obtained about an employee's performance, competencies, or traits. The application of 360 degree feedback can also be made to facilitate effective leadership development.

Companies like Wipro and Motorola have been employing it for identifying their employees' areas of development, and have been using it as an effective tool for leadership development. Wipro had earlier adopted the competency route to leadership development with the focus on the people. Wipro later switched to the PCMM Level 5. Motorola has developed a performance-led leadership development model called 'Totality of Motorola Leadership' (TOML)[84]. It was done by pre-defining competencies and providing customized (individual) developmental planning based on the 360 degree feedback to enhance organizational performance. All the three companies mentioned above have made 360 degree feedback an integral part of their employee development programs.

Johnson & Johnson introduced a model of leadership, called the 'Standard of Leadership', based on the 360 degree feedback in 1996, to ensure business success and market leadership. It was introduced at the top level. Philips believed that the 360 degree feedback should be used only as a developmental tool, and not a substitute for the performance management system.

Philips also used the full circle feedback for identifying 'top potential' category employees. It developed a leadership competency model focusing on six competencies, including determination for high quality results, search for better methods, high performance expectation, focus on the market, self and people development, and developing commitment. The leadership model has been linked with organizational values and goals.

GE introduced the 360 degree feedback during the 1980s, with Jack Welch taking over the CEOship of the corporation. Questionnaires and open reviews were largely used with the help of the then Management Development Professor at Harvard. The 'Crotonville Culture' was gradually expanded to key business areas where the entrenched positions of senior managers were pretty endemic, and the business results were not showing. The outcome was a redefined leadership.

At NIIT, the 360 degree feedback is referred to as the Individual Effectiveness Feedback (IEF) which is web enabled. The person concerned gets the feedback through an auto-generated ca on the inputs from self, peers, team members, and supervisors.

At NIIT, an individual's effectiveness is measured on five dimensions, viz., ownership, shared values, contribution to high performing team and communication. Use of the 360 degree feedba a development tool has helped the employees develop traits and attributes conducive to th performance NIIT culture.

Cross-Cultural and Gender Issues in Leadership

Along with the five perspectives of leadership presented throughout this chapter, cultural values and practices affect what leaders do. Culture shapes the leader's values and norms, which influence his or her decisions and actions. Cultural values also shape the expectations that followers have of their leaders. An executive who acts inconsistently with cultural expectations is more likely to be perceived as an ineffective leader. Furthermore, leaders who deviate from those values may experience various forms of influence to get them to conform to the leadership norms and expectations of the society. In other words, implicit leadership theory, described in the previous section of this chapter, explains differences in leadership practices across cultures.

Over the past few years, 150 researchers from dozens of countries have worked together on Project GLOBE (Global Leadership and Organizational Behavior Effectiveness) to identify the effects of cultural values on leadership.[85] The project organized countries into 10 regional clusters, of which the United States, Great Britain, and similar countries are grouped into the "Anglo" cluster. The results of this massive investigation suggest that some features of leadership are universal and some differ across cultures. Specifically, the GLOBE project reports that "charismatic visionary" is a universally recognized concept and that middle managers around the world believe that it is characteristic of effective leaders. *Charismatic visionary* represents a cluster of concepts including visionary, inspirational, performance orientation, integrity, and decisiveness.[86] In contrast, participative leadership is perceived as characteristic of effective leadership in low power distance cultures but less so in high power distance cultures. For instance, one study reported that Mexican employees expect managers to make decisions affecting their work. Mexico is a high power distance culture, so followers expect leaders to apply their authority rather than delegate their power most of the time.[87] In summary, there are similarities and differences in the concept and preferred practice of leadership across cultures.

Leadership Across Cultures

A cross-cultural study was conducted by Fukushige and Spicer[88] to quantify the differences between Japanese and British followers in respect of their preferences for leadership and work-goals based on Full-Range Leadership Model of Bass and Avolio's[89] and Path-Goal Leadership Theory of House[90].

The research also investigated the relationship between leadership preferences and work-goals and how work-goals potentially influence their leader's behavior. Significant differences were obtained between them: the Japanese followers prefer 'element of variety and adventure in their job' whereas the British followers gave preference to 'sufficient time for your personal or family life'. These differences were related to their respective leadership preferences. Significant differences were obtained for all the twelve leadership styles, except Bass and Avolio's *Management-by-Exception Passive* and House's[90] *Directive Leadership.* The other differences were observed in work-goals on the parameters of element of variety and adventure in the job, opportunities to be high performer, stress-free working environment and opportunities to socialize with other people.

In an exploratory study, Fukushige and Spicer[91] studied suitability of Bass and Avolio's full-range leadership model in the Japanese context and they found that idealized influence attributed and inspirational motivation leadership styles were not endorsed but contingent reward was highly supported by Japanese followers. The Japanese culture-specific potential leadership styles found were liberal, trust, punctual, network, and protective. Path-goal theory's directive, supportive, participative and achievement-oriented leadership styles were found to be significant. Cultural change factors

Microsoft Germany's Gender Leadership Boom Europe's population is shrinking and aging, two trends that worried Achim Berg (second from left in photo) when he was recently hired as CEO of Microsoft Germany. Fortunately, in a country where men still overwhelmingly dominate the executive suite, the former Deutsche Telekom executive has a straightforward solution: Hire more female managers and create a work environment that motivates them to stay. Berg now has five women on the 12-person management board and a growing pool of junior female staff members working their way into leadership positions. Berg also welcomes the gender balance because it brings more diverse leadership styles. "Women have a different management style," Berg claims. Dorothee Belz, Microsoft Germany's director of legal and corporate affairs, agrees. Women, she suggests, look at issues differently and are more willing than men to discuss problems. Berg says that working with more female colleagues has also altered his own leadership style; it has become more consultative, with less forcefulness on "speed and quick results." He has also noticed less politics in executive meetings. "It seems that there is a noticeable decline in territorial behavior. But perhaps we'd be better off consulting a zoologist," says Berg, laughing.[92]

which appeared to influence leadership preferences in Japan were male chauvinism to gender equality, collectivism to individualism, and seniority to meritocracy.

With respect to gender, studies in field settings have generally found that male and female leaders do not differ in their levels of task-oriented or people-oriented leadership. The main explanation is that real-world jobs require similar behavior from male and female job incumbents.[93] However, women do adopt a participative leadership style more readily than their male counterparts. One possible reason is that, compared to boys, girls are often raised to be more egalitarian and less status-oriented, which is consistent with being participative. There is also some evidence that women have somewhat better interpersonal skills than men, and this translates into their relatively greater use of the participative leadership style. A third explanation is that subordinates, on the basis of their own gender stereotypes, expect female leaders to be more participative, so female leaders comply with follower expectations to some extent.

Several recent surveys report that women are rated higher than men on the emerging leadership qualities of coaching, teamwork, and empowering employees.[94] Yet research also suggests that women are evaluated negatively when they try to apply the full range of leadership styles, particularly more directive and autocratic approaches. Thus, ironically, women may be well suited to contemporary leadership roles, yet they often continue to face limitations of leadership through the gender stereotypes and prototypes of leaders that are held by followers.[95] Overall, both male and female leaders must be sensitive to the fact that followers have expectations about how leaders should act, and negative evaluations may go to leaders who deviate from those expectations.

Open Leadership

In the age of social media, which is creating a revolution and impacting organizational set-ups, it is the leaders who have a crucial role to navigate through these changes. A leader not only needs to consider the social media revolution and leverage its power of openness, but also needs to retain control. Sharing is an inherent behavior in human beings, but social media has further fueled this behavior by providing technologies and platforms for connecting with a number of individuals at lightening speed, which is cheaper and easier.

Revolution and changes, which have occurred due to social media, require changes in leadership styles for organizations to thrive and sustain.[96] Li defines open leadership as: "Having the confidence and humility to give up the need to be in control while inspiring commitment from people to accomplish goals." However, there is the fear of losing control concerning *open leadership.*

Dimensions of Open Leadership

The dimensions which have been considered to understand open leadership include (a) views about people–optimistic/pessimistic and (b) views about success–collaborative/independent. Based on these dimensions, there are optimistic leaders and collaborative leaders.

Optimistic Leader Optimistic leaders have the traits of curiosity and humility. They are curious about all aspects (employees, customers, markets, suppliers, industry trends, and the world around) and are always on the drive to find new opportunities, learn new things to improve themselves and others around them. Such leaders consider social technologies to extend their learning in a new way. Humility enables them to change their views based on their exposure. They become self-aware and have confidence to accept mistakes or the need for help.

Collaborative Leader Under open leadership, a collaborative leader needs to be more open, let go on control, but be able to get the things done. It is beyond any title or role in the organizations, and the best collaborators have many different kinds of connections.

Open Leadership Archetypes

Open leadership archetypes (Exhibit 12.5) are discussed below.

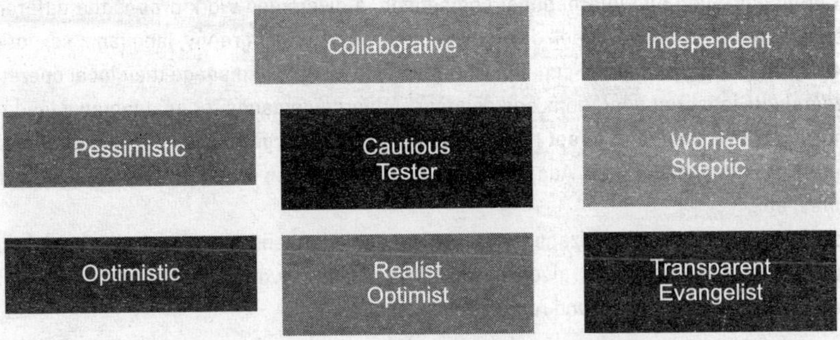

Source: Adapted from: Li Charlene (2010), "Open Leadership Mind-Sets and Traits", in *Open Leadership: How Social Technology Can Transform the Way You Lead*, CA: Josey-Bass, p. 175.

Exhibit 12.5 *Open Leadership Archetypes*

Realist Optimist This is the most effective type of open leadership. Such leaders understand the need for openness and its limitations. He/she can win through tough situations by collaborative approach and overcome impediments through openness and winning trust. Such leaders need not be at the top of an organization. They are open to social technologies, but work along with those who are unenthusiastic about it. Such leaders, having understanding of realities, give importance to people and their own role and position in the organization.

The Worried Skeptics Such leaders are pessimistic and independent. They have the habit of worrying, they are usually people in the top management. They emphasize on individuality, expect a person to take individual responsibility for actions and outcomes, skeptical about accepting and adopting new social media tools, rely heavily on their own excellent analytical and intuitive skills, and are infrequent on open dialogues with important audiences as they fear risk and insecure.

Cautious Testers Such leaders are pessimistic, but they understand the importance of collaborating. They have willingness to collaborate with other people to test options, plans and new ideas, but at the same time are tempered by pessimism. Their associates are willing to have dialogue with them on opportunities, and benefits based on relationship and trust. Their experience of using social technologies is low. Such leaders have the limitation of not abandoning command and control practices.

Transparent Evangelists They are optimistic but individualistic. They are highly technology savvy and believe in the ability of the impact of new technologies and transformation on all aspects of the organization. However, these individuals are independent in their thinking and outlook to adopting technologies. They think of technology from their personal angle and not from the organizational perspective. They believe that organizations cannot be too open.

Best Companies for Leadership Qualities—2010: The Hay Group Study[97] The Hay Group conducted a study on Best Companies for Leadership in 2010. The study covered various companies located in Asia, Europe, North America and Latin America. The important highlights of the study are as follows:

1. *Leadership across the organization:* The best companies for leadership encourage leadership across all the levels and units/subsidiaries. All employees are expected to lead and are motivated to bring in new ideas, and make valuable contributions to the organization. They support flat business structures.
2. *Diversity is an advantage:* Diversity is considered a competitive edge. Equal opportunity is provided to minority groups. In the context of globalization and international competition, a diversified workforce is the differentiator for leader companies from others. They actively seek diversity in the aspects of geography, language, sex, orientation, culture, educational background, etc. Globalized companies recruit local people to manage their local operations.
3. *Adaptable leadership:* Globalized operations and diverse workforce demands for an adaptable leadership. Managers of these organizations are trained to adapt their leadership approach, get mastery on collaborative strategies, and improve upon cross-cultural leadership. Adaptation is also undertaken in other aspects like development techniques, reward structures, etc.
4. *Holistic approach to work:* These organizations value all stakeholders and have interest in social and environmental responsibilities. Utmost importance is given to work-life balance, work towards achieving high environmental standards, and CSR is the key to attract and recruit employees.

Best Companies for Leadership 2010

Global	Asia	Europe	North America	Latin America
General Electric	Samsung Electronics	Unilever	General Electric	Unilever
Procter & Gamble	HSBC Holdings	Banco Santander	Procter & Gamble	LAN
Inter Corp.	Tata Sons	Telefonica	Southwest Airlines	3M Company
Simens	Infosys Technologies	Deutsche Bank	Walmart	General Electric
Banco Santander	Nissan Motor Co. Ltd	HSBC Holdings	Coca-Cola	Cemex
The Coca-Cola Company		Repsol YPF	PepsiCo	IBM
McDonald's Corp.		Volkswagen	Microsoft	Telefonica
Accenture		L'Oreal	IBM	Empresas Polar
Walmart		Danone	Cisco Systems	Votorantim
Southwest Airlines		Vodafone	Johnson & Johnson	Banco Santander

Source: Hay Group (2010), Best Companies for Leadership, http://www.haygroup.com/BestCompaniesForLeadership/research-and-findings/about-the-research.aspx, accessed on 1/3/2011.

Key findings: Continent-wise[98]

Asia In the Asian region, the best companies for leadership distinguished themselves from others as they valued technical expertise in leaders, attracted leaders with international opportunities, gave equal importance to ideas flowing from subsidiaries and headquarters, doled out high pay and bonuses to attract leaders and had social responsibility as crucial for them.

Europe The best companies for leadership in Europe had the following distinguishing features: these shared best practices for leadership across businesses, had programs to strengthen cross-cultural leadership, considered leadership development important in employees' performance, they provided facilities to work from home and actively managed a pool of successors for mission-critical roles.

North America Ninety per cent of the top 10 companies have expat programs, and have same percentage of women in senior positions. In most of the top 10 companies, inspiring leadership is greatly valued. Job rotation is another key feature to provide extensive experience, and international opportunities are used almost twice to attract leaders.

Latin America Seventy per cent of the top 10 companies give priority to work-life balance, thirty percent of the women workforce are in senior positions, there is roughly half support to work-from-home concept, international opportunities are used in 63 percent top companies to lure leaders and leaders are rotated for various roles extensively across the organization.

Chapter Summary

Leadership is defined as the ability to influence, motivate, and enable others to contribute toward the effectiveness and success of the organizations of which they are members. Leaders use influence to motivate followers and arrange the work environment so that they do the job more effectively. Leaders exist throughout the organization, not just in the executive suite.

The competency perspective tries to identify the characteristics of effective leaders. Recent writing suggests that leaders have specific personality characteristics, positive self-concept, drive, integrity, leadership motivation, knowledge of the business, cognitive and practical intelligence, and emotional intelligence. The behavioral perspective of leadership identifies two clusters of leader behavior, people-oriented and task-oriented. People-oriented behaviors include showing mutual trust and respect for subordinates, demonstrating a genuine concern for their needs, and having a desire to look out for their welfare. Task-oriented behaviors include assigning employees to specific tasks, clarifying their work duties and procedures, ensuring they follow company rules, and pushing them to reach their performance capacity.

The contingency perspective of leadership takes the view that effective leaders diagnose the situation and adapt their style to fit that situation. The path-goal model is the prominent contingency theory that identifies four leadership styles—directive, supportive, participative, and achievement-oriented—and several contingencies relating to the characteristics of the employee and of the situation.

Two other contingency leadership theories include the situational leadership theory and Fiedler's contingency theory. Research support is quite weak for both theories. However, a lasting element of Fiedler's theory is the idea that leaders have natural styles and, consequently, companies need to change the leaders' environments to suit their style. Leadership substitutes theory identifies contingencies that either limit the leader's ability to influence subordinates or make a particular leadership style unnecessary.

Transformational leaders create a strategic vision, communicate that vision through framing and use of metaphors, model the vision by 'walking the talk' and acting consistently, and build commitment toward the vision. This contrasts with transactional leadership, which involves linking job performance to valued rewards and ensuring that employees have the resources needed to get the job done. The contingency and behavioral perspectives adopt the transactional view of leadership.

According to the implicit leadership perspective, people have leadership prototypes, which they use to evaluate the leader's effectiveness. Furthermore, people form a romance of leadership; they want to believe that leaders make a difference, so they engage in fundamental attribution error and other perceptual distortions to support this belief in the leader's impact.

Cultural values also influence the leader's personal values, which in turn influence his or her leadership practices. Women generally do not differ from men in the degree of people-oriented or task-oriented leadership. However, female leaders more often adopt a participative style. Research also suggests that people evaluate female leaders on the basis of gender stereotypes, which may result in higher or lower ratings.

Key Terms

Fiedler's contingency model
implicit leadership theory
leadership
leadership substitutes
path-goal leadership theory
servant leadership
shared leadership
situational leadership theory
transactional leadership
transformational leadership

Critical Thinking Questions

1. Why is it important for top executives to value and support leadership demonstrated at all levels of the organization?
2. Find two newspaper ads for management or executive positions. What leadership competencies are mentioned in these ads? If you were on the selection panel, what methods would you use to identify these competencies in job applicants?
3. Consider your favorite teacher. What people-oriented and task-oriented leadership behaviors did he or she use effectively? In general, do you think students prefer an instructor who is more people-oriented or task-oriented? Explain your preference.
4. Your employees are skilled and experienced customer service representatives who perform nonroutine tasks, such as solving unique customer problems or meeting special needs with the company's equipment. Use path-goal theory to identify the most appropriate leadership style(s) you should use in this situation. Be sure to fully explain your answer, and discuss why other styles are inappropriate.
5. Transformational leadership is the most popular perspective of leadership. However, it is far from perfect. Discuss the limitations of transformational leadership.
6. This chapter distinguished charismatic leadership from transformational leadership. Yet charisma is identified by most employees and managers as a characteristic of effective leaders. Why is charisma commonly related to leadership? In your opinion, are the best leaders charismatic? Why or why not?
7. Identify a current political leader (e.g., president, governor, mayor) and his or her recent accomplishments. Now, using the implicit leadership perspective, think of ways that these accomplishments of the leader may be overstated. In other words, explain why they may be due to factors other than the leader.
8. You hear two people debating the merits of women as leaders. One person claims that women make better leaders than do men because women are more sensitive to their employees' needs and involve them in organizational decisions. The other person counters that although these leadership styles may be increasingly important, most women have trouble gaining acceptance as leaders when they face tough situations in which a more autocratic style is required. Discuss the accuracy of the comments made in this discussion.

CASE STUDY 12.1

PROFITEL INC.

As a formerly government-owned telephone monopoly, Profitel enjoyed many decades of minimal competition. Even today, as a publicly traded enterprise, the company's almost exclusive control over telephone copper wiring across the country keeps its profit margins above 40 percent. Competitors in telephone and DSL broadband continue to rely on Profitel's wholesale business, which generates substantially more profit than similar wholesale services in many other countries. However, Profitel has stiff competition in the cellular (mobile) telephone business, and other emerging technologies (voice-over-Internet) threaten Profitel's dominance. Because of these threats, Profitel's board of directors decided to hire an outsider as the new chief executive.

Although several qualified candidates expressed an interest in Profitel's top job, the board selected Lars Peeters, who had been CEO for six years of a publicly traded European telephone company, followed by a brief stint as CEO of a cellular telephone company in the United States until it was acquired by a larger firm. Profitel's board couldn't believe its good fortune; Peeters brought extensive industry knowledge and global experience, a high-octane energy level, self-confidence, decisiveness, and a congenial yet strongly persuasive interpersonal style. He also had a unique "presence," which caused people to pay attention and respect his leadership. The board was also impressed with Peeters's strategy to bolster Profitel's profit margins. This included investing heavily in the latest wireless broadband technology (for both cellular telephone and computer Internet) before competitors could gain a foothold, cutting costs through layoffs and reduction of peripheral services, and putting pressure on the government to deregulate Profitel's traditional and emerging businesses. When Peeters described his strategy to the board, one board member commented that this was the same strategy Peeters used in his previous two CEO postings. Peeters dismissed the comment, saying that each situation is unique.

Peeters lived up to his reputation as a decisive executive. Almost immediately after taking the CEO job at Profitel, he hired two executives from the European company where he had previously worked. Together, over the next two years, they cut the workforce by 5 percent and rolled out the new wireless broadband technology for cell phones and Internet. Costs increased somewhat due to downsizing expenses and the wireless technology rollout. Profitel's wireless broadband subscriber list grew quickly because, in spite of its very high prices, the technology faced limited competition and Profitel was pushing customers off the older technology to the new network. Profitel's customer satisfaction ratings fell, however. A national consumer research group reported that Profitel's broadband offered the country's worst value. Employee morale also declined due to layoffs and the company's public image problems. Some industry experts also noted that Profitel selected its wireless technology without evaluating the alternative emerging wireless technology, which had been gaining ground in other countries. Peeters's aggressive campaign against government regulation also had unintended consequences. Rather than achieving less regulation, criticizing the government and its telecommunications regulator made Profitel look even more arrogant in the eyes of both customers and government leaders.

Profitel's board was troubled by the company's lackluster share price, which had declined 20 percent since Peeters was hired. Some board members also worried that the company had bet on the wrong wireless technology and that subscription levels would stall far below the number necessary to achieve the profits stated in Peeters's strategic plan. This concern came closer to reality when a foreign-owned competitor won a $1 billion government contract to improve broadband services in regional areas of the country. Profitel's proposal for that regional broadband upgrade had specified high prices and limited corporate investment, but Peeters had been confident Profitel would be awarded the contract because of its market dominance and existing infrastructure with the new wireless network. When the government decided otherwise, Profitel's board fired Peeters along with the two executives he had hired from the European company. Now, the board had to figure out what went wrong and how to avoid this problem in the future.

Discussion Questions

1. Which perspective of leadership best explains the problems experienced in this case? Analyze the case using concepts discussed in that leadership perspective.
2. What can organizations do to minimize the leadership problems discussed above?

CASE STUDY 12.2

MACK ATTACK

BusinessWeek

John J. Mack, who had left Morgan Stanley four years earlier, was back as CEO, replacing Philip J. Purcell, who had resigned weeks earlier after mounting criticism that he was mismanaging the once-mighty investment bank. Whereas Purcell was a top-down strategist and tended to hole up in his office, Mack is drawing on his skills as a salesman and operator to make Morgan Stanley as nimble and dynamic as possible. He also hired key people to help him put the new culture in place.

This *BusinessWeek* case study examines the leadership of Morgan Stanley CEO John J. Mack. It describes his actions to change the investment bank's culture and to redirect decision making so that it is more aggressive rather than timid. Read through this *BusinessWeek* article at www.mhhe.com/mcshane5e, and prepare for the discussion questions below.

Discussion Questions

1. On the basis of the information in this case study, describe the competencies that seem strongest in John Mack.
2. To what extent has John Mack exhibited transformational leadership behaviors to shift Morgan Stanley's culture and decision making?

Source: E. Thornton, "Mack Attack," *BusinessWeek*, 3 July 2006, p. 88.

TEAM EXERCISE 12.3

LEADERSHIP DIAGNOSTIC ANALYSIS

PURPOSE To help students learn about the different path-goal leadership styles and understand when to apply each style.

INSTRUCTIONS

1. Students individually write down two incidents in which someone was an effective manager or leader over them. The leader and situation can be from work, a sports team, a student work group, or any other setting where leadership might emerge. For example, students might describe how their supervisor in a summer job pushed them to reach higher performance goals than they would have done otherwise. Each incident should state the actual behaviors that the leader used, not just general statements (e.g., "My boss sat down with me and we agreed on specific targets and deadlines; then he said several times over the next few weeks that I was capable of reaching those goals.") Each incident requires only two or three sentences.
2. After everyone has written his or her two incidents, the instructor will form small groups (typically, four or five students). Each team will answer the following questions for each incident presented in that team:
   a. Which path-goal theory leadership style(s)–directive, supportive, participative, or achievement-oriented–did the leader apply in this incident?
   b. Ask the person who wrote the incident about the conditions that made this leadership style (or these styles, if more than one was used) appropriate in this situation? The team should list these contingency factors clearly and, where possible, connect them to the contingencies described in path-goal theory. (*Note:* The team might identify path-goal leadership contingencies that are not described in the book. These, too, should be noted and discussed.)
3. After the teams have diagnosed the incidents, each team will describe to the entire class the most interesting incident as well as the team's diagnosis of that incident. Other teams will critique the diagnosis. Any leadership contingencies not mentioned in the textbook should also be presented and discussed.

SELF-ASSESSMENT 12.4

WHAT IS YOUR BOSS'S PREFERRED LEADERSHIP STYLE?

PURPOSE This assessment is designed to help you understand two important dimensions of leadership and identify which of these dimensions is more prominent in your supervisor, team leader, or coach or in another person to whom you are accountable.

INSTRUCTIONS Read each of the statements below and circle the response that you believe best describes your supervisor. You may substitute for "supervisor" anyone else to whom you are accountable, such as a team leader, CEO, course instructor, or sports coach. Then use the scoring key in Appendix B at the end of the book to calculate the results for each leadership dimension. After completing this assessment, be prepared to discuss in class the distinctions between these leadership dimensions.

Leadership Dimensions Instrument

My Supervisor . . .	Strongly agree ▼	Agree ▼	Neutral ▼	Disagree ▼	Strongly disagree ▼
1. Focuses attention on irregularities, mistakes, exceptions, and deviations from what is expected of me.	5	4	3	2	1
2. Engages in words and deeds that enhance his or her image of competence.	5	4	3	2	1
3. Monitors performance for errors needing correction.	5	4	3	2	1
4. Serves as a role model for me.	5	4	3	2	1
5. Points out what I will receive if I do what is required.	5	4	3	2	1
6. Instills pride in being associated with him or her.	5	4	3	2	1
7. Keeps careful track of mistakes.	5	4	3	2	1
8. Can be trusted to help me overcome any obstacle.	5	4	3	2	1
9. Tells me what to do to be rewarded for my efforts.	5	4	3	2	1
10. Makes me aware of strongly held values, ideals, and aspirations that are shared in common.	5	4	3	2	1
11. Is alert for failure to meet standards.	5	4	3	2	1
12. Mobilizes a collective sense of mission.	5	4	3	2	1
13. Works out agreements with me on what I will receive if I do what needs to be done.	5	4	3	2	1
14. Articulates a vision of future opportunities.	5	4	3	2	1
15. Talks about special rewards for good work.	5	4	3	2	1
16. Talks optimistically about the future.	5	4	3	2	1

Source: Items and dimensions are adapted from D. N. Den Hartog, J. J. Van Muijen, and P. L. Koopman, "Transactional versus Transformational Leadership: An Analysis of the MLQ," *Journal of Occupational & Organizational Psychology* 70 (March 1997), pp. 19–34. Den Hartog et al. label transactional leadership as "rational-objective leadership" and label transformational leadership as "inspirational leadership." Many of their items may have originated from B. M. Bass and B. J. Avolio, *Manual for the Multifactor Leadership Questionnaire* (Palo Alto, CA: Consulting Psychologists Press, 1989).

4

PART

Organizational Processes

BioWare Corp. was created by three medical doctors who had a passion for developing electronic games. They had some experience in interactive medical education, but starting a company to make commercial games was another matter. Two of the physicians, Ray Muzyka and Greg Zeschuk, became joint chief executive officers of the new company, while the third partner returned to medical practice two years after BioWare was launched. The company was initially organized into a simple team structure in which everyone worked together to create its first game, *Shattered Steel*.

During the development of *Shattered Steel,* Muzyka and Zeschuk started a second game project, called *Baldur's Gate.* The question was, what organizational structure would best support this company for the future? BioWare could simply have two teams working independently on the two games. However, a multiteam structure would duplicate resources, possibly undermine information sharing among people with the same expertise across teams, and weaken employee loyalty to the overall company.

BioWare Corp. cofounders Ray Muzyka (left) and Greg Zeschuk (right) had to choose which organizational structure would best serve the rapidly growing electronics company.

Alternatively, the game developer could create departments around the various specializations, including art, programming, audio, quality assurance, and design. This would allow employees with similar technical expertise to share information and create new ideas within their specialization. However, employees would not have the same level of teamwork or commitment to the final product as they would in a team-based project structure.[1]

13

ORGANIZATIONAL STRUCTURE

Learning Objectives

After reading this chapter, you should be able to:

1. Describe three types of coordination in organizational structures.
2. Justify the optimal span of control in a given situation.
3. Discuss the advantages and disadvantages of centralization and formalization.
4. Distinguish organic from mechanistic organizational structures.
5. Identify and evaluate the six pure types of departmentalization.
6. Describe three variations of divisional structure and explain which one should be adopted in a particular situation.
7. Diagram the matrix structure and discuss its advantages and disadvantages.
8. Compare and contrast network structures with other forms of departmentalization.
9. Identify four characteristics of external environments and discuss the preferred organizational structure for each environment.
10. Summarize the influence of organizational size, technology, and strategy on organizational structure.

organizational structure The division of labor as well as the patterns of coordination, communication, workflow, and formal power that direct organizational activities.

What organizational structure will work best for BioWare? We'll find out in this chapter. **Organizational structure** refers to the division of labor as well as the patterns of coordination, communication, workflow, and formal power that direct organizational activities. The chapter begins by introducing the two fundamental processes in organizational structure: division of labor and coordination. This is followed by a detailed investigation of the four main elements of organizational structure: span of control, centralization, formalization, and departmentalization. The latter part of this chapter examines the contingencies of organizational design, including external environment, organizational size, technology, and strategy.

Throughout this chapter, we hope to show that an organization's structure is much more than an organizational chart diagramming which employees report to which managers. Organizational structure includes reporting relationships, but it also relates to job design, information flow, work standards and rules, team dynamics, and power relationships. Organizational structures are frequently used as tools for organizational change because they establish new communication patterns and align employee behavior with the corporate vision.[2] For example, when Charles Schwab & Co. experienced financial trouble not long ago, founder Charles Schwab (who returned as CEO) held a two-day marathon session in which the company's top executives were asked to redraw the organizational chart in a way that would make the company simpler, more decentralized, and refocused on the customer. Every executive in the room, including those whose jobs would be erased from the new structure, was asked for his or her input.[3] The point we want to emphasize here is that organizational structure reconfigures power, communication patterns, and possibly the company's culture in the long term. As such, altering the organization's structure is an important component of an executive's toolkit for organizational change.[4]

Learning Objectives

After reading the next two sections, you should be able to:

1. Describe three types of coordination in organizational structures.
2. Justify the optimal span of control in a given situation.
3. Discuss the advantages and disadvantages of centralization and formalization.
4. Distinguish organic from mechanistic organizational structures.

Division of Labor and Coordination

All organizational structures include two fundamental requirements: the division of labor into distinct tasks and the coordination of that labor so that employees are able to accomplish common goals.[5] Organizations are groups of people who work interdependently toward some purpose. To efficiently accomplish their goals, these groups typically divide the work into manageable chunks, particularly when there are many different tasks to perform. They also introduce various coordinating mechanisms to ensure that everyone is working effectively toward the same objectives.

Division of Labor

Division of labor refers to the subdivision of work into separate jobs assigned to different people. Subdivided work leads to job specialization, because each job now includes a narrow subset of the tasks necessary to complete the product or service. To produce its first electronic game, BioWare's cofounders divided the work among a dozen or more employees. Some people were responsible for programming; others completed the artwork; still others developed the game's sound effects; and so forth. Today's electronic games are so sophisticated that a project may extend for more than a year and involve several dozen people with highly specialized expertise. As companies get larger, this horizontal division of labor is usually accompanied by vertical division of labor: Some people are assigned the task of supervising employees, others are responsible for managing those supervisors, and so on.

Why do companies divide the work required to build an electronic game into several jobs? As you learned earlier in this book, job specialization increases work efficiency.[6] Job incumbents can master their tasks quickly because work cycles are shorter. Less time is wasted changing from one task to another Training costs are reduced because employees require fewer physical and mental skills to accomplish the assigned work. Finally, job specialization makes it easier to match people with specific aptitudes or skills to the jobs for which they are best suited. Although one person working alone might be able to design an electronic game, doing so would take much longer than having the game designed by a team of specialists. Also, an individual who produces superb animation might deliver only mediocre software coding, whereas a highly skilled team of people would have higher quality across all areas of work.

Coordinating Work Activities

When people divide work among themselves, they require coordinating mechanisms to ensure that everyone works in concert. Coordination is so closely connected to division of labor that the optimal level of specialization is limited by the feasibility of coordinating the work. In other words, an organization should divide work among many people only to the extent that those people can coordinate with each other. Otherwise, individual effort is wasted due to misalignment, duplication, and mistiming of tasks. Coordination also tends to become more expensive and difficult as the division of labor increases, so companies specialize jobs only to the point where it isn't too costly or challenging to coordinate the people in those jobs.[7]

Every organization–from the two-person corner convenience store to the largest corporate entity–uses one or more of the following coordinating mechanisms:[8] informal communication, formal hierarchy, and standardization (see Exhibit 13.1). These forms of coordination align the work of staff within the same department as well as across work units. These coordinating mechanisms are also critical when several organizations work together, such as in joint ventures and humanitarian aid programs.[9]

Coordination through Informal Communication Informal communication is a coordinating mechanism in all organizations. It includes sharing information on mutual tasks as well as forming common mental models so that employees synchronize work activities using the same mental road map.[10] Informal communication is vital in nonroutine and ambiguous situations because employees can exchange a large volume of information through face-to-face communication and other media-rich channels.

Coordination through informal communication is easiest in small firms, such as BioWare when it was a start-up firm, although information technologies have further leveraged this coordinating mechanism in large organizations.[11] Companies employing thousands of people also support informal communication by keeping each production site small. Magna International, the global auto-parts manufacturer, keeps its plants to a maximum size of around 200 employees. Magna's leaders believe that employees have difficulty remembering each other's names in plants that are any larger, a situation that makes informal communication more difficult as a coordinating mechanism.[12]

Form of coordination	Description	Subtypes/strategies
Informal communication	Sharing information on mutual tasks; forming common mental models to synchronize work activities	• Direct communication • Liaison roles • Integrator roles • Temporary teams
Formal hierarchy	Assigning legitimate power to individuals, who then use this power to direct work processes and allocate resources	• Direct supervision • Formal communication channels
Standardization	Creating routine patterns of behavior or output	• Standardized skills • Standardized processes • Standardized output

Sources: Based on information in J. Galbraith, *Designing Complex Organizations* (Reading, MA: Addison-Wesley, 1973), pp. 8–19; H. Mintzberg, *The Structuring of Organizations* (Englewood Cliffs, NJ: Prentice Hall, 1979), chap. 1; D. A. Nadler and M. L. Tushman, *Competing by Design: The Power of Organizational Architecture* (New York: Oxford University Press, 1997), chap. 6.

Exhibit 13.1 *Coordinating Mechanisms in Organizations*

Larger organizations also encourage coordination through informal communication by assigning *liaison roles* to employees, who are expected to communicate and share information with co-workers in other work units. Where coordination is required among several work units, companies create *integrator roles.* These people are responsible for coordinating a work process by encouraging employees in each work unit to share information and informally coordinate work activities. Integrators do not have authority over the people involved in that process, so they must rely on persuasion and commitment. Brand managers at Procter & Gamble have integrator roles because they coordinate work among marketing, production, and design groups.[13]

concurrent engineering
The organization of employees from several departments into a temporary team for the purpose of developing a product or service.

Another way that larger organizations encourage coordination through informal communication is by organizing employees from several departments into temporary teams. This strategy occurs through **concurrent engineering** in the product or service development process. Traditional product development is a sequential arrangement. For example, the marketing department might develop a product strategy, which is passed "over the wall" to design engineers, whose design work is then passed on to manufacturing engineers to figure out a cost-efficient production process and to the purchasing department to source raw materials. This serial process can be cumbersome because its main coordinating mechanism is formal hierarchical communication.

In contrast, concurrent engineering involves forming a cross-functional project team of people from these specialized departments to engage in product development simultaneously. By being assigned to a team, rather than working within their usual specialized departments, employees are given the mandate and opportunity to coordinate with each other using informal communication. As soon as the design engineer begins to form the product specifications, representatives from manufacturing, engineering, marketing, purchasing, and other departments can offer feedback as well as begin their contribution to the process. This coordination usually occurs through information technology, but it also includes plenty of face-to-face communication when the concurrent-engineering team members are located together in the same physical space. Face-to-face communication is a particularly information-rich medium, which allows team members to work on various stages of product development (marketing, design, manufacturing, purchasing, etc.) at the same time. The result: Chrysler, Toyota, Harley-Davidson, and many other organizations have found that the concurrent-engineering process tends to produce higher-quality products with dramatically less development time than does the traditional arrangement.[14]

Coordination through Formal Hierarchy Informal communication is the most flexible form of coordination, but it can become chaotic as the number of interdependencies among employees increases. Consequently, as organizations grow, they rely increasingly on a second coordinating mechanism: formal hierarchy.[15] Hierarchy assigns legitimate power to individuals, who then use this power to direct work processes and allocate resources. In other words, work is coordinated through direct supervision–the chain of command.

The formal hierarchy has traditionally been applauded as the optimal coordinating mechanism for large organizations. A century ago, administrative management scholars argued that organizations are most effective when managers exercise their authority and employees receive orders from only one supervisor. Coordination should occur through the chain of command; that is, up the hierarchy and across to the other work unit. Any organization with a formal structure coordinates work to some extent through this arrangement. For instance, project leaders at BioWare are responsible for ensuring that employees on their computer game project remain on schedule and that their respective tasks are compatible with tasks completed by other team members. The formal hierarchy also coordinates work among executives through the division of organizational activities. If the organization is divided into geographic areas, the structure gives the regional group leaders legitimate power over executives responsible for production, customer service, and other activities in those areas. If the organization is divided into product groups, the heads of those groups have the right to coordinate work across regions.

The formal hierarchy can be efficient for simple and routine situations, but it is not as agile for coordination in complex and novel situations. Communicating through the chain of command is rarely as fast or accurate as direct communication between employees. For instance, we noted earlier that product development–typically a complex and novel activity–tends to occur more quickly and produce higher-quality results when people coordinate mainly through informal communication rather than formal hierarchy. Another concern with formal hierarchy is that managers are able to closely supervise only a limited number of employees. As the business grows, the number of supervisors and layers of management must increase, resulting in a costly bureaucracy. Finally, today's workforce is less tolerant of rigid structures. For instance, Wegmans Food Market is one of the best places to work, partly because the Rochester, New York–based grocery chain minimizes formal hierarchy as a coordinating mechanism.

"Shipwrecked or not, Bradley, we must maintain the chain of command."

Coordination through Standardization Standardization, the third means of coordination, involves creating routine patterns of behavior or output. This coordinating mechanism takes three distinct forms:

- *Standardized processes.* Quality and consistency of a product or service can often be improved by standardizing work activities through job descriptions and procedures.[16] This coordinating mechanism is feasible when the work is routine (such as mass production) or simple (such as making pizzas), but it is less effective in nonroutine and complex work such as product design.

- *Standardized outputs.* This form of standardization involves ensuring that individuals and work units have clearly defined goals and output measures (e.g., customer satisfaction, production efficiency). For instance, to coordinate the work of salespeople, companies assign sales targets rather than specific behaviors.
- *Standardized skills.* When work activities are too complex to standardize through processes or goals, companies often coordinate work effort by extensively training employees or hiring people who have learned precise role behaviors from educational programs. This form of coordination is used in hospital operating rooms. Surgeons, nurses, and other operating room professionals coordinate their work more through training than through goals or company rules.

Division of labor and coordination of work represent the two fundamental ingredients of all organizations. But how work is divided, which coordinating mechanisms are emphasized, who makes decisions, and other issues are related to the four elements of organizational structure.

ELEMENTS OF ORGANIZATIONAL STRUCTURE

Every company is configured in terms of four basic elements of organizational structure. This section introduces three of them: span of control, centralization, and formalization. The fourth element–departmentalization–is presented in the next section.

Span of Control

span of control
The number of people directly reporting to the next level in the hierarchy.

Span of control (also called *span of management*) refers to the number of people directly reporting to the next level in the hierarchy. A narrow span of control exists when very few people report directly to a manager, whereas a wide span exists when a manager has many direct reports.[17] A century ago, French engineer and management scholar Henri Fayol strongly recommended a relatively narrow span of control, typically no more than 20 employees per supervisor and 6 supervisors per manager. Fayol championed formal hierarchy as the primary coordinating mechanism, so he believed that supervisors should closely monitor and coach employees. His views were similar to those of Napoleon and other military leaders, who declared that somewhere between 3 and 10 subordinates is the optimal span of control. These prescriptions were based on the belief that managers simply could not monitor and control any more subordinates closely enough.[18]

Today, we know better. The best-performing manufacturing plants currently have an average of 38 production employees per supervisor.[19] What's the secret here? Did Fayol, Napoleon, and others miscalculate the optimal span of control? The answer is that those sympathetic to hierarchical control believed that employees should perform the physical tasks, whereas supervisors and other management personnel should make the decisions and monitor employees to make sure they performed their tasks. In contrast, the best-performing manufacturing operations today rely on self-directed teams, so direct supervision (formal hierarchy) is supplemented with other coordinating mechanisms. Self-directed teams coordinate mainly through informal communication and specialized knowledge, so formal hierarchy plays a minor role. Many firms that employ doctors, lawyers, and other professionals have a larger span of control because these staff members coordinate their work mainly through standardized skills. For example, more than two dozen people report directly to Cindy Zollinger, president of Boston-based litigation-consulting firm Cornerstone Research. Zollinger explains that this large number of direct reports is possible because she leads professional staff who don't require close supervision. "They largely run themselves," Zollinger explains. "I help them in dealing with obstacles they face, or in making the most of opportunities that they find."[20]

A second factor influencing the best span of control is whether employees perform routine tasks. A wider span of control is possible when employees perform routine jobs, because there is less frequent need for direction or advice from supervisors. A narrow span of control is necessary when employees perform novel or complex tasks, because these employees tend to require more supervisory decisions and coaching. This principle is illustrated in a survey of American property and casualty insurers. The average span of control in commercial-policy processing departments is around 15 employees per supervisor, whereas the span of control is 6.1 in claims service and 5.5 in commercial underwriting. Staff members in the latter two departments perform more technical work, so they have more novel and complex tasks. Commercial-policy processing, on the other hand, is like production work, where tasks are routine and have few exceptions.[21]

A third influence on span of control is the degree of interdependence among employees within the department or team.[22] Generally, a narrow span of control is necessary where employees perform highly interdependent work with others. More supervision is required for highly interdependent jobs because employees tend to experience more conflict with each other, which requires more of a manager's time to resolve. Also, employees are less clear on their personal work performance in highly interdependent tasks, so supervisors spend more time providing coaching and feedback.

Tall versus Flat Structures Span of control is interconnected with organizational size (number of employees) and the number of layers in the organizational hierarchy. Consider two companies with the same number of employees. If Company A has a wider span of control (more direct reports per manager) than Company B, then Company A must have fewer layers of management (i.e., a flatter structure) than does Company B. The reason for this relationship is that a company with a wider span of control necessarily has more employees per supervisor, more supervisors for each middle manager, and so on. This larger number of direct reports, compared to a company with a narrower span of control, is possible only by removing layers of management. The interconnection of span of

The Struggle to Stay Flat When Ken Iverson became CEO of Nucor Corporation in the mid-1960s, he insisted that the Charlotte, North Carolina, steelmaker have only three layers of management below him: Crew supervisors reported to their functional manager (production, shipping, maintenance), who reported to the plant manager, who reported to Iverson. By allowing each plant to operate as an independent business, this flat structure was manageable even as Nucor grew to more than two dozen plants. But today Nucor is America's largest steelmaker in terms of shipments, employing 20,000 people at more than four dozen facilities worldwide. Managing 50 or more direct reports would itself be a full-time job, so Nucor's current chairman and CEO, Dan DiMicco (shown in photo), reluctantly added another layer of management (five executive vice presidents). "I needed to be free to make decisions on trade battles," says DiMicco, adding that he continues to stay involved by checking his own e-mail and meeting with staff at every opportunity. Even with five layers of hierarchy, Nucor is incredibly lean. Many other companies the same size have twice as many levels of management.[23]

control, organizational size (number of employees), and number of management layers also means that as companies employ more people, they must widen the span of control, build a taller hierarchy, or both. Most companies end up building taller structures because they rely on direct supervision to some extent as a coordinating mechanism and there are limits to how many people each manager can coordinate (see Exhibit 13.2).

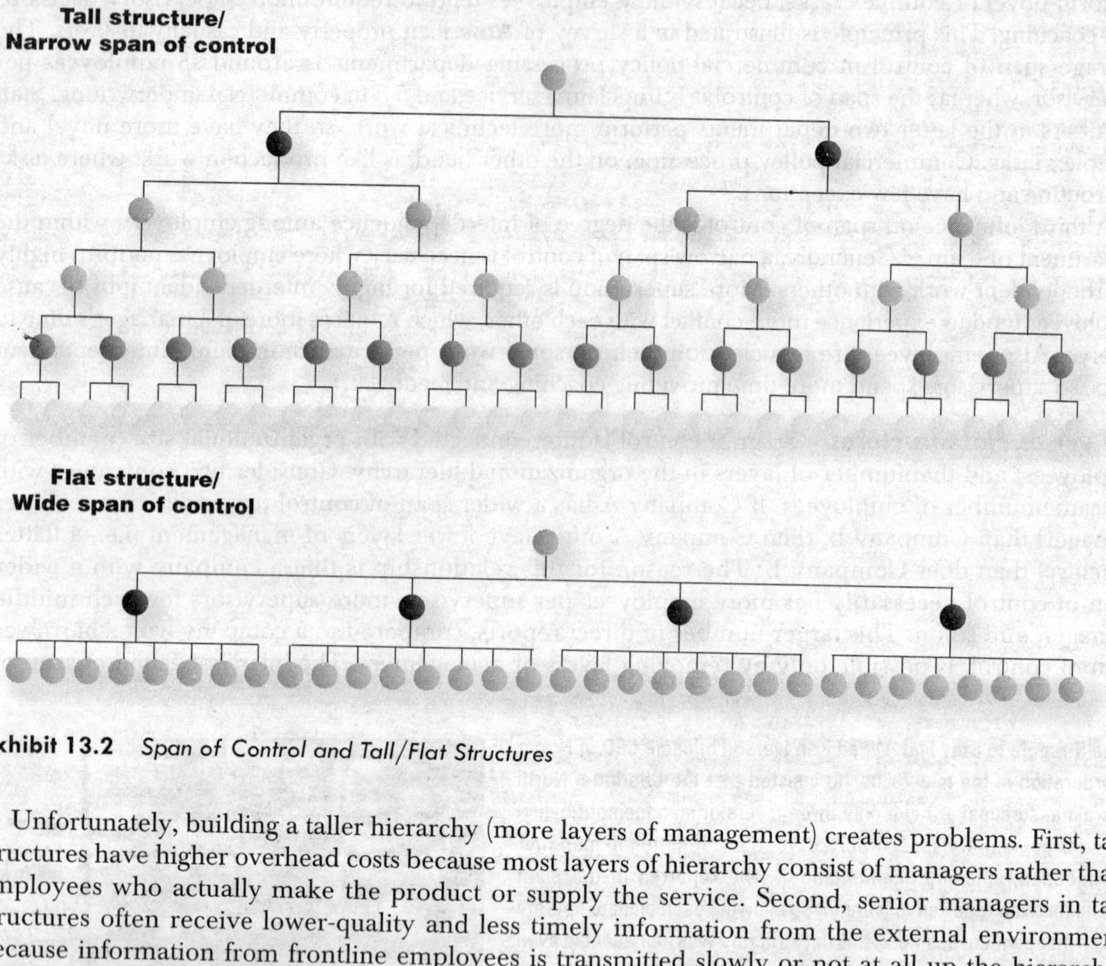

Exhibit 13.2 *Span of Control and Tall/Flat Structures*

Unfortunately, building a taller hierarchy (more layers of management) creates problems. First, tall structures have higher overhead costs because most layers of hierarchy consist of managers rather than employees who actually make the product or supply the service. Second, senior managers in tall structures often receive lower-quality and less timely information from the external environment because information from frontline employees is transmitted slowly or not at all up the hierarchy. Also, the more layers of management through which information must pass, the higher the probability that managers will filter out information that does not put them in a positive light. Finally, tall hierarchies tend to undermine employee empowerment and engagement because they focus power around managers rather than employees.[24]

These problems have prompted leaders to "delayer"–remove one or more levels in the organizational hierarchy.[25] Soon after Mark Hurd was hired as CEO of HP (Hewlett-Packard), he stripped the high-technology company's 11 layers of hierarchy down to 8 layers. He argued that this action reduced costs and would make HP more nimble. BASF's European Seal Sands plant went even further when it was dramatically restructured around self-directed teams. "Seven levels of management have been cut basically to two," says a BASF executive.[26]

Although many companies enjoy reduced costs and more empowered employees when they delayer the organizational hierarchy, some organizational experts warn that there are also negative long-term consequences of cutting out too much middle management.[27] These include undermining necessary managerial functions, increasing workload and stress among management, and restricting managerial career development:

- *Undermines managerial functions.* Critics of delayering point out that all companies need managers to guide work activities, coach subordinates, and manage company growth. Furthermore, managers are needed to make quick decisions and represent a source of appeal over conflicts. These valuable functions are underserved when the span of control becomes too wide.
- *Increases workload and stress.* Delayering increases the number of direct reports per manager and thus significantly increases management workload and corresponding levels of stress. Managers partly reduce the workload by learning to give subordinates more autonomy rather than micromanaging them. However, this role adjustment itself is stressful (same responsibility, but less authority or control), and many companies increase the span of control beyond the point at which many managers are capable of coaching or leading their direct reports.
- *Restricts managerial career development.* Delayering results in fewer managerial jobs, so companies have less maneuverability to develop managerial skills. Promotions are also riskier because they involve a larger jump in responsibility in flatter, compared to taller, hierarchies. Furthermore, having fewer promotion opportunities means that managers experience more career plateauing, which reduces their motivation and loyalty. Chopping back managerial career structures also sends a signal that managers are no longer valued. "Delayering has had an adverse effect on morale, productivity and performance," argues a senior executive in the Australian federal government. "Disenfranchising middle management creates negative perceptions and lower commitment to the organization with consequent reluctance to accept responsibility."[28]

Centralization and Decentralization

centralization
The degree to which formal decision authority is held by a small group of people, typically those at the top of the organizational hierarchy.

Centralization and decentralization are a second element to consider when designing an organizational structure. **Centralization** means that formal decision-making authority is held by a small group of people, typically those at the top of the organizational hierarchy. Most organizations begin with centralized structures, as the founder makes most of the decisions and tries to direct the business toward his or her vision. As organizations grow, however, they diversify and their environments become more complex. Senior executives aren't able to process all the decisions that significantly influence the business. Consequently, larger organizations typically *decentralize;* that is, they disperse decision authority and power throughout the organization.

The optimal level of centralization or decentralization depends on several contingencies that we will examine later in this chapter. However, we also need to keep in mind that different degrees of decentralization can occur simultaneously in different parts of an organization. Nestlé, the Swiss-based food company, has decentralized marketing decisions to remain responsive to local markets, but it has centralized production, logistics, and supply chain management activities to improve cost efficiencies and avoid having too much complexity across the organization. "If you are too decentralized, you can become too complicated–you get too much complexity in your production system," explains a Nestlé executive.[29]

Likewise, 7-Eleven relies on both centralization and decentralization in different parts of the organization. The convenience store chain leverages buying power and efficiencies by centralizing decisions about information technology and supplier purchasing. At the same time, it decentralizes local inventory decisions to store managers so that they can adapt quickly to changing circumstances at the local level. Along with receiving ongoing product training and guidance from regional consultants, store managers have the best information about their customers and can respond quickly to local market needs. "We could never predict a busload of football players on a Friday night, but the store manager can," explains a 7-Eleven executive.[30]

Formalization

formalization
The degree to which organizations standardize behavior through rules, procedures, formal training, and related mechanisms.

Formalization is the degree to which organizations standardize behavior through rules, procedures, formal training, and related mechanisms.[31] In other words, companies become more formalized as they increasingly rely on various forms of standardization to coordinate work. McDonald's Restaurants and most other efficient fast-food chains typically have a high degree of formalization because they rely on standardization of work processes as a coordinating mechanism. Employees have precisely defined roles, right down to how much mustard should be dispensed, how many pickles should be applied, and how long each hamburger should be cooked.

Older companies tend to become more formalized because work activities become routinized, making them easier to document into standardized practices. Larger companies also tend to have more formalization because direct supervision and informal communication among employees do not operate as easily when large numbers of people are involved. External influences, such as government safety legislation and strict accounting rules, also encourage formalization.

Formalization may increase efficiency and compliance, but it can also create problems.[32] Rules and procedures reduce organizational flexibility, so employees follow prescribed behaviors even when the situation clearly calls for a customized response. High levels of formalization tend to undermine organizational learning and creativity. Some work rules become so convoluted that organizational efficiency would decline if they were actually followed as prescribed. Formalization is also a source of job dissatisfaction and work stress. Finally, rules and procedures have been known to take on a life of their own in some organizations. They become the focus of attention rather than the organization's ultimate objectives of producing a product or service and serving its dominant stakeholders.

The challenge that companies face as they get larger and older is to avoid too much formalization. Yahoo seems to be a case in point. A decade ago, the world's most popular Web portal site was a creative hotspot among Web-based companies. Through strategic acquisitions (Flickr, del.icio.us, Yahoo! 360, etc.), the company continues to launch new services, but observers and former staff say that internal innovations have been hampered by creeping bureaucracy. "In a small company [the attitude] is, 'Hey, let's launch it and let's see if the users like it,'" says a senior Yahoo staffer who recently moved to a smaller firm. "There was a time a few years ago where Yahoo had more of that mentality. But as companies get bigger and bigger, many of them reach a point where they can't do that as quickly." Another former Yahoo employee is more blunt: "If you are on the Internet, you have to be fast and you have to take risks. The organizational structure that Yahoo has is completely antithetical to the industry they are in."[33]

mechanistic structure
An organizational structure with a narrow span of control and a high degree of formalization and centralization.

Mechanistic versus Organic Structures

We discussed span of control, centralization, and formalization together because they cluster around two broader organizational forms: mechanistic and organic structures.[34] A **mechanistic structure** is characterized by a narrow span of control and high degree of formalization and centralization. Mechanistic

Growing an Organic TAXI Award-winning TAXI, whose clients include Blue Shield of California, New York Life Insurance, and Molson Coors, is a rising star in the competitive world of creative marketing. One of TAXI's secrets to success has been an organic structure, in contrast to its major competitors, which have more rigid mechanistic hierarchies. "[Other advertising firms] operated on a 19th-century model of many secular departments trying to integrate everything ad hoc. Most cultures were so layered that a great idea was easily crushed," explains TAXI cofounder Paul Lavoie (bottom right in this photo with a few staff from TAXI's New York City office). "We needed a flexible infrastructure, able to move with the pace of change. TAXI started lean and nimble, and remains so today." But as it gained popularity, TAXI faced the challenge of accommodating growth (30 to 40 percent per year) without evolving into yet another mechanistic firm. Its solution was to duplicate itself across several cities, with each unit maintaining an organic structure that actively collaborates with other offices. The company also maintains an organic structure by keeping each business unit relatively small. For example, when its office in Toronto, Canada, reached 150 staff members, TAXI opened a second office in that city, called TAXI 2.[35]

organic structure
An organizational structure with a wide span of control, little formalization, and decentralized decision making.

structures have many rules and procedures, limited decision making at lower levels, tall hierarchies of people in specialized roles, and vertical rather than horizontal communication flows. Tasks are rigidly defined and are altered only when sanctioned by higher authorities. Companies with an **organic structure** have the opposite characteristics. They operate with a wide span of control, decentralized decision making, and little formalization. Tasks are fluid, adjusting to new situations and organizational needs.

As a general rule, mechanistic structures operate better in stable environments because they rely on efficiency and routine behaviors, whereas organic structures work better in rapidly changing (i.e., dynamic) environments because they are more flexible and responsive to the changes. Organic structures are also more compatible with organizational learning, high-performance workplaces, and quality management because they emphasize information sharing and an empowered workforce rather than hierarchy and status.[36] However, the advantages of organic structures, rather than mechanistic structures, in dynamic environments occur only when employees have developed well-established roles and expertise.[37] Without these conditions, employees are unable to coordinate effectively with each other, resulting in errors and gross inefficiencies.

Start-up companies often face this problem, known as the *liability of newness.* Newness makes start-up firms more organic–they tend to be smaller organizations with few rules and considerable delegation of authority. However, employees in new organizations often lack industry experience, and their teams have not developed sufficiently for peak performance. As a result, the organic structures of new companies cannot compensate for the poorer coordination and significantly lower efficiencies caused by the lack of structure from past experience and team mental models. Fortunately, companies can minimize the liability of newness by launching businesses with existing teams of people or with industry veterans guiding the novices. Nitro Group is an example. The upstart ad agency was founded in Shanghai in 2002 and expanded quickly to London, New York, Sydney, and other centers. Each of these offices is highly organic, with fairly young staff, yet each local office is able to draw on the expertise of several experienced staff members to assist with specific accounts. Thus, Nitro enjoys an organic structure yet has the foundations of well-established roles and expertise to deliver the service.[38]

Learning Objectives

After reading this section, you should be able to:

5. Identify and evaluate the six pure types of departmentalization.
6. Describe three variations of divisional structure and explain which one should be adopted in a particular situation.
7. Diagram the matrix structure and discuss its advantages and disadvantages.
8. Compare and contrast network structures with other forms of departmentalization.

FORMS OF DEPARTMENTALIZATION

Span of control, centralization, and formalization are important elements of organizational structure, but most people think about organizational charts when the discussion of organizational structure arises. The organizational chart represents the fourth element in the structuring of organizations, called *departmentalization*. Departmentalization specifies how employees and their activities are grouped together. It is a fundamental strategy for coordinating organizational activities because it influences organizational behavior in the following ways:[39]

- Departmentalization establishes the chain of command–the system of common supervision among positions and units within the organization. It frames the membership of formal work teams and typically determines which positions and units must share resources. Thus, departmentalization establishes interdependencies among employees and subunits.
- Departmentalization focuses people around common mental models or ways of thinking, such as serving clients, developing products, or supporting a particular skill set. This focus is typically anchored around the common budgets and measures of performance assigned to employees within each departmental unit.
- Departmentalization encourages coordination through informal communication among people and subunits. With common supervision and resources, members within each configuration typically work near each other, so they can use frequent and informal interaction to get the work done.

There are almost as many organizational charts as there are businesses, but the six most common pure types of departmentalization are simple, functional, divisional, team-based, matrix, and network.

Simple Structure

Most companies begin with a *simple structure*.[40] They employ only a few people and typically offer only one distinct product or service. There is minimal hierarchy–usually just employees reporting to the owners. Employees perform broadly defined roles because there are insufficient economies of scale to assign them to specialized jobs. The simple structure is highly flexible and minimizes the walls that form between employees in other structures. However, the simple structure usually depends on the owner's direct supervision to coordinate work activities, so it is very difficult to operate as the company grows and becomes more complex.

Functional Structure

functional structure
An organizational structure in which employees are organized around specific knowledge or other resources.

Growing organizations usually introduce a functional structure at some level of the hierarchy or at some time in their history. A **functional structure** organizes employees around specific knowledge or other resources. The opening vignette to this chapter described how the cofounders of BioWare contemplated the functional structure for the electronic game company. Specifically, they considered the possibility of creating departments around the various specializations, including art, programming, audio, quality assurance, and design.

Evaluating the Functional Structure The functional structure creates specialized pools of talent that typically serve everyone in the organization. This provides more economies of scale than are possible if functional specialists are spread over different parts of the organization. It increases employee identity with the specialization or profession. Direct supervision is easier in functional structures because managers oversee people with common issues and expertise.[41]

The functional structure also has limitations.[42] Grouping employees around their skills tends to focus attention on those skills and related professional needs rather than on the company's product, service, or client needs. Unless people are transferred from one function to the next, they might not develop a broader understanding of the business. Compared with other structures, the functional structure usually produces higher dysfunctional conflict and poorer coordination in serving clients or developing products. These problems occur because employees need to work with co-workers in other departments to complete organizational tasks yet they have different subgoals and mental models of ideal work. Together, these problems require substantial formal controls and coordination when people are organized around functions.

Divisional Structure

divisional structure
An organizational structure in which employees are organized around geographic areas, outputs (products or services), or clients.

The **divisional structure** (sometimes called the *multidivisional* or *M-form* structure) groups employees around geographic areas, outputs (products or services), or clients. Exhibit 13.3 illustrates these three variations of divisional structure. The *geographic divisional structure* organizes employees around distinct regions of the country or world. Exhibit 13.3 (*a*) illustrates a geographic divisional structure recently adopted by Barrick Gold Corporation, the world's largest gold-mining company. The *product/service divisional structure* organizes employees around distinct outputs. Exhibit 13.3 (*b*) illustrates a simplified version of this type of structure at Philips. The Dutch electronics company divides its workforce mainly into three divisions: health care products, lighting products, and consumer products. The *client divisional structure* organizes employees around specific customer groups. Exhibit 13.3 (*c*) illustrates a customer-focused divisional structure similar to one adopted by the U.S. Internal Revenue Service.[43]

Which form of divisional structure should large organizations adopt? The answer depends mainly on the primary source of environmental diversity or uncertainty.[44] Suppose an organization has one type of product sold to people across the country. If customer needs vary across regions, or if state governments impose different regulations on the product, then a geographic structure would be best to be more vigilant of this diversity. On the other hand, if the company sells several types of products across the country and customer preferences and government regulations are similar everywhere, then a product structure would likely work best.

Coca-Cola, Nestlé, and many other food and beverage companies are organized mainly around geographic regions because consumer tastes and preferred marketing strategies vary considerably

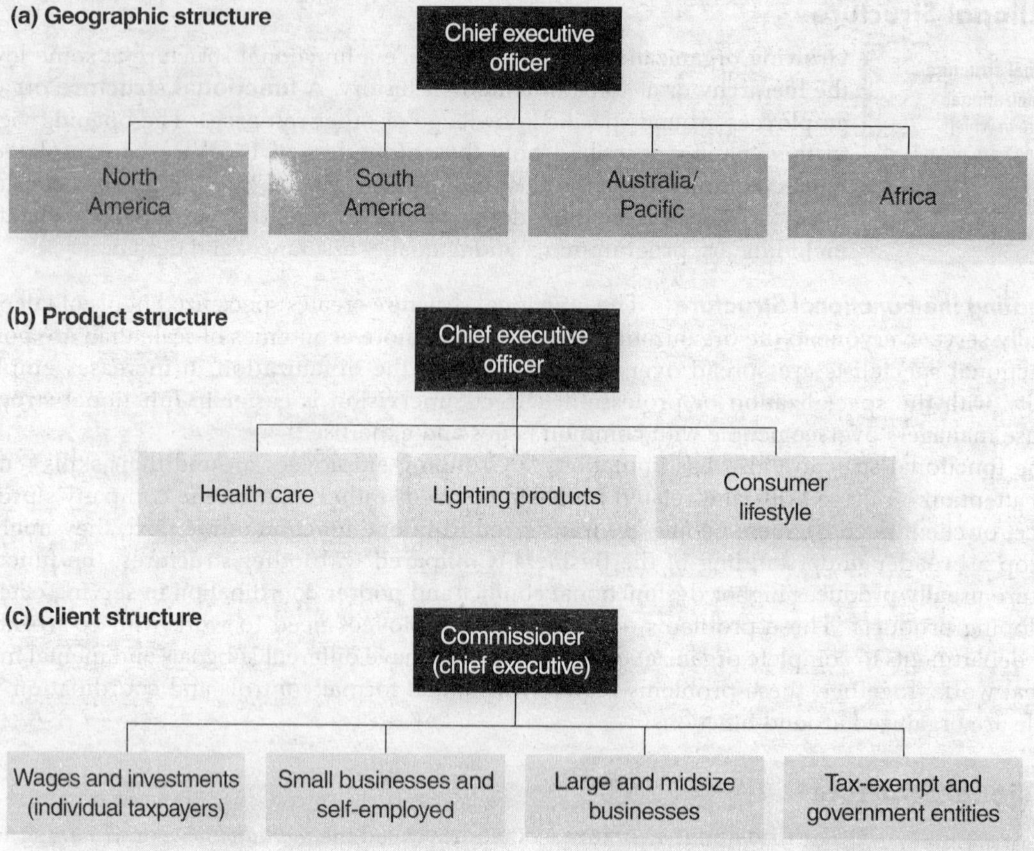

Note: Diagram (*a*) shows the global geographic divisional structure of Barrick Gold Corp.; diagram (*b*) is similar to the product divisions at Philips; diagram (*c*) is similar to the customer-focused structure at the U.S. Internal Revenue Service.

Exhibit 13.3 *Three Types of Divisional Structure*

around the world. Even though McDonald's makes the same Big Mac throughout the world, the company has more fish products in Hong Kong and more vegetarian products in India, in line with traditional diets in those countries. Philips, on the other hand, is organized around products because consumer preferences around the world are similar within each product group. Hospitals from Geneva, Switzerland, to Santiago, Chile, buy similar medical equipment from Philips, whereas the manufacturing and marketing of these products are quite different from Philips' consumer electronics business.

The Globally Integrated Enterprise Many companies are moving away from structures that organize people around geographic clusters.[45] One reason is that clients can purchase products online and communicate with businesses from almost anywhere in the world, so local representation is less critical. Reduced geographic variation is another reason for the shift away from geographic structures; freer trade has reduced government intervention, and consumer preferences for many products and services are becoming more similar (converging) around the world. The third reason is that large companies increasingly have global business customers who demand one global point of purchase, not one in every country or region.

A More Customer-Facing Caterpillar For decades, Caterpillar, Inc., the world's largest manufacturer of construction and mining equipment, enjoyed a cozy dominance in the North American marketplace, resulting in an insular culture focused on fiefdoms of expertise rather than customers or cost efficiency. Reflecting this culture, Caterpillar operated with a functional structure, organizing employees around engineering, marketing, manufacturing, and other business processes with almost no communication across these units. The vice presidents of these departments were so powerful that one CEO described them as "the kingpins of decisions." Several years ago, more agile competitors from Japan and elsewhere threatened Caterpillar's future. Fortunately, the company reacted quickly enough to remain in business. One of its first actions was to jettison the old corporate structure in favor of a divisional structure that paid more attention to customers and efficiency. The new structure essentially demoted the functional vice presidents, who now report to the product and marketing people who previously reported to them.[46]

globally integrated enterprise
An organizational structure in which work processes and executive functions are distributed around the world through global centers, rather than developed in a home country and replicated in satellite countries or regions.

This shift away from geographic and toward product or client-based divisional structures reflects the trend toward the **globally integrated enterprise.**[47] As the label implies, a globally integrated enterprise connects work processes around the world, rather than replicating them within each country or region. This type of organization typically organizes people around product or client divisions. Even functional units–production, marketing, design, human resources, and so on–serve the company worldwide rather than within specific geographic clusters. These functions are sensitive to cultural and market differences and have local representation to support that sensitivity, but local representatives are associates of a global function rather than a local subsidiary copied across several regions. Indeed, a globally integrated enterprise is marked by a dramatic increase in virtual teamwork, because employees are assigned global projects and ongoing responsibilities for work units that transcend geographic boundaries.

The globally integrated enterprise no longer orchestrates its business from a single headquarters in one "home" country. Instead, its divisional and functional operations are led from where the work is concentrated, and this concentration depends on economics (cost of labor, infrastructure, etc.), expertise, and openness (trade, capital flow, knowledge sharing, etc.). For example, IBM has moved toward the globally integrated enterprise structure by locating its global data centers in Colorado, Web site management in Ireland, back-office finance in Brazil, software in India, and procurement in China. IBM's vice president of worldwide engineering, responsible for procurement, recently moved from Armonk, New York, to China, where the procurement center is located. "These people are not leading teams focused on China or India or Brazil or Ireland–or Colorado or Vermont," says IBM CEO Sam Palmisano. "They are leading integrated global operations."[48]

Evaluating the Divisional Structure The divisional form is a building-block structure; it accommodates growth relatively easily and focuses employee attention on products or customers rather than tasks. Different products, services, or clients can be accommodated by sprouting new divisions. These advantages are offset by a number of limitations. First, the divisional structure tends to duplicate resources, such as production equipment and engineering or information technology expertise. Also, unless the division is quite large, resources are not used as efficiently as they are in functional structures where resources are pooled across the entire organization. The divisional structure also creates silos of knowledge. Expertise is spread across several autonomous business units, and this reduces the ability and perhaps motivation of the people in one division to share their knowledge with counterparts in other divisions. In contrast, a functional structure groups experts together, thereby supporting knowledge sharing.

Finally, the preferred divisional structure depends on the company's primary source of environmental diversity or uncertainty. This principle seems to be applied easily enough at Coca-Cola, McDonald's, and Philips, but many global organizations experience diversity and uncertainty in terms of geography, product, *and* clients. Consequently, some organizations revise their structures back and forth or create complex structures that attempt to give all three dimensions equal status. This waffling and complexity generates further complications, because organizational structure decisions shift power and status among executives. If the company switches from a geographic to product structure, people who lead the geographic fiefdoms suddenly get demoted under the product chiefs. In short, leaders of global organizations struggle to find the best divisional structure, often with the result that one or more executives leave and those who remain experience frustration.

Team-Based Structure

team-based structure
An organizational structure built around self-directed teams that complete an entire piece of work.

The opening story to this chapter introduced the organizational structure dilemma that BioWare's cofounders faced when they decided to rapidly expand operations. One of the structural forms they considered was based entirely on teams. This **team-based structure** would have BioWare employees organized around several projects, each with its own autonomous team. Generally, a team-based organizational structure is built around self-directed teams that complete an entire piece of work, such as manufacturing a product or developing an electronic game. This type of structure is usually organic. There is a wide span of control because teams operate with minimal supervision. In extreme situations, there is no formal leader, just someone selected by other team members to help coordinate the work and liaise with top management. Team structures are highly decentralized because almost all day-to-day decisions are made by team members rather than someone further up the organizational hierarchy. Finally, many team-based structures have low formalization because teams are given relatively few rules about how to organize their work. Instead, executives assign quality and quantity output targets and often productivity improvement goals to each team. Teams are then encouraged to use available resources and their own initiative to achieve those objectives.

Team-based structures are usually found within the manufacturing or service operations of larger divisional structures. For example, several GE Aircraft Engines plants are organized as team-based structures, but these plants operate within GE's larger divisional structure. However, a small number of firms apply the team-based structure from top to bottom, including W. L. Gore & Associates and Semco SA, where almost all associates work in teams.

Evaluating the Team-Based Structure The team-based organization represents an increasingly popular structure because it is usually more flexible and responsive to the environment.[49] It tends to reduce costs because teams have less reliance on formal hierarchy (direct supervision). A cross-functional team structure improves communication and cooperation across traditional boundaries. With greater autonomy, this structure also allows quicker and more informed decision making.[50] For this reason, some hospitals have shifted from functional departments to cross-functional teams. Teams composed of nurses, radiologists, anesthetists, a pharmacology representative, possibly social workers, a rehabilitation therapist, and other specialists communicate and coordinate more efficiently, thereby reducing delays and errors.[51]

Against these benefits, the team-based structure can be costly to maintain due to the need for ongoing interpersonal skill training. Teamwork potentially takes more time to coordinate than formal hierarchy during the early stages of team development. Employees may experience more stress due to increased ambiguity in their roles. Team leaders also experience more stress due to increased conflict, loss of functional power, and unclear career progression ladders. In addition, team structures suffer from duplication of resources and potential competition (and lack of resource sharing) across teams.[52]

Matrix Structure

Throughout this chapter we have referred to the dilemma that Ray Muzyka and Greg Zeschuk faced regarding the best choice of an organizational structure for BioWare. The electronic game developer could adopt a functional structure, but this might not generate an optimal level of teamwork or commitment to the final product. Alternatively, BioWare's employees could be organized into a team-based structure. But having several teams would duplicate resources and possibly undermine resource sharing among people with the same expertise across teams.

matrix structure
An organizational structure that overlays two structures (such as a geographic divisional and a functional structure) in order to leverage the benefits of both.

After carefully weighing the various organizational structure options, Muzyka and Zeschuk adopted a **matrix structure** to gain the benefits of both a functional structure and a project-based (team) structure. BioWare's matrix structure, which is similar to the diagram in Exhibit 13.4, is organized around both functions (art, audio, programming, etc.) and team-based game development projects. Employees are assigned to a cross-functional team responsible for a specific game project, yet they also belong to a permanent functional unit from which they are reassigned when their work is completed on a particular project.[53] Muzyka and Zeschuk say the matrix structure encourages employees to think in terms of the final product yet keeps them organized around their expertise to encourage knowledge sharing. "The matrix structure also supports our overall company culture where BioWare is the team,

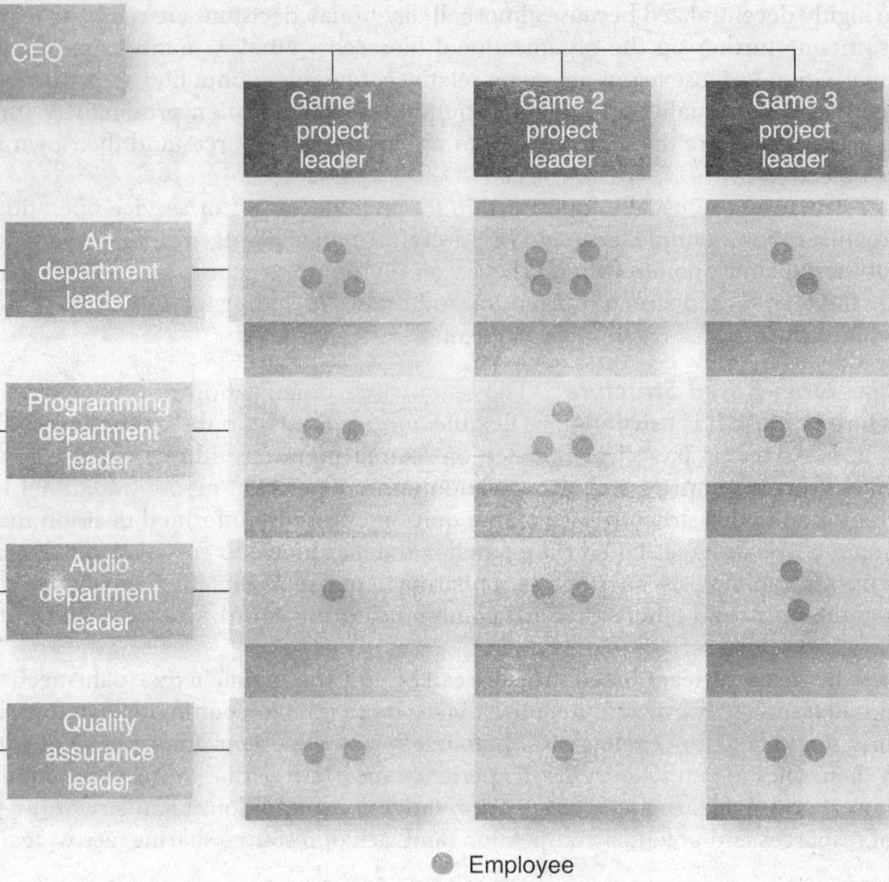

Exhibit 13.4 *Project-Based Matrix Structure (Similar to BioWare's Structure)*

and everyone is always willing to help each other whether they are on the same project or not," they add. BioWare's matrix structure has proved to be a good choice, particularly as the company (which recently became an independent division of Electronic Arts) has grown to almost 400 employees working on more than a half-dozen game projects in Austin, Texas, and Edmonton, Canada.

BioWare's structure, in which project teams overlap with functional departments, is just one form of matrix structure. Another variation, which is common in large global firms, is to have geography on one axis and products/services or client groups on the other. Procter & Gamble recently moved toward this type of global matrix structure with geographic divisions (called "market development organizations") on one axis and "global business units," representing global brands, on the other axis. Previously, P&G had a geographic divisional structure, which gave too much power to country managers and not enough power or priority to globalizing its major brands (e.g., Pantene, Tide, Pringles). P&G's leaders believe that the new matrix structure will balance this power, thereby supporting its philosophy of thinking globally and acting locally.[54]

Evaluating the Matrix Structure The matrix structure usually makes very good use of resources and expertise, making it ideal for project-based organizations with fluctuating workloads. When properly managed, it improves communication efficiency, project flexibility, and innovation, compared to purely functional or divisional designs. It focuses employees on serving clients or creating products yet keeps people organized around their specialization, so knowledge sharing improves and resources are used more efficiently. The matrix structure is also a logical choice when, as in the case of Procter & Gamble, two different dimensions (regions and products) are equally important. Structures determine executive power and what is important; the matrix structure works when two different dimensions deserve equal attention.

In spite of these advantages, the matrix structure has several well-known problems.[55] One concern is that it increases conflict among managers who equally share power. Employees working at the matrix level have two bosses and, consequently, two sets of priorities that aren't always aligned with

Losing Data in the Matrix Soon after Britain's Inland Revenue and Customs/Excise departments merged to become HM Revenue & Customs (HMRC), the combined department experienced a series of errors that violated individual privacy rights. The most serious of these incidents occurred when HMRC staff somehow lost two computer disks containing confidential details of 25 million child welfare claimants. The UK government's investigation into the security lapse concluded that along with resulting from poor security procedures, the error was partly due to "muddled accountabilities" created by the matrix organizational structure under which the new department operated. The investigator's initial briefing stated that the matrix structure and numerous departments made it "difficult to relate roles and responsibilities amongst senior management to accountability." In fact, responsibility for data security was assigned to no less than five departments, each of which reported to different director generals. The final report concluded that "[HMRC] is not suited to the so-called 'constructive friction' matrix type organization [that was] in place at the time of the data loss." HMRC has since changed to a more traditional, single-command organizational structure.[56]

each other. Project leaders might squabble with functional leaders regarding the assignment of specific employees to projects as well as regarding the employee's technical competence. For example, Citigroup, Inc., recently adopted a geographic-product matrix structure and apparently is already experiencing dysfunctional conflict between the regional and product group executives.[57] Aware of these potential conflicts, BioWare holds several "synchronization meetings" each year involving all department directors (art, design, audio, etc.), producers (i.e., game project leaders), and the human resource manager. These meetings sort out differences and ensure that staff members are properly assigned to each game project.

Another challenge is that the existence of two bosses can dilute accountability. In a functional or divisional structure, one manager is responsible for everything, even the most unexpected issues. But in a matrix structure, the unusual problems don't get resolved because neither manager takes ownership of them.[58] Mark Hurd was so concerned about accountability that he replaced Hewlett-Packard's matrix structure soon after becoming CEO. "The more accountable I can make you, the easier it is for you to show you're a great performer," Hurd declared. "The more I use a matrix, the easier I make it to blame someone else."[59] The combination of dysfunctional conflict and ambiguous accountability in matrix structures also explains why some employees experience more stress and some managers are less satisfied with their work arrangements.

Network Structure

BMW and Mercedes aren't eager to let you know this, but some of their vehicles designed and constructed with Germanic precision are neither designed nor constructed by them or in Germany. Much of BMW's X3, for example, was designed by Magna Steyr in Austria. Magna also manufactured the vehicle in Austria until BMW transferred this work to its plant in South Carolina. The contract manufacturer also builds Mercedes's off-road G-class vehicle. Both BMW and Mercedes are hub organizations that own and market their respective brands, whereas Magna and other suppliers are spokes around the hub that provide production, engineering, and other services that get the auto firms' luxury products to customers.[60]

network structure
An alliance of several organizations for the purpose of creating a product or serving a client.

BMW, Mercedes, and many other organizations are moving toward a **network structure** as they design and build a product or serve a client through an alliance of several organizations.[61] As Exhibit 13.5 illustrates, this collaborative structure typically consists of several satellite organizations beehived around a hub or core firm. The core firm orchestrates the network process and provides one or two other core competencies, such as marketing or product development. In our example, BMW or Mercedes is the hub that provides marketing and management, whereas other firms perform many other functions. The core firm might be the main contact with customers, but most of the product or service delivery and support activities are farmed out to satellite organizations located anywhere in the world. Extranets (Web-based networks with partners) and other technologies ensure that information flows easily and openly between the core firm and its array of satellites.[62]

One of the main forces pushing toward a network structure is the recognition that an organization has only a few *core competencies.* A core competency is a knowledge base that resides throughout the organization and provides a strategic advantage. As companies discover their core competency, they "unbundle" noncritical tasks to other organizations that have a core competency at performing those tasks. For instance, BMW decided long ago that its core competency is not facilities management, so it outsourced this function at its British engine plant to Dalkia, which specializes in facility maintenance and energy management.[63]

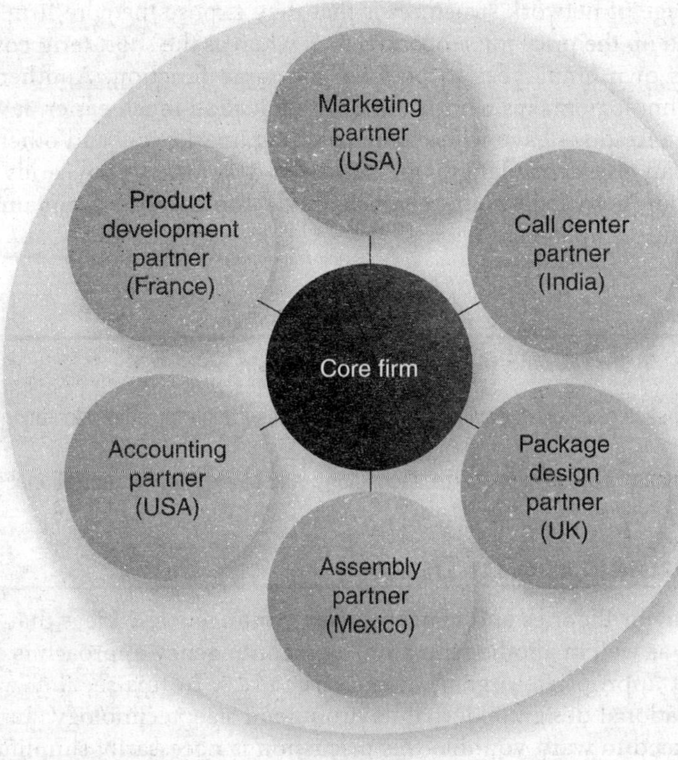

Exhibit 13.5 *A Network Structure*

Companies are also more likely to form network structures when technology is changing quickly and production processes are complex or varied.[64] Many firms cannot keep up with the hyperfast changes in information technology, so they have outsourced their entire information system departments to IBM, EDS, and other firms that specialize in information system services. Similarly, many high-technology firms form networks with Flextronics, Celestica, and other electronic equipment manufacturers that have expertise in diverse production processes.

Evaluating the Network Structure For several years, organizational behavior theorists have argued that organizational leaders must develop a metaphor of organizations as plasmalike organisms rather than rigid machines.[65] Network structures come close to the organism metaphor because they offer the flexibility to realign their structure with changing environmental requirements. If customers demand a new product or service, the core firm forms new alliances with other firms offering the appropriate resources. For example, by working with Magna International, BMW was probably able to develop and launch the X3 vehicle much sooner than would have been the case if it had performed these tasks on its own. When BMW needs a different type of manufacturing, it isn't saddled with nonessential facilities and resources. Network structures also offer efficiencies because the core firm becomes globally competitive as it shops worldwide for subcontractors with the best people and the best technology at the best price. Indeed, the pressures of global competition have made network structures more vital, and computer-based information technology has made them possible.[66]

A potential disadvantage of network structures is that they expose the core firm to market forces. Other companies may bid up the price for subcontractors, whereas the short-term cost would be lower if the company hired its own employees to perform the same function. Another problem is that although information technology makes worldwide communication much easier, it will never replace the degree of control organizations have when manufacturing, marketing, and other functions are in-house. The core firm can use arm's-length incentives and contract provisions to maintain the subcontractor's quality, but these actions are relatively crude compared to maintaining the quality of work performed by in-house employees.

Learning Objectives

After reading this section, you should be able to:

9. Identify four characteristics of external environments and discuss the preferred organizational structure for each environment.
10. Summarize the influence of organizational size, technology, and strategy on organizational structure.

CONTINGENCIES OF ORGANIZATIONAL DESIGN

Most organizational behavior theories and concepts have contingencies: Ideas that work well in one situation might not work as well in another situation. This contingency approach is certainly relevant when choosing the most appropriate organizational structure.[67] In this section, we introduce four contingencies of organizational design: external environment, size, technology, and strategy. Before doing so, however, we need to warn you that this discussion is necessarily simplified because of an unresolved debate among organizational structure experts.[68] The debate centers on the question of whether specific contingencies can be associated with specific elements of structure (centralization, formalization, etc.) or whether we need to examine *configurations* of contingencies with broad typologies of organizational structure (such as organic versus mechanistic). Some writers further suggest that more than two different structural typologies might work equally well in a particular situational configuration. With these caveats in mind, let's examine the four main contingencies of organizational structure.

External Environment

The best structure for an organization depends on its external environment. The external environment includes anything outside the organization, including most stakeholders (e.g., clients, suppliers, government), resources (e.g., raw materials, human resources, information, finances), and competitors. Four characteristics of external environments influence the type of organizational structure best suited to a particular situation: dynamism, complexity, diversity, and hostility.[69]

Dynamic versus Stable Environments Dynamic environments have a high rate of change, leading to novel situations and a lack of identifiable patterns. Organic structures are better suited to this type of environment so that the organization can adapt more quickly to changes, but only if employees are experienced and coordinate well in teamwork.[70] In contrast, stable environments are characterized by regular cycles of activity and steady changes in supply and demand for inputs and outputs. Events are more predictable, enabling the firm to apply rules and procedures. Mechanistic structures are more efficient when the environment is predictable, so they tend to work better than organic structures.

Complex versus Simple Environments Complex environments have many elements, whereas simple environments have few things to monitor. As an example, a major university library operates in a more complex environment than a small-town public library. The university library's clients require several types of services–book borrowing, online full-text databases, research centers, course reserve collections, and so on. A small-town public library has fewer of these demands placed on it. The more complex the environment, the more decentralized the organization should become. Decentralization is a logical response to complexity because decisions are pushed down to people and subunits with the necessary information to make informed choices.

Diverse versus Integrated Environments Organizations located in diverse environments have a greater variety of products or services, clients, and regions. In contrast, an integrated environment has only one client, product, and geographic area. The more diversified the environment, the more the firm needs to use a divisional structure aligned with that diversity. If it sells a single product around the world, a geographic divisional structure would align best with the firm's geographic diversity, for example.

Hostile versus Munificent Environments Firms located in a hostile environment face resource scarcity and more competition in the marketplace. Hostile environments are typically dynamic ones because they reduce the predictability of access to resources and demand for outputs. Organic structures tend to be best in hostile environments. However, when the environment is extremely hostile–such as a severe shortage of supplies or lower market share–organizations tend to temporarily centralize so that decisions can be made more quickly and executives feel more comfortable being in control.[71] Ironically, centralization may result in lower-quality decisions during organizational crises, because top management has less information, particularly when the environment is complex.

Being Big and Small All at Once Johnson & Johnson (J&J) may be best known for Band-Aids and baby powder, but the New Jersey–based company is really a conglomerate of 250 businesses in 57 countries that manufacture and/or market prescription medicines (accounting for 40 percent of its total business), medical devices and diagnostics (the largest such business in the world), and personal care products (toothbrushes, skin creams, shampoos, etc.). Successful companies decentralize when operating in complex and diversified environments, and J&J is no exception. "J&J is probably the reference company for being decentralized," says William Weldon, J&J's chairman and CEO. Weldon points out that the company's decentralized structure allows it be more sensitive and responsive to each unique culture and business setting. "The men and women who run our businesses around the world usually are people who grew up in those markets, understand those markets, and develop themselves in those markets," Weldon explains. Decentralization of a large organization has other advantages. "We are big and we are small all at once," says J&J's Web site. "Each of our operating companies functions as its own small business . . . [yet] they also have access to the know-how and resources of a Fortune 50 company. It's like having dozens of strategic partners at their fingertips."[72]

Organizational Size

Larger organizations should have different structures from smaller organizations.[73] As the number of employees increases, job specialization increases due to a greater division of labor. The greater division of labor requires more elaborate coordinating mechanisms. Thus, larger firms make greater use of standardization (particularly work processes and outcomes) to coordinate work activities. These coordinating mechanisms create an administrative hierarchy and greater formalization. Historically, larger organizations make less use of informal communication as a coordinating mechanism. However, emerging information technologies and increased emphasis on empowerment have caused informal communication to regain its importance in large firms.[74]

Larger organizations also tend to be more decentralized. Executives have neither sufficient time nor expertise to process all the decisions that significantly influence the business as it grows. Therefore, decision-making authority is pushed down to lower levels, where incumbents are able to cope with the narrower range of issues under their control.

Technology

Technology is another factor to consider when designing the best organizational structure for the situation.[75] *Technology* refers to the mechanisms or processes by which an organization turns out its product or service. One technological contingency is *variability*–the number of exceptions to standard procedure that tend to occur. In work processes with low variability, jobs are routine and follow standard operating procedures. Another contingency is *analyzability*–the predictability or difficulty of the required work. The less analyzable the work, the more it requires experts with sufficient discretion to address the work challenges. An organic, rather than a mechanistic, structure should be introduced where employees perform tasks with high variety and low analyzability, such as in a research setting. The reason is that employees face unique situations with little opportunity for repetition. In contrast, a mechanistic structure is preferred where the technology has low variability and high analyzability, such as an assembly line. The work is routine and highly predictable, an ideal situation for a mechanistic structure to operate efficiently.

Organizational Strategy

organizational strategy
The way the organization positions itself in its setting in relation to its stakeholders, given the organization's resources, capabilities, and mission.

Organizational strategy refers to the way the organization positions itself in its setting in relation to its stakeholders, given the organization's resources, capabilities, and mission.[76] In other words, strategy represents the decisions and actions applied to achieve the organization's goals. Although size, technology, and environment influence the optimal organizational structure, these contingencies do not necessarily determine structure. Instead, corporate leaders formulate and implement strategies that shape both the characteristics of these contingencies as well as the organization's resulting structure.

This concept is summed up with the simple phrase "Structure follows strategy."[77] Organizational leaders decide how large to grow and which technologies to use. They take steps to define and manipulate their environments, rather than let the organization's fate be entirely determined by external influences. Furthermore, organizational structures don't evolve as a natural response to these contingencies. Instead, they result from organizational decisions. Thus, organizational strategy influences both the contingencies of structure and the structure itself. If a company's strategy is to compete through innovation, a more organic structure would be preferred because it is easier for employees to share knowledge and be creative. If a company chooses a low-cost strategy, a mechanistic structure is preferred because it maximizes production and service efficiency.[78] Overall, it is now apparent that organizational structure is influenced by size, technology, and environment, but the organization's strategy may reshape these elements and loosen their connection to organizational structure.

Chapter Summary

Organizational structure is the division of labor as well as the patterns of coordination, communication, workflow, and formal power that direct organizational activities. All organizational structures divide labor into distinct tasks and coordinate that labor to accomplish common goals. The primary means of coordination are informal communication, formal hierarchy, and standardization.

The four basic elements of organizational structure are span of control, centralization, formalization, and departmentalization. The optimal span of control—the number of people directly reporting to the next level in the hierarchy—depends on the presence of coordinating mechanisms other than formal hierarchy, as well as on whether employees perform routine tasks and how much interdependence there is among employees within the department.

Centralization occurs when formal decision authority is held by a small group of people, typically senior executives. Many companies decentralize as they become larger and more complex, but some sections of the company may remain centralized while other sections decentralize. Formalization is the degree to which organizations standardize behavior through rules, procedures, formal training, and related mechanisms. Companies become more formalized as they get older and larger. Formalization tends to reduce organizational flexibility, organizational learning, creativity, and job satisfaction.

Span of control, centralization, and formalization cluster into mechanistic and organic structures. Mechanistic structures are characterized by a narrow span of control and a high degree of formalization and centralization. Companies with an organic structure have the opposite characteristics.

Departmentalization specifies how employees and their activities are grouped together. It establishes the chain of command, focuses people around common mental models, and encourages coordination through informal communication among people and subunits. A functional structure organizes employees around specific knowledge or other resources. This fosters greater specialization and improves direct supervision, but it weakens the focus on serving clients or developing products.

A divisional structure groups employees around geographic areas, clients, or outputs. This structure accommodates growth and focuses employee attention on products or customers rather than tasks. However, this structure duplicates resources and creates silos of knowledge. Team-based structures are very flat, with low formalization, and organize self-directed teams around work processes rather than functional specialties. The matrix structure combines two structures to leverage the benefits of both types of structure. However, this approach requires more coordination than functional or pure divisional structures, may dilute accountability, and increases conflict. A network structure is an alliance of several organizations for the purpose of creating a product or serving a client.

The best organizational structure depends on the firm's external environment, size, technology, and strategy. The optimal structure depends on whether the environment is dynamic or stable, complex or simple, diverse or integrated, and hostile or munificent. As organizations increase in size, they become more decentralized and more formalized. The work unit's technology—including variety of work and analyzability of problems—influences whether to adopt an organic or mechanistic structure. These contingencies influence but do not necessarily determine structure. Instead, corporate leaders formulate and implement strategies that shape both the characteristics of these contingencies as well as the organization's resulting structure.

Key Terms

centralization
concurrent engineering
divisional structure
formalization
functional structure
globally integrated enterprise
matrix structure
mechanistic structure
network structure
organic structure
organizational strategy
organizational structure
span of control
team-based structure

Critical Thinking Questions

1. TAXI and Nitro, two creative advertising companies described in this chapter, have organic, team-based structures. What coordinating mechanism likely dominates in this type of organizational structure? Describe the extent and form in which the other two types of coordination might be apparent at TAXI and Nitro.
2. Think about the business school or other organizational unit whose classes you are currently attending. What is the dominant coordinating mechanism used to guide or control the instructor? Why is this coordinating mechanism used the most here?
3. Administrative theorists concluded many decades ago that the most effective organizations have a narrow span of control. Yet today's top-performing manufacturing firms have a wide span of control. Why is this possible? Under what circumstances, if any, should manufacturing firms have a narrow span of control?
4. Leaders of large organizations struggle to identify the best level and types of centralization and decentralization. What should companies consider when determining the degree of decentralization?
5. Diversified Technologies Ltd. (DTL) makes four types of products, each type to be sold to different types of clients. For example, one product is sold exclusively to automobile repair shops, whereas another is used mainly in hospitals. Customer expectations and needs are surprisingly similar throughout the world. The company has separate marketing, product design, and manufacturing facilities in Asia, North America, Europe, and South America because, until recently, each jurisdiction had unique regulations governing the production and sales of these products. However, several governments have begun the process of deregulating the products that DTL designs and manufactures, and trade agreements have opened several markets to foreign-made products. Which form of departmentalization might be best for DTL if deregulation and trade agreements occur?
6. IBM is becoming a globally integrated enterprise. What does this organization look like in terms of its departmentalization? What challenges might face companies that try to adopt the globally integrated enterprise model?
7. From an employee perspective, what are the advantages and disadvantages of working in a matrix structure?
8. Suppose that you have been hired as a consultant to diagnose the environmental characteristics of your college or university. How would you describe the school's external environment? Is the school's existing structure appropriate for this environment?

CASE STUDY 13.1

MACY'S GETS PERSONAL

Macy's, Inc., wants to get more personal with its customers. The world's largest department store is responding to declining sales by introducing a new organizational structure in which local districts and stores have more autonomy to personalize merchandise and marketing for customers in that area. This change is part of its "My Macy's" strategy developed a year earlier, which is aimed at getting customers to feel a personal connection to the Macy's outlets in their area by ensuring that those stores provide merchandise assortments, size ranges, marketing programs, and shopping experiences that are more closely aligned to local needs.

"Improving sales and earnings performance requires innovation in engaging our customer more effectively in every store, as well as reducing total costs," explains Macy's CEO Terry J. Lundgren. "We believe the right answer is to reallocate our resources to place more emphasis and talent at the local market level to differentiate Macy's stores, serve customers, and drive business. In essence, we plan to drive sales growth by improving our knowledge at the local level and then acting quickly on that knowledge. In addition, we believe our new strategies will speed up decision making and simplify the process of working with our vendors."

Macy's new organizational structure consists of 20 districts spread across three regions (East, South, and West). District managers and their small staff of store merchandisers and planners will be responsible for an average of 10 stores rather than 16 to 18 stores in the previous structure. This narrower span of control gives district staff and management the opportunity to work more closely with each store. The district managers, who report to regional heads, will also have more autonomy to make decisions regarding space allocation, service levels, and visual merchandising within each store.

The district store merchandisers will liaise with Macy's central buying executives to understand and act on the merchandise needs of local customers. The district planners will provide market-specific intelligence to division planning offices. The company is introducing new systems technology to help the district and store management more accurately stock local stores with items, brands, garment sizes, and colors preferred by customers who shop at those specific locations. District offices will also receive resources to participate in local events. The new structure will result in about 250 people in district offices, double the previous number at that level. Meanwhile, Macy's is laying off more than 2,000 employees, many of them from regional offices where many decisions were previously made.

Macy's new organizational structure and marketing strategy is something of an about-face. Over the past few years, the company rebranded several local department stores that it has acquired. Burdines in Florida, Stern's in New York, Bon Marché in the Pacific Northwest, Goldsmith's in Memphis, and Kaufmann's in Pittsburgh, among others, are now called Macy's. This rebranding may have weakened the company's personal connection to local customers. Furthermore, until recently, Macy's followed the traditional department store model of standardizing merchandising and marketing regardless of geographic locale. This resulted in advertising winter coats in Miami and swimsuits in Detroit in December.

One retail analyst suggests that Macy's reorganization is an indication that its recent mergers and acquisitions have not worked out as smoothly as planned. "The need for closer supervision exists in this company," says the analyst. "This is a new layer of closer supervision." Another retail expert warns that Macy's needs to carefully get the right balance regarding decentralization and formalization. "Too much localization can inflate costs, while too much standardization triggers staleness. A retailer must understand which business elements should incorporate localization, how costly they are to customize, and how much impact they will have from store to store."

Even with these concerns, Macy's CEO is upbeat about the reorganization. "I'm pretty excited about the new structure," says Lundgren. "It's about growing sales. It's about trying to be more locally in tune with customer preferences. It's about giving our team a small span of control, so they really get educated about what the product needs are for that local consumer."

Discussion Questions

1. What changes has Macy's introduced in terms of the four elements of organizational structure?
2. What contingencies suggest that Macy's new organizational structure is appropriate for its environment?
3. What problems do you think Macy's might experience with the new organizational structure? What factors suggest that the new organizational structure may face problems?

Sources: D. Moin, "Macy's to Cut 2,550 Jobs in Restructuring," *Women's Wear Daily,* 7 February 2008, p. 3; "Macy's Launches New Initiatives to Drive Sales, Earnings," *Business Wire,* 7 February 2008; P. Alexander, "Will Macy's Go Far Enough?" *Advertising Age,* 5 May 2008, p. 30.

CASE STUDY 13.2

MORE THAN COSMETIC CHANGES AT AVON

BusinessWeek After several years of stellar growth and earnings, Avon Products Inc. suddenly experienced declining sales around the world. CEO Andrea Jung, who led the company through its good years, now had to become a turnaround expert. "I'd never done anything like that before," admits Jung. "My first reaction was: 'I get it. I see the numbers, but I just don't know if I, or we, have the stomach for it." One of Jung's strategies was to reorganize Avon so that it would be more nimble and responsive to the market.

This *BusinessWeek* case study describes how Avon CEO Andrea Jung introduced a new organizational structure and made other changes to return the cosmetics company to profitability and growth. Read the full text of this *BusinessWeek* article at www.mhhe.com/mcshane5e, and prepare for the discussion questions below.

Discussion Questions

1. What organizational structure problems did Avon experience prior to the reorganization?
2. What changes did Andrea Jung make to Avon's organizational structure? In your opinion, were these structural changes appropriate? Why or why not?
3. This case study also refers to problems and improvements in managerial decision making. In what way(s) does decision making relate to organizational structure here?

Source: N. Byrnes, "Avon: More than Cosmetic Changes," *BusinessWeek,* 12 March 2007, pp. 62–63.

TEAM EXERCISE 13.3

THE CLUB ED EXERCISE

Cheryl Harvey and Kim Morouney, Wilfred Laurier University

PURPOSE This exercise is designed to help you understand the issues to consider when designing organizations at various stages of growth.

MATERIALS Each student team should have enough overhead transparencies or flip-chart sheets to display several organizational charts.

INSTRUCTIONS Each team discusses the scenario presented. The first scenario is presented below. The instructor will facilitate discussion and notify teams when to begin the next step. The exercise and debriefing require approximately 90 minutes, although fewer scenarios can reduce the time somewhat.

1. Students are placed in teams (typically four or five people).
2. After reading Scenario 1 presented below, each team will design an organizational chart (departmentalization) that is most appropriate for the situation. Students should be able to describe the type of structure drawn and explain why it is appropriate. The structure should be drawn on an overhead

transparency or flip chart for others to see during later class discussion. The instructor will set a fixed time (e.g., 15 minutes) to complete this task.

Scenario 1. Determined never to shovel snow again, you are establishing a new resort business on a small Caribbean island. The resort is under construction and is scheduled to open one year from now. You decide it is time to draw up an organizational chart for this new venture, called Club Ed.

3. At the end of the time allowed, the instructor will present Scenario 2, and each team will be asked to draw another organizational chart to suit that situation. Again, students should be able to describe the type of structure drawn and explain why it is appropriate.
4. At the end of the time allowed, the instructor will present Scenario 3, and each team will be asked to draw another organizational chart to suit that situation.
5. Depending on the time available, the instructor might present a fourth scenario. The class will gather to present their designs for each scenario. During each presentation, teams should describe the type of structure drawn and explain why it is appropriate.

Source: Reprinted with permission of Cheryl Harvey, Wilfrid Laurier University.

SELF-ASSESSMENT 13.4

WHAT ORGANIZATIONAL STRUCTURE DO YOU PREFER?

PURPOSE This exercise is designed to help you understand how an organization's structure influences the personal needs and values of people working in that structure.

INSTRUCTIONS Personal values influence how comfortable you are working in different organizational structures. You might prefer an organization with clearly defined rules or no rules at all. You might prefer a firm where almost any employee can make important decisions or one where important decisions are screened by senior executives. Read each statement below and indicate the extent to which you would like to work in an organization with that characteristic. When finished, use the scoring key in Appendix B at the end of the book to calculate your results. This self-assessment should be completed alone so that you can assess yourself honestly without concerns of social comparison. Class discussion will focus on the elements of organizational design and their relationship to personal needs and values.

Organizational Structure Preference Scale

I would like to work in an organization where . . .	Not at all	A little	Some-what	Very much	Score
1. A person's career ladder has several steps toward higher status and responsibility.	☐	☐	☐	☐	___
2. Employees perform their work with few rules to limit their discretion.	☐	☐	☐	☐	___
3. Responsibility is pushed down to employees who perform the work.	☐	☐	☐	☐	___
4. Supervisors have few employees, so they work closely with each person.	☐	☐	☐	☐	___
5. Senior executives make most decisions to ensure that the company is consistent in its actions.	☐	☐	☐	☐	___
6. Jobs are clearly defined so that there is no confusion over who is responsible for various tasks.	☐	☐	☐	☐	___
7. Employees have their say on issues, but senior executives make most of the decisions.	☐	☐	☐	☐	___
8. Job descriptions are broadly stated or nonexistent.	☐	☐	☐	☐	___
9. Everyone's work is tightly synchronized around top-management operating plans.	☐	☐	☐	☐	___
10. Most work is performed in teams without close supervision.	☐	☐	☐	☐	___
11. Work gets done through informal discussion with co-workers rather than through formal rules.	☐	☐	☐	☐	___
12. Supervisors have so many employees that they can't watch anyone very closely.	☐	☐	☐	☐	___
13. Everyone has clearly understood goals, expectations, and job duties.	☐	☐	☐	☐	___
14. Senior executives assign overall goals, but leave daily decisions to frontline teams.	☐	☐	☐	☐	___
15. Even in a large company, the CEO is only three or four levels above the lowest position.	☐	☐	☐	☐	___

Propelled by a culture of cost efficiency and competitiveness, Dell, Inc., was the unstoppable leader in the computer industry for more than a decade. Experts praised its low-cost, responsive manufacturing and direct-marketing sales model. Founder Michael Dell championed short-term objectives, while Kevin Rollins (until recently Dell CEO) was the architect of efficiency-oriented processes and measures. Dell culture emphasized "winning," meaning that it focused on beating the competition and staying on top through low prices. "There are some organizations where people think they're a hero if they invent a new thing," Rollins said a few years ago. "Being a hero at Dell means saving money."

Dell's competitive and efficiency-focused culture is now becoming a liability to the computer-maker's future.

Although still an efficient manufacturer of low-cost computers, Dell's spectacular success has stalled while HP and other competitors are moving ahead. The reason? Dell's strong culture blinded leaders and most staff to anything other than building low-cost computers, yet the market was shifting toward a preference for style and innovation. "Dell's culture is not inspirational or aspirational," suggests one industry expert. "[Its] culture only wants to talk about execution." A few staff warned that Dell's culture needed to change, but those who dared to criticize the company's deeply ingrained values and assumptions were quickly silenced. "A lot of red flags got waved—but only once," recalls a former Dell manager.

Meanwhile, Dell's fortunes—including public ratings of its culture—were falling. A few years ago, Dell ranked number one on *Fortune* magazine's list of most admired companies in America; two years later, it was off the top 20 list. Similarly, Dell Canada placed fifth on the list of Canada's most admired corporate cultures in 2006. A year later, the company was not mentioned at all; its culture was no longer admired.

These and other concerns motivated founder Michael Dell to return as CEO, replacing Kevin Rollins. Other senior executives have also left the company. "The company was too focused on the short term," Dell admits. He apparently also repeatedly emphasizes to staff that Dell's past culture "is not a religion." Dell is convinced he can turn the company around, and there is some indication his new vision is working. Still, a few critics believe that changing Dell's culture will be a mammoth task. "It's not an easy transition," warns a technology analyst. "You've got to change your mind-set and your culture."[1]

14

ORGANIZATIONAL CULTURE

Learning Objectives

After reading this chapter, you should be able to:

1. Describe the elements of organizational culture.
2. Discuss the importance of organizational subcultures.
3. List four categories of artifacts through which corporate culture is deciphered.
4. Identify three functions of organizational culture.
5. Discuss the conditions under which organizational culture strength improves organizational performance.
6. Compare and contrast four strategies for merging organizational cultures.
7. Identify the four strategies for changing or strengthening an organization's culture.
8. Apply attraction-selection-attrition theory to explain how organizational culture strengthens.
9. Describe the stages of organizational socialization.
10. Explain how realistic job previews assist the socialization process.

organizational culture The values and assumptions shared within an organization.

Dell's current challenges illustrate the perils of ignoring organizational culture. **Organizational culture** consists of the values and assumptions shared within an organization.[2] It defines what is important and unimportant in the company and, consequently, directs everyone in the organization toward the "right way" of doing things. You might think of organizational culture as the organization's DNA–invisible to the naked eye, yet a powerful template that shapes what happens in the workplace.

This chapter begins by identifying the elements of organizational culture and then describing how culture is deciphered through artifacts. This is followed by a discussion of the relationship between organizational culture and performance, including the effects of cultural strength, fit, and adaptability. Then we examine ways to change or strengthen organizational culture. The final section of this chapter turns our attention to the challenges of and solutions to merging organizational cultures.

Learning Objectives

After reading the next two sections, you should be able to:

1. Describe the elements of organizational culture.
2. Discuss the importance of organizational subcultures.
3. List four categories of artifacts through which corporate culture is deciphered.

ELEMENTS OF ORGANIZATIONAL CULTURE

Exhibit 14.1 illustrates how the shared values and assumptions of an organization's culture relate to each other and are associated with artifacts, which are discussed later in this chapter. *Values,* which were described in Chapters 1 and 2, are stable, evaluative beliefs that guide our preferences for outcomes or courses of action in a variety of situations.[3] They are conscious perceptions about what is good or bad, right or wrong. In the context of organizational culture, values are discussed as *shared values,* which are values that people within the organization or work unit have in common and place near the top of their hierarchy of values.[4] At Dell, employees generally hold the shared values of efficiency and competitiveness (winning), whereas other possible values take a lower priority. Organizational culture also consists of *shared assumptions*–a deeper element that some experts believe is the essence of corporate culture. Shared assumptions are nonconscious, taken-for-granted perceptions or ideal prototypes of behavior that are considered the correct way to think and act toward problems and opportunities. Shared assumptions are so deeply ingrained that you probably wouldn't discover them by surveying employees. Only by observing the employees, analyzing their decisions, and debriefing them on their actions would these assumptions rise to the surface.

It has become a popular practice for leaders to identify and publicly state their organization's culture or, more precisely, their shared values. Yahoo, the online portal company, is no exception. Its Web site proudly says that six values represent "what makes it tick": excellence, innovation, customer fixation, teamwork, community, and fun. Korean steelmaker POSCO, which is one of Asia's most admired companies and rated by senior university students as the most desired company to work for in Korea, also proudly describes its six core values: customer focus, execution (achieving goals), integrity, recognizing the value of people, and challenge (an indomitable spirit of transforming the impossible into reality).

Do these values really represent the cultural content of Yahoo and POSCO? Possibly, to some extent. However, these value proclamations represent *espoused values*–the values that leaders say they and their

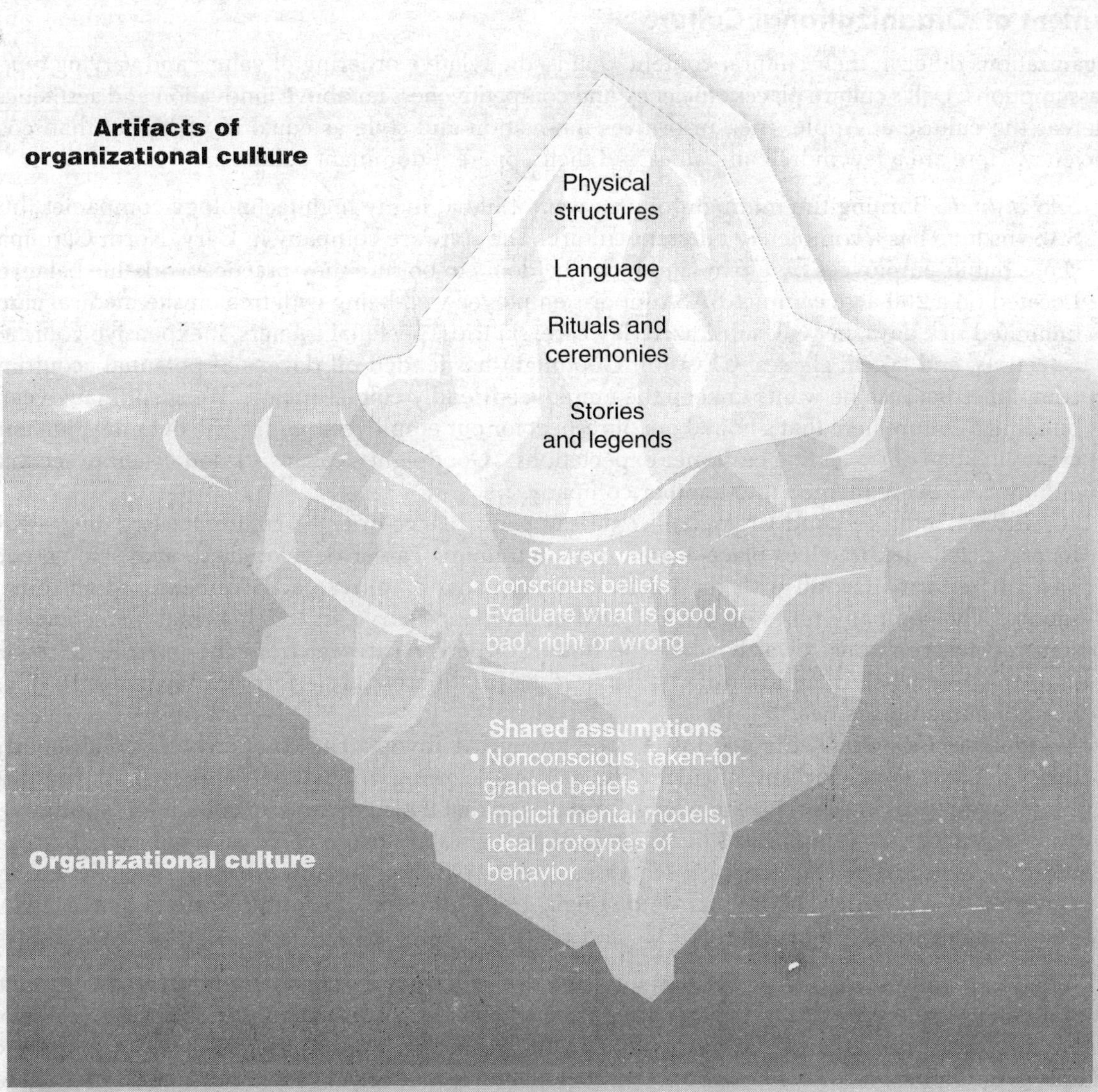

Exhibit 14.1 *Organizational Culture Assumptions, Values, and Artifacts*

staff rely on to guide their decisions and actions.[5] Organizational leaders construct a positive public image by claiming to believe in values that are socially desirable, even when they are not applied (see Chapter 2). An often-cited example is Enron Corp.[6] The Houston-based energy conglomerate listed its cultural values as communication, respect, integrity, and excellence, yet it went bankrupt when its leaders perpetrated one of the world's largest accounting frauds. The problem was that Enron's espoused values were quite different from its enacted values. Another issue is that even if leaders abide by the espoused values, lower-level employees might not share these values. In contrast, organizational culture consists of shared *enacted values*–the values that leaders and employees truly rely on to guide their decisions and actions. These "values-in-use" are apparent by watching people in action.

Content of Organizational Culture

Organizations differ in their cultural content, that is, the relative ordering of values and varying types of assumptions. Dell's culture places efficiency and competitiveness far above innovation and aesthetics, whereas the culture at Apple, Inc., prioritizes innovation and style as equal to or higher than cost efficiency. Here are a few more companies and their apparent dominant cultures:

- *SAS Institute.* Burning the midnight oil is a way of life at many high-technology companies, but SAS Institute has a completely different culture. The software company in Cary, North Carolina, shoos out its employees by 6 p.m. and locks the doors to be sure they practice work–life balance. Located on a 200-acre campus, SAS supports employee well-being with free on-site medical care, unlimited sick days, heavily subsidized day care, ski trips, personal trainers, inexpensive gourmet cafeterias, and tai chi classes. CEO Jim Goodnight has fended off dozens of potential acquiring companies because he wants to keep the employee-friendly culture intact. "We spent many years building a culture here that's honed out of respect for our employees, and is one of innovation and creativity, one of exceeding customer expectations," Goodnight explains. "I don't want to see that end by SAS being merged into another company."[7]
- *ICICI Bank.* India's second-largest bank exudes a performance-oriented culture focused on growth. Its organizational practices place a premium on training, career development, goal setting, and pay for performance, all with the intent of maximizing employee achievement and customer service. The company relies on GE's storied performance curve, in which a small percentage of staff receive generous rewards while the bottom 5 percent are cut from the payroll. "Growth happens only when there are differential rewards for differential performers," explains ICICI's head of human resources.[8]
- *Toyota Motor Company.* Being good isn't good enough at Toyota. The company that continuously raises the bar on production efficiency has a strong learning orientation culture–employees are encouraged to discover and acknowledge mistakes so that the company can continuously improve. Toyota's culture also emphasizes humility. Even as it rises to the top of the auto industry, Toyota's leaders are hesitant to talk up their successes. "We're paranoid against arrogance," explains Ray Tanguay, vice president of Toyota Motor Engineering and Manufacturing North America. "'Not good enough' are key words for us."[9]

Employee-friendly and creative, performance-oriented, efficiency and humility–how many corporate cultural values are there? Many experts have tried to classify corporate culture into a few easy-to-remember categories. One of the most popular and respected models identifies seven corporate cultures (see Exhibit 14.2). Another popular model identifies four organizational cultures organized in a two-by-two table representing internal versus external focus and flexibility versus control. Other models organize cultures around a circle with 8 or 12 categories. These circumplex models suggest that some cultures are opposite to others, such as an avoidance culture versus a self-actualization culture, or a power culture versus a collegial culture.[10]

These organizational culture models and surveys are popular with corporate leaders faced with the messy business of diagnosing their company's culture and identifying what kind of culture they want to develop. Unfortunately, they also present a distorted view of organizational culture. First, these models oversimplify the diversity of cultural values in organizations. The fact is, there are dozens of individual values, and many more combinations of values, so the number of organizational cultures that these models describe likely falls considerably short of the full set. Second, we must remember that organizational culture includes shared assumptions about the right way to do things, not just shared values. Few models take this more subterranean aspect of culture into account.

Organizational culture dimension	Characteristics of the dimension
Innovation	Experimenting, opportunity seeking, risk taking, few rules, low cautiousness
Stability	Predictability, security, rule-oriented
Respect for people	Fairness, tolerance
Outcome orientation	Action-oriented, high expectations, results-oriented
Attention to detail	Precise, analytic
Team orientation	Collaboration, people-oriented
Aggressiveness	Competitive, low emphasis on social responsibility

Source: Based on information in C. A. O'Reilly III, J. Chatman, and D. F. Caldwell, "People and Organizational Culture: A Profile Comparison Approach to Assessing Person-Organization Fit," *Academy of Management Journal* 34, no. 3 (1991), pp. 487–518.

Exhibit 14.2 *Organizational Culture Profile Dimensions and Characteristics*

A third concern is that these organizational culture models and measures typically adopt an "integration" perspective; they assume that most organizations have a fairly clear, unified culture that is easily decipherable.[11] They assert that an organization's culture is inherently measurable because any ambiguity is outside the domain of the culture. The integration perspective further assumes that when an organization's culture changes, it shifts from one unified condition to a new unified condition with only temporary ambiguity or weakness during the transition. These assumptions are probably incorrect or, at best, oversimplified. An organization's culture is usually quite blurry, so much so that it cannot be estimated through employee surveys alone. As we discuss next, organizations consist of diverse subcultures that preclude any potential consensus or consistency in values and assumptions across the organization. Indeed, even these subcultural clusters can be ill-defined because values and assumptions are ultimately unique to every individual. We are not suggesting here that organizational culture is nonexistent; some degree of shared values and assumptions does exist in many organizations. Instead, we warn that popular organizational culture models and measures oversimplify the variety of organizational cultures and falsely presume that organizations can easily be identified within these categories.

Organizational Subcultures

When discussing organizational culture, we are really referring to the *dominant culture,* that is, the values and assumptions shared most consistently and widely by the organization's members. The dominant culture is usually understood and internalized by senior management, but it sometimes exists in spite of senior management's desire for another culture. Furthermore, as mentioned in the previous section, an organization's dominant culture is not as unified or clear as many consultants and business leaders assume. Instead, organizations are composed of *subcultures* located throughout their various divisions, geographic regions, and occupational groups.[12] Some subcultures enhance the dominant culture by espousing parallel assumptions and values; others differ from but do not oppose the dominant culture; still others are called *countercultures* because they embrace values or assumptions that directly oppose the organization's dominant culture. It is also possible that some organizations (including some universities, according to one study) operate with subcultures and no decipherable dominant culture at all.[13]

Subcultures, particularly countercultures, potentially create conflict and dissension among employees, but they also serve two important functions.[14] First, they maintain the organization's standards of performance and ethical behavior. Employees who hold countercultural values are an important source of surveillance and critical review of the dominant order. They encourage constructive conflict and more creative thinking about how the organization should interact with its environment. Subcultures prevent employees from blindly following one set of values and thereby help the organization to abide by society's ethical values.

The second function of subcultures is that they are the spawning grounds for emerging values that keep the firm aligned with the needs of customers, suppliers, society, and other stakeholders. Companies eventually need to replace their dominant values with ones that are more appropriate for the changing environment. If subcultures are suppressed, the organization may take longer to discover and adopt values aligned with the emerging environment.

Deciphering Organizational Culture through Artifacts

artifacts
The observable symbols and signs of an organization's culture.

We can't directly see an organization's cultural assumptions and values. Instead, as Exhibit 14.1 illustrated earlier, we decipher organizational culture indirectly through artifacts. **Artifacts** are the observable symbols and signs of an organization's culture, such as the way visitors are greeted, the organization's physical layout, and how employees are rewarded.[15] A few experts suggest that artifacts are the essence of organizational culture, whereas most others (including the authors of this book) view artifacts as symbols or indicators of culture. Either way, artifacts are important because they reinforce and potentially support changes to an organization's culture.

Artifacts provide valuable evidence about a company's culture.[16] An organization's culture is usually too ambiguous and complex and its cultural assumptions too deeply ingrained to be measured through surveys. Instead, we need to observe workplace behavior, listen to everyday conversations among staff and with customers, study written documents and e-mails, note physical structures and settings, and interview staff about corporate stories. In other words, we need to sample information from a range of organizational artifacts. For example, the Mayo Clinic conducted an assessment of its culture by hiring an anthropologist to decipher the medical organization's culture at its headquarters in Rochester, Minnesota, and to identify ways of transferring that culture to its two newer sites in Florida and Arizona. For six weeks, the anthropologist shadowed employees, posed as a patient in waiting rooms, did countless interviews, and accompanied physicians on patient visits. The final report outlined Mayo's dominant culture and how its satellite operations varied from that culture.[17]

In this section, we review the four broad categories of artifacts: organizational stories and legends, rituals and ceremonies, language, and physical structures and symbols.

Organizational Stories and Legends

Stories permeate strong organizational cultures. Some tales recount heroic deeds, such as Michael Dell's determination in the 1980s to build his computer company, beginning from his dorm room when attending university. Other stories ridicule past events that deviate from the firm's core values. Organizational stories and legends serve as powerful social prescriptions of the way things should (or should not) be done. They add human realism to corporate expectations, individual performance standards, and the criteria for getting fired. Stories also produce emotions in listeners, and this tends to improve listeners' memory of the lesson within the story.[18] Stories have the greatest effect on communicating corporate culture when they describe real people, are assumed to be true, and are known by employees throughout the organization. Stories are also prescriptive–they advise people what to do or not to do.[19]

Rituals and Ceremonies

rituals
The programmed routines of daily organizational life that dramatize the organization's culture.

Rituals are the programmed routines of daily organizational life that dramatize an organization's culture. They include how visitors are greeted, how often senior executives visit subordinates, how people communicate with each other, how much time employees take for lunch, and so on. For instance, BMW's fast-paced culture is quite literally apparent in the way employees walk around the German carmaker's offices. "When you move through the corridors and hallways

Stories of Cirque du Soleil's Daring Culture Cirque du Soleil, the Montreal-based troupe that combines circus with theater, thrives on a culture of daring and creativity. This is apparent in stories about how the troupe was started. In 1980, Gilles Ste-Croix asked the Quebec government for funding to start a street theater group in Baie-Saint-Paul, northwest of Quebec City. When the government rejected the application, Ste-Croix walked 55 miles (90 kilometers) from Baie-Saint-Paul to Quebec City . . . on stilts! The grueling 22-hour trip got the government's attention and financial support. "If you're crazy enough to walk all this way on stilts, we'll give you some money to create jobs," a Quebec government representative apparently said. Without that daring event, Cirque du Soleil probably wouldn't exist today, because Ste-Criox's band of 15 performers included Guy Laliberté, who founded Cirque du Soleil in 1984 with Ste-Croix and others. In 1987, Cirque du Soleil was invited to perform at the Los Angeles Arts Festival, but the festival could not provide funds in advance to cover Cirque du Soleil's costs. Laliberté took a gamble by literally emptying the troupe's bank account to transport the performers and equipment to California. "I bet everything on that one night [at the Los Angeles Arts Festival]," Laliberté recalls. "If we failed, there was no cash for gas to come home." Fortunately, the gamble paid off. Cirque du Soleil was a huge success, which led to more opportunities and successes in the following years.[20]

ceremonies
Planned displays of organizational culture, conducted specifically for the benefit of an audience.

of other companies' buildings, people kind of crawl, they walk slowly," observes a BMW executive. "But BMW people tend to move faster."[21] **Ceremonies** are more formal artifacts than rituals. Ceremonies are planned activities conducted specifically for the benefit of an audience. This would include publicly rewarding (or punishing) employees or celebrating the launch of a new product or newly won contract.

Organizational Language

The language of the workplace speaks volumes about the company's culture. How employees address co-workers, describe customers, express anger, and greet stakeholders are all verbal symbols of cultural values. Employees at The Container Store compliment each other about "being Gumby," meaning that they are being as flexible as the once-popular green toy to help a customer or another employee.[22] When Charles Schwab & Co. acquired U.S. Bank, executives at U.S. Bank winced when they heard Schwab executives use the word "customers"; U.S. Bank staff have "clients," a term that reflects a deeper, longer-term relationship.[23] Language also highlights values held by organizational subcultures. For instance, consultants working at Whirlpool kept hearing employees talk about the appliance company's "PowerPoint culture." This phrase, which names Microsoft's presentation software, is a critique of Whirlpool's hierarchical culture in which communication is one-way (from executives to employees).[24]

Physical Structures and Symbols

Winston Churchill once said, "We shape our buildings; thereafter, they shape us."[25] The former British prime minister was reminding us that buildings both reflect and influence an organization's culture. The size, shape, location, and age of buildings might suggest a company's emphasis on teamwork, environmental friendliness, flexibility, or any other set of values.[26] Wal-Mart's culture of efficiency and frugality is easily apparent from its head office in Bentonville, Arkansas. The world's largest retailer operates out of what looks like an old shopping mall–a low-rise brick structure surrounded by a large parking lot. Oakley, Inc's "interplanetary headquarters" in Foothills Ranch, California, on the other hand, is a vaultlike structure complete with towering metallic walls studded with oversize bolts, representing its secretive and protective culture. "We've always had a fortress mentality," says an executive at the eyewear and clothing company. "What we make is gold, and people will do anything to get it, so we protect it."[27]

Even if the building doesn't make much of a statement, there is a treasure trove of physical artifacts inside. Desks, chairs, office space, and wall hangings (or lack of them) are just a few of the items that might convey cultural meaning.[28] The interior of Wal-Mart's head office symbolizes frugality just as much as does its exterior building structure. Suppliers crowd into a spartan waiting room that could have been copied from offices at the state department of motor vehicles. Visitors pay for their own soft drinks and coffee. Multimillion-dollar contracts are discussed with Wal-Mart buyers in small rooms, each with one fluorescent lightbulb and one framed picture of Wal-Mart founder Sam Walton.[29]

The physical artifacts at the head offices of Mother symbolize a culture quite different from Wal-Mart's. Housed in a converted warehouse in an artsy district of London, the creative agency has a large reception hall with an adjoining casual lounge on one side and a large cafeteria on the other, where staff can get free fruit, cereals, toast, and similar snacks any time they want. A wide staircase leads from reception to the next floor, which has meeting rooms separated only by dividers made of hanging strips of opaque plastic. The top floor of Mother's offices is one room dominated by a massive concrete table around which dozens of staff work. Each of these physical artifacts alone might not say much, but put enough of them together and you can see how they symbolize Mother's edgy creative culture with a strong team orientation.[30]

Learning Objectives

After reading the next section, you should be able to:

4. Identify three functions of organizational culture.
5. Discuss the conditions under which organizational culture strength improves organizational performance.

IS ORGANIZATIONAL CULTURE IMPORTANT?

Does organizational culture improve organizational effectiveness? Leaders at The Container Store, Mayo Clinic, Cirque du Soleil, and other companies think so. "Culture is one of the most precious things a company has, so you must work harder on it than anything else," says Herb Kelleher, founder of Southwest Airlines. Many writers of popular-press management books also assert that the most successful companies have strong cultures. In fact, one popular management book, *Built to Last,* suggests that successful companies are "cultlike" (although not actually cults, the authors are careful to point out).[31] The research evidence, however, is more ambivalent than these proclamations. Specifically, companies with strong cultures tend to be more successful, but only under a particular set of conditions.[32] Before discussing these contingencies, let's examine organizational culture *strength* and its potential benefits.

Corporate culture strength refers to how widely and deeply employees hold the company's dominant values and assumptions. In a strong organizational culture, most employees across all subunits understand and embrace the dominant values. These values and assumptions are also institutionalized through well-established artifacts, thereby making it difficult to change the culture. Furthermore, strong cultures tend to be long-lasting; some can be traced back to the values and assumptions established by the company's founder. In contrast, companies have weak cultures when the dominant values are held

Lee Kum Kee's Secret Sauce to Success Guangdong Nanfang Lee Kum Kee Health Products Co., Ltd., a subsidiary of food products company Lee Kum Kee, has a secret sauce that makes it one of the best places to work in Asia. "Two words explain why we are a Best Employer: corporate culture," says human resource vice president Raymond Lo. "Our unique culture is our competitive edge. It plays a major role in the success of our organization." Lee Kum Kee's core values include pragmatism, integrity, constant entrepreneurship, and sharing the benefits with community. Lo explains that cultural values are so important that leaders must believe in and live them. "The corporate culture must have a soul," he says. "Many companies try to model themselves on successful companies, but unless the chief executive and management truly believe in the culture, it won't work." Lo adds that his company actively works to ensure everyone understands and believes in the company's culture. "We also spend a lot of time in team building in order to nourish our corporate culture."[33]

mainly by a few people at the top of the organization, are barely discernible, and are in flux. A strong corporate culture potentially increases the company's success by serving three important functions (see Exhibit 14.3):

1. *Control system.* Organizational culture is a deeply embedded form of social control that influences employee decisions and behavior.[34] Culture is pervasive and operates nonconsciously. You might think of it as an automatic pilot, directing employees in ways that are consistent with organizational expectations.
2. *Social glue.* Organizational culture is the "social glue" that bonds people together and makes them feel part of the organizational experience.[35] Employees are motivated to internalize the organization's dominant culture because it fulfills their need for social identity. This social glue is increasingly important as a way to attract new staff and retain top performers.
3. *Sense making.* Organizational culture assists the sense-making process.[36] It helps employees to understand what goes on and why things happen in the company. Corporate culture also makes it easier for them to understand what is expected of them and to interact with other employees who know the culture and believe in it. For instance, one recent study reported that organizational culture strength increases role clarity, which reduces stress among sales staff.[37]

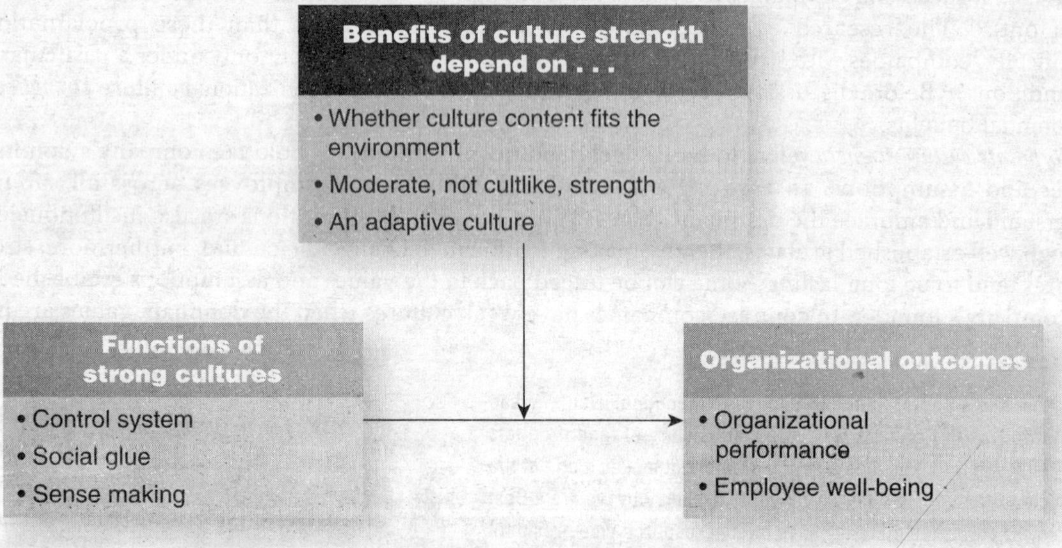

Exhibit 14.3 *Potential Benefits and Contingencies of Culture Strength*

Contingencies of Organizational Culture and Effectiveness

Studies have found only a modestly positive relationship between culture strength and organizational effectiveness because three contingencies need to be considered: (1) whether the culture content is aligned with the environment, (2) whether the culture is not so strong that it becomes cultlike, and (3) whether the culture incorporates an adaptive culture (see Exhibit 14.3).

Culture Content Alignment with Environment One contingency is whether the organization's culture content–its dominant values and assumptions–is aligned with the external environment. Consider the situation that Dell recently faced. As described in the opening vignette to this chapter,

Dell's culture gave the highest priority to cost efficiency and competitiveness, yet these values and assumptions are no longer ideal for the marketplace. Low-cost computers are still popular, but consumers increasingly demand computers that are innovative and look "cool." Dell had a strong culture, but it was no longer the best culture for the external environment.

Avoiding a Corporate Cult A second contingency is the degree of culture strength. Various experts suggest that companies with very strong cultures (i.e., corporate "cults") may be less effective than companies with moderately strong cultures.[38] One reason why corporate cults may undermine organizational effectiveness is that they lock decision makers into mental models, which can blind them to new opportunities and unique problems. They overlook or incorrectly define subtle misalignments between the organization's activities and the changing environment. Dell faced this problem. Kevin Rollins and Michael Dell sensed that the company's culture tolerated competitive staff members even if they didn't collaborate, and it emphasized financial performance far too much (staff even had stock tickers on their computer screens). Yet these leaders never thought about changing this culture. Instead, the program they created a few years ago (called the "Soul of Dell") merely supplemented the company's core values and assumptions. "It's not that we didn't have a culture with the qualities that drive business success," explained a Dell executive at the time. "We just aspired to do better."[39]

The other reason why very strong cultures may be dysfunctional is that they suppress dissenting subcultural values. At Dell, for instance, anyone who questioned the company's almost sacred values and assumptions was quickly silenced, even though the dissenting values could have helped Dell shift more quickly to a better-aligned culture. The challenge for organizational leaders is to maintain not only a strong culture but one that allows subcultural diversity. Subcultures encourage constructive conflict, which improves creative thinking and offers some level of ethical vigilance over the dominant culture. In the long run, a subculture's nascent values could become important dominant values as the environment changes. Corporate cults suppress subcultures, thereby undermining these benefits.

adaptive culture
An organizational culture in which employees are receptive to change, including the ongoing alignment of the organization to its environment and continuous improvement of internal processes.

Culture Is an Adaptive Culture A third contingency between cultural strength and organizational effectiveness is whether the culture content includes an **adaptive culture.**[40] An adaptive culture exists when employees are receptive to change–they assume that the organization needs to continuously adapt to its external environment and that they need to be flexible in their roles within the organization. Employees in an adaptive culture embrace an open-systems perspective, in which the organization's survival and success require ongoing adaptation to the external environment, which itself is continuously changing. They assume that their future depends on monitoring the external environment and serving stakeholders with the resources available. Thus, employees in adaptive cultures have a strong sense of ownership. They take responsibility for the organization's performance and alignment with the external environment.

In an adaptive culture, receptivity to change extends to internal processes and roles. Employees recognize that satisfying stakeholder needs requires continuous improvement of internal work processes. Toyota's culture, described earlier in this chapter, illustrates this aspect of an adaptive culture because it values the continuous improvement of the production process as well as of its products and services. Furthermore, employee support for changing internal work processes involves flexibility in their own work roles. The phrase "That's not my job" is found in nonadaptive cultures. Finally, an adaptive culture has a strong learning orientation because receptivity to change and improvement logically involves support for action-oriented discovery. With a learning orientation, employees welcome new learning opportunities, actively experiment with new ideas and practices, view reasonable mistakes as a natural part of the learning process, and continuously question past practices.[41]

Organizational Culture and Business Ethics

An organization's culture influences more than just the bottom line; it can also affect the ethical conduct of the organization's employees. This makes sense because good behavior is driven by ethical values, and ethical values can become embedded in an organization's dominant culture. A few years ago, Michael Dell and former CEO Kevin Rollins saw this connection between culture and ethics when they launched the "Soul of Dell." Concerned about employee obsession with the company's stock price, the executives tried to shift the company's winning culture into one that emphasizes "winning with integrity."[42] For example, one of the computer maker's revised values was defined as "behaving ethically in every interaction and in every aspect of how we conduct business." Unfortunately, the Soul of Dell initiative probably didn't change the company's culture. Two years after the Soul of Dell cultural change program was launched, the company reported that some executives had manipulated the company books to reach performance targets that would give them a larger bonus.[43]

Learning Objectives

After reading the next two sections, you should be able to:

6. Compare and contrast four strategies for merging organizational cultures.
7. Identify the four strategies for changing or strengthening an organization's culture.
8. Apply attraction-selection-attrition theory to explain how organizational culture strengthens.
9. Describe the stages of organizational socialization.
10. Explain how realistic job previews assist the socialization process.

MERGING ORGANIZATIONAL CULTURES

4C Corporate Culture Clash and Chemistry is a company with an unusual name and mandate. The Dutch consulting firm helps clients to determine whether their culture is aligned ("chemistry") or incompatible with ("clash") a potential acquisition or merger partner. The firm also analyzes the company's culture with its strategy. There should be plenty of demand for 4C's expertise. According to various studies, most corporate mergers and acquisitions fail in terms of subsequent performance of the merged organization. Evidence suggests that such failures occur partly because corporate leaders are so focused on the financial or marketing logistics of a merger that they fail to conduct due-diligence audits on their respective corporate cultures.[44] Some forms of integration (which we discuss later in this section) may allow successful mergers between companies with different cultures. However, research concludes that mergers typically suffer when organizations with significantly divergent corporate cultures merge into a single entity with a high degree of integration.[45]

The marriage of AOL with Time Warner is one of the more spectacular culture clashes. In theory, the world's largest merger offered huge opportunities for converging AOL's dominance in Internet services with Time Warner's deep knowledge of and assets in traditional media. Instead, the two corporate cultures mixed like oil and water. AOL's culture valued youthful, high-flying, quick deal making. People were rewarded with stock options. Time Warner, on the other hand, had a button-down, hierarchical, systematic culture. Executives were older and the reward was a decent retirement package (affectionately known as the "golden rubber band" because people who left invariably returned for the retirement benefit).[46]

Bicultural Audit

bicultural audit
A process of diagnosing cultural relations between companies and determining the extent to which cultural clashes will likely occur.

Organizational leaders can minimize these cultural collisions and fulfill their duty of due diligence by conducting a bicultural audit.[47] A **bicultural audit** diagnoses cultural relations between the companies and determines the extent to which cultural clashes will likely occur. The bicultural audit process begins by identifying cultural differences between the merging companies. Next, the bicultural audit data are analyzed to determine which differences between the two firms will result in conflict and which cultural values provide common ground on which to build a cultural foundation in the merged organization. The final stage involves identifying strategies and preparing action plans to bridge the two organizations' cultures.

A few years ago, pulp-and-paper conglomerate Abitibi-Price applied a bicultural audit before it agreed to merge with rival Stone Consolidated. Specifically, Abitibi developed the Merging Cultures Evaluation Index (MCEI), an evaluation system that helped Abitibi executives compare its culture with other companies in the industry. The MCEI analyzed several dimensions of corporate culture, such as concentration of power versus diffusion of power, innovation versus tradition, wide versus narrow flow of information, and consensus versus authoritative decision making. Abitibi and Stone executives completed the questionnaire to assess their own culture, and then they compared the results. The MCEI results, along with financial and infrastructural information, served as the basis for Abitibi-Price to merge with Stone Consolidated to become Abitibi-Consolidated (now Abitibi Bowater), the world's largest pulp-and-paper firm.[48]

Strategies for Merging Different Organizational Cultures

In some cases, the bicultural audit results in a decision to end merger talks because the two cultures are too different to merge effectively. However, even with substantially different cultures, two companies may form a workable union if they apply the appropriate merger strategy. The four main strategies for merging different corporate cultures are assimilation, deculturation, integration, and separation (see Exhibit 14.4).[49]

Assimilation Assimilation occurs when employees at the acquired company willingly embrace the cultural values of the acquiring organization. Typically, this strategy works best when the acquired company has a weak, dysfunctional culture and the acquiring company's culture is strong and aligned with the external environment. Culture clash is rare with assimilation because the acquired firm's culture is weak and employees are looking for better cultural alternatives. Research in Motion (RIM), the BlackBerry wireless device maker, applies the assimilation strategy by deliberately acquiring only small start-up firms. "Small companies . . . don't have cultural issues," says RIM co-CEO Jim Balsillie, adding that they are typically absorbed into RIM's culture with little fuss or attention.[50]

Deculturation Assimilation is rare. Employees usually resist organizational change, particularly when they are asked to throw away personal and cultural values. Under these conditions, some acquiring companies apply a *deculturation* strategy by imposing their culture and business practices on the acquired organization. The acquiring firm strips away artifacts and reward systems that support the old culture. People who cannot adopt the acquiring company's culture are often terminated.

Merger strategy	Description	Works best when:
Assimilation	Acquired company embraces acquiring firm's culture.	Acquired firm has a weak culture.
Deculturation	Acquiring firm imposes its culture on an unwilling acquired firm.	Rarely works—may be necessary only when acquired firm's culture doesn't work but employees don't realize it.
Integration	Merging companies combine the two or more cultures into a new composite culture.	Existing cultures can be improved.
Separation	Merging companies remain distinct entities with minimal exchange of culture or organizational practices.	Firms operate successfully in different businesses requiring different cultures.

Sources: Based on ideas in A. R. Malekazedeh and A. Nahavandi, "Making Mergers Work by Managing Cultures," *Journal of Business Strategy*, May–June 1990, pp. 55–57; K. W. Smith, "A Brand-New Culture for the Merged Firm," *Mergers and Acquisitions*, 35 (June 2000), pp. 45–50.

Exhibit 14.4 *Strategies for Merging Different Organizational Cultures*

Deculturation may be necessary when the acquired firm's culture doesn't work but employees aren't convinced of this. However, this strategy is difficult to apply effectively because the acquired firm's employees resist the cultural intrusions from the buying firm, thereby delaying or undermining the merger process.

Integration A third strategy is to combine the two or more cultures into a new composite culture that preserves the best features of the previous cultures. Integration is slow and potentially risky because there are many forces preserving the existing cultures. Still, this strategy should be considered when the companies have relatively weak cultures or when their cultures include several overlapping

A Marriage of Cultural Separation A decade ago, McDonald's Restaurants took a controlling interest in Chipotle Mexican Grill, a young start-up restaurant chain with a considerably different approach to doing business. While McDonald's epitomizes fast food, Chipotle is a model of freshly prepared Mexican-style meals. Recognizing that McDonald's culture and practices wouldn't work at Chipotle, founder and CEO Steve Ells convinced the global food giant to keep a distance from the younger restaurant chain's culture. "Chipotle structured the agreement so that McDonald's would essentially become the 'banker' without changing recipes, ingredients, or culture— all the elements to which Chipotle fans and team members are loyal," says Ells. For the most part, McDonald's executives kept to their word, but Ells did have to explain to them on several occasions why the restaurant only serves food that it makes better than anyone else. "They probably did give me grief," Ells admitted. Eventually, McDonald's sold its stake in Chipotle for a tidy profit. "We learned from each other," Ells says of the partnership, "but we use different kinds of food, and we aim for a different kind of experience and culture altogether. So we ended up going our separate ways."[51]

values. Integration also works best when people realize that their existing cultures are ineffective and, therefore, people are motivated to adopt a new set of dominant values.

Separation A separation strategy occurs when the merging companies agree to remain distinct entities with minimal exchange of culture or organizational practices. This strategy is most appropriate when the two merging companies are in unrelated industries or operate in different countries, because the most appropriate cultural values tend to differ by industry and national culture. For example, Cisco Systems followed a separation strategy when it acquired Linksys. The home wireless network company was performing well and was in a different business environment–low-cost mass-market retail–so Cisco made sure that Linksys kept its own culture. Cisco executives were so concerned about this separation that the company formed a team to ensure that Cisco's leaders did not impose their culture and control on the smaller enterprise.[52] Cisco's action are rare, however. Executives in acquiring firms usually have difficulty keeping their hands off the acquired firm. It's not surprising, therefore, that only 15 percent of mergers leave the acquired company as a stand-alone unit.[53]

CHANGING AND STRENGTHENING ORGANIZATIONAL CULTURE

Is it possible to change an organization's culture? Yes, but doing so isn't easy, the change rarely occurs quickly, and often the culture ends up changing (or replacing) corporate leaders. In fact, some writers argue that leaders shouldn't even bother to attempt such a transformation because organizational culture "cannot be managed."[54] This view is more extreme than most, but organizational culture experts generally agree that changing an organization's culture is a considerable challenge. At the same time, under the right conditions, organizational culture can be a powerful influence on the company's success. Over the next few pages, we will highlight four strategies that have had some success at altering corporate cultures. This list, outlined in Exhibit 14.5, is not exhaustive, but each activity seems to work well under the right circumstances.

Actions of Founders and Leaders

An organization's culture begins with its founders.[55] You can see this at Dell, Inc., where founder Michael Dell established a competitive and cost-focused culture. Founders are often visionaries who provide a powerful role model for others to follow. The company's culture sometimes reflects the founder's personality, and this cultural imprint can remain with the organization for decades. For example, some observers say that Dell's culture is so much a part of Michael Dell's personal orientation to life that he might not be the best person to try to change it.

Founders establish an organization's culture, but they and subsequent leaders are sometimes able to reshape that culture by applying transformational leadership and organizational change practices.[56] The recent changes at Procter & Gamble Co. (P&G) illustrate this point. P&G had a very strong hierarchical culture for several decades, yet by applying many of the transformational leadership practices described in Chapter 12, chief executive A. G. Lafley was able to alter that culture into one that is much more customer-focused.

Aligning Artifacts

Artifacts represent more than just the visible indicators of a company's culture. They are also mechanisms that reshape and reinforce the culture. By altering artifacts–or creating new ones–leaders can potentially adjust shared values and assumptions. National Australia Bank (NAB) is a case in point. John Stewart was hired as CEO a few years ago, after rogue trading caused large financial and

Exhibit 14.5 *Strategies for Changing and Strengthening Organizational Culture*

Lululemon Athletica Changes the Leader, Keeps the Culture With its new-age, self-affirmation culture and a focus on healthy lifestyles, Lululemon Athletica Inc. has been a phenomenal success story in the retail industry. The designer of high-end yoga wear opened its first store a decade ago and now boasts more than 80 stores in the United States, Canada, and Australia. Founder Dennis J. ("Chip") Wilson recognized that Lululemon needed a leader with more corporate experience, but he didn't want the new leader to undermine the company's existing culture. He may have found an ideal choice in former Starbucks vice president Christine Day. "[Lululemon is] another premium brand with an exceptional product and a tremendous culture," says Day, who is now Lululemon's chief executive officer. "I feel quite at home." She adds that the decision to join Lululemon required careful thought about the culture fit with her personal values. "For me that's about really being able to live my values both personally and at work," she says.[57]

reputational losses. Investigations of the trading debacle revealed that NAB's culture was too hierarchical, bureaucratic, and profit-focused. Stewart shifted NAB's culture toward one that is more open, accountable, and egalitarian by improving leadership, recruitment, rewards, communication practices, and empowered accountability through decentralization. For example, he cut head-office staff by more than half, devoted considerable time to coaching upcoming executives, and publicly rewarded employees for revealing and learning from their mistakes. "Most of our problems continue to be internal, so my main concern is that we get our cultural change right," explained Stewart, who recently retired. Coincidentally, NAB had just moved into a low-rise campuslike building in Melbourne's docklands area, which also had the effect of supporting an open and egalitarian culture.[58]

Corporate cultures are also altered and strengthened through the artifacts of stories and behaviors. According to Max De Pree, former CEO of furniture manufacturer Herman Miller, Inc., every organization needs "tribal storytellers" to keep the organization's history and culture alive.[59] Leaders play a role by creating memorable events that symbolize the cultural values they want to develop or maintain. At Wall Street investment firm Goldman Sachs, this leadership function is so important that executives are called "culture carriers." Goldman's senior executives live and breathe the company's culture so much that they can effectively transmit and reinforce that culture.[60] Companies also strengthen culture in new operations by transferring current employees who abide by the culture.

Introducing Culturally Consistent Rewards

Reward systems are artifacts that often have a powerful effect on strengthening or reshaping an organization's culture.[61] John Stewart relied on rewards to transform the culture at National Australia Bank. Robert Nardelli also used the rewards lever to change Home Depot's freewheeling culture. Nardelli introduced precise measures of corporate performance and drilled managers with weekly performance objectives related to those metrics. A two-hour weekly conference call became a ritual in which Home Depot's top executives were held accountable for the previous week's goals. These actions reinforced a more disciplined (and centralized) performance-oriented culture.[62]

Attracting, Selecting, and Socializing Employees

attraction-selection-attrition (ASA) theory
A theory which states that organizations have a natural tendency to attract, select, and retain people with values and personality characteristics that are consistent with the organization's character, resulting in a more homogeneous organization and a stronger culture.

Organizational culture is strengthened by attracting and hiring people who already embrace the cultural values. This process, along with weeding out people who don't fit the culture, is explained by **attraction-selection-attrition (ASA) theory.**[63] ASA theory states that organizations have a natural tendency to attract, select, and retain people with values and personality characteristics that are consistent with the organization's character, resulting in a more homogeneous organization and a stronger culture.

- *Attraction.* Job applicants engage in self-selection by avoiding employment in companies whose values seem incompatible with their own values.[64] Companies often encourage this self-selection by actively describing their cultures, but applicants will look for evidence of the company's culture even when it is not advertised. Applicants also inspect organizational artifacts when visiting the company.
- *Selection.* How well the person "fits" in with the company's culture is often a factor in deciding which job applicants to hire. Companies with strong cultures often put applicants through several interviews and other selection tests, in part to better gauge the applicants' values and their congruence with the company's values.[65] Consider Park Place Dealerships. As one of the top-rated luxury-car dealerships in the United States, the Dallas–Fort Worth company relies on interviews and selection tests to carefully screen applicants for their culture fit. "Testing is one piece of our hiring process that enables us to find people who will not only be successful in our culture, but

thrive and enjoy our culture," says Park Place chairman Ken Schnitzer. When Park Place recently acquired a Lexus dealership in California, several people who did not fit the culture left. "We've had some turnover," Schnitzer acknowledges in reference to the Lexus dealership. "We're looking for people to fit into our culture. It's not easy to get hired by Park Place."[66]

- *Attrition*. People are motivated to seek environments that are sufficiently congruent with their personal values and to leave environments that are a poor fit. This occurs because person-organization value congruence supports their social identity and minimizes internal role conflict. Even if employees aren't forced out, many quit when value incongruence is sufficiently high. This likely occurred when Park Place Dealerships acquired the Lexus dealership in California–some staff members left voluntarily or otherwise because they did not fit Park Place's unique culture.[67]

organizational socialization
The process by which individuals learn the values, expected behaviors, and social knowledge necessary to assume their roles in the organization.

Along with their use of attraction, selection, and attrition, organizations rely on organizational socialization to strengthen their cultures. **Organizational socialization** is the process by which individuals learn the values, expected behaviors, and social knowledge necessary to assume their roles in the organization.[68] When a company clearly communicates its culture, job candidates and new hires are more likely to internalize its values quickly and deeply. Socialization is an important process to help newcomers absorb the corporate culture as well as adjust to co-workers, work procedures, and other corporate realities. Thus, the final section of this chapter looks more closely at the organizational socialization process.

Organizational Socialization

Trung Nguyen's first few days of work at Oklahoma-based Integris-Health were filled with orientation sessions. "I was expecting something extremely boring where it was hard to stay awake, like watching hours of videos or PowerPoint slides," admits Nguyen. Instead, the seminars taught him a lot about the company, what it stands for, and the community it serves. "I've lived in Oklahoma for more than 20 years," says Nguyen, who is originally from Vietnam. "And this week, I've learned more about the community that's surrounding me and the health services that care for my loved ones."[69]

Integris-Health successfully brings employees into the organization through orientation sessions and other organizational socialization practices to help newcomers learn about the company and adjust to their role in the company. An important part of this process is helping newcomers become familiar with, and believe in, the organization's culture. "The cultural aspects of our training programs are at least as important as the technical aspects," says an executive at JetBlue, the New York–based discount airline. "The People Department will find the right people and we will inculcate the culture into them and nurture that culture until we release them out into the operation."[70] Research indicates that when employees are effectively socialized into the organization, they tend to perform better, have higher job satisfaction, and remain longer with the organization.[71]

Socialization as a Learning and Adjustment Process

Organizational socialization is a process of both learning and adjustment. It is a learning process because newcomers try to make sense of the company's physical workplace, social dynamics, and strategic and cultural environment. They learn about the organization's performance expectations, power dynamics, corporate culture, company history, and jargon. They also need to form successful and satisfying relationships with other people from whom they can learn the ropes.[72] Thus, effective socialization enables new recruits to form a cognitive map of the physical, social, and strategic and cultural dynamics of the organization without information overload.

Organizational socialization is also a process of adjustment, because individuals need to adapt to their new work environment. They develop new work roles that reconfigure their social identity, adopt new team norms, and practice new behaviors.[73] Research reports that the adjustment process is fairly rapid for many people, usually occurring within a few months. However, newcomers with diverse work experience seem to adjust better than those with limited previous experience, possibly because they have a larger toolkit of knowledge and skills to make the adjustment possible.[74]

Stages of Organizational Socialization

Socialization is a continuous process, beginning long before the first day of employment and continuing throughout one's career within the company. However, it is most intense when people move across organizational boundaries, such as when they first join a company or get transferred to an international assignment. Each of these transitions is a process that can be divided into three stages. Our focus here is on the socialization of new employees, so the three stages are called preemployment socialization, encounter, and role management (see Exhibit 14.6). These stages parallel the individual's transition from outsider to newcomer and then to insider.[75]

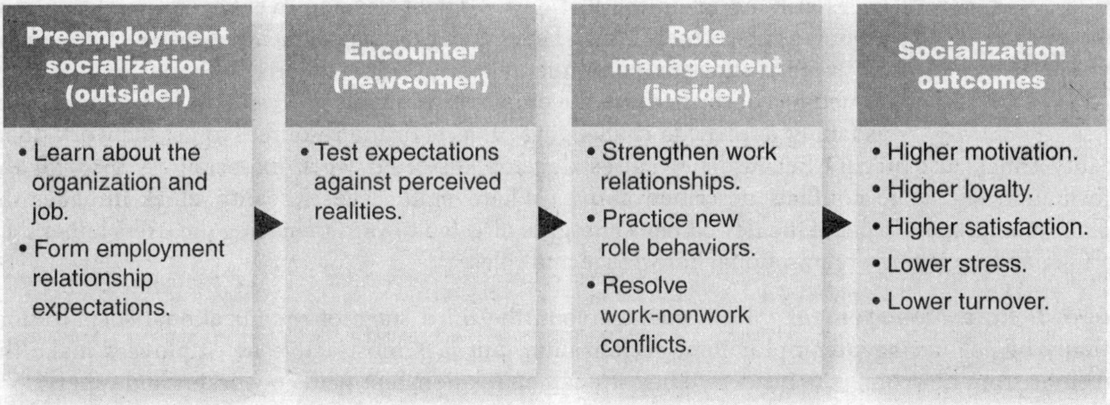

Exhibit 14.6 *Stages of Organizational Socialization*

Stage 1: Preemployment Socialization Think back to the months and weeks before you began working in a new job (or attending a new school). You actively searched for information about the company, formed expectations about working there, and felt some anticipation about fitting into that environment. The preemployment socialization stage encompasses all the learning and adjustment that occurs before the first day of work. In fact, a large part of the socialization adjustment process occurs during this stage.[76]

The main problem with preemployment socialization is that outsiders rely on indirect information about what it is like to work in the organization. This information is often distorted by inherent conflicts during the mating dance between employer and applicant.[77] One conflict occurs between the employer's need to attract qualified applicants and the applicant's need for accurate information to make better employment decisions. Many firms use a "flypaper" approach by describing only positive aspects of the job and company, causing applicants to accept job offers on the basis of incomplete or false expectations.

Another conflict that prevents accurate exchange of information occurs when applicants avoid asking important questions about the company because they don't want to convey an unfavorable image to their prospective employer. For instance, applicants usually don't like to ask about starting salaries and promotion opportunities because it makes them sound greedy or overaggressive. Yet, unless the employer provides this information, applicants might fill in the missing information with false assumptions that produce an inaccurate psychological contract.

Two other types of conflict tend to distort preemployment information for employers. Applicants engage in impression management when seeking employment, and this tends to motivate them to hide negative information, act out of character, and occasionally embellish information about their past accomplishments. At the same time, employers are sometimes reluctant to ask certain questions or use potentially valuable selection devices because they might scare off applicants. Unfortunately, employers are more likely to hire the wrong people when applicants embellish their résumés and when employers are unwilling to ask applicants important questions.

Stage 2: Encounter The first day on the job typically marks the beginning of the encounter stage of organizational socialization. This is the stage in which newcomers test their prior expectations with the perceived realities. Many companies fail the test, resulting in **reality shock**–the stress that results when employees perceive discrepancies between their preemployment expectations and on-the-job reality.[78] Reality shock doesn't necessarily occur on the first day; it might develop over several weeks or even months as newcomers form a better understanding of their new work environment.

reality shock
The stress that results when employees perceive discrepancies between their preemployment expectations and on-the-job reality.

Reality shock is common in many organizations.[79] Unmet expectations sometimes occur because the employer is unable to live up to its promises, such as failing to provide challenging projects or the resources to get the work done. Reality shock also occurs because new hires develop distorted work expectations through the information exchange conflicts described above. Whatever the cause, reality shock impedes the socialization process because the newcomer's energy is directed toward managing the stress rather than learning and accepting organizational knowledge and roles.[80]

Stage 3: Role Management Role management, the third stage of organizational socialization, actually begins during preemployment socialization, but it is most active as employees make the transition from newcomers to insiders. They strengthen relationships with co-workers and supervisors, practice new role behaviors, and adopt attitudes and values consistent with their new positions and the organization. Role management also involves resolving the conflicts between work and nonwork activities, including resolving discrepancies between their existing values and those emphasized by the organizational culture.

Improving the Socialization Process

realistic job preview (RJP)
A method of improving organizational socialization in which job applicants are given a balance of positive and negative information about the job and work context.

One potentially effective way to improve the socialization process is through a **realistic job preview** (**RJP**)–a balance of positive and negative information about the job and work context.[81] Unfortunately, as mentioned earlier, many companies overpromise. They often exaggerate positive features of the job and neglect to mention the undesirable elements in the hope that the best applicants will get "stuck" on the organization. In contrast, an RJP helps job applicants to decide for themselves whether their skills, needs, and values are compatible with the job and organization.

Lindblad's RJP Keeps Newcomer Expectations Shipshape Lindblad Expeditions can't afford to have crew members jump ship soon after starting the job. To minimize reality shock, the 500-employee adventure cruise company gives applicants a DVD showing a realistic picture of what it's like to work on board. The program shows not one but two scenes in which staff members are cleaning toilets. One scene reveals the cramped quarters for crew members. In another scene, a dishwasher talks about washing 5,000 dishes in one day. The video is meant to scare off applicants who cannot adjust easily to the challenges of working on a ship. The realistic job preview video does have this effect, says Lindblad human resource manager Kris Thompson, but the attrition is well worth it if it reduces turnover soon after staff are hired. "If [new hires] get on board and say, 'This is not what I expected,' then shame on us," says Thompson.[82]

RJPs scare away some applicants, but they also tend to reduce turnover and increase job performance.[83] This occurs because RJPs help applicants develop more accurate preemployment expectations, which, in turn, minimize reality shock. RJPs represent a type of vaccination by preparing employees for the more challenging and troublesome aspects of work life. There is also some evidence that RJPs increase organizational loyalty. A possible explanation for this is that companies providing candid information are easier to trust. They also show respect for the psychological contract and concern for employee welfare.[84]

Socialization Agents Ask new employees what most helped them to adjust to their jobs and chances are they will mention helpful co-workers, bosses, or maybe even friends who work for the company. The fact is, much organizational socialization occurs informally through these socialization agents.[85] Supervisors tend to provide technical information, performance feedback, and information about job duties. They also improve the socialization process by giving newcomers reasonably challenging first assignments, buffering them from excessive demands, and helping them form social ties with co-workers.

Co-workers are important socialization agents because they are easily accessible, can answer questions when problems arise, and serve as role models for appropriate behavior. New employees tend to receive this information and support when co-workers integrate them into the work team. Co-workers also aid the socialization process by being flexible and tolerant in their interactions with new hires. The challenge for some companies is helping newcomers to learn from co-workers about the company's culture when opening new stores where most employees are new to the company. At Whole Foods Market, the solution is yoghurt. "One of our secrets is what I refer to as our 'yoghurt culture,'" explains Whole Foods Market cofounder John Mackey. This strategy involves transferring employees who carry Whole Foods Market's unique culture to new stores so that recently hired employees learn and embrace that culture more quickly. "For example, in our Columbus Circle store in New York, about 25% of the team members transferred from existing stores," Mackey recalls. "They were the starting culture for the fermentation that turned Columbus Circle into a true Whole Foods store."[86]

Several organizations rely on a "buddy system," whereby newcomers are assigned to co-workers who act as sources of information and social support. Meridian Technology Center in Stillwater, Oklahoma, relies on a buddy system in the socialization of new staff members. Buddies introduce new hires to other employees, give them campus tours, and generally familiarize them with the physical layout of the workplace. They have lunch with employees on their first day and meet weekly with them for their first two months. Cxtec, the networking and voice technology company in Syracuse, New York, helps new staff meet other employees through food. On the first Friday of each month, new staff members take charge of the doughnut cart, introducing themselves as they distribute the morning snack to the company's 350 employees.[87] Collectively, these practices help newcomers to form social networks, which, as you learned in Chapter 10, are powerful means of gaining information and influence in the organization.

Chapter Summary

Organizational culture consists of the values and assumptions shared within an organization. Shared assumptions are nonconscious, taken-for-granted perceptions or beliefs that have worked so well in the past that they are considered the correct way to think and act toward problems and opportunities. Values are stable, evaluative beliefs that guide our preferences for outcomes or courses of action in a variety of situations.

Organizations differ in their cultural content, that is, the relative ordering of values. There are several classifications of organizational culture, but they tend to oversimplify the wide variety of cultures and completely ignore the underlying assumptions of culture. Organizations have subcultures as well as the dominant culture. Subcultures maintain the organization's standards of performance and ethical behavior. They are also the source of emerging values that replace aging core values.

Artifacts are the observable symbols and signs of an organization's culture. Four broad categories of artifacts include organizational stories and legends, rituals and ceremonies, language, and physical structures and symbols. Understanding an organization's culture requires assessment of many artifacts because they are subtle and often ambiguous.

Organizational culture has three main functions: a form of social control, the "social glue" that bonds people together, and a way to help employees make sense of the workplace. Companies with strong cultures generally perform better than those with weak cultures, but only when the cultural content is appropriate for the organization's environment. Also, the culture should not be so strong that it drives out dissenting values, which may form emerging values for the future. Organizations should have adaptive cultures so that employees support ongoing change in the organization and their own roles.

Organizational culture clashes are common in mergers and acquisitions. This problem can be minimized by performing a bicultural audit to diagnose the compatibility of the organizational cultures. The four main strategies for merging different corporate cultures are integration, deculturation, assimilation, and separation.

Organizational culture is very difficult to change, but culture change is possible and sometimes necessary for a company's continued survival. Four strategies for changing and strengthening an organization's culture are the actions of founders and leaders, aligning artifacts with the desired culture, introducing culturally consistent rewards, and attracting, selecting, and socializing employees.

Attraction-selection-attrition (ASA) theory states that organizations have a natural tendency to attract, select, and retain people with values and personality characteristics that are consistent with the organization's character, resulting in a more homogeneous organization and a stronger culture. Organizational socialization is the process by which individuals learn the values, expected behaviors, and social knowledge necessary to assume their roles in the organization. It is a process of both learning about the work context and adjusting to new work roles, team norms, and behaviors.

Employees typically pass through three socialization stages: preemployment, encounter, and role management. To manage the socialization process, organizations should introduce realistic job previews (RJPs) and recognize the value of socialization agents in the process. RJPs give job applicants a realistic balance of positive and negative information about the job and work context. Socialization agents provide information and social support during the socialization process.

Key Terms

adaptive culture
artifacts
attraction-selection-attrition (ASA) theory
bicultural audit
ceremonies
organizational culture
organizational socialization
realistic job preview (RJP)
reality shock
rituals

Critical Thinking Questions

1. Superb Consultants has submitted a proposal to analyze the cultural values of your organization. The proposal states that Superb has developed a revolutionary new survey to tap the company's true culture. The survey takes just 10 minutes to complete, and the consultants say results can be based on a small sample of employees. Discuss the merits and limitations of this proposal.
2. Some people suggest that the most effective organizations have the strongest cultures. What do we mean by the "strength" of organizational culture, and what possible problems are there with a strong organizational culture?
3. The CEO of a manufacturing firm wants everyone to support the organization's dominant culture of lean efficiency and hard work. The CEO has introduced a new reward system to reinforce this culture and personally interviews all professional and managerial applicants to ensure that they bring similar values to the organization. Some employees who criticized these values had their careers sidelined until they left. Two midlevel managers were fired for supporting contrary values, such as work–life balance. Based on your knowledge of organizational subcultures, what potential problems is the CEO creating?
4. Identify at least two artifacts you have observed in your department or school from each of the four broad categories: (a) organizational stories and legends, (b) rituals and ceremonies, (c) language, (d) physical structures and symbols.
5. "Organizations are more likely to succeed when they have an adaptive culture." What can an organization do to foster an adaptive culture?
6. Suppose you are asked by senior officers of a city government to identify ways to reinforce a new culture of teamwork and collaboration. The senior executive group clearly supports these values, but it wants everyone in the organization to embrace them. Identify four types of activities that would strengthen these cultural values.
7. Socialization is most intense when people pass through organizational boundaries. One example is your entry into the college or university that you are now attending. What learning and adjustment occurred as you moved from outsider to newcomer to insider as a student here.
8. Acme Corp. is planning to acquire Beta Corp., which operates in a different industry. Acme's culture is entrepreneurial and fast-paced, whereas Beta employees value slow, deliberate decision making by consensus. Which merger strategy would you recommend to minimize culture shock when Acme acquires Beta? Explain your answer.

CASE STUDY 14.1

HILLTON'S TRANSFORMATION

Thirty years ago, Hillton was a small city (about 70,000 residents) that served as an outer suburb to a large metropolitan city. The municipality of Hillton treated its employees like family and gave them a great deal of autonomy in their work. Everyone in the organization (including the two labor unions representing employees) implicitly agreed that the leaders and supervisors of the organization should rise through the ranks on the basis of their experience. Few people were ever hired from the outside into middle or senior positions. The rule of employment at Hillton was to learn the job skills, maintain a reasonably good work record, and wait your turn for promotion.

Hillton grew rapidly over the past three decades. As the population grew, so did the municipality's workforce to keep pace with the increasing demand for municipal services. This meant that employees were promoted fairly quickly and were almost assured guaranteed employment. In fact, until recently, Hillton had never laid off any employee. The organization's culture could be described as one of entitlement and comfort. Neither the elected city councilors nor the city manager bothered the departmental managers about their work. There were few cost controls because the rapid growth placed more emphasis on keeping up with the population expansion. The public became somewhat more critical of the city's poor service, including road construction at inconvenient times and the apparent lack of respect some employees showed toward taxpayers.

During these expansion years, Hillton put most of its money into "outside" (also called "hard") municipal services. These included road building, utility construction and maintenance, fire and police protection, recreational facilities, and land use control. This emphasis occurred because an expanding population demanded more of these services and most of Hillton's senior people came from the outside services group. For example, Hillton's city manager for many years was a road development engineer. The "inside" workers (taxation, community services, etc.) tended to have less seniority, and their departments were given less priority.

As commuter and road systems developed, Hillton attracted more upwardly mobile professionals into the community. Some infrastructure demands continued, but now these suburban dwellers wanted more of the soft services, such as libraries, social activities, and community services. They also began complaining about the way the municipality was being run. The population had more than tripled over the past three decades, and it was increasingly apparent that the organization needed more corporate planning, information systems, organization development, and cost control systems. In various ways, residents voiced their concerns that the municipality was not providing the quality of management that they would expect from a city of Hillton's size.

Three years ago, a new mayor and council replaced most of the previous incumbents, mainly on the platform of improving the municipality's management structure. The new council gave the city manager, along with two other senior managers, an early retirement buyout package. Rather than promoting from the lower ranks, the council decided to fill all three positions with qualified candidates from large municipal corporations in the region. The following year, several long-term managers left Hillton and at least half of those positions were filled by people from outside the organization.

In less than two years, Hillton had eight senior or departmental managers hired from other municipalities who played a key role in changing the organization's value system. These eight managers became known (often with negative connotations) as the "professionals." They worked closely with each other to change the way middle and lower-level managers had operated for many years. They brought in a new computer system and emphasized cost controls in areas where managers previously had complete autonomy. Promotions were increasingly based more on merit than seniority.

These managers frequently announced in meetings and newsletters that municipal employees must provide superlative customer service and that Hillton would become one of the most customer-friendly places for citizens and those who do business with the municipality. To this end, the managers were quick to support the public's increasing demand for more soft services, including expanded library services and recreational activities. And when population growth recently flattened out, the city manager and other professionals gained council support to lay off a few of the outside workers due to lack of demand for hard services.

One of the most significant changes was that the outside departments no longer held dominant positions in city management. Most of the professional managers had worked exclusively in administrative and related inside jobs. Two had master of business administration degrees. This led to some tension between the professional managers and the older outside managers.

Even before the layoffs, managers of outside departments resisted the changes more than others did. These managers complained that their employees with the highest seniority were turned down for promotions. They argued for more budget and warned that infrastructure problems would cause liability problems. Informally, these outside managers were supported by the labor union representing outside workers. The union leaders tried to bargain for more job guarantees, whereas the union representing inside workers focused more on improving wages and benefits. Leaders of the outside union made several statements in the local media that the city had "lost its heart" and that the public would suffer from the actions of the new professionals.

Discussion Questions

1. Contrast Hillton's earlier corporate culture with the emerging set of cultural values.
2. Considering the difficulty in changing organizational culture, why does Hillton's management seem to have been successful at this transformation?
3. Identify two other strategies that the city might consider to reinforce the new set of corporate values.

CASE STUDY 14.2

MERCK'S NEW CULTURAL CURE

BusinessWeek

Richard Clark was thrust into the CEO job at Merck & Co. during its darkest hour. The pharmaceutical giant was drowning in liability suits stemming from its arthritis drug Vioxx, which was pulled from the market because of a link to heart attacks and strokes. Meanwhile, two of the company's other blockbuster drugs were getting close to the expiration of their patents. And Merck's labs, which other companies once hailed as a bastion of scientific innovation, were crippled by a culture that buried good ideas under layers of bureaucracy. To revitalize drug development, Clark had to inject a new set of values where Merck's 60,000 employees–scientists, regulatory staff, and salespeople–would be motivated to work together.

This *BusinessWeek* case study describes the actions of CEO Richard Clark to change Merck's culture into one that is more in tune with the current environment. Read the full text of this *BusinessWeek* article at www.mhhe.com/mcshane5e, and prepare for the discussion questions that follow.

Discussion Questions

1. Describe the main features of Merck's past culture, and explain why that culture was not effective.
2. What are the key cultural values that CEO Richard Clark wants to instill in Merck employees? Explain how this new culture is better aligned with the external environment.
3. What strategies has Clark applied to transform Merck's culture? In your opinion, to what extent will each of these strategies be effective at bringing about cultural change?

Source: A. Weintraub, "Is Merck's Medicine Working?" *BusinessWeek,* 30 July 2007, p. 66.

CLASS EXERCISE 14.3

DIAGNOSING CORPORATE CULTURE PROCLAMATIONS

PURPOSE This exercise is designed to help you understand the importance and context in which corporate culture is identified and discussed in organizations.

INSTRUCTIONS This exercise is a take-home activity, although it can be completed in classes where computers and Internet connections are available. The instructor will divide the class into small teams (typically four or five people per team). Each team is assigned a specific industry–such as energy, biotechnology, or computer hardware.

The team's task is to search the Web sites of several companies in the selected industry for company statements about their corporate cultures. Use company Web-site search engines (if they exist) to find documents with key phrases such as "corporate culture" or "company values."

In the next class, or at the end of the time allotted in the current class, students will report on their observations by answering the following three discussion questions.

Discussion Questions

1. What values seem to dominate the corporate cultures of the companies you searched? Are these values similar or diverse across companies in the industry?
2. What was the broader content of the Web pages on which these companies described or mentioned their corporate cultures?
3. Do companies in this industry refer to their corporate cultures on their Web sites more or less than companies in other industries searched by teams in this class?

SELF-ASSESSMENT 14.4

WHAT ARE YOUR CORPORATE CULTURE PREFERENCES?

PURPOSE This self-assessment is designed to help you identify the corporate culture that fits most closely with your personal values and assumptions.

INSTRUCTIONS Read each pair of statements in the Corporate Culture Preference Scale and circle the statement that describes the organization you would prefer to work in. Then use the scoring key in Appendix B at the end of the book to calculate your results for each subscale. The scale does not attempt to measure your preference for every corporate culture–just a few of the more common varieties. Also, keep in mind that none of these corporate cultures is inherently good or bad. The focus here is on how well you fit within each of them. This exercise should be completed alone so that you can assess yourself honestly without concerns of social comparison. Class discussion will focus on the importance of matching job applicants to the organization's dominant values.

Corporate Culture Preference Scale

I would prefer to work in an organization:			
1a.	Where employees work well together in teams.	or	1b. That produces highly respected products or services.
2a.	Where top management maintains a sense of order in the workplace.	or	2b. Where the organization listens to customers and responds quickly to their needs.
3a.	Where employees are treated fairly.	or	3b. Where employees continuously search for ways to work more efficiently.
4a.	Where employees adapt quickly to new work requirements.	or	4b. Where corporate leaders work hard to keep employees happy.
5a.	Where senior executives receive special benefits not available to other employees.	or	5b. Where employees are proud when the organization achieves its performance goals.
6a.	Where employees who perform the best get paid the most.	or	6b. Where senior executives are respected.
7a.	Where everyone gets her or his job done like clockwork.	or	7b. That is on top of innovations in the industry.
8a.	Where employees receive assistance to overcome any personal problems.	or	8b. Where employees abide by company rules.
9a.	That is always experimenting with new ideas in the marketplace.	or	9b. That expects everyone to put in 110 percent for peak performance.
10a.	That quickly benefits from market opportunities.	or	10b. Where employees are always kept informed about what's happening in the organization.
11a.	That can quickly respond to competitive threats.	or	11b. Where most decisions are made by the top executives.
12a.	Where management keeps everything under control.	or	12b. Where employees care for each other.

In the mid-1990s, South Umpqua State Bank, in the foothills of southern Oregon, had $140 million in assets and six branches. Ray Davis, who was hired around that time as Umpqua's new CEO, didn't believe the financial institution would last long if it remained a sleepy community bank, so he initiated a seismic shift in its culture and practices. "We asked the question: why should anyone do business with us?" Davis recalls. "So we set out to differentiate ourselves in customer sales and service." Today, with assets of $8.3 billion and 148 stores from Napa, California, to Bellevue, Washington, Umpqua Bank is the largest regional community bank in the Pacific Northwest. It is also one of America's best places to work and a popular destination for bank executives around the world who want to discover Umpqua's unique model of banking.

Applying effective organizational change practices has helped Umpqua Bank become the largest regional community bank in the Pacific Northwest.

Umpqua Bank's transformation originated with Davis's vision that the bank should provide a unique retail experience supported by a customer-focused and innovative culture. This model of banking was communicated to employees, who received heavy doses of customer service training conducted by the Ritz-Carlton hotel. Rather than performing specialized jobs, employees were trained so that each could provide most customer services (loans, deposits, etc.) within the branch.

Umpqua Bank morphed its branches into retail stores, complete with comfy chairs, coffee bars (serving Umpqua's own brand of coffee), video games, free Wi-Fi, and high-definition TVs showing the financial news. The new design and parallel changes in employee service began as a pilot project at one store with staff members hand-picked by Davis. The executive team hired people whose values were consistent with the bank's new culture. At the same time, the team got "the wrong people off the bus." For example, three of the six original branch managers left the company.

Davis was aware of potential resistance throughout this period of turbulent change. "When you are leading for growth, you know you are going to disrupt comfortable routines and ask for new behavior, new priorities, new skills," he acknowledges. "Even when we want to change, and *do* change, we tend to relax and the rubber band snaps us back into our comfort zones." To prevent employees from returning to their old ways, Davis introduced a "return on quality" (ROQ) measure for each store and department. This composite measure of customer service and performance is calculated monthly and distributed to all employees so that they know their work unit's relative standing in the organization.[1]

15

ORGANIZATIONAL CHANGE

Learning Objectives

After reading this chapter, you should be able to:

1. Describe the elements of Lewin's force field analysis model.
2. Outline six reasons why people resist organizational change.
3. Discuss six strategies for minimizing resistance to change.
4. Outline the conditions for effectively diffusing change from a pilot project.
5. Describe the action research approach to organizational change.
6. Outline the "Four-D" model of appreciative inquiry and explain how this approach differs from action research.
7. Explain how parallel learning structures assist the change process.
8. Discuss three ethical issues in organizational change.
9. Explore the importance of personal change in organizations.

Umpqua Bank's transformation from a sleepy community bank to a regional leader illustrates many of the strategies and practices necessary to successfully change organizations. It reveals how CEO Ray Davis created an urgency to change, minimized resistance to change, built the new model from a pilot project that was later diffused throughout the organization, and introduced systems and structures that reinforced employee behaviors consistent with the new banking model and company culture. Although Umpqua's transformation sounds as though it was a smooth transition, most organizational change is messy, requiring considerable leadership effort and vigilance. As we will describe throughout this chapter, the challenge of change is not so much in deciding which way to go; the challenge is in the execution of this strategy. "We had to pull the train back into the station a few times to make sure everyone was on board," says Umpqua Bank executive Lani Hayward. "We're trying to do something that's never been done before and that's to be a community bank at any size."[2]

This chapter begins by introducing Lewin's model of change and its component parts. This includes sources of resistance to change, ways to minimize this resistance, and ways to stabilize desired behaviors. Next, the chapter examines four approaches to organizational change–action research, appreciative inquiry, large-group interventions, and parallel learning structures. The last section of this chapter considers both cross-cultural and ethical issues in organizational change.

Learning Objectives

After reading the next three sections, you should be able to:

1. Describe the elements of Lewin's force field analysis model.
2. Outline six reasons why people resist organizational change.
3. Discuss six strategies for minimizing resistance to change.
4. Outline the conditions for effectively diffusing change from a pilot project.

Lewin's Force Field Analysis Model

force field analysis
Kurt Lewin's model of systemwide change that helps change agents diagnose the forces that drive and restrain proposed organizational change.

Social psychologist Kurt Lewin developed the force field analysis model to explain how the change process works (see Exhibit 15.1).[3] Although it was developed more than 50 years ago, recent reviews conclude that Lewin's **force field analysis** model remains one of the most widely respected ways of viewing this process.[4]

One side of the force field model represents the *driving forces* that push organizations toward a new state of affairs. These might include new competitors or technologies, evolving workforce expectations, or a host of other environmental changes. Corporate leaders also produce driving forces even when external forces for change aren't apparent. For instance, some experts call for "divine discontent" as a key feature of successful organizations, meaning that leaders continually urge employees to strive for higher standards or new innovations even when the company outshines the competition.

unfreezing
The first part of the change process, in which the change agent produces disequilibrium between the driving and restraining forces.

The other side of Lewin's model represents the *restraining forces* that maintain the status quo. These restraining forces are commonly called "resistance to change" because they appear as employee behaviors that block the change process. Stability occurs when the driving and restraining forces are roughly in equilibrium, that is, they are of approximately equal strength in opposite directions.

Lewin's force field model emphasizes that effective change occurs by **unfreezing** the current situation, moving to a desired condition, and then

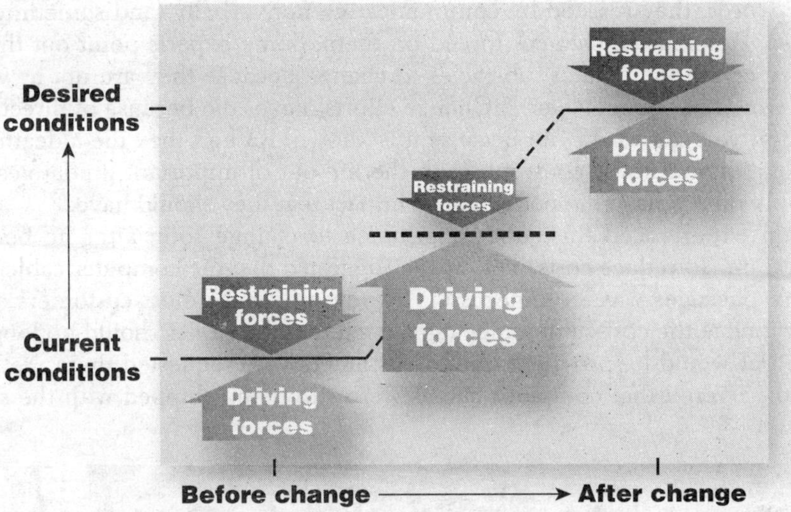

Exhibit 15.1 *Lewin's Force Field Analysis Model*

refreezing
The latter part of the change process, in which systems and conditions are introduced that reinforce and maintain the desired behaviors.

refreezing the system so that it remains in the desired state. Unfreezing involves producing disequilibrium between the driving and restraining forces. As we will describe later, this may occur by increasing the driving forces, reducing the restraining forces, or having a combination of both. Refreezing occurs when the organization's systems and structures are aligned with the desired behaviors. They must support and reinforce the new role patterns and prevent the organization from slipping back into the old way of doing things. Over the next few pages, we use Lewin's model to understand why change is blocked and how the process can evolve more smoothly.

Restraining Forces

Robert Nardelli pushed hard to transform Home Depot from a loose configuration of fiefdoms to a more performance-oriented operation that delivered a consistent customer experience. Change did occur at the world's largest home improvement retailer, but at a price. A large number of talented managers and employees left the company, and some of those remaining continued to resent Nardelli's transformation. Disenchanted staff referred to the company as "Home Despot" because the changes took away their autonomy. Others named it "Home GEpot," a cutting reference to the large number of former GE executives that Nardelli hired into top positions. After five years, the Home Depot board decided to replace Nardelli, partly because he made some unsuccessful strategic decisions and partly because of the aftereffects of Nardelli's changes.[5]

Robert Nardelli, who is now CEO of Chrysler, experienced employee *resistance to change* when at Home Depot. Resistance to change takes many forms, ranging from overt work stoppages to subtle attempts to continue the "old ways." One recent study of bank employees reported that subtle resistance is much more common than overt resistance. Some employees in that study avoided the desired changes by moving into different jobs. Others continued to perform tasks the old way as long as management didn't notice. Even when employees complied with the planned changes, they engaged in resistance by performing their work without corresponding cognitive or emotional support for the change.[6] In other words, they resisted by communicating nonverbally (and sometimes verbally!) to customers that they disliked the changes forced on them. Some experts point out that these subtle forms of resistance create the greatest obstacles to change because they are not as visible as overt resistance. In the words of one manager: "[Change efforts] never die because of direct confrontation. Direct confrontation you can work with because it is known. Rather, they die a death of a thousand cuts. People and issues you never confront drain the life out of important [initiatives] and result in solutions that simply do not have the performance impact that they should have."[7]

John Thompson experienced this subtle resistance to change soon after he became CEO of Symantec Corporation. To reduce costs, Thompson suggested that the computer cable included in all Symantec software packages was an unnecessary expense because most customers already owned these cables. Everyone at the cost-cutting meeting agreed that the cables should no longer be shipped with the software but would be provided free to customers who requested them. Yet several weeks later Thompson discovered that computer cables were still being shipped with the software, so he

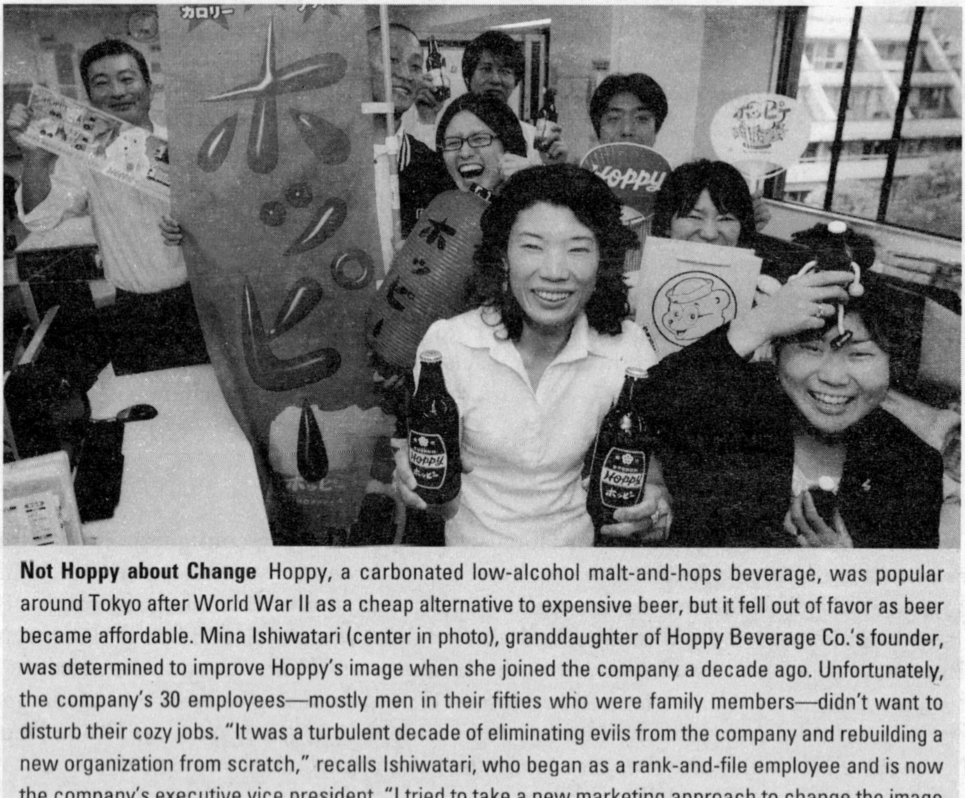

Not Hoppy about Change Hoppy, a carbonated low-alcohol malt-and-hops beverage, was popular around Tokyo after World War II as a cheap alternative to expensive beer, but it fell out of favor as beer became affordable. Mina Ishiwatari (center in photo), granddaughter of Hoppy Beverage Co.'s founder, was determined to improve Hoppy's image when she joined the company a decade ago. Unfortunately, the company's 30 employees—mostly men in their fifties who were family members—didn't want to disturb their cozy jobs. "It was a turbulent decade of eliminating evils from the company and rebuilding a new organization from scratch," recalls Ishiwatari, who began as a rank-and-file employee and is now the company's executive vice president. "I tried to take a new marketing approach to change the image of Hoppy . . . but no one would listen to me." With limited support and budget, Ishiwatari developed a Web site that informed the public about the product, sold it online, and documented Ishiwatari's views in an early Weblog. As the contemporary marketing caught the attention of health-conscious young people, Hoppy sales have doubled to about US$25 million annually, even though it is sold only around Tokyo. Most employees who opposed Ishiwatari's radical changes have since left the company; almost all of the 43 current staff members were hired by Ishiwatari and support her vision of Hoppy's future.[8]

reminded the executive responsible that the team makes these decisions only once. "If you've got a disagreement or a point of view, bring it up when we're going through the discussion," Thompson advised the executive. "Don't hold back and give me this smiley kind of benign agreement. Go back and get it fixed. We're not shipping cables any more."[9]

Employee Resistance as a Resource for Change Although Symantec's CEO was probably frustrated by the executive's passive resistance to change, change agents need to realize that resistance is a common and natural human response. As economist John Kenneth Galbraith once quipped, "In the choice between changing one's mind and proving there's no need to do so, most people get busy on the proof!"[10] Even when people do support change, they typically assume that it is others–not themselves–who need to change. The problem, however, isn't so much that resistance to change exists. The main problem is that change agents typically view resistance as an unreasonable, dysfunctional, and irrational response to a desirable initiative. They often form an "us versus them" perspective without considering that the causes of resistance may, in fact, be traced back to their own actions or inaction.[11]

The emerging view among change management experts is that resistance to change needs to be seen as a resource, rather than as an impediment to change. First, resistance incidents are symptoms of deeper problems in the change process. They are signals that the change agent has not sufficiently addressed the underlying conditions that support effective organizational change.[12] In some situations, employees may be worried about the *consequences* of change, such as how the new conditions will take away their power and status. In other situations, employees show resistance because of concerns about the *process* of change itself, such as the effort required to break old habits and learn new skills.

Second, resistance should be recognized as a form of constructive conflict. As you learned in Chapter 11, constructive conflict can potentially improve decision making, including identifying better ways to improve the organization's success. However, constructive conflict is typically accompanied by dysfunctional relationship conflict. This appears to be the case when change agents see resistance to change as an impediment rather than a resource. They describe the people who resist as the problem, whereas their focus should be on understanding the reasons why these people resist. Thus, by viewing resistance as a form of constructive conflict, change agents may be able to improve the change strategy or change process.

Finally, resistance should be viewed in the context of justice and motivation. Resistance is a form of voice, so, as described in Chapter 5, it potentially improves procedural justice. By redirecting initial forms of resistance into constructive conversations, change agents can increase employee perceptions and feelings of fairness. Furthermore, resistance is motivational; it potentially engages people to think about the change strategy and process. Change agents can harness that motivational force to ultimately strengthen commitment to the change initiative.

Why Employees Resist Change Change management experts have developed a long list of reasons why people do not embrace change.[13] Many of these reasons relate to a lack of motivation, such as exists when employees estimate that the negative consequences that the change might impose on them outweigh the benefits. Another factor is the inability to change due to lack of adequate skills and knowledge. Employees also resist change unwittingly because they lack a sufficiently clear understanding of what is expected of them (i.e., lack of role clarity). Six of the most commonly cited reasons why people resist change are summarized below.[14] Connections 15.1 describes how some of these sources of resistance existed at the FBI in spite of clear evidence that the law enforcement agency needed to develop a new mandate.

- *Direct costs.* People tend to block actions that result in higher direct costs or lower benefits than those in the existing situation. Connections 15.1 describes how some FBI managers likely resisted

15.1 CONNECTIONS

The FBI Meets Its Own Resistance

In 1993, following the first terrorist attack on the World Trade Center, the U.S. Federal Bureau of Investigation (FBI) was given a new mandate: refocus from a reactive law enforcement agency (solving crimes) to a proactive domestic intelligence agency (preventing terrorism). Eight years later, the FBI was still mainly a crime investigation organization with limited intelligence-gathering capabilities. This failure to change was identified as a factor in the FBI's inability to prevent terrorist attacks on the same buildings as well as the Pentagon. One government report even stated that the FBI and the CIA "seem to be working harder and harder just to maintain a status quo that is increasingly irrelevant to the new challenges."

The FBI experienced many sources of resistance in its mandate of transforming from a reactive law enforcement agency into a proactive domestic intelligence agency.

One source of resistance, according to government reports, is that FBI employees and managers are unable or unwilling to change because solving crimes (rather than intelligence gathering) is burned into their mindset, routines, career paths, and decentralized structure. Most FBI field managers were trained in law enforcement, so they continue to give preferential treatment and resources to enforcement rather than terrorist prevention initiatives.

Even if FBI leaders were motivated to become more focused on intelligence gathering, the organization's systems and structures undermine these initiatives. The FBI has been a decentralized organization, where field agents operate without much orchestration from headquarters. Until recently, the FBI also lacked a secure centralized information system (in fact, most of its records were still paper-based), which is essential for intelligence work but less important for criminal investigations. Furthermore, information is so closely guarded further down the ranks (called "close holds") that an information access barrier called "the wall" isolates FBI intelligence officers from the mainstream criminal investigation staff. Overall, these structural characteristics effectively scuttled any attempt to transform the FBI into an intelligence agency.

Resistance to change was also likely due in part to a historic rivalry between the FBI and the Central Intelligence Agency (CIA). Raising the profile and legitimacy of intelligence gathering at the FBI would have acknowledged that the CIA's work was valuable, so some FBI leaders and staff were reluctant to move in that direction.

The FBI is now taking concerted steps to address these barriers to change. But John Miller, the FBI's assistant director of the office of public affairs, admits that the FBI continues to face challenges. "The FBI has no corner on the market of people being resistant to change," he says. "We don't recruit people from Planet Perfect; we recruit human beings."[15]

the bureau's new intelligence mandate because it would necessarily remove some of their resources, personal status, and career opportunities.

- *Saving face.* Some people resist change as a political strategy to "prove" that the decision is wrong or that the person encouraging change is incompetent. This not-invented-here syndrome is widespread, according to change experts. Says one consultant, "Unless they're scared enough to listen, they'll never forgive you for being right and for knowing something they don't."[16]
- *Fear of the unknown.* People resist change out of worry that they cannot adjust to the new work requirements. This fear of the unknown increases the *risk* of personal loss. For example, even if many FBI managers and professionals recognized that the agency should change its mandate, they likely were reluctant to push the changes forward because it is difficult to anticipate how this mandate would affect them personally.
- *Breaking routines.* People typically resist initiatives that force them out of their comfort zones and require them to invest time and energy in learning new role patterns. Umpqua Bank CEO Ray Davis, who was introduced in the opening vignette to this chapter, acknowledged this source of resistance when describing the "rubber band" effect–employees tend to snap back into their comfort zones rather than stick with the new behaviors. Indeed, most employees in one survey admitted they don't follow through with organizational changes because they "like to keep things the way they are" or the changes seem to be too complicated or time wasting.[17] FBI agents likely resisted the organization's new mandate because they were accustomed to working independently on investigations, so it would be a challenge to engage in more information sharing and collaboration across teams and departments.
- *Incongruent team dynamics.* Teams develop and enforce conformity to a set of norms that guide behavior. However, conformity to existing team norms may discourage employees from accepting organizational change. For example, Best Buy introduced the results-only work environment (ROWE), in which employees were evaluated by their results, not their face time. Yet, even though the program allowed employees to wander in to work at any time, deviations were often met with half-humorous barbs from co-workers, such as "Forgot to set your alarm clock again?" These rebukes, which were consistent with the team norms that previously governed face-time violations, undermined the ROWE program. Best Buy's consultants eventually set up sessions that warned employees about these taunts, which they called "sludge."[18]
- *Incongruent organizational systems.* Rewards, information systems, patterns of authority, career paths, selection criteria, and other systems and structures are both friends and foes of organizational change. When properly aligned, they reinforce desired behaviors. When misaligned, they pull people back into their old attitudes and behavior. Even enthusiastic employees lose momentum after failing to overcome the structural confines of the past.

Unfreezing, Changing, and Refreezing

According to Lewin's force field analysis model, effective change occurs by unfreezing the current situation, moving to a desired condition, and then refreezing the system so that it remains in this desired state. Unfreezing occurs when the driving forces are stronger than the restraining forces. This happens by making the driving forces stronger, weakening or removing the restraining forces, or doing a combination of both.

With respect to the first option, driving forces must increase enough to motivate change. Change rarely occurs by increasing driving forces alone, however, because the restraining forces often adjust to counterbalance the driving forces. This is rather like the coils of a mattress. The harder corporate leaders push for change, the stronger the restraining forces push back. This antagonism threatens the change effort by producing tension and conflict within the organization. The preferred option is to both increase the driving forces and reduce or remove the restraining forces. Increasing the driving forces creates an urgency for change, whereas reducing the restraining forces minimizes resistance to change.

Creating an Urgency for Change

It is almost a cliché to say that organizations today operate in more dynamic, fast-paced environments than they did a few decades ago. The environmental pressures represent the driving forces that push employees out of their comfort zones. They energize people to face the risks that change creates. In many organizations, however, corporate leaders buffer employees from the external environment to such an extent that these driving forces are hardly felt by anyone below the top executive level. The result is that employees don't understand why they need to change and leaders are surprised when their change initiatives do not have much effect. The change process therefore necessarily begins by ensuring that employees develop an urgency for change. This typically occurs by informing employees about competitors, changing consumer trends, impending government regulations, and other driving forces in the external environment.[19]

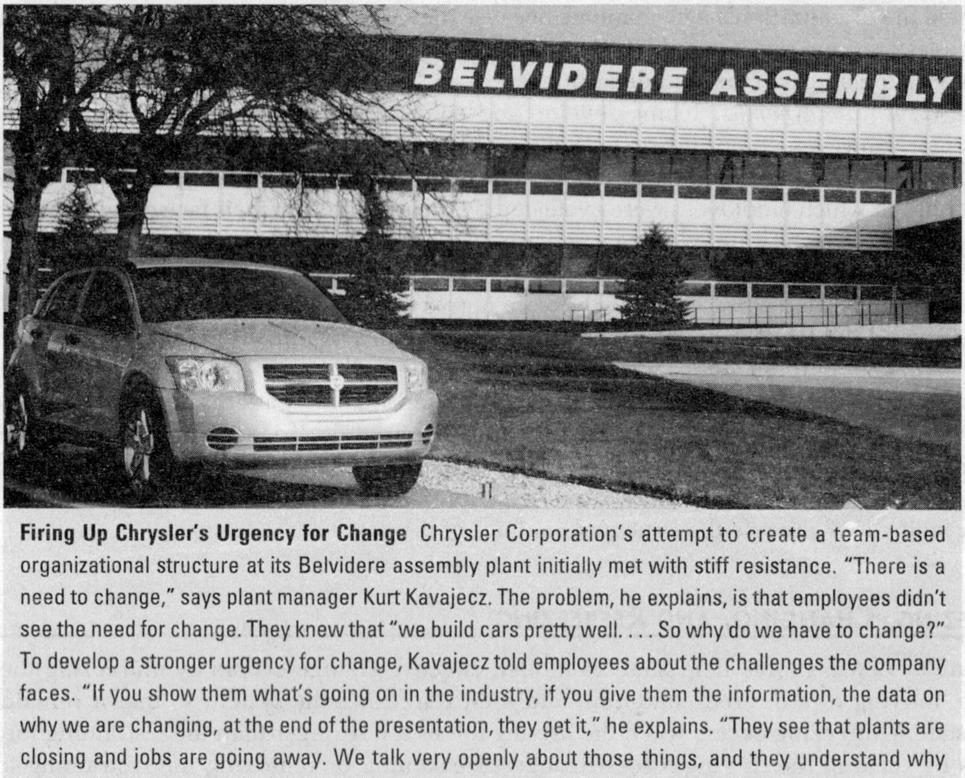

Firing Up Chrysler's Urgency for Change Chrysler Corporation's attempt to create a team-based organizational structure at its Belvidere assembly plant initially met with stiff resistance. "There is a need to change," says plant manager Kurt Kavajecz. The problem, he explains, is that employees didn't see the need for change. They knew that "we build cars pretty well. . . . So why do we have to change?" To develop a stronger urgency for change, Kavajecz told employees about the challenges the company faces. "If you show them what's going on in the industry, if you give them the information, the data on why we are changing, at the end of the presentation, they get it," he explains. "They see that plants are closing and jobs are going away. We talk very openly about those things, and they understand why we're changing." The Chrysler plant eventually introduced team-based work.[20]

Customer-Driven Change Some companies fuel the urgency to change by putting employees in direct contact with customers. Dissatisfied customers represent a compelling driving force for change because of the adverse consequences for the organization's survival and success. Customers also provide a human element that further energizes employees to change current behavior patterns.[21]

Executives at Shell Europe applied customer-driven change when they discovered that middle managers seemed blissfully unaware that Shell wasn't achieving either its financial goals or its customer needs. So, to create an urgency for change, the European managers were loaded onto buses and taken out to talk with customers and employees who work with customers every day. "We called these 'bus rides.' The idea was to encourage people to think back from the customer's perspective rather than from the head office," explains Shell Europe's vice president of retailing. "The bus rides were difficult for a lot of people who, in their work history, had hardly ever had to talk to a customer and find out what was good and not so good about Shell from the customer's standpoint."[22]

Creating an Urgency for Change without External Forces Exposing employees to external forces can strengthen the urgency for change, but leaders often need to begin the change process before problems come knocking at the company's door. "You want to create a burning platform for change even when there isn't a need for one," says Steve Bennett, CEO of financial software company Intuit.[23] Creating an urgency for change when the organization is riding high requires a lot of persuasive influence that helps employees visualize future competitive threats and environmental shifts.

For instance, Apple Computer's iPod dominates the digital music market, but Steve Jobs wants the company to be its own toughest competitor. Just when sales of the iPod Mini were soaring, Jobs challenged a gathering of 100 top executives and engineers to develop a better product to replace it. "Playing it safe is the most dangerous thing we can do," Jobs warned. Nine months later, the company launched the iPod Nano, which replaced the still-popular iPod Mini, before competitors could offer a better alternative.[24]

Experts warn, however, that employees may see the burning-platform strategy as manipulative, a view that produces cynicism about change and undermines trust in the change agent.[25] Also, the urgency for change does not always need to be initiated from a problem-oriented perspective. Instead, as we will describe later in this chapter, effective change agents can adopt a positive orientation by championing a vision of a more appealing future state. By creating a future vision of a better organization, leaders effectively make the current situation less appealing. When the vision connects to employee values and needs, it can be a motivating force for change even when external "problems" are not strong.

Reducing the Restraining Forces

Employee resistance should be viewed as a resource, but its underlying causes–the restraining forces–need to be addressed. As we explained earlier using the mattress-coil metaphor, it is not enough to increase the driving forces because employees often push back harder to offset the opposing force. Exhibit 15.2 summarizes six strategies for addressing the sources of employee resistance. If feasible, communication, learning, employee involvement, and stress management should be attempted first.[26] However, negotiation and coercion are necessary for people who will clearly lose something from the change and in cases where the speed of change is critical.

Communication As Connections 15.1 described, the FBI experienced a high level of resistance to changing into an intelligence-gathering organization. One of the first strategies the FBI leaders are now applying to address that resistance is communicating in every way possible and to as many audiences as possible that the FBI must change, why it must change, and what the new bureau will look like. "The word is out. Terrorism is the No. 1 priority, and intelligence is what the bureau is about," says former assistant attorney general Paul R. Corts, who has worked closely with the FBI during the change process. "You've got to say it, say it, and say it again."

Strategy	Example	When applied	Problems
Communication	Customer complaint letters are shown to employees.	When employees don't feel an urgency for change or don't know how the change will affect them.	Time-consuming and potentially costly.
Learning	Employees learn how to work in teams as company adopts a team-based structure.	When employees need to break old routines and adopt new role patterns.	Time-consuming and potentially costly.
Employee involvement	Company forms task force to recommend new customer service practices.	When the change effort needs more employee commitment, some employees need to save face, and/or employee ideas would improve decisions about the change strategy.	Very time-consuming. Might lead to conflict and poor decisions if employees' interests are incompatible with organizational needs.
Stress management	Employees attend sessions to discuss their worries about the change.	When communication, training, and involvement do not sufficiently ease employee worries.	Time-consuming and potentially expensive. Some methods may not reduce stress for all employees.
Negotiation	Employees agree to replace strict job categories with multiskilling in return for increased job security.	When employees will clearly lose something of value from the change and would not otherwise support the new conditions. Also necessary when the company must change quickly.	May be expensive, particularly if other employees want to negotiate their support. Also tends to produce compliance but not commitment to the change.
Coercion	Company president tells managers to "get on board" the change or leave.	When other strategies are ineffective and the company needs to change quickly.	Can lead to more subtle forms of resistance, as well as long-term antagonism with the change agent.

Sources: Adapted from J. P. Kotter and L. A. Schlesinger, "Choosing Strategies for Change," *Harvard Business Review* 57 (1979), pp. 106–114; P. R. Lawrence, "How to Deal with Resistance to Change," *Harvard Business Review*, May–June 1954, pp. 49–57.

Exhibit 15.2 *Strategies for Minimizing Resistance to Change*

Communication is the highest priority and first strategy required for any organizational change. According to one recent survey, communication (together with involvement) is considered the top strategy for engaging employees in the change process.[27] Communication improves the change process in at least two ways. First, as mentioned earlier, leaders develop an urgency to change by candidly telling employees about the driving forces for change. Whether through town hall meetings with senior management or by directly meeting with disgruntled customers, employees become energized to change. Second, communication can potentially reduce fear of the unknown. The more corporate leaders communicate their vision of the future, the more easily employees can understand their own role in that future. This effort may also begin the process of adjusting team norms to be more consistent with the new reality.

Learning Learning is an important process in most change initiatives because employees require new knowledge and skills to fit the organization's evolving requirements. The FBI is now addressing past resistance to change through heavy investment in training staff in counterterrorism and counterintelligence. In addition, hundreds of FBI executives have been sent to weeklong courses to learn how to coach employees during the change process. Coaching and other forms of learning are time-consuming, but they help employees break routines by teaching them new role patterns.

Employee Involvement Unless the change must occur quickly or employee interests are highly incompatible with the organization's needs, employee involvement is almost an essential part of the change process. Chapter 7 described several potential benefits of employee involvement, all of which are relevant to organizational change. Employees who participate in decisions about the change tend to feel they have more personal responsibility for its successful implementation, rather than being disinterested agents of someone else's decisions.[28] This sense of ownership also minimizes the problems of saving face and fear of the unknown. Furthermore, the complexity of today's work environment demands that more people provide ideas regarding the best direction of the change effort. Employee involvement is such an important component of organizational change that special initiatives have been developed to allow participation in large groups. These change interventions are described later in the chapter.

Stress Management Organizational change is a stressful experience for many people because it threatens self-esteem and creates uncertainty about the future.[29] Communication, learning, and

Employee Involvement Sizzles at Lopez Foods With blue-chip clients such as McDonald's and Wal-Mart, Lopez Foods, Inc. has built an impressive business over the past 15 years. And with annual sales of $500 million, the Oklahoma City–based beef patty and sausage manufacturer has become the 10th-largest Hispanic-owned company in America. To ensure that the next 15 years will be equally successful, CEO Eduardo Sanchez recently introduced a major organizational change initiative aimed at making "a quantum leap" in the company's efficiency and performance. Employee involvement has been a critical component of the change process. The company held several "brown paper" sessions in which the current production process was mapped out on a large wall of brown paper and employees were asked to verify that process and to figure out how to improve it. "We got everyone involved, got sticky [notes], and said, 'Here's the process as-is, and we want to work on the to-be—what's it going to be?'" says assistant vice president Dave Lopez. Sanchez was surprised at the employees' high level of enthusiasm for improving efficiency. "Things we thought would be a hard sell on the employees, they themselves have come up to us and said, 'We can do this better,' or 'We don't need five people here, we only need three,'" says Sanchez.[30]

employee involvement can reduce some of the stressors. However, research indicates that companies also need to introduce stress management practices to help employees cope with the changes.[31] In particular, stress management minimizes resistance by removing some of the direct costs and fear of the unknown of the change process. Stress also saps energy, so minimizing stress potentially increases employee motivation to support the change process.

Negotiation As long as people resist change, organizational change strategies will require some influence tactics. Negotiation is a form of influence that involves the promise of benefits or resources in exchange for the target person's compliance with the influencer's request. This strategy potentially activates those who would otherwise lose out from the change. However, it merely gains compliance rather than commitment to the change effort, so it might not be effective in the long term.

Coercion If all else fails, leaders rely on coercion to change organizations. Coercion can include persistently reminding people of their obligations, frequently monitoring behavior to ensure compliance, confronting people who do not change, and using threats of sanctions to force compliance. Replacing people who will not support the change is an extreme step, but it is fairly common. The opening story to this chapter described how three of the original six branch managers at Umpqua Bank left the company when Ray Davis introduced a radically different model of banking. Similarly, within one year after Robert Nardelli was hired as CEO of Home Depot, most of the retailer's top management team had voluntarily or involuntarily left the company.

Replacing staff is a radical form of organizational unlearning because replacing executives removes knowledge of the organization's past routines. This potentially opens up opportunities for new practices to take hold.[32] At the same time, coercion is a risky strategy because survivors (employees who do not leave) may have less trust in corporate leaders and engage in more political tactics to protect their own job security.

Refreezing the Desired Conditions

Unfreezing and changing behavior won't produce lasting change. People are creatures of habit, so they easily slip back into past patterns. Therefore, leaders need to refreeze the new behaviors by realigning organizational systems and team dynamics with the desired changes.[33] For instance, recall that the FBI experienced resistance to change because organizational structures interfered with the desired future of intelligence gathering. Now the FBI is not only changing; it is institutionalizing these changes through new systems and structures. New career paths have been established for intelligence officers as well as for criminal investigation agents. The compensation system has been redesigned to reward staff who succeed in intelligence work rather than just criminal investigations. The FBI is also slowly developing information systems so that agents can share knowledge quickly with each other and with other agencies.

Change Agents, Strategic Visions, and Diffusing Change

Kurt Lewin's force field analysis model is a useful template to explain the dynamics of organizational change. But it overlooks three ingredients in effective change processes: change agents, strategic visions, and diffusing change.

Change Agents and Strategic Visions

The opening vignette to this chapter described several ways that Umpqua Bank CEO Ray Davis supported organizational change. Perhaps the most important of these was Davis's own skills and behaviors as a transformational leader. He developed an appealing vision of the desired future state, communicated that vision in ways that were meaningful to others, made decisions and acted in ways that were consistent with that vision, and built commitment to that vision.[34] Change agents come in different forms, and more than one person is often required to fulfill these different roles.[35] In most situations, however, transformational leaders are the primary agents of change.

A key element of leading change is a strategic vision. A leader's vision provides a sense of direction and establishes the critical success factors against which the real changes are evaluated. Furthermore, vision provides an emotional foundation to the change because it links the individual's values and self-concept to the desired change.[36] A strategic vision also minimizes employee fear of the unknown and provides a better understanding about what behaviors employees must learn for the desired future.

Diffusion of Change

In Chapter 4, as well as earlier in this chapter, we described Best Buy's results-only work environment (ROWE) initiative, which was introduced to support work–life balance and employment expectations of a younger workforce. ROWE evaluates employees by their results, not their face time. This new arrangement gives employees at the Minneapolis-based retailer the freedom to come to work when it suits them. ROWE is a significant departure from the traditional employment relationship, so Best Buy wisely introduced an early version of it as a pilot project. Specifically, the program was first tested with a retail division of 320 employees that suffered from low morale and high turnover. Only after employee engagement scores increased and turnover fell over several months was the ROWE program expanded to other parts of the organization.[37]

As at Best Buy, change agents often test the transformation process with a pilot project and then diffuse what has been learned from this experience to other parts of the organization. Unlike centralized, systemwide changes, pilot projects are more flexible and less risky.[38] The pilot project approach also makes it easier to select organizational groups that are most ready for change, thus increasing the pilot project's success.

But how do we ensure that the change process started in the pilot project is adopted by other segments of the organization? The MARS model introduced in Chapter 2 offers a useful template for organizing the answer to this question. First, employees are more likely to adopt the practices of a pilot project when they are motivated to do so.[39] This occurs when they see that the pilot project is successful and people in the pilot project receive recognition and rewards for changing their previous work practices. Diffusion also requires supervisor support and reinforcement of the desired behaviors. More generally, change agents need to minimize the sources of resistance to change that we discussed earlier in this chapter.

Second, employees must have the ability–the required skills and knowledge–to adopt the practices introduced in the pilot project. According to innovation diffusion studies, people adopt ideas more readily when they have an opportunity to interact and learn from others who have already applied the new practices.[40] Thus, pilot projects get diffused when employees in the original pilot are dispersed to other work units as role models and knowledge sources.

Third, pilot projects get diffused when employees have clear role perceptions, that is, when they understand how the practices in a pilot project apply to them even though they are in a completely different functional area. For instance, accounting department employees won't easily recognize how they can adopt quality improvement practices developed by employees in the production department. The challenge here is for change agents to provide guidance that is neither too specific, because it might not seem relevant to other areas of the organization, nor too abstract, because this makes the instructions too vague. Finally, employees require supportive situational factors, including the resources and time necessary to adopt the practices demonstrated in the pilot project.

Learning Objectives

After reading the next two sections, you should be able to:

5. Describe the action research approach to organizational change.
6. Outline the "Four-D" model of appreciative inquiry and explain how this approach differs from action research.
7. Explain how parallel learning structures assist the change process.
8. Discuss three ethical issues in organizational change.
9. Explore the importance of personal change in organizations.

FOUR APPROACHES TO ORGANIZATIONAL CHANGE

So far, this chapter has examined the dynamics of change that occur every day in organizations. However, organizational change agents and consultants also apply various structured approaches to organizational change. This section introduces four of the leading approaches: action research, appreciative inquiry, large-group interventions, and parallel learning structures.

Action Research Approach

action research
A problem-focused change process that combines action orientation (changing attitudes and behavior) and research orientation (testing theory through data collection and analysis).

Along with introducing the force field model, Kurt Lewin recommended an **action research** approach to the change process. Action research maintains that meaningful change is a combination of action orientation (changing attitudes and behavior) and research orientation (testing theory).[41] On the one hand, the change process needs to be action-oriented because the ultimate goal is to bring about change. An action orientation involves diagnosing current problems and applying interventions that resolve those problems. On the other hand, the change process is a research study because change agents apply a conceptual framework (such as team dynamics or organizational culture) to a real situation. As with any good research, the change process involves collecting data to diagnose problems more effectively and to systematically evaluate how well the theory works in practice.[42]

Within this dual framework of action and research, the action research approach adopts an open-systems view. It recognizes that organizations have many interdependent parts, so change agents need to anticipate both the intended and the unintended consequences of their interventions. Action research is also a highly participative process because open-systems change requires both the knowledge and the commitment of members within that system. Indeed, employees are essentially co-researchers as well as participants in the intervention. Overall, action research is a data-based, problem-oriented process that diagnoses the need for change, introduces the intervention, and then evaluates and stabilizes the desired changes. The main phases of action research are illustrated in Exhibit 15.3 and described below:[43]

1. *Form client-consultant relationship.* Action research usually assumes that the change agent originates outside the system (such as a consultant), so the process begins by forming the client-consultant relationship. Consultants need to determine the client's readiness for change, including whether people are motivated to participate in the process, are open to meaningful change, and possess the abilities to complete the process.
2. *Diagnose the need for change.* Action research is a problem-oriented activity that carefully diagnoses the problem through systematic analysis of the situation. Organizational diagnosis identifies the appropriate direction for the change effort by gathering and analyzing data about an ongoing system, such as through interviews and surveys of employees and other stakeholders. Organizational diagnosis also

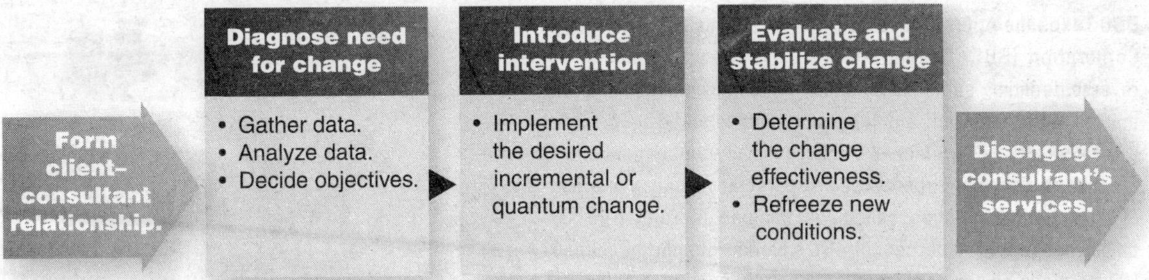

Exhibit 15.3 *The Action Research Process*

includes employee involvement in agreeing on the appropriate change method, the schedule for the actions involved, and the expected standards of successful change.

3. *Introduce intervention.* This stage in the action research model applies one or more actions to correct the problem. It may include any of the prescriptions mentioned in this textbook, such as building more effective teams, managing conflict, building a better organizational structure, or changing the corporate culture. An important issue is how quickly the changes should occur.[44] Some experts recommend *incremental change,* in which the organization fine-tunes the system and takes small steps toward a desired state. Others claim that *quantum change* is often required, in which the system is overhauled decisively and quickly. Quantum change is usually traumatic to employees and offers little opportunity for correction. But incremental change is also risky when the organization is seriously misaligned with its environment, thereby facing a threat to its survival.
4. *Evaluate and stabilize change.* Action research recommends evaluating the effectiveness of the intervention against the standards established in the diagnostic stage. Unfortunately, even when these standards are clearly stated, the effectiveness of an intervention might not be apparent for several years or might be difficult to separate from other factors. If the activity has the desired effect, the change agent and participants need to stabilize the new conditions. This refers to the refreezing process that was described earlier. Rewards, information systems, team norms, and other conditions are redesigned so that they support the new values and behaviors.

The action research approach has dominated organizational change thinking ever since it was introduced in the 1940s. However, some experts complain that the problem-oriented nature of action research–in which something is wrong that must be fixed–focuses on the negative dynamics of the group or system rather than its positive opportunities and potential. This concern with action research has led to the development of a more positive approach to organizational change, called *appreciative inquiry.*[45]

Appreciative Inquiry Approach

appreciative inquiry
An organizational change strategy that directs the group's attention away from its own problems and focuses participants on the group's potential and positive elements.

Appreciative inquiry tries to break out of the problem-solving mentality of traditional change management practices by reframing relationships around the positive and the possible. It searches for organizational (or team) strengths and capabilities and then adapts or applies that knowledge for further success and well-being. Appreciative inquiry is therefore deeply grounded in the emerging philosophy of *positive organizational behavior,* which suggests that focusing on the positive rather than negative aspects of life will improve organizational success and individual well-being. In other words, this approach emphasizes building on strengths rather than trying to directly correct problems.[46]

BBC Takes the Appreciative Journey The British Broadcasting Corporation (BBC) needed more innovative programming to reverse declining audience numbers, but employees complained that the radio, television, and Internet broadcaster did not provide a creative work environment. To discover how to become more creative, the company sponsored an appreciative inquiry process of employee consultation, called Just Imagine. More than 10,000 employees (about 40 percent of BBC's workforce) participated in 200 meetings held over six months. At each meeting, employees were paired to ask each other three questions: (1) What has been the most creative/valued experience in your time at the BBC? (2) What were the conditions that made that experience possible? (3) If those experiences were to become the norm, how would the BBC have to change? The pairs then discussed their interview results in teams of 10 people, and the most powerful stories were shared with others at the meeting. These meetings produced 98,000 ideas, which boiled down to 15,000 unique suggestions and ultimately 35 concrete initiatives. The BBC's executive publicized the results and immediately implemented several recommendations, such as a job swapping and a newcomer orientation program. Greg Dyke, BBC's respected director-general at the time, commented that the appreciative inquiry process provided valuable guidance. "It gave me a powerful mandate for change," he stated. "I could look staff in the eye and say, 'This is what you told us you wanted.'"[47]

Appreciative inquiry typically directs its inquiry toward successful events and successful organizations or work units. This external focus becomes a form of behavioral modeling, but it also increases open dialogue by redirecting the group's attention away from its own problems. Appreciative inquiry is especially useful when participants are aware of their "problems" or already suffer from negativity in their relationships. The positive orientation of appreciative inquiry enables groups to overcome these negative tensions and build a more hopeful perspective of their future by focusing on what is possible.[48]

The "Four-D" model of appreciative inquiry (named after its four stages) shown in Exhibit 15.4 begins with *discovery*–identifying the positive elements of the observed events or organization.[49] This might involve documenting positive customer experiences elsewhere in the organization. Or it might include interviewing members of another organization to discover its fundamental strengths. As participants discuss their findings, they shift into the *dreaming* stage by envisioning what might be possible in an ideal organization. By directing their attention to a theoretically ideal organization or situation, participants feel safer revealing their hopes and aspirations than they would if they were discussing their own organization or predicament.

As participants make their private thoughts public to the group, the process shifts into the third stage, called *designing*. Designing involves the process of dialogue, in which participants listen with selfless receptivity to each other's models and assumptions and eventually form a collective model for thinking within the team. In effect, they create a common image of what should be. As this model takes shape, group members shift the focus back to their own situation. In the final stage of appreciative inquiry,

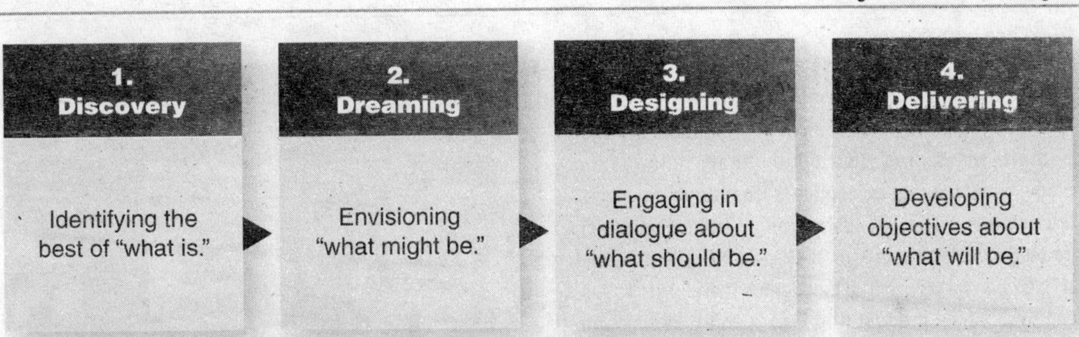

Sources: Based on F. J. Barrett and D. L. Cooperrider, "Generative Metaphor Intervention: A New Approach for Working with Systems Divided by Conflict and Caught in Defensive Perception," *Journal of Applied Behavioral Science* 26 (1990), p. 229; D. Whitney and C. Schau, "Appreciative Inquiry: An Innovative Process for Organization Change," *Employment Relations Today* 25 (Spring 1998), pp. 11–21; J. M. Watkins and B. J. Mohr, *Appreciative Inquiry: Change at the Speed of Imagination* (San Francisco: Jossey-Bass, 2001), pp. 25, 42–45.

Exhibit 15.4 *The Four-D Model of Appreciative Inquiry*

called *delivering* (also known as *destiny*), participants establish specific objectives and direction for their own organization on the basis of their model of what will be.

Appreciative inquiry was developed 20 years ago, but it really gained popularity only within the past few years. Several success stories of organizational change from appreciative inquiry have emerged in a variety of organizational settings, including British Broadcasting Corporation, Castrol Marine, Canadian Tire, Avon México, American Express, Green Mountain Coffee Roasters, and Hunter Douglas.[50] However, experts warn that appreciative inquiry is not always the best approach to changing teams or organizations, and, indeed, it has not always been successful. Appreciative inquiry requires participants who are willing to let go of the problem-oriented approach and leaders who are willing to accept appreciative inquiry's less structured process.[51] Another concern is that research has not yet examined the contingencies of this approach.[52] In other words, we don't yet know under what conditions appreciate inquiry is a useful approach to organizational change and under what conditions it is less effective. Overall, appreciative inquiry has much to offer the organizational change process, but we are just beginning to understand its potential and limitations.

Large-Group Interventions

future search
An organizational change strategy that consists of systemwide group sessions, usually lasting a few days, in which participants identify trends and establish ways to adapt to those changes.

Appreciative inquiry can occur in small teams, but it is often designed to involve a large number of people, such as the 10,000 employees who participated in the process at the British Broadcasting Corporation. As such, appreciative inquiry is often identified as one of several large-group organizational change interventions. Another large-group intervention, known as **future search** (and its variations–*search conferences* and *open-space technology*) "puts the entire system in the room," meaning that the process tries to involve as many employees and other stakeholders as possible associated with the organizational system.[53] Future-search conferences are typically multiday events at which participants are asked to identify trends or issues and establish strategic solutions for those conditions.

For example, Emerson & Cuming's chemical manufacturing facility in Canton, Massachusetts, relied on a future-search conference in which managers, supervisors, and production employees were organized into five stakeholder teams to identify initiatives that would improve the plant's safety,

IKEA Future Searches for the Perfect Sofa IKEA held a three-day future-search event involving more than four dozen stakeholders, including the company president, product design staff, sales and distribution staff, information technology, retail managers, suppliers from three countries, and six customers. The Swedish furniture company, which was growing rapidly, wanted to "build a quicker, leaner, and simpler" pipeline for its product development and distribution. Focusing on a single product (the Ektorp sofa), participants overcame the immense complexity of the system, the language barriers (for most, English was a second language), and apprehension and suspicions about change to map out a new product development process. One year later, IKEA launched a new sofa line (the Fixhult) based on further iterations of the process designed in the future-search workshop.[54]

efficiency, and cooperation. Lawrence Public Schools in Kansas conducted a future-search conference involving parents, teachers, students, community partners, and other stakeholders to help the board allocate resources more effectively. "The goals that were developed at the future search conference reflect what the community envisioned for its school district," says superintendent Randy Weseman. Those goals have since become the foundation of the board's strategic decision making.[55]

Future-search meetings and similar large-group change events potentially minimize resistance to change and assist the quality of the change process, but they also have limitations.[56] One problem is that involving so many people invariably limits the opportunity to contribute and increases the risk that a few people will dominate the process. Another concern is that these events focus on finding common ground, and this may prevent the participants from discovering substantive differences that interfere with future progress. A third issue is that these events generate high expectations about an ideal future state that are difficult to satisfy in practice. Employees become even more cynical and resistant to change if they do not see meaningful decisions and actions resulting from these meetings. The State of Washington Department of Corrections held a future-search event that tried to minimize these problems. The event involved a representation of 75 employees and managers, who reached a consensus on the department's future direction. Department executives were then assigned specific recommendations to ensure that the conference results were put into place.[57]

Parallel Learning Structure Approach

parallel learning structure
A highly participative arrangement composed of people from most levels of the organization who follow the action research model to produce meaningful organizational change.

Parallel learning structures are highly participative arrangements composed of people from most levels of the organization who follow the action research model to produce meaningful organizational change. They are social structures developed alongside the formal hierarchy with the purpose of increasing the organization's learning.[58] Ideally, participants in parallel learning structures are sufficiently free from the constraints of the larger organization so that they can more effectively solve organizational issues.

Royal Dutch/Shell relied on a parallel learning structure to introduce a more customer-focused organization.[59] Rather than try to change the entire organization at once, executives held weeklong "retail boot camps" with six country teams of frontline people (e.g., gas station managers, truck drivers, marketing professionals). Participants learned about competitive trends in their regions and were taught powerful marketing tools to identify new opportunities. The teams then returned home to study their market and develop proposals for improvement. Four months later, boot camp teams returned for a second workshop, at which each proposal was critiqued by Royal Dutch/Shell executives. Each team had 60 days to put its ideas into action; then the teams returned for a third workshop to analyze what worked and what didn't. This parallel learning process did much more than introduce new marketing ideas. It created enthusiasm in participants that spread contagiously to their co-workers, including managers above them, when they returned to their home countries.

Cross-Cultural and Ethical Issues in Organizational Change

One significant concern with some organizational change interventions is that they originate in the United States and other Western countries and may conflict with cultural values in some other countries.[60] A few experts point out that this Western perspective of change is linear, as is Lewin's force field model, discussed earlier. It also assumes that the change process is punctuated by tension and overt conflict. But these assumptions are incompatible with cultures that view change as a natural cyclical process with harmony and equilibrium as the objectives.[61] This dilemma suggests that we need to develop a more contingency-oriented perspective concerning the cultural values of participants.

Some organizational change practices also face ethical issues.[62] One ethical concern is the risk of violating individual privacy rights. The action research model is built on the idea of collecting information from organizational members, yet this requires that employees provide personal information and emotions that they may not want to divulge.[63] A second ethical concern is that some change activities potentially increase management's power by inducing compliance and conformity in organizational members. For instance, action research is a systemwide activity that requires employee participation rather than allowing individuals to get involved voluntarily. A third concern is that some organizational change interventions undermine the individual's self-esteem. The unfreezing process requires that participants disconfirm their existing beliefs, sometimes including their own competence at certain tasks or interpersonal relations.

Organizational change is usually more difficult than it initially seems. Yet the dilemma is that most organizations operate in hyperfast environments that demand continuous and rapid adaptation. Organizations survive and gain competitive advantage by mastering the complex dynamics of moving people through the continuous process of change as quickly as the external environment is changing.

Personal Change for the Road Ahead

In this last section of this textbook we thought it would be a good idea to shift our attention from organizational change to a few practical ideas about personal change and development in organizations. Whether you are just starting your career or are already well ahead along the trail, the following principles should help you improve both your prospects and your long-term career satisfaction. These points do not cover everything you need to remember about developing your career. Instead, they highlight some key strategies that will help you along the road ahead.

Understand Your Needs and Values

The first piece of advice regarding personal growth and development is that you should understand your needs and values. How do you know which path is most fulfilling for you? This involves doing self-assessments of your vocational interests and recounting experiences you have enjoyed. Holland's occupational choice model presented in Chapter 2 helps to align your personality and interests with the work environment. It may also be useful to get feedback from others regarding activities that they notice whether you like or dislike, or that they see what you are excelling at. This applies the Johari Window model described in Chapter 3, where you learn more about yourself through information presented by close associates.

Understand Your Competencies

Knowing yourself also involves knowing what you are capable of doing[64]. Although you might visualize your future as an Albert Einstein, the head of a *Fortune* 500 company, or a political leader of your country, you need to take your potential abilities into account. The more closely the work you perform is aligned with your personal competencies, the more will you develop feelings of satisfaction and empowerment. Self-assessments, performance results, and constructive feedback from friends can help identify your capabilities. Also keep in mind that competencies extend beyond technical skills: employers also look for generic competencies, such as communication, problem solving, and emotional intelligence.

Set Career Goals

Goal setting is a powerful way to motivate and achieve results, and this applies as much to careers as to any other activity. Career goals are benchmarks against which we evaluate our progress and identify strategies to develop our competencies. Career consultant Barbara Moses emphasizes that career goal setting is a fundamental element in becoming a "career activist." It involves writing your own script rather than waiting for someone to write it for you: being vigilant by identifying and preparing for opportunities, and becoming an independent agent by separating your self-identity from your job title, your organization, or what other people think you should be[65].

Maintain Networks

Networking makes a difference in career growth. This observation is supported by several research studies and from evidence in executive placement firms. One large placement firm reported that 64 per cent of the 7,435 clients in its executive career transition program found new employment through networking. As one successful job hunter advises, "Be prepared, know your story, and network, network, network."[66] Some networks are more effective than others, however. Specifically, job seekers tend to be more successful with large nonredundant networks. Networks that extend beyond your current sphere of work are also critical. Careers change much more today than in the past, so you need to establish connections to other fields where you may find yourself someday[67].

Get a Mentor

Thus far our discussion has emphasized self-leadership in personal development. We need to set our own goals, motivate ourselves for career advancement, and visualize where we want to go. But personal development in organizational settings also benefits from the help of others. Mentoring is the process of learning the ropes of organizational life from a senior person within the company. Mentors give protégés more visible and meaningful work opportunities, and they also provide ongoing career guidance. You might think of them as career coaches because they provide ongoing advice and feedback[68].

Organizational Behavior: The Journey Continues

Nearly 100 years ago, American industrialist Andrew Carnegie said: "Take away my people, but leave my factories, and soon grass will grow on the factory floors. Take away my factories, but leave my people, and soon we will have a new and better factory." Carnegie's statement reflects the message woven throughout this textbook: Organizations are not buildings or machinery or financial assets; rather, they are the people in them. Organizations are human entities–full of life, sometimes fragile, always exciting.

Chapter Summary

Lewin's force field analysis model states that all systems have driving and restraining forces. Change occurs through the process of unfreezing, changing, and refreezing. Unfreezing produces disequilibrium between the driving and restraining forces. Refreezing realigns the organization's systems and structures with the desired behaviors.

Restraining forces are manifested as employee resistance to change. Resistance to change should be viewed as a resource, not an inherent obstacle to change. The main reasons why people resist change are direct costs, saving face, fear of the unknown, breaking routines, incongruent team dynamics, and incongruent organizational systems. Resistance to change may be minimized by keeping employees informed about what to expect from the change effort (communicating); teaching employees valuable skills for the desired future (learning); involving them in the change process; helping employees cope with the stress of change; negotiating trade-offs with those who will clearly lose from the change effort; and using coercion (sparingly and as a last resort).

Organizational change also requires driving forces. This means that employees need to have an urgency for change by becoming aware of the environmental conditions that demand change in the organization. The change process also requires refreezing the new behaviors by realigning organizational systems and team dynamics with the desired changes. Every successful change also requires change agents with a clear, well-articulated vision of the desired future state. The change process also often applies a diffusion process in which change begins as a pilot project and eventually spreads to other areas of the organization.

Action research is a highly participative, open-systems approach to change management that combines an action orientation (changing attitudes and behavior) with research orientation (testing theory). It is a data-based, problem-oriented process that diagnoses the need for change, introduces the intervention, and then evaluates and stabilizes the desired changes.

Appreciative inquiry embraces the positive organizational behavior philosophy by focusing participants on the positive and possible. It tries to break out of the problem-solving mentality that dominates organizational change through the action research model. The four stages of appreciative inquiry include discovery, dreaming, designing, and delivering.

Large-group interventions, such as future-search conferences, are highly participative events that typically try to get the entire system into the room. A fourth organizational change approach, called parallel learning structures, relies on social structures developed alongside the formal hierarchy with the purpose of increasing the organization's learning. They are highly participative arrangements, composed of people from most levels of the organization who follow the action research model to produce meaningful organizational change.

One significant concern is that organizational change theories developed with a Western cultural orientation potentially conflict with cultural values in some other countries. Also, organizational change practices can raise one or more ethical concerns, including increasing management's power over employees, threatening individual privacy rights, undermining individual self-esteem, and making clients dependent on the change consultant.

Key Terms

action research
appreciative inquiry
force field analysis
future search
parallel learning structure
refreezing
unfreezing

Critical Thinking Questions

1. Chances are that the school you are attending is currently undergoing some sort of change to adapt more closely to its environment. Discuss the external forces that are driving the change. What internal drivers for change also exist?
2. Use Lewin's force field analysis to describe the dynamics of organizational change at Umpqua Bank (opening vignette to this chapter).
3. Employee resistance is a *symptom*, not a *problem*, in the change process. What are some of the real problems that may underlie employee resistance?
4. Senior management of a large multinational corporation is planning to restructure the organization. Currently, the organization is decentralized around geographic areas so that the executive responsible for each area has considerable autonomy over manufacturing and sales. The new structure will transfer power to the executives responsible for different product groups; the executives responsible for each geographic area will no longer be responsible for manufacturing in their area but will retain control over sales activities. Describe two types of resistance senior management might encounter from this organizational change.
5. Discuss the role of reward systems in organizational change. Specifically, identify where reward systems relate to Lewin's force field model and where they undermine the organizational change process.
6. Web Circuits is a Malaysian-based custom manufacturer for high-technology companies. Senior management wants to introduce lean management practices to reduce production costs and remain competitive. A consultant has recommended that the company start with a pilot project in one department and, when successful, diffuse these practices to other areas of the organization. Discuss the advantages of this recommendation, and identify three ways (other than the pilot project's success) to make diffusion of the change effort more successful.
7. Suppose that you are vice president of branch services at the Bank of East Lansing. You notice that several branches have consistently low customer service ratings even though there are no apparent differences in resources or staff characteristics. Describe an appreciative inquiry process in one of these branches that might help to overcome this problem.
8. This chapter suggests that some organizational change activities face ethical concerns. Yet several consultants actively use these processes because they believe they benefit the organization and do less damage to employees than it seems on the surface. For example, some activities try to open up the employee's hidden area (review the Johari Window discussion in Chapter 3) so that there is better mutual understanding with co-workers. Discuss this argument, and identify where you think organizational change interventions should limit this process.

CASE STUDY 15.1

TRANSACT INSURANCE CORPORATION

Steven L. McShane, University of Western Australia, and Terrance Bogyo, WorkSafeBC

TransAct Insurance Corporation (TIC) provides automobile insurance throughout the southeastern United States. Last year, a new president was hired by TIC's board of directors to improve the company's competitiveness and customer service. After spending several months assessing the situation, the new president introduced a strategic plan to strengthen TIC's competitive position. He also replaced three vice presidents. Jim Leon was hired as vice president of claims, TIC's largest division, with 1,500 employees, 50 claims center managers, and 5 regional directors.

Jim immediately met with all claims managers and directors, and he visited employees at TIC's 50 claims centers. As an outsider, this was a formidable task, but his strong interpersonal skills and uncanny ability to remember names and ideas helped him through the process. Through these visits and discussions, Jim discovered that the claims division had been managed in a relatively authoritarian, top-down manner. He could also see that morale was very low and employee-management relations were guarded. High workloads and isolation (adjusters work in tiny cubicles) were two other common complaints. Several managers acknowledged that the high turnover among claims adjusters was partly due to these conditions.

Following discussions with TIC's president, Jim decided to make morale and supervisory leadership his top priority. He initiated a divisional newsletter with a tear-off feedback form for employees to register their comments. He announced an open-door policy in which any claims division employee could speak to him directly and confidentially without going first to the immediate supervisor. Jim also fought organizational barriers to initiate a flextime program so that employees could design work schedules around their needs. This program later became a model for other areas of TIC.

One of Jim's most pronounced symbols of change was the "Claims Management Credo" outlining the philosophy that every claims manager would follow. At his first meeting with the complete claims management team, Jim presented a list of what he thought were important philosophies and actions of effective managers. The management group was asked to select and prioritize items from this list. They were told that the resulting list would be the division's management philosophy and all managers would be held accountable for abiding by its principles. Most claims managers were uneasy about this process, but they also understood that the organization was under competitive pressure and that Jim was using this exercise to demonstrate his leadership.

The claims managers developed a list of 10 items, such as encouraging teamwork, fostering a trusting work environment, setting clear and reasonable goals, and so on. The list was circulated to senior management in the organization for their comments and approval and sent back to all claims managers for their endorsement. Once this was done, a copy of the final document was sent to every claims division employee. Jim also announced plans to follow up with an annual survey to evaluate each claims manager's performance. This concerned the managers, but most of them believed that the credo exercise was a result of Jim's initial enthusiasm and that he would be too busy to introduce a survey after settling into the job.

One year after the credo had been distributed, Jim announced that the first annual survey would be conducted. All claims employees would complete the survey and return it confidentially to the human resource department where the survey results would be compiled for each claims center manager. The survey asked the extent to which the manager had lived up to each of the 10 items in the credo. Each form also provided space for comments.

Claims center managers were surprised that a survey would be conducted, but they were even more worried about Jim's statement that the results would be shared with employees. What results would employees see? Who would distribute these results? What happens if a manager gets poor ratings from his or her subordinates? "We'll work out the details later," said Jim in response to these questions. "Even if the survey results aren't great, the information will give us a good baseline for next year's survey."

The claims division survey had a high response rate. In some centers, every employee completed and returned a form. Each report showed the claims center manager's average score for each of the 10 items, as well as how many employees rated the manager at each level of the 5-point scale. The reports also included every comment made by employees at that center.

No one was prepared for the results of the first survey. Most managers received moderate or poor ratings on the 10 items. Very few managers averaged above 3.0 (out of the 5 points) on more than a couple of items. This suggested that, at best, employees were ambivalent about whether their claims center manager had abided by the 10 management philosophy items. The comments were even more devastating than the ratings. Comments ranged from mildly disappointed to extremely critical of the claims managers. Employees also described their long-standing frustration with TIC, high workloads, and isolated working conditions. Several people bluntly stated that they were skeptical about the changes that Jim had promised. "We've heard the promises before, but now we've lost faith," wrote one claims adjuster.

The survey results were sent to each claims manager, the regional director, and employees at the claims center. Jim instructed managers to discuss the survey data and comments with their regional manager and directly with employees. The claims center managers, who thought employees would see only the average scores, went into shock when they realized that the reports included individual comments. Some managers went to their regional director, complaining that revealing the personal comments would ruin their careers. Many directors sympathized, but the results were already available to employees.

When Jim heard about these concerns, he agreed that the results were lower than expected and that the comments should not have been shown to employees. After discussing the situation with his directors, he decided that the discussion meetings between claims managers and their employees should proceed as planned. To delay or withdraw the reports would undermine the credibility and trust that Jim was trying to develop with employees. However, the regional director attended the meeting in each claims center to minimize direct conflict between the claims center manager and employees.

Although many of these meetings went smoothly, a few created harsh feelings between managers and their employees. The sources of some comments were easily identified by their content, and this created a few delicate moments in several sessions. A few months after the meetings, two claims center managers quit and three others asked for transfers back to nonmanagement positions in TIC. Meanwhile, Jim wondered how to manage this process more effectively, particularly since employees expected another survey the following year.

Discussion Questions

1. What symptom(s) exist in this case to suggest that something has gone wrong?
2. What are the root causes that have led to these symptoms?
3. What actions should the company take to correct these problems?

CASE STUDY 15.2

INSIDE INTEL

BusinessWeek

For years, Intel thrived on a business model that cofounder Andy Grove perfected and reinforced under his leadership and the leadership of his successor, Craig Barrett. But Intel's latest CEO, Paul Otellini, has different plans. Rather than continuing to build faster chips just for PC computers, Otellini sees bigger opportunities in new "platforms." Otellini also wants to raise the profile of marketing, rather than let engineers determine which products are developed. Even the famous Intel logo (with a lowered "e") is being ditched for a more contemporary design.

This *BusinessWeek* case study reviews the changes that Paul Otellini is introducing at Intel and explains how he is building momentum toward these changes. The article also describes how employees are responding to the changes. Read through this *BusinessWeek* article at www.mhhe.com/mcshane5e, and prepare for the discussion questions that follow.

Discussion Questions

1. What change management strategies has Paul Otellini used to help introduce the various changes at Intel?
2. Discuss evidence that some employees are resisting the changes. What, if anything, can Otellini do to minimize this resistance?

Source: C. Edwards, "Inside Intel," *BusinessWeek*, 9 January 2006, p. 46.

TEAM EXERCISE 15.3

STRATEGIC CHANGE INCIDENTS

PURPOSE This exercise is designed to help you identify strategies for facilitating organizational change in various situations.

INSTRUCTIONS

1. The instructor will place students into teams, and each team will be assigned one of the scenarios presented below.
2. Each team will diagnose its assigned scenario to determine the most appropriate set of change management practices. Where appropriate, these practices should (a) create an urgency to change, (b) minimize resistance to change, and (c) refreeze the situation to support the change initiative. Each of these scenarios is based on real events.
3. Each team will present and defend its change management strategy. Class discussion regarding the appropriateness and feasibility of each strategy will occur after all teams assigned the same scenario have presented. The instructor will then describe what the organizations actually did in these situations.

SCENARIO 1: GREENER TELCO The board of directors at a large telephone company wants its executives to make the organization more environmentally friendly by encouraging employees to reduce waste in the workplace. Government and other stakeholders expect the company to take this action and be publicly successful. Consequently, the managing director wants to significantly reduce paper usage, refuse, and other waste throughout the company's many widespread offices. Unfortunately, a survey indicates that employees do not value environmental objectives and do not know how to "reduce, reuse, recycle." As the executive responsible for this change, you have been asked to develop a strategy that might bring about meaningful behavioral change toward this environmental goal. What would you do?

SCENARIO 2: GO FORWARD AIRLINE A major airline had experienced a decade of rough turbulence, including two bouts of bankruptcy protection, 10 managing directors, and morale so low that employees had removed company logos from their uniforms out of embarrassment. Service was terrible, and the airplanes rarely arrived or left the terminal on time. This was costing the airline significant amounts of money in passenger layovers. Managers were paralyzed by anxiety, and many had been with the firm so long that they didn't know how to set strategic goals that worked. One-fifth of all flights were losing money, and the company overall was near financial collapse (just three months to defaulting on payroll obligations). You and the newly hired managing director must get employees to quickly improve operational efficiency and customer service. What actions would you take to bring about these changes in time?

SELF-ASSESSMENT 15.4

ARE YOU TOLERANT OF CHANGE?

PURPOSE This exercise is designed to help you understand how people differ in their tolerance of change.

INSTRUCTIONS Read each of the statements on page 468 and circle the response that best fits your personal belief. Then use the scoring key in Appendix B at the end of this book to calculate your results. This self-assessment should be completed alone so that you can rate yourself honestly without concerns of social comparison. Class discussion will focus on the meaning of the concept measured by this scale and its implications for managing change in organizational settings.

Tolerance of Change

To what extent does each statement describe you? Indicate your level of agreement by marking the appropriate response on the right.	Strongly agree	Moderately agree	Slightly agree	Neutral	Slightly disagree	Moderately disagree	Strongly disagree
1. An expert who doesn't come up with a definite answer probably doesn't know too much.	☐	☐	☐	☐	☐	☐	☐
2. I would like to live in a foreign country for a while.	☐	☐	☐	☐	☐	☐	☐
3. There is really no such thing as a problem that can't be solved.	☐	☐	☐	☐	☐	☐	☐
4. People who fit their lives into a schedule probably miss most of the joy of living.	☐	☐	☐	☐	☐	☐	☐
5. A good job is one where it is always clear what is to be done and how it is to be done.	☐	☐	☐	☐	☐	☐	☐
6. It is more fun to tackle a complicated problem than to solve a simple one.	☐	☐	☐	☐	☐	☐	☐
7. In the long run, it is possible to get more done by tackling small, simple problems rather than large, complicated ones.	☐	☐	☐	☐	☐	☐	☐
8. Often the most interesting and stimulating people are those who don't mind being different and original.	☐	☐	☐	☐	☐	☐	☐
9. What we are used to is always preferable to what is unfamiliar.	☐	☐	☐	☐	☐	☐	☐
10. People who insist on a yes or no answer just don't know how complicated things really are.	☐	☐	☐	☐	☐	☐	☐
11. A person who leads an even, regular life in which few surprises or unexpected happenings arise really has a lot to be grateful for.	☐	☐	☐	☐	☐	☐	☐
12. Many of our most important decisions are based on insufficient information.	☐	☐	☐	☐	☐	☐	☐
13. I like parties where I know most of the people more than ones where all or most of the people are complete strangers.	☐	☐	☐	☐	☐	☐	☐
14. Teachers or supervisors who hand out vague assignments give people a chance to show initiative and originality.	☐	☐	☐	☐	☐	☐	☐
15. The sooner everyone acquires similar values and ideals, the better.	☐	☐	☐	☐	☐	☐	☐
16. A good teacher is one who makes you wonder about your way of looking at things.	☐	☐	☐	☐	☐	☐	☐

Source: Adapted from S. Budner, "Intolerance of Ambiguity as a Personality Variable," *Journal of Personality* 30 (1962), pp. 29–50.

ADDITIONAL CASES

CASE 1: A MIR KISS?

Steven L. McShane, University of Western Australia

A team of psychologists at Moscow's Institute for Biomedical Problems (IBMP) wanted to learn more about the dynamics of long-term isolation in space. This knowledge would be applied to the International Space Station, a joint project of several countries that would send people into space for more than six months. It would eventually include a trip to Mars that would take up to three years.

IBMP set up a replica in Moscow of the Mir space station. They then arranged for three international researchers from Japan, Canada, and Austria to spend 110 days isolated in a chamber the size of a train car. This chamber joined a smaller chamber where four Russian cosmonauts had already completed half of their 240 days of isolation. This was the first time an international crew was involved in the studies None of the participants spoke English as their first language, yet they communicated throughout their stay in English at varying levels of proficiency.

Judith Lapierre, a French-Canadian, was the only female in the experiment. Along with having a PhD in public health and social medicine, Lapierre had studied space sociology at the International Space University in France and conducted isolation research in the Antarctic. This was her fourth trip to Russia, where she had learned the language. The mission was supposed to have a second female participant from the Japanese space program, but she was not selected by IBMP.

The Japanese and Austrian participants viewed the participation of a woman as a favorable factor, says Lapierre. For example, to make the surroundings more comfortable, they rearranged the furniture, hung posters on the wall, and put a tablecloth on the kitchen table. "We adapted our environment, whereas the Russians just viewed it as something to be endured," she explains. "We decorated for Christmas, because I'm the kind of person who likes to host people."

New Year's Eve Turmoil

Ironically, it was at one of those social events, the New Year's Eve party, that events took a turn for the worse. After drinking vodka (allowed by the Russian space agency), two of the Russian cosmonauts got into a fistfight that left blood splattered on the chamber walls. At one point, a colleague hid the knives in the station's kitchen because of fears that the two Russians were about to stab each other. The two cosmonauts, who generally did not get along, had to be restrained by other men. Soon after that brawl, the Russian commander grabbed Lapierre, dragged her out of view of the television monitoring cameras, and kissed her aggressively–twice. Lapierre fought him off, but the message didn't register. He tried to kiss her again the next morning.

The next day, the international crew complained to IBMP about the behavior of the Russian cosmonauts. The Russian institute apparently took no action against any of the aggressors. Instead, the institute's psychologists replied that the incidents were part of the experiment. They wanted crew members to solve their personal problems with mature discussion, without asking for outside help. "You have to understand that Mir is an autonomous object, far away from anything," Vadim Gushin, the IBMP psychologist in charge of the project, explained after the experiment ended in March. "If the crew can't solve problems among themselves, they can't work together."

Following IBMP's response, the international crew wrote a scathing letter to the Russian institute and the space agencies involved in the experiment. "We had never expected such events to take place in a highly controlled scientific experiment where individuals go through a multistep selection process," they wrote. "If we had known . . . we would not have joined it as subjects." The letter also complained about IBMP's response to their concerns.

Informed of the New Year's Eve incident, the Japanese space program convened an emergency meeting on January 2 to address the incidents. Soon after, the Japanese team member quit, apparently shocked by IBMP's inaction. He was replaced with a Russian researcher on the international team. Ten days after the fight–a little over a month after the international team began the mission–the doors between the Russian and international crew's chambers were barred at the request of the international research team. Lapierre later emphasized that this action was taken because of concerns about violence, not the incident involving her.

A Stolen Kiss or Sexual Harassment?

By the end of the experiment in March, news of the fistfight between the cosmonauts and the commander's attempts to kiss Lapierre had reached the public. Russian scientists attempted to play down the kissing incident by saying that it was one fleeting kiss, a clash of cultures, and a female participant who was too emotional.

"In the West, some kinds of kissing are regarded as sexual harassment. In our culture it's nothing," said Russian psychologist Vadim Gushin in one interview. In another interview, he explained: "The problem of sexual harassment is given a lot of attention in North America but less in Europe. In Russia it is even less of an issue, not because we are more or less moral than the rest of the world; we just have different priorities."

Judith Lapierre says the kissing incident was tolerable compared to this reaction from the Russian scientists who conducted the experiment. "They don't get it at all," she complains. "They don't think anything is wrong. I'm more frustrated than ever. The worst thing is that they don't realize it was wrong."

Norbert Kraft, the Austrian scientist on the international team, also disagreed with the Russian interpretation of events. "They're trying to protect themselves," he says. "They're trying to put the fault on others. But this is not a cultural issue. If a woman doesn't want to be kissed, it is not acceptable."

Sources: G. Sinclair, Jr., "If You Scream in Space, Does Anyone Hear?" *Winnipeg Free Press,* May 5, 2000, p. A4; S. Martin, "Reining in the Space Cowboys," *Globe & Mail,* 19 April 2000, p. R1; M. Gray, "A Space Dream Sours," *Maclean's,* 17 April 2000, p. 26; E. Niiler, "In Search of the Perfect Astronaut," *Boston Globe,* 4 April 2000, p. E4; J. Tracy, "110-Day Isolation Ends in Sullen . . . Isolation," *Moscow Times,* 30 March 2000, p. 1; M. Warren, "A Mir Kiss?" *Daily Telegraph* (London), 30 March 2000, p. 22; G. York, "Canadian's Harassment Complaint Scorned," *Globe & Mail,* 25 March 2000, p. A2; and S. Nolen, "Lust in Space," *Globe & Mail,* 24 March 2000, p. A3.

CASE 2: ARCTIC MINING CONSULTANTS

Steven L. McShane, University of Western Australia, and Tim Neale

Tom Parker enjoyed working outdoors. At various times in the past, he worked as a ranch hand, high steel rigger, headstone installer, prospector, and geological field technician. Now 43, Parker is a geological field technician and field coordinator with Arctic Mining Consultants. He has specialized knowledge and experience in all nontechnical aspects of mineral exploration, including claim staking, line cutting and grid installation, soil sampling, prospecting, and trenching. He is responsible for hiring, training, and supervising field assistants for all of Arctic Mining Consultants' programs. Field assistants are paid a fairly low daily wage (no matter how long they work, which may be up to 12 hours or more) but are provided meals and accommodation. Many of the programs are operated by a project manager who reports to Parker.

Parker sometimes acts as a project manager, as he did on a job that involved staking 15 claims near Eagle Lake, Alaska. He selected John Talbot, Greg Boyce, and Brian Millar, all of whom had previously worked with Parker, as the field assistants. To stake a claim, the project team marks a line with flagging tape and blazes along the perimeter of the claim, cutting a claim post every 500 yards (called a *length*). The 15 claims would require almost 60 miles of line in total. Parker had budgeted seven days (plus mobilization and demobilization) to complete the job. This meant that each of the four stakers (Parker, Talbot, Boyce, and Millar) would have to complete a little over seven lengths each day. The following is a chronology of the project.

Day 1

The Arctic Mining Consultants crew assembled in the morning and drove to Eagle Lake, from where they were flown by helicopter to the claim site. On arrival, they set up tents at the edge of the area to be staked, and they agreed on a schedule for cooking duties. After supper, they pulled out the maps and discussed the job–how long it would take, the order in which the areas were to be staked, possible helicopter landing spots, and the areas that might be more difficult to stake.

Parker pointed out that with only a week to complete the job, everyone would have to average seven and a half lengths per day. "I know that is a lot," he said, "but you've all staked claims before and I'm confident that each of you is capable of it. And it's only for a week. If we get the job done in time, there's a $300 bonus for each man." Two hours later, Parker and his crew members had developed what seemed to be a workable plan.

Day 2

Millar completed six lengths, Boyce six lengths, Talbot eight, and Parker eight. Parker was not pleased with Millar's or Boyce's production. However, he didn't make an issue of it, thinking that they would develop their "rhythm" quickly.

Day 3

Millar completed five and a half lengths, Boyce four, and Talbot seven. Parker, who was nearly twice as old as the other three, completed eight lengths. He also had enough time remaining to walk over and check the quality of stakes that Millar and Boyce had completed and then walk back to his own area for the helicopter pickup back to the tent site.

That night Parker exploded with anger. "I thought I told you that I wanted seven and a half lengths a day!" he shouted at Boyce and Millar. Boyce said that he was slowed down by unusually thick underbrush in his assigned area. Millar said that he had done his best and would try to pick up the pace. Parker did not mention that he had inspected their work. He explained that as far as he was concerned, the field assistants were supposed to finish their assigned area for the day, no matter what.

Talbot, who was sharing a tent with Parker, talked to him later. "I think that you're being a bit hard on them, you know. I know that it has been more by luck than anything else that I've been able to do my quota. Yesterday I only had five lengths done after the first seven hours and there was only an hour before I was supposed to be picked up. Then I hit a patch of really open bush and was able to do three lengths in 70 minutes. Why don't I take Millar's area tomorrow and he can have mine? Maybe that will help."

"Conditions are the same in all of the areas," replied Parker, rejecting Talbot's suggestion. "Millar just has to try harder."

Day 4

Millar did seven lengths and Boyce completed six and a half. When they reported their production that evening, Parker grunted uncommunicatively. Parker and Talbot did eight lengths each.

Day 5

Millar completed six lengths, Boyce six, Talbot seven and a half, and Parker eight. Once again Parker blew up, but he concentrated his diatribe on Millar. "Why don't you do what you say you are going to do? You know that you have to do seven and a half lengths a day. We went over that when we first got here, so why don't you do it? If you aren't willing to do the job, then you never should have taken it in the first place!"

Millar replied by saying that he was doing his best, that he hadn't even stopped for lunch, and that he didn't know how he could possibly do any better. Parker launched into him again: "You have got to work harder! If you put enough effort into it, you will get the area done!"

Later Millar commented to Boyce, "I hate getting dumped on all the time! I'd quit if it didn't mean that I'd have to walk 50 miles to the highway. And besides, I need the bonus money. Why doesn't he pick on you? You don't get any more done than me; in fact, you usually get less. Maybe if you did a bit more he wouldn't be so bothered about me."

"I only work as hard as I have to," Boyce replied.

Day 6

Millar raced through breakfast, was the first one to be dropped off by the helicopter, and arranged to be the last one picked up. That evening the production figures were Millar eight and a quarter lengths, Boyce seven, and Talbot and Parker eight each. Parker remained silent when the field assistants reported their performance for the day.

Day 7

Millar was again the first out and last in. That night, he collapsed in an exhausted heap at the table, too tired to eat. After a few moments, he announced in an abject tone, "Six lengths. I worked like a dog all day and I only got a lousy six lengths!" Boyce completed five lengths, Talbot seven, and Parker seven and a quarter.

Parker was furious. "That means we have to do a total of 34 lengths tomorrow if we are to finish this job on time!" With his eyes directed at Millar, he added: "Why is it that you never finish the job? Don't you realize that you are part of a team, and that you are letting the rest of the team down? I've been checking your lines and you're doing too much blazing and wasting too much time making picture-perfect claim posts! If you worked smarter, you'd get a lot more done!"

Day 8

Parker cooked breakfast in the dark. The helicopter drop-offs began as soon as morning light appeared on the horizon. Parker instructed each assistant to complete eight lengths and, if they finished early, to help the others. Parker said that he would finish the other ten lengths. Helicopter pickups were arranged for one hour before dark.

By noon, after working as hard as he could, Millar had completed only three lengths. "Why bother," he thought to himself, "I'll never be able to do another five lengths before the helicopter comes, and I'll catch the same amount of abuse from Parker for doing six lengths as for seven and a half." So he sat down and had lunch and a rest. "Boyce won't finish his eight lengths either, so even if I did finish mine, I still wouldn't get the bonus. At least I'll get one more day's pay this way."

That night, Parker was livid when Millar reported that he had completed five and a half lengths. Parker had done ten and a quarter lengths, and Talbot had completed eight. Boyce proudly announced that he finished seven and a half lengths, but he sheepishly added that Talbot had helped him with some of it. All that remained were the two and a half lengths that Millar had not completed.

The job was finished the next morning and the crew demobilized. Millar has never worked for Arctic Mining Consultants again, despite being offered work several times by Parker. Boyce sometimes does staking for Arctic, and Talbot works full-time with the company.

CASE 3: BIG SCREEN'S BIG FAILURE

Fiona McQuarrie, University of the Fraser Valley, Canada

Bill Brosnan stared at the financial statements in front of him and shook his head. The losses from *Conquistadors,* the movie that was supposed to establish Big Screen Studios as a major Hollywood power, were worse than anyone had predicted. In fact, the losses were so huge that Brosnan's predecessor, Buck Knox, had been fired as a result of this colossal failure. Brosnan had wanted to be the head of a big movie production company for as long as he could remember, and he was thrilled to have been chosen by the board of directors to be the new president. But he had never expected that the first task in his dream job would be to deal with the fallout from one of the most unsuccessful movies ever.

The driving force behind *Conquistadors* was its director, Mark Frazier. Frazier had made several profitable movies for other studios and had a reputation as being a maverick with a "vision." He was a director with clearly formulated ideas of what his movies should look like, and he also had no hesitations about being forceful with producers, studios, actors, and technical staff to ensure that his idea came to life as he had envisioned it. For several years, while Frazier had been busy on other projects, he had also been working on a script about two Spanish aristocrats in the 16th century who set out for America to find riches and gold and encountered many amazing adventures on their travels. Frazier was something of an amateur historian, and this led to his interest in the real-life stories of the Spanish conquistadors and the idea of bringing those stories to life for a 21st-century audience. But he also felt that creating an epic tale like this would establish him as a serious writer and filmmaker in the eyes of Hollywood, some of whose major powers had dismissed his past work as unimaginative or clichéd.

When Big Screen Studios approached Frazier to see if he would be interested in working for them, the company was going through a rough spot. Through several years of hard work and mostly successful productions, Buck Knox, the president of Big Screen, had established Big Screen as a studio that produced cost-efficient and profitable films. The studio also had a good reputation for being supportive of the creative side of filmmaking; actors, writers, directors, and producers generally felt that Big Screen trusted them enough to give them autonomy in making decisions appropriate for their productions. (Other studios had reputations for keeping an overly tight rein on production budgets and for dictating choices based on cost rather than artistic considerations.) However, in the last two years Big Screen had invested in several major productions–a musical, a horror film, and the sequel to a wildly successful film adaptation of a comic book–that for various reasons had all performed well below expectations. Knox had also heard through the grapevine that several of the studio's board members were prepared to join together to force him out of the presidency if Big Screen did not come up with a hit soon.

Knox knew that Frazier was being wooed by several other studios for his next project, and he decided to contact Frazier to see if he was interested in directing any of the productions Big Screen was considering in the next year or so. After hearing Knox's descriptions of the upcoming productions, Frazier said, "What I'd really be interested in doing is directing this script I've been writing." He described the plot of *Conquistadors* to Knox, and Knox was enchanted by the possibilities–two strong male lead characters, a beautiful woman the men encountered in South America whose affections they fought over, battles, sea journeys, and challenging journeys over mountains and through jungles. However, Knox could also see that this movie might be extremely expensive to produce. He expressed this concern to Frazier, and Frazier replied, "Yes, but it will be an investment that will pay off. I know this movie will work. And I've mentioned it to two other studios and they are interested in it. I would prefer to make it with Big Screen, but if I have to, I will go somewhere else to get it made. That is how strongly I believe in it. However, any studio I work with has to trust me. I won't make the film without adequate financial commitment from the studio, I want final approval over casting, and I won't make the film if I don't get final cut." ("Final cut" means the director, not the studio, edits the version of the movie that is released to theaters and that the studio cannot release a version of the movie that the director does not approve.)

Knox told Frazier that he would get back to him later that week, and he asked Frazier not to commit to any other project until then. He spent several days mulling over the possibilities. Like Frazier, he believed that *Conquistadors* could be a huge success. It certainly sounded like it had more potential than anything else Big Screen had in development. However, Knox was still concerned about the potential cost and the amount of control over the project that Frazier was demanding. Frazier's reputation as a maverick meant that he likely would not compromise on his demands. Knox was also concerned about his own vulnerability if the movie failed. But, on the other hand, Big Screen needed a big hit, and it needed one soon. Big Screen would look very bad if it turned down *Conquistadors* and the movie became a gigantic hit for some other studio. Frazier had a respectable track record of producing moneymakers, so even if he might be difficult to work with, the end product usually was successful. At the end of the week, Knox phoned Frazier and told him that Big Screen was willing to produce *Conquistadors*. Frazier thanked Knox, and he added, "This film is going to redeem me, and it's going to redeem Big Screen as well."

Preproduction on the film started almost immediately after Frazier and the studio negotiated a budget of $50 million. This was slightly higher than Knox had anticipated, but he believed it was not an excessive amount to permit Frazier to realize the grand vision he had described. Knox further reassured himself by assigning John Connor, one of his trusted vice presidents, to act as the studio's liaison with Frazier and to be executive producer on the film. Connor was a veteran of many years in the movie production industry and was experienced in working with directors and budgets. Knox trusted Connor to be able to make Frazier contain the costs of the production within the agreed-on limits.

The first major problem the film encountered involved casting. The studio gave Frazier final approval over casting, as he had requested. Frazier's first signing was Cole Rogan, a famous action star, to be one of the male leads. The studio did not object to this choice; in fact, Knox and Connor felt that Rogan was an asset because he had a reputation as a star who could "open" a film (in other words, audiences would come to a movie just because he was in it). However, Frazier then decided to cast Frank Monaco as the other male lead. Monaco had made only a few films to date, and those were fluffy romantic comedies. Frazier said that Monaco would bring important qualities of vulnerability and innocence to the role, which would be a strong contrast to Rogan's rugged machismo. However, Connor told Knox he saw two major problems with Monaco's casting: Monaco had never proved himself in an epic adventure role, and he was an accomplished enough actor that he would make the rather wooden Rogan look bad. Knox told Connor to suggest to Frazier that Rogan's role be recast. Unfortunately, it turned out that Frazier had signed Rogan to a "pay or play" deal, meaning that if the studio released Rogan from the project, the studio would have to pay him a considerable sum of money. Knox was somewhat bothered that Frazier had made this deal with Rogan without consulting either him or Connor, but he told Connor to instruct Frazier to release Rogan and recast the role, and the studio would just accept the payment to Rogan as part of the production costs. Although Frazier complained, he did as the studio asked and chose as a replacement Marty Jones, an actor who had had some success in films but mostly in supporting roles. However, Jones was thrilled to be cast in a major role, and Connor felt that he would be capable of convincingly playing the part.

A few weeks after casting was completed, Connor called Knox and asked to see him immediately. "Buck," he told him once he arrived at Knox's office, "we have a really big problem." Connor said that Frazier was insisting the majority of the production be filmed in the jungles of South America, where most of the action took place, rather than on a studio soundstage or in a more accessible location that resembled the South American locale. Not only that, but Frazier was also insisting that he needed to bring along most of the crew that had worked on his previous films, rather than staffing the production locally. "Why does he want that? That's going to cost a hell of a lot," Knox said. "I know," Connor said, "but he says it's the only way that the film is going to work. He says it just won't be the same if the actors are in a studio or in some swamp in the southern U.S. According to him, the actors and the crew need to be in the real location to truly understand what the conquistadors went through, and audiences won't believe it's a real South American jungle if the film isn't made in one."

Knox told Connor that Frazier had to provide an amended budget to reflect the increased costs before he would approve the location filming. Connor took the request to Frazier, who complained that the studio was weakening on its promise to support the film adequately, and he added that he might be tempted to take the film to another studio if he was not allowed to film on location in South America. After a few weeks, he produced an amended budget of $75 million. Knox was horrified that the budget for *Conquistadors* had nearly increased by half in a few weeks. He told Connor that he would accept the amended budget only under two conditions: one, that Connor would go on the location shoot to ensure that costs stayed within the amended budget and, two, that if the costs exceeded Frazier's estimates, he would have to pay any excess himself. Frazier again complained that the studio was attempting to compromise his vision, but he grudgingly accepted the modified terms.

Frazier, Connor, and the cast and crew then headed off to the South American jungles for a scheduled two-month shoot. Immediately it became apparent that there was more trouble. Connor, who reported daily to Knox, told him after two weeks had passed that Frazier was shooting scenes several times over–not because the actors or the crew were making mistakes, or because there was something wrong with the scene, but because the output just didn't meet his artistic standards. This attention to detail meant that the filming schedule was nearly a week behind after only the first week's work. Also, because the filming locations were so remote, the cast and crew were spending nearly four hours of a scheduled seven-hour workday traveling to and from location, leaving only three hours in which they could work at regular pay rates. Work beyond those hours meant they had to be paid overtime, and as Frazier's demanding vision required shooting 10 or 12 hours each day, the production was incurring huge overtime costs. As if that wasn't bad enough, the "rushes" (the finished film produced each day) showed that Monaco and Jones didn't have any chemistry as a pair, and Gia Norman, the European actress Frazier had cast as the love interest, had such a heavy accent that most of her lines couldn't be understood.

Knox told Connor that he was coming to the location right away to meet with Frazier. After several days of very arduous travel, Knox, Connor, and Frazier met in the canvas tent that served as the director's office in the middle of the jungle. Knox didn't waste any time with pleasantries. "Mark," he told Frazier, "there is no way you can bring this film in for the budget you have promised or within the deadline you agreed to. John has told me how this production is being managed, and it's just not acceptable. I've done some calculations, and at the rate you are going, this picture is going to cost $85 million and have a running time of four and a half hours. Big Screen is not prepared to support that. We need a film that's a commercially viable length, and we need it at a reasonable cost."

"It needs to be as long as it is," replied Frazier, "because the story has to be told. And if it has to cost this much, it has to cost this much. Otherwise it will look like crap and no one will buy a ticket to see it."

"Mark," replied Knox, "we are prepared to put $5 million more into this picture, and that is it. You have the choice of proceeding under those terms, and keeping John fully informed of the costs so that he can help you stay within the budget. If you don't agree to that, you can leave the production, and we will hire another director and sue you for breach of contract."

Frazier looked as though he was ready to walk into the jungle and head back to California that very minute, but the thought of losing his dream project was too much for him. He muttered, "OK, I'll finish it."

Knox returned to California, nursing several nasty mosquito bites, and Connor stayed in the jungle and reported to him regularly. Unfortunately, it didn't seem like Frazier was paying much attention to the studio's demands. Connor estimated that the shoot would run three months rather than two and that the total cost of the shoot would be $70 million. This left only $10 million of the budget for post-production, distribution, and marketing, which was almost nothing for an epic adventure. To add to Knox's problems, he got a phone call from Richard Garrison, the chairman of Big Screen's board of directors. Garrison had heard gossip about what was going on with *Conquistadors* in the jungles of South America, and he wanted to know what Knox was going to do to curb Frazier's excesses. Knox told Garrison that Frazier was operating under clearly understood requirements and that Connor was on the set to monitor the costs. Unfortunately, Knox thought, Connor was doing a good job of reporting, but he didn't seem to be doing much to correct the problems he was observing.

Frazier eventually came back to California after three and a half months of shooting, and he started editing the several hundred hours of film he had produced. Knox requested that Frazier permit Connor or himself to participate in the editing, but Frazier retorted that permitting that would infringe on his right to "final cut"; he refused to allow anyone associated with the studio to be in the editing room. Knox scheduled a release date for the film in six months' time and asked the studio's publicity department to start working on an ad campaign for the film, but not much could be done on either of these tasks without at least a rough cut of the finished product.

Three weeks into the editing, Connor called Knox. "I heard from Mark today," he said. "He wants to do some reshoots." "Is that a problem?" Knox asked. "No," said Connor, "most of it is interior stuff that we can do here. But he wants to add a prologue. He says that the story doesn't make sense without more development of how the two lead characters sailed from Spain to South America. He wants to hire a ship."

"He wants to *what?*" exclaimed Knox.

"He wants to hire a sailing ship, like the conquistadors traveled on. There are a couple of tall ships that would do, but the one he wants is in dry dock in Mexico and would cost at least a million to make seaworthy and sail up to southern California. And that's on top of the cost of bringing the actors and crew back for a minimum of a week. I suggested to him that we try some special effects or a computerized animation for the scenes of the ship on the ocean, and shoot the shipboard scenes in the studio, but he says that won't be the same and it needs to be authentic."

At this point, Knox was ready to drive over to the editing studios and take care of Frazier himself. Instead, he called Garrison and explained the situation. "I won't commit any more money to this without the board's approval. But we've already invested $80 million into this already, so is a few more million that much of a deal if it gets the damn thing finished and gets Frazier out of our hair? If we tell him no, we'll have to basically start all over again, or just dump the whole thing and kiss $80 million goodbye." At the other end of the line, Garrison sighed, and said, "Do whatever you have to do to get it done."

Knox told Connor to authorize the reshoots, with a schedule of two months and the expectation that Frazier would have a rough cut of the film ready for the studio executives to view in three months. However, because of the time Frazier had already spent on editing, Knox had to change the release date, which meant changing the publicity campaign as well–and releasing the film at the same time that one of Big Screen's major competitors was releasing another epic adventure that was considered a surefire hit. However, Knox felt he had no choice. If he didn't enforce some deadline, Frazier might sit in the editing room and tinker with his dream forever.

Connor supervised the reshoots and reported that they went as well as could be expected. The major problem was that Gia Norman had had plastic surgery on her nose after the first shoot was completed and looked considerably different than she had in the jungles of South America. However, creative lighting, makeup, and costuming managed to minimize the change in her appearance. By all accounts, the (very expensive) sailing ship looked spectacular in the rushes, and Frazier was satisfied that his vision had been sufficiently dramatized.

Amazingly, Frazier delivered the rough cut of the film at the agreed-on time. Knox, Connor, Garrison, and the rest of the studio's executives crowded into the screening room to view the realization of Frazier's dream. Five and a half hours later, they were in shock. No one could deny that the movie looked fantastic and that it was an epic on a grand scale, but there was no way the studio could commercially release a film that was over five hours long–plus Frazier had agreed to produce a movie that was at most two and a half hours long. Knox was at his wits' end. He cornered Garrison in the hallway outside the screening room. "Will you talk to Mark? He won't listen to me, he won't listen to John. But we can't release this. It won't work." Garrison agreed, and contacted Frazier the next day. He reported back to Knox that Frazier, amazingly, had agreed to cut the film to two hours and fifteen minutes. Knox, heartened by this news, proceeded with the previously set release date, which by now was a month away, and got the publicity campaign going.

Two days before the scheduled release date, Frazier provided an advance copy of his shortened version of *Conquistadors* for a studio screening. Knox had asked him to provide a copy sooner, but Frazier said that he could not produce anything that quickly. As a consequence, the version of the film that the studio executives were seeing for the first time was the version that had already had thousands of copies duplicated for distribution to movie theaters all across North America. In fact, those copies were on their way by courier to the theaters as the screening started.

At the end of the screening, the studio executives were stunned. Yes, the movie was shorter, but now it made no sense. Characters appeared and disappeared randomly, the plot was impossible to follow, and the dialogue did not make sense at several key points in the small parts of plot that were discernible. The film was a disaster. Several of the executives present voiced the suspicion that Frazier had deliberately edited the movie this way to get revenge on the studio for not "respecting" his vision and forcing him to reduce the film's length. Others suggested that Frazier was simply a lunatic who never should have been given so much autonomy in the first place.

Knox, Garrison, and Connor held a hastily called meeting the next morning. What could the studio do? Recall the film and force Frazier to produce a more coherent shorter version? Recall the film and release the five-and-a-half-hour version? Or let the shorter version be released as scheduled and hope that it wouldn't be too badly received? Knox argued that the film should be recalled and Frazier should be forced to produce the product he agreed to produce. Connor said that he thought Frazier had been doing his best to do what the studio wanted, based on what Connor saw on the set, and that making Frazier cut the movie so short compromised the vision Frazier wanted to achieve. He said the studio should release the long version and present it as a "special cinematic event." Garrison, as chairman of the board, listened to both sides, and after figuring out the costs of recalling and/or reediting the film–not to mention the less tangible costs of further worsening the film's reputation–said, "Gentlemen, we really don't have any choice. *Conquistadors* will be released tomorrow."

Knox immediately canceled the critics' screenings of *Conquistadors,* scheduled for that afternoon, so that bad reviews would not appear on the day of the film's release. Despite that preemptive step and an extensive advertising campaign, *Conquistadors* was a complete and utter flop. On a total outlay of $90 million, the studio recouped less than $9 million. The reviews of the film were terrible, and audiences stayed away in droves. The only place *Conquistadors* was even close to successful was in some parts of Europe, where film critics called the edited version an example of American studios' crass obsession with making money by compromising the work of a genius. The studio attempted to capitalize on this note of hope by releasing the five-and-a-half-hour version of *Conquistadors* for screening at some overseas film festivals and cinema appreciation societies, but the revenues from these screenings were so small that they made no difference to the overall financial results.

Three months after *Conquistadors* was released, Garrison called Knox in and told him he was fired. Garrison told Knox that the board appreciated what a difficult production *Conquistadors* had been to manage but that the costs of the production had been unchecked to such a degree that the board no longer had confidence in Knox's ability to operate Big Screen Studios efficiently. Connor was offered a very generous early retirement package, and he accepted it. The board then hired Bill Brosnan, a vice president at another studio, as Knox's replacement.

After reviewing *Conquistadors'* financial records and the notes that Knox had kept throughout the production, Brosnan was determined that a disaster like this would not undermine his career as it had Knox's. But what could he do to ensure this would not happen?

CASE 4: BRIDGING THE TWO WORLDS—THE ORGANIZATIONAL DILEMMA

William Todorovic, Indiana-Purdue University, Fort Wayne

I had been hired by Aluminum Elements Corp. (AEC), and it was my first day of work. I was 26 years old, and I was now the manager of AEC's customer service group, which looked after customers, logistics, and some of the raw material purchasing. My superior, George, was the vice president of the company. AEC manufactured most of its products, a majority of which were destined for the construction industry, from aluminum.

As I walked around the shop floor, the employees appeared to be concentrating on their jobs, barely noticing me. Management held daily meetings, at which various production issues were discussed. No one from the shop floor was invited to the meetings, unless there was a specific problem. Later I learned that management had separate washrooms and separate lunchrooms, as well as other perks that floor employees did not have. Most of the floor employees felt that the managers, although polite on the surface, did not really feel they had anything to learn from the floor employees.

John, who worked on the aluminum slitter, a crucial operation required before any other operations could commence, had had a number of unpleasant encounters with George. As a result, George usually sent written memos to the floor in order to avoid a direct confrontation with John. Because the directions in the memos were complex, these memos were often more than two pages in length.

One morning, as I was walking around, I noticed that John was very upset. Feeling that perhaps there was something I could do, I approached John and asked him if I could help. He indicated that everything was just fine. From the looks of the situation, and John's body language, I felt that he was willing to talk but that he knew this was not the way things were done at AEC. Tony, who worked at the machine next to John's, then cursed and said that the office guys cared only about schedules, not about the people down on the floor. I just looked at him, and then I said that I began working here only last week and thought I could address some of their issues. Tony gave me a strange look, shook his head, and went back to his machine. I could hear him still swearing as I left. Later I realized that most of the office staff were also offended by Tony's language.

On the way back to my office, Lesley, a recently hired engineer from Russia, approached me and pointed out that the employees were not accustomed to managers talking to them. Management only issued orders and made demands. As we discussed the different perceptions between office and floor staffs, we were interrupted by a very loud lunch bell, which startled me. I was happy to join Lesley for lunch, but she asked me why I was not eating in the office lunchroom. I replied that if I was going to understand how AEC worked, I had to get to know all the people better. In addition, I realized that this was not how things were done, and wondered about the nature of this apparent division between the management and the floor. In the lunchroom, the other workers were amazed to see me there, commenting that I was just new and had not learned the ropes yet.

After lunch, when I asked George, my supervisor, about his recent confrontation with John, George was surprised that John got upset; he exclaimed, "I just wanted John to know that he did a great job and, as a result, we will be able to ship on time one large order to the West Coast. In fact, I thought I was complimenting him."

Earlier, Lesley had indicated that certain behavior was expected from management, and therefore from me. I reasoned that I do not think that this behavior works and, besides, it is not what I believe or how I care to behave. For the next couple of months, I simply walked around the floor and took every opportunity to talk to the shop floor employees. Often, when the employees related specific information about their workplaces, I felt that it went over my head. Frequently, I had to write down the information and revisit it later. I made a point of listening to them, identifying where they were coming from, and trying to understand them. I needed to keep my mind open to new ideas. Because the shop employees expected me to make requests and demands, I made a point of not doing any of that. Soon enough, the employees became friendly and started to accept me as one of their own, or at least as a different type of management person.

During my third month of work, the employees showed me how to improve the scheduling of jobs, especially those on the aluminum slitter. In fact, the greatest contribution was made by John, who demonstrated better ways to combine the most common slitting sizes and reduce waste by retaining some of the "common-size" material for new orders. Seeing the opportunity, I programmed a spreadsheet to calculate and track inventory. This, in addition to better planning and forecasting, allowed us to reduce our new order turnarounds from four to five weeks to a single day, in by 10 a.m. and out by 5 p.m.

By the time I was employed for four months, I realized that members from other departments were coming to me and asking me to relay messages to the shop employees. When I asked why they were delegating this task to me, they stated that I spoke the same language as the shop employees. Increasingly, I became the messenger for the office-to-floor communications.

One morning, George called me into his office and complimented me on the levels of customer service and the improvements that had been achieved. As we talked, I mentioned that we could not have done it without John's help. "He really knows his stuff, and he is good," I said. I suggested that we consider him for some type of promotion. Also, I hoped that this would be a positive gesture that would improve the communication between the office and shop floor.

George turned and pulled a flyer out of his desk. "Here is a management skills seminar. Do you think we should send John to it?"

"That is a great idea," I exclaimed, "Perhaps it would be good if he were to receive the news from you directly, George." George agreed, and after discussing some other issues, we parted company.

That afternoon, John came into my office, upset and ready to quit. "After all my effort and work, you guys are sending me for training seminars. So, am I not good enough for you?"

CASE 5: FRAN HAYDEN JOINS DAIRY ENGINEERING

Glyn Jones, University of Waikato, New Zealand

Background

Dairy Engineering (NZ) Ltd. has its headquarters in Hamilton, New Zealand, with manufacturing plants in South Auckland and Christchurch. The company manufactures equipment for the dairy industry. In its early years it focused on the domestic market, but in the last five years it has expanded into the export market. The company employs 450 people, which makes it a large company by New Zealand standards.

This case focuses on events in the accounting department at the head office, which is organized into two sections: cost accounting and management information services (MIS). The accounting department is structured as shown in Exhibit 1.

Name	Position	Description
Rob Poor	Chief accountant	Rob is the accounting department manager. He is 40 years old and is a qualified accountant with a chartered accounting (ACA) qualification. He has been with the company for six years. He is an unassuming person regarded as a bit "soft" by his staff.
Vernon Moore	Chief cost accountant	Vernon is 30 years old and is a graduate with an ACA qualification. He joined the company 18 months ago. He is considered an easygoing type and is well liked by his staff.
Peter Bruton	Management accountant	Peter is 37 years old and has a science degree in dairy technology. He is also studying part-time for a management degree through Massey University. He is regarded as "moody" and is not well liked by his staff.

Exhibit 1 *Description of Employees in the Case*

Fran, the New Graduate

Fran Hayden was in the final year of her bachelor of management studies (BMS) degree at the University of Waikato, where she had proved to be a high achiever. Fran was interested in a position with Dairy Engineering because of the opportunity to gain practical experience, the higher starting salary compared to the industry average, and the fact that her boyfriend lived in the community.

Fran sent her curriculum vitae to the company, and two weeks later she was invited to an interview with the chief accountant. She was surprised at the end of the interview to be offered the position of assistant cost accountant. Fran said she would like to think it over. Two weeks later, Fran had still not replied, so Rob telephoned her to ask if she was going to take the position. Although not totally convinced that she would enjoy the job, Fran decided to accept the offer.

The First Day at Work

Like many of her peers, Fran was glad to be leaving university after four years of study. She was looking forward to having money to spend as well as reducing her student debt. In order to "look the part," she had gone further into debt to buy new corporate clothing. On reporting to the accounting department, she got her first shock in the real world. No one was expecting her! Even worse, she discovered that there was no vacancy for her in cost accounting! Instead, she had been assigned to management information systems (MIS).

Mike, a co-worker in MIS, accompanied Fran to the department, where she was introduced to two other colleagues, Tom and Adrian. They seemed to be a friendly bunch, as apparently was her boss, Peter Bruton, who explained that her main duties were to assist with compiling information for the monthly management report known as "Big Brother."

After two weeks the time came for compiling Big Brother. Fran found that her part was almost entirely clerical and consisted of photocopying, collating, binding, punching, and stamping the pages of the report. She then had to hand-deliver copies of the report to the senior manager at headquarters. After Big Brother was completed, Fran found that again she had little to do. She began to wonder why MIS needed four people.

The Big Opportunity

One afternoon, the chief accountant called Fran to his office to tell her about an upcoming management workshop in Auckland on performance measurement. Rob talked about the importance of staff development and said that he would like to see one of his younger staff attend the workshop. He then asked Fran if she would be interested. She jumped at the opportunity. Unfortunately, her boss was away on two weeks' leave at the time, but Rob said he would talk with Peter.

Fran enjoyed the workshop, particularly rubbing shoulders with experienced managers, living in an Auckland hotel, and generally acting the management part. Even before returning to Hamilton, she wrote a detailed report on the workshop for the chief accountant.

On her return to Hamilton, however, she found all was far from well.

On Sunday evening Fran was telephoned by her colleague Mike with some disturbing news. When Peter returned to work to find that Fran was in Auckland, he was furious, complaining that he had not been consulted and that his authority was being undermined.

Peter: Fran is no longer employed in this section.

Fran returned to work full of trepidation, only to find that the expected encounter with her boss did not take place because he was in Christchurch. She handed two copies of her report on the workshop to the chief accountant's secretary before taking the opportunity of her boss's absence to seek the advice of her colleagues:

Fran: I am really worried. What do you think I should do?

Adrian: Stop worrying about it. He's just letting off steam. I have seen this all before. He'll get over it.

Fran: Come on; get serious. He is my boss! He can make things very difficult for me.

Mike: I think you should talk with Rob. After all, he's the one who suggested you go. It's not like it was your idea. He has to stick up for you.

The next day Fran managed to get an appointment with the chief accountant. She started by saying that she found the workshop very useful. She then brought up her fears about Peter's displeasure with her attendance at the workshop, to which the chief accountant responded.

Rob: Well, yes, he was a bit upset, but don't worry, I will sort it out. The report was really good. By the way, I think you should treat it as confidential. Don't show it to anyone or discuss it with anyone. Is that okay? Don't worry about this. I assure you that I will sort it out.

Fran left the meeting feeling reassured but also a bit puzzled, wondering how Rob could have read her report in such a short time.

On Thursday Peter returned to work and just before lunch called Fran into his office, where he proceeded to attack her verbally, saying that she had "connived" behind his back to attend the workshop and that she had never asked for his permission. He said that he realized she was an intelligent "girl" but that she was "sneaky."

Peter: You better know which side your bread is buttered on–that for better or worse, you are in my section. No other section would want you.

He then called Mike in and spoke to him.

Peter: I don't want Fran wasting any more time–she is not to make any private calls from work.

Later, in "confidence," he also spoke to Janet, one of the administration clerks.

Peter: Don't go talking with Fran–she has far too much work to catch up on.

Naturally, Janet did tell Fran!

The following week, Vernon happened to pass Fran in the corridor and stopped to talk with her. Fran had met Vernon only briefly during her first week in the company and was surprised when he asked her why she looked so miserable. She explained, and he said that they should talk with the chief accountant; taking Fran with him, he went to Rob's office. Vernon said that they needed a word, and Fran listened as Vernon outlined the situation to Rob. Fran made it clear that if Peter continued to treat her this way, she would have to ask for a transfer. She also said that there was certainly not enough work in MIS to keep her occupied for more than a day or so each week.

The chief accountant listened, and then he asked her to give him a written report of what had happened since she had joined the company, including the latest incident with her boss. This, he said, would be brought up at the next senior management meeting. On the weekend Fran wrote the report, which included a request for a transfer out of MIS on the basis of the lack of work and her boss's attitude toward her. On Monday morning she handed her report to the chief accountant's secretary.

Fran expected a reply but by early afternoon had heard nothing. At the end of the day, however, Peter called all his staff into his office. He was obviously in a good mood and told them that he had put his plan for revising Big Brother to the management meeting and had received an enthusiastic response. As he spoke, Fran noticed the color draining out of Mike's face. On the way out, he told her that what Peter was describing were *his* revision plans, not Peter's own plans. Mike resolved never to give his boss another one of his ideas.

Mike: He just uses other people's brains–but that's the last time he uses mine.

Fran drove home from work feeling despondent. She wished she had never joined the company. Her job was boring, almost entirely clerical, and it certainly did not require a degree. She was also taking the stresses home, resulting in quarrels with her boyfriend and roommates.

Fran concluded that she had only two alternatives: a transfer or resignation. But to leave her job after less than five months would hardly impress any future employer. In desperation, she went to talk with Vernon, who she thought would be sympathetic, but she received more unwelcome news. He told her about the outcome of the senior management meeting. Contrary to Fran's expectation, the chief accountant had not confronted Peter. In fact, it appeared that he had been eclipsed by Peter's presentation for the revision of Big Brother and the chief accountant had not attempted to raise the issue.

Vernon was frank–she must either transfer or resign. Then, to Fran's surprise, he suggested she apply for a position in his section that would become vacant in three weeks' time. One of his assistant accountants was leaving to go overseas at short notice, and he did not have a replacement. Vernon cautioned, however, that Fran's only chance was to apply directly to the chief accountant; that would force the issue. With a formal, written application before him, the chief accountant would have to make a decision. Just as certainly, Peter would resist the request. Later Fran drafted a letter to Rob requesting that she be transferred from MIS to the upcoming position in cost accounting.

The Confrontation

The next morning, Fran took her request to the chief accountant. After he read it, she was surprised by his comment.

Rob: You really needn't have done this, you know–I intended dealing with the situation.

Fran left Rob's office wondering what to believe. From her desk she watched as Peter made his way across to the chief accountant's office. The meeting was brief. Five minutes later, he left Rob's office, and as he passed by, he spoke to her in a loud voice.

Peter: Fran–you are finished at this company.

Fran saw her colleagues duck their heads down and pretend to be working. No one envied her position. She wondered how, in such a short time, she had ended up in such a situation.

CASE 6: FROM LIPPERT-JOHANSON INCORPORATED TO FENWAY WASTE MANAGEMENT

Lisa V. Williams, Jeewon Cho, and Alicia Boisnier, SUNY at Buffalo

Part One

Catherine O'Neill was very excited to finally be graduating from Flagship University at the end of the semester. She had always been interested in accounting, following from her father's lifelong occupation, and she very much enjoyed the challenging major. She was involved in many highly regarded student clubs in the business school and worked diligently to earn good grades. Now her commitment to the profession would pay off, she hoped, as she turned her attention to her job search. In late fall, she had on-campus interviews with several firms, but her interview with the prestigious Lippert-Johanson Incorporated (LJI) stood out in her mind as offering the most attractive opportunity. That's why Catherine was thrilled to learn she had made it to the next level of interviews, to be held at the firm's main office later that month.

When Catherine entered the elegant lobby of LJI's New York City offices, she was immediately impressed by all there was to take in. Catherine had always been one to pay attention to detail, and her acute observations of her environment had always been an asset. She was able to see how social and environmental cues told her what was expected of her, and she always set out to meet and exceed those expectations. On a tour of the office, she had already begun to size up her prospective workplace.

She appreciated the quiet, focused work atmosphere. She liked how everyone was dressed: Most wore suits, and their conservative apparel supported the professional attitudes that seemed to be omnipresent. People spoke to her in a formal but friendly manner, and they seemed enthusiastic. Some of them even took the time to greet her as she was guided to the conference room for her individual interview. "I like the way this place feels, and I would love to come to work here every day," Catherine thought. "I hope I do well in my interview!"

Before she knew it, Catherine was sitting in a well-appointed office with one of the eight managers in the firm. Sandra Jacobs was the picture of a professional woman, and Catherine naturally took her cue from her about how to conduct herself in the interview. It seemed to go very quickly, although the interview lasted an hour. As soon as Catherine left the office, she could not wait to phone her father about the interview. "I loved it there and I just know I'm a good fit!" she told her proud father. "Like them, I believe it is important to have the highest ethical standards and quality of work. Ms. Jacobs really emphasized the mission of the firm, as well as its policies. She did say that all the candidates have an excellent skill set and are well qualified for the job, so mostly they are going to base their hiring decision on how well they think each of us will fit into the firm. Reputation is everything to an accounting firm. I learned that from you, Dad!"

After six weeks of apprehensive waiting, Catherine's efforts were rewarded when LJI and another firm contacted her with job offers. Catherine knew she would accept the offer from LJI. She saw the firm as very ethical, with the highest standards for work quality and an excellent reputation. Catherine was grateful to have been selected from such a competitive hiring process. "There couldn't be a better choice for me! I'm so proud to become a member of this company!"

Catherine's first few days at LJI were a whirlwind of newcomer experiences. She had meetings with her supervisor to discuss the firm's mission statement, her role in the firm, and what was expected of her. She was also told to spend some time looking at the employee handbook, which covers many important policies of the firm, such as dress code, sick time, grievances, the chain of command and job descriptions, and professional ethics. Everyone relied on the handbook to provide clear guidance about what was expected of each employee. Also, Catherine was informed that she would soon begin participating in continuing professional education, which would allow her to update her skills and knowledge in her field. "This is great," thought Catherine, "I'm so glad to know the firm doesn't just talk about its high standards; it actually follows through with action."

What Catherine enjoyed most about her new job were her warm and welcoming colleagues who invited her to their group lunches beginning on her first day. They talked about work and home; they seemed close, both professionally and personally. She could see that everyone had a similar attitude about work: They cared about their work and the firm, they took responsibility for their own tasks, but they also helped one another out. Catherine also got involved in LJI activities outside work, like the company's baseball and soccer teams, happy hours, picnics, and parties, and she enjoyed the chance to mingle with her co-workers. In what seemed like no time at all, Catherine started to really see herself as a fully integrated member of LJI.

Before tax season started, Catherine attended some meetings of the AICPA and other professional accounting societies. There, she met many accountants from other firms who all seemed very impressed when she told them where she worked. Catherine's pride and appreciation for being a member of LJI grew as she realized how highly regarded the firm was among others in the accounting industry.

Part Two

Over the past seven years, Catherine's career in New York has flourished. Her reputation as one of the top tax accountants in her company is well established, and it is recognized by colleagues outside the firm as well. However, Catherine entered a new chapter of her life when she married Ted Lewis, an oncology intern, who could not turn down an offer of residency at a top cancer center in upstate New York. Wanting to support Ted's once-in-a-lifetime career opportunity, Catherine decided it was time to follow the path of many of her colleagues and leave public accounting for a position that would be more conducive to starting a family. Still, her heart was in the profession, so she took an available position as a controller of a small recycling company located a few miles from Catherine and Ted's new upstate New York home. She knew that with this position she could have children as well as maintain her career.

Fenway Waste Management is small–about 35 employees. There are about 25 people who work in the warehouse, 3 administrative assistants, 2 supervisors, and 5 people in management. Catherine is finding that she has to adjust to her new position and surroundings. Often she has found herself doing work that formally belonged to someone else; because it is a small company, managers seem to wear many hats. This was quite different from what she had experienced at LJI. In addition, the warehouse workers often have to work with greasy materials and sometimes track the grease into the offices. Catherine half-laughed and half-worried when she saw a piece of paper pinned to the wall that said, "Clean Up After Yourself!" She supposed that the nature of the business was why the offices are functional but furnished with old pieces. She couldn't imagine having a business meeting there. Also, for most of the employees, the casual dress matches the causal attitudes. But Catherine continued to wear a dressed-down version of her formal LJI attire, even though her new co-workers considered her overdressed.

With all the changes Catherine has experienced, she has maintained one familiar piece of her past. Although it is not required for her new position, Catherine still attends AICPA meetings and makes a point to continue updating her knowledge of current tax laws. At this year's conference, she told a former colleague, "Being here, I feel so much more like myself–I am so much more connected to these people and this environment than to those at my new job. It's too bad I don't feel this way at Fenway. I guess I'm just more comfortable with professionals who are similar to me."

CASE 7: GLENGARRY REGIONAL MEDICAL CENTER

*Adapted and updated by Steven L. McShane, University of Western Australia, from a case written by Donald D. White and H. William Vroman**

Glengarry Regional Medical Center (GlenMed) is an acute care general hospital located in Scotston, a community of 35,000 in the southwestern United States. GlenMed was founded in 1950 with 35 beds and grew to a capacity of 55 beds within three years. Economic growth in the region, along with a rapid influx of people, resulted in additional expansions, and five years ago the hospital reached its present capacity of 166 beds. The hospital was called Glengarry County Hospital until a few years ago.

The population of Glengarry County has grown steadily from approximately 56,800 in 1985 to 86,600 today. However, the hospital size has remained unchanged over this time. Approximately 500 people are employed at Glengarry. The medical staff consists of 75 doctors and related professionals. A substantial majority of the medical staff members are specialists. Therefore, the hospital offers a wide range of medical services, serving upward of 15,000 inpatients and approximately 19,000 outpatients each year.

*The original version of this case was published in Donald D.White and H. William Vroman, *Action in Organizations, 1977.* Reprinted with permission of Donald D. White.

Three years ago, GlenMed's board of directors concluded that major expansion of the hospital was necessary to adequately serve residents in Scotston and Glengarry County. The situation had become critical by the time this expansion decision was made. Hospital managers and board members had received numerous complaints concerning the hospital's overcrowded conditions. New patients experienced long waits until beds became available; offices and hallways had become overflow storage space. State health department officials warned GlenMed's administration that if equipment and supplies were not removed from hallways, the hospital would not be licensed for the coming year and therefore could lose its accreditation.

GlenMed would expand from 166 to 248 beds, at an estimated cost of $75 million. To more accurately reflect the services available and the population served by the growing medical complex, the board decided to change the hospital's name from Glengarry County Hospital to Glengarry Regional Medical Center. A fund-raising drive raised $9 million, enough funds to launch the expansion. Tax-exempt revenue bonds would provide most of the remaining funding.

Organizational Background

Glengarry Regional Medical Center, like other county hospitals in the state, is governed by a seven-member board of directors. State law provided that the board be appointed by the local county judge. As with any political system, appointments are based on a combination of individual qualifications and the political postures of board members. Historically, the board had not provided strong leadership to the hospital. However, recent appointments, together with strong leadership from a new board chairman, had greatly increased the activity and contribution of the board to the operation of the hospital.

All public hospital administrators face ongoing pressure from various groups, including civic political leaders, patients and their families, medical professionals, and hospital staff members. These pressures can take a toll on hospital leaders, as has been the case at GlenMed. Over the past decade, the hospital has been led by no less than four chief executives, three of them within the past five years. One administrator was asked to resign after the hospital lost more than $1.6 million in two years. His replacement tried to stem the losses, but she left after 18 months. Employees complained that she was autocratic and made erratic decisions. It was later determined that she had a serious illness, which may have contributed to these decisions and actions. Her replacement had been the chief financial officer for the previous two years. He lasted three years as CEO before the board asked him to resign. Although never publicly stated, the board concluded that he lacked initiative to develop the hospital and was around the hospital less often than a typical full-time employee.

While searching for a new CEO, the board appointed Donald Dale as acting CEO. Dale had served as second in command (i.e., assistant administrator) under the previous CEO. During this interim period, Dale worked closely with Louise Ogbonna, GlenMed's human resource director. Both managers were acutely aware of employee morale and motivation problems within the medical center, which they attributed to ineffective leadership over the past few years and ongoing employee concerns about the hospital's next administrator.

Dale and Ogbonna had recently attended a seminar on improving management competencies for health care organizations. They were convinced that Glengarry Regional Medical Center needed to develop management skills, so they contacted Dr. Vinkat Chandry, the university professor and management consultant who had conducted the seminar. Over the next month, the two administrators met on four occasions with Dr. Chandry to discuss the problems and needs of the hospital.

Dale and Ogbonna were emphatic that they wanted to develop a more employee-oriented culture, and they had taken a few steps in that direction. For example, to enhance two-way communication, they created a nonsupervisory employee council that met once a month to discuss with Dale and

Ogbonna problems and conditions throughout the hospital. Each department elected one person to represent it on the council. Initially, most of the communication was from the top down. However, shortly after the council had been created, a core of employees rose to take leadership of the group. They elected a spokesman and requested that they be permitted to meet once a month without either Dale or Ogbonna present. Thereafter, the employee representatives met twice monthly, once with the administrators and once without them.

Louise Ogbonna also suggested to Dr. Chandry that some form of management training should be developed and conducted for department heads and hospital supervisors. Both Dale and Chandry were hesitant about the training program at this time because they didn't want to saddle a new CEO with a program that he or she might not favor. However, Ogbonna felt strongly that the program should be initiated "as soon as possible." Such a program was designed by Dr. Chandry with agreement by Dale and Ogbonna regarding its content. Shortly thereafter, the board announced the selection of Arnold Benson as GlenMed's next CEO. Dale, Ogbonna, and Chandry agreed to postpone the management training program until Benson took over the following month, but Dale indicated from his initial meeting with Benson that the new training initiative would be supported.

A New Leader for the "Troops"

From a pool of 70 applicants, the board selected Arnold Benson as GlenMed's new CEO. At only 36 years old, Benson was among the youngest applicants and the youngest administrator to head the hospital. He held bachelor's and master's degrees in business administration and had considerable experience working in hospital organizations. After serving four years in the Marine Corps, Benson began his health care management career as director of purchasing and human resources in a 78-bed hospital. He then moved to a 156-bed Catholic hospital, where he rose from assistant administrator to associate administrator and finally to CEO, all within three years. Four years ago, Benson accepted the CEO position at a multihospital complex in St. Louis, Missouri, which included 144-bed and 134-bed facilities. There, he had overseen a major expansion of the hospital facilities. In Benson's words, "My objective was to become a professional hospital administrator. I realized that since I did not yet have a master's degree in hospital administration I would have to go with a 'back door approach' by working my way up the ranks."

Benson accepted the CEO job at GlenMed because he wanted to relocate to a smaller, safer community in the southwestern United States. The St. Louis hospital where he worked was in a rough part of the city. Also, the hospital had been a prime target for numerous union drives (none of which was successful). Benson's salary expectations were high, given his considerable experience in hospital administration, so he was pleased when the board made him a reasonable offer to lead Glengarry Regional Medical Center.

Benson was a tall, athletic-looking man whose mild manners and easygoing Texas drawl tended to hide his "down-to-business" approach to administration. Soon after arriving, he realized that he would be facing many problems inside and outside the hospital in the next few months. He knew that the most pressing of these was the hospital expansion. Moreover, it was clear to him that the primary concern of some board members was the hospital's financial health.

Financial concerns plagued Benson from the moment he arrived at GlenMed. During his first weeks on the job, the building program finances consumed almost half his time. In addition, Benson was advised three weeks after his arrival that employees had been promised a 7 percent across-the-board pay increase at the beginning of the year (in a few months). The total cost of the increase was more than $1.2 million. Benson felt that the hospital could not afford this amount of payroll increase, so he reduced the increase to 2 percent.

"When I came aboard, the board charged me with the financial responsibility of the medical center," Benson explained to his managers. "If the troops were to get their pay increase in January, it would throw the entire budget out of kilter. I have only been here three weeks, and quite frankly the current budget didn't get the attention it deserved."

Benson had his clerical assistant send staff an e-mail announcing the decision to cut the amount of the pay increase. He also stressed that the total financial posture of the hospital would be reevaluated. Benson's message was also posted on bulletin boards. Over the following week, several of the posted messages were slashed and rude comments were written on them. Soon after, a rumor circulated that the hospital board of directors planned to buy Benson a new luxury car. Pictures of Mercedes and BMWs were e-mailed around, with suggestions that Benson had expensive taste in automobiles. (In reality, Benson was given the Mercury Grand Marquis purchased for the previous CEO a year earlier.)

Recognizing the discontent over his decision, Benson met with members of the employee advisory council to discuss the pay question. Several members of the group quoted statistics showing that, on the average, blue-collar workers throughout the United States were being paid more than were most hospital employees. Benson replied that it was unfair to quote blue-collar statistics because they are in a different industry, adding that hospital employees earn enough to live comfortably. He then asked the members of the advisory council if they would work harder if they had received the full increase. According to Benson, "When all responded negatively, I told them point blank that it would be foolish to pay people more with no increase in productivity." He reminded those present that he had approved some pay increase and that he planned to put in effect a new compensation plan in the near future.

The employee council also voiced complaints about other conditions at GlenMed. Over the next few weeks, Benson saw to it that many of the problems were corrected to the group's satisfaction. However, when the last "demand" was met, Benson announced that the advisory group was no longer necessary. A question was raised by one of the employees concerning whether the group would be permitted to re-form if subsequent problems arose. Benson replied that it would not be permitted to do so.

Benson was confronted by a second important decision not long after the incident involving the pay increase. The hospital had obtained most of its funds for expansion through tax-exempt revenue bonds. However, the building program excluded much-needed parking lots. Benson therefore found it necessary to ask the local banking community for an additional $5.7 million so that parking lots could be built. Although the bankers agreed to underwrite the project, the feasibility study on which their decision was based indicated that the parking lots would have to generate revenue, whereas all hospital parking was currently provided without charge to the medical staff, employees, and visitors. Benson was concerned about how employees would react to pay parking so soon after learning that their pay increases had been reduced. The commitment to introduce pay parking had been made to the bankers, but Benson postponed announcement of this news.

Management Development Program

In early January, department heads throughout the hospital attended the management development program that Dr. Chandry had developed with the approval of Donald Dale and Louise Ogbonna. The program consisted of seven two-hour sessions held over one month. A similar program would be conducted for supervisors a few months later. The program included many elements of traditional management training, with particular emphasis on interpersonal skill development. Dale and Ogbonna also hoped the program would identify high-potential managers. Attendance in the program was voluntary, but Benson personally recommended that department heads and supervisors should participate. Benson, Dale, and Ogbonna received all materials for the program, but they agreed not to attend the sessions due to concerns that their presence might reduce participation.

One event dramatized the high level of distrust among department heads throughout the hospital. Participants were asked to complete evaluation forms that were to be used in connection with an exercise known as the Johari Window. The purpose of the exercise was to help the managers see themselves more clearly as others saw them and to help others in the group in a similar manner by providing them with "image feedback" information. The theory behind the exercise, together with its purpose, was explained to those present. Each manager was asked to write the name of every department head (including himself or herself) and to list at least one asset and one liability of each person listed. Dr. Chandry requested that the completed forms be returned to him at the beginning of the next session. The name of the individual providing the "feedback" information was not to be placed on the sheet itself. Dr. Chandry explained that he would facilitate the exchange of feedback at the next session by reading the name of a participant followed by the assets and liabilities that were identified by his or her peers.

Dr. Chandry began the next session by asking that all feedback sheets be passed in to him. Much to his surprise, only about half of the sheets were returned, and most of them were insufficiently completed. After a short pause, he asked those present to explain why they had failed to complete the assignment. Following a brief discussion, it was evident that the department heads had decided in another meeting that they would not complete the feedback sheet. Some managers explained that they did not know one another well enough. (Prior to the management program many of the department heads did not know one another by name, although a "get acquainted" exercise was used in the first session.) Others expressed fear that the information assembled on each individual would in some way be used against him or her.

One woman openly expressed concern that other department heads at the meeting might misuse the information. Another head privately suggested that some of those in attendance thought Dr. Chandry himself might take the information to the CEO. The discussion that followed had a cathartic effect on the group. For the first time, many of the managers "opened up" and talked about the lack of communication and trust that existed between the department heads and between the department heads and Benson.

Dr. Chandry ended the session by again explaining that the purpose of the exercise was to "improve our understandings of ourselves as well as of those with whom we associate throughout the hospital." Participants then agreed to complete and return the feedback sheets at the next session. At the next session, the exercise was completed smoothly. Many of the managers commented afterward that they believed that the exercise had been beneficial and had helped to open up the group. One department head did comment, however, "To tell you the truth, I think our refusal to complete the feedback sheets helped to break the ice between us. You know, it is the first time we really ever got together and agreed on something." The remainder of the management development program for departmental managers was well received.

The Retreat

A few days after the department heads' program was completed, Benson asked Dr. Chandry to meet with him. He began their conference by stating that he was pleased with what he had heard about the sessions and was anxious to ensure that the momentum that had been created would not be lost. He asked Dr. Chandry what he thought of bringing all the department heads together for a weekend retreat at a resort area not far from Scotston. Dr. Chandry was pleased with the suggestion, saying that he had considered recommending such an event but was concerned about the hospital's financial situation. Benson replied that the money for the retreat could be found since he anticipated that it would have a positive impact on the hospital's operations.

The following week Benson advised department heads that a retreat had been scheduled for the weekend of February 14 and 15. He went on to explain that the department heads would gather on Friday morning at the hospital and would drive directly to the resort. All expenses would be paid by the medical center. He told them that he hoped that the meeting would permit a free exchange of ideas.

A week before the scheduled retreat, Dr. Chandry met alone with the department heads who attended the training program to conduct a brief follow-up session. As he walked into the room, Dr. Chandry noticed that many managers were voicing their frustrations to one another. Thinking that the concerns were about this follow-up session, Dr. Chandry explained his presence and told them that he was interested in their feedback and application of the management training.

One manager stated that their anger had nothing to do with this meeting or with Dr. Chandry. Others then spoke up, most of them about the upcoming retreat. A few department heads stated that they did not want to attend the retreat. One newly married woman stated that it was Valentine's Day and her husband did not want her to go. Two other heads said they already had plans to attend a previously reserved Valentine's Day event at the country club that Friday evening. As discussion continued, it became apparent that the department heads had been told rather than consulted about the retreat. Some expressed displeasure with being "forced" into going to the retreat and using part of their weekend without first being asked their opinion.

Dr. Chandry listened carefully and explained to the managers that he believed the retreat was a good idea. He told them that he had considered such an event but that the CEO suggested the idea on his own. Furthermore, Dr. Chandry told them that the department heads should give Benson "a chance" during the weekend to see what might come out of the retreat. There were a few supportive comments made by one or two department heads and the meeting broke up.

Dr. Chandry left the meeting both perplexed and concerned. He had not anticipated the frustration that he witnessed from department heads throughout the hospital. As he walked toward the entrance of the hospital, Dr. Chandry asked himself whether he should provide further assistance to Benson before the retreat. He decided to stop in and see the CEO before leaving the hospital.

CASE 8: HIGH NOON AT ALPHA MILLS

Arif Hassan and Thivagar Velayutham, International Islamic University, Malaysia

Alpha Plantations Sdn. Bhd. is an oil palm plantation located in Malaysia. It consists of an oil palm estate and one palm oil mill. It is a wholly owned subsidiary of a British multinational company and was founded with the purpose of supplying crude palm oil for its parent company's detergent manufacturing business. Since its formation, most of the managers have been recruited from the United Kingdom, with many British ex-soldiers and policemen joining up. Ang Siow Lee joined Alpha Mill in 1965 at the age of 15 as a laborer, and he rose through the ranks to become the most senior nonmanagerial staff member at Alpha. Ang was the senior production supervisor in Alpha's palm oil mill. His immediate superior was the mill manager, and he had two junior supervisors to assist him. The mill operated on a three-shift cycle of 25 operators each, and each supervisor (including Ang) was in charge of one shift.

Ang was responsible for the smooth daily palm oil processing operations. He coordinated the activities of all three shifts with the two supervisors, prepared the daily production reports, dealt with short-term human resource planning issues, handled minor discipline issues, and set and evaluated short-term performance targets for all three shifts. In addition, he acted as the "gatekeeper," which meant that any mill personnel who wished to see the mill manager must first see Ang, who tried to solve the problem, which may be anything from house repairs to a request for an advance on wages. In rare cases when Ang could not resolve the issue, the matter was brought to the mill manager. Ang ran a tight ship, and he never let anyone forget it. His superb technical competency helped him keep the mill in top shape. He was accustomed to receiving the highest appraisal ratings from the mill manager, who appreciated his firm, methodical, almost militarily efficient way of running the mill. The palm oil industry in Malaysia faced many challenges in 1999. World oil prices plunged due to oversupply, and palm oil prices hit a 15-year low. This cut the profit margins of all palm oil producers and caused Alpha Mill to post losses regularly.

Captain Chubb, the 54-year-old ex-Royal Engineer and mill manager, was at a loss as to how to improve performance. "We are doing nothing wrong, and have met all our efficiency targets. It's this market that is killing us!" he exasperatedly explained during the annual year-end visit of the directors from London. Very soon, Chubb was given his marching orders. In early 2000 a new mill manager was appointed who was very different from all his predecessors. Ian Davison, a 32-year-old who hailed from Edinburgh, Scotland, was not a career plantation engineer and had never managed an agricultural product processing mill before. He was actually an electronics engineer, with an Ivy League MBA, on the fast track to a top management position. His previous appointment was manager of a detergent factory in Egypt, where he managed to streamline and modernize operations and increase financial performance drastically. Headquarters in London had high hopes that he would be able to do the same with Alpha Mill and return it to profitability. His first action was to analyze operations at Alpha Mill and look for ways to reduce production costs and increase profits. He arrived at the following conclusions:

- Current performance standards allowed too much machine breakdown and changeover time. Better standards were achievable with the latest technology.
- Wastage could be reduced and yield improved drastically by installing machinery based on new technology.
- Personnel numbers were too high–they could be reduced with technology and multitasking, thereby unleashing the full potential of workers.
- Personnel were just "cruising along"–they were not fully committed to achieving better performance.
- Hygiene needs were not being met.
- The old colonial and hierarchical company culture was not conducive to performance improvement.
- Information was not shared across the mill. Operators knew about only their own little area in the mill and almost nothing about the company as a whole.

Davison proposed to remedy the situation with the following initiatives:

- Empower operators by reorganizing the shifts into self-directed production teams, with the supervisors playing the role of "facilitators," and thereby gain commitment.
- Install new technology and automation.
- Adopt more stringent performance measures.

Davison began to implement and execute these initiatives by organizing an excursion to a local picnic spot for the entire factory. After the icebreakers, games, and lunch, he held a briefing session on the beach, where he explained the situation Alpha Mill was in and the need to make changes. He then unveiled his plan for the first time. The response was enthusiastic, although some operators privately confessed to not understanding some of the terminology Davison used. At the end of the excursion, when there was some time allocated for feedback, Ang expressed his full support for Davison's plan. "We in Alpha Mill have full confidence in you, our new leader, and we assure you of our 110 percent support to make your plan a success!" he said at the end of his speech.

When the new machinery had been installed and each shift had been reorganized into self-directed work teams, the plan was put into motion. Whenever the team faced a problem during processing and tried to find a solution using the techniques that had been taught, Ang would step in after some time, issue instructions, and take over the process. "This is a simple problem, no need to waste time over it. Just do it. . . ." His instructions were always followed, and the immediate problem was always solved. However, the production team reverted to the old ways of working, and none of the expected benefits of teaming were realized. Given the new, tighter performance standards and reduced manpower, the team consistently underperformed. Team meetings were one-way affairs at which Ang would tell everyone else what had gone wrong.

Ang's response to this was to push himself harder. He was always the first to arrive and the last to leave. He would spend a lot of time troubleshooting process problems. He pushed his operators even harder, but he felt that he had less of a "handle" on his operators now that they had direct access to the mill manager and most of their minor needs were seen to by him. Sometimes he became annoyed because of his operators' mistakes and would resort to shouting and cursing, which had the immediate effect of moving people in the direction he wanted. This was in contrast to the mere glare that would have sufficed previously.

The continued poor performance of Alpha Mill affected Ang's midyear appraisal rating, which fell from "excellent" to merely "adequate." During the appraisal interview, an annoyed Davison bluntly told Ang that he needed to understand clearly what the initiatives were all about and that he had to let the team take some responsibility, make mistakes, and learn from them. "With your knowledge of this mill, you should be able to provide them with all the technical input they need," he said. Davison also added, "It might help if you treated our people with a little more respect. We aren't living in the 1940s anymore, you know." Ang was thunderstruck by the appraisal but did not raise any objections on the spot. He silently deferred to Davison's judgment and promised to do better. He also reiterated his utmost support for Davison and his plan.

After the midyear appraisal, there was a noticeable change in Ang's demeanor. He became very quiet and began to take a less active role in the daily running of the mill. He was superficially polite to the operators and answered most requests for help with "Get the team together and discuss it among yourselves. Show the boss that you can solve it for yourselves." At first the teams were at a loss and mill performance suffered badly, but within two weeks the team had found its feet and performance began to improve. One of Ang's junior supervisors, Raman, was able to coordinate between production teams to ensure that the performance gains were maintained. The effect on Ang was devastating. He became withdrawn and began to drink more than usual. His presence at team meetings became a mere formality, and he contributed next to nothing, taking a backseat to other team members. He spoke very little to mill personnel and became a mere shadow of his former self.

Davison was very aware of the changes taking place on the mill floor. He decided that it was time to have Ang removed from his position. He began to plan for a reshuffle of Alpha Mill's organization chart: Ang would be promoted to the new position of mill executive, a staff position with a small pay raise. His responsibility would be to advise the mill manager on technical, quality, and efficiency problems faced by the mill. He would be assigned to carry out minor improvement projects and performance audits from time to time. Raman would be promoted as supervisor and report directly to the mill manager. Ang would no longer have any line authority over the production team. This reorganization was quickly approved by head office, and Davison proceeded to lay the groundwork for the announcements and the necessary paperwork. Little did he foresee what was to follow.

Ang was in the head office one morning when the personnel executive's clerk congratulated him on his imminent promotion. A surprised Ang enquired further and learned of the plans that Davison had in store for him. That was the final straw. He rushed back to Alpha Mill just as Davison was about to conduct his noon mill inspection. The confrontation was very loud, acrimonious, and public. It ended with Ang being terminated for insubordination and gross misconduct.

After Ang left, Davison felt that the obstacle to better commitment and morale was gone and that performance would improve greatly. He was very wrong. Team performance began to deteriorate, and no amount of pep talks could improve it. He began to wonder what had gone wrong.

CASE 9: KEEPING SUZANNE CHALMERS

Steven L. McShane, University of Western Australia

Thomas Chan hung up the telephone and sighed. The vice president of software engineering at Advanced Photonics Inc. (API) had just spoken to Suzanne Chalmers, who called to arrange a meeting with Chan later that day. She didn't say what the meeting was about, but Chan almost instinctively knew that Suzanne was going to quit after working at API for the past four years. Chalmers was a software engineer in Internet protocol (IP), the data transmission standard that directs information in the form of fiber-optic light through API's routers. It is very specialized work, and Suzanne was one of API's top talents in that area.

Thomas Chan had been through this before. A valued employee would arrange a private meeting. The meeting would begin with a few pleasantries, and then the employee announces that he or she wants to quit. Some employees say they are leaving because of the long hours and stressful deadlines. They say they need to decompress, get to know the kids again, or whatever. But that's not usually the real reason. Almost every organization in this industry is scrambling to keep up with technological advances and the competition. Employees would just leave one stressful job for another one.

Also, many of the people who leave API join a start-up company a few months later. The start-up firms can be pressure cookers where everyone works 16 hours each day and has to perform a variety of tasks. For example, engineers in these small firms might have to meet customers or work on venture capital proposals rather than focus on specialized tasks related to their knowledge. API now has over 6,000 employees, so it is easier to assign people to work that matches their technical competencies.

No, the problem isn't the stress or long hours, Chan thought. The problem is money–too much money. Most of the people who leave are millionaires. Suzanne Chalmers is one of them. Thanks to generous stock options that have skyrocketed on the stock markets, many employees at API have more money than they can use. Most are under 40 years old, so it's too early for them to retire. But their financial independence gives them less reason to remain with API.

The Meeting

The meeting with Suzanne Chalmers took place a few hours after the telephone call. It began like the others, with the initial pleasantries and brief discussion about progress on the latest fiber-optic router project. Then Suzanne made her well-rehearsed statement: "Thomas, I've really enjoyed working here, but I'm going to leave Advanced Photonics." Suzanne took a breath and then looked at Chan. When he didn't reply after a few seconds, she continued: "I need to take time off. You know, get away to recharge my batteries. The project's nearly done, and the team can complete it without me. Well, anyway, I'm thinking of leaving."

Chan spoke in a calm voice. He suggested that Suzanne should take an unpaid leave for two or maybe three months, complete with paid benefits, and then return refreshed. Suzanne politely rejected that offer, saying that she needs to get away from work for a while. Thomas then asked Suzanne whether she was unhappy with her work environment–whether she was getting the latest computer technology to do her work and whether there were problems with co-workers. The workplace was fine, Suzanne replied. The job was getting a bit routine, but she had a comfortable workplace with excellent co-workers.

Chan then apologized for the cramped workspace, due mainly to the rapid increase in the number of people hired over the past year. He suggested that if Suzanne took a couple of months off, API would give her special treatment when she returned: a larger workspace with a better view of the park behind the campuslike building. She politely thanked Chan for that offer but said it wasn't what she needed. Besides, it wouldn't be fair to have a large workspace when other team members work in smaller quarters.

Chan was running out of tactics, so he tried his last hope: money. He asked whether Suzanne had higher offers. Suzanne replied that she regularly received calls from other companies and some of them offered more money. Most were start-up firms that offered a lower salary but higher potential gains in stock options. Chan knew from market surveys that Suzanne was already paid well in the industry. He also knew that API couldn't compete on share option potential. Employees working in start-up firms sometimes saw their shares increase by five or ten times their initial value, whereas shares at API and other large firms increased more slowly. However, Chan promised Suzanne that he would recommend that she receive a significant raise–maybe 25 percent more–and more stock options. Chan added that Chalmers was one of API's most valuable employees and that the company would suffer if she left the firm.

The meeting ended with Chalmers promising to consider Chan's offer of higher pay and stock options. Two days later, Chan received her resignation in writing. Five months later, Chan learned that after a few months traveling with her husband, Chalmers joined a start-up software firm in the area.

CASE 10: NORTHWEST CANADIAN FOREST PRODUCTS LIMITED

Peter Seidl, British Columbia Institute of Technology, Canada

Northwest Canadian Forest Products Limited owns and operates five sawmills in British Columbia (BC) and Alberta, Canada. These mills produce high-quality lumber for use in the manufacture of window frames, doors, and moldings for markets in the United States and Japan in addition to lower-quality, commodity-type lumber used in the Canadian construction industry. Currently, the president of the company is thinking about the long-term prospects of each of the mills and is paying particular attention to the Jackson Sawmill located in the small town of Jackson, BC.

The Jackson Sawmill was originally built in 1950 and was last upgraded in 1986. The president knows she will soon (in 2007) have to decide whether or not to invest substantial sums of money ($50 million) in new plant and equipment at the Jackson Sawmill. New investment is required in order to keep the mill up-to-date and competitive with similar mills throughout North America. However, the mill has consistently been the poorest performer (in terms of productivity and product quality) in the company since 1986 even though its equipment is of similar age, type, and quality to that found in the other mills.

The president would like to invest the money needed because the alternative to re-investing in Jackson would be to downsize the Jackson Sawmill by reducing production capacity and permanently laying off over half the 200-person workforce. The remaining part of the mill would serve the domestic market only. A new mill would then be built in Alberta in order to serve the more demanding, quality-conscious export markets. A new mill in Alberta would cost more than the $50 million investment required at the Jackson Sawmill. However, the president is willing to seriously consider implementing this alternative because she thinks that the labor relations climate in Alberta is much better than the one found at Jackson.

In fact, she attributes most, if not all, of the problems at Jackson to its poor labor-management relations. During the last round of collective bargaining, there was a strike at all four of the company's BC mills. The strike was, however, much more bitter at Jackson than elsewhere. Company buildings suffered minor damage during the strike at the hands of some striking employees. Since then, there were two separate occasions when the entire workforce walked off the job for a day to protest the company's decision to fire two employees for insubordination.

The Jackson Sawmill has the worst safety record of all the company's mills. There is a joint management-management safety committee (as required by law), but it is viewed as a waste of time by both sides. One management member of the safety committee, Des, the production manager and the second highest manager at the mill, has said: "The union guys start each safety committee meeting by complaining about safety but they just can't wait to complain about everything else they can possibly think of. Their whining and complaining is so predictable that I go to every safety meeting ready for a fight on workload and production issues as well as for a fight on safety. Of course, safety is everyone's responsibility but production issues are none of their business. Production is a management responsibility. Plans, budgets, and other management concerns are very definitely not part of the committee's job. Most of what's said at these meetings isn't worth listening to."

The union is also dissatisfied with the functioning of the safety committee. Ivan, the chief union steward who also serves on the committee, observes: "If the safety committee wasn't mandatory by law, management wouldn't even pretend to listen to us. We put forward our safety concerns but management says that we are mixing safety in with workload and production issues. They only want to talk about what they think are safety issues–like serious accidents. Thankfully, we don't have too many of those! But safety is more than just avoiding major accidents. We get far too many 'little accidents' and 'near-accidents' here. At least that's what management calls them. They just want us to work faster and faster. We complain and complain at the meetings but they just say 'that's a production issue and this is a safety committee.' They accuse us of trying to run the company when we ask for better equipment. They say we don't understand things like costs and limited budgets. We don't care about their budgets, we've got work issues to talk about and we'll keep speaking out for the crew no matter what. That's what the union is for."

Big Bad John, one of the mill's toughest and most experienced supervisors, describes his job as follows: "The job of supervisor is to keep a close watch on every move the crew makes. If I look away for a second, some guy is going to be doing something wrong–either with the equipment or with the logs. They're always making mistakes. Lots of mistakes! Some of these guys are just plain dumb. And lazy, too! Any chance they can get to steal some company time, they take. They start work late, they take long lunch breaks, they talk too much during their shifts. A minute here, a minute there–it all adds up. The younger guys are the worst. They always want to talk back to me, they can't follow my orders like most of the older guys can. Lousy attitude, that's what they've got."

Vic, the youngest union steward, gives his view of labor-management relations: "The supervisors and the managers, they know it all. They think they're so smart. They treat the guys on the crew like children. Almost everyone on the crew has a high school education. Some even have college backgrounds. Most are raising families. We're not stupid! Sure, some guys come in late and miss a day of work now and then. Who can blame them? The pace of work is exhausting. How can you do a good job when you're tired and rushing all the time?" He adds: "Of course, we're not perfect. We make mistakes just like everyone else does. But nobody ever explains anything to the crew members. The supervisors just watch everyone like hawks and jump all over them, criticize them, and make them feel stupid when they use a piece of equipment the wrong way. We're always so rushed and busy here that the senior crew members don't have much time to explain things to the newer workers, the younger guys. Also, the equipment could be in better shape, that would help."

The production manager, Des, observes that "the union just doesn't understand–or even care about–the connection between the poor work ethic, the poor attitude on the part of the crew members here, and the mill's mediocre productivity and product quality. The union and the crew only take their very narrow 'employee-view' of how things are done around here. They don't understand the bigger picture. Well, it's very competitive out there. They don't understand what tight budgets, increasing costs, declining quality, missed production targets, and complaining customers mean to a business. They just sit back and complain about our management style. What they don't realize is that their attitude makes our management style necessary. Complaining is easy, no responsibility is needed. Managing, on the other hand, is challenging. And it's especially tough to control and manage this particular crew. We've currently got 30 unresolved grievances–that's a lot of formal complaints for a mill of our size. Some of the union stewards actually go out among the crew and look for grievances just because they're mad they can't run the mill the way they want to. Sometimes I think the stewards want to create grievances where no real problems exist. They want to create headaches for those of us in management."

The president of the company has recently informed Digby, the mill's new general manager (he started at Jackson last month after a career in eastern Canada), of the decision she will soon have to make regarding the mill's future. She told Digby that significant improvements in mill productivity and product quality are required if the mill is to receive the $50 million investment in new plant and equipment. Without such improvements, the mill would be downsized and over half of the workforce would be permanently laid off. Half the supervisory and managerial personnel would also lose their jobs.

Digby has just telephoned Moe (the president of the local union who does not work at the mill but who is very familiar with developments at the mill) to tell him about the message from the company president. Upon hearing of the potential job losses, Moe was troubled and asked to meet with Digby to discuss the situation. However, Moe was also somewhat skeptical because the previous general manager once told him that some permanent layoffs would occur unless productivity was improved. No layoffs subsequently occurred. Therefore, Moe is uncertain if the company is serious about these potential future layoffs or merely bluffing in order to get the employees to work harder.

CASE 11: PERFECT PIZZERIA

John E. Dittrich and Robert A. Zawacki

Perfect Pizzeria in Southville, deep in southern Illinois, is the chain's second-largest franchise. The headquarters is located in Phoenix, Arizona. Although the business is prospering, it has employee and managerial problems.

Each operation has one manager, an assistant manager, and from two to five night managers. The managers of each pizzeria work under an area supervisor. There are no systematic criteria for being a manager or becoming a manager trainee. The franchise has no formalized training period for the manager. No college education is required. The managers for whom the case observer worked during a four-year period were relatively young (ages 24 to 27), and only one had completed college. They came from the ranks of night managers, assistant managers, or both. The night managers were chosen for their ability to perform the duties of the regular employees. The assistant managers worked a two-hour shift during the luncheon period five days a week to gain knowledge about bookkeeping and management. Those becoming managers remained at that level unless they expressed interest in investing in the business.

The employees were mostly college students, with a few high school students performing the less challenging jobs. Because Perfect Pizzeria was located in an area with few job opportunities, it was relatively easy for it to fill its employee quotas. All the employees, with the exception of the manager, were employed part-time. Consequently, they earned only the minimum wage.

The Perfect Pizzeria system is devised so that food and beverage costs and profits are set up according to a percentage. If the percentage of food unsold or damaged in any way is very low, the manager gets a bonus. If the percentage is high, the manager does not receive a bonus; rather, he or she receives only his or her normal salary.

There are many ways in which the percentage can fluctuate. Because the manager cannot be in the store 24 hours a day, some employees make up for their paychecks by helping themselves to the food. When a friend comes in to order a pizza, extra ingredients are put on the friend's pizza. Occasional nibbles by 18 to 20 employees throughout the day at the meal table also raise the percentage figure. An occasional bucket of sauce may be spilled or a pizza accidentally burned. Sometimes the wrong-size pizza may be made.

In the event of an employee mistake or a burned pizza by the oven person, the expense is supposed to come from the individual. Because of peer pressure, the night manager seldom writes up a bill for the erring employee. Instead, the establishment takes the loss, and the error goes unnoticed until the end of the month when the inventory is taken. That's when the manager finds out that the percentage is high and that there will be no bonus.

In the present instance, the manager took retaliatory measures. Previously, each employee was entitled to a free pizza, salad, and all the soft drinks he or she could drink for every six hours of work. The manager raised this figure from six to twelve hours of work. However, the employees had received these six-hour benefits for a long time. Therefore, they simply took advantage of the situation whenever the manager or the assistant was not in the building. Although the night managers theoretically had complete control of the operation in the evenings, they did not command the respect that the manager or assistant manager did. That was because night managers received the same pay as the regular employees, could not reprimand other employees, and were basically the same age or sometimes even younger than the other employees.

Thus, apathy grew within the pizzeria. There seemed to be a further separation between the manager and his workers, who started out to be a closely knit group. The manager made no attempt to alleviate the problem, because he felt it would iron itself out. Either the employees who were dissatisfied would quit or they would be content to put up with the new regulations. As it turned out, there was a rash of employee dismissals. The manager had no problem in filling the vacancies with new workers, but the loss of key personnel was costly to the business.

With the large turnover, the manager found he had to spend more time in the building, supervising and sometimes taking the place of inexperienced workers. This was in direct violation of the franchise regulation, which stated that a manager would act as a supervisor and at no time take part in the actual food preparation. Employees were not placed under strict supervision with the manager working alongside them. The operation no longer worked smoothly because of differences between the remaining experienced workers and the manager concerning the way in which a particular function should be performed.

Within a two-month period, the manager was again free to go back to his office and leave his subordinates in charge of the entire operation. During this two-month period, in spite of the differences between experienced workers and the manager, the unsold/damaged food percentage returned to the previous low level and the manager received a bonus each month. The manager felt that his problems had been resolved and that conditions would remain the same, since the new personnel had been properly trained.

It didn't take long for the new employees to become influenced by the other employees. Immediately after the manager returned to his supervisory role, the unsold/damaged food percentage began to rise. This time the manager took a bolder step. He cut out *any* benefits that the employees had–no free pizzas, salads, or drinks. With the job market at an even lower ebb than usual, most employees were forced to stay. The appointment of a new area supervisor made it impossible for the manager to work behind the counter, because the supervisor was centrally located in Southville.

The manager tried still another approach to alleviate the rising unsold/damaged food percentage problem and maintain his bonus. He placed a notice on the bulletin board, stating that if the percentage remained at a high level, a lie detector test would be given to all employees. All those found guilty of taking or purposefully wasting food or drinks would be immediately terminated. This did not have the desired effect on the employees, because they knew if they were all subjected to the test, all would be found guilty and the manager would have to dismiss all of them. This would leave him in a worse situation than ever.

Even before the following month's unsold/damaged food percentage was calculated, the manager knew it would be high. He had evidently received information from one of the night managers about the employees' feelings toward the notice. What he did not expect was that the percentage would reach an all-time high. That is the state of affairs at the present time.

Source: John E. Dittrich and Robert A. Zawacki, ***People and Organizations*** (Plano, TX: Business Publications, 1981), pp. 126–128. Used by permission of McGraw-Hill/Irwin.

CASE 12: SIMMONS LABORATORIES

Adapted by William Starbuck from a case written by Alex Bavelas

Brandon Newbridge was sitting alone in the conference room of the laboratory. The rest of the group had gone. One of the secretaries had stopped and talked for a while about her husband's coming enrollment in graduate school, then went home. Brandon, alone in the laboratory, slid a little farther down in his chair, looking with satisfaction at the results of the first test run of the new photon unit.

He liked to stay after the others had gone. His appointment as project head was still new enough to give him a deep sense of pleasure. His eyes were on the graphs before him, but in his mind he could hear Dr. William Goh, the project head, saying again, "There's one thing about this place you can bank on. The sky is the limit for anyone who can produce!" Newbridge felt again the tingle of happiness and embarrassment. Well, dammit, he said to himself, he had produced. He wasn't kidding anybody. He had come to Simmons Laboratories two years ago. During a routine testing of some rejected Clanson components, he had stumbled on the idea of the photon correlator, and the rest just happened. Goh had been enthusiastic: A separate project had been set up for further research and development of the device, and Newbridge had gotten the job of running it. The whole sequence of events still seemed a little miraculous to him.

He shrugged out of the reverie and bent determinedly over the sheets when he heard someone come into the room behind him. He looked up expectantly; Goh often stayed late himself and now and then dropped in for a chat. This always made the day's end especially pleasant for Newbridge. It wasn't Goh. The man who had come in was a stranger. He was tall and thin. He wore steel-rimmed glasses and had a very wide leather belt with a large brass buckle. Lucy remarked later that it was the kind of belt the Pilgrims must have worn.

The stranger smiled and introduced himself. "I'm Lester Zapf. Are you Brandon Newbridge?" Newbridge said yes, and they shook hands. "Doctor Goh said I might find you in. We were talking about your work, and I'm very much interested in what you are doing." Newbridge waved to a chair.

Zapf didn't seem to belong in any of the standard categories of visitors: customer, visiting fireman, stockholder. Newbridge pointed to the sheets on the table. "There are the preliminary results of a test we're running. We have a new gadget by the tail, and we're trying to understand it. It's not finished, but I can show you the section we're testing."

He stood up, but Zapf was deep in the graphs. After a moment, Zapf looked up with an odd grin. "These look like plots of a Jennings surface. I've been playing around with some autocorrelation functions of surfaces–you know that stuff." Newbridge, who had no idea what he was referring to, grinned back and nodded, and immediately felt uncomfortable. "Let me show you the monster," he said, and he led the way to the workroom.

After Zapf left, Newbridge slowly put the graphs away, feeling vaguely annoyed. Then, as if he had made a decision, he quickly locked up and took the long way out so that he would pass Goh's office. But the office was locked. Newbridge wondered whether Goh and Zapf had left together.

The next morning, Newbridge dropped into Goh's office, mentioned that he had talked with Zapf, and asked who he was.

"Sit down for a minute," Goh said. "I want to talk to you about him. What do you think of him?" Newbridge replied truthfully that he thought Zapf was very bright and probably very competent. Goh looked pleased.

"We're taking him on," he said. "He's had a very good background in a number of laboratories, and he seems to have ideas about the problems we're tackling here." Newbridge nodded in agreement, instantly wishing that Zapf would not be placed with him.

"I don't know yet where he will finally land," Goh continued, "but he seems interested in what you are doing. I thought he might spend a little time with you by way of getting started." Newbridge nodded thoughtfully. "If his interest in your work continues, you can add him to your group."

"Well, he seemed to have some good ideas even without knowing exactly what we are doing," Newbridge answered. "I hope he stays; we'd be glad to have him."

Newbridge walked back to the lab with mixed feelings. He told himself that Zapf would be good for the group. He was no dunce; he'd produce. Newbridge thought again of Goh's promise when he had promoted him: "The man who produces gets ahead in this outfit." The words seemed to carry the overtones of a threat now.

That day Zapf didn't appear until midafternoon. He explained that he had had a long lunch with Goh, discussing his place in the lab. "Yes," said Newbridge, "I talked with Jerry this morning about it, and we both thought you might work with us for a while."

Zapf smiled in the same knowing way that he had smiled when he mentioned the Jennings surfaces. "I'd like to," he said.

Newbridge introduced Zapf to the other members of the lab. Zapf and Link, the group's mathematician, hit it off well and spent the rest of the afternoon discussing a method for analyzing patterns that Link had been worrying about over the last month.

It was 6:30 when Newbridge finally left the lab that night. He had waited almost eagerly for the end of the day to come–when they would all be gone and he could sit in the quiet rooms, relax, and think it over. "Think what over?" he asked himself. He didn't know. Shortly after 5 p.m., they had almost all gone except Zapf, and what followed was almost a duel. Newbridge was annoyed that he was being cheated out of his quiet period and finally resentfully determined that Zapf should leave first.

Zapf was sitting at the conference table reading, and Newbridge was sitting at his desk in the little glass-enclosed cubby he used during the day when he needed to be undisturbed. Zapf had gotten the last year's progress reports out and was studying them carefully. The time dragged. Newbridge doodled on a pad, the tension growing inside him. What the hell did Zapf think he was going to find in the reports?

Newbridge finally gave up, and they left the lab together. Zapf took several of the reports with him to study in the evening. Newbridge asked him if he thought the reports gave a clear picture of the lab's activities.

"They're excellent," Zapf answered with obvious sincerity. "They're not only good reports; what they report is damn good, too!" Newbridge was surprised at the relief he felt and grew almost jovial as he said good-night.

Driving home, Newbridge felt more optimistic about Zapf's presence in the lab. He had never fully understood the analysis that Link was attempting. If there was anything wrong with Link's approach, Zapf would probably spot it. "And if I'm any judge," he murmured, "he won't be especially diplomatic about it."

He described Zapf to his wife, who was amused by the broad leather belt and brass buckle.

"It's the kind of belt that Pilgrims must have worn," she laughed.

"I'm not worried about how he holds his pants up," he laughed with her. "I'm afraid that he's the kind that just has to make like a genius twice each day. And that can be pretty rough on the group."

Newbridge had been asleep for several hours when he was jerked awake by the telephone. He realized it had rung several times. He swung off the bed muttering about damn fools and telephones. It was Zapf. Without any excuses, apparently oblivious of the time, he plunged into an excited recital of how Link's patterning problem could be solved.

Newbridge covered the mouthpiece to answer his wife's stage-whispered "Who is it?" "It's the genius," replied Newbridge.

Zapf, completely ignoring the fact that it was two in the morning, went on in a very excited way, starting in the middle of an explanation of a completely new approach to some of the photon lab problems that he had stumbled on while analyzing past experiments. Newbridge managed to put some enthusiasm in his own voice and stood there, half-dazed and very uncomfortable, listening to Zapf talk endlessly about what he had discovered. It was probably not only a new approach but also an analysis that showed the inherent weakness of the previous experiment and how experimentation along that line would certainly have been inconclusive. The following day Newbridge spent the entire morning with Zapf and Link, the mathematician, the customary morning meeting of Newbridge's group having been called off so that Zapf's work of the previous night could be gone over intensively. Zapf was very anxious that this be done, and Newbridge was not too unhappy to call the meeting off for reasons of his own.

For the next several days Zapf sat in the back office that had been turned over to him and did nothing but read the progress reports of the work that had been done in the last six months. Newbridge caught himself feeling apprehensive about the reaction that Zapf might have to some of his work. He was a little surprised at his own feelings. He had always been proud–although he had put on a convincingly modest face–of the way in which new ground in the study of photon measuring devices had been broken in his group. Now he wasn't sure, and it seemed to him that Zapf might easily show that the line of research they had been following was unsound or even unimaginative.

The next morning (as was the custom) the members of the lab, including the secretaries, sat around a conference table. Newbridge always prided himself on the fact that the work of the lab was guided and evaluated by the group as a whole, and he was fond of repeating that it was not a waste of time to include secretaries in such meetings. Often, what started out as a boring recital of fundamental assumptions to a naive listener uncovered new ways of regarding these assumptions that would not have occurred to the researcher, who had long ago accepted them as a necessary basis for his work.

These group meetings also served Brandon in another sense. He admitted to himself that he would have felt far less secure if he had had to direct the work out of his own mind, so to speak. With the group meeting as the principle of leadership, it was always possible to justify the exploration of blind alleys because of the general educative effect on the team. Zapf was there; Lucy and Martha were there; Link was sitting next to Zapf, their conversation concerning Link's mathematical study apparently continuing from yesterday. The other members, Bob Davenport, Georgia Thurlow, and Arthur Oliver, were waiting quietly.

Newbridge, for reasons that he didn't quite understand, proposed for discussion this morning a problem that all of them had spent a great deal of time on previously, with the conclusion that a solution was impossible–there was no feasible way of treating the problem in an experimental fashion. When Newbridge proposed the problem, Davenport remarked that there was hardly any use of going over it again and that he was satisfied that there was no way of approaching the problem with the equipment and the physical capacities of the lab.

This statement had the effect of a shot of adrenaline on Zapf. He said he would like to know what the problem was in detail. Walking to the blackboard, he began writing down the "factors" as various members of the group began discussing the problem and simultaneously listing the reasons why it had been abandoned.

Very early in the description of the problem it was evident that Zapf was going to disagree about the impossibility of attacking it. The group realized this, and finally the descriptive materials and their recounting of the reasoning that had led to its abandonment dwindled away. Zapf began his statement, which, as it proceeded, might well have been prepared the previous night, although Newbridge knew this was impossible. He couldn't help being impressed with the organized and logical way that Zapf was presenting ideas that must have occurred to him only a few minutes before.

Zapf had some things to say, however, that left Newbridge with a mixture of annoyance and irritation and, at the same time, a rather smug feeling of superiority over Zapf in at least one area. Zapf held the opinion that the way that the problem had been analyzed was very typical of group thinking. With an air of sophistication that made it difficult for a listener to dissent, he proceeded to comment on the American emphasis on team ideas, satirically describing the ways in which they led to a "high level of mediocrity."

During this time Newbridge observed that Link stared studiously at the floor, and he was very conscious of Thurlow's and Davenport's glances toward him at several points of Zapf's little speech. Inwardly, Newbridge couldn't help feeling that this was one point at least in which Zapf was off on the wrong foot. The whole lab, following Goh's lead, talked, if not practiced, the theory of small research teams as the basic organization for effective research. Zapf insisted that the problem could be approached and that he would like to study it for a while himself.

Newbridge ended the morning session by remarking that the meetings would continue and that the very fact that a supposedly insoluble experimental problem was now going to get another chance was another indication of the value of such meetings. Zapf immediately remarked that he was not at all averse to meetings to inform the group about the progress of its members. The point he wanted to make was that creative advances were seldom accomplished in such meetings–they were made by an individual "living with" a problem closely and continuously, in a rather personal relationship with it.

Newbridge went on to say to Zapf that he was very glad that Zapf had raised these points and that he was sure the group would profit by reexamining the basis on which they had been operating. Newbridge agreed that individual effort was probably the basis for making major advances. He considered the group meetings useful primarily because they kept the group together and they helped the weaker members of the group keep up with the ones who were able to advance more easily and quickly in the analysis of problems.

It was clear as days went by and meetings continued that Zapf came to enjoy them because of the pattern that the meetings assumed. It became typical for Zapf to hold forth, and it was unquestionably clear that he was more brilliant, better prepared on the various subjects that were germane to the problem being studied, and more capable of going ahead than anyone else there. Newbridge grew increasingly disturbed as he realized that his leadership of the group had been, in fact, taken over.

Whenever the subject of Zapf was mentioned in occasional meetings with Goh, Newbridge would comment only on the ability and obvious capacity for work that Zapf had. Somehow he never felt that he could mention his own discomforts, not only because they revealed a weakness on his part but also because it was quite clear that Goh himself was considerably impressed with Zapf's work and with the contacts he had with him outside the photon laboratory.

Newbridge now began to feel that perhaps the intellectual advantages that Zapf had brought to the group did not quite compensate for what he felt were evidences of a breakdown in the cooperative spirit he had seen in the group before Zapf's arrival. More and more of the morning meetings were skipped. Zapf's opinion concerning the abilities of others in the group, except for Link, was obviously low. At times during morning meetings or in smaller discussions he had been on the point of rudeness, refusing to pursue an argument when he claimed it was based on another person's ignorance of the facts involved. His impatience with others led him to also make similar remarks to Goh. Newbridge inferred this from a conversation with Goh in which Goh asked whether Davenport and Oliver were going to be kept on; his failure to mention Link, the mathematician, led Newbridge to feel that this was the result of private conversations between Zapf and Goh.

It was not difficult for Newbridge to make quite a convincing case of whether the brilliance of Zapf was sufficient recompense for the beginning of this breaking up of the group. He spoke privately with Davenport and with Oliver, and it was quite clear that both of them were uncomfortable because of Zapf. Newbridge didn't press the discussion beyond the point of hearing them say that they did feel awkward and that it was sometimes difficult to understand the arguments Zapf advanced but often embarrassing to ask him to fill in the basis for his arguments. Newbridge did not interview Link in this manner.

About six months after Zapf had joined the photon lab, a meeting was scheduled in which the sponsors of the research were visiting to get some idea of the work and its progress. It was customary at these meetings for project heads to present the research being conducted in their groups. The members of each group were invited to other meetings that were held later in the day and open to all, but the special meetings were usually made up only of project heads, the head of the laboratory, and the sponsors.

As the time for the special meeting approached, it seemed to Newbridge that he must avoid the presentation at all costs. His reasons for this were that he could not trust himself to present the ideas and work that Zapf had advanced because of his apprehension about whether he could present them in sufficient detail and answer such questions about them as might be asked. On the other hand, he did not feel he could ignore these newer lines of work and present only the material that he had done or that had been started before Zapf's arrival. He felt also that it would not be beyond Zapf at all, in his blunt and undiplomatic way–if he were at the meeting, that is–to comment on his [Newbridge's] presentation and reveal Newbridge's inadequacy. It also seemed quite clear that it would not be easy to keep Zapf from attending the meeting, even though he was not on the administrative level of those invited.

Newbridge found an opportunity to speak to Goh and raised the question. He told Goh that, with the meetings coming up and with the interest in the work and with Zapf's contributions to the work, Zapf would probably like to come to the meetings but there was a question of how the others in the group would feel if only Zapf were invited. Goh passed this over very lightly by saying that he didn't think the group would fail to understand Zapf's rather different position and that Zapf certainly should be invited. Newbridge immediately said he agreed: Zapf should present the work because much of it was work he had done, and this would be a nice way to recognize Zapf's contributions and to reward him, because he was eager to be recognized as a productive member of the lab. Goh agreed, and so the matter was decided.

Zapf's presentation was very successful and in some ways dominated the meeting. He attracted the interest and attention of many of those who had come, and a long discussion followed his presentation. Later in the evening–with the entire laboratory staff present–in the cocktail period before the dinner, a little circle of people formed around Zapf. One of them was Goh himself, and a lively discussion took place concerning the application of Zapf's theory. All of this disturbed Newbridge, but his reaction and behavior were characteristic. He joined the circle, praised Zapf to Goh and to others, and remarked on the brilliance of the work.

Newbridge, without consulting anyone, began at this time to take some interest in the possibility of a job elsewhere. After a few weeks he found that a new laboratory of considerable size was being organized in a nearby city and that the kind of training he had would enable him to get a project-head job equivalent to the one he had at the lab with slightly more money.

He immediately accepted it and notified Goh by letter, which he mailed on a Friday night to Goh's home. The letter was quite brief, and Goh was stunned. The letter merely said that he had found a better position, that he didn't want to appear at the lab any more for personal reasons, that he would be glad to come back at a later time to assist if there was any mix-up in the past work, that he felt sure Zapf could supply any leadership that the group required, and that his decision to leave so suddenly was based on personal problems–he hinted at problems of health in his family, his mother and father. All of this was fictitious, of course. Goh took it at face value but still felt that this was very strange behavior and quite unaccountable, for he had always felt his relationship with Newbridge had been warm and that Newbridge was satisfied and, in fact, quite happy and productive.

Goh was considerably disturbed, because he had already decided to place Zapf in charge of another project that was going to be set up very soon. He had been wondering how to explain this to Newbridge, in view of the obvious help Newbridge was getting from Zapf and the high regard in which he held him. Goh had, indeed, considered the possibility that Newbridge could add to his staff another person with the kind of background and training that had been unique in Zapf and had proved so valuable.

Goh did not make any attempt to meet Newbridge. In a way, he felt aggrieved about the whole thing. Zapf, too, was surprised at the suddenness of Newbridge's departure. When Goh asked Zapf whether he preferred to stay with the photon group instead of heading the new project for the Air Force, Zapf chose the Air Force project and went on to that job the following week. The photon lab was hard hit. The leadership of the lab was given to Link with the understanding that this would be temporary until someone could come in to take over.

Source: Adaptation of Bob Knowlton case written by Alex Baveals, revised in 2000 by William Starbuck. Reprinted with permission of William Starbuck.

CASE 13: TREETOP FOREST PRODUCTS

Steven L. McShane, University of Western Australia, and David Lebeter

Treetop Forest Products, Inc. is a sawmill operation in Oregon that is owned by a major forest products company but operates independently of headquarters. It was built 30 years ago and completely updated with new machinery five years ago. Treetop receives raw logs from the area for cutting and planing into building-grade lumber, mostly 2-by-4 and 2-by-6 pieces of standard lengths. Higher-grade logs leave Treetop's sawmill department in finished form and are sent directly to the packaging department. The remaining 40 percent of sawmill output consists of cuts from lower-grade logs, requiring further work by the planing department.

Treetop has 1 general manager, 16 supervisors and support staff, and 180 unionized employees. The unionized employees are paid an hourly rate specified in the collective agreement, whereas management and support staff are paid a monthly salary. The mill is divided into six operating departments: boom, sawmill, planer, packaging, shipping, and maintenance. The sawmill, boom, and packaging departments operate a morning shift starting at 6 a.m. and an afternoon shift starting at 2 p.m. Employees in these departments rotate shifts every two weeks. The planer and shipping departments operate only morning shifts. Maintenance employees work the night shift (starting at 10 p.m.).

Each department, except for packaging, has a supervisor on every work shift. The planer supervisor is responsible for the packaging department on the morning shift, and the sawmill supervisor is responsible for the packaging department on the afternoon shift. However, the packaging operation is housed in a separate building from the other departments, so supervisors seldom visit the packaging department. This is particularly true for the afternoon shift because the sawmill supervisor is the farthest distance from the packaging building.

Packaging Quality

Ninety percent of Treetop's product is sold on the open market through Westboard Co., a large marketing agency. Westboard represents all forest products mills owned by Treetop's parent company, as well as several other clients in the region. The market for building-grade lumber is very price-competitive because there are numerous mills selling a relatively undifferentiated product. However, some differentiation does occur in product packaging and presentation. Buyers will look closely at the packaging when deciding whether to buy from Treetop or another mill.

To encourage its clients to package their products better, Westboard sponsors a monthly package quality award. The marketing agency samples and rates its clients' packages daily, and the sawmill with the highest score at the end of the month is awarded a plaque. Package quality is a combination of how the lumber is piled (e.g., defects turned in), where the bands and dunnage are placed, how neatly the stencil and seal are applied, the stencil's accuracy, and how neatly and tightly the plastic wrap is attached.

Treetop Forest Products won Westboard's package quality award several times over the past five years and received high ratings in the months that it didn't win. However, the mill's ratings have started to decline over the past year or two, and several clients have complained about the appearance of the finished product. A few large customers switched to competitors' lumber, saying that the decision was based on the substandard appearance of Treetop's packaging when it arrived in their lumberyard.

Bottleneck in Packaging

The planing and sawmilling departments have significantly increased productivity over the past couple of years. The sawmill operation recently set a new productivity record on a single day. The planer operation has increased productivity to the point where last year it reduced operations to just one (rather than two) shift per day. These productivity improvements are due to better operator training, fewer machine breakdowns, and better selection of raw logs. (Sawmill cuts from high-quality logs usually do not require planing work.)

Productivity levels in the boom, shipping, and maintenance departments have remained constant. However, the packaging department has recorded decreasing productivity over the past couple of years, with the result that a large backlog of finished product is typically stockpiled outside the packaging building. The morning shift of the packaging department is unable to keep up with the combined production of the sawmill and planer departments, so the unpackaged output is left for the afternoon shift. Unfortunately, the afternoon shift packages even less product than the morning shift, so the backlog continues to build. The backlog adds to Treetop's inventory costs and increases the risk of damaged stock.

Treetop has added Saturday overtime shifts as well as extra hours before and after the regular shifts for the packaging department employees to process this backlog. Last month, the packaging department employed 10 percent of the workforce but accounted for 85 percent of the overtime. This is frustrating to Treetop's management because time-and-motion studies recently confirmed that the packaging department is capable of processing all of the daily sawmill and planer production without overtime. Moreover, with employees earning one and a half or two times their regular pay on overtime, Treetop's cost competitiveness suffers.

Employees and supervisors at Treetop are aware that people in the packaging department tend to extend lunch by 10 minutes and coffee breaks by 5 minutes. They also typically leave work a few minutes before the end of the shift. This abuse has worsened recently, particularly on the afternoon shift. Employees who are temporarily assigned to the packaging department also seem to participate in this time-loss pattern after a few days. Although they are punctual and productive in other departments, these temporary employees soon adopt the packaging crew's informal schedule when assigned to that department.

CASE 14: KV KAMATH: A VISIONARY LEADER IN THE BANKING SECTOR

Dr. Radha R. Sharma & Phillip Abraham, Management Development Institute, India

K V Kamath has become the synonym of modern banking in India. Kamath, CEO, ICICI Bank is credited with driving not only ICICI Bank's growth, but also that of the entire financial services sector in the country. With the reverse merger of ICICI to ICICI Bank, he transformed ICICI from an industrial project finance institution into India's most comprehensive financial services powerhouse with interests in retail banking, insurance, online trading and BPO among others, thus transforming the face of Indian Banking Industry. Today, ICICI Bank is one of the largest private sector banks in India. At a time when banking was synonymous with the physical banking approach of public sector banks, Kamath took the banking services to the next level as he introduced the ATM mode of banking and internet banking that was duplicated by all other banks in India.[1]

K V Kamath

Kamath born on December 2, 1947, spent his early years in Mangalore, Karnataka. After completing higher secondary and pre-university education from St. Aloysius, he joined the Karnataka Regional Educational College (KREC) for a Bachelor's degree in Mechanical Engineering. After graduating from there in 1969, he joined Indian Institute of Management, Ahmedabad (IIM-A) for a Master's Degree in Business Administration. That was the time when ICICI, born with a mandate initiated by World Bank, was in a phase of revamp and hired a batch of young graduates. Thus Kamath started his career with ICICI in the Project Finance Division.

To enrich his career, Kamath moved on to different departments to acquire varied experiences which included setting up of new businesses such as leasing, venture capital, credit rating as well as handling general management positions. As part of his general management responsibilities he initiated and implemented ICICI's computerization programme. In 1988, Kamath joined the Asian Development Bank, Manila in their Private Sector Department. His principal work experience at ADB was in various projects in China, India, Indonesia, Philippines, Bangladesh and Vietnam. He was the ADB representative on the boards of several companies and this experience offered him considerable insight into the working of global firms. During his years in South East Asia, Kamath worked in most of the developing countries in the region including China, Thailand, Philippines, Indonesia and Vietnam, and this provided a rich experience in terms of exposure to a variety of business situations, many of them typical to emerging markets.

The Second Innings

Kamath's second innings with ICICI commenced in 1996 with his appointment as Managing Director and Chief Executive Officer. Around the same time India had started experiencing the preliminary effects of liberalization initiated during 1991. ICICI started its banking subsidiary, ICICI Banking Corporation, which was later renamed ICICI Bank Ltd. Under Kamath, growth of ICICI has been phenomenal and it has written new sagas in the history of Indian banking industry by growing leaps and bounds from 1996 to 2008. ICICI bank is the largest private sector bank in India in market capitalization and second largest overall in terms of assets. This is not merely a story of growth of an Indian Corporate; it is also an illustration of clearly envisaged leadership strategy.

Were it not for Kamath's ability to think the unthinkable, ICICI might have continued to languish as a development finance institution. But his second inning has been creating waves in the financial sector in a big way, whether it was insurance, retail lending, internet banking, online trading, business process outsourcing or commodities trading. Thus, he has been a leader who could identify and ride the next big wave. He will be remembered for introducing the ATM culture in India and more importantly, for his vision to anticipate the death of the stand-alone term 'lending institution'[2]. He charted a course for ICICI Bank in a new business zone and created the country's second largest private bank with assets of over Rs. 100,000 crore, thus demonstrating value creation for the group and its stakeholders.[2]

Kamath, after taking over the reins of ICICI Bank had a clear vision and mission right from the beginning. He had envisioned targeting the Indian Middle class with a slew of convenience friendly banking strategies that would create a new level for services in banking thus creating a niche for ICICI Bank in the minds of the consumers. The visionary banker saw an encashable opportunity in the retail banking space. ICICI's strategy and product offering recognized the changing demands of a growing middle-class.

Talent Management

It was on top of Kamath's mind to enable the bank to surge ahead and capture vital market share. He needed to create leaders within the organization who could foresee the opportunities ahead of others.

As Kamath puts it "To build a successful business, you have to be able to pick entrepreneurs very early and get them embedded into the business. They need to go out into the ecosystem, demonstrate their abilities, nurture the business and build it up. We have succeeded in doing this." Thus, he has had belief in his people with raw intellect and entrepreneurial capability.[3] This belief led to two processes being institutionalized in ICICI—the bank's phenomenal talent screening process and its courage to bet on young and bright executives much ahead in their careers. Thus, a strong system was put in place to spot and groom more leaders.

It was ICICI which pioneered in recognizing female talent. As Kamath puts in "women leaders are also taken on board based on the intellect, ability and entrepreneurial skills to lead teams." Three of the five members of the bank's Executive Board are women. As a CEO he has been picking up leaders with ability, intellect and the entrepreneurial ability to lead teams and he values women's "ability to think in a much more detached manner than men." 13 of its 40 top managers are female employees. According to Kamath "Almost all the leaders we have picked have succeeded and most have been women". These women defined the odds and adopted an aggressive, risk taking attitude to make ICCI Bank India's most diversified and customer oriented bank.

Women find ICICI culture very conducive, free from gender bias, which encourages women employees by allowing flexible timings, and protection of position and seniority upon availing maternity leave, etc.

The bank has institutionalized a talent screening process to deal with its bulging size. With the numbers of employees rising and bank expanding to various national and international markets, a talent screening process had to be put in place. The process involves creating a list of talent which is empanelled as leadership talent. Talent is then categorized and they would have the first strike at the new roles. To be recognized as a leadership talent, one needs to be a performer. In this way bank has created a pool of 2000 people out of 15000 odd people at a point of time. "The assumption is that unless you are a performer, you won't have credibility as a leader," said Ram Kumar, Head, Human Resources at ICICI.

This is all about leading people in the right way. The ICICI Style of grooming leaders includes taking very deliberate and calculated decisions—training people to take challenges, pressures and risks, accepting failures as a part of the process, building a holistic perspective and expanding horizons of employees, and accountability and high performance appraisal.

Today, the bank is strongly positioned across the spectrum of banking products—from top end wealth management business to micro finance. The 1000 odd branches of ICICI bank have accelerated customer acquisition and deliver products to cater to every segment of the society. ICICI's future strategy is two-fold and organic. First, it needs to capitalize on the globalization of Indian economy by setting up global network; second, it requires to widen its geographical spread by increasing the numbers of branches and to reach out to the rural market. But, the question arises regarding the time till which ICICI will overlook inorganic growth, considering its enormous size and the size of group companies of various kinds.

This case has been prepared by Professor (Dr) Radha R Sharma and Abraham Phillip, a student of 15-month full-time management program at Management Development Institute, India, as the basis for class discussion rather than to illustrate either effective or ineffective handling of an administrative situation.

References

1. Courtesy *The Economic Times*, http://www.123oye.com/google-news/hot-ceo/icici.htm
2. Business Leader of the year: K V Kamath. 4 Oct, 2007, http://economictimes.indiatimes.com/articleshow/2429981.cms
3. ICICI's K.V. Kamath Shapes a Business Plan in Rural India's Uncertain Financial Terrain, Published: July 26, 2006 in Knowledge@Wharton

CASE 15: CORE VALUES IN ACTION—AMERICAN EXPRESS CASE STUDY FROM POLAND

Dr. Agata Stachowicz-Stanusch, The Silesian University of Technology, Faculty of Organization and Management, Poland

American Express (AmEx) is one of the best known and most admired companies in the world. It is known not only for its services and customer care but also for its exceptional working environment created through consistent implementation of the company's core values into everyday life. It was founded in 1850 by Henry Wells, William Fargo and John Butterfield. Currently, the company operates in more than 130 countries worldwide and employs over 58,300 staff.[1]

In the very beginning, the company developed without any visionary strategy and it was all the more a matter of fortune and came down to taking advantage of opportunities. Yet ever since it was founded, AmEx has operated within a set of certain principles, hard-and-fast rules that are binding to all company's employees. The rules have been slightly modified over the 150-year history, but most importantly, all company's activities have had to be conducted in accordance with these rules.

Originally, when AmEx was providing courier services, its founders arrived at a conclusion that a courier company could only be successful if it implemented such values as:

- Security
- Trust
- Vigilance
- Excellent service[2]

Since the company was founded in 1850, these values have been symbolized by a watchdog (usually depicted as a bulldog). All company materials featured the dog that was supposed to remind of what should be of utmost importance to American Express. These values were not just empty words but served as signposts to those working at AmEx.

In 1855, an incident occurred that went down in history—a shipment of 50 thousand gold coins was stolen. The perpetrators were caught but the coins were never retrieved. Their owner received the equivalent amount of money, even though it made a dent in the young company's budget. This occurrence was one of the foundations upon which American Express started to build its corporate image as a trustworthy company that was particular about the broadly defined security of its customers.[3] The current history of AmEx shows that it is a company with a character. From the darkest hours and days after 9/11 attacks, arose some of the finest moments in American Express' long history. The employees maintained their professional focus and exhibited an unwavering strength of character, despite the overwhelming human loss, physical destruction and emotional anguish that enveloped them. They proved without question that the values and attributes of American Express and its brand—including trust, compassion, teamwork, resilience and an unparalleled commitment to customer service—are far more real and enduring than bricks, mortar, glass or steel.[4]

In order to reflect the articulated values even better, AmEx President J.C. Fargo compiled a set of principles, regulations and instructions for employees. It included both technical rules of business conduct and employee-behavior patterns. It was a forerunner to the currently existing and binding AmEx Code of Conduct. The rules for equal treatment of customers went down in history. "Irrespective of whether they are rich or poor, man or woman or child, black or white, bringing big or small profit to the company—they must be treated politely and respectfully".[5]

On entering the financial and tourist services sector, the company slightly modified its key values. They now encompassed:

- Security
- Integrity
- Strength
- Protection
- Service

In 1951, they were also linked to a new symbol—a Roman centurion whose image appears on American Express travellers cheques and credit cards even today.

Today, the key values of American Express are known as the "American Express Blue Box Values". Blue Box is the present-day logo of American Express. The values were put down in 1990 by American Express Financial Advisors and taken up by the entire corporation.[6] The American Express Blue Box Values reflect the following creed:

"All our actions and decisions must be based on and guided by these values:

- Placing the interests of customers first;
- Constant pursuit of quality in everything we do;
- Treating our people with respect and dignity;
- Operating in a manner that reflects the highest standards of integrity;
- Teamwork—from the smallest unit to the enterprise in its entirety;
- Being good citizens in the communities in which we live and work.

By living these values, we provide our customers with remarkable service, hold a leadership position in our sector and deliver a satisfactory return to our shareholders."

AmEx has produced two documents to guide its employees in their everyday work, giving them a basis containing behavior patterns to look up to. The documents are the Code of Conduct and the Compliance Program. The Blue Box Values are obviously at the core of both documents*.

The Code of Conduct is one of the most important documents and a significant part of corporate culture and values. It sets forth the basic principles of business ethics and certain legal requirements applicable to all AmEx employees. The Code of Conduct does not apply to AmEx employees only; those who perform contract work for AmEx without being its employees are often required to adhere to it. Adherence to the Code of Conduct is a condition included in the employment contract or agreements. The Code of Conduct regulates issues including but not limited to:

- Behavior congruent with business ethics;
- Caring about employees' safety, health and working environment;
- Accepting and giving gifts;
- Protection of information about clients and company's employees;
- Intellectual property protection within the company, including patents and brand.

The Code of Conduct constitutes a basis for the Compliance Program which is yet another vital document that codifies the company's policy on important issues in detail. It addresses such problems as:

- Intellectual property and patent protection
- Media cooperation policy

*Information compiled based on interview with American Express Corporate Card Department employees in Poland

- Employee dispute resolution policy
- Anti-money laundering regulations

Each new employee becomes acquainted with and made aware of the company's values, Code of Conduct and Compliance Program by an HR officer before they start work. He or she also receives printed materials regarding these issues, while the managers must sign a special agreement on the acceptance of these documents. During the first six months of employment, a new employee undergoes dedicated training to understand the AmEx values, practices, conduct and policies even better.[7]

Due to the fact that there is no document which could describe all probable situations and also life is full of unpredictable occurrences, employees are also instructed on what to do in situations in which they are not certain about whether a particular action is in line with the core values, Code of Conduct or company policy (even though the Code of Conduct gives examples of actions and their compliance with the adopted principles). Employees can seek advice from their managers, the HR officer, the Compliance Officer (employed by each organizational unit within the company) or the Ombudsperson. The AmEx Ombudspersons constitute an independent, separate body (the Ombudspersons Office) whose task is to represent employees, resolve conflicts and ensure that the company's activities are in line with the key values, Code of Conduct or Compliance Program. The main characteristic of the ombudspersons' work is confidentiality. Any employee who turns to the Ombudsperson can be certain that all information revealed to them would be kept secret and confidential. The Ombudspersons have their own independent e-mail messaging system, independent phone lines and their offices are equipped with sound-proof rooms. They are also not exposed to pressure exerted by managers as they only report to the CEO. The budget allocated to their activity is also independent from the corporation's budget and the funds are paid out by an independent foundation established for this purpose. One might say they constitute the "second, independent authority within the corporation". Employees can turn to the ombudspersons with various problems they are unable to solve on their own or when they have noticed other employees acting against the principles adopted by the company. For example, an employee does not know if it is consistent with the company policy that his wife works for an AmEx vendor or an employee feels he or she is subject to discrimination in the internal promotion process or an employee has noticed or has been asked to do something that seems contrary to the company policy. If this is the case, the ombudsman can use a number of actions and powers, beginning with providing advice and ending with conducting "internal investigations".

Besides, there is a simple guide for employees who have to make a difficult decision regarding ethical issues. The employees know that in such a situation they should ask themselves several questions such as:

- Do I compromise my own value system in any way by making this decision?
- Do I wish that my action becomes a widely adopted practice within the corporation?
- How would I feel if my action were described on the first page of a local newspaper?
- Could the company lose customers or shareholders if they found out its employees had taken such a decision?
- Will I feel comfortable if I tell my spouse, parents or children about the decision I have made?

Another body to supervise the adopted policies and behavior patterns are the so-called Compliance Officers who operate in each business unit of the enterprise. They work with an aim to check the procedures, processes, practices, decisions, documentation, etc. for compliance with the values, behavior and policies approved by the company (meaning with the Blue Box Values, the Code of Conduct and the Compliance Program).

It is obvious that the existence of these units is to set limits to behavior that is contrary to corporate values, conduct standards or internal procedures. Should these be violated, disciplinary actions may be taken. Such actions may be taken against:

- Employees who have agreed to, directed, approved of or taken part in actions violating the regulations in force,
- Employees who have deliberately not informed, withheld or suppressed facts about a violation of the adopted rules,
- Employees who have taken retaliatory actions against those employees who disclosed unlawful activity,
- Managers who were aware of improper practices committed by their employees but did not react to such acts.

Before anyone gets punished, things need to go a long way toward clarifying all circumstances in order to obtain 100% certainty about the person's guilt (e.g. both the accused person's opinion and that of the supervisor are taken into account). As a general rule, there is no such thing as bad employees, there is only bad personnel management, and if an employee makes a mistake, it is usually a result of poor training.

To ensure the core values or the Code of Conduct are not infringed, AmEx tries to employ only such persons whose personal value system is in line with the corporate values. Therefore, one of the elements in employee recruitment consists in checking his or her suitability with regard to the company's core values and yet another one is training. This is how behavior that is contrary to the company policy is partly eliminated in advance.

On the other hand, there is a full range of awards and recognitions for those who act in line with the company's policy values. One award is called "Rings of Reward" and it is granted for outstanding service to the company.

The awards are granted in public during formal meetings or business unit gatherings. Beside awards, there is also an employee assessment system (yearly evaluation and period employee performance reviews) to analyze the employees' achievements, their approach to the obligatory values and behavior standards as well as the accomplishment of targets set. During the evaluation, the particular employee performs a self-assessment and his or her supervisor produces their own version; both versions are confronted and a commonly agreed evaluation is submitted for approval to the HR officer. The evaluation result serves as the basis for determining the annual bonus, salary increase or promotion.

American Express deeply believes that the way managers behave largely determines the way the employees behave. They are in a way a role model. Therefore, they expect a lot from their managers at American Express. By performing their functions, the managers must meet the highest standards of integrity in relationships with their employees, customers, vendors and the entire business environment. Hence, the managers must take seriously the corporation's requirement to act in line with the adopted rules. To help them achieve this goal, the managers receive the so-called Compliance Goals beside the standard business goals. Their task is to increase efficiency in the implementation of management through values and to reach the highest level of action adherence with the adopted rules, procedures and practices. If the compliance targets are not met, the business unit's efficiency and productivity are evaluated as poor, which further unfavorably affects the managers' bonus. A reverse situation will obviously have a positive impact on salaries and their premiums.

One of the most revered values is "treating our people with respect and dignity".[8] It is manifested through a number of actions, practices and procedures. The company has developed special programs to ensure equal treatment for employees, equal internal promotion opportunities, objective employee assessment, as well as to ensure better preventive measures for health and safety at work. They must be in accordance with local law requirements and meet the highest possible safety and employee protection standards. Employees are made aware of safety procedures as well as informed on how to avoid risk at workplace and how to report misconduct. They are encouraged to come up with new ideas to enhance workplace safety. Employees are also obliged to keep all information about other company employees confidential. They may not disclose any information about other employees (in particular such as those regarding pay, employee assessment, performance, absence, etc.) either to some other AmEx employees or persons outside the company. Another proof for acting in accordance with this value is striving to employ staff irrespective of their gender, race, skin color, age, nationality, religion, sexual orientation, marital status or citizenship. In this respect, AmEx is considered to be one of the most exemplary organizations in the world. It is also evident that the company policy forbids anyone from taking advantage of their position to intimidate or harass employees, not even to mention sexual undertones. Religious beliefs, political views and sexual preferences are not to be discussed in the company, because this could hurt someone's feelings. The Code of Conduct precisely regulates also those issues related to devoting time to political and charitable activities. It is important, too, that any case of any form of discrimination may result in disciplinary termination. Employees are trained so that they avoid stereotypes and treat everyone equally. Employees should approach others without prejudice and making judgments about them. It is particularly important in certain cultures such as India (where people coming from different castes might work in one AmEx office) or in Arab countries (where religious issues play vital role). AmEx allocates special funds for employee team-building and programs that are supposed to fight existing stereotypes and prejudice.

The company also sponsors private team-building events for employees from particular departments or larger organizational units. AmEx has established action patterns and standards in accord with the key values that are binding on employees holding particular positions. This means that for the Market Coordinator, for example (who is responsible for coordination of market activities between several markets and the company's headquarters), that they have to analyze on an ongoing basis what consequences a particular decision made for one market could bring for those responsible for other markets. An unauthorized decision may lead to a conflict of interests; hence the need for constant struggle to reach as broad a compromise as possible, but taking costs and financial profits into account at the same time.

American Express is known for its respect for employees and customers just as well as for its charitable activities which reflect the value defined as "Being good citizens in the communities in which we live and work".

It is no surprise at American Express that thousands of employees give gifts to the needy. It is no surprise, either, that thousands of AmEx employees devote their spare time after work, weekends and other occasions (such as holidays) to hand out meals to the homeless, to teach disabled children on a voluntary basis, to provide advice to victims of violence or to build low-cost houses for the homeless. There are special employee programs at American Express to encourage charity work. Under one of them an employee can get 30% of their regular pay for one year if they decide to volunteer for a charity organization.

Questions for Discussion:

1. Identify opportunities and risks related to development of strong corporate culture based on core values for modern, global corporation.
2. Does the fact that an organization has and implements in its daily life its core values guarantee that such organization is ethical and corruption resistant?

3. What actions, practices and tools can be applied by a modern organization to ensure more effective implementation of behaviors consistent with its core values?
4. Identify your own core values and the core values of your organization and provide specific actions that should be taken to apply these values in daily life.

References

1. American Express (2009), "Who we are", http://about.americanexpress.com/oc/whoweare/
2. Massengill, R. (1999), "Becoming American Express, 150 Years of Reinvention and Customer Service", American Express Company, New York, p. 6.
3. Massengill, R. (1999), "Becoming American Express, 150 Years of Reinvention and Customer Service", American Express Company, New York, p. 13.
4. Richardson, F. (2002), "Remembrance and Renewal, American Express after 9/11", American Express Company, p. 8.
5. Massengill, R. (1999), "Becoming American Express, 150 Years of Reinvention and Customer Service", American Express Company, New York, p. 39.
6. Massengill, R. (1999), "Becoming American Express, 150 Years of Reinvention and Customer Service", American Express Company, New York, p. 186.
7. Stachowicz-Stanusch, A. (2007), "Potęga wartości. Jak zbudować nieśmiertelną firmę", Helion, Gliwice, pp. 145–158.
8. Massengill, R. (1999), "Becoming American Express, 150 Years of Reinvention and Customer Service", American Express Company, New York, p. 112.

VIDEO CASES

VIDEO CASES FOR PART ONE

Wal-Mart's Public Image Campaign

After years of criticism from various groups, Wal-Mart is paying more attention to its stakeholders. "We've talked to environmentalists; we've talked to NGOs; we've talked to people in neighborhoods. We've really reached out to say: What should we be doing differently?" says Mona Williams, Wal-Mart's VP of corporate communications. In Aurora, Colorado, the world's largest retailer has introduced numerous environmental initiatives, including solar and wind energy and recycled tires. Wal-Mart also claims that it has removed managers who acted unethically due to pressures to reduce costs. "We are light-years ahead of where we were even two or three years ago," says Williams. This PBS program details some of the initiatives Wal-Mart has developed to change its relationship with stakeholders. We also hear from critics who explain why Wal-Mart's recent public image campaign doesn't correct the company's underlying problems.

Discussion Questions

1. Which stakeholders does Wal-Mart seem to be serving better now than in the past? Why does this shift make a difference to Wal-Mart?
2. Are the ongoing criticisms about Wal-Mart justified? Is it possible to satisfy stakeholders more fully than Wal-Mart is currently attempting to do?

Good Business Deeds

You might not expect to see British American Tobacco, McDonald's, and Microsoft at a meeting on corporate social responsibility, but in their own way these firms are taking steps to become better employers and citizens in the community. This video program describes how these and other firms are embracing values and corporate social responsibility. It particularly highlights a few firms that serve as role models in this regard. One of these is Greyston Bakery, a multimillion-dollar gourmet operation that takes people who need help and turns them into contributing members of the organization and society. Another is Eileen Fisher Company, which promotes good labor practices both at home and overseas and helps customers meet their needs. At each firm, the company's values are aligned more closely with employee values than is the case at a typical organization.

Discussion Questions

1. Employees at Greyston Bakery, Eileen Fisher Company, Feed the Children, Green@Work, and other organizations described in this video program seem to have a strong congruence of their personal values with the organization's values. What are the apparent benefits of this value congruence?
2. Discuss the implications of corporate social responsibility in terms of organizational effectiveness.

VIDEO CASES FOR PART TWO

Johnson & Johnson: (A) Creating a Global Learning Organization: The Credo; (B) Management Fundamentals Training at Johnson & Johnson

Johnson & Johnson (J&J) is a family-oriented health care and personal products company with about 330 operating units and more than 150,000 employees around the world. The company is well known for "the Credo," a set of value statements introduced in 1938 to help J&J's executives and employees make better decisions. The Credo helps J&J staff to continuously be aware of and serve the needs of its core stakeholders. It also serves as the glue that holds the company's geographically and industrially diverse operating units together. This program introduces Johnson & Johnson's Credo and shows how the company instills the Credo values in its managers.

Discussion Questions

1. Why does Johnson & Johnson place so much importance on the Credo?
2. How does Johnson & Johnson ensure that managers understand and apply the Credo in their daily decisions and actions?

Pike Place Fish Market

Fifteen years ago, Pike Place Fish Market in Seattle had unhappy employees and was in financial trouble. Rather than close shop, owner John Yokoyama sought help from consultant Jim Bergquist to improve his leadership and energize the workforce. Rather than rule as a tyrant, Yokoyama learned how to actively involve employees in the business. Soon, employees felt more empowered and gained more enjoyment from their work. They also began to actively have fun at work, doing things such as setting goals as a game, throwing fish to each other as sport, and pretending they are "world famous."

Today, thanks to these and other strategies described in this video case, Pike Place *is* world famous. The little shop has become a tourist attraction, and customers from California to New York call in orders.

Discussion Questions

1. On the basis of the model of emotions and attitudes in Chapter 4, explain how the changes at Pike Place Fish Market improved job satisfaction and reduced turnover. How did these attitude changes affect customer satisfaction?
2. Goal setting is discussed as an important activity at Pike Place. Evaluate the effectiveness of the firm's goal setting process in the context of the characteristics of effective goals described in Chapter 5 of this textbook.
3. How is coaching applied at Pike Place, and how does this coaching influence employee performance?

Stress in Japan

Stress from overwork has become an epidemic in Japan. This video program consists of two segments that illustrate the degree to which some Japanese employees are overworked, as well as the consequences of their overwork. The first segment follows a typical day of a Japanese manager, from his two-hour morning commute to his late-night working hours. The program also shows that he is under constant pressure to improve efficiency and experiences a heavy burden and responsibility to do better. The second segment describes how *karoshi*–death from overwork–took the life of 23-year-old Yoshika. It reconstructs Yoshika's work life as a graphic artist up to the time when she died suddenly on the job due to a brain hemorrhage.

Discussion Questions

1. Identify the various sources of stress (i.e., stressors) that the Japanese manager in the first segment likely experiences each day. Does he do anything to try to manage his stress?
2. What conditions led up to the *karoshi* death of Yoshika? Are these conditions commonly found in the country where you live?

Clockless Office: Best Buy's Rowe Program

Kelly McDevitt has a busy job as online promotions manager for Best Buy. But McDevitt doesn't have to worry about punching a time clock because of the retailer's results-only work environment (ROWE). "I don't count my hours–I don't have hours," she says. McDevitt attends office meetings, but even attending those events is optional. "It's not how many hours somebody puts in face time at the office; it's are they getting their work done" explains Calli Ressler. This *BusinessWeek* TV program describes the ROWE initiative, explains why it was introduced, and outlines its apparent benefits.

Discussion Questions

1. Why would productivity jump at Best Buy under ROWE, compared to the traditional employment arrangement where employees are expected to be at the office?
2. What effect would the ROWE program have on workplace stress? Explain your answer.
3. What are the limitations and risks of the ROWE program? Which jobs and employees would be poorly suited to this work arrangement?

VIDEO CASES FOR PART THREE

Team Work: Team Activities for Co-workers

Companies have more ways than ever before to help employees with team building. Cooking classes, hula hoops, human-size Chinese checkers, and horse riding are just a few of the activities that help employees work more effectively together. This NBC program reveals three team-building activities–rodeos, field games, and hula hoops. We also hear the opinions of participants in these activities.

Discussion Questions

1. This program shows employees in three team-building activities: rodeo, field games, and hula hoops. Which of these three appeals to you the most as a team-building activity? Explain why.
2. What individual and team-building skills do participants believe will be improved by the hula hoops?
3. To what extent would each of these activities influence team dynamics back on the job? What conditions might further improve the transfer of team dynamics from these activities to the workplace?

Generation Next Changes the Face of the Workplace

Jo Muse is baffled. The CEO of Muse Communications received requests from younger staff for vacation time after just two months on the job. "Why do you think that you can work places for a couple months and then get a vacation?" Muse asks his Generation-X and -Y staff. "And unpaid! You don't care if you get paid. What's up with that?" Baby-boomer managers such as Jo Muse face the challenge of figuring out the needs and expectations of young employees. The differences–which range from subtle to stark–also produce conflict in the workplace. "There is a clash," suggests 24-year-old X-ray technician Doan Phan. Phan points to differences in technology skills as one source of conflict. Another is the urgency to change the workplace. "We want to bring in new ideas. We want to change things," Phan says. This PBS program peeks into several organizations to see how younger- and older-generation employees are getting along. The program examines how Gen-X and -Y employees view their employment differently than do baby boomers. It also describes the actions of companies that are addressing these conflicts and changing expectations.

Discussion Questions

1. In this program, in what ways are Generation-X and -Y employees depicted differently from baby-boomer employees? Are the differences a reasonably accurate representation of generational differences in the workplace today?
2. What steps have Deloitte and other companies taken to adjust to the expectations of younger employees and to reduce potential generational conflict in the workplace?

Celebrity CEO Charisma

Does the cult of CEO charisma really make a difference to company profits? This NBC program takes a brief look at chief executives who acted like superheroes but failed to deliver, as well as a few low-key executives who really made a difference. The program hears from Harvard Business School professor Rakesh Khurana, author of *Searching for a Corporate Savior,* a book warning that charismatic leaders are not necessarily effective leaders.

Discussion Questions

1. Why do company boards tend to hire charismatic CEOs?
2. What can corporate boards do to minimize the charisma effect when filling chief executive officer and other senior executive positions?

Southwest CEO: Get to Know Gary Kelly

Southwest Airlines remains one of the most successful airlines in the United States. Its secret to success? Treat customers as kings and queens, and treat employees even better. This video program shows how Southwest Airlines CEO Gary Kelly keeps in touch with day-to-day activities at the airline. It also describes some of the challenges that Kelly and his executive team have ahead of them.

Discussion Questions

1. Discuss the transactional and transformational leadership of Gary Kelly.
2. How does Gary Kelly's leadership reinforce Southwest Airlines' organizational culture?

VIDEO CASE FOR PART FOUR

Lindblad Expeditions: Under the Surface

Traveling around the world for six months as a crew member of an expedition ship is a dream job in many respects. But as this recruitment video from Lindblad Expeditions describes, working on the National Geographic *Sea Bird* and other cruise ships requires a dedicated crew, and that means a real working day. This video program provides viewers with a realistic picture of what it is like to work on board one of these vessels. Crew members offer their candid thoughts about why they joined and what they experienced, including the most exciting and most arduous aspects of the job.

Discussion Questions

1. In your opinion, is this program effective in providing a realistic job preview of working life on board an expedition cruise ship? Why or why not?
2. Discuss the effectiveness of this video program in terms of the learning and adjustment of new employees. Are the risks of discouraging some job applicants offset by the positive effects on those who apply and are hired?
3. If you were responsible for the hiring and induction of new employees at Lindblad Expeditions or a similar organization, what other means would you apply to ensure that employees experience an effective socialization process?

Ricardo Semler: Brazil's Caring Capitalist

This video program gives the viewer a rare glimpse inside the fabled operations of the Brazilian conglomerate, SEMCO SA. Two decades ago, Ricardo Semler transformed his father's rigidly hierarchical shipbuilding supplies business into an organization that embraces egalitarianism and worker autonomy. Today, almost all of SEMCO's 3,000 employees set their own work schedules. They are encouraged to move around to different workstations, in part so that supervisors have difficulty knowing who is at work and who has gone home. Employees are also key decision makers, choosing everything from the office furniture to how much they should get paid. But SEMCO is not a laid-back country club. Employees are rewarded for how well their work unit performs, so co-workers will not tolerate those who fail to pull their weight. Also, although employees can set their own salaries, those who ask for too much money find themselves without a team willing to keep them on the payroll. This video program also describes Ricardo Semler's recent initiatives in education and ecotourism, both of which also give employees authority and responsibility.

Discussion Questions

1. Describe SEMCO's organizational culture. What artifacts are mentioned in this program that represent and reinforce this culture? What strategies or practices does SEMCO apply to specifically support its culture?
2. SEMCO is apparently a very successful company. Which of the four perspectives of organizational effectiveness described in Chapter 1 best explain this organization's success?
3. SEMCO SA is featured in Chapter 12 of this book as an example of shared leadership. What information in this video program indicated that SEMCO encourages shared leadership?

Appendix A

Theory Building and Systematic Research Methods

Theory Building

People need to make sense of their world, so they form theories about the way the world operates. A **theory** is a general set of propositions that describes interrelationships among several concepts. We form theories for the purpose of predicting and explaining the world around us.[1] What does a good theory look like? First, it should be stated as clearly and simply as possible so that the concepts can be measured and there is no ambiguity regarding the theory's propositions. Second, the elements of the theory must be logically consistent with each other, because we cannot test anything that doesn't make sense. Third, a good theory provides value to society; it helps people understand their world better than they would without the theory.[2]

Theory building is a continuous process that typically includes the inductive and deductive stages shown in Exhibit A.1.[3] The inductive stage draws on personal experience to form a preliminary theory, whereas the deductive stage uses the scientific method to test the theory.

The inductive stage of theory building involves observing the world around us, identifying a pattern of relationships, and then forming a theory from these personal observations. For example, you might casually notice that new employees want their supervisor to give direction, whereas this leadership style irritates long-service employees. From these observations, you form a theory about the effectiveness of directive leadership. (See Chapter 12 for a discussion of this leadership style.)

Positivism versus Interpretivism Research requires an interpretation of reality, and researchers tend to perceive reality in one of two ways. A common view, called **positivism,** is that reality exists independent of people. It is "out there" to be discovered and tested. Positivism is the foundation for

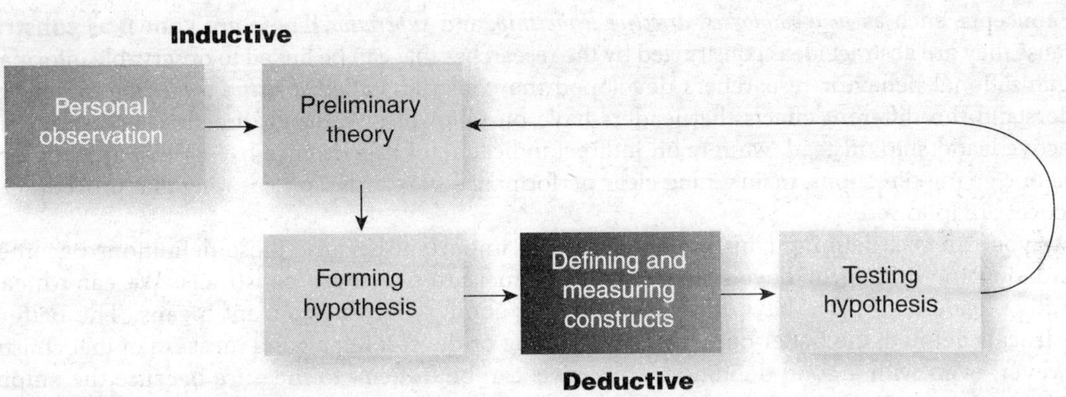

Exhibit A.1 *Theory Building and Theory Testing*

most quantitative research (statistical analysis). It assumes that we can measure variables and that those variables have fixed relationships with other variables. For example, the positivist perspective says that we could study whether a supportive style of leadership reduces stress. If we find evidence that it does, then someone else studying leadership and stress would "discover" the same relationship.

Interpretivism takes a different view of reality. It suggests that reality comes from shared meaning among people in a particular environment. For example, supportive leadership is a personal interpretation of reality, not something that can be measured across time and people. Interpretivists rely mainly on qualitative data, such as observation and nondirective interviews. They particularly listen to the language people use to understand the common meaning that people have toward various events or phenomena. For example, they might argue that you need to experience and observe supportive leadership to effectively study it. Moreover, you can't really predict relationships because the specific situation shapes reality.[4]

Most OB scholars identify themselves somewhere between the extreme views of positivism and interpretivism. Many believe that inductive research should begin with an interpretivist angle. We should consider a new topic with an open mind and search for the shared meaning among people in the situation being studied. In other words, researchers should let the participants define reality rather than let the researcher's preconceived notions shape that reality. This process involves gathering qualitative information and letting this information shape the theory.[5] After the theory emerges, researchers shift to the positivist perspective by quantitatively testing relationships in that theory.

Theory Testing: The Deductive Process Once a theory has been formed, we shift into the deductive stage of theory building. This process includes forming hypotheses, defining and measuring constructs, and testing hypotheses (see Exhibit A.1). **Hypotheses** make empirically testable declarations that certain variables and their corresponding measures are related in a specific way proposed by the theory. For instance, to find support for the directive leadership theory described earlier, we need to form and then test a specific hypothesis from that theory. One such hypothesis might be "New employees are more satisfied with supervisors who exhibit a directive rather than nondirective leadership style." Hypotheses are indispensable tools of scientific research, because they provide the vital link between the theory and empirical verification.

Defining and Measuring Constructs Hypotheses are testable only if we can define and then form measurable indicators of the concepts stated in the hypotheses. Consider the hypothesis in the previous paragraph about new employees and directive leadership. To test this hypothesis, we first need to define the concepts, such as *new employees, directive leadership,* and *supervisor.* These are known as **constructs,** because they are abstract ideas constructed by the researcher that can be linked to observable information. Organizational behavior researchers developed the construct called *directive leadership* to help them understand the different effects that leaders have on followers. We can't directly see, taste, or smell directive leadership; instead, we rely on indirect indicators of its existence by, for example, observing someone giving directions, maintaining clear performance standards, and ensuring that procedures and practices are followed.

As you can see, defining constructs well is very important because these definitions become the foundation for finding or developing acceptable measures of those constructs. We can't measure directive leadership if we have only a vague idea about what this concept means. The better the construct is defined, the better our chances of finding or developing a good measure of that construct. However, even with a good definition, constructs can be difficult to measure because the empirical representation must capture several elements in the definition. A measure of directive leadership must be able to identify not only people who give directions but also those who maintain performance standards and ensure that procedures are followed.

Testing Hypotheses The third step in the deductive process is to collect data for the empirical measures of the variables. Following our directive leadership example, we might conduct a formal survey in which new employees indicate the behavior of their supervisors and their attitudes toward their supervisors. Alternatively, we might design an experiment in which people work with someone who applies either a directive or a nondirective leadership style. When the data have been collected, we can use various procedures to statistically test our hypotheses.

A major concern in theory building is that some researchers might inadvertently find support for their theory simply because they use the same information used to form the theory during the inductive stage. Consequently, the deductive stage must collect new data that are completely independent of the data used during the inductive stage. For instance, you might decide to test your theory of directive leadership by studying employees in another organization. Moreover, the inductive process may have relied mainly on personal observation, whereas the deductive process might use survey questionnaires. By studying different samples and using different measurement tools, we minimize the risk of conducting circular research.

Using the Scientific Method Earlier, we said that the deductive stage of theory building follows the scientific method. The **scientific method** is a systematic, controlled, empirical, and critical investigation of hypothetical propositions about the presumed relationships among natural phenomena.[6] There are several elements to this definition, so let's look at each one. First, scientific research is *systematic* and *controlled* because researchers want to rule out all but one explanation for a set of interrelated events. To rule out alternative explanations, we need to control them in some way, such as by keeping them constant or removing them entirely from the environment.

Second, we say that scientific research is *empirical* because researchers need to use objective reality–or as close as we can get to it–to test a theory. They measure observable elements of the environment, such as what a person says or does, rather than relying on their own subjective opinion to draw conclusions. Moreover, scientific research analyzes these data using acceptable principles of mathematics and logic.

Third, scientific research involves *critical investigation.* This means that the study's hypotheses, data, methods, and results are openly described so that other experts in the field can properly evaluate the research. It also means that scholars are encouraged to critique and build on previous research. The scientific method encourages the refinement and eventually the replacement of a particular theory with one that better suits our understanding of the world.

Grounded Theory: An Alternative Approach The scientific method dominates the quantitative approach to systematic research, but another approach, called **grounded theory,** dominates research using qualitative methods.[7] Grounded theory is a process of developing knowledge through the constant interplay of data collection, analysis, and theory development. It relies mainly on qualitative methods to form categories and variables, analyze relationships among these concepts, and form a model based on the observations and analysis. Grounded theory combines the inductive stages of theory development by cycling back and forth between data collection and analysis to converge on a robust explanatory model. This ongoing reciprocal process results in theory that is grounded in the data (thus, the name "grounded theory").

Like the scientific method, grounded theory is a systematic and rigorous process of data collection and analysis. It requires specific steps and documentation, and it adopts a positivist view by assuming that the results are generalizable to other settings. However, grounded theory also takes an interpretivist view by building categories and variables from the perceived realities of the subjects rather than from an assumed universal truth.[8] It also recognizes that personal biases are not easily removed from the research process.

Selected Issues in Organizational Behavior Research

There are many issues to consider in theory building, particularly when we use the deductive process to test hypotheses. Some of the more important issues are sampling, causation, and ethical practices in organizational research.

Sampling in Organizational Research When finding out why things happen in organizations, we typically gather information from a few sources and then draw conclusions about the larger population. If we survey several employees and determine that older employees are more loyal to their company, then we would like to generalize this statement to all older employees in our population, not just those whom we surveyed. Scientific inquiry generally requires that researchers engage in **representative sampling,** that is, sampling a population in such a way that we can extrapolate the results of the sample to the larger population.

One factor that influences representativeness is whether the sample is selected in an unbiased way from the larger population. Let's suppose that you want to study organizational commitment among employees in your organization. A casual procedure might result in sampling too few employees from the head office and too many located elsewhere in the country. If head office employees actually have higher loyalty than employees located elsewhere, the biased sampling would cause the results to underestimate the true level of loyalty among employees in the company. If you repeat the process again next year but somehow overweight employees from the head office, the results might wrongly suggest that employees have increased their organizational commitment over the past year. In reality, the only change may be the direction of sampling bias.

How do we minimize sampling bias? The answer is to randomly select the sample. A randomly drawn sample gives each member of the population an equal probability of being chosen, so there is less likelihood that a subgroup within that population will dominate the study's results.

The same principle applies to random assignment of subjects to groups in experimental designs. If we want to test the effects of a team development training program, we need to randomly place some employees in the training group and randomly place others in a group that does not receive training. Without this random selection, each group might have different types of employees, so we wouldn't know whether the training explains the differences between the two groups. Moreover, if employees respond differently to the training program, we couldn't be sure that the training program results are representative of the larger population. Of course, random sampling does not necessarily produce a perfectly representative sample, but we do know that it is the best approach to ensure unbiased selection.

The other factor that influences representativeness is sample size. Whenever we select a portion of the population, there will be some error in our estimate of the population values. The larger the sample, the less error will occur in our estimate. Let's suppose that you want to find out how employees in a 500-person firm feel about smoking in the workplace. If you asked 400 of those employees, the information would provide a very good estimate of how the entire workforce in that organization feels. If you survey only 100 employees, the estimate might deviate more from the true population. If you ask only 10 people, the estimate could be quite different from what all 500 employees feel.

Notice that sample size goes hand in hand with random selection. You must have a sufficiently large sample size for the principle of randomization to work effectively. In our example of attitudes toward smoking, we would do a poor job of random selection if our sample consisted of only 10 employees from the 500-person organization. The reason is that these 10 people probably wouldn't capture the diversity of employees throughout the organization. In fact, the more diverse the population, the larger the sample size should be to provide adequate representation through random selection.

Causation in Organizational Research Theories present notions about relationships among constructs. Often, these propositions suggest a causal relationship, namely, that one variable has an effect on another variable. When discussing causation, we refer to variables as being independent or dependent. *Independent variables* are the presumed causes of *dependent variables,* which are the presumed effects. In our earlier example of directive leadership, the main independent variable (there might be others) would be the supervisor's directive or nondirective leadership style because we presume that it causes the dependent variable (satisfaction with supervision).

In laboratory experiments (described later), the independent variable is always manipulated by the experimenter. In our research on directive leadership, we might have subjects (new employees) work with supervisors who exhibit directive or nondirective leadership behaviors. If subjects are more satisfied under the directive leaders, we would be able to infer an association between the independent and dependent variables.

Researchers must satisfy three conditions to provide sufficient evidence of causality between two variables.[9] The first condition of causality is that the variables are empirically associated with each other. An association exists whenever one measure of a variable changes systematically with a measure of another variable. This condition of causality is the easiest to satisfy because there are several well-known statistical measures of association. A research study might find, for instance, that heterogeneous groups (in which members come from diverse backgrounds) produce more creative solutions to problems. This might be apparent because the measure of creativity (such as number of creative solutions produced within a fixed time) is higher for teams that have a high score on the measure of group heterogeneity. They are statistically associated or correlated with each other.

The second condition of causality is that the independent variable precedes the dependent variable in time. Sometimes, this condition is satisfied through simple logic. In our group heterogeneity example, it doesn't make sense to say that the number of creative solutions caused the group's heterogeneity, because the group's heterogeneity existed before the group produced the creative solutions. In other situations, however, the temporal relationship among variables is less clear. One example is the ongoing debate about job satisfaction and organizational commitment. Do companies develop more loyal employees by increasing their job satisfaction, or do changes in organizational loyalty cause changes in job satisfaction? Simple logic does not answer these questions; researchers must use sophisticated longitudinal studies to build up evidence of a temporal relationship between these two variables.

The third requirement for evidence of a causal relationship is that the statistical association between two variables cannot be explained by a third variable. There are many associations that we quickly dismiss as being causally related. For example, there is a statistical association between the number of storks in an area and the birthrate in that area. We know that storks don't bring babies, so something else must cause the association between these two variables. The real explanation is that both storks and birthrates have a higher incidence in rural areas.

In other studies, the third-variable effect is less apparent. Many years ago, before polio vaccines were available, a study in the United States reported a surprisingly strong association between consumption of a certain soft drink and the incidence of polio. Was polio caused by drinking this pop, or did people with polio have a unusual craving for this beverage? Neither. Both polio and consumption of the pop drink were caused by a third variable: climate. There was a higher incidence of polio in the summer months and in warmer climates, and people drink more liquids in these climates.[10] As you can see from this example, researchers have a difficult time supporting causal inferences because third-variable effects are sometimes difficult to detect.

Ethics in Organizational Research Organizational behavior researchers need to abide by the ethical standards of the society in which the research is conducted. One of the most important ethical considerations is the individual subject's freedom to participate in the study. For example, it is inappropriate to force employees to fill out a questionnaire or attend an experimental intervention for research purposes only. Moreover, researchers have an obligation to tell potential subjects about any possible risks inherent in the study so that participants can make an informed choice about whether to be involved.

Finally, researchers must be careful to protect the privacy of those who participate in the study. This usually includes letting people know when they are being studied as well as guaranteeing that their individual information will remain confidential (unless publication of identities is granted). Researchers maintain anonymity through careful security of data. The research results usually aggregate data in numbers large enough that they do not reveal the opinions or characteristics of any specific individual. For example, we would report the average absenteeism of employees in a department rather than state the absence rate of each person. When researchers are sharing data with other researchers, it is usually necessary to specially code each case so that individual identities are not known.

Research Design Strategies

So far, we have described how to build a theory, including the specific elements of empirically testing the theory within the standards of scientific inquiry. But what are the different ways to design a research study so that we get the data necessary to achieve our research objectives? There are many strategies, but they mainly fall under three headings: laboratory experiments, field surveys, and observational research.

Laboratory Experiments A **laboratory experiment** is any research study in which independent variables and variables outside the researcher's main focus of inquiry can be controlled to some extent. Laboratory experiments are usually located outside the everyday work environment, such as in a classroom, simulation lab, or any other artificial setting in which the researcher can manipulate the environment. Organizational behavior researchers sometimes conduct experiments in the workplace (called *field experiments*) in which the independent variable is manipulated. However, the researcher has less control over the effects of extraneous factors in field experiments than he or she has in laboratory situations.

Advantages of Laboratory Experiments There are many advantages of laboratory experiments. By definition, this research method offers a high degree of control over extraneous variables that would otherwise confound the relationships being studied. Suppose we wanted to test the effects of directive leadership on the satisfaction of new employees. One concern might be that employees are influenced by how much leadership is provided, not just the type of leadership style. An experimental design would allow us to control how often the supervisor exhibited this style so that this extraneous variable does not confound the results.

second advantage of lab studies is that the independent and dependent variables can be developed more precisely than is possible in a field setting. For example, the researcher can ensure that supervisors in a lab study apply specific directive or nondirective behaviors, whereas real-life supervisors would e a more complex mixture of leadership behaviors. By using more precise measures, we are more certain that we are measuring the intended construct. Thus, if new employees are more satisfied with supervisors in the directive leadership condition, we are more confident that the independent variable was directive leadership rather than some other leadership style.

A third benefit of laboratory experiments is that the independent variable can be distributed more evenly among participants. In our directive leadership study, we can ensure that approximately half of the subjects have a directive supervisor and the other half have a nondirective supervisor. In natural settings, we might have trouble finding people who have worked with a nondirective leader, and consequently we might have difficulty determining the effects of this condition.

Disadvantages of Laboratory Experiments With these powerful advantages, you might wonder why laboratory experiments are the least appreciated form of organizational behavior research.[11] One obvious limitation of this research method is that it lacks realism, and thus the results might be different in the real world. One argument is that laboratory experiment subjects are less involved than their counterparts in an actual work situation. This is sometimes true, although many lab studies have highly motivated participants. Another criticism is that the extraneous variables controlled in the lab setting might produce a different effect of the independent variable on the dependent variables. This might also be true, but remember that the experimental design controls variables in accordance with the theory and its hypotheses. Consequently, this concern is really a critique of the theory, not the lab study.

Finally, there is the well-known problem that participants are aware they are being studied and this causes them to act differently than they normally would. Some participants try to figure out how the researcher wants them to behave and then deliberately try to act that way. Other participants try to upset the experiment by doing just the opposite of what they believe the researcher expects. Still others might act unnaturally simply because they know they are being observed. Fortunately, experimenters are well aware of these potential problems and are usually (although not always) successful at disguising the study's true intent.

Field Surveys **Field surveys** collect and analyze information in a natural environment–an office, a factory, or some other existing location. The researcher takes a snapshot of reality and tries to determine whether elements of that situation (including the attitudes and behaviors of people in that situation) are associated with each other as hypothesized. Everyone does some sort of field research. You might think that people from some states are better drivers than others, so you "test" your theory by looking at the way people with out-of-state license plates drive. Although your methods of data collection might not satisfy scientific standards, this is a form of field research because it takes information from a naturally occurring situation.

Advantages and Disadvantages of Field Surveys One advantage of field surveys is that the variables often have a more powerful effect than they would in a laboratory experiment. Consider the effect of peer pressure on the behavior of members within the team. In a natural environment, team members would form very strong cohesive bonds over time, whereas a researcher would have difficulty replicating this level of cohesiveness and corresponding peer pressure in a lab setting.

Another advantage of field surveys is that the researcher can study many variables simultaneously, thereby permitting a fuller test of more complex theories. Ironically, this is also a disadvantage of field surveys because it is difficult for the researcher to contain his or her scientific inquiry. There is a tendency to shift from deductive hypothesis testing to more inductive exploratory browsing through the data. If these two activities become mixed together, the researcher can lose sight of the strict covenants of scientific inquiry.

The main weakness with field surveys is that it is very difficult to satisfy the conditions for causal conclusions. One reason is that the data are usually collected at one point in time, so the researcher must rely on logic to decide whether the independent variable really preceded the dependent variable. Contrast this with the lab study in which the researcher can usually be confident that the independent variable was applied before the dependent variable occurred. Increasingly, organizational behavior studies use longitudinal research to provide a better indicator of temporal relations among variables, but this is still not as precise as the lab setting. Another reason why causal analysis is difficult in field surveys is that extraneous variables are not controlled as they are in lab studies. Without this control, there is a higher chance that a third variable might explain the relationship between the hypothesized independent and dependent variables.

Observational Research In their study of brainstorming and creativity, Robert Sutton and Andrew Hargadon observed 24 brainstorming sessions at IDEO, a product design firm in Palo Alto, California. They also attended a dozen "Monday morning meetings," conducted 60 semistructured interviews with IDEO executives and designers, held hundreds of informal discussions with these people, and read through several dozen magazine articles about the company.[12]

Sutton's and Hargadon's use of observational research and other qualitative methods was quite appropriate for their research objective, which was to reexamine the effectiveness of brainstorming beyond the number of ideas generated. Observational research generates a wealth of descriptive accounts about the drama of human existence in organizations. It is a useful vehicle for learning about the complex dynamics of people and their activities, such as brainstorming. (The results of Sutton and Hargadon's study are discussed in the decision-making chapter.)

Participant observation takes the observation method one step further by having the observer take part in the organization's activities. This experience gives the researcher a fuller understanding of the activities, compared to just watching others participate in those activities.

In spite of its intuitive appeal, observational research has a number of weaknesses. The main problem is that the observer is subject to the perceptual screening and organizing biases that we discuss in Chapter 3 of this textbook. There is a tendency to overlook the routine aspects of organizational life, even though they may prove to be the most important data for research purposes. Instead, observers tend to focus on unusual information, such as activities that deviate from what the observer expects. Because observational research usually records only what the observer notices, valuable information is often lost.

Another concern with the observation method is that the researcher's presence and involvement may influence the people whom he or she is studying. This can be a problem in short-term observations, but in the long term people tend to return to their usual behavior patterns. With ongoing observations, such as Sutton and Hargadon's study of brainstorming sessions at IDEO, employees eventually forget that they are being studied.

Finally, observation is usually a qualitative process, so it is more difficult to empirically test hypotheses with the data. Instead, observational research provides rich information for the inductive stages of theory building. It helps us to form ideas about the way things work in organizations. We begin to see relationships that lay the foundation for new perspectives and theory. We must not confuse this inductive process of theory building with the deductive process of theory testing.

Notes

[1]F.N. Kerlinger, *Foundations of Behavioral Research* (New York: Holt, Rinehart & Winston, 1964), p. 11.

[2]J.B. Miner, *Theories of Organizational Behavior* (Hinsdale, IL: Dryden, 1980), pp. 7–9.

[3]Ibid., pp. 6–7.

[4]J. Mason, *Qualitative Researching* (London: Sage, 1996).

[5]A. Strauss and J. Corbin, eds., *Grounded Theory in Practice* (London: Sage, 1997); B.G. Glaser and A. Strauss, *The Discovery of Grounded Theory: Strategies for Qualitative Research* (Chicago: Aldine, 1967).

[6]Kerlinger, *Foundations of Behavioral Research,* p. 13.

[7]Strauss and Corbin, *Grounded Theory in Practice;* Glaser and Strauss, *The Discovery of Grounded Theory.*

[8]W.A. Hall and P. Callery, "Enhancing the Rigor of Grounded Theory: Incorporating Reflexivity and Relationality," *Qualitative Health Research* 11 (March 2001), pp. 257–272.

[9]P. Lazarsfeld, *Survey Design and Analysis* (New York: Free Press, 1955).

[10]This example is cited in D.W. Organ and T.S. Bateman, *Organizational Behavior,* 4th ed. (Homewood, IL: Irwin, 1991), p. 42.

[11]Ibid., p. 45.

[12]R.I. Sutton and A. Hargadon, "Brainstorming Groups in Context: Effectiveness in a Product Design Firm," *Administrative Science Quarterly* 41 (1996), pp. 685–718.

Appendix B

Scoring Keys for Self-Assessment Activities

The following pages provide scoring keys for self-assessments that are fully presented in this textbook. These self-assessments, as well as the self-assessments that are only summarized in this book, can also be scored automatically at the student Online Learning Center.

Chapter 2

Scoring Key for "Are You Introverted or Extroverted?"

Scoring Instructions: Use the table shown here to assign numbers to each box you checked. For example, if you checked "Moderately inaccurate" for statement 1 ("I feel comfortable around people"),

For statement items 1, 2, 6, 8, 9	For statement items 3, 4, 5, 7, 10
Very accurate description of me = 4	Very accurate description of me = 0
Moderately accurate = 3	Moderately accurate = 1
Neither accurate nor inaccurate = 2	Neither accurate nor inaccurate = 2
Moderately inaccurate = 1	Moderately inaccurate = 3
Very inaccurate description of me = 0	Very inaccurate description of me = 4

you would assign a "1" to that statement. After assigning numbers for all 10 statements, add up the numbers to estimate your extroversion-introversion personality.

Interpreting Your Score: *Extroversion* characterizes people who are outgoing, talkative, sociable, and assertive. It includes several facets, such as friendliness, gregariousness, assertiveness, activity level, excitement seeking, and cheerfulness. The opposite of extroversion is *introversion,* which refers to the personality characteristics of being quiet, shy, and cautious. Extroverts get their energy from the outer world (people and things around them), whereas introverts get their energy from the internal world, such as personal reflection on concepts and ideas. Introverts are more inclined to direct their interests to ideas rather than to social events.

This is the short version of the IPIP Introversion-Extroversion Scale, so it estimates overall introversion-extroversion but not specific facets within the personality dimension. Scores range from 0 to 40. Low scores indicate introversion; high scores indicate extroversion. The norms in the following table are estimated from results of early adults (under 30 years old) in Scotland and undergraduate psychology students in the United States. However, introversion-extroversion norms vary from one group to the next; the best norms are likely based on the entire class you are attending or on past students in this course.

IPIP introversion-extroversion	Interpretation
35 to 40	High extroversion
28 to 34	Moderate extroversion
21 to 27	Between extroversion and introversion
7 to 20	Moderate introversion
0 to 6	High introversion

Chapter 3

Scoring Key for "How Much Personal Structure Do You Need?"

Scoring Instructions: Use the table below to assign numbers to each box you checked. For example, if you checked "Moderately disagree" for statement 3 ("I enjoy being spontaneous"), you would assign a "5" to that statement. After assigning numbers for all 12 statements, add up your scores to estimate your personal need for structure.

For statement items 1, 5, 6, 7, 8, 9, 10, 12	For statement items 2, 3, 4, 11
Strongly agree = 6	Strongly agree = 1
Moderately agree = 5	Moderately agree = 2
Slightly agree = 4	Slightly agree = 3
Slightly disagree = 3	Slightly disagree = 4
Moderately disagree = 2	Moderately disagree = 5
Strongly disagree = 1	Strongly disagree = 6

Interpreting Your Score: Some people need to "make sense" of things around them more quickly or completely than do other people. This personal need for perceptual structure relates to selective attention as well as perceptual organization and interpretation. For instance, people with a strong personal need for closure might form first impressions, fill in missing pieces, and rely on stereotyping more quickly than people who don't mind incomplete perceptual situations.

This scale, called the personal need for structure (PNS) scale, assesses the degree to which people are motivated to structure their world in a simple and unambiguous way. Scores range from 12 to 72, with higher scores indicating a high personal need for structure. PNS norms vary from one group to the next. For instance, a study of Finnish nurses reported a mean PNS score of 34, whereas a study of 236 male and 303 female undergraduate psychology students in the United States had a mean score of 42. The norms in the following table are based on scores from these undergraduate students.

Personal need for structure scale	Interpretation
58 to 72	High need for personal structure
47 to 57	Above-average need for personal structure
38 to 46	Average need for personal structure
27 to 37	Below-average need for personal structure
12 to 26	Low need for personal structure

Chapter 4

Scoring Key for "Are You Committed to Your School?"

Scoring Instructions: Use the table below to assign numbers to each box you checked. Insert the number for each statement on the appropriate line below the table. For example, if you checked "Moderately disagree" for statement 1 ("I would be very happy . . ."), you would write a "2" on the line with "(1)" underneath it. After assigning numbers for all 12 statements, add up your scores to estimate your affective and continuance school commitment.

For statement items 1, 2, 3, 4, 6, 8, 10, 11, 12	For statement items 5, 7, 9
Strongly agree = 7	Strongly agree = 1
Moderately agree = 6	Moderately agree = 2
Slightly agree = 5	Slightly agree = 3
Neutral = 4	Neutral = 4
Slightly disagree = 3	Slightly disagree = 5
Moderately disagree = 2	Moderately disagree = 6
Strongly disagree = 1	Strongly disagree = 7

Affective commitment:

___ + ___ + ___ + ___ + ___ + ___ = ___
(1) (3) (5) (7) (9) (11)

Continuance commitment:

___ + ___ + ___ + ___ + ___ + ___ = ___
(2) (4) (6) (8) (10) (12)

Interpreting Your Affective Commitment Score: This scale measures both affective commitment and continuance commitment. *Affective commitment* refers to a person's emotional attachment to, identification with, and involvement in a particular organization. In this scale, the organization is the school you are attending. How high or low is your affective commitment? The ideal would be to compare your score with the collective results of other students in your class. You can also compare your score with the following results, which are based on a sample of employees.

Affective commitment score	Interpretation
Above 37	High level of affective commitment
32 to 36	Above-average level of affective commitment
28 to 31	Average level of affective commitment
20 to 27	Below-average level of affective commitment
Below 20	Low level of affective commitment

Interpreting Your Continuance Commitment Score: *Continuance commitment* occurs when employees believe it is in their own personal interest to remain with the organization. People with a high continuance commitment have a strong calculative bond with the organization. In this scale, the organization is the school you are attending. How high or low is your continuance commitment? The ideal would be to compare your score with the collective results of other students in your class. You can also compare your score with the following results, which are based on a sample of employees.

Continuance commitment score	Interpretation
Above 32	High level of continuance commitment
26 to 31	Above-average level of continuance commitment
21 to 25	Average level of continuance commitment
13 to 20	Below-average level of continuance commitment
Below 12	Low level of continuance commitment

Chapter 5

Scoring Key for "What Needs Are Most Important to You?"

Scoring Instructions: Use the table below to assign numbers to each box you checked. Insert the number for each statement on the appropriate line below the table. For example, if you checked "Moderately inaccurate" for statement 1 ("I would rather be myself than be well thought of"), you would write a "3" on the line with "(1)" underneath it. After assigning numbers for all 15 statements, add up your scores to estimate your results for the two learned needs measured by this scale.

For statement items 2, 3, 4, 5, 6, 8, 9, 12, 14, 15	For statement items 1, 7, 10, 11, 13
Very accurate description of me = 4	Very accurate description of me = 0
Moderately accurate = 3	Moderately accurate = 1
Neither accurate nor inaccurate = 2	Neither accurate nor inaccurate = 2
Moderately inaccurate = 1	Moderately inaccurate = 3
Very inaccurate description of me = 0	Very inaccurate description of me = 4

Need for achievement:

___ + ___ + ___ + ___ + ___ + ___ + ___ = ___
(2) (3) (6) (7) (9) (12) (14)

Need for social approval:

___ + ___ + ___ + ___ + ___ + ___ + ___ + ___ = ___
(1) (4) (5) (8) (10) (11) (13) (15)

Although everyone has the same innate drives, our secondary or learned needs vary on the basis of our self-concept. This self-assessment provides an estimate of your need strength on two secondary needs: need for achievement and need for social approval.

Interpreting Your Need for Achievement Score: This scale, formally called *achievement striving,* estimates the extent to which you are motivated to take on and achieve challenging personal goals. This includes a desire to perform better than others and to reach one's potential. The scale ranges from 0 to 28. How high or low is your need for achievement? The ideal would be to compare your score with the collective results of other students in your class. Otherwise, the following exhibit offers a rough set of norms with which you can compare your score on this scale.

Need for achievement score	Interpretation
24 to 28	High level of need for achievement
18 to 23	Above-average level of need for achievement
12 to 17	Average level of need for achievement
6 to 11	Below-average level of need for achievement
0 to 5	Low level of need for achievement

Interpreting Your Need for Social Approval Score: The need for social approval scale estimates the extent to which you are motivated to seek favorable evaluation from others. Founded on the drive to bond, the need for social approval is a secondary need in that people vary in this need on the basis of their self-concept, values, personality, and possibly socialized social norms. This scale ranges from 0 to 32. How high or low is your need for social approval? The ideal would be to compare your score with the collective results of other students in your class. Otherwise, the following exhibit offers a rough set of norms with which you can compare your score on this scale.

Need for social approval score	Interpretation
28 to 32	High need for social approval
20 to 27	Above-average need for social approval
12 to 19	Average need for social approval
6 to 11	Below-average need for social approval
0 to 5	Low need for social approval

Chapter 6

Scoring Key for "What Is Your Attitude toward Money?"

Scoring Instructions: This instrument presents three dimensions with a smaller set of items from the original money attitude scale. To calculate your score on each dimension, write the number that you circled in the scale above the corresponding item number in the scoring key at the bottom of this page. For example, write the number you circled for the scale's first statement ("I sometimes purchase things . . .") on the line above "(1)." Then add up the numbers for that dimension. The money attitude total score is calculated by adding up all scores on all dimensions.

Interpreting Your Score: The three money attitude scale dimensions measured here, as well as the total score, are defined as follows:

Money as power/prestige: People with higher scores on this dimension tend to use money to influence and impress others.

Retention time: People with higher scores on this dimension tend to be careful financial planners.

Money anxiety: People with higher scores on this dimension tend to view money as a source of anxiety.

Money attitude total: This is a general estimate of how much respect and attention you give to money.

Money attitude dimension	Calculation	Your score
Money as power/prestige	____ + ____ + ____ + ____ = (1) (4) (7) (10)	____
Retention time	____ + ____ + ____ + ____ = (2) (5) (8) (11)	____
Money anxiety	____ + ____ + ____ + ____ = (3) (6) (9) (12)	____
Money attitude total	Add up all dimension scores =	____

The below table shows how a sample of MBA students scored on the money attitude scale. The table shows percentiles, that is, the percentage of people with the same or lower score. For example, the table indicates that a score of 12 on the retention scale is quite low because only 20 percent of the MBA students scored at this level or lower (80 percent scored higher). However, a score of 12 on the prestige scale is quite high because 80 percent of the MBA students scored at or below this number (only 20 percent scored higher).

Percentile (% with scores at or below this number)	Prestige score	Retention score	Anxiety score	Total money score
Average score	9.89	14.98	12.78	37.64
Highest score	17	20	18	53
90	13	18	16	44
80	12	17	15	42
70	11	17	14	40
60	10	16	14	39
50	10	15	13	38
40	9	14	12	36
30	8	14	11	34
20	7	12	10	32
10	7	11	8	29
Lowest score	4	8	6	23

Chapter 7

Scoring Key for "Do You Have a Creative Personality?"

Scoring Instructions: Assign a positive point (+1) after each of the following words that you checked off in the self-assessment:

Capable	____	Inventive	____
Clever	____	Original	____
Confident	____	Reflective	____
Egotistical	____	Resourceful	____
Humorous	____	Self-confident	____
Individualistic	____	Sexy	____
Informal	____	Snobbish	____
Insightful	____	Unconventional	____
Intelligent	____	Wide interests	____

Assign a negative point (−1) after each of the following words that you checked off in the self-assessment:

Affected	____	Cautious	____
Commonplace	____	Mannerly	____

Conservative	____	Narrow interests	____
Conventional	____	Sincere	____
Dissatisfied	____	Submissive	____
Honest	____	Suspicious	____

Words without a check mark receive a zero. Add up the total score, which will range from −12 to +18.

Interpreting Your Score: This instrument estimates your creative potential as a personal characteristic. The scale recognizes that creative people are intelligent and persistent and possess an inventive thinking style. Creative personality varies somewhat from one occupational group to the next. The table below provides norms based on undergraduate and graduate university students.

Creative disposition	Interpretation
Above +9	You have a high creative personality
+1 to +9	You have an average creative personality
Below +1	You have a low creative personality

Chapter 8

Scoring Key for "What Team Roles Do You Prefer?"

Scoring Instructions: Write the score circled for each item on the appropriate line below (statement numbers are in parentheses), and add up each scale.

Encourager	___ (6) +	___ (9) +	___ (11) =	___
Gatekeeper	___ (4) +	___ (10) +	___ (13) =	___
Harmonizer	___ (3) +	___ (8) +	___ (12) =	___
Initiator	___ (1) +	___ (5) +	___ (14) =	___
Summarizer	___ (2) +	___ (7) +	___ (15) =	___

Interpreting Your Score: The five team roles measured here are based on scholarship over the years. The following table defines these five roles and presents the range of scores for high, medium, and low levels of each role. These norms are based on results from a sample of MBA students.

Team role and definition	Interpretation
Encourager: People who score high on this dimension have a strong tendency to praise and support the ideas of other team members, thereby showing warmth and solidarity to the group.	High: 12 and above Medium: 9 to 11 Low: 8 and below
Gatekeeper: People who score high on this dimension have a strong tendency to encourage all team members to participate in the discussion.	High: 12 and above Medium: 9 to 11 Low: 8 and below
Harmonizer: People who score high on this dimension have a strong tendency to mediate intragroup conflicts and reduce tension.	High: 11 and above Medium: 9 to 10 Low: 8 and below
Initiator: People who score high on this dimension have a strong tendency to identify goals for the meeting, including ways to work on those goals.	High: 12 and above Medium: 9 to 11 Low: 8 and below
Summarizer: People who score high on this dimension have a strong tendency to keep track of what was said in the meeting (i.e., act as the team's memory).	High: 10 and above Medium: 8 to 9 Low: 7 and below

Chapter 9

Scoring Key for "Are You an Active Listener?"

Scoring Instructions: Use the table below to score the response you circled for each statement. Write the score for each item on the appropriate line below the table (statement numbers are in parentheses), and add up each subscale. For example, if you checked "Very much" for statement 1 ("I keep an open mind . . ."), you would write a "3" on the line with "(1)" underneath it. Then calculate the overall active listening inventory score by summing all subscales.

For statement items 3, 4, 6, 7, 10, 13	For statement items 1, 2, 5, 8, 9, 11, 12, 14, 15
Not at all = 3	Not at all = 0
A little = 2	A little = 1
Somewhat = 1	Somewhat = 2
Very much = 0	Very much = 3

Avoiding interruption (AI)	___ (3)	+ ___ (7)	+ ___ (15)	= ___
Maintaining interest (MI)	___ (6)	+ ___ (9)	+ ___ (14)	= ___
Postponing evaluation (PE)	___ (1)	+ ___ (5)	+ ___ (13)	= ___
Organizing information (OI)	___ (2)	+ ___ (10)	+ ___ (12)	= ___
Showing interest (SI)	___ (4)	+ ___ (8)	+ ___ (11)	= ___
Active listening (total score)				___

Interpreting Your Score: The five active listening dimensions and the overall active listening scale measured here are defined below, along with the range of scores for high, medium, and low levels of each dimension based on a sample of MBA students.

Active listening dimension and definition	Score interpretation
Avoiding interruption: People with high scores on this dimension have a strong tendency to let a speaker finish his or her statements before responding.	High: 8 to 9 Medium: 5 to 7 Low: Below 5
Maintaining interest: People with high scores on this dimension have a strong tendency to remain focused and concentrate on what a speaker is saying even when the conversation is boring or the information is well known.	High: 6 to 9 Medium: 3 to 5 Low: Below 3
Postponing evaluation: People with high scores on this dimension have a strong tendency to keep an open mind and avoid evaluating what the speaker is saying until the speaker has finished.	High: 7 to 9 Medium: 4 to 6 Low: Below 4
Organizing information: People with high scores on this dimension have a strong tendency to actively organize the speaker's ideas into meaningful categories.	High: 8 to 9 Medium: 5 to 7 Low: Below 5
Showing interest: People with high scores on this dimension have a strong tendency to use nonverbal gestures or brief verbal acknowledgments to demonstrate that they are paying attention to the speaker.	High: 7 to 9 Medium: 5 to 6 Low: Below 5

Active listening dimension and definition	Score interpretation
Active listening (total): People with high scores on this total active listening scale have a strong tendency to actively sense a sender's signals, evaluate them accurately, and respond appropriately.	High: Above 31 Medium: 26 to 31 Low: Below 26

Note: The active listening inventory does not explicitly measure two other dimensions of active listening, namely, empathizing and providing feedback. Empathizing is difficult to measure with behaviors; providing feedback involves behaviors similar to showing interest.

Chapter 10

Scoring Key for "How Do You Influence Your Boss?"

Scoring Instructions: To calculate your scores on the upward influence scale, write the number circled for each statement on the appropriate line below (statement numbers are in parentheses), and add up each scale.

Assertiveness	___ (8)	+ ___ (15)	+ ___ (16)	= ___
Exchange	___ (2)	+ ___ (5)	+ ___ (13)	= ___
Coalition formation	___ (1)	+ ___ (11)	+ ___ (18)	= ___
Upward appeal	___ (4)	+ ___ (12)	+ ___ (17)	= ___
Ingratiation	___ (3)	+ ___ (6)	+ ___ (9)	= ___
Persuasion	___ (7)	+ ___ (10)	+ ___ (14)	= ___

Interpreting Your Score: *Influence* refers to any behavior that attempts to alter someone's attitudes or behavior. There are several types of influence, including the following six measured by this instrument: assertiveness, exchange, coalition formation, upward appeal, ingratiation, and persuasion. This instrument assesses your preference for using each type of influence on your boss or other people at higher levels in the organization. Each scale has a potential score ranging from 3 to 15 points. A higher score on a scale indicates that you have a higher preference for that particular tactic. The six upward influence dimensions measured here are defined below, along with the range of scores for high, medium, and low levels of each tactic.

Influence tactic and definition	Score interpretation
Assertiveness: Assertiveness involves actively applying legitimate and coercive power to influence others. This tactic includes persistently reminding others of their obligations, frequently checking their work, confronting them, and using threats of sanctions to force compliance.	High: 8 to 15 Medium: 5 to 7 Low: 3 to 4
Exchange: Exchange involves the promise of benefits or resources in exchange for the target person's compliance with your request. This tactic also includes reminding the target of past benefits or favors with the expectation that the target will now make up for that debt. Negotiation is also part of the exchange strategy.	High: 10 to 15 Medium: 6 to 9 Low: 3 to 5
Coalition formation: Coalition formation occurs when a group of people with common interests band together to influence others. This tactic pools the power and resources of many people, so the coalition potentially has more influence than would be the case if each person operated alone.	High: 11 to 15 Medium: 7 to 10 Low: 3 to 6
Upward appeal: Upward appeal occurs when you rely on support from a higher-level person to influence others. In effect, this is a form of coalition in which one or more members are people with higher authority or expertise.	High: 9 to 15 Medium: 6 to 8 Low: 3 to 5
Ingratiation: Flattering your boss in front of others, helping your boss with his or her work, agreeing with your boss's ideas, and asking for your boss's advice are all examples of ingratiation. This tactic increases the perceived similarity of the source of ingratiation to the target person.	High: 13 to 15 Medium: 9 to 12 Low: 3 to 8
Persuasion: Persuasion refers to using logical and emotional appeals to change others' attitudes. According to several studies, it is also the most common upward influence strategy.	High: 13 to 15 Medium: 9 to 12 Low: 3 to 8

Chapter 11

Scoring Key for the Dutch Test for Conflict Handling

Scoring Instructions: To calculate your scores on the Dutch test for conflict handling, write the number circled for each statement on the appropriate line below (statement numbers are in parentheses), and add up each scale.

Yielding	___ (1)	+ ___ (6)	+ ___ (11)	+ ___ (16)	= ___
Compromising	___ (2)	+ ___ (7)	+ ___ (12)	+ ___ (17)	= ___
Forcing	___ (3)	+ ___ (8)	+ ___ (13)	+ ___ (18)	= ___
Problem solving	___ (4)	+ ___ (9)	+ ___ (14)	+ ___ (19)	= ___
Avoiding	___ (5)	+ ___ (10)	+ ___ (15)	+ ___ (20)	= ___

Interpreting Your Score: The five conflict-handling dimensions are defined below, along with the range of scores for high, medium, and low levels of each dimension.

Conflict-handling dimension and definition	Score interpretation
Yielding: Yielding involves giving in completely to the other side's wishes or at least cooperating with little or no attention to your own interests. This style involves making unilateral concessions or unconditional promises and offering help with no expectation of reciprocal help.	High: 14 to 20 Medium: 9 to 13 Low: 4 to 8
Compromising: Compromising involves looking for a position in which your losses are offset by equally valued gains. It involves matching the other party's concessions, making conditional promises or threats, and actively searching for a middle ground between the interests of the two parties.	High: 17 to 20 Medium: 11 to 16 Low: 4 to 10
Forcing: Forcing involves trying to win the conflict at the other's expense. It includes "hard" influence tactics, particularly assertiveness, to get one's own way.	High: 15 to 20 Medium: 9 to 14 Low: 4 to 8

Conflict-handling dimension and definition	Score interpretation
Problem solving: Problem solving tries to find a mutually beneficial solution for all parties. Information sharing is an important feature of this style because all parties need to identify common ground and potential solutions that satisfy all of them.	High: 17 to 20 Medium: 11 to 16 Low: 4 to 10
Avoiding: Avoiding tries to smooth over or avoid conflict situations altogether. It represents a low concern for both self and the other party. In other words, avoiders try to suppress thinking about the conflict.	High: 13 to 20 Medium: 8 to 12 Low: 4 to 7

Chapter 12

Scoring Key for "What's Your Boss's Approach to Leadership?"

Transactional Leadership

Scoring Instructions: Add up scores for the odd-numbered items (i.e., 1, 3, 5, 7, 9, 11, 13, 15). The maximum score is 40.

Interpreting Your Score: Transactional leadership is "managing"–helping organizations to achieve their current objectives more efficiently, such as by linking job performance to valued rewards and ensuring that employees have the resources needed to get the job done. The following table shows the range of scores for high, medium, and low levels of transactional leadership.

Transactional leadership score	Interpretation
32 to 40	The person you evaluated seems to be a highly transactional leader.
25 to 31	The person you evaluated seems to be a moderately transactional leader.
Below 25	The person you evaluated seems to display few characteristics of a transactional leader.

Transformational Leadership

Scoring Instructions: Add up scores for the even-numbered items (i.e., 2, 4, 6, 8, 10, 12, 14, 16). The maximum score is 40. A higher score indicates that your supervisor has a strong inclination toward transformational leadership.

Interpreting Your Score: Transformational leadership involves changing teams or organizations by creating, communicating, and modeling a vision for the organization or work unit and inspiring employees to strive for that vision. The following table shows the range of scores for high, medium, and low levels of transformational leadership.

Transformational leadership score	Interpretation
32 to 40	The person you evaluated seems to be a highly transformational leader.
25 to 31	The person you evaluated seems to be a moderately transformational leader.
Below 25	The person you evaluated seems to display few characteristics of a transformational leader.

Chapter 13

Scoring Key for "What Organizational Structure Do You Prefer?"

Scoring Instructions: Use the table below to assign numbers to each response you circled. Insert the number for each statement on the appropriate line below the table. For example, if you checked "Not at all" for item 1 ("A person's career ladder . . ."), you would write a "0" on the line with "(1)" underneath it. After assigning numbers for all 15 statements, add up the scores to estimate your degree of preference for a tall hierarchy, formalization, and centralization. Then calculate the overall score by summing all scales.

For statement items 2, 3, 8, 10, 11, 12, 14, 15	For statement items 1, 4, 5, 6, 7, 9, 13
Not at all = 3	Not at all = 0
A little = 2	A little = 1
Somewhat = 1	Somewhat = 2
Very much = 0	Very much = 3

Tall hierarchy (H)	___ + (1)	___ + (4)	___ + (10)	___ + (12)	___ = (15)	___ (H)
Formalization (F)	___ + (2)	___ + (6)	___ + (8)	___ + (11)	___ = (13)	___ (F)
Centralization (C)	___ + (3)	___ + (5)	___ + (7)	___ + (9)	___ = (14)	___ (C)
Total score (mechanistic)	___ + (H)	___ + (F)	___ = (C)	___ Total		

Interpreting Your Score: The three organizational structure dimensions and the overall score are defined below, along with the range of scores for high, medium, and low levels of each dimension based on a sample of MBA students.

Organizational structure dimension and definition	Interpretation
Tall hierarchy: People with high scores on this dimension prefer to work in organizations with several levels of hierarchy and a narrow span of control (few employees per supervisor).	High: 11 to 15 Medium: 6 to 10 Low: Below 6
Formalization: People with high scores on this dimension prefer to work in organizations where jobs are clearly defined with limited discretion.	High: 12 to 15 Medium: 9 to 11 Low: Below 9
Centralization: People with high scores on this dimension prefer to work in organizations where decision making occurs mainly among top management rather than being spread out to lower-level staff.	High: 10 to 15 Medium: 7 to 9 Low: Below 7
Total score (mechanistic): People with high scores on this dimension prefer to work in mechanistic organizations, whereas those with low scores prefer to work in organic organizational structures. Mechanistic structures are characterized by a narrow span of control and high degree of formalization and centralization. Organic structures have a wide span of control, little formalization, and decentralized decision making.	High: 30 to 45 Medium: 22 to 29 Low: Below 22

Chapter 14

Scoring Key for "What Are Your Corporate Culture Preferences?"

Scoring Instructions: On each line below, write a "1" if you circled the statement and a "0" if you did not. Then add up the scores for each subscale.

Interpreting Your Score: These corporate cultures may be found in many organizations, but they represent only four of many possible organizational cultures. Also, keep in mind that none of these cultures is inherently good or bad. Each is effective in different situations. The four corporate cultures are defined below, along with the range of scores for high, medium, and low levels of each dimension based on a sample of MBA students.

Control culture	___ +	___ +	___ +	___ +	___ +	___ =	___
	(2a)	(5a)	(6b)	(8b)	(11b)	(12a)	
Performance culture	___ +	___ +	___ +	___ +	___ +	___ =	___
	(1b)	(3b)	(5b)	(6a)	(7a)	(9b)	
Relationship culture	___ +	___ +	___ +	___ +	___ +	___ =	___
	(1a)	(3a)	(4b)	(8a)	(10b)	(12b)	
Responsive culture	___ +	___ +	___ +	___ +	___ +	___ =	___
	(2b)	(4a)	(7b)	(9a)	(10a)	(11a)	

Corporate culture dimension and definition	Score interpretation
Control culture: This culture values the role of senior executives to lead the organization. Its goal is to keep everyone aligned and under control.	High: 3 to 6 Medium: 1 to 2 Low: 0
Performance culture: This culture values individual and organizational performance and strives for effectiveness and efficiency.	High: 5 to 6 Medium: 3 to 4 Low: 0 to 2
Relationship culture: This culture values nurturing and well-being. It considers open communication, fairness, teamwork, and sharing to be a vital part of organizational life.	High: 6 Medium: 4 to 5 Low: 0 to 3
Responsive culture: This culture values its ability to keep in tune with the external environment, including being competitive and realizing new opportunities.	High: 6 Medium: 4 to 5 Low: 0 to 3

Chapter 15

Scoring Key for "Are You Tolerant of Change?"

Scoring Instructions: Use the table below to assign numbers to each box you checked. For example, if you checked "Moderately disagree" for statement 1 ("An expert who doesn't come up . . ."), you would write a "6" beside that statement. After assigning numbers for all 16 statements, add up your scores to estimate your tolerance for change.

For statement items 2, 4, 6, 8, 10, 12, 14, 16	For statement items 1, 3, 5, 7, 9, 11, 13, 15
Strongly agree = 7	Strongly agree = 1
Moderately agree = 6	Moderately agree = 2
Slightly agree = 5	Slightly agree = 3
Neutral = 4	Neutral = 4
Slightly disagree = 3	Slightly disagree = 5
Moderately disagree = 2	Moderately disagree = 6
Strongly disagree = 1	Strongly disagree = 7

Interpreting Your Score: This measurement instrument is formally known as the *tolerance of ambiguity scale.* Although it was developed 40 years ago, the instrument is still used today in research. People with a high tolerance of ambiguity are comfortable with uncertainty, sudden change, and new situations. These are characteristics of the hyperfast changes occurring in many organizations today. The table below indicates the range of scores for high, medium, and low tolerance for change. These norms are based on results for MBA students.

Tolerance for change score	Interpretation
81 to 112	You seem to have a high tolerance for change.
63 to 80	You seem to have a moderate level of tolerance for change.
Below 63	You seem to have a low degree of tolerance for change. Instead, you prefer stable work environments.

GLOSSARY

A

ability The natural aptitudes and learned capabilities required to successfully complete a task. (2)

absorptive capacity The ability to recognize the value of new information, assimilate it, and use it for value-added activities. (1)

achievement-nurturing orientation A cross-cultural value describing the degree to which people in a culture emphasize competitive versus cooperative relations with other people. (2)

action research A problem-focused change process that combines action orientation (changing attitudes and behavior) and research orientation (testing theory through data collection and analysis). (15)

adaptive culture An organizational culture in which employees are receptive to change, including the ongoing alignment of the organization to its environment and continuous improvement of internal processes. (14)

alternative dispute resolution (ADR) An orderly process of third-party dispute resolution, typically including mediation followed by arbitration. (11)

anchoring and adjustment heuristic A natural tendency for people to be influenced by an initial anchor point such that they do not sufficiently move away from that point as new information is provided. (7)

appreciative inquiry An organizational change strategy that directs the group's attention away from its own problems and focuses participants on the group's potential and positive elements. (15)

artifacts The observable symbols and signs of an organization's culture. (14)

attitudes The cluster of beliefs, assessed feelings, and behavioral intentions toward a person, object, or event (called an *attitude object*). (4)

attraction-selection-attrition (ASA) theory A theory which states that organizations have a natural tendency to attract, select, and retain people with values and personality characteristics that are consistent with the organization's character, resulting in a more homogeneous organization and a stronger culture. (14)

attribution process The perceptual process of deciding whether an observed behavior or event is caused largely by internal or external factors. (3)

autonomy The degree to which a job gives employees the freedom, independence, and discretion to schedule their work and determine the procedures used in completing it. (6)

availability heuristic A natural tendency to assign higher probabilities to objects or events that are easier to recall from memory, even though ease of recall is also affected by nonprobability factors (e.g., emotional response, recent events). (7)

B

balanced scorecard (BSC) A goal-setting and reward system that translates the organization's vision and mission into specific, measurable performance goals related to financial, customer, internal, and learning/growth (i.e., human capital) processes. (5, 6)

behavior modification A theory that explains learning in terms of the antecedents and consequences of behavior. (3)

bicultural audit A process of diagnosing cultural relations between companies and determining the extent to which cultural clashes will likely occur. (14)

bounded rationality The view that people are bounded in their decision-making capabilities, including access to limited information, limited information processing, and tendency toward satisficing rather than maximizing when making choices. (7)

brainstorming A freewheeling, face-to-face meeting where team members aren't allowed to criticize but are encouraged to speak freely, generate as many ideas as possible, and build on the ideas of others. (8)

Brooks's law The principle that adding more people to a late software project only makes it later. Also called the *mythical man-month.* (8)

C

categorical thinking Organizing people and objects into preconceived categories that are stored in our long-term memory. (3)

centrality A contingency of power pertaining to the degree and nature of interdependence between the power holder and others. (10)

centralization The degree to which formal decision authority is held by a small group of people, typically those at the top of the organizational hierarchy. (13)

ceremonies Planned displays of organizational culture, conducted specifically for the benefit of an audience. (14)

coalition A group that attempts to influence people outside the group by pooling the resources and power of its members. (10)

cognitive dissonance A condition that occurs when we perceive an inconsistency between our beliefs, feelings, and behavior. (4)

collectivism A cross-cultural value describing the degree to which people in a culture emphasize duty to groups to which people belong and to group harmony. (2)

communication The process by which information is transmitted and understood between two or more people. (9)

competencies Skills, knowledge, aptitudes, and other personal characteristics that lead to superior performance. (2)

concurrent engineering The organization of employees from several departments into a temporary team for the purpose of developing a product or service. (13)

conflict A process in which one party perceives that his or her interests are being opposed or negatively affected by another party. (11)

conscientiousness A personality dimension describing people who are careful, dependable, and self-disciplined. (2)

constructive conflict A type of conflict in which people focus their discussion on the issue while maintaining respect for people having other points of view. (8, 11)

contact hypothesis A theory stating that the more we interact with someone, the less prejudiced or perceptually biased we will be against that person. (3)

continuance commitment An employee's calculative attachment to the organization, whereby the employee is motivated to stay only because leaving would be costly. (4)

corporate social responsibility (CSR) Organizational activities intended to benefit society and the environment beyond the firm's immediate financial interests or legal obligations. (1)

counterproductive work behaviors (CWBs) Voluntary behaviors that have the potential to directly or indirectly harm the organization. (1)

countervailing power The capacity of a person, team, or organization to keep a more powerful person or group in the exchange relationship. (10)

creativity The development of original ideas that make a socially recognized contribution. (7)

D

decision making The conscious process of making choices among alternatives with the intention of moving toward some desired state of affairs. (7)

deep-level diversity Differences in the psychological characteristics of employees, including personalities, beliefs, values, and attitudes. (1)

distributive justice Perceived fairness in the individual's ratio of outcomes to contributions compared with a comparison other's ratio of outcomes to contributions. (5)

divergent thinking Reframing a problem in a unique way and generating different approaches to the issue. (7)

divisional structure An organizational structure in which employees are organized around geographic areas, outputs (products or services), or clients. (13)

drives Hardwired characteristics of the brain that correct deficiencies or maintain an internal equilibrium by producing emotions to energize individuals. (5)

E

electronic brainstorming A recent form of brainstorming that relies on networked computers for submitting and sharing creative ideas. (8)

emotional contagion The nonconscious process of "catching" or sharing another person's emotions by mimicking that person's facial expressions and other nonverbal behavior. (9)

emotional dissonance The conflict between required and true emotions. (4)

emotional intelligence (EI) A set of abilities to perceive and express emotion, assimilate emotion in thought, understand and reason with emotion, and regulate emotion in oneself and others. (4)

emotional labor The effort, planning, and control needed to express organizationally desired emotions during interpersonal transactions. (4)

emotions Physiological, behavioral, and psychological episodes experienced toward an object, person, or event that create a state of readiness. (4)

empathy A person's understanding of and sensitivity to the feelings, thoughts, and situations of others. (3)

employee engagement The employee's emotional and cognitive motivation, self-efficacy to perform the job, perceived clarity of the organization's vision and his or her specific role in that vision, and belief that he or she has the resources to get the job done. (5)

employee involvement The degree to which employees influence how their work is organized and carried out. (7)

employee stock ownership plan (ESOP) A reward system that encourages employees to buy company stock. (6)

empowerment A psychological concept in which people experience more self-determination, meaning, competence, and impact regarding their role in the organization. (6)

equity sensitivity An individual's outcome/input preferences and reaction to various outcome/input ratios. (5)

equity theory A theory explaining how people develop perceptions of fairness in the distribution and exchange of resources. (5)

ERG theory A needs hierarchy theory consisting of three fundamental needs–existence, relatedness, and growth. (5)

escalation of commitment The tendency to repeat an apparently bad decision or allocate more resources to a failing course of action. (7)

ethical sensitivity A personal characteristic that enables people to recognize the presence of an ethical issue and determine its relative importance. (2)

ethics The study of moral principles or values that determine whether actions are right or wrong and outcomes are good or bad. (1)

evaluation apprehension A decision-making problem that occurs when individuals are reluctant to mention ideas that seem silly because they believe (often correctly) that other team members are silently evaluating them. (8)

evidence-based management The practice of making decisions and taking actions based on research evidence. (1)

exit-voice-loyalty-neglect (EVLN) model The four ways, as indicated in the name, that employees respond to job dissatisfaction. (4)

expectancy theory A motivation theory based on the idea that work effort is directed toward behaviors that people believe will lead to desired outcomes. (5)

extroversion A personality dimension describing people who are outgoing, talkative, sociable, and assertive. (2)

F

false-consensus effect A perceptual error in which we overestimate the extent to which others have beliefs and characteristics similar to our own. (3)

Fiedler's contingency model Developed by Fred Fiedler, an early contingency leadership model that suggests that leader effectiveness depends on whether the person's natural leadership style is appropriately matched to the situation. (12)

five-factor model (FFM) The five abstract dimensions representing most personality traits: conscientiousness, emotional stability, openness to experience, agreeableness, and extroversion. (2)

force field analysis Kurt Lewin's model of systemwide change that helps change agents diagnose the forces that drive and restrain proposed organizational change. (15)

formalization The degree to which organizations standardize behavior through rules, procedures, formal training, and related mechanisms. (13)

four-drive theory A motivation theory that is based on the innate drives to acquire, bond, learn, and defend and that incorporates both emotions and rationality. (5)

functional structure An organizational structure in which employees are organized around specific knowledge or other resources. (13)

fundamental attribution error The tendency to see the person rather than the situation as the main cause of that person's behavior. (3)

future search An organizational change strategy that consists of systemwide group sessions, usually lasting a few days, in which participants identify trends and establish ways to adapt to those changes. (15)

G

gainsharing plan A team-based reward that calculates bonuses from the work unit's cost savings and productivity improvement. (6)

general adaptation syndrome A model of the stress experience, consisting of three stages: alarm reaction, resistance, and exhaustion. (4)

global mindset The capacity for complex perceiving and thinking characterized by superior awareness of and openness to different ways that others perceive their environment. (3)

globalization Economic, social, and cultural connectivity with people in other parts of the world. (1)

globally integrated enterprise An organizational structure in which work processes and executive functions are distributed around the world through global centers, rather than developed in a home country and replicated in satellite countries or regions. (13)

goal setting The process of motivating employees and clarifying their role perceptions by establishing performance objectives. (5)

grapevine An unstructured and informal network founded on social relationships rather than organizational charts or job descriptions. (9)

groupthink The tendency of highly cohesive groups to value consensus at the price of decision quality. (8)

H

halo effect A perceptual error whereby our general impression of a person, usually based on one prominent characteristic, colors our perception of other characteristics of that person. (3)

high-performance work practices (HPWP) A perspective which holds that effective organizations incorporate several workplace practices that leverage the potential of human capital. (1)

human capital The stock of knowledge, skills, and abilities among employees that provides economic value to the organization. (1)

I

implicit favorite A preferred alternative that the decision maker uses repeatedly as a comparison with other choices. (7)

implicit leadership theory A theory stating that people evaluate a leader's effectiveness in terms of how well that person fits preconceived beliefs about the features and behaviors of effective leaders (leadership prototypes) and that people tend to inflate the influence of leaders on organizational events. (12)

impression management The practice of actively shaping our public images. (10)

individualism A cross-cultural value describing the degree to which people in a culture emphasize independence and personal uniqueness. (2)

influence Any behavior that attempts to alter someone's attitudes or behavior. (10)

information overload A condition in which the volume of information received exceeds the person's capacity to process it. (9)

ingratiation Any attempt to increase liking by, or perceived similarity to, some targeted person. (10)

inoculation effect A persuasive communication strategy of warning listeners that others will try to influence them in the future and that they should be wary about the opponent's arguments. (10)

intellectual capital A company's stock of knowledge, including human capital, structural capital, and relationship capital. (1)

intuition The ability to know when a problem or opportunity exists and to select the best course of action without conscious reasoning. (7)

J

job burnout The process of emotional exhaustion, cynicism, and reduced personal accomplishment that results from prolonged exposure to stressors. (4)

job characteristics model A job design model that relates the motivational properties of jobs to specific personal and organizational consequences of those properties. (6)

job design The process of assigning tasks to a job, including the interdependency of those tasks with other jobs. (6)

job enlargement The practice of adding more tasks to an existing job. (6)

job enrichment The practice of giving employees more responsibility for scheduling, coordinating, and planning their own work. (6)

job evaluation Systematically rating the worth of jobs within an organization by measuring their required skill, effort, responsibility, and working conditions. (6)

job rotation The practice of moving employees from one job to another. (6)

job satisfaction A person's evaluation of his or her job and work context. (4)

job specialization The result of division of labor in which work is subdivided into separate jobs assigned to different people. (6)

Johari Window A model of mutual understanding that encourages disclosure and feedback to increase our own open area and reduce the blind, hidden, and unknown areas. (3)

L

leadership Influencing, motivating, and enabling others to contribute toward the effectiveness and success of the organizations of which they are members. (12)

leadership substitutes A theory identifying contingencies that either limit a leader's ability to influence subordinates or make a particular leadership style unnecessary. (12)

lean management A cluster of practices to improve organizational efficiency by continuously reducing waste, unevenness, and overburden in the production process. (1)

learning A relatively permanent change in behavior (or behavioral tendency) that occurs as a result of a person's interaction with the environment. (3)

learning orientation An individual attitude and organizational culture in which people welcome new learning opportunities, actively experiment with new ideas and practices, view reasonable mistakes as a natural part of the learning process, and continuously question past practices. (3)

legitimate power An agreement among organizational members that people in certain roles can request certain behaviors of others. (10)

locus of control A person's general belief about the amount of control he or she has over personal life events. (2)

M

Machiavellian values The beliefs that deceit is a natural and acceptable way to influence others and that getting more than one deserves is acceptable. (10)

management by walking around (MBWA) A communication practice in which executives get out of their offices and learn from others in the organization through face-to-face dialogue. (9)

Maslow's needs hierarchy theory A motivation theory of needs arranged in a hierarchy, whereby people are motivated to fulfill a higher need as a lower one becomes gratified. (5)

matrix structure An organizational structure that overlays two structures (such as a geographic divisional and a functional structure) in order to leverage the benefits of both. (13)

mechanistic structure An organizational structure with a narrow span of control and a high degree of formalization and centralization. (13)

media richness A medium's data-carrying capacity, that is, the volume and variety of information that can be transmitted during a specific time. (9)

mental imagery The process of mentally practicing a task and visualizing its successful completion. (6)

mental models Visual or relational images in our mind that represent the external world. (3)

moral intensity The degree to which an issue demands the application of ethical principles. (2)

motivation The forces within a person that affect his or her direction, intensity, and persistence of voluntary behavior. (2, 5)

motivator-hygiene theory Herzberg's theory stating that employees are primarily motivated by growth and esteem needs, not by lower-level needs. (6)

multisource (360-degree) feedback Information about an employee's performance collected from a full circle of people, including subordinates, peers, supervisors, and customers. (5)

Myers-Briggs Type Indicator (MBTI) An instrument designed to measure the elements of Jungian personality theory, particularly preferences regarding perceiving and judging information. (2)

N

need for achievement (nAch) A need in which people want to accomplish reasonably challenging goals and desire unambiguous feedback and recognition for their success. (5)

need for affiliation (nAff) A need in which people seek approval from others, conform to their wishes and expectations, and avoid conflict and confrontation. (5)

need for power (nPow) A need in which people want to control their environment, including people and material resources, to benefit either themselves (personalized power) or others (socialized power). (5)

needs Goal-directed forces that people experience. (5)

negotiation The process whereby two or more conflicting parties attempt to resolve their divergent goals by redefining the terms of their interdependence. (11)

network structure An alliance of several organizations for the purpose of creating a product or serving a client. (13)

neuroticism A personality dimension describing people with high levels of anxiety, hostility, depression, and self-consciousness. (2)

nominal group technique A variation of brainstorming consisting of three stages: Participants (1) silently and independently document their ideas, (2) collectively describe these ideas to the other team members without critique, and then (3) silently and independently evaluate the ideas presented. (8)

norms The informal rules and shared expectations that groups establish to regulate the behavior of their members. (8)

O

open systems A perspective which holds that organizations depend on the external environment for resources, affect that environment through their output, and consist of internal subsystems that transform inputs to outputs. (1)

organic structure An organizational structure with a wide span of control, little formalization, and decentralized decision making. (13)

organizational (affective) commitment The employee's emotional attachment to, identification with, and involvement in a particular organization. (4)

organizational behavior (OB) The study of what people think, feel, and do in and around organizations. (1)

organizational citizenship behaviors (OCBs) Various forms of cooperation and helpfulness to others that support the organization's social and psychological context. (1)

organizational culture The values and assumptions shared within an organization. (14)

organizational effectiveness A broad concept represented by several perspectives, including the organization's fit with the external environment, internal-subsystems configuration for high performance, emphasis on organizational learning, and ability to satisfy the needs of key stakeholders. (1)

organizational efficiency The amount of outputs relative to inputs in the organization's transformation process. (1)

organizational learning A perspective which holds that organizational effectiveness depends on the organization's capacity to acquire, share, use, and store valuable knowledge. (1)

organizational memory The storage and preservation of intellectual capital. (1)

organizational politics Behaviors that others perceive as self-serving tactics for personal gain at the expense of other people and possibly the organization. (10)

organizational socialization The process by which individuals learn the values, expected behaviors, and social knowledge necessary to assume their roles in the organization. (14)

organizational strategy The way the organization positions itself in its setting in relation to its stakeholders, given the organization's resources, capabilities, and mission. (13)

organizational structure The division of labor as well as the patterns of coordination, communication, workflow, and formal power that direct organizational activities. (13)

organizations Groups of people who work interdependently toward some purpose. (1)

P

parallel learning structure A highly participative arrangement composed of people from most levels of the organization who follow the action research model to produce meaningful organizational change. (15)

path-goal leadership theory A contingency theory of leadership based on the expectancy theory of motivation that relates several leadership styles to specific employee and situational contingencies. (12)

perception The process of receiving information about and making sense of the world around us. (3)

personality The relatively enduring pattern of thoughts, emotions, and behaviors that characterize a person, along with the psychological processes behind those characteristics. (2)

persuasion The use of facts, logical arguments, and emotional appeals to change another person's beliefs and attitudes, usually for the purpose of changing the person's behavior. (9, 10)

positive organizational behavior A perspective of organizational behavior that focuses on building positive qualities and traits within individuals or institutions as opposed to focusing on what is wrong with them. (3)

postdecisional justification The tendency to support the selected alternative in a decision by forgetting or downplaying the negative features of that alternative, emphasizing its positive features, and doing the opposite for alternatives not selected. (7)

power The capacity of a person, team, or organization to influence others. (10)

power distance A cross-cultural value describing the degree to which people in a culture accept unequal distribution of power in a society. (2)

primacy effect A perceptual error in which we quickly form an opinion of people on the basis of the first information we receive about them. (3)

procedural justice Perceived fairness of the procedures used to decide the distribution of resources. (5)

process losses Resources (including time and energy) expended toward team development and maintenance rather than the task. (8)

production blocking A time constraint in team decision making due to the procedural requirement that only one person may speak at a time. (8)

profit-sharing plan A reward system that pays bonuses to employees on the basis of the previous year's level of corporate profits. (6)

prospect theory A natural tendency to feel more dissatisfaction from losing a particular amount than satisfaction from gaining an equal amount. (7)

psychological harassment Repeated and hostile or unwanted conduct, verbal comments, actions, or gestures that affect an employee's dignity or psychological or physical integrity and that result in a harmful work environment for the employee. (4)

R

rational choice paradigm The view in decision making that people should–and typically do–use logic and all available information to choose the alternative with the highest value. (7)

realistic job preview (RJP) A method of improving organizational socialization in which job applicants are given a balance of positive and negative information about the job and work context. (14)

reality shock The stress that results when employees perceive discrepancies between their preemployment expectations and on-the-job reality. (14)

recency effect A perceptual error in which the most recent information dominates our perception of others. (3)

referent power The capacity to influence others on the basis of an identification with and respect for the power holder. (10)

refreezing The latter part of the change process, in which systems and conditions are introduced that reinforce and maintain the desired behaviors. (15)

relationship conflict A type of conflict in which people focus on characteristics of other individuals, rather than on the issues, as the source of conflict. (11)

representativeness heuristic A natural tendency to evaluate probabilities of events or objects by the degree to which they resemble (are representative of) other events or objects rather than on objective probability information. (7)

resilience The capability of individuals to cope successfully in the face of significant change, adversity, or risk. (4)

rituals The programmed routines of daily organizational life that dramatize the organization's culture. (14)

role A set of behaviors that people are expected to perform because of the positions they hold in a team and organization. (8)

role perceptions The extent to which people understand the job duties (roles) assigned to or expected of them. (2)

S

satisficing Selecting an alternative that is satisfactory or "good enough," rather than the alternative with the highest value (maximization). (7)

scenario planning A systematic process of thinking about alternative futures and what the organization should do to anticipate and react to those environments. (7)

scientific management The practice of systematically partitioning work into its smallest elements and standardizing tasks to achieve maximum efficiency. (6)

selective attention The process of attending to some information received by our senses and ignoring other information. (3)

self-concept An individual's self-beliefs and self-evaluations. (2)

self-directed teams (SDTs) Cross-functional work groups that are organized around work processes, complete an entire piece of work requiring several interdependent tasks, and have substantial autonomy over the execution of those tasks. (8)

self-efficacy A person's belief that he or she has the ability, motivation, correct role perceptions, and favorable situation to complete a task successfully. (2)

self-fulfilling prophecy The perceptual process in which our expectations about another person cause that person to act in a way that is consistent with those expectations. (3)

self-leadership The process of influencing oneself to establish the self-direction and self-motivation needed to perform a task. (6)

self-reinforcement Reinforcement that occurs when an employee has control over a reinforcer but doesn't "take" it until completing a self-set goal. (3)

self-serving bias The tendency to attribute our favorable outcomes to internal factors and our failures to external factors. (3)

self-talk The process of talking to ourselves about our own thoughts or actions. (6)

servant leadership The view that leaders serve followers, rather than vice versa; leaders help employees fulfill their needs and are coaches, stewards, and facilitators of employee performance. (12)

sexual harassment Unwelcome conduct of a sexual nature that detrimentally affects the work environment or leads to adverse job-related consequences for its victims. (4)

shared leadership The view that leadership is broadly distributed, rather than assigned to one person, such that people within the team and organization lead each other. (12)

situational leadership theory A commercially popular but poorly supported leadership model stating that effective leaders vary their style (telling, selling, participating, delegating) with the "readiness" of followers. (12)

skill variety The extent to which employees must use different skills and talents to perform tasks within their jobs. (6)

social capital The knowledge and other resources available to people or social units (teams, organizations) from a durable network that connects them to others. (8, 10)

social identity theory A theory that explains self-concept in terms of the person's unique characteristics (personal identity) and membership in various social groups (social identity). (2)

social learning theory A theory stating that much learning occurs by observing others and then modeling the behaviors that lead to favorable outcomes and avoiding behaviors that lead to punishing consequences. (3)

social loafing The problem that occurs when people exert less effort (and usually perform at a lower level) when working in teams than when working alone. (8)

span of control The number of people directly reporting to the next level in the hierarchy. (13)

stakeholders Individuals, organizations, and other entities who affect, or are affected by, the organization's objectives and actions. (1)

stereotyping The process of assigning traits to people on the basis of their membership in a social category. (3)

stock option A reward system that gives employees the right to purchase company stock at a future date at a predetermined price. (6)

strength-based coaching A positive organizational behavior approach to coaching and feedback that focuses on building and leveraging the employee's strengths rather than trying to correct his or her weaknesses. (5)

stress An adaptive response to a situation that is perceived as challenging or threatening to a person's well-being. (4)

stressors Any environmental conditions that place a physical or emotional demand on a person. (4)

subjective expected utility The probability (expectation) of satisfaction (utility) resulting from choosing a specific alternative in a decision. (7)

substitutability A contingency of power pertaining to the availability of alternatives. (10)

surface-level diversity The observable demographic or physiological differences in people, such as their race, ethnicity, gender, age, and physical disabilities. (1)

T

tacit knowledge Knowledge that is embedded in our actions and ways of thinking and is transmitted only through observation and experience. (3)

task identity The degree to which a job requires completion of a whole or an identifiable piece of work. (6)

task interdependence The extent to which team members must share materials, information, or expertise in order to perform their jobs. (8)

task significance The degree to which a job has a substantial impact on the organization and/or larger society. (6)

team-based structure An organizational structure built around self-directed teams that complete an entire piece of work. (13)

team building A process that consists of formal activities intended to improve the development and functioning of a work team. (8)

team cohesion The degree of attraction people feel toward the team and their motivation to remain members. (8)

teams Groups of two or more people who interact and influence each other, are mutually accountable for achieving common goals associated with organizational objectives, and perceive themselves as a social entity within an organization. (8)

third-party conflict resolution Any attempt by a relatively neutral person to help conflicting parties resolve their differences. (11)

transactional leadership Leadership that helps organizations achieve their current objectives more efficiently, such as by linking job performance to valued rewards and ensuring that employees have the resources needed to get the job done. (12)

transformational leadership A leadership perspective that explains how leaders change teams or organizations by creating, communicating, and modeling a vision for the organization or work unit and inspiring employees to strive for that vision. (12)

trust A psychological state comprising the intention to accept vulnerability on the basis of positive expectations of the intent or behavior of another person. (4, 8)

U

uncertainty avoidance A cross-cultural value describing the degree to which people in a culture tolerate ambiguity (low uncertainty avoidance) or feel threatened by ambiguity and uncertainty (high uncertainty avoidance). (2)

unfreezing The first part of the change process, in which the change agent produces disequilibrium between the driving and restraining forces. (15)

upward appeal A type of influence in which someone with higher authority or expertise is called on in reality or symbolically to support the influencer's position. (10)

V

values Relatively stable, evaluative beliefs that guide a person's preferences for outcomes or courses of action in a variety of situations. (1)

virtual teams Teams whose members operate across space, time, and organizational boundaries and are linked through information technologies to achieve organizational tasks. (8)

virtual work Work performed away from the traditional physical workplace by means of information technology. (1)

W

wikis Collaborative Web spaces at which anyone in a group can write, edit, or remove material from the Web site. (9)

win-lose orientation The belief that conflicting parties are drawing from a fixed pie, so the more one party receives, the less the other party will receive. (11)

win-win orientation The belief that conflicting parties will find a mutually beneficial solution to their disagreement. (11)

work–life balance The degree to which a person minimizes conflict between work and nonwork demands. (1)

workaholic A person who is highly involved in work, feels compelled to work, and has a low enjoyment of work. (4)

References

Chapter 1

1. "The Pixar Principle," *The Age*(Melbourne, AU), 28 May 2006; C. Eller, "Ed Catmull: Pixar's Superhero Shakes Up Disney," *Los Angeles Times,* 12 June 2006; W.C. Taylor and P. LaBarre, "How Pixar Adds a New School of Thought to Disney," *New York Times,* 29 January 2006; B. Barnes, "Disney and Pixar: The Power of the Prenup," *New York Times,* 1 June 2008; S. Leith, "How Pixar Found Its Shiny Metal Soul," *Sunday Telegraph* (London), 22 June 2008; H. Rao and R.I. Sutton, "Innovation Lessons from Pixar: An Interview with Oscar-Winning Director Brad Bird," *McKinsey Quarterly,* April 2008, pp. 1–9.

2. M. Warner, "Organizational Behavior Revisited," *Human Relations* 47 (October 1994), pp. 1151–1166; R. Westwood and S. Clegg, "The Discourse of Organization Studies: Dissensus, Politics, and Paradigms," in *Debating Organization: Point-Counterpoint in Organization Studies,* ed. R. Westwood and S. Clegg (Malden, MA: Blackwell, 2003), pp. 1–42.

3. Some of the historical bases of OB mentioned in this paragraph are described in J.A. Conger, "Max Weber's Conceptualization of Charismatic Authority: Its Influence on Organizational Research," *The Leadership Quarterly* 4, no. 3–4 (1993), pp. 277–288; R. Kanigel, *The One Best Way: Frederick Winslow Taylor and the Enigma of Efficiency* (New York: Viking, 1997); J.H. Smith, "The Enduring Legacy of Elton Mayo," *Human Relations* 51, no. 3 (1998), pp. 221–249; T. Takala, "Plato on Leadership," *Journal of Business Ethics* 17 (May 1998), pp. 785–798; J.A. Fernandez, "The Gentleman's Code of Confucius: Leadership by Values," *Organizational Dynamics* 33, no. 1 (February 2004), pp. 21–31.

4. T.R. Mitchell and W.G. Scott, "The Universal Barnard: His Micro Theories of Organizational Behavior," *Public Administration Quarterly,* Fall 1985, pp. 239–259; A.M. Davis, "Liquid Leadership: The Wisdom of Mary Parker Follett (1868–1933)," http://sunsite.utk.edu/FINS/Mary_Parker_Follett/Fins-MPF-03.txt, 1997 (accessed 18 July 2008).

5. H.M. Parsons, "Hawthorne: An early OBM experiment," *Journal of Organizational Behavior Management,* 12(1) (1992).

6. C.E. Turner, "Test room studies in employee effectiveness," *The American Journal of Public Health* (June 1933), p. 584.

7. D. Katz and R.L. Kahn, *The Social Psychology of Organizations* (New York: Wiley, 1966), chap. 2; R.N. Stern and S.R. Barley, "Organizations as Social Systems: Organization Theory's Neglected Mandate," *Administrative Science Quarterly* 41 (1996), pp. 146–162.

8. L.E. Greiner, "A Recent History of Organizational Behavior," in *Organizational Behaviour,* ed. S. Kerr (Columbus, OH: Grid, 1979), pp. 3–14; J. Micklethwait and A. Wooldridge, *The Company: A Short History of a Revolutionary Idea* (New York: Random House, 2003).

9. B. Schlender, "The Three Faces of Steve," *Fortune,* 9 November 1998, pp. 96–101.

10. S.L. Rynes et al., "Behavioral Coursework in Business Education: Growing Evidence of a Legitimacy Crisis," *Academy of Management Learning & Education* 2, no. 3 (2003), pp. 269–283; R.P. Singh and A.G. Schick, "Organizational Behavior: Where Does It Fit in Today's Management Curriculum?" *Journal of Education for Business* 82, no. 6 (July 2007), p. 349.

11. P.R. Lawrence and N. Nohria, *Driven: How Human Nature Shapes Our Choices* (San Francisco: Jossey-Bass, 2002), chap. 6.

12. P.R. Lawrence "Historical Development of Organizational Behavior," in *Handbook of Organizational Behavior,* ed. L.W. Lorsch (Englewood Cliffs, NJ: Prentice Hall, 1987), pp. 1–9; S.A. Mohrman, C.B. Gibson, and A.M. Mohrman Jr., "Doing Research That Is Useful to Practice: A Model and Empirical Exploration," *Academy of Management Journal* 44 (April 2001), pp. 357–375. For a contrary view, see: A.P. Brief and J.M. Dukerich, "Theory in Organizational Behavior: Can It Be Useful?" *Research in Organizational Behavior* 13 (1991), pp. 327–352.

13. M.S. Myers, *Every Employee a Manager* (New York: McGraw-Hill, 1970).

14. D. Yankelovich, "Got to Give to Get," *Mother Jones* 22 (July 1997), pp. 60–63; D. MacDonald, "Good Managers Key to Buffett's Acquisitions," *Montreal Gazette,* 16 November 2001. The two studies on OB and financial performance are B.N. Pfau and I.T. Kay, *The Human Capital Edge* (New York: McGraw-Hill, 2002); I.S. Fulmer, B.Gerhart, and K.S. Scott, "Are the 100 Best Better? An Empirical Investigation of the Relationship between Being a 'Great Place to Work' and Firm Performance," *Personnel Psychology* 56, no. 4 (Winter 2003), pp. 965–993.

15. Rolf P. Lynton and Udai Pareek, *Training for Orgaisational Transformation* 1 and 2, (New Delhi: Sage, 2000)

16. T.W. Adorno, et al., *The Authoritarian Personality* (New York: Harper, 1950); J.B.P. Sinha, *The Nurturant Task Leader* (New Delhi: Concept, 1980).

17. S. Kakar, "Authority Patterns of Subordinates' Behaviour in Indian Organizations", *Administrative Science Quarterly* 16 (1971), pp. 298--307; *Ibid.* J.B.P. Sinha.

18. J.B.P. Sinha, "Organizational Dynamics" In U.P. Pareek (ed.), *A Survey of Research in Psychology* 2 (1971–76), pp. 417-77, (Bombay: Popular Prakashan).

19. A.K. Singh. 'Organizational Development in India: Past Trends and Current Challenges', in A.K. Singh et al., (eds.) *Designing and Developing Organizations for Tomorrow*, pp. 27–45 (2001), (New Delhi: Response)

20. A.K. Rice, *Productivity and Social Organization: The Ahmedabad Experiment*, (London: Tavistock, 1958).

21. N. De, *Alternative Design of Human Organization*, (New Delhi: Sage, 1985).

22. J.B.P. Sinha, "Psychic Relevance of Work in Indian Culture," *Dynamic Psychiatry* 18 (1985), pp. 134--41.

23. S.R. Ganesh, "Quality of Life in Indian Organizations", Working paper No. 407 (1982), Indian Institute of Management-Ahmedabad, (New Delhi: Indian Council of Social Science Research).

24. K.M. Srinivas, *Pilgrimage to Indian Ethos Management: A Look at Indigenous Approaches to Organizational Development*, Indian Institute of Management–Calcutta, (Calcutta: Management Centre for Human Values, 2000).

25. S.K. Chakraborty, *Managerial Effectiveness and Quality of Work Life: Indian Insights*, (New Delhi: Tata McGraw-Hill, 1987); S.K. Chakraborty, *Managerial Transformation by Values: A Corporate Pilgrimage*, (New Delhi: Sage, 1993).

26. S. Sharma, *New Mantras in Corporate Corridors: From Ancient Roots to Global Routes.* (New Delhi: New Age International, 2007).

27. P. Garg and I. Parikh, Young *Managers at the Cross-Roads: The Trishanku Complex.* (New Delhi: Sage, 1992).

28. D.W. Orme-Johnson et al., "Maharishi's Vedic Psychology: The Science of the Cosmic Psyche" In H.S.R. Kao and D. Sinha (eds.), *Asian Perspectives on Psychology* (1997), pp. 282--308, (New Delhi: Sage)

29. N. Pande and R.K. Naidu, "Anasakti and Health: A Study of Non-Attachment," *Psychology and Developing Societies*, 4 (1992), pp. 89--104.

30. Radha R. Sharma, "Emotional Intelligence as a Mediator in Executive Burnout," *Academy of Human Resource Development*, (Minnesota, USA: Cutting Edge Monograph, 2006), pp.7--13.

31. G. Misra, "Implications of Culture for Psychological Knowledge," In J.W. Berry et al. (eds.), *Psychology in Human and Social Development: Lessons from Different Cultures* (2003), pp. 31–67, (New Delhi: Sage).

32. J. Pandey, "Ingratiation as a Social Behaviour," In J. Pandey (ed.) *Perspectives on Experimental Social Psychology* (1981), pp. 157-85. (New Delhi: Concept).

33. R.C. Tripathi, 'Machiavellianism and Social Manipulation' In J.Pandey (ed.), *Perspectives on Experimental Social Psychology* (1981), pp. 137--56. (New Delhi: Concept).

34. U. Jain, *Psychological Consequences of Crowding,* (New Delhi: Sage, 1987); J. Pandey, "Socio-Psychological Dimensions of Experiences and Consequences of Crowding," In J.C. Lasry et al. (eds), *Latest Contributions to Cross-Cultural Psychology* (1999), (Lisse: Swets & Zetlinger).

35. R. Agarwal and G. Misra, "Variations in Achievement Cognitions: Role of Ecology, Age and Gender," *International Journal of Intercultural Relations* 13 (1989), pp. 93--107; P. Mehta, *People's Development, Motivation and Work Organization.* (New Delhi: Participation and Development Centre, 1991).

36. L. Krishnan, "Distributive Justice in the Indian Perspective," In H.S.R. Kao and D. Sinha (eds), *Asian Perspectives on Psychology (1997),* pp. 25--39. (New Delhi: Sage).

37. R. A. Shweder et al., "Culture and Moral Development," In J. Singer, R.A. Shweder and G. Herdt (eds), *Cultural Psychology: Essays in Comparative Human Development* (1990), pp. 136-204. (New York: Cambridge University Press).

38. U. Pareek, *Organization Behaviour Process* (Jaipur: Rawat, 1988).

39. J.B.P. Sinha, *Multinationals in India: Managing the Interface of Cultures,* (New Delhi: Sage, 2004).

40. R.N. Kanungo and A.M. Jaeger, "Introduction: The Need for Indigenous Management in Development in Developing Countries" In R.N. Kanungo and A.M. Jaeger (eds*), Management in Developing Countries* (1990), pp. 1--22. (London and New York: Routledge); M. Mendonca and R.N. Kanungo. "Motivation through Effective Reward Management in Developing Countries" In R.N. Kanungo and M. Mendonca (eds), *Work Motivation: Models for Developing Countries* (1994), pp. 49--83. (New Delhi: Sage).

41. *Op cit.* J.B.P. Sinha, (1980).

42. Subhash Sharma, "Corporate Gita," In *New Mantras in Corporate Corridors: From Ancient Roots to Global Routes* (2007), pp. 109–135, New Delhi: New Age International).

43. *Ibid.*

44. *Ibid.*

45. J.B.P. Sinha, "Indian Cultural Context," In *Culture and Organizational Behaviour* (2008), pp. 29–49, (New Delhi: Sage).

46. *Ibid.*

47. E.C. Banfield, *The Moral Basis of a Background Society,* p 89 (Glenco, IL: The Free Press, 1958).

48. A. Ronald, *Understanding Indians,* Paper presented at the International Conference on Understanding India (3-5 Nov 2005), (Aarhus, Denmark).

49. Mohrman, Gibson, and Mohrman Jr., "Doing Research That Is Useful to Practice"; J.P. Walsh et al., "On the Relationship between Research and Practice: Debate and Reflections," *Journal of Management Inquiry* 16, no. 2 (June 2007), pp. 128–154. Similarly, in 1961, Harvard business professor Fritz Roethlisberger proposed that the field of OB is concerned with human behavior "from the points of view of both (a) its determination . . . and (b) its improvement." See P.B. Vaill, "F.J. Roethlisberger and the Elusive Phenomena of Organizational Behavior," *Journal of Management Education* 31, no. 3 (June 2007), pp. 321–338.

50. R.H. Hall, "Effectiveness Theory and Organizational Effectiveness," *Journal of Applied Behavioral Science* 16, no. 4 (October 1980), pp. 536–545; K. Cameron, "Organizational Effectiveness: Its Demise and Re-emergence through Positive Organizational Scholarship," in *Great Minds in Management,* ed. K.G. Smith and M.A. Hitt (New York: Oxford University Press, 2005), pp. 304–330.

51. J.L. Price, "The Study of Organizational Effectiveness," *The Sociological Quarterly* 13 (1972), pp. 3–15.

52. S.C. Selden and J.E. Sowa, "Testing a Multi-dimensional Model of Organizational Performance: Prospects and Problems," *Journal of Public Administration Research and Theory* 14, no. 3 (July 2004), pp. 395–416.

53. F.E. Kast and J.E. Rosenweig, "General Systems Theory: Applications for Organization and Management," *Academy of Management Journal 15, no. 4* (1972), pp. 447–465; P.M. Senge, *The Fifth Discipline: The Art and Practice of the Learning Organization* (New York: Doubleday Currency, 1990); A. De Geus, *The Living Company* (Boston: Harvard Business School Press, 1997); R.T. Pascale, M. Millemann, and L. Gioja, *Surfing on the Edge of Chaos* (London: Texere, 2000).

54. V.P. Rindova and S. Kotha, "Continuous 'Morphing': Competing through Dynamic Capabilities, Form, and Function," *Academy of Management Journal* 44 (2001), pp. 1263–1280; J. McCann, "Organizational Effectiveness: Changing Concepts for Changing Environments," *Human Resource Planning* 27, no. 1 (2004), pp. 42–50.

55. J. Arlidge, "McJobs That All the Family Can Share," *Daily Telegraph* (London), 26 January 2006, p. 1.

56. C. Ostroff and N. Schmitt, "Configurations of Organizational Effectiveness and Efficiency," *Academy of Management Journal* 36, no. 6 (1993), p. 1345. There are different ways of defining efficiency, as well as some disagreement whether work efficiency and productivity are the same thing.

57. J.P. Womack and D.T. Jones, *Lean Thinking,* 2d ed. (New York: Free Press, 2003); J.K. Liker, *The Toyota Way* (New York: McGraw-Hill, 2004); T. Melton, "The Benefits of Lean Manufacturing: What Lean Thinking Has to Offer the Process Industries," *Chemical Engineering Research and Design* 83, no. 6 (2005), pp. 662–673.

58. F.A. Kennedy and S.K. Widener, "A Control Framework: Insights from Evidence on Lean Accounting," *Management Accounting Research,* in press (2008).

59. NHS Federation, "NHS Chief Vows to Cut Waste and Look to Toyota in Efficiency Drive" (news release), 14 June 2006, (London); D. Jones and A. Mitchell, *Lean Thinking for the NHS* (London: NHS Confederation, 2006); M. McCarthy, "Can Car Manufacturing Techniques Reform Health Care?" *Lancet* 367, no. 9507 (28 January 2006), pp. 290–291; "Nissan 'Shot in the Arm' for Healthcare Sector," Newcarinfo.co.uk, 13 February 2007; I. Green, "Drive for Success," *Nursing Standard* 21, no. 38 (30 May 2007), pp. 62–63.

60. P.S. Adler et al., "Performance Improvement Capability: Keys to Accelerating Performance Improvement in Hospitals," *California Management Review* 45, no. 2 (2003), pp. 12–33; J. Jamrog, M. Vickers, and D. Bear, "Building and Sustaining a Culture That Supports Innovation," *Human Resource Planning* 29, no. 3 (2006), pp. 9–19. Klaus Kleinfeld's quotation is from "Siemens CEO Klaus Kleinfeld: 'Nobody's Perfect, but a Team Can Be,'" *Knowledge@Wharton,* 19 April 2006.

61. K.E. Weick, *The Social Psychology of Organizing* (Reading, MA: Addison-Wesley, 1979); S. Brusoni and A. Prencipe, "Managing Knowledge in Loosely Coupled Networks: Exploring the Links between Product and Knowledge Dynamics," *Journal of Management Studies* 38, no. 7 (November 2001), pp. 1019–1035; D. Pinelle and C. Gutwin, "Loose Coupling and Healthcare Organizations: Deployment Strategies for Groupware," *Computer Supported Cooperative Work* 15, no. 5–6 (2006), pp. 537–572.

62. G. Huber, "Organizational Learning: The Contributing Processes and Literature," *Organizational Science* 2 (1991), pp. 88–115; D.A. Garvin, *Learning in Action: A Guide to Putting the Learning Organization to Work* (Boston: Harvard Business School Press, 2000); H. Shipton, "Cohesion or Confusion? Towards a Typology for Organizational Learning Research," *International Journal of Management Reviews* 8, no. 4 (2006), pp. 233–252.

63. W.C. Bogner and P. Bansal, "Knowledge Management as the Basis of Sustained High Performance," *Journal of Management Studies* 44, no. 1 (2007), pp. 165–188; D. Jiménez-Jiménez and J.G. Cegarra-Navarro, "The Performance Effect of Organizational Learning and Market Orientation," *Industrial Marketing Management* 36, no. 6 (2007), pp. 694–708.

64. M. Liedtke, "Google vs. Yahoo: Heavyweights Attack from Different Angles," *Associated Press Newswires,* 18 Dec-ember 2004; R. Basch, "Doing Well by Doing Good," *Searcher Magazine,* January 2005, pp. 18–28; A. Ignatius and L.A. Locke, "In Search of the Real Google," *Time,* 20 February 2006, p. 36.

65. W. Cohen and D. Levinthal, "Absorptive Capacity: A New Perspective on Learning and Innovation," *Administrative Science Quarterly* 35 (1990), pp. 128–152; G. Todorova and B. Durisin, "Absorptive Capacity: Valuing a Reconceptualization," *Academy of Management Review* 32, no. 3 (2007), pp. 774–786.

66. M. Rogers, "Absorptive Capacity and Economic Growth: How Do Countries Catch Up?" *Cambridge Journal of Economics* 28, no. 4 (July 2004), pp. 577–596.

67. T.A. Stewart, *Intellectual Capital: The New Wealth of Organizations* (New York: Currency/Doubleday, 1997); H. Saint-Onge and D. Wallace, *Leveraging Communities of Practice for Strategic Advantage* (Boston: Butterworth-Heinemann, 2003), pp. 9–10; J.A. Johannessen, B. Olsen, and J. Olaisen, "Intellectual Capital as a Holistic Management Philosophy: A Theoretical Perspective," *International Journal of Information Management* 25, no. 2 (2005), pp. 151–171.

68. M.N. Wexler, "Organizational Memory and Intellectual Capital," *Journal of Intellectual Capital* 3, no. 4 (2002), pp. 393–414.

69. M.E. McGill and J.W. Slocum Jr., "Unlearn the Organization," *Organizational Dynamics* 22, no. 2 (1993), pp. 67–79; A.E. Akgün, G.S. Lynn, and J.C. Byrne, "Antecedents and Consequences of Unlearning in New Product Development Teams," *Journal of Product Innovation Management* 23 (2006), pp. 73–88.

70. J. Pfeffer, *The Human Equation: Building Profits by Putting People First* (Boston: Harvard University Press, 1998); E. Appelbaum et al., *Manufacturing Advantage: Why High-Performance Work Systems Pay Off* (Ithaca, NY: Cornell University Press, 2000); G.S. Benson, S.M. Young, and E.E. Lawler III, "High-Involvement Work Practices and Analysts' Forecasts of Corporate Earnings," *Human Resource Management* 45, no. 4 (2006), pp. 519–537; L. Sels et al., "Unravelling the HRM-Performance Link: Value-Creating and Cost-Increasing Effects of Small Business HRM," *Journal of Management Studies* 43, no. 2 (2006), pp. 319–342.

71. M.A. Huselid, "The Impact of Human Resource Management Practices on Turnover, Productivity, and Corporate Financial Performance," *Academy of Management Journal* 38, no. 3 (1995), p. 635; B.E. Becker and M.A. Huselid, "Strategic Human Resources Management: Where Do We Go from Here?" *Journal of Management* 32, no. 6 (December 2006), pp. 898–925; J. Combs et al., "How Much Do High-Performance Work Practices Matter? A Meta-Analysis of Their Effects on Organizational Performance," *Personnel Psychology* 59, no. 3 (2006), pp. 501–528.

72. J. Barney, "Firm Resources and Sustained Competitive Advantage," *Journal of Management* 17, no. 1 (1991), pp. 99–120.

73. E.E. Lawler III, S.A. Mohrman, and G.E. Ledford Jr., *Strategies for High Performance Organizations* (San Francisco: Jossey-Bass, 1998); S.H. Wagner, C.P. Parker, and D. Neil, "Employees That Think and Act Like Owners: Effects of Ownership Beliefs and Behaviors on Organizational Effectiveness," *Personnel Psychology* 56, no. 4 (Winter 2003), pp. 847–871; P.J. Gollan, "High Involvement Management and Human Resource Sustainability: The Challenges and Opportunities," *Asia Pacific Journal of Human*

Resources 43, no. 1 (April 2005), pp. 18–33; Y. Liu et al., "The Value of Human Resource Management for Organizational Performance," *Business Horizons* 50 (2007), pp. 503–511; P. Tharenou, A.M. Saks, and C.Moore, "A Review and Critique of Research on Training and Organizational-Level Outcomes," *Human Resource Management Review* 17, no. 3 (2007), pp. 251–273.

74. S. Fleetwood and A. Hesketh, "HRM-Performance Research: Under-Theorized and Lacking Explanatory Power," *International Journal of Human Resource Management* 17, no. 12 (December 2006), pp. 1977–1993.

75. J. Godard, "High Performance and the Transformation of Work? The Implications of Alternative Work Practices for the Experience and Outcomes of Work," *Industrial and Labor Relations Review* 54, no. 4 (July 2001), pp. 776–805; G. Murray et al., eds., *Work and Employment Relations in the High-Performance Workplace* (London: Continuum, 2002); B. Harley, "Hope or Hype? High Performance Work Systems," in *Participation and Democracy at Work: Essays in Honour of Harvie Ramsay,* ed. B. Harley, J. Hyman, and P. Thompson (Houndsmills, UK: Palgrave Macmillan, 2005), pp. 38–54.

76. A.L. Friedman and S. Miles, *Stakeholders: Theory and Practice* (New York: Oxford University Press, 2006); M.L. Barnett, "Stakeholder Influence Capacity and the Variability of Financial Returns to Corporate Social Responsibility," *Academy of Management Review* 32, no. 3 (2007), pp. 794–816; R.E. Freeman, J.S. Harrison, and A.C. Wicks, *Managing for Stakeholders: Survival, Reputation, and Success* (New Haven, CT: Yale University Press, 2007).

77. C. Eden and F. Ackerman, *Making Strategy: The Journey of Strategic Management* (London: Sage, 1998).

78. T.A. Hemphill, "Rejuvenating Wal-Mart's Reputation," *Business Horizons* 48, no. 1 (2005), pp. 11–21; A. Bianco, *The Bully of Bentonville: How the High Cost of Wal-Mart's Everyday Low Prices Is Hurting America* (New York: Random House, 2006); C. Fishman, *The Wal-Mart Effect* (New York: Penguin, 2006). For a description of Wal-Mart's recent corrective actions on environmentalism, see E.L. Plambeck and L. Denend, "Wal*Mart," *Stanford Social Innovation Review* 6, no. 2 (Spring 2008), pp. 53–59.

79. G.R. Salancik and J. Pfeffer, *The External Control of Organizations: A Resource Dependence Perspective* (New York: Harper & Row, 1978); T. Casciaro and M.J. Piskorski, "Power Imbalance, Mutual Dependence, and Constraint Absorption: A Closer Look at Dependence Theory," *Administrative Science Quarterly* 50 (2005), pp. 167–199; N. Roome and F. Wijen, "Stakeholder Power and Organizational Learning in Corporate Environmental Management," *Organization Studies* 27, no. 2 (2005), pp. 235–263.

80. R.E. Freeman, A.C. Wicks, and B. Parmar, "Stakeholder Theory and 'The Corporate Objective Revisited,'" *Organization Science* 15, no. 3 (May–June 2004), pp. 364–369; D. Balser and J. McClusky, "Managing Stakeholder Relationships and Nonprofit Organization Effectiveness," *Nonprofit Management & Leadership* 15, no. 3 (Spring 2005), pp. 295–315; Friedman and Miles, *Stakeholders: Theory and Practice,* chap. 3.

81. B.M. Meglino and E.C. Ravlin, "Individual Values in Organizations: Concepts, Controversies, and Research," *Journal of Management* 24, no. 3 (1998), pp. 351–389; B.R. Agle and C.B. Caldwell, "Understanding Research on Values in Business," *Business and Society* 38, no. 3 (September 1999), pp. 326–387; A. Bardi and S.H. Schwartz, "Values and Behavior: Strength and Structure of Relations," *Personality and Social Psychology Bulletin* 29, no. 10 (October 2003), pp. 1207–1220; S. Hitlin and J.A. Pilavin, "Values: Reviving a Dormant Concept," *Annual Review of Sociology* 30 (2004), pp. 359–393.

82. R.M. Patten, "From Implicit to Explicit: Putting Corporate Values and Personal Accountability Front and Centre," *Ivy Business Journal* Sep–Oct 2004, pp. H1–H4.

83. Middle East Company News, "Accountability, Teamwork, and Continuous Improvement Define Core Operating Values at DED," Middle East Company News (news release), (Dubai: 4 January 2005).

84. M. van Marrewijk, "Concepts and Definitions of CSR and Corporate Sustainability: Between Agency and Communion," *Journal of Business Ethics* 44 (May 2003), pp. 95–105; Barnett, "Stakeholder Influence Capacity."

85. L.S. Paine, *Value Shift* (New York: McGraw-Hill, 2003); A. Mackey, T.B. Mackey, and J.B. Barney, "Corporate Social Responsibility and Firm Performance: Investor Preferences and Corporate Strategies," *Academy of Management Review* 32, no. 3 (2007), pp. 817–835.

86. S. Zadek, *The Civil Corporation: The New Economy of Corporate Citizenship* (London: Earthscan, 2001); S. Hart and M. Milstein, "Creating Sustainable Value," *Academy of Management Executive* 17, no. 2 (2003), pp. 56–69.

87. "Canadians Inclined to Punish Companies Deemed Socially Irresponsible, Study Suggests," *Canadian Press,* 23 April 2005; M. Johne, "Show Us the Green, Workers Say," *Globe & Mail,* 10 October 2007, p. C1; Aspen Institute, *Where Will They Lead? MBA Student Attitudes about Business & Society* (Washington, DC: Aspen Institute, April 2008).

88. PRNewswire, "Lockheed Martin Is Top Choice as Ideal Employer for Engineering Students" (news release), Bethesda, MD, 15 May 2006.

89. A. Fox, "Corporate Social Responsibility Pays Off," *HRMagazine* 52, no. 8 (August 2007), pp. 42–47.

90. Ministry of Corporate Affairs (2009). CSR Voluntary Guidelines. www.mca.gov.in/.../CSR_Voluntary_Guidelines_24dec2009.pdf (accessed on 10/2/2011).

91. Sanjay K. Agarwal, "Chapter 1: Introduction," In *Corporate Social Responsibility in India,* (New Delhi: Response, 2008).

92. TERI-BCSD. About TERI-BCSD India. http://bcsd.teri.res.in/index.php?option=com_content&task=view&id=106&Itemid=173 (accessed 10/2/2011).

93. *IB Times* Staff Reporter, *Top Five MBA Programs in Ethics and CSR*, 7 Dec 2010, http://www.ibtimes.com/articles/89470/20101207/mba-csr-ethics-stanford-harvard-insead-tuck-wharton.htm (accessed on 10/12/2010).

94. Columbia Business School: Innovative Programs, *The Individual, Business and Society (IBS) Curriculum*, http://www4.gsb.columbia.edu/mba/academics/innovative (accessed on 8/3/2001)

95. Ross School of Business: Course Descriptions, Full Time MBA. http://www.bus.umich.edu/CourseManagement/ViewCourseDescriptions.asp?Term=F11&Dept=B A&Program=MBA (accessed on 8/3/2011).

96. Kellog Graduate School of Management, Northwestern University: Core Curriculum, Full Time MBA Program, http://www.kellog.northwestern.edu/Programs/FullTimeMBA/Academics/Core_Curriculum.aspx (accessed on 8/3/2011)

97. IESE Business School: Second Year Courses, MBA Program, http://www.iese.edu/en/files/secondYearCourses_tcm4-26445.pdf (accessed on 8/3/2011); IESE Business School, First Year Courses, http://www.iese.edu/en/MBA_Programs/programs/MBA/the_program/academics/courses.asp (accssed on 8/3/2011).

98. Yale School of Management: Electives, MBA program (2011). http://mba.yale.edu/MBA/curriculum/electives/index.shtml, accessed on 8/3/2011; Yale School of Management (2011). Curriculum.MBA for Executives: Leadership in Healthcare. http://mbae.som.yale.edu/program-curriculum.aspx (accessed on 8/3/2011).

99. Radha R. Sharma, "A Survey of Perception of Management Students about CSR," (unpublished) Management Development Institute, Gurgaon (2003).

100. http://www.123eng.com/forum/viewtopic.php?t=13615, 22. 5.08

101. Radha R. Sharma, "Corporate Social Responsibility in Management Education: Who is responsible?", *Indian Journal of Training & Development*, xxxiv:3, July-Sep 2004.

102. *Business Standard*, Government to Observe Annual India Corporate Week (2009). http://www.businessstandard.com/india/news/govt-to-observe-annual-%5Cindia-corporate-week%5C/376685 (accessed on 10/2/2011); *Press Information Bureau*, India Corporate Week 2010–A Curtain Raiser, http://www.pib.nic.in/newsite/erelease.aspx?relid=67691 (accessed on 10/2/2011).

103. www.ficci-sedf.org/fsedf/what-we-do/CSR-Award%20report.pdf

104. FICCI-SEDF (2010), *BusinessWorld* FICCI--SEDF Corporate Social Responsibility Award 2009-2010. http://www.ficci-sedf.org/award10-11/prev-winners.htm (accessed on 10/2/2011).

105. Golden Peacock Award, Golden Peacock Award for Corporate Social Responsibility. http://www.goldenpeacockawards.com/awards/award-for-corporate-social-responsibility.html (accessed on 10/2/2011); Golden Peacock Award (2010), Golden Peacock Award--Guidelines & Application Form, http://www.goldenpeacockawards.com/pdf/2010/GPACSR-2010.pdf (accessed on 10/2/2011).

106. CII-ITC (2010), Sustainability Award, http://www.sustainabledevelopment.in/sustainablity_awards/overview2009.htm (accessed on 10/2/2011).

107. TERI: Selection Process, http://www.teriin.org/awards/intro_selection.htm (accessed on 10/2/2011); TERI: 8th TERI Corporate Awards 2008-09, http://www.teriin.org/awards/winner_social.htm (accessed on 10/2/2011).

108. Asian Forum CSR, *The Organization behind the CSR Awards*, http://www.asianforumcsr.com/awards/awards.htm (accessed on 10/2/2011); *Op. cit.* Sanjay K. Agarwal (2008).

109. J.P. Campbell, "The Definition and Measurement of Performance in the New Age," in *The Changing Nature of Performance: Implications for Staffing, Motivation, and Development,* ed. D.R. Ilgen and E.D. Pulakos (San Francisco: Jossey-Bass, 1999), pp. 399–429; R.D. Hackett, "Understanding and Predicting Work Performance in the Canadian Military," *Canadian Journal of Behavioural Science* 34, no. 2 (2002), pp. 131–140.

110. D.W. Organ, "Organizational Citizenship Behavior: It's Construct Clean-up Time," *Human Performance* 10 (1997), pp. 85–97; S.J. Motowidlo, "Some Basic Issues Related to Contextual Performance and Organizational Citizenship Behavior in Human Resource Management," *Human Resource Management Review* 10, no. 1 (2000), pp. 115–126; J.A. LePine, A. Erez, and D.E. Johnson, "The Nature and Dimensionality of Organizational Citizenship Behavior: A Critical Review and Meta-Analysis," *Journal of Applied Psychology* 87 (February 2002), pp. 52–65.

111. K. Lee and N.J. Allen, "Organizational Citizenship Behavior and Workplace Deviance: The Role of Affect and Cognitions," *Journal of Applied Psychology* 87, no. 1 (2002), pp. 131–142.

112. M. Rotundo and P. Sackett, "The Relative Importance of Task, Citizenship, and Counterproductive Performance to Global Ratings of Job Performance: A Policy-Capturing Approach," *Journal of Applied Psychology* 87 (February 2002), pp. 66–80; P.D. Dunlop and K. Lee, "Workplace Deviance, Organizational Citizenship Behaviour, and Business Unit Performance: The Bad

Apples Do Spoil the Whole Barrel," *Journal of Organizational Behavior* 25 (2004), pp. 67–80. For discussion of various counterproductive workplace issues, see J. Langan-Fox, C.L. Cooper, and R.J. Klimoski, eds., *Research Companion to the Dysfunctional Workplace* (Cheltenham, UK: Edward Elgar, 2007).

113. B. Carey, "Truckload's New Recruiting Routes," *Traffic World,* 22 August 2005; D. Simanoff, "Hotels Plagued by Staff Vacancies," *Tampa Tribune,* 30 January 2006, p. 1; L. Smyrlis, "A Growing Concern," *Canadian Transportation and Logistics,* October 2007, p. 18.

114. Watson Wyatt, "U.S. Workers Cite Hypocrisy and Favoritism–Rather Than Financial Misdeeds–As Biggest Ethical Lapses at Work" (news release), Washington, DC, 12 January 2005; Watson Wyatt, *WorkCanada 2004/2005–Pursuing Productive Engagement* (Toronto: Watson Wyatt, January 2005).

115. Basch, "Doing Well by Doing Good,"; K. Coughlin, "Goooood Move," *Star-Ledger* (Newark, NJ), 5 June 2005, p. 1.

116. D.A. Harrison and J.J. Martocchio, "Time for Absenteeism: A 20-Year Review of Origins, Offshoots, and Outcomes," *Journal of Management* 24 (Spring 1998), pp. 305–350; C.M. Mason and M.A. Griffin, "Group Absenteeism and Positive Affective Tone: A Longitudinal Study," *Journal of Organizational Behavior* 24 (2003), pp. 667–687; A. Vaananen et al., "Job Characteristics, Physical and Psychological Symptoms, and Social Support as Antecedents of Sickness Absence among Men and Women in the Private Industrial Sector," *Social Science & Medicine* 57, no. 5 (2003), pp. 807–824.

117. http://en.wikipedia.org/wiki/Offshore outsourcing; A. McCue, "Indian outsourcers to launch European invasion, 2006," www.silicon.com; http://en.wikipedia.org/wiki/Offshore_outsourcing; Gibson, India 2.0 Aims to Sustain Its Global IT Influence eWeek (2006).

118. http://en.wikipedia.org/wiki/Offshore_outsourcing (Q4: 2006), Mandatory Multisourcing Discipline, *Business Trends Quarterly.*

119. Linda Cohen and Allie Young, *Multisourcing: Moving beyond outsourcing to achieve growth and agility,* (Mass, HBSP: 2005).

120. http://en.wikipedia.org/wiki/Offshore_outsourcing, Mandatory Multisourcing Discipline (2006); http://www.bpoindia.org/research/bpo-in-india.shtml (accsesed on 25/4/2008).

121. http://www.destinyinfotek.com/24.4.08; Google Eyes India R&D Facility for 2004", by Keith Regan, *E Commerce Times*", 12 Dec 2003.

122. http://www.callcenterindia.blogspot.com, 17 Feb and 31 March 2005.

123. J. Sullivan, *Eight Elements of a Successful Employment Brand,* ER Daily, 23 February 2004, www.erexchange.com/articles/db/52CB45FDADFAA4CD2BBC366659E26892A.asp (accessed on 20/12/2010).

124. L. Moroko and M.D. Uncles, "Characteristics of Successful Employer Brands," *Journal of Brand Management* (2008), 6:3, pp. 160--75.

125. *Ibid.*

126. R.W. Mosley, Customer Experience, Organizational Culture and the Employer Brand," *Brand management* (2007), 15:2, pp. 123–34.

127. Great Place to Work Institute, India's Best Companies to Work For (2010), http://www.greatplacetowork.com/what we do/lists-in-2010.htm (accessed on 26/2/2011).

128. Michelle E. Mor Barak, Managing Diversity: Toward a Globally Inclusive Workplace," 2nd ed., California: Sage, 2005), chap 11, http://www.managingglobaldiversity.com/pdf/6 chap11 overview.pdf (accessed on 3/2/2011).

129. Chen Yu-Shan, "The Positive Effect of Green Intellectual Capital on Competitive Advantages of Firms," *Journal of Business Ethics* 77 (2008), pp. 271–286.

130. D. Ulrich, "Intellectual Capital = CompetenceXCommitment," *Sloan Management Review* 39:2 (1998), pp. 15–26.

131. Gregory Unruh Gregory and Richard Ettenson, "Winning in the Green Frenz," *Harvard Business Review* 88:11 (Nov 2010), pp. 110-115.

132. Atanu Chaudhury et al, "Necessity Breeds Opportunity: Constraints, Innovation and Competitive Advantage (2009)" http://www.deloitte.com/assets/Dcom-SouthAfrica/Local%20Assets/Documents/Necessity%20%Opportunity.pdf.

133. E.M. Rogers, *Diffusion of Innovation,* 3rd ed., (New York: Free Press, 1983).

134. R.T. Sieet al., "Study on the Relations Between Management Innovation and Customer Citizenship Behaviors," *Journal of Small Business and Enterprose* 12:2 (2007), pp 33–35.

135. C. Julia Naranjo-Valencia et al., "Innovation or Imitation? The Role of Organizational Culture," *Management Decision* 49:1 (2011), pp. 55–72.

136. Rakesh Basant Rakesh (2006). "Bangalore Cluster: Evolution, Growth and Challenges (Working Paper)," Indian Institute of Management-Ahmedabad, www.iimahd.ernet.in/publications/data/2006-05-02rbasant.pdf (accessed on 28/1/2011); "TCI

Global Competitiveness Conference," Ideas incorporated based on Session on Prosperity through Collaboration and Clusters, In *Competitiveness, Innovative Clusters and Prosperity,* 29 Nov – 3 Dec, 2010, organized by Management Development Institute, Gurgaon, India.

137. UNIDO, "General Review Study of Small & Medium Enterprise (SME) Clusters in India," United Nations Industrial Development Organization, Geneva (2001). www.unido.org/fileadmin/import/userfiles/russof/small.pdf, *(accessed on 28/1/2011).*

138. Michael E. Porter, "Clusters and Cluster Development," Institute for Strategy and Competitiveness, http://www.isc.hbs.edu/econ-clusters.htm (accessed on 28/1/2011).

139. Jeffrey G Covin and Morgan P Miles. "Corporate Entrepreneurship and the Pursuit of Competitive Advantage," *Entrepreneurship Theory and Practice* 23:3 (1999), pp.47--63.

140. M.H. Morris and D.F. Kuratko, *Corporate Entrepreneurship,* (Orlando, Florida: Harcourt College Publishers, 2002).

141. D.F. Kuratko et al., "Corporate Entrepreneurship Behavior Among Managers: A Review of Theory, Research and Practice," In J.A. Katz et al. (eds), *Corporate Entrepreneurship, Advances in Entrepreneurship: Firm Emergence and Growth* 7 (2004).

142. M.H. Morris et al., *Corporate Entrepreneurship and Innovation,* 2nd ed, p. 259 (Ohio: Thomson South-Western, 2008).

143. Arti Shivastava, Social Entrepreneurship in India–The Complete Guide to Funding, Profitable Sectors (2011)," http://www.pluggd.in/social-entrepreneurship-in-india-funds-profitable-sectors-297/ (accessed on 21/3/2011); Trevis S. Certo and Miller Toyah, "Social Entrepreneurship: Key Issues and Concepts," *Business Horizons* 2008, http://wwwts.au.edu.tw (accessed on 21/3/2011).

144. J. Austin et al., "Social and Commercial Entrepreneurship: Same, Different or Both?" *Entrepreneurship Theory and Practice* 30:1 (2006), pp 1–22.

145. J. Austin et al., "Corporate Social Entrepreneurship: The New Frontier," In M. Epstein and K. Hanson. Westport (eds), *The Accountable Corporation,* Vol 3: Corporate Social Responsibility (2006), (CT: Praeger).

146. J. Austin, "Social Partnering in Latin America: Lessons Drawn from Collaborations of Businesses and Civil Society Organizations," David Rockefeller Center for Latin American Studies (2004), distributed by *Harvard University Press* Cambridge, (MA: Harvard University).

147. J. Austin and Reficco Ezequiel, "Corporate Social Entrepreneurship (working paper)," *Harvard Business School* (2009), http://www.csrglobal.cn/upload/image/302212.pdf (accessed on 22/2/2011).

148. J. Austin et al.,. "Social Entrepreneurship: It's For Corporations, Too," In A Nicholls (ed.) *Social Entrepreneurship: New Paradigms of Sustainable Social Change* (2005), (Oxford, UK: Oxford University Press).

149. C. Rangarajan, *Responding To Globalization: India's Answer* (2006), http://eac.gov.in/aboutus/chspe/55GLOBALIZATION%20AND%20CHALLENGES%20BEFORE%20INDIA-Gen%20(single%20space).doc; Chandrasekaran Balakrishan, *Impact of Globalisation on Developing Countries and India* (2004), http://economics.about.com/od/globalizationtrade/l/aaglobalization.htm; Rajen Mehrotra, *Globalisation and its Impact on Indian Industry,* ILO, 4 Jan 2005, New Delhi, http://www.gmupolicy.net/india/GlobalCompetitiveBusinessNov04.ppt#8

150. " 'Huge Responsibility' on GlobalCo to Perform," *New Zealand Herald,* 18 June 2001; "A Major Player on the World Milk Stage," *Weekly Times* (Sydney), 8 September 2004, p. 91; K. Newman, "Greener Pastures," *MIS New Zealand,* September 2004, p. 18; D. Blayney et al., *U.S. Dairy at a Global Crossroads* (Washington, DC: U.S. Department of Agriculture, Economic Research Service, November 2006).

151. S. Fischer, "Globalization and Its Challenges," *American Economic Review,* May 2003, pp. 1–29. For discussion of the diverse meanings of "globalization," see M.F. Guillén, "Is Globalization Civilizing, Destructive or Feeble? A Critique of Five Key Debates in the Social Science Literature," *Annual Review of Sociology* 27 (2001), pp. 235–260.

152. The ongoing debate regarding the advantages and disadvantages of globalization are discussed in Guillén, "Is Globalization Civilizing, Destructive or Feeble?"; D. Doane, "Can Globalization Be Fixed?" *Business Strategy Review* 13, no. 2 (2002), pp. 51–58; J. Bhagwati, *In Defense of Globalization* (New York: Oxford University Press, 2004); M. Wolf, *Why Globalization Works* (New Haven, CT: Yale University Press, 2004).

153. K. Ohmae, *The Next Global Stage* (Philadelphia: Wharton School, 2005).

154. R. House, M. Javidan, and P. Dorfman, "Project GLOBE: An Introduction," *Applied Psychology: An International Journal* 50 (2001), pp. 489–505; M.M. Javidan et al., "In the Eye of the Beholder: Cross Cultural Lessons in Leadership from Project GLOBE," *Academy of Management Perspectives* 20, no. 1 (February 2006), pp. 67–90.

155. BBC News, *Jet Airways Lays off 800 Staff* (15 Oct 2008). http://news.bbc.co.uk/2/hi/7670874.stm. accessed on 16/12/2010; Jayanti Ghosh, "Global Crisis and Beyond Sustainable Growth Trajectories for the Developing World," *International Labour Review* 149:2 (2010); Joseph Stiglitz, "The Global Crisis, Social Protection and Jobs" *International Labour Review,* 148:1-2 (2009), http://www.ilo.org/public/english/revue/download/pdf/s1_stiglitz2009_1_2.pdf (accessed on 6/12/2010); Rajeshwari Sharma, *Lay-offs*

Needn't be the FirstOption (2 Feb 2008), http://www.livemint.com/2009/02/02205740/layoffs-needn8217t-be-the-f.html (accessed on 16/12/2010).

156. PR Newswire, "For the Second Time in Three Years Verizon Ranked No. 1 on DiversityInc Magazine's List of Top 50 Companies for Diversity" (news release), New York, 2 April 2008; Verizon, *Doing the Work: 2007 Verizon Corporate Responsibility Report* (New York: Verizon, 2008).

157. M.F. Riche, "America's Diversity and Growth: Signposts for the 21st Century," *Population Bulletin* (June 2000), pp. 3–43; U.S. Census Bureau, *Statistical Abstract of the United States: 2004–2005* (Washington, DC: U.S. Census Bureau, May 2005).

158. D.A. Harrison et al., "Time, Teams, and Task Performance: Changing Effects of Surface- and Deep-Level Diversity on Group Functioning," *Academy of Management Journal* 45, no. 5 (2002), pp. 1029–1046.

159. R. Zemke, C. Raines, and B. Filipczak, *Generations at Work: Managing the Clash of Veterans, Boomers, Xers, and Nexters in Your Workplace* (New York: Amacom, 2000); M.R. Muetzel, *They're Not Aloof, Just Generation X* (Shreveport, LA: Steel Bay, 2003); S.H. Applebaum, M. Serena, and B.T. Shapiro, "Generation X and the Boomers: Organizational Myths and Literary Realities," *Management Research News* 27, no. 11–12 (2004), pp. 1–28; N. Howe and W. Strauss, "The Next 20 Years: How Customer and Workforce Attitudes Will Evolve," *Harvard Business Review* (July–August 2007), pp. 41–52.

160. O.C. Richard, "Racial Diversity, Business Strategy, and Firm Performance: A Resource-Based View," *Academy of Management Journal* 43 (2000), pp. 164–177; D.D. Frink et al., "Gender Demography and Organization Performance: A Two-Study Investigation with Convergence," *Group & Organization Management* 28 (March 2003), pp. 127–147; T. Kochan et al., "The Effects of Diversity on Business Performance: Report of the Diversity Research Network," *Human Resource Management* 42 (2003), pp. 3–21; R.J. Burke and E. Ng, "The Changing Nature of Work and Organizations: Implications for Human Resource Management," *Human Resource Management Review* 16 (2006), pp. 86–94.

161. D. Porras, D. Psihountas, and M. Griswold, "The Long-Term Performance of Diverse Firms," *International Journal of Diversity* 6, no. 1 (2006), pp. 25–34; R.A. Weigand, "Organizational Diversity, Profits and Returns in U.S. Firms," *Problems & Perspectives in Management*, no. 3 (2007), pp. 69–83.

162. C. Hymowitz, "The New Diversity," *Wall Street Journal*, 14 November 2005, R1.

163. R.J. Ely and D.A. Thomas, "Cultural Diversity at Work: The Effects of Diversity Perspectives on Work Group Processes and Outcomes," *Administrative Science Quarterly* 46 (June 2001), pp. 229–273; Kochan et al., "The Effects of Diversity on Business Performance"; D. van Knippenberg and S.A. Haslam, "Realizing the Diversity Dividend: Exploring the Subtle Interplay between Identity, Ideology and Reality," in *Social Identity at Work: Developing Theory for Organizational Practice*, ed. S.A. Haslam et al. (New York: Taylor and Francis, 2003), pp. 61–80; D. van Knippenberg, C.K.W. De Dreu, and A.C. Homan, "Work Group Diversity and Group Performance: An Integrative Model and Research Agenda," *Journal of Applied Psychology* 89, no. 6 (2004), pp. 1008–1022; E. Molleman, "Diversity in Demographic Characteristics, Abilities and Personality Traits: Do Faultlines Affect Team Functioning?" *Group Decision and Negotiation* 14, no. 3 (2005), pp. 173–193.

164. A. Birritteri, "Workplace Diversity: Realizing the Benefits of an All-Inclusive Employee Base," *New Jersey Business*, November 2005, 36.

165. Verizon, *Making Connections: Verizon Corporate Responsibility Report*, (New York: Verizon, December 2004); J. Carlton, "Dig In: At Google, a Global Workforce Translates into a Global Cafeteria Menu," *The Wall Street Journal*, 14 November 2005, p. R9; P. Goffney, "Champions of Diversity: The Path to Corporate Enlightenment," *Essence*, May 2005, pp. 149–57.

166. M.F. Riche, "America's Diversity and Growth: Signposts for the 21st Century," *Population Bulletin* (June 2000), pp. 3–43; U.S. Census Bureau, *Statistical Abstract of the United States: 2004–2005* (Washington: U.S. Census Bureau, May 2005).

167. Association of American Medical Colleges, "Table 1: Women Applicants, Enrollees–Selected Years 1949–1950 through 2002–2003" (14 July 2003), http://www.aamc.org/members/wim/statistics/stats03/start.htm (accessed 20 June 2005); U.S. Census Bureau, *Statistical Abstract of the United States: 2004–2005*, (Table no. 570, p. 371).

168. W.G. Bennis and R.J. Thomas, *Geeks and Geezers* (Boston: Harvard Business School Press, 2002), pp. 74–79; E.D.Y. Greenblatt, "Work–Life Balance: Wisdom or Whining," *Organizational Dynamics* 31, no. 2 (2002), pp. 177–93.

169. Basch, "Doing Well by Doing Good"; Coughlin, "Goooood Move."

170. M.V. Roehling et al., "The Nature of the New Employment Relationship(s): A Content Analysis of the Practitioner and Academic Literatures," *Human Resource Management* 39 (2000), pp. 305–20; W.R. Boswell et al., "Responsibilities in the 'New Employment Relationship': An Empirical Test of an Assumed Phenomenon," *Journal of Managerial Issues* 13 (Fall 2001), 307–27; M. Fugate, A.J. Kinicki, and B.E. Ashforth, "Employability: A Psycho-Social Construct, Its Dimensions, and Applications," *Journal of Vocational Behavior* 65, no. 1 (2004), pp. 14–38.

171. M. Jenkins, "Yours for the Taking," *Boeing Frontiers*, June 2004, http://www.boeing.com/news/frontiers/index.html.

172. B.A. Lautsch, "Uncovering and Explaining Variance in the Features and Outcomes of Contingent Work," *Industrial & Labor Relations Review* 56 (October 2002), pp. 23–43; S. Ang, L. Van Dyne, and T.M. Begley, "The Employment Relationships of Foreign

Workers versus Local Employees: A Field Study of Organizational Justice, Job Satisfaction, Performance, and OCB," *Journal of Organizational Behavior* 24 (2003), pp. 561–83; A.L. Kalleberg, "Flexible Firms and Labor Market Segmentation," Work and Occupations 30, no. 2 (May 2003), pp. 154–75; B.A. Lautsch, "The Influence of Regular Work Systems on Compensation for Contingent Workers," *Industrial Relations* 42, no. 4 (October 2003), pp. 565–88; Connelly and Gallagher, "Emerging Trends in Contingent Work Research"; B. Pocock, J. Buchanan, and I. Campbell, "Meeting the Challenge of Casual Work in Australia: Evidence, Past Treatment and Future Policy," *Australian Bulletin of Labour* 30, no. 1 (March 2004), pp. 16–32.

173. S. de Castro and Y.-C. Tham, "Home Work," *Digital Life*, 8 February 2005.

174. Australian Telework Advisory Committee (ATAC), *Telework–International Developments (Paper III)* (Canberra: Commonwealth of Australia, March 2005); M. Conlin, "The Easiest Commute of All," *Business Week*, 12 December 2005, p. 78.

175. "AT&T Telecommute Survey Indicates Productivity Is Up," AT&T News release, (New York: 6 August 2002); L. Duxbury and C. Higgins, "Telecommute: A Primer for the Millennium Introduction," in *The New World of Work: Challenges and Opportunities*, ed. C.L. Cooper and R.J. Burke (Oxford: Blackwell, 2002), pp. 157–99; V. Illegems and A. Verbeke, "Telework: What Does It Mean for Management?" *Long Range Planning* 37 (2004), pp. 319–34; S. Raghuram and B.Wiesenfeld, "Work–Nonwork Conflict and Job Stress among Virtual Workers," *Human Resource Management* 43, no. 2/3 (Summer/Fall 2004), pp. 259–77.

176. D.E. Bailey and N.B. Kurland, "A Review of Telework Research: Findings, New Directions, and Lessons for the Study of Modern Work," *Journal of Organizational Behavior* 23 (2002), pp. 383–400; D.W. McCloskey and M. Igbaria, "Does 'Out of Sight' Mean 'Out of Mind'? An Empirical Investigation of the Career Advancement Prospects of Telecommuters," *Information Resources Management Journal* 16 (April–June 2003), pp. 19–34; Sensis, *Sensis® Insights Report: Teleworking*, (Melbourne: Sensis, June 2005).

177. J. Lipnack and J. Stamps, *Virtual Teams: People Working across Boundaries with Technology* (New York: John Wiley & Sons, 2001); L.L. Martins, L.L. Gilson, and M.T. Maynard, "Virtual Teams: What Do We Know and Where Do We Go from Here?" *Journal of Management* 30, no. 6 (2004), pp. 805–35; G. Hertel, S. Geister, and U. Konradt, "Managing Virtual Teams: A Review of Current Empirical Research," *Human Resource Management Review* 15, no. 1 (2005), pp. 69–95.

178. Priscilla H. Douglas, Affinity Groups--Catalyst for Inclusive Organizations," *Employment Relations Today* 34:4, pp. 11--18 (2008); Gorge A. Gonzalez, "Diversity Change in Organizations: A Systematic, Multilevel and Nonlinear Process," *The Journal of Applied Behavioral Science*, 46:2 (2010), pp. 197–219; Neha Pal, India Incorporation to go for Inclusive Growth, *Financial Express*, 2008, http://www.financialexpress.com/news/india-inc-to-go-for-inclusive-growth/383501/0 (accessed on 1/2/2011); Flannery G. Stevens et al., "Unlocking the Benefits of Diversity: All Inclusive Multiculturalism and Positive Organizational Change," *The Journal of Applied Behavioral Science*, 44:1 (2008) pp. 116–133.

179. World Bank, *What is Inclusive Growth?* (2009), http://siteresources.worldbank.org/INDEBTDEPT/Resources/468980-218567884549/WhatIsInclusiveGrowth20081230.pdf (accessed on 31/1/2011).

180. N.M. Pless and T. Maak, "Building an Inclusive Diversity Culture: Principles, Process and Practice," *Journal of Business Ethics* 54 (2004), pp 129–147.

181. Rediff, *Some Must Have Skills for the Future* (2008), http://www.rediff.com/money/2008/jan/16spec.htm (accessed on 14/2/2011).

182. Gartner, *Gartner Says the World of Work Will Witness 10 Changes During the Next 10 Years* (2010), http://www.gartner.com/it/page.jsp?id=1416513 (accessed on 12/2/2011).

183. *India's Population* (2011), http://www.indiaonlinepages.com/population/india/india-current-population.html (accessed on 4/4/2011).

184. Sujata Aggarwal (2006). *The Workplace of the Future*, Tata Group Communication (2006) http://www.tata.com/careers/articles/inside.aspx?artid=xTlZ3G8Rit8= (accessed on 14/2/2011).

185. Gary M. Oslon and Judith S. Oslon, "Distance Matters," *Human–Computer Interaction* 15 (2000), pp. 139–178; Gary M Oslon et al. (eds), *Scientific Research on the Internet*, (Cambridge, MA: MIT Press, 2008).

186. C.E. Amiot et al., "Status, Equity and Social Justification During an Intergroup Merger: A Longitudinal Study," *British Journal of Social Psychology* 46 (2007), pp. 557–77.

187. D.J. Terry et al., "Employee Adjustment to an Organizational Merger: Stress, Coping and Intergroup Differences," *Stress Medicine* 12 (1996), pp. 105–122.

188. Myeong-Gu Seo and Sharon N Hill, "Understanding the Human Side of Merger and Acquisition: An Integrative Framework," *Journal of Applied Behavioral Science* Dec 2005, 41:4, pp. 422–443.

189. *Ibid.*

190. P. Very et al., Relative Standing and the Performance of Recently Acquired European Firms. Strategic Management Journal, 18:8 (1997), pp. 593–614.

191. P. Goulet and D.M. Schweiger, "Managing Culture and Human Resources in Mergers and Acquisitions," In G.K. Stahl and I. Bjorkman (eds), *Handbook of Research in International Human Resource Management*, pp. 405–429, (London: Edward Elgar Ltd, 2006).

192. T.J. Larkin and S. Larkin, "Reaching and Changing Frontline Employees," *Harvard Business Review*, 74:3 (1996), pp 95–107.

193. Deepak K. Datta et al., "Causes and Effects of Employees Downsizing: A Review and Synthesis," *Journal of Management*, 36:1 (2010), pp 281–348.

194. L. Story and E. Dash, "For Wall Street Workers, axe falls quietly", *The New York Times* May 16, 2008; DC Weiss "Humor Columnist Takes Aim at Stealth Layoffs," *ABA Journal* 23 May 2008.

195. Op cit. Deepak K. Datta et al (2010).

196. *Ibid.*

197. *Ibid.*

198. J.P. Guthrie and D.K. Datta, "Dumb and Dumber: The Impact of Downsizing on Firm Performance as Moderated by Industry Conditions," *Organization Science* 19 (2008), pp. 108–123.; Franco Gandolfi "Unravelling Downsizing – What do we know about the phenomenon?" *Review of International Comparative Management* 10:3 (2009).

199. F. Gandolfi and P. Neck, "Consequences, Payoffs, and Falloutof Downsizing (A literature review of corporate downsizing: Part 3)," *Review of International Comparative Management*, 9:1 (2008), pp. 55–78.

200. J. Brockner, "The Effects of Work Layoffs in Survivors: Research, Theory and Practice. Research in Organizational Behavior, 10 (1998), pp. 213–255.

201. J. McGregor, "The Stealth Layoff", *BusinessWeek* 16 May 2008, http://www.businessweek.com/careers/managementiq/archives/2008/05/the_stealth_lay.html (accessed on 16/2/2011).

202. M.N. Zald, "More Fragmentation? Unfinished Business in Linking the Social Sciences and the Humanities," *Administrative Science Quarterly* 41 (1996), pp. 251–261. Concerns about the "trade deficit" in OB are raised in C. Heath and S.B. Sitkin, "Big-B versus Big-O: What Is Organizational about Organizational Behavior?" *Journal of Organizational Behavior* 22 (2001), pp. 43–58.

203. J. Pfeffer and R.I. Sutton, *Hard Facts, Dangerous Half-Truths, and Total Nonsense* (Boston: Harvard Business School Press, 2006); D.M. Rousseau and S. McCarthy, "Educating Managers from an Evidence-Based Perspective," *Academy of Management Learning & Education* 6, no. 1 (2007), pp. 84–101.

204. C.M. Christensen and M.E. Raynor, "Why Hard-Nosed Executives Should Care about Management Theory," *Harvard Business Review*, September 2003, pp. 66–74. For an excellent critique of the "one best way" approach in early management scholarship, see P.F. Drucker, "Management's New Paradigms," *Forbes*, 5 October 1998, pp. 152–177.

205. H.L. Tosi and J.W. Slocum Jr., "Contingency Theory: Some Suggested Directions," *Journal of Management* 10 (1984), pp. 9–26.

206. D.M. Rousseau and R.J. House, "Meso Organizational Behavior: Avoiding Three Fundamental Biases," in *Trends in Organizational Behavior*, ed. C.L. Cooper and D.M. Rousseau (Chichester, UK: John Wiley, 1994), pp. 13–30.

Chapter 2

1. R. Langlois, "Fairmont Hotels: Business Strategy Starts with People," *Canadian HR Reporter*, 5 November 2001, p. 19; V. Galt, "A World of Opportunity for Those in Mid-Career," *Globe & Mail*, 7 June 2006, p. C1; M.T. Bitti, "Rewards of Hard Work," *National Post*, 17 October 2007, p. WK2.

2. L.L. Thurstone, "Ability, Motivation, and Speed," *Psychometrika* 2, no. 4 (1937), pp. 249–254; N.R.F. Maier, *Psychology in Industry*, 2d ed. (Boston: Houghton Mifflin, 1955); V.H. Vroom, *Work and Motivation* (New York: Wiley, 1964); J.P. Campbell et al., *Managerial Behavior, Performance, and Effectiveness* (New York: McGraw-Hill, 1970).

3. E.E. Lawler III and L.W. Porter, "Antecedent Attitudes of Effective Managerial Performance," *Organizational Behavior and Human Performance* 2 (1967), pp. 122–142; M.A. Griffin, A. Neal, and S.K. Parker, "A New Model of Work Role Performance: Positive Behavior in Uncertain and Interdependent Contexts," *Academy of Management Journal* 50, no. 2 (April 2007), pp. 327–347.

4. Only a few literature reviews have included all four factors. These include J.P. Campbell and R.D. Pritchard, "Motivation Theory in Industrial and Organizational Psychology," in *Handbook of Industrial and Organizational Psychology*, ed. M.D. Dunnette (Chicago: Rand McNally, 1976), pp. 62–130; T.R. Mitchell, "Motivation: New Directions for Theory, Research, and Practice," *Academy of Management Review* 7, no. 1 (January 1982), pp. 80–88; G.A.J. Churchill et al., "The Determinants of Salesperson Performance: A Meta-Analysis," *Journal of Marketing Research (JMR)* 22, no. 2 (1985), pp. 103–118; R.E. Plank and D.A. Reid, "The Mediating Role of Sales Behaviors: An Alternative Perspective of Sales Performance and Effectiveness," *Journal of Personal Selling & Sales Management* 14, no. 3 (Summer 1994), pp. 43–56. The *MARS* acronym was coined by senior officers in the Singapore armed forces. Chris Perryer at the University of Western Australia suggests the full model should be called the "MARS BAR" because the outcomes might be labeled "behavior and results"!

5. C.C. Pinder, *Work Motivation in Organizational Behavior* (Upper Saddle River, NJ: Prentice Hall, 1998); G.P. Latham and C.C. Pinder, "Work Motivation Theory and Research at the Dawn of the Twenty-First Century," *Annual Review of Psychology* 56 (2005), pp. 485–516.

6. L.M. Spencer and S.M. Spencer, *Competence at Work: Models for Superior Performance* (New York: Wiley, 1993); R. Kurz and D. Bartram, "Competency and Individual Performance: Modelling the World of Work," in *Organizational Effectiveness: The Role of Psychology,* ed. I.T. Robertson, M. Callinan, and D. Bartram (Chichester, UK: John Wiley, 2002), pp. 227–258; D. Bartram, "The Great Eight Competencies: A Criterion-Centric Approach to Validation," *Journal of Applied Psychology* 90, no. 6 (2005), pp. 1185–1203; H. Heinsman et al., "Competencies through the Eyes of Psychologists: A Closer Look at Assessing Competencies," *International Journal of Selection and Assessment* 15, no. 4 (December 2007), pp. 412–427.

7. P. Tharenou, A.M. Saks, and C. Moore, "A Review and Critique of Research on Training and Organizational-Level Outcomes," *Human Resource Management Review* 17, no. 3 (2007), pp. 251–273.

8. Canada Newswire, "Canadian Organizations Must Work Harder to Productively Engage Employees" (news release), 25 January 2005.

9. K.F. Kane, "Special Issue: Situational Constraints and Work Performance," *Human Resource Management Review* 3 (Summer 1993), pp. 83–175; S.B. Bacharach and P. Bamberger, "Beyond Situational Constraints: Job Resources Inadequacy and Individual Performance at Work," *Human Resource Management Review* 5, no. 2 (1995), pp. 79–102; G. Johns, "Commentary: In Praise of Context," *Journal of Organizational Behavior* 22 (2001), pp. 31–42.

10. H. Cho, "Super Bowl of Retail Days," *Baltimore Sun,* 23 November 2006; A. Cheng, "Black Friday Kicks Off Retailers' Biggest Selling Season," *Dow Jones Business News,* 24 November 2007; J. Davis, "Training Helps Sales Staff Cope with Black Friday," *Rocky Mountain News* (Denver), 20 November 2007, p. Bus3. Black Friday is so-called because it apparently marks the first day of the year when many retailers become profitable–i.e., their books go "in the black."

11. J.P. Campbell, "The Definition and Measurement of Performance in the New Age," In *The Changing Nature of Performance: Implications for Staffing, Motivation, and Development,* D.R. Ilgen and E.D. Pulakos (eds) (San Francisco: Jossey-Bass, 1999), pp. 399–429; R.D. Hackett, "Understanding and Predicting Work Performance in the Canadian Military," *Canadian Journal of Behavioural Science* 34:2 (2002), pp. 131–40.

12. D.W. Organ, "Organizational Citizenship Behavior: It's Construct Clean-up Time," *Human Performance* 10 (1997), pp. 85–97; J.A. LePine, A. Erez, and D.E. Johnson, "The Nature and Dimensionality of Organizational Citizenship Behavior: A Critical Review and Meta-Analysis," *Journal of Applied Psychology* 87 (February 2002), pp. 52–65; B. Erickson, "Nature Times Nurture: How Organizations Can Optimize Their People's Contributions," *Journal of Organizational Excellence* 24, no. 1 (Winter 2004), pp. 21–30; M.A. Vey and J.P. Campbell, "In-Role or Extra-Role Organizational Citizenship Behavior: Which Are We Measuring?" *Human Performance* 17:1 (2004), pp. 119–35.

13. M. Rotundo and P. Sackett, "The Relative Importance of Task, Citizenship, and Counterproductive Performance to Global Ratings of Job Performance: A Policy-Capturing Approach," *Journal of Applied Psychology* 87 (February 2002), pp. 66–80; P. D. Dunlop and K. Lee, "Workplace Deviance, Organizational Citizenship Behaviour, and Business Unit Performance: The Bad Apples Do Spoil the Whole Barrel," *Journal of Organizational Behavior* 25 (2004), pp. 67–80.

14. B. Carey, "Truckload's New Recruiting Routes," *Traffic World,* 22 August 2005; D. Simanoff, "Hotels Plagued by Staff Vacancies," *Tampa Tribune,* 30 January 2006, p. 1.

15. Watson Wyatt, "U.S. Workers City Hypocrisy and Favoritism–Rather Than Financial Misdeeds–as Biggest Ethical Lapses at Work," Watson Wyatt News release (Washington, DC: 12 January 2005); Watson Wyatt, *WorkCanada 2004/2005–Pursuing Productive Engagement* (Toronto: Watson Wyatt, January 2005).

16. T.R. Mitchell, B.C. Holtom, and T.W. Lee, "How to Keep Your Best Employees: Developing an Effective Retention Policy," *Academy of Management Executive* 15 (November 2001), pp. 96–108.

17. http://www.bpoindia.org/research/attrition-rate-big-challenge.shtml; http:// en.wikipedia.org/wiki/Turnover_%28employment%29; http://en.wikipedia.org/wiki/Likert_scale; http://www.naukrihub.com/hr-today/bpo-attrition-problem.html; http://retention.naukrihub.com/attrition-rate-in-asia.htmlReferences, 13. 5.08; http://www.bpoindia.org/research/attrition-rate-big-challenge.shtml; http://www.citehr.com/why-employees-leave-organisations-azim-premji-vt2059.html

18. http://www.hewittassociates.com/Intl/AP/en-AP/AboutHewitt/Newsroom/PressReleases/2006/october-11-06.aspx

19. B.R. Sharma and M. Mohapatra, "Drivers of Organizational Commitment among Managers of Industrial Organizations: A Case Study," *Global Business Review* 9:1 (Jan-June 2008), pp. 51–63.

20. B.K. Punia, "Employee Empowerment and Retention," *Vision* (Jan-June 2004), pp. 81-91.

21. Kirtika Suneja and Shivani Shinde, *Economic Times* 23 May 2008, p.1.

22. Personality researchers agree on one point about the definition of personality: It is difficult to pin down. A definition necessarily captures one perspective of the topic more than others, and the concept of personality is itself very broad. The definition presented here is based on C.S. Carver and M.F. Scheier, *Perspectives on Personality,* 6th ed. (Boston: Allyn & Bacon, 2007); D.C. Funder, *The Personality Puzzle,* 4th ed. (New York: Norton, 2007).

23. D.P. McAdams and J.L. Pals, "A New Big Five: Fundamental Principles for an Integrative Science of Personality," *American Psychologist* 61, no. 3 (2006), pp. 204–217.

24. B. Reynolds and K. Karraker, "A Big Five Model of Disposition and Situation Interaction: Why a 'Helpful' Person May Not Always Behave Helpfully," *New Ideas in Psychology* 21 (April 2003), pp. 1–13; W. Mischel, "Toward an Integrative Science of the Person," *Annual Review of Psychology* 55 (2004), pp. 1–22.

25. B.W. Roberts and A. Caspi, "Personality Development and the Person-Situation Debate: It's Déjà Vu All Over Again," *Psychological Inquiry* 12, no. 2 (2001), pp. 104–109.

26. K.L. Jang, W.J. Livesley, and P.A. Vernon, "Heritability of the Big Five Personality Dimensions and Their Facets: A Twin Study," *Journal of Personality* 64, no. 3 (1996), pp. 577–591; N.L. Segal, *Entwined Lives: Twins and What They Tell Us about Human Behavior* (New York: Plume, 2000); T. Bouchard and J. Loehlin, "Genes, Evolution, and Personality," *Behavior Genetics* 31, no. 3 (May 2001), pp. 243–273; G. Lensvelt-Mulders and J. Hettema, "Analysis of Genetic Influences on the Consistency and Variability of the Big Five across Different Stressful Situations," *European Journal of Personality* 15, no. 5 (2001), pp. 355–371; P. Borkenau et al., "Genetic and Environmental Influences on Person 3 Situation Profiles," *Journal of Personality* 74, no. 5 (2006), pp. 1451–1480.

27. Segal, *Entwined Lives,* pp. 116–118. For critiques of the genetics perspective of personality, see J. Joseph, "Separated Twins and the Genetics of Personality Differences: A Critique," *American Journal of Psychology* 114, no. 1 (Spring 2001), pp. 1–30; P. Ehrlich and M.W. Feldman, "Genes, Environments & Behaviors," *Daedalus* 136, no. 2 (Spring 2007), pp. 5–12.

28. B.W. Roberts and W.F. DelVecchio, "The Rank-Order Consistency of Personality Traits from Childhood to Old Age: A Quantitative Review of Longitudinal Studies," *Psychological Bulletin* 126, no. 1 (2000), pp. 3–25; A. Terracciano, P.T. Costa, and R.R. McCrae, "Personality Plasticity after Age 30," *Personality and Social Psychology Bulletin* 32, no. 8 (August 2006), pp. 999–1009.

29. M. Jurado and M. Rosselli, "The Elusive Nature of Executive Functions: A Review of Our Current Understanding," *Neuropsychology Review* 17, no. 3 (2007), pp. 213–233.

30. W. Immen, "Prospective Hires Put to the Test," *Globe & Mail,* 26 January 2005, p. C1.

31. R.M. Guion and R.F. Gottier, "Validity of Personnel Measures in Personnel Selection," *Personnel Psychology* 18 (1965), pp. 135–64; N. Schmitt et al., "Meta-Analyses of Validity Studies Published between 1964 and 1982 and the Investigation of Study Characteristics," *Personnel Psychology* 37 (1984), pp. 407–22.

32. P.G. Irving, "On the Use of Personality Measures in Personnel Selection," *Canadian Psychology* 34 (April 1993), pp. 208–14.

33. B.W. Roberts and E.M. Pomerantz, "On Traits, Situations, and Their Integration: A Developmental Perspective," *Personality & Social Psychology Review* 8, no. 4 (2004), pp. 402–416; W. Fleeson, "Situation-Based Contingencies Underlying Trait-Content Manifestation in Behavior," *Journal of Personality* 75, no. 4 (2007), pp. 825–862.

34. J.M. Digman, "Personality Structure: Emergence of the Five-Factor Model," *Annual Review of Psychology* 41 (1990), pp. 417–440; O.P. John and S. Srivastava, "The Big Five Trait Taxonomy: History, Measurement, and Theoretical Perspectives," in *Handbook of Personality: Theory and Research,* ed. L.A. Pervin and O.P. John (New York: Guildford Press, 1999), pp. 102–138; A. Caspi, B.W. Roberts, and R.L. Shiner, "Personality Development: Stability and Change," *Annual Review of Psychology* 56, no. 1 (2005), pp. 453–484; McAdams and Pals, "A New Big Five."

35. J. Hogan and B. Holland, "Using Theory to Evaluate Personality and Job-Performance Relations: A Socioanalytic Perspective," *Journal of Applied Psychology* 88, no. 1 (2003), pp. 100–112; D.S. Ones, C. Viswesvaran, and S. Dilchert, "Personality at Work: Raising Awareness and Correcting Misconceptions," *Human Performance* 18, no. 4 (2005), pp. 389–404.

36. M.R. Barrick and M.K. Mount, "Yes, Personality Matters: Moving on to More Important Matters," *Human Performance* 18, no. 4 (2005), pp. 359–372.

37. M.R. Barrick, M.K. Mount, and T.A. Judge, "Personality and Performance at the Beginning of the New Millennium: What Do We Know and Where Do We Go Next?" *International Journal of Selection and Assessment* 9, no. 1–2 (2001), pp. 9–30; T.A. Judge and R. Ilies, "Relationship of Personality to Performance Motivation: A Meta-Analytic Review," *Journal of Applied Psychology* 87, no. 4 (2002), pp. 797–807; A. Witt, L.A. Burke, and M.R. Barrick, "The Interactive Effects of Conscientiousness and Agreeableness on Job Performance," *Journal of Applied Psychology* 87 (February 2002), pp. 164–169; J. Moutafi, A. Furnham, and J. Crump, "Is Managerial Level Related to Personality?" *British Journal of Management* 18, no. 3 (2007), pp. 272–280.

38. K.M. DeNeve and H. Cooper, "The Happy Personality: A Meta-Analysis of 137 Personality Traits and Subjective Well-Being," *Psychological Bulletin* 124 (September 1998), pp. 197–229; R. Ilies, M.W. Gerhardt, and H. Le, "Individual Differences in Leadership Emergence: Integrating Meta-Analytic Findings and Behavioral Genetics Estimates," *International Journal of Selection and Assessment* 12, no. 3 (September 2004), pp. 207–219; B. Kozak, J. Strelau, and J.N.V. Miles, "Genetic Determinants of Individual Differences in Coping Styles," *Anxiety, Stress & Coping* 18, no. 1 (March 2005), pp. 1–15.

39. C.G. Jung, *Psychological Types,* trans. H.G. Baynes (Princeton, NJ: Princeton University Press, 1971); I.B. Myers, *The Myers-Briggs Type Indicator* (Palo Alto, CA: Consulting Psychologists Press, 1987).

40. Subhash Sharma, *The Way of the Theory K. In New Mantras in Corporate Corridors: From Ancient Roots to Global Routes,* (New Delhi: New Age International, 2007), pp. 189–214.

41. M. Snyder, *Public Appearances/Private Realities: The Psychology of Self-Monitoring* (New York: W. H. Freeman, 1987).

42. R.J. Ellis and S.E. Cronshaw, "Self-Monitoring and Leader Emergence: A Test of Moderator Effects," *Small Group Research* 23 (1992), pp. 113–29; M. Kilduff and D.V. Day, "Do Chameleons Get Ahead? The Effects of Self-Monitoring on Managerial Careers," *Academy of Management Journal* 37 (1994), pp. 1047–60; M.A. Warech et al., "Self-Monitoring and 360-Degree Ratings," *Leadership Quarterly* 9 (Winter 1998), pp. 449–73; A. Mehra, M. Kilduff, and D.J. Brass, "The Social Networks of High and Low Self-Monitors: Implications for Workplace Performance," *Administrative Science Quarterly* 46 (March 2001), pp. 121–46.

43. J.L. Holland, *Making Vocational Choices: A Theory of Careers* (Englewood Cliffs, NJ: Prentice Hall, 1973).

44. G.D. Gottfredson and J.L. Holland, "A Longitudinal Test of the Influence of Congruence: Job Satisfaction, Competency Utilization, and Counterproductive Behavior," *Journal of Counseling Psychology* 37 (1990), pp. 389–98; A. Furnham, "Vocational Preference and P-O Fit: Reflections on Holland's Theory of Vocational Choice," *Applied Psychology: An International Review* 50 (2001), pp. 5–29.

45. J. Tupponce, "Listening to Those Inner Voices," *Richmond Times-Dispatch*, 11 May 2003, p. S3.

46. Furnham, "Vocational Preference and P-O Fit: Reflections on Holland's Theory of Vocational Choice"; R.P. Tett and D.D. Burnett, "A Personality Trait-Based Interactionist Model of Job Performance," *Journal of Applied Psychology* 88, no. 3 (2003), pp. 500–517; W. Yang, G.S. Stokes, and C.H. Hui, "Cross-Cultural Validation of Holland's Interest Structure in Chinese Population," *Journal of Vocational Behavior* (2005), In Press.

47. G.D. Gottfredson, "John L. Holland's Contributions to Vocational Psychology: A Review and Evaluation," *Journal of Vocational Behavior* 55, no. 1 (1999), pp. 15–40.

48. J.D. Campbell, S. Assanand, and A. Di Paula, "The Structure of the Self-Concept and Its Relation to Psychological Adjustment," *Journal of Personality* 71, no. 1 (2003), pp. 115–140; M. J. Constantino et al., "The Direct and Stress-Buffering Effects of Self-Organization on Psychological Adjustment," *Journal of Social & Clinical Psychology* 25, no. 3 (2006), pp. 333–360.

49. C. Sedikides and A.P. Gregg, "Portraits of the Self," in *The Sage Handbook of Social Psychology*, ed. M.A. Hogg and J. Cooper (London: Sage, 2003), pp. 110–138; M.R. Leary, "Motivational and Emotional Aspects of the Self," *Annual Review of Psychology* 58, no. 1 (2007), pp. 317–344.

50. D.A. Moore, "Not So above Average after All: When People Believe They Are Worse than Average and Its Implications for Theories of Bias in Social Comparison," *Organizational Behavior and Human Decision Processes* 102, no. 1 (2007), pp. 42–58.

51. D.A. Moore and P.J. Healy, "The Trouble with Overconfidence," *Psychological Review* 115, no. 2 (2008), pp. 502–517.

52. N.J. Hiller and D.C. Hambrick, "Conceptualizing Executive Hubris: The Role of (Hyper-)Core Self-Evaluations in Strategic Decision-Making," *Strategic Management Journal* 26, no. 4 (2005), pp. 297–319; U. Malmendier and G. Tate, "CEO Overconfidence and Corporate Investment," *The Journal of Finance* 60, no. 6 (2005), pp. 2661–2700; J.A. Doukas and D. Petmezas, "Acquisitions, Overconfident Managers and Self-Attribution Bias," *European Financial Management* 13, no. 3 (2007), pp. 531–577.

53. W.B. Swann Jr., "To Be Adored or to Be Known? The Interplay of Self-Enhancement and Self-Verification," in *Foundations of Social Behavior*, ed. R.M. Sorrentino and E.T. Higgins (New York: Guildford, 1990), pp. 408–448; W.B. Swann Jr., P.J. Rentfrow, and J.S. Guinn, "Self-Verification: The Search for Coherence," in *Handbook of Self and Identity*, ed. M.R. Leary and J.Tagney (New York: Guilford, 2002), pp. 367–383.

54. Leary, "Motivational and Emotional Aspects of the Self."

55. T.A. Judge and J.E. Bono, "Relationship of Core Self-Evaluations Traits–Self-Esteem, Generalized Self-Efficacy, Locus of Control, and Emotional Stability–With Job Satisfaction and Job Performance: A Meta-Analysis," *Journal of Applied Psychology* 86, no. 1 (2001), pp. 80–92; T.A. Judge and C. Hurst, "Capitalizing on One's Advantages: Role of Core Self-Evaluations," *Journal of Applied Psychology* 92, no. 5 (2007), pp. 1212–1227. We have described the three most commonly noted components of self-evaluation. The full model also includes emotional stability (low neuroticism). However, the core self-evaluation model has received limited research and its dimensions are being debated. For example, see R.E. Johnson, C.C. Rosen, and P.E. Levy, "Getting to the Core of Core Self-Evaluation: A Review and Recommendations," *Journal of Organizational Behavior* 29 (2008), pp. 391–413.

56. W.B. Swann Jr., C. Chang-Schneider, and K.L. McClarty, "Do People's Self-Views Matter? Self-Concept and Self-Esteem in Everyday Life," *American Psychologist* 62, no. 2 (2007), pp. 84–94.

57. S. Lath, "Johnson & Johnson: Living by Its Credo," *Business Today* (India), 5 November 2006, pp. 126–129; R. Alsop, "How Boss's Deeds Buff a Firm's Reputation," *Wall Street Journal*, 21 January 2007, p. B1; F. Catteeuw, E. Flynn, and J. Vonderhorst, "Employee Engagement: Boosting Productivity in Turbulent Times," *Organization Development Journal* 25, no. 2 (Summer 2007), pp. P151–P157; C.J. Corace, "Engagement–Enrolling the Quiet Majority," *Organization Develop-ment Journal* 25, no. 2 (Summer 2007), pp. P171–P175; F. van de Ven, "Fulfilling the Promise of Career Development: Getting to the 'Heart' of the Matter," *Organization Development Journal* 25, no. 3 (Fall 2007), pp. P45–P51.

58. A. Bandura, *Self-Efficacy: The Exercise of Control* (New York: Freeman, 1997).

59. G. Chen, S.M. Gully, and D. Eden, "Validation of a New General Self-Efficacy Scale," *Organizational Research Methods* 4, no. 1 (January 2001), pp. 62–83.

60. P.E. Spector, "Behavior in Organizations as a Function of Employee Locus of Control," *Psychological Bulletin* 91 (1982), pp. 482–497; K. Hattrup, M.S. O'Connell, and J.R. Labrador, "Incremental Validity of Locus of Control after Controlling for Cognitive Ability and Conscientiousness," *Journal of Business and Psychology* 19, no. 4 (2005), pp. 461–481; T.W.H. Ng, K.L. Sorensen, and L.T. Eby, "Locus of Control at Work: A Meta-Analysis," *Journal of Organizational Behavior* 27 (2006), pp. 1057–1087.

61. H. Tajfel, *Social Identity and Intergroup Relations* (Cambridge, UK: Cambridge University Press, 1982); B.E. Ashforth and F. Mael, "Social Identity Theory and the Organization," *Academy of Management Review* 14 (1989), pp. 20–39; M.A. Hogg and D.J. Terry, "Social Identity and Self-Categorization Processes in Organizational Contexts," *Academy of Management Review* 25 (January 2000), pp. 121–140; S.A. Haslam, R.A. Eggins, and K.J.Reynolds, "The ASPIRe Model: Actualizing Social and Personal Identity Resources to Enhance Organizational Outcomes," *Journal of Occupational and Organizational Psychology* 76 (2003), pp. 83–113.

62. Sedikides and Gregg, "Portraits of the Self." The history of the social self in human beings is described in M.R. Leary and N.R. Buttermore, "The Evolution of the Human Self: Tracing the Natural History of Self-Awareness," *Journal for the Theory of Social Behaviour* 33, no. 4 (2003), pp. 365–404.

63. M.R. Edwards, "Organizational Identification: A Conceptual and Operational Review," *International Journal of Management Reviews* 7, no. 4 (2005), pp. 207–230; D.A. Whetten, "Albert and Whetten Revisited: Strengthening the Concept of Organizational Identity," *Journal of Management Inquiry* 15, no. 3 (September 2006), pp. 219–234.

64. J.BP. Sihna, (2008), Self and Personality, in Culture and Organizational Behaviour, pp. 81–109, (New Delhi: Sage, 2008).

65. A.C. Paranjpe, *Self and Identity in Modern Psychology and Indian Thought*, (New York: Plenum Press, 1998).

66. S. Vivekananda, *The Yogas and Other Works*. (ed S. Nikhiland), (New York: Ramkrishna – Vivekananda Centre, 1953).

67. R.N. Kanungo, and M. Mendonca, *Ethical Dimensions of Leadership*, (Thousand Oaks, CA: Sage, 1996).

68. H.R. Markus and S. Kitayama, "Culture and the Self: Implications for Cognition, Emotion, and Motivation," *Psychological Review* (1991), pp. 224--53.

69. A. Roland, *In Search of Self in India and Japan: Towards a Cross-Cultural Psychology*, (Princeton, NJ: Princeton University Press, 1988).

70. S. Freud, *A General Introduction to Psycholoanalysis*, (Prema Giants: New York, 1917/49).

71. T.A. Harris, I'm OK-You're OK: A Practical Guide to Transactional Analysis (1969), (New York: Harper and Row).

72. B.M. Meglino and E.C. Ravlin, "Individual Values in Organizations: Concepts, Controversies, and Research," *Journal of Management* 24, no. 3 (1998), pp. 351–389; B.R. Agle and C.B. Caldwell, "Understanding Research on Values in Business," *Business and Society* 38, no. 3 (September 1999), pp. 326–387; S. Hitlin and J.A. Pilavin, "Values: Reviving a Dormant Concept," *Annual Review of Sociology* 30 (2004), pp. 359–393.

73. D. Lubinski, D.B. Schmidt, and C.P. Benbow, "A 20-Year Stability Analysis of the Study of Values for Intellectually Gifted Individuals from Adolescence to Adulthood," *Journal of Applied Psychology* 81 (1996), pp. 443–451.

74. B. Kabanoff and J. Daly, "Espoused Values in Organizations," *Australian Journal of Management* 27, Special issue (2002), pp. 89–104.

75. Hitlin and Pilavin, "Values: Reviving a Dormant Concept"; A. Pakizeh, J.E. Gebauer, and G.R. Maio, "Basic Human Values: Inter-Value Structure in Memory," *Journal of Experimental Social Psychology* 43, no. 3 (2007), pp. 458–465.

76. S.H. Schwartz, "Universals in the Content and Structure of Values: Theoretical Advances and Empirical Tests in 20 Countries," *Advances in Experimental Social Psychology* 25 (1992), pp. 1–65; S.H. Schwartz, "Are There Universal Aspects in the Structure and Contents of Human Values?" *Journal of Social Issues* 50 (1994), pp. 19–45; D. Spini, "Measurement Equivalence of 10 Value Types from the Schwartz Value Survey across 21 Countries," *Journal of Cross-Cultural Psychology* 34, no. 1 (January 2003), pp. 3–23; S.H. Schwartz and K. Boehnke, "Evaluating the Structure of Human Values with Confirmatory Factor Analysis," *Journal of Research in Personality* 38, no. 3 (2004), pp. 230–255.

77. G.R. Maio and J.M. Olson, "Values as Truisms: Evidence and Implications," *Journal of Personality and Social Psychology* 74, no. 2 (1998), pp. 294–311; G.R. Maio et al., "Addressing Discrepancies between Values and Behavior: The Motivating Effect of Reasons," *Journal of Experimental Social Psychology* 37, no. 2 (2001), pp. 104–117; B. Verplanken and R.W. Holland, "Motivated Decision Making: Effects of Activation and Self-Centrality of Values on Choices and Behavior," *Journal of Personality and Social Psychology* 82, no. 3 (2002), pp. 434–447; A. Bardi and S.H. Schwartz, "Values and Behavior: Strength and Structure of Relations," *Personality and Social Psychology Bulletin* 29, no. 10 (October 2003), pp. 1207–1220; M.M. Bernard and G.R. Maio, "Effects of Introspection about Reasons for Values: Extending Research on Values-as-Truisms," *Social Cognition* 21, no. 1 (2003), pp. 1–25.

78. K. Hornyak, "Upward Move: Cynthia Schwalm," *Medical Marketing & Media,* June 2008, p. 69. For research on the consequences on value congruence, see A.L. Kristof, "Person-Organization Fit: An Integrative Review of Its Conceptualizations,

Measurement, and Implications," *Personnel Psychology* 49, no. 1 (Spring 1996), pp. 1–49; M.L. Verquer, T.A. Beehr, and S.H. Wagner, "A Meta-Analysis of Relations between Person-Organization Fit and Work Attitudes," *Journal of Vocational Behavior* 63 (2003), pp. 473–489; J.W. Westerman and L.A. Cyr, "An Integrative Analysis of Person-Organization Fit Theories," *International Journal of Selection and Assessment* 12, no. 3 (September 2004), pp. 252–261; D. Bouckenooghe et al., "The Prediction of Stress by Values and Value Conflict," *Journal of Psychology* 139, no. 4 (2005), pp. 369–382.

79. T. Simons, "Behavioral Integrity: The Perceived Alignment between Managers' Words and Deeds as a Research Focus," *Organization Science* 13, no. 1 (January–February 2002), pp. 18–35; Watson Wyatt, "Employee Ratings of Senior Management Dip, Watson Wyatt Survey Finds" (news release), New York, 4 January 2007.

80. K.A. McDonald, "Meyners Does a Reality Check," *Journal of Accountancy* 201, no. 2 (2006), p. 51.

81. T.A. Joiner, "The Influence of National Culture and Organizational Culture Alignment on Job Stress and Performance: Evidence from Greece," *Journal of Managerial Psychology* 16 (2001), pp. 229–242; Z. Aycan, R.N. Kanungo, and J.B.P. Sinha, "Organizational Culture and Human Resource Management Practices: The Model of Culture Fit," *Journal of Cross-Cultural Psychology* 30 (July 1999), pp. 501–526.

82. D. Oyserman, H.M. Coon, and M. Kemmelmeier, "Rethinking Individualism and Collectivism: Evaluation of Theoretical Assumptions and Meta-Analyses," *Psychological Bulletin* 128 (2002), pp. 3–72; P.C. Earley and C.B. Gibson, "Taking Stock in Our Progress on Individualism-Collectivism: 100 Years of Solidarity and Community," *Journal of Management* 24 (May 1998), pp. 265–304; F.S. Niles, "Individualism-Collectivism Revisited," *Cross-Cultural Research* 32 (November 1998), pp. 315–341.

83. Oyserman, Coon, and Kemmelmeier, "Rethinking Individualism and Collectivism"; Also see F. Li and L. Aksoy, "Dimensionality of Individualism–Collectivism and Measurement Equivalence of Triandis and Gelfand's Scale," *Journal of Business and Psychology* 21, no. 3 (2007), pp. 313–329. The relationship between individualism and collectivism is still being debated, but most experts now agree that individualism and collectivism have serious problems with conceptualization and measurement.

84. G. Hofstede, *Culture's Consequences: Comparing Values, Behaviors, Institutions, and Organizations across Nations,* 2d ed. (Thousand Oaks, CA: Sage, 2001).

85. Dalcher Darren, "The Paradox of Uncertainty: When Less Means More?", *CEPIS UPGRADE,* XI:5 (October 2010), www.cepis.org/upgrade/media/UPGRADE_5_2010_UPENET1.pdf *(accessed on 16/2/2011).*

86. Hofstede, *Culture's Consequences.* Hofstede used the terms *masculinity* and *femininity* for *achievement* and *nurturing orientation,* respectively. We have adopted the latter two terms to minimize the sexist perspective of these concepts.

87. J.S. Osland et al., "Beyond Sophisticated Stereotyping: Cultural Sensemaking in Context," *Academy of Management Executive* 14 (February 2000), pp. 65–79; S.S. Sarwono and R.W. Armstrong, "Microcultural Differences and Perceived Ethical Problems: An International Business Perspective," *Journal of Business Ethics* 30 (March 2001), pp. 41–56; M. Voronov and J.A. Singer, "The Myth of Individualism-Collectivism: A Critical Review," *Journal of Social Psychology* 142 (August 2002), pp. 461–480; N. Jacob, "Cross-Cultural Investigations: Emerging Concepts," *Journal of Organizational Change Management* 18, no. 5 (2005), pp. 514–528.

88. S. Prabhupada, *Bhagavad-Gita as it is,* 2nd ed., (Mumbai: Bhaktivedanta Book Trust, 1989).

89. Asia Society, 2006 http://askasia.org/teachers/essays/essay.php?no=104

90. http:///www.infosys.com/about/vision_and_mission.asp; http:www.bluecloud.org/13.html

91. C. Savoye, "Workers Say Honesty Is Best Company Policy," *Christian Science Monitor,* 15 June 2000; J.M. Kouzes and B.Z. Posner, *The Leadership Challenge,* 3d ed. (San Francisco: Jossey-Bass, 2002); J. Schettler, "Leadership in Corporate America," *Training & Development,* September 2002, pp. 66–73.

92. P.L. Schumann, "A Moral Principles Framework for Human Resource Management Ethics," *Human Resource Management Review* 11 (Spring–Summer 2001), pp. 93–111; J. Boss, *Analyzing Moral Issues,* 3d ed. (New York: McGraw-Hill, 2005), chap. 1; M.G. Velasquez, *Business Ethics: Concepts and Cases,* 6th ed. (Upper Saddle River, NJ: Prentice Hall, 2006), chap. 2.

93. T. J. Jones, "Ethical Decision Making by Individuals in Organizations: An Issue-Contingent Model," *Academy of Management Review* 16 (1991), pp. 366–395; B.H. Frey, "The Impact of Moral Intensity on Decision Making in a Business Context," *Journal of Business Ethics* 26 (August 2000), pp. 181–195; D.R. May and K.P. Pauli, "The Role of Moral Intensity in Ethical Decision Making," *Business and Society* 41 (March 2002), pp. 84–117.

94. J.R. Sparks and S.D. Hunt, "Marketing Researcher Ethical Sensitivity: Conceptualization, Measurement, and Exploratory Investigation," *Journal of Marketing* 62 (April 1998), pp. 92–109.

95. K.F. Alam, "Business Ethics in New Zealand Organizations: Views from the Middle and Lower Level Managers," *Journal of Business Ethics* 22 (November 1999), pp. 145–153; K. Blotnicky, "Is Business in Moral Decay?" *Chronicle-Herald* (Halifax), 11 June 2000; B. Stoneman and K.K. Holliday, "Pressure Cooker," *Banking Strategies,* January–February 2001, p. 13.

96. B. Farrell, D.M. Cobbin, and H.M. Farrell, "Codes of Ethics: Their Evolution, Development and Other Controversies," *Journal of Management Development* 21, no. 2 (2002), pp. 152–163; G. Wood and M. Rimmer, "Codes of Ethics: What Are They Really and What Should They Be?" *International Journal of Value-Based Management* 16, no. 2 (2003), p. 181.

97. S. Greengard, "Golden Values," *Workforce Management,* March 2005, pp. 52–53; K. Tyler, "Do the Right Thing," *HRMagazine,* February 2005, pp. 99–102.

98. K. Whitney, "Ernst & Young Ethics Training: Part of the Company Fabric," *Chief Learning Officer,* July 2007, p. 32.

99. T.F. Lindeman, "A Matter of Choice," *Pittsburgh Post-Gazette,* 30 March 2004; J. Fortier, "Trust in the Workplace," *Ottawa Business Journal,* 4 January 2007.

100. E. Aronson, "Integrating Leadership Styles and Ethical Perspectives," *CANADIAN JOURNAL OF ADMINISTRATIVE SCIENCES* 18 (December 2001), pp. 266–276; D.R. May et al., "Developing the Moral Component of Authentic Leadership," *ORGANIZATIONAL DYNAMICS* 32 (2003), pp. 247–260. The Vodafone director quotation is from R. Van Lee, L. Fabish, and N. McGaw, "The Value of Corporate Values," *STRATEGY1BUSINESS,* no. 39 (Summer 2005), pp. 1–13.

101. Subhash Sharma, "TQOM: Total Quality of Management," In *New Mantras in Corporate Corridors: From Ancient Roots to Global Routes* (2007), pp. 225–234, (New Delhi: New Age International).

102. Paul Krugman, "Greed is Bad," *The New York Times,* 4 June 2002. http://nytimes.com/2002/06/04/opinion/greed-is-bad.html (accessed on 16/2/2011).

103. R.L. Peterson. "The Neuroscience of Investing: MRI of the Reward System," *Brain Research Bulletin* 67 (2005), pp 391–97.

104. Shaker A. Zahra et al., "The Antecedents and Consequences of Top Management Fraud," *Journal of Management* 31 (2005), pp. 803–828.

105. S.L. Robinson and R.J. Bennett, "A Typology of Deviant Workplace Behavior: A Multidimensional Scaling Study," *Academy of Management Journal,* 38 (1995), pp. 555–72.

Chapter 3

1. IBM, "Sam Palmisano Discusses IBM's New Corporate Service Corps," (news release), Armonk, NY, 25 July 2007; G. Hills and A. Mahmud, *Volunteering for Impact: Best Practices in International Corporate Volunteering* (Boston: FSG Social Impact Advisors, September 2007); IBM, "IBM's Corporate Service Corps Heading to Six Emerging Countries to Spark Socio-Economic Growth While Developing Global Leaders" (news release), Armonk, NY, 26 March 2008; M. Jackson, "Corporate Volunteers Reaching Worldwide," *Boston Globe,* 4 May 2008, p. 3.

2. O. Levy et al., "What We Talk about When We Talk about 'Global Mindset': Managerial Cognition in Multinational Corporations," *Journal of International Business Studies* 38, no. 2, pp. 231–258; S.J. Black, W.H. Mobley, and E. Weldon, "The Mindset of Global Leaders: Inquisitiveness and Duality," in *Advances in Global Leadership* (JAI, 2006), pp. 181–200; S. Beechler and D. Baltzley, "Creating a Global Mindset," *Chief Learning Officer* 7, no. 6 (2008), pp. 40–45.

3. The effect of the target in selective attention is known as "bottom-up selection"; the effect of the perceiver's psychodynamics on this process is known as "top-down selection." See C.E. Connor, H.E. Egeth, and S. Yantis, "Visual Attention: Bottom-Up versus Top-Down," *Current Biology* 14, no. 19 (2004), pp. R850–R852; E.I. Knudsen, "Fundamental Components of Attention," *Annual Review of Neuroscience* 30, no. 1 (2007), pp. 57–78.

4. A. Mack et al., "Perceptual Organization and Attention," *Cognitive Psychology* 24, no. 4 (1992), pp. 475–501; A.R. Damasio, *Descartes' Error: Emotion, Reason, and the Human Brain* (New York: Putnam Sons, 1994); C. Frith, "A Framework for Studying the Neural Basis of Attention," *Neuropsychologia* 39, no. 12 (2001), pp. 1367–1371; N. Lavie, "Distracted and Confused? Selective Attention under Load," *Trends in Cognitive Sciences* 9, no. 2 (2005), pp. 75–82; M. Shermer, "The Political Brain," *Scientific American* 295, no. 1 (July 2006), p. 36; D. Westen, *The Political Brain: The Role of Emotion in Deciding the Fate of the Nation* (Cambridge, MA: PublicAffairs, 2007).

5. Confirmation bias is defined as "unwitting selectivity in the acquisition and use of evidence." R.S. Nickerson, "Confirmation Bias: A Ubiquitous Phenomenon in Many Guises," *Review of General Psychology* 2, no. 2 (1998), pp. 175–220. This occurs in a variety of ways, including overweighting positive information, perceiving only positive information, and restricting cognitive attention to a favored hypothesis. Research has found that confirmation bias is typically unconscious and driven by emotions.

6. S. Lewandowsky et al., "Memory for Fact, Fiction, and Misinformation: The Iraq War 2003," *Psychological Science* 16, no. 3 (2005), pp. 190–195.

7. D.J. Simons and C.F. Chabris, "Gorillas in Our Midst: Sustained Inattentional Blindness for Dynamic Events," *Perception* 28 (1999), pp. 1059–1074.

8. K.A. Lane, J. Kang, and M.R. Banaji, "Implicit Social Cognition and Law," *Annual Review of Law and Social Science* 3, no. 1 (2007).

9. E. Byron, "To Master the Art of Solving Crimes, Cops Study Vermeer," *Wall Street Journal,* 27 July 2005, p. A1; K.A. Findley and M. Scott, "The Multiple Dimensions of Tunnel Vision in Criminal Cases," *Wisconsin Law Review* 2 (2006), pp. 291–397; D.K.

Rossmo, "Criminal Investigative Failures," *FBI Law Enforcement Bulletin* 75, no. 9 (2006), pp. 1–8; M. Allen, "Unsolved Killings," *Roanoke Times* (Virginia), 10 August 2008.

10. C.N. Macrae and G.V. Bodenhausen, "Social Cognition: Thinking Categorically about Others," *Annual Review of Psychology* 51 (2000), pp. 93–120. For literature on the automaticity of the perceptual organization and interpretation process, see J.A. Bargh, "The Cognitive Monster: The Case against the Controllability of Automatic Stereotype Effects," in *Dual Process Theories in Social Psychology,* ed. S. Chaiken and Y. Trope (New York: Guilford, 1999), pp. 361–382; J.A. Bargh and M. J. Ferguson, "Beyond Behaviorism: On the Automaticity of Higher Mental Processes," *Psychological Bulletin* 126, no. 6 (2000), pp. 925–945; M. Gladwell, *Blink: The Power of Thinking without Thinking* (New York: Little, Brown, 2005).

11. E.M. Altmann and B.D. Burns, "Streak Biases in Decision Making: Data and a Memory Model," *Cognitive Systems Research* 6, no. 1 (2005), pp. 5–16. For a discussion of cognitive closure and perception, see A.W. Kruglanski, *The Psychology of Closed Mindedness* (New York: Psychology Press, 2004).

12. N. Ambady and R. Rosenthal, "Half a Minute: Predicting Teacher Evaluations from Thin Slices of Nonverbal Behavior and Physical Attractiveness," *Journal of Personality and Social Psychology* 64, no. 3 (March 1993), pp. 431–441. For other research on thin slices, see N. Ambady and R. Rosenthal, "Thin Slices of Expressive Behavior as Predictors of Interpersonal Consequences: A Meta-Analysis," *Psychological Bulletin* 111, no. 2 (1992), pp. 256–274; N. Ambady et al., "Surgeons' Tone of Voice: A Clue to Malpractice History," *Surgery* 132, no. 1 (July 2002), pp. 5–9.

13. P.M. Senge, *The Fifth Discipline: The Art and Practice of the Learning Organization* (New York: Doubleday Currency, 1990), chap. 10; P.N. Johnson-Laird, "Mental Models and Deduction," *Trends in Cognitive Sciences* 5, no. 10 (2001), pp. 434–442; A.B. Markman and D. Gentner, "Thinking," *Annual Review of Psychology* 52 (2001), pp. 223–247; T. J. Chermack, "Mental Models in Decision Making and Implications for Human Resource Development," *Advances in Developing Human Resources* 5, no. 4 (2003), pp. 408–422.

14. M.A. Hogg et al., "The Social Identity Perspective: Intergroup Relations, Self-Conception, and Small Groups," *Small Group Research* 35, no. 3 (June 2004), pp. 246–276; J. Jetten, R. Spears, and T. Postmes, "Intergroup Distinctiveness and Differentiation: A Meta-Analytic Integration," *Journal of Personality and Social Psychology* 86, no. 6 (2004), pp. 862–879.

15. J.W. Jackson and E.R. Smith, "Conceptualizing Social Identity: A New Framework and Evidence for the Impact of Different Dimensions," *Personality and Social Psychology Bulletin* 25 (January 1999), pp. 120–135.

16. L. Falkenberg, "Improving the Accuracy of Stereotypes within the Workplace," *Journal of Management* 16 (1990), pp. 107–118; S.T. Fiske, "Stereotyping, Prejudice, and Discrimination," in *Handbook of Social Psychology,* ed. D.T. Gilbert, S.T. Fiske, and G. Lindzey, 4th ed. (New York: McGraw-Hill, 1998), pp. 357–411; Macrae and Bodenhausen, "Social Cognition."

17. C.N. Macrae, A.B. Milne, and G.V. Bodenhausen, "Stereotypes as Energy-Saving Devices: A Peek inside the Cognitive Toolbox," *Journal of Personality and Social Psychology* 66 (1994), pp. 37–47; J.W. Sherman et al., "Stereotype Efficiency Reconsidered: Encoding Flexibility under Cognitive Load," *Journal of Personality and Social Psychology* 75 (1998), pp. 589–606; Macrae and Bodenhausen, "Social Cognition."

18. L. Sinclair and Z. Kunda, "Motivated Stereotyping of Women: She's Fine If She Praised Me but Incompetent If She Criticized Me," *Personality and Social Psychology Bulletin* 26 (November 2000), pp. 1329–1342; J.C. Turner and S.A. Haslam, "Social Identity, Organizations, and Leadership," in *Groups at Work: Theory and Research,* ed. M.E. Turner (Mahwah, NJ: Lawrence Erlbaum, 2001), pp. 25–65.

19. Kingsley R. Browne, *Biology at Work: Rethinking Sexual Equality* (Rutgers University Press, 2002).

20. Ann M. Morrison and Mary-Ann Von Glinow, "Women and Minorities in Management," *American Psychologist* 45:2, February 1990, pp. 200-208.

21. M. Linehan et al., The Growth of Female Expatriation and Male Spouses in Europe: The Challenges for International Human Resource Management, *The International Journal of Applied Human Resource Management* **1:1** (2000), pp. 37-48.

22. Gary S. Insch et al., "The Expatriate Glass Ceiling: The Second Layer of Glass," *Journal of Business Ethics* 83 (2008), pp. 19–28.

23. N. Korac-Kakabadse and A. Kouzmin, "Glass and Concrete Ceilings", *Women in Management Review,* 12:5 (1997), pp. 182–195.

24. Alexis Herman (1989) http://www.advancingwomen.com/wk_glassceiling2.html (accessed on 31/05/2011).

25. Alice Eagly, "Women and the Labyrinth of Leadership," *Harvard Business Review,* Sep 2007, 85:9 (2007), pp. 63–71.

26. A.L. Friedman and S.R. Lyne, "The Beancounter Stereotype: Towards a General Model of Stereotype Generation," *Critical Perspectives on Accounting* 12, no. 4 (2001), pp. 423–451.

27. "Employers Face New Danger: Accidental Age Bias," *Omaha World-Herald,* 10 October 2005, p. D1; "Tiptoeing through the Employment Minefield of Race, Sex, and Religion? Here's Another One," *North West Business Insider* (Manchester, UK), February 2006.

28. S.O. Gaines and E.S. Reed, "Prejudice: From Allport to Dubois," *American Psychologist* 50 (February 1995), pp. 96–103; Fiske, "Stereotyping, Prejudice, and Discrimination"; M. Hewstone, M. Rubin, and H. Willis, "Intergroup Bias," *Annual Review of Psychology* 53 (2002), pp. 575–604.

29. M. Weinstein, "Racism, Sexism, Ageism: Workplace Not Getting Any Friendlier," *Training,* May 2006, p. 11.

30. M. Patriquin, "Quebec Farm Segregated Black Workers," *Globe & Mail,* 30 April 2005, p. A1; S. Foley, "The Women Who Took on a Banking Giant and Won a $33m Sexism Case," *The Independent* (London), 5 April 2008.

31. J.A. Bargh and T.L. Chartrand, "The Unbearable Automaticity of Being," *American Psychologist* 54, no. 7 (July 1999), pp. 462–479; S.T. Fiske, "What We Know Now about Bias and Intergroup Conflict, the Problem of the Century," *Current Directions in Psychological Science* 11, no. 4 (August 2002), pp. 123–128. For recent evidence that shows that intensive training can minimize stereotype activation, see K. Kawakami et al., "Just Say No (to Stereotyping): Effects of Training in the Negation of Stereotypic Associations on Stereotype Activation," *Journal of Personality and Social Psychology* 78, no. 5 (2000), pp. 871–888; E.A. Plant, B.M. Peruche, and D.A. Butz, "Eliminating Automatic Racial Bias: Making Race Non-Diagnostic for Responses to Criminal Suspects," *Journal of Experimental Social Psychology* 41, no. 2 (2005), p. 141.

32. J.A. Bargh and T.L. Chartrand, "The Unbearable Automaticity of Being," *American Psychologist* 54, no. 7 (July 1999), pp. 462–79; S.T. Fiske, "What We Know Now About Bias and Intergroup Conflict, the Problem of the Century," *Current Directions in Psychological Science* 11, no. 4 (August 2002), pp. 123–28. For recent evidence that shows that intensive training can minimize stereotype activation, see K. Kawakami et al., "Just Say No (to Stereotyping): Effects of Training in the Negation of Stereotypic Associations on Stereotype Activation," *Journal of Personality and Social Psychology* 78, no. 5 (2000), pp. 871–88; and E.A. Plant, B.M. Peruche, and D.A. Butz, "Eliminating Automatic Racial Bias: Making Race Non-Diagnostic for Responses to Criminal Suspects," *Journal of Experimental Social Psychology* 41, no. 2 (2005), pp. 141–56.

33. M. Bendick, M.L. Egan, and S.M. Lofhjelm, "Workforce Diversity Training: From Anti-Discrimination Compliance to Organizational Development HR," *Human Resource Planning* 24 (2001), pp. 10–25; L. Roberson, C.T. Kulik, and M.B. Pepper, "Using Needs Assessment to Resolve Controversies in Diversity Training Design," *Group & Organization Management* 28, no. 1 (March 2003), pp. 148–74; D.E. Hogan and M. Mallott, "Changing Racial Prejudice through Diversity Education," *Journal of College Student Development* 46, no. 2 (March/April 2005), pp. 115–25.

34. P. Babcock, "Detecting Hidden Bias," *HRMagazine,* February 2006, p. 50.

35. P. Ford, "Next French Revolution: A Less Colorblind Society," *Christian Science Monitor,* 14 November 2005, p. 1; J.W. Anderson, "French Firm Tests Colorblind Hiring," *Washington Post,* 29 January 2006, p. A20; L. Ash, "Escaping France's Ghettoes," *BBC Radio: Crossing Continents* (London), 29 March 2007; P. Gumbel, "The French Exodus," *Time International,* 16 April 2007, p. 18; A. Sage, "L'Oreal Accused of Discrimination in 'All-White' Campaign," *The Times* (London), 16 May 2007, p. 57; D. Vidal, "Affirmative Action Bypasses Those at the Bottom of the Pile," *Le Monde Diplomatique,* May 2007. As an interesting twist, L'Oreal now lists Hamid Senni as one of its consultants on workplace diversity.

36. T.F. Pettigrew, "Intergroup Contact Theory," *Annual Review of Psychology* 49 (1998), pp. 65–85; S. Brickson, "The Impact of Identity Orientation on Individual and Organizational Outcomes in Demographically Diverse Settings," *Academy of Management Review* 25 (January 2000), pp. 82–101; J. Dixon and K. Durrheim, "Contact and the Ecology of Racial Division: Some Varieties of Informal Segregation," *British Journal of Social Psychology* 42 (March 2003), pp. 1–23.

37. B.F. Reskin, "The Proximate Causes of Employment Discrimination," *Contemporary Sociology* 29 (March 2000), pp. 319–28.

38. H.H. Kelley, *Attribution in Social Interaction* (Morristown, NJ: General Learning Press, 1971).

39. J.M. Feldman, "Beyond Attribution Theory: Cognitive Processes in Performance Appraisal," *Journal of Applied Psychology* 66 (1981), pp. 127–148.

40. J.M. Crant and T.S. Bateman, "Assignment of Credit and Blame for Performance Outcomes," *Academy of Management Journal* 36 (1993), pp. 7–27; B. Weiner, "Intrapersonal and Interpersonal Theories of Motivation from an Attributional Perspective," *Educational Psychology Review* 12 (2000), pp. 1–14; N. Bacon and P. Blyton, "Worker Responses to Teamworking: Exploring Employee Attributions of Managerial Motives," *International Journal of Human Resource Management* 16, no. 2 (February 2005), pp. 238–255.

41. Fundamental attribution error is part of a larger phenomenon known as correspondence bias. See D.T. Gilbert and P.S. Malone, "The Correspondence Bias," *Psychological Bulletin* 117, no. 1 (1995), pp. 21–38.

42. I. Choi, R.E. Nisbett, and A. Norenzayan, "Causal Attribution across Cultures: Variation and Universality," *Psychological Bulletin* 125, no. 1 (1999), pp. 47–63; D.S. Krull et al., "The Fundamental Fundamental Attribution Error: Correspondence Bias in Individualist and Collectivist Cultures," *Personality and Social Psychology Bulletin* 25, no. 10 (October 1999), pp. 1208–1219; R.E. Nisbett, *The Geography of Thought: How Asians and Westerners Think Differently . . . and Why* (New York: Free Press, 2003), chap. 5.

43. F. Lee and L.Z. Tiedens, "Who's Being Served? 'Self-Serving' Attributions in Social Hierarchies," *Organizational Behavior and Human Decision Processes* 84, no. 2 (2001), pp. 254–287; E.W.K. Tsang, "Self-Serving Attributions in Corporate Annual Reports:

A Replicated Study," *Journal of Management Studies* 39, no. 1 (January 2002), pp. 51–65; N.J. Roese and J.M. Olson, "Better, Stronger, Faster: Self-Serving Judgment, Affect Regulation, and the Optimal Vigilance Hypothesis," *Perspectives on Psychological Science* 2, no. 2 (2007), pp. 124–141.

44. Similar models are presented in D. Eden, "Self-Fulfilling Prophecy as a Management Tool: Harnessing Pygmalion," *Academy of Management Review* 9 (1984), pp. 64–73; R.H.G. Field and D.A. Van Seters, "Management by Expectations (MBE): The Power of Positive Prophecy," *Journal of General Management* 14 (Winter 1988), pp. 19–33; D.O. Trouilloud et al., "The Influence of Teacher Expectations on Student Achievement in Physical Education Classes: Pygmalion Revisited," *European Journal of Social Psychology* 32 (2002), pp. 591–607.

45. D. Eden, "Interpersonal Expectations in Organizations," in *Interpersonal Expectations: Theory, Research, and Applications* (Cambridge, UK: Cambridge University Press, 1993), 154–178.

46. D. Eden, "Pygmalion Goes to Boot Camp: Expectancy, Leadership, and Trainee Performance," *Journal of Applied Psychology* 67 (1982), pp. 194–199; R.P. Brown and E.C. Pinel, "Stigma on My Mind: Individual Differences in the Experience of Stereotype Threat," *Journal of Experimental Social Psychology* 39, no. 6 (2003), pp. 626–633.

47. S. Madon, L. Jussim, and J. Eccles, "In Search of the Powerful Self-Fulfilling Prophecy," *Journal of Personality and Social Psychology* 72, no. 4 (April 1997), pp. 791–809; A.E. Smith, L. Jussim, and J. Eccles, "Do Self-Fulfilling Prophecies Accumulate, Dissipate, or Remain Stable over Time?" *Journal of Personality and Social Psychology* 77, no. 3 (1999), pp. 548–565; S. Madon et al., "Self-Fulfilling Prophecies: The Synergistic Accumulative Effect of Parents' Beliefs on Children's Drinking Behavior," *Psychological Science* 15, no. 12 (2005), pp. 837–845.

48. W.H. Cooper, "Ubiquitous Halo," *Psychological Bulletin* 90 (1981), pp. 218–244; K.R. Murphy, R.A. Jako, and R.L. Anhalt, "Nature and Consequences of Halo Error: A Critical Analysis," *Journal of Applied Psychology* 78 (1993), pp. 218–225; T.H. Feeley, "Comment on Halo Effects in Rating and Evaluation Research," *Human Communication Research* 28, no. 4 (October 2002), pp. 578–586. For a variation of the classic halo effect in business settings, see P. Rosenzweig, *The Halo Effect . . . And the Eight Other Business Delusions That Deceive Managers* (New York: Free Press, 2007).

49. C.L. Kleinke, *First Impressions: The Psychology of Encountering Others* (Englewood Cliffs, NJ: Prentice Hall, 1975); E.A. Lind, L. Kray, and L. Thompson, "Primacy Effects in Justice Judgments: Testing Predictions from Fairness Heuristic Theory," *Organizational Behavior and Human Decision Processes* 85 (July 2001), pp. 189–210; O. Ybarra, "When First Impressions Don't Last: The Role of Isolation and Adaptation Processes in the Revision of Evaluative Impressions," *Social Cognition* 19 (October 2001), pp. 491–520; S.D. Bond et al., "Information Distortion in the Evaluation of a Single Option," *Organizational Behavior and Human Decision Processes* 102, no. 2 (2007), pp. 240–254.

50. D.D. Steiner and J.S. Rain, "Immediate and Delayed Primacy and Recency Effects in Performance Evaluation," *Journal of Applied Psychology* 74 (1989), pp. 136–142; K.T. Trotman, "Order Effects and Recency: Where Do We Go from Here?" *Accounting & Finance* 40 (2000), pp. 169–182; W. Green, "Impact of the Timing of an Inherited Explanation on Auditors' Analytical Procedures Judgements," *Accounting and Finance* 44 (2004), pp. 369–392.

51. R.W. Clement and J. Krueger, "The Primacy of Self-Referent Information in Perceptions of Social Consensus," *British Journal of Social Psychology* 39 (2000), pp. 279–299; R.L. Gross and S.E. Brodt, "How Assumptions of Consensus Undermine Decision Making," *Sloan Management Review*, January 2001, pp. 86–94; J. Oliver et al., "Projection of Own on Others' Job Characteristics: Evidence for the False Consensus Effect in Job Characteristics Information," *International Journal of Selection and Assessment* 13, no. 1 (2005), pp. 63–74.

52. D. Eden et al., "Implanting Pygmalion Leadership Style through Workshop Training: Seven Field Experiments," *Leadership Quarterly* 11 (2000), pp. 171–210; S.S. White and E.A. Locke, "Problems with the Pygmalion Effect and Some Proposed Solutions," *Leadership Quarterly* 11 (Autumn 2000), pp. 389–415; M. Bendick, M.L. Egan, and S.M. Lofhjelm, "Workforce Diversity Training: From Anti-Discrimination Compliance to Organizational Development HR," *Human Resource Planning* 24 (2001), pp. 10–25; L. Roberson, C.T. Kulik, and M.B. Pepper, "Using Needs Assessment to Resolve Controversies in Diversity Training Design," *Group & Organization Management* 28, no. 1 (March 2003), pp. 148–174; D.E. Hogan and M. Mallott, "Changing Racial Prejudice through Diversity Education," *Journal of College Student Development* 46, no. 2 (March–April 2005), pp. 115–125.

53. B. George, *Authentic Leadership* (San Francisco: Jossey-Bass, 2004); W.L. Gardner et al., "'Can You See the Real Me?' A Self-Based Model of Authentic Leader and Follower Development," *Leadership Quarterly* 16 (2005), pp. 343–372; B. George, *True North* (San Francisco: Jossey-Bass, 2007).

54. For a discussion of the Implicit Association Test, including critique, see H. Blanton et al., "Decoding the Implicit Association Test: Implications for Criterion Prediction," *Journal of Experimental Social Psychology* 42, no. 2 (2006), pp. 192–212; A.G. Greenwald, B.A. Nosek, and N. Sriram, "Consequential Validity of the Implicit Association Test: Comment on Blanton and Jaccard (2006)," *American Psychologist* 61, no. 1 (2006), pp. 56–61; W. Hofmann et al., "Implicit and Explicit Attitudes and Interracial Interaction: The Moderating Role of Situationally Available Control Resources," *Group Processes & Intergroup Relations* 11, no. 1 (January 2008), pp. 69–87.

55. P. Babcock, "Detecting Hidden Bias," *HRMagazine,* February 2006, p. 50.

56. T.W. Costello and S.S. Zalkind, *Psychology in Administration: A Research Orientation* (Englewood Cliffs, NJ: Prentice Hall, 1963), pp. 45–46; J.M. Kouzes and B.Z. Posner, *The Leadership Challenge,* 4th ed. (San Francisco: Jossey-Bass, 2007), chap. 3.

57. J. Luft, *Group Processes* (Palo Alto, CA: Mayfield, 1984). For a variation of this model, see J. Hall, "Communication Revisited," *California Management Review* 15 (Spring 1973), pp. 56–67.

58. L.C. Miller and D.A. Kenny, "Reciprocity of Self-Disclosure at the Individual and Dyadic Levels: A Social Relations Analysis," *Journal of Personality and Social Psychology* 50 (1986), pp. 713–719.

59. J. Dixon and K. Durrheim, "Contact and the Ecology of Racial Division: Some Varieties of Informal Segregation," *British Journal of Social Psychology* 42 (March 2003), pp. 1–23; P.J. Henry and C.D. Hardin, "The Contact Hypothesis Revisited: Status Bias in the Reduction of Implicit Prejudice in the United States and Lebanon," *Psychological Science* 17, no. 10 (2006), pp. 862–868; T.F. Pettigrew and L.R. Tropp, "A Meta-Analytic Test of Intergroup Contact Theory," *Journal of Personality and Social Psychology* 90, no. 5 (2006), pp. 751–783; C. Tredoux and G. Finchilescu, "The Contact Hypothesis and Intergroup Relations 50 Years On: Introduction to the Special Issue," *South African Journal of Psychology* 37, no. 4 (2007), pp. 667–678; T.F. Pettigrew, "Future Directions for Intergroup Contact Theory and Research," *International Journal of Intercultural Relations* 32, no. 3 (2008), pp. 187–199.

60. G. Thomas, "Fyfe Rewrites the Tune atANZ," *Air Transport World,* September 2007, p. 61.

61. W. Frey, "Rubbish Boy Doing Well as Junk Man," *Metro-Vancouver,* 25 April 2005, 11; PR Newswire, "Domino's Pizza Named One of Michigan's 'Cool Places toWork' " (news release), Ann Arbor, 10September 2007.

62. W.G. Stephen and K.A. Finlay, "The Role of Empathy in Improving Intergroup Relations," *Journal of Social Issues* 55 (Winter 1999), pp. 729–743; S.K. Parker and C.M. Axtell, "Seeing Another Viewpoint: Antecedents and Outcomes of Employee Perspective Taking," *Academy of Management Journal* 44 (December 2001), pp. 1085–1100; G.J. Vreeke and I.L. van der Mark, "Empathy, an Integrative Model," *New Ideas in Psychology* 21, no. 3 (2003), pp. 177–207.

63. I. Nonaka and H. Takeuchi, *The Knowledge-Creating Company* (New York: Oxford University Press, 1995); P. Duguid, " 'The Art of Knowing': Social and Tacit Dimensions of Knowledge and the Limits of the Community of Practice," *The Information Society* 21 (2005), pp. 109–118.

64. B.F. Skinner, *About Behaviorism* (New York: Knopf, 1974); J. Komaki, T. Coombs, and S. Schepman, "Motivational Implications of Reinforcement Theory," in *Motivation and Leadership at Work,* ed. R.M. Steers, L.W. Porter, and G.A. Bigley (New York: McGraw-Hill, 1996), pp. 34–52; R.G. Miltenberger, *Behavior Modification: Principles and Procedures* (Pacific Grove, CA: Brooks/Cole, 1997).

65. T.K. Connellan, *How to Improve Human Performance* (New York: Harper & Row, 1978), pp. 48–57; F. Luthans and R. Kreitner, *Organizational Behavior Modification and Beyond* (Glenview, IL: Scott, Foresman, 1985), pp. 85–88.

66. Miltenberger, *Behavior Modification,* chaps. 4–6.

67. Punishment can also include removing a pleasant consequence, such as when employees must switch from business-class to economy-class flying when their sales fall below the threshold for top-tier sales "stars."

68. T.R. Hinkin and C.A. Schriesheim, " 'If You Don't Hear from Me You Know You Are Doing Fine,' " *Cornell Hotel & Restaurant Administration Quarterly* 45, no. 4 (November 2004), pp. 362–372.

69. L.K. Trevino, "The Social Effects of Punishment in Organizations: A Justice Perspective," *Academy of Management Review* 17 (1992), pp. 647–676; L.E. Atwater et al., "Recipient and Observer Reactions to Discipline: Are Managers Experiencing Wishful Thinking?" *Journal of Organizational Behavior* 22, no. 3 (May 2001), pp. 249–270.

70. G.P. Latham and V.L. Huber, "Schedules of Reinforcement: Lessons from the Past and Issues for the Future," *Journal of Organizational Behavior Management* 13 (1992), pp. 125–149; B.A. Williams, "Challenges to Timing-Based Theories of Operant Behavior," *Behavioural Processes*62 (April 2003), pp. 115–123.

71. S. Overman, "Many Offer Basic Wellness Initiatives, Few Track Results," *Employee Benefit News,* 15 April 2006; H. Wecsler, "Sick Day Incentive Plan Favored by NLR Board," *Arkansas Democrat Gazette,* 17 February 2006, p. 14.

72. ExxonMobil, "UK and Ireland Corporate Citizenship," August 2004; Wecsler, "Sick Day Incentive Plan Favored by NLR Board."

73. M. Colias, "Obese Police," *Crain's Chicago Business,* 26 February 2007, p. 1; D. Gibson, "Investing in Employees' Health," *Lane Report* (Kentucky), December 2007, p. 28.

74. Bargh and Ferguson, "Beyond Behaviorism." Some writers argue that behaviorists long ago accepted the relevance of cognitive processes in behavior modification. See I. Kirsch et al., "The Role of Cognition in Classical and Operant Conditioning," *Journal of Clinical Psychology* 60, no. 4 (April 2004), pp. 369–392.

75. A. Bandura, *Social Foundations of Thought and Action: A Social Cognitive Theory* (Englewood Cliffs, NJ: Prentice Hall, 1986).

76. A. Pescuric and W.C. Byham, "The New Look of Behavior Modeling," *Training & Development* 50 (July 1996), pp. 24–30.

77. M.E. Schnake, "Vicarious Punishment in a Work Setting," *Journal of Applied Psychology* 71 (1986), pp. 343–345; Trevino, "The Social Effects of Punishment in Organizations"; J.B. DeConinck, "The Effect of Punishment on Sales Managers' Outcome Expectancies and Responses to Unethical Sales Force Behavior," *American Business Review* 21, no. 2 (June 2003), pp. 135–140.

78. A. Bandura, "Self-Reinforcement: Theoretical and Methodological Considerations," *Behaviorism* 4 (1976), pp. 135–155; C.A. Frayne and J.M. Geringer, "Self-Management Training for Improving Job Performance: A Field Experiment Involving Salespeople," *Journal of Applied Psychology* 85, no. 3 (June 2000), pp. 361–372; J.B. Vancouver and D.V. Day, "Industrial and Organisation Research on Self-Regulation: From Constructs to Applications," *Applied Psychology: An International Review* 54, no. 2 (April 2005), pp. 155–185.

79. D.A. Kolb, *Experiential Learning* (Englewood Cliffs, NJ: Prentice Hall, 1984); S. Gherardi, D. Nicolini, and F. Odella, "Toward a Social Understanding of How People Learn in Organizations," *Management Learning* 29 (September 1998), pp. 273–297; D.A. Kolb, R.E. Boyatzis, and C. Mainemelis, "Experiential Learning Theory: Previous Research and New Directions," in *Perspectives on Thinking, Learning, and Cognitive Styles,* ed. R. J. Sternberg and L.F. Zhang (Mahwah, NJ: Lawrence Erlbaum, 2001), pp. 227–248.

80. W.E. Baker and J.M. Sinkula, "The Synergistic Effect of Market Orientation and Learning Orientation on Organizational Performance," *Academy of Marketing Science Journal* 27, no. 4 (Fall 1999), pp. 411–427; Z. Emden, A. Yaprak, and S.T. Cavusgil, "Learning from Experience in International Alliances: Antecedents and Firm Performance Implications," *Journal of Business Research* 58, no. 7 (2005), pp. 883–892.

81. R. Farson and R. Keyes, "The Failure-Tolerant Leader," *Harvard Business Review* 80 (August 2002), pp. 64–71; T.C. Li, "Loyalty Pays Off for Chief of Malaysia's CIMB," *Wall Street Journal Asia,* 23 June 2008, p. 36.

82. J. Jusko, "Always Lessons to Learn," *Industry Week* (15 February 1999), p. 23; R. Farson and R. Keyes, "The Failure-Tolerant Leader," *Harvard Business Review* 80 (August 2002), pp. 64–71.

83. I. Teotonio, "Rescuers Pull 'Victims' from Rubble," *Toronto Star,* 8 April 2005, pp. B01, B03.

84. J.A. Conger and K. Xin, "Executive Education in the 21st Century," *Journal of Management Education* (February 2000), pp. 73–101; R.M. Fulmer, P. Gibbs, and M. Goldsmith, "Developing Leaders: How Winning Companies Keep on Winning," *Sloan Management Review* (October 2000), pp. 49–59; "Strategies Needed to Nurture Top Talent," *South China Morning Post (Hong Kong),* 7 August 2004, p. 4; M.J. Marquardt, "Harnessing the Power of Action Learning," *T+D,* June 2004, pp. 26–32.

85. M. Cheong, "Risk Awareness on the Table," *South China Morning Post* (Hong Kong), 10 June 2008, p. 10; H. Takeda, "Medical Risk and Quality Management through Informatics," paper presented at Saudi e-Health Conference, Saudi Arabia, 19 March 2008.

Chapter 4

1. C. Foster, "Turning Ha-Ha into A-Ha!" *Employee Benefit News Canada,* December 2007; M. Labash, "Are We Having Fun Yet?" *Weekly Standard,* 17 September 2007; Mott MacDonald, *Meridian: Mott MacDonald Annual Review 2006–2007* (Croydon, UK: Mott MacDonald, 2007); F. Oliver, "Greetings From: The Happiest Place in the World," *Professional Builder,* August 2007, p. 44; "Mott MacDonald: Multidisciplinary Consultancy," *Sunday Times: 100 Best Companies to Work For 2008* (London), 9 March 2008, p. 18; C. Eggleston, "Dixon Schwabl #1 to Work for in America," *R-News* (Rochester, NY), 23 June 2008; Great Place to Work Institute, *They Made It Happen: Dixon Schwabl Is #1* (San Francisco: Great Place to Work Institute, 23 June 2008); S. Leonard, "Keeping Staff Happy Is the Bottom Line," *Sunday Times: Best Companies Guide 2009* (London), 29 June 2008, p. 8; Mott MacDonald, *Meridian: Mott MacDonald Annual Review 2007–2008* (Croydon, UK: Mott MacDonald, 2008).

2. The centrality of emotions in marketing, economics, and sociology is discussed in G. Loewenstein, "Emotions in Economic Theory and Economic Behavior," *American Economic Review* 90, no. 2 (May 2000), pp. 426–432; D.S. Massey, "A Brief History of Human Society: The Origin and Role of Emotion in Social Life," *American Sociological Review* 67 (February 2002), pp. 1–29; J. O'Shaughnessy and N. J. O'Shaughnessy, *The Marketing Power of Emotion* (New York: Oxford University Press, 2003).

3. The definition presented here is constructed from the following sources: N.M. Ashkanasy, W.J. Zerbe, and C.E.J. Hartel, "Introduction: Managing Emotions in a Changing Workplace," in *Managing Emotions in the Workplace,* ed. N.M. Ashkanasy, W. J. Zerbe, and C. E. J. Hartel (Armonk, NY: Sharpe, 2002), pp. 3–18; H.M. Weiss, "Conceptual and Empirical Foundations for the Study of Affect at Work," in *Emotions in the Workplace,* ed. R.G. Lord, R.J. Klimoski, and R. Kanfer (San Francisco: Jossey-Bass, 2002), pp. 20–63. However, the meaning of emotions is still being debated. See, for example, M. Cabanac, "What Is Emotion?" *Behavioral Processes* 60 (2002), pp. 69–83.

4. R. Kanfer and R.J. Klimoski, "Affect and Work: Looking Back to the Future," in *Emotions in the Workplace,* ed. R.G. Lord, R.J. Klimoski, and R. Kanfer (San Francisco: Jossey-Bass, 2002), pp. 473–490; J.A. Russell, "Core Affect and the Psychological Construction of Emotion," *Psychological Review* 110, no. 1 (2003), pp. 145–172.

5. R.B. Zajonc, "Emotions," in *Handbook of Social Psychology,* ed. D.T. Gilbert, S.T. Fiske, and L. Gardner (New York: Oxford University Press, 1998), pp. 591–634.

6. N.A. Remington, L.R. Fabrigar, and P.S. Visser, "Reexamining the Circumplex Model of Affect," *Journal of Personality and Social Psychology* 79, no. 2 (2000), pp. 286–300; R.J. Larsen, E. Diener, and R.E. Lucas, "Emotion: Models, Measures, and Individual Differences," in *Emotions in the Workplace,* ed. R.G. Lord, R.J. Klimoski, and R. Kanfer (San Francisco: Jossey-Bass, 2002), pp. 64–113; L.F. Barrett et al., "The Experience of Emotion," *Annual Review of Psychology* 58, no. 1 (2007), pp. 373–403.

7. A.H. Eagly and S. Chaiken, *The Psychology of Attitudes* (Orlando, FL: Harcourt Brace Jovanovich, 1993); A.P. Brief, *Attitudes in and around Organizations* (Thousand Oaks, CA: Sage, 1998). There is an amazing lack of consensus on the definition of attitudes. This book adopts the three-component model, whereas some experts define attitude as only the "feelings" component, with "beliefs" as a predictor and "intentions" as an outcome. Some writers specifically define attitudes as an "evaluation" of an attitude object, whereas others distinguish attitudes from evaluations of an attitude object. For some of these definitional variations, see I. Ajzen, "Nature and Operation of Attitudes," *Annual Review of Psychology* 52 (2001), pp. 27–58; D. Albarracín et al., "Attitudes: Introduction and Scope," in *The Handbook of Attitudes,* ed. D. Albarracín, B.T. Johnson, and M.P. Zanna (Mahwah, NJ: Lawrence Erlbaum, 2005), pp. 3–20; W.A. Cunningham and P.D. Zelazo, "Attitudes and Evaluations: A Social Cognitive Neuroscience Perspective," *Trends in Cognitive Sciences* 11, no. 3 (2007), pp. 97–104.

8. C.D. Fisher, "Mood and Emotions While Working: Missing Pieces of Job Satisfaction?" *Journal of Organizational Behavior* 21 (2000), pp. 185–202; Cunningham and Zelazo, "Attitudes and Evaluations"; M.D. Lieberman, "Social Cognitive Neuroscience: A Review of Core Processes," *Annual Review of Psychology* 58, no. 1 (2007), pp. 259–289.

9. S. Orbell, "Intention-Behavior Relations: A Self-Regulation Perspective," in *Contemporary Perspectives on the Psychology of Attitudes,* ed. G. Haddock and G.R. Maio (East Sussex, UK: Psychology Press, 2004), pp. 145–168.

10. H.M. Weiss and R. Cropanzano, "Affective Events Theory: A Theoretical Discussion of the Structure, Causes, and Consequences of Affective Experiences at Work," *Research in Organizational Behavior* 18 (1996), pp. 1–74; J. Wegge et al., "A Test of Basic Assumptions of Affective Events Theory (AET) in Call Centre Work," *British Journal of Management* 17 (2006), pp. 237–254.

11. J.A. Bargh and M.J. Ferguson, "Beyond Behaviorism: On the Automaticity of Higher Mental Processes," *Psychological Bulletin* 126, no. 6 (2000), pp. 925–945; R.H. Fazio, "On the Automatic Activation of Associated Evaluations: An Overview," *Cognition and Emotion* 15, no. 2 (2001), pp. 115–141; M. Gladwell, *Blink: The Power of Thinking without Thinking* (New York: Little, Brown, 2005).

12. A.R. Damasio, *Descartes' Error: Emotion, Reason, and the Human Brain* (New York: Putnam Sons, 1994); A. Damasio, *The Feeling of What Happens* (New York: Harcourt Brace, 1999); P. Ekman, "Basic Emotions," in *Handbook of Cognition and Emotion,* ed. T. Dalgleish and M. Power (San Francisco: Jossey-Bass, 1999), pp. 45–60; J.E. LeDoux, "Emotion Circuits in the Brain," *Annual Review of Neuroscience* 23 (2000), pp. 155–184; R.J. Dolan, "Emotion, Cognition, and Behavior," *Science* 298, no. 5596 (8 November 2002), pp. 1191–1194.

13. N. Schwarz, "Emotion, Cognition, and Decision Making," *Cognition and Emotion* 14, no. 4 (2000), pp. 433–440; M.T. Pham, "The Logic of Feeling," *Journal of Consumer Psychology* 14, no. 4 (2004), pp. 360–369.

14. G.R. Maio, V.M. Esses, and D.W. Bell, "Examining Conflict between Components of Attitudes: Ambivalence and Inconsistency Are Distinct Constructs," *Canadian Journal of Behavioural Science* 32, no. 2 (2000), pp. 71–83.

15. P.C. Nutt, *Why Decisions Fail* (San Francisco: Berrett-Koehler, 2002); S. Finkelstein, *Why Smart Executives Fail* (New York: Viking, 2003); P.C. Nutt, "Search during Decision Making," *European Journal of Operational Research* 160 (2005), pp. 851–876.

16. Weiss and Cropanzano, "Affective Events Theory."

17. P.C. Nutt, *Why Decisions Fail* (San Francisco: Berrett-Koehler, 2002); S. Finkelstein, *Why Smart Executives Fail* (New York: Viking, 2003); P.C. Nutt, "Search during Decision Making," *European Journal of Operational Research* 160 (2005), pp. 851–76.

18. Op. Cit. Weiss and Cropanzano

19. L. Festinger, *A Theory of Cognitive Dissonance* (Evanston, IL: Row, Peterson, 1957); G.R. Salancik, "Commitment and the Control of Organizational Behavior and Belief," in *New Directions in Organizational Behavior,* ed. B.M. Staw and G.R. Salancik (Chicago: St. Clair, 1977), pp. 1–54; A.D. Galinsky, J. Stone, and J. Cooper, "The Reinstatement of Dissonance and Psychological Discomfort Following Failed Affirmation," *European Journal of Social Psychology* 30, no. 1 (2000), pp. 123–147.

20. T.A. Judge, E.A. Locke, and C.C. Durham, "The Dispositional Causes of Job Satisfaction: A Core Evaluations Approach," *Research in Organizational Behavior* 19 (1997), pp. 151–188; Massey, "A Brief History of Human Society."

21. C.M. Brotheridge and A.A. Grandey, "Emotional Labor and Burnout: Comparing Two Perspectives of 'People Work,'" *Journal of Vocational Behavior* 60 (2002), pp. 17–39; P.G. Irving, D.F. Coleman, and D.R. Bobocel, "The Moderating Effect of Negative Affectivity in the Procedural Justice-Job Satisfaction Relation," *Canadian Journal of Behavioural Science* 37, no. 1 (January 2005), pp. 20–32.

22. J. Schaubroeck, D.C. Ganster, and B. Kemmerer, "Does Trait Affect Promote Job Attitude Stability?" *Journal of Organizational Behavior* 17 (1996), pp. 191–196; C. Dormann and D. Zapf, "Job Satisfaction: A Meta-Analysis of Stabilities," *Journal of Organizational Behavior* 22 (2001), pp. 483–504.

23. R. Corelli, "Dishing Out Rudeness," *Maclean's,* 11 January 1999, pp. 44–47; D. Matheson, "A Vancouver Cafe Where Rudeness Is Welcomed," *Canada AM, CTV Television,* 11 January 2000.

24. B.E. Ashforth and R.H. Humphrey, "Emotional Labor in Service Roles: The Influence of Identity," *Academy of Management Review* 18 (1993), pp. 88–115. For a recent review of the emotional labor concept, see T.M. Glomb and M.J. Tews, "Emotional Labor: A Conceptualization and Scale Development," *Journal of Vocational Behavior* 64, no. 1 (2004), pp. 1–23.

25. J.A. Morris and D.C. Feldman, "The Dimensions, Antecedents, and Consequences of Emotional Labor," *Academy of Management Review* 21 (1996), pp. 986–1010; D. Zapf, "Emotion Work and Psychological Well-Being: A Review of the Literature and Some Conceptual Considerations," *Human Resource Management Review* 12 (2002), pp. 237–268.

26. K.B. Mathis, "Puttin' on the Ritz," *Florida Times-Union* (Jacksonville), 22 January 2006, p. G1.

27. "Imagekampagne 'Das Schönste Lächeln Für Unsere Gäste,'" (Berlin, 2006), www.berlin.de/fifawm2006/stadt/imagekampagne/index.php (accessed 19 September 2008); S. Dowling, "Teaching Berlin How to Smile," *Spiegel Online,* 11 January 2006, www.spiegel.de/international/0,1518,390118,00.html; M. Lim, "World Cup a Chance to 'Sell' New Germany," *Straits Times* (Singapore), 2 June 2006.

28. E. Forman, "'Diversity Concerns Grow as Companies Head Overseas,' Consultant Says," *Sun-Sentinel* (Fort Lauderdale, FL), 26 June 1995. Cultural differences in emotional expression are discussed in F. Trompenaars, "Resolving International Conflict: Culture and Business Strategy," *Business Strategy Review* 7, no. 3 (Autumn 1996), pp. 51–68; F. Trompenaars and C. Hampden-Turner, *Riding the Waves of Culture,* 2d ed. (New York: McGraw-Hill, 1998), chap. 6; A.E. Raz and A. Rafaeli, "Emotion Management in Cross-Cultural Perspective: 'Smile Training' in Japanese and North American Service Organizations," *Research on Emotion in Organizations* 3 (2007), pp. 199–220.

29. This relates to the automaticity of emotion, which is summarized in P. Winkielman and K.C. Berridge, "Unconscious Emotion," *Current Directions in Psychological Science* 13, no. 3 (2004), pp. 120–123; K.N. Ochsner and J.J. Gross, "The Cognitive Control of Emotions," *Trends in Cognitive Sciences* 9, no. 5 (May 2005), pp. 242–249.

30. W.J. Zerbe, "Emotional Dissonance and Employee Well-Being," in *Manag-ing Emotions in the Workplace,* ed. N.M. Ashkanasy, W. J. Zerbe, and C.E.J. Hartel (Armonk, NY: Sharpe, 2002), pp. 189–214; R. Cropanzano, H.M. Weiss, and S.M.Elias, "The Impact of Display Rules and Emotional Labor on Psychological Well-Being at Work," *Research in Occupational Stress and Well Being* 3 (2003), pp. 45–89.

31. J. Verdon, "They Can Hardly Contain Themselves," *The Record* (Bergen, NJ), 21 April 2007, p. A15; S. Leonard and M. Clayton, "Long Hours Hurt Business and Families," *Sunday Times: Best Companies Guide 2009* (London), 29 June 2008, p. 12.

32. Brotheridge and Grandey, "Emotional Labor and Burnout"; Zapf, "Emotion Work and Psychological Well-Being"; J.M. Diefendorff, M.H. Croyle, and R.H. Gosserand, "The Dimensionality and Antecedents of Emotional Labor Strategies," *Journal of Vocational Behavior* 66, no. 2 (2005), pp. 339–357.

33. K.K. Spors, "Top Small Workplaces 2007," *Wall Street Journal,* 1 October 2007, p. R1.

34. J.D. Mayer, P. Salovey, and D.R.Caruso, "Models of Emotional Intelligence," in *Handbook of Human Intelligence,* 2d ed., ed. R.J. Sternberg (New York: Cambridge University Press, 2000), pp. 396–420. This definition is also recognized in C. Cherniss, "Emotional Intelligence and Organizational Effectiveness," in *The Emotionally Intelligent Workplace,* ed. C. Cherniss and D. Goleman (San Francisco: Jossey-Bass, 2001), pp. 3–12; M. Zeidner, G. Matthews, and R.D.Roberts, "Emotional Intelligence in the Workplace: A Critical Review," *Applied Psychology: An International Review* 53, no. 3 (2004), pp. 371–399.

35. These four dimensions of emotional intelligence are discussed in detail in D. Goleman, R. Boyatzis, and A. McKee, *Primal Leadership* (Boston: Harvard Business School Press, 2002), chap. 3. Slight variations of this model are presented in R. Boyatzis, D. Goleman, and K.S. Rhee, "Clustering Competence in Emotional Intelligence," in *The Handbook of Emotional Intelligence,* ed. R. Bar-On and J.D.A. Parker (San Francisco: Jossey-Bass, 2000), pp. 343–362; D. Goleman, "An EI-Based Theory of Performance," in *The Emotionally Intelligent Workplace,* ed. C. Cherniss and D. Goleman (San Francisco: Jossey-Bass, 2001), pp. 27–44.

36. Which model best represents EI and its abilities is debated in several sources, including several chapters in K.R. Murphy, ed., *A Critique of Emotional Intelligence: What Are the Problems and How Can They Be Fixed?* (Mahwah, NJ: Lawrence Erlbaum, 2006).

37. H.A. Elfenbein and N. Ambady, "Predicting Workplace Outcomes from the Ability to Eavesdrop on Feelings," *Journal of Applied Psychology* 87, no. 5 (2002), pp. 963–971.

38. The hierarchical nature of the four EI dimensions is discussed by Goleman, but it is more explicit in the Salovey and Mayer model. See D.R. Caruso and P. Salovey, *The Emotionally Intelligent Manager* (San Francisco: Jossey-Bass, 2004).

39. C. Fox, "Shifting Gears," *Australian Financial Review,* 13 August 2004, p. 28; J. Thomson, "True Team Spirit," *Business Review Weekly,* 18 March 2004, p. 92.

40. P.N. Lopes et al., "Emotional Intelligence and Social Interaction," *Personality and Social Psychology Bulletin* 30, no. 8 (August 2004), pp. 1018–1034; C.S. Daus and N.M. Ashkanasy, "The Case for the Ability-Based Model of Emotional Intelligence in Organizational Behavior," *Journal of Organizational Behavior* 26 (2005), pp. 453–466; J.E. Barbuto Jr., and M.E. Burbach, "The Emotional Intelligence of Transformational Leaders: A Field Study of Elected Officials," *Journal of Social Psychology* 146, no. 1 (2006), pp. 51–64; M.A. Brackett et al., "Relating Emotional Abilities to Social Functioning: A Comparison of Self-Report and Performance Measures of Emotional Intelligence," *Journal of Personality and Social Psychology* 91, no. 4 (2006), pp. 780–795; D.L. Reis et al., "Emotional Intelligence Predicts Individual Differences in Social Exchange Reasoning," *NeuroImage* 35, no. 3 (2007), pp. 1385–1391.

41. Some studies have reported situations where EI has a limited effect on individual performance. For example, see A.L. Day and S.A. Carroll, "Using an Ability-Based Measure of Emotional Intelligence to Predict Individual Performance, Group Performance, and Group Citizenship Behaviors," *Personality and Individual Differences* 36 (2004), pp. 1443–1458; Z. Ivcevic, M.A. Brackett, and J.D. Mayer, "Emotional Intelligence and Emotional Creativity," *Journal of Personality* 75, no. 2 (2007), pp. 199–236; J.C. Rode et al., "Emotional Intelligence and Individual Performance: Evidence of Direct and Moderated Effects," *Journal of Organizational Behavior* 28, no. 4 (2007), pp. 399–421.

42. D. McGinn, "The Emotional Workplace," *National Post,* 18 August 2007, p. FW3.

43. Goleman, Boyatzis, and McKee, *Primal Leadership;* S.C. Clark, R. Callister, and R. Wallace, "Undergraduate Management Skills Courses and Students' Emotional Intelligence," *Journal of Management Education* 27, no. 1 (February 2003), pp. 3–23; Lopes et al., "Emotional Intelligence and Social Interaction"; H.A. Elfenbein, "Learning in Emotion Judgments: Training and the Cross-Cultural Understanding of Facial Expressions," *Journal of Nonverbal Behavior* 30, no. 1 (2006), pp. 21–36; C.-S. Wong et al., "The Feasibility of Training and Development of EI: An Exploratory Study in Singapore, Hong Kong and Taiwan," *Intelligence* 35, no. 2 (2007), pp. 141–150.

44. R. Johnson, "Can You Feel It?" *People Management,* 23 August 2007, pp. 34–37.

45. D.A. Harrison, D.A. Newman, and P.L. Roth, "How Important Are Job Attitudes? Meta-Analytic Comparisons of Integrative Behavioral Outcomes and Time Sequences," *Academy of Management Journal* 49, no. 2 (2006), pp. 305–325.

46. E.A. Locke, "The Nature and Causes of Job Satisfaction," in *Handbook of Industrial and Organizational Psychology,* ed. M. Dunnette (Chicago: Rand McNally, 1976), pp. 1297–1350; H.M. Weiss, "Deconstructing Job Satisfaction: Separating Evaluations, Beliefs and Affective Experiences," *Human Resource Management Review,* no. 12 (2002), pp. 173–194. Some definitions still include emotion as an element of job satisfaction, whereas the definition presented in this book views emotion as a cause of job satisfaction. Also, this definition views job satisfaction as a "collection of attitudes," not several "facets" of job satisfaction.

47. Ipsos-Reid, "Ipsos-Reid Global Poll Finds Major Differences in Employee Satisfaction around the World" (news release), Toronto, 8 January 2001; International Survey Research, *Employee Satisfaction in the World's 10 Largest Economies: Globalization or Diversity?* (Chicago: International Survey Research, 2002); Watson Wyatt Worldwide, "Malaysian Workers More Satisfied with Their Jobs Than Their Companies' Leadership and Supervision Practices" (news release), Kuala Lumpur, 30 November 2004; Kelly Global Workforce Index, *American Workers Are Happy with Their Jobs and Their Bosses* (Troy, MI: Kelly Services, November 2006).

48. T.W. Smith, *Job Satisfaction in America: Trends and Socio-Demographic Correlates,* (Chicago: National Opinion Research Center/University of Chicago, August 2007).

49. PR News, "Hudson Employment Index Data Suggest U.S. Workers Will Jump Ship" (news release), New York, 7 January 2004; Watson Wyatt Worldwide, "Malaysian Workers More Satisfied with Their Jobs Than Their Companies' Leadership and Supervision Practices" (news release); K. Keis, "HR Needs Happy Staff to Show Its Success," *Canadian HR Reporter,* 14 February 2005, p. 14.

50. H. Rao and R.I. Sutton, "Innovation Lessons from Pixar: An Interview with Oscar-Winning Director Brad Bird," *McKinsey Quarterly* (April 2008), pp. 1–9.

51. M.J. Withey and W.H. Cooper, "Predicting Exit, Voice, Loyalty, and Neglect," *Administrative Science Quarterly,* no. 34 (1989), pp. 521–539; W.H. Turnley and D.C. Feldman, "The Impact of Psychological Contract Violations on Exit, Voice, Loyalty, and Neglect," *Human Relations,* no. 52 (July 1999), pp. 895–922. Subdimensions of silence and voice also exist. See L. Van Dyne, S. Ang, and I.C. Botero, "Conceptualizing Employee Silence and Employee Voice as Multidimensional Constructs," *Journal of Management Studies* 40, no. 6 (September 2003), pp. 1359–1392.

52. T.R. Mitchell, B.C. Holtom, and T.W. Lee, "How to Keep Your Best Employees: Developing an Effective Retention Policy," *Academy of Management Executive* 15 (November 2001), pp. 96–108; C.P. Maertz and M.A. Campion, "Profiles of Quitting:

Integrating Process and Content Turnover Theory," *Academy of Management Journal* 47, no. 4 (2004), pp. 566–582; K. Morrell, J. Loan-Clarke, and A. Wilkinson, "The Role of Shocks in Employee Turnover," *British Journal of Management* 15 (2004), pp. 335–349; B.C. Holtom, T.R. Mitchell, and T.W. Lee, "Increasing Human and Social Capital by Applying Job Embeddedness Theory," *Organizational Dynamics* 35, no. 4 (2006), pp. 316–331.

53. A.A. Luchak, "What Kind of Voice Do Loyal Employees Use?" *British Journal of Industrial Relations* 41 (March 2003), pp. 115–134.

54. A.O. Hirschman, *Exit, Voice, and Loyalty: Responses to Decline in Firms, Organizations, and States* (Cambridge, MA: Harvard University Press, 1970); E.A. Hoffmann, "Exit and Voice: Organizational Loyalty and Dispute Resolution Strategies," *Social Forces* 84, no. 4 (June 2006), pp. 2313–2330.

55. J.D. Hibbard, N. Kumar, and L.W. Stern, "Examining the Impact of Destructive Acts in Marketing Channel Relationships," *Journal of Marketing Research* 38 (February 2001), pp. 45–61; J. Zhou and J.M. George, "When Job Dissatisfaction Leads to Creativity: Encouraging the Expression of Voice," *Academy of Management Journal* 44 (August 2001), pp. 682–696.

56. M.J. Withey and I.R. Gellatly, "Situational and Dispositional Determinants of Exit, Voice, Loyalty and Neglect," *Proceedings of the Administrative Sciences Association of Canada, Organizational Behaviour Division* (June 1998); D.C. Thomas and K. Au, "The Effect of Cultural Differences on Behavioral Responses to Low Job Satisfaction," *Journal of International Business Studies* 33, no. 2 (2002), pp. 309–326; S.F. Premeaux and A.G. Bedeian, "Breaking the Silence: The Moderating Effects of Self-Monitoring in Predicting Speaking Up in the Workplace," *Journal of Management Studies* 40, no. 6 (2003), pp. 1537–1562.

57. T.A. Judge et al., "The Job Satisfaction–Job Performance Relationship: A Qualitative and Quantitative Review," *Psychological Bulletin* 127 (2001), pp. 376–407; L. Saari and T.A. Judge, "Employee Attitudes and Job Satisfaction," *Human Resource Management* 43, no. 4 (Winter 2004), pp. 395–407. Other studies report stronger correlations with job performance when both the belief and feeling components of job satisfaction are consistent with each other and when overall job attitude (satisfaction and commitment combined) is being measured. See D.J. Schleicher, J.D. Watt, and G.J. Greguras, "Reexamining the Job Satisfaction-Performance Relationship: The Complexity of Attitudes," *Journal of Applied Psychology* 89, no. 1 (2004), pp. 165–177; Harrison, Newman, and Roth, "How Important Are Job Attitudes?"

58. G. Thomas, "Air NZ Execs Switch Roles to Embrace Change," *The Australian,* 17 August 2007, p. 35; D. Moss, "Catering to a Creative Workforce," *HRMagazine,* July 2008, p. 33.

59. J.I. Heskett, W.E. Sasser, and L.A.Schlesinger, *The Service Profit Chain* (New York: Free Press, 1997); D.J. Koys, "The Effects of Employee Satisfaction, Organizational Citizenship Behavior, and Turnover on Organizational Effectiveness: A Unit-Level, Longitudinal Study," *Personnel Psychology* 54 (April 2001), pp. 101–114; W.C. Tsai and Y.M. Huang, "Mechanisms Linking Employee Affective Delivery and Customer Behavioral Intentions," *Journal of Applied Psychology* 87, no. 5 (2002), pp. 1001–1008; T. DeCotiis et al., "How Outback Steakhouse Created a Great Place to Work, Have Fun, and Make Money," *Journal of Organizational Excellence* 23, no. 4 (Autumn 2004), pp. 23–33; G.A. Gelade and S. Young, "Test of a Service Profit Chain Model in the Retail Banking Sector," *Journal of Occupational and Organizational Psychology* 78 (2005), pp. 1–22.

60. HCL Technologies: "Employees First", http://www.hcltech.com/employee-first/ (accessed on 28/2/2011).

61. P. Guenzi and O. Pelloni, "The Impact of Interpersonal Relationships on Customer Satisfaction and Loyalty to the Service Provider," *International Journal of Service Industry Management* 15, no. 3–4 (2004), pp. 365–384; S.J. Bell, S. Auh, and K. Smalley, "Customer Relationship Dynamics: Service Quality and Customer Loyalty in the Context of Varying Levels of Customer Expertise and Switching Costs," *Journal of the Academy of Marketing Science* 33, no. 2 (Spring 2005), pp. 169–183; P.B. Barger and A.A. Grandey, "Service with a Smile and Encounter Satisfaction: Emotional Contagion and Appraisal Mechanisms," *Academy of Management Journal* 49, no. 6 (2006), pp. 1229–1238.

62. R.T. Mowday, L.W. Porter, and R.M. Steers, *Employee Organization Linkages: The Psychology of Commitment, Absenteeism, and Turnover* (New York: Academic Press, 1982).

63. J.P. Meyer, "Organizational Commitment," *International Review of Industrial and Organizational Psychology* 12 (1997), pp. 175–228. Along with affective and continuance commitment, Meyer identifies "normative commitment," which refers to employee feelings of obligation to remain with the organization. This commitment has been excluded so that students focus on the two most common perspectives of commitment.

64. R.D. Hackett, P. Bycio, and P.A. Hausdorf, "Further Assessments of Meyer and Allen's (1991) Three-Component Model of Organizational Commitment," *Journal of Applied Psychology* 79 (1994), pp. 15–23.

65. J.P. Meyer et al., "Affective, Continuance, and Normative Commitment to the Organization: A Meta-Analysis of Antecedents, Correlates, and Consequences," *Journal of Vocational Behavior* 61 (2002), pp. 20–52; M. Riketta, "Attitudinal Organizational Commitment and Job Performance: A Meta-Analysis," *Journal of Organizational Behavior* 23 (2002), pp. 257–266.

66. J.P. Meyer et al., "Organizational Commitment and Job Performance: It's the Nature of the Commitment That Counts," *Journal of Applied Psychology* 74 (1989), pp. 152–156; A.A. Luchak and I.R. Gellatly, "What Kind of Commitment Does a Final-Earnings Pension Plan Elicit?" *Relations Industrielles* 56 (Spring 2001), pp. 394–417; Z.X. Chen and A.M. Francesco, "The Relationship between the Three Components of Commitment and Employee Performance in China," *Journal of Vocational Behavior* 62, no. 3 (2003), pp. 490–510; D.M. Powell and J.P. Meyer, "Side-Bet Theory and the Three-Component Model of Organizational Commitment," *Journal of Vocational Behavior* 65, no. 1 (2004), pp. 157–177.

67. E.W. Morrison and S.L. Robinson, "When Employees Feel Betrayed: A Model of How Psychological Contract Violation Develops," *Academy of Management Review* 22 (1997), pp. 226–256; J.E. Finegan, "The Impact of Person and Organizational Values on Organizational Commitment," *Journal of Occupational and Organizational Psychology* 73 (June 2000), pp. 149–169.

68. D.M. Cable and T.A. Judge, "Person-Organization Fit, Job Choice Decisions, and Organizational Entry," *Organizational Behavior and Human Decision Processes* 67, no. 3 (1996), pp. 294–311; T.J. Kalliath, A.C. Bluedorn, and M.J. Strube, "A Test of Value Congruence Effects," *Journal of Organizational Behavior* 20, no. 7 (1999), pp. 1175–1198; J.W. Westerman and L.A. Cyr, "An Integrative Analysis of Person-Organization Fit Theories," *International Journal of Selection and Assessment* 12, no. 3 (September 2004), pp. 252–261.

69. D.M. Rousseau et al., "Not So Different after All: A Cross-Discipline View of Trust," *Academy of Management Review* 23 (1998), pp. 393–404.

70. S. Ashford, C. Lee, and P. Bobko, "Content, Causes, and Consequences of Job Insecurity: A Theory-Based Measure and Substantive Test," *Academy of Management Journal* 32 (1989), pp. 803–829; C. Hendry and R. Jenkins, "Psychological Contracts and New Deals," *Human Resource Management Journal* 7 (1997), pp. 38–44.

71. T.S. Heffner and J.R. Rentsch, "Organizational Commitment and Social Interaction: A Multiple Constituencies Approach," *Journal of Vocational Behavior* 59 (2001), pp. 471–490.

72. E. White, "Know Your Duties, the Firm to Reduce New-Job Surprises," *The Wall Street Journal*, 27 December 2005, p. A16.

73. P. Kruger, "Betrayed by Work," *Fast Company*, November 1999, p. 182.

74. S.L. Robinson, M.S. Kraatz, and D.M. Rousseau, "Changing Obligations and the Psychological Contract: A Longitudinal Study," *Academy of Management Journal* 37 (1994), pp. 137–52; Morrison and Robinson, "When Employees Feel Betrayed: A Model of How Psychological ContractViolation Develops."

75. D.M. Rousseau, *Psychological Contracts in Organizations* (Thousand Oaks, CA: Sage, 1995); M. Janssens, L. Sels, and I. Van den Brande, "Multiple Types of Psychological Contracts: A Six-Cluster Solution," *Human Relations* 56, no. 11 (2003), pp. 1349–78.

76. P.R. Sparrow, "Reappraising Psychological Contracting: Lessons for the Field of Human Resource Development from Cross-Cultural and Occupational Psychology Research," *International Studies of Management & Organization* 28 (March 1998), pp. 30–63; D.C. Thomas, K. Au, and E.C. Ravlin, "Cultural Variation and the Psychological Contract," *Journal ofOrganizational Behavior* 24 (2003), pp. 451–71.

77. "Officials Worry as Younger Japanese Embrace 'Freeting,'" *Taipei Times* (Korea), 4 June 2003, p. 12; "Ministry Scheme Lets You Test-Drive a Job," *Yomiuri Shimbun* (Tokyo), 22 April 2005; C. Fujioka, "Idle Young Adults Threaten Japan's Workforce," *Reuters News*, 28 February 2005; "40% of Students Accept Becoming 'Freeters' to Realize Dreams: Survey,"*Kyodo News* (Tokyo), 2 May 2006.

78. W.H. Whyte, *Organization Man* (New York: Simon & Schuster, 1956), p. 129; C. Hendry and R. Jenkins, "Psychological Contracts and New Deals," *Human Resource Management Journal* 7 (1997), pp. 38–44.

79. L. Uchitelle, "As Job Cuts Spread, Tears Replace Anger," *The New York Times*, 5 August 2001. Psychological contract expectations of young employees are discussed in P. Herriot and C. Pemberton, "Facilitating New Deals," *Human Resource Management Journal* 7 (1997), pp. 45–56; and P.R. Sparrow, "Transitions in the Psychological Contract: Some Evidence from the Banking Sector," *Human Resource Management Journal* 6 (1996), pp. 75–92.

80. N. Davidson, "Vancouver Developer Looks to Make Video Games without Burning Out Staff," *Canadian Press*, 21 February 2006. Some quotations are from Propaganda's Web site: www.propagandagames.go.com.

81. J.C. Quick et al., *Preventive Stress Management in Organizations* (Washington, DC: American Psychological Association, 1997), pp. 3–4; R.S. DeFrank and J.M. Ivancevich, "Stress on the Job: An Executive Update," *Academy of Management Executive* 12 (August 1998), pp. 55–66; A.L. Dougall and A. Baum, "Stress, Coping, and Immune Function," in *Handbook of Psychology*, ed. M. Gallagher andR.J. Nelson (Hoboken, NJ: Wiley, 2003), pp. 441–455. There are at least three schools of thought regarding the meaning of stress, and some reviews of the stress literature describe these schools without pointing to any one as the preferred definition. One reviewer concluded that the stress concept is so broad that it should be considered an umbrella concept, capturing a broad array of phenomena and providing a simple term for the public to use. See T.A. Day, "Defining Stress as a Prelude to Mapping Its Neurocircuitry: No Help from Allostasis," *Progress in Neuro-Psychopharmacology and Biological Psychiatry* 29, no. 8 (2005), pp. 1195–1200; R. Cropanzano and A. Li, "Organizational Politics and Workplace Stress," in *Handbook of*

Organizational Politics, ed. E. Vigoda-Gadot and A. Drory (Cheltenham, UK: Edward Elgar, 2006), pp. 139–160; R.L. Woolfolk, P.M. Lehrer, and L.A. Allen, "Conceptual Issues Underlying Stress Management," in *Principles and Practice of Stress Management,* ed. P.M. Lehrer, R.L. Woolfolk, and W.E. Sime (New York: Guilford Press, 2007), pp. 3–15.

82. Finegan, "The Impact of Person and Organizational Values on Organizational Commitment"; Dougall and Baum, "Stress, Coping, and Immune Function"; R.S. Lazarus, *Stress and Emotion: A New Synthesis* (New York: Springer, 2006); L.W. Hunter and S.M.B. Thatcher, "Feeling the Heat: Effects of Stress, Commitment, and Job Experience on Job Performance," *Academy of Management Journal* 50, no. 4 (2007), pp. 953–968.

83. T. Haratani, "Job Stress Trends in Japan" in *Job Stress Trends in East Asia (Proceedings of the First East-Asia Job Stress Meeting),* ed. A. Tsutsumi (Tokyo: Waseda University, 8 January, 2000), pp. 4–10; "New Survey: Americans Stressed More than Ever," *PR Newswire,* 26 June 2003; Mind, *Stress and Mental Health in the Workplace* (London: Mind, May 2005); M. Shields, "Stress and Depression in the Employed Population," *Health Reports (Statistics Canada)* 17, no. 4 (October 2006), pp. 11–32; W. Lester, "A World of Stress," *Daily News* (South Africa), 6 February 2007.

84. Quick et al., *Preventive Stress Management in Organizations,* pp. 5–6; B.L. Simmons and D.L. Nelson, "Eustress at Work: The Relationship between Hope and Health in Hospital Nurses," *Health Care Management Review* 26, no. 4 (October 2001), pp. 7ff.

85. H. Selye, "A Syndrome Produced by Diverse Nocuous Agents," *Nature* 138, no. 1 (4 July 1936), p. 32; H. Selye, *Stress without Distress* (Philadelphia: Lippincott, 1974). The earliest use of the word *stress* is reported in R.M.K. Keil, "Coping and Stress: A Conceptual Analysis," *Journal of Advanced Nursing* 45, no. 6 (2004), pp. 659–665.

86. S.E. Taylor, R.L. Repetti, and T. Seeman, "Health Psychology: What Is an Unhealthy Environment and How Does It Get under the Skin?" *Annual Review of Psychology* 48 (1997), pp. 411–447.

87. D. Ganster, M. Fox, and D. Dwyer, "Explaining Employees' Health Care Costs: A Prospective Examination of Stressful Job Demands, Personal Control, and Physiological Reactivity," *Journal of Applied Psychology* 86 (May 2001), pp. 954–964; M. Kivimaki et al., "Work Stress and Risk of Cardiovascular Mortality: Prospective Cohort Study of Industrial Employees," *British Medical Journal* 325 (19 October 2002), pp. 857–860; S. Andrew and S. Ayers, "Stress, Health, and Illness," in *The Sage Handbook of Health Psychology,* ed. S. Sutton, A. Baum, and M. Johnston (London: Sage, 2004), pp. 169–196; A. Rosengren et al., "Association of Psychosocial Risk Factors with Risk of Acute Myocardial Infarction in 11,119 Cases and 13,648 Controls from 52 Countries (the INTERHEART Study): Case-Control Study," *The Lancet* 364, no. 9438 (11 September 2004), pp. 953–962.

88. R.C. Kessler, "The Effects of Stressful Life Events on Depression," *Annual Review of Psychology* 48 (1997), pp. 191–214; L. Greenburg and J. Barling, "Predicting Employee Aggression against Coworkers, Subordinates and Supervisors: The Roles of Person Behaviors and Perceived Workplace Factors," *Journal of Organizational Behavior* 20 (1999), pp. 897–913; M. Jamal and V.V. Baba, "Job Stress and Burnout among Canadian Managers and Nurses: An Empirical Examination," *Canadian Journal of Public Health* 91, no. 6 (November–December 2000), pp. 454–458; L. Tourigny, V.V. Baba, and T.R. Lituchy, "Job Burnout among Airline Employees in Japan: A Study of the Buffering Effects of Absence and Supervisory Support," *International Journal of Cross Cultural Management* 5, no. 1 (April 2005), pp. 67–85; M.S. Hershcovis et al., "Predicting Workplace Aggression: A Meta-Analysis," *Journal of Applied Psychology* 92, no. 1 (2007), pp. 228–238.

89. D. Ganster, M. Fox, and D. Dwyer, "Explaining Employees' Health Care Costs: A Prospective Examination of Stressful Job Demands, Personal Control, and Physiological Reactivity," *Journal of Applied Psychology* 86 (May 2001), pp. 954–64.

90. R.C. Kessler, "The Effects of Stressful Life Events on Depression," *Annual Review of Psychology* 48 (1997), pp. 191–214; M. Jamal and V.V. Baba, "Job Stress and Burnout among Canadian Managers and Nurses: An Empirical Examination," *Canadian Journal of Public Health* 91, no. 6 (November-December 2000). pp. 454–58.

91. C. Maslach, W.B. Schaufeli, and M.P. Leiter, "Job Burnout," *Annual Review of Psychology* 52 (2001), pp. 397–422; J.R.B. Halbesleben and M.R. Buckley, "Burnout in Organizational Life," *Journal of Management* 30, no. 6 (2004), pp. 859–79.

92. Radha R. Sharma, *Determinants of Executive Burnout in India,* Unpublished Research Report, WHO; Ministry of Health, Govt. of India, (2005); Radha R. Sharma, "Indian Model of Executive Burnout Journal, *Vikalpa,* IIM-Ahmedabad, 32:2 (2007), pp. 23–38.

93. Radha R. Sharma, "Executive burnout: Contribution of Role-related Factors," *Indian Journal of Industrial Research,* 38:1 (2002), pp. 81–95.

94. M. Jamal, "Job Stress and Job Performance Controversy: An Empirical Assessment," *Organizational Behavior and Human Performance* 33 (1984), pp. 1–21; G. Keinan, "Decision Making under Stress: Scanning of Alternatives under Controllable and Uncontrollable Threats," *Journal of Personality and Social Psychology* 52 (1987), pp. 638–44. The positive effects of moderate stress are reported in L. Van Dyne, K.A. Jehn, and A. Cummings, "Differential Effects of Strain on Two Forms of Work Performance: Individual Employee Sales and Creativity," *Journal of Organizational Behavior* 23, no. 1 (2002), pp. 57–74; E. Chajut and D. Algom, "Selective Attention Improves under Stress: Implications for Theories of Social Cognition," *Journal of Personality and Social Psychology* 85, no. 2 (2003), pp. 231–48.

95. R.D. Hackett and P. Bycio, "An Evaluation of Employee Absenteeism as a Coping Mechanism among Hospital Nurses," *Journal of Occupational & Organizational Psychology* 69 (December 1996), pp. 327–38; A. Vaananen et al., "Job Characteristics, Physical and Psychological Symptoms, and Social Support as Antecedents of Sickness Absence among Men and Women in the Private Industrial Sector," *Social Science & Medicine* 57, no. 5 (September 2003), pp. 807–24; L. Tourigny, V.V. Baba, and T.R. Lituchy, "Job Burnout among Airline Employees in Japan: A Study of the Buffering Effects of Absence and Supervisory Support," *International Journal of Cross Cultural Management* 5, no. 1 (April 2005), pp. 67–85.

96. L. Greenburg and J. Barling, "Predicting Employee Aggression against Coworkers, Subordinates, and Supervisors: The Roles of Person Behaviors and Perceived Workplace Factors," *Journal of Organizational Behavior* 20 (1999), pp. 897–913; H. Steensma, "Violence in the Workplace: The Explanatory Strength of Social (In)Justice Theories," in *The Justice Motive in Everyday Life*, ed. M. Ross and D.T. Miller (New York: Cambridge University Press, 2002), pp. 149–67; J.D. Leck, "Violence in the Canadian Workplace," *Journal of the American Academy of Business* 7, no. 2 (September 2005), pp. 308–15.

97. K. Danna and R.W. Griffin, "Health and Well-Being in the Workplace: A Review and Synthesis of the Literature," *Journal of Management*, Spring 1999, pp. 357–384.

98. N. Wager, G. Fieldman, and T. Hussey, "The Effect on Ambulatory Blood Pressure of Working under Favourably and Unfavourably Perceived Supervisors," *Occupational and Environmental Medicine* 60, no. 7 (1 July 2003), pp. 468–74. For further details on the stressful effects of bad bosses, see E.K. Kelloway et al., "Poor Leadership," in *Handbook of Workplace Stress*, ed. J. Barling, E.K. Kelloway, and M. Frone (Thousand Oaks, CA: Sage, 2005), pp. 89–112.

99. Bureau of Labor Statistics, "National Census of Fatal Occupational Injuries in 2004," U.S. Department of Labor news release (Washington, DC: 25 August 2005); N. Paton, "Nurses on the Verge of Breakdown," *Occupational Health*, April 2006, p. 4.

100. 13. H.-H. Pai, "'Our Eyes Have Been Opened by the Abuse'" *The Guardian* (London), 29 April 2006, p. 2.

101. This is a slight variation of the definition in the Quebec antiharassment legislation. See www.cnt.gouv.qc.ca. For related definitions and discussion of workplace incivility, see H. Cowiea et al., "Measuring Workplace Bullying," *Aggression and Violent Behavior* 7 (2002), pp. 33–51; C.M. Pearson and C.L. Porath, "On the Nature, Consequences and Remedies of Workplace Incivility: No Time for 'Nice'? Think Again," *Academy of Management Executive* 19, no. 1 (February 2005), pp. 7–18.

102. "HR Bullied Just as Much as Anyone Else," *Personnel Today*, November 2005, p. 3; Pearson and Porath, "On the Nature, Consequences and Remedies of Workplace Incivility"; S. Toomey, "Bullying Alive and Kicking," *The Australian*, 16 July 2005, p. 9; J. Przybys, "How Rude!" *Las Vegas Review-Journal*, 25 April 2006, p. 1E.

103. U.S. Equal Employment Opportunity Commission, *Sexual Harassment Charges: EEOC & FEPAs Combined: FY 1997-FY 2007 (Washington, DC: EEOC, 2008)*, http:// www.eeoc.gov/stats/harass.html (accessed 27 October 2008). For a legal discussion of types of sexual harassment, see: B. Lindemann and D.D. Kadue, *Sexual Harassment in Employment Law* (Washington, DC: BNA Books, 1999), pp. 7–9.

104. E.K. Kelloway and J. Barling, "Job Characteristics, Role Stress, and Mental Health," *Journal of Occupational Psychology* 64 (1991), pp. 291–304; M. Siegall and L.L. Cummings, "Stress and Organizational Role Conflict," *Genetic, Social, and General Psychology Monographs* 12 (1995), pp. 65–95; J. Lait and J.E. Wallace, "Stress at Work: A Study of Organizational-Professional Conflict and Unmet Expectations," *Relations Industrielles* 57, no. 3 (Summer 2002), pp. 463–87; E. Grunfeld et al., "Job Stress and Job Satisfaction of Cancer Care Workers," *Psycho-Oncology* 14, no. 1 (May 2005), pp. 61–69.

105. A.M. Saks and B.E. Ashforth, "Proactive Socialization and Behavioral Self-Management," *Journal of Vocational Behavior* 48 (1996), pp. 301–23; A. Nygaard and R. Dahlstrom, "Role Stress and Effectiveness in Horizontal Alliances," *Journal of Marketing* 66 (April 2002), pp. 61–82.

106. Past predictions of future work hours are described in B.K. Hunnicutt, *Kellogg's Six-Hour Day* (Philadelphia: Temple University Press, 1996).

107. N. Chesley, "Blurring Boundaries? Linking Technology Use, Spillover, Individual Distress, and Family Satisfaction," *Journal of Marriage and Family* 67, no. 5 (2005), pp. 1237–1248; T. Taylor, "Hard-Working Canadians Find It Tough to Disconnect," *Calgary Herald*, 18 May 2005, p. A10; R. Parloff, "Secrets of Greatness–How I Work: Amy W. Schulman," *Fortune*, 20 March 2006, p. 66; F.C.J. Morris, "Technology Addicted Employees," *New Jersey Law Journal*, 2 March 2007.

108. E. Galinsky et al., *Overwork in America: When the Way We Work Becomes Too Much* (New York: Families and Work Institute, March 2005); J. MacBride-King, *Wrestling with Workload: Organizational Strategies for Success* (Ottawa: Conference Board of Canada, 2005); R.G. Netemeyer, J.G. Maxham III, and C. Pullig, "Conflicts in the Work–Family Interface: Links to Job Stress, Customer Service Employee Performance, and Customer Purchase Intent," *Journal of Marketing* 69 (April 2005), pp. 130–145.

109. R. Drago, D. Black, and M. Wooden, *The Persistence of Long Work Hours*, Melbourne Institute Working Paper Series (Melbourne: Melbourne Institute of Applied Economic and Social Research, University of Melbourne, August 2005).

110. C.B. Meek, "The Dark Side of Japanese Management in the 1990s: Karoshi and Ijime in the Japanese Workplace," *Journal of Managerial Psychology* 19, no. 3 (2004), pp. 312–331; J. Shi, "Beijing's High Flyers Dying to Get Ahead," *South China Morning Post* (Hong Kong), 8 October 2005, p. 8; N. You, "Mantra: Work for Life, Rather than Live to Work," *China Daily*, 26 March 2005.

111. A. Bakker, E. Demerouti, and W. Verbeke, "Using the Job Demands-Resources Model to Predict Burnout and Performance," *Human Resources Management* 43, no. 1 (2004), pp. 83–104;

W.B. Schaufeli, "Job Demands, Job Resources, and Their Relationship with Burnout and Engagement: A Multisample Study," *Journal of Organizational Behavior* 25 (2004), pp. 293–315; A. Bakker and E. Demerouti, "The Job Demands-Resources Model: State of the Art," *Journal of Managerial Psychology* 22, no. 3 (2007), p. 309.

112. R. Karasek and T. Theorell, *Healthy Work: Stress, Productivity, and the Reconstruction of Working Life* (New York: Basic Books, 1990); N. Turner, N. Chmiel, and M. Walls, "Railing for Safety: Job Demands, Job Control, and Safety Citizenship Role Definition," *Journal of Occupational Health Psychology* 10, no. 4 (2005), pp. 504–512.

113. R.J. Burke and C.L. Cooper, *The Organization in Crisis: Downsizing, Restructuring, and Privatization* (Oxford, UK: Blackwell, 2000); M. Kivimaki et al., "Factors Underlying the Effect of Organizational Downsizing on Health of Employees: Longitudinal Cohort Study," *British Medical Journal* 320 (8 April 2000), pp. 971–75; M. Sverke, J. Hellgren, and K. N"swall, "No Security: A Meta-Analysis and Review of Job Insecurity and Its Consequences," *Journal of Occupational Health Psychology* 7 (July 2002), pp. 242–64; R.J. Burke, "Correlates of Nursing Staff Survivor Responses to Hospital Restructuring and Downsizing," *Health Care Manager* 24, no. 2 (2005), pp. 141–49.

114. C. Higgins and L. Duxbury, *The 2001 National Work-Life Conflict Study: Report One, Final Report* (Ottawa: Health Canada, March 2002); M. Shields, "Shift Work and Health," *Health Reports (Statistics Canada)* 13 (Spring 2002), pp. 11–34.

115. E.K. Kelloway, B.H. Gottlieb, and L. Barham, "The Source, Nature, and Direction of Work and Family Conflict: A Longitudinal Investigation," *Journal of Occupational Health Psychology* 4 (October 1999), pp. 337–46; C.M. Brotheridge and R.T. Lee, "Impact of Work-Family Interference on General Well-Being: A Replication and Extension," *International Journal of Stress Management* 12, no. 3 (2005), pp. 203-21.

116. A.S. Wharton and R.J. Erickson, "Managing Emotions on the Job and at Home: Understanding the Consequences of Multiple Emotional Roles," *Academy of Management Review* (1993), pp. 457–86.

117. B. Keil, "The 10 Most Stressful Jobs in NYC," New York Post, 6 April 1999, p. 50; A. Smith et al., *The Scale of Occupational Stress: A Further Analysis of the Impact of Demographic Factors and Type of Job* (Sudbury, Suffolk: United Kingdom, Health & Safety Executive, 2000).

118. S.J. Havlovic and J.P. Keenen, "Coping with Work Stress: The Influence of Individual Differences," *Handbook on Job Stress* (special issue)," *Journal of Social Behavior and Personality* 6 (1991), pp. 199–212.

119. S.S. Luthar, D. Cicchetti, and B. Becker, "The Construct of Resilience: A Critical Evaluation and Guidelines for Future Work," *Child Development* 71, no. 3 (May–June 2000), pp. 543–562; F. Luthans, "The Need for and Meaning of Positive Organizational Behavior," *Journal of Organizational Behavior* 23 (2002), pp. 695–706; G.A. Bonanno, "Loss, Trauma, and Human Resilience: Have We Underestimated the Human Capacity to Thrive after Extremely Aversive Events?" *American Psychologist* 59, no. 1 (2004), pp. 20–28.

120. M. Beasley, T. Thompson, and J. Davidson, "Resilience in Response to Life Stress: The Effects of Coping Style and Cognitive Hardiness," *Personality and Individual Differences* 34, no. 1 (2003), pp. 77–95; M.M. Tugade, B.L. Fredrickson, and L. Feldman Barrett, "Psychological Resilience and Positive Emotional Granularity: Examining the Benefits of Positive Emotions on Coping and Health," *Journal of Personality* 72, no. 6 (2004), pp. 1161–1190; I. Tsaousis and I. Nikolaou, "Exploring the Relationship of Emotional Intelligence with Physical and Psychological Health Functioning," *Stress and Health* 21, no. 2 (2005), pp. 77–86; L. Campbell-Sills, S.L. Cohan, and M.B. Stein, "Relationship of Resilience to Personality, Coping, and Psychiatric Symptoms in Young Adults," *Behaviour Research and Therapy* 44, no. 4 (April 2006), pp. 585–599.

121. J.T. Spence and A.S. Robbins, "Workaholism: Definition, Measurement and Preliminary Results," *Journal of Personality Assessment* 58 (1992), pp. 160–178; R.J. Burke, "Workaholism in Organizations: Psychological and Physical Well-Being Consequences," *Stress Medicine* 16, no. 1 (2000), pp. 11–16; I. Harpaz and R. Snir, "Workaholism: Its Definition and Nature," *Human Relations* 56 (2003), pp. 291–319; R.J. Burke, A.M. Richardson, and M. Martinussen, "Workaholism among Norwegian Senior Managers: New Research Directions," *International Journal of Management* 21, no. 4 (December 2004), pp. 415–426.

122. R.J. Burke and G. MacDermid, "Are Workaholics Job Satisfied and Successful in Their Careers?" *Career Development International* 4 (1999), pp. 277–282; R.J. Burke and S. Matthiesen, "Short Communication: Workaholism among Norwegian Journalists: Antecedents and Consequences," *Stress and Health* 20, no. 5 (2004), pp. 301–308.

123. S.-A. Chia and E. Toh, "Give Employees a Break," *Straits Times* (Singapore), 23 July 2005.

124. M. Siegall and L.L. Cummings, "Stress and Organizational Role Conflict," *Genetic, Social, and General Psychology Monographs* 12 (1995), pp. 65–95.

125. W.E. Ormond, J.L. Keown-Gerrard, and T. Kline, "Stress Audits as a Precursor to Stress Management Workshops: An Evaluation of the Process," *Human Resource Development Quarterly* 14, no. 1 (Spring 2003), pp. 111–116; "Employee Wellness," *Canadian HR Reporter*, 23 February 2004, pp. 9–12.

126. L.T. Eby et al., "Work and Family Research in IO/OB: Content Analysis and Review of the Literature (1980–2002)," *Journal of Vocational Behavior* 66, no. 1 (2005), pp. 124–197.

127. S.R. Madsen, "The Effects of Home-Based Teleworking on Work-Family Conflict," *Human Resource Development Quarterly* 14, no. 1 (2003), pp. 35–58.

128. Organization for Economic Co-operation and Development, *Babies and Bosses: Reconciling Work and Family Life,* vol. 4 (Canada, Finland, Sweden and the United Kingdom) (Paris: OECD, 2005); B. Pettit and J. Hook, "The Structure of Women's Employment in Comparative Perspective," *Social Forces* 84, no. 2 (December 2005), pp. 779–801; J. Heymann et al., *The Work, Family, and Equity Index: How Does the United States Measure Up?* Project on Global Working Families (Montreal: Institute for Health and Social Policy, June 2007).

129. M. Secret, "Parenting in the Workplace: Child Care Options for Consideration," *Journal of Applied Behavioral Science* 41, no. 3 (September 2005), pp. 326–347.

130. S. Overman, "Sabbaticals Benefit Companies as Well as Employees," *Employee Benefit News,* 15 April 2006.

131. S. Moreland, "Strike Up Creativity," *Crain's Cleveland Business,* 14 April 2003, p. 3; J. Saranow, "Anybody Want to Take a Nap?" *Wall Street Journal,* 24 January 2005, p. R5.

132. M. Waung, "The Effects of Self-Regulatory Coping Orientation on Newcomer Adjustment and Job Survival," *Personnel Psychology* 48 (1995), pp. 633–650; M.H. Abel, "Humor, Stress, and Coping Strategies," *Humor: International Journal of Humor Research* 15, no. 4 (2002), pp. 365–381; N.A. Kuiper et al., "Humor Is Not Always the Best Medicine: Specific Components of Sense of Humor and Psychological Well-Being," *Humor: International Journal of Humor Research* 17, no. 1–2 (2004), pp. 135–168; E.J. Romero and K.W. Cruthirds, "The Use of Humor in the Workplace," *Academy of Management Perspectives* 20, no. 2 (2006), pp. 58–69; M. McCreaddie and S. Wiggins, "The Purpose and Function of Humor in Health, Health Care and Nursing: A Narrative Review," *Journal of Advanced Nursing* 61, no. 6 (2008), pp. 584–595.

133. M. Conlin, "Smashing the Clock," *BusinessWeek,* 11 December 2006, pp. 60–68; L. Gresham, "A New Dawn," *Employee Benefits News,* March 2007; B. Ward, "Power to the People," *Star-Tribune* (Minneapolis–St. Paul), 1 June 2008, p. 1E.

134. W.M. Ensel and N. Lin, "Physical Fitness and the Stress Process," *Journal of Community Psychology* 32, no. 1 (January 2004), pp. 81–101.

135. S. Armour, "Rising Job Stress Could Affect Bottom Line," *USA Today,* 29 July 2003; V.A. Barnes, F.A. Treiber, and M.H. Johnson, "Impact of Transcendental Meditation on Ambulatory Blood Pressure in African-American Adolescents," *American Journal of Hypertension* 17, no. 4 (2004), pp. 366–369; P. Manikonda et al., "Influence of Non-Pharmacological Treatment (Contemplative Meditation and Breathing Technique) on Stress Induced Hypertension–A Randomized Controlled Study," *American Journal of Hypertension* 18, no. 5, Supplement 1 (2005), pp. A89–A90.

136. L. Chordes, "Here's to Your Health," *Best's Review,* April 2006, pp. 52–55; D. Gill, "Get Healthy . . . or Else," *Inc.,* April 2006, pp. 35–38; J. Wojcik, "Pitney Bowes Tool Encourages Workers to Live Healthier," *Business Insurance,* 3 April 2006, p. 4.

137. S.E. Taylor et al., "Biobehavioral Responses to Stress in Females: Tend-and-Befriend, Not Fight-or-Flight," *Psychological Review* 107, no. 3 (July 2000), pp. 411–429; R. Eisler and D.S. Levine, "Nurture, Nature, and Caring: We Are Not Prisoners of Our Genes," *Brain and Mind* 3 (2002), pp. 9–52.

138. Leonard L. Berry et al., "What's the Hard Return on Employees Wellness Programs?" *Harvard Business Review* (Dec 2010), http://www.wellsteps.com/admin/attachments/728485616c6e21dab8b106198da4bdaf.pdf, accessed on 24/2/2011.

139. Buck Survey: "Working Well: A Global Survey of Health Promotion and Workplace Wellness Strategies," (Executive Summary, 2009), http://www.vielife.com/downloads/research/gw/Global_Wellness_2009_ExecSumm_English.pdf , accessed on 24/2/2011.

Chapter 5

1. E. Pofeldt, "What Makes a Great Boss?" *Fortune,* 16 October 2006, p. 192B; "Employee Engagement–Design for Working," *Human Resources,* February 2008, p. 54; A. McCall, "24 Rackspace," *Sunday Times: 100 Best Companies to Work For 2008,* 9 March 2008, p. 38; Rackspace Hosting, "2008 Racker Letter to Investors," San Antonio, TX, 7 August 2008.

2. C.C. Pinder, *Work Motivation in Organizational Behavior* (Upper Saddle River, NJ: Prentice Hall, 1998); R.M. Steers, R.T. Mowday, and D.L. Shapiro, "The Future of Work Motivation Theory," *Academy of Management Review* 29 (2004), pp. 379–387.

3. W.H. Macey and B. Schneider, "The Meaning of Employee Engagement," *Industrial and Organizational Psychology* 1 (2008), pp. 3–30.

4. N.P. Rothbard, "Enriching or Depleting? The Dynamics of Engagement in Work and Family Roles," *Administrative Science Quarterly* 46, no. 4 (December 2001), pp. 655–684; R. Baumruk, "The Missing Link: The Role of Employee Engagement in

Business Success," *Workspan,* November 2004, p. 48; F.D. Frank, R.P. Finnegan, and C.R. Taylor, "The Race for Talent: Retaining and Engaging Workers in the 21st Century," *Human Resource Planning* 27, no. 3 (January 2004), p. 12; D.R. May, R.L. Gilson, and L.M. Harter, "The Psychological Conditions of Meaningfulness, Safety and Availability and the Engagement of the Human Spirit at Work," *Journal of Occupational and Organizational Psychology* 77 (March 2004), pp. 11–37; A.M. Saks, "Antecedents and Consequences of Employee Engagement," *Journal of Managerial Psychology* 21, no. 7 (2006), pp. 600–619; F. Catteeuw, E. Flynn, and J. Vonderhorst, "Employee Engagement: Boosting Productivity in Turbulent Times," *Organization Development Journal* 25, no. 2 (Summer 2007), pp. P151–P157.

5. G. Ginsberg, ed., *Essential Techniques for Employee Engagement,* The Practitioner's Guide To . . . (London: Melcrum, 2007).

6. M. Millar, "Getting the Measure of Its People," *Personnel Today,* 14 December 2004, p. 6; K. Ockenden, "Inside Story," *Utility Week,* 28 January 2005, p. 26; Saks, "Antecedents and Consequences of Employee Engagement"; Scottish Executive Social Research, *Employee Engagement in the Public Sector: A Review of the Literature* (Edinburgh: Scottish Executive Social Research, May 2007).

7. "Event Brief of Q2 2006 JCPenney Earnings Conference Call," *Voxant Fair Disclosure Wire,* 10 August 2006; S. Edelson, "The Penney Program," *Women's Wear Daily,* 12 February 2007, p. 1; J. Engen, "Are Your Employees Truly Engaged?" *Chief Executive,* March 2008, p. 42.

8. Business Wire, "Towers Perrin Study Finds, Despite Layoffs and Slow Economy, a New, More Complex Power Game Is Emerging between Employers and Employees" (news release), New York, 30 August 2001; "Gallup Study: Feeling Good Matters in the Workplace," *Gallup Management Journal,* 12 January 2006; "Few Workers Are 'Engaged' at Work and Most Want More from Execs," *Dow Jones Business News* (San Francisco), 22 October 2007.

9. Business Wire, "Towers Perrin Study Finds"; K.V. Rondeau and T.H. Wagar, "Downsizing and Organizational Restructuring: What Is the Impact on Hospital Performance?" *International Journal of Public Administration* 26 (2003), pp. 1647–1668.

10. C. Lachnit, "The Young and the Dispirited," *Workforce* 81 (August 2002), p. 18; S.H. Applebaum, M. Serena, and B.T. Shapiro, "Generation X and the Boomers: Organizational Myths and Literary Realities," *Management Research News* 27, no. 11–12 (2004), pp. 1–28. Motivation and needs across generations are also discussed in R. Zemke and B. Filipczak, *Generations at Work: Managing the Clash of Veterans, Boomers, Xers, and Nexters in Your Workplace* (New York: AMACOM, 2000).

11. The confusing array of definitions about drives and needs has been the subject of criticism for a half century. See, for example, R.S. Peters, "Motives and Motivation," *Philosophy* 31 (1956), pp. 117–130; H. Cantril, "Sentio, Ergo Sum: 'Motivation' Reconsidered," *Journal of Psychology* 65, no. 1 (January 1967), pp. 91–107; G.R. Salancik and J. Pfeffer, "An Examination of Need-Satisfaction Models of Job Attitudes," *Administrative Science Quarterly* 22, no. 3 (September 1977), pp. 427–456.

12. A. Blasi, "Emotions and Moral Motivation," *Journal for the Theory of Social Behaviour* 29, no. 1 (1999), pp. 1–19; D.W. Pfaff, *Drive: Neurobiological and Molecular Mechanisms of Sexual Motivation* (Cambridge, MA: MIT Press, 1999); T.V. Sewards and M.A. Sewards, "Fear and Power-Dominance Drive Motivation: Neural Representations and Pathways Mediating Sensory and Mnemonic Inputs, and Outputs to Premotor Structures," *Neuroscience and Biobehavioral Reviews* 26 (2002), pp. 553–579; K.C. Berridge, "Motivation Concepts in Behavioral Neuroscience," *Physiology & Behavior* 81, no. 2 (2004), pp. 179–209. We distinguish drives from emotions, but future research may find that the two concepts are not so different as is stated here.

13. K. Passyn and M. Sujan, "Self-Accountability Emotions and Fear Appeals: Motivating Behavior," *Journal of Consumer Research* 32, no. 4 (2006), pp. 583–589; S.G. Barsade and D.E. Gibson, "Why Does Affect Matter in Organizations?" *Academy of Management Perspectives* 21, no. 2 (February 2007), pp. 36–59.

14. G. Loewenstein, "The Psychology of Curiosity: A Review and Reinterpretation," *Psychological Bulletin* 116, no. 1 (1994), pp. 75–98; R.E. Baumeister and M.R. Leary, "The Need to Belong: Desire for Interpersonal Attachments as a Fundamental Human Motivation," *Psychological Bulletin* 117 (1995), pp. 497–529; A.E. Kelley, "Neurochemical Networks Encoding Emotion and Motivation: An Evolutionary Perspective," in *Who Needs Emotions? The Brain Meets the Robot,* ed. J.-M. Fellous and M.A. Arbib (New York: Oxford University Press, 2005), pp. 29–78.

15. S. Hitlin, "Values as the Core of Personal Identity: Drawing Links between Two Theories of Self," *Social Psychology Quarterly* 66, no. 2 (2003), pp. 118–137; D.D. Knoch and E.E. Fehr, "Resisting the Power of Temptations: The Right Prefrontal Cortex and Self-Control," *Annals of the New York Academy of Sciences* 1104, no. 1 (2007), p. 123; B. Monin, D.A. Pizarro, and J.S. Beer, "Deciding versus Reacting: Conceptions of Moral Judgment and the Reason-Affect Debate," *Review of General Psychology* 11, no. 2 (2007), pp. 99–111.

16. N.M. Ashkanasy, W.J. Zerbe, and C.E.J. Härtel, "A Bounded Emotionality Perspective on the Individual in the Organization," in *Emotions in Organizational Behavior,* ed. C.E.J. Härtel, W.J. Zerbe, and N.M. Ashkanasy (Mahwah, NJ: Lawrence Erlbaum, 2005), pp. 113–117.

17. A.H. Maslow, "A Theory of Human Motivation," *Psychological Review* 50 (1943), pp. 370–396; A.H. Maslow, *Motivation and Personality* (New York: Harper & Row, 1954).

18. D.T. Hall and K.E. Nougaim, "An Examination of Maslow's Need Hierarchy in an Organizational Setting," *Organizational Behavior and Human Performance* 3, no. 1 (1968), p. 12; M.A. Wahba and L.G. Bridwell, "Maslow Reconsidered: A Review of Research on the Need Hierarchy Theory," *Organizational Behavior and Human Performance* 15 (1976), pp. 212–240; E.L. Betz, "Two Tests of Maslow's Theory of Need Fulfillment," *Journal of Vocational Behavior* 24, no. 2 (1984), pp. 204–220;P.A. Corning, "Biological Adaptation in Human Societies: A 'Basic Needs' Approach," *Journal of Bioeconomics* 2, no. 1 (2000), pp. 41–86.

19. K. Dye, A.J. Mills, and T.G. Weatherbee, "Maslow: Man Interrupted–Reading Management Theory in Context," *Management Decision* 43, no. 10 (2005), pp. 1375–1395.

20. A.H. Maslow, "A Preface to Motivation Theory," *Psychosomatic Medicine* 5 (1943), pp. 85–92.

21. W.L. Lee, "Net Value: That Loving Feeling," *The Edge Financial Daily* (Malaysia), 25 April 2005; N. Mwaura, "Honour Staff for Good Work," *Daily Nation* (Nairobi, Kenya), 27 September 2005; "Firms Told to Buy Loyalty and Not Time," *The Kingdom* (Killarney, Ireland), 10 January 2008; L. Jakobson, "Amgen: A Culture of Recognition in Record Time," *Incentive,* 7 August 2008.

22. A.H. Maslow, *Maslow on Management* (New York: Wiley, 1998).

23. F.F. Luthans, "Positive Organizational Behavior: Developing and Managing Psychological Strengths," *The Academy of Management Executive* 16, no. 1 (2002), pp. 57–72; S.L. Gable and J. Haidt, "What (and Why) Is Positive Psychology?" *Review of General Psychology* 9, no. 2 (2005), pp. 103–110; M.E.P. Seligman et al., "Positive Psychology Progress: Empirical Validation of Interventions," *American Psychologist* 60, no. 5 (2005), pp. 410–421.

24. C.P. Alderfer, *Existence, Relatedness, and Growth* (New York: Free Press, 1972).

25. J. Rauschenberger, N. Schmitt, and J.E. Hunter, "A Test of the Need Hierarchy Concept by a Markov Model of Change in Need Strength," *Administrative Science Quarterly* 25, no. 4 (December 1980), pp. 654–670; J.P. Wanous and A.A. Zwany, "A Cross-Sectional Test of Need Hierarchy Theory," *Organizational Behavior and Human Performance* 18 (1977), pp. 78–97.

26. B.A. Agle and C.B. Caldwell, "Understanding Research on Values in Business," *Business and Society* 38 (September 1999), pp. 326–387; B. Verplanken and R.W. Holland, "Motivated Decision Making: Effects of Activation and Self-Centrality of Values on Choices and Behavior," *Journal of Personality and Social Psychology* 82, no. 3 (2002), pp. 434–447; S. Hitlin and J.A. Pilavin, "Values: Reviving a Dormant Concept," *Annual Review of Sociology* 30 (2004), pp. 359–393.

27. F. Herzberg et al., *The Motivation to Work,* (New York: Wiley, 1957).

28. A. Maslow, *Motivation & Personality,* (New York: Harper & Row, 1954).

29. D.E. Guest, "Motivation after Herzberg," unpublished paper delivered at Compensation Forum, London (1992).

30. D.C. McClelland, *The Achieving Society* (New York: Van Nostrand Reinhold, 1961); D.C. McClelland and D.H. Burnham, "Power Is the Great Motivator," *Harvard Business Review* 73 (January–February 1995), pp. 126–139; D. Vredenburgh and Y. Brender, "The Hierarchical Abuse of Power in Work Organizations," *Journal of Business Ethics* 17 (September 1998), pp. 1337–1347; S. Shane, E.A. Locke, and C.J. Collins, "Entrepreneurial Motivation," *Human Resource Management Review* 13, no. 2 (2003), pp. 257–279.

31. McClelland, *The Achieving Society.*

32. Shane, Locke, and Collins, "Entrepreneurial Motivation."

33. McClelland and Burnham, "Power Is the Great Motivator"; J.L. Thomas, M.W. Dickson, and P.D. Bliese, "Values Predicting Leader Performance in the U.S. Army Reserve Officer Training Corps Assessment Center: Evidence for a Personality-Mediated Model," *The Leadership Quarterly* 12, no. 2 (2001), pp. 181–196.

34. Vredenburgh and Brender, "The Hierarchical Abuse of Power in Work Organizations."

35. D. Miron and D.C. McClelland, "The Impact of Achievement Motivation Training on Small Business," *California Management Review* 21 (1979), pp. 13–28.

36. Lawrence and Nohria, *Driven: How Human Nature Shapes Our Choices,* Chapter 11.

37. R. Turcsik, "The Prince of Tidewater," *Progressive Grocer,* 15 April 2003.

38. P.R. Lawrence and N. Nohria, *Driven: How Human Nature Shapes Our Choices* (San Francisco: Jossey-Bass, 2002).

39. L. Gaertner et al., "The 'I,' the 'We,' and the 'When': A Meta-Analysis of Motivational Primacy in Self-Definition," *Journal of Personality and Social Psychology* 83, no. 3 (2002), pp. 574–591; M.R. Leary, "Motivational and Emotional Aspects of the Self," *Annual Review of Psychology* 58, no. 1 (2007), pp. 317–344.

40. Baumeister and Leary, "The Need to Belong."

41. J. Litman, "Curiosity and the Pleasures of Learning: Wanting and Liking New Information," *Cognition and Emotion* 19, no. 6 (2005), pp. 793–814; T.G. Reio, Jr., et al., "The Measurement and Conceptualization of Curiosity," *Journal of Genetic Psychology* 167, no. 2 (2006), pp. 117–135.

42. W.H. Bexton, W. Heron, and T.H. Scott, "Effects of Decreased Variation in the Sensory Environment," *Canadian Journal of Psychology* 8 (1954), pp. 70–76; Loewenstein, "The Psychology of Curiosity."

43. A.R. Damasio, *Descartes' Error: Emotion, Reason, and the Human Brain* (New York: Putnam Sons, 1994); J.E. LeDoux, "Emotion Circuits in the Brain," *Annual Review of Neuroscience* 23 (2000), pp. 155–184; P. Winkielman and K.C. Berridge, "Unconscious Emotion," *Current Directions in Psychological Science* 13, no. 3 (2004), pp. 120–123.

44. Lawrence and Nohria, *Driven,* pp. 145–147.

45. Ibid., chap. 11.

46. S.K. Roy and G.A. Raja, *Motivational and Organisational Effectiveness* In (1997) Roy, S.K. and Menon, A.S. (Eds.) New Delhi: Sri Ram Centre of Industrial Relations, pp. 104–35.

47. P. Kalyansundram and M.T. Arason, "A Study of the Motivational Climate in an Industry," *Managmement and Labour studies* 17:2 (1992), pp. 19–28.

48. B.R. Sharma and K. Kaur, "Determinants of Managerial Motivation in Public Sector Manufacturing Organizations," *Indian Journal of Industrial Relations* 36:2 (2000), pp. 140–158.

49. Radha R. Sharma and B.R. Sharma, "Organisational Commitment and Motivation of Managerial Staff," *Productivity* 44:2, Jul–Sep 2003, pp. 251–257.

50. Expectancy theory of motivation in work settings originated in V.H. Vroom, *Work and Motivation* (New York: Wiley, 1964). The version of expectancy theory presented here was developed by Edward Lawler. Lawler's model provides a clearer presentation of the model's three components. P-to-O expectancy is similar to "instrumentality" in Vroom's original expectancy theory model. The difference is that instrumentality is a correlation whereas P-to-O expectancy is a probability. See J.P. Campbell et al., *Managerial Behavior, Performance, and Effectiveness* (New York: McGraw-Hill, 1970); E.E. Lawler III, *Motivation in Work Organizations* (Monterey, CA: Brooks-Cole, 1973); D.A. Nadler and E.E. Lawler, "Motivation: A Diagnostic Approach," in *Perspectives on Behavior in Organizations,* 2d ed., ed. J.R. Hackman, E.E. Lawler III, and L.W. Porter (New York: McGraw-Hill, 1983), pp. 67–78.

51. M. Zeelenberg et al., "Emotional Reactions to the Outcomes of Decisions: The Role of Counterfactual Thought in the Experience of Regret and Disappointment," *Organizational Behavior and Human Decision Processes* 75, no. 2 (1998), pp. 117–141; B.A. Mellers, "Choice and the Relative Pleasure of Consequences," *Psychological Bulletin* 126, no. 6 (November 2000), pp. 910–924; R.P. Bagozzi, U.M. Dholakia, and S. Basuroy, "How Effortful Decisions Get Enacted: The Motivating Role of Decision Processes, Desires, and Anticipated Emotions," *Journal of Behavioral Decision Making* 16, no. 4 (October 2003), pp. 273–295.

52. Nadler and Lawler, "Motivation."

53. P.W. Mulvey et al., *The Knowledge of Pay Study: E-Mails from the Frontline* (Scottsdale, AZ: WorldatWork, 2002); Watson Wyatt, "WorkMalaysia," (Kuala Lumpur: Watson Wyatt, 2004), www.watsonwyatt.com/asia-pacific/research/workasia/workmy_keyfindings.asp (accessed 2 December 2005); Watson Wyatt, *WorkCanada 2004/2005–Pursuing Productive Engagement* (Toronto: Watson Wyatt, January 2005); Kelly Services, "Majority of Canada's Workers Happy, Bosses among Best in World" (news release), Toronto, 28 Novem-ber 2006; Hudson, *Rising above the Average: 2007 Compensation & Benefits Report* (New York: June 2007).

54. T. Matsui and T. Terai, "A Cross-Cultural Study of the Validity of the Expectancy Theory of Motivation," *Journal of Applied Psychology* 60 (1975), pp. 263–265; D.H.B. Welsh, F. Luthans, and S.M. Sommer, "Managing Russian Factory Workers: The Impact of U.S.-Based Behavioral and Participative Techniques," *Academy of Management Journal* 36 (1993), pp. 58–79.

55. This limitation was recently acknowledged by Victor Vroom, who had introduced expectancy theory in his 1964 book. See G.P. Latham, *Work Motivation: History, Theory, Research, and Practice* (Thousand Oaks, CA: Sage, 2007), pp. 47–48.

56. M.L. Ambrose and C.T. Kulik, "Old Friends, New Faces: Motivation Research in the 1990s," *Journal of Management* 25 (May 1999), pp. 231–92; C.L. Haworth and P.E. Levy, "The Importance of Instrumentality Beliefs in the Prediction of Organizational Citizenship Behaviors," *Journal of Vocational Behavior* 59 (August 2001), pp. 64–75; Y. Chen, A. Gupta, and L. Hoshower, "Marketing Students' Perceptions of Teaching Evaluations: An Application of Expectancy Theory," *Marketing Education Review* 14, no. 2 (Summer 2004), pp. 23–36.

57. T. Matsui and I. Terai, "A Cross-Cultural Study of the Validity of the Expectancy Theory of Motivation," *Journal of Applied Psychology* 60 (1979), pp. 263–65; D.H.B. Welsh, F. Luthans, and S.M. Sommer, "Managing Russian Factory Workers: The Impact of U.S.-Based Behavioral and Participative Techniques," *Academy of Management Journal* 36 (1993), pp. 58–79.

58. Pande and Naidu, 1992

59. S.K. Chakraborty, *Managerial Effectiveness and Quality of Work Life: Indian Insights.* (New Delhi: Tata McGraw-Hill, 1987).

60. C.K. Prahalad and R.A. Mashelkar (2010). "Innovation's Holy Grail," *Harvard Business Review* Jul–Aug 2010.

61. S. Zeller, "Good Calls," *Government Executive,* 15 May 2005; C. Bailor, "Checking the Pulse of the Contact Center," *Customer Relationship Management,* November 2007, pp. 24–29.

62. A. Shin, "What Customers Say and How They Say It," *Washington Post,* 18 October 2006, p. D01; D. Ververidis and C. Kotropoulos, "Emotional Speech Recognition: Resources, Features, and Methods," *Speech Communication* 48, no. 9 (2006), pp. 1162–1181.

63. G.P. Latham, "Goal Setting: A Five-Step Approach to Behavior Change," *Organizational Dynamics* 32, no. 3 (2003), pp. 309–318; E.A. Locke and G.P. Latham, *A Theory of Goal Setting and Task Performance* (Englewood Cliffs, NJ: Prentice Hall, 1990). The acronym *SMART* refers to goals that are specific, measurable, acceptable, relevant, and timely. However, this list duplicates some characteristics (e.g., specific goals are measurable *and* timely) and overlooks the characteristics of challenging and feedback-related.

64. "NYC Speeds Transformation of Yellow Cabs to Green," *Reuters News,* 17 July 2008; M. Barbaro, "Bloomberg Encourages Staff to Watch the Clock," *New York Times,* 18 August 2008.

65. A. Li and A.B. Butler, "The Effects of Participation in Goal Setting and Goal Rationales on Goal Commitment: An Exploration of Justice Mediators," *Journal of Business and Psychology* 19, no. 1 (Fall 2004), pp. 37–51.

66. Locke and Latham, *A Theory of Goal Setting and Task Performance,* chaps. 6 and 7; J. Wegge, "Participation in Group Goal Setting: Some Novel Findings and a Comprehensive Model as a New Ending to an Old Story," *Applied Psychology: An International Review* 49 (2000), pp. 498–516.

67. M. London, E.M. Mone, and J.C. Scott, "Performance Management and Assessment: Methods for Improved Rater Accuracy and Employee Goal Setting," *Human Resource Management* 43, no. 4 (Winter 2004), pp. 319–336; G.P. Latham and C.C. Pinder, "Work Motivation Theory and Research at the Dawn of the Twenty-First Century," *Annual Review of Psychology* 56 (2005), pp. 485–516.

68. Houghton Mifflin Company, "Multifaceted Leader Brings Unique Vision to Urban District," 2007, www.beyond-the-book.com/leadership/leadership_030707.html (accessed 11 September 2008); Richmond Pubic Schools, *Balanced Scorecard–Strategic Objectives, Measures and Projects* (Richmond, VA: Richmond Public Schools, 7 November 2007).

69. E. White, "For Relevance, Firms Revamp Worker Reviews," *Wall Street Journal,* 17 July 2006, p. B1.

70. S.P. Brown, S. Ganesan, and G. Challagalla, "Self-Efficacy as a Moderator of Information-Seeking Effectiveness," *Journal of Applied Psychology* 86, no. 5 (2001), pp. 1043–1051; P.A. Heslin and G.P. Latham, "The Effect of Upward Feedback on Managerial Behaviour," *Applied Psychology: An International Review* 53, no. 1 (2004), pp. 23–37; D. Van-Dijk and A.N. Kluger, "Feedback Sign Effect on Motivation: Is It Moderated by Regulatory Focus?" *Applied Psychology: An International Review* 53, no. 1 (2004), pp. 113–135; J.E. Bono and A.E. Colbert, "Understanding Responses to Multi-Source Feedback: The Role of Core Self-Evaluations," *Personnel Psychology* 58, no. 1 (Spring 2005), pp. 171–203.

71. P. Drucker, *The Effective Executive* (Oxford, UK: Butterworth-Heinemann, 2007), p. 22.

72. M. Buckingham, *Go Put Your Strengths to Work* (New York: Free Press, 2007); S.L. Orem, J. Binkert, and A.L. Clancy, *Appreciative Coaching: A Positive Process for Change* (San Francisco: Jossey-Bass, 2007); S. Gordon, "Appreciative Inquiry Coaching," *International Coaching Psychology Review* 3, no. 2 (March 2008), pp. 19–31.

73. A. Terracciano, P.T. Costa, and R.R. McCrae, "Personality Plasticity after Age 30," *Personality and Social Psychology Bulletin* 32, no. 8 (August 2006), pp. 999–1009; Leary, "Motivational and Emotional Aspects of the Self."

74. M. Buckingham and D.O. Clifton, *Now, Discover Your Strengths* (New York: Free Press, 2001).

75. R. White, "Building on Employee Strengths at Sony Europe," *Strategic HR Review* 5, no. 5 (2006), pp. 28–31.

76. D. Hendry, "Game-Playing: The Latest Business Tool," *Globe & Mail,* 17 November 2006, p. C11.

77. L. Hollman, "Seeing the Writing on the Wall," *Call Center* (August 2002), p. 37; S.E. Ante, "Giving the Boss the Big Picture," *BusinessWeek,* 13 February 2006, p. 48.

78. S. Bowness, "Full-Circle Feedback," *Profit,* May 2006, p. 77.

79. S. Brutus and M. Derayeh, "Multisource Assessment Programs in Organizations: An Insider's Perspective," *Human Resource Development Quarterly* 13 (July 2002), pp. 187–202.

80. F.P. Morgeson, T.V. Mumford, and M.A. Campion, "Coming Full Circle: Using Research and Practice to Address 27 Questions about 360-Degree Feedback Programs," *Consulting Psychology Journal* 57, no. 3 (2005), pp. 196–209; J.W. Smither, M. London, and R.R. Reilly, "Does Performance Improve Following Multisource Feedback? A Theoretical Model, Meta-Analysis, and Review of Empirical Findings," *Personnel Psychology* 58, no. 1 (2005), pp. 33–66; L.E. Atwater, J.F. Brett, and A.C. Charles, "Multisource Feedback: Lessons Learned and Implications for Practice," *Human Resource Management* 46, no. 2 (Summer 2007), pp. 285–307.

81. A.S. DeNisi and A.N. Kluger, "Feedback Effectiveness: Can 360-Degree Appraisals Be Improved?" *Academy of Management Executive* 14 (February 2000), pp. 129–139; M.A. Peiperl, "Getting 360-Degree Feedback Right," *Harvard Business Review* 79 (January 2001), pp. 142–147; M.-G. Seo, L.F. Barrett, and J.M. Bartunek, "The Role of Affective Experience in Work Motivation," *Academy of Management Review* 29 (2004), pp. 423–449.

82. S.J. Ashford and G.B. Northcraft, "Conveying More (or Less) Than We Realize: The Role of Impression Management in Feedback Seeking," *Organizational Behavior and Human Decision Processes* 53 (1992), pp. 310–334; J.R. Williams et al., "Increasing Feedback Seeking in Public Contexts: It Takes Two (or More) to Tango," *Journal of Applied Psychology* 84 (December 1999), pp. 969–976.

83. J.B. Miner, "The Rated Importance, Scientific Validity, and Practical Usefulness of Organizational Behavior Theories: A Quantitative Review," *Academy of Management Learning and Education* 2, no. 3 (2003), pp. 250–268. Also see C.C. Pinder, *Work Motivation in Organizational Behavior* (Upper Saddle River, NJ: Prentice Hall, 1997), p. 384.

84. P.M. Wright, "Goal Setting and Monetary Incentives: Motivational Tools That Can Work Too Well," *Compensation and Benefits Review* 26 (May–June 1994), pp. 41–49; E.A. Locke and G.P. Latham, "Building a Practically Useful Theory of Goal Setting and Task Motivation: A 35-Year Odyssey," *American Psychologist* 57, no. 9 (2002), pp. 705–717.

85. Latham, *Work Motivation,* p. 188.

86. "Power Station Workers Upset over 'Unfair' Pay," *Hobart Mercury* (Australia), 26 September 2008.

87. J. Greenberg and E.A. Lind, "The Pursuit of Organizational Justice: From Conceptualization to Implication to Application," in *Industrial and Organizational Psychology: Linking Theory with Practice,* ed. C.L. Cooper and E.A. Locke (London: Blackwell, 2000), pp. 72–108; R. Cropanzano and M. Schminke, "Using Social Justice to Build Effective Work Groups," in *Groups at Work: Theory and Research,* ed. M.E. Turner (Mahwah, NJ: Lawrence Erlbaum, 2001), pp. 143–171; D.T. Miller, "Disrespect and the Experience of Injustice," *Annual Review of Psychology* 52 (2001), pp. 527–553.

88. J.S. Adams, "Toward an Understanding of Inequity," *Journal of Abnormal and Social Psychology,* 67 (1963), pp. 422–436; R.T. Mowday, "Equity Theory Predictions of Behavior in Organizations," in *Motivation and Work Behavior,* 5th ed., ed. L.W. Porter and R.M. Steers (New York: McGraw-Hill, 1991), pp. 111–131; R.G. Cropanzano and J. Greenberg, "Progress in Organizational Justice: Tunneling through the Maze," in *International Review of Industrial and Organizational Psychology,* ed. C.L. Cooper and I.T. Robertson (New York: Wiley, 1997), pp. 317–372; L.A. Powell, "Justice Judgments as Complex Psychocultural Constructions: An Equity-Based Heuristic for Mapping Two- and Three-Dimensional Fairness Representations in Perceptual Space," *Journal of Cross-Cultural Psychology* 36, no. 1 (January 2005), pp. 48–73.

89. C.T. Kulik and M.L. Ambrose, "Personal and Situational Determinants of Referent Choice," *Academy of Management Review* 17 (1992), pp. 212–237; G. Blau, "Testing the Effect of Level and Importance of Pay Referents on Pay Level Satisfaction," *Human Relations* 47 (1994), pp. 1251–1268.

90. T.P. Summers and A.S. DeNisi, "In Search of Adams' Other: Reexamination of Referents Used in the Evaluation of Pay," *Human Relations* 43 (1990), pp. 497–511.

91. Y. Cohen-Charash and P.E. Spector, "The Role of Justice in Organizations: A Meta-Analysis," *Organizational Behavior and Human Decision Processes* 86 (November 2001), pp. 278–321.

92. Canadian Press, "Pierre Berton, Canadian Cultural Icon, Enjoyed Long and Colourful Career," *Times Colonist* (Victoria, B.C.), 30 November 2004.

93. K.S. Sauleya and A.G. Bedeian, "Equity Sensitivity: Construction of a Measure and Examination of Its Psychometric Properties," *Journal of Management* 26 (September 2000), pp. 885–910; G. Blakely, M. Andrews, and R. Moorman, "The Moderating Effects of Equity Sensitivity on the Relationship between Organizational Justice and Organizational Citizenship Behaviors," *Journal of Business and Psychology* 20, no. 2 (2005), pp. 259–273.

94. M. Ezzamel and R. Watson, "Pay Comparability across and within UK Boards: An Empirical Analysis of the Cash Pay Awards to CEOs and Other Board Members," *Journal of Management Studies* 39, no. 2 (March 2002), pp. 207–232; J. Fizel, A.C. Krautman, and L. Hadley, "Equity and Arbitration in Major League Baseball," *Managerial and Decision Economics* 23, no. 7 (October–November 2002), pp. 427–435.

95. B. Murphy, "Rising Fortunes," *Milwaukee Journal Sentinel,* 10 October 2004, p. 1; S. Greenhouse, "How Costco Became the Anti-Wal-Mart," *New York Times,* 17 July 2005, p. BU1; "#19 James Dimon," *Forbes,* 3 May 2007; R. Wartzman, "Put a Cap on CEO Pay," *BusinessWeek,* 12 September 2008.

96. Greenberg and Lind, "The Pursuit of Organizational Justice"; K. Roberts and K.S. Markel, "Claiming in the Name of Fairness: Organizational Justice and the Decision to File for Workplace Injury Compensation," *Journal of Occupational Health Psychology* 6 (October 2001), pp. 332–347; J.B. Olson-Buchanan and W.R. Boswell, "The Role of Employee Loyalty and Formality in Voicing Discontent," *Journal of Applied Psychology* 87, no. 6 (2002), pp. 1167–1174.

97. R. Hagey et al., "Immigrant Nurses' Experience of Racism," *Journal of Nursing Scholarship* 33 (Fourth Quarter 2001), pp. 389–395; Roberts and Markel, "Claiming in the Name of Fairness"; D.A. Jones and D.P. Skarlicki, "The Effects of Overhearing Peers Discuss an Authority's Fairness Reputation on Reactions to Subsequent Treatment," *Journal of Applied Psychology* 90, no. 2 (2005), pp. 363–372.

98. Miller, "Disrespect and the Experience of Injustice."

99. M.L. Ambrose, M.A. Seabright, and M. Schminke, "Sabotage in the Workplace: The Role of Organizational Injustice," *Organizational Behavior and Human Decision Processes* 89, no. 1 (2002), pp. 947–965.

100. N.D. Cole and G.P. Latham, "Effects of Training in Procedural Justice on Perceptions of Disciplinary Fairness by Unionized Employees and Disciplinary Subject Matter Experts," *Journal of Applied Psychology* 82 (1997), pp. 699–705 D.P. Skarlicki and G.P. Latham, "Increasing Citizenship Behavior within a Labor Union: A Test of Organizational Justice Theory," *Journal of Applied Psychology* 81 (1996), pp. 161–69.

Chapter 6

1. J. Hope and R. Fraser, *Beyond Budgeting: How Managers Can Break Free from the Annual Performance Trap* (Boston: Harvard Business School Press, 2003); J. Hope, *Reinventing the CFO: How Financial Managers Can Transform Their Roles and Add Greater Value* (Boston: Harvard Business School Press, 2006); O. Hammarström, *Handelsbanken, Sweden: Make Work Pay–Make Work Attractive*, Attractive Workplace for All: Company Cases (Dublin, Ireland: Eurofound, October 2007); R.M. Lindsay and T. Libby, "Svenska Handelsbanken: Controlling a Radically Decentralized Organization without Budgets," *Issues in Accounting Education* 22, no. 4 (November 2007), pp. 625–640; Svenska Handelsbanken, *Annual Report 2007* (Stockholm: Svenska Handelsbanken, April 2008).

2. M.C. Bloom and G.T. Milkovich, "Issues in Managerial Compensation Research," in *Trends in Organizational Behavior*, ed. C.L. Cooper and D.M. Rousseau (Chichester, UK: Wiley, 1996), pp. 23–47.

3. S.E.G. Lea and P. Webley, "Money as Tool, Money as Drug: The Biological Psychology of a Strong Incentive," *Behavioral and Brain Sciences* 29, no. 2 (2006), pp. 161–209; D. Valenze, *The Social Life of Money in the English Past* (New York: Cambridge University Press, 2006); G.M. Rose and L.M. Orr, "Measuring and Exploring Symbolic Money Meanings," *Psychology and Marketing* 24, no. 9 (2007), pp. 743–761.

4. D.W. Krueger, "Money, Success, and Success Phobia," in *The Last Taboo: Money as Symbol and Reality in Psychotherapy and Psychoanalysis*, ed. D.W. Krueger (New York: Brunner/Mazel, 1986), pp. 3–16.

5. P.F. Wernimont and S. Fitzpatrick, "The Meaning of Money," *Journal of Applied Psychology* 56, no. 3 (1972), pp. 218–226; T.R. Mitchell and A.E. Mickel, "The Meaning of Money: An Individual-Difference Perspective," *Academy of Management Review* (July 1999), pp. 568–578; R. Trachtman, "The Money Taboo: Its Effects in Everyday Life and in the Practice of Psychotherapy," *Clinical Social Work Journal* 27, no. 3 (1999), pp. 275–288; S. Lea, "Money: Motivation, Metaphors, and Mores," *Behavioral and Brain Sciences* 29, no. 2 (2006), pp. 196–209; Lea and Webley, "Money as Tool, Money as Drug"; T.L.-P. Tang et al., "The Love of Money and Pay Level Satisfaction: Measurement and Functional Equivalence in 29 Geopolitical Entities around the World," *Management and Organization Review* 2, no. 3 (2006), pp. 423–452.

6. A. Furnham and R. Okamura, "Your Money or Your Life: Behavioral and Emotional Predictors of Money Pathology," *Human Relations* 52 (September 1999), pp. 1157–1177.

7. Tang et al., "The Love of Money and Pay Level Satisfaction"; T. Tang et al., "To Help or Not to Help? The Good Samaritan Effect and the Love of Money on Helping Behavior," *Journal of Business Ethics* (2007); T. Tang and Y.-J. Chen, "Intelligence vs. Wisdom: The Love of Money, Machiavellianism, and Unethical Behavior across College Major and Gender," *Journal of Business Ethics* 82, no. 1 (2008), pp. 1–26.

8. R. Lynn, *The Secret of the Miracle Economy* (London: SAE, 1991), cited in Furnham and Okamura, "Your Money or Your Life."

9. A. Furnham, B.D. Kirkcaldy, and R. Lynn, "National Attitudes to Competitiveness, Money, and Work among Young People: First, Second, and Third World Differences," *Human Relations* 47 (January 1994), pp. 119–132; S.H. Ang, "The Power of Money: A Cross-Cultural Analysis of Business-Related Beliefs," *Journal of World Business* 35 (March 2000), pp. 43–60; G. Dell'Orto and K.O. Doyle, "Poveri Ma Belli: Meanings of Money in Italy and in Switzerland," *American Behavioral Scientist* 45, no. 2 (October 1, 2001), pp. 257–271; K.O. Doyle, "Introduction: Ethnicity and Money," *American Behavioral Scientist* 45, no. 2 (October 1, 2001), pp. 181–190; V.K.G. Lim, "Money Matters: An Empirical Investigation of Money, Face and Confucian Work Ethic," *Personality and Individual Differences* 35 (2003), pp. 953–970; T.L.-P. Tang, A. Furnham, and G.M.-T. Davis, "A Cross-Cultural Comparison of the Money Ethic, the Protestant Work Ethic, and Job Satisfaction: Taiwan, the USA, and the UK," *International Journal of Organization Theory and Behavior* 6, no. 2 (Summer 2003), pp. 175–194.

10. D.G. Gardner, L. Van Dyne, and J.L. Pierce, "The Effects of Pay Level on Organization-Based Self-Esteem and Performance: A Field Study," *Journal of Occupational and Organizational Psychology* 77 (2004), pp. 307–322; S.L. Rynes, B. Gerhart, and K.A. Minette, "The Importance of Pay in Employee Motivation: Discrepancies between What People Say and What They Do," *Human Resource Management* 43, no. 4 (Winter 2004), pp. 381–394; B.S. Frey, "Awards as Compensation," *European Management Journal* 4 (2007), pp. 6–14.

11. J.S. Mill, *Utilitarianism*, 7th ed. (London: Longmans, Green, 1879; Project Gutenberg EBook), chap. 4.

12. "Seniority Pay System Seeing Revival," *Kyodo News* (Tokyo), 29 March 2004; R.J. Palabrica, "13th Month Pay," *Philippine Daily Inquirer,* 30 November 2007; B. Weberg, "Building the Perfect Perks," *State Legislatures* 34, no. 7 (July 2008), pp. 65–66.

13. D.M. Figart, "Equal Pay for Equal Work: The Role of Job Evaluation in an Evolving Social Norm," *Journal of Economic Issues* 34 (March 2000), pp. 1–19.

14. E.E. Lawler III, *Rewarding Excellence: Pay Strategies for the New Economy* (San Francisco: Jossey-Bass, 2000), pp. 30–35, 109–119; R. McNabb and K. Whitfield, "Job Evaluation and High Performance Work Practices: Compatible or Conflictual? *Journal of Management Studies* 38 (March 2001), pp. 293–312.

15. P.K. Zingheim and J.R. Schuster, "Competencies and Rewards: Substance or Just Style?" *Compensation Benefits Review* 35, no. 5 (2003), pp. 40–44.

16. City of Flagstaff, Arizona, skill-based pay information is derived from the job advertisement "108-08–Multi Skilled Worker–Plant Operator–Plant Technician" (8 August 2008) and "2008–2009 City of Flagstaff Pay Plan: Skill Based Pay" (retrieved 8 September 2008).

17. R.J. Long, "Paying for Knowledge: Does It Pay?" *Canadian HR Reporter,* 28 March 2005, pp. 12–13; J.D. Shaw et al., "Success and Survival of Skill-Based Pay Plans," *Journal of Management* 31, no. 1 (February 2005), pp. 28–49; E.C. Dierdorff and E.A. Surface, "If You Pay for Skills, Will They Learn? Skill Change and Maintenance under a Skill-Based Pay System," *Journal of Management* 34, no. 4 (August 2008), pp. 721–743.

18. Zingheim and Schuster, "Competencies and Rewards"; F. Giancola, "Skill-Based Pay–Issues for Consideration," *Benefits & Compensation Digest* 44, no. 5 (2007), pp. 1–15.

19. E.B. Peach and D.A. Wren, "Pay for Performance from Antiquity to the 1950s," *Journal of Organizational Behavior Management* (1992), pp. 5–26.

20. L. Spiers, "Piece by Piecemeal," *Lawn & Landscape Magazine,* 5 August 2003; C. Petrie, "PCCW Puts the Focus on Rewarding Staff," *South China Morning Post* (Hong Kong), 17 July 2004, p. 4; H.-H. Pai, "'Our Eyes Have Been Opened to the Abuse'," *The Guardian* (London), 29 April 2006, p. 2.

21. "Using Incentive Plans Wisely," *Receivables Report for America's Health Care Financial Managers* 23, no. 6 (2008), pp. 9–11.

22. G. Hamel, *The Future of Management* (Boston: Harvard Business School Press, 2007), pp. 73–75.

23. J.D. Ketcham and M.F. Furukawa, "Hospital-Physician Gainsharing in Cardiology," *Health Affairs* 27, no. 3 (2008), pp. 803–812.

24. L.R. Gomez-Mejia, T.M. Welbourne, and R.M. Wiseman, "The Role of Risk Sharing and Risk Taking under Gainsharing," *Academy of Management Review* 25 (July 2000), pp. 492–507; K.M. Bartol and A. Srivastava, "Encouraging Knowledge Sharing: The Role of Organizational Reward Systems," *Journal of Leadership & Organizational Studies* 9 (Summer 2002), pp. 64–76.

25. V.L. Parker, "Org Charts Turn Around with Teams," *News & Observer* (Raleigh, NC), 21 July 2005, p. D1; N. Byrnes and M. Arndt, "The Art of Motivation," *BusinessWeek,* 1 May 2006, p. 56; M. Bolch, "Rewarding the Team," *HRMagazine,* February 2007, pp. 91–93; P. Glader, "Nucor Bets on Growth in North America," *Wall Street Journal,* 3 January 2007, p. A3.

26. J. Berg, "Hard-Earned Rewards Boost Team Spirit," *njbiz* 19, no. 18 (May 2006), pp. 22–22.

27. C. Rosen, J. Case, and M. Staubus, "Every Employee an Owner [Really]," *Harvard Business Review* 83, no. 6 (June 2005), pp. 122–130; R.A. Wirtz, "Employee Ownership: Economic Miracle or ESOPs Fable?" *The Region* (Magazine of the Federal Reserve Bank of Minneapolis), June 2007, pp. 22–41.

28. K.K. Spors, "Top Small Workplaces 2007: What Makes a Great Workplace?" *Wall Street Journal,* 1 October 2007, p. R1.

29. J. Chelius and R.S. Smith, "Profit Sharing and Employment Stability," *Industrial and Labor Relations Review* 43 (1990), pp. 256s–273s; S.H. Wagner, C.P. Parker, and N.D. Christiansen, "Employees That Think and Act Like Owners: Effects of Ownership Beliefs and Behaviors on Organizational Effectiveness," *Personnel Psychology* 56, no. 4 (Winter 2003), pp. 847–871; G. Ledford, M. Lucy, and P. LeBlanc, "The Effects of Stock Ownership on Employee Attitudes and Behavior: Evidence from the Rewards of Work Studies," *Perspectives* (Sibson), January 2004.

30. A.J. Maggs, "Enron, ESOPs, and Fiduciary Duty," *Benefits Law Journal* 16, no. 3 (Autumn 2003), pp. 42–52; C. Brodzinski, "ESOP's Fables Can Make Coverage Risky," *National Underwriter P & C,* 13 June 2005, pp. 16–17.

31. J. Pfeffer, *The Human Equation* (Boston: Harvard Business School Press, 1998); B.N. Pfau and I.T. Kay, *The Human Capital Edge* (New York: McGraw-Hill, 2002); D. Guest, N. Conway, and P. Dewe, "Using Sequential Tree Analysis to Search for 'Bundles' of HR Practices," *Human Resource Management Journal* 14, no. 1 (2004), pp. 79–96. The problems with performance-based pay are discussed in W.C. Hammer, "How to Ruin Motivation with Pay," *Compensation Review* 7, no. 3 (1975), pp. 17–27; A. Kohn, *Punished by Rewards* (Boston: Houghton Mifflin, 1993); M. O'Donnell and J. O'Brian, "Performance-Based Pay in the Australian Public Service," *Review of Public Personnel Administration* 20 (Spring 2000), pp. 20–34; M. Beer and M.D. Cannon, "Promise and Peril of Implementing Pay-for-Performance," *Human Resource Management* 43, no. 1 (Spring 2004), pp. 3–48.

32. M. Buckingham and D.O. Clifton, *Now, Discover Your Strengths* (New York: Free Press, 2001).

33. S. Kerr, "Organization Rewards: Practical, Cost-Neutral Alternatives That You May Know, but Don't Practice," *Organizational Dynamics* 28 (Summer 1999), pp. 61–70.

34. J.S. DeMatteo, L.T. Eby, and E. Sundstrom, "Team-Based Rewards: Current Empirical Evidence and Directions for Future Research," *Research in Organizational Behavior* 20 (1998), pp. 141–183; S. Rynes, B. Gerhart, and L. Parks, "Personnel Psychology: Performance Evaluation and Pay for Performance," *Annual Review of Psychology* 56 (2005), pp. 571–600.

35. "Dream Teams," *Human Resources Professional* (November 1994), pp. 17–19.

36. "There's Only One Lesson to Learn from UBS," *Euromoney,* May 2008, p. 9; *Shareholder Report on UBS's Write-Downs* (Zurich, Switzerland: UBS, 18 April 2008); U. Harnischfeger, "UBS Says Excess of Ambition Led to Its Miscues on Subprime Loans," *New York Times,* 22 April 2008, p. C3; S. Reed, "Behind the Mess at UBS," *BusinessWeek,* no. 4073 (3 March 2008), pp. 30–31.

37. H. Connon, "Overhyped, Overpaid and Overextended," *The Observer* (London), 20 March 2005, p. 4; J. Harris and P. Bromiley, "Incentives to Cheat: The Influence of Executive Compensation and Firm Performance on Financial Misrepresentation," *Organization Science* 18, no. 3 (May 2007), pp. 350–367.

38. E.E. Lawler III, *High-Involvement Management* (San Francisco: Jossey-Bass, 1986), p. 120.

39. A. Holecek, "Griffith, Ind., Native Takes over as Steel Plant Manager," *Northwest Indiana Times* (Munster, IN), 25 May 2003.

40. F.F. Reichheld, *The Loyalty Effect* (Boston: Harvard Business School Press, 1996), p. 236.

41. D.R. Spitzer, "Power Rewards: Rewards That Really Motivate," *Management Review* (May 1996), pp. 45–50. For a classic discussion on the unintended consequences of pay, see S. Kerr, "On the Folly of Rewarding A, While Hoping for B," *Academy of Management Journal* 18 (1975), pp. 769–783.

42. "Strong Leaders Make Great Workplaces," *CityBusiness,* 28 August 2000; P.M. Perry, "Holding Your Top Talent," *Research Technology Management* 44 (May 2001), pp. 26–30.

43. J.R. Edwards, J.A. Scully, and M.D. Brtek, "The Nature and Outcomes of Work: A Replication and Extension of Interdisciplinary Work-Design Research," *Journal of Applied Psychology* 85, no. 6 (2000), pp. 860–868; F.P. Morgeson and M.A. Campion, "Minimizing Tradeoffs When Redesigning Work: Evidence from a Longitudinal Quasi-Experiment," *Personnel Psychology* 55, no. 3 (Autumn 2002), pp. 589–612.

44. P. Siekman, "This Is Not a BMW Plant," *Fortune,* 18 April 2005, p. 208.

45. H. Fayol, *General and Industrial Management,* trans. C. Storrs (London: Pitman, 1949); E.E. Lawler III, *Motivation in Work Organizations* (Monterey, CA: Brooks/Cole, 1973), chap. 7; M.A. Campion, "Ability Requirement Implications of Job Design: An Interdisciplinary Perspective," *Personnel Psychology* 42 (1989), pp. 1–24.

46. F.C. Lane, *Venice: A Maritime Republic* (Baltimore: Johns Hopkins University Press, 1973), pp. 361–364; R.C. Davis, "Arsenal and *Arsenalotti:* Workplace and Community in Seventeenth-Century Venice," in *The Workplace before the Factory,* ed. T.M. Safley and L.N. Rosenband (Ithaca, NY: Cornell University Press, 1993), pp. 180–203.

47. A. Smith, *An Inquiry into the Nature and Causes of the Wealth of Nations,* 5th ed. (London: Methuen, 1904), pp. 8–9.

48. F.W. Taylor, *The Principles of Scientific Management* (New York: Harper & Row, 1911); R. Kanigel, *The One Best Way: Frederick Winslow Taylor and the Enigma of Efficiency* (New York: Viking, 1997).

49. C.R. Walker and R.H. Guest, *The Man on the Assembly Line* (Cambridge, MA: Harvard University Press, 1952); W.F. Dowling, "Job Redesign on the Assembly Line: Farewell to Blue-Collar Blues?" *Organizational Dynamics,* Autumn 1973, pp. 51–67; Lawler III, *High-Involvement Management.*

50. M. Keller, *Rude Awakening* (New York: Harper Perennial, 1989), p. 128.

51. F. Herzberg, B. Mausner, and B.B. Snyderman, *The Motivation to Work* (New York: Wiley, 1959).

52. S.K. Parker, T.D. Wall, and J.L. Cordery, "Future Work Design Research and Practice: Towards an Elaborated Model of Work Design," *Journal of Occupational and Organizational Psychology* 74 (November 2001), pp. 413–440. For a decisive critique of motivator-hygiene theory, see N. King, "Clarification and Evaluation of the TwoFactor Theory of Job Satisfaction," *Psychological Bulletin* 74 (1970), pp. 18–31.

53. J.R. Hackman and G. Oldham, *Work Redesign* (Reading, MA: Addison-Wesley, 1980).

54. D. Whitford, "A Human Place to Work," *Fortune,* 8 January 2001, pp. 108–119.

55. C. Hosford, "Flying High" (cover story), *Incentive* 181, no. 12 (December 2007), pp. 14–20; C. Hosford, "Training Programs Benefit Rolls-Royce," *B to B,* 16 July 2007, p. 14.

56. J.E. Champoux, "A Multivariate Test of the Job Characteristics Theory of Work Motivation," *Journal of Organizational Behavior* 12, no. 5 (September 1991), pp. 431–446; R.B. Tiegs, L.E. Tetrick, and Y. Fried, "Growth Need Strength and Context

Satisfactions as Moderators of the Relations of the Job Characteristics Model," *Journal of Management* 18, no. 3 (September 1992), pp. 575–593.

57. "Region Positioned among DCX Leaders in Advanced Manufacturing," *Toledo Business Journal,* August 2004, p. 1; M. Connelly, "Chrysler Boosts Belvidere Flexibility," *Automotive News,* 13 February 2006, p. 44.

58. M.A. Campion and C.L. McClelland, "Follow-Up and Extension of the Interdisciplinary Costs and Benefits of Enlarged Jobs," *Journal of Applied Psychology* 78 (1993), pp. 339–351; N.G. Dodd and D.C. Ganster, "The Interactive Effects of Variety, Autonomy, and Feedback on Attitudes and Performance," *Journal of Organizational Behavior* 17 (1996), pp. 329–347.

59. J.R. Hackman et al., "A New Strategy for Job Enrichment," *California Management Review* 17, no. 4 (1975), pp. 57–71; R.W. Griffin, *Task Design: An Integrative Approach* (Glenview, IL: Scott Foresman, 1982).

60. P.E. Spector and S.M. Jex, "Relations of Job Characteristics from Multiple Data Sources with Employee Affect, Absence, Turnover Intentions, and Health," *Journal of Applied Psychology* 76 (1991), pp. 46–53; P. Osterman, "How Common Is Workplace Transformation and Who Adopts It?" *Industrial and Labor Relations Review* 47 (1994), pp. 173–188; R. Saavedra and S.K. Kwun, "Affective States in Job Characteristics Theory," *Journal of Organizational Behavior* 21 (2000), pp. 131–146.

61. Hackman and Oldham, *Work Redesign,* pp. 137–138.

62. A. Hertting et al., "Personnel Reductions and Structural Changes in Health Care: Work–Life Experiences of Medical Secretaries," *Journal of Psychosomatic Research* 54 (February 2003), pp. 161–170.

63. "Running a Business: Managing a Handelsbanken Branch," *A View from the Top* (Handelsbanken Maidstone newsletter), Winter 2007, p. 1; "The Sunday Times 100 Best Companies to Work For 2008" (Chester, UK: Svenska Handelsbanken, 10 March 2008), www.handelsbanken.co.uk (accessed 11 September 2008).

64. This definition is based mostly on G.M. Spreitzer and R.E. Quinn, *A Company of Leaders: Five Disciplines for Unleashing the Power in Your Workforce* (San Francisco: Jossey-Bass, 2001). However, most elements of this definition appear in other discussions of empowerment. See, for example, R. Forrester, "Empowerment: Rejuvenating a Potent Idea," *Academy of Management Executive* 14 (August 2000), pp. 67–80; W.A. Randolph, "Re-thinking Empowerment: Why Is It So Hard to Achieve?" *Organizational Dynamics* 29 (November 2000), pp. 94–107; S.T. Menon, "Employee Empowerment: An Integrative Psychological Approach," *Applied Psychology: An International Review* 50 (2001), pp. 153–180.

65. The positive relationship between these structural empowerment conditions and psychological empowerment is reported in H.K.S. Laschinger et al., "A Longitudinal Analysis of the Impact of Workplace Empowerment on Work Satisfaction," *Journal of Organizational Behavior* 25, no. 4 (June 2004), pp. 527–545.

66. C.S. Koberg et al., "Antecedents and Outcomes of Empowerment," *Group and Organization Management* 24 (1999), pp. 71–91; Y. Melhem, "The Antecedents of Customer-Contact Employees' Empowerment," *Employee Relations* 26, no. 1–2 (2004), pp. 72–93.

67. B.J. Niehoff et al., "The Influence of Empowerment and Job Enrichment on Employee Loyalty in a Downsizing Environment," *Group and Organization Management* 26 (March 2001), pp. 93–113; J. Yoon, "The Role of Structure and Motivation for Workplace Empowerment: The Case of Korean Employees," *Social Psychology Quarterly* 64 (June 2001), pp. 195–206; T.D. Wall, J.L. Cordery, and C.W. Clegg, "Empowerment, Performance, and Operational Uncertainty: A Theoretical Integration," *Applied Psychology: An International Review* 51 (2002), pp. 146–169.

68. R. Semler, *The Seven-Day Weekend* (London: Century, 2003); L.M. Fisher, "Ricardo Semler Won't Take Control," *strategy1business,* no. 41 (Winter 2005), pp. 1–11; "Concept of Managerial Control 'Is an Illusion'–Semler," *All Africa* (Johannesburg), 28 August 2007.

69. G.M. Spreitzer, "Social Structural Characteristics of Psychological Empowerment," *Academy of Management Journal* 39 (April 1996), pp. 483–504; J. Godard, "High Performance and the Transformation of Work? The Implications of Alternative Work Practices for the Experience and Outcomes of Work," *Industrial & Labor Relations Review* 54 (July 2001), pp. 776–805; P.A. Miller, P. Goddard, and H.K. Spence Laschinger, "Evaluating Physical Therapists' Perception of Empowerment Using Kanter's Theory of Structural Power in Organizations," *Physical Therapy* 81 (December 2001), pp. 1880–1888.

70. J.-C. Chebat and P. Kollias, "The Impact of Empowerment on Customer Contact Employees' Role in Service Organizations," *Journal of Service Research* 3 (August 2000), pp. 66–81; H.K.S. Laschinger, J. Finegan, and J. Shamian, "The Impact of Workplace Empowerment, Organizational Trust on Staff Nurses' Work Satisfaction and Organizational Commitment," *Health Care Management Review* 26 (Summer 2001), pp. 7–23.

71. G. Hohmann, "Bayer to Add 24 Jobs at Institute," *Charleston Gazette,* 6 August 2008, p. P1A.

72. P. Mannion, "Never Lose Focus," *Electronic Engineering Times,* 30 May 2005, p. 1; "Bosses Love Team Workers," *Lancashire Evening Post* (UK), 25 May 2006.

73. C.P. Neck and C.C. Manz, "Thought Self-Leadership: The Impact of Mental Strategies Training on Employee Cognition, Behavior, and Affect," *Journal of Organizational Behavior* 17 (1996), pp. 445–467.

74. C.C. Manz, "Self-Leadership: Toward an Expanded Theory of Self-Influence Processes in Organizations," *Academy of Management Review* 11 (1986), pp. 585–600; C.C. Manz and C. Neck, *Mastering Self-Leadership,* 3d ed. (Upper Saddle River, NJ: Prentice Hall, 2004); C.P. Neck and J.D. Houghton, "Two Decades of Self-Leadership Theory and Research," *Journal of Managerial Psychology* 21, no. 4 (2006), pp. 270–295.

75. O.J. Strickland and M. Galimba, "Managing Time: The Effects of Personal Goal Setting on Resource Allocation Strategy and Task Performance," *Journal of Psychology* 135 (July 2001), pp. 357–367.

76. R.M. Duncan and J.A. Cheyne, "Incidence and Functions of Self-Reported Private Speech in Young Adults: A Self-Verbalization Questionnaire," *Canadian Journal of Behavioral Science* 31 (April 1999), pp. 133–136.

77. J.E. Driscoll, C. Copper, and A. Moran, "Does Mental Practice Enhance Performance?" *Journal of Applied Psychology* 79 (1994), pp. 481–492; C.P. Neck, G.L. Stewart, and C.C. Manz, "Thought Self-Leadership as a Framework for Enhancing the Performance of Performance Appraisers," *Journal of Applied Behavioral Science* 31 (September 1995), pp. 278–302. Some research separates mental imagery from mental practice, whereas most studies combine both into one concept.

78. A. Joyce, "Office Perks: Re-energize to Get through the Blahs," *Washington Post,* 28 August 2005, p. F05.

79. A. Wrzesniewski and J.E. Dutton, "Crafting a Job: Revisioning Employees as Active Crafters of Their Work," *Academy of Management Review* 26 (April 2001), pp. 179–201.

80. M.I. Bopp, S.J. Glynn, and R.A. Henning, *Self-Management of Performance Feedback during Computer-Based Work by Individuals and Two-Person Work Teams,* paper presented at the APA-NIOSH conference, March 1999.

81. A.W. Logue, *Self-Control: Waiting until Tomorrow for What You Want Today* (Englewood Cliffs, NJ: Prentice Hall, 1995).

82. Neck and Manz, "Thought Self-Leadership"; A.M. Saks and B.E. Ashforth, "Proactive Socialization and Behavioral Self-Management," *Journal of Vocational Behavior* 48 (1996), pp. 301–323; L. Morin and G. Latham, "The Effect of Mental Practice and Goal Setting as a Transfer of Training Intervention on Supervisors' Self-Efficacy and Communication Skills: An Exploratory Study," *Applied Psychology: An International Review* 49 (July 2000), pp. 566–578; J.S. Hickman and E.S. Geller, "A Safety Self-Management Intervention for Mining Operations," *Journal of Safety Research* 34 (2003), pp. 299–308.

83. S. Ming and G.L. Martin, "Single-Subject Evaluation of a Self-Talk Package for Improving Figure Skating Performance," *Sport Psychologist* 10 (1996), pp. 227–238; J. Bauman, "The Gold Medal Mind," *Psychology Today* 33 (May 2000), pp. 62–69; L.J. Rogerson and D.W. Hrycaiko, "Enhancing Competitive Performance of Ice Hockey Goaltenders Using Centering and Self-Talk," *Journal of Applied Sport Psychology* 14, no. 1 (2002), pp. 14–26; A. Papaioannou et al., "Combined Effect of Goal Setting and Self-Talk in Performance of a Soccer-Shooting Task," *Perceptual and Motor Skills* 98, no. 1 (February 2004), pp. 89–99; R.A. Hamilton, D. Scott, and M.P. MacDougall, "Assessing the Effectiveness of Self-Talk Interventions on Endurance Performance," *Journal of Applied Sport Psychology* 19, no. 2 (2007), pp. 226–239. For a review of the self-talk research, including limitations of this self-leadership strategy, see J. Hardy, "Speaking Clearly: A Critical Review of the Self-Talk Literature," *Psychology of Sport and Exercise* 7 (2006), pp. 81–97.

84. S. Williams, "Personality and Self-Leadership," *Human Resource Management Review* 7, no. 2 (1997), pp. 139–155; J. Houghton et al., "The Relationship between Self-Leadership and Personality: A Comparison of Hierarchical Factor Structure," *Journal of Managerial Psychology* 19, no. 4 (2004), pp. 427–441; R.W. Renn et al, "The Roles of Personality and Self-Defeating Behaviors in Self-Management Failure," *Journal of Management* 31, no. 5 (2005), pp. 659–679.

85. J.D. Houghton and S.K. Yoho, "Toward a Contingency Model of Leadership and Psychological Empowerment: When Should Self-Leadership Be Encouraged?" *Journal of Leadership & Organizational Studies* 11, no. 4 (2005), pp. 65–83; J.D. Houghton and D.L. Jinkerson, "Constructive Thought Strategies and Job Satisfaction: A Preliminary Examination," *Journal of Business and Psychology* 22 (2007), pp. 45–53.

Chapter 7

1. N. Cohen, "Google's Lunchtime Betting Game," *New York Times,* 7 January 2008, p. 4; R. Dye, "The Promise of Prediction Markets: A Roundtable," *McKinsey Quarterly,* April 2008, pp. 82–93; A. Fawcett, "Job Searchers," Sydney Morning Herald, 5 April 2008, p. 5; M. Helft, "The Human Hands behind the Google Money Machine," *New York Times,* 2 June 2008, p. 1; B. Iyer and T.H. Davenport, "Reverse Engineering Google's Innovation Machine," *Harvard Business Review* 86, no. 4 (2008), pp. 58–68; V. Khanna, "The Voice of Google," *Business Times Singapore,* 12 January 2008.

2. "Google: Inside the Googleplex," *The Economist,* 10 September 2007, p. 1; Iyer and Davenport, "Reverse Engineering Google's Innovation Machine."

3. F.A. Shull Jr., A.L. Delbecq, and L.L. Cummings, *Organizational Decision Making* (New York: McGraw-Hill, 1970), p. 31.

4. R.E. Nisbett, *The Geography of Thought: How Asians and Westerners Think Differently–and Why* (New York: Free Press, 2003); R. Hanna, "Kant's Theory of Judgment," *Stanford Encyclopedia of Philosophy,* 2004, http://plato.stanford.edu/entries/kant-judgment/

(accessed 31 March 2008); D. Baltzly, “Stoicism,” *Stanford Encyclopedia of Philosophy,* 2008, http://plato.stanford.edu/entries/stoicism/ (accessed 30 March 2008).

5. J.G. March and H.A. Simon, *Organizations* (New York: Wiley, 1958).

6. This model is adapted from several sources, including H.A. Simon, *The New Science of Management Decision* (New York: Harper & Row, 1960); H. Mintzberg, D. Raisinghani, and A. Théorêt, “The Structure of ‘Unstructured’ Decision Processes,” *Administrative Science Quarterly* 21 (1976), pp. 246–275; W.C. Wedley and R.H.G. Field, “A Predecision Support System,” *Academy of Management Review* 9 (1984), pp. 696–703.

7. P.F. Drucker, *The Practice of Management* (New York: Harper & Brothers, 1954), pp. 353–357; B.M. Bass, *Organizational Decision Making* (Homewood, IL: Irwin, 1983), chap. 3.

8. L.R. Beach and T.R. Mitchell, “A Contingency Model for the Selection of Decision Strategies,” *Academy of Management Review* 3 (1978), pp. 439–449; I.L. Janis, *Crucial Decisions* (New York: Free Press, 1989), pp. 35–37; W. Zhongtuo, “Meta-Decision Making: Concepts and Paradigm,” *Systematic Practice and Action Research* 13, no. 1 (February 2000), pp. 111–115.

9. N. Schwarz, “Social Judgment and Attitudes: Warmer, More Social, and Less Conscious,” *European Journal of Social Psychology* 30 (2000), pp. 149–176; N.M. Ashkanasy and C.E.J. Hartel, “Managing Emotions in Decision-Making,” in *Managing Emotions in the Workplace,* ed. N.M. Ashkanasy, W.J. Zerbe, and C.E.J. Hartel (Armonk, NY: Sharpe, 2002); S. Maitlis and H. Ozcelik, “Toxic Decision Processes: A Study of Emotion and Organizational Decision Making,” *Organization Science* 15, no. 4 (July–August 2004), pp. 375–393.

10. A. Howard, “Opinion,” *Computing* (8 July 1999), p. 18.

11. A.R. Damasio, *Descartes’ Error: Emotion, Reason, and the Human Brain* (New York: Putnam Sons, 1994); P. Winkielman and K.C. Berridge, “Unconscious Emotion,” *Current Directions in Psychological Science* 13, no. 3 (2004), pp. 120–123, [illegible]echara and A.R. Damasio, “The Somatic Marker Hypothesis: A Neural Theory of Economic Decision,” *Games and Economic Behavior* 52, no. 2 (2005), pp. 336–372.

12. T.K. Das and B.S. Teng, “Cognitive Biases and Strategic Decision Processes: An Integrative Perspective,” *Journal of Management Studies* 36, no. 6 (November 1999), pp. 757–778; P. Bijttebier, H. Vextommen, and G.V. Steene, “Assessment of Cognitive Coping Styles: A Closer Look at Situation-Response Inventories,” *Clinical Psychology Review* 21, no. 1 (2001), pp. 85–104; P.C. Nutt, “Expanding the Search for Alternatives during Strategic Decision-Making,” *Academy of Management Executive* 18, no. 4 (November 2004), pp. 13–28.

13. J. Brandtstadter, A. Voss, and K. Rothermund, “Perception of Danger Signals: The Role of Control,” *Experimental Psychology* 51, no. 1 (2004), pp. 24–32; M. Hock and H.W. Krohne, “Coping with Threat and Memory for Ambiguous Information: Testing the Repressive Discontinuity Hypothesis,” *Emotion* 4, no. 1 (2004), pp. 65–86.

14. “NASA Managers Differed over Shuttle Strike,” *Reuters,* 22 July 2003; Columbia Accident Investigation Board, *Report,* Vol. 1 (Washington, DC: Government Printing Office, August 2003); C. Gibson, “*Columbia:* The Final Mission,” *NineMSN,* 13 July 2003; S. Jefferson, “NASA Let Arrogance on Board,” *Palm Beach Post,* 30 August 2003; R.J. Smith, “NASA Culture, *Columbia* Probers Still Miles Apart,” *Washington Post,* 22 August 2003, p. A3.

15. O.W. Linzmayer, *Apple Confidential 2.0: The Definitive Story of the World’s Most Colorful Company* (San Francisco: No Starch Press, 2004), pp. 109–114.

16. P.C. Nutt, *Why Decisions Fail* (San Francisco: Berrett-Koehler, 2002); S. Finkelstein, *Why Smart Executives Fail* (New York: Viking, 2003).

17. E. Witte, “Field Research on Complex Decision-Making Processes–The Phase Theorum,” *International Studies of Management and Organization* 56 (1972), pp. 156–182; J.A. Bargh and T.L. Chartrand, “The Unbearable Automaticity of Being,” *American Psychologist* 54, no. 7 (July 1999), pp. 462–479.

18. R. Rothenberg, “Ram Charan: The Thought Leader Interview,” *strategy 1 business,* Fall 2004.

19. “Over the Last Ten Years, Google Has Become a Poster Child,” *Computer Weekly,* 9 September 2008, p. 188.

20. H.A. Simon, *Administrative Behavior,* 2d ed. (New York: Free Press, 1957); H.A. Simon, “Rational Decision Making in Business Organizations,” *American Economic Review* 69, no. 4 (September 1979), pp. 493–513.

21. D. Sandahl and C. Hewes, “Decision Making at Digital Speed,” *Pharmaceutical Executive* 21 (August 2001), p. 62.

22. Simon, *Administrative Behavior,* pp. xxv, 80–84.

23. P.O. Soelberg, “Unprogrammed Decision Making,” *Industrial Management Review* 8 (1967), pp. 19–29; J.E. Russo, V.H. Medvec, and M.G. Meloy, “The Distortion of Information during Decisions,” *Organizational Behavior and Human Decision Processes* 66 (1996), pp. 102–110. This is consistent with the observations by Milton Rokeach, who famously stated, “Life is ipsative, because decisions in everyday life are inherently and phenomenologically ipsative decisions.” M. Rokeach, “Inducing Changes and Stability in Belief Systems and Personality Structures,” *Journal of Social Issues* 41, no. 1 (1985), pp. 153–171.

24. A.L. Brownstein, "Biased Predecision Processing," *Psychological Bulletin* 129, no. 4 (2003), pp. 545–568.

25. T. Gilovich, D. Griffin, and D. Kahneman, *Heuristics and Biases: The Psychology of Intuitive Judgment* (Cambridge, UK: Cambridge University Press, 2002); D. Kahneman, "Maps of Bounded Rationality: Psychology for Behavioral Economics," *American Economic Review* 93, no. 5 (December 2003), pp. 1449–1475.

26. A. Tversky and D. Kahneman, "Judgment under Uncertainty: Heuristics and Biases," *Science* 185, no. 4157 (27 September 1974), pp. 1124–1131; I. Ritov, "Anchoring in Simulated Competitive Market Negotiation," *Organizational Behavior and Human Decision Processes* 67, no. 1 (1996), p. 16; D. Ariely, G. Loewenstein, and A. Prelec, "Coherent Arbitrariness": Stable Demand Curves without Stable Preferences," *Quarterly Journal of Economics* 118 (2003), p. 73; N. Epley and T. Gilovich, "Are Adjustments Insufficient?" *Personality and Social Psychology Bulletin* 30, no. 4 (April 2004), pp. 447–460; J.D. Jasper and S.D. Christman, "A Neuropsychological Dimension for Anchoring Effects," *Journal of Behavioral Decision Making* 18 (2005), pp. 343–369; S.D. Bond et al., "Information Distortion in the Evaluation of a Single Option," *Organizational Behavior and Human Decision Processes* 102 (2007), pp. 240–254.

27. A. Tversky and D. Kahneman, "Availability: A Heuristic for Judging Frequency and Probability," *Cognitive Psychology* 5 (1973), pp. 207–232.

28. D. Kahneman and A. Tversky, "Subjective Probability: A Judgment of Representativeness," *Cognitive Psychology* 3, no. 3 (1972), p. 430; T. Gilovich, *How We Know What Isn't So: The Fallibility of Human Reason in Everyday Life* (New York: Free Press, 1991); B.D. Burns, "Heuristics as Beliefs and as Behaviors: The Adaptiveness of the 'Hot Hand,'" *Cognitive Psychology* 48 (2004), pp. 295–331; E.M. Altmann and B.D. Burns, "Streak Biases in Decision Making: Data and a Memory Model," *Cognitive Systems Research* 6, no. 1 (2005), p. 5.

29. H.A. Simon, "Rational Choice and the Structure of Environments," *Psychological Review* 63 (1956), pp. 129–138.

30. S. Botti and S.S. Iyengar, "The Dark Side of Choice: When Choice Impairs Social Welfare," *Journal of Public Policy and Marketing* 25, no. 1 (2006), pp. 24–38; K.D. Vohs et al., "Making Choices Impairs Subsequent Self-Control: A Limited-Resource Account of Decision Making, Self-Regulation, and Active Initiative," *Journal of Personality and Social Psychology* 94, no. 5 (2008), pp. 883–898.

31. S.S. Iyengar and M.R. Lepper, "When Choice Is Demotivating: Can One Desire Too Much of a Good Thing?" *Journal of Personality and Social Psychology* 79, no. 6 (2000), pp. 995–1006.

32. A. Tofler, *Future Shock* (New York: Random House, 1970), p. 264.

33. S.S. Iyengar, G. Huberman, and W. Jiang, "How Much Choice Is Too Much? Contributions to 401(K) Retirement Plans," in *Pension Design and Structure: New Lessons from Behavioral Finance,* ed. O. Mitchell and S. Utkas (Oxford, UK: Oxford University Press, 2004), pp. 83–95; J. Beshears et al., "Simplification and Saving," 2006, http://ssrn.com/paper=1086462; J. Choi, D. Laibson, and B. Madrian, *Reducing the Complexity Costs of 401(K) Participation through Quick Enrollment* (National Bureau of Economic Research, January 2006).

34. P.C. Nutt, "Search during Decision Making," *European Journal of Operational Research* 160 (2005), pp. 851–876.

35. P. Winkielman et al., "Affective Influence on Judgments and Decisions: Moving Towards Core Mechanisms," *Review of General Psychology* 11, no. 2 (2007), pp. 179–192.

36. J.P. Forgas, "Affective Intelligence: Towards Understanding the Role of Affect in Social Thinking and Behavior," in *Emotional Intelligence in Everyday Life,* ed. J.V. Ciarrochi, J.P. Forgas, and J.D. Mayer (New York: Psychology Press, 2001), pp. 46–65; J.P. Forgas and J.M. George, "Affective Influences on Judgments and Behavior in Organizations: An Information Processing Perspective," *Organizational Behavior and Human Decision Processes* 86 (September 2001), pp. 3–34; G. Loewenstein and J.S. Lerner, "The Role of Affect in Decision Making," in *Handbook of Affective Sciences,* ed. R.J. Davidson, K.R. Scherer, and H.H. Goldsmith (New York: Oxford University Press, 2003), pp. 619–642; J.S. Lerner, D.A. Small, and G. Loewenstein, "Heart Strings and Purse Strings: Carryover Effects of Emotions on Economic Decisions," *Psychological Science* 15, no. 5 (2004), pp. 337–341; M.T. Pham, "Emotion and Rationality: A Critical Review and Interpretation of Empirical Evidence," *Review of General Psychology* 11, no. 2 (2007), pp. 155–178.

37. M.T. Pham, "The Logic of Feeling," *Journal of Consumer Psychology* 14 (September 2004), pp. 360–369; N. Schwarz, "Metacognitive Experiences in Consumer Judgment and Decision Making," *Journal of Consumer Psychology* 14 (September 2004), pp. 332–349.

38. L. Sjöberg, "Intuitive vs. Analytical Decision Making: Which Is Preferred?" *Scandinavian Journal of Management* 19 (2003), pp. 17–29.

39. M. Lyons, "Cave-In Too Close for Comfort, Miner Says," *Saskatoon StarPhoenix,* 6 May 2002.

40. W.H. Agor, "The Logic of Intuition," *Organizational Dynamics* (Winter 1986), pp. 5–18; H.A. Simon, "Making Management Decisions: The Role of Intuition and Emotion," *Academy of Management Executive,* February 1987, pp. 57–64; O. Behling and N.L. Eckel, "Making Sense out of Intuition," *Academy of Management Executive* 5 (February 1991), pp. 46–54. This process is also known as naturalistic decision making. For a discussion of research on naturalistic decision making, see the special issue in *Organization*

Studies: R. Lipshitz, G. Klein, and J.S. Carroll, "Introduction to the Special Issue: Naturalistic Decision Making and Organizational Decision Making: Exploring the Intersections," *Organization Studies* 27, no. 7 (2006), pp. 917–923.

41. M.D. Lieberman, "Intuition: A Social Cognitive Neuroscience Approach," *Psychological Bulletin* 126 (2000), pp. 109–137; G. Klein, *Intuition at Work* (New York: Currency/Doubleday, 2003); E. Dane and M.G. Pratt, "Exploring Intuition and Its Role in Managerial Decision Making," *Academy of Management Review* 32, no. 1 (2007), pp. 33–54.

42. Klein, *Intuition at Work*, pp. 12–13, 16–17.

43. Y. Ganzach, A.N. Kluger, and N. Klayman, "Making Decisions from an Interview: Expert Measurement and Mechanical Combination," *Personnel Psychology* 53 (Spring 2000), pp. 1–20; A.M. Hayashi, "When to Trust Your Gut," *Harvard Business Review* 79 (February 2001), pp. 59–65. Evidence of high failure rates from quick decisions is reported in Nutt, *Why Decisions Fail;* Nutt, "Search during Decision Making"; P.C. Nutt, "Investigating the Success of Decision Making Processes," *Journal of Management Studies* 45, no. 2 (March 2008), pp. 425–455.

44. P. Goodwin and G. Wright, "Enhancing Strategy Evaluation in Scenario Planning: A Role for Decision Analysis," *Journal of Management Studies* 38 (January 2001), pp. 1–16; R. Bradfield et al., "The Origins and Evolution of Scenario Techniques in Long Range Business Planning," *Futures* 37, no. 8 (2005), pp. 795–812; G. Wright, G. Cairns, and P. Goodwin, "Teaching Scenario Planning: Lessons from Practice in Academe and Business," *European Journal of Operational Research,* in press (2008).

45. J. Pfeffer and R.I. Sutton, "Knowing 'What' to Do Is Not Enough: Turning Knowledge into Action," *California Management Review* 42, no. 1 (Fall 1999), pp. 83–108; R. Charan, C. Burke, and L. Bossidy, *Execution: The Discipline of Getting Things Done* (New York: Crown Business, 2002). The survey of managerial competencies is reported in D. Nilsen, B. Kowske, and A. Kshanika, "Managing Globally," *HRMagazine,* August 2005, 111–115.

46. R.N. Taylor, *Behavioral Decision Making* (Glenview, IL: Scott, Foresman, 1984), pp. 163–166.

47. G. Whyte, "Escalating Commitment to a Course of Action: A Reinterpretation," *Academy of Management Review* 11 (1986), pp. 311–321; J. Brockner, "The Escalation of Commitment to a Failing Course of Action: Toward Theoretical Progress," *Academy of Management Review* 17, no. 1 (January 1992), pp. 39–61.

48. J. Lorinc, "Power Failure," *Canadian Business,* November 1992, pp. 50–58; M. Fackler, "Tokyo's Newest Subway Line a Saga of Hubris, Humiliation," *Associated Press Newswires,* 20 July 1999; M. Keil and R. Montealegre, "Cutting Your Losses: Extricating Your Organization When a Big Project Goes Awry," *Sloan Management Review,* 41, no. 3 (Spring 2000), pp. 55–68; I. Swanson, "Holyrood Firms Face Grilling over Costs," *Evening News* (Edinburgh), 6 June 2003, p. 2; Lord Fraser of Carmyllie QC, *The Holyrood Inquiry* (Edinborough: Scottish Parliamentary Corporate Body, 2004).

49. F.D. Schoorman and P.J. Holahan, "Psychological Antecedents of Escalation Behavior: Effects of Choice, Responsibility, and Decision Consequences," *Journal of Applied Psychology* 81 (1996), pp. 786–793.

50. D. Collins, "Senior Officials Tried to Stop Spending," *Irish Examiner,* 5 October 2005; M. Sheehan, "Throwing Good Money after Bad," *Sunday Independent* (Dublin), 9 October 2005; "Computer System Was Budgeted at Eur9m . . . It's Cost Eur170m . . . Now Health Chiefs Want a New One," *Irish Mirror,* 7 July 2007, p. 16; E. Kennedy, "Health Boss Refuses to Ditch Ill-Fated PPARS System," *Irish Independent,* 5 February 2007.

51. G. Whyte, "Escalating Commitment in Individual and Group Decision Making: A Prospect Theory Approach," *Organizational Behavior and Human Decision Processes* 54 (1993), pp. 430–455; D.J. Sharp and S.B. Salter, "Project Escalation and Sunk Costs: A Test of the International Generalizability of Agency and Prospect Theories," *Journal of International Business Studies* 28, no. 1 (1997), pp. 101–121.

52. M. Keil, G. Depledge, and A. Rai, "Escalation: The Role of Problem Recognition and Cognitive Bias," *Decision Sciences* 38, no. 3 (August 2007), pp. 391–421.

53. J.D. Bragger et al., "When Success Breeds Failure: History, Hysteresis, and Delayed Exit Decisions," *Journal of Applied Psychology* 88, no. 1 (2003), pp. 6–14. A second logical reason for escalation, called the Martingale strategy, is described in J.A. Aloysius, "Rational Escalation of Costs by Playing a Sequence of Unfavorable Gambles: The Martingale," *Journal of Economic Behavior & Organization* 51 (2003), pp. 111–129.

54. I. Simonson and B.M. Staw, "De-escalation Strategies: A Comparison of Techniques for Reducing Commitment to Losing Courses of Action," *Journal of Applied Psychology* 77 (1992), pp. 419–426; W. Boulding, R. Morgan, and R. Staelin, "Pulling the Plug to Stop the New Product Drain," *Journal of Marketing Research,* no. 34 (1997), pp. 164–176; B.M. Staw, K.W. Koput, and S.G. Barsade, "Escalation at the Credit Window: A Longitudinal Study of Bank Executives' Recognition and Write-Off of Problem Loans," *Journal of Applied Psychology,* 82, no. 1 (1997), pp. 130–142; M. Keil and D. Robey, "Turning around Troubled Software Projects: An Exploratory Study of the Deescalation of Commitment to Failing Courses of Action," *Journal of Management Information Systems* 15 (Spring 1999), pp. 63–87.

55. D. Ghosh, "De-escalation Strategies: Some Experimental Evidence," *Behavioral Research in Accounting,* 9 (1997), pp. 88–112.

56. I. Macwhirter, "Let's Build a Parliament," *The Scotsman,* 17 July 1997, p. 19; Swanson, "Holyrood Firms Face Grilling over Costs"; Lord Fraser of Carmyllie QC, *The Holyrood Inquiry.*

57. M. Gardner, "Democratic Principles Making Businesses More Transparent," *Christian Science Monitor,* 19 March 2007, p. 13.

58. M. Fenton-O'Creevy, "Employee Involvement and the Middle Manager: Saboteur or Scapegoat?" *Human Resource Management Journal,* 11, no. 1 (2001), pp. 24–40. Also see V.H. Vroom and A.G. Jago, *The New Leadership: Managing Participation in Organizations* (Englewood Cliffs, NJ: Prentice Hall, 1988).

59. Some of the early OB writing on employee involvement includes C. Argyris, *Personality and Organization* (New York: Harper & Row, 1957); D. McGregor, *The Human Side of Enterprise* (New York: McGraw-Hill, 1960); R. Likert, *New Patterns of Management* (New York: McGraw-Hill, 1961).

60. A.G. Robinson and D.M. Schroeder, *Ideas Are Free* (San Francisco: Berrett-Koehler, 2004).

61. S.W. Crispin, "Workers' Paradise," *Far Eastern Economic Review,* 17 April 2003, pp. 40–41; "Thai Carbon Black: Worker-Driven Focus Key to Firm's Success," *The Nation* (Thailand), 3 June 2004.

62. R.J. Ely and D.A. Thomas, "Cultural Diversity at Work: The Effects of Diversity Perspectives on Work Group Processes and Outcomes," *Administrative Science Quarterly* 46 (June 2001), pp. 229–273; E. Mannix and M.A. Neale, "What Differences Make a Difference? The Promise and Reality of Diverse Teams in Organizations," *Psychologieal Science in the Public Interest* 6, no. 2 (2005), pp. 31–55.

63. D. Berend and J. Paroush, "When Is Condorcet's Jury Theorem Valid?" *Social Choice and Welfare* 15, no. 4 (1998), pp. 481–488; C.R. Sunstein, *Infotopia: How Many Minds Produce Knowledge* (Oxford, UK: Oxford University Press, 2006), chap. 1.

64. K.T. Dirks, L.L. Cummings, and J.L. Pierce, "Psychological Ownership in Organizations: Conditions under Which Individuals Promote and Resist Change," *Research in Organizational Change and Development,* no. 9 (1996), pp. 1–23; J.P. Walsh and S.-F. Tseng, "The Effects of Job Characteristics on Active Effort at Work," *Work & Occupations,* 25, no. 1 (February 1998), pp. 74–96; B. Scott-Ladd and V. Marshall, "Participation in Decision Making: A Matter of Context?" *Leadership & Organization Development Journal* 25, no. 8 (2004), pp. 646–662.

65. Thomas H. Davenport, and Jeanne G. Harris, "Automated Decision Making Comes of Age," *MIT Sloan Management Review* Summer 46:4 (2005), pp. 83–89; Thomas H. Davenport, "Competing on Analytics," *Harvard Business Review* (2006).

66. J. Zhou and C.E. Shalley, "Research on Employee Creativity: A Critical Review and Directions for Future Research," *Research in Personnel and Human Resources Management* 22 (2003), pp. 165–217; M.A. Runco, "Creativity," *Annual Review of Psychology* 55 (2004), pp. 657–687.

67. G. Wallas, *The Art of Thought* (New York: Harcourt Brace Jovanovich, 1926). For recent applications of Wallas's classic model, see T. Kristensen, "The Physical Context of Creativity," *Creativity and Innovation Management* 13, no. 2 (June 2004), pp. 89–96; U.-E. Haner, "Spaces for Creativity and Innovation in Two Established Organizations," *Creativity and Innovation Management* 14, no. 3 (2005), pp. 288–298.

68. R.S. Nickerson, "Enhancing Creativity," in *Handbook of Creativity,* ed. R.J. Sternberg (New York: Cambridge University Press, 1999), pp. 392–430.

69. R.I. Sutton, *Weird Ideas That Work* (New York: Free Press, 2002), p. 26.

70. For a thorough discussion of insight, see R.J. Sternberg and J.E. Davidson, *The Nature of Insight* (Cambridge, MA: MIT Press, 1995).

71. Jonathan S. Fienstien, *The Nature of Creative Development,* (Stanford Business Books, 2006, 572 pp).

72. Yusuf Shahid, "From Creativity to Innovation," *Technology in Society* 31 (2009), pp. 1–8.

73. Bettina Von Stamm, "What are Innovation, Creativity and Design?" In *Managing Innovation, Design and Creativity,* Bettina Von Stamm (ed), (UK: John Wiley & Sons, 2008).

74. Amabile et. Al., "Assessing the Work Environment for Creativity," *Academy of Management Journal* 39 (1996), pp. 1154–84.

75. R.J. Sternberg and L.A. O'Hara, "Creativity and Intelligence," in *Handbook of Creativity,* ed. R.J. Sternberg (New York: Cambridge University Press, 1999), pp. 251–272; S. Taggar, "Individual Creativity and Group Ability to Utilize Individual Creative Resources: A Multilevel Model," *Academy of Management Journal* 45 (April 2002), pp. 315–330.

76. S. Litt, "Church's Transformation into Business Offers Answer to Many People's Prayers," *Plain Dealer* (Cleveland), 12 September 2003, p. E1; K. Palmer, "Design of the Times," *Smart Business Cleveland,* September 2003, p. 37; M. Smith, "A New Class: They're Creative, Driven and They're Here," *Inside Business,* April 2003, p. 48; D. Trattner, "Old Church Provides Inspiration for Designers," *Plain Dealer* (Cleveland), 2 January 2006, p. E3; A. Fisher, "Ideas Made Here," *Fortune,* 11 June 2007, p. 35; M.R. Kropko, "Designing Men," *Charleston Gazette,* 5 November 2007, p. P2C; J. Morgan, Lewis, "Wizards of Wal-Mart," *Inside Business,* March 2007, p. 34; L. Taxel, "It Takes Two," *Continental In-Flight Magazine,* April 2007.

77. G.J. Feist, "The Influence of Personality on Artistic and Scientific Creativity," in *Handbook of Creativity,* ed. R.J. Sternberg (New York: Cambridge University Press, 1999), pp. 273–296; Sutton, *Weird Ideas That Work,* pp. 8–9, chap. 10; T. Åsterbro, S.A.

Jeffrey, and G.K. Adomdza, "Inventor Perseverance after Being Told to Quit: The Role of Cognitive Biases," *Journal of Behavioral Decision Making* 20 (2007), pp. 253–272.

78. R.W. Weisberg, "Creativity and Knowledge: A Challenge to Theories," in *Handbook of Creativity,* ed. R.J. Sternberg (New York: Cambridge University Press, 1999), pp. 226–250.

79. Sutton, *Weird Ideas That Work,* pp. 121, 153–154; C. Andriopoulos, "Six Paradoxes in Managing Creativity: An Embracing Act," *Long Range Planning* 36 (2003), pp. 375–388.

80. T. Koppell, *Powering the Future* (New York: Wiley, 1999), p. 15.

81. R.J. Sternberg and T.I. Lubart, *Defying the Crowd: Cultivating Creativity in a Culture of Conformity* (New York: Free Press, 1995); Feist, "The Influence of Personality on Artistic and Scientific Creativity"; S.J. Dollinger, K.K. Urban, and T.A. James, "Creativity and Openness to Experience: Validation of Two Creative Product Measures," *Creativity Research Journal* 16, no. 1 (2004), pp. 35–47; C.E. Shalley, J. Zhou, and G.R. Oldham, "The Effects of Personal and Contextual Characteristics on Creativity: Where Should We Go from Here?" *Journal of Management* 30, no. 6 (2004), pp. 933–958; T.S. Schweizer, "The Psychology of Novelty-Seeking, Creativity and Innovation: Neurocognitive Aspects within a Work-Psychological Perspective," *Creativity and Innovation Management* 15, no. 2 (2006), pp. 164–172.

82. M.D. Mumford, "Managing Creative People: Strategies and Tactics for Innovation," *Human Resource Management Review* 10 (Autumn 2000), pp. 313–351; T.M. Amabile et al., "Leader Behaviors and the Work Environment for Creativity: Perceived Leader Support," *Leadership Quarterly* 15, no. 1 (2004), pp. 5–32; Shalley, Zhou, and Oldham, "The Effects of Personal and Contextual Characteristics on Creativity"; T.C. DiLiello and J.D. Houghton, "Creative Potential and Practised Creativity: Identifying Untapped Creativity in Organizations," *Creativity and Innovation Management* 17, no. 1 (2008), pp. 37–46.

83. R. Westwood and D.R. Low, "The Multicultural Muse: Culture, Creativity and Innovation," *International Journal of Cross Cultural Management* 3, no. 2 (2003), pp. 235–259.

84. "Samsung CEO Yun Picks Google as New Role Model," *Korea Times,* 1 October 2007.

85. T.M. Amabile, "Motivating Creativity in Organizations: On Doing What You Love and Loving What You Do," *California Management Review* 40 (Fall 1997), pp. 39–58; A. Cummings and G.R. Oldham, "Enhancing Creativity: Managing Work Contexts for the High Potential Employee," *California Management Review,* 40, no. 1 (Fall 1997), pp. 22–38.

86. T.M. Amabile, "Changes in the Work Environment for Creativity during Downsizing," *Academy of Management Journal* 42 (December 1999), pp. 630–640.

87. J. Moultrie et al., "Innovation Spaces: Towards a Framework for Understanding the Role of the Physical Environment in Innovation," *Creativity & Innovation Management* 16, no. 1 (2007), pp. 53–65.

88. J.M. Howell and K. Boies, "Champions of Technological Innovation: The Influence of Contextual Knowledge, Role Orientation, Idea Generation, and Idea Promotion on Champion Emergence," *Leadership Quarterly* 15, no. 1 (2004), pp. 123–143; Shalley, Zhou, and Oldham, "The Effects of Personal and Contextual Characteristics on Creativity."

89. A. Hiam, "Obstacles to Creativity–and How You Can Remove Them," *Futurist* 32 (October 1998), pp. 30–34.

90. M.A. West, *Developing Creativity in Organizations* (Leicester, UK: BPS Books, 1997), pp. 33–35.

91. S. Hemsley, "Seeking the Source of Innovation," *Media Week,* 16 August 2005, p. 22.

92. J. Neff, "At Eureka Ranch, Execs Doff Wing Tips, Fire Up Ideas," *Advertising Age,* 9 March 1998, pp. 28–29.

93. A. Hargadon and R.I. Sutton, "Building an Innovation Factory," *Harvard Business Review* 78 (May–June 2000), pp. 157–166; T. Kelley, *The Art of Innovation* (New York: Currency Doubleday, 2001), pp. 158–162.

94. M. Burton, "Open Plan, Open Mind," *Director,* March 2005, pp. 68–72; A. Benady, "Mothers of Invention," *The Independent* (London), 27 November 2006; B. Murray, "Agency Profile: Mother London," *Ihaveanidea,* 28 January 2007, www.ihaveanidea.org.

95. K.S. Brown, "The Apple of Jonathan Ive's Eye," *Investor's Business Daily,* 19 September 2003.

Chapter 8

1. C. Fishman, "The Anarchist's Cookbook," *Fast Company,* July 2004, p. 70; J. Mackey, "Open Book Company," *Newsweek,* 28 November 2005, p. 42; D. Jacobson, "Best-Kept Secrets of the World's Best Companies: Gainsharing," *Business 2.0,* April 2006, p. 82; A. Kimball-Stanley, "Bucking the Trend in Benefits," *Providence Journal* (Rhode Island), 14 May 2006, p. H01; K. Zimbalist, "Green Giant," *Time,* 24 April 2006, p. 24.

2. "Interview: David Bryce–Part 3 of 3," *Service Untitled,* 13 October 2006, www.serviceuntitled.com/interview-david-bryce-part-3-of-3/2006/10/13/; D. Hechler, "Teamwork Is Job One at Ford," *Fulton County Daily Report* (Atlanta), 16 May 2006, p. 16; "Mayor Announces Plan to Reduce Pot-Hole Wait Times to Two Days," *US Fed News,* 7 August 2008; T. Tan, "Playing to Win," *Publishers Weekly,* 28 July 2008.

3. M.E. Shaw, *Group Dynamics,* 3d ed. (New York: McGraw-Hill, 1981), p. 8; S.A. Mohrman, S.G. Cohen, and A.M. Mohrman Jr., *Designing Team-Based Organizations: New Forms for Knowledge Work* (San Francisco: Jossey-Bass, 1995), pp. 39–40; E. Sundstrom, "The Challenges of Supporting Work Team Effectiveness," in *Supporting Work Team Effectiveness,* ed. E. Sundstrom and Associates (San Francisco: Jossey-Bass, 1999), pp. 6–9.

4. R.A. Guzzo and M.W. Dickson, "Teams in Organizations: Recent Research on Performance and Effectiveness," *Annual Review of Psychology* 47 (1996), pp. 307–338; D.A. Nadler, "From Ritual to Real Work: The Board as a Team," *Directors and Boards* 22 (Summer 1998), pp. 28–31; L.R. Offermann and R.K. Spiros, "The Science and Practice of Team Development: Improving the Link," *Academy of Management Journal* 44 (April 2001), pp. 376–392.

5. B.D. Pierce and R. White, "The Evolution of Social Structure: Why Biology Matters," *Academy of Management Review* 24 (October 1999), pp. 843–853; P.R. Lawrence and N. Nohria, *Driven: How Human Nature Shapes Our Choices* (San Francisco: Jossey-Bass, 2002); J.R. Spoor and J.R. Kelly, "The Evolutionary Significance of Affect in Groups: Communication and Group Bonding," *Group Processes & Intergroup Relations* 7, no. 4 (2004), pp. 398–412.

6. M.A. Hogg et al., "The Social Identity Perspective: Intergroup Relations, Self-Conception, and Small Groups," *Small Group Research* 35, no. 3 (June 2004), pp. 246–276; N. Michinov, E. Michinov, and M.-C. Toczek-Capelle, "Social Identity, Group Processes, and Performance in Synchronous Computer-Mediated Communication," *Group Dynamics: Theory, Research, and Practice* 8, no. 1 (2004), pp. 27–39; M. Van Vugt and C.M. Hart, "Social Identity as Social Glue: The Origins of Group Loyalty," *Journal of Personality and Social Psychology* 86, no. 4 (2004), pp. 585–598.

7. S. Schacter, *The Psychology of Affiliation* (Stanford, CA: Stanford University Press, 1959), pp. 12–19; R. Eisler and D.S. Levine, "Nurture, Nature, and Caring: We Are Not Prisoners of Our Genes," *Brain and Mind* 3 (2002), pp. 9–52; A.C. DeVries, E.R. Glasper, and C.E. Detillion, "Social Modulation of Stress Responses," *Physiology & Behavior* 79, no. 3 (August 2003), pp. 399–407; S. Cohen, "The Pittsburgh Common Cold Studies: Psychosocial Predictors of Susceptibility to Respiratory Infectious Illness," *International Journal of Behavioral Medicine* 12, no. 3 (2005), pp. 123–131.

8. Cohen, "The Pittsburgh Common Cold Studies"; M.T. Hansen, M.L. Mors, and B. Løvås, "Knowledge Sharing in Organizations: Multiple Networks, Multiple Phases," *Academy of Management Journal* 48, no. 5 (2005), pp. 776–793; R. Cross et al., "Using Social Network Analysis to Improve Communities of Practice," *California Management Review* 49, no. 1 (2006), pp. 32–60; P. Balkundi et al., "Demographic Antecedents and Performance Consequences of Structural Holes in Work Teams," *Journal of Organizational Behavior* 28, no. 2 (2007), pp. 241–260; W. Verbeke and S. Wuyts, "Moving in Social Circles: Social Circle Membership and Performance Implications," *Journal of Organizational Behavior* 28, no. 4 (2007), pp. 357–379.

9. "Teamwork and Collaboration Major Workplace Trends," *Ottawa Business Journal,* 18 April 2006; S. Wuchty, B.F. Jones, and B. Uzzi, "The Increasing Dominance of Teams in Production of Knowledge," *Science* 316 (18 May 2007), pp. 1036–1039.

10. S. Beatty, "Bass Talk: Plotting Plaid's Future," *Wall Street Journal,* 9 September 2004, p. B1.

11. M. Moldaschl and W. Weber, "The 'Three Waves' of Industrial Group Work: Historical Reflections on Current Research on Group Work," *Human Relations* 51 (March 1998), pp. 347–388. Several popular books in the 1980s encouraged teamwork, based on the Japanese economic miracle. These books include W. Ouchi, *Theory Z: How American Management Can Meet the Japanese Challenge* (Reading, MA: Addison-Wesley, 1981); R.T. Pascale and A.G. Athos, *Art of Japanese Management* (New York: Simon and Schuster, 1982).

12. C.R. Emery and L.D. Fredenhall, "The Effect of Teams on Firm Profitability and Customer Satisfaction," *Journal of Service Research* 4 (February 2002), pp. 217–229; G.S. Van der Vegt and O. Janssen, "Joint Impact of Interdependence and Group Diversity on Innovation," *Journal of Management* 29 (2003), pp. 729–751.

13. R.E. Baumeister and M.R. Leary, "The Need to Belong: Desire for Interpersonal Attachments as a Fundamental Human Motivation," *Psychological Bulletin* 117 (1995), pp. 497–529; S. Chen, H.C. Boucher, and M.P. Tapias, "The Relational Self Revealed: Integrative Conceptualization and Implications for Interpersonal Life," *Psychological Bulletin* 132, no. 2 (2006), pp. 151–179; J.M. Feinberg and J.R. Aiello, "Social Facilitation: A Test of Competing Theories," *Journal of Applied Social Psychology* 36, no. 5 (2006), pp. 1087–1109; A.M. Grant, "Relational Job Design and the Motivation to Make a Prosocial Difference," *Academy of Management Review* 32, no. 2 (2007), pp. 393–417; N.L. Kerr et al., "Psychological Mechanisms Underlying the Kohler Motivation Gain," *Personality & Social Psychology Bulletin* 33, no. 6 (2007), pp. 828–841.

14. E.A. Locke et al., "The Importance of the Individual in an Age of Groupism," in *Groups at Work: Theory and Research,* ed. M.E. Turner (Mahwah, NJ: Lawrence Erlbaum, 2001), pp. 501–528; N.J. Allen and T.D. Hecht, "The 'Romance of Teams': Toward an Understanding of Its Psychological Underpinnings and Implications," *Journal of Occupational and Organizational Psychology* 77 (2004), pp. 439–461.

15. I.D. Steiner, *Group Process and Productivity* (New York: Academic Press, 1972); N.L. Kerr and S.R. Tindale, "Group Performance and Decision Making," *Annual Review of Psychology* 55 (2004), pp. 623–655.

16. D. Dunphy and B. Bryant, "Teams: Panaceas or Prescriptions for Improved Performance?" *Human Relations* 49 (1996), pp. 677–699. For a discussion of Brooks's Law, see F.P. Brooks, ed., *The Mythical Man-Month: Essays on Software Engineering,* 2d ed. (Reading, MA: Addison-Wesley, 1995).

17. J. Gruber, "More Aperture Dirt," *Daring Fireball*, 4 May 2006, daringfireball.net/2006/05/more_aperture_dirt (accessed 7 June 2006); J. Gruber, "Aperture Dirt," *Daring Fireball*, 28 April 2006, daringfireball.net/2006/04/aperture_dirt, (accessed 30 April 2006).

18. S.J. Karau and K.D. Williams, "Social Loafing: A Meta-Analytic Review and Theoretical Integration," *Journal of Personality and Social Psychology* 65 (1993), pp. 681–706; R.C. Liden et al., "Social Loafing: A Field Investigation," *Journal of Management* 30 (2004), pp. 285–304; L.L. Chidambaram, "Is Out of Sight, Out of Mind? An Empirical Study of Social Loafing in Technology-Supported Groups," *Information Systems Research* 16, no. 2 (2005), pp. 149–168; U.-C. Klehe and N. Anderson, "The Moderating Influence of Personality and Culture on Social Loafing in Typical versus Maximum Performance Situations," *International Journal of Selection and Assessment* 15, no. 2 (2007), pp. 250–262.

19. M. Erez and A. Somech, "Is Group Productivity Loss the Rule or the Exception? Effects of Culture and Group-Based Motivation," *Academy of Management Journal* 39 (1996), pp. 1513–1537; Kerr and Tindale, "Group Performance and Decision Making."

20. E. Kidwell and N. Bennett, "Employee Propensity to Withhold Effort: A Conceptual Model to Intersect Three Avenues of Research," *Academy of Management Review* 19 (1993), pp. 429–56; J.M. George, "Asymmetrical Effects of Rewards and Punishments: The Case of Social Loafing," *Journal of Occupational and Organizational Psychology* 68 (1995), pp. 327–38; T.A. Judge and T.D. Chandler, "Individual-Level Determinants of Employee Shirking," *Relations Industrielles* 51 (1996), pp. 468–86.

21. G.P. Shea and R.A. Guzzo, "Group Effectiveness: What Really Matters?" *Sloan Management Review* 27 (1987), pp. 33–46; J.R. Hackman et al., "Team Effectiveness in Theory and in Practice," in *Industrial and Organizational Psychology: Linking Theory with Practice*, ed. C.L. Cooper and E.A. Locke (Oxford, UK: Blackwell, 2000), pp. 109–129.

22. M.A. West, C.S. Borrill, and K.L. Unsworth, "Team Effectiveness in Organizations," *International Review of Industrial and Organizational Psychology* 13 (1998), pp. 1–48; R. Forrester and A.B. Drexler, "A Model for Team-Based Organization Performance," *Academy of Management Executive* 13 (August 1999), pp. 36–49; J.E. McGrath, H. Arrow, and J.L. Berdahl, "The Study of Groups: Past, Present, and Future," *Personality 8 Social Psychology Review* 4, no. 1 (2000), pp. 95–105; M.A. Marks, J.E. Mathieu, and S.J. Zaccaro, "A Temporally Based Framework and Taxonomy of Team Processes," *Academy of Management Review* 26, no. 3 (July 2001), pp. 356–376.

23. J.S. DeMatteo, L.T. Eby, and E. Sundstrom, "Team-Based Rewards: Current Empirical Evidence and Directions for Future Research," *Research in Organizational Behavior* 20 (1998), pp. 141–183; E.E. Lawler III, *Rewarding Excellence: Pay Strategies for the New Economy* (San Francisco: Jossey-Bass, 2000), pp. 207–214; G. Hertel, S. Geister, and U. Konradt, "Managing Virtual Teams: A Review of Current Empirical Research," *Human Resource Management Review* 15 (2005), pp. 69–95.

24. These and other environmental conditions for effective teams are discussed in R. Wageman, "Case Study: Critical Success Factors for Creating Superb Self-Managing Teams at Xerox," *Compensation and Benefits Review* 29 (September–October 1997), pp. 31–41; Sundstrom, "The Challenges of Supporting Work Team Effectiveness"; J.N. Choi, "External Activities and Team Effectiveness: Review and Theoretical Development," *Small Group Research* 33 (April 2002), pp. 181–208; T.L. Doolen, M.E. Hacker, and E.M. Van Aken, "The Impact of Organizational Context on Work Team Effectiveness: A Study of Production Team," *IEEE Transactions on Engineering Management* 50, no. 3 (August 2003), pp. 285–296; S.D. Dionne et al., "Transformational Leadership and Team Performance," *Journal of Organizational Change Management* 17, no. 2 (2004), pp. 177–193.

25. L. Hirsh, "Manufacturing in Action," *Press-Enterprise* (Riverside, CA), 21 June 2008, p. E01.

26. A. Niimi, "The Slow and Steady Climb toward True North" (Toyota Motor Manufacturing North America news release), 7 August 2003; L. Adams, "Medrad Works and Wins as a Team," *Quality Magazine*, October 2004, p. 42; J. Teresko, "Toyota's Real Secret," *Industry Week*, 1 February 2007.

27. M.A. Campion, E.M. Papper, and G.J. Medsker, "Relations between Work Team Characteristics and Effectiveness: A Replication and Extension," *Personnel Psychology* 49 (1996), pp. 429–452; D.C. Man and S.S.K. Lam, "The Effects of Job Complexity and Autonomy on Cohesiveness in Collectivistic and Individualistic Work Groups: A Cross-Cultural Analysis," *Journal of Organizational Behavior* 24 (2003), pp. 979–1001.

28. G.S. Van der Vegt, J.M. Emans, and E. Van de Vliert, "Patterns of Interdependence in Work Teams: A Two-Level Investigation of the Relations with Job and Team Satisfaction," *Personnel Psychology* 54 (Spring 2001), pp. 51–69; R. Wageman, "The Meaning of Interdependence," in *Groups at Work: Theory and Research*, ed. M.E. Turner (Mahwah, NJ: Lawrence Erlbaum, 2001), pp. 197–217; S.M. Gully et al., "A Meta-Analysis of Team-Efficacy, Potency, and Performance: Interdependence and Level of Analysis as Moderators of Observed Relationships," *Journal of Applied Psychology* 87, no. 5 (Oct 2002), pp. 819–832; M.R. Barrick et al., "The Moderating Role of Top Management Team Interdependence: Implications for Real Teams and Working Groups," *Academy of Management Journal* 50, no. 3 (2007), pp. 544–557.

29. L. Gratton and T.J. Erickson, "Ways to Build Collaborative Teams," *Harvard Business Review* (November 2007), pp. 100–109.

30. G. Stasser, "Pooling of Unshared Information during Group Discussion," in *Group Process and Productivity*, ed. S. Worchel, W. Wood, and J.A. Simpson (Newbury Park, CA: Sage, 1992); J.R. Katzenbach and D.K. Smith, *The Wisdom of Teams: Creating the High-Performance Organization* (Boston: Harvard University Press, 1993), pp. 45–47.

31. J. O'Toole, "The Power of Many: Building a High-Performance Management Team," *ceoforum.com.au,* March 2003.

32. Fishman, "The Anarchist's Cookbook."

33. P. Wise, "How Shell Finds Student World's Brightest Sparks," *Financial Times* (London), 8 January 2004, p. 12; "Shell Oil Introduces Undergrads to Gourami Business Challenge" (University of Texas at Austin news release), 15 August 2005; S. Ganesan, "Talent Quest," *Malaysia Star,* 28 January 2007; J. Porretto, "Wanted: Engineers," *The Commercial Appeal,* 4 September 2007, p. B3.

34. F.P. Morgeson, M.H. Reider, and M.A. Campion, "Selecting Individuals in Team Settings: The Importance of Social Skills, Personality Characteristics, and Teamwork Knowledge," *Personnel Psychology* 58, no. 3 (2005), pp. 583–611; V. Rousseau, C. Aubé, and A. Savoie, "Teamwork Behaviors: A Review and an Integration of Frameworks," *Small Group Research* 37, no. 5 (2006), pp. 540–570. For a detailed examination of the characteristics of effective team members, see M.L. Loughry, M.W. Ohland, and D.D. Moore, "Development of a Theory-Based Assessment of Team Member Effectiveness," *Educational and Psychological Measurement* 67, no. 3 (June 2007), pp. 505–524.

35. C.O.L.H. Porter et al., "Backing Up Behaviors in Teams: The Role of Personality and Legitimacy of Need," *Journal of Applied Psychology* 88, no. 3 (2003), pp. 391–403; C.E. Hårtel and D. Panipucci, "How 'Bad Apples' Spoil the Bunch: Faultlines, Emotional Levers, and Exclusion in the Workplace," *Research on Emotion in Organizations* 3 (2007), pp. 287–310.

36. D. van Knippenberg, C.K.W. De Dreu, and A.C. Homan, "Work Group Diversity and Group Performance: An Integrative Model and Research Agenda," *Journal of Applied Psychology* 89, no. 6 (2004), pp. 1008–1022; E. Mannix and M.A. Neale, "What Differences Make a Difference? The Promise and Reality of Diverse Teams in Organizations," *Psychological Science in the Public Interest* 6, no. 2 (2005), pp. 31–55.

37. D.C. Lau and J.K. Murnighan, "Interactions within Groups and Subgroups: The Effects of Demographic Faultlines," *Academy of Management Journal* 48, no. 4 (August 2005), pp. 645–659; R. Rico et al., "The Effects of Diversity Faultlines and Team Task Autonomy on Decision Quality and Social Integration," *Journal of Management* 33, no. 1 (February 2007), pp. 111–132.

38. The NTSB and NASA studies are summarized in J.R. Hackman, "New Rules for Team Building," *Optimize* (July 2002), pp. 50–62.

39. B.W. Tuckman and M.A.C. Jensen, "Stages of Small-Group Development Revisited," *Group and Organization Studies* 2 (1977), pp. 419–442; B.W. Tuckman, "Developmental Sequence in Small Groups," *Group Facilitation* (Spring 2001), pp. 66–81.

40. D.L. Miller, "The Stages of Group Development: A Retrospective Study of Dynamic Team Processes," *Canadian Journal of Administrative Sciences* 20, no. 2 (2003), pp. 121–134.

41. G.R. Bushe and G.H. Coetzer, "Group Development and Team Effectiveness: Using Cognitive Representations to Measure Group Development and Predict Task Performance and Group Viability," *Journal of Applied Behavioral Science* 43, no. 2 (June 2007), pp. 184–212.

42. J.E. Mathieu and G.F. Goodwin, "The Influence of Shared Mental Models on Team Process and Performance," *Journal of Applied Psychology* 85 (April 2000), pp. 273–284; J. Langan-Fox and J. Anglim, "Mental Models, Team Mental Models, and Performance: Process, Development, and Future Directions," *Human Factors and Ergonomics in Manufacturing* 14, no. 4 (2004), pp. 331–352; B.C. Lim and K.J. Klein, "Team Mental Models and Team Performance: A Field Study of the Effects of Team Mental Model Similarity and Accuracy," *Journal of Organizational Behavior* 27 (2006), pp. 403–418; R. Rico, M. Sánchez-Manzanares, and C. Gibson, "Team Implicit Coordination Processes: A Team Knowledge-Based Approach," *Academy of Management Review,* 33 (2008), pp. 163–184.

43. W.B. Scott, "Blue Angels," *Aviation Week & Space Technology,* 21 March 2005, pp. 50–57.

44. A.P. Hare, "Types of Roles in Small Groups: A Bit of History and a Current Perspective," *Small Group Research* 25 (1994), pp. 443–448; A. Aritzeta, S. Swailes, and B. Senior, "Belbin's Team Role Model: Development, Validity and Applications for Team Building," *Journal of Management Studies* 44, no. 1 (January 2007), pp. 96–118.

45. S.H.N. Leung, J.W.K. Chan, and W.B. Lee, "The Dynamic Team Role Behavior: The Approaches of Investigation," *Team Performance Management* 9 (2003), pp. 84–90; G.L. Stewart, I.S. Fulmer, and M.R. Barrick, "An Exploration of Member Roles as a Multilevel Linking Mechanism for Individual Traits and Team Outcomes," *Personnel Psychology* 58, no. 2 (2005), pp. 343–365.

46. W.G. Dyer, *Team Building: Current Issues and New Alternatives,* 3d ed. (Reading, MA: Addison-Wesley, 1995); C.A. Beatty and B.A. Barker, *Building Smart Teams: Roadmap to High Performance* (Thousand Oaks, CA: Sage, 2004).

47. Langan-Fox and Anglim, "Mental Models, Team Mental Models, and Performance"; J.E. Mathieu et al., "Scaling the Quality of Teammates' Mental Models: Equifinality and Normative Comparisons," *Journal of Organizational Behavior* 26 (2005), pp. 37–56.

48. "German Businesswoman Demands End to Fun at Work," *Reuters,* 9 July 2003.

49. R.W. Woodman and J.J. Sherwood, "The Role of Team Development in Organizational Effectiveness: A Critical Review," *Psychological Bulletin* 88 (1980), pp. 166–186.

50. L. Mealiea and R. Baltazar, "A Strategic Guide for Building Effective Teams," *Personnel Management* 34, no. 2 (Summer 2005), pp. 141–160.

51. G.E. Huszczo, "Training for Team Building," *Training and Development Journal* 44 (February 1990), pp. 37–43; P. McGraw, "Back from the Mountain: Outdoor Management Development Programs and How to Ensure the Transfer of Skills to the Workplace," *Asia Pacific Journal of Human Resources* 31 (Spring 1993), pp. 52–61.

52. D.C. Feldman, "The Development and Enforcement of Group Norms," *Academy of Management Review* 9 (1984), pp. 47–53; E. Fehr and U. Fischbacher, "Social Norms and Human Cooperation," *Trends in Cognitive Sciences* 8, no. 4 (2004), pp. 185–190.

53. N. Ellemers and F. Rink, "Identity in Work Groups: The Beneficial and Detrimental Consequences of Multiple Identities and Group Norms for Collaboration and Group Performance," *Advances in Group Processes* 22 (2005), pp. 1–41.

54. J.J. Dose and R.J. Klimoski, "The Diversity of Diversity: Work Values Effects on Formative Team Processes," *Human Resource Management Review* 9, no. 1 (Spring 1999), pp. 83–108.

55. S. Taggar and R. Ellis, "The Role of Leaders in Shaping Formal Team Norms," *Leadership Quarterly* 18, no. 2 (2007), pp. 105–120.

56. D.J. Beal et al., "Cohesion and Performance in Groups: A Meta-Analytic Clarification of Construct Relations," *Journal of Applied Psychology* 88, no. 6 (2003), pp. 989–1004; S.W.J. Kozlowski and D.R. Ilgen, "Enhancing the Effectiveness of Work Groups and Teams," *Psychological Science in the Public Interest* 7, no. 3 (2006), pp. 77–124.

57. K.A.Jehn, G.B. Northcraft, and M.A. Neale, "Why Differences Make a Difference: A Field Study of Diversity, Conflict, and Performance in Workgroups," *Administrative Science Quarterly* 44, no. 4 (1999), pp. 741–763; van Knippenberg, De Dreu, and Homan, "Work Group Diversity and Group Performance." For evidence that diversity/similarity does not always influence cohesion, see S.S. Webber and L.M. Donahue, "Impact of Highly and Less Job-Related Diversity on Work Group Cohesion and Performance: A Meta-Analysis," *Journal of Management* 27, no. 2 (2001), pp. 141–162.

58. E. Aronson and J. Mills, "The Effects of Severity of Initiation on Liking for a Group," *Journal of Abnormal and Social Psychology* 59 (1959), pp. 177–181; J.E. Hautaluoma and R.S. Enge, "Early Socialization into a Work Group: Severity of Initiations Revisited," *Journal of Social Behavior & Personality* 6 (1991), pp. 725–748.

59. B. Mullen and C. Copper, "The Relation between Group Cohesiveness and Performance: An Integration," *Psychological Bulletin* 115 (1994), pp. 210–227.

60. M. Rempel and R.J. Fisher, "Perceived Threat, Cohesion, and Group Problem Solving in Intergroup Conflict," *International Journal of Conflict Management* 8 (1997), pp. 216–234; M.E. Turner and T. Horvitz, "The Dilemma of Threat: Group Effectiveness and Ineffectiveness under Adversity," in *Groups at Work: Theory and Research,* ed. M.E. Turner (Mahwah, NJ: Lawrence Erlbaum, 2001), pp. 445–470.

61. W. Piper et al., "Cohesion as a Basic Bond in Groups," *Human Relations* 36 (1983), pp. 93–108; C.A. O'Reilly, D.E. Caldwell, and W.P. Barnett, "Work Group Demography, Social Integration, and Turnover," *Administrative Science Quarterly* 34 (1989), pp. 21–37.

62. Mullen and Copper, "The Relation between Group Cohesiveness and Performance"; A.V. Carron et al., "Cohesion and Performance in Sport: A Meta-Analysis," *Journal of Sport and Exercise Psychology* 24 (2002), pp. 168–188; Beal et al., "Cohesion and Performance in Groups."

63. C. Langfred, "Is Group Cohesiveness a Double-Edged Sword? An Investigation of the Effects of Cohesiveness on Performance," *Small Group Research* 29 (1998), pp. 124–143; K.L. Gammage, A.V. Carron, and P.A. Estabrooks, "Team Cohesion and Individual Productivity: The Influence of the Norm for Productivity and the Identifiability of Individual Effort," *Small Group Research* 32 (February 2001), pp. 3–18.

64. S.L. Robinson, "Trust and Breach of the Psychological Contract," *Administrative Science Quarterly* 41 (1996), pp. 574–599; D.M. Rousseau et al., "Not So Different after All: A Cross-Discipline View of Trust," *Academy of Management Review* 23 (1998), pp. 393–404; D.L. Duarte and N.T. Snyder, *Mastering Virtual Teams: Strategies, Tools, and Techniques That Succeed,* 2d ed. (San Francisco: Jossey-Bass, 2000), pp. 139–155.

65. D.J. McAllister, "Affect- and Cognition-Based Trust as Foundations for Interpersonal Cooperation in Organizations," *Academy of Management Journal* 38, no. 1 (February 1995), pp. 24–59; M. Williams, "In Whom We Trust: Group Membership as an Affective Context for Trust Development," *Academy of Management Review* 26, no. 3 (July 2001), pp. 377–396.

66. O.E. Williamson, "Calculativeness, Trust, and Economic Organization," *Journal of Law and Economics* 36, no. 1 (1993), pp. 453–486.

67. E.M. Whitener et al., "Managers as Initiators of Trust: An Exchange Relationship Framework for Understanding Managerial Trustworthy Behavior," *Academy of Management Review* 23 (July 1998), pp. 513–530; J.M. Kouzes and B.Z. Posner, *The Leadership Challenge,* 3d ed. (San Francisco: Jossey-Bass, 2002), chap. 2; T. Simons, "Behavioral Integrity: The Perceived Alignment between Managers' Words and Deeds as a Research Focus," *Organization Science* 13, no. 1 (January–February 2002), pp. 18–35.

68. S.L. Jarvenpaa and D.E. Leidner, "Communication and Trust in Global Virtual Teams," *Organization Science* 10 (1999), pp. 791–815; M.M. Pillutla, D. Malhotra, and J. Keith Murnighan, "Attributions of Trust and the Calculus of Reciprocity," *Journal of Experimental Social Psychology* 39, no. 5 (2003), pp. 448–455.

69. K.T. Dirks and D.L. Ferrin, "The Role of Trust in Organizations," *Organization Science* 12, no. 4 (July–August 2004), pp. 450–467.

70. J.R. Dunn and M.E. Schweitzer, "Feeling and Believing: The Influence of Emotion on Trust," *Journal of Personality and Social Psychology* 88, no. 5 (May 2005), pp. 736–48; H. Gill et al., "Antecedents of Trust: Establishing a Boundary Condition for the Relation between Propensity to Trust and Intention to Trust," *Journal of Business and Psychology* 19, no. 3 (Spring 2005), pp. 287–302.

71. M. Connelly, "Chrysler Wants to Put Team Assembly in All Plants," *Automotive News,* 30 May 2005, p. 53; J. Leute, "Union, Management Work in Lockstep at Belvidere, Ill., Plant," *Janesville Gazette* (Janesville, WI), 18 July 2005; J. Smith, "Building Cars, Building Teams," *Plant Engineering,* December 2005, pp. 41–50; M. Connelly, "Chrysler Boosts Belvidere Flexibility," *Automotive News,* 13 February 2006, p. 44; C. Vander Doelen, "Chrysler Boss Urges Workers, Managers to Espouse Change," *Winnipeg Free Press,* 13 January 2006, p. E11; B. Vavra, "Stick with the Game Plan," *Plant Engineering,* 15 December 2007, p. 26.

72. Mohrman, Cohen, and Mohrman, Jr., *Designing Team-Based Organizations*; D.E. Yeatts and C. Hyten, *High-Performing Self-Managed Work Teams: A Comparison of Theory and Practice* (Thousand Oaks, CA: Sage, 1998); E.E. Lawler, *Organizing for High Performance* (San Francisco: Jossey-Bass, 2001); R.J. Torraco, "Work Design Theory: A Review and Critique with Implications for Human Resource Development," *Human Resource Development Quarterly* 16, no. 1 (Spring 2005), pp. 85–109.

73. Mackey, "Open Book Company."

74. P. Panchak, "Production Workers Can Be Your Competitive Edge," *Industry Week,* October 2004, p. 11; S.K. Muthusamy, J.V. Wheeler, and B.L. Simmons, "Self-Managing Work Teams: Enhancing Organizational Innovativeness," *Organization Development Journal* 23, no. 3 (Fall 2005), pp. 53–66.

75. Emery and Fredenhall, "The Effect of Teams on Firm Profitability and Customer Satisfaction"; A. Krause and H. Dunckel, "Work Design and Customer Satisfaction: Effects of the Implementation of Semi-Autonomous Group Work on Customer Satisfaction Considering Employee Satisfaction and Group Performance (translated abstract)," *Zeitschrift fur Arbeits-Und Organisationspsychologie* 47, no. 4 (2003), pp. 182–193; H. van Mierlo et al., "Self-Managing Teamwork and Psychological Well-Being: Review of a Multilevel Research Domain," *Group & Organization Management* 30, no. 2 (April 2005), pp. 211–235.

76. E.L. Trist et al., *Organizational Choice* (London: Tavistock, 1963); N. Adler and P. Docherty, "Bringing Business into Sociotechnical Theory and Practice," *Human Relations* 51, no. 3 (1998), pp. 319–45; R.J. Torraco, "Work Design Theory: A Review and Critique with Implications for Human Resource Development," *Human Resource Development Quarterly* 16, no. 1 (Spring 2005), pp. 85–109.

77. The main components of sociotechnical systems are discussed in M. Moldaschl and W. G. Weber, "The 'Three Waves' of Industrial Group Work: Historical Reflections on Current Research on Group Work," *Human Relations* 51 (March 1998), pp. 259–87; and W. Niepce and E. Molleman, "Work Design Issues in Lean Production from Sociotechnical System Perspective: Neo-Taylorism or the Next Step in Sociotechnical Design?" *Human Relations* 51, no. 3 (March 1998), pp. 259–87.

78. E. Ulich and W.G. Weber, "Dimensions, Criteria, and Evaluation of Work Group Autonomy," in *Handbook of Work Group Psychology,* ed. M.A. West (Chichester, UK: John Wiley and Sons, 1996), pp. 247–82.

79. K.P. Carson and G.L. Stewart, "Job Analysis and the Sociotechnical Approach to Quality: A Critical Examination," *Journal of Quality Management* 1 (1996), pp. 49–65; C.C. Manz and G.L. Stewart, "Attaining Flexible Stability by Integrating Total Quality Management and Socio-Technical Systems Theory," *Organization Science* 8 (1997), pp. 59–70.

80. C.R. Emery and L.D. Fredendall, "The Effect of Teams on Firm Profitability and Customer Satisfaction," *Journal of Service Research* 4 (February 2002), pp. 217–29; I.M. Kunii, "He Put the Flash Back in Canon," *Business Week* (16 September 2002), p. 40; A. Krause and H. Dunckel, "Work Design and Customer Satisfaction: Effects of the Implementation of Semi-Autonomous Group Work on Customer Satisfaction Considering Employee Satisfaction and Group Performance (Translated Abstract)," *Zeitschrift fur Arbeits-und Organisationspsychologie* 47, no. 4 (2003), pp. 182–93.

81. J.P. Womack, D.T. Jones, and D. Roos, *The Machine That Changed the World* (New York: MacMIllan, 1990); P.S. Adler and R.E. Cole, "Designed for Learning: A Tale of Two Auto Plants," *Sloan Management Review* 34 (Spring 1993), pp. 85–94; C. Berggren, "Volvo Uddevalla: A Dead Horse or a Car Dealer's Dream?" in *Actes du GERPISA* (May 1993), pp. 129–43; J.Å. Granath, "Torslanda to Uddevalla Via Kalmar: A Journey in Production Practice in Volvo," Paper presented at Seminário Internacional Reestruturação Produtiva, Flexibilidade do Trabalho e Novas Competências Profissionais COPPE/UFRJ, Rio de Janeiro, Brasil, 24–25 August 1998; Emery and Fredendall, "The Effect of Teams on Firm Profitability and Customer Satisfaction" ; J. Boudreau et al., "On the Interface between Operations and Human Resources Management," *Manufacturing & Service Operations Management* 5, no. 3 (Summer 2003), pp. 179–202.

82. C.E. Nicholls, H.W. Lane, and M.B. Brechu, "Taking Self-Managed Teams to Mexico," *Academy of Management Executive* 13 (August 1999), pp. 15–25; B.L. Kirkman and D.L. Shapiro, "The Impact of Cultural Values on Job Satisfaction and Organizational Commitment in Self-Managing Work Teams: The Mediating Role of Employee Resistance," *Academy of Management Journal* 44 (June 2001), pp. 557–69.

83. C.C. Manz, D.E. Keating, and A. Donnellon, "Preparing for an Organizational Change to Employee Self-Management: The Managerial Transition," *Organizational Dynamics* 19 (Autumn 1990), pp. 15–26; J.D. Orsburn and L. Moran, *The New Self-Directed Work Teams: Mastering the Challenge* (New York: McGraw-Hill, 2000), Chapter 11. The Robert Frost quotation is found at www.quoteland.com.

84. M. Fenton-O'Creevy, "Employee Involvement and the Middle Manager: Saboteur or Scapegoat?" *Human Resource Management Journal* 11 (2001), pp.24–40; R. Wageman, "How Leaders Foster Self-Managing Team Effectiveness," *Organization Science* 12, no. 5 (September–October 2001), pp. 559–77; C. Douglas and W. L. Gardner, "Transition to Self-Directed Work Teams: Implications of Transition Time and Self-Monitoring for Managers' Use of Influence Tactics," *Journal of Organizational Behavior* 25 (2004), pp. 47–65. The TRW quotation is found in J. Jusko, "Always Lessons to Learn," Industry Week (15February 1999), pp. 23–30.

85. D. Stafford, "Sharing the Driver's Seat," *Kansas City Star*, 11 June 2002, p. D1.

86. G. Garda, K. Lindstrom, and M. Dallnera, "Toward a Learning Organization: The Introduction of a Client-Centered Team-Based Organization in Administrative Surveying Work," *Applied Ergonomics* 34 (2003), pp. 97–105.

87. R. Hodson, "Dignity in the Workplace under Participative Management: Alienation and Freedom Revisited," *American Sociological Review* 61 (1996), pp. 719–38; R. Yonatan and H. Lam, "Union Responses to Quality Improvement Initiatives: Factors Shaping Support and Resistance," *Journal of Labor Research* 20 (Winter 1999), pp. 111–31.

88. Moldaschl and Weber, "The 'Three Waves' of Industrial Group Work"; W. Niepce and E. Molleman, "Work Design Issues in Lean Production from a Sociotechnical System Perspective: Neo-Taylorism or the Next Step in Sociotechnical Design?" *Human Relations* 51, no. 3 (March 1998), pp. 259–287.

89. "Medical Marvel," *Works Management* (Best Factory Awards Supplement), October 2007, pp. 21–22.

90. E. Ulich and W.G. Weber, "Dimensions, Criteria, and Evaluation of Work Group Autonomy," in *Handbook of Work Group Psychology,* ed. M.A. West (Chichester, UK: Wiley, 1996), pp. 247–282.

91. K.P. Carson and G.L. Stewart, "Job Analysis and the Sociotechnical Approach to Quality: A Critical Examination," *Journal of Quality Management* 1 (1996), pp. 49–65; C.C. Manz and G.L. Stewart, "Attaining Flexible Stability by Integrating Total Quality Management and Socio-Technical Systems Theory," *Organization Science* 8 (1997), pp. 59–70.

92. J. Gordon, "Do Your Virtual Teams Deliver Only Virtual Performance?" *Training,* June 2005, pp. 20–24.

93. J. Lipnack and J. Stamps, *Virtual Teams: People Working across Boundaries with Technology* (New York: Wiley, 2001); B.S. Bell and W.J. Kozlowski, "A Typology of Virtual Teams: Implications for Effective Leadership," *Group & Organization Management* 27 (March 2002), pp. 14–49; Hertel, Geister, and Konradt, "Managing Virtual Teams."

94. G. Gilder, *Telecosm: How Infinite Bandwidth Will Revolutionize Our World* (New York: Free Press, 2001); L.L. Martins, L.L. Gilson, and M.T. Maynard, "Virtual Teams: What Do We Know and Where Do We Go from Here?" *Journal of Management* 30, no. 6 (2004), pp. 805–835.

95. Martins, Gilson, and Maynard, "Virtual Teams." The quotation is found in S. Gasper, "Virtual Teams, Real Benefits," *Network World,* 24 September 2001, p. 45.

96. D. Robb, "Global Workgroups," *Computerworld,* 15 August 2005, pp. 37–38.

97. D. Robey, H.M. Khoo, and C. Powers, "Situated Learning in Cross-Functional Virtual Teams," *Technical Communication* (February 2000), pp. 51–66.

98. Lureya and Raisinghani, "An Empirical Study of Best Practices in Virtual Teams."

99. S. Alexander, "Virtual Teams Going Global," *InfoWorld* (13 November 2000), pp. 55–56.

100. S. Prashad, "Building Trust Tricky for 'Virtual' Teams," *Toronto Star,* 23 October 2003, p. K06.

101. S. Van Ryssen and S.H. Godar, "Going International without Going International: Multinational Virtual Teams," *Journal of International Management* 6 (2000), pp. 49–60.

102. B.J. Alge, C. Wiethoff, and H.J. Klein, "When Does the Medium Matter? Knowledge-Building Experiences and Opportunities in Decision-Making Teams," *Organizational Behavior and Human Decision Processes* 91, no. 1 (2003), pp. 26–37; D. Robey, K.S. Schwaig, and L. Jin, "Intertwining Material and Virtual Work," *Information & Organization* 13 (2003), pp. 111–29; U. Bernard, R. Gfrörer, and B. Staffelbach, "Der Einfluss Von Telearbeit Auf Das Team: Empirisch Analysiert Am Beispiel Eines Versicherungsunternehmens (translated abstract)," *Zeitschrift für Personalforschung* 19, no. 2 (2005), pp. 120–38.

103. "Leading a Virtual Team: Agilent's Grant Marshall," ceoforum.com.au, March 2005; "Supporting Australian Innovation," *Electronics News,* 11 January 2005; M. Conlin, "The Easiest Commute of All," *Business Week,* 12 December 2005, p. 78.

104. Martins, Gilson, and Maynard, "Virtual Teams"; G. Hertel, U. Konradt, and K. Voss, "Competencies for Virtual Teamwork: Development and Validation of a Web-Based Selection Tool for Members of Distributed Teams," *European Journal of Work and Organizational Psychology* 15, no. 4 (2006), pp. 477–504.

105. "Sumaya Kazi: Creating a Culture of Connections," *brassmagazine.com*, November 2007, pp. 11–14; A. van Diggelen, "Dynamics Super Connector," *Silicon Valley/San Jose Business Journal*, 2 February 2007.

106. G. Buckler, "Staking One for the Team," *Computing Canada*, 22 October 2004, p. 16.

107. V.H. Vroom and A.G. Jago, *The New Leadership* (Englewood Cliffs, NJ: Prentice Hall, 1988), pp. 28–29.

108. M. Diehl and W. Stroebe, "Productivity Loss in Idea-Generating Groups: Tracking Down the Blocking Effects," *Journal of Personality and Social Psychology* 61 (1991), pp. 392–403; R.B. Gallupe et al., "Blocking Electronic Brainstorms," *Journal of Applied Psychology* 79 (1994), pp. 77–86; B.A. Nijstad, W. Stroebe, and H.F.M. Lodewijkx, "Production Blocking and Idea Generation: Does Blocking Interfere with Cognitive Processes?" *Journal of Experimental Social Psychology* 39, no. 6 (November 2003), pp. 531–548; B.A. Nijstad and W. Stroebe, "How the Group Affects the Mind: A Cognitive Model of Idea Generation in Groups," *Personality & Social Psychology Review* 10, no. 3 (2006), pp. 186–213.

109. B.E. Irmer, P. Bordia, and D. Abusah, "Evaluation Apprehension and Perceived Benefits in Interpersonal and Database Knowledge Sharing," *Academy of Management Proceedings* (2002), pp. B1–B6.

110. I.L. Janis, *Groupthink: Psychological Studies of Policy Decisions and Fiascoes*, 2d ed. (Boston: Houghton Mifflin, 1982); J.K. Esser, "Alive and Well after 25 Years: A Review of Groupthink Research," *Organizational Behavior and Human Decision Processes* 73, no. 2–3 (1998), pp. 116–141.

111. J.N. Choi and M.U. Kim, "The Organizational Application of Groupthink and Its Limitations in Organizations," *Journal of Applied Psychology* 84, no. 2 (April 1999), pp. 297–306; W.-W. Park, "A Comprehensive Empirical Investigation of the Relationships among Variables of the Groupthink Model," *Journal of Organizational Behavior* 21, no. 8 (December 2000), pp. 873–887; D.D. Henningsen et al., "Examining the Symptoms of Groupthink and Retrospective Sensemaking," *Small Group Research* 37, no. 1 (February 2006), pp. 36–64.

112. D. Miller, *The Icarus Paradox: How Exceptional Companies Bring About Their Own Downfall* (New York: HarperBusiness, 1990); S. Finkelstein, *Why Smart Executives Fail* (New York: Viking, 2003); K. Tasa and G. Whyte, "Collective Efficacy and Vigilant Problem Solving in Group Decision Making: A Non-linear Model," *Organizational Behavior and Human Decision Processes* 96, no. 2 (March 2005), pp. 119–129.

113. D. Isenberg, "Group Polarization: A Critical Review and Meta-Analysis," *Journal of Personality and Social Psychology* 50 (1986), pp. 1141–51; C. McGarty et al., "Group Polarization as Conformity to the Prototypical Group Member," *British Journal of Social Psychology* 31 (1992), pp. 1–20; C.R. Sunstein, "Deliberative Trouble? Why Groups Go to Extremes," *Yale Law Journal* 110, no. 1 (October 2000), pp. 71–119.

114. D. Friedman, "Monty Hall's Three Doors: Construction and Deconstruction of a Choice Anomaly," *American Economic Review* 88 (September 1998), pp. 933–46; D. Kahneman, "Maps of Bounded Rationality: Psychology for Behavioral Economics," *American Economic Review* 93, no. 5 (December 2003), pp. 1449–75.

115. H. Collingwood, "Best-Kept Secrets of the World's Best Companies: Outside-In R&D," *Business 2.0*, April 2006, p. 82.

116. K.M. Eisenhardt, J.L. Kahwajy, and L.J. Bourgeois III, "Conflict and Strategic Choice: How Top Management Teams Disagree," *California Management Review* 39 (1997), pp. 42–62; R. Sutton, *Weird Ideas That Work* (New York: Free Press, 2002); C.J. Nemeth et al., "The Liberating Role of Conflict in Group Creativity: A Study in Two Countries," *European Journal of Social Psychology* 34, no. 4 (2004), pp. 365–374. For a discussion on how all conflict is potentially detrimental to teams, see C.K.W. De Dreu and L.R. Weingart, "Task versus Relationship Conflict, Team Performance, and Team Member Satisfaction: A Meta-Analysis," *Journal of Applied Psychology* 88 (August 2003), pp. 587–604; P. Hinds and D.E. Bailey, "Out of Sight, Out of Sync: Understanding Conflict in Distributed Teams," *Organization Science* 14, no. 6 (2003), pp. 615–632.

117. K. Darce, "Ground Control: NASA Attempts a Cultural Shift," *Seattle Times*, 24 April 2005, p. A3; R. Shelton, "NASA Attempts to Change Mindset in Wake of *Columbia* Tragedy," *Macon Telegraph* (Macon, GA), 7 July 2005.

118. B. Mullen, C. Johnson, and E. Salas, "Productivity Loss in Brainstorming Groups: A Meta-Analytic Integration," *Basic and Applied Psychology* 12 (1991), pp. 2–23. The original description of brainstorming appeared in A.F. Osborn, *Applied Imagination* (New York: Scribner, 1957).

119. R.I. Sutton and A. Hargadon, "Brainstorming Groups in Context: Effectiveness in a Product Design Firm," *Administrative Science Quarterly* 41 (1996), pp. 685–718; T. Kelley, *The Art of Innovation* (New York: Currency Doubleday, 2001); V.R. Brown and P.B. Paulus, "Making Group Brainstorming More Effective: Recommendations from an Associative Memory Perspective," *Current Directions in Psychological Science* 11, no. 6 (2002), pp. 208–212; K. Leggett Dugosh and P.B. Paulus, "Cognitive and Social Comparison Processes in Brainstorming," *Journal of Experimental Social Psychology* 41, no. 3 (2005), pp. 313–320.

120. R.B. Gallupe, L.M. Bastianutti, and W.H. Cooper, "Unblocking Brainstorms," *Journal of Applied Psychology* 76 (1991), pp. 137–142; W.H. Cooper et al., "Some Liberating Effects of Anonymous Electronic Brainstorming," *Small Group Research* 29, no. 2 (April 1998), pp. 147–178; A.R. Dennis, B.H. Wixom, and R.J. Vandenberg, "Understanding Fit and Appropriation Effects in Group Support Systems via Meta-Analysis," *MIS Quarterly* 25, no. 2 (June 2001), pp. 167–193; D.M. DeRosa, C.L. Smith, and D.A. Hantula, "The Medium Matters: Mining the Long-Promised Merit of Group Interaction in Creative Idea Generation Tasks in a Meta-Analysis of the Electronic Group Brainstorming Literature," *Computers in Human Behavior* 23, no. 3 (2007), pp. 1549–1581.

121. A.L. Delbecq, A.H. Van de Ven, and D.H. Gustafson, *Group Techniques for Program Planning: A Guide to Nominal Group and Delphi Processes* (Middleton, WI: Green Briar Press, 1986).

122. S. Frankel, "NGT 1 MDS: An Adaptation of the Nominal Group Technique for Ill-Structured Problems," *Journal of Applied Behavioral Science* 23 (1987), pp. 543–551; H. Barki and A. Pinsonneault, "Small Group Brainstorming and Idea Quality: Is Electronic Brainstorming the Most Effective Approach?" *Small Group Research* 32, no. 2 (April 2001), pp. 158–205.

123. S. Frankel, "NGT + MDS: An Adaptation of the Nominal Group Technique for Ill-Structured Problems," *Journal of Applied Behavioral Science* 23 (1987), pp. 543–51; H. Barki and A. Pinsonneault, "Small Group Brainstorming and Idea Quality: Is Electronic Brainstorming the Most Effective Approach?" *Small Group Research* 32, no. 2 (April 2001), pp. 158–205.

124. Graham, "Teambuilding Reveals Its Serious Side."

125. W.G. Dyer, *Team Building: Current Issues and New Alternatives*, 3rd ed. (Reading, MA: Addison-Wesley, 1995); C.A. Beatty and B.A. Barker, *Building Smart Teams: Roadmap to High Performance* (Thousand Oaks, CA: Sage Publications, 2004).

126. J. Murray, "Office Hours," *The Guardian* (London), 5 September 2005, p. 4; S. Williams, "Thanks, but No Thanks," *Australian Financial Review*, 20 August 2005, p. 32; "Lockheed Volunteers Get Bush Nod," *Los Angeles Daily News*, 9 May 2006, p. AV2.

127. M. Beer, *Organizational Change and Development: A Systems View* (Santa Monica, CA: Goodyear, 1980), pp. 143–46; E. Sundstrom, K.P. De Meuse, and D. Futrell, "Work Teams: Applications and Effectiveness," *American Psychologist* 45 (1990), pp. 120–33.

128. J. Langan-Fox and J. Anglim, "Mental Models, Team Mental Models, and Performance: Process, Development, and Future Directions," *Human Factors and Ergonomics in Manufacturing* 14, no. 4 (2004), pp. 331–52; J.E. Mathieu et al., "Scaling the Quality of Teammates' Mental Models: Equifinality and Normative Comparisons," *Journal of Organizational Behavior* 26 (2005), pp. 37–56.

129. R. Beckhard, "The Confrontation Meeting," *Harvard Business Review* 45, no. 4 (1967), pp. 159–65; H.D. Glover, "Organizational Change and Development: The Consequences of Misuse," *Leadership & Organization Development Journal* 13, no. 1 (1992), pp. 9–16. For recent discussion about problems with confrontation in teams, see M.A. Von Glinow, D.L. Shapiro, and J.M. Brett, "Can We *Talk*, and Should We? Managing Emotional Conflict in Multinational Teams," *Academy of Management Review* 29, no. 4 (2004), pp. 578–92.

130. "German Businesswoman Demands End to Fun at Work," *Reuters* (9 July 2003).

131. R.W. Woodman and J.J. Sherwood, "The Role of Team Development in Organizational Effectiveness: A Critical Review," *Psychological Bulletin* 88 (1980), pp. 166–86.

132. L. Mealiea and R. Baltazar, "A Strategic Guide for Building Effective Teams," *Personnel Management* 34, no. 2 (Summer 2005), pp. 141–60.

133. G.E. Huszczo, "Training for Team Building," *Training and Development Journal* 44 (February 1990), pp. 37–43; P. McGraw, "Back from the Mountain: Outdoor Management Development Programs and How to Ensure the Transfer of Skills to the Workplace," *Asia Pacific Journal of Human Resources* 31 (Spring 1993), pp. 52–61.

Chapter 9

1. J. Bennett and M. Beith, "Alternate Universe," *Newsweek*, 30 July 2007; S. Hatch, "Virtual Worlds, Real Meetings," *Corporate Meetings & Incentives*, February 2007, pp. 12–17; N. Paton, "Managers Struggle to Keep Tabs on Gossipy Avatars," *The Edge* (Singapore), 23 June 2008; M.K. Pratt, "Avatars Get Down to Business," *Computerworld*, 23 June 2008, pp. 22–29.

2. C. Barnard, *The Functions of the Executive* (Cambridge, MA: Harvard University Press, 1938).

3. M.T. Hansen, M.L. Mors, and B. Løvås, "Knowledge Sharing in Organizations: Multiple Networks, Multiple Phases," *Academy of Management Journal* 48, no. 5 (2005), pp. 776–793; R. Du, S. Ai, and Y. Ren, "Relationship between Knowledge Sharing and Performance: A Survey in Xu'an, China," *Expert Systems with Applications* 32 (2007), pp. 38–46; S.R. Murray and J. Peyrefitte, "Knowledge Type and Communication Media Choice in the Knowledge Transfer Process," *Journal of Managerial Issues* 19, no. 1 (Spring 2007), pp. 111–133.

4. S. Hamm, "International Isn't Just IBM's First Name," *BusinessWeek*, 28 January 2008.

5. N. Ellemers, R. Spears, and B. Doosje, "Self and Social Identity," *Annual Review of Psychology* 53 (2002), pp. 161–186; S.A. Haslam and S. Reicher, "Stressing the Group: Social Identity and the Unfolding Dynamics of Responses to Stress," *Journal of Applied Psychology* 91, no. 5 (2006), pp. 1037–1052; M.T. Gailliot and R.F. Baumeister, "Self-Esteem, Belongingness, and Worldview Validation: Does Belongingness Exert a Unique Influence upon Self-Esteem?" *Journal of Research in Personality* 41, no. 2 (2007), pp. 327–345.

6. S. Cohen, "The Pittsburgh Common Cold Studies: Psychosocial Predictors of Susceptibility to Respiratory Infectious Illness," *International Journal of Behavioral Medicine* 12, no. 3 (2005), pp. 123–131; B.N. Uchino, "Social Support and Health: A Review of Physiological Processes Potentially Underlying Links to Disease Outcomes," *Journal of Behavioral Medicine* 29, no. 4 (2006), pp. 377–387.

7. D. Kirkpatrick, "It's Not a Game," *Fortune*, 5 February 2007, pp. 34–38.

8. C.E. Shannon and W. Weaver, *The Mathematical Theory of Communication* (Urbana, IL: University of Illinois Press, 1949); R.M. Krauss and S.R. Fussell, "Social Psychological Models of Interpersonal Communication," in *Social Psychology: Handbook of Basic Principles*, ed. E.T. Higgins and A. Kruglanski (New York: Guilford Press, 1996), pp. 655–701.

9. J.R. Carlson and R.W. Zmud, "Channel Expansion Theory and the Experiential Nature of Media Richness Perceptions," *Academy of Management Journal* 42 (April 1999), pp. 153–170.

10. P. Shachaf and N. Hara, "Behavioral Complexity Theory of Media Selection: A Proposed Theory for Global Virtual Teams," *Journal of Information Science* 33 (2007), pp. 63–75.

11. N.B. Ducheneaut and L.A. Watts, "In Search of Coherence: A Review of E-Mail Research," *Human-Computer Interaction* 20, no. 1–2 (2005), pp. 11–48.

12. W. Lucas, "Effects of E-Mail on the Organization," *European Management Journal* 16, no. 1 (February 1998), pp. 18–30; D.A. Owens, M.A. Neale, and R.I. Sutton, "Technologies of Status Management: Status Dynamics in E-Mail Communications," *Research on Managing Groups and Teams* 3 (2000), pp. 205–230; N.B. Ducheneaut, "Ceci n'est pas un Objet? Talking about Objects in E-Mail," *Human-Computer Interaction* 18, no. 1–2 (2003), pp. 85–110.

13. N.B. Ducheneaut, "The Social Impacts of Electronic Mail in Organizations: A Case Study of Electronic Power Games Using Communication Genres," *Information, Communication & Society* 5, no. 2 (2002), pp. 153–188; N. Panteli, "Richness, Power Cues and Email Text," *Information & Management* 40, no. 2 (2002), pp. 75–86.

14. N. Epley and J. Kruger, "When What You Type Isn't What They Read: The Perseverance of Stereotypes and Expectancies over E-Mail," *Journal of Experimental Social Psychology* 41, no. 4 (2005), pp. 414–422.

15. J.B. Walther, "Language and Communication Technology: Introduction to the Special Issue," *Journal of Language and Social Psychology* 23, no. 4 (December 2004), pp. 384–396; J.B. Walther, T. Loh, and L. Granka, "Let Me Count the Ways: The Interchange of Verbal and Nonverbal Cues in Computer-Mediated and Face-to-Face Affinity," *Journal of Language and Social Psychology* 24, no. 1 (March 2005), pp. 36–65; K. Byron, "Carrying Too Heavy a Load? The Communication and Miscommunication of Emotion by Email," *Academy of Management Review* 33, no. 2 (2008), pp. 309–327.

16. Williams, "Apologies and Rows by Email Are a New Sin for Hi-Tech Cowards"; E. Horng, "No-E-Mail Fridays Transform Office," *ABC News*, 7 April 2007; M. Jackson, "Some Firms Get Innovative in Effort to Boost Face-to-Face Connections," *Boston Globe*, 21 October 2007, p. 3; M. Richtel, "Lost in E-Mail, Tech Firms Face Self-Made Beast," *New York Times*, 14 June 2008; D. Schaper, "An E-Mail Vacation: Taking Fridays Off," *NPR Morning Edition*, 20 June 2008.

17. S. Williams, "Apologies and Rows by Email Are a New Sin for Hi-Tech Cowards," *Western Mail* (Cardiff, Wales), 1 April 2006, p. 11.

18. G. Hertel, S. Geister, and U. Konradt, "Managing Virtual Teams: A Review of Current Empirical Research," *Human Resource Management Review* 15 (2005), pp. 69–95; H. Lee, "Behavioral Strategies for Dealing with Flaming in an Online Forum," *Sociological Quarterly* 46, no. 2 (2005), pp. 385–403.

19. K. Cox, "Irving Oil Fuels Its Leaders," *Globe & Mail*, 21 April 2004, p. C1.

20. D.D. Dawley and W.P. Anthony, "User Perceptions of E-Mail at Work," *Journal of Business and Technical Communication* 17, no. 2 (April 2003), pp. 170–200; "Email Brings Costs and Fatigue," *Western News* (University of Western Ontario, London, Canada), 9 July 2004; G.F. Thomas and C.L. King, "Reconceptualizing E-Mail Overload," *Journal of Business and Technical Communication* 20, no. 3 (July 2006), pp. 252–287; S. Carr, "Email Overload Menace Growing," *Silicon.com*, 12 July 2007.

21. W.M. Bulkeley, "Playing Well with Others: How IBM's Employees Have Taken Social Networking to an Unusual Level," *Wall Street Journal*, 18 June 2007, p. R10; M. Rauch, "Virtual Reality," *Sales & Marketing Management* 159, no. 1 (January 2007), pp. 18–23.

22. A.F. Cameron and J. Webster, "Unintended Consequences of Emerging Communication Technologies: Instant Messaging in the Workplace," *Computers in Human Behavior* 21, no. 1 (2005), pp. 85–103.

23. H. Green, "The Water Cooler Is Now on the Web," *BusinessWeek*, 1 October 2007, p. 78; N.J. Hoover, "Social Experiment," *InformationWeek*, 24 September 2007, p. 40; C. Boulton, "IBM's Social Beehive and Discovery Search," *www.eWeek.com*, 21 January 2008.

24. C. Wagner and A. Majchrzak, "Enabling Customer-Centricity Using Wikis and the Wiki Way," *Journal of Management Information Systems* 23, no. 3 (2006), pp. 17–43; R.B. Ferguson, "Build a Web 2.0 Platform and Employees Will Use It," *eWeek*, 20 June 2007; C. Karena, "Working the Wiki Way," *Sydney Morning Herald*, 6 March 2007.

25. K. Grayson, "Best Buy Employee Site a Model for Big Firms," *Minneapolis/St. Paul Business Journal*, 2 May 2008; P. Krill, "Web 2.0 Scores Successes in the Enterprise," *InfoWorld Daily News*, 18 June 2008.

26. L.Z. Tiedens and A.R. Fragale, "Power Moves: Complementarity in Dominant and Submissive Nonverbal Behavior," *Journal of Personality and Social Psychology* 84, no. 3 (2003), pp. 558–568.

27. P. Ekman and E. Rosenberg, *What the Face Reveals: Basic and Applied Studies of Spontaneous Expression Using the Facial Action Coding System* (Oxford, England: Oxford University Press, 1997); P. Winkielman and K.C. Berridge, "Unconscious Emotion," *Current Directions in Psychological Science* 13, no. 3 (2004), pp. 120–123.

28. E. Hatfield, J.T. Cacioppo, and R.L. Rapson, *Emotional Contagion* (Cambridge, UK: Cambridge University Press, 1993); S.G. Barsade, "The Ripple Effect: Emotional Contagion and Its Influence on Group Behavior," *Administrative Science Quarterly* 47 (December 2002), pp. 644–675; M. Sonnby-Borgstrom, P. Jonsson, and O. Svensson, "Emotional Empathy as Related to Mimicry Reactions at Different Levels of Information Processing," *Journal of Nonverbal Behavior* 27 (Spring 2003), pp. 3–23; S.G. Barsade and D.E. Gibson, "Why Does Affect Matter in Organizations?" *Academy of Management Perspectives* (February 2007), pp. 36–59; S.K. Johnson, "I Second That Emotion: Effects of Emotional Contagion and Affect at Work on Leader and Follower Outcomes," *Leadership Quarterly* 19, no. 1 (2008), pp. 1–19.

29. J.R. Kelly and S.G. Barsade, "Mood and Emotions in Small Groups and Work Teams," *Organizational Behavior and Human Decision Processes* 86 (September 2001), pp. 99–130.

30. L.K. Treviño, J. Webster, and E.W. Stein, "Making Connections: Complementary Influences on Communication Media Choices, Attitudes, and Use," *Organization Science* 11, no. 2 (2000), pp. 163–182; B. Barry and I.S. Fulmer, "The Medium Is the Message: The Adaptive Use of Communication Media in Dyadic Influence," *Academy of Management Review* 29, no. 2 (2004), pp. 272–292; J.W. Turner et al., "Exploring the Dominant Media: How Does Media Use Reflect Organizational Norms and Affect Performance?" *Journal of Business Communication* 43, no. 3 (July 2006), pp. 220–250; M.B. Watson-Manheim and F. Bélanger, "Communication Media Repertoires: Dealing with the Multiplicity of Media Choices," *MIS Quarterly* 31, no. 2 (2007), pp. 267–293.

31. R.C. King, "Media Appropriateness: Effects of Experience on Communication Media Choice," *Decision Sciences* 28, no. 4 (1997), pp. 877–910.

32. K. Griffiths, "KPMG Sacks 670 Employees by E-Mail," *The Independent* (London), 5 November 2002, p. 19; "Shop Worker Sacked by Text Message," *The Post* (Claremont/Nedlands, Western Australia), 28 July 2007, p. 1, 78.

33. R.L. Daft and R.H. Lengel, "Information Richness: A New Approach to Managerial Behavior and Organization Design," *Research in Organizational Behavior* 6 (1984), pp. 191–233; R.H. Lengel and R.L. Daft, "The Selection of Communication Media as an Executive Skill," *Academy of Management Executive* 2 (1988), pp. 225–232.

34. R.E. Rice, "Task Analyzability, Use of New Media, and Effectiveness: A Multi-Site Exploration of Media Richness," *Organization Science* 3 (1992), pp. 475–500.

35. J.W. Turner and N.L. Reinsch Jr., "The Business Communicator as Presence Allocator," *Journal of Business Communication* 44, no. 1 (2007), pp. 36–58; N.L. Reinsch Jr., J.W. Turner, and C.H. Tinsley, "Multicommunicating: A Practice Whose Time Has Come?" *Academy of Management Review* 33, no. 2 (2008), pp. 391–403.

36. "Employer Snapshots: 2008," *Toronto Star*, 13 October 2007; H. Schachter, "Strange but True: Some Staff Meetings Are Actually Efficient," *Globe & Mail*, 23 July 2007.

37. Carlson and Zmud, "Channel Expansion Theory and the Experiential Nature of Media Richness Perceptions"; N. Kock, "Media Richness or Media Naturalness? The Evolution of Our Biological Communication Apparatus and Its Influence on Our Behavior toward E-Communication Tools," *IEEE Transactions on Professional Communication* 48, no. 2 (June 2005), pp. 117–130.

38. D. Muller, T. Atzeni, and F. Butera, "Coaction and Upward Social Comparison Reduce the Illusory Conjunction Effect: Support for Distraction-Conflict Theory," *Journal of Experimental Social Psychology* 40, no. 5 (2004), pp. 659–665; L.P. Robert and A.R. Dennis, "Paradox of Richness: A Cognitive Model of Media Choice," *IEEE Transactions on Professional Communication* 48, no. 1 (2005), pp. 10–21.

39. M. McLuhan, *Understanding Media: The Extensions of Man* (New York: McGraw-Hill, 1964).

40. K. Griffiths, "KPMG Sacks 670 Employees by E-Mail," *The Independent* (London), 5 November 2002, p. 19; P. Nelson, "Work Practices," *Personnel Today*, 12 November 2002, p. 2.

41. E.V. Wilson, "Perceived Effectiveness of Interpersonal Persuasion Strategies in Computer-Mediated Communication," *Computers in Human Behavior* 19, no. 5 (2003), pp. 537–552; K. Sassenberg, M. Boos, and S. Rabung, "Attitude Change in Face-to-Face and Computer-Mediated Communication: Private Self-Awareness as Mediator and Moderator," *European Journal of Social Psychology* 35 (2005), pp. 361–374; P. Di Blasio and L. Milani, "Computer-Mediated Communication and Persuasion: Peripheral vs. Central Route to Opinion Shift," *Computers in Human Behavior* 24, no. 3 (2008), pp. 798–815.

42. J. Kruger et al., "Egocentrism over E-Mail: Can We Communicate as Well as We Think?" *Journal of Personality and Social Psychology* 89, no. 6 (2005), pp. 925–936.

43. D. Goleman, R. Boyatzis, and A. McKee, *Primal Leaders* (Boston: Harvard Business School Press, 2002), pp. 92–95.

44. D. Woodruff, "Crossing Culture Divide Early Clears Merger Paths," *Asian Wall Street Journal,* 28 May 2001, p. 9.

45. T. Walsh, "Nardelli Brags on VIP Recruits, Game Plan," *Detroit Free Press,* 8 September 2007.

46. R.M. Krauss, "The Psychology of Verbal Communication," in *International Encyclopedia of the Social and Behavioral Sciences,* ed. N. Smelser and P. Baltes (London: Elsevier, 2002), pp. 16161–16165.

47. L.L. Putnam, N. Phillips, and P. Chapman, "Metaphors of Communication and Organization," in *Handbook of Organization Studies,* ed. S.R. Clegg, C. Hardy, and W.R. Nord (London: Sage, 1996), pp. 373–408; G. Morgan, *Images of Organization,* 2d ed. (Thousand Oaks, CA: Sage, 1997); M. Rubini and H. Sigall, "Taking the Edge Off of Disagreement: Linguistic Abstractness and Self-Presentation to a Heterogeneous Audience," *European Journal of Social Psychology* 32 (2002), pp. 343–351.

48. T. Koski, "Reflections on Information Glut and Other Issues in Knowledge Productivity," *Futures* 33 (August 2001), pp. 483–495.

49. A.G. Schick, L.A. Gordon, and S. Haka, "Information Overload: A Temporal Approach," *Accounting, Organizations & Society* 15 (1990), pp. 199–220; A. Edmunds and A. Morris, "The Problem of Information Overload in Business Organisations: A Review of the Literature," *International Journal of Information Management* 20 (2000), pp. 17–28; R. Pennington, "The Effects of Information Overload on Software Project Risk Assessment," *Decision Sciences* 38, no. 3 (August 2007), pp. 489–526.

50. D.C. Thomas and K. Inkson, *Cultural Intelligence: People Skills for Global Business* (San Francisco: Berrett-Koehler, 2004), chap. 6; D. Welch, L. Welch, and R. Piekkari, "Speaking in Tongues," *International Studies of Management & Organization* 35, no. 1 (Spring 2005), pp. 10–27.

51. S. Ohtaki, T. Ohtaki, and M.D. Fetters, "Doctor-Patient Communication: A Comparison of the USA and Japan," *Family Practice* 20 (June 2003), pp. 276–282; M. Fujio, "Silence during Intercultural Communication: A Case Study," *Corporate Communications* 9, no. 4 (2004), pp. 331–339.

52. D.C. Barnlund, *Communication Styles of Japanese and Americans: Images and Realities* (Belmont, CA: Wadsworth, 1988); H. Yamada, *American and Japanese Business Discourse: A Comparison of Interaction Styles* (Norwood, NJ: Ablex, 1992), chap. 2; H. Yamada, *Different Games, Different Rules* (New York: Oxford University Press, 1997), pp. 76–79.

53. M. Griffin, "The Office, Australian Style," *Sunday Age* (22 June 2003), p. 6.

54. 34. S. Ohtaki, T. Ohtaki, and M.D. Fetters, "Doctor–Patient Communication: A Comparison of the USA and Japan," *Family Practice* 20 (June 2003), pp. 276–82; M. Fujio, "Silence during Intercultural Communication: A Case Study," *Corporate Communications* 9, no. 4 (2004), pp. 331–39.

55. P. Harris and R. Moran, *Managing Cultural Differences* (Houston: Gulf, 1987); H. Blagg, "A Just Measure of Shame?" *British Journal of Criminology* 37 (Autumn 1997), pp. 481–501; R.E. Axtell, *Gestures: The Do's and Taboos of Body Language around the World,* rev. ed. (New York: Wiley, 1998).

56. D.C. Barnlund, *Communication Styles of Japanese and Americans: Images and Realities* (Belmont,CA: Wadsworth, 1988); Yamada, *American and Japanese Business Discourse: A Comparison of Interaction Styles,* Chapter 2; H. Yamada, *Different Games, Different Rules* (New York: Oxford University Press, 1997), pp. 76–79.

57. D. Tannen, *You Just Don't Understand: Men and Women in Conversation* (New York: Ballantine Books, 1990); D. Tannen, *Talking from 9 to 5* (New York: Avon, 1994); M. Crawford, *Talking Difference: On Gender and Language* (Thousand Oaks, CA: Sage, 1995), pp. 41–44; L.L. Namy, L.C. Nygaard, and D. Sauerteig, "Gender Differences in Vocal Accommodation: The Role of Perception," *Journal of Language and Social Psychology* 21, no. 4 (December 2002), pp. 422–432; H. Itakura and A.B.M. Tsui, "Gender and Conversational Dominance in Japanese Conversation," *Language in Society* 33, no. 2 (2004), pp. 223–248.

58. A. Mulac et al., "Uh-Huh. What's That All About?' Differing Interpretations of Conversational Backchannels and Questions as Sources of Miscommunication across Gender Boundaries," *Communication Research* 25 (December 1998), pp. 641–668; N.M. Sussman and D.H. Tyson, "Sex and Power: Gender Differences in Computer-Mediated Interactions," *Computers in Human Behavior* 16 (2000), pp. 381–394; D.R. Caruso and P. Salovey, *The Emotionally Intelligent Manager* (San Francisco: Jossey-Bass, 2004), p. 23; D. Fallows, *How Women and Men Use the Internet* (Washington, DC: Pew Internet and American Life Project, 28 December 2005).

59. K. Davis and J.W. Newstrom, *Human Behavior at Work: Organizational Behavior,* 7th ed. (New York: McGraw-Hill, 1985), p. 413.

60. The three components of listening discussed here are based on several recent studies in the field of marketing, including S.B. Castleberry, C.D. Shepherd, and R. Ridnour, "Effective Interpersonal Listening in the Personal Selling Environment: Conceptualization, Measurement, and Nomological Validity," *Journal of Marketing Theory and Practice* 7 (Winter 1999), pp. 30–38; L.B. Comer and T. Drollinger, "Active Empathetic Listening and Selling Success: A Conceptual Framework," *Journal of Personal Selling & Sales Management* 19 (Winter 1999), pp. 15–29; K. de Ruyter and M.G.M. Wetzels, "The Impact of Perceived Listening Behavior in Voice-to-Voice Service Encounters," *Journal of Service Research* 2 (February 2000), pp. 276–284.

61. S.P. Means, "Playing at Pixar," *Salt Lake Tribune* (Utah), 30 May 2003, p. D1; G. Whipp, "Swimming against the Tide," *Daily News of Los Angeles,* 30 May 2003, p. U6.

62. Thomas Harris, *I'm OK–You're OK,* Arrow, 288pp, 1995; Amy Thomas Harris, *Staying OK,* Arrow, 297pp, 1995.

63. "JAL Reform Step Ejects Execs from Private Rooms," *Japan Times,* 17 May 2007.

64. A. Leaman and B. Bordass, "Productivity in Buildings: The Killer Variables," *Building Research & Information* 27, no. 1 (1999), pp. 4–19; T.J. Allen, "Architecture and Communication among Product Development Engineers," *California Management Review* 49, no. 2 (Winter 2007), pp. 23–41; F. Becker, "Organizational Ecology and Knowledge Networks," *California Management Review* 49, no. 2 (Winter 2007), pp. 42–61.

65. M. Gardner, "Democratic Principles Make Businesses More Transparent," *Christian Science Monitor,* 19 March 2007, p. 13.

66. G. Evans and D. Johnson, "Stress and Open-Office Noise," *Journal of Applied Psychology* 85 (2000), pp. 779–783; F. Russo, "My Kingdom for a Door," *Time Magazine,* 23 October 2000, p. B1.

67. S.P. Means, "Playing at Pixar," *Salt Lake Tribune* (Utah), 30 May 2003, p. D1; G. Whipp, "Swimming against the Tide," *Daily News of Los Angeles,* 30 May 2003, p. U6.

68. E. Cone, "Rise of the Blog," *CIO Insight,* April 2005, p. 54; M. Delio, "The Enterprise Blogosphere," *InfoWorld,* 28 March 2005, pp. 42–47.

69. S. Greengard, "Employee Surveys: Ask the Right Questions, Probe the Answers for Insight," *Workforce Management,* December 2004, p. 76; A. Kover, "And the Survey Says…" *Industry Week,* September 2005, pp. 49–52.

70. R. Rodwell, "Regular Staff Meetings Help Build Morale," *South China Morning Post* (Hong Kong), 27 August 2005, p. 4.

71. T. Fenton, "Inside the WorldBlu List: 1-800-Got-Junk?'s CEO on Why 'Being Democratic Is Extremely Important to Maintaining Our Competitive Advantage,' " (Atlanta: WorldBlu, 3 January 2008). The original term is "management by *wandering* around," but this has been replaced with *walking around* over the years. See W. Ouchi, *Theory Z* (New York: Avon Books, 1981), pp. 176–177; T. Peters and R. Waterman, *In Search of Excellence* (New York: Harper & Row, 1982), p. 122.

72. D. Thomas, "HR Challenges . . . I'm Lovin' It," *Personnel Today,* 6 September 2005, p. 11.

73. R. Rousos, "Trust in Leaders Lacking at Utility," *The Ledger* (Lakeland, FL), 29 July 2003, p. B1; B. Whitworth and B. Riccomini, "Management Communication: Unlocking Higher Employee Performance," *Communication World,* March–April 2005, pp. 18–21.

74. K. Davis, "Management Communication and the Grapevine," *Harvard Business Review* 31 (September–October 1953), pp. 43–49; W.L. Davis and J.R. O'Connor, "Serial Transmission of Information: A Study of the Grapevine," *Journal of Applied Communication Research* 5 (1977), pp. 61–72.

75. H. Mintzberg, *The Structuring of Organizations* (Englewood Cliffs, NJ: Prentice Hall, 1979), pp. 46–53; D. Krackhardt and J.R. Hanson, "Informal Networks: The Company Behind the Chart," *Harvard Business Review* 71 (July–August 1993), pp. 104–111.

76. C.J. Walker and C.A. Beckerle, "The Effect of State Anxiety on Rumor Transmission," *Journal of Social Behaviour & Personality* 2 (August 1987), pp. 353–360; R.L. Rosnow, "Inside Rumor: A Personal Journey," *American Psychologist* 46 (May 1991), pp. 484–496; M. Noon and R. Delbridge, "News from Behind My Hand: Gossip in Organizations," *Organization Studies* 14 (1993), pp. 23–36.

77. N. Nicholson, "Evolutionary Psychology: Toward a New View of Human Nature and Organizational Society," *Human Relations* 50 (September 1997), pp. 1053–1078; R.F. Baumeister, L. Zhang, and K.D. Vohs, "Gossip as Cultural Learning," *Review of General Psychology* 8, no. 2 (2004), pp. 111–121; E.K. Foster, "Research on Gossip: Taxonomy, Methods, and Future Directions," *Review of General Psychology* 8, no. 2 (2004), pp. 78–99.

Chapter 10

1. D.A. Brown, *A Matter of Trust* (Ottawa: Government of Canada, 15 June 2007); N. Greenaway, "Ex-RCMP Boss Showed 'Lack of Leadership,' " *Ottawa Citizen,* 11 December 2007; T. MacCharles, "High Cost of Whistleblowing," *Toronto Star,* 30 June 2007; K. May, "Budget Check Led to RCMP Slush Fund," *Ottawa Citizen,* 14 April 2007.

2. J.R.P. French and B. Raven, "The Bases of Social Power," in *Studies in Social Power,* ed. D. Cartwright (Ann Arbor: University of Michigan Press, 1959), pp. 150–167; A.D. Galinsky et al., "Power and Perspectives Not Taken," *Psychological Science* 17, no. 12

(2006), pp. 1068–1074. Also see H. Mintzberg, *Power in and around Organizations* (Englewood Cliffs, NJ: Prentice Hall, 1983), chap. 1; J. Pfeffer, *Managing with Power* (Boston: Harvard Business University Press, 1992), pp. 17, 30.

3. R.A. Dahl, "The Concept of Power," *Behavioral Science* 2 (1957), pp. 201–218; R.M. Emerson, "Power-Dependence Relations," *American Sociological Review* 27 (1962), pp. 31–41; A.M. Pettigrew, *The Politics of Organizational Decision-Making* (London: Tavistock, 1973).

4. R. Gulati and M. Sytch, "Dependence Asymmetry and Joint Dependence in Interorganizational Relationships: Effects of Embeddedness on a Manufacturer's Performance in Procurement Relationships," *Administrative Science Quarterly* 52, no. 1 (2007), pp. 32–69.

5. French and Raven, "The Bases of Social Power"; P. Podsakoff and C. Schreisheim, "Field Studies of French and Raven's Bases of Power: Critique, Analysis, and Suggestions for Future Research," *Psychological Bulletin* 97 (1985), pp. 387–411; P.P. Carson and K.D. Carson, "Social Power Bases: A Meta-Analytic Examination of Interrelationships and Outcomes," *Journal of Applied Social Psychology* 23 (1993), pp. 1150–1169.

6. C. Barnard, *The Function of the Executive* (Cambridge, MA: Harvard University Press, 1938); C. Hardy and S.R. Clegg, "Some Dare Call It Power," in *Handbook of Organization Studies*, ed. S.R. Clegg, C. Hardy, and W.R. Nord (London: Sage, 1996), pp. 622–641.

7. A.I. Shahin and P.L. Wright, "Leadership in the Context of Culture: An Egyptian Perspective," *Leadership & Organization Development Journal* 25, no. 5–6 (2004), pp. 499–511; Y.J. Huo et al., "Leadership and the Management of Conflicts in Diverse Groups: Why Acknowledging versus Neglecting Subgroup Identity Matters," *European Journal of Social Psychology* 35, no. 2 (2005), pp. 237–254.

8. L.S. Sya, "Flying to Greater Heights," *New Sunday Times* (Kuala Lumpur), 31 July 2005, p. 14; M. Bolch, "Rewarding the Team," *HRMagazine*, February 2007, pp. 91–93.

9. J.M. Peiro and J.L. Melia, "Formal and Informal Interpersonal Power in Organisations: Testing a Bifactorial Model of Power in Role-Sets," *Applied Psychology* 52, no. 1 (2003), pp. 14–35.

10. P.F. Drucker, "The New Workforce," *The Economist* (3 November 2001), pp. 8–12.

11. R.B. Cialdini and N.J. Goldstein, "Social Influence: Compliance and Conformity," *Annual Review of Psychology* 55 (2004), pp. 591–621.

12. C.K. Hofling et al., "An Experimental Study in Nurse-Physician Relationships," *Journal of Nervous and Mental Disease* 143, no. 2 (1966), pp. 171–180.

13. K. Miyahara, "Charisma: From Weber to Contemporary Sociology," *Sociological Inquiry* 53, no. 4 (Fall 1983), pp. 368–388; J.D. Kudisch and M.L. Poteet, "Expert Power, Referent Power, and Charisma: Toward the Resolution of a Theoretical Debate," *Journal of Business & Psychology* 10 (Winter 1995), pp. 177–195; D. Ladkin, "The Enchantment of the Charismatic Leader: Charisma Reconsidered as Aesthetic Encounter," *Leadership* 2, no. 2 (May 2006), pp. 165–179.

14. G. Yukl and C.M. Falbe, "Importance of Different Power Sources in Downward and Lateral Relations," *Journal of Applied Psychology* 76 (1991), pp. 416–423; B.H. Raven, "Kurt Lewin Address: Influence, Power, Religion, and the Mechanisms of Social Control," *Journal of Social Issues* 55 (Spring 1999), pp. 161–186.

15. P.L. Dawes, D.Y. Lee, and G.R. Dowling, "Information Control and Influence in Emergent Buying Centers," *Journal of Marketing* 62, no. 3 (July 1998), pp. 55–68; D. Willer, "Power-at-a-Distance," *Social Forces* 81, no. 4 (2003), pp. 1295–1334; D.J. Brass et al., "Taking Stock of Networks and Organizations: A Multilevel Perspective," *Academy of Management Journal* 47, no. 6 (December 2004), pp. 795–817.

16. C.R. Hinings et al., "Structural Conditions of Intraorganizational Power," *Administrative Science Quarterly* 19 (1974), pp. 22–44. Also see C.S. Saunders, "The Strategic Contingency Theory of Power: Multiple Perspectives," *Journal of Management Studies* 27 (1990), pp. 1–21.

17. D. Brady, "The It Girl," *Canadian Business*, 5 November 2007, pp. 43–46; A. McMains, "TBWA Confirms DeCourcy Hire," *AdWeek*, 21 August 2007, www.adweek.com/aw/national/article_display.jsp?vnu_content_id=1003628468; "The Judges," *Advertising Age's Creativity*, May 2008, p. 100; N. Bussey, "TBWA Forms Digital Agency for Adidas," *Campaign*, 26 September 2008, p. 2; D. Kaplan, "Interview: Colleen DeCourcy, CDO, TBWA," *paidcontent.org*, 1 June 2008; D. Long, "Digital Thinkers: Judge and Jury," *New Media Age*, 27 March 2008, p. 29.

18. D.J. Hickson et al., "A Strategic Contingencies' Theory of Intraorganizational Power," *Administrative Science Quarterly* 16 (1971), pp. 216–227; Hinings et al., "Structural Conditions of Intraorganizational Power"; R.M. Kanter, "Power Failure in Management Circuits," *Harvard Business Review* (July–August 1979), pp. 65–75.

19. Hickson et al., "A Strategic Contingencies' Theory of Intraorganizational Power"; J.D. Hackman, "Power and Centrality in the Allocation of Resources in Colleges and Universities," *Administrative Science Quarterly* 30 (1985), pp. 61–77; D.J. Brass and M.E. Burkhardt, "Potential Power and Power Use: An Investigation of Structure and Behavior," *Academy of Management Journal* 36 (1993), pp. 441–470.

20. D. Gates, "Simmering Strike Scorching Both Sides," *Seattle Times,* 29 September 2008, p. A1; J. Wallace and A. James, "Strike Time," *Seattle Post-Intelligencer,* 6 September 2008, p. A1.

21. S.D. Harrington and B. Ivry, "For Commuters, a Day to Adapt," *The Record* (Bergen, NJ), 21 December 2005, p. A1; S. McCarthy, "Transit Strike Cripples New York," *Globe & Mail* (Toronto), 21 December 2005, p. A17.

22. Kanter, "Power Failure in Management Circuits"; B.E. Ashforth, "The Experience of Powerlessness in Organizations," *Organizational Behavior and Human Decision Processes* 43 (1989), pp. 207–242; L. Holden, "European Managers: HRM and an Evolving Role," *European Business Review* 12 (2000).

23. D.C. Hambrick and E. Abrahamson, "Assessing Managerial Discretion across Industries: A Multimethod Approach," *Academy of Management Journal* 38, no. 5 (1995), pp. 1427–1441; M.A. Carpenter and B.R. Golden, "Perceived Managerial Discretion: A Study of Cause and Effect," *Strategic Management Journal* 18, no. 3 (1997), pp. 187–206.

24. J. Voight, "When Credit Is Not Due," *Adweek,* 1 March 2004, p. 24.

25. R. Madell, "Ground Floor," *Pharmaceutical Executive (Women in Pharma Supplement),* June 2000, pp. 24–31.

26. D. Krackhardt and J.R. Hanson, "Informal Networks: The Company behind the Chart," *Harvard Business Review* 71 (July–August 1993), pp. 104–111; P.S. Adler and S.-W. Kwon, "Social Capital: Prospects for a New Concept," *Academy of Management Review* 27, no. 1 (2002), pp. 17–40.

27. A. Mehra, M. Kilduff, and D. J. Brass, "The Social Networks of High and Low Self-Monitors: Implications for Workplace Performance," *Administrative Science Quarterly* 46 (March 2001), pp. 121–146.

28. D. Bushey and M. Joll, "Social Network Analysis Comes to Raytheon," *The Monitor* (Raytheon news magazine), 2006; J. McGregor, "The Office Chart That Really Counts," *BusinessWeek,* 27 February 2006, p. 48; J. Reingold, "What's Your OQ?" *Fortune,* 23 July 2007, pp. 98–106; T. Cox, "Map Quest," *Quality Progress,* May 2008, p. 44.

29. B.R. Ragins and E. Sundstrom, "Gender and Power in Organizations: A Longitudinal Perspective," *Psychological Bulletin* 105 (1989), pp. 51–88; M. Linehan, "Barriers to Women's Participation in International Management," *European Business Review* 13 (2001).

30. A. DeFelice, "Climbing to the Top," *Accounting Technology* 24, no. 1 (2008), pp. 12–18.

31. D.M. McCracken, "Winning the Talent War for Women: Sometimes It Takes a Revolution," *Harvard Business Review* (November–December 2000), pp. 159–167.

32. D. Keltner, D.H. Gruenfeld, and C. Anderson, "Power, Approach, and Inhibition," *Psychological Review* 110, no. 2 (2003), pp. 265–284; B. Simpson and C. Borch, "Does Power Affect Perception in Social Networks? Two Arguments and an Experimental Test," *Social Psychology Quarterly* 68, no. 3 (2005), pp. 278–287; Galinsky et al., "Power and Perspectives Not Taken."

33. "Many Nails in Zaccardelli's Coffin," *Toronto Star,* 11 December 2006, p. A18; A. Mayeda, "Top Mountie Unhorsed," *Montreal Gazette,* 7 December 2006, p. A1; B. Laghi and O. Moore, "Mounties Say Top Ranks Covered Up Mismanagement of Pension Fund," *Globe & Mail,* 29 March 2007, p. A1.

34. K. Atuahene-Gima and H. Li, "Marketing's Influence Tactics in New Product Development: A Study of High Technology Firms in China," *Journal of Product Innovation Management* 17 (2000), pp. 451–470; A. Somech and A. Drach-Zahavy, "Relative Power and Influence Strategy: The Effects of Agent/Target Organizational Power on Superiors' Choices of Influence Strategies," *Journal of Organizational Behavior* 23 (2002), pp. 167–179.

35. D. Kipnis, S.M. Schmidt, and I. Wilkinson, "Intraorganizational Influence Tactics: Explorations in Getting One's Way," *Journal of Applied Psychology* 65 (1980), pp. 440–452; A. Rao and K. Hashimoto, "Universal and Culturally Specific Aspects of Managerial Influence: A Study of Japanese Managers," *Leadership Quarterly* 8 (1997), pp. 295–312; L.A. McFarland, A.M. Ryan, and S.D. Kriska, "Field Study Investigation of Applicant Use of Influence Tactics in a Selection Interview," *Journal of Psychology* 136 (July 2002), pp. 383–398.

36. Cialdini and Goldstein, "Social Influence."

37. Rao and Hashimoto, "Universal and Culturally Specific Aspects of Managerial Influence." Silent authority as an influence tactic in non-Western cultures is also discussed in S.F. Pasa, "Leadership Influence in a High Power Distance and Collectivist Culture," *Leadership & Organization Development Journal* 21 (2000), pp. 414–426.

38. Laghi and Moore, "Mounties Say Top Ranks Covered Up Mismanagement of Pension Fund."

39. "Be Part of the Team If You Want to Catch the Eye," *Birmingham Post* (UK), 31 August 2000, p. 14; S. Maitlis, "Taking It from the Top: How CEOs Influence (and Fail to Influence) Their Boards," *Organization Studies* 25, no. 8 (2004), pp. 1275–1311.

40. A.T. Cobb, "Toward the Study of Organizational Coalitions: Participant Concerns and Activities in a Simulated Organizational Setting," *Human Relations* 44 (1991), pp. 1057–1079; E.A. Mannix, "Organizations as Resource Dilemmas: The Effects of Power Balance on Coalition Formation in Small Groups," *Organizational Behavior and Human Decision Processes* 55

(1993), pp. 1–22; D.J. Terry, M.A. Hogg, and K.M. White, "The Theory of Planned Behavior: Self-Identity, Social Identity and Group Norms," *British Journal of Social Psychology* 38 (September 1999), pp. 225–244.

41. Brown, *A Matter of Trust,* pp. 11–12.

42. M. Hiltzik, "Apple CEO's Visions Don't Guarantee Sustained Gains," *Los Angeles Times,* 14 April 2003, p. C1; D. Gilmor, "Opinion: Apple Could Use a Polishing of Jobs-Led Arrogance with Press," *PR Week,* 14 January 2008, p. 11. The origin of "reality distortion field" is described at www.folklore.org.

43. A.P. Brief, *Attitudes in and around Organizations* (Thousand Oaks, CA: Sage, 1998), pp. 69–84; D.J. O'Keefe, *Persuasion: Theory and Research* (Thousand Oaks, CA: Sage, 2002).

44. These and other features of message content in persuasion are detailed in R. Petty and J. Cacioppo, *Attitudes and Persuasion: Classic and Contemporary Approaches* (Dubuque, IA: W.C. Brown, 1981); M. Pfau, E.A. Szabo, and J. Anderson, "The Role and Impact of Affect in the Process of Resistance to Persuasion," *Human Communication Research* 27 (April 2001), pp. 216–252; O'Keefe, *Persuasion,* chap. 9; R. Buck et al., "Emotion and Reason in Persuasion: Applying the ARI Model and the CASC Scale," *Journal of Business Research* 57, no. 6 (2004), pp. 647–656; W.D. Crano and R. Prislin, "Attitudes and Persuasion," *Annual Review of Psychology* 57 (2006), pp. 345–374.

45. N. Rhodes and W. Wood, "Self-Esteem and Intelligence Affect Influenceability: The Mediating Role of Message Reception," *Psychological Bulletin* 111, no. 1 (1992), pp. 156–171.

46. D. Strutton and L.E. Pelton, "Effects of Ingratiation on Lateral Relationship Quality within Sales Team Settings," *Journal of Business Research* 43 (1998), pp. 1–12; R. Vonk, "Self-Serving Interpretations of Flattery: Why Ingratiation Works," *Journal of Personality and Social Psychology* 82 (2002), pp. 515–526.

47. C.A. Higgins, T.A. Judge, and G.R. Ferris, "Influence Tactics and Work Outcomes: A Meta-Analysis," *Journal of Organizational Behavior* 24 (2003), pp. 90–106.

48. D. Strutton, L.E. Pelton, and J. Tanner Jr., "Shall We Gather in the Garden: The Effect of Ingratiatory Behaviors on Buyer Trust in Salespeople," *Industrial Marketing Management* 25 (1996), pp. 151–162; J. O'Neil, "An Investigation of the Sources of Influence of Corporate Public Relations Practitioners," *Public Relations Review* 29 (June 2003), pp. 159–169.

49. M.C. Bolino and W.H. Turnley, "More than One Way to Make an Impression: Exploring Profiles of Impression Management," *Journal of Management* 29 (2003), pp. 141–160.

50. T. Peters, "The Brand Called You," *Fast Company,* August 1997, www.fastcompany.com/magazine/10/brandyou.html; J. Sills, "Becoming Your Own Brand," *Psychology Today* 41, no. 1 (February 2008), pp. 62–63.

51. S.L. McShane, "Applicant Misrepresentations in Résumés and Interviews in Canada," *Labor Law Journal,* January 1994, pp. 15–24; S. Romero and M. Richtel, "Second Chance," *New York Times,* 5 March 2001, p. C1; P. Sabatini, "Fibs on Résumés Commonplace," *Pittsburgh Post-Gazette,* 24 February 2006.

52. J. Laucius, "Internet Guru's Credentials a True Work of Fiction," *Ottawa Citizen,* 12 June 2001.

53. A.W. Gouldner, "The Norm of Reciprocity: A Preliminary Statement," *American Sociological Review* 25 (1960), pp. 161–178.

54. Y. Fan, "Questioning *Guanxi:* Definition, Classification, and Implications," *International Business Review* 11 (2002), pp. 543–561; D. Tan and R.S. Snell, "The Third Eye: Exploring *Guanxi* and Relational Morality in the Workplace," *Journal of Business Ethics* 41 (December 2002), pp. 361–384; W.R. Vanhonacker, "When Good *Guanxi* Turns Bad," *Harvard Business Review* 82, no. 4 (April 2004), pp. 18–19.

55. C.M. Falbe and G. Yukl, "Consequences for Managers of Using Single Influence Tactics and Combinations of Tactics," *Academy of Management Journal* 35 (1992), pp. 638–652.

56. R.C. Ringer and R.W. Boss, "Hospital Professionals' Use of Upward Influence Tactics," *Journal of Managerial Issues* 12 (2000), pp. 92–108

57. G. Blickle, "Do Work Values Predict the Use of Intraorganizational Influence Strategies?" *Journal of Applied Social Psychology* 30, no. 1 (January 2000), pp. 196–205; P.P. Fu et al., "The Impact of Societal Cultural Values and Individual Social Beliefs on the Perceived Effectiveness of Managerial Influence Strategies: A Meso Approach," *Journal of International Business Studies* 35, no. 4 (July 2004), pp. 284–305.

58. This definition of organizational politics has become the dominant perspective over the past 15 years. See G.R. Ferris and K.M. Kacmar, "Perceptions of Organizational Politics," *Journal of Management* 18 (1992), pp. 93–116; R. Cropanzano et al., "The Relationship of Organizational Politics and Support to Work Behaviors, Attitudes, and Stress," *Journal of Organizational Behavior* 18 (1997), pp. 159–180; E. Vigoda, "Stress-Related Aftermaths to Workplace Politics: The Relationships among Politics, Job Distress, and Aggressive Behavior in Organizations," *Journal of Organizational Behavior* 23 (2002), pp. 571–591. However, organizational politics was previously viewed as influence tactics outside the formal role that could be either selfish or altruistic. This older definition is less common today, possibly because it is incongruent with popular views of politics and because it

overlaps too much with the concept of influence. For the older perspective of organizational politics, see J. Pfeffer, *Power in Organizations* (Boston: Pitman, 1981); Mintzberg, *Power in and around Organizations.*

59. K.M. Kacmar and R.A. Baron, "Organizational Politics: The State of the Field, Links to Related Processes, and an Agenda for Future Research," in *Research in Personnel and Human Resources Management,* ed. G.R. Ferris (Greenwich, CT: JAI Press, 1999), pp. 1–39; L.A. Witt, T.F. Hilton, and W.A. Hochwarter, "Addressing Politics in Matrix Teams," *Group & Organization Management* 26 (June 2001), pp. 230–247; Vigoda, "Stress-Related Aftermaths to Workplace Politics."

60. D. Tannen, *Talking from 9 to 5* (New York: Avon, 1994), Chapter 2; M. Crawford, *Talking Difference: On Gender and Language* (Thousand Oaks, CA: Sage, 1995), pp. 41–44.

61. S. Mann, "Politics and Power in Organizations: Why Women Lose Out," *Leadership & Organization Development Journal* 16 (1995), pp. 9–15; E.H. Buttner and M. McEnally, "The Interactive Effect of Influence Tactic, Applicant Gender, and Type of Job on Hiring Recommendations," Sex Roles 34 (1996), pp. 581–91; L.L. Carli, "Gender, Interpersonal Power, and Social Influence," *Journal of Social Issues* 55 (Spring 1999), pp. 81–99.

62. C. Hardy, *Strategies for Retrenchment and Turnaround: The Politics of Survival* (Berlin: Walter de Gruyter, 1990), chap. 14; M.C. Andrews and K.M. Kacmar, "Discriminating among Organizational Politics, Justice, and Support," *Journal of Organizational Behavior* 22 (2001), pp. 347–366.

63. S. Blazejewski and W. Dorow, "Managing Organizational Politics for Radical Change: The Case of Beiersdorf-Lechia S.A., Poznan," *Journal of World Business* 38 (August 2003), pp. 204–223.

64. L.W. Porter, R.W. Allen, and H.L. Angle, "The Politics of Upward Influence in Organizations," *Research in Organizational Behavior* 3 (1981), pp. 120–122; R.J. House, "Power and Personality in Complex Organizations," *Research in Organizational Behavior* 10 (1988), pp. 305–357.

65. R. Christie and F. Geis, *Studies in Machiavellianism* (New York: Academic Press, 1970); S.M. Farmer et al., "Putting Upward Influence Strategies in Context," *Journal of Organizational Behavior* 18 (1997), pp. 17–42; K.S. Sauleya and A.G. Bedeian, "Equity Sensitivity: Construction of a Measure and Examination of Its Psychometric Properties," *Journal of Management* 26 (September 2000), pp. 885–910.

66. G.R. Ferris et al., "Perceptions of Organizational Politics: Prediction, Stress-Related Implications, and Outcomes," *Human Relations* 49 (1996), pp. 233–263.

Chapter 11

1. L. Belkin, "When Whippersnappers and Geezers Collide," *New York Times,* 26 July 2007; J.J. Deal, *Retiring the Generation Gap: How Employees Young and Old Can Find Common Ground* (San Francisco: Jossey-Bass, 2007); L. Gravett and R. Throckmorton, *Bridging the Generation Gap* (Franklin Lakes, NJ: Career Press, 2007); D. Kadlec, "Don't Trust Anyone under Thirty," *Money,* November 2007, pp. 50–52; P. Fogg, "When Generations Collide," *Chronicle of Higher Education* 54, no. 45 (2008), pp. B18–B20; B. Ott, N. Blacksmith, and K. Royal, "What Generation Gap? Job Seekers from Different Generations Often Look for the Same Things from Prospective Employers, According to Recent Gallup Research," *Gallup Management Journal Online,* 2008, pp. 1–4; N. Weil, "Welcome to the Generation Wars," *CIO,* 1 February 2008.

2. D. Tjosvold, *Working Together to Get Things Done* (Lexington, MA: Lexington, 1986), pp. 114–115; J.A. Wall and R.R. Callister, "Conflict and Its Management," *Journal of Management* 21 (1995), pp. 515–558; M.A. Rahim, "Toward a Theory of Managing Organizational Conflict," *International Journal of Conflict Management* 13, no. 3 (2002), pp. 206–235; D. Tjosvold, "Defining Conflict and Making Choices about Its Management," *International Journal of Conflict Management* 17, no. 2 (2006), pp. 87–95.

3. For example, see L. Urwick, *The Elements of Administration,* 2d ed. (London: Pitman, 1947); C. Argyris, "The Individual and Organization: Some Problems of Mutual Adjustment," *Administrative Science Quarterly* 2, no. 1 (1957), pp. 1–24; K.E. Boulding, "Organization and Conflict," *Conflict Resolution* 1, no. 2 (June 1957), pp. 122–134; R.R. Blake, H.A. Shepard, and J.S. Mouton, *Managing Intergroup Conflict in Industry* (Houston: Gulf, 1964).

4. C.K.W. De Dreu and L.R. Weingart, "A Contingency Theory of Task Conflict and Performance in Groups and Organizational Teams," in *International Handbook of Organizational Teamwork and Cooperative Working,* ed. M.A. West, D. Tjosvold, and K.G. Smith (Chichester, UK: Wiley, 2003), pp. 151–166; K.A. Jehn and C. Bendersky, "Intragroup Conflict in Organizations: A Contingency Perspective on the Conflict-Outcome Relationship," *Research in Organizational Behavior* 25 (2003), pp. 187–242.

5. N. Oudeh, "Functional Harmony–Assessing the Impact of Conflict on Organizational Health," paper presented at Workplace Health in a Tight Labour Market, Toronto, 7 March 2007.

6. M.P. Follett, "Constructive Conflict," in *Dynamic Administration: The Collected Papers of Mary Parker Follett,* ed. H.C. Metcalf and L. Urwick (New York: Harper and Brothers, 1942), pp. 30–37.

7. Rahim, "Toward a Theory of Managing Organizational Conflict"; M. Duarte and G. Davies, "Testing the Conflict-Performance Assumption in Business-to-Business Relationships," *Industrial Marketing Management* 32 (2003), pp. 91–99. Although

the 1970s marked a point when the benefits conflict became widely acknowledged, this view was expressed earlier by some writers. See L.A. Coser, *The Functions of Social Conflict* (New York: Free Press, 1956); J.A. Litterer, "Conflict in Organization: A Reexamination," *Academy of Management Journal* 9 (1966), pp. 178–186; H. Assael, "Constructive Role of Interorganizational Conflict," *Administrative Science Quarterly* 14, no. 4 (1969), pp. 573–582. A much earlier statement in support of conflict comes from American poet and journalist Walt Whitman, who wrote in 1860: "Have you learned lessons only of those who admired you, and were tender with you, and stood aside for you? Have you not learned great lessons from those who braced themselves against you, and disputed the passage with you?" Cited in D. Taras and P. Steel, "We Provoked Business Students to Unionize: Using Deception to Prove an IR Point," *British Journal of Industrial Relations* 45, no. 1 (March 2007), pp. 179–198.

8. K.M. Eisenhardt, J.L. Kahwajy, and L. J. Bourgeois III, "How Management Teams Can Have a Good Fight," *Harvard Business Review*, July–August 1997, pp. 77–85; K.M. Eisenhardt, J.L. Kahwajy, and L. J. Bourgeois III, "Conflict and Strategic Choice: How Top Management Teams Disagree," *California Management Review* 39 (Winter 1997), pp. 42–62; T. Greitemeyer et al., "Information Sampling and Group Decision Making: The Effects of an Advocacy Decision Procedure and Task Experience," *Journal of Experimental Psychology–Applied* 12, no. 1 (March 2006), pp. 31–42; U. Klocke, "How to Improve Decision Making in Small Groups: Effects of Dissent and Training Interventions," *Small Group Research* 38, no. 3 (June 2007), pp. 437–468.

9. H. Guetzkow and J. Gyr, "An Analysis of Conflict in Decision-Making Groups," *Human Relations* 7, no. 3 (August 1954), pp. 367–382; L.H. Pelled, K.M. Eisenhardt, and K.R. Xin, "Exploring the Black Box: An Analysis of Work Group Diversity, Conflict, and Performance," *Administrative Science Quarterly* 44 (March 1999), pp. 1–28; Jehn and Bendersky, "Intragroup Conflict in Organizations." The notion of two types of conflict dates back to the 1950s, but it became the dominant perspective in the 1990s. We have avoided using the "cognitive" and "affective" conflict labels because each type of conflict includes both cognitive and emotional elements.

10. C.K.W. De Dreu, "When Too Little or Too Much Hurts: Evidence for a Curvilinear Relationship between Task Conflict and Innovation in Teams," *Journal of Management* 32, no. 1 (February 2006), pp. 83–107.

11. C.K.W. De Dreu and L.R. Weingart, "Task versus Relationship Conflict, Team Performance, and Team Member Satisfaction: A Meta-Analysis," *Journal of Applied Psychology* 88 (August 2003), pp. 587–604; A.C. Mooney, P. J. Holahan, and A.C. Amason, "Don't Take It Personally: Exploring Cognitive Conflict as a Mediator of Affective Conflict," *Journal of Management Studies* 44, no. 5 (2007), pp. 733–758.

12. J. Yang and K.W. Mossholder, "Decoupling Task and Relationship Conflict: The Role of Intergroup Emotional Processing," *Journal of Organizational Behavior* 25 (2004), pp. 589–605.

13. A. Grove, "How to Make Confrontation Work for You," in *The Book of Management Wisdom*, ed. P. Krass (New York: Wiley, 2000), pp. 83–89; B. Schlender, "Inside Andy Grove's Latest Crusade," *Fortune*, 23 August 2004, p. 68; J. Detar, "Andy Grove, Intel's Inside Man," *Investor's Business Daily*, 24 July 2007.

14. A.C. Amason and H. J. Sapienza, "The Effects of Top Management Team Size and Interaction Norms on Cognitive and Affective Conflict," *Journal of Management* 23, no. 4 (1997), pp. 495–516.

15. L. Pondy, "Organizational Conflict: Concepts and Models," *Administrative Science Quarterly* 2 (1967), pp. 296–320; K.W. Thomas, "Conflict and Negotiation Processes in Organizations," in *Handbook of Industrial and Organizational Psychology*, 2nd ed., ed. M.D. Dunnette and L.M. Hough (Palo Alto, CA: Consulting Psychologists Press, 1992), pp. 651–718.

16. H. Barki and J. Hartwick, "Conceptualizing the Construct of Interpersonal Conflict," *International Journal of Conflict Management* 15, no. 3 (2004), pp. 216–244.

17. M.A. Von Glinow, D.L. Shapiro, and J.M. Brett, "Can We Talk, and Should We? Managing Emotional Conflict in Multicultural Teams," *Academy of Management Review* 29, no. 4 (2004), pp. 578–592.

18. G.E. Martin and T. J. Bergman, "The Dynamics of Behavioral Response to Conflict in the Workplace," *Journal of Occupational & Organizational Psychology* 69 (December 1996), pp. 377–387; J.M. Brett, D.L. Shapiro, and A.L. Lytle, "Breaking the Bonds of Reciprocity in Negotiations," *Academy of Management Journal* 41 (August 1998), pp. 410–424.

19. Murphy, "Microsoft's Midlife Crisis."

20. M.A. Von Glinow, D.L. Shapiro, and J.M. Brett, "Can We Talk, and Should We? Managing Emotional Conflict in Multicultural Teams," *Academy of Management Review* 29, no. 4 (2004), pp. 578–92.

21. G.E. Martin and T.J. Bergman, "The Dynamics of Behavioral Response to Conflict in the Workplace," *Journal of Occupational & Organizational Psychology* 69 (December 1996), pp. 377–87; J.M. Brett, D.L. Shapiro, and A.L. Lytle, "Breaking the Bonds of Reciprocity in Negotiations," *Academy of Management Journal* 41 (August 1998), pp. 410–24.

22. H. Witteman, "Analyzing Interpersonal Conflict: Nature of Awareness, Type of Initiating Event, Situational Perceptions, and Management Styles," *Western Journal of Communications* 56 (1992), pp. 248–80; Wall and Callister, "Conflict and Its Management."

23. A. Grove, "How to Make Confrontation Work for You," in *The Book of Management Wisdom*, ed. P. Krass (New York: John Wiley & Sons, 2000), pp. 83–89; B. Schlender, "Inside Andy Grove's Latest Crusade," *Fortune*, 23 August 2004, p. 68.

24. M. Rempel and R.J. Fisher, "Perceived Threat, Cohesion, and Group Problem Solving in Intergroup Conflict," *International Journal of Conflict Management* 8 (1997), pp. 216–34.

25. B. Dudley, "Bring Back the Dazzle," *Seattle Times*, 23 September 2005; J. Greene, "Troubling Exits at Microsoft," *BusinessWeek*, 26 September 2005, p. 98; A. Linn, "Microsoft Reorganizes to Compete Better with Google, Yahoo," *Associated Press Newswires*, 21 September 2005; V. Murphy, "Microsoft's Midlife Crisis," *Forbes*, 3 October 2005, p. 88; L. Vaas, "Microsoft Expands Bureaucracy, Crowns MSN King," *eWeek*, 20 September 2005; J.L. Yang, "Microsoft's New Brain," *Fortune*, 1 May 2006, p. 56.

26. R.E. Walton and J.M. Dutton, "The Management of Conflict: A Model and Review," *Administrative Science Quarterly* 14 (1969), pp. 73–84; S.M. Schmidt and T.A. Kochan, "Conflict: Toward Conceptual Clarity," *Administrative Science Quarterly* 17, no. 3 (September 1972), pp. 359–370.

27. J.A. McMullin, T. Duerden Comeau, and E. Jovic, "Generational Affinities and Discourses of Difference: A Case Study of Highly Skilled Information Technology Workers," *British Journal of Sociology* 58, no. 2 (2007), pp. 297–316.

28. P. Hinds and D.E. Bailey, "Out of Sight, Out of Sync: Understanding Conflict in Distributed Teams," *Organization Science* 14, no. 6 (2003), pp. 615–632; P. Hinds and M. Mortensen, "Understanding Conflict in Geographically Distributed Teams: The Moderating Effects of Shared Identity, Shared Context, and Spontaneous Communication," *Organization Science* 16, no. 3 (May–June 2005), pp. 290–307.

29. M. Landler, "Twist in the Intrigue at VW May Help Chief Keep His Job," *New York Times*, 21 April 2006, p. 5; R. Hutton, "Porsche Ready to Swallow VW," *Autocar*, 7 November 2007; "German Carmaker Family Feud Plays Out in VW Boardroom," *Deutsche Welle*, 18 September 2008; D. Hawranek, "Clans, Executives Sharpen Knives Backstage at Porsche and VW," *Spiegel Online*, 11 March 2008; N.D. Schwartz, "Porsche Takes a Controlling Interest in VW," *New York Times*, 17 September 2008.

30. R. Wageman and G. Baker, "Incentives and Cooperation: The Joint Effects of Task and Reward Interdependence on Group Performance," *Journal of Organizational Behavior* 18, no. 2 (1997), pp. 139–158; G.S. van der Vegt, B.J.M. Emans, and E. van de Vliert, "Patterns of Interdependence in Work Teams: A Two-Level Investigation of the Relations with Job and Team Satisfaction," *Personnel Psychology* 54, no. 1 (2001), pp. 51–69.

31. P.C. Earley and G.B. Northcraft, "Goal Setting, Resource Interdependence, and Conflict Management," in *Managing Conflict: An Interdisciplinary Approach*, ed. M.A. Rahim (New York: Praeger, 1989), pp. 161–170; K. Jehn, "A Multimethod Examination of the Benefits and Detriments of Intragroup Conflict," *Administrative Science Quarterly* 40 (1995), pp. 245–282.

32. A. Risberg, "Employee Experiences of Acquisition Processes," *Journal of World Business* 36 (March 2001), pp. 58–84.

33. Jehn and Bendersky, "Intragroup Conflict in Organizations."

34. M. Hewstone, M. Rubin, and H. Willis, "Intergroup Bias," *Annual Review of Psychology* 53 (2002), pp. 575–604; J. Jetten, R. Spears, and T. Postmes, "Intergroup Distinctiveness and Differentiation: A Meta-Analytic Integration," *Journal of Personality and Social Psychology* 86, no. 6 (2004), pp. 862–879.

35. Follett, "Constructive Conflict"; Blake, Shepard, and Mouton, *Managing Intergroup Conflict in Industry;* T. Ruble and K. Thomas, "Support for a Two-Dimensional Model of Conflict Behavior," *Organizational Behavior and Human Performance* 16 (1976), pp. 143–155; C.K.W. De Dreu et al., "A Theory-Based Measure of Conflict Management Strategies in the Workplace," *Journal of Organizational Behavior* 22 (2001), pp. 645–668; Rahim, "Toward a Theory of Managing Organizational Conflict."

36. Jehn, "A Multimethod Examination of the Benefits and Detriments of Intragroup Conflict."

37. G.A. Callanan, C.D. Benzing, and D.F. Perri, "Choice of Conflict-Handling Strategy: A Matter of Context," *Journal of Psychology* 140, no. 3 (2006), pp. 269–288.

38. D.W. Johnson et al., "Effects of Cooperative, Competitive, and Individualistic Goal Structures on Achievement: A Meta-Analysis," *Psychological Bulletin* 89 (1981), pp. 47–62; Rahim, "Toward a Theory of Managing Organizational Conflict."

39. R.A. Friedman et al., "What Goes Around Comes Around: The Impact of Personal Conflict Style on Work Conflict and Stress," *International Journal of Conflict Management* 11, no. 1 (2000), pp. 32–55; X.M. Song, J. Xile, and B. Dyer, "Antecedents and Consequences of Marketing Managers' Conflict-Handling Behaviors," *Journal of Marketing* 64 (January 2000), pp. 50–66; M. Song, B. Dyer, and R. J. Thieme, "Conflict Management and Innovation Performance: An Integrated Contingency Perspective," *Academy of Marketing Science* 34, no. 3 (2006), pp. 341–356; L.A. DeChurch, K.L. Hamilton, and C. Haas, "Effects of Conflict Management Strategies on Perceptions of Intragroup Conflict," *Group Dynamics* 11, no. 1 (2007), pp. 66–78.

40. C.K.W. De Dreu and A.E.M. Van Vianen, "Managing Relationship Conflict and the Effectiveness of Organizational Teams," *Journal of Organizational Behavior* 22 (2001), pp. 309–328; R. J. Lewicki et al., *Negotiation*, 4th ed. (Burr Ridge, IL: McGraw-Hill/Irwin, 2003), pp. 35–36.

41. D. Cox, "Goodenow's Downfall," *Toronto Star,* 29 July 2005, p. A1; A. Maki, "NHLPA's New Leader Is a Peacemaker, Not Warrior," *Globe & Mail,* 29 July 2005, p. S1; M. Spector, "Players: He Is Your Father," *National Post,* 29 July 2005, p. B8; "Report: Saskin Had Friends at NHL Head Office," *CanWest News Service,* 13 October 2007; C. Masisak, "For Kelly, It's a Big Job," *Washington Times,* 4 December 2007; R. Westhead, "Report: 'Big Brother' Spied on NHL Players," *Toronto Star,* 30 May 2007; M. Spector, "NHLPA Enjoys Breath of Fresh Air," *Globe & Mail,* 12 January 2008.

42. M.W. Morris and H.-Y. Fu, "How Does Culture Influence Conflict Resolution? Dynamic Constructivist Analysis," *Social Cognition* 19 (June 2001), pp. 324–349; C.H. Tinsley, "How Negotiators Get to Yes: Predicting the Constellation of Strategies Used across Cultures to Negotiate Conflict," *Journal of Applied Psychology* 86, no. 4 (2001), pp. 583–593; J.L. Holt and C.J. DeVore, "Culture, Gender, Organizational Role, and Styles of Conflict Resolution: A Meta-Analysis," *International Journal of Intercultural Relations* 29, no. 2 (2005), pp. 165–196.

43. D.A. Cai and E.L. Fink, "Conflict Style Differences between Individualists and Collectivists," *Communication Monographs* 69 (March 2002), pp. 67–87; C.H. Tinsley and E. Weldon, "Responses to a Normative Conflict among American and Chinese Managers," *International Journal of Conflict Management* 3, no. 2 (2003), pp. 183–194; F.P. Brew and D.R. Cairns, "Styles of Managing Interpersonal Workplace Conflict in Relation to Status and Face Concern: A Study with Anglos and Chinese," *International Journal of Conflict Management* 15, no. 1 (2004), pp. 27–57.

44. N. Brewer, P. Mitchell, and N. Weber, "Gender Role, Organizational Status, and Conflict Management Styles," *International Journal of Conflict Management* 13 (2002), pp. 78–95; N.B. Florea et al., "Negotiating from Mars to Venus: Gender in Simulated International Negotiations," *Simulation & Gaming* 34 (June 2003), pp. 226–248; Holt and DeVore, "Culture, Gender, Organizational Role, and Styles of Conflict Resolution."

45. K. Lewin, *Resolving Social Conflicts* (New York: Harper, 1948).

46. J.D. Hunger and L.W. Stern, "An Assessment of the Functionality of the Superordinate Goal in Reducing Conflict," *Academy of Management Journal* 19, no. 4 (1976), pp. 591–605; M. Sherif, "Superordinate Goals in the Reduction of Intergroup Conflict," *American Journal of Sociology* 63, no. 4 (1958), pp. 349–356.

47. Sherif, "Superordinate Goals in the Reduction of Intergroup Conflict"; Eisenhardt, Kahwajy, and Bourgeois III, "How Management Teams Can Have a Good Fight"; Song, Xile, and Dyer, "Antecedents and Consequences of Marketing Managers' Conflict-Handling Behaviors."

48. H.C. Triandis, "The Future of Workforce Diversity in International Organisations: A Commentary," *Applied Psychology: An International Journal* 52, no. 3 (2003), pp. 486–495.

49. "Can the New CEO End a Culture Clash after a Merger?" *Financial Times,* 10 September 2008, p. 16.

50. T.F. Pettigrew, "Intergroup Contact Theory," *Annual Review of Psychology* 49 (1998), pp. 65–85; S. Brickson, "The Impact of Identity Orientation on Individual and Organizational Outcomes in Demographically Diverse Settings," *Academy of Management Review* 25 (January 2000), pp. 82–101; J. Dixon and K. Durrheim, "Contact and the Ecology of Racial Division: Some Varieties of Informal Segregation," *British Journal of Social Psychology* 42 (March 2003), pp. 1–23.

51. Triandis, "The Future of Workforce Diversity in International Organisations."

52. Von Glinow, Shapiro, and Brett, "Can We Talk, and Should We?"

53. P.O. Walker, "Decolonizing Conflict Resolution: Addressing the Ontological Violence of Westernization," *American Indian Quarterly* 28, no. 3/4 (July 2004), pp. 527–49; Native Dispute Resolution Network, "Glossary of Terms" (Tucson, Arizona, 2005), http://nativenetwork.ecr.gov (accessed 15 September 2005).

54. E. Horwitt, "Knowledge, Knowledge, Who's Got the Knowledge," *Computerworld,* 8 April 1996, pp. 80, 81, 84.

55. For a critical view of the problem-solving style in negotiation, see J.M. Brett, "Managing Organizational Conflict," *Professional Psychology: Research and Practice* 15 (1984), pp. 664–678.

56. R.E. Fells, "Developing Trust in Negotiation," *Employee Relations* 15 (1993), pp. 33–45; R.E. Fells, "Overcoming the Dilemmas in Walton and McKersie's Mixed Bargaining Strategy," *Industrial Relations* (Laval) 53 (March 1998), pp. 300–325.

57. R. Stagner and H. Rosen, *Psychology of Union-Management Relations* (Belmont, CA: Wadsworth, 1965), pp. 95–96, 108–110; R.E. Walton and R.B. McKersie, *A Behavioral Theory of Labor Negotiations: An Analysis of a Social Interaction System* (New York: McGraw-Hill, 1965), pp. 41–46; L. Thompson, *The Mind and Heart of the Negotiator* (Upper Saddle River, NJ: Prentice Hall, 1998), chap. 2.

58. J.W. Salacuse and J.Z. Rubin, "Your Place or Mine? Site Location and Negotiation," *Negotiation Journal* 6 (January 1990), pp. 5–10; J. Mayfield et al., "How Location Impacts International Business Negotiations," *Review of Business* 19 (December 1998), pp. 21–24.

59. J. Margo, "The Persuaders," *Boss Magazine,* 29 December 2000, p. 38. For a full discussion of the advantages and disadvantages of face-to-face and alternative negotiation situations, see M.H. Bazerman et al., "Negotiation," *Annual Review of Psychology* 51 (2000), pp. 279–314.

60. A.F. Stuhlmacher, T.L. Gillespie, and M.V. Champagne, "The Impact of Time Pressure in Negotiation: A Meta-Analysis," *International Journal of Conflict Management* 9, no. 2 (April 1998), pp. 97–116; C.K.W. De Dreu, "Time Pressure and Closing of the Mind in Negotiation," *Organizational Behavior and Human Decision Processes* 91 (July 2003), pp. 280–295. However, one recent study reported that speeding up these concessions leads to better negotiated outcomes. See D.A. Moore, "Myopic Prediction, Self-Destructive Secrecy, and the Unexpected Benefits of Revealing Final Deadlines in Negotiation," *Organizational Behavior and Human Decision Processes* 94, no. 2 (2004), pp. 125–139.

61. Lewicki et al., *Negotiation,* pp. 298–322.

62. S. Doctoroff, "Reengineering Negotiations," *Sloan Management Review* 39 (March 1998), pp. 63–71; D.C. Zetik and A.F. Stuhlmacher, "Goal Setting and Negotiation Performance: A Meta-Analysis," *Group Processes & Intergroup Relations* 5 (January 2002), pp. 35–52.

63. B. McRae, *The Seven Strategies of Master Negotiators* (Toronto: McGraw-Hill Ryerson, 2002), pp. 7–11.

64. L.L. Thompson, "Information Exchange in Negotiation," *Journal of Experimental Social Psychology* 27 (1991), pp. 161–179.

65. L. Thompson, E. Peterson, and S.E. Brodt, "Team Negotiation: An Examination of Integrative and Distributive Bargaining," *Journal of Personality and Social Psychology* 70 (1996), pp. 66–78; Y. Paik and R.L. Tung, "Negotiating with East Asians: How to Attain 'Win-Win' Outcomes," *Management International Review* 39 (1999), pp. 103–122.

66. D.J. O'Keefe, *Persuasion: Theory and Research* (Thousand Oaks, CA: Sage, 2002).

67. Lewicki et al., *Negotiation,* pp. 90–96; S. Kwon and L.R. Weingart, "Unilateral Concessions from the Other Party: Concession Behavior, Attributions, and Negotiation Judgments," *Journal of Applied Psychology* 89, no. 2 (2004), pp. 263–278.

68. D. Malhotra, "The Fine Art of Making Concessions," *Negotiation* (January 2006), pp. 3–5.

69. J.J. Zhao, "The Chinese Approach to International Business Negotiation," *Journal of Business Communication,* July 2000, pp. 209–237; N. Crundwell, "U.S.-Russian Negotiating Strategies," *BISNIS Bulletin,* October 2003, pp. 5–6.

70. J.Z. Rubin and B.R. Brown, *The Social Psychology of Bargaining and Negotiation* (New York: Academic Press, 1976), chap. 9.

71. L.L. Putnam, "Beyond Third Party Role: Disputes and Managerial Intervention," *Employee Responsibilities and Rights Journal* 7 (1994), pp. 23–36; A.R. Elangovan, "The Manager as the Third Party: Deciding How to Intervene in Employee Disputes," in *Negotiation: Readings, Exercises, and Cases,* 3d ed., ed. R.J. Lewicki, J.A. Litterer, and D. Saunders (New York: McGraw-Hill, 1999), pp. 458–469. For a somewhat different taxonomy of managerial conflict intervention, see P.G. Irving and J.P. Meyer, "A Multidimensional Scaling Analysis of Managerial Third-Party Conflict Intervention Strategies," *Canadian Journal of Behavioural Science* 29, no. 1 (January 1997), pp. 7–18. A recent review describes 10 species of third-party intervention, but these consist of variations of the three types described here. See D.E. Conlon et al., "Third Party Interventions across Cultures: No 'One Best Choice,'" in *Research in Personnel and Human Resources Management* (Greenwich, CT: JAI Press, 2007), pp. 309–349.

72. B.H. Sheppard, "Managers as Inquisitors: Lessons from the Law," in *Bargaining inside Organizations,* ed. M.H. Bazerman and R.J. Lewicki (Beverly Hills, CA: Sage, 1983); N.H. Kim, D.W. Sohn, and J.A. Wall, "Korean Leaders' (and Subordinates') Conflict Management," *International Journal of Conflict Management* 10, no. 2 (April 1999), pp. 130–153; D.J. Moberg, "Managers as Judges in Employee Disputes: An Occasion for Moral Imagination," *Business Ethics Quarterly* 13, no. 4 (2003), pp. 453–477.

73. R. Karambayya and J.M. Brett, "Managers Handling Disputes: Third Party Roles and Perceptions of Fairness," *Academy of Management Journal* 32 (1989), pp. 687–704; R. Cropanzano et al., "Disputant Reactions to Managerial Conflict Resolution Tactics," *Group & Organization Management* 24 (June 1999), pp. 124–153.

74. A.R. Elangovan, "Managerial Intervention in Organizational Disputes: Testing a Prescriptive Model of Strategy Selection," *International Journal of Conflict Management* 4 (1998), pp. 301–335; P.S. Nugent, "Managing Conflict: Third-Party Interventions for Managers," *Academy of Management Executive* 16, no. 1 (February 2002), pp. 139–154.

75. J.P. Meyer, J.M. Gemmell, and P.G. Irving, "Evaluating the Management of Interpersonal Conflict in Organizations: A Factor-Analytic Study of Outcome Criteria," *Canadian Journal of Administrative Sciences* 14 (1997), pp. 1–13; L.B. Bingham, "Employment Dispute Resolution: The Case for Mediation," *Conflict Resolution Quarterly* 22, no. 1–2 (2004), pp. 145–174; M. Hyde et al., "Workplace Conflict Resolution and the Health of Employees in the Swedish and Finnish Units of an Industrial Company," *Social Science & Medicine* 63, no. 8 (2006), pp. 2218–2227.

76. W.H. Ross and D.E. Conlon, "Hybrid Forms of Third-Party Dispute Resolution: Theoretical Implications of Combining Mediation and Arbitration," *Academy of Management Review* 25, no. 2 (2000), pp. 416–427; W.H. Ross, C. Brantmeier, and T. Ciriacks, "The Impact of Hybrid Dispute-Resolution Procedures on Constituent Fairness Judgments," *Journal of Applied Social Psychology* 32, no. 6 (June 2002), pp. 1151–1188.

77. Department of Defense, U.S. Air Force, "AMC Uses Alternative Dispute Resolution to Solve Workplace Conflicts" (news release), Scott Air Force Base, Illinois, 13 July 2005.

78. L.B. Bingham et al., "Mediating Employment Disputes at the United States Postal Service: A Comparison of In-House and Outside Neutral Mediator Models," *Review of Public Personnel Administration* 20, no. 1 (January 2000), pp. 5–19; T.

Nabatchi, L.B. Bingham, and D.H. Good, "Organizational Justice and Workplace Mediation: A Six Factor Model," *International Journal of Conflict Management* 18, no. 2 (2007), pp. 148–174. Information was also received from the USPS Web site: www.usps.com/redress/.

79. S.L. Hayford, "Alternative Dispute Resolution," *Business Horizons* 43 (January–February 2000), pp. 2–4; O. Rabinovich-Einy, "Beyond IDR: Resolving Hospital Disputes and Healing Ailing Organizations through ITR," *St. John's Law Review* 81, no. 1 (January 2007), pp. 173–202; T.M. Marcum and E.A. Campbell, "Peer Review in Employment Disputes: An Employee Right or an Employee Wrong?" *Journal of Workplace Rights* 13, no. 1 (2008), pp. 41–58.

Chapter 12

1. "Driving the Engine," *Broadcasting & Cable* 133, no. 16 (21 April 2003), p. 6A; S. Pappu, "The Queen of Tween," *Atlantic Monthly,* November 2004, pp. 118–125; A. Becker, "The Wonderful World of Sweeney," *Broadcasting & Cable,* 25 February 2008, p. 19; J.R. Littlejohn, "Distinguished Vanguard Award for Leadership," *Multichannel News,* 19 May 2008.

2. R. House, M. Javidan, and P. Dorfman, "Project GLOBE: An Introduction," *Applied Psychology: An International Review* 50 (2001), pp. 489–505; R. House et al., "Understanding Cultures and Implicit Leadership Theories across the Globe: An Introduction to Project GLOBE," *Journal of World Business* 37 (2002), pp. 3–10.

3. Bill George, "Mindful Leadership: Compassion, Contemplation and Meditation Develop Effective Leaders," *The European Financial Review* (16 Oct 2010), http://www.europeanfinancialreview.com/?p=1855 (accessed on 26/2/2011).

4. R.G. Isaac, W.J. Zerbe, and D.C. Pitt, "Leadership and Motivation: The Effective Application of Expectancy Theory," *Journal of Managerial Issues* 13 (Summer 2001), pp. 212–226; C.L. Pearce and J.A. Conger, eds., *Shared Leadership: Reframing the Hows and Whys of Leadership* (Thousand Oaks, CA: Sage, 2003); J.S. Nielson, *The Myth of Leadership* (Palo Alto, CA: Davies-Black, 2004); J.A. Raelin, "We the Leaders: In Order to Form a Leaderful Organization," *Journal of Leadership & Organizational Studies* 12, no. 2 (2005), pp. 18–30.

5. J.A. Raelin *Creating Leaderful Organizations: How to Bring Out Leadership in Everyone* (San Francisco: Berrett-Koehler, 2003).

6. A. Deutschman, "The Fabric of Creativity," *Fast Company,* December 2004, p. 54; P.J. Kiger, "Power to the Individual," *Workforce Management,* 27 February 2006, pp. 1–7; G. Hamel, *The Future of Management* (Boston: Harvard Business School Press, 2007), chap. 5.

7. "Powered by Frontline People, *mployee Engagement Today,* September 2007; C. Hosford, "Flying High," *Incentive* 181, no. 12 (December 2007), pp. 14–20.

8. Many of these perspectives are summarized in R.N. Kanungo, "Leadership in Organizations: Looking Ahead to the 21st Century," *Canadian Psychology* 39 (Spring 1998), pp. 71–82; G.A. Yukl, *Leadership in Organizations,* 6th ed. (Upper Saddle River, NJ: Pearson Education, 2006).

9. The history of the trait perspective of leadership, as well as current research on this topic, is nicely summarized in S.J. Zaccaro, C. Kemp, and P. Bader, "Leader Traits and Attributes," in *The Nature of Leadership,* ed. J. Antonakis, A.T. Cianciolo, and R.J. Sternberg (Thousand Oaks, CA: Sage, 2004), pp. 101–124.

10. R.M. Stogdill, *Handbook of Leadership* (New York: Free Press, 1974), chap. 5.

11. J. Intagliata, D. Ulrich, and N. Smallwood, "Leveraging Leadership Competencies to Produce Leadership Brand: Creating Distinctiveness by Focusing on Strategy and Results," *Human Resources Planning* 23, no. 4 (2000), pp. 12–23; J.A. Conger and D.A. Ready, "Rethinking Leadership Competencies," *Leader to Leader* (Spring 2004), pp. 41–47; Zaccaro, Kemp, and Bader, "Leader Traits and Attributes."

12. This list is based on S.A. Kirkpatrick and E.A. Locke, "Leadership: Do Traits Matter?" *Academy of Management Executive* 5 (May 1991), pp. 48–60; R.M. Aditya, R.J. House, and S. Kerr, "Theory and Practice of Leadership: Into the New Millennium," in *Industrial and Organizational Psychology: Linking Theory with Practice,* ed. C.L. Cooper and E.A. Locke (Oxford, UK: Blackwell, 2000), pp. 130–165; D. Goleman, R. Boyatzis, and A. McKee, *Primal Leaders* (Boston: Harvard Business School Press, 2002); T.A. Judge et al., "Personality and Leadership: A Qualitative and Quantitative Review," *Journal of Applied Psychology* 87, no. 4 (August 2002), pp. 765–780; T.A. Judge, A.E. Colbert, and R. Ilies, "Intelligence and Leadership: A Quantitative Review and Test of Theoretical Propositions," *Journal of Applied Psychology* 89, no. 3 (June 2004), pp. 542–552; Zaccaro, Kemp, and Bader, "Leader Traits and Attributes."

13. M. Popper et al., "The Capacity to Lead: Major Psychological Differences between Leaders and Nonleaders," *Military Psychology* 16, no. 4 (2004), pp. 245–263.

14. B. George, *Authentic Leadership* (San Francisco: Jossey-Bass, 2004); W.L. Gardner et al., "'Can You See the Real Me?' A Self-Based Model of Authentic Leader and Follower Development," *Leadership Quarterly* 16 (2005), pp. 343–372; B. George, *True North* (San Francisco: Jossey-Bass, 2007), chap. 4; M.E. Palanski and F.J. Yammarino, "Integrity and Leadership: Clearing the Conceptual Confusion," *European Management Journal* 25, no. 3 (2007), pp. 171–184.

15. R. Charan, C. Burke, and L. Bossidy, *Execution: The Discipline of Getting Things Done* (New York: Crown Business, 2002); D. Nilsen, B. Kowske, and A. Kshanika, "Managing Globally," *HRMagazine,* August 2005, pp. 111–115.

16. The large-scale studies are reported in C. Savoye, "Workers Say Honesty Is Best Company Policy," *Christian Science Monitor,* 15 June 2000; J.M. Kouzes and B.Z. Posner, *The Leadership Challenge,* 3d ed. (San Francisco: Jossey-Bass, 2002), chap. 2; J. Schettler, "Leadership in Corporate America," *Training & Development,* September 2002, pp. 66–73.

17. M. Dolliver, "Deflating a Myth," *Brandweek,* 12 May 2008, pp. 30–32. For other surveys on low perceived integrity of business leaders, see Watson Wyatt Worldwide, "Asia-Pacific Workers Satisfied with Jobs Despite Some Misgivings with Management and Pay" (news release) Singapore, 16 November 2004; J. Cremer, "Asian Workers Give Low Marks to Leaders," *South China Morning Post* (Hong Kong), 30 July 2005, p. 8; D. Jones, "Optimism Puts Rose-Colored Tint in Glasses of Top Execs," *USA Today,* 16 December 2005, p. B1; E. Pondel, "Friends & Bosses?" *Seattle Post-Intelligencer,* 10 April 2006, p. C1.

18. R. Davidovitz et al., "Leaders as Attachment Figures: Leaders' Attachment Orientations Predict Leadership-Related Mental Representations and Followers' Performance and Mental Health," *Journal of Personality and Social Psychology* 93, no. 4 (2007), pp. 632–650.

19. J.B. Miner, "Twenty Years of Research on Role Motivation Theory of Managerial Effectiveness," *Personnel Psychology* 31 (1978), pp. 739–760; R.J. House and R.N. Aditya, "The Social Scientific Study of Leadership: Quo Vadis?" *Journal of Management* 23 (1997), pp. 409–473.

20. J. Hedlund et al., "Identifying and Assessing Tacit Knowledge: Understanding the Practical Intelligence of Military Leaders," *Leadership Quarterly* 14, no. 2 (2003), pp. 117–140; R.J. Sternberg, "A Systems Model of Leadership: WICS," *American Psychologist* 62, no. 1 (2007), pp. 34–42.

21. J. George, "Emotions and Leadership: The Role of Emotional Intelligence," *Human Relations* 53 (August 2000), pp. 1027–1055; Goleman, Boyatzis, and McKee, *Primal Leaders;* R.G. Lord and R.J. Hall, "Identity, Deep Structure and the Development of Leadership Skill," *Leadership Quarterly* 16, no. 4 (August 2005), pp. 591–615; C. Skinner and P. Spurgeon, "Valuing Empathy and Emotional Intelligence in Health Leadership: A Study of Empathy, Leadership Behaviour and Outcome Effectiveness," *Health Services Management Research* 18, no. 1 (February 2005), pp. 1–12.

22. R. Jacobs, "Using Human Resource Functions to Enhance Emotional Intelligence," in *The Emotionally Intelligent Workplace,* ed. C. Cherniss and D. Goleman (San Francisco: Jossey-Bass, 2001), pp. 161–163; Conger and Ready, "Rethinking Leadership Competencies."

23. R.G. Lord and D.J. Brown, *Leadership Processes and Self-Identity: A Follower-Centered Approach to Leadership* (Mahwah, NJ: Lawrence Erlbaum, 2004); R. Bolden and J. Gosling, "Leadership Competencies: Time to Change the Tune?" *Leadership* 2, no. 2 (May 2006), pp. 147–163.

24. P.G. Northouse, *Leadership: Theory and Practice,* 3d ed. (Thousand Oaks, CA: Sage, 2004), chap. 4; Yukl, *Leadership in Organizations,* chap. 3.

25. A.K. Korman, "Consideration, Initiating Structure, and Organizational Criteria–A Review," *Personnel Psychology* 19 (1966), pp. 349–362; E.A. Fleishman, "Twenty Years of Consideration and Structure," in *Current Developments in the Study of Leadership,* ed. E.A. Fleishman and J.C. Hunt (Carbondale: Southern Illinois University Press, 1973), pp. 1–40; T.A. Judge, R.F. Piccolo, and R. Ilies, "The Forgotten Ones? The Validity of Consideration and Initiating Structure in Leadership Research," *Journal of Applied Psychology* 89, no. 1 (2004), pp. 36–51; Yukl, *Leadership in Organizations,* pp. 62–75.

26. V.V. Baba, "Serendipity in Leadership: Initiating Structure and Consideration in the Classroom," *Human Relations* 42 (1989), pp. 509–525.

27. S. Kerr et al., "Towards a Contingency Theory of Leadership Based upon the Consideration and Initiating Structure Literature," *Organizational Behavior and Human Performance* 12 (1974), pp. 62–82; L.L. Larson, J.G. Hunt, and R.N. Osborn, "The Great Hi-Hi Leader Behavior Myth: A Lesson from Occam's Razor," *Academy of Management Journal* 19 (1976), pp. 628–641.

28. R. Tannenbaum and W.H. Schmidt, "How to Choose a Leadership Pattern," *Harvard Business Review,* May–June 1973, pp. 162–180.

29. R.P. Vecchio, J.E. Justin, and C.L. Pearce, "The Utility of Transactional and Transformational Leadership for Predicting Performance and Satisfaction within a Path-Goal Theory Framework," *Journal of Occupational and Organizational Psychology* 81 (2008), pp. 71–82.

30. For a thorough study of how expectancy theory of motivation relates to leadership, see Isaac, Zerbe, and Pitt, "Leadership and Motivation."

31. R.J. House, "A Path-Goal Theory of Leader Effectiveness," *Administrative Science Quarterly* 16 (1971), pp. 321–338; M.G. Evans, "Extensions of a Path-Goal Theory of Motivation," *Journal of Applied Psychology* 59 (1974), pp. 172–178; R.J. House and T.R. Mitchell, "Path-Goal Theory of Leadership," *Journal of Contemporary Business,* Autumn 1974, pp. 81–97; M.G. Evans, "Path Goal Theory of Leadership," in *Leadership,* ed. L.L. Neider and C.A. Schriesheim (Greenwich, CT: Information Age, 2002), pp. 115–138.

32. Various thoughts on servant leadership are presented in L.C. Spears and M. Lawrence, eds., *Focus on Leadership: Servant-Leadership* (New York: Wiley, 2002).

33. D. Tarrant, "The Leading Edge," *The Bulletin,* 15 November 2005; "2006 Movers & Shakers," *Financial Planning,* January 2006, p. 1.

34. R.J. House, "Path-Goal Theory of Leadership: Lessons, Legacy, and a Reformulated Theory," *Leadership Quarterly* 7 (1996), pp. 323–352.

35. M. Bong, "You, Me, and Sushi," *Tiger Tales* (Tiger Airways magazine), November 2006; "Apex-Pal Unveils New Growth Strategies for the Year," *Channel News Asia,* 2 April 2008; C. Prystay, "Sushi for All," *Forbes Asia,* 10 March 2008; N. Theresianto, "Apex-Pal Expands Its Sakae Sushi Empire," *Edge Singapore,* 11 February 2008; L. Wei, "Tête à Tête with Mr Douglas Foo," *Newsmag F&B,* April 2008.

36. J. Indvik, "Path-Goal Theory of Leadership: A Meta-Analysis," *Academy of Management Proceedings* (1986), pp. 189–192; J.C. Wofford and L.Z. Liska, "Path-Goal Theories of Leadership: A Meta-Analysis," *Journal of Management* 19 (1993), pp. 857–876.

37. J.D. Houghton and S.K. Yoho, "Toward a Contingency Model of Leadership and Psychological Empowerment: When Should Self-Leadership Be Encouraged?" *Journal of Leadership & Organizational Studies* 11, no. 4 (2005), pp. 65–83.

38. R.T. Keller, "A Test of the Path-Goal Theory of Leadership with Need for Clarity as a Moderator in Research and Development Organizations," *Journal of Applied Psychology* 74 (1989), pp. 208–212.

39. C.A. Schriesheim and L.L. Neider, "Path-Goal Leadership Theory: The Long and Winding Road," *Leadership Quarterly* 7 (1996), pp. 317–321.

40. P. Hersey and K.H. Blanchard, *Management of Organizational Behavior: Utilizing Human Resources,* 5th ed. (Englewood Cliffs, NJ: Prentice Hall, 1988).

41. R.P. Vecchio, "Situational Leadership Theory: An Examination of a Prescriptive Theory," *Journal of Applied Psychology* 72 (1987), pp. 444–451; W. Blank, J.R. Weitzel, and S.G. Green, "A Test of the Situational Leadership Theory," *Personnel Psychology* 43 (1990), pp. 579–597; C.L. Graeff, "Evolution of Situational Leadership Theory: A Critical Review," *Leadership Quarterly* 8 (1997), pp. 153–170.

42. F.E. Fiedler, *A Theory of Leadership Effectiveness* (New York: McGraw-Hill, 1967); F.E. Fiedler and M.M. Chemers, *Leadership and Effective Management* (Glenview, IL: Scott, Foresman, 1974).

43. F.E. Fiedler, "Engineer the Job to Fit the Manager," *Harvard Business Review* 43, no. 5 (1965), pp. 115–122.

44. For a summary of criticisms, see Yukl, *Leadership in Organizations,* pp. 217–218.

45. N. Nicholson, *Executive Instinct* (New York: Crown, 2000).

46. This observation has also been made by C.A. Schriesheim, "Substitutes-for-Leadership Theory: Development and Basic Concepts," *Leadership Quarterly* 8 (1997), pp. 103–108.

47. D.F. Elloy and A. Randolph, "The Effect of Superleader Behavior on Autonomous Work Groups in a Government Operated Railway Service," *Public Personnel Management* 26 (Summer 1997), pp. 257–272; C.C. Manz and H. Sims Jr., *The New SuperLeadership: Leading Others to Lead Themselves* (San Francisco: Berrett-Koehler, 2001).

48. M.L. Loughry, "Coworkers Are Watching: Performance Implications of Peer Monitoring," *Academy of Management Proceedings* (2002), pp. O1–O6.

49. C.C. Manz and C. Neck, *Mastering Self-Leadership,* 3d ed. (Upper Saddle River, NJ: Prentice Hall, 2004).

50. P.M. Podsakoff and S.B. MacKenzie, "Kerr and Jermier's Substitutes for Leadership Model: Background, Empirical Assessment, and Suggestions for Future Research," *Leadership Quarterly* 8 (1997), pp. 117–132; S.D. Dionne et al., "Neutralizing Substitutes for Leadership Theory: Leadership Effects and Common-Source Bias," *Journal of Applied Psychology* 87, no. 3 (June 2002), pp. 454–464; J.R. Villa et al., "Problems with Detecting Moderators in Leadership Research Using Moderated Multiple Regression," *Leadership Quarterly* 14, no. 1 (February 2003), pp. 3–23; S.D. Dionne et al., "Substitutes for Leadership, or Not," *Leadership Quarterly* 16, no. 1 (2005), pp. 169–193.

51. J.M. Burns, *Leadership* (New York: Harper & Row, 1978); B.J. Avolio and F.J. Yammarino, eds., *Transformational and Charismatic Leadership: The Road Ahead* (Greenwich, CT: JAI Press, 2002); B.M. Bass and R.E. Riggio, *Transformational Leadership,* 2d ed. (Mahwah, NJ: Lawrence Erlbaum, 2006).

52. V.L. Goodwin, J.C. Wofford, and J.L. Whittington, "A Theoretical and Empirical Extension to the Transformational Leadership Construct," *Journal of Organizational Behavior,* 22 (November 2001), pp. 759–774.

53. A. Zaleznik, "Managers and Leaders: Are They Different?" *Harvard Business Review* 55, no. 5 (1977), pp. 67–78; W. Bennis and B. Nanus, *Leaders: The Strategies for Taking Charge* (New York: Harper & Row, 1985). For a recent discussion regarding managing versus leading, see G. Yukl and R. Lepsinger, "Why Integrating the Leading and Managing Roles Is Essential for Organizational Effectiveness," *Organizational Dynamics* 34, no. 4 (2005), pp. 361–375.

54. Both transformational and transactional leadership improve work unit performance. See B.M. Bass et al., "Predicting Unit Performance by Assessing Transformational and Transactional Leadership," *Journal of Applied Psychology* 88 (April 2003), pp. 207–218. This point is also argued in Yukl and Lepsinger, "Why Integrating the Leading and Managing Roles Is Essential for Organizational Effectiveness."

55. For a discussion on the tendency to slide from transformational to transactional leadership, see W. Bennis, *An Invented Life: Reflections on Leadership and Change* (Reading, MA: Addison-Wesley, 1993).

56. R.J. House, "A 1976 Theory of Charismatic Leadership," in *Leadership: The Cutting Edge,* ed. J.G. Hunt and L.L. Larson (Carbondale: Southern Illinois University Press, 1977), pp. 189–207; J.A. Conger, "Charismatic and Transformational Leadership in Organizations: An Insider's Perspective on These Developing Streams of Research," *Leadership Quarterly* 10 (Summer 1999), pp. 145–179.

57. J.E. Barbuto, Jr., "Taking the Charisma Out of Transformational Leadership," *Journal of Social Behavior & Personality* 12 (September 1997), pp. 689–697; Y.A. Nur, "Charisma and Managerial Leadership: The Gift That Never Was," *Business Horizons* 41 (July 1998), pp. 19–26; M.D. Mumford and J.R. Van Doorn, "The Leadership of Pragmatism–Reconsidering Franklin in the Age of Charisma," *Leadership Quarterly* 12, no. 3 (Fall 2001), pp. 279–309; A. Fanelli, "Bringing Out Charisma: CEO Charisma and External Stakeholders," *Academy of Management Review* 31, no. 4 (2006), pp. 1049–1061; M.J. Platow et al., "A Special Gift We Bestow on You for Being Representative of Us: Considering Leader Charisma from a Self-Categorization Perspective," *British Journal of Social Psychology* 45, no. 2 (2006), pp. 303–320.

58. B. Shamir et al., "Correlates of Charismatic Leader Behavior in Military Units: Subordinates' Attitudes, Unit Characteristics, and Superiors' Appraisals of Leader Performance," *Academy of Management Journal* 41, no. 4 (1998), pp. 387–409; R.E. De Vries, R.A. Roe, and T.C.B. Taillieu, "On Charisma and Need for Leadership," *European Journal of Work and Organizational Psychology* 8 (1999), pp. 109–133; R. Khurana, *Searching for a Corporate Savior: The Irrational Quest for Charismatic CEOs* (Princeton, NJ: Princeton University Press, 2002).

59. K. Brooker and J. Schlosser, "The Un-CEO," *Fortune,* 16 September 2002, pp. 88–93; B. Nussbaum, "The Power of Design," *BusinessWeek,* 17 May 2004, p. 86; N. Buckley, "The Calm Reinventor," *Financial Times* (London), 29 January 2005, p. 11; S. Ellison, "Women's Touch Guides P&G Chief's Firm Hand in Company Turnaround," *Wall Street Journal Europe,* 1 June 2005, p. A1; S. Hill Jr., "P&G's Turnaround Proves Listening to Customer Pays," *Manufacturing Business Technology,* July 2005, p. 64; J. Tylee, "Procter's Creative Gamble," *Campaign,* 18 March 2005, pp. 24–26.

60. D. Olive, "The 7 Deadly Chief Executive Sins," *Toronto Star,* 17 February 2004, p. D01.

61. Y. Berson et al., "The Relationship between Vision Strength, Leadership Style, and Context," *Leadership Quarterly* 12, no. 1 (2001), pp. 53–73.

62. N. Nilekani, "How I Develop NextGeneration Leaders," *Economic Times* (India), 25 November 2005.

63. Bennis and Nanus, *Leaders,* pp. 27–33, 89; I.M. Levin, "Vision Revisited," *Journal of Applied Behavioral Science* 36 (March 2000), pp. 91–107; R.E. Quinn, *Building the Bridge As You Walk on It: A Guide for Leading Change* (San Francisco: Jossey-Bass, 2004), chap. 11; J.M. Strange and M.D. Mumford, "The Origins of Vision: Effects of Reflection, Models, and Analysis," *Leadership Quarterly* 16, no. 1 (2005), pp. 121–148.

64. J.R. Baum, E.A. Locke, and S.A. Kirkpatrick, "A Longitudinal Study of the Relation of Vision and Vision Communication to Venture Growth in Entrepreneurial Firms," *Journal of Applied Psychology* 83 (1998), pp. 43–54; S.L. Hoe and S.L. McShane, "Leadership Antecedents of Informal Knowledge Acquisition and Dissemination," *International Journal of Organisational Behaviour* 5 (2002), pp. 282–291.

65. "Canadian CEOs Give Themselves Top Marks for Leadership!" *Canada News Wire,* 9 September 1999; L. Manfield, "Creating a Safety Culture from Top to Bottom," *WorkSafe Magazine,* February 2005, pp. 8–9.

66. J.A. Conger, "Inspiring Others: The Language of Leadership," *Academy of Management Executive* 5 (February 1991), pp. 31–45; G.T. Fairhurst and R.A. Sarr, *The Art of Framing: Managing the Language of Leadership* (San Francisco, CA: Jossey-Bass, 1996); A.E. Rafferty and M.A. Griffin, "Dimensions of Transformational Leadership: Conceptual and Empirical Extensions," *Leadership Quarterly* 15, no. 3 (2004), pp. 329–354.

67. D.E. Berlew, "Leadership and Organizational Excitement," *California Management Review* 17, no. 2 (Winter 1974), pp. 21–30; Bennis and Nanus, *Leaders,* pp. 43–55; T. Simons, "Behavioral Integrity: The Perceived Alignment between Managers' Words and Deeds as a Research Focus," *Organization Science* 13, no. 1 (January–February 2002), pp. 18–35.

68. J. Benson and A. Becker, "Synergy: Easy as ABC," *Broadcasting & Cable* 135, no. 41 (2005), pp. 10–12.

69. M. Webb, "Executive Profile: Peter C. Farrell," *San Diego Business Journal,* 24 March 2003, p. 32; P. Benesh, "He Likes Them Breathing Easy," *Investor's Business Daily,* 13 September 2005, p. A04. For a discussion of trust in leadership, see C.S. Burke et al., "Trust in Leadership: A Multi-Level Review and Integration," *Leadership Quarterly* 18, no. 6 (2007), pp. 606–632. The survey on leading by example is reported in J.C. Maxwell, "People Do What People See," *BusinessWeek,* 19 November 2007, p. 32.

70. J. Barling, T. Weber, and E.K. Kelloway, "Effects of Transformational Leadership Training on Attitudinal and Financial Outcomes: A Field Experiment," *Journal of Applied Psychology* 81 (1996), pp. 827–832.

71. A. Bryman, "Leadership in Organizations," in *Handbook of Organization Studies,* ed. S.R. Clegg, C. Hardy, and W.R. Nord (Thousand Oaks, CA: Sage, 1996), pp. 276–292.

72. B.S. Pawar and K.K. Eastman, "The Nature and Implications of Contextual Influences on Transformational Leadership: A Conceptual Examination," *Academy of Management Review* 22 (1997), pp. 80–109; C.P. Egri and S. Herman, "Leadership in the North American Environmental Sector: Values, Leadership Styles, and Contexts of Environmental Leaders and Their Organizations," *Academy of Management Journal* 43, no. 4 (2000), pp. 571–604.

73. J.R. Meindl, "On Leadership: An Alternative to the Conventional Wisdom," *Research in Organizational Behavior* 12 (1990), pp. 159–203; L.R. Offermann, J.J.K. Kennedy, and P.W. Wirtz, "Implicit Leadership Theories: Content, Structure, and Generalizability," *Leadership Quarterly* 5, no. 1 (1994), pp. 43–58; R.J. Hall and R.G. Lord, "Multi-Level Information Processing Explanations of Followers' Leadership Perceptions," *Leadership Quarterly* 6 (1995), pp. 265–287; O. Epitropaki and R. Martin, "Implicit Leadership Theories in Applied Settings: Factor Structure, Generalizability, and Stability over Time," *Journal of Applied Psychology* 89, no. 2 (2004), pp. 293–310.

74. R.G. Lord et al., "Contextual Constraints on Prototype Generation and Their Multilevel Consequences for Leadership Perceptions," *Leadership Quarterly* 12, no. 3 (2001), pp. 311–338; T. Keller, "Parental Images as a Guide to Leadership Sensemaking: An Attachment Perspective on Implicit Leadership Theories," *Leadership Quarterly* 14 (2003), pp. 141–160; K.A. Scott and D.J. Brown, "Female First, Leader Second? Gender Bias in the Encoding of Leadership Behavior," *Organizational Behavior and Human Decision Processes* 101 (2006), pp. 230–242.

75. R. Ilies, M.W. Gerhardt, and H. Le, "Individual Differences in Leadership Emergence: Integrating Meta-Analytic Findings and Behavioral Genetics Estimates," *International Journal of Selection and Assessment* 12, no. 3 (September 2004), pp. 207–219.

76. S.F. Cronshaw and R.G. Lord, "Effects of Categorization, Attribution, and Encoding Processes on Leadership Perceptions," *Journal of Applied Psychology* 72 (1987), pp. 97–106; J.L. Nye and D.R. Forsyth, "The Effects of Prototype-Based Biases on Leadership Appraisals: A Test of Leadership Categorization Theory," *Small Group Research* 22 (1991), pp. 360–379.

77. R. Weber et al., "The Illusion of Leadership: Misattribution of Cause in Coordination Games," *Organization Science* 12, no. 5 (2001), pp. 582–98; N. Ensari and S.E. Murphy, "Cross-Cultural Variations in Leadership Perceptions and Attribution of Charisma to the Leader," *Organizational Behavior and Human Decision Processes* 92 (2003), pp. 52–66; M.L.A. Hayward, V.P. Rindova, and T.G. Pollock, "Believing One's Own Press: The Causes and Consequences of CEO Celebrity," *Strategic Management Journal* 25, no. 7 (July 2004), pp. 637–53.

78. Meindl, "On Leadership: An Alternative to the Conventional Wisdom," p. 163.

79. J. Pfeffer, "The Ambiguity of Leadership," *Academy of Management Review* 2 (1977), pp. 102–12.

80. L.M. Fisher, "Ricardo Semler Won't Take Control," *strategy+business,* no. 41 (Winter 2005), pp. 1–11.

81. Meindl, "On Leadership"; J. Felfe and L.-E. Petersen, "Romance of Leadership and Management Decision Making," *European Journal of Work and Organizational Psychology* 16, no. 1 (2007), pp. 1–24; B. Schyns, J.R. Meindl, and M.A. Croon, "The Romance of Leadership Scale: Cross-Cultural Testing and Refinement," *Leadership* 3, no. 1 (February 2007), pp. 29–46.

82. J. Pfeffer, "The Ambiguity of Leadership," *Academy of Management Review* 2 (1977), pp. 102–112.

83. R. Weber et al., "The Illusion of Leadership: Misattribution of Cause in Coordination Games," *Organization Science* 12, no. 5 (2001), pp. 582–598; N. Ensari and S.E. Murphy, "Cross-Cultural Variations in Leadership Perceptions and Attribution of Charisma to the Leader," *Organizational Behavior and Human Decision Processes* 92 (2003), pp. 52–66; M.L.A. Hayward, V.P. Rindova, and T.G. Pollock, "Believing One's Own Press: The Causes and Consequences of CEO Celebrity," *Strategic Management Journal* 25, no. 7 (July 2004), pp. 637–653.

84. Radha R. Sharma, *360 Degree Feedback: Competency Mapping and Assessment Centre,* (New Delhi: Tata McGraw-Hill, 2002).

85. Six of the Project GLOBE clusters are described in a special issue of the *Journal of World Business,* 37 (2000). For an overview of Project GLOBE, see House, Javidan, and Dorfman, "Project GLOBE"; House et al., "Understanding Cultures and Implicit Leadership Theories across the Globe."

86. J.C. Jesiuno, "Latin Europe Cluster: From South to North," *Journal of World Business* 37 (2002), p. 88. Another GLOBE study, of Iranian managers, also reported that "charismatic visionary" stands out as a primary leadership dimension. See A. Dastmalchian, M. Javidan, and K. Alam, "Effective Leadership and Culture in Iran: An Empirical Study," *Applied Psychology: An International Review* 50 (2001), pp. 532–558.

87. D.N. Den Hartog et al., "Culture Specific and Cross-Culturally Generalizable Implicit Leadership Theories: Are Attributes of Charismatic/Transformational Leadership Universally Endorsed?" *Leadership Quarterly* 10 (1999), pp. 219–256; F.C. Brodbeck et al., "Cultural Variation of Leadership Prototypes across 22 European Countries," *Journal of Occupational and Organizational Psychology* 73 (2000), pp. 1–29; E. Szabo et al., "The Europe Cluster: Where Employees Have a Voice," *Journal of World Business*

37 (2002), pp. 55–68. The Mexican study is reported in C.E. Nicholls, H.W. Lane, and M.B. Brechu, "Taking Self-Managed Teams to Mexico," *Academy of Management Executive* 13 (August 1999), pp. 15–25.

88. A. Fukushige and D.P. Spicer, "Leadership and Followers Work-goals: A Comparison Between Japan and the UK," *International Journal of Human Resource Management*, forthcoming (IJHRM_1457_final, 2011).

89. B.M. Bass and B.J. Avolio, *Full Range Leadership Development: Manual for the Multifactor Leadership Questionnaire*, (Palo Alto, CA: Mindgarden, 1997); B.M. Bass, "Does the Transactional-Transformational Paradigm Transcend Organizational and National Boundaries?", *American Psychologist* 52 (1997), pp. 130–9.

90. R.J. House, "A Path-Goal Theory of Leader Effectiveness," *Administrative Science Quarterly* 16 (1971), pp. 321–8.

91. A. Fukushige and David P. Spicer, "Leadership preferences in Japan:
an Exploratory Study," *Leadership & Organization Development Journal* 28:6 (2007), pp. 508–530.

92. R. Fend, "Wir Sind Die Firma (We Are the Company)," *Financial Times Deutschland,* 2 October 2008, p. 31; N. Klawitter et al., "Die Natur Der Macht (The Nature of Power)," *Der Spiegel,* 22 September 2008, p. 52; M. Schiessl, "Microsoft Reaps the Rewards of Female Managers," *Spiegel Online,* 8 February 2008, www.spiegel.de/international/business/0,1518,533852,00.html.

93. G.N. Powell, "One More Time: Do Female and Male Managers Differ?" *Academy of Management Executive* 4 (1990), pp. 68–75; M.L. van Engen and T.M. Willemsen, "Sex and Leadership Styles: A Meta-Analysis of Research Published in the 1990s," *Psychological Reports* 94, no. 1 (February 2004), pp. 3–18.

94. R. Sharpe, "As Leaders, Women Rule," *BusinessWeek,* 20 November 2000, p. 74; M. Sappenfield, "Women, It Seems, Are Better Bosses," *Christian Science Monitor,* 16 January 2001; A.H. Eagly and L.L. Carli, "The Female Leadership Advantage: An Evaluation of the Evidence," *Leadership Quarterly* 14, no. 6 (December 2003), pp. 807–834; A.H. Eagly, M.C. Johannesen-Schmidt, and M.L. van Engen, "Transformational, Transactional, and Laissez-Faire Leadership Styles: A Meta-Analysis Comparing Women and Men," *Psychological Bulletin* 129 (July 2003), pp. 569–591.

95. A.H. Eagly, S.J. Karau, and M.G. Makhijani, "Gender and the Effectiveness of Leaders: A Meta-Analysis," *Psychological Bulletin* 117 (1995), pp. 125–145; J.G. Oakley, "Gender-Based Barriers to Senior Management Positions: Understanding the Scarcity of Female CEOs," *Journal of Business Ethics* 27 (2000), pp. 821–834; N.Z. Stelter, "Gender Differences in Leadership: Current Social Issues and Future Organizational Implications," *Journal of Leadership Studies* 8 (2002), pp. 88–99; M.E. Heilman et al., "Penalties for Success: Reactions to Women Who Succeed at Male Gender-Typed Tasks," *Journal of Applied Psychology* 89, no. 3 (2004), pp. 416–427; A.H. Eagly, "Achieving Relational Authenticity in Leadership: Does Gender Matter?" *Leadership Quarterly* 16, no. 3 (June 2005), pp. 459–474.

96. Li Charlene, Open Leadership Mind-Sets and Traits. In *Open Leadership: How Social Technology Can Transform the Way You Lead,* pp. 175, (CA: Josey Bass, 2010).

97. Hay Group (2010), *Best Companies for Leadership* (2010), http://www.haygroup.com/BestCompaniesForLeadership/research-and-findings/about-the-research.aspx (accessed on 1/3/2011).

98. Hay Group, *Key Global Findings From The Hay Group 2010 Best Companies for Leadership Study* (2010), http://www.haygroup.com/BestCompaniesForLeadership/research-and-findings/key-findings.aspx (accessed on 1/3/2011).

Chapter 13

1. R. Muzyka and G. Zeschuk, "Managing Multiple Projects," *Game Developer,* March 2003, pp. 34–42; M. Saltzman, "The Ex-Doctors Are In," *National Post,* 24 March 2004, p. AL4; R. McConnell, "For Edmonton's BioWare, Today's the Big Day," *Edmonton Journal,* 14 April 2005, p. C1; D. Gladstone and S. Molloy, "Doctors & Dragons," *Computer Gaming World,* December 2006.

2. S. Ranson, R. Hinings, and R. Greenwood, "The Structuring of Organizational Structure," *Administrative Science Quarterly* 25 (1980), pp. 1–14; K. Walsh, "Interpreting the Impact of Culture on Structure," *Journal of Applied Behavioral Science* 40, no. 3 (September 2004), pp. 302–322.

3. B. Morris, "Charles Schwab's Big Challenge," *Fortune,* 30 May 2005, pp. 60–69.

4. J.-E. Johanson, "Intraorganizational Influence," *Management Communication Quarterly* 13 (February 2000), pp. 393–435.

5. H. Mintzberg, *The Structuring of Organizations* (Englewood Cliffs, NJ: Prentice Hall, 1979), pp. 2–3.

6. E.E. Lawler III, *Motivation in Work Organizations* (Monterey, CA: Brooks/Cole, 1973); M.A. Campion, "Ability Requirement Implications of Job Design: An Interdisciplinary Perspective," *Personnel Psychology* 42 (1989), pp. 1–24.

7. G.S. Becker and K.M. Murphy, "The Division-of-Labor, Coordination Costs and Knowledge," *Quarterly Journal of Economics* 107, no. 4 (November 1992), pp. 1137–1160; L. Borghans and B. Weel, "The Division of Labour, Worker Organisation, and Technological Change," *Economic Journal* 116, no. 509 (2006), pp. F45–F72.

8. Mintzberg, *The Structuring of Organizations,* chap. 1; D.A. Nadler and M.L. Tushman, *Competing by Design: The Power of Organizational Architecture* (New York: Oxford University Press, 1997), chap. 6; J.R. Galbraith, *Designing Organizations: An Executive Guide to Strategy, Structure, and Process* (San Francisco: Jossey-Bass, 2002), chap. 4.

9. J. Stephenson Jr., "Making Humanitarian Relief Networks More Effective: Operational Coordination, Trust and Sense Making," *Disasters* 29, no. 4 (2005), p. 337.

10. A. Willem, M. Buelens, and H. Scarbrough, "The Role of Inter-unit Coordination Mechanisms in Knowledge Sharing: A Case Study of a British MNC," *Journal of Information Science* 32, no. 6 (2006), pp. 539–561; R.R. Gulati, "Silo Busting," *Harvard Business Review* 85, no. 5 (2007), pp. 98–108.

11. Borghans and Weel, "The Division of Labour, Worker Organisation, and Technological Change."

12. T. Van Alphen, "Magna in Overdrive," *Toronto Star,* 24 July 2006.

13. For a discussion of the role of brand manager at Procter & Gamble, see C. Peale, "Branded for Success," *Cincinnati Enquirer,* 20 May 2001, p. A1. Details about how to design integrator roles in organizational structures are presented in Galbraith, *Designing Organizations,* pp. 66–72.

14. M. Hoque, M. Akter, and Y. Monden, "Concurrent Engineering: A Compromise Approach to Develop a Feasible and Customer-Pleasing Product," *International Journal of Production Research* 43, no. 8 (2005), pp. 1607–1624; S.M. Sapuan, M.R. Osman, and Y. Nukman, "State of the Art of the Concurrent Engineering Technique in the Automotive Industry," *Journal of Engineering Design* 17, no. 2 (2006), pp. 143–157; D.H. Kincade, C. Regan, and F.Y. Gibson, "Concurrent Engineering for Product Development in Mass Customization for the Apparel Industry," *International Journal of Operations & Production Management* 27, no. 6 (2007), pp. 627–649.

15. A.H. Van De Ven, A.L. Delbecq, and R.J. Koenig Jr., "Determinants of Coordination Modes within Organizations," *American Sociological Review* 41, no. 2 (1976), pp. 322–338.

16. Y.-M. Hsieh and A. Tien-Hsieh, "Enhancement of Service Quality with Job Standardisation," *Service Industries Journal* 21 (July 2001), pp. 147–166.

17. For recent discussion of span of control, see N.A. Theobald and S. Nicholson-Crotty, "The Many Faces of Span of Control: Organizational Structure across Multiple Goals," *Administration Society* 36, no. 6 (January 2005), pp. 648–660; R.M. Meyer, "Span of Management: Concept Analysis," *Journal of Advanced Nursing* 63, no. 1 (2008), pp. 104–112.

18. H. Fayol, *General and Industrial Management,* trans. C. Storrs (London: Pitman, 1949); D.D. Van Fleet and A.G. Bedeian, "A History of the Span of Management," *Academy of Management Review* 2 (1977), pp. 356–372; D.A. Wren, A.G. Bedeian, and J.D. Breeze, "The Foundations of Henri Fayol's Administrative Theory," *Management Decision* 40, no. 9 (2002), pp. 906–918.

19. D. Drickhamer, "Lessons from the Leading Edge," *Industry Week,* 21 February 2000, pp. 23–26.

20. G. Anders, "Overseeing More Employees–with Fewer Managers–Consultants Are Urging Companies to Loosen Their Supervising Views," *Wall Street Journal,* 24 March 2008, p. B6.

21. J. Greenwald, "Ward Compares the Best with the Rest," *Business Insurance,* 26 August 2002, p. 16.

22. J.H. Gittell, "Supervisory Span, Relational Coordination and Flight Departure Performance: A Reassessment of Postbureaucracy Theory," *Organization Science* 12, no. 4 (July–August 2001), pp. 468–483.

23. P. Glader, "It's Not Easy Being Lean," *Wall Street Journal,* 19 June 2006, p. B1; Nucor Corporation, "About Us," Charlotte, NC, 2008, www.nucor.com/indexinner.aspx?finpage=aboutus (accessed 2 September 2008).

24. T.D. Wall, J.L. Cordery, and C.W. Clegg, "Empowerment, Performance, and Operational Uncertainty: A Theoretical Integration," *Applied Psychology: An International Review* 51 (2002), pp. 146–169.

25. J. Morris, J. Hassard, and L. McCann, "New Organizational Forms, Human Resource Management and Structural Convergence? A Study of Japanese Organizations," *Organization Studies* 27, no. 10 (2006), pp. 1485–1511.

26. "BASF Culling Saves (GBP) 4m," *Personnel Today,* 19 February 2002, p. 3; A. Lashinsky, "The Hurd Way," *Fortune,* 17 April 2006, p. 92.

27. Q.N. Huy, "In Praise of Middle Managers," *Harvard Business Review* 79 (September 2001), pp. 72–79; C.R. Littler, R. Wiesner, and R. Dunford, "The Dynamics of Delayering: Changing Management Structures in Three Countries," *Journal of Management Studies* 40, no. 2 (2003), pp. 225–256; H.J. Leavitt, *Top Down: Why Hierarchies Are Here to Stay and How to Manage Them More Effectively* (Cambridge, MA: Harvard Business School Press, 2005); L. McCann, J. Morris, and J. Hassard, "Normalized Intensity: The New Labour Process of Middle Management," *Journal of Management Studies* 45, no. 2 (2008), pp. 343–371.

28. Littler, Wiesner, and Dunford, "The Dynamics of Delayering."

29. S. Wetlaufer, "The Business Case against Revolution: An Interview with Nestle's Peter Brabeck," *Harvard Business Review* 79, no. 2 (February 2001), pp. 112–119; H.A. Richardson et al., "Does Decentralization Make a Difference for the Organization? An Examination of the Boundary Conditions Circumscribing Decentralized Decision-Making and Organizational Financial

Performance," *Journal of Management* 28, no. 2 (2002), pp. 217–244; G. Masada, "To Centralize or Decentralize?" *Optimize,* May 2005, pp. 58–61.

30. J.G. Kelley, "Slurpees and Sausages: 7-Eleven Holds School," *Richmond Times-Dispatch* (Virginia), 12 March 2004, p. C1; S. Marling, "The 24-Hour Supply Chain," *InformationWeek,* 26 January 2004, p. 43.

31. Mintzberg, *The Structuring of Organizations,* chap. 5

32. W. Dessein and T. Santos, "Adaptive Organizations," *Journal of Political Economy* 114, no. 5 (2006), pp. 956–995; A.A.M. Nasurdin et al., "Organizational Structure and Organizational Climate as Potential Predictors of Job Stress: Evidence from Malaysia," *International Journal of Commerce and Management* 16, no. 2 (2006), pp. 116–129; C.-J. Chen and J.-W. Huang, "How Organizational Climate and Structure Affect Knowledge Management–The Social Interaction Perspective," *International Journal of Information Management* 27, no. 2 (2007), pp. 104–118.

33. C. Holahan, "Bidding Yahoo Adieu," *BusinessWeek,* 23 June 2008, p. 23.

34. T. Burns and G. Stalker, *The Management of Innovation* (London: Tavistock, 1961).

35. P. Lavoie, "TAXI," *Campaign,* 12 October 2007, p. 15; L. Sylvain, "TAXI Deconstructed," *Strategy,* June 2007, p. 50; S. Vranica, "For Small Agency, a Battle to Shed 'Boutique Stigma,' " *Wall Street Journal,* 8 August 2007, p. B2D.

36. J. Tata, S. Prasad, and R. Thom, "The Influence of Organizational Structure on the Effectiveness of TQM Programs," *Journal of Managerial Issues* 11, no. 4 (Winter 1999), pp. 440–453; A. Lam, "Tacit Knowledge, Organizational Learning and Societal Institutions: An Integrated Framework," *Organization Studies* 21 (May 2000), pp. 487–513.

37. W.D. Sine, H. Mitsuhashi, and D.A. Kirsch, "Revisiting Burns and Stalker: Formal Structure and New Venture Performance in Emerging Economic Sectors," *Academy of Management Journal* 49, no. 1 (2006), pp. 121–132.

38. R. Gardner, "Charismatic Clarke Brings His Client Service Approach to UK," *Campaign,* 8 October 2004, p. 18; N. O'Leary, "Chris Clarke Is Coming for Your Business," *Adweek,* 9 April 2007, pp. 8, 39; S. Russell, "Global Ambitions," *B&T,* 8 June 2007, p. 17.

39. Mintzberg, *The Structuring of Organizations,* p. 106.

40. Ibid., chap. 17.

41. Galbraith, *Designing Organizations,* pp. 23–25.

42. E.E. Lawler III, *Rewarding Excellence: Pay Strategies for the New Economy* (San Francisco: Jossey-Bass, 2000), pp. 31–34.

43. These structures were identified from corporate Web sites and annual reports. These organizations typically rely on a mixture of other structures, so the charts shown have been adapted for learning purposes.

44. M. Goold and A. Campbell, "Do You Have a Well-Designed Organization?" *Harvard Business Review* 80 (March 2002), pp. 117–124.

45. G.L. Neilson and B.A. Pasternack, "The Cat That Came Back," *strategy 1business,* no. 40 (17 August 2005), pp. 1–14.

46. J.R. Galbraith, "Structuring Global Organizations," in *Tomorrow's Organization,* ed. S.A. Mohrman et al. (San Francisco: Jossey-Bass, 1998), pp. 103–129; C. Homburg, J.P. Workman Jr., and O. Jensen, "Fundamental Changes in Marketing Organization: The Movement toward a Customer-Focused Organizational Structure," *Academy of Marketing Science Journal* 28 (Fall 2000), pp. 459–478; T.H. Davenport, J.G. Harris, and A.K. Kohli, "How Do They Know Their Customers So Well?" *Sloan Management Review* 42 (Winter 2001), pp. 63–73; J.R. Galbraith, "Organizing to Deliver Solutions," *Organizational Dynamics* 31 (2002), pp. 194–207.

47. S.J. Palmisano, "The Globally Integrated Enterprise," *Foreign Affairs* 85, no. 3 (May–June 2006), pp. 127–136; S. Palmisano, "The Globally Integrated Enterprise," *Vital Speeches of the Day* 73, no. 10 (2007), pp. 449–453.

48. "IBM Moves Engineering VP to China as Part of Global Focus," *Manufacturing Business Technology,* September 2007, p. 13; J. Bonasia, "Globalization: Learning to Close the Continental Divide," *Investor's Business Daily,* 7 September 2007.

49. J.R. Galbraith, E.E. Lawler III, and Associates, *Organizing for the Future: The New Logic for Managing Complex Organizations* (San Francisco: Jossey-Bass, 1993); R. Bettis and M. Hitt, "The New Competitive Landscape," *Strategic Management Journal* 16 (1995), pp. 7–19.

50. P.C. Ensign, "Interdependence, Coordination, and Structure in Complex Organizations: Implications for Organization Design," *Mid-Atlantic Journal of Business* 34 (March 1998), pp. 5–22.

51. M.M. Fanning, "A Circular Organization Chart Promotes a Hospital-Wide Focus on Teams," *Hospital & Health Services Administration* 42 (June 1997), pp. 243–254; L.Y. Chan and B.E. Lynn, "Operating in Turbulent Times: How Ontario's Hospitals Are Meeting the Current Funding Crisis," *Health Care Management Review* 23 (June 1998), pp. 7–18.

52. R. Cross, "Looking before You Leap: Assessing the Jump to Teams in Knowledge-Based Work," *Business Horizons,* September 2000; M. Fenton-O'Creevy, "Employee Involvement and the Middle Manager: Saboteur or Scapegoat?" *Human Resource*

Management Journal 11 (2001), pp. 24–40; G. Garda, K. Lindstrom, and M. Dallnera, "Towards a Learning Organization: The Introduction of a Client-Centered Team-Based Organization in Administrative Surveying Work," *Applied Ergonomics* 34 (2003), pp. 97–105; C. Douglas and W.L. Gardner, "Transition to Self-Directed Work Teams: Implications of Transition Time and Self-Monitoring for Managers' Use of Influence Tactics," *Journal of Organizational Behavior* 25 (2004), pp. 47–65.

53. R.C. Ford and W.A. Randolph, "Cross-Functional Structures: A Review and Integration of Matrix Organization and Project Management," *Journal of Management* 18 (1992), pp. 267–294.

54. N. Buckley, "P&G Shakes Up Its Global Units," *Financial Times* (London), 19 May 2004; "Merely Splitting Hairs," *Marketing Week,* 17 February 2005, p. 26. Procter & Gamble's structure is actually more complex than we have described here. Its "four pillars" also include global business services and corporate functions. See P&G Corporate Info, Corporate Structure, Four Pillars, www.pg.com/jobs/corporate_structure/four_pillars.shtml.

55. G. Calabrese, "Communication and Co-operation in Product Development: A Case Study of a European Car Producer," *R & D Management* 27 (July 1997), pp. 239–252; T. Sy and L.S. D'Annunzio, "Challenges and Strategies of Matrix Organizations: Top-Level and Mid-Level Managers' Perspectives," *Human Resource Planning* 28, no. 1 (2005), pp. 39–48.

56. D. Enrich, "Citigroup Will Revamp Capital-Markets Group," *Wall Street Journal,* 23 August 2008, p. B7.

57. Nadler and Tushman, *Competing by Design,* chap. 6; M. Goold and A. Campbell, "Structured Networks: Towards the Well-Designed Matrix," *Long Range Planning* 36, no. 5 (October 2003), pp. 427–439.

58. D. Ciampa and M. Watkins, "Rx for New CEOs," *Chief Executive,* January 2008.

59. K. Poynter, *Data Security at HMRC* (Progress Report to Chancellor of the Exchequer and HM Treasury), 14 December 2007; V. Houlder, "The Merger That Exposed a Taxing Problem for Managers," *Financial Times,* 11 July 2008, p. 12; K. Poynter, *Review of Information Security at HM Revenue and Customs* (London: HM Treasury, Government of the United Kingdom, June 2008).

60. P. Siekman, "This Is Not a BMW Plant," *Fortune,* 18 April 2005, p. 208; "Magna's Austria Plant to Lose Production of BMW X3," *Reuters,* 16 May 2007.

61. R.F. Miles and C.C. Snow, "The New Network Firm: A Spherical Structure Built on a Human Investment Philosophy," *Organizational Dynamics* 23, no. 4 (1995), pp. 5–18; C. Baldwin and K. Clark, "Managing in an Age of Modularity," *Harvard Business Review* 75 (September–October 1997), pp. 84–93.

62. J. Hagel III and M. Singer, "Unbundling the Corporation," *Harvard Business Review* 77 (March–April 1999), pp. 133–141; R. Hacki and J. Lighton, "The Future of the Networked Company," *McKinsey Quarterly* 3 (2001), pp. 26–39.

63. J. Dwyer, "Mind How You Go," *Facilities Management,* May 2008, pp. 22–25.

64. M.A. Schilling and H.K. Steensma, "The Use of Modular Organizational Forms: An Industry-Level Analysis," *Academy of Management Journal* 44 (December 2001), pp. 1149–1168.

65. G. Morgan, *Images of Organization,* 2d ed. (Newbury Park, CA: Sage, 1996); G. Morgan, *Imagin-I-Zation: New Mindsets for Seeing, Organizing and Managing* (Thousand Oaks, CA: Sage, 1997).

66. H. Chesbrough and D.J. Teece, "When Is Virtual Virtuous? Organizing for Innovation," *Harvard Business Review* (January–February 1996), pp. 65–73; P.M.J. Christie and R. Levary, "Virtual Corporations: Recipe for Success," *Industrial Management* 40 (July 1998), pp. 7–11.

67. L. Donaldson, *The Contingency Theory of Organizations* (Thousand Oaks, CA: Sage, 2001); J. Birkenshaw, R. Nobel, and J. Ridderstrâle, "Knowledge as a Contingency Variable: Do the Characteristics of Knowledge Predict Organizational Structure?" *Organization Science* 13, no. 3 (May–June 2002), pp. 274–289.

68. A.D. Meyer, A.S. Tsui, and C.R. Hinings, "Configurational Approaches to Organizational Analysis," *Academy of Management Journal* 36, no. 6 (December 1993), pp. 1175–1195; K.K. Sinha and A.H. Van De Ven, "Designing Work within and between Organizations," *Organization Science* 16, no. 4 (July–August 2005), pp. 389–408.

69. P.R. Lawrence and J.W. Lorsch, *Organization and Environment* (Homewood, IL: Irwin, 1967); Mintzberg, *The Structuring of Organizations,* chap. 15.

70. Burns and Stalker, *The Management of Innovation;* Lawrence and Lorsch, *Organization and Environment.*

71. Mintzberg, *The Structuring of Organizations,* p. 282.

72. S. Warner, "From Band-Aids to Biotech," *New York Times,* 10 April 2005, p. 1; "Johnson & Johnson CEO William Weldon: Leadership in a Decentralized Company," *Knowledge@Wharton,* 25 June 2008; Johnson & Johnson, "Our Management Approach," New Brunswick, NJ, 2008, www.jnj.com/connect/about-jnj/management-approach/ (accessed 2 September 2008).

73. D.S. Pugh and C.R. Hinings, *Organizational Structure: Extensions and Replications* (Farnborough, England: Lexington Books, 1976); Mintzberg, *The Structuring of Organizations,* chap. 13.

74. Galbraith, *Designing Organizations,* pp. 52–55; G. Hertel, S. Geister, and U. Konradt, "Managing Virtual Teams: A Review of Current Empirical Research," *Human Resource Management Review* 15 (2005), pp. 69–95.

75. C. Perrow, "A Framework for the Comparative Analysis of Organizations," *American Sociological Review* 32 (1967), pp. 194–208; D. Gerwin, "The Comparative Analysis of Structure and Technology: A Critical Appraisal," *Academy of Management Review* 4, no. 1 (1979), pp. 41–51; C.C. Miller et al., "Understanding Technology-Structure Relationships: Theory Development and Meta-Analytic Theory Testing," *Academy of Management Journal* 34, no. 2 (1991), pp. 370–399.

76. R.H. Kilmann, *Beyond the Quick Fix* (San Francisco: Jossey-Bass, 1984), p. 38.

77. A.D. Chandler, *Strategy and Structure* (Cambridge, MA: MIT Press, 1962).

78. D. Miller, "Configurations of Strategy and Structure," *Strategic Management Journal* 7 (1986), pp. 233–249.

Chapter 14

1. L.M. Fisher, "How Dell Got Soul," *strategy1business,* Fall 2004, pp. 1–14; N. Byrnes, P. Burrows, and L. Lee, "Dark Days at Dell," *BusinessWeek,* 4 September 2006, p. 26; M. Kessler, "Dell Reverses, Steps into Wal-Mart," *USA Today,* 25 May 2007, p. B1; S. Lohr, "Can Michael Dell Refocus His Namesake?" *New York Times,* 9 September 2007, p. 1; D. Zehr, "Dell Challenge: New Ideas and Less Red Tape," *Austin American-Statesman,* 4 February 2007, p. A1; Waterstone Human Capital and National Post, *Canada's 10 Most Admired Corporate Cultures, 2007* (Toronto: Waterstone Human Capital and National Post, February 2008).

2. A. Williams, P. Dobson, and M. Walters, *Changing Culture: New Organizational Approaches* (London: Institute of Personnel Management, 1989); E.H. Schein, "What Is Culture?" in *Reframing Organizational Culture,* ed. P.J. Frost et al. (Newbury Park, CA: Sage, 1991), pp. 243–253.

3. B.M. Meglino and E.C. Ravlin, "Individual Values in Organizations: Concepts, Controversies, and Research," *Journal of Management* 24, no. 3 (1998), pp. 351–389; B.R. Agle and C.B. Caldwell, "Understanding Research on Values in Business," *Business and Society* 38, no. 3 (September 1999), pp. 326–387; S. Hitlin and J.A. Pilavin, "Values: Reviving a Dormant Concept," *Annual Review of Sociology* 30 (2004), pp. 359–393.

4. N.M. Ashkanasy, "The Case for Culture," in *Debating Organization,* ed. R. Westwood and S. Clegg (Malden, MA: Blackwell, 2003), pp. 300–310.

5. B. Kabanoff and J. Daly, "Espoused Values in Organisations," *Australian Journal of Management* 27, special issue (2002), pp. 89–104.

6. K. Axtman, "Inside the Culture and Collapse of Enron," *Christian Science Monitor* 96, no. 222 (12 October 2004), p. 3; D. Tourish and N. Vatcha, "Charismatic Leadership and Corporate Cultism at Enron: The Elimination of Dissent, the Promotion of Conformity and Organizational Collapse," *Leadership* 1, no. 4 (November 2005), pp. 455–480.

7. B. Darrow, "James Goodnight, Founder and CEO, SAS Institute," *Computer Reseller News,* 12 December 2005, p. 23; "Doing Well by Being Rather Nice," *Economist,* 1 December 2007, p. 84 (http://search.ebscohost.com/login.aspx?direct=true&db=f5h&AN=27728242&site=ehost-live); "SAS Turned Down 'Numerous' Acquisition Inquiries This Year, Says CEO," *CMP TechWeb,* 17 December 2007.

8. S. Shrinate, "Performance Appraisal: The 10% Rule," *Business Today* (India), 5 December 2004, p. 160; G.S. Alexander, "Expert Hand to Help Pick Kamath's Successor at ICICI," *Economic Times* (India), 3 October 2008; A. Dhall, "ICICI Bank: Measuring Success in Global Standards," *Economic Times* (India), 14 September 2008.

9. C. Vander Doelen, "Toyota Hiring in Woodstock," *Windsor Star,* 30 November 2007; D. Welch, "Staying Paranoid at Toyota," *BusinessWeek,* 2 July 2007, p. 80; H. Takeuchi, E. Osono, and N. Shimizu, "The Contradictions That Drive Toyota's Success," *Harvard Business Review* 86, no. 6 (2008), pp. 96–104.

10. C.A. O'Reilly III, J. Chatman, and D.F. Caldwell, "People and Organizational Culture: A Profile Comparison Approach to Assessing Person-Organization Fit," *Academy of Management Journal* 34 (1991), pp. 487–516; J.J. van Muijen, "Organizational Culture," in *A Handbook of Work and Organizational Psychology: Organizational Psychology,* 2d ed., ed. P.J.D. Drenth, H. Thierry, and C.J. de Wolff (East Sussex, UK: Psychology Press, 1998), pp. 113–132; P.A. Balthazard, R.A. Cooke, and R.E. Potter, "Dysfunctional Culture, Dysfunctional Organization: Capturing the Behavioral Norms That Form Organizational Culture and Drive Performance," *Journal of Managerial Psychology* 21, no. 8 (2006), pp. 709–732; C. Helfrich et al., "Assessing an Organizational Culture Instrument Based on the Competing Values Framework: Exploratory and Confirmatory Factor Analyses," *Implementation Science* 2, no. 1 (2007), p. 13. For recent reviews of organizational culture survey instruments, see T. Scott et al., "The Quantitative Measurement of Organizational Culture in Health Care: A Review of the Available Instruments," *Health Services Research* 38, no. 3 (2003), pp. 923–945; D.E. Leidner and T. Kayworth, "A Review of Culture in Information Systems Research: Toward a Theory of Information Technology Culture Conflict," *MIS Quarterly* 30, no. 2 (2006), pp. 357–399; S. Scott-

Findlay and C.A. Estabrooks, "Mapping the Organizational Culture Research in Nursing: A Literature Review," *Journal of Advanced Nursing* 56, no. 5 (2006), pp. 498–513.

11. J. Martin, P.J. Frost, and O.A. O'Neill, "Organizational Culture: Beyond Struggles for Intellectual Dominance," in *Handbook of Organization Studies,* 2d ed., ed. S. Clegg et al. (London: Sage, 2006), pp. 725–753; N.E. Fenton and S. Inglis, "A Critical Perspective on Organizational Values," *Nonprofit Management and Leadership* 17, no. 3 (2007), pp. 335–347; K. Haukelid, "Theories of (Safety) Culture Revisited–An Anthropological Approach," *Safety Science* 46, no. 3 (2008), pp. 413–426.

12. J. Martin and C. Siehl, "Organizational Culture and Counterculture: An Uneasy Symbiosis," *Organizational Dynamics* (Autumn 1983), pp. 52–64; G. Hofstede, "Identifying Organizational Subcultures: An Empirical Approach," *Journal of Management Studies* 35, no. 1 (1990), pp. 1–12; E. Ogbonna and L.C. Harris, "Organisational Culture in the Age of the Internet: An Exploratory Study," *New Technology, Work and Employment* 21, no. 2 (2006), pp. 162–175.

13. H. Silver, "Does a University Have a Culture?" *Studies in Higher Education* 28, no. 2 (2003), pp. 157–169.

14. A. Sincl..., "Approaches to Organizational Culture and Ethics," *Journal of Business Ethics* 12 (1993), pp. 63–73; A. Boisnier and J. Chatman, "The Role of Subcultures in Agile Organizations," in *Leading and Managing People in Dynamic Organizations,* ed. R. Petersen and E. Mannix (Mahwah, NJ: Lawrence Erlbaum, 2003), pp. 87–112; C. Morrill, M.N. Zald, and H. Rao, "Covert Political Conflict in Organizations: Challenges from Below," *Annual Review of Sociology* 29, no. 1 (2003), pp. 391–415.

15. J.S. Ott, *The Organizational Culture Perspective* (Pacific Grove, CA: Brooks/Cole, 1989), chap. 2; J.S. Pederson and J.S. Sorensen, *Organizational Cultures in Theory and Practice* (Aldershot, England: Gower, 1989), pp. 27–29; M.O. Jones, *Studying Organizational Symbolism: What, How, Why?* (Thousand Oaks, CA: Sage, 1996).

16. E.H. Schein, "Organizational Culture," *American Psychologist* (February 1990), pp. 109–119; A. Furnham and B. Gunter, "Corporate Culture: Definition, Diagnosis, and Change," *International Review of Industrial and Organizational Psychology* 8 (1993), pp. 233–261; E.H. Schein, *The Corporate Culture Survival Guide* (San Francisco: Jossey-Bass, 1999), chap. 4.

17. M. Doehrman, "Anthropologists–Deep in the Corporate Bush," *Daily Record* (Kansas City, MO), 19 July 2005, p. 1.

18. C.J. Boudens, "The Story of Work: A Narrative Analysis of Workplace Emotion," *Organization Studies* 26, no. 9 (2005), pp. 1285–1306; S. Denning, *The Leader's Guide to Storytelling* (San Francisco: Jossey-Bass, 2005).

19. A.L. Wilkins, "Organizational Stories as Symbols Which Control the Organization," in *Organizational Symbolism,* ed. L.R. Pondy et al. (Greenwich, CT: JAI Press, 1984), pp. 81–92; R. Zemke, "Storytelling: Back to a Basic," *Training* 27 (March 1990), pp. 44–50; J.C. Meyer, "Tell Me a Story: Eliciting Organizational Values from Narratives," *Communication Quarterly* 43 (1995), pp. 210–224; W. Swap et al., "Using Mentoring and Storytelling to Transfer Knowledge in the Workplace," *Journal of Management Information Systems* 18 (Summer 2001), pp. 95–114.

20. M. Miller, "The Acrobat," *Forbes,* 15 March 2004, pp. 100–103; R. Ouzounian, "Cirque's Dream Factory," *Toronto Star,* 1 August 2004.

21. "The Ultimate Chairman," *Business Times Singapore,* 3 September 2005.

22. D. Roth, "My Job at The Container Store," *Fortune,* 10 January 2000, pp. 74–78.

23. R. Frank and S. Craig, "White-Shoe Shuffle," *Wall Street Journal,* 15 September 2004, p. A1.

24. R.E. Quinn and N.T. Snyder, "Advance Change Theory: Culture Change at Whirlpool Corporation," in *The Leader's Change Handbook,* ed. J.A. Conger, G.M. Spreitzer, and E.E. Lawler III (San Francisco: Jossey-Bass, 1999), pp. 162–193.

25. Churchill apparently made this statement on October 28, 1943, in the British House of Commons, when London, damaged by bombings in World War II, was about to be rebuilt.

26. G. Turner and J. Myerson, *New Workspace, New Culture: Office Design as a Catalyst for Change* (Aldershot, UK: Gower, 1998).

27. P. Roberts, "The Empire Strikes Back," *Fast Company,* no. 22 (February–March 1999), pp. 122–131; H. Nguyen, "Oakley Shades for Her Eyes Only," *Orange County Register* (Santa Ana, CA), 11 May 2006. Details and photos are also found at: www.oakley.com; and americahurrah.com/Oakley/Entry.htm.

28. K.D. Elsbach and B.A. Bechky, "It's More than a Desk: Working Smarter through Leveraged Office Design," *California Management Review* 49, no. 2 (Winter 2007), pp. 80–101.

29. A. D'Innocenzio, "Wal-Mart's Town Becomes New Address for Corporate America," *Associated Press,* 19 September 2003; J. Useem, "One Nation under Wal-Mart," *Fortune,* 3 March 2003, pp. 65–78.

30. M. Burton, "Open Plan, Open Mind," *Director,* March 2005, pp. 68–72; B. Murray, "Agency Profile: Mother London," *Ihaveanidea,* 28 January 2007, www.ihaveanidea.org.

31. J.C. Collins and J.I. Porras, *Built to Last: Successful Habits of Visionary Companies* (London: Century, 1994); T.E. Deal and A.A. Kennedy, *The New Corporate Cultures* (Cambridge, MA: Perseus Books, 1999); R. Barrett, *Building a Values-Driven Organization: A Whole System Approach to Cultural Transformation* (Burlington, MA: Butterworth-Heinemann, 2006); J.M. Kouzes and B.Z. Posner, *The Leadership Challenge,* 4th ed. (San Francisco: Jossey-Bass, 2007), chap. 3.

32. C. Siehl and J. Martin, "Organizational Culture: A Key to Financial Performance?" in *Organizational Climate and Culture,* ed. B. Schneider (San Francisco, CA: Jossey-Bass, 1990), pp. 241–281; G.G. Gordon and N. DiTomasco, "Predicting Corporate Performance from Organizational Culture," *Journal of Management Studies* 29 (1992), pp. 783–798; J.P. Kotter and J.L. Heskett, *Corporate Culture and Performance* (New York: Free Press, 1992); C.P.M. Wilderom, U. Glunk, and R. Maslowski, "Organizational Culture as a Predictor of Organizational Performance," in *Handbook of Organizational Culture and Climate,* ed. N.M. Ashkanasy, C.P.M. Wilderom, and M.F. Peterson (Thousand Oaks, CA: Sage, 2000), pp. 193–210; A. Carmeli and A. Tishler, "The Relationships between Intangible Organizational Elements and Organizational Performance," *Strategic Management Journal* 25 (2004), pp. 1257–1278; S. Teerikangas and P. Very, "The Culture-Performance Relationship in M&A: From Yes/No to How," *British Journal of Management* 17, no. S1 (2006), pp. S31–S48.

33. A. Krishnan, "CEOs from the Best Provide Insights Gained from Hewitt Best Employers Study," *The Edge* (Malaysia), 21 July 2008.

34. J.C. Helms Mills and A.J. Mills, "Rules, Sensemaking, Formative Contexts, and Discourse in the Gendering of Organizational Culture," in *International Handbook of Organizational Climate and Culture,* ed. N. Ashkanasy, C. Wilderom, and M. Peterson (Thousand Oaks, CA: Sage, 2000), pp. 55–70; J.A. Chatman and S.E. Cha, "Leading by Leveraging Culture," *California Management Review* 45 (Summer 2003), pp. 20–34.

35. B. Ashforth and F. Mael, "Social Identity Theory and the Organization," *Academy of Management Review* 14 (1989), pp. 20–39.

36. M.R. Louis, "Surprise and Sensemaking: What Newcomers Experience in Entering Unfamiliar Organizational Settings," *Administrative Science Quarterly* 25 (1980), pp. 226–251; S.G. Harris, "Organizational Culture and Individual Sensemaking: A Schema-Based Perspective," *Organization Science* 5 (1994), pp. 309–321.

37. J.W. Barnes et al., "The Role of Culture Strength in Shaping Sales Force Outcomes," *Journal of Personal Selling & Sales Management* 26, no. 3 (Summer 2006), pp. 255–270.

38. C.A. O'Reilly III and J.A. Chatman, "Culture as Social Control: Corporations, Cults, and Commitment," *Research in Organizational Behavior* 18 (1996), pp. 157–200; B. Spector and H. Lane, "Exploring the Distinctions between a High Performance Culture and a Cult," *Strategy & Leadership* 35, no. 3 (2007), pp. 18–24.

39. Fisher, "How Dell Got Soul," p. 6.

40. Kotter and Heskett, *Corporate Culture and Performance;* J.P. Kotter, "Cultures and Coalitions," *Executive Excellence* 15 (March 1998), pp. 14–15; B.M. Bass and R.E. Riggio, *Transformational Leadership,* 2d ed. (New York: Routledge, 2006), chap. 7. The term *adaptive culture* has a different meaning in organizational behavior than it has in cultural anthropology, where it refers to nonmaterial cultural conditions (such as ways of thinking) that lag the material culture (physical artifacts). For the anthropological perspective, see W. Griswold, *Cultures and Societies in a Changing World,* 3d ed. [Thousand Oaks, CA: Pine Forge Press (Sage), 2008], p. 66.

41. W.E. Baker and J.M. Sinkula, "The Synergistic Effect of Market Orientation and Learning Orientation on Organizational Performance," *Academy of Marketing Science Journal* 27, no. 4 (Fall 1999), pp. 411–427; Z. Emden, A. Yaprak, and S.T. Cavusgil, "Learning from Experience in International Alliances: Antecedents and Firm Performance Implications," *Journal of Business Research* 58, no. 7 (2005), pp. 883–892.

42. A. Maitland and K. Rollins, "The Two-in-a-Box World of Dell," *Financial Times* (London), 20 March 2003, p. 14.

43. D. Ho, "Michael Dell Says He Had No Role in Accounting Scandal," *Cox News Service,* 6 September 2007.

44. M.L. Marks, "Adding Cultural Fit to Your Diligence Checklist," *Mergers & Acquisitions* 34, no. 3 (November–December 1999), pp. 14–20; Schein, *The Corporate Culture Survival Guide,* chap. 8; M.L. Marks, "Mixed Signals," *Across the Board,* May 2000, pp. 21–26; J.P. Daly, R.W. Pouder, and B. Kabanoff, "The Effects of Initial Differences in Firms' Espoused Values on Their Postmerger Performance," *Journal of Applied Behavioral Science* 40, no. 3 (September 2004), pp. 323–343.

45. Teerikangas and Very, "The Culture-Performance Relationship in M&A"; G.K. Stahl and A. Voigt, "Do Cultural Differences Matter in Mergers and Acquisitions? A Tentative Model and Examination," *Organization Science* 19, no. 1 (January 2008), pp. 160–176.

46. A. Klein, "A Merger Taken AO-Ill," *Washington Post,* 21 October 2002, p. E1; A. Klein, *Stealing Time: Steve Case, Jerry Levin, and the Collapse of AOL Time Warner* (New York: Simon & Schuster, 2003).

47. C.A. Schorg, C.A. Raiborn, and M.F. Massoud, "Using a 'Cultural Audit' to Pick M&A Winners," *Journal of Corporate Accounting & Finance,* May–June 2004, pp. 47–55; W. Locke, "Higher Education Mergers: Integrating Organisational Cultures and Developing Appropriate Management Styles," *Higher Education Quarterly* 61, no. 1 (2007), pp. 83–102.

48. S. Greengard, "Due Diligence: The Devil in the Details," *Workforce,* October 1999, p. 68; Marks, "Adding Cultural Fit to Your Diligence Checklist."

49. A.R. Malekazedeh and A. Nahavandi, "Making Mergers Work by Managing Cultures," *Journal of Business Strategy* (May–June 1990), pp. 55–57; K.W. Smith, "A Brand-New Culture for the Merged Firm," *Mergers and Acquisitions* 35 (June 2000), pp. 45–50.

50. T. Hamilton, "RIM on a Roll," *Toronto Star,* 22 February 2004, p. C01.

51. R. Brand, "Chipotle Founder Had Big Dreams," *Rocky Mountain News* (Denver), 23 December 2006, p. 1C; M. Heffernan, "Dreamers: Chipotle Founder Steve Ells," *Reader's Digest,* 15 September 2008; B. Krummert, "There Will Be Lines," *Restaurant Hospitality,* August 2008, p. 42.

52. I. Mount, "Be Fast, Be Frugal, Be Right," *Inc.* 26, no. 1 (January 2004), pp. 64–70; S. Anthony and C. Christensen, "Mind over Merger," *Optimize,* February 2005, pp. 22–27.

53. Hewitt Associates, "Mergers and Acquisitions May Be Driven by Business Strategy–but Often Stumble over People and Culture Issues" (PR Newswire news release), Lincolnshire, IL, 3 August 1998.

54. J. Martin, "Can Organizational Culture Be Managed?" in *Organizational Culture,* ed. P.J. Frost et al. (Beverly Hills, CA: Sage, 1985), pp. 95–98.

55. E.H. Schein, "The Role of the Founder in Creating Organizational Culture," *Organizational Dynamics* 12, no. 1 (Summer 1983), pp. 13–28; R. House, M. Javidan, and P. Dorfman, "Project GLOBE: An Introduction," *Applied Psychology: An International Review* 50 (2001), pp. 489–505; R. House et al., "Understanding Cultures and Implicit Leadership Theories across the Globe: An Introduction to Project GLOBE," *Journal of World Business* 37 (2002), pp. 3–10.

56. A.S. Tsui et al., "Unpacking the Relationship between CEO Leadership Behavior and Organizational Culture," *Leadership Quarterly* 17 (2006), pp. 113–137; Y. Berson, S. Oreg, and T. Dvir, "CEO Values, Organizational Culture and Firm Outcomes," *Journal of Organizational Behavior* (in press).

57. R. Gluyas, "Back to Grass Roots: Stewart's Culture Shock," *The Australian,* 4 November 2006, p. 33; L. Carapiet, "NAB's John Stewart Knows His ABCs," *Australian Banking & Finance,* December 2007, p. 6; S. Dellaportas, B.J. Cooper, and P. Braica, "Leadership, Culture and Employee Deceit: The Case of the National Australia Bank," *Corporate Governance: An International Review* 15, no. 6 (2007), pp. 1442–1452; M. Stevens, "Success and Succession: Stewart Bloodied but Unbowed," *The Australian,* 31 July 2008, p. 19.

58. B. Bouw, "Zen and the Art of Retailing," *Globe & Mail,* 30 November 2007; D. Flavelle, "Yoga-Wear Icon Brews Up New Top Executive," *Toronto Star,* 3 April 2008; J. Wells, "Now It's Her Chance to Stretch," *Globe & Mail,* 3 April 2008.

59. M. De Pree, *Leadership Is an Art* (East Lansing: Michigan State University Press, 1987).

60. B. McLean, "Inside the Money Machine," *Fortune,* 6 September 2004, p. 84.

61. J. Kerr and J.W. Slocum Jr., "Managing Corporate Culture through Reward Systems," *Academy of Management Executive* 1 (May 1987), pp. 99–107; J.M. Higgins et al., "Using Cultural Artifacts to Change and Perpetuate Strategy," *Journal of Change Management* 6, no. 4 (2006), pp. 397–415.

62. S. Brimble, "Apex Distribution Enters Next Level of Growth through Product Diversification," *On Stream,* Summer 2006, pp. 12–16; R. Charan, "Home Depot's Blueprint for Culture Change," *Harvard Business Review,* April 2006, pp. 61–70.

63. B. Schneider, "The People Make the Place," *Personnel Psychology* 40, no. 3 (1987), pp. 437–453; B. Schneider et al., "Personality and Organizations: A Test of the Homogeneity of Personality Hypothesis," *Journal of Applied Psychology* 83, no. 3 (June 1998), pp. 462–470; T.R. Giberson, C.J. Resick, and M.W. Dickson, "Embedding Leader Characteristics: An Examination of Homogeneity of Personality and Values in Organizations," *Journal of Applied Psychology* 90, no. 5 (2005), pp. 1002–1010.

64. T.A. Judge and D.M. Cable, "Applicant Personality, Organizational Culture, and Organization Attraction," *Personnel Psychology* 50, no. 2 (1997), pp. 359–394; D.S. Chapman, et al., "Applicant Attraction to Organizations and Job Choice: A Meta-Analytic Review of the Correlates of Recruiting Outcomes," *Journal of Applied Psychology* 90, no. 5 (2005), pp. 928–944; A.L. Kristof-Brown, R.D. Zimmerman, and E.C. Johnson, "Consequences of Individuals' Fit at Work: A Meta-Analysis of Person-Job, Person-Organization, Person-Group, and Person-Supervisor Fit," *Personnel Psychology* 58, no. 2 (2005), pp. 281–342; C. Hu, H.-C. Su, and C.-I.B. Chen, "The Effect of Person-Organization Fit Feedback via Recruitment Web Sites on Applicant Attraction," *Computers in Human Behavior* 23, no. 5 (2007), pp. 2509–2523.

65. A. Kristof-Brown, "Perceived Applicant Fit: Distinguishing between Recruiters' Perceptions of Person-Job and Person-Organization Fit," *Personnel Psychology* 53, no. 3 (Autumn 2000), pp. 643–671; A.E.M. Van Vianen, "Person-Organization Fit: The Match between Newcomers' and Recruiters' Preferences for Organizational Cultures," *Personnel Psychology* 53 (Spring 2000), pp. 113–149.

66. S. Cruz, "Park Place Lexus Mission Viejo Seeing Improvements," *Orange County Business Journal,* 12 May 2008, p. 15; C. Hall, "'Emotional Intelligence' Counts in Job Hires," *Dallas Morning News,* 20 August 2008.

67. D.M. Cable and J.R. Edwards, "Complementary and Supplementary Fit: A Theoretical and Empirical Integration," *Journal of Applied Psychology* 89, no. 5 (2004), pp. 822–834.

68. J. Van Maanen, "Breaking In: Socialization to Work," in *Handbook of Work, Organization, and Society,* ed. R. Dubin (Chicago: Rand McNally, 1976).

69. P. Burkes Erickson, "Welcoming Employees: Making That First Day a Great Experience," *Daily Oklahoman,* 15 July 2007.

70. S. Huettel, "Soaring Ahead," *St. Petersburg Times,* 24 October 2005; E.P. Lima, "Winning Cultures," *Air Transport World,* February 2006, p. 54.

71. D.G. Allen, "Do Organizational Socialization Tactics Influence Newcomer Embeddedness and Turnover?," *Journal of Management* 32, no. 2 (April 2006), pp. 237–256; A.M. Saks, K.L. Uggerslev, and N.E. Fassina, "Socialization Tactics and Newcomer Adjustment: A Meta-Analytic Review and Test of a Model," *Journal of Vocational Behavior* 70, no. 3 (2007), pp. 413–432.

72. G.T. Chao et al., "Organizational Socialization: Its Content and Consequences," *Journal of Applied Psychology* 79 (1994), pp. 450–463; H.D. Cooper-Thomas and N. Anderson, "Organizational Socialization: A Field Study into Socialization Success and Rate," *International Journal of Selection and Assessment* 13, no. 2 (2005), pp. 116–128.

73. N. Nicholson, "A Theory of Work Role Transitions," *Administrative Science Quarterly* 29 (1984), pp. 172–191; B.E. Ashforth, D.M. Sluss, and A.M. Saks, "Socialization Tactics, Proactive Behavior, and Newcomer Learning: Integrating Socialization Models," *Journal of Vocational Behavior* 70, no. 3 (2007), pp. 447–462; T.N. Bauer, "Newcomer Adjustment during Organizational Socialization: A Meta-Analytic Review of Antecedents, Outcomes, and Methods," *Journal of Applied Psychology* 92, no. 3 (2007), pp. 707–721; A. Elfering et al., "First Years in Job: A Three-Wave Analysis of Work Experiences," *Journal of Vocational Behavior* 70, no. 1 (2007), pp. 97–115.

74. J.M. Beyer and D.R. Hannah, "Building on the Past: Enacting Established Personal Identities in a New Work Setting," *Organization Science* 13 (November–December 2002), pp. 636–652; H.D.C. Thomas and N. Anderson, "Newcomer Adjustment: The Relationship between Organizational Socialization Tactics, Information Acquisition and Attitudes," *Journal of Occupational and Organizational Psychology* 75 (December 2002), pp. 423–437.

75. L.W. Porter, E.E. Lawler III, and J.R. Hackman, *Behavior in Organizations* (New York: McGraw-Hill, 1975), pp. 163–167; Van Maanen, "Breaking In: Socialization to Work"; D.C. Feldman, "The Multiple Socialization of Organization Members," *Academy of Management Review* 6 (1981), pp. 309–318.

76. B.E. Ashforth and A.M. Saks, "Socialization Tactics: Longitudinal Effects on Newcomer Adjustment," *Academy of Management Journal* 39 (1996), pp. 149–178; J.D. Kammeyer-Mueller and C.R. Wanberg, "Unwrapping the Organizational Entry Process: Disentangling Multiple Antecedents and Their Pathways to Adjustment," *Journal of Applied Psychology* 88, no. 5 (2003), pp. 779–794.

77. Porter, Lawler III, and Hackman, *Behavior in Organizations,* chap. 5.

78. Louis, "Surprise and Sensemaking."

79. S.L. Robinson and D.M. Rousseau, "Violating the Psychological Contract: Not the Exception but the Norm," *Journal of Organizational Behavior* 15 (1994), pp. 245–259.

80. D.L. Nelson. "Organizational Socialization: A Stress Perspective," *Journal of Occupational Behavior* 8 (1987), pp. 311–324; Elfering et al., "First Years in Job."

81. J.P. Wanous, *Organizational Entry* (Reading, MA: Addison-Wesley, 1992); J.A. Breaugh and M. Starke, "Research on Employee Recruitment: So Many Studies, So Many Remaining Questions," *Journal of Management* 26, no. 3 (2000), pp. 405–434.

82. J.M. Phillips, "Effects of Realistic Job Previews on Multiple Organizational Outcomes: A Meta-Analysis," *Academy of Management Journal* 41 (December 1998), pp. 673–690.

83. Y. Ganzach et al., "Social Exchange and Organizational Commitment: Decision-Making Training for Job Choice as an Alternative to the Realistic Job Preview," *Personnel Psychology* 55 (Autumn 2002), pp. 613–637.

84. E. Simon, "Employers Study Applicants' Personalities," *Associated Press,* 5 November 2007. Also see the Lindblad RJP video at www.expeditions.com/Theater17.asp?Media=475.

85. C. Ostroff and S.W.J. Koslowski, "Organizational Socialization as a Learning Process: The Role of Information Acquisition," *Personnel Psychology* 45 (1992), pp. 849–874; Cooper-Thomas and Anderson, "Organizational Socialization"; A. Baber and L. Waymon, "Uncovering the Unconnected Employee," *T&D,* May 2008, pp. 60–66.

86. C. Fishman, "The Anarchist's Cookbook," *Fast Company,* July 2004, p. 70; "World's Finest Food Retailers: Whole Foods, Not Holy Food," *The Grocer,* 12 November 2005, p. 32.

87. L. Buchanan et al., "That's Chief Entertainment Officer," *Inc.* 29, no. 8 (August 2007), pp. 86–94; Burkes Erickson, "Welcoming Employees."

Chapter 15

1. J.R. Engen, "Stirring It Up," *Bank Director Magazine,* Fourth Quarter 2002; L. Conley, "Cultural Phenomenon," *Fast Company,* April 2005, pp. 76–77; R. Davis, *Leading for Growth: How Umpqua Bank Got Cool and Created a Culture of Greatness* (San Francisco:

Jossey-Bass, 2007); L. Bielski, "Still Pushing the Envelope," *ABA Banking Journal*, October 2008, p. 36; S. Woodward, "Umpqua, the Unbank," *Oregonian*, 30 March 2008, p. D1.

2. J.B. Bernstel, "A New Blend of Bank," *ABA Bank Marketing*, March 2006, pp. 14–19.

3. K. Lewin, *Field Theory in Social Science* (New York: Harper & Row, 1951).

4. D. Coghlan and T. Brannick, "Kurt Lewin: The 'Practical Theorist' for the 21st Century," *Irish Journal of Management* 24, no. 2 (2003), pp. 31–37; B. Burnes, "Kurt Lewin and the Planned Approach to Change: A Re-appraisal," *Journal of Management Studies* 41, no. 6 (September 2004), pp. 977–1002.

5. D. Howell, "Nardelli Nears Five-Year Mark with Riveting Record," *DSN Retailing Today*, 9 May 2005, pp. 1, 38; R. Charan, "Home Depot's Blueprint for Culture Change," *Harvard Business Review*, April 2006, pp. 61–70; R. DeGross, "Five Years of Change: Home Depot's Results Mixed under Nardelli," *Atlanta Journal-Constitution*, 1 January 2006, p. F1; B. Grow, D. Brady, and M. Arndt, "Renovating Home Depot," *BusinessWeek*, 6 March 2006, pp. 50–57.

6. S. Chreim, "Postscript to Change: Survivors' Retrospective Views of Organizational Changes," *Personnel Review* 35, no. 3 (2006), pp. 315–335.

7. M. Johnson-Cramer, S. Parise, and R. Cross, "Managing Change through Networks and Values," *California Management Review* 49, no. 3 (Spring 2007), pp. 85–109.

8. K. Shimizu, "Hoppy Enjoying Comeback after Radical Shift in Management," *Japan Times*, 15 August 2007.

9. G.L. Neilson, B.A. Pasternack, and K.E. Van Nuys, "The Passive-Aggressive Organization," *Harvard Business Review* 83, no. 10 (2005), pp. 82–92.

10. Variations of this often-cited quotation are found in several books, articles, and Web sites, but unfortunately none cite the original source. This quotation is from D.R. Henderson, "The New Industrial Economist," *Wall Street Journal*, 2 May 2006.

11. B.J. Tepper et al., "Subordinates' Resistance and Managers' Evaluations of Subordinates' Performance," *Journal of Management* 32, no. 2 (April 2006), pp. 185–209; J.D. Ford, L.W. Ford, and A. D'Amelio, "Resistance to Change: The Rest of the Story," *Academy of Management Review* 33, no. 2 (2008), pp. 362–377.

12. E.B. Dent and S.G. Goldberg, "Challenging 'Resistance to Change,'" *Journal of Applied Behavioral Science* 35 (March 1999), pp. 25–41; D.B. Fedor, S. Caldwell, and D.M. Herold, "The Effects of Organizational Changes on Employee Commitment: A Multilevel Investigation," *Personnel Psychology* 59, no. 1 (2006), pp. 1–29.

13. For an excellent review of the resistance-to-change literature, see R.R. Sharma, *Change Management: Concepts and Applications* (New Delhi: Tata McGraw-Hill, 2007), chap. 4.

14. D. Eggen, "FBI Fails to Transform Itself, Panel Says," *Washington Post*, 7 June 2005, p. A04; C. Ragavan and C.S. Hook, "Fixing the FBI," *U.S. News & World Report*, 28 March 2005, pp. 18–24, 26, 29–30; Commission on the Intelligence Capabilities of the United States Regarding Weapons of Mass Destruction, *Report to the President of the United States*, Washington, DC., 31 March 2005; J.J. Brazil, "Mission: Impossible?" *Fast Company*, April 2007, pp. 92–97, 108–109.

15. D.A. Nadler, "The Effective Management of Organizational Change," in *Handbook of Organizational Behavior*, ed. J.W. Lorsch (Englewood Cliffs, NJ: Prentice Hall, 1987), pp. 358–369; R. Maurer, *Beyond the Wall of Resistance: Unconventional Strategies to Build Support for Change* (Austin, TX: Bard Books, 1996); P. Strebel, "Why Do Employees Resist Change?" *Harvard Business Review*, May–June 1996, pp. 86–92; D.A. Nadler, *Champions of Change* (San Francisco: Jossey-Bass, 1998).

16. V. Newman, "The Psychology of Managing for Innovation," *KM Review* 9, no. 6 (2007), pp. 10–15.

17. *Bosses Want Change but Workers Want More of the Same!* (Sydney: Talent2, 29 June 2005).

18. C. Ressler and J. Thompson, *Why Work Sucks and How to Fix It* (New York: Portfolio, 2008), chap. 2.

19. T.G. Cummings, "The Role and Limits of Change Leadership," in *The Leader's Change Handbook*, ed. J.A. Conger, G.M. Spreitzer, and E.E. Lawler III (San Francisco: Jossey-Bass, 1999), pp. 301–320; J.P. Kotter and D.S. Cohen, *The Heart of Change* (Boston: Harvard Business School Press, 2002), pp. 15–36; J.P. Kotter, *A Sense of Urgency* (Boston: Harvard Business School Press, 2008).

20. J. Smith, "Building Cars, Building Teams," *Plant Engineering*, December 2005, pp. 41–50.

21. L.D. Goodstein and H.R. Butz, "Customer Value: The Linchpin of Organizational Change," *Organizational Dynamics* 27 (June 1998), pp. 21–35.

22. I.J. Bozon and P.N. Child, "Refining Shell's Position in Europe," *McKinsey Quarterly*, no. 2 (2003), pp. 42–51.

23. D. Darlin, "Growing Tomorrow," *Business 2.0*, May 2005, p. 126.

24. L. Grossman and S. Song, "Stevie's Little Wonder," *Time*, 19 September 2005, p. 63; S. Levy, "Honey, I Shrunk the iPod. A Lot," *Newsweek*, 19 September 2005, p. 58.

25. T.F. Cawsey and G. Deszca, *Toolkit for Organizational Change* (Los Angeles: Sage, 2007), p. 104.

26. J.P. Kotter and L.A. Schlesinger, "Choosing Strategies for Change," *Harvard Business Review,* March–April 1979, pp. 106–114.

27. B. Nanus and S.M. Dobbs, *Leaders Who Make a Difference* (San Francisco: Jossey-Bass, 1999); Kotter and Cohen, *The Heart of Change,* pp. 83–98. The recent survey is reported in M. Meaney and C. Pung, "Creating Organizational Transformations: McKinsey Global Survey Results," *McKinsey Quarterly,* July 2008, pp. 1–7.

28. K.T. Dirks, L.L. Cummings, and J.L. Pierce, "Psychological Ownership in Organizations: Conditions under Which Individuals Promote and Resist Change," *Research in Organizational Change and Development* 9 (1996), pp. 1–23; A. Cox, S. Zagelmeyer, and M. Marchington, "Embedding Employee Involvement and Participation at Work," *Human Resource Management Journal* 16, no. 3 (2006), pp. 250–267.

29. D. Blossom, "Lopez Foods Looks to Beef Up Profits, Take Bite into International Breakfasts," *Daily Oklahoman,* 9 April 2008; A. Hanacek, "Star Power," *National Provisioner* 222, no. 2 (February 2008), pp. 22–29.

30. N.T. Tan, "Maximising Human Resource Potential in the Midst of Organisational Change," *Singapore Management Review* 27, no. 2 (2005), pp. 25–35.

31. M. McHugh, "The Stress Factor: Another Item for the Change Management Agenda?" *Journal of Organizational Change Management* 10 (1997), pp. 345–362; D. Buchanan, T. Claydon, and M. Doyle, "Organisation Development and Change: The Legacy of the Nineties," *Human Resource Management Journal* 9 (1999), pp. 20–37.

32. D. Nicolini and M.B. Meznar, "The Social Construction of Organizational Learning: Conceptual and Practical Issues in the Field," *Human Relations* 48 (1995), pp. 727–746.

33. E.E. Lawler III, "Pay Can Be a Change Agent," *Compensation & Benefits Management* 16 (Summer 2000), pp. 23–26; Kotter and Cohen, *The Heart of Change,* pp. 161–177; M.A. Roberto and L.C. Levesque, "The Art of Making Change Initiatives Stick," *MIT Sloan Management Review* 46, no. 4 (Summer 2005), pp. 53–60.

34. R.E. Quinn, *Building the Bridge as You Walk on It: A Guide for Leading Change* (San Francisco: Jossey-Bass, 2004), chap. 11.

35. R. Caldwell, "Models of Change Agency: A Fourfold Classification," *British Journal of Management* 14 (June 2003), pp. 131–142.

36. Kotter and Cohen, *The Heart of Change,* pp. 61–82; D.S. Cohen and J.P. Kotter, *The Heart of Change Field Guide* (Boston: Harvard Business School Press, 2005).

37. J. Thottam, "Reworking Work," *Time,* 25 July 2005, p. 50; Ressler and Thompson, *Why Work Sucks and How to Fix It,* pp. 20, 45–48.

38. M. Beer, R.A. Eisenstat, and B. Spector, *The Critical Path to Corporate Renewal* (Boston: Harvard Business School Press, 1990).

39. R.E. Walton, "Successful Strategies for Diffusing Work Innovations," *Journal of Contemporary Business,* Spring 1977, pp. 1–22; R.E. Walton, *Innovating to Compete: Lessons for Diffusing and Managing Change in the Workplace* (San Francisco: Jossey-Bass, 1987); Beer, Eisenstat, and Spector, *The Critical Path to Corporate Renewal,* chap. 5.

40. E.M. Rogers, *Diffusion of Innovations,* 4th ed. (New York: Free Press, 1995).

41. P. Reason and H. Bradbury, *Handbook of Action Research* (London: Sage, 2001); Coghlan and Brannick, "Kurt Lewin"; C. Huxham and S. Vangen, "Researching Organizational Practice through Action Research: Case Studies and Design Choices," *Organizational Research Methods* 6 (July 2003), pp. 383–403.

42. V.J. Marsick and M.A. Gephart, "Action Research: Building the Capacity for Learning and Change," *Human Resource Planning* 26 (2003), pp. 14–18.

43. L. Dickens and K. Watkins, "Action Research: Rethinking Lewin," *Management Learning* 30 (June 1999), pp. 127–140; J. Heron and P. Reason, "The Practice of Co-operative Inquiry: Research 'with' Rather Than 'on' People," in *Handbook of Action Research,* ed. P. Reason and H. Bradbury (Thousand Oaks, CA: Sage, 2001), pp. 179–188.

44. D.A. Nadler, "Organizational Frame Bending: Types of Change in the Complex Organization," in *Corporate Transformation: Revitalizing Organizations for a Competitive World,* ed. R.H. Kilmann, T.J. Covin, and Associates (San Francisco: Jossey-Bass, 1988), pp. 66–83; K.E. Weick and R.E. Quinn, "Organizational Change and Development," *Annual Review of Psychology* 50 (1999), pp. 361–386.

45. T.M. Egan and C.M. Lancaster, "Comparing Appreciative Inquiry to Action Research: OD Practitioner Perspectives," *Organization Development Journal* 23, no. 2 (Summer 2005), pp. 29–49.

46. F.F. Luthans, "Positive Organizational Behavior: Developing and Managing Psychological Strengths," *Academy of Management Executive* 16, no. 1 (2002), pp. 57–72; N. Turner, J. Barling, and A. Zacharatos, "Positive Psychology at Work," in *Handbook of Positive Psychology,* ed. C.R. Snyder and S. Lopez (Oxford, UK: Oxford University Press, 2002), pp. 715–730; K. Cameron, J.E. Dutton, and R.E. Quinn, eds., *Positive Organizational Scholarship: Foundation of a New Discipline* (San Francisco: Berrett-Koehler, 2003); J.I. Krueger and D.C. Funder, "Towards a Balanced Social Psychology: Causes, Consequences, and Cures for the Problem-Seeking Approach to Social Behavior and Cognition," *Behavioral and Brain Sciences* 27, no. 3 (June 2004), pp. 313–327;

S.L. Gable and J. Haidt, "What (and Why) Is Positive Psychology?" *Review of General Psychology* 9, no. 2 (2005), pp. 103–110; M.E.P. Seligman et al., "Positive Psychology Progress: Empirical Validation of Interventions," *American Psychologist* 60, no. 5 (2005), pp. 410–421.

47. S. Berrisford, "Using Appreciative Inquiry to Drive Change at the BBC," *Strategic Communication Management* 9, no. 3 (2005), pp. 22–25; M.-Y. Cheung-Judge and E.H. Powley, "Innovation at the BBC," in *The Handbook of Large Group Methods,* ed. B.B. Bunker and B.T. Alban (New York: Wiley, 2006), pp. 45–61.

48. D. Whitney and D.L. Cooperrider, "The Appreciative Inquiry Summit: Overview and Applications," *Employment Relations Today* 25 (Summer 1998), pp. 17–28; J.M. Watkins and B.J. Mohr, *Appreciative Inquiry: Change at the Speed of Imagination* (San Francisco: Jossey-Bass, 2001).

49. F.J. Barrett and D.L. Cooperrider, "Generative Metaphor Intervention: A New Approach for Working with Systems Divided by Conflict and Caught in Defensive Perception," *Journal of Applied Behavioral Science* 26 (1990), pp. 219–239; Whitney and Cooperrider, "The Appreciative Inquiry Summit"; Watkins and Mohr, *Appreciative Inquiry,* pp. 15–21.

50. M. Schiller, "Case Study: Avon México," in *Appreciative Inquiry: Change at the Speed of Imagination,* ed. J.M. Watkins and B.J. Mohr (San Francisco: Jossey-Bass, 2001), pp. 123–126; D. Whitney and A. Trosten-Bloom, *The Power of Appreciative Inquiry: A Practical Guide to Positive Change* (San Francisco: Berrett-Koehler, 2003); P. Babcock, "Seeing a Brighter Future," *HRMagazine* 50, no. 9 (September 2005), p. 48; D.S. Bright, D.L. Cooperrider, and W.B. Galloway, "Appreciative Inquiry in the Office of Research and Development: Improving the Collaborative Capacity of Organization," *Public Performance & Management Review* 29, no. 3 (2006), p. 285; D. Gilmour and A. Radford, "Using OD to Enhance Shareholder Value: Delivering Business Results in BP Castrol Marine," *Organization Development Journal* 25, no. 3 (2007), pp. P97- P102.

51. T.F. Yaeger, P.F. Sorensen, and U. Bengtsson, "Assessment of the State of Appreciative Inquiry: Past, Present, and Future," *Research in Organizational Change and Development* 15 (2004), pp. 297–319; G.R. Bushe and A.F. Kassam, "When Is Appreciative Inquiry Transformational? A Meta-Case Analysis," *Journal of Applied Behavioral Science* 41, no. 2 (June 2005), pp. 161–181.

52. G.R. Bushe, "Five Theories of Change Embedded in Appreciative Inquiry" in *18th Annual World Congress of Organization Development,* Dublin, Ireland, July 14–18, 1998.

53. M. Weisbord and S. Janoff, *Future Search: An Action Guide to Finding Common Ground in Organizations and Communities* (San Francisco: Berrett-Koehler, 2000); R.M. Lent, M.T. McCormick, and D.S. Pearce, "Combining Future Search and Open Space to Address Special Situations," *Journal of Applied Behavioral Science* 41, no. 1 (March 2005), pp. 61–69; S. Janoff and M. Weisbord, "Future Search as 'Real-Time' Action Research," *Futures* 38, no. 6 (2006), pp. 716–722.

54. N. Aronson, E. Axelrod, and S. Crowther, "Lawrence Public Schools: Institutionalized Goals," in *Future Search in School District Change,* ed. R. Schweitz, K. Martens, and N. Aronson (Lanham, MD: Scarecrow Education, 2005), pp. 3–18; R. Lent, J. Van Patten, and T. Phair, "Creating a World-Class Manufacturer in Record Time," in *The Handbook of Large Group Methods,* ed. B.B. Bunker and B.T. Alban (New York: Wiley, 2006), pp. 112–124.

55. For a critique of future-search conferences and similar whole-system events, see A. Oels, "Investigating the Emotional Roller-Coaster Ride: A Case Study–Based Assessment of the Future Search Conference Design," *Systems Research and Behavioral Science* 19 (July–August 2002), pp. 347–355; M.F.D. Polanyi, "Communicative Action in Practice: Future Search and the Pursuit of an Open, Critical and Non-coercive Large-Group Process," *Systems Research and Behavioral Science* 19 (July 2002), pp. 357–366; A. De Grassi, "Envisioning Futures of African Agriculture: Representation, Power, and Socially Constituted Time," *Progress in Development Studies* 7, no. 2 (2007), pp. 79–98.

56. M. Weisbord and S. Janoff, "Faster, Shorter, Cheaper May Be Simple; It's Never Easy," *Journal of Applied Behavioral Science* 41, no. 1 (March 1, 2005), pp. 70–82.

57. T. Shapley, "Trying to Fix What Everyone Else Has Broken," *Seattle Post-Intelligencer,* 16 November 2005, p. B8.

58. G.R. Bushe and A.B. Shani, *Parallel Learning Structures* (Reading, MA: Addison-Wesley, 1991); E.M. Van Aken, D.J. Monetta, and D.S. Sink, "Affinity Groups: The Missing Link in Employee Involvement," *Organization Dynamics* 22 (Spring 1994), pp. 38–54.

59. D.J. Knight, "Strategy in Practice: Making It Happen," *Strategy & Leadership* 26 (July–August 1998), pp. 29–33; R.T. Pascale, "Grassroots Leadership–Royal Dutch/Shell," *Fast Company,* no. 14 (April–May 1998), pp. 110–120; R.T. Pascale, "Leading from a Different Place," in *The Leader's Change Handbook,* ed. J.A. Conger, G.M. Spreitzer, and E.E. Lawler III (San Francisco: Jossey-Bass, 1999), pp. 301–320; R. Pascale, M. Millemann, and L. Gioja, *Surfing on the Edge of Chaos* (London: Texere, 2000).

60. C.-M. Lau, "A Culture-Based Perspective of Organization Development Implementation," *Research in Organizational Change and Development* 9 (1996), pp. 49–79.

61. T.C. Head and P.F. Sorenson, "Cultural Values and Organizational Development: A Seven-Country Study," *Leadership and Organization Development Journal* 14 (1993), pp. 3–7; R.J. Marshak, "Lewin Meets Confucius: A Review of the OD Model of Change," *Journal of Applied Behavioral Science* 29 (1993), pp. 395–415; C.M. Lau and H.Y. Ngo, "Organization Development and

Firm Performance: A Comparison of Multinational and Local Firms," *Journal of International Business Studies* 32, no. 1 (2001), pp. 95–114.

62. M. McKendall, "The Tyranny of Change: Organizational Development Revisited," *Journal of Business Ethics* 12 (February 1993), pp. 93–104; C.M.D. Deaner, "A Model of Organization Development Ethics," *Public Administration Quarterly* 17 (1994), pp. 435–446.

63. G.A. Walter, "Organization Development and Individual Rights," *Journal of Applied Behavioral Science* 20 (1984), pp. 423–439.

64. B. Moses, "Give People Belief in the Future," *Workforce*, June 2000, pp. 134–41.

65. B. Moses, "Career Activists Take Command," *Globe & Mail*, 20 March 2000, p. B6.

66. Drake Beam Morin, *1999 DBM Career Transition Study* (Drake Beam Morin, November 2000); F.T. McCarthy, "CareerEvolution," *The Economist*, 29 January 2000.

67. B. Moses, *The Good News about Careers: How You'll Be Working in the Next Decade* (San Francisco: Jossey-Bass, 1999); S.E. Sullivan, "The Changing Nature of Careers: A Review and Research Agenda," *Journal of Management* 25 (May 1999), pp. 457–84.

68. S.C. Van Collie, "Moving up through Mentoring," *Workforce*, March 1998, pp. 36–40; N. Beech and A. Brockbank, "Power/Knowledge and Psychosocial Dynamics in Mentoring," *Management Learning* 30 (March 1999), pp. 7–24.

PHOTO CREDITS

CHAPTER 1

page 2: Red Prouser / Reuters / Landov

page 5 (left): Courtesy of Schlesinger Library, Radcliffe Institute for Advanced Study, Harvard University

page 5 (right): © AP Images

page 15: © Jim Varney Photography

page 21: Courtesy of Lockheed Martin Corporation

page 31: Courtesy of Camenzind Evolution

CHAPTER 2

page 74: © National Post, Nathan Denette

page 79: Reprinted with permission of the Rocky Mountain News; Photo by JUDY DEHAAS / Rocky Mountain News

page 94: © India Today Group. Reprinted with permission

page 109: © James Leynse / Corbis

CHAPTER 3

page 122: Courtesy of John S. Leiter

page 126: © Ashley Cooper / Corbis

page 131: © John Angerson

page 136: © Scott Adams / Dist. By United Feature Syndicate, Inc.

page 139: © Kenny Rodger / The New Zealand Herald

page 143: Courtesy of Humana, Inc. and Virgin HealthMiles, Inc.

CHAPTER 4

page 154: Courtesy of Mott MacDonald

page 157: Copyright © Ted Goff, www.tedgoff.com, used with permission

page 162: © Wolfgang Kumm / dpa / Landov

page 165: © GM Corp.

page 181: Photo by Mikael Kjellstrom / Calgary Herald, May 18, 2005

page 187: Courtesy of Mark Wells

CHAPTER 5

page 198: © 2008 Rackspace US, Inc., Used under license

page 201: © AP Images

page 205: Courtesy of Sarova Panafric Hotel

page 218: Photo by Edward Reed, Courtesy of New York City Office of the Mayor

page 221: © Jens Kalaene / DPA / Landov

page 225: © The New Yorker Collection 2001 Barbara Smaller from cartoonbank.com. All rights reserved
page 226: © Chris Mueller / Redux Pictures

Chapter 6

page 236: © Francis Dean / The Image Works
page 243: © Will Crockett, Shoot Smarter
page 246: © Robert Caplin / Bloomberg News / Landov
page 251: Courtesy of Rolls-Royce plc.
page 255: Courtesy of Semco
page 256: Courtesy of Bayer CropScience

Chapter 7

page 268: © Matthew Staver / Bloomberg News / Landov Images
page 273: Courtesy of NASA
page 274: Copyright © Randy Glasbergen. Reprinted with special permission from www.glasbergen.com
page 279: © Stockbyte / Alamy
page 283: © Irish Times LTD
page 285: © OnAsia Images / Yvan Cohen
page 290: © Chris Mueller / Redux

Chapter 8

page 308: Courtesy of Whole Foods Market
page 316: Courtesy of La-Z-Boy Inc.
page 320: Shell Gourami Business Challenge, Langkawi August 2008, by www.affendy.com
page 324: U.S. Navy Photo by Michelle Wisniewski
page 335: Dean Smith / camera crew photography
page 339: Photo courtesy of brass | MEDIA Inc.
page 343: Johnson Space Center / NASA

Chapter 9

page 356: Courtesy of International Business Machines Corporation. Unauthorized use not permitted.
page 363: The Boston Globe
page 364: © Nancy Kuehn, The Minneapolis Business Journal
page 368: © Tim Fraser
page 370: Copyright © Ted Goff, www.tedgoff.com, used with permission
page 373: © Mark M. Lawrence / Corbis
page 381: Photo courtesy of Kowloon Shangri-LA

Chapter 10

page 392: Jean Levac / Ottawa Citizen Group, Inc.
page 399: © Erwin Brown
page 402: Courtesy of Karl J. Arunski, Raytheon
page 405: © David Paul Morris / Getty Images
page 407: Copyright © Ted Goff, www.tedgoff.com, used with permission

Chapter 11

page 420: © ImageState / PunchStock
page 425: © Reza Estakhrian / Getty Images
page 429: © Stephan Schraps / AFP / Getty Images
page 434: © AP Images
page 440: © Dave Carpenter, www.CartoonStock.com
page 443: © AP Images

Chapter 12

page 454: © AP Images
page 457: © Bill Cramer
page 463: © Theresa Barraclough / AFP / Getty Images
page 468: © AP Images
page 477: © Mathias Woltmann

Chapter 13

page 488: © The Edmonton Journal
page 493: © Edward Smith / Artizans.com, Reprinted with permission
page 495: © AP Images
page 499: Photo by Christopher Barth, Courtesy of TAXI New York
page 503: Robert Gilhooly / Bloomberg News / Landov Photos
page 507: © Kevin Foy / Alamy
page 511: © AP Images

Chapter 14

page 520: © Frederic Larson / San Francisco Chronicle
page 527: © The Canadian Press
page 529: © AP Images
page 534: © AP Images
page 536: © The Canadian Press
page 541: Photos courtesy of Lindblad Expeditions

Chapter 15

page 548: Courtesy of Umpqua Bank
page 552: The Japan Times
page 554: © AP Images
page 556: © AP Images
page 559: © Vito Palmisano
page 564: BananaStock / PictureQuest
page 566: © Sichov / SIPA Press

Organization Index

NAME INDEX

C

E

F

G

H

L

P

X

Y

Z

SUBJECT INDEX

B

C

D

E

F

N

O

P

Q

R

S

T

URL INDEX